1850 1875 1900

1831–1905
Mary Mapes Dodge,
Hans Brinker, 1865

1832–1888
Louisa May Alcott,
Little Women, 1868

1832–1898
Lewis Carroll, *Alice's
Adventures in
Wonderland*, 1865

1835–1910
Mark Twain, *The
Adventures of Tom
Sawyer*, 1876

1844–1912
Andrew Lang, Scottish
collector of folklore, *The
Blue Fairy Book*, 1889

1848–1908
Joel Chandler Harris,
*Uncle Remus, His Songs
and His Sayings*, 1880

1849–1924
Frances Hodgson
Burnett, *The Secret
Garden*, 1910

1850–1894
Robert Louis
Stevenson, *A Child's
Garden of Verses*, 1885;
Treasure Island, 1883

1854–1916
Joseph Jacobs, collector,
English Fairy Tales, 1890

1856–1919
L. Frank Baum, *The
Wonderful Wizard of Oz*,
1900

1858–1924
Edith Nesbit, *The Red
House*, 1903

1859–1932
Kenneth Grahame, *The
Wind in the Willows*, 1908

1860–1937
James M. Barrie, *Peter
Pan*, 1904

1865–1936
Rudyard Kipling, *The
Jungle Books*, 1894–95

1867–1957
Laura Ingalls Wilder,
*Little House in the Big
Woods*, 1932

1873–1956
Walter De la Mare,
poet, *Peacock Pie*, 1913

1874–1942
Lucy M. Montgomery,
Anne of Green Gables,
1909

1878–1967
Carl Sandburg, poet,
Rootabaga Stories, 1922

1882–1956
A. A. Milne, Winnie
the Pooh series of
stories and verse, 1924–
1928

1891–1967
Esther Forbes, *Johnny
Tremain*, 1943

1892–1973
J. R. R. Tolkien, *The
Hobbit*, 1937; *The Lord of
the Rings*, 1954–55

1898–1963
C. S. Lewis (Narnia
series), *The Lion, the
Witch, and the Wardrobe*,
1950

1899–1937
Jean deBrunhoff, *The
Story of Babar*, 1931

1899–1985
E. B. White, *Charlotte's
Web*, 1952

1902–1967
Langston Hughes,
poet, *Don't You Turn
Back*, 1969

1903–
Mary Norton, *The
Borrowers*, 1952

LITERATURE
AND THE CHILD

SECOND EDITION

LITERATURE AND THE CHILD

SECOND EDITION

BERNICE E. CULLINAN
New York University

Harcourt Brace Jovanovich, Publishers

San Diego   New York   Chicago   Austin   Washington, D.C.

London   Sydney   Tokyo   Toronto

To Mary Karrer
1944–1987

Words, once my stock, are wanting to commend
So great a poet and so good a friend.

John Dryden, Epistle to Peter Antony Motteux, 1698

Cover and part openers copyright © Trina Schart Hyman. Text illustrations by Pat Rogondino.

Copyright © 1989, 1981 by Harcourt Brace Jovanovich, Inc.

ISBN: 0-15-551111-4

Library of Congress Catalog Card Number: 88-80623

Printed in the United States of America

Copyrights and Acknowledgments and Illustration Credits appear on pages 722–29, which constitute a continuation of the copyright page.

Preface

The riches of our literary heritage are as abundant for children as they are for adults. *Literature and the Child*, Second Edition, embraces that heritage and is written for those who will help pass on the literature to the generations to come. Without a teacher, parent, or librarian to share the joys of good books, children are unlikely to discover them on their own. This text, therefore, discusses the outstanding books of yesterday and today and suggests ways to introduce them to young readers. It provides a comprehensive, activity-based literature program for children at the nursery, elementary, and junior high school levels.

In response to users and reviewers of the First Edition, we have reorganized and streamlined the sequence of the chapters. This new edition brings the book thoroughly up-to-date both with recent research in the field of children's literature and with the latest trends and titles in children's books.

The text is divided into three segments. Part I, "The Child," describes the developmental foundations, according to Piagetian theory, of the study of children's literature. So teachers can select books that are appropriate to children's developmental levels, these early chapters outline children's social, emotional, and cognitive growth and emphasize the role books can play in that growth. The placement of these chapters within the book also creates a natural progression into the study of the books themselves.

Part II, "The Books," is organized according to genre and builds around themes that complement and expand the school curriculum. Picture books (Chapter 4) are examined from the perspective of the young child in an expanding world, emphasizing the child's personal and social focus. Chapter 5 studies folklore, with its recurring themes and patterned stories, through archetypes. Fantasy and science fiction (Chapter 6) are explored via their imaginative themes of the known and the unknown, the seen and the unseen. Poetry and verse, the heart of all literary experience, are presented in Chapter 7 mainly in terms of the pleasure they give through their meaning, music, and rhythm. Chapter 8 considers realistic fiction, which is both a mirror of life and a window to it, primarily from the perspective of children's and adolescents' emerging awareness of themselves as individuals in the larger world. Historical fiction and biography (Chapter 9) are discussed in relation to the curriculum. Teaching units organize particular eras from the prehistoric to the contemporary. Similar units for classroom use are offered for nonfiction in Chapter 10. Criteria for evaluating books within their respective genres are provided in each chapter.

Part III, "The World of Children's Books," contains chapters on the literature of many cultures and on the history of children's literature. To reflect the multicultural world in which we live, Chapter 11 focuses on five racial and ethnic groups and their contributions to children's literature. Although such books and poems are discussed in the genre chapters, this chapter highlights outstanding examples of works that portray the unique cultural values of each group. The chapter concludes with a unifying theme of living together in a world of peace where groups of all cultures work and live together. Chapter 12, on the history of children's literature, provides a look into the roots of children's stories and the development of our literary heritage. Although this historical information can be taught at any point in the course, placing the chapter at the end of the text allows readers to see where literature is today before seeing where it has been. A time line of key authors, illustrators, and books appears on the endpapers of this text and highlights the historical progression of the world of children's literature.

SPECIAL FEATURES

Because readers found them to be so helpful in the First Edition, we have continued to provide suggestions for teaching ideas and student activities to extend children's literary experiences. The "Teaching Ideas" offer information for engaging the students' interests in the books or topics under discussion, and the "Activity: Teacher to Student" projects suggest ways to generate students' insights about themselves and the interrelatedness of literature and their world.

Also like the First Edition of *Literature and the Child*, profiles of outstanding authors and illustrators of children's books appear throughout the book. These vignettes provide a glimpse into the lives and beliefs of those who dedicate their work to bringing beauty and wonder into children's lives. They help teachers and children know that real people create the books—a concept that helps demystify the writing process.

New to this edition are "Landmark" boxes, which are discussions of books that were instrumental in establishing the standards of each genre. Located at the beginning of each genre chapter, the landmarks highlight the books that are representative of a level of excellence to which most books aspire.

The end of each chapter contains recommendations for further reading, plus professional references, notes, and a complete reference list of all the titles mentioned in the chapter. Extensive reference information for teachers' use in planning units of study appears in the appendices.

To supplement the text, an *Instructor's Manual*, by S. Lee Galda and Deborah Wooten, is also available. The manual provides content outlines; activities for individuals, for small groups, and for the entire class; test questions; references; and additional readings for each chapter of the text.

ACKNOWLEDGMENTS

The story of a book grows as the book grows and as more people participate in its development. My first thanks go to William J. Wisneski, who had the vision to see what *Literature and the Child* could become, and to Julia Berrisford, who enriched that vision for the Second Edition.

My deepest gratitude goes to Dr. Arlene M. Pillar for her dedication to high-quality literature and for her friendship through the years. To my colleagues at New York University, John Mayher, Gordon Pradl, and Trika Smith-Burke; to students at New York University, Lisa Mack and Dimitra Dreyer; to teachers in New York City, Hindy List and Shelley Harwayne; and to colleagues across the country in Baytown, Texas, Hilda Lauber and Mary Sirmons; in Cypress-Fairbanks, Houston, Dr. Patricia Smith; in Merced, California, Teresa Pitta and Nanette Rahilly; in San Diego, Dr. Jacqueline Chaparro; in Sacramento, Francie Alexander and Dr. Barbara Schmidt; in New Orleans, Gwen Kershaw; and in Worthington, Ohio, Vicki Frost, Paula Baur, Lillian Webb, and Laurie Secord—for each of these I feel particular gratitude.

Colleagues at other schools kindly consented to review portions of the manuscript in its various stages. I extend to these people my sincere appreciation: Patricia Cianciolo, Michigan State University; Patricia Hanley, University of South Florida, Tampa; James Jacobs, Brigham Young University; Shirley Lukenbill, University of Texas, Austin; and Rosemary Roehl, St. Cloud State University.

Specific thanks go to people who read and critiqued sections: Laurence Pringle for the nonfiction chapter; Dr. Rudine Sims Bishop for the section on black-American literature; Dr. Marcia Posner for the section on Jewish Americans; Dr. M. Jean Greenlaw and Marc Grabler for the chapter on fantasy and science fiction; Dr. Margaret Anzul and Dr. S. Lee Galda for the sections on response to literature; Dr. Barbara Worth and Dr. Phyllis Povell for the history of children's literature; Dr. Angela Jaggar for the sections on language and multicultural literature; Diane Person for the sections on fantasy and realistic and historical fiction; and nephew Tim Cullinan, a naturalist, for the section on wildlife management. Then there are those who suggested outstanding books I might have missed: Dr. Constantine Georgiou on international literature, Allan DeFina and Lucy Rubin on peace education, Jim Trelease on books for reading aloud, and Dr. Beatrice Teitel on predictable books.

The librarians at Port Washington Library answered all sorts of questions at all hours of the day. They are Corinne Camarata and Carey Ayres, also Rachel Fox, who developed the list of holiday books; plus Lucy Salerno, Priscilla Ciccariello, and Vera Fiddler. My thanks also go to Nancy Curtin of the Manhasset Library and Caroline Ward from the Nassau County Library who provided the right source at the right time.

Arranging for permissions is an onerous and detailed task, but Deborah Wooten managed it with grace and charm. She also worked with S. Lee Galda in developing the *Instructor's Manual* that accompanies this edition. K. C. Kelly tackled the bibliographies with amazing skill and good humor. Dr. Joan Kindy read page proofs with a keen eye for detail.

Family and friends endure a lot when one in their midst spends endless hours at the computer or in the library. For me, it has been my husband, Paul

Cullinan; son, Jim Ellinger; daughter and family, Janie and Alan Carley with Kali and Jason; Jeanne Brown; Scott and Angela Jaggar; and Joan and Hal Kindy.

I wish to extend special thanks to Trina Schart Hyman, who drew the wonderful cover illustration and the part openers. The imaginative progression of the part openers captures the message that we become the books we read.

Finally, the staff at HBJ devoted themselves to producing a book worthy of the beauty in the literature described within. Sincere thanks go to Sarah Helyar Smith, manuscript editor; Lisa W. Doss, production editor; Diane Pella, designer; Candace Young, art editor; Lesley Lenox, production manager; and Eleanor Garner, permissions editor.

Contents

PART III THE WORLD OF CHILDREN'S BOOKS

11 *Literature of Many Cultures*

LITERATURE
AND THE CHILD

SECOND EDITION

THE CHILD

PART I

1

The Study of Children's Literature

Hello Book!

Hello book!
What are you up to?
Keeping yourself to yourself,
shut in between your covers,
a prisoner high on a shelf.
Come on book!
What is your story?
Haven't you ever been read?
Did you think
    I would just pass by you,
And pick me a comic instead?
No way book!
I'm your reader.
I open you up. Set you free.
Listen, I know a secret!
Will you share
    your secrets with me?[1]

N. M. Bodecker

hildren's literature is an exciting area to study; its value has many dimensions. Parents notice that reading a good story to a child is the secret to a peaceful bedtime. Teachers recognize that a good story encourages young readers to stick with a book until it is mastered. Librarians are aware that a story time filled with exciting fare lures children into the library to check out books on their own. Reading theorists have shown that the single most important activity for building the knowledge required for eventual success in reading is reading aloud to children.[2] Cognitive psychologists realize that a narrative (or story) is structured the same way the human mind is structured; there is a match between the way we organize our minds and the way we construct stories.[3]

Others note that a child's imagination is fostered by the invitation to pretend found in imaginative literature. It is clear that we transmit much of our cultural heritage through literature. Still others appreciate that our vocabularies are enriched and expanded by the books we read. And even more perceive that we gain a better understanding of ourselves when we read. Child development specialists recognize that literature helps children realize their potential during a particular stage of development and fosters progress toward the next stage.

Yes, the books children read are formative in their lives; it is our responsibility to know their books.

Thousands of children's books are published each year in America, and certainly few can read them all, let alone catch up on the more than 50,000 already in print. Therefore, we need to develop guidelines for choosing the best. Whether or not children benefit from the best inevitably depends upon the adults in their lives who know them and know their books.

Children surrounded by adults who read become avid readers themselves: in this as in so many other areas, children do as we do—not as we say or tell them to do. Readers are made in childhood; the models we provide and the books we select influence children in lasting ways. If you are one of the lucky ones who, as a child, could climb onto a lap and share a book with someone special or read late into the night under the covers, then you know firsthand the enriching role that books can play. Equipped with knowledge of and love for books and children, you can lead children to the joys and unforgettable experiences of literature.

Many times, teaching reading and teaching literature are considered separate entities in school curricula, despite their interdependence. Often, the reading program is directed toward teaching decoding and practical skills while the literature program is aimed at reading appreciation and reading as an art. Research indicates, however, that we lead children into reading most successfully when the two programs are merged. All reading is

Reading for pleasure, the most important kind.

concept development, and learning to read better and reading literature for appreciation are a single organic process; separations are artificial and detrimental.

The ultimate goals of a reading teacher and of a literature teacher are the same: both want students to read a wide variety of literary and expository material for many purposes, one of which is reading as a source of enjoyment. Too often, reading to gain information or, worse yet, simply to decode is stressed rather than to gain meaning. This emphasis thereby outweighs reading as a pleasurable activity, so that children think of reading as saying words aloud or as a means of acquiring facts. Little is gained by teaching students the mechanical skills of reading and, in the process, teaching them to hate reading. Students who pass through school with high scholastic standing but who never voluntarily read for information or pleasure represent hidden failures of education. They become *aliterates*—those who know how to read but do not read. They may glance

at the headlines of a newspaper but most often reach for the TV schedule. Aliterates are no better off than illiterates, who cannot read at all.[4] Avoidance of reading signals a lack of value for reading; voluntary or freely elected reading indicates that the process is valued and enjoyed. When reading and literature programs are successful, enthusiasm for reading parallels and enhances the skills of reading.

Louise Rosenblatt, in *The Reader, the Text, the Poem,* defines two types of reading—efferent and aesthetic. Efferent reading is done for the practical purpose of gaining knowledge from the text—something we need to know, learn, remember for practical purposes—much like your reading of this textbook. Aesthetic reading is done for the joy of the experience—a total engagement with the text for the sheer pleasure therein.[5] In much teaching of literature, we ask students to read efferently (to recall characters, events, and metaphors) instead of encouraging aesthetic reading (giving oneself over to the literary experience) and allowing

The age-old phenomenon of sibling rivalry unmistakably expressed. (Text and art excerpts from *I'll Fix Anthony,* written by Judith Viorst, illustrated by Arnold Lobel.)

the reader the right to determine what to make of it.

When children make independent choices about how to spend their time, they turn to reading if it is a source of pleasure. The degree to which enjoyment effectively motivates reading depends largely on the strength of the pleasurable experiences associated with books. Children who have satisfying experiences with books continue to turn to them. One purpose of this text is to introduce books that show children that reading is worth the effort. The selection is guided by C. S. Lewis's precepts that "no book is really worth reading at the age of ten which is not equally (and often far more) worth reading at the age of fifty" and that the only imaginative works we ought to outgrow are those it would have been better not to have read at all.[6]

The definition of literature—all instances in which language is used imaginatively—is qualified implicitly to include the characteristics of permanence and excellence. Although children's books, like adult books, vary greatly in quality, the imaginative expression of human experience that is part of the mainstream of universal literature appears in literature for children as well. As Myles McDowell observes, a good children's book makes a complex experience available to its readers, whereas a good adult book draws attention to the inescapable complexity of experience.[7]

Perhaps the most distinct characteristic of children's literature is that it addresses the social, emotional, and cognitive developmental levels of its readers. Guidelines for content, characterization, structure, point of view, theme, and style of a book appropriate for a particular child differ according to the developmental and conceptual levels of the child who happens to be reading it. Thus, we cannot just say, "This is a good book," but must ask ourselves, "Good for whom?" For example, Judith Viorst's *I'll Fix Anthony* (P) always evokes a lively and empathetic response from readers in the primary grades because sibling rivalry is a near-universal experience. The nature of the response varies, however, according to the developmental level of the reader and of the place he or she holds in the sibling lineup. Recently, two brothers, about 20 months apart in age, read *I'll Fix Anthony* on the same day. The 7-year-old commented with a chuckle, "What he doesn't know is that Anthony will *always* be bigger than he is!" The 5-year-old at first said nothing, but later in the day was overheard chanting to himself, "When I'm six we'll have a skipping contest and I'll skip faster. Then we'll have a jumping contest and I'll jump higher. When I'm six I'll be able to tell time. . . ." It was clear that his identification with the book was very strong and that he was vicariously enjoying a triumph over the "Anthony" in his life, with almost total recall of the story. Both responses to the story were equally valid, each child responding from his own vantage point. The developmental level of the reader, thus, is a major factor when selecting a good book. Through knowing books and children, we can select the books that have the most value for the child at a given time.

LITERATURE IN RELATION TO THE READER'S DEVELOPMENT

Literature speaks of the mysteries of the human condition, although in books for children, treatment of these themes is adjusted according to the age-related interests and capacities of the audience. Like music, art, drama, and dance as creative expression, prose and verse for children sift experience and interpret life. And although we may tire of them, the books that do this, and that children ask for time and time again, are breathtakingly fresh for each new generation.

Theorists emphasize that an examination of a literary piece must consider the process involved in responding to the text. A literary experience is not created solely by a text, but by a reader interacting with that text. Renowned critic Wolfang Iser states that a literary work is more than the text, for the text takes on life only when it is "realized," and further, that realization is influenced by the individual dispo-

sition of the reader, who is in turn acted upon by different patterns of the text.[8] The convergence of text and reader brings a literary work into existence; it cannot be identified totally with the reality of the text *or* with the individual disposition of the reader. The literary experience, then, shaped by interaction of reader and text, becomes a "virtual" experience—one the reader has himself or herself. Readers add to their stock of experiences through the many possible lives they lead in the books they read; books *are* experiences. James Britton goes so far as to say that reading is not a vicarious experience; we become the books we read.[9]

A text may be realized in several different ways, depending on the cast of mind of the reader. A literary text must, by definition, allow readers to fill in conceptual gaps for themselves, to make inferences, build metaphors, and create characters. In filling these gaps, a reader, creating meaning from a text, makes choices. These choices invest the text with a more personal meaning but also exclude all those choices not made. Thus, no reader can ever exhaust the full potential of any text. There is, therefore, no one correct reading for a text, but merely readings that are more or less complete, both in terms of encompassing the information presented explicitly in the text and in making use of those gaps in the text that allow the reader to create a personal meaning.

The importance of interaction between reader and text can be seen in the following account of a discussion by a group of sixth-grade students who had just finished reading Ursula Le Guin's *A Wizard of Earthsea* (I–A) and had previously read several books in "The Chronicles of Narnia" series (I–A) by C. S. Lewis and two of Madeleine L'Engle's space fantasies, *A Wrinkle in Time* (I–A) and *A Wind in the Door* (I–A).

MICHELLE: I liked Narnia best—it was so magicky.

JON-PAUL: Well, I liked it a lot, but not the

best. For me, *A Wrinkle in Time* was best—
"It," you know, the Naked Brain, and the
shadowed planets, and all that.

TEACHER: There was a shadow in *A Wizard of
Earthsea,* and the "black thing" caused shadowed or dark planets in *A Wrinkle in Time.*
Somehow, the bad thing, the evil in several of
the books we read, seems to be pictured in
some way by blackness or shadows.

SARAH: Except for Narnia, and there it wasn't
a black witch but a white witch. The evil spell
was snow and winter.

HEDY: That's because nothing could grow or be
alive then. Aslan brought the Spring.

SARAH: But still whatever it appeared like,
there was a battle against the forces of evil.

TEACHER: What about *A Wizard of Earthsea?*

JON-PAUL: Well, like we read, the shadow that
was following Ged was really the evil in himself, but he didn't recognize it until the end. I
don't really understand that very well, but I
understand it some.

TEACHER: In *A Wind in the Door* you could be
"x-ed" if you weren't trying to be your real
self. Again, the picture the author gives us
to imagine in our own minds is rather similar:
If you are "x-ed," what has happened to
you?

JON-PAUL: You become annihilated. You don't
exist any more. If you were a planet, where
you used to be there was just a black hole of
nothingness in the universe.

SARAH: And for Ged, if he didn't recognize
that there *was* a bad side to his own nature, it
could destroy him. He would be "x-ed" by his
shadow, and he wouldn't be living any more,
but just the power of evil could live in his
body.

TEACHER: We talked a lot when we were reading the books by Madeleine L'Engle about the
theme of her books—that the central idea was
the battle between good and evil in the universe. What would you say is the theme of
the other fantasies?

HEDY: Well, in Narnia it was sort of the same
because Aslan was good and the White Witch
was evil.

SARAH: I see it! I see it! I just finished reading
Susan Cooper's *The Dark is Rising,* and it's the

same theme in that book, too. It's the light
against the dark. It's good against evil. *They're
all about the same thing!*[10]

The other children sat in silence, mulling
over this idea. They understood Sarah in a
way. Certainly, they understood momentarily
the words she was saying, though possibly
they would soon forget them. They clearly
would need time to read and reflect more before they could understand deeply this aspect
of what literature is. Try as Sarah might to explain to them the meaning of her personal
insights, it is difficult if not impossible to do.
Sarah's life has been changed and mere explanation will not affect her classmates. She can
report how the literary works affect her, but
her classmates will not know the new reality
Sarah has discovered until they themselves discover it. Each reader derives his own meaning
from a work through direct participation; another's explanation remains a hazy outline until the images become clear firsthand.

Sarah had taken one of those rare steps to
a new level of understanding. From now on,
every book she reads cannot only be a delightful world in itself, but can relate in some way
to other books. She is on that threshold where
every human experience she reads about, and
thus enters into vicariously, will begin to relate
somehow to all human experience, and where
human experience transmuted into literature
begins to relate to all other literature. Northrop
Frye explains it this way:

All themes and characters and stories you
encounter in literature belong to one big interlocking family. . . . You keep associating
your literary experiences together: you're always being reminded of some other story
you read or movie you saw or character that
impressed you. For most of us, most of the
time, this goes on unconsciously, but the
fact that it does go on suggests that perhaps
in literature you don't just read one novel or

poem after another, but that there's a real subject to be studied, as there is in science, and that the more you read, the more you learn about literature as a whole.[11]

When children compare a particular work with others similar to it in some way, even at the primary-school level, they begin to develop an understanding of the unity of literature. Moss and Stott suggest that all stories belong to one interlocking family of stories.[12] Extending Northrop Frye's proposition that authors often imitate others' stories or build upon the conventions and patterns from literature, Moss and Stott show how many stories are based on similar patterns. For example, they state that in nearly all children's stories, characters make physical journeys, journeys that conclude either in a new setting (linear), or at the point of departure (circular). "Beauty and the Beast" and Hans Christian Andersen's "Inchelina" are illustrative of the linear story pattern, in that the resolution of the story problem leaves the characters at a destination far from the point of origin. "Hansel and Gretel" is illustrative of the circular story; the protagonists return to the place of origin, but there are changes in the relationships among the characters. Moss and Stott suggest that the organizing principles of conflict, genre classifications, and the quest for identity provide avenues for comparing stories in addition to the linear and circular journey patterns.

Young children learn to look at literature in this way when they are immersed in stories with similar patterns. They quickly see the pattern of "three" when they hear "The Three Little Pigs," "The Three Billy Goats Gruff," and "Goldilocks and the Three Bears," (with 3 each of chairs, beds, and bowls of porridge) read aloud. They will also recognize that *Moss Gown* (P–I) by William Hooks has elements from the "Cinderella" story they have heard before. Recognizing patterns helps a child to understand and appreciate literature.

Reading, then, is an active process of constructing meanings, in which the reader's imagination is engaged with a text created by an author. Stories that spell out every last detail leave little room for the reader to participate. At the other extreme, stories that are very abstract and complex may not allow the reader access to them. In the first case, the reader becomes bored; in the second, there is never any engagement with the text. For these reasons, we not only search for good books but must also continually ask, "Good for whom?" A focus on literature must include a focus on the reader.

Since a literary experience is evoked only when a reader creates meaning from the words on the page, we cannot select literature solely on the basis of literary merit and apart from a consideration of the reader who will experience it. When we consider books for children, the child as interpreter is ever present as the other half of the equation.

The sweep of a child's development from birth to adolescence is large, and the breadth of literature appropriate to each developmental level is tremendous. Choosing literary experiences that are meaningful requires a knowledge of child development as well as a knowledge of books. In this text, concepts of general developmental stages in the child's construction of reality, derived from the work of Jean Piaget and others, inform the guidelines used for selecting literature. Each book discussed is designated N, P, I, or A, the letters corresponding to school and age levels as follows:

N (Nursery), birth to age 4—Nursery school
P (Primary), ages 5 to 9—Grades K–3
I (Intermediate), ages 10 to 12—Grades 4–6
A (Advanced), ages 13 to 15—Grades 7–9

Developmental stages are *not* applied rigidly since we know each child develops in an individual way. Further, no stage is discrete; rather it overlaps and is incorporated into the next in an ever-spiraling sequence of development. Children at every stage draw upon the ways they learned at all prior stages and use their growing fund of knowledge to learn new things. Earlier stages are never left behind. In situations that are strange or unfamiliar, children regress to less mature thought in working their way toward understanding. Interpret grade level assignments flexibly.

CHOOSING LITERATURE FOR CHILDREN

Selecting books for children requires a knowledge of child development. The books should take into account children's cognitive development, language development, and concept of morality as well as the social dimensions in which they learn and interact with literature. By observing children's responses to literature and other media, we can become aware of the broad patterns of intellectual organization that structure their thinking. We also learn to make judgments about the appropriateness of specific books. When we observe their social development—the way they respond to people and books and adopt feelings and beliefs about themselves—we can be more effective in selecting appropriate books.

A critical reason for selecting age-appropriate books is not only to assure that the best books are read but that they will ever be read at all. Once children pass a certain age, they will not be seen reading what they consider to be "baby books." If we miss the children's golden years of 2 to 4 when Margaret Wise Brown's *Goodnight Moon* (N) strikes a responsive chord, they may never see the charm of it later. If we lose the chance to share Maurice Sendak's *Where the Wild Things Are* (P) when children are 5 to 7, they may never experience its magic. Fifth grade students will not be caught reading Arnold Lobel's *Frog and Toad Are Friends* (P), nor will junior high school stu-

So Mother Bear made something
for Little Bear.
"See, Little Bear," she said,
"I have something for my little bear.
Here it is.

12

Books must be selected that are appropriate for the age of the child. (From *Little Bear* by Else Minarik, illustrated by Maurice Sendak.)

dents be seen reading E. B. White's *Charlotte's Web* (P–I). There are over 50,000 children's books in print; a child could read omnivorously and still never read a significant book. Most importantly, unless children read some of the really good books, they will probably not become lifelong readers.

Cognitive Development

Piaget's description of intellectual development offers one of the most fully explicated frameworks for analyzing changes underlying thought processes. He views the acquisition of knowledge as a gradual developmental process in which children actively experience and organize concepts about their environment. Therefore, the child is seen as an active, dynamic being who interacts with the environment to create knowledge. We cannot pour knowledge into the child as we would liquid into an empty vessel, but we can create situations in which the child finds meaning without help. We, as human beings, have a natural bent to search for meaning; that meaning is shaped by our current store of knowledge.

Our accumulated store of prior experience, called our cognitive structure, is made up of *schemata* (plural for schema). Schemata, according to Piaget, are images representing reality that we hold in thought, although they are not transformed by thought. In simpler terms, a schema is a conceptual framework for understanding something; it is a network of associations and experiences surrounding a subject. It stands to reason that the richer the background of experience with a subject, the richer the concepts and schemata.

Piaget believes the process of adaptation includes assimilation and accommodation. Assimilation involves using concepts already stored in the mind to deal with new information in the environment; accommodation involves modifying these structures so that the new information can be incorporated into the existing cognitive structures. Through the processes of assimilation and accommodation, we continually develop new structures that enable us to make further sense of the world.

Piaget views development as movement through four main stages: sensorimotor, preoperational, concrete operations, and formal operations.[13] The sensorimotor, preverbal stage lasts approximately from the first 18 months to 2 years of life. Children learn through their senses and motor movements; they feel, grasp, taste, touch, smell, see, and hear people and objects in their environment. During this stage, books that are congruent with their real life experiences make sense to them. Board books

and participation books, such as Kunhardt's *Pat the Bunny* (N), incorporate experiences appropriate for this age. At the same time, a child is learning language, which is learned *only* in context, because of the needs it serves. Children learn language to tell people what they want, to relate to others, to find out about their world, and to create an imaginary life. Books provide infinite opportunities to engage a child in talk about meaningful things.

The preoperational stage (approximately 2 to 7 years) is characterized by the beginnings of language and, therefore, of thought and symbolic representation. Still there is as yet no concept of conservation of quantity or recognition of reversible operations. For example, if we pour liquid from a short, fat glass into a tall, slender glass, children will think there is more in the tall, slender glass. Children see stories as true: stories present the world as it is, not as it might be. Magic is believable and contradictions are not questioned.

Kindergarten teacher Vivian Paley taperecorded children's stories and conversations during a school year and observed that 5-year-olds accept magical explanations without question. From *Wally's Stories:*

> One day at lunch Wally says, "I'm going to be a mother lion when I grow up."
> "A mother lion?" I ask. "Can you become a mother lion?"
> "Sure. The library has everything. Even magic. When I'm eight I can learn magic. That's how."
> "Why a mother lion?"
> "Because I would have babies and do the mommy work. They stay home and take care of babies. Daddy lions go to work and have to walk fast."
> Deana has been listening. "People can't turn into animals."
> "That's true," Wally says.
> "You changed your mind, Wally?" I ask.
> "It *is* true, what she said. But I'm going to use magic."

"Oh, I didn't hear him say that." Deana leans forward. "If he uses magic he might. Maybe. It's very hard to do." . . . [Another child enters the discussion.]

"What if he uses magic?"

"Oh, I though you meant ordinary. He could do it with magic," says Earl.[14]

Paley comments:

Magic weaves in and out of everything the children say and do. The boundaries between what the child thinks and what the adult sees are never clear to the adult, but the child does not expect compatibility. The child himself is the ultimate magician. He credits God and lesser powers, but it is the child who confirms the probability of events. If he can imagine something, it exists.[15]

Arthur Applebee interviewed 6- and 9-year-old children about the reality of stories and found, astonishingly, that for 6-year-olds, the stories are real. Here are some examples (responses in italics):

Heidi (6 years, 0 months)   Where does Cinderella live?—*With her two ugly sisters.*—Where is that?—*I think it's in an old house.*—Could we go for a visit?—*(No.)*—Why not?— . . . *Cause they'll say Cinderella can't come she'll have to wash up the plates and all the dishes and wash the floor.*—Hmm, do you think we could go visit the ugly sisters?—*(Yes.)*—We could? Where would we go?— . . . —Do you think it's near or far away?—*Far away.*[16]

Joseph (6 years, 3 months) Is Cinderella a real person?—*No.*—Was she ever a real person?—*Nope, she died.*—Did she used to be alive?—*Yes.*—When did she live?—*A long time ago, when I was one years old.*—Are stories always about things that really happened?—*Yes.*—When did the things in *Little Red Riding Hood* happen?—*A long time ago when I was a baby, they happened. There was witches and that, a long time ago. So when they started witch . . . they saw two good people and they made some more good people, so did the more horrible people. And they made more good people and the bad people got drowned.*—Are there still people like that?—*Nope, they were all killed, the police got them.*[17]

The concrete operations stage (about 7 to 11 years) is a time when children distinguish between reality and fantasy in literature. They are able to classify objects and ideas and become more systematic in the way they organize their storehouse of knowledge about their world. Children in this stage, called concrete thinkers by Piaget, can comprehend some abstractions. They seem to accept contradictions in their own view of reality. By the age of 9, their views about the believability of Cinderella and other storybook characters have, for the most part, changed.

Amanda (9 years) Where does Cinderella live?—(long pause) *I know she lives in a house with her two ugly sisters.*—Could we go there?—*No!*—Why not?—*Because it isn't true!*[18]

Finally, in the fourth stage (around age 11), children reach the level of formal or hypothetic-deductive operations; that is, they can now reason on hypotheses as well as on objects. They can reason logically, deal with abstractions, consider alternate ways of viewing a situation, and tolerate ambiguity. For example, Lev, a 13-year-old, demonstrated that he had attained the level of formal operations in his thinking when he acknowledged that Ursula Le Guin used the shadow character symbolically in *A Wizard of Earthsea*.[19] Lev showed that he understood that the shadow represented evil in Ged, the central character, when he explained, "The shadow represented the evil side of Ged, the other side of him. It was the world of shadow and death, the anti-Ged. If Ged was the right hand, the shadow would be the left hand . . . matter and antimatter, sort of." Mature students in this study were able to generalize from the story to their own lives and talk about the underside of human nature. Recognizing the multiple interpretations of metaphor and symbols is clearly age related. Thus, Lev not only tolerated the ambiguity but in discussions of its use he saw it as a desirable part of the complexity of the plot.

What does all this say to the literature teacher? Most important, the methods teachers use need to be informed by a knowledge of cognitive developmental stages. This not only directs their choice of books for specific age groups but also tells them what expectations are reasonable with respect to kinds of response and levels of response.

Each child's response depends upon the level of cognitive and emotional development attained, his or her construct of the world, and the conviction with which each holds those constructs. Because young children see literature as a representation of the real world, they are more likely to accept it as true. Applebee points out:

> For very young children the world of stories is part of the world in which they live; its events are as important and meaningful to them as anything else that happens. The separation of these worlds when they are finally confronted with the distinction between fact and fantasy is often relatively distressing; for a while, at least, a story is accepted only if the child thinks it is true. Slightly older children, once they have reconciled themselves to the distinction between fact and fantasy, continue to view stories from a single perspective: the events in a story remain made-up correlatives of events in the world.[20]

Eventually, children begin to view a story as a representation of one of many possible worlds and are able to construe it as one alternative of many. Therefore, the stages of response differ developmentally and individually—variables that any literature teacher must

consider. (See the accompanying table on story selection according to developmental stage.)

Language Development

Studies of child language development provide a broad base for inferences about appropriate literary experiences.[21] Although many others are possible, three principles guide our discussion of language and literature. First, children develop language naturally as they interact with language users—when they are immersed in language and expected to respond to it. Stories told or read to children give them opportunities to hear words in use and, in the process, to support, expand, and stimulate their own experiments with language. As children listen to language they gradually assimilate meanings and eventually express meanings through their own sounds. Language development is a natural process of generalizing and discriminating finer meanings and sounds. As children learn, books can help at every stage to fulfill their need to make sense of language and of the world.

We also know that, in language development, comprehension generally exceeds production. Though they may not be using sentences in their own speech production, children understand sentences and draw meaning from the contexts in which they are heard. For example, when asked, "Where's your teddy bear?" a child can pick up the toy or point to it long before he or she can say the words. Similarly, the 6-year-old who responds to a question with "I know it in my head but I can't say it," understands more than he can say. Through experience, children assimilate meaning and associate words as labels that they use to express meaning. Books, which provide experience beyond the immediate environment, contribute to the meaning base of language. Through books we learn to comprehend many more words than we actually use;

GUIDE TO STORY SELECTION ACCORDING TO DEVELOPMENTAL STAGE

Age Characteristics	Story Characteristics	Suggested Books
Infants and Toddlers (Approximately Birth to Age 2)		
Explores through senses	Provides tactile, auditory, and visual experiences	*Pat the Bunny* (Kunhardt)
Learns by hands-on approach	Invites participation	*Hand Rhymes* (Brown)
Learns language as label	Patterned language	*Brown Bear, Brown Bear* (Martin)
	Brief rhythmic song games	Mother Goose rhymes
	Objects associated with words	*Dressing* (Oxenbury)
Nursery and Early Childhood (Approximately 2 to 4)		
Builds concepts through direct experiences	Deals with simple concepts	*Shapes, Shapes, Shapes* (Hoban)
Learns word and thing are different	Identifies objects	ABC books
Sees self as center of world	Focuses on child	*Max's Bath* (Wells)
	Celebrates routine	*Goodnight Moon* (Brown)
Learns language rapidly	Repetitive and rhythmic language	*Millions of Cats* (Gág)
Begins to develop sense of story	Simple plots	*Is Anyone Home?* (Maris)
	Structured plots	*The Three Little Pigs*
Sees events as discrete	Cumulative plot structure	*This Is the House That Jack Built*
Early Primary (Approximately Age 5 to 7)		
Expresses normal fears	Reassuring themes	*Knots on a Counting Rope* (Martin and Archambault)
Develops self-identity	Deals with importance of self	*Dandelion* (Freeman)
Has rich imaginative life	Presents fantasy believably	*Tale of Peter Rabbit* (Potter)
Has developed sense of story	Clear plot sequence	*Rosie's Walk* (Hutchins)
	Predictable plots	*The Three Bears*
Has eye-for-an-eye morality	Shows justice prevailing	*I'll Fix Anthony* (Viorst)
Develops powers of observation	Gives attention to details	*Who's Counting* (Tafuri)
Primary (Approximately Age 7 to 9)		
Recognizes differing points of view	Clear identification of point of view	*The Ghost-Eye Tree* (Martin and Archambault)
Develops independence in reading	Some easy-to-read vocabulary	*Little Bear* (Minarik)
Prefers realism and law-and-order rules	Realistic settings and events	*Ramona Quimby, Age Eight* (Cleary)
Recognizes existence of multiplicity of meaning	Multiple layers of meaning	*Frederick* (Lionni)
Begins to manipulate ideas and actions mentally	Characters with whom to identify	*Worse Than Willy!* (Stevenson)
"Conserves," remembers, organizes knowledge	Episodic (longer stories with chapters)	*Charlotte's Web* (White)

GUIDE TO STORY SELECTION *(continued)*

Age Characteristics	Story Characteristics	Suggested Books
Intermediate (Approximately Age 9 to 12)		
Begins to recognize symbolic meaning and figurative language	Multiple layers of meaning Figurative language	*A Stranger Came Ashore* (Hunter) *Tuck Everlasting* (Babbitt)
Sees humor in language	Play with idiosyncrasies of language	*The Westing Game* (Raskin)
Has bizarre sense of humor	Silliness and nonsense	*How to Eat Fried Worms* (Rockwell)
Sees relationships between events and feelings	Identifiable character motivation	*Sarah Plain and Tall* (MacLachlan)
Strengthens independence in reading	Episodic, simple narratives	*Tales of a Fourth Grade Nothing* (Blume)
Plays team games	Action-filled suspense and sports	*The Hockey Machine* (Christopher)
Likes adventure and suspense	Intrigue and mystery	*Encylopedia Brown* (Sobol)
Concerned with self	Deals with personal and social concerns	*Are You There, God? It's Me, Margaret* (Blume)
Intermediate-Advanced (Approximately Age 11 to 13)		
Considers alternative realities	Represents alternatives to real world	*A Wrinkle in Time* (L'Engle)
Becomes aware of mortality	Confronts death and other painful issues	*Bridge to Terabithia* (Paterson)
Understands figurative language	Interesting language use	*The Phantom Tollbooth* (Juster)
Understands complexity	Complex plot structure	*The Blue Sword* (McKinley)
Becomes aware of social injustice	Confronts issues of prejudice	*Roll of Thunder, Hear My Cry* (Taylor)
Generalizes from past experience	Reflects historical conflicts	*My Brother Sam Is Dead* (Collier and Collier)
Develops compassion	Presents emotional and social conflict	*Dicey's Song* (Voigt)
Advanced (Approximately Age 13 and Beyond)		
Accepts responsibility for behavior	Deals with issues	*Wolf of Shadows* (Strieber)
Appreciates subtle humor	Understated humor	*The Not-Just-Anybody Family* (Byars), *The Year of the Gopher* (Naylor)
Recognizes moral conflicts	Presents moral issues	*The Chocolate War* (Cormier)
Seeks role models and heroes	Biographic material and heroic characters	*Traitor* (Fritz) *Lincoln* (Freedman)
Accepts alternate realities	Offers imaginative fantasy and science fiction	*A Wizard of Earthsea* (Le Guin)

books expand vocabulary by providing new words in a context that helps children understand them.

Finally, language learning never ends. As students mature, language skills increase and awareness grows in direct proportion to experiences. Older students come to recognize that written material and society affect each other and that language is used for a variety of purposes. Along the way they come to understand the persuasive uses of language, the figurative uses of language, the existence of different points of view, and the influence of literature. From wide exposure to many uses of language, then, students recognize the need to evaluate what they read and hear. Young children interpret metaphoric language through physical resemblances between things; later they may recognize conceptual or psychological links. As their metaphoric competence increases, students can be helped by books to extend their ability to comprehend the subtleties and ambiguities of language.

Moral Development

One specific aspect of development that affects response to literature is moral development. Jean Piaget's pioneering work in the psychology of development provides a scaffolding upon which researchers such as Lawrence Kohlberg and his associates have built a theory about children's reasoning concerning right and wrong, good and bad. Their conceptualization of children's comprehension of morality views growth as movement through a series of invariant stages. The developmentally early stage, called a morality of constraint, is oriented toward obedience to adult rules and attention to external physical consequences.

In *Child and Tale*, F. André Favat explores comparisons between the characteristics of the child and the characteristics of the fairy tale.[22] Just as magic and animism suffuse the world of the fairy tale, so do they suffuse the world of the child. During the morality of constraint stage, children find acceptable the harsh fate that invariably befalls wrong-doers. They consider it just when the scoundrel cook in ''The Pink'' is forced to eat live coals for having deceived the king or when the maid-in-waiting is put naked into a barrel stuck with nails and dragged along the streets for having posed as the true princess in ''The Goose Girl.'' Favat concludes that fairy tales embody an accurate representation of the child's conception of morality.

As the child develops, the morality of constraint is replaced gradually by a morality of cooperation learned through interaction with other children and a developing sense of mutual respect. As they come to understand the role of motives in their own and others' actions, they can understand the motives of characters in their stories. They are pleased that Peter Rabbit escapes from Mr. McGregor's garden instead of being eaten and they accept the punishment of being put to bed with camomile tea as appropriate for his misbehavior.

In a study of children's moral development in response to fables, Arlene Pillar found that students at the morality of cooperation stage were concerned about their peers' reaction to misconduct.[23] They believed that the shepherd boy should not cry ''Wolf!'' because it was not nice, you would get punished, and no one would like you. One said, ''Then nobody will be your friend.''

Literature is replete with moral dilemmas that can elicit discussions of values. James Miller, Jr., explains:

> Literature properly presented should confront the student (like life itself) with a multiplicity of ethical systems and moral perspectives. This expansion and deepening of the student's moral awareness constitutes the education of his moral imagination. It is one important (but not the sole) aim of literary study.[24]

Probing children's reasoning behind a moral position and their resulting defense of it can help them develop the strength of their own convictions; they also examine the values they hold. Teachers aware of their own values (which may or may not be similar to their students') help students probe the multiple ethical systems and moral perspectives by withholding personal judgments and providing an atmosphere where divergent views are respected. This is an area in which teachers help students learn *how* to think; they do not tell them *what* to think. This stance, along with questions that tap and expand the structure of children's reasoning, can facilitate a fuller response to literature.

Social Dimensions of Response to Literature

There are three things about the social dimensions of a child's response to literature that every teacher ought to know. First, learning occurs in a social context dependent upon interaction, and literature plays an important role in that context. Second, children grow in their ability to understand literature as they gain life experience and are able to view literature from an objective stance. Third, a teacher's influence on children's response to literature is a powerful determinant.

Social development provides another window into a child's world and the role of literature in it. Children develop feelings and beliefs about themselves and their world through interaction with those around them. They find out who they are and the role they are to play by interpreting the verbal and nonverbal messages significant others give to them. Children develop a positive self-concept if people around them show them they are loved and valued. In a similar way, they develop a positive attitude toward books if books are treated as a source of pleasure and knowledge. When children experience sharing books with a loving caregiver from early on, they develop pos-

itive feelings about books and the joy that can come from them. The social context in which children grow shapes their view of the world and the role of literature in it.

Northrop Frye underscores the role of literature in educating the imagination and shows the necessity of imagination in creating a social vision.[25] He believes that the fundamental job of the imagination in ordinary life is to produce, out of the society we *have* to live in, a vision of the society we *want* to live in. In this sense, we live in two worlds: our ordinary world and our ideal world. One world is around us, the other is a vision inside our minds, born and fostered by the imagination, yet real enough for us to try to make the world we see conform to its shape.

Frye goes on to say that the quest of human beings is to discover their identities and their place within their societies, to discover who they are and where they belong. The story that is told so often is of how man once lived in a golden age or a garden of Eden, how that world was lost, and how someday we may be able to get it back again. This feeling of lost identity and regaining it is the framework of all literature.

Literature plays a strong role in helping children envision a world they do not see. E. B. White's *Charlotte's Web* (P–I), an ode to friendship, explores relationships in a fantasy world that have lasting meaning in the real world. Lloyd Alexander's *The Book of Three* (I–A) series follows Taran's quest for his lost identity and celebrates an individual's joy of knowing who he or she is. Literature feeds the imagination; it helps us create a vision of society to work toward.

Children grow in their ability to understand literature as they gain life experience and are able to view literature from an objective view. James Britton explains the difference as one of the ways we use language—as a participant and as a spectator.[26] Although we continue to use both participant and spectator stances all our lives, we become more adept as spectators as we learn more about literature.

Britton describes reading a literary text as a special kind of language act. He distinguishes between using language as a participant—that is, to get things done in the real world—and using language as a spectator. As a spectator, the reader is freed from the constraints of action and can savor feelings, contemplate forms, and evaluate literature objectively. Literature is the written form of spectator role language; thus, it is understood and appreciated more fully when a reader approaches a literary text from a spectator stance. D. W. Harding observes that, as a spectator, a reader lives through a story as a virtual experience, withholding judgments until the story is completed.[27]

In a study of the developmental patterns of response to literature, Lee Galda found that one dimension that distinguished older readers (grades 8–9) from younger readers (grades 4–5) was the ability of the older children to consistently view the texts as works of art separate from life.[28] The younger readers compared the characters in Betsy Byars's *The Summer of the Swans* (I) to their own lives. They complained of the lack of exact fit with their own worlds: the characters were "kind of like us," but "they don't act like we act at my house," "they don't fight like real brothers and sisters." The older readers were more objective when they criticized the book; they understood how literature works. When one girl commented that Charlie's retardation "wasn't necessary" to the story, another countered with "Well, the story did need it because it sort of changed the relationship between Sara and Charlie." Rather than dismissing parts of stories they found extraneous, the older readers could go beyond their personal reactions to see how parts functioned in the story as a whole. In summary, Galda states,

> There was a greater understanding of the inter-relatedness of literary elements in the older readers than there was in the younger readers. Along with this was a diminishing tendency to judge a book according to its fit with one's personal perception of reality. Thus, even fantasy comes to be understood as being about recognizable people with familiar problems, as being *true* even if not *real*.[29]

Students in the Galda study were moving from a participant stance toward a spectator stance as they gained more experience in life and in reading literature.

The teacher's attitude toward literature is also a major factor in how children respond to a given book and to books in general. In a study of children's responses to literature in an elementary school, Janet Hickman observed the power of teachers, among other things, to stimulate or to dissuade response to books.[30] Spending four months as a participant observer in an open-classroom, open-space school with K–1, 2–3, and 4–5 grades, Hickman recorded both spontaneous and solicited responses to literature. *Where the Sidewalk Ends* (P–I–A) by Shel Silverstein was shared among children across all grade levels and stimulated several instances of spontaneous response, such as acting out some of the verses, reading favorites to a friend or to anyone who would listen, and choosing an appropriate verse to comment upon real-life events. Another book, used for focused response as a research tool, did *not* lead to spontaneous response; there were no pictures drawn, no stories written about it, and no dramas planned around it. None of the children went beyond the required talk about this book. Hickman reflected upon the reasons and observed that *Where the Sidewalk Ends* was a part of the body of literature of common interest to teachers and children. Teachers had expressed their own approving, amused responses, had encouraged children's contact with the book, and more by attention than intention, had lent a special sanction to its use. On the other hand, the teachers absented themselves from any discussions of the book

Telling stories is a primary human activity; children tell stories to make sense of their world.

used for research purposes and avoided bringing it up with students. Hickman concludes:

> Whether or not they were totally conscious of it, teachers wielded a great deal of power over children's responses to literature. In choosing the books that would be in their classroom areas, in choosing the way such books would be presented and discussed, in providing ready access to the books, and in suggesting and demonstrating appropriate modes of responding, teachers influenced both the quantitative and qualitative aspects of the responses expressed by children.[31]

The social context in which children learn about literature is a strong determinant of the way they will respond to it. Teachers who create an inviting literacy environment by surrounding children with books, reading aloud, and sharing enthusiasm about books, will find that students respond positively to literature.

Developing a Sense of Story

Read Steven Kellogg's *Can I Keep Him?* (P), a tightly structured story with a repetitive phrase, to a group of 5-year-olds; by the time you reach the third page, they will be "reading" it with you. Hearing only the first three pages, children can recognize the story structure and predict what is coming next. In *Brown Bear, Brown Bear* (P), Bill Martin Jr invites children to respond to the oft-repeated question "What do you see?" They quickly discover the story pattern and can join in with the reading after hearing the first few pages. They are not memorizing the text—as so many very young children do who "read and reread" their favorite story (even when it is held upside down)—but know intuitively how the story works. Children acquire such intuition by hearing many stories and developing expectations about them; this is called developing a sense of story.

In addition to developing an understanding of the sequential structure of stories, children learn to use the content of stories to organize what they encounter of the world. Their vision of reality is shaped by the stories they tell themselves. Telling ourselves stories is a primary human activity, engaged in by adults as well as children. Each of us selectively perceives the world from a unique vantage point, and we tell ourselves stories about what we perceive. Children who are sent to bed in a dark room may fear the monsters that lie hidden there, and no amount of logical reassurance convinces them that the stories they have told themselves about the presence of monsters are unfounded. Philosophical treatises debate what reality actually is, but there is a consensus that one's own reality is what one perceives it to be; it is largely shaped by what we choose to believe.

James Britton describes "storying" as serving an assimilative function through which we balance out inner needs with external realities.[32] Children's make-believe play and the stories they tell (often based on the stories they read) are among the activities in which they improvise freely upon events in the actual world, and in doing so, they enable themselves to return and meet the demands of real life more adequately. Britton sees play and imaginative storytelling as areas of free activity that lie between the world of shared and verifiable experience and the world of inner necessity. The essential purpose of this kind of play is to relate inner needs to the demands of the external world. Children who hear or read stories of

A good example of a sequentially structured story is *The Doorbell Rang*, written and illustrated by Pat Hutchins. Each time the doorbell rings, more children have come to share Ma's cookies.

witches and fairy godmothers (symbols that may embody and work upon the hate and love that are part of a close, dependent relationship) adapt or use in their own stories these symbols to accommodate their own needs.

Research into the stories children tell shows that their sense of story grows as they mature. Arthur Applebee found that children's stories change from disconnected strings to sequential orderings and eventually contain distinct "story markers."[33] One such marker is evident when young children signal that they are telling a story by giving a title. Another appears when they begin their stories with a formal opening, such as "once upon a time," and end with a closing phrase such as "they lived happily ever after." Most children use recognizable opening and closing story frames by the time they are 5 years old. Many children at this age also use the past tense when they tell a story, and some alter their speaking tone into a dramatic "story voice." The fact that these story markers appear regularly in children's oral language indicates the extent to which they have assimilated literature and dramatically illustrates the potential power of literature to affect language as well as cognitive and affective development.

The stories children enjoy change as the children mature intellectually and accumulate experience. Applebee identified the patterns evident in children's stories and found predictable characteristics at each level of thinking from preoperational, through concrete operational, to formal operational thought, as defined by Piaget and discussed above. When asked about a story, young children usually respond with a detailed retelling of the narrative; they have great difficulty in summarizing a story. Asked what stories are about, they will often respond with a short list of the characters: "Lisa knows stories are about 'Cinderella, Humpty Dumpty, and Jack and Jill.' . . . And Ernest answers in the same vein [when asked]: 'What kind of story would you like?' 'Bears, The

Three Bears.' . . . 'What is it about?' 'Three Bears, and Goldilocks, and her mother.' "[34]

Yet when Ernest is asked to tell the story of the three bears, he gives a detailed, accurate retelling of the story, and even imitates the deep-, middle-, and high-toned voices of the characters. Even though he gives the list of characters as the response to the question of what the story is about, there is no question that he knows the story in its entirety.

As children mature further and their cognitive development reaches the concrete operational stage, their original stories and retellings tend to include summaries and categories of behavior as well as lists of characters. When asked to "tell about" *Bridge to Terabithia* (I), by Katherine Paterson, a 10-year-old responded: "It's about a boy who likes to run but Leslie beats him. Then Jesse and Leslie become good friends and build Terabithia. Then Leslie dies and Jesse takes his sister there." This ability to summarize reflects the concrete operations of serial ordering and classification, operations that a simple retelling does not require.

As children move toward the formal operational mode of thinking, their comprehension of a story is revealed through analogy. For example, a fourth grader equated story with gossip: "Reading something is like the same as hearing from somebody, 'Oh, did you hear what happened?' or something like that." They may recognize a character's motives, as when they understand that Mafatu is driven by his need to overcome his fear of the sea in Armstrong Sperry's *Call It Courage* (I). Students who read Lois Lowry's *Rabble Starkey* (I–A) will identify with Rabble and admire her tenacity to hold onto the people and places that lend stability to her life. Although they may not be able to tolerate the adversity that Rabble faces, identifying with her may strengthen their resolve to behave courageously in the future. Their generalizations about a work entail a consideration of its theme and point of view. They can deal with the ambiguity of two things being true at the same time, even where they are contradictory. They recognize that the point of view from which we view events affects our perception of them. For example, they can recognize that the story in Cynthia Voigt's *Dicey's Song* (A) would be told much differently were it from the grandmother's point of view rather than from the adolescent's. Many students interpret the theme of Voigt's story as the need for better communication between people who love each other, whereas others may see it as a story of a girl growing up and becoming less self-centered. Students at the formal operations level of thinking can also compare books that develop a similar theme. This reflects the ability to consider several realities rather than just one and to engage in critical judgments in the light of these possibilities.

Fostering Creative Interaction

Teachers who are aware of the changing nature of a child's concept of story can provide experiences with literature that both build upon and expand that concept by suggesting books that clarify and reconcile the complexities of the world and stretch their minds. Although children generally like well-crafted books, which build suspense, avoid anticlimaxes, and have memorable themes, they also enjoy ''formula'' stories. They enjoy fantasy in the early grades, realistic books and mysteries in the middle grades, and both realism and fantasy in junior high and high school.

Northrop Frye, respected Canadian critic, suggests that we cannot change a student's mind by telling him that one book is better than another, especially if he prefers the latter. Students need to be given time to mature in their reading choices:

> When I was at school we had to read *Lorna Doone*, and a girl beside me used to fish a love-story magazine out of her desk and read it on her knee when the teacher wasn't looking. She

obviously regarded these stories as much hotter stuff than *Lorna Doone*, and perhaps they were, but I'd be willing to bet something that they told exactly the same kind of story. To see these resemblances in structure will not, by itself, give any sense of comparative value, any notion why Shakespeare is better than the television movie. In my opinion value-judgments in literature should not be hurried. It does a student little good to be told that A is better than B, especially if he prefers B at the time. He has to feel values for himself, and should follow his individual rhythm in doing so. In the meantime, he can read almost anything in any order, just as he can eat mixtures of food that would have his elders reaching for the baking soda. A sensible teacher or librarian can soon learn how to give guidance to a youth's reading that allows for undeveloped taste and still doesn't turn him into a gourmet or a dyspeptic before his time.[35]

Teachers do make a difference, however, and the books they share with children can be influential in fostering new interests, shifting focuses, and developing latent tastes. Stories that are full of action, with characters approximately the same age as or a little older than the readers appeal to them. Biographies, informational books, and realistic animal stories become increasingly popular from the upper elementary grades on. However, these general interests are just that—general. It is important to have a variety of books on hand, and while Nancy Drew mysteries should not be discouraged, other, more complex stories should be encouraged.

In addition to providing a variety of reading experiences, teachers should encourage a variety of responses. Children need time to absorb any learning experience, and this is especially true for literature. Response can take many forms, including quiet reflection. The outward response to a book may be through art, drama, or oral or written language activities. Sometimes the perfect follow-up is obvious; other times teachers need to guide.

Flexible teachers who have a large collection of ideas and activities are prepared to give children choices. Activities that are centered around books and that release children's spontaneity encourage children to read more. When given the opportunity, children spin off on their own, stretching their imaginations to limits beyond ours. The spark from a freely developed project may ignite many imaginative fires.

Teachers who want to foster children's creative interactions with stories must allow the readers to respond to the text in a way that makes the text meaningful to them. One child may be fascinated by the ghostly legend of the sea in Natalie Babbitt's *The Eyes of the Amaryllis* (I), another by the character of the grandmother, another by the problem the granddaughter has in dividing her loyalty between her father and her grandmother. Children should be allowed to explore their own ideas as well as to share the responses of others, and to discuss all responses in the light of the text itself. A teacher who wants to hear only one kind of response to a story will soon have children who read "for the teacher" rather than for themselves. If we applaud the narrowly focused, one right answer, that is what we will be given. A teacher who encourages each child to work out a personal response, to share that response with others, and to return to the text for verification will soon have students who read for pleasure, immersing themselves in the stories and becoming critically aware.

Another way of encouraging fully developed and individual responses to literature is to teach children to be critically flexible. A story can be viewed from many different perspectives. Sometimes one perspective does not allow for full comprehension of a text, and the ability to view the story in another light may increase both understanding and enjoyment. Natalie Babbitt's *Tuck Everlasting* (I) might be construed as a philosophical question about the worth of eternal life, a character study of Win-

nie Foster, or a thematic statement about choices made in life. All three interpretations are plausible. Singly, each represents a limited evocation of the possibilities of the text; together they enable a more comprehensive response.

It should be evident at this point that our responses to stories inevitably will *not* be the same as the responses of our students. Our own responses change over time as our life experiences change. For example, our response to *The Adventures of Huckleberry Finn* would not be the same today as it was when we first read it at age 12 or 13. Rather than impose our own reading and interpretation of a text upon our students, we should make an effort to listen to their responses. Our job is to provide a rich supply of literature and give students many occasions to talk about what they read—but not to decide beforehand how they should respond to it. We can nurture the gift of imagination by letting students know that many interpretations are possible.

In this same vein, the teacher's response is crucial. The teacher who gushes about how lovely, touching, and sensitive a book is may find students turning away in disgust. Similarly, adopting an affected, overly dramatic stage voice when reading poetry or prose turns students away from what we want them to know and enjoy. Sincere enthusiasm and genuine enjoyment, however, are likely to be contagious.

THE MULTIDIMENSIONAL VIEW OF LITERATURE

There are many valid extraliterary reasons for using children's books in schools. For example, teachers can help foster concept development by incorporating in their teaching plans books that explore specific concepts, or they can enhance understanding of a historical period by including historical fiction and biography with factual books of history. Knowing books leads to endless possibilities for discovery.

Literature means many things to many people; each unique perspective, however, is equally valid. We dare not believe that our view of literature is the only view, lest, like the blind men of Hindostan—each of whom identified a different part of an elephant as the whole creature—each of us be partly in the right but all of us in the wrong. The proper perspective seems to vary according to the purpose; our purpose is to develop awareness in students so they have access to many different views.[36]

When we teach literature, we relate a book to all others we know and to our lives. We may emphasize parts of a story that might remind our students of an ancient Greek myth, or we may focus on a character who reflects ourselves or a character met in another book. Through personal response and relating books to life, children become aware of the eternal stream of literature and of life and are encouraged to develop a sense of wonder, a pondering of other ways of seeing, thinking, feeling, and being. Opening up a book to children in this way will lead them beyond understanding that single piece of literature to an illumination of their lives in relation to the world and a broader spectrum of humanity.

The teacher who is able to approach a piece of literature in a variety of ways encourages students to respond with versatility. We can look at stories for theme, archetype, or element; as a mirror or window on life; or in a developmentally expanding frame. We teach children to be flexible by being flexible in our own approach to literature, for they follow our actions more than our words. When we play with possibilities affably, we foster children's ability to respond to books in fulfilling ways.

The following multidimensional view of Ursula Le Guin's *A Wizard of Earthsea* (I–A) can be exemplary; it takes many turns. The book tells the story of Ged, who, when his village is

The stark, bold line drawing of Ged suggests the strength he must show in his encounters with evil. (From *A Wizard of Earthsea* by Ursula Le Guin, illustrated by Ruth Robbins.)

attacked by marauding warriors, discovers that he has magical powers. He devotes his life to perfecting his skill, but plagued by overwhelming pride, sometimes flaunts his powers before he fully masters them. When Jasper, a fellow student of magic, challenges him, Ged attempts to show greater skill than he possesses and in the process calls forth a spirit from the land of the dead. This nameless shadow beast roams Ged's world and haunts him endlessly. His struggle to evade the shadow and his inevitable confrontation with it are told in a compelling style.

If we look at the story for recurring patterns and themes, we see reflections of ancient mythology and biblical literature—as Ged is named in the River Ar:

On the day the boy was thirteen years old, a day in the early splendour of autumn while still the bright leaves are on the trees, Ogion returned to the village from his rovings over Gont Mountain, and the ceremony of Passage was held. The witch took from the boy his name Duny, the name his mother had given him as a baby. Nameless and naked he walked into the cold springs of the Ar where it rises among rocks under the high cliffs. As he entered the water clouds crossed the sun's face and great shadows slid and mingled over the water of the pool about him. He crossed to the far bank, shuddering with cold but walking slow and erect as he should through that icy, living water. As he came to the bank Ogion, waiting, reached out his hand and clasping the boy's arm whispered to him his true name: Ged. Thus was he given his name by one very wise in the uses of power.[37]

The ritual described suggests religious ceremonies of passage such as the Jewish bar mitzvah at the thirteenth birthday, or confirmation in Christian rites, or perhaps baptism. The idea of naming and the value of one's name is used in a way to convey the power of naming in the biblical sense.[38] Ged makes frequent references to the importance of his name: he says, "By my name, I will do it," and "Unless I can learn the word that masters it: its name." The power of Ged's name glows again near the end of the story:

In silence, man and shadow met face to face, and stopped. Aloud and clearly, breaking that old silence, Ged spoke the shadow's name, and in the same moment the shadow spoke without lips or tongue, saying the same word: "Ged." And the two voices were one voice.[39]

Ged's friend, Vetch, watches the struggle between man and his shadow and fears that the evil thing might take Ged's form. He remains silent as he wonders what will come.

Now when he saw his friend and heard him speak, his doubt vanished. And he began to see the truth, that Ged had neither lost nor won but, naming the shadow of his death with his own name, had made himself whole: a man: who, knowing his whole true self, cannot be used or possessed by any power other than himself, and whose life therefore is lived for life's sake and never in the service of ruin, or pain, or hatred, or the dark. In the *Creation of Ea* which is the oldest song, it is said, "Only in silence the word, only in dark the light, only in dying life: bright the hawk's flight on the empty sky."[40]

Traces of mythological and biblical archetypes emanate from Le Guin's powerful story. Ged is the seventh son of a seventh son, a position that bears ancient significance. His journey emerges from the struggle between good and evil within him and echoes the biblical Jacob's struggle with the devil. The promise of eternal life after death rings through theology and through this story.

From a psychological point of view, the shadow that haunts Ged is symbolic of the unconscious or of the dark underside of a person's being. Jungian or Freudian psychoanalysts would interpret the shadow in many ways.

At first it was shapeless, but as it drew nearer it took on the look of a man. An old man it seemed, grey and grim, coming towards Ged; but even as Ged saw his father the smith in that figure, he saw that it was not an old man but a young one. It was Jasper: Jasper's insolent handsome young face, and silver-clasped grey cloak, and stiff stride. . . . It brightened, and in its light the look of Jasper fell from the figure that approached, and it became Pechvarry. But Pechvarry's face was all bloated and pallid like the face of a drowned man, and he reached out his hand strangely as if beckoning. . . . Then the thing that faced him changed utterly, spreading out to either side as if it opened enormous thin wings, and it writhed, and swelled, and shrank again. Ged saw in it for an instant, Skiorh's white face, and then a pair of clouded, staring eyes, and then suddenly a fearful face he did not know, man or monster.[41]

Each of the people the shadow represents is one that Ged wrongs or one for whom he has been less than he could be. Ged needs to return to himself—to what Jung calls the inferior side of oneself, or the shadow—and to see his behavior in a clear light. It is the shadow Ged tries to flee and only when he faces it does he become whole.[42] The shadow as an image of guilt becomes evident, as do other literary symbols, the more widely and thoughtfully one reads. There is a strong possibility, however, that such esoteric symbolism may elude many readers. Still this does not deny the validity of using psychological insights to discuss the book with those who can grasp the additional layers of meaning.

Looking at *A Wizard of Earthsea* sociologically, teachers can help mature readers see Ged as a prototype of the adolescent who wavers between adult capabilities and childish needs. For some readers, the theme is about the misuse of power that learning bestows. Ged struggles with power: flaunts it to impress Jasper, misuses it, and finally accepts responsibility for it. In another sense, the story shows the need for balance and equilibrium in life and the effect that one person can have on the entire world.

A structural look at the story for motifs or recurring images would focus on the play between light and dark. The nameless evil shadow that haunts Ged repeatedly lunges at him from darkness. Light, sunshine, and brightness of day force the shadow to recede. Transparent whiteness, grayness, fog, and mist that obscure vision convey strong visual images. The ship that carries Ged to the island of Roke, *Shadow*, forebodes danger.

We see from this multidimensional discussion of Ursula Le Guin's novel that many interpretations are possible. The type of exploration that a teacher chooses to pursue is determined by the literary background of the students and the goals of the instruction. Teachers who are intrigued by this compelling story can help students discover its relevance for their lives. *The Tombs of Atuan* (I–A) and *The Farthest Shore* (I–A) are sequels to *A Wizard of Earthsea*.

Teachers who are aware of numerous possibilities for exploring books can expand children's thinking. Some books lend themselves to one view more readily than others. Some children, responding in a characteristic mode, may choose only one view; others, more experienced in response, may consider many dimensions. An informed teacher can open many windows for viewing books.

TYPES OF LITERATURE

Until they have read widely and have discussed what they read, children are generally unaware that there are different types of books or that stories can be categorized. Indeed, it is not important to label books for children, because each book is an experience unlike any other. However, literary forms provide a frame of reference for exploring books and studying the field; they help simplify the task of presenting literature in meaningful and varied ways. Given the very large number of children's books in print, the student of children's literature would be overwhelmed were the books to be treated as an amorphous mass.

Classification schemes for children's books are fraught with problems. Formal literary divisions are inadequate because format sometimes takes precedence over content and tone, as in the case of the picture book. Divisions by content or mode are problematic, too; for example, books grouped as animal stories may have fantasy, realistic, and factual books among them. At best, boundaries within any system are indistinct.

He planted himself in the center of the road, raised one hand to stop the traffic, and then beckoned with the other, the way policemen do, for Mrs. Mallard to cross over.

In picture books, the text and illustrations blend to tell the story. (From *Make Way for Ducklings,* written and illustrated by Robert McCloskey.)

Literature can also be divided into poetry and prose, or fiction and nonfiction. It can be divided along the lines of genre; as contemporary or traditional; as short story, novel, or drama; or as tragedy, romance, comedy. Genre classification groups share a number of characteristics, such as types of characters, settings, actions, and overall form or structure. This book primarily uses genre classifications, with the exception of picture books, which are based on format, and multicultural books, which are based on content.

Various distinguishing features help categorize the genres. For example, ancient stories with no known author are designated as *folklore;* stories focusing on events that could happen today are works of *realistic fiction;* stories that are set in the past, *historical;* those that could not happen in the real world, *fantasy;* and those that might happen in the future, *science fiction.* Children discover the distinctions gradually as they read widely and have books read to them.

Picture Books

The classification of picture books is based on format: picture books tell a story through a unique combination of text and illustration so that meaning conveyed in the text is extended by the illustrations. The content may be realistic, fanciful, or factual, but the format of text and illustration combined defines it as a picture book. An example is Robert McCloskey's popular *Make Way for Ducklings* (P).

As children become increasingly aware of an aesthetic world, picture books come to be appreciated for their art. Children are sensitive to color and pattern. As they create their own pictures, they become aware of pictures others create. Books that draw attention to the aesthetic world are in keeping with the ever-expanding interests of the child.

Picture books are also appreciated for the stories they tell. Young children are egocentric, fascinated with themselves and their own needs, interests, and concerns. Because young children have their primary experiences in and are dependent upon the home and family, books that help them explore their personal world are uniquely suited to their needs and interests.

As children mature, they begin to expand beyond their personal world of self, home, and family into a broader social world. They perceive friends, school, and neighborhood as integral parts of their lives and relationships. They expand their interests beyond the familiar and immediate to show an interest in other children and adults. Books that deal with the child's social world are congruent with developmental interests. Thus, art, story, and children's interests are three avenues by which to explore picture books.

Some of the features that characterize picture books are the following:

Integration of words and pictures
Numerous illustrations
Brief and uncomplicated plot

Folklore

Folklore has no single identifiable author; the stories were passed through the generations by word of mouth before they were ever written down. As people told the stories to one another, they were changed and molded to suit the teller's style or fancy. Folklore is a broad category encompassing many types. For example, the Mother Goose nursery rhymes, which delight the ear of the young child even before the meaning of the words is known, are a part of folklore. Folk and fairy tales, which mirror the language and values of a culture, constitute another major category of folk literature. Fables, too—those simply told and highly condensed morality tales that often use animal characters to embody human virtues and vices—belong to the folklore tradition.

In addition, classical mythology, which reverberates with symbolic meaning, makes up a

Folk literature comprises stories passed down from one generation to the next. They may convey morality, explain earthly and celestial phenomena, or impart values. (From *Hermes, Lord of Robbers,* translated by Penelope Proddow and illustrated by Barbara Cooney.)

large portion of folk literature. Some of the great myths explain the origin of the earth, the phenomena of nature, and the relation between humans and their gods according to the beliefs of the people who created them. Legends are exaggerated hero tales grown hardly recognizable through retellings that embellished the initial grain of truth. The American version of hero tales, called *tall tales,* exaggerates the strength, the size, and the riches of America. Our Paul Bunyan, John Henry, and Pecos Bill epitomize American values in the same manner as Robin Hood and King Arthur epitomize those of the English.

Recurring themes, motifs, and patterns involving characters, images, incidents, and conventional story shapes are evident in traditional literature. The struggle between light and dark, a lost child, a superhuman character, an image of eternal spring, the transformation of a frog into a prince, or the repetitive cycle of a story pattern are examples of archetypes.

Features that characterize the major forms of folklore are the following:

FOLK TALES

Simple repetitive plots
Stereotyped characters symbolizing good or evil
Obvious themes illuminating human values
Repeated use of the numbers three and seven
Repetitive and rhythmic language

FABLES

Single-incident plots
Animal characters symbolizing human traits
Explicitly stated morals
Didactic language

MYTHS

Explanations of the origins and cycles of the
    universe
Gods and mortals as characters
Symbolic language

TALL TALES

Regional settings and dialect
Heroic themes
Earthy wit and humor
Exaggerated size and deeds

Fantasy

Fantasy is distinguished by the imaginary nature of places and events: surreal worlds in which animals talk, inanimate objects have feelings, time is manipulated, or humans accomplish superhuman feats. Plot, character, and incident make believable whatever the fantasy writers say is so within the framework they set. E. B. White's *Charlotte's Web* (P–I) is a

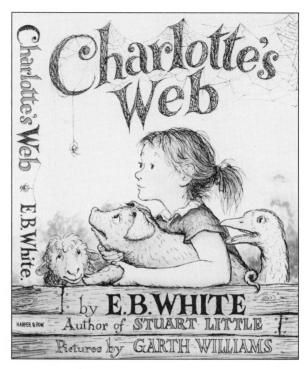

The unlikely friendship of a spider and a pig is woven into a memorable fantasy. (From *Charlotte's Web*, by E. B. White, illustrated by Garth Williams.)

well-known fantasy. Fantasy can embrace themes of eternal or universal truths that reflect human concerns.

Children can learn about fantasy through noticing the devices used to create it—miniature people, as in Mary Norton's *The Borrowers* (I); time warp, as in Philippa Pearce's *Tom's Midnight Garden* (I); or talking animals, as in Kenneth Grahame's *The Wind in the Willows* (I).

Among the features that characterize fantasy are the following:

Imaginary worlds made believable
Characters who possess supernatural qualities
Themes often dealing with the struggle between
    good and evil
Language sometimes used symbolically

Science Fiction

Science fiction employs imaginative extrapolation of fact and theory: stories project what could happen in another time through logical extension of established theories and scientific principles. Science fiction describes worlds that are not only plausible, but may exist someday; it also considers the impact of science on life. Early science fiction writers extrapolated primarily from technology, but the genre now attracts writers who incorporate sociology and anthropology. Science fiction themes often question the effect of progress upon the quality of life and examine the values of contemporary society. John Christopher's *The White Mountains* (I–A) is a popular piece of science fiction, and Madeleine L'Engle's *A Wrinkle in Time* (I) is considered a classic in the field.

Science fiction readers are intrigued with the consideration of alternative futures. Science fiction writers themselves say they are not attempting to predict the future; instead, they consider many potential futures. They also say that although science fiction readers do not know what the future holds, they won't be surprised when it gets here.

The characteristic features of science fiction are as follows:

Alternate views of the future
Extrapolation from facts and theories
Consideration of impact of technology on life

Poetry and Verse

Poetry is the shorthand of beauty. As Emerson suggested long ago, it says the most important things in the simplest way. And as Sandburg explains, "Poetry is a phantom script telling how rainbows are made and why they go away."[43] Poetry is distilled language that captures the essence of an idea or experience and encompasses the universe in its vision.

Much poetry is metrical, rhythmic, and rhymed, appealing to the ear as well as to the mind and the emotions. Taking many forms, the best poetry and verse—from nonsense rhymes and limericks through lyrical and narrative poetry—always shapes a taken-for-granted ordinary into thoughts extraordinary.

Some fine examples of poetry and verse for children are David McCord's *A Star in the Pail* (P), Aileen Fisher's *Listen, Rabbit!* (P–I), Karla Kuskin's discussion of the ideas that grow into poems in *Near the Window Tree* (I), Myra Cohn Livingston's *Worlds I Know* (I), and Robert Louis Stevenson's *A Child's Garden of Verses* (P–I–A).

Sometimes mystifying, often difficult, poetry can enrich life and fire the imagination. Poetry engages the heart for reasons that reason may never know. Children love poetry: it echoes their language and their concept of the world. If young children are discovering turtles, for example, they should hear Vachel Lindsay's

There was a little turtle.
He lived in a box.
He swam in a puddle.
He climbed on the rocks.[44]

Older students, occupied with plans for their future, should hear Louise Driscoll's "Hold Fast Your Dreams," which says:

Within your heart
Keep one still, secret spot
Where dreams may go
And sheltered so
May thrive and grow—
Where doubt and fear are not[45]

Whatever the occasion, poetry infuses greater meaning and imparts a sense of joy in the process.

Among the distinctive features of poetry are the following:

This lamp in my window
Glows warmly, shines bright.
It guides friends and strangers
Who travel at night.

Through only a few words, poetry can create an image and stir an emotion, and thoughtful illustrations solidify that image. (From *Whiskers and Rhymes* by Arnold Lobel).

Condensed language calling attention to itself
Extensive use of figurative language
Clearly discernible forms
Manipulation of sounds and structures

Realistic Fiction

Fiction set in modern times, with events that could occur, is called realistic fiction (or contemporary realism). Although plot, character, and incident are created and manipulated according to an author's design, all remain within the realm of the possible. Sue Ellen Bridgers's *Permanent Connections* (A) is illustrative of contemporary realism. Katherine Paterson's *Bridge to Terabithia* (I) is beautifully written realistic fiction.

Children with a strong desire for realistic books are sometimes looking for clues about what life might hold for them. Reading about

children a few years older than they serves as a rehearsal for anticipated experiences. Books often provide a mirror for the reader; they also become a window through which to view other lives.

Numerous studies show that a country's social and political philosophies are evident in its children's books. Obviously, the social concerns that impinge upon authors are reflected in their work and show in the problems and conflicts they write about. In earlier books, the problems were often solved when virtue was rewarded, justice triumphed, and good overcame evil. More recently, this is not the case. Realistic fiction is frequently open-ended; the problem is not resolved and the central character accepts a less-than-perfect world.

Among the distinguishing characteristics of contemporary realism are the following:

An illusion of reality, a believable slice of life
Characters who represent the full range of
  humanity
Real-world settings
Themes dealing with basic truths of human
  nature
Language similar to natural spoken language

Historical Fiction

Historical fiction is categorized by the time of the setting and the believability of events: the stories are set in the historical past with events that could possibly have occurred. An author creates plot, character, and incident and casts them into an authentic historical setting that is true to the facts of history. Esther Forbes's *Johnny Tremain* (I–A) is a well-known historical novel.

Children who read about the past through historical fiction gain a richer and more immediate understanding of life than they do through a book of historical facts. Many children learn more about life on the frontier

The Courage of Sarah Noble, a stirring example of historical fiction, depicts the life of a frontier family. (Written by Alice Dalgliesh, illustrated by Leonard Weisgard.)

through Laura Ingalls Wilder's "Little House" series (P–I) than through their school textbooks.

Teachers can enrich the school curriculum by including books of historical fiction with textbooks. Many different books about a historical time can give readers rich insights about life and provide them with the unique opportunity of evaluating divergent reports of the same event.

Features that characterize historical fiction are as follows:

An illusion of reality set in the past
Believable characters
Real-world settings in the historical past
Themes dealing with basic conflicts of humans
Language reflecting the historical period and
  people

Biography

Biography tells the story of a person's life in part or in its entirety. It bears the imprint of the author; although the story of a person's life provides the basic facts, the writer interprets, selects, and organizes elements to create an aesthetic work. Jean Fritz wrote about her childhood in China in *Homesick: My Own Story* (I). Carl Sandburg's extensive biography, *Abe Lincoln Grows Up* (A), is another outstanding example. Russell Freedman casts a new light on *Lincoln* (I–A) in a photobiography that won the 1988 Newbery Award.

Distinguishing features of biography include the following:

A plot structured around a person's life
Themes often dealing with a struggle for success
Emphasis on the strength and moral fiber of the
  subject

Nonfiction

Informational books aimed at explaining a subject are categorized as *nonfiction*. They present information in a variety of formats: in picture books and photographic essays, as reproductions of original documents, as how-to-do-it manuals, or as direct expository texts. Nonfiction outnumbers fiction in most children's libraries, yet until recently, little critical attention was given to it. History, science, mathematics, arts and crafts, and social sciences are but a few of the topics included in nonfiction. Russell Freedman's *Indian Chiefs* (I), Rhoda Blumberg's *The Incredible Journey of Lewis and Clark*

A Superb View of the United States Squadron, Under the Command of Commodore Perry, Bound for the East shows the fleet that returned to Japan on February 13, 1854.

Nonfiction informs readers about a subject. In the case of *Commodore Perry in the Land of the Shogun,* by Rhoda Blumberg, the story tells of adventure in far-off places that is reminiscent of fiction.

(I), and Patricia Lauber's *Volcano: The Eruption and Healing of Mount St. Helens* (I) are excellent examples of nonfiction.

Organizing a unit in the science and social studies curricula requires teachers to locate numerous books on a topic. Selecting the books involves attending to the recency, adequacy, accuracy, and authenticity of the information in them. More subtle, yet equally important, is the author's passionate interest in the subject.

Characteristic features of nonfiction books are as follows:

Concentration on facts and concepts
Logical presentation of information
Expository language

Books for Multicultural Understanding

Books for multicultural understanding portray an ethnic or racial group accurately and show that each human being is connected to all other humans through a common humanity. Human needs, emotions, and desires are similar; books can help us appreciate the similarities while at the same time help us appreciate and celebrate uniqueness among cultural groups. *So Far From the Bamboo Grove* (I–A), by Yoko K. Watkins, is an excellent book to develop understanding about an Asian culture.

The United States was once called a "melting pot" where peoples of many nations came to live together in harmony. The metaphor of a "salad bowl" is more apt today; people of many cultures blend together while each retains its distinctive features and flavorings.

The distinguishing characteristics of multiethnic literature are the following:

Presentation of an ethnic group through positive and authentic images
Portrayal of individuals with unique thoughts and emotions

So Far from the Bamboo Grove, by Yoko Kawashima Watkins, shows the universality of human needs, emotions, and desires.

KEEPING UP WITH NEW CHILDREN'S BOOKS

The field of children's literature is enormous and continually growing. Teachers and librarians need to recognize outstanding examples of various genres and know how to keep up with new publications. There are between 2,000 and 4,000 books for children published each year; and more than 50,000 children's books in print.

Review Journals

The best sources of information are the review journals: *The Horn Book Magazine, Bulletin of the Center for Children's Books (BCCB), School Library Journal (SLJ),* and *Booklist.* Addresses for each are found in the "Book Selection Aids" appendix.

The Horn Book Magazine, published six times a year, contains discriminating reviews of high-quality new books and articles by authors, illustrators, publishers, teachers, librarians, critics, editors, and others interested in the field of children's literature. The magazine was founded in 1924 by Bertha Mahoney Miller.

Bulletin of the Center for Children's Books (BCCB), published monthly except August, contains reviews of new titles that are evaluated as "recommended," "acceptable," "marginal," "not recommended," or "for special collections or unusual readers only." Starred reviews signal an outstanding book. Except for preschool years, a reading grade level range is given rather than the age of child. Curriculum uses, such as music, science, or art, and developmental values, such as growing up or friendship, are given where appropriate. The Center for Children's Books was initiated at the University of Chicago in 1945 by Frances Henne and Alice Brooks McGuire.

School Library Journal (SLJ), published 11 times a year, contains reviews written by practicing school and public librarians. In addition to the reviews of books, the journal contains reviews of audiovisual materials and computer software for children and adolescents, articles on a range of subjects of interest to people in the field, and a lively letters-to-the-editor column. SLJ was established in 1953.

Booklist, a journal of the American Library Association, (ALA) is published twice monthly from September through June and monthly in July and August. Each issue contains reviews of books, audiovisual materials, and computer software. Reviews are written by staff members who seek opinions from practicing school and public librarians. *Booklist* was established in 1903 by the ALA.

A list of additional book selection aids is found in Appendix B.

The Newbery Medal is awarded annually for the most distinguished contribution to literature for children.

The Caldecott Medal is given annually to the illustrator of the most distinguished children's picture book.

Children's Book Awards

The excitement in the children's book world reaches fever pitch in mid-January when it is Newbery and Caldecott selection time. The selection committees have read all the books published all year and meet in long sessions deliberating which books will be the winners of these two prestigious awards. Waiting to hear who won the Newbery and Caldecott is like waiting for the announcement of the winner of the Pulitzer Prize, the Nobel Peace Prize, the Emmy, or the Oscar.

Why are these awards so important? Experts are declaring that the winners are the outstanding examples of children's literature for the year. The awards have significant educational, social, cultural, and financial impact. Receiving one of the awards means the books will be read by and will influence generations of schoolchildren around the world. In America alone, every public and school library will purchase the award-winning books. Winning one of the awards, therefore, also guarantees considerable financial reward for the author and the publisher. The awards are given widespread media attention, and the winning authors commonly receive numerous speaking invitations.

The John Newbery Medal Frederic G. Melcher, editor of *Publisher's Weekly* Magazine, donated and named this award as a tribute to John Newbery (1713–1767) who was the first English publisher of books for children. The award, administered by the Association for Library Services to Children of the American Library Association, was established in 1922 and has been awarded annually ever since. The Newbery Medal is given for the most distinguished contribution to literature for children published in the United States during the year. The judgment is based on the literary quality of the text. A list of winners and honor books is in Appendix A.

The Randolph Caldecott Medal In 1937, Melcher proposed the establishment of an award for picture books. This award was named in honor of Randolph Caldecott (1846–1886), an English illustrator who was one of the first to put action and liveliness into illustrations for children. This award, also administered by the Association for Library Services to Children of the ALA, was established in 1938 and is awarded annually. The Caldecott Medal is given to the illustrator of the most distinguished picture book published in the United

States during the year. The selection is based on the quality of the illustrations. A list of winners and honor books is in Appendix A.

Other awards for children's books are described below, and the winners of each are listed in Appendix A.

The Hans Christian Andersen Award was established in 1956 by the International Board on Books for Young People. It is given every two years to an author who has made an important international contribution to children's literature. Since 1966 an illustrator's award has been given also.

The International Reading Association Children's Book Award was established in 1975. It is given for the first or second book of a promising new writer who shows unusual promise in the children's book field.

The National Council of Teachers of English Award for Excellence in Poetry for Children was established in 1977. It is given every three years to a living American poet in recognition of his or her entire body of work.

The Laura Ingalls Wilder Award, administered by the Association of Library Service to Children of the ALA, was established in 1954. It is given every three years to an author or illustrator who has made a substantial and lasting contribution to children's literature.

The *Children's Books: Awards and Prizes,* a comprehensive listing of award winners, is published every two or three years by the Children's Book Council. The 1986 edition lists 55 awards in the United States selected by adults and 28 selected by young readers, 29 awards granted in the British Commonwealth, and 13 international and multinational awards.

In addition to these individual awards, teachers and librarians will want to be aware of various lists of outstanding books published annually. The National Council of Teachers of English develops an annual list of books that are particularly suited for language study. The list is published in *Language Arts. Outstanding Science Trade Books for Children* is published by the National Science Teachers Association, and *Notable Children's Trade Books in the Field of Social Studies* is published by the National Council of Social Studies.

Finally, children get to vote for books they like in *Children's Choices,* sponsored by the International Reading Association and the Children's Book Council. This list appears annually in the October issue of *The Reading Teacher.*

PROFESSIONAL REFERENCES

Anderson, Richard, et al. *Becoming a Nation of Readers: The Report of the Commission on Reading.* Washington, D.C.: National Institute of Education, U.S. Department of Education, 1985.

Applebee, Arthur N. *The Child's Concept of Story: Ages Two to Seventeen.* Chicago: University of Chicago Press, 1978.

Association for Library Service to Children. *Notable Children's Books, 1976–1980.* Chicago: American Library Association, 1986.

Book Industry Study Group, Inc. *Consumer Research Study on Reading and Book Purchasing.* Summary Report presented at the Library of Congress. April 1984.

The Booklist. American Library Association. 50 East Huron St., Chicago, Ill. 60611.

Britton, James. *Language and Learning.* New York: Penguin Books, 1970.

Bulletin of the Center for Children's Books (BCCB). Subscription: The University of Chicago Press.

Journals Division, P.O. Box 37005, Chicago, Ill. 60637.

Cameron, Eleanor. "High Fantasy: Wizard of Earthsea." *Horn Book Magazine* 47, no. 2 (April 1971): 129–38.

The Children's Book Council, eds. *Children's Books: Awards and Prizes.* New York: Children's Book Council, 1986.

Elleman, Barbara. *Popular Reading for Children 2: A Collection of Booklist Titles.* Chicago: American Library Association, 1986.

Helbig, Althea K., and Agnes Regan Perkins. *The Dictionary of American Children's Fiction, 1960–1984.* Westport, Conn.: Greenwood Press, 1987.

Holland, Norman. *Five Readers Reading.* New Haven: Yale University Press, 1975.

The Horn Book Magazine. Park Square Building, 31 St. James Ave., Boston, Mass. 02116.

Iser, Wolfgang. *The Implied Reader.* Baltimore: Johns Hopkins University Press, 1974.

Kingman, Lee, ed. *Newbery and Caldecott Medal Books, Volume 5, 1976–1985.* Boston: Horn Book 1986.

Le Guin, Ursula. "Child and Shadow." *Quarterly Journal of the Library of Congress,* 32, no. 2 (April 1975): 139–48.

Le Guin, Ursula. "Child and Shadow." *Quarterly Journal of the Library of Congress,* 32, no. 2 (April 1975): 139–48.

Lewis, C. S. *Essays Presented to Charles Williams.* London: Oxford University Press, 1947.

McDowell, Myles. "Fiction for Children and Adults: Some Essential Differences." *Children's Literature in Education,* 10 (March 1973): 50–63.

Meek, Margaret, Aidan Warlow, and Griselda Barton, eds. *The Cool Web: The Pattern of Children's Reading.* New York: Atheneum, 1978.

Monson, Dianne, ed. *Adventuring with Books: A Booklist for Pre-K—Grade 6.* Urbana, Ill.: National Council of Teachers of English, 1985.

Moss, Anita, and Jon C. Stott. *The Family of Stories: An Anthology of Children's Literature.* New York: Holt, Rinehart, & Winston, 1986.

Nakamura, Joyce, ed. *Children's Authors and Illustrators: An Index to Biographical Dictionaries,* 4th ed. Detroit: Gale Research, 1986.

Paley, Vivian Gussin. *Wally's Stories.* Cambridge: Harvard University Press, 1981.

Pradl, Gordon M., ed. *Prospect & Retrospect: Selected Essays of James Britton.* Upper Montclair, N.J.: Boynton Cook, 1982.

Ripple, R. E., and V. N. Rockcastle, eds. *Piaget Rediscovered: A Report of the Conference on Cognition Studies and Curriculum Development.* Ithaca: Cornell University Press, 1964.

Robinson, Robert D. "The Three Little Pigs: From Six Directions." *Elementary English,* 45, no. 3 (March 1968): 354–59, 366.

Roginski, Jim. *Behind the Covers: Interviews with Authors and Illustrators of Books for Children and Young Adults.* Littleton, Colo.: Libraries Unlimited, 1985.

Rosenblatt, Louise. *Literature as Exploration.* 3rd ed. 1938. Reprint. New York: Noble & Noble, 1976.

———. *The Reader, the Text, the Poem.* Carbondale: Southern Illinois University Press, 1978.

School Library Journal (SLJ). Subscription: R. R. Bowker, Subscription Dept., P.O. Box 1426, Riverton, N.J. 08077.

Sutherland, Zena. *The Best in Children's Books: The University of Chicago Guide to Children's Literature, 1979–1984.* Chicago: University of Chicago Press, 1986.

Tompkins, Jane P., ed. *Reader-Response Criticism: From Formalism to Post-Structuralism.* Baltimore: Johns Hopkins University Press, 1980.

NOTES

1. N. M. Bodecker, "Hello Book," from a Bookmark for Children's Book Week (New York: Children's Book Council, 1978).

2. Richard Anderson et al., *Becoming a Nation of Readers: The Report of the Commission on Reading,* (Washington, D.C.: National Institute of Education, U.S. Department of Education, 1985), 23.

3. Barbara Hardy, "Narrative as a Primary Act of Mind," in *The Cool Web: The Pattern of Children's Reading,* ed. Margaret Meek, Aidan Warlow, and Griselda Barton (New York: Atheneum, 1978), 12–23.

4. Estimates of illiteracy in America range from 1 percent, according to a general information publication that bases its statistics on federal censuses; to 4 percent, according to the Book Industry Study Group; to 13 percent, according to American Demographics. The difference between these figures is so great because the criteria used by such research organizations vary. One study, for instance, may label literacy as reading at the fourth grade level; another, at the tenth grade level. Whatever the exact percentage, even 1 percent illiteracy is too high. (See *The World Almanac and Book of Facts, 1988* [New York: World Almanac, 1988], 732; Book Industry Study Group, *The 1983 Consumer Research Study on Reading and Book Purchasing,* Summary Report presented at the Library of Congress, April 11, 1984; and Cheryl Russell et al., "Matters of Note About Demographics: I Need to See Your Children," *American Demographics* 8, no. 10 (October 1986): 77.

5. Louise Rosenblatt, *The Reader, the Text, the Poem* (Carbondale: Southern Illinois University Press, 1978), 24.

6. C. S. Lewis, "On Stories," in

Essays Presented to Charles Williams (London: Oxford University Press, 1947), 100.

7. Myles McDowell, "Fiction for Children and Adults: Some Essential Differences," *Children's Literature in Education,* 10 (March 1973): 51.

8. Wolfgang Iser, "The Reading Process: A Phenomenological Approach," in *The Implied Reader* (Baltimore: Johns Hopkins University Press, 1974), 274–94. For further explication of the transaction between the reader and the text, see Wolfgang Iser, *The Act of Reading: A Theory of Aesthetic Response* (Baltimore: Johns Hopkins University Press, 1978); Suzanne K. Langer, *Mind: An Essay on Human Feeling,* Vol. 1 (Baltimore: Johns Hopkins University Press, 1967); Louise Rosenblatt, *Literature as Exploration,* 3rd ed. (1938; reprint, New York: Noble & Noble, 1976); Rosenblatt, *The Reader;* Norman Holland, *Five Readers Reading* (New Haven: Yale University Press, 1975); and Jane P. Tompkins, ed., *Reader-Response Criticism: From Formalism to Post Structuralism* (Baltimore: Johns Hopkins University Press, 1980).

9. James Britton, "The Role of Fantasy," in *Prospect and Retrospect: Selected Essays of James Britton,* ed. Gordon M. Pradl (Montclair, N.J.: Boynton Cook, 1982), 38–45.

10. Margaret Anzul, Madison Elementary School, Madison, N.J., 1978.

11. Northrop Frye, *The Educated Imagination* (Bloomington: Indiana University Press, 1970), 48–49.

12. Anita Moss and Jonathan Stott, *The Family of Stories* (New York: Holt, Rinehart & Winston, 1986).

13. Jean Piaget, "Development and Learning." In *Piaget Rediscovered: A Report of the Conference on Cognitive Studies and Curriculum Development,* ed. R. E. Ripple and V. N. Rockcastle (Ithaca: Cornell University Press, 1964), 9–10.

14. Vivian Gussin Paley, *Wally's Stories* (Cambridge: Harvard University Press, 1981), 7–8.

15. Ibid., 29–30.

16. Arthur Applebee, *The Child's Concept of Story,* (Chicago: University of Chicago Press, 1978), 42.

17. Ibid., 44.

18. Ibid., 45.

19. Bernice Cullinan, Kathy Harwood, and Lee Galda, "The Reader and the Story: Comprehension and Response," *Journal of Research and Development in Education,* 16, no. 3 (Spring 1983): 36.

20. Applebee, *Child's Concept of Story,* 132.

21. For a detailed discussion of language and development of a sense of story, see James Britton, *Language and Learning* (Harmondsworth, Eng.: Penguin Books, 1970); and Applebee, *Child's Concept of Story.*

22. F. André Favat. *Child and Tale: The Origins of Interest.* Research Report no. 19 (Urbana, Ill.: National Council of Teachers of English, 1977).

23. Arlene M. Pillar, "Aspects of Moral Judgment in Response to Fables," *Journal of Research and Development in Education,* 16, no. 3 (Spring 1983): 47–54.

24. James Miller, Jr., "Literature and the Moral Imagination," *Response to Literature,* ed. James R. Squire (Urbana, Ill.: National Council of Teachers of English, 1968), 30.

25. Northrop Frye, *The Educated Imagination,* 55.

26. James Britton, *Language and Learning* (London: Penguin Press, 1970).

27. D. W. Harding, "Psychological Processes in the Reading of Fiction," in *The Cool Web,* 58–72.

28. S. Lee Galda, *Children Evaluating Literature: Patterns of Response Across Grades Four Through Nine,* Final report, the University of Georgia Research Foundation, the Elva-Knight-International Reading Association, and the College of Education, University of Georgia, 1986.

29. Ibid., 18.

30. Janet Hickman, "Everything Considered: Response to Literature in an Elementary School Setting," *Journal of Research and Development in Education,* 16, no. 3 (Spring 1983): 8–13.

31. Ibid., 12.

32. Britton, *Language and Learning,* 11.

33. Arthur N. Applebee, "Studies in the Spectator Role: An Approach to Response in Literature," in *Researching Response to Literature and the Teaching of Literature,* ed. Charles R. Cooper (New York: Atheneum, 1978), 92–99.

34. Arthur Applebee, "Where Does Cinderella Live?" in *The Cool Web,* 55.

35. Frye, *The Educated Imagination,* 115–16.

36. Robert D. Robinson, "The Three Little Pigs: From Six Directions," *Elementary English* (now *Language Arts*), 45, no. 3 (March 1968): 354–59, 366.

37. Ursula Le Guin, *A Wizard of Earthsea* (1968; reprint, New York: Puffin, Viking Penguin, 1971), 25.

38. The archetypal patterns are discussed at length in Eleanor Cameron, "High Fantasy: Wizard of Earthsea," *Horn Book*

Magazine 47, no. 2 (April 1971): 129–38.

39. Le Guin, *A Wizard of Earthsea*, 197–98.
40. Ibid., 199–200.
41. Ibid., 197.
42. Ursula Le Guin discusses her own interpretation of *A Wizard of Earthsea* in "Child and Shadow," *Quarterly Journal of* the Library of Congress, 32, no. 2 (April 1975): 139–48.
43. Lee Bennett Hopkins, ed., *Rainbows Are Made: Poems by Carl Sandburg*, illustrated by Fritz Eichenberg (San Diego: Harcourt Brace Jovanovich, 1982), 46.
44. Vachel Lindsay, "The Little Turtle," in *The Arbuthnot An-* thology of Children's Literature, 4th ed., ed. Zena Sutherland et al. (New York: Lothrop, Lee & Shepard, 1976), 42.
45. Louise Driscoll, "Hold Fast Your Dreams," in *Time for Poetry*, 3rd ed., comp. May Hill Arbuthnot and Shelton Root (Glenview, Ill.: Scott, Foresman, 1967), 192.

CHILDREN'S BOOKS CITED

Alexander, Lloyd. *The Book of Three*. New York: Dell, 1980.

Andersen, Hans Christian. "Inchelina." In *The Family of Stories*. Edited by Anita Moss and Jonathan Stott. New York: Holt, Rinehart & Winston, 1984.

Babbitt, Natalie. *The Eyes of The Amaryllis*. New York: Farrar, Straus & Giroux, 1977.

———. *Tuck Everlasting*. New York: Farrar, Straus & Giroux, 1975.

Blumberg, Rhoda, *Commodore Perry in the Land of the Shogun*. New York: Lothrop, Lee & Shepard, 1985.

———. *The Incredible Journey of Lewis and Clark*. New York: Lothrop, Lee & Shepard, 1987.

Blume, Judy. *Are You There, God? It's Me, Margaret*. New York: Bradbury Press, 1970.

———. *Tales of a Fourth Grade Nothing*. Illustrated by Roy Doty. New York: Dutton, 1972.

Bodecker, N. M. "Hello Book" from a bookmark for Children's Book Week. Children's Book Council, 1978.

Bridgers, Sue Ellen, *Permanent Connections*. New York: Harper & Row, 1987.

Brown, Marc. *Hand Rhymes*. New York: Dutton, 1985.

Brown, Margaret Wise. *Goodnight Moon*. Illustrated by Clement Hurd. New York: Harper & Row, 1947.

Byars, Betsy. *The Not-Just-Anybody Family*. Illustrated by Jacqueline Rogers. New York: Delacorte, 1986.

———. *The Summer of the Swans*. New York: Penguin, 1981.

Christopher, John. *The White Mountains*. New York: Macmillan, 1967.

Christopher, Matt. *The Hockey Machine*. Boston: Little, Brown, 1985.

Cleary, Beverly. *Ramona Quimby, Age Eight*. Illustrated by Alan Tiegreen. New York: Morrow, 1981.

Collier, James Lincoln, and Christopher Collier. *My Brother Sam Is Dead*. New York: Four Winds, 1974.

Cooper, Susan. *The Dark Is Rising*. Ilustrated by Alan Cober. New York: Atheneum, 1973.

Cormier, Robert. *The Chocolate War*. New York: Pantheon, 1974.

———. *I Am the Cheese*. New York: Pantheon, 1977.

Crane, Walter. *The House That Jack Built*. London: Dent, 1866.

Dalgliesh, Alice. *The Courage of Sarah Noble*. Illustrated by Leonard Weisgard. New York: Scribner's, 1954.

Driscoll, Louise. "Hold Fast Your Dreams." In *Time for Poetry*. Edited by May Hill Arbuthnot and Shelton Root. Glenview, Ill.: Scott, Foresman, 1967.

Fisher, Aileen. *Listen, Rabbit*. Illustrated by Symeon Shimin. New York: Crowell. 1964.

Forbes, Esther. *Johnny Tremain*. Illustrated by Lynd Ward. Boston: Houghton Mifflin, 1946.

Freedman, Russell. *Indian Chiefs*. New York: Holiday, 1987.

———. *Lincoln: A Photobiography*. New York: Clarion, 1987.

Freeman, Don. *Dandelion*. Illustrated by Don Freeman. New York: Viking Press, 1964.

Fritz, Jean. *Traitor: The Case of Benedict Arnold*. New York: Putnam, 1981.

———. *Homesick: My Own Story*. Illustrated by Margot Tomes. New York: Putnam, 1982.

———. *Why Don't You Get A Horse, Sam Adams?* Illustrated by Trina Schart Hyman. New York: Coward, 1974.

Gág, Wanda. *Millions of Cats*. New York: Coward, 1928.

Galdone, Paul. *The Three Bears*. New York: Clarion, 1985.

———. *The Three Little Pigs*. New York: Clarion, 1984.

Grahame, Kenneth. *The Wind in the Willows*. Illustrated by E. H. Shepard. New York: Scribners, 1933.

Greenaway, Kate. *Mother Goose: Or the Old Nursery Rhymes*. 1881. Reprint. New York: Warne, 1900.

Grimm, Jakob and Wilhelm. *Grimm's Fairy Tales*. Illustrated by George Cruikshank. Translated by Edgar Taylor. London: Baldwin, 1823.

Hoban, Tana. *Shapes, Shapes, Shapes.* New York: Greenwillow, 1986.

Hooks, William. *Moss Gown.* Illustrated by Donald Carrick. New York: Clarion, 1987.

Hopkins, Lee Bennett, ed. *Rainbows Are Made: Poems by Carl Sandburg.* Illustrated by Fritz Eichenberg. San Diego: Harcourt Brace Jovanovich, 1984.

Hunter, Mollie. *A Stranger Came Ashore.* New York: Harper & Row, 1975.

Hutchins, Pat. *The Doorbell Rang.* New York: Greenwillow, 1986.

———. *Rosie's Walk.* New York: Macmillan, 1968.

Juster, Norton. *The Phantom Tollbooth.* New York: Random, 1961.

Kellogg, Steven. *Can I Keep Him?* New York: Dial, 1971.

Kunhardt, Dorothy. *Pat the Bunny.* 1940. Reprint. New York: Golden Press-Western, 1962.

Kuskin, Karla. *Near the Window Tree.* New York: Harper & Row, 1975.

Lauber, Patricia. *Volcano: The Eruption and Healing of Mount St. Helens.* New York: Bradbury Press, 1986.

Lee, Harper. *To Kill a Mockingbird.* New York: Lippincott, 1960.

Le Guin, Ursula. *The Farthest Shore.* Illustrated by Gail Garraty. New York: Atheneum, 1972.

———. *The Tombs of Atuan.* Illustrated by Gail Garraty. New York: Atheneum, 1971.

———. *A Wizard of Earthsea.* Illustrated by Ruth Robbins. Boston: Parnassus, 1968.

L'Engle, Madeleine. *A Wind in the Door.* New York: Farrar, Straus & Giroux, 1973.

———. *A Wrinkle in Time.* New York: Farrar, Straus & Giroux, 1962.

Lewis, C. S. *The Chronicles of Narnia: The Lion, the Witch & the Wardrobe.* New York: Macmillan, 1951.

Lindsay, Vachel. "The Little Turtle." In *The Arbuthnot Anthology of Children's Literature,* 4th ed. Edited by Zena Sutherland et al. New York: Lothrop, Lee & Shepard, 1976.

Lionni, Leo. *Frederick.* New York: Pantheon, 1967.

Livingston, Myra Cohn. *Worlds I Know and Other Poems.* New York: Atheneum, McElderry, 1985.

Lobel, Arnold. *Frog and Toad Are Friends.* New York: Harper & Row, 1970.

———. *Whiskers and Rhymes.* New York: Greenwillow Books, 1985.

Lowry, Lois. *Rabble Starkey.* Boston: Houghton Mifflin, 1987.

McCloskey, Robert. *Make Way for Ducklings.* New York: Viking, 1941.

McKinley, Robin. *The Blue Sword.* New York: Greenwillow, 1982.

MacLachlan, Patricia. *Sarah Plain and Tall.* New York: Harper & Row, 1985.

Maris, Ron. *Is Anyone Home?* New York: Greenwillow, 1986.

Martin, Bill, Jr. *Brown Bear, Brown Bear, What Do You See?* Illustrated by Eric Carle. New York: Holt, Rinehart & Winston, 1983.

——— and John Archambault. *The Ghost-Eye Tree.* Illustrated by Ted Rand. New York: Holt, Rinehart, & Winston, 1985.

———. *Knots on a Counting Rope.* Illustrated by Ted Rand. New York: Henry Holt, 1987.

Minarik, Else. *Little Bear.* Illustrated by Maurice Sendak. New York: Harper & Row, 1957.

Naylor, Phyllis Reynolds. *The Year of the Gopher.* New York: Atheneum, 1987.

Norton, Mary. *The Borrowers.* Illustrated by Beth and Joe Krush. New York: Harcourt, 1953.

Oxenbury, Helen. *Dressing.* New York: Wanderer, 1981.

Paterson, Katherine. *Bridge to Terabithia.* Illustrated by Donna Diamond. New York: Crowell, 1977.

Pearce, Philippa. *Tom's Midnight Garden.* Illustrated by Susan Einzig. Philadelphia: Lippincott, 1959.

Potter, Beatrix. *The Tale of Peter Rabbit.* London: Warne, 1902.

Proddow, Penelope. *Hermes, Lord of Robbers.* Illustrated by Barbara Cooney. New York: Doubleday, 1971.

Rackham, Arthur. *Mother Goose Nursery Rhymes.* New York: Viking Press, 1975.

Raskin, Ellen. *The Westing Game.* New York: Dutton, 1978.

Rockwell, Thomas. *How to Eat Fried Worms.* Illustrated by Emily McCully. New York: Watts, 1973.

Sandburg, Carl. *Abe Lincoln Grows Up.* Illustrated by James Daugherty. 1931. Reprint. San Diego: Harcourt Brace Jovanovich, 1974.

Sendak, Maurice. *Where the Wild Things Are.* New York: Harper & Row, 1963.

Silverstein, Shel. *Where the Sidewalk Ends.* New York: Harper & Row, 1974.

Sobol, Donald. *Encyclopedia Brown, Boy Detective.* Nashville: Nelson, 1963.

Sperry, Armstrong. *Call It Courage.* New York: Macmillan, 1940.

Stevens, Janet. *The House That Jack Built: A Mother Goose Nursery Rhyme.* New York: Holiday, 1985.

Stevenson, James. *Worse Than Willy!* New York: Greenwillow, 1984.

Stevenson, Robert Louis. *A Child's Garden of Verses.* Illustrated by Jessie Willcox Smith. New York: Scribners, n.d.

Strieber, Whitley. *Wolf of Shadows.*

New York: Knopf, 1985.

Tafuri, Nancy. *Who's Counting?* New York: Greenwillow, 1986.

Taylor, Mildred. *Roll of Thunder, Hear My Cry.* Illustrated by Jerry Pinkney. New York: Dial, 1976.

Twain, Mark. *The Adventures of Huckleberry Finn.* New York: Bantam, 1986.

Viorst, Judith. *I'll Fix Anthony.* Illustrated by Arnold Lobel. New York: Harper & Row, 1969.

Voigt, Cynthia. *Dicey's Song.* New York: Atheneum, 1982.

Watkins, Yoko Kawashima. *So Far from the Bamboo Grove.* New York: Lothrop, Lee & Shepard, 1986.

Wells, Rosemary. *Max's Bath.* New York: Dial, 1985.

White, E. B. *Charlotte's Web.* Illustrated by Garth Williams. New York: Harper & Row, 1952.

Wilder, Laura Ingalls. Little House Books. 9 vols. Illustrated by Garth Williams, New York: Harper & Row, 1953.

2

Literature in the Classroom

Books Fall Open

Books fall open,
you fall in,
delighted where
you've never been;
hear voices not once
heard before,
reach world on world
through door on door;
find unexpected
keys to things
locked up beyond
imaginings.
What *might* you be,
perhaps *become*,
because one book
is somewhere? Some
wise delver into
wisdom, wit,
and wherewithal
has written it.

True books will venture,
dare you out,
whisper secrets,
maybe shout
across the gloom
to you in need,
who hanker for
a book to read.[1]

David McCord

avid McCord's lyrical prediction "books fall open,/you fall in" conjures up an image of what we believe should be happening in homes, schools, and libraries. Books do lead to worlds unknown and to things beyond imagining. Children's literature lies at the heart of the elementary school curriculum; its use is informed by theory and research and based on sound practices that teachers and librarians have developed through experience. A solid body of research—some of it grounded in child development, some in whole language learning, and some in cognitive psychology—undergirds the use of literature for learning.

A TRANSACTIONAL VIEW OF READING

Readers construct meaning as they interact with a text.[2] Instead of absorbing "the one right meaning" from a text, readers bring their own background knowledge to bear and create their unique meanings based upon an interaction with the text.[3] This was demonstrated most visibly in studies by Steffensen, Joag-Dev, and Anderson.[4] In an illustrative study, the researchers presented a text (a letter) about a Indian wedding and one about an American wedding to a group of people from India and a group from the United States. Both groups read the same words but took very different meanings from their readings. The Americans read both accounts as a report of a joyous occasion: they reported that the bride looked beautiful and that romance filled the air. The readers from India, however, viewed the occasion as a solemn affair; they noted the hierarchy of the seating arrangements for guests, the importance of the dowry and financial arrangements, and the sacrifice the bride was making. Each group of readers brought different background experiences and expectations about weddings to the reading and, therefore, took very different meanings from it although they had read the same words.

A Response Approach to Literature

A response approach to literature is one that values equally the diversity and uniqueness of what a child has to say about a book. It encourages versatility of perceptions by the child and assumes that each reader—child and adult—creates his or her own meaning in interaction with a text. Teachers who insist upon one preconceived "right" response inhibit children's thinking and deny them the joy of a personal discovery. The response view advocates using informed judgment first to determine where a child is and then to open the doorway to greater literary experiences.

Two conceptual constructs central to the response approach are reader response theory and developmental psychology. Reader response theory grows from the ideas of Louise Rosenblatt first advanced in *Literature as Exploration* and later in *The Reader, the Text, the Poem*. Before Rosenblatt's work, educators believed that a writer embeds meaning in a text and a reader works at extracting it, that the correct meaning waits to be discovered by the clever reader. A major proponent of this view was I. A. Richards, who, in his *Practical Criticism*, pursued the idea by carefully analyzing reader responses to various poems and pointing out the many "misinterpretations." Richards lamented the fact that a reader's predisposition and experience could lead away from the "one right meaning" of a poem.

Rosenblatt, on the other hand, casts the reader into a much more important and active role. She sees the literary work existing in the "live circuit set up between reader and text: the reader infuses intellectual and emotional meanings into what he reads."[5] It is a circular process in which the reader responds to the words on the page and at the same time draws upon personal experiences in order to create individual meaning. For Rosenblatt, the validity of each person's response is established by verification with the text. Thus, a response is invalid if contradicted by the text. Such a flexible position leaves room for a wide range of responses—all valid. Furthermore, in the classroom it leads to lively discussions as children share with each other their unique perceptions of a piece of literature enjoyed in common.

The work of Wolfgang Iser (see Chapter 1), compatible with Rosenblatt's, describes the relation between reader and author. Insofar as a writer uses particular narrative techniques, he circumscribes the impression a reader takes from his work. If he paints a totally explicit picture, according to Iser, the text is dull because there are no gaps to activate the readers' imaginations, to allow them to make inferences and individually realize the intentions of a text. If the author sketches too briefly, the reader is required to fill in too many gaps, feels dissatisfied, and may tire of the effort. This implies that a single work will have many, more or less complete, realizations, as many as there are readers filling in the gaps.

What does this mean for the literature teacher? Initially, it means that we need to cre-

ate an environment in which readers can take risks in expressing their responses, and that this can best be achieved if we entertain a variety of possibilities and do not impose our own interpretations as the "one right answer" or by moralizing about the issues involved. For example, children discussing Katherine Paterson's *The Great Gilly Hopkins* (I) have strong feelings about the ending of the story. Some insist that Gilly should have stayed in the secure world provided by Maime Trotter. Others are equally vehement that Gilly rightfully belongs with her grandmother or that Courtney, her natural mother, really wants her and will return to claim her. The sensitive dicussion leader will draw out such readers' responses and their underlying reasoning, sometimes asking, for example, "What is it in the book that makes you feel that way?"

Also, small-group discussions should be encouraged. When children hear interpretations different from their own, they gradually learn that a story can have many interpretations and that their own perception is as valid as those of their friends. Exposure to others' interpretations can also encourage students to entertain alternate possibilities. Teachers, responsible for directing the course of discussion, can help engender respect for divergent views and encourage students to think about things in ways they had not thought before.

A developmental perspective aligned with reader response theory provides further insight for the literature teacher.[6] James Squire, one of the early researchers, studied the responses of adolescents to four short stores. Among other findings, Squire found that adolescents tend to "happiness bind" (the inclination to interpret a happy ending in spite of contrary evidence in the text), that readers who became deeply involved in a story were more likely to consider the literary values of the story, and that adolescent readers need assistance in interpreting fiction.

Other early researchers, Alan Purves and Victoria Rippere, devised a means of analyzing

bumpity,
bumpity,

hold on tight,

A-1 This oversized board book contains plain white backgrounds filled with droll round-headed infants of various ethnic groups. The sturdy construction withstands frequent and rough handling by toddlers. (*Say Goodnight* by Helen Oxenbury. New York: Macmillan, Aladdin Books, 1987.)

rocking horse

A-2 Lisa McCue has extended the life of Don Freeman's *Corduroy* in board books and miniature-sized pudgy books. The sturdy construction and colorful illustrations appeal to infants and toddlers. (*Corduroy on the Go*. New York: Viking Penguin, 1987.)

Books for the Very Young

The largest increase in the publication of children's books lies in books for the very young. With great versatility in format and modes of illustration as well as creative design, authors and illustrators have created a wealth of resources to use with children from birth on. The materials used range from hard board books to soft flannel pages, from pop-up books to toy books of all sorts. Straightforward informational books, concept books, and simple story books grace bookstore and library shelves to introduce the pleasures of reading from the beginning of a child's life.

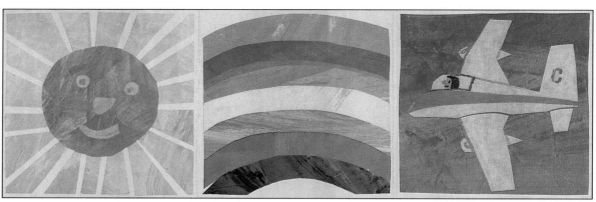

A-3 Eric Carle's accordion-folded cardboard sections are designed to be free-standing in a child's playpen or crib. The colorful scenes of his collages call attention to the natural beauty of a child's world. (*All Around Us*. Boston: Picture Book Studio, 1986.)

LET'S SEE WHAT PUNCHINELLO WILL DO TONIGHT!

A-4 Tomie dePaola's toy book opens to scenes of *Giorgio's Village* with intricate settings and movable characters. Such books stimulate curiosity in a child's exploration of the story. (New York: Putnam's, 1982.)

A-5 The story in this oversized board book proceeds from front to back and then on around again. Bold images with only a few simple words characterize books that toddlers turn to time and again. (*Fat Mouse* by Harry Stevens. New York: Viking Kestrel, 1987.)

A-6 Janet and Allan Ahlberg use a fresh and imaginative approach in clever sequels to traditional nursery tales. *The Jolly Postman* delivers letters, contained in envelope pages, from one storybook character to another. (Boston: Little, Brown, 1986.)

A-7 This is actually a pillow made from soft flannel with a goodnight story in its pages. It suggests security and warmth. (*My Pillow Book* by Angela Ackerman. New York: Random House, 1988.)

A-8 This informational book uses colorful characters on spacious pages to show the step-by-step process of how a home is built. (*Building a House* by Byron Barton. New York: Greenwillow, 1981.)

A-9 This concept book contains photographs of familiar objects in strong, uncluttered images with striking color. (*Red, Blue, Yellow Shoe* by Tana Hoban. New York: Greenwillow, 1986.)

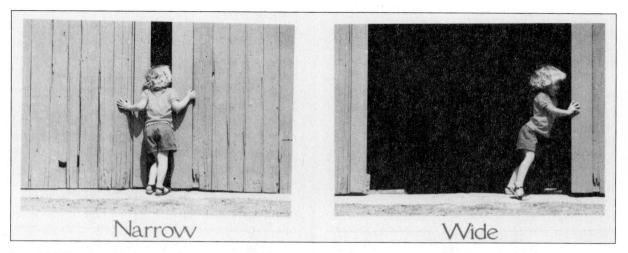

Narrow   Wide

Bruce McMillan uses his camera to capture scenes for children who are at a stage of active conceptual development. (From *Becca Backward, Becca Frontward* by Bruce McMillan.)

the content of individuals' oral and written responses to literature.[7] The four categories describe the posture of the person writing about literature: the state of involvement, the perception, the interpretation of meaning or significance, and the evaluation of the literary work. Many studies followed with researchers expanding and revising the Purves categories and clearly establishing the study of the developmental effects of response to literature.[8]

At the same time response to literature studies were growing, new developments in the field of reading theory were underway. Psycholinguists and cognitive psychologists agreed that individuals' reading comprehension was affected by how their knowledge and expectations interacted with the material they were reading—that is, the text. Frank Smith summarized this new approach to reading: meaning does not reside in a text; rather, it is created in the mind of the reader in interaction with the text.[9]

Recognizing a need for a kind of inquiry to describe responses more adequately, researchers began to view response from a developmental perspective. For example, Arthur Applebee began to look at children's responses to literature, tracing their concept of story as they grew.[10] He found that their use of conventions, attitudes toward story, and organizational patterns reflected general cognitive developmental trends. (See Chapter 1 for discussion of stages of cognitive development.) Preoperational children, for example, cannot analyze themes or author's motives and, rather than summarizing a story in broad, generalized terms, will retell it in great detail, embellishing the original with their unique poetic version. On the other hand, children at the stage of formal operations are able to analyze and generalize from stories, concentrating on how the work interacts with their view of the world.

Research on Response to Literature

The seminal study in reader response is considered to be I. A. Richards's *Practical Criticism*, published in 1929. Richards's study, cited earlier, was an attempt to introduce a new kind of documentation to those interested in the contemporary state of culture. Over a period of several years, he distributed selections from a group of 13 poems to his students, requesting that they reread them and comment upon them over the coming week. He gave no hints beforehand other than a comment that the selections were "perhaps a mixed lot." Richards analyzed the responses by categorizing what he regarded as "barriers" that readers place in the way of understanding the meanings of the poems. (These so-called barriers were actually the readers' life experiences.) He searched for ways of teaching literature that would make uniform the readers' interpretations of the selections.

Richards's work inspired several decades of teaching for close textual analysis after the model designated as *New Criticism.* Richards and the New Critics believed that there was an objectively "correct" interpretation of a text. Disagreement began to rise, however. Rosenblatt's *Literature as Exploration,* published in 1938, called attention to the role of the reader, the process by which readers interpret literature, and the contributions the reader's intellectual and emotional functioning might make toward the experience of literature. Rosenblatt's ideas, set forth again in *The Reader, the Text, the Poem* (1978), have been widely accepted as the more reasonable view.

Many studies have built upon Rosenblatt's transactional theory. For example, Shelley Rubin and Howard Gardner investigated children's comprehension of story, metaphor, and language conventions in a series of studies at Harvard, called Project Zero. In one developmental study, "Once Upon a Time: The Development of Sensitivity to Story Structure," Rubin and Gardner examined the story competence of first, third, and sixth grade students by reading an incomplete, specially constructed fairy tale to the subjects.[11] One group of students at each grade level heard a version of the fairy tale in which all character motivation had been deleted; the other group heard a version with character motivation included. Asking students to retell the story after three days showed some strong developmental patterns. The first graders' recountings were more sparse, and their labeling of characters was more polemic (good–bad, wicked witch–nice

princess) than those of the older students. On the whole, the ones who heard the motivation-deleted version retold a more complete version than the ones who heard the motivation-included version. Rubin and Gardner suggested that the fuller version was overwhelming to the young students. Third graders became most actively involved in the task and told the most exhaustive endings. They incorporated themes, characters, and events from other fairy tales in their retellings and enjoyed the process most. Sixth graders who heard the motivation-deleted version of the fairy tale filled in from their own knowledge of character motivation when they retold it three days later, but the ones who heard the motivation-included version always performed better in the way they solved the story problem and in-

Children interpret stories according to their own developmental levels. Katherine Patterson's *Bridge to Terabithia* raises an issue that challenges children at several developmental levels.

tegrated their own endings. It is clear that age and experience with fairy tales influence students' responses to the experimental tasks.

Bernice Cullinan, Kathy Harwood, and Lee Galda studied developmental factors in fourth, sixth, and eighth grade children's responses to more complicated literature.[12] The participants were interviewed individually and in groups of three after reading one realistic and one fantasy novel. In the realistic novel, *Bridge to Terabithia* (I), Leslie, a central character, dies, but in their retellings, not a single fourth grader mentioned the death. When encouraged to tell more by nondirective probes, such as "Anything else?" children added other details from the story but studiously avoided any mention of Leslie's death. When a child in the group questioned "whether she really died," others insisted she had "come back to life," and was right there with Jesse at the end of the story. Their strong expectations for a happy ending, called "happiness binding" by Squire,[13] caused them to read a happy ending into the story.

The sixth grade readers comprehended the story at a literal and occasionally at an interpretive level. They included Leslie's death in the retelling but expressed shock that it had happened. "I never read a book like this before where a good person dies," they said. The girls accepted the story as believable and gripping, but the boys were disdainful of the emotional intensity of the novel: they saw Jesse as an emotional sissy and Leslie as a daredevil showoff. Some said the book sounded "like a Hollywood romance or a soap opera."

The eighth grade girls read the novel as a romance and hoped that they might someday be the kind of friend to some boy, often a particular boy, that Leslie was to Jesse. The eighth grade boys, on the other hand, reacted very differently in the individual interview and the group discussion. Individually, they characterized the relationship between the boy and girl as idyllic, but in the group they demeaned both characters as "countrified" and immature. Con-

cern for their macho image affected their responses in front of their peers.

The fourth graders saw no special meaning in the metaphor of the bridge in the title. They said flatly, "It's just about building a bridge." The sixth graders were tentative: "It could have been the bridge of their friendship." The eighth graders saw many possible meanings. One noted, "She was his bridge to a better life." Another said, "It was like a bridge between the real world and the make-believe. And I thought that when she died, she was half in the real world and half in the make-believe world."

The fourth grade students were not able to read with understanding *A Wizard of Earthsea* (I-A), even though they could read the words at a literal level. One child complained about the long sentences, saying "they just rumbled by like a jumbled bunch of words." They misread *"loosing* the shadow" when Ged unleashes a shadow of death from under the earth, and said, "I didn't understand that part about him *losing* his shadow." By reading the novel before they were developmentally ready for it, even though it was for experimental purposes, it has undoubtedly been ruined for them forever.

The sixth grade students comprehended *A Wizard of Earthsea* adequately. The boys liked the book better than the girls did, although some avid science fiction and fantasy readers said, "I like my evil to be more aggressive, like Sauron in *The Lord of the Rings,* or General Woundwort in *Watership Down.*" They complained that the shadow "was sneaky and went around getting inside people," whereas the evil in the other books "lined up their troops and went out after 'em."

The eighth grade students comprehended *A Wizard of Earthsea* at both a literal and interpretive level; they were also able to see meaning in the story for their own lives. One said, "I guess I have a shadow side, too, but I don't want to know about that right now."

When asked about the meaning of the shadow in *A Wizard of Earthsea*, the fourth graders mumbled, "I don't remember that part." The sixth graders saw the shadow as evil.

This study confirmed that children's developmental levels as well as their backgrounds of reading and life experiences are the most influential factors in their responses to literature. They did not comprehend aspects of the novels for which they had no basis of understanding.

Anthony Petrosky also studied reader response from a developmental perspective in adolescents.[14] His case studies of four 14- and 15-year-olds corroborated findings that age and reading experience influence response markedly. Petrosky also demonstrated the usefulness of group discussions in helping readers clarify and validate their responses. Talking about a story with significant others, he found, influences responses to it, and as Norman Holland and G. Mills separately had contended,[15] helps filter out responses inappropriate to the text. Such discussion may also expand responses since readers take in statements about the work as they take in the work itself. These findings suggest that discussion after reading is one good way to help children clarify their responses. As one child echoed the thoughts of all of us, "I never thought about it that way, but now it makes a lot of sense."

James Britton argues against piecemeal analysis of stories children read, taking the position that it interferes with comprehension of a work as an integrated whole.[16] When asked to remember each tiny detail, children lose the overarching meaning; the same thing happens if they are asked to discuss the story bit by bit. Teachers' questions, then, need to be broad, open-ended ones rather than the kind that seek specific details.

Ways in which discussion can support the understanding of literature are also described by Margaret Anzul in her study of children in a literature discussion group during their fifth and sixth grade years.[17] Anzul focused on children's growth in aesthetic reading within a transactional context in which the teaching was inductive, based on the readers' responses. Transcripts of the class sessions showed that students were increasingly able to sustain independent discussions of literature and to move to higher levels of thinking, such as interpretive and evaluative. Anzul observed "moments of passion" among her students when they would become emotionally involved in the discussion, raise their voices, and speak emphatically as they discussed their response to a story. When these moments occurred, the emotional as well as the cognitive involvement in the stories led to sustained interpretive and analytical talk on the part of the readers.

Anzul concluded that meaningful involvement over time with significant works of literature contributed to students' ability to discuss and interpret new works. Students learned "more than they were taught" as they spontaneously appropriated literary knowledge as they needed it. Literary conventions, such as symbol, metaphor, point of view, and irony were explored as they came across such conventions in their reading.

S. Lee Galda explored uniqueness in patterns of response and the effect of group discussion on individual response in a study of 11-year-old girls.[18] She found that each child had a characteristic way of responding and that some were more open to the possibilities in stories than others. She also found that they sometimes used labels to express literary concepts that were ill-formed, whereas at other times they struggled to express intuitively known concepts for which they had no labels.

From studies of this kind we know how children's responses to literature can serve as guides to teachers; their responses tell us what literary concepts need to be taught and what basic experiences with literature need to be provided. No hierarchical list exists of literary concepts to be taught in a predetermined order, but concepts and labels that are necessary for children to discuss literature should be provided when the children have a need to know them. Galda gives the example of two children who talked about the way Katherine Paterson "broke moods" when she moved from direct dialogue to a third-person narrator in *Bridge to Terabithia* (I). It was apparent that these children were dealing with the effect of point of view on narration, but they did not have the words to discuss it. Children's responses, then, can inform teachers about what to teach and when to teach it.

What else does this say to the literature teacher? Most important, the methods teachers use need to be informed by a knowledge of cognitive and emotional developmental stages. This not only directs the choice of books for specific age groups but also tells teachers what expectations are reasonable with respect to kinds and levels of response. Teachers need to remember that as children mature, their dependence upon stories as truth lessens.[19] Children should be allowed to accept the distinction between fact and fiction on their own terms.

CREATING THE ENVIRONMENT FOR CHILDREN TO RESPOND TO LITERATURE

Activities described throughout this text are chosen to help readers develop a deeper understanding of and a greater appreciation for books. Because children's literature is so rich and varied, it can be used to enhance every area of the curriculum. More important, though, are those experiences that keep literature central. The activities are intended to bring readers back to books and guide them to others. Connie and Harold Rosen state the case well:

> It is as though there is a deep lack of confidence in the power of literature to do its work and a profound conviction that unless literature can be converted into the hard currency of familiar school learning it has not earned its keep.

What will take children more deeply into the experience of the book? This is the question we should be asking rather than by what means can I use this book as a launching-pad into any one of a dozen endeavors which leave the book further and further behind, at best a distant sound, at worst forgotten entirely.[20]

Children will eagerly read, learn, and create in an atmosphere in which books are valued and celebrated; when they are around people who prize reading, they learn to love to read. The two most important factors in helping children become avid readers are time for reading books that they choose and listening to good books read aloud by enthusiastic readers.

Every classroom needs an inviting reading corner furnished with a soft rug, perhaps a rocking chair, pillows, or other comfortable places to sit, adequate light, and pleasing things to look at. It also should have, of course, a good and continually changing collection of books. In addition, children need freedom to explore many kinds of materials by themselves in the school library.

Research and practical experience show that most children who become involved in activities related to books read more than those who do not. The phenomenon is cyclical—reading leads to engagement and involvement, which lead to deeper understanding, more enjoyment, and hence, more reading.

Extension activities allow children the time to savor and absorb books. It is important to ponder a book for a while before beginning another; students need a chance to linger in the spell cast by a good book. This may mean *doing nothing* or it may mean using creative learning activities. Response and reflection are important ingredients of a child's complete learning experience; give time for both.

Using and Misusing

There is a rhyme that goes "Mother said, 'Oh, stop a bit!/This is overdoing it!' This injunction also applies to activities designed to extend the

Children need the freedom to explore many kinds of materials by themselves in the school library.

understanding and appreciation of literature—in particular to the urge to turn every book encounter into a concrete project. We should avoid overdoing a good thing, for in our zeal we may be engendering boredom instead of interest.

Children can be encouraged to respond to literature in many ways. They discover the intrinsic pleasure in extended activities when there are many to choose from. There is always the danger, however, that teachers may become so enthusiastic about activities that they spend time on them that might better be spent reading more books. The aesthetic nature of the reading experience requires personal involvement; the impact of the book determines the response one makes. Reading is a private affair that calls upon the emotions of the reader. Some books should be explored, others read, closed, and forever locked in the reader's heart. A sensitive teacher knows when a reader wants to make this choice.

Creating Enthusiasm for Books

The teacher or librarian is the most critical factor in creating an environment for learning

through literature. Enthusiasm for reading is contagious; teachers and librarians could start an epidemic! A case in point is Elly Kazin, a third grade teacher in East Williston, New York. Elly registered casually for a course in children's literature at Adelphi University. But something magical happened in that course; not only did Elly Kazin get excited about children's literature, so did her 30 third grade students.

How did it happen? Professor Barbara Goldman, who teaches the course, explains it this way:

> Elly involved her students in what she was learning. She told them, "Let's take this course together, and this is what *we* have to do!" Whenever I gave an assignment to the college students, Elly took it back to her third graders. For example, writing annotations for thirty picture books with complete bibliographic data, summaries, and comparisons to other books was turned over to her students.[21]

Here is an example of an annotation done by one of the children in her class:

Auther—Bernard Waber
Title—*Ira Sleeps Over*
Year—1972
Summary—A boy sleeps over his frinds house fer the frish time end needs to find out whether or not to take his teddy bear.
Plot—Whether or not he shoud take his teddy bear.
Main characters—Ira, Reggie
Illustrations—colorful
Interesting words—clunky p. 35, creeky p. 35
Similar book—*Best Friends* by Steven Kellogg
Books by the same author—*The House on 88th Street*
Lyle Finds His Mother
Lovable Lyle

When Professor Goldman assigned an examination of folklore, Elly again turned the assignment over to her students. They each selected one folktale to examine in depth and searched the school and public libraries for variants. One student brought in several variations of *Little Red Riding Hood* (P), including those illustrated by Bernadette Watts, Paul Galdone, Trina Schart Hyman, and William Stobbs. They shared their folktales with each other, discussed the characteristics of folktales, and compared the different variants. They used this knowledge to write their own stories in folklore style.

When Professor Goldman assigned an in-depth study of one author or illustrator, Elly gave the assignment to her students. Each child in the class became an expert on one author or illustrator. One child proudly proclaimed, "I've read everything Charlotte Zolotow has written—and that's a lot!" Another was an Ezra Jack Keats expert; another specialized in Tomie dePaola; another, in Maurice Sendak. When Goldman visited the class, one child slipped quietly to her and asked, "How's our teacher doing?" Professor Goldman made it clear that they were all doing quite well. In fact, at the end of the course, she presented each child with a facsimile certificate for successfully "completing" the college course.

The spark that Professor Goldman generated was magnified and spread to 30 children who became avid readers. The librarians in the school and public libraries knew these children; they were always asking for more books. The parents were amazed at the spurt of reading energy they saw in their children.

From this experience and others, we know that excitement about literature is indeed contagious. Children are inherently motivated when their teacher is enthusiastic. There is a magnifying effect when one is learning about literature and teaching it to children simultaneously.

There are many ways to create a reading environment in the classroom or library. Enthusiasm for books is primary, but this needs to be extended into the physical environment of the room. Following are three ways to establish a book-centered atmosphere.

Centers

Centers are focal spots in a classroom or library that are developed around a topic or theme. Some may be permanent; others may be seasonal. The Literature Center pictured was done in conjunction with a fourth grade unit on the kinds of fiction.[22]

Realistic fiction: It could happen.
Historical fiction: It might have happened.
Fantasy: It couldn't happen.
Science fiction: It might happen.

Book jackets and stacks of books of each type of fiction were placed under each category. As students read, they began to classify their books according to the categories. Folders listing some examples of each type of fiction were available for reference. Students also searched for authors who have written in more than one of these categories—for example, Mollie Hunter's books include a *Sound of Chariots* (realistic), *The Stronghold* (historical), and *A Furl of Fairy*

In Coal Country, by Judith Hendershot, is a popular choice for historical fiction in the form of a picture book. (Illustrated by Thomas B. Allen.)

Wind (fantasy). Students listed books of each type they had read and did a project on their favorites. In addition, they began to identify one noted author of each type of fiction, such as Jean Fritz (historical), Betsy Byars (realistic), Lloyd Alexander (fantasy), and H. M. Hoover (science fiction). Finally, students were asked to recall some picture books in each category. For realistic, they found Keats's *The Snowy Day* (P) and *Peter's Chair* (P); for fantasy, they found Sendak's *Where the Wild Things Are* (P) and *In the Night Kitchen* (P).

Sustained Silent Reading

Students need time to read; giving them time is part of creating an environment for literature. Several approaches to extended silent reading are popular. Sustained Silent Reading (SSR) is a plan wherein 20 to 30 minutes are set aside each day when everybody in the school reads: the principal, the custodian, the teachers, and all the students. There are many variations of the program: DEAR, Drop Everything And Read; USSR, Uninterrupted Sustained Silent Reading; or READ, Read Everything And Dream.

We know that reading independently improves reading fluency, but research suggests that students do not have enough time to read in school. C. W. Fisher et al. found that students spend up to 70 percent of the time allocated for reading instruction doing seatwork—workbooks and skill sheets—many of which are unrelated to reading and are actually detrimental to children's attitude toward reading.[23]

Dolly Cinquino described her daughter storming in the door from school complaining, "Mom, I *hate* reading!" Her mother countered, "But you love reading your Little House and Beverly Cleary books here at home." "Yes, I know that, but I *hate* reading!" What she hated was the class at school called "Reading," which obviously had nothing to do with really reading books. Classroom research shows that the amount of time devoted to worksheets does nothing to improve reading proficiency.[24] The

amount of independent silent reading children do in school, however, is significantly related to gains in reading achievement.[25] Researchers estimate that the typical primary school child reads silently only 7 or 8 minutes per day. By the middle grades, silent reading time may average 15 minutes per school day.[26]

Mary Sirmons, second grade teacher in Baytown, Texas, describes her own classroom, which differs markedly from the typical classrooms described above. She reports how much her students of varying ability levels have read during the past few years.

Since September, 1982, I have been involved in an innovative reading program with my second-grade students. Each year I obtain a teacher's book loan from our local public library where I am allowed to check out 150 books for a 60-day period. I bring the books into the classroom, place them on wooden display racks with the front, not the spine, of the book showing. I encourage the students to check them out daily.

I explain the reading program to the students' parents at the beginning of each year and ask them to encourage their child to read at home on a regular basis. At the end of the

Classrooms need to have a good and continually changing collection of books, and children need the time and freedom to be able to explore the books.

1985–86 school year, I had used this program with groups of students on four different reading ability levels.

During 1982–83, my accelerated group of 30 students read slightly over 12,000 books. This was an average of 400 books per student. The following (1983–84) year, my high-average group of 26 students read 8,654 books (Average—332). In 1984–85, the average group of 25 students read a total of 6,529 books (Average—261). In 1985–86, my low group of 22 students read a total of 3,352 books (Average—152). This makes an accumulated total of over 30,000 books read during the four years.

Book-sharing activities are planned throughout the year and as a culminating activity for the program, I give the students a free-book party during the last week of school. On this day, students come dressed as their favorite book character. Each child is given free books which I have received as bonuses from orders placed to book clubs during the year.[27]

Bulletin Boards

Teachers do not need to be ad writers to create bulletin boards that draw attention to books; they create meaningful ones about books important to them. Boards devoted to one theme at a time are best, since doing too much in too small a space results in confusion and clutter. If the central purpose of the display is immediately recognizable, the viewer is attracted to observe details.

Bulletin boards that feature changing displays of book jackets, information on authors, realia associated with books, and children's interpretations of books promote reading. Posters about books, maps, book marks, and other relevant materials are available, often free, from publishers.

Vibrant color, texture, large size, and movement contribute to the effectiveness of bulletin boards. A balloon with a passenger basket assures that books can take you any-where, and an owl may ask "Who-o-o-?" or command "Be Wise! Read!" Keys may open doors to, and clocks may signal time for, varieties of experiences with literature, while cut-paper ships with white burlap sails can announce "Smooth Sailing," "Shipping Out," or "Launching" lively books.

Students can help create bulletin board displays, too. For instance, an older group constructed logs from heavy wrapping paper and arranged these as a bonfire with leaping red foil flames. They called their display "Burning Issues in Books." Among the book jackets used were Chana Byers Abells's *The Children We Remember* (I), Israel Bernbaum's *My Brother's Keeper* (I), Roberto Innocenti's *Rose Blanche* (I), Toshi Maruki's *Hiroshima No Pika* (I), Milton Meltzer's *Ain't Gonna Study War No More* (A), Huynk Quang Nhuong's *The Land I Lost* (I), and Whitley Strieber's *Wolf of Shadows* (A).

Some teachers feature different writers in an author-of-the-month display. Biographical material (available from publishers) often includes a photograph as well as a personal statement by the author. Students can research additional information or write brief summaries of their books for the bulletin board, or they can suggest activities to extend the enjoyment of the author's books.

A "Poet-Tree" is a variation of this kind of display. Leaves made of construction paper or index cards can be attached to a tree sketched on a bulletin board or to a large tree branch that has been secured in a bucket of plaster. The tree can feature works of one poet, seasonal poems, or poems on a theme.

The sign on or near the tree calls attention to a bulletin board. Cut from a bright color that contrasts with the background, the letters should be large and clear. The message serves as a teaser; it should be simple and easily understood by children. Subtle word play or convoluted constructions may be confusing to those too young to understand the meaning or symbolism. The following captions have been used successfully to entice readers to these units:

Humor: What's So Funny?
Nonfiction: Books About Real Things
Imaginative Stories: Let's Pretend
Pets: It's Raining Cats and Dogs
Siblings: One Sister for Sale
Bears: VIB's—Very Important Bears
Historical Fiction: Time Ago Tales
Time Fantasy: Tesser Through Time
World War II: Never To Forget
Biography: Real People

PRESENTING LITERATURE

One of the most important roles a teacher has—and one of the most exciting—is sharing good literature with children. Children show their excitement eagerly and enthusiastically as they respond to literature they hear and see and turn to books themselves as a source of pleasure. They beg you to read a story again and to keep on reading. They begin to recognize authors and illustrators and ask for their books. They share their own enthusiasm for reading with their classmates by eagerly talking about books.

Teachers and librarians who surround children with books and poetry will observe these natural responses and, with careful planning, can stimulate even more. Students will begin to compare different versions of a folktale or contrast the print and media versions of a story. They will find poetry that goes with a book or topic. When teachers give book talks, share audiovisual presentations, and read aloud good books and poetry, they are showing children that reading is worth the effort.

Reading Stories and Poems Aloud

Reading aloud is one of the most common and easiest means of sharing books and poetry—

and a rich experience for all when done well. Once considered a suitable time filler or a calming activity after lunch recess, it is now known to have a positive impact on students' reading development.[28] And reading aloud to older students extends their horizons, introduces literature they might not read on their own, offers alternate worlds and life-styles, and provides a model of a good reader.

Some of the most convincing research, showing that reading aloud to children plays a part in early literacy development, has been conducted since 1980.[29] Gordon Wells, for instance, shows dramatic differences between a child who had been read to and one who had not.[30] Rosie, who scored lowest on all tests administered, including the test of knowledge of literacy, never had stories read to her before

she started school. By comparison, Jonathan had had approximately 6,000 book and story experiences before starting school and by age 10 had far exceeded all other children in literacy development. "Probably the most striking finding from the whole of the longitudinal study," Wells notes, "has been the very strong relationship between knowledge of literacy at age 5 and all later assessments of school achievements."[31] Several other writers have synthesized the research about reading aloud and its effect on children learning to read and write.[32] The wealth of evidence caused the Commission on Reading to conclude that "The single most important activity for building the knowledge required for eventual success in reading is reading aloud to children."[33]

The teachers in P.S. 321, District 15, in Brooklyn, New York, reiterated the reasons for reading aloud by listing them on a chart hanging in their Teacher Resource Room:

WHY READ ALOUD

Reading aloud
  Introduces new words
  Introduces more complex sentence structures
  Exposes students to more standard forms of
    English
  Exposes students to various styles of written
    language
  Develops a sense of story
  Motivates children to read better
  Provides structure and motivation for creative
    writing
  Enriches students' general knowledge
  Adds pleasure to the day

There are some important guidelines to consider when selecting books to read aloud, the most important of which is to select well-written stories. Books of quality abound, and it is a waste of precious time to read second-rate materials. Sometimes teachers read an inferior book "because the children love it," but students will love good books even more. Select books for reading aloud that will influence and expand their literary tastes.

Find out which books are already familiar by asking children to list their favorites, and then build from there, selecting books that children will probably not discover on their own. By all means read them Roald Dahl's *James and the Giant Peach* (I) unless, of course, most of them have already read this book on their own. Save reading-aloud time for the special books they should know. (See the list of suggestions in the Teaching Activity, "Books For Reading Aloud.") Introduce children to all of an author's books by reading aloud from *one* of them. For example, read Beverly Cleary's *Ramona the Pest* (P-I), but let students discover Cleary's other characters on their own.

Reading from outstanding examples of all types of literature—realistic fiction, historical fiction, fantasy, folklore, and poetry—can help expand children's literary tastes. Reading some books slightly above students' reading abilities extends their language; they usually comprehend more than they can read. However, a good book can be spoiled for children by reading it to them before they can understand its subtleties. Most books can be understood on several levels, but it would be a waste to read E. B. White's *Charlotte's Web* (P-I) to first-grade children, who will only interpret it on a literal level as a funny story about a pig. It is far better to save it until children can appreciate the deeper meanings of friendship, sacrifice, and love in the story.

Some books are best reserved for private reading. For example, Judy Blume says that she thinks her book *Are You There God? It's Me, Margaret* (I), because it is an account of a personal experience, is best shared by just her and the individual reader, whereas her book *Blubber* (I) begs to be read aloud because it deals with group behavior.

When reading aloud to children, know your material before you begin. Practice reading is important, especially in poetry, where the phrasing and cadence carry so much of the meaning. (The end of a line, for example, may not be the end of a phrase.) Listening to poets reading their own work on recordings can be useful; they know how it should sound. One such recording, "Poetry Parade" (Weston Woods), offers David McCord, Aileen Fisher, Karla Kuskin, and Harry Behn reading their poetry. There are other good reasons for practice sessions: Arlene Mosel's *Tikki Tikki Tembo* (P-I), contains a name that is repeated throughout the story—Tikki tikki tembo no sa rembo-chari bari ruchi-pip peri pembo; its rhythmic cadence and ear-tickling sounds carry the story and would be spoiled were the reader to stumble over it.

It is important to be thoroughly familiar with the content of the material read aloud. Some books contain words and incidents that might be offensive in some communities or that are best kept as a private interchange between author and individual reader. You can avoid embarrassment in a group by being alert to sensitive issues. Jean George's *Julie of the Wolves* (I-A) contains a brief "rape" scene in which a young husband attempts to consummate a marriage that had been prearranged in childhood. The story holds together without this incident and is otherwise an excellent choice for reading aloud to fifth and sixth grade students. Some teachers prefer to omit this passage when reading aloud in order to avoid embarrassing preteens into self-conscious snickering. Not all books or all scenes are for group sharing.

When reading, use a natural voice, with inflections and modulations befitting the story. Avoid greatly exaggerated voice changes and overly dramatic gestures. Read slowly, enunciate clearly, project your voice directly, and maintain eye contact with your listeners as much as possible. Teachers who read aloud with their noses in the book soon lose their audience.

There are different points of view about reading picture books aloud to children. Some believe that the illustrations are integral to the text and that children need to see them while hearing the words. Bill Martin believes that listening to a story and looking at the pictures are two different things that children should experience separately.[34] Your decision will rest on the qualities of the particular book you choose. If you feel that the illustrations are needed to make sense of the story, hold the book open and to one side as you read. Young children like to sit on the floor clustered close to you; this adds to the intimacy of the story experience. Face them away from distractions such as bright windows or doorways, so that their full attention can be on the story. If you choose to read the book aloud and then show the pictures, this extends the enjoyment—and there is nothing wrong with reading through a favorite book two or three times.

Read aloud time should not be optional. Teachers who permit students to draw, read their own books, or do quiet seatwork diminish the importance of reading aloud by implying that it does not deserve students' full attention.

Make story time a highlight of the day—a special treat that you share. Your enthusiasm and special preparations for the occasion set the tone; once you have begun, the magic of the story takes over.

Jim Trelease brought the values of reading aloud to the attention of parents and educators in *The Read-Aloud Handbook*.[35] He states that the desire to read is not inborn, but fostered, and that daily reading aloud has an effect comparable to that of a television commercial. If a television commercial can cause a child to want a particular hamburger or breakfast cereal, how much more important it is to feed and nurture the mind of a child by developing curiosity, emotional strength, and imagination by daily reading aloud. Margaret Mary Kimmel and Elizabeth Segel, in *For Reading Out Loud!*,[36] report that reading aloud from literature meaningful to children is widely acknowledged to be the most effective way to foster a lifelong love of books and reading. Trelease as well as Kimmel and Segel demonstrate techniques and include a list of recommended titles for reading aloud.

Reading aloud is central to every school day and should continue through adolescence, at least. Nursery and primary school teachers read aloud two or three times a day. One kindergarten teacher, Kristen Kerstetter, explains:

> I read to my children a lot—a whole lot! I'll read anywhere from one to three stories at a time. Sometimes I'll reread a favorite story twice. And I read two and three times a day including reading to the whole group, to small groups of four or five children and to individual children. I'll read stories over and over again, just the way children hear bedtime stories. It is not unusual for me to read a book twenty times in one month![37]

Poetry is particularly suited to reading aloud. There is a wealth of poetry that can extend and enrich every classroom experience. Long before children study poetry as a separate topic they need to hear it, read it, and feel it. Poetry should be as much a part of the school day as recess.

A personal collection of poetry is a vital tool for teachers and librarians. Despite the abundance of poems on every topic, it is often difficult to have the right poem ready at the right moment. A card file has many advantages: poems on cards can be grouped or regrouped according to need and are readily available for use. Far better than searching desperately for a specific poem about snow five minutes before reading Ezra Jack Keats's *The Snowy Day* (N-P) to a group of children is to be able to turn to your collection and immediately find Dorothy Aldis's "Snow":

> The fenceposts wear marshmallow hats
> On a snowy day:
> Bushes in their night gowns
> Are kneeling down to pray—
> And all the trees have silver skirts
> And want to dance away.[38]

Poetry collections grow and continue to be used throughout one's professional career. Categorize the poetry file by seasons, animals, feelings, or other topics related to the curriculum.

A copy of a special poem that harmonizes with a story can be pasted inside the front cover of the book. For example, Dorothy Aldis's "Whistles," which begins

> I want to learn to whistle.
> I've always wanted to[39]

is a perfect complement to Ezra Jack Keats's *Whistle for Willie* (P-I), while Harry Behn's "Hallowe'en":

> Tonight is the night
> When dead leaves fly
> Like witches on switches
> Across the sky, . . .[40]

belongs with any number of Halloween stories.

There are poems that extend the enjoyment of books for older readers, too. Mary O'Neill's "My Friend Leona," in her collection *People I'd Like to Keep* (I), includes these lines:

> She says she has dresses
> Too sweet to be seen
> But the ones she wears
> Are scrimped and mean. . . .[41]

which beg to be read with Eleanor Estes's *The Hundred Dresses* (I), one of the earliest books to deal realistically with prejudice. After reading Betsy Byars's *The TV Kid* (I), read Shel Silverstein's "Jimmy Jet and His TV Set" in *Where the Sidewalk Ends* (P-I), about a boy addicted to television, who

> . . . watched all day, he watched all night
> Till he grew pale and lean, . . .[42]

Children like to start their own poetry collections. These might take the same form as the teacher's, but more often poems are collected in a notebook or journal that allows room for additions, personal illustrations, and poems they write themselves.

In addition to poetry that is related to books, teachers should read aloud from a variety of poetry collections. Some outstanding examples appear in the following list, others are found in Chapter 7.

TEACHING ACTIVITY

BOOKS FOR READING ALOUD: A LITERATURE CURRICULUM   The following list of books is organized according to the age group for whom they hold greatest interest. These books have an energy that makes them seem timeless and fresh as they are read and reread, and are ones it would be a loss not to have experienced.

One basis for selection is that the books have lasting value. Undoubtedly, among the great many books published annually there are additional outstanding ones, but the ones cited here contain special experiences basic to a literary education.

We believe that, as children read books from this list, they begin to build a strong foundation for a lifelong love of reading. The choices reflect our personal and professional taste and belief that these books have the potential for becoming children's favorites for all time. It is informed by our work with children and our knowledge of their literature. While some good books must certainly have been overlooked, we are certain that the ones ultimately selected represent the finest writing for children today. Although not all those listed are of equal merit, all possess marks of quality that distinguish them from the mass of unenduring books and make them worthy of literary study.

Designation according to age of reader is, of course, flexible; all of us have seen how children will read well beyond their normal level when a book strikes to the center of their interest. Most of the books can be read aloud—and most students comprehend at a higher listening level than reading level. Finally, these books stand a good chance of becoming champion repeaters among readers because, although they may demand more, they also pay a richer dividend in joy.

NURSERY (N)

Bang, *Ten, Nine, Eight*
Brown, *Goodnight Moon*
Crews, *Truck*
Dabcovich, *Sleepy Bear*
dePaola, *Tomie dePaola's Mother Goose* (verse)
Hoban, *Is It Larger? Is It Smaller?*
Maris, *Is Anyone Home?*
Tafuri, *Have You Seen My Duckling?*
Watson, *Father Fox's Pennyrhymes* (verse)
Wildsmith, *Brian Wildsmith's Mother Goose* (verse)

NURSERY–PRIMARY (N–P)

Asbjørnsen and Moe, *The Three Billy Goats Gruff*
Burningham, *Mr. Gumpy's Outing*
Carle, *The Very Hungry Caterpillar*
De Angeli, *Marguerite de Angeli's Book of Nursery and Mother Goose Rhymes* (verse)
Emberley, *Drummer Hoff*
Freeman, *Corduroy*
Gág, *Millions of Cats*
Grimm, *Little Red Riding Hood*
Hutchins, *You'll Soon Grow into Them, Titch*
Keats, *Peter's Chair*
Kraus, *Leo the Late Bloomer*
Martin, *Brown Bear, Brown Bear, What Do You See?*
McCloskey, *Blueberries for Sal*
McCord, *All Small* (poetry)
Potter, *The Tale of Peter Rabbit*

Seuss, *Horton Hatches the Egg*
Slobodkina, *Caps for Sale*
Wood, *The Napping House*

PRIMARY (P)

Bang, *Dawn*
Bemelmans, *Madeline*
Bryan, *The Cat's Purr*
Cooney, *Miss Rumphius*
dePaola, *Strega Nona*
Grimm, *Hansel and Gretel*
Hall, *Ox-Cart Man*
Hoban, *Bread and Jam for Frances*
Hoberman, *A House Is a House for Me* (poetry)
Hogrogian, *One Fine Day*
Larrick, *When the Dark Comes Dancing: A Bedtime Poetry Book* (poetry)
Levinson, *Watch the Stars Come Out*
Lionni, *Swimmy*
Martin, *Foolish Rabbit's Big Mistake*
McCloskey, *Make Way for Ducklings*
Milne, *When We Were Very Young* (poetry)
Sendak, *Where the Wild Things Are*
Zolotow, *I Know a Lady*

PRIMARY–INTERMEDIATE (P–I)

Aardema, *Why Mosquitoes Buzz in People's Ears*
Andersen, *Thumbelina*
Cleary, *Ramona and Her Father*
Grimm, *The Sleeping Beauty*
Grimm, *Snow White and the Seven Dwarfs*

Jukes, *Blackberries in the Dark*
Kuskin, *The Dallas Titans Get Ready for Bed*
Kuskin, *Near the Window Tree* (poetry)
Louie, *Yeh Shen: A Cinderella Story from China*
MacLachlan, *Sarah, Plain and Tall*
McCord, *One at a Time* (poetry)
Steptoe, *The Story of Jumping Mouse*
White, *Charlotte's Web*
Wilder, *Little House in the Big Woods*

INTERMEDIATE (I)

Babbitt, *Tuck Everlasting*
Byars, *The Pinballs*
Fritz, *Homesick: My Own Story*
Grimm, *The Juniper Tree and Other Tales from Grimm*
Hamilton, *The People Could Fly*
Hunter, *A Stranger Came Ashore*
King-Smith, *Babe: The Gallant Pig*
Lasky, *The Night Journey*
L'Engle, *A Wrinkle in Time*
Lewis, *The Lion, the Witch, and the Wardrobe*
Lunn, *The Root Cellar*
Merriam, *Fresh Paint* (poetry)
Milne, *Winnie the Pooh*
Norton, *The Borrowers*
Paterson, *Bridge to Terabithia*
Raskin, *The Westing Game*
Singer, *Zlateh the Goat and Other Stories*
Steig, *Abel's Island*
Yagawa, *The Crane Wife*

INTERMEDIATE–ADVANCED
  (I–A)

Alexander, *Westmark*
Brooks, *Queen Eleanor:
  Independent Spirit of the
  Medieval World: A Biography of
  Eleanor of Aquitaine*
Cleaver, *Where the Lilies Bloom*
Collier, *my brother Sam is dead*
Conrad, *Prairie Songs*
Cooper, *The Dark Is Rising*
Dunning, *Reflections on a Gift of
  Watermelon Pickle . . . and
  Other Modern Verse* (poetry)
Fox, *One-Eyed Cat*
George, *Julie of the Wolves*
Hunter, *The Third Eye*

Le Guin, *A Wizard of Earthsea*
Maruki, *Hiroshima No Pika*
O'Brien, *Z for Zachariah*
O'Dell, *Island of the Blue Dolphins*
Paton Walsh, *The Green Book*
Rawls, *Where the Red Fern Grows*
Reiss, *The Upstairs Room*
Sandburg, *Rainbows Are Made:
  Poems by Carl Sandburg*
  (poetry)
Speare, *The Sign of the Beaver*
Taylor, *Roll of Thunder, Hear My
  Cry*
Tolkien, *The Hobbit*
Voigt, *Dicey's Song*

ADVANCED (A)

Adams, *Watership Down*

Brooks, *Midnight Hour Encores*
Cormier, *The Chocolate War*
Engdahl, *Enchantress from the
  Stars*
Fleischman, *Rear View Mirrors*
Hoover, *The Delikon*
Janeczko, *Pocket Poems: Selected
  for a Journey* (poetry)
McKinley, *The Blue Sword*
McKinley, *The Hero and the
  Crown*
Sutcliff, *The Light Beyond the
  Forest*
Sutcliff, *The Road to Camlann: The
  Death of King Arthur*
Voigt, *A Solitary Blue*
Whitman, *American Bard*
  (poetry)

Storytelling

Storytelling is a higher art than reading aloud and, as with most good things, requires more work and greater talent. Although storytelling is too individual a process for outright imitation to be useful, watching a gifted storyteller in action can provide clues to techniques that charm listeners.

Since your feelings about a story can become evident in the telling, tell a story you like. Block the story into parts. (Folk tales, which are frequently composed of three episodes, are easy to remember.) Try seeing the story in scenes and hearing the language in your mind. Memorize the major sequence of events but vary the story in your own style as you tell it. Word-for-word memory is seldom necessary, except for key phrases, for every storyteller adds a personal touch.

Put key phrases on cards ("prompt notes"), and refer to them to jog the memory during practice sessions. Because the magic of many stories lies in the language, there will usually be some phrases that should be preserved; for example, "I'm going to blow your house away" just will not substitute for "Then I'll huff and I'll puff and I'll blow your house down." Nor will "Little tree, give me new clothes" do for "Shiver and quiver, my little tree, silver and gold throw down on me."

Practice your story. Tell it in front of a mirror, record it (and listen critically), tell it to one person, and then tell it to a small group. Try to use prompt notes less and less frequently until you no longer need them. The story may change as you continue to tell it, but that is a natural part of the process as you make the story your own. Tell the story as often as you can. Live audiences give instant feedback, so you can know immediately where you need to heighten the drama, draw out or shorten the climax, add or expand a descriptive passage.

Children are brutally honest, but patient, critics who will help you perfect your skill. Occasionally, simple props or figures cut from felt can be used during a story, but the magic of the story itself is what holds listeners. For example, with a beginning such as "One day a

Storytelling captures the audience's imagination.

fox was digging behind a stump of an old tree and found a bumble bee. He put it in his bag, threw his bag over his shoulder, and traveled,"[43] you capture your audience, now eager to learn what happened to that bee and that fox. This story, "Travels of a Fox," appears in Veronica Hutchinson's *Chimney Corner Stories*. The same story has been published in a single edition, *What's in Fox's Sack?* illustrated by Paul Galdone.

The story of a fox's travels is popular with storytellers. It has also been both collected and published in a single-edition picture book. (From *What's in Fox's Sack?*, illustrated by Paul Galdone.)

Collections of stories selected by talented storytellers such as *Storytelling: Art and Technique,* by Augusta Baker and Ellin Greene, or *Handbook for Storytellers,* by Caroline Feller Bauer, provide excellent guidance. Eileen Colwell's collection that begins with *Tell Me a Story* and Anne Pellowski's *The Story Vine* also contain valuable materials and techniques.

Storytellers of a generation ago leave a valuable legacy of materials and techniques. Ruth Sawyer, in *The Way of the Storyteller,* discusses the history of folklore, the preparation of tales for telling, and includes the "fairy gold" of some of her favorite stories. Recordings of Ruth Sawyer reading Christmas stories from her book *Joy to the World* and Frances Clarke Sayers telling some of Carl Sandburg's *Rootabaga Stories* and some stories by Hans Christian Andersen are available (Weston Woods). Marie L. Shedlock's *The Art of the Storyteller* also contains essential material for beginning storytellers.

Book Talks and Book Reviews

Book talks and book reviews are variations of a form; their purpose differs and, therefore, their form differs. A book talk is an oral presentation by a teacher or librarian about one or more books to introduce the books and to induce students to read them. A book review is a critical analysis, spoken or written, of a book. A book talk does not give away the plot; instead, just enough of the story is told to entice readers to read the book on their own. Book reviews critically analyze the literary elements and give an evaluative statement about the book's merit. Teachers and librarians read book reviews to see if they want to purchase a book.

Here are some excerpts from a book review that followed reading Jarrell's *Snow White and the Seven Dwarfs* (P-I), illustrated by Nancy Ekholm Burkert, and Paul Hein's *Snow White* (P-I), illustrated by Trina Schart Hyman.

Look at the illustrations to see how each artist depicts the characters. First, look at the two versions of Snow White's mother, the queen, pricking her finger. Burkert shows her from a distance through a casement castle window, slightly regal and remote. In contrast, Hyman shows her from inside the room as a dreaming, wistful young woman.

On the next page, Hyman shows the stepmother in the very same room, but she has made some changes: she has replaced the dead queen's devotional shrine with a magical mirror. She has also changed the atmosphere in the room from a homelike scene with tea and sewing to one filled with medicinal herbs, candles, and the mirror; the stepmother holds a tiny black kitten.

Hyman first shows the stepmother as a beautiful young woman, but as the story progresses and jealousy consumes her, the facial expressions and body are contorted. Notice especially that as her face shows in the mirror her emotions are reflected in the frame around it. The cunningly carved imps and furies in the frame become increasingly demonic. The figure at the base is an ancient and ugly naked hag.

Burkert never shows the stepmother's face; her figure appears only twice, and then from behind, in settings filled with symbols of evil.

Audiovisual Presentations

Audiovisual materials that are used to present literature to children are not substitutes for books; they create a totally different literary experience. A group of nursery school children giggled as they watched *Rosie's Walk* (Weston Woods), a film based on Pat Hutchins's picture book. They saw the fox sneak up behind Rosie the hen, jump to pounce upon her, land on a garden rake, and get smacked on the nose with the rake handle. The background country music enlivens Rosie's perky walk, the slyness of the crafty fox, and the trauma of each boomeranging blow. The children immediately

Trina Schart Hyman portrays Snow White's mother, the queen, from inside the room and as a dreaming, wistful young woman. (From *Snow White* by the Brothers Grimm, translated by Paul Heins and illustrated by Trina Schart Hyman.)

Nancy Ekholm Burkert views the queen, Snow White's mother, from outside the castle window. An atmosphere of medieval times in the austere castle walls and the remote and ermine-gowned queen set the time and place of the story before the reader reaches the first page. (From *Snow White and the Seven Dwarfs, A Tale from the Brothers Grimm,* translated by Randall Jarrell and illustrated by Nancy Ekholm Burkert.)

ran for the book of the same title so they could relive the excitement of the film story, and they continued to reread it for weeks.

Films should illuminate books and leave room for the imaginative participation of the audience. Many filmmakers, conscientious about the work they produce, take great pains to remain faithful to the original story. Because the filmmaker needs a great deal more art than appears in most picture books, the original artwork is often painstakingly recreated in a style that suits the graphic requirements of the film medium, while embodying the styles of the original artist; in some cases, the original artist creates the drawings for the film productions. An informative film about the intricate and imaginative process of animation is *Gene Deitch: The Picture Book Animated* (Weston Woods).

Unfortunately, there are some audiovisual adaptations of literature that insult the audience and sensationalize the work. Some of the most offensive are media presentations of folklore with cartoonlike illustrations, simplified plot retellings, and unadorned moralistic preachments. Full-length novels condensed into filmstrips often degenerate into a series of inconsequential pictures that rob children of the joy of creating their own mental images. Rather than inviting participation in creating images, some films spell out details unequivocally, undermining the subtle essence of characterization and expressive language and diminishing the emotional power of the work. Evocative prose is reduced to a full-color slide show that requires a passive sponge instead of an active participant. The child's imagination, experience, and emotions are deadened and left to dull.

Audiovisual presentations and media interpretations, therefore, are an asset to a literature program as long as they complement the books and draw children back to literature. Evaluate audiovisual materials for use in a literature program first by considering the literary value of the work; a good film cannot improve a bad book. Next, consider if the treatment is appropriate to the literary work. Does it enrich and expand the book's original purpose without sensationalizing it into something beyond the author's intent? A good example is Robert McCloskey's *Time of Wonder* (P) (Weston Woods), which is presented with his original illustrations and appropriate music to capture the book's sensitive tribute to nature.

A third point concerns appropriateness to the audience. Diluting a work of art to make it accessible to a younger audience changes the author's purpose and deceives children. A particularly conspicuous example of this is the Walt Disney Productions treatment of A. A. Milne's *Winnie the Pooh* (P-I). The film replaces Ernest Shepard's original winsome illustrations with cartoons, reduces Milne's poetic language to stilted dialogue, and adds an unnecessary character, a groundhog, who repeats, "I'm not in the book." Unfortunately, 4- and 5-year-old children having seen the films think they now know Winnie the Pooh, Eeyore, Tigger, Kanga, Piglet, and the others. Unless they are introduced to the original work at an appropriate age, these children have been robbed of the joy of really knowing these lovable characters.

Finally, in addition to maintaining the integrity of the original work, audiovisual mate-

In an effort to make A. A. Milne's stories available to a younger audience, Disney has adapted the characters and adventures. Unfortunately, becoming familiar with the Disney versions spoils the stories for older children who wish to read the books.

rials should be technically excellent; clear sound and visual reproduction are vital. They should also be durable enough to hold up to repeated use.

Selection, then, may be even more critical for audiovisual materials than for books.[44] The excellent films of poetry and color based on Mary O'Neill's *Hailstones and Halibut Bones* (P-I) (Sterling Educational Films), the animated drawings based on Leo Lionni's *Swimmy* (P) (Connecticut Films), and the live-action videotape of Isaac Bashevis Singer's *Zlateh the Goat* (I) (Weston Woods) show that outstanding literary

PROFILE

Morton Schindel

I'm a storyteller in today's media. Making films based on great books for children offers challenge and imposes responsibility. For in the age of telecommunications, filmed adaptations of outstanding stories, created with fidelity to the original, will inevitably find their way to larger and larger audiences among successive generations of children.[45]

Energetic teachers and librarians attending conventions in and around New York sometimes visit Weston Woods Studios in Connecticut. The founder, Morton Schindel, makes those visits to the multimedia world of children's literature memorable. He opens his door to those who believe as Walter De la Mare that "Only the rarest kind of best is good enough for the very young."

Recipient of the 1979 Regina Medal and a 1985 Academy Award nomination, Schindel uses a variety of media to draw young readers to fine literature. Through sound filmstrips, cassettes, motion pictures, video, and recordings, he makes books sing and nourishes interest in reading. He feels that while none of these media duplicates the child's private pleasure in holding his own book, they *can* transmit with integrity what the author and illustrator have to say. As a result of his work, children beyond number have delighted in literature they might never have known and are encouraged to pursue these stories in books.

We know that children eagerly seek books from libraries once they have seen filmed or televised versions. Schindel is reassuring about the positive role films can

experiences are created in many excellent forms. The teacher's job is to select without compromise: the same standards for excellence apply to all presentations of literature.

The greatest advantage of audiovisual presentations is their flexibility: many more children can share a literary experience at the same time than with a book. This is especially true in the case of small books, such as those of Beatrix Potter, which are simply not suitable for sharing with a large group of children. Busy

teachers do not have as much time to share books as they or the children would like. Sound filmstrip viewers and video players set up for individuals or small groups allow many children to use them at any time.

Media presentations do not, of course, replace oral reading by teachers. They can, however, supplement a strong read-aloud program. Children return to the media presentations of stories time and again for pleasure and reinforcement. Further, students with certain

play in leading children back to books.

> I've seen over and over again how book and film can become companions in motivating youngsters toward reading. Once the film has opened the book to a child, he will want to hold it in his hands and dwell to his heart's content on the words and pictures that have some special meaning to him.[46]

Teachers, parents, and librarians testify to the truth of his statement; his finely crafted films provide a channel that flows toward books rather than away from them.

Schindel developed the iconographic technique for photographing picture stories. This type of filmmaking imparts an illusion of motion to still pictures through camera movement abetted by careful juxtaposition of sound elements. Looking at a book the way children might when they read, Schindel's cameras have made more than 350 outstanding picture books come to life. His work has garnered many film festival awards and has been dubbed in many languages, winning an international following.

With his production of high-quality audiovisual materials, Schindel extends and complements the lively art of picture books. He recognizes how critical certain early experiences are for learning how to read.

> The words in a book (and even the pictures, we are beginning to realize) are symbols that require skills to decode and perceive. And yet, it is a time when youngsters' minds are most open and absorbent that they have the greatest reading limitations and are therefore least able to share the heritage that is preserved for them in books. It has been my task as a communicator in the audio-visual media to bridge this gap, to use with as much taste and integrity as I could muster the techniques that make it possible to open books to children before they are able to read by themselves.[47]

Morton Schindel sees himself as a partner with both authors and illustrators, and with teachers, librarians, and parents in bringing to children the literary heritage in the pages of good books.

learning disabilities often learn best when they hear and see the words at the same time. This provides important practice in fusing the printed letters and words into comprehensible language patterns.

LEARNING ABOUT LITERATURE

In an integrated literature-based curriculum, many types of learning occur simultaneously. Each time you read a story aloud, children learn to listen, to reason, and to respond to oral presentations. They are also observing models for their own writing. When children retell a story, they are learning speaking skills, organization, sequence, and dramatic presentation. When they read on their own, children are learning to become fluent readers, to enjoy literature, and to build a storehouse of language and story possibilities. And when they write their own stories, they are becoming more proficient writers, selecting significant details, organizing thoughts, and expressing the thoughts with clarity. All of this is well and good, but children should learn something about their literature in the process. The following sections present ways of helping students become aware of the features of their literature.

Experiencing literature and studying literature are *not* the same, yet both have a place in elementary school. Even before learning to read independently, children have rich literary experiences. For the youngest child, literature attracts for the pure pleasure it brings, and teachers will rarely have any agenda for modifying attitudes or achieving behavioral objectives. Even while listening for pure pleasure, however, children unconsciously internalize a sense of the total form of a literary work.

The *study* of literature does not begin until *after* the literature is experienced: someone tells, reads, or dramatizes a story, and a fortunate child just enjoys it. When the time comes for children to look at literature analytically and to make abstractions about its forms, structures, archetypes, and patterns, they have joyful experiences upon which to draw.

With older children, enjoyment is still uppermost, and the study of literature is sensitively introduced only as it adds to their appreciation and insight. The study of literature does *not* replace the original literary experience; neither does study always need to follow the experience. There is a time and a place for both.

As Northrop Frye explains,

> In all our literary experience there are two kinds of response. There is the direct experience of the work itself, while we're reading a book or seeing a play, especially for the first time. This experience is uncritical, or rather pre-critical, so it's not infallible. If our experience is limited, we can be roused to enthusiasm or carried away by something that we can later see to have been second-rate or even phony. Then there is the conscious, critical response we make after we've finished reading or left the theatre, where we compare what we've experienced with other things of the same kind, and form a judgment of value and proportion on it. This critical response, with practice, gradually makes our pre-critical responses more sensitive and accurate, or improves our taste, as we say. But behind our responses to individual works, there's a bigger response to our literary experience as a whole, as a total possession.[48]

Children can come to recognize similarities between the sisters in "Cap O'Rushes" and the stepsisters in "Cinderella." Later, this recognition can contribute insights concerning the behavior of the daughters in *King Lear* and in William Hooks's *Moss Gown* (P). They see the same rags-to-riches theme in "Cinderella" and in the Horatio Alger stories, and although they may not be able to verbalize it, they recognize the theme as an expression of wish fulfillment. They see the underdog fighting against great odds in "Jack and the Beanstalk," "Jack the Giant Killer," and "David and Goliath," and add to their expectations of what stories are all about.

Concomitantly, they meet increasingly complex forms in their experience with simple narratives—from cumulative repetition of "The Gingerbread Boy," to the parallel plots in McCloskey's *Blueberries for Sal* (N-P), to slightly more complex plots of detective stories such as Sobol's *Encyclopedia Brown* (P-I), to the alternating narrators in Zindel's *The Pigman* (A), to the story within a story in Chambers's *Breaktime* (A). Children can appreciate increasingly complex literature only as long as their cognitive capacity increases. A teacher's job, then, is to provide a rich experience so that children begin to build their own personal literary storehouse of understanding.

The following sections discuss some of the elements of literature. Informed teachers introduce the terms as a part of the total literary experience. For example, one might introduce the term *setting* when discussing the forest in which "Little Red Riding Hood" takes place.

Setting

Setting is where a story takes place. A setting may represent the real world with verisimilitude, it may portray a totally fanciful world of the author's invention, or it may create a sense that the story could have occurred at any place and time. Setting reveals character: describing a person's home partially describes the person. As is true for other components, setting is woven into the fabric of the story.

Some stories could take place in almost any setting. Others are possible only because the characters are in a particular place at a particular time. For example, Robert McCloskey's *Time of Wonder* (P-I) could take place only on an island at the end of summer. Historical novels, too, depend heavily upon setting, as in the story of *Boris* (I), by Jaap ter Haar, dramatically shaped by events of the siege of Leningrad during World War II. Theme, plot, and character, all woven into the physical and social fabric of time and place, interact with setting.

Plot Structure

Plot structure is the way a story is organized. Children, notorious plot readers, want to find out what *happens,* and will discard a book that has little or no action. Plot action, carried forward through incident and dialogue, is generally more lively in children's books than in adult novels, with their introspection and reminiscence. Plot sequence may be presented through a straightforward chronology, flashbacks, or multiple concurrent scenes. As children develop their concept of story, they choose to read stories with more complex plots.

Children enjoy *surprise endings;* skilled writers use them cleverly. *Just Like Everyone Else* (P) by Karla Kuskin, *Teeny Tiny* (P) by Jill Bennett, and *Cat on the Mat* (N-P) by Brian Wildsmith for young children all have just the right twist for the ending. *White Dynamite and Curly Kidd* by Bill Martin and John Archambault is the story of a young cowpoke eager to follow in Dad's

Sal picks blueberries in McCloskey's classic story, sometimes called the perfect picture book for its deft blend of text and illustration. (From *Blueberries for Sal* by Robert McCloskey.)

footsteps in a rodeo. Only on the final page do we discover that the young cowpoke is a girl.

Chain tales or *cumulative tales* have a structure that can be made visible to young children. *The House That Jack Built* (P) by Paul Galdone, *One Fine Day* (P) by Nonny Hogrogian, and *I Know an Old Lady* (P) retold by Nadine Westcott are folktales that use this structure.

Flashbacks are a more complex structural device and are found in intermediate grade literature. Betsy Byars's *The Midnight Fox* (I), Kathryn Lasky's *The Night Journey* (I), and Emily Neville's *Berries Goodman* (I) hinge the story on looking back to events of the past.

Some skilled writers use a letter format to structure their stories. *Dear Mr. Henshaw* (I) is based on what Beverly Cleary had lying around the house—literally—letters to an author from children. Cleary uses this device, as well as diary entries, to tell an engaging story.

Sequence is made visible by using wordless, or nearly wordless, picture books, such as *Rosie's Walk* (P). If you cut apart two copies of a wordless book, mount the pages on construction paper, and laminate the pieces, children can put the pages in the right order. They can check themselves, if you number the backs of the pieces. With *Rosie's Walk*, you can map the story starting with an overview of the farm and following her hair-raising jaunt. Hogrogian's *One Fine Day* (P) also adapts well to mapping.

Characterization

Characterization refers to the techniques—description, dialogue, incident, introspection, or revelation of thoughts—authors use to make a character memorable. What most sharply defines a character is what the author tells us

As children learn more about literature, they love to share their newfound understanding with friends.

about him. Among the other things that contribute to the portrait an author paints of a protagonist are what she has him think, say, and do, and what others have to say to and about him. In the very first chapter of *Call It Courage* (I-A), Armstrong Sperry uses all these ways to establish character. Well-developed characters seem real to children and often become part of their fantasy life. Many children know Madeline, Charlotte, and Ramona Quimby as real people and true friends.

Well-developed characters are fully drawn; after reading you can almost predict what they would do in a new situation. Generally, only the main character will be well developed in a children's story. Secondary characters are often "flat"; only one dimension is spelled out.

Children quickly build expectations about how certain characters will behave. From their very earliest experiences with folklore, they know that the wolf is an evil character. Some stories depend upon this understanding. Children will not appreciate the humor of *Mr. and Mrs. Pig's Evening Out* (P) by Mary Rayner unless they have this previous knowledge about wolves.

Point of View

Point of view is the perspective from which a story is told, and it affects all other components of the story. In many books, a central character tells the story in the first person—as an observer or as a participant in events. A third-person, omniscient narrator reports events, describes scenes, and reveals thoughts of characters as an all-seeing eye. Sometimes different chapters are told from the point of view of different characters. Young children, in an egocentric stage of development, imagine themselves into the roles of characters; older children can maintain multiple points of view and comprehend the complexity brought about by conflict in points of view.

Assuming a different point of view is a difficult task for young children. Until about 8 or 9 years of age, they have not yet reached the level of thought required for taking another's perspective and simply cannot remove themselves from egocentric thinking characteristic of the preoperational stage. Telling a story from a different point of view is a good language activity for them and one that provides some insights for the teacher. The following are excerpts from two retellings by children of "The Three Billy Goats Gruff" from the point of view of the troll.

> MATT (age 5):
>   The Three Little Billy Goats—up on a hill—uh—eating some grass. He want to cross the water and get some more grass—and get big and fat—and they found a bridge and they wanted to go cross. They better not 'cause the mean old troll is under it. . . . [Later] I'm gonna come and eat you up. He knocked the—the troll got—lost his balance and—crashed in the water. And the troll dropped—and he drownded.

> STEVE (age 7½):
>   Once these three goats wanted to cross a bridge and the—um—Should I say me?—Um—um—I came up and started to scream at him. He said—and the goat said—um—to wait for his other brother. . . . [Later] I better get this one. . . . and he said "Oh, no, you're not going to eat me up" and then he hit him with his horns and he fell into the water. [Teacher: Who did he hit?] . . . Oh, me. Then, uh, uh, I fell in the water and the other—he started tramping across the bridge and they ate all the grass they wanted.[49]

Neither 5-year-old Matt nor 7½-year-old Steve can maintain the troll's point of view. Even though both manage to assume it fleetingly, they revert to the third-person narrator—the form they hear most often. You will need to know your students well before asking them to tell a story from a different point of view; you also need to remember that taking another role is a developmental task that is learned naturally—it is *not* something you teach.

Two picture books that can be used to call attention to perspective or point of view are *Fish Is Fish* and *Dear Daddy*. *Fish Is Fish* (P) by Leo Lionni is a story of a minnow and a tadpole who become friends. When the tadpole grows into a frog, he leaves the pond but returns one day to tell his friend, the minnow grown into a fish, about all that he has seen. When the frog describes birds, the fish pictures them in his mind as large feathered fish. He imagines cows to look like fish-shaped animals and people to look like fish walking upright. The illustrations show that the fish can only see the world in terms of what he knows. Phillipe Dupasquier uses letters from a child to her father in *Dear Daddy* (P). Sophie's father is away at sea on a cargo ship. As we see what Sophie writes to him, we see what is happening at her home in large illustrations across a spread. Across the top of the page, we see what her father is doing at sea. The contrasting points of view merge when the father returns home.

Language Style

Style refers to the manner in which authors use words to tell a story. The order of words, the sounds of words, and the meanings of words artfully shaped by an author make life radiate from literature. Sounds that fall felicitously on the ear create visual images that distinguish great literature from the mundane.

Children become sensitive to literary language when they hear it read aloud and have some attention called to it. Elinor Horwitz evokes a feeling of mystical splendor about the magic of the night in *When the Sky Is Like Lace* (P), in which the made-up word, "bimulous" conjures up a mood of wonder. Language becomes a plaything when children are read

poems, such as "Eletelephony" by Laura Richards, "Tiddley Pom", by A. A. Milne, and "Jabberwocky" by Lewis Carroll.

Edward Lear exemplifies a master wordsmith at work. Readers savor his language in *The Pelican Chorus & the Quangle Wangle's Hat* (P-I) when he describes the Quangle Wangle sitting on a "Crumpetty Tree" wearing his hat with "ribbons and bibbons" on every side. Or in *The Pobble Who Has No Toes* (P-I) when he describes him:

> And when he came to observe his feet,
> Formerly garnished with toes so neat,
> His face at once became forlorn
> On perceiving that all his toes were gone![50]

Literary concepts can and should be taught to children, but only when the children are ready to learn them—when they have a need to know and an experiential base upon which to anchor the concepts. Labels without concepts are detrimental to children's growth in the study of literature and often obscure the areas of study that need to be emphasized. Teachers aware of literary concepts *and* the levels of children's development can provide information and support when it is appropriate.

RESPONDING TO LITERATURE

Students respond to literature in a variety of ways; sometimes their silence is an eloquent testimony to the power of a book. Reflection is an appropriate response at times, but at other times, you may want to encourage a tangible response by having the children participate in a creative activity. The following sections—writing, oral language, drama, and art—contain suggestions for you to select from, much as a shopping list. Choose from them or let them trigger your own creative ideas.

Creating a web of possibilities is an effective way to plan for a response to literature. The concept of *webbing*, developed in England

and popularized in America by Charlotte S. Huck, is sometimes called semantic mapping, a sunburst, or a schematic design. Huck and Janet Hickman edit a quarterly, *The Web*,[51] in which they review new books and include a web of possibilities for integrating literature into the curriculum. The idea of webbing, consonant with schema theory, shows the visible connections within a network of ideas. Webs can be built around a central theme or topic, a single book, or the work of one author or illustrator.

Creating a web of possibilities can be done in a group—of teachers, librarians, or students—brainstorming activities and related books to enrich an area of study. See some examples of webs in Chapters 10 and 11.

Writing

Literature can be integrated into every area of the curriculum; the values of literature extend far beyond appreciation and enjoyment, although these are primary. When they read on their own, children build a storehouse of language and story possibilities. The stories they read and hear are created by some of the most skilled writers of all times. These well-written stories and poems serve as models for children in their own writing.

When children write, they draw upon the stories they know as they select significant details, organize their thoughts, and express them with clarity. Children who write also read differently from those who do not write. When students are learning the craft of writing, they are sensitive to what other writers do; and so they adopt some of the strategies as their own. Similarly, children who read are better writers than those who do not read. Tway and Calder used recognized criteria to evaluate students' writing and found that those who had read widely wrote richer compositions.[52]

Hearing and reading good stories develops vocabularies, sharpens a sensitivity to language, and fine-tunes a sense of writing styles.

According to Moffett,[53] we draw upon our storehouse of prior verbal experience when we write. If that experience has been rich with good literature, the storehouse will be fuller. And the only source of knowledge sufficiently rich and reliable for learning about written language, explains Frank Smith, is the writing already done by others.[54] We learn to write by reading what others have written; we enrich our repertoire of language possibilities by reading what others have said. Nick Aversa, a middle school teacher, gives a good illustration of this effect: "We read *My Life and Hard Times* by James Thurber and then I saw aspects of Thurber's style cropping up in students' writing the rest of the year. The literature we read is actually a demonstration of good writing; students try on other writers' style in the process of creating their own."[55]

When children read well-crafted stories, they intuitively develop a sense of beginnings, middles, and endings. They also observe how changing the point of view alters a story, how an author develops characterization, how the setting influences events, and how the same story can be told in a variety of ways. Teachers and librarians can help young writers become aware of structure by calling attention to it in the books the class reads. For example, Shelley Harwayne, teacher trainer and codirector of a writing project, responded to a student's draft of a story that seemed to lack any structure:

> Tommy, I've noticed you building with the blocks, and sometimes you put a red one, then a yellow one, then a red one, then a yellow one. You sort of make a pattern. Well authors do that, too. Remember when we read *My Mom Travels a Lot* (P) by Caroline Bauer and noticed that the narrator told one good thing and then one bad thing about her mom's traveling? That's a pattern just like your red and yellow blocks. We noticed the same pattern in *Fortunately* (P) by Remy Charlip and *Kevin's Grandma* (P) by Barbara Williams. Think about it; it might work in your writing.[56]

Child-Made Books Books provide countless ways to stimulate written language. When they write simple captions on their drawings about stories and create their own books based on books they have read, children are refining their writing skills. Just as children learn to read by reading, so do they learn to write by writing.

One day 6-year-old Beth rushed up to her librarian shouting "I made a story. Let's put it in a book and make it real!" Indeed, a story in a book does seem more real: there is a certain dignity to written pages bound between covers. Beth's story was a simple one about a puppy. When she put her words into a handmade book, added illustrations, and signed her name to the title page—"because I'm the author"—the book in her eyes became worthy of the most esteemed literary prize.

Blank books such as the one Beth used can be made beforehand and held ready for the youngsters who will make them into "real" books. Pages from wallpaper sample books (usually discarded by decorating stores), stapled or sewn over folded paper, make colorful book covers, which can be left in a convenient spot ready for young authors.

Keeping a journal develops and extends writing skills. Individual or group diaries can record events, thoughts, ideas, and plans. One primary teacher, for instance, had as a permanent member of her class a stuffed animal, Paddington. The bear's diary stayed with him at all times so that his activities and feelings could be recorded. On weekends, Paddington went home with different students, who were responsible for writing in the diary so that the rest of the class would know what they—and Paddington—had done.

Some children may want to use the letters of the alphabet as a framework for a story, as many authors have done. Nancy Jewell, in *ABC Cat* (P), follows the antics of a cat by starting each page with the next letter of the alphabet. Trina Schart Hyman uses the letters of the alphabet to illustrate a child using objects beginning with that letter in *A Little Alphabet* (P). Lilian Obligado uses the alphabet as a frame for innumerable alliterative phrases in *Faint Frogs Feeling Feverish and Other Terrifically Tantalizing Tongue Twisters* (P). Terry Berger uses the alphabet as the framework for *Ben's ABC Day* (P). Jane Bayer uses it for a well-loved ball bouncing or jump rope game in *A My Name Is Alice* (P) that follows the pattern, "A my name is Alice and my husband's name is Alex. We come from Alaska and we sell ants."[57]

Sophisticated child-made books can be constructed of simple materials. Respect for children's work is shown when it is bound in a durable binding and placed on library shelves for others to enjoy. Steps in making a book are as follows:

1. Fold in half the sheets of paper that are to become the pages of the book. Nest the sheets together so that the folded edges become the spine of the book.
2. Stitch the pages (along the crease made by folding) on a sewing machine or by hand.
3. Cut a piece of oak tag or carboard one-half inch larger all around than the open pages.
4. Select fabric, contact paper, or heavy wallpaper for decorating the cover. (Illustrations and the title can be pasted onto the fabric and made more durable by putting them through a laminator.) Lay the cardboard on the piece of covering material chosen. Cut the material at least one inch larger than the pages and cardboard all around.
5. Fold the covering material over the edges of the cardboard and glue it into place.
6. Paste the first and last sheets of paper to the covers to join the stitched pages to the cover.

Another type of book that children can make is the *zig-zag book*. It is made from one long strip of paper that is folded in a zig-zag manner, like a fan. This form of book is useful for stories that are sequential or cyclical, such as a child's autobiography, the seasons, the life of an animal or a plant, and so forth. The size

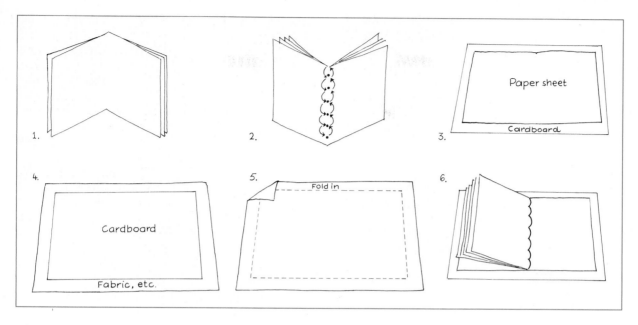

of the book, of course, depends on the size of paper that is available. If we use, for instance, a sheet of paper that is 12 by 18 inches, the book will have four pages on each side that are 4½- by 6-inches wide.

1. Select a long sheet of construction paper and cut in half lengthwise.
2. Carefully fold the long strip in a zig-zag fashion into four equal panels.
3. Follow the directions in the stitched book instructions for the book covers.

Children who want to know more about how books are made can read Greenfeld's *Books: From Writer to Reader* (I-A) and Aliki's *How a Book Is Made* (P-I). Each describes the research and writing and follows the process through agents, editors, illustrators, designers, printers, and book promoters to delivery for sale at a bookstore. After reading these, children may want to make a display for the class showing the progression of a book from the author's idea through the completed book. Publishers will sometimes send sample press

sheets, dummies, and folded and gathered pages of unbound books upon request.

The Literature Newsletter A classroom newsletter devoted entirely to literature that children enjoy can provide an outlet for sharing books, book reviews, and other children's writing stimulated by their reading. It can also offer editorials, crossword puzzles, art work stimulated by books, an advice column directed to book characters, book-related cartoons, and feature articles on an author or illustrator of the month. The format can vary from a single sheet duplicated for all class members (or others in the school) to one with many pages covering a variety of topics. One school that was being visited by an author announced the event in its newsletter, which was enlarged and displayed on a huge bulletin board in the central hall, with headlines covering the entire entryway. A newsletter requires editors, reporters, feature writers, book reviewers, and art editors recruited from class members, whereas typing, printing, and duplicating may require help

A child-created book will often hold as much interest for other children as those fashioned by adults.

from parents or school aides, depending upon the age and skills of the group.

Creative Book-Reporting Book reports are fun when they tap children's creative potential; they are valuable when they help a child to understand a book better by clarifying thoughts and feelings. Above all, as in the activities described in this book, the prime goal is to develop in children an enduring love of literature; everything else is secondary and is aimed at achieving this. Being required to read a teacher-selected book and write a report about it has turned more children away from reading than perhaps any other activity. The traditional book reports we are force-fed—drudgery for the child who writes them, time consuming for the teacher who reads and grades them, and boring for the children who must listen to them read aloud—subvert our primary goal.

Book reports should take children back to the book and give them a chance to linger in the story just a little longer. Many ways of re-

porting about books are enjoyable and meaningful to the child and valuable to the teacher, who can discern from them what the child has gained from the book.

Presented below are some ideas that are certain to suggest others and that, put on index cards, could become the nucleus of a literature activity box of ideas for children's projects.

All aspects of the language arts are integrated in these ideas. Remember, however, that children need choices. Some may like to put themselves in imaginative situations as they discuss books read; others may prefer just to talk about a book; and still others may choose to keep the reading experience personal. Be flexible. Encourage them to use these ideas as a springboard for others that may be more important to them. It is illuminating to put yourself in their place; if you ask yourself what a particular idea is good for, you are on the right track. If it leads to thoughtful consideration of a book by the student or to further reading, then it has a place in your plans.

Devise a television or newspaper announcement to advertise a book. Include words and pictures.

Make puppet characters, write a play about a book, and put on a puppet show.

Choose a character in a book and write a new story about him or her.

Write an account of what you would have done or how you would have acted had you been one of the characters in a book you read.

Write about the author or illustrator of a book.

Write a summary of a book, telling what you especially like or dislike about it.

Compare two books about the same subject.

Compare two books by the same author.

Write a story about the funniest incident in a book.[58]

Oral Language

Oral language is central to many book extension activities. These range from the spontaneous recommendations of a book by its reader to structured panel discussions about books by one author. Oral language activities need not take long; they can fit easily into those five spare minutes when the children put on their boots faster than you anticipated.

The Book Buddies system invites oral response to reading. In it, after a child completes reading a book, she selects a partner, and the two go off into a hall or corner where the reader gives a brief summary, discusses the parts that were good, and answers questions from the partner.

Storytelling by Children Children's writing skills seldom match their oral language skills before the end of their elementary-school years. Storytelling activities contribute to their sense of story and provide opportunities for developing and expanding language. A strong read-aloud program is vital; children will use the literary language they hear in creating their own stories.

Wordless books are an excellent stimulus to storytelling. Because the story line depends entirely upon the illustrations, children become much more aware of the details in the pictures; they do not make a quick scan of them. These books provide a story structure—plot, characters, theme—as with any conventional books, and so provide the necessary framework on which to build their stories. Children can tell such stories to each other, to a group, or into a recorder. Storytelling can be done with partners, in which case each takes the role of one or more of the characters as they interpret the story. In group storytelling, children pass a book along, each telling the story from one page. From the experience gained, children learn how the elements of the story interconnect and build on each other.

Tape recorders are indispensable for wordless book activities. When children record their stories, these become available for other children to listen to while looking at the book. Each storyteller's version of the book will be different, so that variety is thus added to the classroom collection. In addition to using tape recorders for recording stories based on books, children can use them in dictating original stories, making background sound tracks for stories read aloud, and recording choral speaking (discussed below), as dialogue for puppet shows, and for other dramatic activities.

Choral Speaking Choral speaking, that is, groups speaking in unison, can be adapted for any age level—for the youngest it may mean joining in as a refrain is read aloud; for older students it may involve the impromptu reading of a poem. Very young children unconsciously chime in when you read aloud passages that strike a sympathetic chord. For example, children quickly pick up and repeat the refrain when you read Maurice Sendak's *Chicken Soup with Rice* (N-P). Rhythm and repetition in language, conducive to choral speaking, is found in abundance in literature for every age group.

When introducing choral speaking, read aloud two or three times the story or poem being used, so that the rhythm of the language can be absorbed by your listeners. Encourage them to follow along with hand clapping until the beat is established. Favorite poems and refrains from stories, unconsciously committed to memory from repeated group speaking, stay in the mind as treasures to be savored for years. Stories with a repeatable refrain and euphonious language include Charlotte Pomerantz's *The Piggy in the Puddle* (P), Ruth Krauss's *A Very Special House* (N-P), Karla Kuskin's *Just Like Everyone Else* (P), Julian Scheer's *Rain Makes Applesauce* (P), and Judith Viorst's *I'll Fix Anthony* (P). A. A. Milne's poetry, including the phrase "James James Morrison Morrison Weatherby George Dupree," in the poem called "Disobedience," from *When We Were Very Young*,[59] is favorite material for choral speaking.

Leader-group response verses exploit the strong rhythm and melody of our language; the response is a phrase, chorus, or an action related to the story, as in this from Margaret Taylor Burroughs's *Did You Feed My Cow?*:

LEADER:	RESPONSE:
Did you feed my Cow?	Yes, ma'am!
Will you tell me how?	Yes, ma'am!
Oh, what did you give her?	Corn and hay.
Oh, what did you give her?	Corn and hay.[60]

Bob Barton, gifted storyteller and drama leader, tells others how he prepares for working with groups and shares some of his material guaranteed to bring success in *Tell Me Another*. Similarly, David Booth and Charles Lundy provide a practical guide for working with young people and stories in *Improvisation*.

Discussion Books become a valued stimulus for discussion, but as we have already pointed out, they can also lead to quiet contemplation; not every book needs to be examined. An important skill that teachers and librarians develop is the ability to recognize when discussion is appropriate and when it is not. No rules

In January
it's so nice
while slipping
on the sliding ice
to sip hot chicken soup
with rice.
Sipping once
sipping twice
sipping chicken soup
with rice.

Maurice Sendak's *Chicken Soup with Rice* lends itself to choral speaking.

can be given for this; it is sensed by those who base decisions on knowledge of children in the group.

For discussion that *is* warranted, there are important guidelines. The purpose of the discussion determines the type of questions, and children's responses, in turn, are largely determined by the types of questions, as the classic study *Critical Reading Ability of Elementary School Children* showed.[61] Questions in which the aim is to clarify feelings are very different from those intended to expand understanding about literary techniques. Discussions to clarify information or to relate experiences from books to children's lives are equally valid.

Questioning is a primary tool for teachers; good questions elicit high-level thinking from children, and poorly framed ones invite surface thinking. The hierarchy of literal, interpretive, and critical levels of reading and thinking is paralleled in questioning.

Literal questions elicit recall of factual information explicitly stated in the printed material. Such questions based on the familiar "Goldilocks and the Three Bears" might be: Where did the three bears go? What did Goldilocks do in their house?

Interpretive questions seek information inferred from the text. They are best answered by reading between the lines and synthesizing information from two or more stated facts. Interpretive questions for the Goldilocks story could be: Why did Goldilocks go into the bears' house? Why did she fall asleep in Baby Bear's bed?

Critical questions intended to elicit evaluation of what is stated in the text invite judgments about the quality of writing and authenticity of information; they also encourage hypothesizing beyond the story—tasks requiring higher-level thinking. This level of question is not answered fully by personal opinion; the basis for the judgment is also given. Critical questions for Goldilocks (where two versions have been read) could include: Which version

do you like best and why? What is another possible ending for the story? What did Goldilocks tell her parents when she got home? Why do you think she told them that? How does the repetition of three (three bowls of porridge, three chairs, three beds) fit the pattern of other folk tales? What other stories use the same pattern? See Benjamin Bloom's *Taxonomy of Educational Objectives Handbook I: Cognitive Domain*, which describes ways of ordering knowledge and helps teachers become aware of the levels of questions they ask.

Drama

Children engage in imaginative play instinctively. They re-create what they see on television, in everyday life, and in their stories. "Let's pretend" games are children's natural way of expressing their thoughts and feelings in the guise of characters and roles. Informal dramatic play led by teachers and librarians uses children's natural desire to pretend and can be the forerunner of numerous drama experiences.

There are many forms of drama to be explored in the elementary classroom.[62] Variations, often called *creative dramatics*, include pantomime, using body movements and expression but no words; interpreting, enacting, or recreating a story or a scene; and improvising, extending, and extrapolating beyond a story or a poem.

In *pantomime*, a story or meaning is conveyed solely through facial expressions, shrugs, frowns, gestures, and other forms of body language. Situations, stories, or characters pantomimed should be ones that the children are familiar with or recognize easily. For example, after reading Beatrix Potter's *The Tale of Peter Rabbit* (N-P), pantomime the scene in which Peter, going about the garden nibbling the vegetables, is spotted and chased by Mr. McGregor.

A good time for *acting out* or creating a story can be immediately following a reading aloud session. After reading aloud "The Three Billy Goats Gruff," for example, the teacher might ask, "Who wants to be the Troll? . . . the biggest billy goat? . . . the middle billy goat? . . . the littlest billy goat?" Discuss with the children how the troll sounds when he asks, "Who's that tripping over my bridge?" how he shows his anger, and how each of the billy goats sounds as he answers the troll.

Interpretation can be introduced with a question from the teacher, such as "Who wants to read the parts of each character in the story we just read?" In Nonny Hogrogian's *One Fine Day* (N-P), for example, one child would read the part of the fox, while others read the parts of the old woman, the cow, the field, the stream, the fair maiden, and others met in the bargaining. This activity, sometimes called Readers Theatre, builds enthusiasm for reading and develops oral reading skills.

Improvisation goes beyond acting out the basic story line. It could be initiated with the teacher saying, "Let's pretend that Goldilocks comes back to visit the three bears the next day." Goldilocks might bring her parents along and a cake for the bears to apologize for snooping around their house. A discussion with the group of what Goldilocks might say, how the bears might answer, and what might happen if they become friends can help move things along. Additional ideas may follow: suppose, for example, Goldilocks invites the bears to visit *her*; what might happen on this visit?

Improvisation can be developed further by exploring characterization. You might say, "Suppose Pippi Longstocking is coming to visit our class," or "What would Frances [in *A Bargin for Frances* (P), by Russell Hoban] say if you wanted to trade your old battered tea set for her new one with the blue willow design?" Well-developed characters, such as Homer Price, Madeline, Curious George, and George and Martha, help lead to extensions into new situations.

Children don't have to be the actors in the story; sometimes puppets can add a new dimension to the tale.

Role-playing is a variation of drama, usually done with short vignettes or specific incidents from stories. For example, intermediate grade students might role-play episodes from Jean George's *My Side of the Mountain* (I), such as the one in which Sam Gribley walks into the library to get maps from Miss Turner or runs into an old lady in the mountains, or the one in which the news reporter comes to interview the wild boy. Discuss the way Sam feels, the way he talks, and the reasons he wants to avoid telling his questioners too much about himself. Brief role-playing episodes often become scenes in more fully developed presentations.

Readers Theatre In Readers Theatre, students read orally from scripts that are based on selections from literature. Performances are not formal: lines are not memorized; there are virtually no sets, costumes, or staging; and participants do not move about the stage. A few gestures or changes in position are permitted but the real effect must come from the readers' oral interpretation of characters and narration.

In *Readers Theatre: Story Dramatization in the Classroom*, Shirlee Sloyer suggests the following steps in preparing a Readers Theatre performance.

1. Select a story with lots of dialogue and a strong plot. The best stories have a taut plot with an "and then" quality to pique your interest and make you want to know what will happen next.
2. Discuss the number of characters needed, including one or more narrators who read the parts between the dialogue.
3. Adapt the story to a play script format and assign roles.
4. When roles are assigned, students do not need to be told to practice their oral reading; they will do so on their own, especially if they can practice with a partner or a director who can advise them on whether the character is coming through in the reading.

5. For the finished production, performers may sit or stand side by side, with the narrators off to one side and slightly closer to the audience. Readers stand statue-still holding their scripts. When not in a scene, readers may turn around or lower their heads.[63]

Some stories can be used verbatim as Readers Theatre scripts. For example, Bill Martin Jr and John Archambault's *The Ghost-Eye Tree* (P-I) needs no adaptation to be turned into a script. Two narrators, a boy, his sister, and a milkman quickly pick up the eerie tone and lilting melody of "One dark and windy autumn night/when the sun had long gone down,/ Mama asked my sister and me/to take the road/ to the end of the town/to get a bucket of milk."[64] Maurice Sendak's *Pierre* (P); Judith Viorst's *Alexander and the Terrible, Horrible, No Good, Very Bad Day* (P); and Martin and Archambault's *White Dynamite and Curly Kidd* (P-I) and *Barn Dance* (P-I) also can be read as scripts directly from the text.

Story Theater Story Theater is interpretive oral reading combined with acting out a story. It works well with simple poems, folktales, and stories that contain plenty of action but not much dialogue. One or more narrators read aloud the selection while, simultaneously, a group of players performs the action described in the reading. The following steps will guide you.

1. Story Theater begins with attentive reading and discussion of the story. Movement or mime is encouraged as a natural extension of action suggested in the text; for example, "Show me how the rabbit moves."
2. Assign roles or choose from volunteers.
3. Players develop their parts as they listen to the oral readers' rendition of the story; oral readers practice their skill until they can vary their pace to accommodate the pace of the players.
4. The final production is a combination of oral reading and mimed action.

Some stories that work well as Story Theater are *Madeline* (P) by Ludwig Bemelmans, *The King's Stilts* (P-I) by Dr. Seuss, and *May I Bring a Friend* (P) by Beatrice De Regniers.

Dramatization differs depending upon the purposes and goals of the experience—primarily according to whether it is done as a performance for others or for the joy of the participants themselves. A guiding rule in this area, no less than in others, is to hold the children's benefit as the highest value. This is not to say that performances for others should not be given, only that they not be given at the cost of exploiting children as performers.

Art

Art activities can be as extensive as your creativity and energy permit. Resources expand when you have access to an art specialist; in any case, your classroom should house numerous supplies and examples of children's artistic work. Art projects related to books are used regularly, not saved for special occasions. A well-stocked art center leads to inventive projects in classrooms and libraries. Paper, fabric, yarn, buttons, socks, plastic bottles, paper bags, cardboard tubes, dowels, rods, wire, styrofoam balls, egg cartons, toothpicks, and pipe cleaners all have potential in the hands of ingenious children and teachers. Needles and thread, glue and tape, and, of course, scissors, crayons, paints, and paint brushes are also needed. Items available free or for a nominal price can often be obtained from neighborhood shops. Art materials are often available to teachers who search grocery, hardware, discount, and other stores for them. Pizza rounds (cardboard trays), five-gallon ice cream drums, boxes, and display materials, for example, often make good classroom art supplies.

Collage Collage is an artful arrangement of various types of materials into a picture. Encourage children to use a variety of media. Simple collage techniques of cutting or tearing paper or fabric and arranging these with other materials make original composite scenes.

Books by Ezra Jack Keats, the master of collage, and stories set in the outdoors provide good subjects for collage pictures. Jim Arnosky's *Watching Foxes* (P), *Sketching Outdoors in Spring* (P-I), and *Deer at the Brook* (P) inspire children to create collage pictures of woodland scenes with dried grass, feathers, and twigs. Fairy tales can be interpreted with a variety of materials; surely Cinderella deserves a bit of lace on her fancy ballgown.

Wall Hangings Wall hangings are composite pictures made on fabric and hung from a dowel rod. Burlap squares, a yard of plain muslin, or terry cloth toweling provide the background for creative expression in stitchery or appliqué. Shapes of the characters or objects cut from other material are stitched or glued onto the fabric. E. B. White's *Charlotte's Web* (P-I) is the basis for a wall hanging that occupies a place of honor in one school library. The background is a medium brown burlap with lines, representing the corner of the barn, drawn in with black marker. Wilbur the pig is made of tan burlap that has Wilbur's image traced on it (made by enlarging an illustration from the book with an opaque projector). The spider web with "Some Pig" in it is embroidered with black string, while Charlotte, the spider herself, is made from fuzzy black fur with pipe cleaner legs. The pieces are glued to the background and dried grass or straw is added to complete the wall hanging.

Mosaics Mosaics are made of small bits of colored paper arranged into designs or figures. Leo Lionni's *Pezzetino* (P) leads naturally into mosaics. The animals in Verna Aardema's *Why Mosquitoes Buzz in People's Ears* (P), illustrated by Leo and Diane Dillon, walking with their hubbubbing and swishing sounds, were recreated in mosaics by a group of primary chil-

A first grade class created mosaics to illustrate their favorite story.

The "flying-one" from Leo Lionni's *Pezzetino* (which means "small piece"), who finds that he is unique and does not need to be a part of something else. (From *Pezzetino*, by Leo Lionni.)

dren. They enjoyed hearing the delicious-sounding words from the book several times and, since it was impossible to re-create the Dillons' majestic art, used another medium to portray the animals. Mosaics of the animals were attached to a mural of junglelike grass and trees.

Flannel Boards A flannel board is a large piece of fiberboard or plywood covered with flannel, felt, or any textured fabric. Characters and objects cut from pieces of flannel, paper, or fabric are placed on the board to tell a story. Heavy felt is the most durable but is also the most difficult to cut; however, once cut, pieces can be reused endlessly. Construction paper or oak tag can be substituted for fabric, but a piece of flannel or sandpaper must be glued to the back of each piece if it is to stick to the flannel board.

The best stories to use on the flannel board have a reasonable number of simple characters and objects that can be replicated and manipulated easily. Traditional and literary folktales that have a sequential accumulation of charac-

ters and action are especially adaptable for flannel board retellings.

Other simple stories that can be used include the following:

Brown Bear in a Brown Chair (P) by Irina Hale   Make each new piece of clothing that Brown Bear demands—a coat, a ribbon, trousers. If they are made from felt scraps, they can be put on or taken off as the Brown Bear changes his mind.

Caps for Sale (P) by Esphyr Slobodkina   Use felt to make hats of each color to stack on top of the man's head. The hats, the monkeys, the man, a tree, and a few houses are all that are necessary.

Corduroy (P) by Don Freeman   Tape a button to the back of the bear so that you can "sew" it on at the appropriate time.

It Could Always Be Worse (P) by Margot Zemach   Cut shapes to represent the man, his wife, children, the rabbi, and the animals so they can be visibly piled on top of one another as the crowded condition worsens.

Little Blue and Little Yellow (P) by Leo Lionni   Cut the pieces from sheets of translucent colored acetate or cellophane so that the blue and yellow pieces form green where they overlap. The

Stories that move sequentially are well suited for roller movies.

acetate sticks to the flannel, so there is no need to glue sandpaper or felt to the back.

The Man Who Didn't Wash His Dishes (P) by Phyllis Krasilovsky   Many small pieces shaped like dishes, ashtrays, pots, and pans are needed to show the man's dilemma as he struggles to stack them.

The Old Woman and Her Pig (P) by Paul Galdone   Cut the pieces for this cumulative tale: the old woman, the pig, the stick, dog, fire.

Roller Movies   A roller movie is a cardboard carton with an opening cut for the screen. Push two pieces of dowel rod or broomstick through the carton walls just inside and parallel to the opening—one just above and one below it. Draw the illustrations for a story on a long strip of shelf paper or window shade cut slightly wider than the box opening, or tape separate pieces together. Attach an end to each roller and scroll the strip onto the roller to which the last illustration was attached. Each scene will show through the screen as you turn the rollers. The long strip of paper is best prepared when rolled out full length on the floor, so the sequence of the story can be planned in the illustrations. Roller movies al-low children to present a continually changing visual accompaniment to their storytelling.

Stories easily adapted to the roller movie screen are those that move sequentially from one scene to the next, such as Crockett Johnson's *Harold and the Purple Crayon* (P). Other stories easily adaptable to the roller movie include cumulative tales such as Nonny Hogrogian's *One Fine Day* (P) and Jack Kent's *The Fat Cat* (P), as well as Ron Maris's *Is Anyone Home* (N-P), Don Freeman's *The Chalk Box Story* (P), and Martha Alexander's *Blackboard Bear* (P).

Filmstrips and Slides   Damaged or out-of-date filmstrips and slides can be bleached and reused by students to create their own audio-visual presentations. Clear acetate strips can also be purchased for filmstrips or cut apart to mount in slide frames. Students plan their presentation on a mimeographed story board and transfer the images to the acetate. Because fine-motor control is necessary to make pictures small enough, rather than attempting to letter a running commentary on the acetate, one can be recorded to be played along with the visual presentation. Fine-tipped felt marking pens or grease pencils are used to make the drawings.

PROFESSIONAL REFERENCES

Applebee, Arthur. *The Child's Concept of Story.* Chicago: University of Chicago Press, 1978.

Barton, Bob. *Tell Me Another.* Portsmouth, N.H.: Heinemann, 1986.

Baker, Augusta, and Ellin Greene. *Storytelling: Art and Technique,* 2nd ed. New York: R. R. Bowker, 1987.

Bauer, Carolyn Feller. *Celebrations: Read Aloud Holiday and Theme Book Programs.* Bronx, N.Y.: H. W. Wilson, 1985.

———. *Handbook for Storytellers.* Chicago: American Library Association, 1977.

———. *This Way to Books.* Bronx, N.Y.: H. W. Wilson, 1983.

Bloom, Benjamin, et al. *Taxonomy of Educational Objectives, Handbook 1: Cognitive Domain.* New York: David McKay, 1956.

Booth, David, and Charles Lundy. *Improvisation: Learning Through Drama.* Orlando: Academic Press, 1984.

Britton, James. "Composition in Context." Lecture delivered at New York University, July 1979.

Calder, James William. "The Effects of Story Structure Instruction on Third-Graders' Concept of Story, Reading Comprehension, Response to Literature, and Written Composition." Ph.D. diss., University of Washington, 1984.

Chomsky, Carol. "Stages in Language Development and Reading Exposure." *Harvard Educational Review* 42 (February 1972): 1–33.

Colwell, Eileen. *Tell Me a Story.* New York: Penguin, 1962.

———. *Tell Me Another Story.* New York: Penguin, 1964.

———. *Time for a Story.* New York: Penguin, 1967.

Cullinan, Bernice E., ed. *Children's Literature in the Reading Program.* Newark, Del.: International Reading Association, 1987.

———, Kathy Harwood, and S. Lee Galda. "The Reader and the Story: Comprehension and Response." *Journal of Research and Development in Education,* 16, no. 3 (Spring 1983): 29–38.

Cunningham, Roger T. "Developing Question-Asking Skills." in *Developing Teacher Competencies,* edited by James Weigand, 81–127. Englewood Cliffs, N.J.: Prentice-Hall, 1971.

Deitch, Gene. *Gene Deitch: Animating Picture Books.* Signature Collection. Sound Filmstrip. Weston, Conn.: Weston Woods.

Dishaw, M. "Descriptions of Allocated Time to Content Areas for the A-B Period." Beginning Teacher Evaluation Study. Technical note IV-11a. Far West Regional Laboratory for Educational Research and Development, San Francisco, 1977.

Durkin, Dolores. *Children Who Read Early.* New York: Teachers College Press, 1966.

Fisher, C. W., et al. "Teaching and Learning in Elementary Schools: A Summary of the Beginning Teacher Evaluation Study." Panel presented at the Far West Regional Laboratory for Educational Research and Development, San Francisco, 1978.

Frye, Northrop. *The Educated Imagination.* Bloomington: Indiana University Press, 1970.

Galda, S. Lee. "Assuming the Spectator Stance: An Examination of the Responses of Three Young Readers." In *Research in the Teaching of English* 16, no. 1 (February 1982): 1–20.

———. "Three Children Reading Stories: A New Approach to Response to Literature in Preadolescents." Ph.D. diss., New York University, 1980.

Goodman, Kenneth S. "Unity in Reading." in *Theoretical Models and Processes of Reading,* 3rd ed. Edited by Harry Singer and Robert B. Ruddell. Newark, Del.: International Reading Association, 1985.

Heathcote, Dorothy. "Learning, Knowing, and Languaging in Drama." *Language Arts* 60, no. 6 (September 1983): 695–701.

Holland, Norman N. *Five Readers Reading.* New Haven: Yale University Press, 1975.

Hunt, Mary Alice, ed. *A Multimedia Approach to Children's Literature,* 3rd ed. Chicago: American Library Association, 1983.

Iser, Wolfgang. *The Act of Reading: A Theory of Aesthetic Response.* Baltimore: Johns Hopkins University Press, 1978.

McCaslin, Nellie. *Creative Drama in the Classroom,* 4th ed. New York: Longman, 1984.

Kerstetter, Kristen, and Charlotte S. Huck. "Developing Readers." In *Children's Literature in the Reading Program.* Edited by Bernice E. Cullinan. Newark, Del.: International Reading Association, 1987, 30–40.

Kimmel, Margaret Mary, and Elizabeth Segel. *For Reading Out Loud! A Guide to Sharing Books with Children.* New York: Delacorte, 1983.

Mills, G. *Hamlet's Castle: The Study of Literature as a Social Experience.* Austin: University of Texas Press, 1976.

Moffett, James. *Teaching the Universe of Discourse.* 1968. Reprint.

Boston: Houghton Mifflin, 1983.

Petrosky, Anthony R. "Genetic Epistemology and Psychoanalytic Ego Psychology: Clinical Support for the Study of Response to Literature." *Research in the Teaching of English* 11 (1977): 28–38.

Pillar, Arlene. "Individualizing Book Reviews." *Elementary English* (now *Language Arts*), 52, no. 4 (April 1975): 467–69.

Purves, Alan C., and Richard Beach. *Literature and the Reader: Research in Response to Literature, Reading Interests, and the Teaching of Literature.* Urbana, Ill.: National Council of Teachers of English, 1972.

Richards, I. A. *Practical Criticism: A Study of Literary Judgment.* 1929. Reprint. New York: Harcourt Brace Jovanovich, 1956.

Rosen, Connie and Harold. *The Language of Primary School Children.* London: Penguin, Education for the Schools Council, 1973.

Rosenblatt, Louise M. *Literature as Exploration.* 1983. Reprint. Oklahoma City: Noble & Noble, 1976.

———. *The Reader, the Text, the Poem.* Carbondale: Southern Illinois University Press, 1978.

Ross, Ramon. *Storyteller.* Westerville, Oh.: Charles E. Merrill, 1972.

Sawyer, Ruth. *The Way of the Storyteller.* New York: Viking, 1962.

Shedlock, Marie L. *The Art of the Storyteller.* Mineola, N.Y.: Dover, 1951.

Siks, Geraldine Brain. *Drama with Children.* New York: Harper &

Row, 1977.

Slade, Peter. *Introduction to Child Drama.* London and Toronto: Hodder & Stoughton, 1976.

Sloyer, Shirlee. *Readers Theatre: Story Dramatization in the Classroom.* Urbana, Ill.: National Council of Teachers of English, 1982.

Smith, Frank. *Writing and the Writer.* New York: Holt, Rinehart & Winston, 1982.

Squire, James R. *The Response of Adolescents while Reading Four Short Stories.* Urbana, Ill.: National Council of Teachers of English, 1964.

Steffensen, Margaret S., Chitra Joag-Dev, and Richard C. Anderson. "A Cross-Cultural Perspective on Reading Comprehension." *Reading Research Quarterly* 15, no. 1 (1979): 10–29.

Trelease, Jim. *The Read-Aloud Handbook,* Rev. ed. New York: Viking-Penguin, 1985.

Tway, Eileen. "A Study of the Feasibility of Training Teachers to Use the Literature Rating Scale in Evaluating Children's Fiction Writing." Ph.D. diss., Syracuse University, 1970.

Ward, Winifred, *Playmaking with Children from Kindergarten Through Junior High School,* 2nd ed. East Norwalk, Conn.: Appleton, 1957.

Wolf, Willavene, C. S. Huck, and M. L. King. *Critical Reading Ability of Elementary School Children.* U.S. Office of Education Report, Project no. 5-1040. Contract no. OE-4-10-187. Washington D.C., 1967.

NOTES

1. David McCord, "Books Fall Open," in *One at a Time* (Boston: Little Brown, 1977), 343.
2. Kenneth S. Goodman, "Unity in Reading," in *Theoretical Models and Processes of Reading,* 3rd ed., eds. Harry Singer and Robert B. Ruddell (Newark, Del.: International Reading Association, 1985), 813–40.
3. Louise M. Rosenblatt, *Literature as Exploration,* 3rd ed. (1938; rpt. New York: Noble and Noble, 1976); *The Reader, the Text, the Poem* (Carbondale:

Southern Illinois University Press, 1978); and "Viewpoints: Transaction Versus Interaction—A Terminological Rescue Operation," *Research in the Teaching of English* 19, no. 1 (February 1985): 96–107.

4. Margaret S. Steffensen, Chitra Joag-Dev, and Richard C. Anderson, "A Cross-Cultural Perspective on Reading Comprehension," *Reading Research Quarterly* 15, no. 1 (1979): 10–29.

5. Louise M. Rosenblatt, *Literature as Exploration*, 25.

6. James R. Squire, *The Responses of Adolescents While Reading Four Short Stories* (Urbana, Ill.: National Council of Teachers of English, 1964).

7. Alan C. Purves and Victoria Rippere, *Elements of Writing about a Literary Work: A Study of Response to Literature* (Urbana, Ill.: National Council of Teachers of English, 1968).

8. Some of the studies of reader response that followed Purves and Squire are: Charles R. Cooper, ed., *Researching Response to Literature and the Teaching of Literature: Points of Departure* (Norwood, N.J.: Ablex, 1985); S. Lee Galda, "Assuming the Spectator Stance: An Examination of the Responses of Three Young Readers," *Research in the Teaching of English* 16, no. 1 (February 1982): 1–20; Susan I. Hepler, "Patterns of Response to Literature: A One-Year Study of a Fifth and Sixth Grade Classroom" Ph.D. diss., Ohio State University, Columbus, 1982; Janet A. Hickman, "A New Perspective on Response to Literature: Research in an Elementary School Setting," *Research in the Teaching of English* 15, no. 4 (December 1981): 343–54. Alan C. Purves and Richard Beach, *Literature and the Reader: Research in Response to Literature, Reading Interests, and the Teaching of Literature* (Urbana, Ill.: National Council of Teachers of English, 1972); Nancy L. Roser, "Research Currents: Relinking Literature and Literacy," *Language Arts* 64, no. 1 (January 1987): 90–97; Jane P. Tompkins, ed., *Reader-Response Criticism: From Formalism to Post-Structuralism* (Baltimore: Johns Hopkins University Press, 1980).

9. Frank Smith, *Understanding Reading: A Psycholinguistic Analysis of Reading and Learning to Read* (New York: Holt, Rinehart & Winston, 1971); *Reading Without Nonsense* (New York: Teachers College Press, 1979). (First published in 1978 by Cambridge University Press, under the title *Reading*); and *Essays into Literacy* (Portsmouth, N.H.: Heinemann), 1983).

10. Arthur N. Applebee, *The Child's Concept of Story: Ages Two to Seventeen* (Chicago: University of Chicago Press, 1978).

11. Shelley Rubin and Howard Gardner, "Once Upon a Time: The Development of Sensitivity to Story Structure," *Researching Response to Literature and the Teaching of Literature: Points of Departure*, ed. Charles R. Cooper (Norwood, N.J.: Ablex, 1985), 169–89.

12. Bernice E. Cullinan, Kathy T. Harwood, and S. Lee Galda, "The Reader and the Story: Comprehension and Response," *Journal of Research and Development in Education* 16, no. 3 (Spring 1983): 29–38.

13. Squire, *The Responses of Adolescents*.

14. Anthony R. Petrosky, "Genetic Epistemology and Psychoanalytic Ego Psychology: Clinical Support for the Study of Response to Literature," *Research in the Teaching of English*, 11 (Spring 1977): 28–38.

15. Norman N. Holland, *Five Readers Reading* (New Haven: Yale University Press, 1975); G. Mills, *Hamlet's Castle: The Study of Literature as a Social Experience* (Austin: University of Texas Press, 1976).

16. James Britton, "Composition in Context," Lecture presented at the 1979 Summer Institute, sponsored by the English Education Program in the Department of Communication Arts and Sciences, School of Education, Health, Nursing, and the Arts Professions (SEHNAP), New York University, July 24, 1979.

17. Margaret Anzul, "Exploring Literature with Children Within a Transactional Framework" Ph.D. diss., New York University, 1988.

18. S. Lee Galda, "Three Children Reading Stories: A Developmental Approach to Response to Literature in Preadolescents," Ph.D. diss., New York University, 1980.

19. Arthur Applebee, *The Child's Concept of Story* (Chicago: University of Chicago Press, 1978), 132.

20. Connie and Harold Rosen, *The Language of Primary School Children* (London: Penguin, Education for the Schools Council, 1973), 195.

21. Barbara Goldman, Adjunct Professor, Adelphi University, Long Island, N.Y., personal communication, March 25, 1986.

22. Adapted from "Elementary Library Literature Curriculum," Worthington City Schools, Ohio, 1985.

23. C. W. Fisher, et al., *Teaching and Learning in Elementary Schools: A Summary of the Beginning Teacher Evaluation Study* (San Francisco: Far West Re-

gional Laboratory for Educational Research and Development, 1978); and J. Ingham, *Books and Reading Development* (London: Heinemann, 1981).

24. G. Leinhardt, N. Zigmond, and W. W. Cooley, "Reading Instruction and Its Effects," *American Educational Research Journal* 18 (1981): 343–61; Barak Rosenshine and Robert Stevens, "Classroom Instruction in Reading," in *Handbook of Reading Research*, ed. P. David Pearson (New York: Longman, 1984), 745–98.

25. Richard L. Allington, "Oral Reading," in *Handbook of Reading Research*, ed. P. David Pearson (New York: Longman, 1984), 829–64.

26. M. Dishaw, *Descriptions of Allocated Time to Content Areas for the A-B Period*, Beginning Teacher Evaluation Study, Technical note IV–IIa (San Francisco: Far West Regional Laboratory for Educational Research and Development, 1977).

27. Mary Sirmons, teacher, Baytown, Texas, Personal communication, April 1986. Reading Supervisor, Hilda Lauber.

28. See, for example, some early studies: Carol Chomsky, "Stages in Language Development and Reading Exposure," *Harvard Educational Review* 42 (February 1972): 1–33; Margaret M. Clark, *Young Fluent Readers* (London: Heinemann, 1976); and Dolores Durkin, *Children Who Read Early* (New York: Teachers College Press, 1966).

29. See Glenda L. Bissex, *Gnys At Wrk: A Child Learns to Write and Read* (Cambridge: Harvard University Press, 1980); Dorothy Butler and Marie Clay, *Reading Begins at Home* (Exeter, N.H.: Heinemann Educational Books, 1982); David B. Doake,

"Book Experience and Emergent Reading Behavior in Preschool Children," Ph.D. diss., University of Alberta, 1981; David B. Doake. "Reading-Like Behavior: Its Role in Learning to Read," in *Observing the Language Learner*, eds. Angela M. Jaggar and M. Trika Smith-Burke (Newark, Del.: International Reading Association, 1985), 82–98; Jerome C. Harste, Virginia A. Woodward, and Carolyn L. Burke, *Language Stories and Literacy Lessons* (Portsmouth, N.H.: Heinemann, 1984); Linda Leonard Lamme, *Growing Up Reading* (Washington, D.C.: Acropolis Books, 1985); Judith A. Schickedanz, *More Than the ABCs: The Early Stages of Reading and Writing* (Washington, D.C.: National Association for the Education of Young Children, 1986); Denny Taylor, *Family Literacy: Young Children Learning to Read and Write* (Portsmouth, N.H.: Heinemann, 1983); Denny Taylor and Dorothy S. Strickland, *Family Storybook Reading* (Portsmouth, N.H.: Heinemann, 1986); and Gordon Wells, *The Meaning Makers* (Portsmouth, N.H.: Heinemann, 1986).

30. Wells, *The Meaning Makers*.

31. Ibid., 147.

32. See, for instance, Bernice E. Cullinan, ed., *Children's Literature in the Reading Program* (Newark, Del.: International Reading Association, 1987); Nigel Hall, *The Emergence of Literacy* (Portsmouth, N.H.: Heinemann Educational Books, 1987); Margaret Mary Kimmel and Elizabeth Segel, *For Reading Out Loud! A Guide to Sharing Books with Children* (New York: Delacorte Press, 1983); Bernard Spodek, *Today's Kindergarten* (New York: Teachers College Press, 1986); William

H. Teale, "Toward a Theory of How Children Learn to Read and Write Naturally," *Language Arts* 59, no. 6 (September 1982): 555–70; and Jim Trelease, *The Read-Aloud Handbook*, (New York: Viking Penguin, 1985).

33. Richard Anderson, Elfrieda Hiebert, Judith Scott, and Ian Wilkinson, *Becoming a Nation of Readers: The Report of the Commission on Reading* (Champaign, Ill.: Center for the Study of Reading, 1985), 23.

34. Statement by Bill Martin Jr in a class presentation; New York University, Fall 1986; Bernice Cullinan, teacher.

35. Trelease, *The Read-Aloud Handbook*.

36. Kimmel and Segel, *For Reading Out Loud!*

37. Kristen Kerstetter and Charlotte S. Huck, "Developing Readers," *Children's Literature in the Reading Program*, ed. Bernice E. Cullinan (Newark, Del.: International Reading Association, 1987), 32–33.

38. Dorothy Aldis, "Snow," in *Time for Poetry*, 3rd ed., comps. May Hill Arbuthnot and Shelton Root (Chicago: Scott, Foresman, 1952), 168.

39. Dorothy Aldis, "Whistles," in *Time for Poetry*, 97.

40. Harry Behn, "Hallowe'en," in *Time for Poetry*, 164.

41. Mary O'Neill, "My Friend Leona," in *People I'd Like to Keep*, illus. Paul Galdone (New York: Doubleday, 1964), 42–47.

42. Shel Silverstein, "Jimmy Jet and His TV Set," in *Where the Sidewalk Ends* (New York: Harper & Row, 1974), 28.

43. Veronica Hutchinson, "Travels of a Fox," in *Chimney Corner Stories*, illus. Lois Lenski (New York: Putnam's, 1905), 91.

44. Mary Alice Hunt, ed., *A Multimedia Approach to Children's*

Literature, 3rd ed. (Chicago: American Library Association, 1983).

45. Letter to Bernice Cullinan from Morton Schindel, July 15, 1980.
46. Morton Schindel, "Making Reading Central to the Lives of All Children," *TAIR Newsletter,* Publication of the Texas Association for the Improvement of Reading, January 1979, 6.
47. Ibid., 4.
48. Northrop Frye, *The Educated Imagination* (1964; reprint, Bloomington: Indiana University Press, 1970), 104–105.
49. Quoted from students at Worthington Hills Elementary School, Worthington, Ohio.
50. Edward Lear, *The Pobble Who Has No Toes,* illus. Kevin W. Maddison (New York: Viking, 1978) n.p.
51. Charlotte S. Huck and Janet Hickman, eds., *The Web,* The Ohio State University, Room 200 Ramseyer Hall, 29 West Woodruff, Columbus, Ohio 43210.
52. Eileen Tway, "A Study of the Feasibility of Training Teachers to Use the Literature Rating Scale in Evaluating Children's Fiction Writing," Ph.D. diss., Syracuse University, 1970;

James William Calder, "The Effects of Story Structure Instruction on Third-Graders' Concept of Story, Reading Comprehension, Response to Literature, and Written Composition," Ph.D. diss., University of Washington, 1984.
53. James Moffett, *Teaching the Universe of Discourse* (1968; reprint, Boston: Houghton Mifflin, 1983).
54. Frank Smith, *Writing and the Writer* (New York: Holt, 1982).
55. Nick Aversa, teacher, Great Neck South Middle School, Great Neck, N.Y.
56. Shelley Harwayne, codirector, Teachers College Writing Project and Teacher Trainer, District 15, Brooklyn, N.Y.
57. Jane Bayer, *A My Name Is Alice,* illus. Steven Kellogg (New York: Dial, 1984), n.p.
58. Adapted from Arlene Pillar, "Individualizing Book Reviews," *Elementary English* (now *Language Arts*) 52, no. 4 (April 1975): 467–69.
59. A. A. Milne, "Disobedience," in *When We Were Very Young* (New York: Dutton, 1924), 32.
60. Margaret Taylor Burroughs, *Did You Feed My Cow?: Rhymes and Games from City Streets and Country Lanes,* illus. Joe E.

De Velasco (Chicago: Follett, 1969), 2.
61. Willavene Wolf, Charlotte S. Huck, and Martha L. King, *Critical Reading Ability of Elementary School Children,* U.S. Office of Education Report, Project no. 5-1040, Contract no. OE-4-10-187 (Washington, D.C.: G.P.O., 1967).
62. Dorothy Heathcote, "Learning, Knowing, and Languaging in Drama," *Language Arts* 60, no. 6 (September 1983): 695–701; Nellie McCaslin, *Creative Drama in the Classroom,* 4th ed. (New York: Longman, 1984); Geraldine Brain Siks, *Drama with Children,* (New York: Harper & Row, 1977); Peter Slade, *Introduction to Child Drama* (London and Toronto: Hodder & Stoughton, 1976); Winifred Ward, *Playmaking with Children from Kindergarten Through Junior High School,* 2nd ed. (New York: Appleton, 1957).
63. Shirlee Sloyer, *Readers Theatre: Story Dramatization in the Classroom* (Urbana, Ill.: National Council of Teachers of English, 1982).
64. Bill Martin Jr and John Archambault, *The Ghost-Eye Tree,* illus. Ted Rand (New York: H. Holt, 1985).

CHILDREN'S BOOKS CITED

Aardema, Verna. *Why Mosquitoes Buzz in People's Ears.* Illus. Leo and Diane Dillon. New York: Dial, 1975.

Abell, Chana Byers. *The Children We Remember.* New York: Greenwillow, 1986.

Adams, Richard. *Watership Down.* New York: Macmillan, 1974.

Alexander, Lloyd. *Westmark.* New York: Dutton, 1981.

Alexander, Martha. *Blackboard Bear.* New York: Dial, 1969.

Aldis, Dorothy. *All Together.* Illus. Marjorie Flack, Magaret Frieman, and Helen D. Jameson. New York: Putnam, 1925.

Aliki. *How a Book Is Made.* New York: Crowell, 1986.

Andersen, Hans Christian. *Thumbelina.* Retold by Amy Ehrlich, illus. Susan Jeffers. New York: Dial, 1979.

Arnosky, Jim. *Deer at the Brook.* New York: Lothrop, 1986.

———. *Sketching Outdoors in Spring*

New York: Lothrop, 1987.

———. *Watching Foxes.* New York: Lothrop, 1984.

Asbjørnsen, Peter Christian, and Jorgen E. Moe. *The Three Billy Goats Gruff.* Illus. Paul Galdone. New York: Clarion, 1981.

Babbitt, Natalie. *Tuck Everlasting.* New York: Farrar, Straus & Giroux, 1975.

Bang, Molly. *Dawn.* New York: Morrow, 1983.

———. *Ten, Nine, Eight.* New

York: Greenwillow, 1983.

Bauer, Caroline Feller. *My Mom Travels a Lot*. Illus. Nancy Winslow Parker. New York: Warne, 1981.

Bayer, Jane. *A, My Name Is Alice*. Illus. Steven Kellogg. New York: Dial, 1984.

Behn, Harry. "Hallowe'en." In *Time for Poetry*, 3rd ed. Edited by May Hill Arbuthnot and Shelton Root. Glenview, Ill.: Scott, Foresman, 1952.

Bemelmans, Ludwig. *Madeline*. New York: Viking, 1939.

Bennett, Jill. *Teeny Tiny*. Illus. Tomie dePaola. New York: Putnam, 1986.

Berger, Terry. *Ben's ABC Day*. Photos by Alice Kandell. New York: Lothrop, Lee & Shepard, 1982.

Bernbaum, Israel. *My Brother's Keeper*. New York: Putnam, 1985.

Blume, Judy. *Are You There, God? It's Me, Margaret*. New York: Bradbury, 1970.

———. *Blubber*. New York: Bradbury, 1974.

Brooks, Bruce. *Midnight Hour Encores*. New York: Harper & Row, 1986.

Brooks, Polly S. *Queen Eleanor: Independent Spirit of the Medieval World: A Biography of Eleanor of Aquitaine*. Philadelphia: Lippincott, 1983.

Brown, Margaret Wise. *Goodnight Moon*. Illus. Clement Hurd. New York: Harper & Row, 1947.

Bryan, Ashley. *The Cat's Purr*. New York: Atheneum, 1985.

Burningham, John. *Mr. Gumpy's Outing*. New York: Holt, Rinehart & Winston, 1971.

Burroughs, Margaret Taylor. *Did You Feed My Cow?: Rhymes and Games from City Streets and Country Lanes*. Illus. Joe E. De Velasco. Chicago: Follett, 1969.

Byars, Betsy. *The Midnight Fox*. Illus. Ann Grifalconi. New York: Viking, 1968.

———. *The Pinballs*. New York: Harper & Row, 1977.

———. *The TV Kid*. Illus. Richard

Cuffari. New York: Viking, 1976.

Carle, Eric. *The Very Hungry Caterpillar*. Philadelphia: Collins, 1969.

Carroll, Lewis. *Jabberwocky*. New York: Warne, 1977.

Chambers, Aidan. *Breaktime*. New York: Harper & Row, 1979.

Charlip, Remy. *Fortunately*. 1964. Reprint; New York: Four Winds, 1980.

Cleary, Beverly. *Dear Mr. Henshaw*. Illus. Paul O. Zelinsky. New York: Morrow, 1983.

———. *Ramona and Her Father*. Illus. Alan Tiegreen. New York: Morrow, 1977.

———. *Ramona the Pest*. Illus. Louis Darling. New York: Morrow, 1968.

Cleaver, Vera and Bill. *Where the Lilies Bloom*. Philadelphia: Lippincott, 1969.

Collier, James Lincoln, and Christopher Collier. *my brother Sam is dead*. New York: Four Winds, 1974.

Conrad, Pam. *Prairie Songs*. New York: Harper & Row, 1985.

Cooney, Barbara. *Miss Rumphius*. New York: Viking, 1982.

Cooper, Susan. *The Dark Is Rising*. Illus. Alan Cober. New York: Atheneum, 1973.

Cormier, Robert. *The Chocolate War*. New York: Pantheon, 1974.

Crews, Donald. *Truck*. New York: Greenwillow, 1980.

Dabcovich, Lydia. *Sleepy Bear*. New York: Dutton, 1982.

Dahl, Roald. *James and the Giant Peach*. Illus. Nancy Ekholm Burkert. New York: Knopf, 1961.

De Angeli, Marguerite. *Marguerite De Angeli's Book of Nursery and Mother Goose Rhymes*. New York: Doubleday, 1954.

dePaola, Tomie. *Strega Nona*. Englewood Cliffs, N.J.: Prentice Hall, 1975.

———. *Tomie dePaola's Mother Goose*. New York: Putnam, 1985.

De Regniers, Beatrice Schenk. *May I Bring a Friend?* Illus. Beni Montresor. New York: Atheneum, 1964.

Dunning, Stephen. *Reflections on a Gift of Watermelon Pickle and Other Modern Verse*. Comps. Stephen Dunning et al. New York: Lothrop, Lee & Shepard, 1967.

Dupasquier, Phillipe. *Dear Daddy*. New York: Bradbury, 1985.

Emberley, Barbara. *Drummer Hoff*. Illus. Ed Emberley. Englewood Cliffs, N.J.: Prentice-Hall, 1967.

Engdahl, Sylvia. *Enchantress from the Stars*. Illus. Rodney Shackell. New York: Atheneum, 1970.

Estes, Eleanor. *The Hundred Dresses*. Illus. Louis Slobodkin. New York: Harcourt Brace, 1944.

Fleischman, Paul. *Rear View Mirrors*. New York: Harper, 1986.

Fox, Paula. *One-Eyed Cat*. New York: Bradbury, 1984.

Freeman, Don. *The Chalk Box Story*. Philadelphia: Lippincott, 1976.

———. *Corduroy*. New York: Viking, 1968.

Fritz, Jean. *Homesick: My Own Story*. Illus. Margot Tomes. New York: Putnam, 1982.

Gág, Wanda. *Millions of Cats*. New York: Coward, 1928.

Galdone, Paul, illus. *The House That Jack Built*. New York: McGraw-Hill, 1961.

———. *The Old Woman and Her Pig*. New York: McGraw-Hill, 1961

———. *What's in Fox's Sack?* New York: Clarion, 1982.

George, Jean Craighead. *Julie of the Wolves*. Illus. John Schoenherr. New York: Harper & Row, 1972.

———. *My Side of the Mountain*. New York: Dutton, 1959.

Greenfeld, Howard. *Books: From Writer to Reader*. New York: Crown, 1976.

Grimm, Jakob and Wilhelm. *Hansel and Gretel*. Retold by Rika Lesser, illus. Paul O. Zelinsky. New York: Dodd Mead, 1984.

———. *The Juniper Tree and Other Tales from Grimm*. Trans. Lore Segal and Randall Jarrell, illus. Maurice Sendak. New York: Farrar, Straus & Giroux, 1973.

———. *Little Red Riding Hood*. Illus. William Stobbs. New York:

Walck, 1973.

———. *Little Red Riding Hood*. Illus. Paul Galdone. New York: McGraw-Hill, 1974.

———. *Little Red Riding Hood*. Illus. Trina Schart Hyman. New York: Holiday House, 1983.

———. *Little Red Riding Hood*. Illus. Bernadette Watts. New York: World, 1968.

———. *The Sleeping Beauty, from the Brothers Grimm*. Trans. and illus. Trina Schart Hyman. Boston: Little, Brown, 1977.

———. *Snow White*. Trans. Paul Heins, illus. Trina Schart Hyman. Boston: Little, Brown, 1974.

———. *Snow White and the Seven Dwarfs*. Trans. Randall Jarrell, illus. Nancy Ekholm Burkert. New York: Farrar, Straus & Giroux, 1972.

Haar, Jaap Ter. *Boris*. New York: Delacorte, 1966.

Hale, Irina. *Brown Bear in a Brown Chair*. New York: Atheneum, McElderry, 1983.

Hall, Donald. *Ox Cart Man*. Illus. Barbara Cooney. New York: Viking, 1979.

Hamilton, Virginia. *The People Could Fly*. Illus. Leo and Diane Dillon. New York: Knopf, 1985.

Hendershot, Judith. *In Coal Country*. Illus. Thomas B. Allen. New York: Knopf, 1987.

Hoban, Russell. *A Bargain for Frances*. Illus. Lillian Hoban. New York: Harper & Row, 1970.

———. *Bread and Jam for Frances*. Illus. Lillian Hoban. New York: Harper & Row, 1964.

Hoban, Tana. *Dig, Drill, Dump, Fill*. New York: Greenwillow, 1975.

———. *Is It Larger? Is It Smaller?* New York: Greenwillow, 1985.

Hoberman, Mary Ann. *A House Is a House for Me*. Illus. Betty Fraser. New York: Viking, 1978.

Hogrogian, Nonny. *One Fine Day*. New York: Macmillan, 1971.

Hooks, William H. *Moss Gown*. Illus. Donald Carrick. New York:

Clarion, 1987.

Hoover, Helen. *The Delikon*. New York: Viking, 1977.

Horwitz, Elinor Lander. *When the Sky Is Like Lace*. Illus. Barbara Cooney. Philadelphia: Lippincott, 1975.

Hunter, Mollie. *A Furl of Fairy Wind*. Illus. Stephen Gammell. New York: Harper & Row, 1977.

———. *A Sound of Chariots*. New York: Harper & Row, 1972.

———. *A Stranger Came Ashore*. New York: Harper & Row, 1975.

———. *The Stronghold*. New York: Harper & Row, 1974.

———. *The Third Eye*. New York: Harper & Row, 1979.

Hutchins, Pat. *Rosie's Walk*. New York: Macmillan, 1968.

———. *You'll Soon Grow into Them, Titch*. New York: Greenwillow, 1983.

Hutchinson, Veronica. "Travels of a Fox." in *Chimney Corner Stories*. Illus. Lois Lenski. New York: Putnam's, 1905.

Hyman, Trina Schart. *A Little Alphabet*. Boston: Little, Brown, 1980.

Innocenti, Roberto. *Rose Blanche*. Mankato, Minn.: Creative Education, 1986.

Janeczko, Paul B. *Pocket Poems: Selected for a Journey*. New York: Bradbury, 1985.

Johnson, Crockett. *Harold and the Purple Crayon*. New York: Harper & Row, 1981.

Jukes, Mavis. *Blackberries in the Dark*. Illus. Thomas B. Allen. New York: Knopf, 1985.

Keats, Ezra Jack. *Peter's Chair*. New York: Harper & Row, 1967.

———. *The Snowy Day*. New York: Viking, 1962.

———. *Whistle for Willie*. New York: Viking, 1964.

Kellogg, Steven. *Best Friends*. New York: Dial, 1986.

Kent, Jack. *The Fat Cat: A Danish Folktale*. New York: Parents, 1974.

King-Smith, Dick. *Babe: The Gallant Pig*. Illus. Mary Rayner. New York: Crown, 1985.

Krasilovsky, Phyllis. *The Man Who Didn't Wash His Dishes*. Illus. Barbara Cooney. New York: Doubleday, 1950.

Kraus, Robert. *Leo the Late Bloomer*. Illus. Jose Aruego. New York: Windmill, 1971.

Krauss, Ruth. *A Very Special House*. Illus. Maurice Sendak. New York: Harper & Row, 1953.

Kuskin, Karla. *The Dallas Titans Get Ready for Bed*. Illus. Marc Simont. New York: Harper & Row, 1986.

———. *Just Like Everyone Else*. New York: Harper & Row, 1959.

———. *Near the Window Tree*. New York: Harper & Row, 1975.

Larrick, Nancy. *When the Dark Comes Dancing: A Bedtime Poetry Book*. Illus. John Wallner. New York: Philomel, 1983.

Lasky, Kathryn. *The Night Journey*. Illus. Trina Schart Hyman. New York: Warne, 1981.

Lear, Edward. *The Pelican Chorus and the Quangle Wangle's Hat*. Illus. Kevin W. Maddison. New York: Viking, 1981.

———. *The Pobble Who Has No Toes*. Illus. Kevin W. Maddison. New York: Viking, 1977.

Le Guin, Ursula. *A Wizard of Earthsea*. Illus. Ruth Robbins. Boston: Parnassus, 1968.

L'Engle, Madeleine. *A Wrinkle in Time*. New York: Farrar, Straus & Giroux, 1962.

Levinson, Riki. *Watch the Stars Come Out*. Illus. Diane Goode. New York: Dutton, 1985.

Lewis, C. S. *The Lion, the Witch, and the Wardrobe*. Illus. Pauline Baynes. New York: Macmillan, 1951.

Lionni, Leo. *Fish Is Fish*. New York: Random House, 1970.

———. *Little Blue and Little Yellow*. New York: Astor-Honor, 1959.

———. *Pezzetino*. New York: Pantheon, 1975.

———. *Swimmy*. New York: Pantheon, 1963.

Louie, Ai-Ling. *Yeh-Shen: A Cinderella Story from China*. Illus. Ed Young. New York: Philomel,

1982.

Lunn, Janet. *The Root Cellar*. New York: Scribner's, 1983.

McCloskey, Robert. *Blueberries for Sal*. New York: Viking, 1948.

———. *Make Way for Ducklings*. New York: Viking, 1941.

———. *Time of Wonder*. New York: Viking, 1957.

McCord, David. *All Small*. Boston: Little, Brown, 1986.

———. *One at a Time*. Illus. Henry Kane. Boston: Little, Brown, 1977.

McKinley, Robin. *The Blue Sword*. New York: Greenwillow, 1982.

———. *The Hero and the Crown*. New York: Greenwillow, 1984.

MacLachlan, Patricia. *Sarah, Plain and Tall*. New York: Harper & Row, 1985.

McMillan, Bruce. *Becca Backward, Becca Frontward*. New York: Lothrop, Lee & Shepard, 1986.

Maris, Ron. *Is Anyone Home?* New York: Greenwillow, 1986.

Martin, Bill, Jr. *Brown Bear, Brown Bear, What Do You See?* Illus. Eric Carle, New York: Holt, 1983.

———, and John Archambault. *Barn Dance*. Illus. Ted Rand. New York: Holt, 1986.

———. *The Ghost-Eye Tree*. Illus. Ted Rand. New York: Holt, 1985.

———. *White Dynamite and Curly Kidd*. Illus. Ted Rand. New York: Holt, 1986.

Martin, Rafe. *Foolish Rabbit's Big Mistake*. Illus. Ed Young. New York: Putnam's, 1985.

Maruki, Toshi. *Hiroshima No Pika*. New York: Lothrop, 1982.

Meltzer, Milton. *Ain't Gonna Study War No More*. New York: Harper & Row, 1985.

Merriam, Eve. *Fresh Paint*. Illus. David Frampton. New York: Macmillan, 1986.

Milne, A. A. "Disobedience." In *When We Were Very Young*. New York: Dutton, 1924.

———. *Winnie the Pooh*. Illus. E. H. Shephard. New York: Dutton, 1926.

Mosel, Arlene. *Tikki Tikki Tembo*. Illus. Blair Lent. New York: Holt, Rinehart & Winston, 1968.

Neville, Emily C. *Berries Goodman*. New York: Harper & Row, 1965.

Nhuong, Huynk Quang. *The Land I Lost*. New York: Harper & Row, 1982.

Norton, Mary. *The Borrowers*. Illus. Beth and Joe Krush. New York: Harcourt Brace, 1953.

Obligado, Lilian. *Faint Frogs Feeling Feverish & Other Terrifically Tantalizing Tongue Twisters*. New York: Viking, 1983.

O'Brien, Robert C. *Z for Zachariah*. New York: Atheneum, 1975.

O'Dell, Scott. *Island of the Blue Dolphins*. Boston: Houghton Mifflin, 1960.

O'Neill, Mary. *Hailstones and Halibut Bones*. Illus. John Wallner. New York: Doubleday, 1989.

———. "My Friend Leona." In *People I'd Like to Keep*. Illus. Paul Galdone. New York: Doubleday, 1964.

Paterson, Katherine. *Bridge to Terabithia*. Illus. Donna Diamond. New York: Crowell, 1977.

———. *The Great Gilly Hopkins*. New York: Crowell, 1978.

Paton Walsh, Jill. *The Green Book*. Illus. Lloyd Bloom. New York: Farrar, Straus & Giroux, 1982.

Pellowski, Anne. *The Story Vine: A Source Book of Unusual and Easy-to-Tell Stories from Around the World*. Illus. by Lynn Sweat. New York: Macmillan, 1984.

"Poetry Parade." David McCord, Aileen Fisher, Karla Kuskin, and Harry Behn. Weston Conn.: Weston Woods. Recording.

Pomerantz, Charlotte. *The Piggy in the Puddle*. Illus. James Marshall. New York: Macmillan, 1974.

Potter, Beatrix. *The Tale of Peter Rabbit*. London: Warne, 1902.

Raskin, Ellen. *The Westing Game*. New York: Dutton, 1978.

Rawls, Wilson. *Where The Red Fern Grows: The Story of Two Dogs and a Boy*. New York: Doubleday, 1961.

Rayner, Mary. *Mr. and Mrs. Pig's Evening Out*. New York: Atheneum, 1976.

Reiss, Johanna. *The Upstairs Room*. New York: Crowell, 1972.

Richards, Laura. "Eletelephony." In *Random House Book of Poetry for Children*, selected and introduced by Jack Prelutsky, illustrated by Arnold Lobel, 192. New York: Random House, 1983.

Sandburg, Carl. *Rainbows Are Made: Poems by Carl Sandburg*. Edited by Lee Bennett Hopkins. San Diego: Harcourt Brace Jovanovich, 1984.

———. *Rootabaga Stories*. Illus. Maud and Miska Pertersham. New York: Harcourt, 1922.

Sawyer, Ruth. *Joy to the World*. Illus. Trina Schart Hyman. Boston: Little, Brown, 1966.

Scheer, Julian. *Rain Makes Applesauce*. Illus. Marvin Bileck. New York: Holiday, 1964.

Sendak, Maurice. *Chicken Soup with Rice*. New York: Harper & Row, 1962.

———. *In the Night Kitchen*. New York: Harper & Row, 1970.

———. *Pierre*. New York: Harper & Row, 1962.

———. *Where the Wild Things Are*. New York: Harper & Row, 1963.

Seuss, Dr. *Horton Hatches the Egg*. New York: Random House, 1940.

———. *The King's Stilts*. New York: Random House, 1939.

Silverstein, Shel. "Jimmy Jet and His TV Set." In *Where the Sidewalk Ends*. New York: Harper & Row, 1974.

Singer, Isaac Bashevis. *Zlateh the Goat and Other Stories*. Illus. Maurice Sendak. New York: Harper & Row, 1966.

Slobodkina, Esphyr. *Caps for Sale*. Reading, Mass.: Addison Wesley, 1947.

Sobol, Donald. *Encyclopedia Brown, Boy Detective*. Illus. Leonard Shortall. Nashville, Tenn.: Nelson, 1963

Speare, Elizabeth George. *The Sign of the Beaver*. Boston: Houghton Mifflin, 1983.

Sperry, Armstrong. *Call It Courage*. New York: Macmillan, 1940.

Steig, William. *Abel's Island*. New York: Farrar, Straus & Giroux, 1976.

Steptoe, John. *The Story of Jumping Mouse*. New York: Lothrop, Lee & Shepard, 1984.

Strieber, Whitley. *Wolf of Shadows*. New York: Knopf, 1985.

Sutcliff, Rosemary. *The Light Beyond the Forest*. Illus. Shirley Felts. New York: Dutton, 1980.

———. *The Road to Camlann: The Death of King Arthur*. New York: Dutton, 1982.

Tafuri, Nancy. *Have You Seen My Duckling?* New York: Greenwillow, 1984.

Taylor, Mildred. *Roll of Thunder, Hear My Cry*. Illus. Jerry Pinkney. New York: Dial, 1976.

Tolkien, J. R. R. *The Hobbit*. 1937. Reprint. Boston: Houghton Mifflin, 1984.

———. *The Lord of the Rings*. Boston: Houghton Mifflin, 1974.

Viorst, Judith. *Alexander and the Terrible, Horrible, No Good, Very Bad Day*. Illus. Ray Cruz. New York: Atheneum, 1972.

———. *I'll Fix Anthony*. Illus. Arnold Lobel. New York: Harper & Row, 1969.

Voigt, Cynthia. *Dicey's Song*. New York: Atheneum, 1982.

———. *A Solitary Blue*. New York: Atheneum, 1983.

Waber, Bernard. *Ira Sleeps Over*. Boston: Houghton Mifflin, 1972.

———. *Lovable Lyle*. Boston: Houghton Mifflin, 1969.

———. *Lyle Finds His Mother*. Boston: Houghton Mifflin, 1974.

———. *The House on East Eighty-Eighth Street*. Boston: Houghton Mifflin, 1962.

Watson, Clyde. *Father Fox's Pennyrhymes*. Illus. Wendy Watson. New York: Crowell, 1971.

Westcott, Nadine Bernard. *I Know an Old Lady*. Boston: Little, Brown, 1980.

White, E. B. *Charlotte's Web*. Illus. Garth Williams. New York: Harper & Row, 1952.

Wilder, Laura Ingalls. *Little House in the Big Woods*. Illus. Garth Williams. New York: Harper & Row, 1953.

Wildsmith, Brian. *Brain Wildsmith's Mother Goose*. New York: Watts, 1964.

———. *Cat on the Mat*. New York: Oxford University Press, 1982.

Williams, Barbara. *Kevin's Grandma*. New York: Dutton, 1975.

Whitman, Walt. *American Bard*. New York: Viking, 1982.

Wood, Audrey. *The Napping House*. Illus. Don Wood. San Diego: Harcourt Brace Jovanovich, 1984.

Yagawa, Sumiko. *The Crane Wife*. Trans. Katherine Paterson, illus. Suekichi Akaba. New York: Morrow, 1981.

Zemach, Margot. *It Could Always Be Worse: A Yiddish Folktale*. New York: Farrar, Straus & Giroux, 1977.

Zindel, Paul. *The Pigman*. New York: Harper & Row, 1968.

Zolotow, Charlotte. *I Know a Lady*. Illus. James Stevenson. New York: Greenwillow, 1984.

3

Language Development and Literature

Books

Like their looks?
Readers read them in nooks,
in a hammock, in bed, up the
   stair,
in a chair, on the porch; anywhere
on the floor, by the shore,
in a plane, on a train;
by the pool, a big rock,
in a room with no clock;
in a bus, trailer, tent;
in a Laundromat meant
for a book; under trees;
on long trips overseas;
in their bath in a tub —
I suppose turning on with their
   toes
the hot water. Who knows?
Books don't tell you to scrub.

You exist? Want to *be?*
Not with comics, cheap movies,
   commercial TV.

No, you won't! Only books — the
   real books —
set their hooks in your brain:
without them, you'll slide down
   the drain;
and at twenty,
as plenty today do,
have Mickey-Mouse minds,
as (I hate to say) *they* do.

One tells by the looks
of most people if books
are a part of their life.
Papers, magazines, rife
in this world, help to kill
time *and* books. But until
you can judge for yourself
of the best on the shelf,
books won't feed you. They *can:*
boy and girl; woman, man.

Just begin when you're young:
when a book in your eye
seems as tall as the sky;
when words, *words* in their flight
are as birds in your sight;
when it thrills you to find
you are using your mind,
and inside it is what
someone else hasn't got.

You! Begin when you're young,
when the tip of your tongue
is still limber. Books reach
with the splendor of speech.
Who can say things well said
is well read.[1]

David McCord

nce, when flying home from a meeting, I sat across the aisle from a father and his two sons, ages 3 and 4. The father distributed two handfuls of crackers to make the long ride less tiresome for the boys. The instant the portions were handed out, the younger one said, "Mikey, how much you got?" Mikey showed his brother who seemed satisfied and who said, "Oh. I gots the same much as you." Obviously the younger boy understands the concepts of "how much," equal portions, and the verb "to get," although he has not yet mastered the variations in the way they are expressed.

Children understand more than they can say and, for many years, more than they can read. As children hear stories and poems read aloud, they build a linguistic storehouse of story patterns and language possibilities that contribute toward a framework of meanings, patterns, and sounds. As these are internalized, the child draws upon the concept, or *schema*, to generate a personal language. The language children encounter, including experiences with books, affects their concept development at every level. It shapes their perception of reality, and although language itself is based on what they perceive, their concept of reality, in turn, is affected by the language they learn.

The most fully developed and beautiful forms of language are found in literature. Literature *is* language, and children's language grows through experience with literature. Children learn naturally in an environment that is filled with language in use; what they learn is what they hear or read. It follows that the richer the environment, the more fully developed a child's language will be. Books provide myriad opportunities for children to talk about life.

Children often mimic words and phrases they meet in books, and since language in literature is modeled by writers who use it well, it becomes an excellent means for expanding vocabulary. A. A. Milne's refrain in "The King's Breakfast", "I only want a little bit of butter for my bread!" lives long beyond nursery years.[2]

Older children grow to appreciate the way language can be used to express their own feelings. In *Julia and the Hand of God* (I), by Eleanor Cameron, the tousled young heroine envies her immaculate friend Maisie, who "slipped sideways through the days instead of flying head-on the way Julia did." Words such as these help children form their thoughts into meaningful, descriptive phrases. Rich literary experiences give children the words they need to express elusive feelings—and having the words to label experience means having a powerful tool for communicating.

Children gradually grow beyond mere fascination with interesting language into the double-edged pleasure of appreciating language interacting with form. As a 12-year-old exclaimed after discovering the intricate word play in Ellen Raskin's *The Westing Game* (I), "How did she *do* that! The whole book tricks you with one verse of a song!" His admiration was based not only upon the clever use of words, but upon the centrality of the word play as a plot device. Teachers who share literature with children give them a gift of words.

Mutual joy in delicious words, acknowledged by a teacher's knowing smile, encourages children to make language their toy when they are young and spurs them, as they mature, to become word collectors who value the nuances in beautiful word images. It is not mere coincidence that people who have large vocabularies read a great deal. In fact, researchers believe that the tremendous number of words that elementary school children add to their vocabularies daily come mainly from the books they read and the books read to them.[3] McCord's poetic statement, "Who can say things well said/is well read," reaffirms the research findings.

Literature parallels every level of language competence, from labeling (participation books) to subtle and sophisticated novelistic imagery and complex poetic symbols. As they grow older, children meet increasingly complex language in their books: they move from " 'Not I,' said the cat. 'Not I,' said the dog" (*Little Red Hen* retold by Galdone); through "They roared their terrible roars and gnashed their terrible teeth and rolled their terrible eyes" (*Where the Wild Things Are* by Sendak); and then on to watching a "mermaid morning" (*The Eyes of the Amaryllis* by Babbitt); and searching for "shadows that haunt one's soul" (*A Wizard of Earthsea* by Le Guin).

There is a great store of literature to share with the young, but the wealth could go unused if adults disregard their responsibilities. Adults must sing the songs, say the rhymes, tell the tales, and read the stories to children to make literature and all its benefits central to children's lives.[4] This chapter summarizes how children learn the oral and written forms of language, identifies criteria for selecting books that enhance early language development, and describes the types of books appropriate for children from infancy into the primary grades. Picture books, Mother Goose nursery rhymes, and folktales, which are also vital materials for young children, are discussed in Chapters 4 and 5.

ORAL LANGUAGE

How do children learn language? Until the mid-1960s, most psycholinguists believed that children learned language innately—that is, humans had an inner capacity that made it possible for them to learn language. Others believed that children learned to talk by imitating the language models around them, but this theory was discredited as we observed children using language constructions they had never heard. For example, at bedtime one disgruntled 3-year-old said, "Why did you bring that book up here that I don't want to be read out of for?" It is highly unlikely he had ever heard such a sentence! Current language researchers and theorists believe that children actively construct the language they use by generating their own rule systems. Children process language and intuitively discover the underlying grammatical structures that give meaning to it. Children do not learn rules; instead they internalize the patterns and use them as they construct their language. Interacting with book language, with its rich vocabulary and strong rhythm, can enrich the process. Children, for instance, will quickly correct the animals' unexpected sounds in Charles Causley's *"Quack!" Said the Billy-Goat* (N-P).

Early language researchers underestimated the child's role in creating language and in shaping the interaction in which it is based. Although we had thought children learn language by imitating adults and by being corrected when they made mistakes, Noam Chomsky's work altered our thinking.[5] Instead of viewing the child as a passive recipient of language, he made us see the child as an active generator of language. He showed, through examples of immature speech, that children apply rules indiscriminately as they are learning language. When children say "goed," "bringded," or "wented," they are in a normal stage of overgeneralizing; they use rules even when the rules do not fit. Here is an example to show how a child continues to overgeneralize the past tense ending for regular verbs *(-ed)* despite her mother's attempts to get her to change:

CHILD: My teacher holded the rabbits and we patted them.
MOTHER: Did you say your teacher held the rabbits?
CHILD: Yes.
MOTHER: What did you say she did?
CHILD: She holded the baby rabbits and we patted them.
MOTHER: Did you say she held them tightly?
CHILD: No, she holded them loosely.[6]

From the evidence collected, we began to see learning language as a constructive process: children create rules for language, test those rules, and refine them until they eventually approximate adult language forms. Language is self-generated, self-regulated, and self-evaluated. Children make increasingly closer approximations to adult norms as they master the rules. Primary—or native—language, therefore, cannot be taught. It is discovered—created and re-created by each and every language learner. The adult's role is to stimulate, demonstrate, encourage, and reward a child's approximations, much as in Eve Rice's *Ebbie* (N-P). Adults can also share books that make a game of language, such as Paul Coltman's *Tog the Ribber* (P-I) and Lewis Carroll's *Jabberwocky* (P), both delightful confabulations.

A decade after Chomsky's ground-breaking work, Michael Halliday forced us to look again at language, this time at language as function.[7]

He categorized the reasons we use language and showed children's development as they master its various uses. His work pushed us to acknowledge the social dimensions of language and made us aware of the effect of context. Through Halliday's work, we came to realize that language is more than form. Language is first and foremost a tool that serves important purposes in our lives. Primarily, it is a means of communicating, but it is also an important tool for learning. We use it to establish relationships, to obtain what we need, to find out about our world, and to create an imaginary life. According to Halliday, children know what language is because they know what language does.

A child uses language to establish and confirm a relationship in Charlotte Zolotow's *Say It!* (P). As mother and child walk through falling leaves in a lovely countryside, the child keeps demanding, "Say it! Come on, say it!" Each time the mother responds with a comment about the scenery or the wild, wondrous day and the child says "No, not that." Finally, the child shrieks, "Say it say it say it!" and the mother says, "I love you I love you I love you." When the child admits that is what she wanted her to say, the mother replies "That's what I've been saying all the time."

Language is a means of accomplishing what we want to do and say. From this view, the emphasis is never upon language itself; language, therefore, is just the tool that the learner is using. As children use language, they learn language. Halliday explains that the process is threefold: learning language, learning through language, and learning about language.[8] All three processes are largely subconscious; they are self-constructed in social interchange. Furthermore, they are learned simultaneously; they cannot be broken apart or separated.

Children in the nursery and early primary years are very literal in the language they speak and understand. They have not yet had enough experience with language to learn about different meanings of the same word. For example, 5-year-old Katie was drawn into her first game of T-Ball, a game in which the ball is placed on a tee instead of being pitched. In Katie's game, first base was a car fender; second base, a tree; and third base, a bush. When Katie came up to bat, she took a swing and hit the ball hard. She ran rapidly to the car fender and stopped. Her friend Nicky jumped up and down yelling, "Go on, Katie! Run home! Run home!" At this, Katie bolted across the street, ran past two houses and tore up the steps of her own front porch. Needless to say, Nicky was disappointed. Katie's understanding of "Run home!" was grounded in the only experience she had had with those words, but she learned a new meaning for them that day.

As children learn to deal with the subtleties of language, they begin to see that others may intend meanings that differ from their own. In literature as in life, children sort out meanings through experience. In Beverly Cleary's *Ramona the Pest* (P-I), Ramona is excited about her first day at kindergarten. When her teacher leads her by the hand to one of the tables and chairs and says, "Sit here for the present," Ramona is doubly excited:

> A present! thought Ramona, and knew at once she was going to like Miss Binney. . . . Nobody had told her she was going to get a present the very first day. What kind of present could it be, she wondered, trying to remember if Beezus had ever been given a present by her teacher.[9]

Ramona stays glued to her chair all day. When her teacher finally explains what she meant, Ramona is chagrined:

> "Oh." Ramona was so disappointed she had nothing to say. Words were so puzzling. *Present* should mean a present just as *attack* should mean to stick tacks in people.[10]

We could say Ramona misunderstood the teacher; on the other hand, we could say the teacher did not understand Ramona.

As Ramona, like other children, interacts with a widening circle of adults and children, she gradually develops a larger repertoire of meanings from which she draws.

WRITTEN LANGUAGE

Children learn language as a whole and as a part of the context in which it is used, not as isolated sounds or skills. They listen to and observe the spoken language and create schemata that they then apply universally. As the children grow and are exposed to more complex language, they refine the schemata to accommodate more sophisticated concepts, such as irregular verbs, metaphorical uses of language, and multiple meanings of words. Children apply these broad schemata as they learn both the oral forms of language (listening and talking) and the written forms of language (reading and writing); they are active learners. Roger Shuy explains:

> Good language learners begin with a function, a need to get something done with language, and move gradually toward acquiring the forms which reveal that function. They learn holistically, not by isolated skills. Such learners worry more about getting things done with language than with the surface correctness of it. . . . They experiment freely and try things out unashamedly.[11]

EMERGENT READING

Emergent reading is a term used to describe the early stages in a child's growth toward literacy; it precedes the conventional reading of print.[12] The term is used to describe young children's attempts to read the same book repeatedly in which the re-enactments gradually sound more like the text of the actual book. Ann Valentino, a teacher in New York City, described the way

Gina, age 3, read a book aloud to her without missing a single word. Valentino, duly impressed, said, "Gina, that's wonderful! How did you do that?" Gina answered demurely, "I guess I just learned it in my heart and it went to my head!"[13] We used to think such behavior was merely charming or clever and dismissed it by saying "she just memorized it." We now know that such behavior demonstrates an important step in learning to read.

Leanore Canepa, a student at New York University, babysat with 4-year-old Josh for several months and, as part of a class assignment, observed his behavior during his nightly bedtime story.[14] Josh had been read to every night since he was an infant and attended a nursery school where he was exposed to print in the form of stories, labels, and language experience charts. One of the stories he asked Leanore to read repeatedly was Bemelmans' *Madeline*. When Leanore asked him to read along early in her stint with him, this is what happened. The text of the book and Josh's version are given.

TEXT	JOSH'S VERSION
In an old house in Paris that was covered with vines	in a old house
lived twelve little girls in two straight lines.	twelve little girls
In two straight lines they broke their bread	twelve straight lines

Toward the end of her stay with Josh, Leanore tape-recorded his reading of *Madeline* again. This time he turned the pages alone, looked at the pictures, and read the following version.

TEXT	JOSH'S VERSION
In an old house in Paris that was covered with vines	Old house in Paris covered with vines
lived twelve little girls in two straight lines.	live twelve girls
In two straight lines they broke their bread	In two lines they broke bread
and brushed their teeth	and then brushed their teeth
and went to bed.	and then went to bed.
They smiled at the good	and they smiled
and frowned at the bad	and frowned at bad guys
and sometimes they were very sad.[15]	

It is clear that Josh's approximations were becoming more like the printed text. He began to focus on meaning rather than mere repetition of words.

Ludwig Bemelman's *Madeline* is a favorite among children with its rhythm and rhyme and its confident heroine.

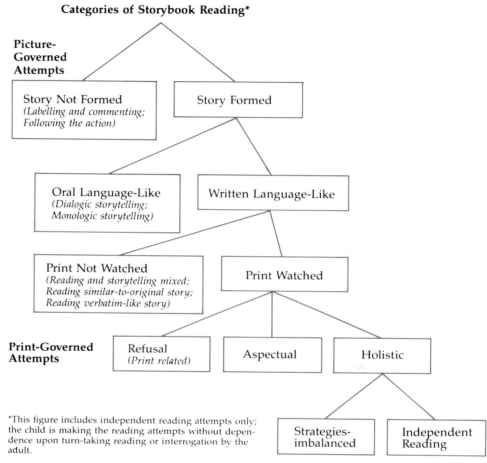

Categories of Storybook Reading*

Picture-Governed Attempts

Story Not Formed
(Labelling and commenting; Following the action)

Story Formed

Oral Language-Like
(Dialogic storytelling; Monologic storytelling)

Written Language-Like

Print Not Watched
(Reading and storytelling mixed; Reading similar-to-original story; Reading verbatim-like story)

Print Watched

Print-Governed Attempts

Refusal
(Print related)

Aspectual

Holistic

Strategies-imbalanced

Independent Reading

*This figure includes independent reading attempts only; the child is making the reading attempts without dependence upon turn-taking reading or interrogation by the adult.

Tree structure of categories of classification scheme for emergent reading of favorite storybooks

Elizabeth Sulzby observed many children (ages roughly 2½ to 6½) to see if she could describe patterns in children's storybook reading.[16] Her goal was to characterize the various developmental stages of emergent reading. She conducted individual interviews in which she asked the children to read to her, and from these identified 10 different types of reading behavior that *precede* independent conventional reading of print. (See the tree diagram above that she developed from her findings.)

Sulzby called the earliest stages of storybook reading labeling, commenting, and fol-lowing the action. In *labeling*, children turn to a page, point to a pictured object, and give its name or a descriptor, for example "doggie, horse." In *commenting*, they give some information about the labeled object, such as "Brush him teefs. Go to bed," or even a fuller sentence: "He's a monster." In *following the action*, they report the activity in the picture as happening now: "See, there he goes. He's gonna catch him. But he don't see him."

Children progress from labeling, commenting, and following the action—in which they only look at the pictures and tell no story—to a form of *dialogue storytelling,* in which they speak for the characters but rarely use dialogue markers (such as he said, she said). As children advance toward *independent reading,* they continue to read the pictures, then mix reading and storytelling, read a simplified story that is similar to the original story, and later, repeat the story verbatim. Their language begins to sound like written language during these stages of storybook reading and generally is more complex and formal than their ordinary conversation or storytelling. Teachers of young children can observe their own students interacting with books as they progress through various developmental stages.

In the last stages of Sulzby's classification system for emergent reading, children attend to the print. It is interesting that children at this stage often refuse to try to read; in fact, as they become aware of the print and realize they must read the print instead of the pictures, they are afraid to try. Some children simply explain "I don't know the words" or "I can't read yet—I need you to help me." Later, children may focus on one or two aspects of print to the exclusion of others. They may focus on a few words they recognize or on a few letters and associated sounds. In this stage, some children go over a page picking out words they know, such as "the," "and," "cat," and "dog."

At the final phase preceding *independent reading,* children may tend to omit unknown words, substitute other words that they already know, sound out words excessively, and often not correct nonsense words that they may formulate. Sulzby calls this "strategy-imbalanced reading" because it is evident that the child demonstrates sporadic control of various strategies but prefers some more than others. Reading independently is distinguished from reading with strategies imbalanced by the amount of self-regulation exhibited. A child may substitute words for ones not recognized but still achieve the meaning the author intended.

Sulzby cautions that care be taken in using her classification system in a hierarchical manner. As with any stage theory, generalizations about specific children are risky. Individual children progress in unique ways, although there is enough reasonable evidence to say that the patterns identified by Sulzby are developmental. The descriptions of behavior at various stages are useful for teachers who are observing children's language and reading development.

Early Writing

Reading and writing are complementary; through these two processes the child comes to understand how sounds, letters, and words relate. Research in children's early writing followed numerous studies of early reading. Reports of children who read early frequently cited the fact that early readers were also ones who liked to make marks on paper.[17] Durkin called the children she identified as early readers "paper and pencil kids." Such reports led others to investigate the direct relation between reading and writing. Carol Chomsky found that children wrote first and read later.[18] Clay, Henderson, and Read separately studied the writing of young children and found identifiable patterns in their markings and spellings.[19] Children begin by making random marks, move to circles, then to linear markings that show they have learned directionality, and eventually to marks that look like letters of the alphabet. As children try to form words, they often write the beginning letter of the word. At this stage, children adopt a letter name strategy. If they do not know how to spell a word, they will invent a spelling using the sounds they hear.[20] Invented spellings are developmentally incomplete; they are not random or incorrect.

Kindergarten teacher Jeanne McPadden exposes her students to print and encourages them to take risks with invented spellings.[21] Children have a copy of the alphabet on their

desks so they may refer to it; they also use books and printed charts and songs. Children who have access to a variety of written materials and are encouraged to experiment with writing make generalizations about writing and spelling and infer the rules that operate. When children are encouraged to see themselves as literate people, they make sense of reading and writing to fulfill their own purposes.

On January 28, 1986, children in Mc-Padden's kindergarten wrote about the explosion of the space shuttle *Challenger*.

MICHAEL: This . is . wan . the . spay . ship . crasht . and . won . of . the . pepl . that . woz . a . techr   (This is when the spaceship crashed and one of the people that was a teacher.)

LAUREN: th spacsip crasht it fal in to th wodr
(The spaceship crashed. It fell into the water.)[22]

The language contained in literature serves as a pattern for children's writing. Rather than learning various discourse forms and styles through drill exercises, children draw upon the styles and forms of the authors they read. This is not to say that children should write to a prescribed pattern. They will intuitively use the forms they find pleasing; the style in which they write will become more complex as they grow older, read more widely, and write more extensively.

Learning Conditions for Literacy Development

Children learn language in an environment filled with language in use. When surrounded by talk, children learn to talk. The conditions that support learning to speak can be applied to learning how to read and write. Brian Cambourne describes several conditions under which children learn to talk and postulates that each one is relevant to all forms of language learning.[23] Four of the conditions are discussed here.

Condition 1: Immersion Children are immersed in a flood of language from the moment they are born. They are literally bathed in the sounds, meanings, and rhythms of the language they are learning. The language that continually flows around them is always meaningful, usually purposeful, and whole.

How does this apply to learning written language—that is, reading and writing? Children learn the meaning of print when they are immersed in it. Each time a sign or a label is pointed out, the child receives a demonstration of its meaning: stories, McDonalds' signs, and cereal boxes. These countless demonstrations help a child associate meaning with print; and thus, the child draws from these demonstrations and makes generalizations about them. Children who are encouraged to make marks on paper have the further advantage of associating meaning with print; they attribute meaning to the marks which eventually begin to look like letters of the alphabet.

Condition 2: Expectation and Opportunity for Use

If you ask the parents of an infant whether or not they expect their child to learn to talk and walk, they will be shocked. Of course, their child will talk and walk! Expectations are very subtle forms of communication to which learners respond. If we give the impression that learning to read, write, spell, or speak is difficult, children will respond accordingly. On the other hand, if we provide appropriate learning conditions and expect children to master these forms of language, they will do it.

Children determine the order of what they learn about their language; they adopt conventions and forms at their own rate. We need to provide ample opportunities for them to use whatever is being demonstrated and allow time for practice. Children are not restricted to 20 minutes a day in learning to talk; neither should they be in learning to read and write. Learning anything takes practice; and the more we practice, the better we get.

Condition 3: Approximation

Adults reward children not just for being right but for being close when they are learning to talk. When a child calls her grandmother "Bammaw," she is not corrected but hugged and praised instead. When close approximations are accepted in learning to write (as in invented spelling) and in learning to read (as in emergent reading) children willingly take risks in their new learning.

Condition 4: Feedback and Modeling

Children move from immature language forms—for instance, "Dat cup" to "That's a cup"—as people around them provide feedback of a very special kind. The child's approximation is accepted and a response is given to the meaning in a conventional expanded form. The child is not told, "No, that's not the way to say it." We respond to the content, not the form. The same conditions prevail when children are learning to read and to write: we praise what they are doing right and respond to the meaning, not the form.

How do these conditions operate in the home and school? Much depends upon the family into which a child is born. Some families begin reading to a child when he or she is only a few hours old. Doake captured his son Raja's responses to books on film during his first year.[24] His parents began reading to him when he was 6 hours old and continued to read daily. By 5 months, Raja had an attention span of 40 minutes; by 9 months, it had increased to 75 minutes. During Raja's eleventh month, he recognized some of his favorite books by name when asked to bring one to a parent.

As discussed earlier, the Commission on Reading concluded, in *Becoming a Nation of Readers*, that the single most important activity for building the knowledge required for eventual success in reading is reading aloud to children.[25] Jim Trelease, in *The Read-Aloud Handbook*, says parents need to do with books what McDonalds does with its hamburgers: advertise![26] Show children that there is something wonderful inside books and let them know that they deserve a reading break each day. And

Laura Jones found that students wanted to read a book by themselves once they heard it read aloud by the teacher.[27]

Two of the most convincing studies of the effect of reading aloud come from work done in New Zealand and England. In *Cushla and Her Books,* Dorothy Butler describes the startling effects that reading aloud had on a child with multiple handicaps.[28] After doctors had predicted severe retardation, Cushla's parents read aloud to her to soothe her through long nights and painful hospitalization. Cushla astounded her parents and her doctors by eventually learning to read on her own at a level beyond her actual age. Gordon Wells focused on 6 of the 32 children he studied from shortly after their first birthdays until the last year of their elementary schooling. The results were clear: the frequency of listening to stories significantly predicted the children's later educational achievement. Wells states:

> And this was not simply the result of the children's having acquired a larger vocabulary. Children who had been read to were better able to narrate an event, describe a scene, and follow instructions. But perhaps what was most important . . . was the greater ease with which they appeared to be able to understand the teachers' use of language.[29]

For some children, school may be the first and only place they encounter books. For others, school will extend an already rich experience with books. Moira McKenzie notes that in terms of becoming literate, the children who are least successful in school are often the ones most dependent upon what the school offers.[30]

In a study of family literacy, Denny Taylor found that, for successful readers, storybook sharing was an intricate part of the fabric of family life.[31] Successful readers grew up in an environment where literacy was the only option.

Marilyn Cochran-Smith found that some storybooks have features that invite interactive patterns of response.[32] For example, *What Do You Say, Dear?* (P) by Sesyle Joslin uses a stylistic feature of direct address which invites the audience to participate actively in creating its meaning. Such stylistic features reflect the way children learn to make sense of oral language in dialogue with adults.

CRITERIA FOR SELECTING BOOKS FOR LANGUAGE DEVELOPMENT

Books for language development cover a broad range of genres and styles. In fact, considering children's voracious appetite for language, almost any book could be used for language development in some productive way. We have a surfeit of riches, however, so we can be selective in the ones we choose.

Books provide models of language in use; they demonstrate the meanings of concepts and represent aspects of the world a child is coming to know. We need to match the book to the level of the child's mental and physical development. Books that children can understand enrich their concept development and, in turn, will provide comprehensible language models. Toddlers can label the people in Oxenbury's *Family* (N) and *Dressing* (N). Four- and 5-year-olds can lift the flaps in Eric Hill's series about Spot. Look for books that (1) have sturdy pages and durable bindings, such as those found in board books, and (2) present concepts in a clear, uncomplicated manner.

The illustrations and design determine the visual appeal of a book. Bright, bold colors and carefully arranged art draw a child toward the meaning a book conveys. Ann Jonas's work is exemplary in *Holes and Peeks* (N), which depicts in clear, bold shapes household objects that may frighten or delight a child. Janet and Allan Ahlberg's *Peek-A-Boo!* (N) contains visual subplots and intriguing details that invite a child to play its game. Look for books that (1) invite participation and (2) have good illustrations and an appealing, artistic design.

Rhythmic, melodic language flows naturally and falls softly on the ear. Books with interesting language will enrich a child's vocabulary and show him or her how language in a book can sound. The rhythm of Shirley Hughes's *Bathwater's Hot* (N) will be echoed by children who hear it read aloud. Choose books that (1) read well when read aloud and (2) contain pleasing language used gracefully.

The gift of imagination is the most precious gift of all, and books that stimulate the imagination contribute to language development. Books that ask "What if?" nurture the magical possibilities in life and are worth sharing with children. Satomi Ichikawa's *Nora's Castle* (P) invites the child to imagine what could happen in a deserted castle. Search for books that (1) encourage children to see possibilities beyond the literal level of the real world and (2) create interesting visual images.

BOOKS FOR THE VERY YOUNG

Books for Babies

Baby books are 10- to 12-page books, often made from sturdy cardboard, which are aimed at 1-, 2-, and 3-year-olds. Phyllis J. Fogelman, president and publisher of Dial Books, pioneered the genre of high-quality board books after she saw the construction and the less desirable content of the books available on the mass market. Fogelman states that baby books

> must be clear, simple, and direct, designed to catch a toddler's attention immediately and hold it. Whether there are words or not, the artwork must tell the story clearly and not rely on minute detail. If there is no plot, each picture must be a story in itself and yet still fit together with the others to make a coherent, unified book. There are usually only twelve pages to work with in board books, including the front and back covers, and yet the story must be one that will not cost children their patience and parents their sanity after dozens of readings.[33]

The notable change in quality is apparent in cloth books, shape books, pudgy books, lift-the-flap books, toy books, and bathtub books, in addition to the most popular board books. Books of this type are appropriate for children who are in the labeling and identification stage, who are in the earliest stages of reading—pointing to pictures and labeling them. Helen

TEACHING IDEA

SHARE A BOOK (N)   Introduce books as early as you wish, as long as making use of them is a pleasurable experience for you and the child. Clear, representational pictures are better than complicated or abstract designs for this age group. Talk to the child about the pictures as you turn the pages, and as much as possible relate what is in the pictures to things that are in the child's real world.

Rachel Isadora's books, *I Touch, I See,* and *I Hear* (all N), tell about familiar objects and people in a young child's world. The child will join in to say the lollipop is "sticky," the cereal is "gooey," and the teddy bear is "soft."

The best way to share a book is to have the child in the adult's lap, with the book held directly in front of the child to focus attention on the pages. The child learns while the adult and child are turning the pages, enjoying the experience together, and treating the book as a valued object.

Oxenbury has produced several series of baby books: one series, which begins with *I Can* (N), shows what a child can do; another, which includes *Dressing* (N), shows clothing and names for each piece that baby wears. Oxenbury's wordless series begins with *Mother's Helper* (N), in which a plump toddler rides the vacuum cleaner. And still another, *Grandma and Grandpa*, concentrates on important people in a child's life.

Participation Books

Participation books provide concrete visual and tactile materials for children to explore—textures to touch, flaps to lift, "flowers" to smell, and pieces to manipulate.

Dorothy Kunhardt's *Pat the Bunny* (N), a classic, has appealed to young children since 1940. The book shows Paul and Judy doing many things and develops the idea that the child can do lots of things, too. Judy feels Daddy's scratchy face, and the toddler can feel

Daddy's scratchy face—a bit of sandpaper—in the picture. There is also a place to stick a finger into Mommy's ring, a piece of cloth to raise and lower in a peek-a-boo game, and scented-paper "flowers" to smell—all intended to engage the child in play and conversation.

Eric Hill introduced a lovable character in books for young children. First appearing in *Where's Spot?* (N), the irrepressible puppy strikes out alone and has the reader searching for him by lifting flaps and opening doors. We search for Spot again in *Spot Goes to School* (N), and in *Spot Goes to the Farm* (N), we search for his ball when it bounces away. In these books, flaps are more than a gimmick to fascinate children, they are an integral part of the story. There are several books about Spot, even one that can be taken into the bathtub. *Spot Goes Splash* (N) is an inflated vinyl book with illustrations of the places he likes to splash. He splashes in puddles and at the beach, but his favorite splash is in the bathtub every night.

Participation books involve the child in some activity. In Marc Brown's brightly illus-

Eric Hill's series of Spot books delight young children and invite them to participate in the story. (From *Spot Goes to the Farm*.)

trated *Hand Rhymes* and *Finger Rhymes* (both N-P), the activities are finger plays. Eric Carle created several books in a series, called *My Very First Book of . . .* , in which children match the lower half of a page with the top half. In *My Very First Book of Shapes* (N), spiral-bound cardboard half pages contain shapes of familiar objects on the bottom and solid black matching shapes on the top half. The child turns the pages to find the top and bottom that go together.

Each Peach Pear Plum (N-P) by Janet and Allan Ahlberg is a visually delightful interpretation of the game "I Spy." On a double-page spread, a two-line verse introduces a familiar nursery character which can be found by sharp-eyed children in the facing picture. Tom Thumb, Mother Hubbard, Cinderella, and other nursery rhyme characters are hidden in the attractive illustrations. *The Baby's Catalogue,* by the same authors, chronicles the activities of the babies in five families.

Beginning Stories

Beginning stories have a simple plot line. Young children progress from labeling and pointing to a stage in which they can attend to short, uncomplicated stories. Ann Jonas provides some of the best stories about familiar childhood experiences, which she captures in clear, bright illustrations. In *Now We Can Go* (N-P), a determined child clutches a tote bag and yells, "Wait a minute! I'm not ready." Then in ritualistic fashion, the child takes each toy from the toy box and puts it into his tote bag. When the toy box is empty and the bag is full, he announces, "Now we can go!" *Where Can It Be?* (N-P) shows the dilemma when a small boy's special blanket cannot be found. We lift the tablecloth, open the refrigerator, and search the house to no avail. Finally, friend Debra walks in with the sought-after object—he had left it at her house. Jonas's strong, vivid colors and simple plots create appealing picture books for young children.

Karla Kuskin, award-winning poet, tells a story in verse about a child who would like to have a pet—any kind will do—in *Something Sleeping in the Hall* (N-P). The child wants "Something big,/something small,/something sleeping in the hall. . . . " The whimsical verses reveal the child considering a number of animals to fill that role.

Anne Rockwell tells simple stories enriched with bright, clear illustrations in a series of board books: *At Night, In the Morning, At the Playground,* and *In the Rain* (all N). Each book highlights the familiar activities and objects in a small child's world with an unadorned text describing them. Anne and Harlow Rockwell capture a child's delight in exploring new territories in *My Back Yard* and *When I Go Visiting* (both N).

Rosemary Wells introduces an engaging, impish young rabbit, Max, and his sister, Ruby, who appear in many books. It is clear that Max has a mind of his own. When Ruby tries to teach him to say a new word, in *Max's First Word* (N), he insists on repeating only one word, "Bang!" Ruby tries "Cup, say cup. Egg, say egg." When she gives him an apple and says, "Yum, yum, Max. Say yum, yum," Max surprises Ruby and us by shouting, "Delicious!" In *Max's Breakfast* (N), Ruby tries to get Max to eat his egg. Max hides his plate, he hides himself, and he resists coaxing until Ruby shows him how tasty the egg is by eating it herself. Max watches timorously and then shouts happily, "All gone!" when the plate is clean.

Nancy Tafuri's *Have You Seen My Duckling?* (N-P) became a favorite of 18-month-old Anna. Her mother told a story as they shared the nearly wordless book saying, "The mother swims back to the nest and the ducklings say, 'Oh, Mommy, our sister has gone. She's chasing a butterfly.' 'Oh, dear,' says Mommy Duck. 'Let's all go look for her.' So they all went swimming off to look for their sister. First Mommy Duck met a bird and said, 'Have you seen my duckling?' The bird said 'No, I haven't seen your duckling—but Anna knows where she is!'" Giggling with delight, Anna pointed to the duckling and said, "There she is!" This kind of sharing involves Anna and makes the experience more enjoyable for mother and child. At 2½ years, Anna could tell the entire story herself even engaging in dialogue with herself, saying "Anna knows where she is!"[34]

Alphabet Books

Alphabet books present the ABCs in a variety of ways. In *John Burningham's ABC* (N-P), the individual letter of the alphabet, in small case and capitals, and a single word are the only text on each page. The spacious pages are filled with the watercolor and crayon drawings of a lumpy child who mimics an alligator, plays with a bear, rides on a cow, and so forth through the alphabet.

Arnold Lobel wrote the words and Anita Lobel drew the pictures in a magnificent alphabet book, *On Market Street* (N-P). The simple story line shows a young boy shopping for presents on Market Street and we see what he bought from A to Z. Each display is constructed from the very objects for sale: the Apple lady is made entirely from apples, the Bookman from books, the Clock lady from clocks and the Doughnut lady from doughnuts, and so on. This unusual artistic approach was inspired by seventeenth-century French trade engravings.

Applebet: An ABC (N-P) by Clyde and Wendy Watson is a story set in rhyme with a little hide-and-seek game tucked in for delight. We follow the apple that Bet picked as it goes on the cart all the way to a country fair and zigzags back home again. Bet and her mother are the people we watch through a riotous day, but we cannot go on before we find the apple hidden somewhere on the page.

Shirley Hughes underscores the role books play in children's lives in *Lucy & Tom's a.b.c.* (N-P). She fills the pages with scenes from a

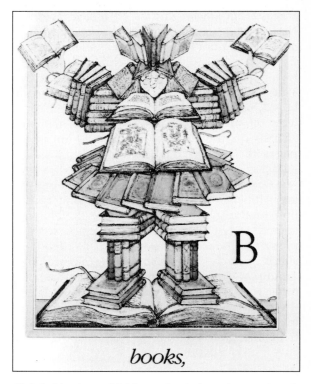

books,

Alphabet books are highly creative in how they teach and illustrate the ABCs. (From *On Market Street* by Arnold Lobel, illustrated by Anita Lobel.)

busy family's life as she uses the alphabet to structure her story. For example, the following appears for the letter *b:*

> **b** is for **b**ooks and **b**ed. Lucy and Tom nearly always have a story read to them at bedtime. Tom knows most of his favorite stories by heart. When he's in bed he can look at the pictures and read aloud to himself. Lucy keeps some of her special books under her pillow, just in case.[35]

Barbara Lalicki compiled the words—some poetry, some prose—and Margot Tomes illustrated them in a beautiful alphabet book, *If There Were Dreams to Sell* (P). Each letter of the alphabet is represented by a word that may be

In Suse MacDonald's *Alphabatics,* the letters begin to bounce and revolve as they turn into the object they represent.

found in Mother Goose, Coleridge, Longfellow, Tolkien, and other classic writers. The outstanding art, however, distinguishes the book as Margot Tomes's delicate, magical illustrations illuminate the ABCs.

Alphabet books serve many useful purposes, only one of which is related to learning the alphabet. Two- to 4-year-old children will point to and label objects on the page; 5-year-olds may say the letter names and words that start with each letter; and 6-year-olds may read the letters, words, or story to confirm their knowledge of letter and sound correspondences. Whichever way they are used, alphabet books help to develop children's awareness of words on a page and play a useful part in language learning in addition to the pleasurable hours they provide a child.

Outstanding illustrators use the alphabet as a structural frame to display their skills, to tell a story, to play with letter sounds and words, to collect nonsense verse, and to delight the imagination. No one need settle for a mediocre alphabet book because there are magnificent

ones available. One of the best, *Anno's Alphabet* (P), by Mitsumasa Anno, is appropriately subtitled *An Adventure in Imagination,* and the aptness becomes evident when you open the book. A wood-carved question mark, a tree, an axe, a vise, a saw, and a wood carver's tool foreshadow what is to come. Each letter is represented by one large object, but there are many related ones hidden in the borders of the page. The book becomes a treasure hunt and a genuine adventure in imagination as children try to find the objects and guess the relationships of all the things Anno has put into his alphabet.

In *Jambo Means Hello* (P), Tom and Muriel Feelings show that an alphabet book can be much more than just a representation of letters. Their book gives Swahili words and concepts for the letters and develops a sense of the majesty and dignity of the people who created the Swahili language. The magnificent illustrations extend the meanings of the words and convey the warmth and sense of community felt among these African people.

ACT 2

The **B** was badly Bitten.

Chris Van Allsburg's *The Z Was Zapped* places the letter in a sentence and provides imaginative illustrations of what happens to the letter.

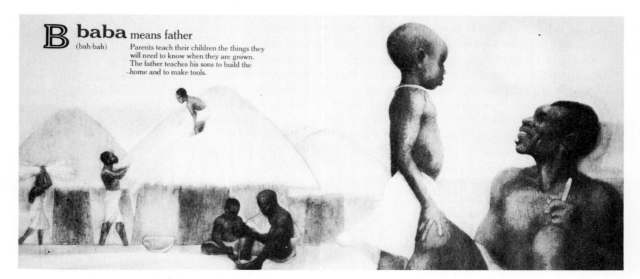

An alphabet book that uses transliterated Swahili terms: "baba means father" in Swahili. Customs of East African life are depicted in detailed double-spread paintings for each letter. (Excerpted from the book *Jambo Means Hello: Swahili Alphabet Book* by Tom and Muriel Feelings. Illustrated by Tom Feelings.)

The voracious caterpillar leaves holes in the page large enough for children's fingers as they count. (From *The Very Hungry Caterpillar* by Eric Carle.)

In a companion to this alphabet book, Tom and Muriel Feelings give the Swahili words for numbers in *Moja Means One* (P). Artful illustrations with a soft chalklike texture extend one's awareness of customs of the African people in this counting book.

Counting Books

Counting books contain numbers and groups of objects to represent them. They contribute to children's cognitive structuring by reinforcing their grasp of quantity and seriation. Like alphabet books, counting books are used for much more than learning to count. They may also help children learn to add or subtract, or just to enjoy the visual portrayal of numerical concepts. Children delight in pointing to the objects displayed and checking to see if the illustrator presented the exact number of items for each numeral. The best illustrations for young children avoid distracting clutter so that the objects can be identified and counted without confusion. With such books, children rehearse counting until they have learned it by heart.

Books for very young children often make counting a game or invite the child to participate, the way Eric Carle does in *The Very Hungry Caterpillar* (N-P). The hungry caterpillar eats holes right through the pages, and the holes lure children to stick tiny fingers through them as they count. The caterpillar finally changes into a huge brilliant butterfly that opens its wings across the entire spread of the final pages. A miniature edition of *The Very Hungry Caterpillar* measures about 4 by 5 inches and contains exactly the same story that has captured the hearts of more than 4 million readers.

Molly Bang's *Ten, Nine, Eight* (N-P) is actually a lullaby that starts with number 10 and counts down to 1. A loving black father reaches out to his daughter as she runs to him in her nightgown. Father is in a rocking chair near the girl's crib and as she snuggles into his lap, the countdown begins: "10 small toes all washed

Molly Bang uses a lullaby to teach children how to count backward. This page from her *Ten, Nine, Eight* chants "3 loving kisses on cheeks and nose."

Animal Numbers, by Bert Kitchen, encourages the young reader to count the baby animals frolicking around their mothers. In this case, two signets echo their mother's form as she creates the image of the numeral.

and warm." After toes, we count stuffed animals, window panes, shoes, and more until the lullaby closes with "2 strong arms around a fuzzy bear's head" and "1 big girl all ready for bed." The beauty and warmth of a loving father-daughter relationship emanate from the vibrant paintings in full color.

Bert Kitchen's *Animal Alphabet* (N-P) received critical acclaim when it was published, and his *Animal Numbers* (N-P) was equally praised. *Animal Numbers* displays each animal mother with a numeral that represents the number of infants in her brood. Children can count the 1 baby kangaroo in its mother's pouch, the 4 baby woodpecker fledglings, the 9 squiggly baby caterpillars, the 10 Irish setter puppies, and up to 100 tadpoles swimming with mother frog. The work of a museum-quality painter and graphic artist elevates a counting book to a high art form, and it is appreciated by all ages.

Tana Hoban uses shiny plastic numerals and letters in 26 *Letters and 99 Cents* (P-I), a counting book turned from front to back and

an alphabet book turned from back to front. Clear spacious pages show the numerals with the correct number of bright pennies aligned. For the numerals 5 and up, two choices are shown, such as the five pennies but also a nickel. For 6 there are six pennies or a nickel and a penny. For the numeral 10, there are three choices: ten pennies, two nickels, or one dime. The combinations continue to 99 cents to show that there is more than one way to equal a numeral with coins. Hoban's photography is startling in its clarity and purity of form.

One Duck, Another Duck (N-P) by Charlotte Pomerantz shows how Grandmother Owl teaches her grandson to count. On a late afternoon visit to a pond, Danny counts a family of ducks, "One duck, another duck, another duck. . . ." With Grandmother's help, he manages to change to "One duck, another duck . . . two ducks; another duck . . . three ducks; another duck. . . ." A family of swans presents a new group to be counted, and later Danny resolves to count the stars as he and his grandmother go home. *One Duck, Another Duck* was illustrated by José Aruego and Ariane Dewey.

Nancy Tafuri wrote and illustrated *Who's Counting* (N-P). This counting book features a rambunctious puppy hidden on each page that young counters will spot as they proceed through one squirrel, two birds, three moles, and so on. Tafuri's conception of space and simplicity of design has a strong visual impact. Her subtle plot line invites children to tell the story which might be missed by unobservant adults.

John Burningham's *1 2 3* (N-P) pictures fat-cheeked children climbing into a tree, one after another until there are 10. The final climber, however, looking something like a tiger, chases the 10 children and claims the tree as his alone. Both numerals and the word for each number are given.

1 Hunter (N-P) by Pat Hutchins is a visual puzzle in which animals are camouflaged in the forest. The animals see the hunter, but the hunter never sees them. Children like to be in on the joke, and so they delight in pointing out what the hunter does not see in this counting book that invites participation.

Eric Carle conveys the passage of time in *The Very Busy Spider* and *The Grouchy Ladybug* (both N-P). The spider starts early in the morning to spin a thin, silky thread on a fence post near a farmyard. All day long the spider ignores invitations from the farm animals to do other things. Instead, she continues to spin her web, catches a pesky fly for supper, and sleeps as night falls. This book demands touching and feeling: the spider and her web are raised on the page so that you can feel the delicate strands as they grow. In *The Grouchy Ladybug*, different animals provoke the ladybug throughout the day. Cleverly die-cut pages demonstrate the relative size of the animals from small to large. The time of day is depicted in numerals on a clock and written out in the text as well as shown visually as the sun moves through its daytime path.

Concept Books

Concept books are simple informational books for young children. They contribute to the child's expanding language by providing numerous examples of an idea. Some present

TEACHING IDEAS

COUNTING IN THE CLASSROOM (N)   Children enjoy exploring counting books and, within a short period, are reciting the numbers as they go. Read to small groups or to individual children so that each can check to see if the illustrator has the correct number of objects for each numeral. (A few have made mistakes!)

ACTIVITY: TEACHER TO STUDENT

MAKE A BOOK (P)   Staple together several pieces of plain paper or make holes in them and tie with a ribbon to form a book. Write down numbers and tell a story about each one. Draw pictures that show the number of things in your story. Or you might draw pictures to go along with a counting song like "This Old Man" or rope-skipping counting songs.

PROFILE

Nancy Tafuri

Nancy Tafuri had a mother who read to her, as Nancy says, "long before it was fashionable to do so."[36] She said, "I adored snuggling up to my mother while she would read (or I read to her) the same favorites over and over. Maybe that, coupled with crayons and endless hours of coloring and the love of nature, has helped form my destined fate." Those hours with her mother sharing books created

a feeling of closeness and warmth that she now tries to convey in her own work. Tafuri envisions a child and a parent sharing her books, so she puts small objects and little subplots there for the child to discover.

Tafuri, born in New York City, was an only child until she was 10. Her mother encouraged her interest in books and never tired of sharing them with her. She studied at the School of Visual Arts in New York where she met her husband. They now live on a 98 acre farm in an eight-room house built in 1790.

The first book Tafuri illustrated was *The Piney Woods Peddler* (P) by George Shannon. For that book, she traveled to the Amish country in Pennsylvania and "holed up" in an old grist mill which, she says, was "kind of spooky." There she used local residents and her own husband as models.

The ideas for many of city-bred Tafuri's books now come from the nature and wildlife (she calls them wildlings) around her country home. *Rabbit's Morning, Early Morning in the Barn*, and *All Year Long* (all N-P) are based on her own observations of wildlife and chil-

such abstract ideas as shape, color, size, or sound through many illustrations. John Riess's *Colors, Numbers,* and *Shapes* (all N-P) are good examples of this. Others tell a story based on concepts such as time or emotions. Aliki, for instance, catalogues children's *Feelings* (N-P) in a collection of vignettes and cartoons. She depicts children who feel sad, lonely, or happy and the situation that caused the emotion.

Tana Hoban's concept books are exemplary. She views the world through a photog-

rapher's eye, and, in *Look Again* (P-I) and *Take Another Look* (P-I), invites the reader to do just that. A plain white page with a small opening becomes a frame that reveals only a small part of a larger photograph to come. The invitation to predict what is coming is clear, although no words are used. On the first page of *Look Again,* children see a network of filaments and speculate that the item might be a spiderweb or a milkweed. On the next page they discover a huge dandelion puff enlarged to fill the

dren in the rural area in which she lives. She explains,

> The frolicsome puppy in *Who's Counting?* [N-P] originated from my own dog. Although he is a keeshond, I made the one in the book a frisky Labrador Retriever. My dog does everything the dog in this book does. He sticks his nose into his water dish and doesn't realize he has to take it out of the water to breathe. He romps over everything with no idea that he's trampling flowers. He frightens ducks and geese and wonders why they won't play with him.

Tafuri credits her husband for the idea of *Have You Seen My Duckling?* (N-P). Together they watched mallards on the pond near their home when he remarked, "There's a book for you, Nancy." In this book as in other Tafuri books, words are minimal. Bright, clear-cut illustrations dominate the pages and tell the story. Tafuri says, "Words are not my thing. One of my books has only 9 words—cut down from 100. I tell my stories in pictures."

Tafuri puts the subtle subplots in her illustrations. While the mother mallard in *Have You Seen My Duckling?* searches the pond's environs for her baby, children quickly find it on each page. In *Across the Stream* (N-P), written by Mirra Ginsburg, Tafuri has a fox follow the mother hen and her chicks who cross the stream to safety atop a family of ducks. In *Do Not Disturb,* (N-P) a later book, campers annoy forest creatures all day, and in retaliation, the animals awaken the campers at night. The family realizes that they have been inconsiderate, and in a futile attempt for peace and quiet, they hang out a sign that says "Do not disturb." Tafuri also illustrated *All Asleep* (N-P), poems written by Charlotte Pomerantz, and several other books.

Nancy Tafuri loves writing and illustrating books for very young children because, she explains, "they have such vivid imaginations. They take everything in." Tafuri's sense of simplicity is just the right ingredient in books for young children.

whole page and, on the next, a child blowing away the dandelion filaments as she holds the flower in her hand. The changing perspectives involve the child in imaginative guessing and show the many dimensions of a dandelion. The book develops the idea of careful observation and shows how perspective changes perception.

Donald Crews's *Truck* (N) has several levels of potential interest. The subtle story line is insignificant to the very young child, who will go through the book repeatedly pointing to the signs along the road that the truck travels and naming the vehicles, whereas older ones will read the road signs and try to figure out the origin, route, and destination of the huge truckload of tricycles. Children who are alert to the signs in their environment will turn to the book again and again to confirm the words they recognize and to demonstrate to themselves their growing repertoire of words they can read.

Vivid colors and strong shapes make things easy to recognize. (From *Truck* by Donald Crews.)

Karen Gundersheimer has produced two simple concept books about shapes and colors for the very young child. In *Colors to Know* (N), an elflike child holds a huge red heart, rides on a bright yellow duck, and climbs inside a sparkling blue mitten. In *Shapes to Show* (N), two mice find recognizable shapes in their daily world: a circle in a beach ball, a triangle in a mask, and a rectangle in a book. These tiny books provide models for children and enrich their language development.

John Burningham helps to develop the concept of *Opposites* (N) in a book filled with humor and good fun. A boy looks suspiciously at a cat as they each hold a pail of water. The word on this page is "dry." On the facing page, the word is "wet" after the boy and the cat have tossed water on each other. "Hard" and "soft" compare sleeping on a park bench with sleeping on a sofa. "Heavy" and "light" compare holding an elephant and a balloon. Simple, funny pictures reinforce the comparisons in a humorous way.

Anne Rockwell's *The Emergency Room* (N) is a story that develops the concept of a place children may encounter. The same author uses a story to show what happens around a commonplace event in *Our Garage Sale* (N). These stories extend beyond simple objects and word labels to develop a broader understanding of places and events important to children.

Tana Hoban is unsurpassed in her use of photography in concept books for young children. The list of credits, awards, and honors runs long for her ingenious books on colors, shapes, sizes, and textures. She sees the magnificent in ordinary things around us and captures it on film so that children can see it, too.

Full-color photographs in her *Is It Larger? Is it Smaller?* (N-P) present the concept of size. Through a series of comparisons without words, Hoban calls attention to differences. A child's sneakers appear beside an adult's pair; a doll tea set, beside a regular sized teapot. *Shapes, Shapes, Shapes* (N-P) contains the familiar and introduces some of the less familiar shapes, such as star, hexagon, and parallelogram. Hoban has produced many other excellent books, including *Is It Red? Is It Yellow? Is It Blue?* (N-P) and *I Walk and Read* (N-P), which facilitate language and concept development.

BOOKS FOR EMERGING READERS

Levels of books for children correspond to the developmental stages of childhood. When children need more complex and sophisticated books than the ones described above, there are many available to fill this need. *Predictable* books are well-suited to the child who is beginning to pay attention to print. *Wordless* books are appropriate for children who are developing a sense of story and learning language rapidly. *Nonfiction* provides many opportunities for children to add to their store of knowledge about the world.

Predictable Books

In predictable books, children anticipate what is going to happen because of the books' highly

TEACHING IDEAS

EMOTIONS (N-P)   Show the animated 16-mm. film "One Was Johnny" or "Really Rosie" (both available from Weston Woods) based on "Nutshell Library" characters (Maurice Sendak, Harper & Row, 1962). You might begin by talking about Johnny's feelings as the parade of characters interrupts his reading. Johnny shows his displeasure by standing on a chair and threatening to eat them all if they are not gone by the time he has counted backward from 10. Children will quickly learn the song "Really Rosie" by Carole King and will sing along on replays of the film or rereadings of the book.

EXPANDING LANGUAGE CONCEPTS: OPPOSITES (N-P)   Books provide opportunities to reinforce concept development and to build new concepts by showing examples of what something is, is not, and does, or what its attributes are. While sharing these books with children, adults are modeling language, expanding upon the words used in the books, and making progressively finer distinctions. Children may imitate these words and eventually assimilate them into their own language system.

Building the concept of opposites through repeated examples is done in several books, including Peter Spier's *Fast-Slow High-Low* (N-P), a treasure house of humor and detail, and John Burningham's delightful *Opposites* (N-P).

ACTIVITY: TEACHER TO STUDENT

WORD SEARCH (P)   Make up a list of opposites and write them in pairs in a book you have made. (Make the book out of sheets of paper held together with a piece of cord or ribbon pulled through a hole in the corner of the sheets, or staple the sheets together along the edge.) Draw pictures that show the meanings of the words.

---

patterned structure. Many 4- and 5-year-old children can read them on their own after hearing them read aloud only once. The books are structured with repetitive language patterns, cumulative story plots, or strongly patterned phrases.

Reading involves sampling, predicting, and confirming.[37] Readers select the most useful syntactic, semantic, and graphophonemic information from print in order to make a prediction about what it says.[38] They hypothesize the most probable meaning based on the information sampled and then confirm it by checking to see if it makes sense, matches the letter-sound correspondences, and sounds like language (syntax). Predictable books are ideal fare for beginning readers because they match expectations at every step along the way.

The gemstone of predictable books, and perhaps the one that accounts for the recognition of the type, is Bill Martin Jr's *Brown Bear, Brown Bear, What Do You See?* (N-P). The answer to the title question is "I see a redbird looking at me." Children familiar with the

"Redbird,
redbird.
What do you see?"

"I see a yellow duck
looking at me."

Through rhythm, rhyme, and a strong, simple pattern, a predictable book encourages children to create expectations. (From *Brown Bear, Brown Bear, What Do You See?* by Bill Martin Jr)

book will know what the next question is going to be: "Redbird, redbird, what do you see?" The rhythm, rhyme, and repetition confirm children's predictions. Through the book, each animal in turn is asked until, finally, children are asked the same question. The last illustration is a full-page collage of everything seen in the book. Eric Carle's bold vivid shapes add to the predictability and the beauty of the book.

Brian Wildsmith's *Cat on the Mat* (N) has a predictable sentence pattern in which only one word is changed on each page. A contented cat sits alone on a bright red-fringed mat. The cat looks askance at the dog who comes next and grows furious as other animals invade the mat. Each new word, the name of the new animal that joins the cat on the mat, is predictable because the child can see it in the picture. Finally, the cat's self-control disappears, and with a "Sssppstt!" the cat chases away the intruders. The final page completes the cycle as the self-satisfied cat sits alone once more and the text reads again, "The cat sat on the mat."

Predictable books range from ones with the very simple repetition of a phrase, as in *Jump, Frog, Jump!* (N-P) by Robert Kalan, to ones with a repeated phrase and a more sophisti-

cated text, as in Ashley Wolff's *Only the Cat Saw* (N-P). Other books are predictable because of the sequence and the context clues, as in *Sleepy Bear* (N-P) by Lydia Dabcovich. This story follows the bear's hibernation with the minimal text stating, "It's getting cold. Leaves are falling. Birds are leaving." Vicki Frost, a kindergarten teacher, remarks, "When my students learn to read *Sleepy Bear*, their parents stop saying, 'Oh, she just memorized the story.' They realize the children really do know how to read."[39]

The context and the sequence help young children read Ron Maris's books *Are You There, Bear?* and *Is Anyone Home?* as well as *This Is the Bear* (all N-P) by Sarah Hayes. In *Is Anyone Home?* inviting gates and doors open on half pages as the child says, "I know who lives here." The sequence of the days of the week and the rhythm of the language help children read Janina Domanska's *Busy Monday Morning* (N-P), a Polish folk song which follows the pattern, "On Monday morning, busy Monday morning, Father mowed the hay and so did I. We mowed hay together he and I." The rhythmic rollicking language and the question and answer format of Robert Kraus's book *Whose*

"Help! Help!" cried the Court when the moon shone bright.
"King Bidgood's in the bathtub, and he won't get out!
Oh, who knows what to do?
Who knows what to do?"

Another form of predictable book is the cumulative story, which builds phrase upon phrase and leads to an entertaining climax. One prominent example is Audrey Wood's *King Bidgood's in the Bathtub,* which garnered a Caldecott honor award for Don Wood's illustrations.

Mouse Are You? (N-P) helps children read the book after hearing it only a few times. Children who have loved this book will want to read the sequels *Where Are You Going, Little Mouse?* and *Come Out and Play, Little Mouse* (both N-P).

The Big Sneeze (N-P) by Ruth Brown follows the tradition of a chain tale, a formula that enhances predictability. A simple fly lands on a sleeping farmer's nose, causing him to sneeze. The sneeze tosses the fly into the spider's web which attracts a cat that wakes a dog that scatters the hens that panic the donkey that brings the farmer's wife. The farmer, dripping with splattered eggs, protests, "I only sneezed!"

Cumulative stories build phrase on phrase, event on event, to a climax and then unravel. They are predictable in that each phrase or event is repeated as new ones accumulate. Audrey Wood wrote and Don Wood illustrated a cumulative tale, *The Napping House* (N-P), in which spectacular foreshadowing leads through a rainy garden into the napping house where everyone is sleeping. The sumptuous illustration on the second page of the story contains all of the characters who will play a role, but the casual observer may not notice them the first time through the book. One by one, the characters climb on to the bed for a nap until a tiny flea bites the mouse and awakens everybody. The resplendent blue tones and chalk images make the book memorable. The same author and illustrator team produced *King Bidgood's in the Bathtub* (P) with its repetitive phrase "And he won't get out!" This time the foreshadowing on title and dedication pages shows a young boy lugging a heavy cask of water up treacherous castle stairs. Soon the problem is clear: "King Bidgood's in the bathtub, and he won't get out! Oh, who knows what to do?" Several members of the king's court suggest solutions but it is the lowly page who finally solves the problem in his own ingenious way. The caliber of the illustrations merited a Caldecott honor book award for Don Wood.

Other high-quality predictable books include: *The Rose in My Garden* (P) by Arnold and Anita Lobel; *A Dark Dark Tale* (N-P) by Ruth Brown; *Where's the Bear?* (N-P) by Charlotte Pomerantz; and *Have You Seen My Duckling?* (N-P) by Nancy Tafuri.

Wordless Books

Wordless books tell a story through illustration alone. They are used at many levels: very young children who do not yet read can tell the stories through the pictures; beginning readers, through their developing concept of story, are able to narrate the books; intermediate grade students use them as models for story writing; and junior high school students use them to delineate the elements of fiction.

Mercer Mayer has created some of the best wordless books. One of them, *Frog, Where Are You?* (N-P), deals with the problems a boy faces because of the behavior of his impetuous pet frog. *Frog Goes to Dinner* (N-P) is a favorite because of the slapstick comedy and uninhibited behavior of the frog. The irrepressible frog hides in the boy's pocket when the family goes to dinner at a fancy restaurant and creates havoc by jumping into a salad, a glass of champagne, and a saxophone. The family is disgruntled when they are evicted from the restaurant, but the reader shares the smirks of delight observed on the boy's face *and* the frog's face when they are sent to their room. Mayer also wrote about an amorous elephant

The beginning illustration in *Frog, Where Are You?* can be the beginning of a valuable composition experience for children. (Written by Mercer Mayer.)

who learns that true love does not run smoothly when a severe case of hiccups ruins a romantic boat ride in *Hiccup!* (N-P). Another of his books, *Ah-Choo!* (N-P), shows the catastrophes a sneeze can cause.

Jan Ormerod's work is distinctive for its clarity, its use of light and shadows, and its portrayal of parental love and shared responsibility. Ormerod created two wordless books, *Sunshine* (N-P) and *Moonlight* (N-P). In *Sunshine*, a small girl helps her sleepy parents get off to a slow and then hectic start in the morning. In *Moonlight*, the same girl creates a boat from a melon rind, toothpicks, and napkins while her father does the dinner dishes. She takes her melon boat to the bathtub and dallies as she gets ready for bed. After her mother brushes her hair, she repeats the ritual for her doll and teddy bear. Dad's bedtime story and goodnight kiss are just the beginning of numerous attempts to get her into bed; she uses one ploy after another to get to stay up later. Dad finally carries her to her bed and promptly falls asleep himself. The girl joins Mom back in the living room where each reads a book until Mom falls asleep. Finally, the parents awaken and carry the by-now-sleeping child back to her own bed.

Brinton Turkle reverses the characters in the story of "Goldilocks and the Three Bears" in *Deep in the Forest* (N-P). In this droll, wordless book, Baby Bear wanders through the forest, finds Goldilocks's home, eats her porridge, rocks in her chair, and bounces on her bed before he falls asleep in it. Of course, Goldilocks and her parents discover him and the damage he has wrought when they return from their

TEACHING IDEA

BIG BOOKS   Big books are oversized editions of children's books. Large-sized print enables a group of children to see the words and to read along with the teacher. Choose a big book, such as *Mrs. Wishy Washy* (Wright Group Story Box), or create one of your own. Bring your students together for story time and show them the big book. Ask them to predict as much of the story as they can from the pictures without relying on the text. Read the story aloud as you follow the words with a pointer. Ask students to join in with you as you read the repetitive refrains, such as "wishy washy, wishy washy." Give students a chance to take turns pointing to the words as others read the story over again. Finally, ask students to identify features of words they recognize, words repeated on a page, and other conventions of print they notice.

One way to encourage children to read along is to have them create their own big books by borrowing from other stories or writing their own.

PROFILE

Jan Ormerod

Jan Ormerod grew up in Australia, lived in England for 7 years, and then returned to Australia. Her daughter, Sophie, was the model for the little girl in *Sunshine* and *Moonlight* (both N-P) and Laura, Sophie's younger sister, was the baby in *Silly Goose* (N-P).

Ormerod's family generates many creative sparks and appears in her books regularly. She explains,

I was trained as a graphic designer and taught art education. My husband, Paul, worked primarily as a college librarian, but he became a children's librarian—just at the right time—when our daughter Sophie was born. When Paul brought children's books home for Sophie, he hooked me too! Sophie was absolutely fascinated by stories that coped with the complexities of her life, and she showed great enjoyment in looking at pictures of other children. Her response motivated me. I became interested in recording stories.[40]

Her first book, *Sunshine*, was published in 1981. Later, she continues,

When Laura was born, Sophie was seven. I was just delighted to see their relationship; they looked so beautiful together I wanted to draw them. *101 Things to Do with a Baby* (N-P) comes directly from our family experience. In one series of pictures, the father is holding the baby and the text doesn't say anything about the older child's jealousy and wish to be held. The expression of great satisfaction on her face and resigned amusement on her father's face when he pays attention to her has to be looked for and interpreted. The joy and the jealousy are all part of life's rich mix.

walk in the forest. When you observe children exploring this book alone, you can detect the instant they recognize it as a reversal of their beloved story.

Pat Hutchins, John Goodall, Paula Winter, and Peter Spier are other masters of the wordless book form. In *Changes, Changes* (N-P), Hutchins creates a world, characters, and a story from a pile of building blocks. The magic of the story has been caught on film (Weston Woods), and children re-create it endlessly in block corners, roller movies, murals, taped retellings with sound effects, and written stories. Books by Spier, Goodall, and Winter are listed

Ormerod watched Laura crawling about the house exploring just the same way the cat did and conceived the idea for *Our Ollie* (N) who sleeps like a cat, yawns like a hippopotamus, sits like a frog, and hugs like a bear. Books in the same series include *Young Joe, Silly Goose,* and *Just Like Me* (all N).

''Sophie often reads to me now,' Ormerod says.

She has picked up the feeling that to communicate with books and about books is a very warm and intense way to share ideas. This starts at the very beginning, in infancy. A book is rarely looked at by a child alone. The parent and the child share the story. Some of the best times I have with my girls come while sharing books. That's the way the books are conceived in my mind—as a joint experience. I have great sympathy for, and I identify with, young parents. I'm talking to them as well as to their children.

In speaking about her books, she explains, ''I'm talking about my own experience as a mother and I'm talking about my own children's experiences—not in a directly biographical way, but certainly all of my information comes from my own private life.'' Further, ''I'm very conscious of doing all of my books on more than one level because I'm aware that I'm talking to very young children, and almost inevitably that young child will be with an adult, and they'll be looking at the book and talking about the book together.''

Jan Ormerod never intentionally starts with a message for her readers; she has to be strongly interested in the ''brain teaser'' matter of the design problems: as she says ''of fitting a large pregnant lady, a baby and a cat into a rectangle, eight by four. I love that part of it.'' She also has to have a good story to work with, ''and I have to be very interested in the drawings—I have to get a lot of delight from doing the drawings. And if those three elements are there, often, a message just sort of sneaks in through the back door.''

To sum up her work, she says, ''I really work as a person who loves to draw, and a person who loves to design—and a person who loves to observe young kids going about their business.'' Ormerod's observations add to the wealth of children's literature.

in the Recommended Reading Section at the end of the chapter.

Emily McCully introduces a large family of mice in *Picnic* (N-P) and continues their adventures in a companion volume, *First Snow* (N-P). In the first story, the youngest mouse and her doll bounce unnoticed off the back of the truck as the family drives through a lush green woodland. The mouse wanders through the wooded area clutching her doll, eating berries, and feeling very lonesome and sad. Meanwhile, the family arrives at the lakeside picnic spot and proceeds to have a good time. When they prepare to eat and finally discover she is

Children can express their own sense of story with wordless books. (From *Picnic* by Emily McCully.)

missing, they retrace their path. The lost little mouse hears the truck coming and runs toward her family for a tearful reunion. Suddenly she discovers that she dropped her beloved doll in the wilderness, and knowing the feeling of being left behind, returns to find her.

Picnic combines many of the elements important in books for young children: it is an engaging story with bright colorful illustrations; it is a wordless book, but it invites language as the child pores over the minute details and subplots; children will want to count the mice children in each scene; and finally, it is a predictable book with a satisfying, happy ending.

The narration that children produce for wordless books can be written on large charts and become their reading instruction material. Moreover, children who watch their own words being put onto paper learn intuitively the relation between print and sound. This means of teaching, called the language experience approach, provides a meaningful founda-

tion for reading, especially when accompanied by a strong reading-aloud program based on good literature. Mary Anne Hall,[41] Sylvia Ashton-Warner,[42] Roger Landrum,[43] and many others have used this approach. The child's own familiar words in turn become the material used for reading instruction. The method assumes that a child will know what he says, will see what he has said when it is written, and will then be able to read his own words with meaning. Literature experiences that are shared and recorded in homemade books or on large charts for reference provide a strong base for beginning reading since the words used are integral to students' listening and speaking vocabularies.

Nonfiction

Nonfiction for young children presents factual information in straightforward, expository prose expanded by clear, realistic illustrations. The books may or may not have a story line. The production of this type of book flourished in the 1980s—perhaps a reflection of the trend of parents' desires to start their children's education very early.

Gail Gibbons produces some of the best informational books for young children. She researches her topics carefully and checks the accuracy of her information with experts. She writes in an intelligible, straightforward style and illustrates with bright, instructive pictures. A favorite with librarians, *Check It Out! The Book About Libraries* (P), describes different kinds of libraries and how to use them. *The Milk Makers* (P) shows different breeds of cows, and describes the anatomical and physiological functions of a cow in the milk-making process. She describes hand milking and milking machines, cooling tanks, milk tank trucks, dairy processing, packaging, and market delivery. (A book that makes the process clear to even younger children is Donald Carrick's book called *Milk* [N-P].) Some of Gibbons's other books include

Department Store, The Post Office Book: Mail and How It Moves, Up Goes the Skyscraper!, and *Flying* (all P).

Byron Barton, another artist who produces outstanding nonfiction for young children, designs strong, bold illustrations etched in black to provide clear visual images. *Airplanes* (N-P) shows jets, seaplanes, crop dusters, helicopters, and cargo and passenger planes. The format is similar in *Boats, Trucks,* and *Trains* (all N-P), all subjects young children like to explore. *Building a House* (N-P) uses bold pictures and a brief text to explain how to build a house from the foundation up. The final scene shows the family moving in to make the house a home—the human dimension and the purpose for all the construction.

The Milk Makers, by Gail Gibbons, combines bold, colorful illustrations with simple, descriptive text in her nonfiction book for young readers.

TEACHING IDEA

STORY SEQUENCE (P-I)   Wordless books can be used to reinforce the concept of story sequence. Buy two paperback copies of the same title and cut the books apart. Mount each page (making sure that you have each front and back) on construction paper and laminate them. Children can then put the story in sequence by arranging the pages in order. Some good books to use include those by Mercer Mayer, Pat Hutchins, Peter Spier, John Goodall, and Paula Winter. Sequencing can also be practiced with Ruth Krauss's *The Backward Day* (P), in which a small child reverses the order of his daily routine. Although this is not a wordless book, children gain the same storytelling experience when they draw individual pictures of each event and then arrange drawings in either the logical order of a normal day, or in the (more fun) mixed-up pattern of the book.

ACTIVITIES: TEACHER TO STUDENT

TAPE-RECORDED STORYTELLING (P-I)   Choose a wordless book and tell its story into a tape recorder. Mercer Mayer's series, which starts with *A Boy, a Dog, and a Frog* (P) is especially fun. After you have made the recording, you can share your story and the book with other children.

DRAMATIZATION (P-I)   Choose parts and dramatize Emily McCully's *Picnic* (N-P) and *First Snow* (N-P). If there are parts where there is no character talking, choose a narrator to tell those parts.

TEACHING IDEA

ENRICHING CONCEPT DEVELOPMENT (N-P)   Children's concept development proceeds from a specific example to wide (and often inaccurate) generalizations. For instance, a child learns the word "Daddy" and may call all men "Daddy" until finer distinctions are made. Well-illustrated informational books can help young children see visible differences and can help them learn to make finer distinctions and more accurate generalizations. Share the following books to enrich children's concepts about their world.

TOOLS: Gibbons, *Tool Book*
Robbins, *Tools*
Rockwell and Rockwell, *The Toolbox*
Turn to the page on hammers in each book. Do they look alike? What can hammers be used for? How do you use them? Compare other tools.

BUILDINGS: Barton, *Building a House*
Gibbons, *Up Goes the Skyscraper!*
Compare the steps in building a house and a skyscraper. How are the procedures the same? What is different?

LIBRARY: Gibbons, *Check It Out!*
Rockwell, *I Like the Library*
What did you learn about libraries? What differs in the books?

BOATS: Barton, *Boats*
Crews, *Harbor*
Gibbons, *Boat Book*
Maestro and Maestro, *Ferryboat*
Rockwell, *Boats*
What kinds of boats do you see? What kinds of work do boats do? What goes on in a harbor?

TOWN AND   Chwast, *Tall City, Wide Country: A Book to Read Forward and*
COUNTRY: *Backward*
Provensen and Provensen, *Town and Country*
Robbins, *City/Country*
How are the city and the country different? What kinds of things happen in the city? in the country?

AIRPLANES: Barton, *Airplanes*
Barton, *Airport*
Crews, *Flying*
Gibbons, *Flying*
Provensen and Provensen, *The Glorious Flight*
What kinds of airplanes do you see? What kinds of work do airplanes do? What kind of trouble did early pilots have?

CARS AND   Barton, *Trucks*
TRUCKS: Cole, *Cars and How They Go*
            Crews, *Truck*
            Rockwell, *Cars*
            Siebert, *Truck Song*

Compare the information in each book. How are cars and trucks alike? What makes
  them different?

Masayuki Yabuuchi creates nature books with realistic paintings that are outstanding for their artistic beauty alone. Crisp, rich illustrations with almost photographic detail make the familiar animals seem nearly real. Yabuuchi invites readers to participate by using a question-and-answer format in *Whose Footprints?* and *Whose Baby?* (both P). The footprints appear on one page with the question but we must turn the page to find the answer. A similar format is used to portray baby animals and their parents. *Animal Mothers* (text by Atsushi Komori) and *Animals Sleeping* (both P) introduce animal behavior by relating it to things children know about themselves. A mother cat carries her kitten in her soft mouth, and a lioness transports her cub in the same gentle manner. Animals asleep and awake, dormant and in action, set the stage for the question-and-answer game in *Animals Sleeping*.

Many informational books are illustrated with photographs that capture reality and provide the visual accuracy necessary for understanding. Joanna Cole's *My Puppy Is Born* (P) is illustrated with excellent photographs by Jerome Wexler. Heiderose Fischer-Nagel's *A Kitten Is Born* (P) and *A Puppy is Born* (P) are also illustrated with excellent color photographs. The portrayal of the birth process is candid in each of these books.

Beginning-to-Read Books

Beginning-to-read books are ones that emerging readers can read on their own; they combine the controlled vocabulary of the basal reader with creative storytelling. We should not overwhelm beginning readers by presenting large vocabularies to them all at once, and so restrictions are set on the words used—but the stories themselves are good stories. Many beginning-to-read books have strong characterization, worthy themes, and tight plots. The sentences are generally simple, without a lot of embedded clauses, and the language is often direct dialogue. The lines are printed so that sentence breaks occur according to natural phrasing, with meaningful chunks of language grouped together. This plus a limited number of different words and interesting stories ensures a happy introduction to reading.

Some early books written with a controlled vocabulary were stilted and bland, but gradually authors mastered the form so that we now have many excellent beginning-to-read books that tell good stories in a natural way.

Else Minarik was one of the first to create good stories within the constraints of a restricted vocabulary. *Little Bear, Father Bear Comes Home, Little Bear's Friend, Little Bear's Visit,* and *A Kiss for Little Bear* (all P) reveal the lovable, childlike nature of Little Bear. In one story, Little Bear wears his new space helmet on an imaginary trip to the moon. When he arrives he finds a house just like his own, a table just like his at home, and a Mother Bear just like his mother. This Mother Bear on the moon invites him for lunch because her own Little Bear has gone to Earth that day. The two continue the fantasy play until Little Bear wants to

PROFILE

Gail Gibbons

Gail Gibbons has opened up an entirely new field of literature for young children. She has made nonfiction accessible to the very youngest child. Gail Gibbons was born in Illinois and graduated from the University of Illinois with a Bachelor of Fine Arts. While she was still in high school, she asked her parents for a typewriter, supposedly to use for homework, but really to type her own stories. She began writing and illustrating at a very early age.

Of her writing, she explains,

When I begin to write a book, I spend a lot of time researching the subject. I go to libraries, talk to many people who know about the subject, and I talk to my editors, too. When I begin to write, I tend to overwrite at first because I have so much information. Then, I spend time rewriting and rewriting the book until it sounds just right. I try to make the text as simple as possible.[44]

When asked about her illustration, she says, "I feel that writing and illustrating a book is like putting a puzzle together: Once the words are there, I begin to make pictures to fit the words." She continues,

My artwork tends to be very colorful. I used to do television graphics for the news and for a children's show called "Take a Giant Step." I still do television graphics and in television the artwork must be very simple and bold and colorful. The image must be read quickly because it will only be seen on television for a short period of time. This style of art has carried over into my book illustration. I feel that when I'm explaining something, it should be easily understood by looking at the pictures.

be reassured that she is really his Mother Bear and that he is in his very own home. Minarik's stories present exciting plots with plenty of action, and develop clear, vivid themes. Maurice Sendak's visual interpretation makes Little Bear even more appealing.

Arnold Lobel made beginning reading more fun when he created Frog and Toad and, in doing so, loosened the restrictions of the beginning-to-read form. His two amphibian friends evoke unrepressed giggles from beginning readers who view Frog and Toad's naiveté

In *Frog and Toad Are Friends,* one of many human embarrassments is portrayed when Toad fears—correctly—that others will laugh at the sight of him in a bathing suit. (From *Frog and Toad Are Friends,* written and illustrated by Arnold Lobel.)

with a feeling of superiority. *Frog and Toad Are Friends* (P), a Caldecott Honor Book, and *Frog and Toad Together* (P), a Newbery Honor Book, are particularly distinguished because these prestigious awards are rarely given to restricted-vocabulary books. Only once before had a beginning-to-read book been so recognized—when Minarik's *Little Bear's Visit* was named a Caldecott Honor Book for Sendak's illustrations. Lobel's *Frog and Toad Are Friends* (P), the first book in the series, shows Toad anxious to get under the water so no one can see him in his bathing suit because he feels so silly. Anyone who feels self-conscious will identify with Toad's feelings. The affectionate teasing between Lobel's all-too-human characters continues in *Days with Frog and Toad, Frog and Toad All Year,* and *Frog and Toad Together* (all P).

Two writers new to the beginning-to-read field are worthy of mention. Jean Van Leeuwen has created two humorous series about pigs: *Tales of Amanda Pig* (P) and *Tales of Oliver Pig* (P). Amanda was the tagalong in the Oliver books, but she asserts her independence as she grows up. In *Tales of Amanda Pig,* she refuses to eat her egg, saying that it stares back at her with "its funny yellow eye." In *More Tales of Amanda Pig* (P), the engaging family celebrates a birthday, entertains guests, and has other good times.

Barbara Porte, who writes in a more serious vein but with subtle humor, has produced a series about a logical and winsome child: *Harry's Dog* (P), *Harry's Visit* (P), and *Harry's Mom* (P). In *Harry's Dog,* Harry tries to conceal a dog from his allergic father. Before long, however, the coughing, sneezing Dad locates the cause of his reaction and orders the dog out of the house. Harry gives numerous reasons that the dog should stay but none are convincing to his red-eyed father. Fortunately, Aunt Rose, who also loves dogs and empathizes with Harry, comes up with a solution to the problem. In *Harry's Mom,* Harry's mother has died and he locates a dictionary definition that tells him he is an orphan. Although his father is alive and well, the dictionary said that an orphan is a child without a father *or* a mother. The touching story shows Harry finding out as much as he can about his mother from his father, grandparents, and aunt. The sensitive theme is not generally treated in beginning-to-read books. Many other beginning-to-read books are listed in the Recommended Reading section at the end of the chapter.

Despite the fact that there are hundreds of beginning-to-read books of literary quality, children should also have access to regular picture books that do not restrict vocabulary, control phrase length, or conform to the other constraints of this form. In order to see if several well-known picture books—that is, with unrestricted vocabularies—differed greatly from the

PROFILE

Donald Crews

Donald Crews is recognized for strong, clean colors and bright, unambiguous shapes in his numerous books for young children. Clear shapes of freight trains, boats, bicycles, and trucks stand out on spacious pages artfully designed. Crews was trained and worked in graphic design before his entry into children's book illustration; his hallmark is strong design and bold typography.

As a youngster, Crews took the train for a visit to his grandmother's farm in Florida every year. He loved the train ride and found the adventure to Florida exciting. It is understandable that he brought vivid images to his rendition of *Freight Train* (P). His talent in graphics plus his use of an airbrush technique give *Freight Train* the feeling of solidity as well as movement and speed.

He is innovative in his approach to illustration. For *Carousel* (P), he prepared three paintings: one of the empty carousel, one of the calliope, and one of the carousel with children. These were prepared as full-color collages. The carousel with children was then photographed and the camera was moved to simulate motion. Pages with onomatopoetic words—such as "boom," "beboom," and "toot"—were also prepared as full-color art and similarly photographed to show movement. As you turn the pages of the book, it appears as if the carousel loaded with children gains speed and actually moves through the spaces.

Crews attended Newark Arts High School and Cooper Union in New York City where he graduated in 1959. From then until his induction into the Army he worked in design. He was assistant art director of *Dance* magazine and on the staff of a small design studio. He served in the Army from 1962 to 1964, spending 18 months in Germany. Toward the end of his service he set himself the project of writing and illustrating a children's book to add to his portfolio. The result was *We Read: A to Z*. When he finally showed it to an editor at Harper & Row, for whom he had been doing book jackets, his career in children's books was launched. *Ten Black Dots* (P), a counting book, came next, then several books for which he did illustrations only, and a decade later, *Freight Train*. He received a Caldecott Honor Book award for *Freight Train* in 1979 and for *Truck* in 1981. Since then he has produced *Parade, Carousel, Harbor, Light, Bicycle Race, School Bus, Flying,* and others.

Donald Crews is married to another talented author-artist, Ann Jonas. They live in Brooklyn, New York, with their daughters, Nina and Amy. They share a studio in their home, do freelance art and designing, and create many wonderful books for children.

beginning-to-read books in the number of different words used, Alden J. Moe[45] analyzed 75 books. Whereas beginning-to-read books use 10 to 250 different words, Moe found only 30 different words in Barbara Emberley's *Drummer Hoff* (N-P), 31 in Pat Hutchins's *Don't Forget the Bacon* (P), 48 in Robert Kraus's *Herman the Helper* (P), and 64 in Martha Alexander's *Blackboard Bear* (P). Moe does not claim that the number of different words is the only factor in readability, but he does show that many standard picture books can be used in beginning reading programs, especially if the teacher initially reads them aloud to the children.

Chapter Books

Chapter books have a continuous story about a central character; the story is divided into self-contained episodes—chapters that can stand alone. Children are proud to be able to read alone, and will soon march into a library and ask for a "real" book—"a book with chapters." Seeing older children reading, they think of thick books as a sign of growing up, and that only "little kids" read beginning-to-read books; they want to demonstrate that they are beyond that stage. We know that, beyond the child's ego satisfaction, there are other benefits to be gained from reading a broader range of materials. The new words and structures encountered in their leisure reading will help children continue to grow in reading ability and experience.

The child making the transition to unlimited reading needs special consideration beyond readability of the material. Books that serve as a transition between picture books and

TEACHING IDEA

USING NEW WORD POWER (P)   Beginning readers are proud of their newly developed skill and take every opportunity to flaunt it. They are enthusiastic about activities that give them a chance to use their new word power and, at the same time, confirm their grasp of what they know. Word games, matching games, parallel stories, and crossword puzzles are enjoyable ways for them to show their word mastery. Harper & Row, Publishers, have several packets of crossword puzzles for primary grade children with word clues based on their series of I Can Read books.

ACTIVITY: TEACHER TO STUDENT

WORD PUZZLES (P)   Do some crossword puzzles and then see if you can make up your own. Use titles and characters from your favorite books. You can also devise matching games with book titles and characters, or 20-question-type guessing games in which you give clues from books:

1. Little Bear   a. Fixed lunch for an earthling.
2. Mother Bear   b. Was shy in a bathing suit.
3. Frog   c. Wrote a letter to his friend.
4. Toad   d. Made birthday soup.

PROFILE

Arnold Lobel

Frog took the box outside. He shouted in a loud voice, "HEY BIRDS, HERE ARE COOKIES!"

Birds came from everywhere. They picked up all the cookies in their beaks and flew away.

"Now we have no more cookies to eat," said Toad sadly. "Not even one."

"Yes," said Frog, "but we have lots and lots of will power."

"You may keep it all, Frog," said Toad. "I am going home now to bake a cake."[46]

Frog and Toad, Arnold Lobel's famous friends, reveal human frailties familiar to us all. Organized list makers, compulsive gardeners, voracious cookie eaters, and brave foes of dragons and monsters, Frog and Toad and Lobel become lasting friends of children the very first time they meet.

Frog and Toad's idiosyncrasies thrive in their comfortable relationship. Even when Toad, who would rather have cookies than willpower, goes home to bake his cake, you know that he will return to share it with friend Frog. Lobel shares his whimsies in the last of the series, *Days With Frog and Toad*. Arnold Lobel describes his discovery of Frog and Toad:

> I remember sitting on the front porch rooting around in my paper bag of life experiences until I hit upon frogs and toads. They look a good deal alike but are still very different. A frog seems to smile, while a toad is clearly a more introverted, slow-moving, worrisome creature.[47]

A beginning-to-read book is not easy to write. "Writing," Lobel said, "is very painful for me." He continued:

> It is very hard for me to sit in a chair and do nothing until I have something to write down. I have to force myself not to think in visual terms, because I know if I start to think of pictures, I'll cop out on the text. When I think the text is perfect, I take a look at it as the illustrator, and sometimes the illustrator asks for a rewrite. With *Grasshopper on the Road* the illustrator/me got the writer/me to rewrite the whole thing, and then the illustrator had to do a whole new series of drawings.[48]

Yet he found that sticking to a beginning-to-read vocabulary was no problem at all, since most of us, he said, including himself, have easy-to-read minds.

Lobel illustrated Jack Prelutsky's *The Random House Book of Poetry* (P-I-A) and *The Random House Book of Mother Goose*, both distinguished collections made memorable by his artistic interpretation. He received the Caldecott Award in 1981 for *Fables*. The recipient of numerous other awards, Lobel was born in Los Angeles and raised by his grandparents in Schenectady, New York. He was a lonely and rather unhappy child, but he became one of the most outstanding and best-loved illustrators of the 1980s. He died on December 7, 1987.

novels are close in appearance to that of the textbooks the child is reading: print is large and well-spaced, and there are some illustrations, though not on every page.

Characters and events link the episodes, so that children who are beginning to retain the continuity of a story over a period of several days obtain experience in remembering and building onto story lines. The stories develop one or more characters engaged in a number of interesting episodes and are often laced with humor.

Studies of reading preference consistently show that humor is a quality that appeals to children of all ages.[49] The type of humor that children respond to changes as they mature, but humor per se remains a constant in their book choices. The International Reading Association and the Children's Book Council co-sponsor a project in which children across the nation evaluate newly published books annually.[50] The resulting lists show that humorous books are among the favorites each year.

Many children have an insatiable appetite for reading. Unfortunately, the supply of quality transitional books, including humorous books, is small, and librarians often struggle to find enough books for them.

Some authors who meet the needs of children who are developing independence in reading are Beverly Cleary, Eleanor Clymer, Matt Christopher, Scott Corbett, Natalie Savage Carlson, Rebecca Caudill, Molly Cone, and Elizabeth Coatsworth—all of whose names, curiously, begin with *C*, a possibly mnemonic fact discovered by my daughter Janie, who spent many happy hours at the public library's *C* shelf.

Beverly Cleary's work has wide appeal and lasting value. *Henry Huggins* (P-I), the first in a series, introduces the ingenious Henry, who carries his dog home in a box on the bus. The dog is enough of a personality to be featured in a book of his own, *Ribsy* (P-I), in which he continues to lead the way into trouble and fun. We also meet Beezus, Henry's friend, in the

Beverly Cleary's series of Ramona stories has proven to be immensely popular with children who are graduating to chapter books. (From Cleary's *Ramona and Her Father,* illustrated by Alan Tiegreen.)

earlier books and later follow her and her sister's exploits in *Beezus and Ramona* (P-I). Ramona, another star character, emerges here and merits having several more books with her as the focus (all P-I): *Ramona the Pest; Ramona the Brave; Ramona and Her Father; Ramona and Her Mother; Ramona Quimby, Age 8;* and *Ramona Forever.*

Ramona and Her Father (P-I) is a Newbery Honor book, a notable fact in that this award is rarely given to books that appeal to the transitional reader. In this story, Ramona, now an impish second grade student, approaches her world with an enthusiasm and naiveté that endears her to the readers, who laugh at her gullibility, having themselves passed that stage so very recently. She assumes much more responsibility for her unemployed father, family finances, and her father's smoking than she can possibly handle, but her undaunted spirit makes the reader cheer her on. Cleary's characters mirror children who live down the street in many neighborhoods across America; therein lies part of the secret of their universal appeal.

Scott Corbett writes about a boy named Kirby in one of the many Corbett series. In this group of books, it is not so much character development (as in Beverly Cleary's books) as plot that works repeatedly. An eccentric old woman gives Kirby an amazing chemistry set that works wonders in *The Lemonade Trick* (I), *The Disappearing Dog Trick* (I), *The Hairy Horror Trick* (I), and many other books in the series. Readers striking out for independence find the exaggerated humor and ridiculous situations leading to a variety of disasters hilarious and engaging.

Third and fourth grade students with an over-riding enthusiasm for sports devour the books of Matt Christopher, the prolific author of over 60 books, each with a central character struggling and training hard to become a good athlete. Christopher inevitably involves his character in a highly tense game that often involves sportsmanship and concludes with a hard-won victory. *Ice Magic* (P-I), *Soccer Halfback* (P-I), and *Football Fugitive* (P-I) are favorites.

Mysteries are also a favorite part of the reading fare for children who are gaining some measure of independence in reading. In *Encyclopedia Brown, Boy Detective* (P-I), Donald Sobol has created a character who logically and methodically tracks down clues to solve mysterious events. Sobol's books are especially enjoyable because the reader is invited—since all the facts are given in the text—to participate in solving the cases along with the hero. For those readers who want to check their answers with the young detective's, the solutions are given at the end of the stories. Favorites in this series include *Encyclopedia Brown Takes the Case* (P-I) and *Encyclopedia Brown Tracks Them Down* (P-I).

Two series of mystery stories that need no introduction to children are the Nancy Drew and Hardy Boys stories. Harriet Stratemeyer Adams, using the pseudonym Carolyn Keene, wrote all but the first 3 of the over 80 Nancy Drew mysteries. These widely read books have been translated into a number of languages, reprinted, mass marketed, sold through book clubs, and adapted into a television series. They, like so many of the series books, have little by way of literary quality, but they do appeal to children. Since these books have simple, predictable plots, children can read through them rapidly, and often go through a collecting phase with the books as they do with baseball cards, pennants, and other memorabilia. The collecting and series-reading stage is a normal developmental phase that children should be allowed to pursue. Most teachers will use any type of book to get children into reading, but do try to lead them gradually toward books of more lasting value. This is a process that is achieved gradually, as children learn to trust the teacher's judgment; this, in turn, comes from finding that books recommended are truly interesting and exciting. Thus, as long as series books are only a part of a child's total reading, they can be considered a stepping stone to books of higher literary quality.

Children who have passed through the transitional phase often can recognize for themselves what it is that makes the Nancy Drew and Hardy Boys books so appealing. The books are exciting, full of danger and intrigue, and the hero or heroine comes out the victor. Mature readers can see that therein lies the lack of distinction: as one sixth grade girl put it, "Nancy Drew always wins." There is a sameness, and eventually a boredom, because the reader knows that these books do not reflect the real world, but do provide escape reading, much as gothic romances do for adults.

In dealing with such popular books of limited literary quality, librarians struggle to decide whether to make them available in schools. As with most things in life, there is no single right answer. If the books serve to get nonreaders into the reading habit and show them the enjoyment of reading, then of course they should be used. If, however, children have access to these books outside of school, they should be given heartier fare in school.

Children learning to read are engaged in an exhilarating experience; it is an adventure that never ends, for we continue to learn to read throughout life. Mark Twain's *Huckleberry Finn*, read when one is an adult, carries a very different meaning from when we read it at 12. One reason for this is that we use our experience to create meaning from the printed page, and so read differently as we gain more experiences on which to draw. Learning to read is not something that happens once; it is a lifetime skill.

For children learning to read, books contain intangible assets, the greatest of which is the joy the book brings to the reader. When interesting books are provided, children struggling to learn to read find out that reading is worth the effort. In *The Uses of Enchantment*, Bruno Bettleheim, speaking of fairy tales, but in a comment applicable to other types of literature as well, says

> The acquisition of skills, including the ability to read, becomes devalued when what one has learned to read adds nothing of importance to one's life. . . . The idea that learning to read may enable one later to enrich one's life is experienced as an empty promise when the stories the child listens to, or is reading at the moment, are vacuous.[51]

The wealth of fine books that exists ensures that children can be surprised by joy at every stage in the process of learning to read. Learning to read with good literature translates to a promise fulfilled.

RECOMMENDED READING

Baby Books

Burningham, John. *The Blanket.* New York: Crowell, 1976.

———. *The Dog.* New York: Crowell, 1976.

———. *Jangle Twang. Skip Trip. Slam Bang. Sniff Shout. Wobble Pop* (set). New York: Viking, 1984.

Isadora, Rachael. *I Hear. I See. I Touch* (set). New York: Greenwillow, 1985.

Oxenbury, Helen. *The Car Trip.* New York: Dial, 1983.

———. *The Check Up.* New York: Dial, 1983.

———. *Family. Friends. Playing. Working* (set). New York: Simon & Schuster, 1981.

Participation Books

Ahlberg, Janet, and Allan Ahlberg. *Peek-a-Boo!* New York: Viking, 1981.

Campbell, Rod. *Dear Zoo.* New York: Four Winds, 1983.

Hill, Eric. *Spot's Birthday Party.* New York: Putnam's, 1982.

———. *Spot's First Christmas.* New York: Putnam's, 1983.

———. *Spot's First Walk.* New York: Putnam's, 1981.

———. *Spot Goes to the Beach.* New York: Putnam's, 1985.

Pienkowski, Jan. *Haunted House.* New York: Dutton, 1979.

Beginning Stories

Chorao, Kay, comp. *The Baby's Story Book.* New York: Dutton, 1985.

Ginsburg, Mirra. *Across the Stream.* Illustrated by Nancy Tafuri. New York: Greenwillow, 1982.

Kellogg, Steven. *Chicken Little.* New York: Morrow, 1985.

Ormerod, Jan. *The Story of Chicken Little.* New York: Lothrop, Lee & Shepard, 1986.

Oxenbury, Helen. *Our Dog.* New York: Dial, 1984.

———. *Shopping Trip. Good Night, Good Morning. Beach Day. Monkey See, Monkey Do* (set). New York: Dial, 1982.

———. *Eating Out. The Birthday Party. The Dancing Class* (set). New York: Dial, 1983.

Wells, Rosemary. *Max's First Word. Max's Toys. Max's Ride. Max's New Suit* (set). New York: Dial, 1979.

———. *Max's Bath. Max's Bedtime. Max's Birthday. Max's Breakfast* (set). New York: Dial, 1985.

Wolde, Gunilla. *Betsy's Baby Brother*. New York: Random House, 1975.
————. *This Is Betsy*. New York: Random House, 1975.

ABC Books

Azarian, Mary. *A Farmer's Alphabet*. Boston: Godine, 1981.

Baskin, Hosea et al. *Hosie's Alphabet*. Illustrated by Leonard Baskin. New York: Viking, 1972.

Bayer, Jane. *A My Name Is Alice*. Illustrated by Steven Kellogg. New York: Dial, 1984.

Brown, Marcia. *All Butterflies*. New York: Scribner's, 1974.

Cleaver, Elizabeth. *ABC*. New York: Atheneum, 1985.

Crowther, Robert. *The Most Amazing Hide and Seek Alphabet Book*. New York: Viking, 1978.

Duke, Kate. *The Guinea Pig ABC*. New York: Dutton, 1983.

Gundersheimer, Karen, *ABC Say with Me*. New York: Harper & Row, 1984.

Hague, Kathleen. *Alphabears*. Illustrated by Michael Hague. New York: Holt, 1984.

Hoban, Tana. *A, B, See!* New York: Greenwillow, 1982.

Hoguet, Susan Ramsay. *I Unpacked My Grandmother's Trunk*. New York: Dutton, 1983.

Isadora, Rachel. *City Seen from A to Z*. New York: Greenwillow, 1983.

Kitamura, Satoshi. *What's Inside: The Alphabet Book*. New York: Farrar, Straus & Giroux, 1985.

Matthiesen, Thomas. *ABC, an Alphabet Book*. New York: Putnam's, 1981.

Neumeier, Marty and Byron Glaser. *Action Alphabet*. New York: Greenwillow, 1985.

Provensen, Alice, and Martin Provensen. *A Peaceable Kingdom: The Shaker Abecedarius*. New York: Viking, 1978.

Stevenson, James. *Grandpa's Great City Tour: An Alphabet Book*. New York: Greenwillow, 1983.

Wildsmith, Brian. *Brian Wildsmith's ABC*. New York: Watts, 1963.

Counting Books

Anno, Mitsumasa, *Anno's Counting Book*. New York: Crowell, 1977.

Ernst, Lisa Campbell. *Up to Ten and Down Again*. New York: Lothrop, Lee & Shepard, 1986.

Gundersheimer, Karen. *1, 2, 3, Play with Me*. New York: Harper & Row, 1984.

Hague, Kathleen. *Numbears: A Counting Book*. Illustrated by Michael Hague. New York: Holt, 1986.

Hoban, Tana. *1, 2, 3*. New York: Greenwillow, 1985.

————. *Count and See*. New York: Macmillan, 1972.

————. *More Than One*. New York: Greenwillow, 1981.

McMillan, Bruce. *Counting Wildflowers*. New York: Lothrop, Lee & Shepard, 1986.

Wadsworth, Olive A. *Over in the Meadow: A Counting-Out Rhyme*. Illustrated by Mary Maki Rae. New York: Viking, 1985.

Concept Books

Burningham, John. *John Burningham's Colors*. New York: Crown, 1986.

Clifton, Lucille. *Everett Anderson's Year*. Illustrated by Ann Grifalconi. New York: Holt, Rinehart & Winston, 1974.

Hoban, Tana. *Circles, Triangles and Squares*. New York: Macmillan, 1974.

————. *I Read Signs*. New York: Greenwillow, 1983.

————. *Is It Rough? Is It Smooth? Is It Shiny?* New York: Greenwillow, 1984.

————. *Over, Under and Through and Other Spatial Concepts*. New York: Macmillan, 1973.

————. *Push, Pull, Empty, Full: A Book of Opposites*. New York: Macmillan, 1972.

————. *Round & Round & Round*. New York: Greenwillow, 1983.

————. *What Is it?* New York: Greenwillow, 1985.

Jonas, Ann. *Round Trip*. New York: Greenwillow, 1983.

Oxenbury, Helen. *I Hear. I See. I Touch* (set). New York: Random House, 1986.

Rockwell, Anne, and Harlow Rockwell. *The Supermarket*. New York: Macmillan, 1979.

Rockwell, Harlow. *My Doctor*. New York: Macmillan, 1973.

————. *My Dentist*. New York: Macmillan, 1975.

Predictable Books

Kalan, Robert. *Blue Sea*. Illustrated by Donald Crews. New York: Greenwillow, 1979.

————. *Rain*. Illustrated by Donald Crews. New York: Greenwillow, 1978.

Keyworth, C. L. *New Day*. Illustrated by Carolyn Bracken. New York: Morrow, 1986.

Lester, Alison. *Clive Eats Alligators*. Boston: Houghton Mifflin, 1986.

Maestro, Betsy, and Guilio Maestro. *The Key to the Kingdom*. San Diego: Harcourt Brace Jovanovich, 1982.

Mother Goose. *The House That Jack Built*. Illustrated by Janet Stevens. New York: Holiday House, 1985.

Pearson, Tracey Campbell. *Sing a Song of Sixpence*. New York: Dial, 1985.

————. *Old MacDonald Had a Farm*. New York: Dial, 1984.

Sendak, Maurice. *Chicken Soup with Rice*. New York: Harper & Row, 1962.

West, Colin. *"Pardon," Said the Giraffe*. New York: Harper & Row, 1986.

Wordless Books

Briggs, Raymond. *The Snowman.* Boston: Little, Brown, 1985.

Goodall, John S. *An Edwardian Summer.* New York: Atheneum, 1976.

———. *Naughty Nancy.* New York: Atheneum. 1975.

———. *The Story of an English Village.* New York: Atheneum, 1979.

———. *The Surprise Picnic.* New York: Atheneum, 1977.

Hutchins, Pat. *Changes, Changes.* New York: Macmillan, 1971.

Krahn, Fernando. *Sebastian and the Mushroom.* New York: Delacorte, 1976.

———. *Who's Seen the Scissors?* New York: Dutton, 1975.

MacGregor, Marilyn. *Baby Takes a Trip.* New York: Four Winds, 1985.

Mayer, Mercer. *Oops!* New York: Dial, 1977.

———, and Marianna Mayer. *One Frog Too Many.* New York: Dial, 1975.

Prater, John. *The Gift.* New York: Viking, 1986.

Vincent, Gabrielle, *Ernest and Celestine's Patchwork Quilt.* New York: Greenwillow, 1985.

Winter, Paula. *The Bear and the Fly.* New York: Crown, 1976.

———. *Sir Andrew.* New York: Crown, 1980.

Young, Ed. *The Other Bone.* New York: Harper & Row, 1984.

———. *Up a Tree.* New York: Harper & Row, 1983.

Informational Books

Gibbons, Gail. *Fill It Up! All about Service Stations.* New York: Crowell, 1985.

———. *New Road!* New York: Crowell, 1983.

Lilly, Kenneth. *Animals in the Country.* New York: Simon & Schuster, 1982.

McMillan, Bruce. *Here a Chick, There a Chick.* New York: Lothrop, Lee & Shepard, 1983.

Patent, Dorothy Hinshaw. *Baby Horses.* Photographs by William Munoz. New York: Dodd, 1985.

Schwartz, David M. *How Much Is a Million?* Illustrated by Steven Kellogg. New York: Lothrop, Lee & Shepard, 1985.

Beginning to Read Books

Bonsall, Crosby. *And I Mean It, Stanley.* New York: Harper & Row, 1974.

Gackenbach, Dick. *Hattie Rabbit.* New York: Harper & Row, 1976.

Gage, Wilson, *Down in the Boondocks.* New York: Greenwillow, 1977.

———. *Squash Pie.* New York: Greenwillow, 1976.

Hoban, Lillian. *Arthur's Pen Pal.* New York: Harper & Row, 1976.

———. *Arthur's Prize Reader.* New York: Harper & Row, 1978.

Hopkins, Lee Bennett. *Surprises.* Illustrated by Megan Lloyd. New York: Harper & Row, 1984.

Lobel, Arnold. *Grasshopper on the Road.* New York: Harper Junior Books, 1986.

———. *Mouse Soup.* New York: Harper & Row, 1977.

———. *Mouse Tales.* New York: Harper & Row, 1972.

———. *Owl at Home.* New York: Harper & Row, 1975.

———. *Uncle Elephant.* New York: Harper & Row, 1981.

Sendak, Maurice. *Pierre.* New York: Harper & Row, 1962.

Sharmat, Marjorie Weinman. *Mooch the Messy.* Illustrated by Ben Schecter. New York: Harper & Row, 1976.

———. *Sophie and Gussie.* Illustrated by Lillian Hoban. New York: Macmillan, 1973.

Chapter Books

Adler, David. *The Fourth Floor Twins and the Skyscraper Parade.*
Illustrated by Irene Trivas. New York: Viking, 1986.

———. *Cam Jansen and the Mystery of the Dinosaur Bones.* Illustrated by Susanna Natti, New York: Viking, 1981.

———. *Cam Jansen and the Mystery of the Stolen Corn Popper.* Illustrated by Susanna Natti. New York: Viking, 1986.

Corbett, Scott. *The Foolish Dinosaur Fiasco.* Illustrated by Jon McIntosh. Boston: Little, Brown, 1978.

Hurwitz, Johanna. *Busybody Nora.* Illustrated by Susan Jeschke. New York: Morrow, 1976.

———. *New Neighbors for Nora.* Illustrated by Susan Jeschke. New York: Morrow, 1979.

———. *Nora and Mrs. Mind-Your-Own-Business.* Illustrated by Susan Jeschke. New York: Morrow, 1982.

Hutchins, Pat. *Follow That Bus!* Illustrated by Laurence Hutchins. New York: Greenwillow, 1977.

Rockwell, Thomas. *How to Eat Fried Worms.* Illustrated by Emily McCully. New York: Watts, 1973.

Simon, Seymour. *Einstein Anderson: Science Sleuth.* New York: Viking, 1980.

———. *Einstein Anderson Sees Through the Invisible Man.* Illustrated by Fred Winkowski. New York: Viking, 1983.

Poetry

Aldis, Dorothy. *All Together.* New York: Putnam's, 1952.

Brewton, John E., and Lorraine A. Brewton. *They've Discovered a Head in the Box for the Bread.* Illustrated by Fernando Krahn. New York: Crowell, 1978.

Cole, William. *An Arkful of Animals.* Illustrated by Lynn Munsinger. Boston: Houghton Mifflin, 1978.

———. *Oh, How Silly!* Illustrated

by Tomi Ungerer. New York: Viking, 1970.

Fowke, Edith, ed. *Sally Go Round the Sun; 300 Children's Songs, Rhymes, and Games.* Illustrated by Judith Gwyn Brown. Englewood Cliffs, N.J.: Prentice-Hall, 1977.

Livingston, Myra Cohn. *Listen, Children, Listen.* San Diego: Harcourt Brace Jovanovich, 1974.

———. *Speak Roughly to Your Little Boy.* Illustrated by Joseph Low. San Diego: Harcourt Brace Jovanovich, 1971.

———. *What a Wonderful Bird the Frog Are.* San Diego: Harcourt Brace Jovanovich, 1973.

Lobel, Arnold. *Whiskers & Rhymes.*

Greenwillow, 1985.

McCord, David. *One at a Time.* Illustrated by Henry B. Kane. Boston: Little, Brown, 1986.

Nash, Ogden. *Custard the Dragon.* Illustrated by Linell Nash. Boston: Little, Brown, 1961.

O'Neill, Mary. *Hailstones and Halibut Bones.* Illustrated by John Wallner. New York: Doubleday, 1989.

Prelutsky, Jack. *Nightmares: Poems to Trouble Your Sleep.* Illustrated by Arnold Lobel. Greenwillow, 1976.

Sutherland, Zena, ed. *Arbuthnot Anthology of Children's Literature,* 4th ed. Glenview, Ill.: Scott, Foresman, 1976.

Tashjian, Virginia. *Juba This and Juba That.* Illustrated by Victoria De Larrea. Boston: Little, Brown, 1969.

———. *With a Deep Sea Smile: Story Hour Stretchers for Large or Small Groups.* Illustrated by Rosemary Wells. Boston: Little, Brown, 1974.

Wallace, Daisy. *Monster Poems.* Illustrated by Kay Charao. New York: Holiday House, 1976.

———. *Ghost Poems.* Illustrated by Tomie de Paola. New York: Holiday House, 1979.

Zemach, Margot. *Hush Little Baby.* New York: Dutton, 1976.

PROFESSIONAL REFERENCES

Anderson, Richard, et al. *Becoming a Nation of Readers: The Report of the Commission on Reading.* Washington, D.C.: The National Institute of Education, U.S. Department of Education, 1985.

Ashton-Warner, Sylvia. *Teacher.* New York: Simon & Schuster, 1966.

Bellugi, Ursula. "Learning the Language." *Psychology Today* 4 (1970): 32–35, 66.

Bettelheim, Bruno. *The Uses of Enchantment: The Meaning and Importance of Fairy Tales.* New York: Knopf, 1976.

Butler, Dorothy. *Cushla and Her Books.* New York: Horn Book, 1980.

———, and Marie Clay. *Reading Begins at Home: Preparing Children for Reading Before They Go to School.* Portsmouth, N.H.: Heinemann, 1979.

Cambourne, Brian. "Language, Learning & Literacy." In *Towards a Reading-Writing Classroom.* Edited by Andrea Butler and Jan Turbill. Portsmouth, N.H.: Hei-

nemann, 1984.

Chomsky, Carol. "Write First, Read Later." *Childhood Education* 46, no. 6 (March 1971): 296–99.

Chomsky, Noam. *Aspects of a Theory of Syntax.* Cambridge: M.I.T. Press, 1965.

Clark, Margaret M. "Language and Reading: Research Trends." In *Problems of Language and Learning.* Edited by Alan Davies. Portsmouth, N.H.: Heinemann, 1975.

Clay, Marie M. *Reading: The Patterning of Complex Behavior.* Portsmouth, N.H.: Heinemann, 1972.

———. *What Did I Write?* Portsmouth, N.H.: Heinemann, 1975.

Clark, Margaret M. *Young Fluent Readers.* Portsmouth, N.H.: Heinemann, 1976.

Cochran-Smith, Marilyn. *The Making of a Reader.* Norwood, N.J.: Ablex, 1984.

Doake, David. "Reading-Like Behavior: Its Role in Learning to Read." In *Observing the Language Learner.* Edited by Angela M. Jaggar and M. Trika Smith-Burke. Newark, Del.: Interna-

tional Reading Association; and Urbana, Ill.: National Council of Teachers of English, 1985.

Durkin, Dolores. *Children Who Read Early: Two Longitudinal Studies.* New York: Teachers College Press, 1966.

Fogelman, Phyllis J. "Baby Books." Lecture presented at the New York Public Library Early Childhood Course. New York, May 9, 1987.

Foreman-Peck, Lorraine, "Evaluating Children's Talk About Literature: A Theoretical Perspective." *Children's Literature in Education* 16, no. 4 (Winter 1985): 203–18.

Goodman, Kenneth S. "Reading: A Psycholinguistic Guessing Game." In *Theoretical Models and Processes of Reading.* Edited by Harry Singer & Robert Ruddell. Newark, Del.: International Reading Association, 1976.

Hall, Mary Anne. *Teaching Reading as a Language Experience.* Westerville, Ohio: Merrill, 1970.

Halliday, M. A. K. *Learning How to*

Mean. New York: Elsevier, North-Holland, 1977.

————. "Three Aspects of Children's Language Development: Learning Language, Learning Through Language, Learning About Language." In *Oral and Written Language Development Research: Impact on the Schools.* Edited by Yetta Goodman, Myna Haussler, and Dorothy Strickland. Urbana, Ill.: National Council of Teachers of English, 1982.

Henderson, Edmund. "The Role of Skills in Teaching Reading." *Theory into Practice* 17, no. 5 (Dec. 1977): 348–56.

Jaggar, Angela M., and M. Trika Smith-Burke, eds. *Observing the Language Learner.* Newark, Del.: International Reading Association and Urbana, Ill.: National Council of Teachers of English, 1985.

Landrum, Roger, et al. *A Day Dream I Had at Night and Other Stories: Teaching Children How to Make Their Own Readers.* New York: Teachers and Writers Collaborative, 1971.

Larrick, Nancy. *A Parent's Guide to Children's Reading.* New York: Bantam, 1982.

McCullough, David W. "Arnold Lobel and Friends: An Interview." *New York Times Book Review,* 11 (Nov. 1979): 54.

McKenzie, Moira. *Journeys into Literacy.* Huddersfield, Engl.: Schofield & Sims, 1986.

————. "The Beginnings of Literacy." in *Theory into Practice* 17, no. 5, (Dec. 1977): 315–24.

Moe, Alden J. "Using Picture Books For Reading Vocabulary Development." In *Using Literature in the Classroom.* Edited by John Warren Stewig and Sam L.

Sebesta. Urbana, Ill.: National Council of Teachers of English, 1978.

Read, Charles. "Preschool Children's Knowledge of English Phonology." *Harvard Educational Review* 41 (February 1971): 1–34.

Sherry, Roger. "A Holistic View of Language." *Research in the Teaching of English* 15 (May 1981): 101–11.

Smith, Frank. *Understanding Reading,* 2nd ed. New York: Holt, Rinehart & Winston, 1978.

Sulzby, Elizabeth. "Children's Emergent Reading of Favorite Storybooks: A Developmental Study." In *Reading Research Quarterly* 20, no. 4 (1985): 458–81.

Trelease, Jim. *The Read-Aloud Handbook,* rev. ed. New York: Viking-Penguin, 1985.

NOTES

1. David McCord, "Books," *One at a Time,* illus. Henry B. Kane (Boston: Little, Brown, 1986), 199–201.
2. A. A. Milne, "The King's Breakfast," *When We Were Very Young,* illus. Ernest H. Shepard (New York: Dutton, 1924), 64–69.
3. Richard Anderson et al., *Becoming a Nation of Readers; The Report on the Commission of Reading* (Washington D.C.: National Institute of Education, 1985), 77–78. For a summary of research about literacy and learning, see *What Works* (Washington, D.C.: U.S. Department of Education, 1986), 9–11.
4. Bernice E. Cullinan and Carolyn W. Carmichael, eds., *Literature and Young Children* (Urbana, Ill.: National Council of Teachers of English, 1977), 1.
5. Noam Chomsky, *Aspects of a Theory of Syntax* (Cambridge: M.I.T. Press, 1965).
6. Ursula Bellugi, "Learning the Language," *Psychology Today* 4 (1970): 32–35, 66.
7. M. A. K. Halliday, *Learning How to Mean* (New York: Elsevier North-Holland, 1977).
8. M. A. K. Halliday, "Three Aspects of Children's Language Development: Learning Language, Learning Through Language, Learning About Language," in *Oral and Written Language Development Research: Impact on the Schools,* ed. Yetta Goodman, Myna Haussler, and Dorothy Strickland (Urbana, Ill.: National Council of Teachers of English, 1982), 7–19.
9. Beverly Cleary, *Ramona the Pest,* illus. Louis Darling (New York: Morrow, 1968), 17.
10. Ibid., 27.
11. Roger Shuy, "A Holistic View of Language," *Research in the Teaching of English* 15 (May 1981): 107.
12. Marie M. Clay, *Reading: The Patterning of Complex Behavior* (Portsmouth, N.H.: Heinemann, 1972), 66–76. See also Don Holdaway, *The Foundations of Literacy* (Sydney: Ashton Scholastic, 1979).
13. Ann Valentino, teacher, Children's Energy Center, New York City, personal report, 1987.
14. Leonore Canepa, student project, New York University, 1986.
15. Ludwig Bemelmans, *Madeline* (New York: Viking, 1939), n.p.
16. Elizabeth Sulzby, "Children's

Emergent Reading of Favorite Storybooks: A Developmental Study," *Reading Research Quarterly* 20, no. 4 (Summer 1985): 458–81.

17. Margaret M. Clark, *Young Fluent Readers* (Portsmouth, N.H.: Heinemann, 1976), Clay, *Reading: The Patterning of Complex Behavior*; Dolores Durkin, *Children Who Read Early: Two Longitudinal Studies* (New York: Teachers College Press, 1966).

18. Carol Chomsky, "Write First, Read Later," *Childhood Education* 47, no. 6 (March 1971): 296–99.

19. Marie M. Clay, *What Did I Write?* (Portsmouth, N.H.: Heinemann, 1975); Edmund Henderson, "The Role of Skills in Teaching Reading," *Theory into Practice*, 17, no. 5 (December 1977): 348–56; and Charles Read, "Preschool Children's Knowledge of English Phonology," *Harvard Education Review*, 41 (February 1971): 1–34. These are the original studies. Their conclusions have been reaffirmed by more recent research, such as Bernice E. Cullinan and Dorothy S. Strickland, "The Early Years: Language, Literature, and Literacy in Classroom Research," *The Reading Teacher* 39, no. 8 (April 1986): 798–806; John T. Guthrie, "Preschool Literacy Learning," *The Reading Teacher* 37, no. 3 (December 1983): 318–20; Martha L. King and Victor M. Rentel, "A Longitudinal Study of Coherence in Children's Written Narratives," Final report, NIE-G-8-0063, Research Foundation, Ohio State University, 1983; Martha L. King and Victor M. Rentel, "Transition to Writing," Final report, NIE-G-79-0039, Research Foundation, Ohio State University, 1982; Martha L. King et al., "How Children Learn to

Write: A Longitudinal Study," Final report, NIE-G-79-0137, Research Foundation, Ohio State University, 1981; Linda Leonard Lamme, *Growing Up Writing* (Washington, D.C.: Acropolis Books, 1984); Judith A. Schickedanz, *More Than the ABCs: The Early Stages of Reading and Writing* (Washington, D.C.: National Association for the Education of Young Children, 1986); Judith A. Schickedanz and Maureen Sullivan, "Mom, What Does U-F-F Spell?" *Language Arts* 61, no. 1 (January 1984): 7–17; Charles A. Temple, Ruth G. Nathan, and Nancy A. Burris, *The Beginnings of Writing* (Boston: Allyn & Bacon, 1982).

20. Henderson, "The Role of Skills in Teaching Reading," *Theory into Practice* 17, no. 5 (Dec. 1977): 348–56.

21. Jeanne McPadden, kindergarten teacher, P.S. 321, Brooklyn, New York 1985–86.

22. Michael and Lauren were kindergarten students at P.S. 321, Brooklyn, New York, 1985–86.

23. Brian Cambourne, "Language, Learning and Literacy," in *Toward a Reading-Writing Classroom*, ed. Andrea Butler and Jan Turbill, (Portsmouth, N.H.: Heinemann, 1984), 5–9.

24. David Doake, "Reading-Like Behavior: Its Role in Learning to Read," in *Observing the Language Learner*, ed. Angela Jaggar and M. Trika Smith-Burke (Newark, Del.: International Reading Association; and Urbana, Ill.: National Council of Teachers of English, 1985), 82–98. Doake talks about Raja in his "Learning to Read: It Starts in the Home," in *Roles in Literacy Learning.: A New Perspective*, ed. Duane R. Tovey and James E. Kerber (Newark, Del.: International Reading Association, 1986), 2–9.

25. Anderson, *Becoming a Nation of Readers*, 23–24.

26. Jim Trelease, *The Read-Aloud Handbook*, rev. ed. (New York: Viking, 1985), 7.

27. Laura Jones, "Children's Choices: Is Reading Aloud or Promoting Individualized Reading the Most Effective Approach?" *Louisiana Library Bulletin* 49, no. 2 (Fall 1986): 83–84.

28. Dorothy Butler, *Cushla and Her Books* (Boston: Horn Book, 1980).

29. Gordon Wells, *The Meaning Makers: Children Learning Language and Using Language to Learn* (Portsmouth, N.H.: Heinemann, 1986), 157.

30. Moira McKenzie, "The Beginnings of Literacy," *Theory into Practice* 17, no. 5 (December 1977): 315–24.

31. Denny Taylor, *Family Literacy: Young Children Learning to Read and Write* (Portsmouth, N.H.: Heinemann, 1983),

32. Marilyn Cochran-Smith, *The Making of a Reader* (Norwood, N.J.: Ablex, 1984).

33. Phyllis J. Fogelman, Early Literacy Project, New York Public Library, May 29, 1987. Early Childhood Resource and Information Center, 66 Leroy St., New York, N.Y. 10014.

34. Anna Pellegrini, daughter of Lee and Tony Pellegrini, personal correspondence, July 10, 1987.

35. Shirley Hughes, *Lucy & Tom's a.b.c.* (New York: Viking, 1986), n.p.

36. Interview with Nancy Tafuri by Bernice Cullinan, at American Library Association Annual Convention, New York City, June 28, 1986.

37. Kenneth S. Goodman, "Transactional Psycholinguistics Model: Unity in Reading," in *Theoretical Models and Processes of Reading*, 3rd ed, edited by

Harry Singer and Robert B. Ruddell (Newark, Del.: International Reading Association, 1985), 813–40; Frank Smith, *Understanding Reading*, 2nd ed. (New York: Holt, Rinehart & Winston, 1978).

38. Margaret C. Clark, "Language and Reading: Research Trends," in *Problems of Language and Learning*, ed. A. Davis (Portsmouth, N.H.: Heinemann, 1975).

39. Vicki Frost, kindergarten teacher, Worthington Hills School, Worthington, Ohio, personal report, March 24, 1987.

40. Interview with Jan Ormerod, New York City, May 12, 1986, plus personal correspondence and Lothrop promotional material.

41. Mary Anne Hall, *Teaching Reading as a Language Experience* (Columbus, Ohio: Merrill, 1970).

42. Sylvia Ashton-Warner, *Teacher* (New York: Simon & Schuster, 1966).

43. Roger Landrum et al., *A Day Dream I Had at Night and Other Stories: Teaching Children How to Make Their Own Readers* (New York: Teachers and Writers Collaborative, 1971).

44. Promotional material on Gail Gibbons from Harcourt Brace Jovanovich and Holiday House.

45. Alden J. Moe, "Using Picture Books for Reading Vocabulary Development," in *Using Literature in the Classroom*, ed. John Warren Stewig and Sam L. Sebesta (Urbana, Ill.: National Council of Teachers of English, 1978), 13–19.

46. Excerpt from Arnold Lobel's *Frog and Toad Together* (New York: Harper & Row, 1972), 40–41.

47. David W. McCullough, "Arnold Lobel and Friends: An Interview," *New York Times Book Review*, 11 (November 1979), 54.

48. Ibid.

49. Ginger Caughman, "Children Become Critics Through Children's Choices," *Louisiana Library Association Bulletin* 49, no. 2 (Fall 1986): 85–86; Ann V. Kent, "Reflections on a Gift of Books," *Louisiana Library Association Bulletin* 49, no. 2 (Fall 1986): 73–75; Dianne L. Monson, "Children's Responses to Humorous Stories" (Ph.D. diss., University of Minnesota, 1966); Nancie Munn, "Choosing Books that Appeal to Children," *Louisiana Library Association Bulletin* 49, no. 2 (Fall 1986): 79–81; George W. Norvell, *What Boys and Girls Like to Read* (Morristown, N.J.: Silver Burdett, 1958); and Bernice J Wolfson, Gary Manning and Maryann Manning, "Revisiting What Children Say Their Reading Interests Are," *Reading World* 24, no. 2 (1984): 4–10.

50. Since 1974, five regional teams of literature specialists, teachers, and librarians annually field test approximately 800 books with nearly 10,000 children. Each year, the results of that selection process are published in the October issue of *The Reading Teacher* as "Children's Choices."

51. Bruno Bettelheim, *The Uses of Enchantment: The Meaning and Importance of Fairy Tales* (New York: Knopf, 1976), 4.

CHILDREN'S BOOKS CITED

Ahlberg, Janet. *The Baby's Catalogue*. Illustrated by Janet Ahlberg and Allan Ahlberg. Boston: Little, Brown, 1983.

———, and Allan Ahlberg. *Each Peach Pear Plum*. New York: Viking, 1978.

———. *Peek-A-Boo*. New York: Viking, 1981.

Alexander, Martha. *Blackboard Bear*. New York: Dial, 1969.

Aliki. *Feelings*. New York: Greenwillow, 1984.

Anno, Mitsumasa. *Anno's Alphabet*. New York: Crowell, 1975.

Babbitt, Natalie. *The Eyes of the Amaryllis*. New York: Farrar, Straus & Giroux, 1977.

Bang, Molly. *Ten, Nine, Eight*. New York: Greenwillow, 1983.

Barton, Byron. *Airplanes*. New York: Crowell, 1986.

———. *Airport*. Illustrated by Byron Barton. New York: Crowell, 1982.

———. *Boats*. New York: Crowell, 1986.

———. *Building a House*. New York: Greenwillow, 1981.

———. *Trains*. New York: Crowell, 1986.

———. *Trucks*. New York: Crowell, 1986.

Bemelmans, Ludwig. *Madeline*. New York: Penguin, 1977.

Brown, Marc. *Finger Rhymes*. New York: Dutton, 1980.

———. *Hand Rhymes*. New York: Dutton, 1985.

Brown, Ruth. *The Big Sneeze*. New York: Lothrop, Lee & Shepard, 1985.

———. *A Dark Dark Tale*. New York: Dial, 1981.

Burningham, John. *John Burningham's 1 2 3*. New York: Crown, 1986.

———. *John Burningham's ABC*. New York: Crown, 1986.

———. *John Burningham's Opposites*. New York: Crown, 1986.

Cameron, Eleanor. *Julia and the Hand of God*. Illustrated by Gail Owens. New York: Dutton, 1977.

Carle, Eric. *The Grouchy Ladybug.* New York: Crowell, 1977.

———. *My Very First Book of Shapes.* New York: Crowell, 1974.

———. *The Very Busy Spider.* New York: Philomel, 1984.

———. *The Very Hungry Caterpillar.* New York: Philomel, 1969.

———. *The Very Hungry Caterpillar,* miniature edition. New York: Putnam's, 1986.

Carrick, Donald. *Milk.* New York: Greenwillow, 1985.

Carroll, Lewis. *Jabberwocky.* Illustrated by Jane Breskin Zalben. New York: Warne, 1977.

Causley, Charles. *''Quack!'' Said the Billy-Goat.* Illustrated by Barbara Firth. Philadelphia: Lippincott, 1986.

Christopher, Matt. *Ice Magic.* Illustrated by Byron Goto. Boston: Little, Brown, 1973.

———. *Soccer Halfback.* Illustrated by Larry Johnson. Boston: Little, Brown, 1978.

———. *Football Fugitive.* Illustrated by Larry Johnson. Boston: Little, Brown, 1976.

Chwast, Seymour. *Tall City, Wide Country.* New York: Viking, 1983.

Cleary, Beverly. *Henry Huggins.* Illustrated by Louis Darling. New York: Morrow, 1950.

———. *Beezus and Ramona.* Illustrated by Louis Darling. New York: Dell, 1979.

———. *Ramona and Her Father.* Illustrated by Alan Tiegreen. New York: Morrow, 1977.

———. *Ramona and Her Mother.* Illustrated by Alan Tiegreen. New York: Dell, 1980.

———. *Ramona Forever.* Illustrated by Alan Tiegreen. New York: Dell, 1985.

———. *Ramona Quimby, Age 8.* Illustrated by Alan Tiegreen. New York: Dell, 1982.

———. *Ramona the Brave.* New York: Dell, 1984.

———. *Ramona the Pest.* Illustrated by Louis Darling. New York: Dell, 1982.

———. *Ribsy.* New York: Morrow, 1964.

Cole, Joanna. *Cars and How They Go.* Illustrated by Gail Gibbons. New York: Crowell, 1983.

———. *My Puppy Is Born.* Photography by Jerome Wexler. New York: Morrow, 1983.

Coltman, Paul. *Tog the Ribber or Granny's Tale.* New York: Farrar, Straus & Giroux, 1985.

Corbett, Scott. *The Disappearing Dog Trick.* Illustrated by Paul Galdone. Boston: Little, Brown, 1963.

———. *The Hairy Horror Trick.* Illustrated by Paul Galdone. Boston: Little, Brown, 1969.

———. *The Lemonade Trick.* Boston: Little, Brown, 1960.

Crews, Donald. *Bicycle Race.* New York: Greenwillow, 1985.

———. *Carousel.* New York: Greenwillow, 1982.

———. *Flying.* New York: Greenwillow, 1987.

———. *Freight Train.* New York: Greenwillow, 1978.

———. *Harbor.* New York: Greenwillow, 1982.

———. *Light.* New York: Greenwillow, 1981.

———. *Parade.* New York: Greenwillow, 1983.

———. *School Bus.* New York: Greenwillow, 1984.

———. *Ten Black Dots.* New York: Greenwillow, 1986 (1968).

———. *Truck.* New York: Greenwillow, 1980.

———. *We Read: A to Z.* New York: Greenwillow, 1984.

Dabcovich, Lydia. *Sleepy Bear.* New York: Dutton, 1982.

Domanska, Janina, ed. *Busy Monday Morning.* New York: Greenwillow, 1985.

Emberley, Barbara. *Drummer Hoff.* Illustrated by Ed Emberley. Englewood Cliffs: N.J.: Prentice-Hall, 1967.

Feelings, Muriel. *Jambo Means Hello: Swahili Alphabet Book.* Illustrated by Tom Feelings. New York: Dial, 1974.

———. *Moja Means One.* Illustrated by Tom Feelings. New York: Dial, 1971.

Fischer-Nagel, Heiderose. *A Kitten Is Born.* Translated by Andrea Martin. Photography by Heiderose Fischer-Nagel and Andreas Fischer-Nagel. New York: Putnam, 1983.

———, and Andreas Fischer-Nagel. *A Puppy Is Born.* Translated by Andrea Martin. New York: Putnam, 1985.

Galdone, Paul. *Little Red Hen.* New York: Clarion, 1973.

Gibbons, Gail. *Boat Book.* New York: Holiday House, 1983.

———. *Check It Out! The Book about Libraries.* San Diego: Harcourt Brace Jovanovich, 1985.

———. *The Milk Makers.* New York: Macmillan, 1985.

———. *Department Store.* New York: Crowell, 1984.

———. *Flying.* New York: Holiday House, 1986.

———. *The Post Office Book: Mail and How It Moves.* New York: Crowell, 1982.

———. *Tool Book.* New York: Holiday House, 1982.

———. *Up Goes the Skyscraper.* New York: Four Winds, 1986.

Ginsburg, Mirra. *Across the Stream.* Illustrated by Nancy Tafuri. New York: Greenwillow, 1982.

Gundersheimer, Karen. *Colors to Know.* New York: Harper & Row, 1986.

———. *Shapes to Show.* New York: Harper & Row, 1986.

Hayes, Sarah. *This Is the Bear.* Philadelphia: Lippincott, 1986.

Hill, Eric. *Spot Goes Splash.* New York: Putnam's, 1984.

———. *Spot Goes to School.* New York: Putnam's, 1984.

———. *Spot Goes to the Circus.* New York: Putnam's, 1986.

————. *Spot Goes to the Farm.* New York: Putnam's, 1987.

————. *Where's Spot?* New York: Putnam's, 1980.

Hoban, Tana. *I Walk and Read.* New York: Greenwillow, 1984.

————. *Is It Larger? Is It Smaller?* New York: Greenwillow, 1985.

————. *Is It Red? Is It Yellow? Is It Blue?* New York: Greenwillow, 1978.

————. *Look Again.* New York: Macmillan, 1971.

————. *Shapes, Shapes, Shapes.* New York: Greenwillow, 1986.

————. *Take Another Look.* New York: Greenwillow, 1981.

————. *26 Letters and 99 Cents.* New York: Greenwillow, 1987.

Hughes, Shirley. *Bathwater's Hot.* New York: Lothrop, Lee & Shepard, 1985.

————. *Lucy & Tom's a.b.c.* New York: Viking, 1986.

Hutchins, Pat. *1 Hunter.* New York: Greenwillow, 1982.

————. *Changes, Changes.* New York: Macmillan, 1971.

————. *Don't Forget the Bacon.* New York: Greenwillow, 1976.

Ichikawa, Satomi. *Nora's Castle.* New York: Philomel, 1986.

Isadora, Rachel. *I Hear. I See. I Touch.* (set) New York: Greenwillow, 1985.

Jonas, Ann. *Holes and Peeks.* New York: Greenwillow, 1984.

————. *Now We Can Go.* New York: Greenwillow, 1986.

————. *Where Can It Be?* New York: Greenwillow, 1986.

Joslin, Sesyle. *What Do You Say, Dear?* Illustrated by Maurice Sendak. New York: Scholastic, 1980.

Kalan, Robert. *Jump, Frog, Jump!* Illustrated by Byron Barton. New York: Greenwillow, 1981.

Keats, Ezra Jack. *The Snowy Day.* New York: Viking, 1962.

Kitchen, Bert. *Animal Alphabet.* New York: Dial, 1984.

————. *Animal Numbers.* New York: Dial, 1987.

Komari, Atsushi. *Animal Mothers.* Illustrated by Masayuki Yabuuchi. New York: Philomel, 1983.

Kraus, Robert. *Come Out and Play, Little Mouse.* New York: Greenwillow, 1987.

————. *Herman the Helper.* Illustrated by José Aruego and Ariane Dewey. New York: Windmill, 1974.

————. *Where Are You Going, Little Mouse?* Illustrated by José Aruego and Ariane Dewey. New York: Greenwillow, 1986.

————. *Whose Mouse Are You?* Illustrated by José Aruego. New York: Macmillan, 1970.

Krauss, Ruth. *The Backward Day.* Illustrated by Marc Simont. New York: Harper & Row, 1950.

Kunhardt, Dorothy. *Pat the Bunny.* 1940. Reprint. Racine, Wis.: Western, 1968.

Kuskin, Karla. *Something Sleeping in the Hall.* New York: Harper & Row, 1985.

Lalicki, Barbara, comp. *If There Were Dreams to Sell.* Illustrated by Margot Tomes. New York: Lothrop, Lee & Shepard, 1984.

Le Guin, Ursula. *A Wizard of Earthsea.* Illustrated by Ruth Robbins. Boston: Parnassus, 1968.

Lobel, Arnold. *Days with Frog and Toad.* New York: Harper & Row, 1979.

————. *Fables.* New York: Harper & Row, 1980.

————. *Frog and Toad All Year.* New York: Harper & Row, 1976.

————. *Frog and Toad Are Friends.* New York: Harper & Row, 1970.

————. *Frog and Toad Together.* New York: Harper & Row, 1972.

————. *Grasshopper on the Road.* New York: Harper Junior Books, 1986.

————. *On Market Street.* Illustrated by Anita Lobel. New York: Greenwillow, 1981.

————. *The Random House Book of Mother Goose.* New York: Random House, 1986.

————. *The Rose in My Garden.* Illustrated by Anita Lobel. New York: Greenwillow, 1984.

McCord, David. *One at a Time.* Boston: Little, Brown, 1986.

McCully, Emily Arnold. *First Snow.* New York: Harper & Row, 1985.

————. *Picnic.* New York: Harper & Row, 1985.

MacDonald, Suse. *Alphabatics.* New York: Bradbury Press, 1986.

Maestro, Betsy, and Guilio Maestro. *Ferryboat.* New York: Crowell, 1986.

Maris, Ron. *Are You There, Bear?* New York: Greenwillow, 1985.

————. *Is Anyone Home?* New York: Greenwillow, 1985.

Martin, Bill, Jr. *Brown Bear, Brown Bear, What Do You See?* Illustrated by Eric Carle. New York: Holt, 1983.

Mayer, Mercer. *Ah-Choo!* New York: Dial, 1966.

————. *A Boy, A Dog, and a Frog.* New York: Dial, 1967.

————. *Frog Goes to Dinner.* New York: Dial, 1974.

————. *Frog, Where Are You?* New York: Dial, 1969.

————. *Hiccup!* New York: Dial, 1976.

Milne, A. A. "The King's Breakfast." In *When We Were Very Young.* Illustrated by Ernest H. Shepard. London: Dutton, 1924.

Minarik, Else H. *Father Bear Comes Home.* Illustrated by Maurice Sendak. New York: Harper & Row, 1959.

————. *A Kiss for Little Bear.* Illustrated by Maurice Sendak. New York: Harper & Row, 1968.

————. *Little Bear.* Illustrated by Maurice Sendak. New York: Harper & Row, 1957.

————. *Little Bear's Friend.* Illustrated by Maurice Sendak. New York: Harper & Row, 1960.

————. *Little Bear's Visit.* Illustrated by Maurice Sendak. New York: Harper & Row, 1961.

Ormerod, Jan. *101 Things to Do with a Baby.* New York: Lothrop, Lee & Shepard, 1984.

———. *Just Like Me.* New York: Lothrop, Lee & Shepard, 1986.

———. *Silly Goose.* New York: Lothrop, Lee & Shepard, 1986.

———. *Moonlight.* New York: Lothrop, Lee & Shepard, 1986.

———. *Our Ollie.* New York: Lothrop, Lee & Shepard, 1986.

———. *Sunshine.* New York: Lothrop, Lee & Shepard, 1981.

———. *Young Joe.* New York: Lothrop, Lee & Shepard, 1985.

Oxenbury, Helen. *Dressing.* New York: Simon & Schuster, 1981.

———. *Family.* New York: Simon & Schuster, 1981.

———. *Grandma and Grandpa.* New York: Dial, 1984.

———. *I Can.* New York: Random House, 1986.

———. *Mother's Helper.* New York: Dial, 1982.

Pearson, Tracey Campbell. *A·Apple Pie.* New York: Dial, 1987.

Pomerantz, Charlotte. *All Asleep.* Illustrated by Nancy Tafuri, New York: Greenwillow, 1984.

———. *One Duck, Another Duck.* Illustrated by José Aruego and Ariane Dewey. New York: Greenwillow, 1984.

———. *Where's the Bear?* Illustrated by Byron Barton. New York: Greenwillow, 1984.

Porte, Barbara Ann. *Harry's Dog.* New York: Greenwillow, 1984.

———. *Harry's Mom.* Illustrated by Yossi Abolafia. New York: Greenwillow, 1985.

———. *Harry's Visit.* Illustrated by Yossi Abolafia. New York: Greenwillow, 1983.

Prelutsky, Jack. *The Random House Book of Poetry.* Illustrated by Arnold Lobel. New York: Random House, 1983.

Provensen, Alice, and Martin Provensen. *The Glorious Flight.* New York: Viking, 1983.

———. *Town and Country.* New York: Crown, 1985.

Raskin, Ellen. *The Westing Game.* New York: Dutton, 1978.

Reiss, John J. *Colors.* New York: Bradbury, 1969.

———. *Numbers.* New York: Bradbury, 1971.

———. *Shapes.* New York: Bradbury, 1974.

Rice, Eve. *Ebbie.* New York: Greenwillow, 1975.

Robbins, Ken. *City/Country: A Car Trip.* New York: Viking, 1985.

———. *Tools.* New York: Four Winds, 1983.

Rockwell, Anne. *At Night.* New York: Crowell, 1986.

———. *At the Playground.* New York: Crowell, 1986.

———. *Boats.* New York: Dutton, 1982.

———. *Cars.* New York: Dutton, 1984.

———. *The Emergency Room.* Illustrated by Harlow Rockwell. New York: Macmillan, 1985.

———. *I Like the Library.* New York: Dutton, 1977.

———. *In the Morning.* New York: Crowell, 1986.

———. *In the Rain.* New York: Crowell, 1986.

———. *Our Garage Sale.* Illustrated by Harlow Rockwell. New York: Greenwillow, 1984.

Rockwell, Anne and Harlow Rockwell. *My Back Yard.* New York: Macmillan, 1984.

———. *The Toolbox.* New York: Macmillan, 1971.

———. *When I Go Visiting.* New York: Macmillan, 1984.

Sendak, Maurice. *One Was Johnny.* Film. Weston, Conn.: Weston Woods.

———. *Really Rosie.* Film. Weston, Conn.: Weston Woods.

———. *Where the Wild Things Are.* New York: Harper & Row, 1963.

Shannon, George. *The Piney Woods Peddler.* Illustrated by Nancy Tafuri. New York: Greenwillow, 1981.

Siebert, Diane. *Truck Song.* Illustrated by Byron Barton. New York: Crowell, 1984.

Sobol, Donald J. *Encyclopedia Brown, Boy Detective.* New York: Lodestar Books, 1963.

———. *Encyclopedia Brown Takes the Case.* Illustrated by Leonard Shortall. New York: Lodestar Books, 1973.

———. *Encyclopedia Brown Tracks Them Down.* Illustrated by Leonard Shortall. New York: Lodestar Books, 1971.

Spier, Peter. *Fast-Slow High-Low.* New York: Doubleday, 1972.

Tafuri, Nancy. *All Year Long.* New York: Greenwillow, 1983.

———. *Do Not Disturb.* New York: Greenwillow, 1987.

———. *Early Morning in the Barn.* New York: Greenwillow, 1983.

———. *Have You Seen My Duckling?* New York: Penguin, 1986.

———. *Rabbit's Morning.* New York: Greenwillow, 1985.

———. *Who's Counting?* New York: Greenwillow, 1986.

Turkle, Brinton. *Deep in the Forest.* New York: Dutton, 1976.

Van Allsburg, Chris. *The Z Was Zapped.* Boston: Houghton Mifflin, 1987.

Van Leeuwen, Jean. *More Tales of Amanda Pig.* Illustrated by Ann Schweninger. New York: Dial, 1985.

———. *Tales of Amanda Pig.* Illustrated by Ann Schweninger. New York: Dial, 1983.

———. *Tales of Oliver Pig.* Illustrated by Arnold Lobel. New York: Dial, 1979.

Watson, Clyde. *Applebet: An ABC.* Illustrated by Wendy Watson. New York: Farrar, Straus & Giroux, 1982.

Wells, Rosemary. *Max's Breakfast.* New York: Dial, 1985.

———. *Max's First Word.* New

York: Dial, 1979.

Wildsmith, Brian. *Cat on the Mat.* New York: Oxford University Press, 1982.

Wolff, Ashley. *Only the Cat Saw.* New York: Dodd, 1985.

Wood, Audrey. *King Bidgood's in the Bathtub.* Illustrated by Don Wood. San Diego: Harcourt Brace Jovanovich, 1985.

———. *The Napping House.* Illustrated by Don Wood. San Diego: Harcourt Brace Jovanovich, 1984.

Wright Group Story Box. *Mrs. Wishy Washy.* San Diego: Wright Group Publishing, 1984.

Yabuuchi, Masayuki. *Whose Baby?* New York: Philomel, 1985.

———. *Animals Sleeping.* New York: Philomel, 1983.

———. *Whose Footprints?* New York: Philomel, 1985.

Zolotow, Charlotte. *Say It!* Illustrated by James Stevenson. New York: Greenwillow, 1980.

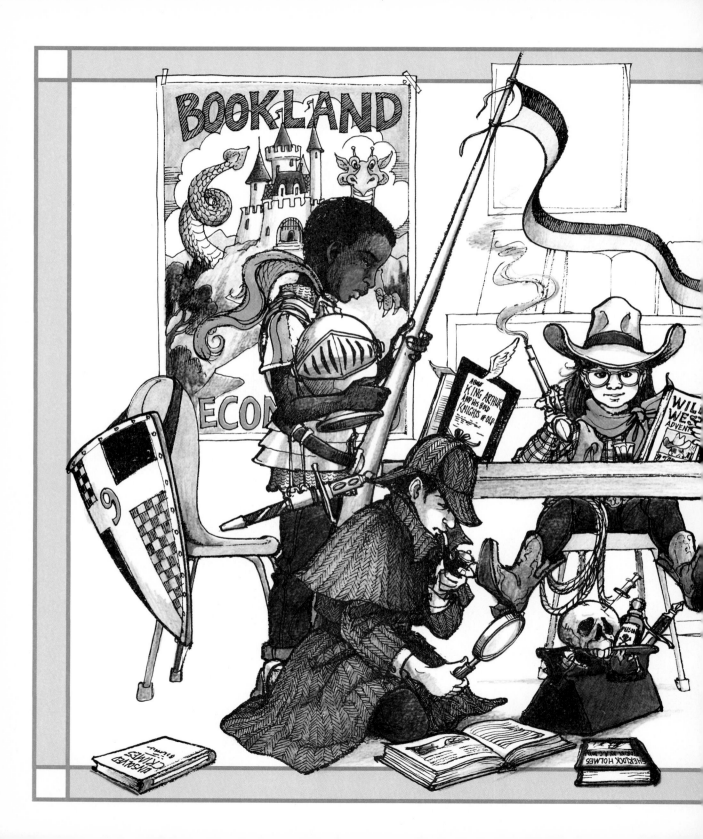

THE BOOKS

PART II

4

Picture Books

Watch Out

Okay everybody, listen to this:
I am tired of being smaller
Than you
And them
And him
And trees and buildings.
So watch out
All you gorillas and adults
Beginning tomorrow morning
Boy
Am I going to be taller.

Karla Kuskin[1]

ooks that tell a story through a combination of text and illustration are commonly called *picture books*. They are unique in the field of children's literature because format rather than content determines their definition. And though there are many fine picture books for older children, generally we think of them as stories for younger boys and girls. Patricia Cianciolo describes picture books as "a unique combination of graphic art and narrative in which the sense of story is completed and more frequently extended by the illustrations. A good picture book—one that is both interesting and attractive—offers a child pleasure, enlightenment, and a creative aesthetic experience."[2]

There are picture books that correspond to every developmental stage of childhood. Many of those particularly appropriate for very young children, and especially rich for their stimulus of language, we have discussed in Chapter 3. In Chapter 4, we address the books that parallel the child's expanding world as it grows beyond egocentricity to encompass family, then school, friends, and others in the child's social world, and eventually the world beyond. The child's horizons come to include nature, pets, and in the aesthetic world, art, dance, and literature. Children are explorers who reach out to people and events in their environment to find meanings for themselves.

The underlying framework for this chapter shows the correspondences between the books and the developmental characteristics of children. This perspective, then, serves as a guide for selecting the right book at the right time, and is reflected in the structure of the chapter, which begins with the child's inner world and follows through the various stages of expanding interest.

As discussed in Chapter 3, children learn through a continual process of relating the unfamiliar and the new to what they already know. And what they learn is an integrated whole. They cannot separate their thoughts into cognitive and emotional parts, for, as Frank Smith explains, "it is in the child's nature to express and develop innate intellectual capacities, integrating all experience into an intricate view of life that includes hopes and fears, loves and hates, beliefs and expectations, and attitudes toward other people and toward himself."[3]

The child, associating what is learned with the context surrounding it, forms a schema of ideas. For example, a child cuddled on an adult's lap while being read to not only learns the content of the story, but associates with reading the pleasures of the moment—the warmth of a loving adult, security, and the shared laughter or joy.

Past feelings coupled with the context of the present come to bear upon the act of learning. That is, children and adults associate past and present feelings with any supposedly simple, objective fact that is being taught. Teachers use this understanding of learning to draw

LANDMARK

Picture Books: The Tale of Peter Rabbit, *1902*

Beatrix Potter (1866–1943) wrote *The Tale of Peter Rabbit* as a letter to 5-year-old Noel Moore, the son of her former governess. Many of her letters to Noel and to other children were full of her own doings and the doings of her pets, including her rabbit, Peter. They were also full of tiny exquisite pictures. Sometimes, when things were duller than usual in Miss Potter's life, the letters contained no news, simply a story. So it was in this letter of September 4, 1893.

> My dear Noel,
> I don't know what to write to you, so I shall tell you a story about four little rabbits, whose names were Flopsy, Mopsy, Cottontail and Peter.
> They lived with their Mother in a sand bank under the root of a big fir tree.
> "Now, my dears," said old Mrs. Bunny, "you may go into the field or down the lane, but don't go into Mr. McGregor's garden . . . ."[4]

Beatrix Potter wrote letters to many of her friends' children; some of them contained the stories she was later to publish. She submitted *The Tale of Peter Rabbit* to Frederick Warne & Co., but it was courteously rejected. After the story was turned down by at least six other publishers, she decided to publish it herself.

The size of the book was determined according to Beatrix Potter's ideas of what a small child's book should be—no more than five inches by four with only one or two sentences per page and a picture each time you turned the page. In December 1901, she had 250 copies printed at her own expense; she sold these to obliging aunts for one and two pence a copy. The day her first edition was published, Warne & Co. wrote and offered to print *Peter Rabbit* if she would do color illustrations instead of the black and white ones it now contained.

Beatrix Potter's sense of what a child would like holds true today. The book has sold more copies than any other children's book—approximately 15 million copies—and has been translated into at least 16 languages. It captures a child's interest today as quickly as it did a century ago. It is truly a landmark in children's picture books.

The simplicity of the story, the charm of the paintings, and the child's size of the book have made Beatrix Potter's *The Tale of Peter Rabbit* a favorite for generations.

upon the prior knowledge children possess and relate the new to the known. In a cumulative fashion, children perceive the world and respond to events in terms of their past experiences and current predilections. When we involve children's interests and provide ways for them to use what they already know, they are empowered to learn.

Books become a part of children's lives and provide a basis for them to compare, share, and learn; books offer vicarious experiences for children to draw upon as they encounter new people and events in their expanding world. For example, a child who trembles at the first crash of thunder might find comfort in Mary Szilagyi's *Thunderstorm* (P), a gentle story of a little girl and her dog who are both frightened by the cracking and flashing of an approaching storm. As her mother comforts the child, she in turn soothes the dog, and the three sit close to share a book as they wait for the storm to pass.

Children gain confidence through stories when they meet characters who share their feelings. Tomie de Paola's *Oliver Button Is a Sissy* (P) tells about a small boy who is teased because he does not like to play football or other rough-and-tumble games. Instead, he likes to jump rope, draw pictures, and play dress-up. Most especially, Oliver likes to dance, and when he enters a talent contest, the other children change their assessment of him to "Oliver Button is a star!" This book shows that conformity need not be the rule; it also expands children's knowledge and understanding of people in their world.

CRITERIA FOR SELECTING PICTURE BOOKS

There are several qualities to look for in selecting picture books. Since learning is a continuous reaching out and integrating of both direct and vicarious experiences, in general one should select books that reflect, extend, or enrich the child's expanding world. As a basis for selection, the illustrations are of prime importance. Look for illustrations (1) that catch and hold the reader's interest, and (2) that have distinguished art that works with the text to amplify the story.

Young children's language is heavily influenced by the language they read and hear. Children are word collectors; they like to play with words and have fun with their sounds. On hearing John Burningham's *Mr. Gumpy's Outing* (N-P), children will echo Mr. Gumpy's "mucking about." The "bimulous" of "bimulous night," from Elinor Horwitz's *When the Sky Is Like Lace* (P), will also find echoes in the group. Thus, books selected should contain (1) intrinsically interesting words used in interesting ways that build excitement and drama, and (2) language that has an internal rhythm, a melody, and a natural beat.

Young children find it natural to identify with storybook characters. They giggle when the heroine in Ludwig Bemelmans' *Madeline* (P) shows how to frighten Miss Clavel by walking on the rail of the bridge rather than on the sidewalk with the other girls; they pull up their shirts and look at their own stomachs when she shows off her appendectomy scar. Through simple fantasy play, they become Madeline as she dares to do the things they pretend to do. Thus, we look for (1) characters well developed in text and illustration, and (2) characters who actively make things happen.

Children do not like long, descriptive monologues; they want things to happen. Their own retelling of stories is essentially a moving from one action to the next via connective phrases such as "and then." Young children find it difficult to follow complex, convoluted plots with flashbacks and subplots and are bored with lengthy descriptions of the setting. They want to know the time—present, past, or future—in which the tale is told, and they want a definite recognizable ending. We look, then, for (1) a clear plot—one visible in both text and illustration and that moves forward logically; and (2) a recognizable climax and a satisfying resolution.

Theme and mood are important aspects of children's books. The underlying message—the main idea the author is trying to convey, a theme—may be interpreted differently by different readers; there is no one right answer. But although good themes are neither blatantly stated nor so subtle they elude the reader, picture books should have (1) a readily identifiable theme that evolves naturally from plot and character, and (2) illustrations that extend the theme and establish the mood.

THE CHILD'S INNER WORLD

In a supportive environment, children soon come to know that they are unique and capable of expressing themselves and of making choices. This individuation process begins when children first perceive themselves as distinct beings. Until about the age of 4, children perceive others egocentrically; that is, others exist only in relation to themselves. Children begin to understand, however, that they are not the only ones who have needs and feelings. Much later they learn that others perceive things differently from them, and they begin to develop a concept of self based upon reflections from others. Many picture books address such developmental characteristics and appeal to children who are in a corresponding stage.

For example, Shirley Hughes describes a small boy's innocent mistake and subsequent ingenuity in *Alfie Gets in First* (N-P). Alfie, racing ahead of his mother and baby sister as they return from shopping, runs in the door and shouts "I won!" Unfortunately the door slams

TEACHING IDEA

LOOSE-TOOTH CENTER (P)   First experiences are important to young children. Even though the event may be one that is universal, for a child it is a brand-new experience. The first loose tooth is an especially significant milestone, symbolizing a step from babyhood to childhood. Books build on the excitement of first experiences and give children the opportunity to compare their experiences with those related in the stories.

Make a loose-tooth center that features a large cardboard tooth. Smaller cutout teeth bear the names of each child who has lost a first tooth. In addition, when a child comes to school with a brand new gaping hole in his mouth, attach a piece of yarn to a cardboard tooth that says "I lost one" and allow the child to wear this around his neck for the day. Place the following books (all P) in the center as the class reads them, so that the children can go back and look at them on their own:

Bate, *Little Rabbit's Loose Tooth*
Brown, *Arthur's Tooth*
Cooney, *The Wobbly Tooth*
Hoban, *Arthur's Loose Tooth*
McCloskey, *One Morning in Maine*
Pomerantz, *The Mango Tooth*

shut while his mother carries Annie Rose up the steps. The door is locked and Mother's key is inside. Just as the milkman brings a ladder to reach an open upstairs window, Alfie solves the problem himself.

Children in the preschool years, then, are busy learning about themselves—who they are and what they can do—and about others, but only as those others affect them. As they perceive people reacting and responding to them, children learn to adjust their actions to elicit the desired responses.

Children's self-concept develops as a direct result of interaction with the environment. Part of this environment is composed of the kinds of reactions young children receive from others. Given positive reactions and reinforcement, they feel good about themselves. When they see that their actions meet with approval, they are encouraged to explore, to express themselves, and to discover their world. Conversely, disapproval and negative feedback may cause children to pull in their boundaries and make them unwilling to take risks.

Children need to know that their feelings are acceptable. Marjorie Sharmat describes the fears and forebodings a young boy suffers as he faces the family's move "out West" in *Gila Monsters Meet You at the Airport* (P). His wild imaginings, based on exaggerated stereotypes, are matched when he meets a boy at the airport who dreads moving east because there are gangsters in the streets and alligators in the sewers. Knowing that joy, sadness, fear, and anger are natural helps children learn to accept their emotions and control them. In picture books, they find others who are afraid, sad, joyous, or angry and associate the characters' feelings with their own. Dealing with emotions, talking about them, and learning how to live with them are vital to an overall sense of well-being. Felice Holman's poem expresses the feelings of those times a child is given too much overt understanding and just wants to be left alone:

LEAVE ME ALONE

Loving care!
Too much to bear.
Leave me alone!

Don't brush my hair,
Don't pat my head,
Don't tuck me in
Tonight in bed,

Don't ask me if I want a sweet,
Don't fix my favorite things to eat,
Don't give me lots of good advice,
And most of all just don't be nice.

But when I've wallowed well in sorrow,
Be nice to me again tomorrow.

FELICE HOLMAN[5]

Self-Concept

Books can mirror the primary experiences that shape children's actions, reactions, and feelings, and can help children reflect upon them. Charlotte Zolotow's *Someone New* (P) illustrates this process dramatically. A young boy feels a sense of unrest when things seem to be changing. He no longer likes the wallpaper he chose for his room, nor does he want to play with his familiar toys. Only gradually does he realize that it is he who is changing. Stories like this play an important role for the child experiencing the conflicts of growing up; they enrich understanding when they relate to one's own life. In addition to providing new experiences, stories also show children that their thoughts, feelings, and reactions are not unusual—that they are like other people and a part of the human race.

In *Titch* (N-P), Pat Hutchins tells about a boy who always gets the smallest toys. His self-worth is boosted when his tiny seed grows into a large plant, symbolizing the fact that Titch, too, will grow. Growth in humans and in nature are visualized harmoniously in text and illustration in a sequel, *You'll Soon Grow into Them, Titch* (N-P). While Titch grows too large for his clothes, trees begin to blossom, bulbs begin to bloom, and baby birds hatch from eggs. Mother's tummy grows noticeably, too, making evident a forthcoming event. When she brings the new baby home, Titch, who has worn mostly hand-me-downs, gives the baby his own outgrown clothes. When he sees that they are still too big for the baby, Titch echoes words often spoken to him: "He'll soon grown into them!"

One of the most important steps in the development of self-concept is the understanding that each of us is important. The advice to "be yourself" is heard often and is a necessary part in the development of children's feelings about themselves. In a world where conformity is pervasive, children need to know that they are valued for their uniqueness, not because they conform to the standards of a group.

Anthony Browne's *Willy the Wimp* (P) is a scrawny chimpanzee in a world of gorillas. When he reads an advertisement for a body-building kit in a comic book, he sends for it and begins a regimen of exercise and diet that promises a new physique and a new image. No longer a wimp, Willy rescues a damsel in distress but reverts to old habits when he bumps into a lamp post and says "Oh, excuse me." Browne's very funny apes appear again in *Willy the Champ* (P). This time, Willy seems resigned to the fact that he is not very athletic. While the gorillas speed by on their racing bikes, he slowly cruises on his old-fashioned, balloon-tired girl's bicycle. He prefers to read and listen to music, and strolls through the park while the others play games. He even cries at Lassie movies. But Willy becomes the hero once again when Buster Nose appears— huge and tough in his studded leather vest and dark sunglasses. Buster throws a vicious punch, Willy ducks—and Buster hits the brick wall with his fist. Then Willy stands up, knocking Buster smack on the chin. Buster goes home to his mother while the gorillas lift a triumphant Willy to their shoulders.

Robert Kraus's story, *Leo the Late Bloomer* (N-P) should be required reading for all who would work with children. Leo is a young tiger who cannot do anything right: he can't read, he can't write, he can't draw, he is a sloppy eater, and he never says a word. Leo's father worries as he watches all the other animals perform those simple tasks, but Leo's mother assures him that Leo is just a late bloomer. Leo's father keeps watching for signs of blooming, but although the seasons come and go, it

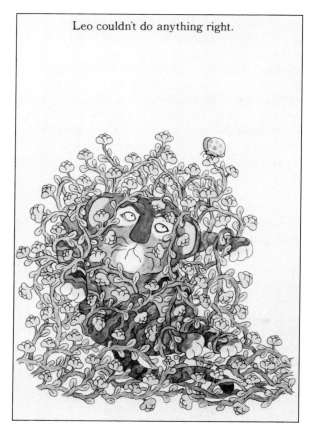

Leo couldn't do anything right.

Children need to know that, in time, they too will grow and will be able to do the things asked of them. (From Robert Kraus's *Leo the Late Bloomer*, illustrated by José Aruego.)

TEACHING IDEA

BLOOMERS (N-P)   Young children eagerly join in once others begin sharing their own "late blooming" problems. After you read *Leo the Late Bloomer* (N-P) by Robert Kraus, ask children to talk about the things they can do now that they could not do last year and then about the things that they cannot do yet. Have them make pictures of their successes and place these on a large bulletin board with the caption "We've bloomed!"

Other books to share with this story include:

Aruego, *Look What I Can Do* (N-P)
Asch, *Bear's Bargain* (N-P)
Brandenburg, *Otto Is Different* (P)
Cohen, *When Will I Read?* (P)
Keats, *Whistle for Willie* (P)
Kuskin, *Herbert Hated Being Small* (P)
Weiss, *Hank and Oogie* (P)

---

seems that Leo will not bloom. In his own good time, of course, he does. He reads, he writes, he draws, and he eats neatly. And he speaks: "And it wasn't just a word. It was a whole sentence. And that sentence was . . . 'I made it!'"

Many books have as their themes the importance of being true to oneself. The title character in Don Freeman's *Dandelion* (P) is a lion who spruces himself up for a party, only to be turned away because his hostess does not recognize him. When a sudden rainstorm ruins his fancy hairstyle and new clothes, Dandelion returns to the party looking himself and is greeted warmly. Children enter into lively discussions about the ways in which people try to impress others. In *"You Look Ridiculous," Said the Rhinoceros to the Hippopotamus* (P), Bernard Waber tells about a sad hippopotamus who longs to look like his friends. True to the title, the hippo imagines what it would be like to have spots like the leopard, a mane like the lion, a shell like the turtle, and many other unlikely attributes—all at the same time. Children enjoy dramatizing these stories of pretense.

Leo Lionni's *Alexander and the Wind-Up Mouse* (P) shows that while we may envy others for lives that seem to be better than ours, given the chance to change, we usually choose to be ourselves. Alexander, a real mouse, envies Willy, a toy mouse, because he is loved by and kept close to Annie while everyone chases Alexander away. But when Alexander sees that Willy is to be thrown away with the trash after Annie's new birthday toys arrive, Willy's life does not seem so idyllic. A lizard witch and a magic purple pebble give Alexander a rare choice—and the choice he makes is one children applaud.

Leo Lionni says that his stories have messages he wants readers to remember; they are not light fluff to be read and cast aside. Certainly the lasting thought from reading *Cornelius* (P) is that it is alright to be oneself no matter how much one differs from others. Cornelius could see things no other crocodile had ever seen before, but his friends were unimpressed when he demonstrated his new skills. Even though they scoffed and said "So what?" they tried to imitate Cornelius.

Each of these books enables children to see characters trying to be something other than what they really are. Discussing children's reactions to the stories leads to explorations on how they would solve the problems themselves.

Since the 1960s, the roles of men and women in our society have expanded dramati-

TEACHING IDEA

POETRY ABOUT ME (N-P) Start a collection of poems that deal with children's feelings. Put them in a big book or simply in a file box. Invite children to illustrate some of the poems. There are many to be found, including these in Dorothy Aldis's *All Together* (N-P): "Bad," "Big," "Everybody Says," "The Sad Shoes," "When I Was Lost," and "Whistles." Also look in Karla Kuskin's *The Rose on My Cake* (P) and *Near the Window Tree* (P-I), and in A. A. Milne's two books of poems, *Now We Are Six* (N-P) and *When We Were Very Young* (N-P).

ACTIVITY: TEACHER TO STUDENT

NOW I AM SIX (P)

THE END

When I was One,
I had just begun.

When I was Two,
I was nearly new.

When I was Three,
I was hardly Me.

When I was Four,
I was not much more.

When I was Five,
I was just alive.

But now I am Six, I'm as clever as clever.
So I think I'll be six now for ever and ever.
A. A. MILNE[6]

This poem talks about how one child felt about being 6 years old. What can you do now that you couldn't do before? Would you like to "be six now for ever and ever"? Why? Draw a picture of yourself now and a picture of you when you were one and "had just begun." Memorize the poem and surprise your parents by saying it on your sixth birthday.

Stories such as Rachel Isadora's *Max* help to dispel the traditional sex-role stereotypes.

cally; children's books reflect the changes. Until recently, the traditional mother, often complete with apron, was portrayed as the keeper of the home—doing the cooking, laundry, cleaning, and caring for the children. The father was shown rushing off to work, briefcase in hand, and returning home only to mow the lawn, service the car, and paint the garage. Children in the family engaged in similarly sex-assigned activities: big brother played baseball while little sister tended to her dolls. This standard idyllic family was seen in advertising, television, and children's books. Deliberate attempts to change the stereotyped image include many so-called bandaid books, which have such strong messages that the stories are overshadowed by the statements. These stories lack realism, characterization, and imagination, and in many cases actually undermine the movement to provide a balanced view of society today. Other books, however, offer a positive picture; they qualify as literature on their own and, at the same time, give the reader something to think about.

Rachel Isadora's *Max* (P) is a picture story about a boy who stops off at his sister's dance class on the way to baseball practice. Unable to remain a passive observer, Max mimics the dancers' movements and later finds that the leaps, splits, and stretches help improve his performance on the baseball field. His mimicry is so successful that he also becomes a member of the dance class.

Bill Martin Jr and and John Archambault tell a rollicking tale of a youngster who travels the rodeo circuit in *White Dynamite and Curly Kidd* (P). As Curly Kidd gets ready to ride "the meanest bull in the whole United States" he explains to his proud offspring how he overcomes his fear. Lucky Kidd shouts encouragement during the ride, and when it is over, throws her hat into the air in jubilation. The rhythmic dialogue and Ted Rand's exuberant full color paintings will entice young cowboys and cowgirls.

Fear Children develop many fears as a normal part of growing up. Fears can arise from a general insecurity and anxiety about the world; young children's sense of reality is not yet strong enough to sort out the various phenomena confronting them, and they may express uncertainty through fear. Books can be an element in coming to terms with fears by presenting experiences similar to those of children, who then compare their actions and feelings with those of the characters in the stories. Books, therefore, can play a role in lessening fears by helping children learn about their inner world. Christopher believes that the pond is *Dark and Full of Secrets* (P) in Carol and Donald Carrick's story. Despite reassurances given to him to the contrary, he fears the monstrous things that lurk beneath the surface. When he ventures out with a mask and snorkel, he sees a peaceful world of crayfish, minnows, and bass. When he realizes that he is far from the pond's edge, he momentarily panics, but quickly realizes that he is able to get back by himself. Christopher's long-standing dread and urgent fear are vividly portrayed in word and illustration. In *The Climb* (P), the Carricks tell another story of a child's fear, this time when a steep hill stands in the way.

Being afraid is one thing, but worrying that others will know you are scared is another. Marjorie Sharmat's *Frizzy the Fearful* (P) suffers from both dilemmas and gradually learns to overcome them. His new-found courage is slow and sometimes painful in this believable story.

Children's fears frequently manifest themselves at night, with wolves, monsters, and ghosts being the common focuses. Simply telling a child that there are no monsters is ineffective; the fear is real to the child. Bill Martin Jr and John Archambault portray a child's fear of walking past *The Ghost-Eye Tree* (P), an ancient oak that seems to waver in the wind and reach out to grab a frightened boy. His sister plays the protector until she, too, hears the howling wind and sees the moon framed by the tree's gnarled branches. Ted Rand's haunting illustrations play with the light and shadow of the spooky night. William Pène DuBois also captures the dark in Mark Strand's *The Night Book* (P), a comforting fantasy in which the moon takes a frightened little girl on a nighttime journey of discovery. With her dog along for security, she sees flowers, birds, insects, and people she has never seen during the day.

Even children who no longer have nighttime fears appreciate *Clyde Monster* (P), by Robert Crowe, which is a marvelous reversal of the traditional monster story. Clyde is an adorable monster creature who is afraid to go to bed because people might be hiding in his cave waiting to get him. His parents tell him that monsters and people made a deal a long time ago: people don't scare monsters and monsters don't scare people. The reassurance convinces Clyde, who goes into his cave—still with a bit of caution: "But could you leave the rock open just a little?"

Mercer Mayer's *There's a Nightmare in My Closet* (P) shows a small boy overcoming his fear—but not his fantasy—when he comforts a monster who has a nightmare. Mayer's ugly but lovable creature who climbs into bed with the child may reassure the frightened listener that, although the monster is "real," it is nothing to be afraid of.

A toy or blanket often serves a useful purpose for a child who is trying to overcome fears. This alter ego provides companionship, security, and comfort, and can be the vehicle through which a child plays out unconscious fears. *Geraldine's Blanket* (P) by Holly Keller shows a creative solution to a common childhood concern. Geraldine carries her baby blanket around until it is an embarrassment to everyone around her. Mother uses all sorts of ploys to get her to give up the ragged blanket but finally Geraldine herself comes up with a compromise: she makes the blanket into a dress for her doll.

Nicki Weiss's *Hank and Oogie* (P) tells of the special relationship between a small boy and his stuffed hippopotamus. Oogie goes everywhere with Hank despite his parents' casual suggestions that sometimes Oogie should stay home. Only after he gets involved in kindergarten is Hank willing to part with his friend. An understanding mother helps him place Oogie on his bedroom shelf, where Oogie can still be the last thing Hank sees each night.

Children sometimes transfer their own fears to a stuffed animal or other object. Martha Alexander's *I'll Protect You from the Jungle Beasts* (P) illustrates this kind of role substitution. A small pajama-clad boy and his teddy bear are walking through the woods amidst frightening growls and roars. "Oh, yes, Teddy, there are lions and tigers and elephants in this forest—big ones. But don't worry, I'll protect you from the jungle beasts." As they get deeper into the woods—and the possibility that they are lost seems real—the boy continues to comfort his friend who, by now, is growing in size. Almost imperceptibly, Teddy becomes the comforter and carries the boy home to their safe, warm bed. Children who empathize with the boy understand his conversation with, and transfer of feelings to, the teddy bear. They also recognize that the whole experience is a dream, foreshadowed by showing the boy in his pajamas and confirmed on the last page when he awakens in his bed beside his normal-sized teddy bear.

Another boy who needs his teddy bear for protection is found in Bernard Waber's *Ira Sleeps Over* (P). Ira is invited to sleep at his friend Reggie's house, but his sister keeps planting seeds of doubt about the experience. How will Ira feel without his teddy bear? He's never slept without him. Reggie will laugh, not only at the bear, but at his name—Tah Tah. Torn between his sister's taunts and the fear of sleeping without his teddy bear, Ira vacillates between taking him and not taking him. Big sister wins, but when Reggie starts telling ghost stories and sneaks his own teddy bear — Foo Foo—out of his dresser drawer, Ira returns

"He won't laugh," I said.

Books about fearful events tell how other children react to these events and help the young readers to understand and come to terms with their own feelings. (From *Ira Sleeps Over* by Bernard Waber.)

to his home next door to get Tah Tah. This very funny story can provoke a lively discussion of "When I *used* to have a teddy bear . . ." in which children readily relate their experiences (past and present).

Rosemary Wells's *Peabody* (P) is Annie's constant companion from the moment she receives the teddy bear for her birthday. She dresses him, takes him places, and talks to him; she also spends a great deal of time protecting him from her younger brother, Robert. When on her next birthday Annie receives a huge talking and walking doll, she lays Peabody aside, forgotten and unloved. Robert is still up to his old tricks, however, and when he puts the doll in a bathtub full of water she is ruined forever. Annie, of course, returns to Peabody in this early lesson in poetic justice.

The bear of all bears, in A. A. Milne's *Winnie the Pooh* (I), is a well-developed character who suffers from being "a bear of very little brain." The author developed the stories around a stuffed bear belonging to his son and added a menagerie of companions in the stories. The joys and troubles that come from being loved by Christopher Robin are the basis for two collections of poetry and two of stories. The stories contain subtle word play and humor that put them beyond the range of most primary children, but many of the poems appeal to the teddy bear set, especially this one:

US TWO

Wherever I am, there's always Pooh,
There's always Pooh and Me.
Whatever I do, he wants to do,
"Where are you going today?" says Pooh:
"Well that's very odd 'cos I was too.
Let's go together," says Pooh, says he.
"Let's go together," says Pooh.

A. A. MILNE[7]

Children who own teddy bears are certain that the bears have feelings, too. The teddy bear often reflects their own feelings of need for love, reassurance, and solitude. In Don Freeman's *Corduroy* (N-P), a lonely teddy bear in a department store fears that his lost button will keep someone from selecting him. He is finally purchased by a small girl who is also looking for a friend. Young children feel a special affection for this bear. When Freeman wrote the sequel *A Pocket for Corduroy* (N-P), one group of kindergarten children insisted on having a party to celebrate the new book.

Bedtime Although it is not possible to prevent all fears from surfacing—and indeed this is not desirable—a feeling of security allays many nighttime fears. Children are reassured through pleasurable experiences in previously

The bedtime classic *Goodnight Moon*, by Margaret Wise Brown, provides reassurance and coziness to young readers. (Illustrated by Clement Hurd.)

frightening situations. For example, children who fear the dark learn to be less fearful when they hear pleasant bedtime stories told in the dark.

Many books serve to soothe children and provide them with the sense of security necessary for an overall good feeling about themselves. One such book that has comforted several generations of children is Margaret Wise Brown's *Goodnight Moon* (N). The moon appears in the window as it travels across the sky while the bunny bids each object in the room goodnight.

Jane Howard blends dream and imagination in *When I'm Sleepy* (N-P). In very simple text, a small girl wonders how it would be to sleep in a nest or a cave, perched on the branch of a tree, or high on a rocky mountain ledge. Lynne Cherry's luminous full-color paintings extend the words to show the child snuggling up next to the animals who actually inhabit those places: birds, bears, goats, and more. Imagination fades into dream as the child falls asleep in her own bed—surrounded by her vast collection of stuffed animals.

ACTIVITY: TEACHER TO STUDENT

TEDDY BEAR WEEK (N-P)   Bring your favorite stuffed animals to school during Teddy Bear Week, but do not be surprised if they need to go home each night. Read stories to your bears, write letters between them, and tell others of some adventures they have had. Read lots of stories and poems about bears, and compare your bears with the ones in books. Have a bread and honey party to highlight the week. Make a V.I.B. (Very Important Bear) bulletin board featuring jackets from teddy bear books and your drawings of teddy bears.

Responsibility

The development of moral reasoning progresses through sequential and qualitatively differentiated stages. As they grow older, children learn to distinguish between good and bad, and between right and wrong. The beginnings of conscience are sparked when a child feels remorse for his bad behavior. Marjorie Weinman Sharmat's young hero tells a lie in *A Big Fat Enormous Lie* (P) and feels the pangs of guilt creep over him. David McPhail's lively illustrations show an ugly green creature—the lie—lurking behind a tree, and as the pressure mounts, the boy talks to the lie. The book cleverly shows how guilt often manifests itself in real physical discomfort when Lie plops itself on top of the boy: "Is that you sitting on my stomach, Lie? That hurts."

As children internalize concepts of right and wrong, they perceive that their actions affect others as well as themselves. Whereas the boy who told the "big, fat enormous lie" was the only one who actually suffered, Evaline Ness, in *Sam, Bangs, and Moonshine* (P), shows that a lie can bring real danger to others. Sam (short for Samantha) lives with her father and her cat, Bangs, on a small island near a large harbor. Her best friend, Thomas, is an innocent younger child who idolizes Sam and believes all her wild tales. Her father's efforts to convince Sam that her fantasies are lies—moonshine, he calls them—only push her

deeper into her dream world. She sends Thomas to a nearby island to search for her baby kangaroo—another figment—and, when the tide comes in early, Thomas and Bangs are nearly drowned. "There's good MOONSHINE and bad MOONSHINE, . . . the important thing is to know the difference," her father tells her. Sam finally realizes that she must take responsibility for her actions.

Marjorie Sharmat combines humor and pathos in several books to show that people (in the guise of animals) are responsible for changing their own behaviors. *Attilla the Angry* (P) is a bad-tempered squirrel who is constantly offending his friends. He goes to a meeting of Angry Animals Anonymous and resolves to mend his ways. At first he overreacts but eventually learns moderation. Other behavior weaknesses are apparent in the titles of Sharmat's books (all P): *Bartholomew the Bossy, Sasha the Silly, Grumley the Grouch, I'm Terrific!,* and *Mooch the Messy.*

Nosey Mrs. Rat (P) by Jeffrey Allen spoofs through exaggeration the stereotype of the neighborhood gossip. Shirley Rat made a hobby of knowing what was going on even if it involved peeking in windows, reading other people's mail, or listening in on telephone conversations. She made life especially miserable for Brewster Blackstone who lived next door: she tracked him down when he played hooky and reported to his father when Brewster flunked history. Finally Brewster retaliates by

ACTIVITY: TEACHER TO STUDENT

BABYSITTER'S HANDBOOK (I) When you babysit, an excellent way to capture your charges' attention, gain their appreciation, and get them ready for bed is to read to them. Start a collection of poems and stories that you can use when you babysit. Several collections of bedtime poems (all N–P) will be useful.

Chorao, *The Baby's Bedtime Book*
Field, *Wynken, Blynken and Nod,* illus. Susan Jeffers
Field, *Wynken, Blynken and Nod,* illus. Barbara Cooney
Hopkins, *And God Bless Me: Prayers, Lullabies and Dream-Poems*
Hopkins, *Go to Bed! A Book of Bedtime Poems*

Kuskin, *Night Again*
Larrick, *When the Dark Comes Dancing*
Pomerantz, *All Asleep*
Stevenson, *The Moon*
Winter, *Hush, Little Baby*
Yolen, *The Lullaby Songbook*

---

capturing Mrs. Rat on film and showing it to all the neighbors. Mrs. Rat takes to her bed avowing "I'll never snoop again," but on the last page of the book she muses, "Well, perhaps for special occasions." James Marshall's cartoon illustrations underscore the slapstick humor.

Imagination

Children's imaginative lives are an important part of their early years. Adults can sometimes get a glimpse of that fantasy world by observing the child at play with an imaginary friend or a favorite toy that has been invested with life. The importance of these symbolic beings is attested to by nursery school teachers or custodians who have received frantic requests to unlock a building at night from parents trying to retrieve a left-behind toy.

Children develop a vivid imaginative life by attributing human characteristics to inanimate objects. A child's favorite teddy bear or blanket becomes a source of security during infancy through a process in which the child invests the object with meaning.[8] Parents and teachers can have very little direct effect on a child's imaginative play, but they can contribute to an environment that is conducive to it.

Playing "let's pretend" games, discussing dreams, and making up stories convey to the child the message that imaginative stories are acceptable.

Adults who fear that too much fantasy will affect a child's sense of reality need not worry; a lively imagination is a central part of the developmental process. Imaginative stories provide a source of pleasure as well as a focal point for children's developing imagination and sense of story. In fact, children who have been deprived of traditional fairy tales and other imaginative stories will create their own.[9]

Some of the most distinguished literature for children builds upon the imaginative life of the central characters. In these stories stuffed animals come to life, fancy runs free, creatures hide under beds, and imaginary friends are real. A. A. Milne's poem "Binker" epitomizes the supportive alter ego created by some children. Christopher Robin can always count on his friend to understand:

> Binker, what I call him—is a secret of my own,
> And Binker is the reason why I never feel alone.[10]

Chris Van Allsburg, twice winner of the coveted Caldecott Medal for his superb art in

A Caldecott Medal winner, *Jumanji*, by Chris Van Allsburg, encourages children to imagine what adventures they can experience in their own living rooms.

Jumanji (P) and *The Polar Express* (P-I), as well as a Caldecott Honor award for *The Garden of Abdul Gasazi* (P-I), makes the transition very smooth between the real world and the imaginary. *Jumanji* revolves around a game in which wild animals come to life and torrential rains drench the living room when two children try to relieve their boredom. In *The Polar Express*, a small boy waits on Christmas Eve to hear the magical jingle of Santa's sleigh bells. Instead, he hears the chugging of a freight train which stops in front of his home. He boards the train and spends a magical evening at the North Pole where Santa gives him a bell from the reindeer's harness. His sadness at discovering he has lost the bell changes to wonder the next morning when he awakens to find the bell has been wrapped and placed under the Christmas tree. A poignant ending shows that the sleigh bell still rings for all those who believe; for oth-

ers it is silent. In *The Garden of Abdul Gasazi* (P), Van Allsburg makes a visual statement with his illustrations that carry the major theme of the book. In a story that hinges on the ability of Abdul Gasazi to make magic, the final, full-page, dramatic panorama alone affirms that, indeed, he is a magic maker. Van Allsburg's gift in design parallels the magic he portrays in story.

Crocodarling (P) by Mary Rayner is a stuffed crocodile who is very real to his small owner, Sam. When the milk is spilled, it was knocked over by Crocodarling's tail, of course. And Sam must walk slowly because the pavement hurts Crocodarling's feet. At nursery school Crocodarling causes the squabbles—never Sam. A kind teacher and tolerant mother help Sam begin to rely less on his toy as he makes friends with the other children.

Anthony Browne gives vent to a child's imagination in *Gorilla* (P). Hannah has never

PROFILE

Chris Van Allsburg

In 1986, Chris Van Allsburg joined a very elite group when he became only the sixth illustrator to receive a second Caldecott Medal. To him, this award suggests that the success of art rests in its power to communicate, to transfer the imaginative into the concrete. Imagination and technical skill are equally important to him:

> Illustrating is simply a matter of drawing something I've already experienced in my mind's eye. Because I see the story unfold as if it were on film, the challenge is deciding precisely which moment should be illustrated and from which point of view.[11]

To Van Allsburg a vivid imagination is a gift we should envy. He thinks it unfortunate that most of the true believers in Santa Claus are under 8 years old. He also thinks that those who believe in fantastic propositions, such as Bigfoot and the Loch Ness monster, live in a far superior world. With tongue firmly in cheek, he insists that his view of the fantastic is ruled by logic:

> When I conceived of the North Pole in *The Polar Express*, it was logic that insisted it be a vast collection of factories. I don't see this as a whim of mine or even as an act of imagination. How could it look any other way, given the volume of toys produced there every year?[12]

Chris Van Allsburg grew up in Michigan where he enjoyed drawing, reading, and—briefly—stamp collecting. By the time he reached sixth grade, however, he gave in to peer pressure and pursued football and other more accepted interests. Not until college did he take up art again, and then only as a lark. The urge to create won out over a career in law and now, in addition to books, he creates magnificent sculptures. He also teaches at the Rhode Island School of Design (from which he received an M.F.A.), where he introduces his students to the two main elements of illustration: imagination and technique.

seen a live gorilla but is infatuated with them. Her father seems always to be busy, so when he gives her a toy gorilla for her birthday she fantasizes the toy as a father figure who takes her to the zoo, to a movie, and then dancing.

Her fantasy becomes reality when her father actually takes her to the zoo. This moving story with its bright, surrealistic illustrations portrays profound truths and the intensity of real emotional needs in a single-parent home.

Ann Jonas makes an ordinary trip to school an extraordinary experience by vivifying a child's unfettered imagination in *The Trek* (P). Through amazing artistic skill, Jonas camouflages animals in shrubs, sidewalks, and other common landmarks. Tigers lurk in a clump of iris, alligators crawl along stone walks, and giraffes hide in dappled tree trunks. The watermelons posing as crocodiles in a fruit stand are truly inventive. Children can test their visual acuity by checking to see if they have discovered all the animals that are listed at the back of the book. This is reminiscent of Dr. Seuss's classic *And to Think That I Saw It on Mulberry Street* (P), in which Marco's lively imagination creates a wonderful parade passing through his quiet neighborhood.

Emily Herman tells a story just made for cool October nights. Lee is sure that *Hubknuckles* (P), a ghostly apparition that appears on Halloween, is only Ma or Pa dressed up in a sheet. She's just a little scared as she goes out into the moonlit night to dance with him beneath the trees. In a deliciously spooky ending, she returns to the house to find both Ma and Pa indoors, while Hubknuckles still glides through the quiet night.

Magic plays an important role in children's imaginative lives. Piaget explains that until about the age of 7, children accept magic without question; they believe in enchantments, transformations, and spells. It is natural, therefore, that many stories depend upon magical elements to convey the plot as well as the theme.

William Steig's work exemplifies some of the most creative use of magic in imaginative stories. Several of his books hinge on the transformation of the central character. In *Sylvester and the Magic Pebble* (P), a young burro makes an unfortunate wish on a magic pebble and turns into a large rock. He lies mute and helpless through the long winter while his parents search desperately for their lost son. A chance picnic in the spring takes them, unknowingly,

Magic is a key ingredient to imaginative stories, in this case transforming Sylvester, a burro, into a rock and finally back to a burro once again. (From *Sylvester and the Magic Pebble* by William Steig.)

to Sylvester's side, where they find the magic pebble and place it on top of the rock. Sylvester returns to his natural state and the family has a joyful reunion. Similar transformations occur in *The Amazing Bone* (P) and *Solomon the Rusty Nail* (P). Steig's pastel watercolors combine pathos with humor, which he integrates with imaginative text to earn many honors, including the Caldecott Medal for *Sylvester and the Magic Pebble*.

Perhaps the best-known imaginative story of all is Maurice Sendak's *Where the Wild Things Are* (P). Max is sent to bed without his supper for being naughty and in his isolation creates one of the most marvelous experiences contained in children's literature. The slender text flows like music while the illustrations grow in

PROFILE

William Steig

They started homeward at noon, having drunk quarts of sarsaparilla to quench their thirst. If all went well—and why shouldn't it?—they'd be back at the farm by three o'clock, as Farmer Palmer had promised.

It was August and the hot sun glittered through a haze. They chatted as they moved along. Ebenezer opined that rain would have a cooling effect, and Farmer Palmer was of the same opinion.[13]

Something always seems not to go well for the animals in William Steig's colorful books. But the mishaps that befall Farmer Palmer, Abel's estrangement from Amanda, the bamboozling of Minstrel Roland by the fox, and Sylvester's metamorphosis are all just so many disasters that are reversed by endurance and perseverance. William Steig's stories affirm for children the place of persistence and patience in winning things not easily won. In his acceptance speech for the Caldecott Medal, he said:

Art, including juvenile literature, has the power to make any spot on earth the living center of the universe; . . . it helps us

size as Max's imagination grows. Sendak's classic tale echoes the child's feelings of rejection, his journey from a safe home, and the creation of a fantasy world in which the child is king: "And when he came to the place where the wild things are they roared their terrible roars and gnashed their terrible teeth and rolled their terrible eyes and showed their terrible claws till Max said 'BE STILL!'" Eventually Max tires of being king of all the wild things and wants to be where someone loves him best of all, and so he returns "across days and in and out of weeks" to his very own room. The supper waiting for him, with the tag phrase "and it was still hot," restores Max to a safe home and his mother's love, made visible in her provision of warm food. Sendak's *In the Night Kitchen* (P) and *Outside Over There* (P) also embody memorable imaginative journeys.

An environment in which children tell stories contributes to language growth and encourages the developing imagination. Unfortunately, children are sometimes admonished not to make up stories and are not given opportunities to recognize the place for real and the place for make believe. Teachers' attitudes toward storytelling and fantasy affect children's willingness to take risks in making up fanciful

to know life in a way that still keeps before us the mystery of things. It enhances the sense of wonder. And wonder is respect for life. Art also stimulates the adventurousness and the playfulness that keep us moving in a lively way and that lead to useful discovery.[14]

William Steig's art has the power to keep the mystery of things before us as it promotes a sense of wonder in illustrations that extend his unpretentious wit. Children sense the playfulness that permeates the text and is sprinkled generously throughout the illustrations.

Steig explains that his books often start as visual images; when he wrote *Roland the Minstrel Pig,* for example, he imagined a picture of a pig hanging on a string. *Sylvester and the Magic Pebble* was to be a book with magic in it because children like magic, and he does too.

William Steig has won numerous awards. He received the Caldecott Medal for *Sylvester and the Magic Pebble* in 1970, a Caldecott Honor Book Award for *The Amazing Bone* in 1977, and Newbery Honor Book Awards for *Abel's Island* in 1977 and for *Doctor DeSoto* in 1983. He also received the American Book Award for *Doctor DeSoto* in 1983 and had the same book selected for the International Board on Books for Youth Honor List in 1984. His works have been selected for the New York Times Best Illustrated Books, the Christopher Award, the Georgia Children's Book Award, the William Allen White Award, and many others.

Born in Manhattan and educated in the New York City public schools, Steig had a formidable career as a magazine cartoonist before he started writing books for children. His work is seen frequently in *The New Yorker*.

tales; an inviting smile or a twinkle in the eye tell children that it is safe to tell a wild tale. Reading many stories in which a character's imagination runs rampant further verifies for them the appropriateness of imaginative storytelling.

Humor

Children love to laugh and will find plenty of cause for deep chuckles in their books. Authors create humor through exaggeration, slapstick, and incongruity and portray silly characters who blatantly disregard normal behavior.

Some primary age children to whom a librarian read *The Stupids Step Out* (P), by Harry Allard, thoroughly enjoyed the ridiculous characters and their antics. The children giggled when they heard the Stupids name their dog "Kitty" and laughed outright when the Stupids wanted to avoid the funny-looking people they saw in a mirror. When the Stupids ate a mashed potato and butterscotch sundae, the children's laughter drowned out the librarian's. Allard continues the adventures of this outrageous family in *The Stupids Have a Ball* (P), in which the Stupids celebrate their children's horrendously bad report cards. In *The Stupids Die* (P),

PROFILE

Maurice Sendak

If I had been lucky I would have been a Renaissance child living in Florence. I would have been up early every morning to watch Michelangelo chiseling away in his backyard.[15]

This statement captures Maurice Sendak's feeling about his art, which is central to his life. Sendak says that his stories and pictures stem from his observations as a youngster from a doorstep on a Brooklyn street, delineated clearly in his *Really Rosie* (where even the address on the door is that of his child-

hood home). In a television interview, Sendak explained: ''As a metaphor you might say that I've been doing that continuously. I mean everything has come out of that doorstep or that door. It ends up by having been one theme that you repeat endlessly.''[16]

Sendak is a self-taught artist and storyteller who studied formally only briefly—at the Art Students League in New York City. He celebrates the old masters as better teachers than contemporary ones. An indefatigable worker, he competes with himself to perfect his skill. Sample work pages in his *Maurice Sendak Fantasy Sketches* reflect how he practices his craft—at breakneck speed, and often to a boisterous classical music accompaniment.

Maurice Sendak and Walt Disney's Mickey Mouse celebrated their fiftieth birthdays together. Disney's art (and the images evoked by William Blake's poetry) made a lasting impression on him. The forces influencing Sendak's style crystallized in *Where the Wild Things Are.* There was never any doubt, as he was growing up, about what he wanted to do, and even while still in high school, he worked for All-American Comics on the ''Mutt and Jeff'' strip. Winner of the Caldecott Medal and the Hans Christian Andersen Award, as well as the Lewis Carroll

the family believes the world has ended when the lights suddenly go out. The dog and cat replace the fuse, but the silly Stupids just think they are now in heaven instead of in their own world.

Steve Kellogg's lovable and rambunctious Great Dane, Pinkerton, wreaks havoc wherever

he goes with his galloping stride and lowly intellect. He creates absolute chaos when he mixes up all the commands at obedience school in *Pinkerton, Behave!* (P), but redeems himself when he catches a burglar, albeit not the way he was trained to do. His escapades are hilariously told in understated text in *A Rose for*

Young children identify with Max, who creates an imaginative world after he is scolded and sent to bed without his supper. (From *Where the Wild Things Are* by Maurice Sendak.)

Shelf Award, numerous citations of merit, and other national and international awards, Sendak has gained worldwide acclaim.

Sendak is the first to say that art alone is not enough to make a good children's book. He doesn't appreciate compliments solely about his pictures because, for his work, the text is vital. While good pictures are imaginative, he says, pictures must come from the text. Illustrations for a bad book will be bad pictures. A really good book brings out the best in him; he has to be truly excited by the words to create illustrations. He states, "I'm a reader primarily, secondly I'm an illustrator."[17]

Sendak's *In the Night Kitchen* was his goodbye to New York when he moved from the city to his present home in some quiet woods in Connecticut. The book was drawn from remembrances of early childhood. Images—such as the bottle of milk (Sendak's transformation of the Empire State Building) and Mickey and his plane (reminiscent of the shooting of King Kong in the film)—come from the movies and comics of childhood; these remain indelible in his memory.

When asked what one should look for in a picture book, Sendak replied:

> Originality of vision. Someone who has something to say that might be very commonplace, but who says it in a totally original and fresh way, who has a point of view, who has a genius for expressing the prosaic in a magical way. Do not look for pyrotechnics, for someone who can make a big slambang picture book out of very little, but look for the genuinely talented person who thinks originally.[18]

Pinkerton (P) and *Tallyho, Pinkerton* (P). Kellogg's cartoon illustrations fill the pages with a riotous jumble of color and activity. His characters wear mischievous grins and wide-eyed innocent expressions. The illustrator is at his best, however, with delightfully scary monsters. *The Mysterious Tadpole* (P) grows from a tiny fish into a huge creature that fills the town swimming pool. *The Island of the Skog* (P) is actually home to a tiny furry creature who constructs a giant disguise to frighten invading mice. In *Ralph's Secret Weapon* (P), a monstrous sea serpent threatens the Navy until a small boy tosses his Aunt Georgina's special banana

TEACHING IDEA

GIANTS (P) After reading several stories about giants, have students compile a list of descriptive words. Encourage them to go beyond "big," "huge," and "scary."

Have one child stand on a table or bookcase while the rest of the boys and girls sit on the floor. Discuss the perspective from each point of view.

Have children work in pairs or small groups to build a huge paper giant. The head, arms, hands, torso, legs, and feet can each be made with separate pieces of craft paper, then the parts can be combined and attached to a classroom wall.

The following books (all P) build upon this theme:

De la Mare, *Molly Whuppie*
dePaola, *Fin M'Coul: The Giant of Knockmany Hill*
dePaola, *The Mysterious Giant of Barletta*
De Regniers, *Jack and the Beanstalk*
Fritz, *The Good Giants and the Bad Pukwudgies*

Jacobs, *Jack and the Beanstalk*
Lobel, *Giant John*
Odor, *Learning About Giants*
Yolen, *The Giants' Farm*

spinach cream cake overboard. Steven Kellogg tells wonderful stories that stretch the imagination and bring great bursts of laughter from children.

Dr. Seuss created a number of very funny characters and made them most memorable with his exaggerated cartoon illustrations. Who can forget poor Horton, the elephant who sat and sat atop a tree in *Horton Hatches the Egg* (P) or *Yertle the Turtle* (P), *The Lorax* (P), and *Thidwick the Big-Hearted Moose* (P)? These and the infamous *The Cat in the Hat* series (N-P) have endeared themselves to generations of children.

TEACHING IDEA:

WHAT'S SO FUNNY? (P-I) When you work with children you soon realize that their humor is sometimes difficult to comprehend. They laugh at jokes you would rather not even hear, while they stare blankly at something you find extremely funny. To help children identify some of the qualities that make a story laughable, discuss the elements of humor and have students categorize the books under the appropriate headings. You could begin with some examples:

Exaggeration: Kahl, *The Duchess Bakes a Cake*
Silliness: Allard, *The Stupids Step Out*
        Galdone, *The Three Sillies*
Language play: Hutchins, *Don't Forget the Bacon*
        Parish, *Amelia Bedelia*

Overstatement: Kent, *The Fat Cat: A Danish Folktale*
Incongruity: Oxenbury, *Pig Tale*
        Rayner, *Mr. and Mrs. Pig's Evening Out*

As society has grown and changed over the centuries, so have families. An interesting contrast in family experiences is Donald Hall's *Ox-Cart Man,* which portrays rural, nineteenth-century New England life, and Shirley

Hughes's *An Evening at Alfie's,* which tells of tribulations in modern life. (*Ox-Cart Man* is illustrated by Barbara Cooney, and *An Evening at Alfie's* is illustrated by Shirley Hughes.)

THE CHILD'S FAMILY WORLD

The home is a child's first school; it has a lasting influence on every child's intellectual, personal, and social development. Family patterns have changed dramatically in the recent past, and as society changes, so too do children's books. Children's lives are affected by divorce, adoption, new babies, working mothers, stepparents, and grandparents. There are books that address each of these.

Donald Hall's *Ox-Cart Man* (P), exquisitely illustrated by Barbara Cooney, recalls a simpler time for the family. The cycle of the changing seasons and the attendant activities bind a New England family to the soil and to each other. In October, the ox-cart man fills his cart with everything he and his family have made or grown during the year and takes it to Portsmouth Market. He sells the shawl his wife made, mittens his daughter knitted, birch brooms made by his son, shingles he split himself, and even his cart and, after kissing him goodbye on the nose, his ox. The pastoral

scenes evoke the simple beauty of time and place.

In contrast, Shirley Hughes portrays a thoroughly modern family in *An Evening at Alfie's* (N-P). When their parents go out for the evening, a babysitter comes to stay with Alfie and Annie Rose. Chaos reigns when plumbing problems lead to a flooded living room and Alfie must help the babysitter deal with both the dripping ceiling and his crying baby sister. The illustrations, too, provide contrast to the gentle calm of *Ox-Cart Man.* Here bright colors and visual confusion spill from every page as the small British youngster tries to help restore order to his home.

Cynthia Rylant's *The Relatives Came* (P-I) shows the joy and confusion surrounding a family reunion. Stephen Gammell was named a Caldecott Honor recipient for his exuberant illustrations which add warmth and cheerfulness to the book. A crumpled family travels in a clunky car across winding roads and treacherous hills to visit their cousins. The relatives arrive to hugs and kisses, feasting, and crowded makeshift sleeping arrangements, as well as games and quiet sharing. The vivid portrayal of the love in an extended family is heartwarming.

The Best Town in the World (P-I) by Byrd Baylor is a poetic reminiscence of a father's childhood. In his hometown, the berries were always riper, the water tastier, and the summers longer than any place else in the world. People in his town did things the way they wanted to; they even spelled words the way they wanted to spell them. The narrator wonders why more people did not live there if it was the best town in the world, but his father explains that, too: if more people lived there it would not be the best town anymore.

Aunts and uncles are special people who frequently serve as extended family to children. Patricia MacLachlan tells a heartwarming story about an aunt and uncle who care for Emma and Zachary while their parents are away in *Seven Kisses in a Row* (P). The aunt and uncle know absolutely nothing about caring for children, but they learn fast—fast enough to know that they are to give seven kisses for a morning greeting and to recognize feigned illness when the last day arrives and Emma does not want to leave.

Brandenberg and Aliki describe the kind of aunt all children would like in *Aunt Nina and Her Nephews and Nieces* (P) and *Aunt Nina's Visit* (P). In the first book, six lucky nieces and nephews come for a visit to celebrate the cat's birthday. They romp through the house and garden, dress up in old clothes, and explore the dusty attic, but they never see the birthday cat. Just before the mouse-shaped cake is cut, they discover Fluffy the cat hidden beneath a blanket—with six brand new kittens. In *Aunt Nina's Visit*, the nieces and nephews are all together to stage a puppet show. They suddenly realize there will be no audience since they are all in the show. Fortunately, Aunt Nina arrives in time to serve as an appreciative audience, and to distribute six kittens.

Crescent Dragonwagon creates a vivid memory as *Jemima Remembers* (P-I) a very special summer vacation spent with her aunt. Together they reflect upon the sights, smells, and feelings of a time to be remembered and cherished.

Families

Judith Viorst presents life from the viewpoint of the child at the center of a nuclear family. In *Alexander Who Used to Be Rich Last Sunday* (P), Grandma comes to visit and gives a dollar to Alexander, who also appears in *Alexander and the Terrible, Horrible, No Good, Very Bad Day* (P). She also gives a dollar each to Nick and Anthony, who save, invest, and work to make their dollars grow. But Alexander loses and spends his bit by bit. He is fined for saying a word boys are not supposed to say and for kicking things boys are not supposed to kick. He loses a bet that he can "hold his breath 'till 300," flushes three cents down the toilet, and loses five cents down a crack in the porch. He sees the rest of his money disappear at a garage sale where he buys a candle stub, a one-eyed bear, and a deck of cards. He tries to make more money by pulling one of his teeth, checking coin-return slots in public telephones, and returning nonreturnable bottles to the store. Finally, broke, he invites his grandma and grandpa to come back soon. In this book, as in many with traditional families, the action centers on the child's activities, not on family structure.

In Robert McCloskey's *Blueberries for Sal* (N-P), a parallel plot develops as Sal and her mother, berry picking along a hillside, meet a mother bear and her baby who are eating the berries. Little Sal and the little bear wander off, then meet up with each others' mothers, who are "old enough to be shy" of each other. When mothers and children are appropriately sorted, they all go home, "eating blueberries all the way." This classic tale continues to be a favorite with young children.

Julian, a black boy, lively and enchanting, is the narrator in *The Stories Julian Tells* (P-I) and

Techniques of Illustration

In picture books, the illustrations combine to create a visual story that supports and enhances the written story. The storytelling quality of the art sparks the imagination.

The art in picture books uses a wide range of media, techniques, and styles. The medium may be watercolor, oil, ink, pastel, charcoal, tissue, fabric, acetate, or any number of substances. The technique may be painting, etching, carving, air brushing, collage, or many other forms. The technique of the artist's style manipulates the medium and evokes the mood.

The following are some of the most successful uses of techniques in children's books today.

B-1 The unusual medium of stitchery shapes the forms and classic patterns of a Greek myth. (*Song to Demeter* by Cynthia and William Birrer. New York: Lothrop, Lee & Shepard, 1987.)

B-2 The soft tones obtained by the delicate layering of pastels evoke a mood of mystery and a willingness to believe that not all things need to be explained. (*The Polar Express* by Chris Van Allsburg. Boston: Houghton Mifflin, 1985.)

B-3 Using art and craft techniques, Jeannie Baker combines bits of fabric, shell, clay, and twigs to illustrate shoreline discoveries. (*Where the Forest Meets the Sea*. New York: Greenwillow, 1987.)

B-4 Photographs capture color, line, shapes, and textures to illustrate concepts in a book for the very young. (*Dots, Spots, Speckles, and Stripes* by Tana Hoban. New York: Greenwillow, 1987.)

B-5 Luminous watercolors accentuated by pencil and black line portray a child's walk through the jungle. (*Junglewalk* by Nancy Tafuri. New York: Greenwillow, 1988.)

B-6 Beloved Frog and Toad literally hop from the page through the magic of paper engineering in the pop-up book. (*The Frog and Toad Pop-Up Book* by Arnold Lobel. New York: Harper & Row, 1986.)

B-7 Full-color gouache paintings, strong in their simplicity, evoke the security a child feels at bedtime. (*A Week of Lullabies* by Helen Plotz, illus. by Marisabina Russo. New York: Greenwillow, 1988.)

B-8 Cartoonlike narrative frames convey the passage of time by calendar and weather changes as an illustrator works on a book. (*How a Book Is Made* by Aliki. New York: Crowell, 1986.)

B-9 A Japanese artist illustrates a Japanese folktale in a traditional mood using line and wash on textured paper. (*The Crane Wife* retold by Sumiko Yagawa, trans. by Katherine Paterson, and illus. by Suekichi Akaba. New York: Morrow, 1981.)

B-10 Leo Lionni conveys a complex message by using simple collages from torn shapes of colored paper. (*Six Crows*. New York: Knopf, 1988.)

B-11 The craft of plasticene is taken to high art in a collage made from shapes artfully arranged. (*The New Baby Calf* by Edith Newlin Chase and Barbara Reid. New York: Scholastic, 1984.)

B-12 The effective use of oils creates contrasts in light and shadow that reflect the good and evil played out in the struggle between a loving mother and a grotesque witch. (*Heckedy Peg* by Audrey and Don Wood. San Diego: Harcourt Brace Jovanovich, 1987.)

B-13 Strikingly dramatic watercolors evoke a sense of wonder on the cold, silent night that a girl goes with her father to search for an owl. (*Owl Moon* by Jane Yolen, illus. by John Schoenherr. New York: Philomel, 1987.)

More Stories Julian Tells (P-I), both by Ann Cameron. Julian relates the problems created when he and his younger brother Huey eat a pudding made by their father as a surprise for mother. Julian convinces Huey that cats can be ordered from a catalog, and squabbles with him in brotherly fashion. The mild humor seen in everyday life, a wise and patient father, and creative play enrich a child's understanding of families in these longer stories that serve as a bridge to chapter books.

Mothers and fathers, important people in children's lives, are important people in children's books. Both are portrayed as providers or playmates, and friends or taskmasters, who mete out rewards and punishments. Some overpower and protect while others encourage independence, but all show loving concern for the central child character.

How My Parents Learned to Eat (P) by Ina Friedman is told by a small child whose father was an American sailor stationed in Yokohama when he met his Japanese wife. Wanting to impress each other, they both learned to adjust their style of eating, one with a fork and one with chopsticks. The story concludes with both kinds of utensils being used in their home now and their daughter comfortable with both in this sensitive view of an Asian-American family.

Lucille Clifton captures a child's unfounded fears of being discarded in *Amifika* (N-P). Amifika hears his mother preparing for his father's return from years in the Army and planning to get rid of something the father will not miss in the crowded apartment. Amifika worries to himself: "If I don't remember him, how he gon' remember me? . . . I be what Mama get rid of. Like she said, he can't miss what he don't remember. I be the thing they get rid of." Amifika tries to avoid the inevitable by hiding: "If they get rid of me, they have to find me first." He hides in the yard in a space between a tree and a fence, his eyes wet and tired as he lies against the tree feeling forlorn and unloved. He awakens in the strong, loving

When his mother cleans house in preparation for his father's return, Amifika hides because he fears he will be discarded along with other unwanted things. (Illustration by Thomas Di Grazia from *Amifika* by Lucille Clifton.)

arms of his father who covers him with kisses and says, "Wake up, boy. Do you remember me?"

> And all of a sudden the dark warm place came together in Amifika's mind and he jumped in the man's arms and squeezed his arms around the man's neck just like his arms remembered something. "You my own Daddy! My Daddy!" he hollered at the top of his voice and kept hollering as his Daddy held him and danced and danced all around the room.[19]

The warm-hearted family that surrounds Amifika is sensitively portrayed in the chalklike illustrations by Thomas Di Grazia.

The trend today is for both parents to work outside the home. Children are cared for in day-care centers, in after-school programs, by neighbors, or by extended family. An ever-increasing phenomenon is that of children being raised by other children; young people themselves are often responsible for the primary care of their younger brothers and sisters. This affects the children's school work as well as their social and emotional life. A discussion with classmates and with a teacher who may herself be a working mother may have far-reaching positive effects both at school and at home.

Vera Williams tells a story of mutual concern between a child and her mother in *A Chair for My Mother* (P). After a fire destroys their furniture, the two begin saving coins in a big glass jar. The mother puts in the tips from her job as a waitress while the little girl adds her few pennies and nickels until, finally, there is enough money. They take Grandma with them to the furniture store where they find the perfect big, comfortable chair. A single parent appears in this story, but no issue is made of the fact. The bright illustrations include borders containing important elements of the story in this Caldecott Honor book. The same family appears in *Something Special for Me* (P), in which the money jar is filled once more for a present for the child, and also in *Music, Music for Everyone* (P).

Strong bonds of affection and the power of love are shown in a fanciful tale by Rosemary Wells, *Hazel's Amazing Mother* (P). Hazel, a young badger, is accosted by bullies as she strolls with the doll her mother made so lovingly. Just when it appears that the doll will be ruined, her mother magically appears to chase the scoundrels away. The *deus ex machina* resolution pictures metaphorically the strength of a mother's love when a child is in trouble.

Fathers appear in a variety of roles in picture books for young children: as a loving care giver in Molly Bang's *Ten, Nine, Eight* (N-P), as a participant in household chores and child rearing in Jan Ormerod's *Sunshine* (N-P) and *Moonlight* (N-P) (all discussed in chapter 3); and as the major homemaker in *Jam: A True Story* (P) by Margaret Mahy. In *Jam*, Mrs. Castle is an atomic scientist while Mr. Castle stays at home with the three children. Mr. Castle is so efficient that he even has time left over for special projects. When ripe plums fall from the tree, Mr. Castle decides to make jam; he continues making jam until every container in the house is filled to overflowing. The family eats jam throughout the year and, at times, they even use it for glue and caulking. Just when they foresee a respite from their jam diet, they hear the soft plunk of ripe plums falling from the tree—a new crop. Sticky red jam marks appear throughout the book, and delicately drawn pots of jam fill the endpapers.

TEACHING IDEA

CHANGING FAMILIES (P-I)   Read Marge Blaine's *The Terrible Thing That Happened at Our House* illustrated by John C. Wallner (P-I). Mother, "who used to be a real mother and stayed home all the time," goes back to being a science teacher. The father begins to help with the household chores, but that interferes with the fun he used to have with the children. The young narrator finally explodes and tells everyone how she feels. They have a family meeting to discuss the problem and come up with a variety of suggestions that enable them to enjoy being a family again. The illustrations in this book are particularly funny; when chaos reigns in the house the pictures spill all over the page. On a long strip of craft paper have students make a mural of the "terrible things" that happen in their houses as a result of both parents working.

David McPhail tells of a strong father-daughter relationship in two different books and in two different ways. In a fanciful tale, *Emma's Pet* (P), young Emma Bear searches for a soft cuddly pet. Her wide-eyed gray cat will not cooperate, so Emma tries a bug, a mouse, a bird, a frog, a snake, a fish, and a dog. None of them is exactly what she wants, except the dog who belongs to someone else, so it seems she will have no pet. When her resources are exhausted, she finds the biggest, softest, cuddliest thing she can find—her father—who gives her a big bear hug.

In a more realistic book by McPhail, *Farm Morning* (P), a small girl awakens her father and proceeds to help him with the morning chores. His patience is tested as she helps with the milking and squirts milk on the floor. She tries collecting eggs, but drops them, and then echoes the sounds of the sheep and geese while he, slightly bemused, tolerates her ineptness. When at last they go inside for breakfast, he says "What would I do without you?" McPhail's jewel-like watercolor illustrations dominate the pages and convey the bonds of affection between the girl and her father.

Mavis Jukes features children and their stepparents in two stories. In *Like Jake and Me* (P-I), young Alex offers to help his stepfather, Jake, split wood but his offer is refused. Jake is not unkind, but he is intent upon what he is doing. An unexpected bond develops between the two when Alex spots a spider on Jake's clothes. Readers will enjoy the very funny conversation that ensues: Alex describes the spider in vague detail, but Jake thinks he is talking about something else. Finally Alex removes the spider from the terrified Jake and the two begin to appreciate each others' differences.

In *No One Is Going to Nashville* (P-I) Jukes tells of the relationship that develops between a girl and her stepmother. Sonia, who spends weekends with her father and stepmother, finds a dog near the house and calls him Max. Her father says "no dog;" and in a phone call to her mother, she finds that no pets are allowed in their apartment, so Sonia reluctantly agrees to place an ad in the paper. When someone comes to take Max, it is the stepmother who balks at giving the dog away. She puts Max in Sonia's arms and says, "from your Wicked Stepmother and from your father, with love. Discussion closed." The strong emotional message of love and acceptance shines through the understated text.

Children of divorce often feel that they are different from other children; they feel that one parent or the other does not love them, and sometimes they feel responsible for the divorce. Jeannette Caines's *Daddy* (P) shows none of the bitterness surrounding divorce, but only Windy's joy when she sees her father on Saturdays:

> Before Daddy comes to get me
> I get wrinkles in my stomach.
> Sometimes I have wrinkles every night
> and at school, worrying about him.
> Then on Saturday morning
> he rings one short and one long,
> and my wrinkles go away.[20]

Windy's father teases, plays, and romps with her to make each Saturday a joyous time. Paula, her father's new wife, joins in the fun in an openly loving way that avoids the stereotypic portrayal of a stepmother.

Although few books deal with adoption, the ones that do show it in a positive way—the adopted child being much wanted and much loved. In *Abby* (P), for example, Jeannette Caines writes of a child who begs to look at her baby book to see her first words and the names of her first visitors. Abby asks questions about her brother's reaction to her, where she came from (Manhattan), how old she was when they adopted her, and what she was wearing. Her mother discusses her adoption openly and describes her brother's reactions in a realistic way. When Kevin tells Abby that he will share her for show and tell at school, Abby wants to know what he will say about her. Kevin answers "that you're adopted, that we get to keep you forever, and that I gave you my fire engine for your birthday." This openly loving story reassures listeners that adoption is a desirable thing.

Two photo essays, *We Don't Look Like Our Mom and Dad* (P-I) by Harriet Sobol and *Being Adopted* (P-I) by Maxine Rosenberg, depict candidly the problems of adjustment and overriding happiness surrounding multiracial adoption. Loving families acknowledge the concerns but reassure readers of the love and permanence of adoption.

New Baby

Reaction to a new baby in the family is not a new subject in children's books, but authors continue to treat it with ingenuity. A typical plot involves the excitement surrounding the new baby, the gradual disenchantment with this interloper who takes center stage, and eventual acceptance.

Ezra Jack Keats gives a vital spark to the age-old problem in *Peter's Chair* (N-P). Peter feels that his rights and possessions are usurped by the new baby girl: every time he turns around, something that has always been his is turned over to the baby. In a last-ditch effort to keep something, he grabs his favorite chair and runs away to camp on the front step. Surprised to find that he no longer fits in his chair, he finally accepts the role of big brother and even helps his father paint his special chair a bright pink for the new baby sister.

Five-year-old Max narrated the story of his sister's birth to his mother, Kathryn Lasky, in *A Baby for Max* (N-P), and his father, Christopher Knight, took the pictures. The pregnancy, preparation, visits to the doctor, and finally the trip to the hospital are all described, as well as the return home with infant Meribah. Max's reactions to the birth and to his dethronement from being the center of attention are sensi-

Kathryn Lasky's *A Baby for Max* photographically tells the story of 5-year-old Max's preparation for and gradual acceptance of his new baby sister. (Photographs by Christopher Knight.)

tively captured in the text and photographs of this unique family story.

Vicki Holland's photodocumentary *We Are Having a Baby* (N-P) covers the period from before the birth through acceptance of the new baby by a sibling. The young narrator describes events and feelings from her point of view—not always a happy one. A caring father steps in to soothe and reassure her when fears and jealousies overwhelm her. The final photo shows the child holding the baby in her arms with the caption, "He's my brother."

Pat Hutchins, in *The Very Worst Monster* (P), tells a hilarious spoof of the new baby in the monster family. Hazel, big sister, is jealous of the newborn, Billy. Everyone coos at the ugly baby, praises his nastiness, and admires his fangs. Hazel declares each time that she is bad, too, and tries to demonstrate just how evil she can be. When Billy wins the Worst Monster Baby in the World contest after he tried to eat the judge, Hazel attempts to give him away. Her parents are shocked, and call her "the

TEACHING IDEA

MY EXPANDING FAMILY (N-P)   Children often feel tremendous disappointment when a new baby turns out to be a great deal less than what they imagine the parents had promised. Someone to play with? Hogwash! The baby is just a lump that screams, cries, and demands too much attention. It can't even look at a book, as is shown so well in Dorothy Aldis's poem:

LITTLE

I am the sister of him   So every morning I show him
And he is my brother.   My doll and my book;
He is too little for us   But every morning he still is
To talk to each other.   Too little to look.[21]

DOROTHY ALDIS

Teachers of primary grade children will want to keep a collection of "new baby" books in their classrooms. Some of the best include the following:

Alexander, *Nobody Asked Me if I Wanted a Baby Sister* (N-P)
Alexander, *When the New Baby Comes, I'm Moving Out* (N-P)
Ancona, *It's a Baby* (N-P)
Byars, *Go and Hush the Baby* (N-P)
Clifton, *Everett Anderson's Nine Month Long* (N-P)
Cole, *The New Baby at Your House* (N-P)

Greenfield, *She Come Bringing Me that Little Baby Girl* (P)
Hoban, *A Baby Sister for Frances* (P)
Hutchins, *You'll Soon Grow into Them, Titch* (N-P)
Keller, *Too Big!* (N-P)
Rogers, *The New Baby* (N-P)
Walter, *My Mama Needs Me* (N-P)

ACTIVITY: TEACHER TO STUDENT

NEW BABY BOOKS (N-P)   Can you remember when your younger brother or sister was a new baby? What did your parents tell you before the baby was born? What did you think the new baby would be like? Were you right? How did you feel when the new baby came home?

After you discuss your experiences, take a sheet of drawing paper and make a picture of something a new baby does. Write a one- or two-line caption describing your picture. Your teacher can make a book of all the pictures and keep it in the classroom library.

worst monster in the world." To this Hazel smugly replies, "I told you I was."

Brothers and Sisters

Anyone who has a brother or a sister knows that the relationship is a love-hate one: at times fun and wonderful, but at other times awful. Siblings as adversaries and siblings as friends appear frequently in children's books. Judith Viorst, who builds stories upon the boisterous lives of her own sons, captures the humor and hostility in *I'll Fix Anthony* (P). A younger brother brags about how he is going to fix his arrogant big brother, Anthony, who makes life miserable. Even though his mother says that Anthony really loves him, he is more inclined to believe Anthony, who says he stinks. In his fantasizing, Anthony will get German measles, then mumps, and then a virus. And Anthony will lose all races, games, and contests, and will sink to the bottom of the swimming pool; even if he stays afloat he'll go "glug glug." And he'll sit home by the phone while the popular hero storyteller accepts sleep-over invitations. "But right now," he says, "I have to run. . . . When I'm six I'll fix Anthony."

Brothers and sisters are notorious rivals. They bicker, they fight, they tease, they whine, they complain, and they criticize. They hate—and they love. Shel Silverstein captures the feelings of one sibling who offers to sell his sister:

FOR SALE

One sister for sale!
One sister for sale!
One crying and spying young sister for sale!
I'm really not kidding,
So who'll start the bidding?
Do I hear a dollar?
A nickel?
A penny?
Oh, isn't there, isn't there, isn't there any
One kid who will buy this old sister for sale,
This crying and spying young sister for sale?

SHEL SILVERSTEIN[22]

Peter Spier shows the ingenuity of three siblings who are left to their own devices to create entertainment for themselves. *Oh, Were They Ever Happy!* (P) refers to their parents' reaction when they arrive home to see their newly painted house—a rainbow of color from every paint can in the neighborhood. In *Bored! Nothing to Do!* (P) two brothers build an airplane from assorted windows, tools, furniture, and machinery. Both books are nearly wordless; the stories are told through Spier's richly detailed and wildly funny drawings.

Grandparents

Grandparents are alive and well in children's books; they are no longer vague shadows merging with the background. Barbara Williams gives grandmothers a new image in *Kevin's Grandma* (P). A child tells his friend Kevin about his grandmother: she gives him piano lessons, drives a station wagon, belongs to a music club, and leads an active life. But Kevin counters each conventional activity with the offbeat things *his* grandmother does: Kevin's grandmother arm wrestles, drives a motorcycle, studies karate, scuba dives, and climbs mountains. There is no rocking chair and knitting image here—grandmothers are active people.

Tomie dePaola refers to his old-fashioned Italian grandmother in *Watch Out for Chicken Feet in Your Soup* (P). From the moment Joey and his friend arrive at Joey's grandmother's door and hear her welcome "Joey mio bambino! How nice you come to see grandma" through "Zuppa, nice chicken soup," the demonstrative, affectionate grandma prevails. Tomie dePaola says he wrote this book in honor of his Italian grandmother shortly after writing one about his Irish grandmother—*Nana Upstairs and Nana Downstairs* (P), which will be discussed shortly. He jokingly confides, "She came to me in a dream and said, 'A-when you write a book about me?'" With such nice tributes to his forebears, readers are sorry Tomie dePaola has only two grandmothers.

"No one makes cookies like Grandma" said Ma in *The Doorbell Rang* (P) by Pat Hutchins. Ma had just made a batch of cookies herself and as Victoria and Sam divide them up—six each—the doorbell rings and two of their friends enter the kitchen. "That's three each," the children say. The doorbell keeps ringing and more friends keep arriving until there is only one cookie for each child. (There is a little math lesson here in the midst of the fun.) The doorbell rings once more as the children stare longingly at their one cookie. But when Ma opens the door, there stands Grandma with a huge tray of freshly baked cookies. In a cyclical twist of plot, Ma says, "And no one makes cookies like Grandma," as the doorbell rings each time. Bright humorous illustrations add to the hilarity of the story.

The Crack-of-Dawn Walkers (P) by Amy Hest communicates the love and special relationship between a little girl and her grandfather as they walk through the early morning snow to the corner store to get the newspaper. After stops for hot chocolate, hot rolls, and candy, Sadie tries to delay the return home for she knows that next week will be her brother's turn. "For now, Grandfather, we ought to pretend I never have to share you, and that you and I are the only morning walkers." Amy Schwartz conveys the special feelings of love in soft, unpretentious drawings.

Good as New (P) by Barbara Douglass is a heartwarming story of a grandfather's ingenuity in solving a small crisis. When teasing bullies throw Grady's beloved teddy bear in the mud, it seems that the bear will have to be thrown away. Grandfather rescues the treasured bear and, much to Grady's dismay, takes out his knife. After a few snips, the old stuffing is removed and the bear gets a good scrubbing. While the flattened bear hangs on the line to dry—one ear on each side—the two go to town to buy new filling. Soon the old bear is as good as new.

Several books about grandparents deal with the realistic truths of aging and death. Children respond to these stories with strong feeling and sensitive empathy. Many have experienced the illness and death of their own grandparents and can appreciate the warm remembrances that books can recall.

Tomie dePaola tells a touching story of role reversal in *Now One Foot, Now the Other* (P). It was Grandpa Bob who held Bobby's hands when he learned to walk and who told stories and played special games with him. After Bob suffers a stroke, Bobby refuses to believe his parents when they tell him that Bob does not know them or will never get better. At first frightened by the sick old man, Bobby begins

ACTIVITY: TEACHER TO STUDENT

FOR SALE (P-I) After reading "For Sale," letter a large copy of the poem on craft paper and make it the center of a bulletin board. Write your own advertisement for your brother or sister. You may follow the format and create a new poem, or perhaps add a personalized second verse to this one. You might have fun writing an imaginary lost-and-found ad for your brother or sister. For example:

Lost: One brother who always gets into my things and leaves gooey messes all over the house. He always says "Me too" when I'm playing with my friends, and he doesn't get scolded when he does things that I'm not supposed to do. If found, keep him.

to talk to him and to play their old games until one day Bob smiles in recognition. Very slowly over the next few months, Bob recovers until one day we read, "'You. Me. Walk,' said Bob. Bobby knew exactly what Bob wanted to do. Bobby stood in front of Bob and let Bob lean on his shoulders. 'OK, Bob. Now one foot.' Bob moved one foot. 'Now the other foot.' Bob moved the other foot."[23] This story provides a sensitive and loving picture of a difficult family situation.

Helen Griffith tells a similar story in *Georgia Music* (P). A young girl spends the summer with her grandfather on his Georgia farm. Together they work and play, taking special pleasure in the sounds of crickets and grasshoppers whirring and scratching in the leaves. They especially enjoy the evenings when Grandfather plays a harmonica to entertain the creatures who have given them such pleasure during the day. The girl goes home in the fall, looking forward to another summer in Georgia, but Grandfather is not well when she returns. He sits listlessly on the porch while weeds grow around the cabin. The girl and her mother take him home with them, but he has little interest in the things around him. One day the girl picks up his harmonica and, as the days go by, she learns to re-create the sounds she heard on the Georgia farm. The sparkle returns to the old man's eyes as he listens to the sounds of

his home. Stevenson's water colors enrich the heartwarming story.

Tomie dePaola recalls a boy's loving reminiscence of two special people he visited each Sunday. Tommy's grandmother always seemed to be standing by the big black stove in the kitchen, while his great-grandmother was always in bed upstairs, and so he called them *Nana Upstairs and Nana Downstairs* (P). He loved to visit his 94-year-old great-grandmother while they ate candy and told each other stories. One day his mother told him that Nana Upstairs had died and that she would not be there anymore. When he saw a falling star a few nights later, his mother said that perhaps it was a kiss from Nana Upstairs. "A long time later," the story continues, "when Tommy had grown up, Nana Downstairs was old and in bed just like Nana Upstairs. Then she died too. And one night, when he looked out his bedroom window, Tommy saw another star fall gently through the sky. 'Now you are both Nana Upstairs,' he thought."[24]

Blackberries in the Dark (P-I) by Mavis Jukes is perhaps one of the most touching and heartrending stories of all. Austin goes to his grandparents' farm for his first visit since his grandfather's death. He and his grandmother grieve together as it seems everything they touch brings aching memories. Seeing the dusty photographs of himself stapled over the work-

TEACHING IDEA

REMEMBERING (P-I)   In several outstanding stories, grandparents reminisce about their own childhood. After sharing some of these tales, ask children to interview their own grandparents or older relatives so that they can begin their own family histories.

Cohen, *Gooseberries to Oranges* (P-I)
Harvey, *Immigrant Girl: Becky of Eldridge Street* (P-I)
Laurence, *The Olden Days Coat* (P-I)

Levinson, *I Go with My Family to Grandma's* (P)
Levinson, *Watch the Stars Come Out* (P)

bench is an especially wrenching time for Austin, and his grandmother comforts him as they cling to each other in shared grief. When Austin goes to pick blackberries that grow near the creek, he longs for the times his grandfather took him fishing. Suddenly he hears a crashing noise and looks up to see Grandma clambering through the bushes, clad in Grandpa's old fishing gear. Together they recall bits of Grandpa's advice and share their first attempt at fly fishing. When they return home, a new level of sharing begins—a time when the past is treasured as a jewel that will brighten the days ahead.

Charlotte Zolotow's *My Grandson Lew* (P) is based on a child's memory of a close relationship with his grandfather. Lew awakens one night to talk with his mother about his grandfather, recalling pleasant things they had done together. Lew remembers visits, being carried through a museum, and his grandfather's scratchy whiskers. Lew's mother tells him that his grandfather has died—she had not told him before because she thought he did not remember him. Lew and his mother share their memories and talk about how much they miss him. "But now we will remember him together and neither of us will be so lonely as we would be if we had to remember him alone."

Several books portray a relationship between a child and an older person, not always a grandparent. Sometimes these relationships start tenuously, as in Cynthia Rylant's *Miss Maggie* (P); others are well-established, as in *I Know a Lady* (P) by Charlotte Zolotow. Miss Maggie is an aging recluse who lives across the field from Nat and his grandmother. Occasionally he takes her a jug of buttermilk or a kettle of beans, but not without checking first to see if she really has a black snake hanging from the rafters as some folks say. One snowy day Nat realizes there is no smoke coming from Miss Maggie's chimney and knows that something must be wrong. He cautiously enters the house only to find the old woman sitting on the floor

Mavis Jukes's *Blackberries in the Dark* is a sensitive story of how a boy and his grandmother grieve for and finally accept the death of his grandfather. (Illustrated by Thomas B. Allen.)

in her freezing kitchen, grieving for her dead pet starling, Henry. Nat persuades her to go with him to his own home where she is cared for kindly. In a satisfying ending, Nat gives Miss Maggie a small black snake named Henry which shows that acceptance and love have sealed the friendship between the two. The quiet dignity of Di Grazia's subdued illustrations match the gentle tone of the story.

Zolotow tells of the ongoing friendship between Sally and her neighbor in *I Know a Lady*. Sally describes a kindly woman who shares daffodils from her garden in the spring, zinnias

ACTIVITY: TEACHER TO STUDENT

Mother's Mother   Mother's Father   Father's Mother   Father's Father

Mother   Father

Brother   YOU   Sister

PLANT YOUR FAMILY TREE (P-I) Fill in names in the blanks to make your family tree.

Now fill in the missing words:

1. Your mother's parents and your father's parents are your _____.
2. Your parents' brothers and sisters are your _____ and _____.
3. If your aunts and uncles have children, they are your _____.
4. Your parents' other children are your _____ and _____.

TEACHING IDEA

QUILTS TELL STORIES (P) Quilts are often made from scraps of cloth taken from clothing worn long ago. Bits of family history are reflected in the shapes and patterns stiched into the design. Read the following stories (all P):

Coerr, *The Josefina Story Quilt*   Johnston, *The Quilt Story*
Fair, *The Bedspread*   Jonas, *The Quilt*
Flournoy, *The Patchwork Quilt*   Roth and Phang, *Patchwork Tales*

Have children design quilt squares with patterns that tell something about themselves: families, interests, pets, hobbies, and favorite things.

in the summer, and chrysanthemums in the fall. She gives the children candy apples at Halloween, cookies at Christmas, and cakes at Easter. Sally wonders what the old lady was like as a child and if she had a special friend, and then vows that when she is old, she too will be nice to children. James Stevenson portrays the elderly lady with just the right touch of dignity and grace. His scratchy lines and watercolors enrich a gentle story.

THE CHILD'S SOCIAL WORLD

Social development intersects all other areas of growth; it is both dependent on and necessary to the child's total development. Friendships with others develop slowly and may not really be possible until children develop an identifiable self-concept. Until about the age of 2, children often engage in solitary play even when other children are present. Later, in parallel play, they are aware of other children and may even play alongside them, with the same toys, but remain independently engaged. Recent research suggests that children at this age are socially aware even though there is little interaction between them.

By the time children enter school, they are beginning to interact; it is here that group play is common. Identification with and success in a peer group follows as children slowly begin to sort out special friends from within the group.

Friends

Friendship is a mixture of good and bad times and usually encounters many stumbling blocks. Some young children become notorious as fighters as they try simultaneously to declare their independence as a person and develop relationships with others.

John Steptoe's *Stevie* (P) portrays a friendship between two boys. Stevie stays with Robert's mother while his own mother works. The older boy's resentment toward Stevie is evident from the beginning and it grows as Stevie intrudes upon Robert's possessions and his independence. When Stevie's mother abruptly takes him away, Robert realizes that the relationship had been important. The strong line illustrations heighten the emotional impact of the sensitive story.

Few other books for children about friendship are so solemn; the great majority focus on the humorous foibles of the characters. In *George and Martha* (P) and several subsequent books, James Marshall creates an endearing pair of hippopotamus friends who engage in ridiculously funny antics. Marshall's *Yummers* (P) is a delightful story about Emily Pig and her friend Eugene Turtle. Emily makes resolutions to stop nibbling, and Eugene tries to help by diverting her attention from food. Unfortunately, each diversion is strenuous and produces extreme hunger pangs, so that Emily is forced to eat to recover her strength. Her understanding friend stands by her through all her problems. Their story is continued in *Yummers, Too* (P).

In Marjorie Weinman Sharmat's *I'm Not Oscar's Friend Anymore* (P), the hero, having had a disagreement with Oscar, goes through a recital of all the afflictions Oscar deserves. Eventually, he decides to give Oscar one more chance to apologize and finds that Oscar doesn't even remember the incident that started all the trouble. Children readily identify with the situation and are able to give many examples from their own short-lived disagreements with their friends.

Janice May Udry's *Let's Be Enemies* (P) has become a classic for its understated simplicity. James and John fight over things such as pretzels and crayons, but when the sun comes out the two forget their grievances and go off arm in arm to roller skate. Even young children see the humor as the two small boys exchange barbs and complaints.

Alfie Gives a Hand (N-P) by Shirley Hughes is one of a number of excellent books about small Alfie. In this one, Alfie goes to a birthday party for one of his nursery school classmates. This is Alfie's first party without his parents and so he takes his security blanket along and keeps it close to his side, even though it gets a bit "mixed up with the Jell-O and potato chips, and covered in sticky crumbs." Bernard, the host, becomes so rambunctious that he frightens a small shy girl and Alfie bravely stashes aside his blanket and takes the little girl's hand to join in a joyful game of Ring Around a Rosy. The initial act of friendship—reaching out to another in need—makes Alfie stronger; he

"I came to tell you that I'm not your friend any more."

"Well then, I'm not *your* friend either."

Two small boys argue over petty things, but when the sun comes out they forget their disagreements and enjoy their friendship once again in *Let's Be Enemies* by Janice May Udry. (Illustrated by Maurice Sendak.)

decides that the next time he may leave his blanket at home, after all.

Elizabeth Winthrop explores friendship and the conflicts from jealousy and possessiveness in *Katharine's Doll* (P). Molly is Katharine's best friend, so when Katharine receives a beautiful doll from her grandmother, they both play with it day after day. One day, Katharine questions Molly about who she came to play with—her or the doll. This breach separates the two girls and terminates the friendship. As Katharine plays alone with her doll, she comes to realize that a doll cannot play "Chopsticks," turn cartwheels, or—most important—be a best friend. Lee Bennett Hopkins's collection of poems, *Best Friends* (P), can enrich the exploration of a friendship theme.

A few books focus on a friendship with a disabled person. For example, Lucille Clifton has Sam tell about *My Friend Jacob* (P), a men-

tally retarded teenager. Sam learns many things from Jacob, and he helps his friend remember things. Remembering is difficult for Jacob, but he is very good at basketball. Jacob always makes a basket on the first try. Jacob also knows the names of every kind of car that goes by. The two friends celebrate their birthdays together: Sam's cake has 8 candles and Jacob's has 17. Sam teaches Jacob how to knock at a door rather than walk right in or stand until someone notices him. Lucille Clifton says she wrote this book because she has a young friend like Jacob who, "like all people, are a bit short on one side and quite tall on others" and who want to be treated the same as everyone else.

George Ancona took the outstanding photographs for Maxine Rosenberg's photodocumentary *My Friend Leslie: The Story of a Handicapped Child* (P-I). A true story about a real child, this book emphasizes what Leslie *can* do rather than what she cannot. Although Leslie has multiple disabilities, she leads a full life.

School

Going to school expands the child's social world, and the excitement of first days at school is recreated in many children's books. Children's questions—Will I have a friend? Who is my teacher? What will I do?—appear as titles and subjects of favorite picture books. Children have pictures of the world different from the ones adults have; ingenious authors present the world as a child might see it.

Miriam Cohen has written a wonderful series of books that feature a multiethnic first grade classroom. Young readers will look forward to the adventures of Jim, Paul, Annamarie, and the others in *Starring First Grade, Lost in the Museum, When Will I Read?, First Grade Takes a Test, No Good in Art* (all P), and several others. In *Liar, Liar, Pants on Fire!* (P), a new boy tries to impress his classmates by exaggerating his abilities. An understanding teacher helps the others understand Alex's

She is busy drawing a fire truck she saw on her way to school.

Willaby draws a fire truck she saw on the way to school when she is supposed to be writing a get-well card to her teacher. (From *Willaby* by Rachel Isadora.)

need for acceptance and together they welcome him into their school.

A slender text and magnificent drawings convey a child's love for her teacher and for drawing in *Willaby* (P) by Rachel Isadora. Panoramic scenes of the classroom show all the other children writing, but Willaby is drawing; others are playing, but Willaby is drawing. When Miss Finney, her teacher, is absent, the substitute has the children write get-well notes to her, but Willaby is so engrossed in drawing a picture of a firetruck that she forgets to write a note. When the substitute collects the notes, Willaby hurriedly stuffs the unsigned firetruck picture into the packet. She worries throughout the weekend that Miss Finney will not know she sent her a card. When Willaby reluctantly arrives at school, however, a note on her desk assures her that Miss Finney did indeed recognize her mark of distinction—her drawing.

Isadora's art carries so much of the story line and characterization that the story would be greatly diminished without it. Touches of pink make Willaby and her work stand out in the otherwise monochromatic charcoal scenes.

Subtle humor, as when Willaby wears decorated rain boots while everyone else has plain ones, pervades the appealing illustrations.

Patricia Reilly Giff, a former reading teacher, has written several books about Ronald Morgan, a bumbling and lovable child who typifies many she worked with in her own classrooms. In *Today Was a Terrible Day* (P), everything goes wrong for Ronald: he forgets to have his mother sign his homework, he cannot do his workbook page, he is caught squirting water and he messes up in reading group—the dumb group. He ends the day by knocking over the plants, which he had forgotten to water. When his teacher, irritated with him, hands him a note, he is sure he is in big trouble. But the note says, "Dear Ronald, I'm sorry you had a sad day. Tomorrow will be a happy day because it's my birthday. You and I will make it happy. Love, Miss Tyler."[25] Not only is she not mad at him, but Ronald reads the whole note by himself! And just for good measure, he takes her a new plant for her birthday. In *The Almost Awful Play* (P), Ronald plays the role of a cat, and despite numerous mishaps during the weeks of preparation, saves the day in the big performance when part of the scenery collapses. Ronald gets new glasses in *Watch Out, Ronald Morgan* (P) and celebrates his birthday a day early so he can have a school party in *Happy Birthday, Ronald Morgan* (P).

Next Year I'll Be Special (P), also by Patricia Reilly Giff, is a small child's soliloquy about how wonderful school will be when she goes to second grade. Her teacher, who will be beautiful, will ask Marilyn which jobs she prefers and will immediately advance her to the top reading group. And, best of all, there will be no homework; they can read library books instead! Her friends will vie for her attention and she will receive Valentines from all of them. It is obvious that first grade is not quite so good.

Children starting school for the first time have a natural fear of the unknown. Piet Rabbit worries about big kids and bullies, friends, his new teacher, and what he will be expected to know in Robert Quackenbush's *First Grade Jitters* (P). He wonders if any of his friends from kindergarten will be in his class, if he will be expected to read, spell, and do arithmetic, and he even worries that he will not understand what the teacher says. Of course, when school begins he finds that his fears were unwarranted, but children will know that they were very real at the time.

Rosemary Wells touches on acceptance and making friends in *Timothy Goes to School* (P). His mother made him a brand-new sunsuit for the first day of school, but his friend Claude says, "Nobody wears a sunsuit on the first day of school." The next day Timothy wears a new jacket, but Claude says " You're not supposed to wear party clothes on the second day of school." Claude not only passes judgment on everything Timothy wears, he also shines at school work and plays the saxophone. When Timothy overhears Violet complaining about Grace, who is just as opinionated as Claude, he and Violet strike up a friendship based on acceptance rather than competition.

Harry Allard's *Miss Nelson Is Missing* (P-I) tells about one teacher's solution to a disruptive class. The children throw spitballs and paper airplanes, whisper, giggle, and do not do their work. Miss Nelson says that something will have to be done about the situation, and the next morning a stern substitute, Miss Viola Swamp, arrives. Miss Swamp loads the children with work, forbids all foolishness, and makes them toe the line so firmly that they long for their sweet and loving Miss Nelson. The children promise to reform when they realize that the mean, crotchety teacher is really Miss Nelson in disguise. Miss Nelson appears again in *Miss Nelson Is Back* (P) and *Miss Nelson Has a Field Day* (P). These books have become standard fare for teachers who need to give a little positive reinforcement at times.

THE CHILD'S NATURAL WORLD

Children learn about nature as they explore their ever-widening worlds. Firsthand experiences are primary, of course, but books can deepen and extend children's awareness of the natural world.

Nature

Books can draw attention to nature in sensitive and thoughtful ways; many do not tell a story as much as establish a mood or celebrate natural beauty. Barbara Cooney's *Miss Rumphius* (P-I) is one of the most beautiful books published in recent years. It is the life story of Alice Rumphius, who helped in her grandfather's workshop where he carved figureheads and painted pictures of sailing ships. Alice helped her grandfather paint the blue skies and told him all of the things she would do when she grew up. "That is all very well, little Alice," said her grandfather, "but there is a third thing you must do." When Alice asked what that was, he said, "You must do something to make the world more beautiful." Miss Rumphius did all the things she planned in her life, and as she grew older, found that she could fulfill her promise to her grandfather by planting lupine seeds along the stony coast where she lived. The challenge is passed on to the narrator of the story, Miss Rumphius's niece, and then on to readers who can write about what they will do to make the world more beautiful.

Byrd Baylor and Peter Parnall combine their talents in several picture books that explore the close relationship between people and their land. *The Desert Is Theirs* (P-I) speaks quietly in text and eloquently in illustration about the harmony of birds, insects, animals, and men—"Desert People who call the earth their mother."

Another book about life in the desert by Baylor and Parnall is *I'm in Charge of Celebrations*

(P), a young girl's soliloquy of some of the special events in her life. Although insignificant to others, each happening is cause for joy to the desert child. Dust Devil Day, Coyote Day, and Triple Rainbow Day—108 in all (besides the ones they close school for) are all cause for celebration.

Uri Shulevitz conveys images evoked by an ancient Chinese poem with breathtaking simplicity in *Dawn* (P). Here, an old man and his grandson awaken at the edge of a lake as the day slowly gathers light. The miracle of dawn breaks over the lake, and the sun suddenly bursts forth over a mountain that stands guard over the water. The poetic text relates how the lake shivers and how vapors slowly and lazily begin to rise. It is when the two row to the center of the lake that the startling light spreads over their world in a vivid moment of dawn.

Peter Spier's wordless book *Rain* (N-P) is a glorious celebration of a summer thunder shower. On the very first page, a dark cloud appears in the corner of the sky as two children play in their sandbox, unaware of the approaching storm. When the first raindrops fall, they run inside for raincoats and an umbrella, then go back outside to revel in the delicious wet world. Children will pore over the many detailed drawings and delight in their discovery of sparkling spider webs, drooping flowers, splashy puddles, overflowing downspouts, sheltered birds, and swimming ducks.

Another book by Spier, *Dreams* (P), conveys through pictures the wondrous images two imaginative children find in the sky. White puffy clouds become dragons and demons, ships and planes on a lazy summer afternoon. In a similar story, Brinton Turkle's *The Sky Dog* (P), a child lies on the sand watching the fluffy white clouds. One resembles a dog, and when a stray dog appears on the beach, the boy is convinced that the "sky dog" has come to him.

A related informational book by Tomie dePaola laces fact wth humor. *The Cloud Book* (P) introduces common cloud forms and accurate weather information within a slight story frame.

Seasons

Young children's sense of time is marked by events more than hours, and their understanding of seasons hinges on observation of falling leaves, snow, spring flowers, or holidays. When we talk with children about spring, summer, fall, and winter, they gradually relate their experiences to the labels we use.

Charlotte Zolotow celebrates the wonders of nature throughout the year in a very simple text illustrated by Nancy Tafuri in *The Song* (N-P), while Alice and Martin Provensen create a panorama of nature's bounty in *The Year at Maple Hill Farm* (N-P). Heidi Goennel describes the things young children like to do during the different *Seasons* (N-P). Bold, colorful illustrations appear three-dimensional in this book for beginning readers.

John Burningham's *Seasons* (P), an unusually beautiful treatment of the four seasons, gives added meaning to abstract words. Summer seems to shine from the pages in vivid contrast to the stark coldness of the winter scenes. Aileen Fisher's *I Like Weather* (P), a lilting story poem, extols the glories of the many faces of nature—"with different kinds of smells and sounds and looks and feels and ways." Such poems and picture books supply images that can help children conceptualize intangible experiences.

The first snow of a season is an occasion that never fails to excite children with its endless possibilities for creative play. In Ezra Jack Keats's *The Snowy Day* (N-P), Peter crunches through the snow, making intriguing patterns of tracks with his feet. He uses a stick to make a new design and then smacks the stick against a snow-covered tree to plop snow on his head. Readers certainly understand Peter's

TEACHING IDEA

LET IT SNOW! (P)   There are many books and poems that extol the virtues of snow. With some of these titles as models, children can be encouraged to write their own stories and verse:

Briggs, *The Snowman* (N-P)
Burton, *Katy and the Big Snow* (N-P)
Craft, *The Winter Bear* (P)
Delton, *A Walk on a Snowy Night* (P)
Gundersheimer, *Happy Winter* (N-P)
Hader and Hader, *The Big Snow* (P)
Keats, *The Snowy Day* (N-P)
Martin, *Island Winter* (P)
McCully, *First Snow* (P)
Radin, *A Winter Place* (P)
Tresselt, *White Snow, Bright Snow* (P)

The scene in which Peter knocks snow from a tree, in Ezra Jack Keats's *The Snowy Day*, is given a third dimension in this diorama of the event.

ACTIVITY: TEACHER TO STUDENT

SNOWMEN (P)   Create a snow scene in a diorama made from a cardboard carton or a shoe box. Used crumpled newspapers to form hills and valleys, an aluminum pie tin to hold a pond or puddle, and sticks and twigs to form trees. Cover everything with cotton batting, cotton balls, or a fluffy mixture made with whipped soap flakes to resemble snow. Ivory flakes, or a similar soap product, mixed with just a little water turns to a fluffy paste when beaten with a mixer. Add small figures to your diorama to make the scene realistic. Find (or make from clay) little dolls and animals that look like the characters in winter stories. Make background scenes on the walls of the diorama and display it with the books.

disappointment when he discovers that the snowball he saves in his pocket melts inside the warm house.

Raymond Briggs's *The Snowman* (N-P), a beautiful wordless book with soft pastel illus-trations, blends fantasy and reality. A small boy carefully builds a snowman, which comes to life in the magic of the night and his dreams. The two explore the gadgetry of the house before they go off on a marvelous flight, to return only as the warming sun appears on the horizon.

Lucille Clifton describes a child at a beginning level of understanding of seasons in *The Boy Who Didn't Believe in Spring* (P). King Shabazz has never seen spring and scoffs when his mother talks about crops coming up. Determined to find the mysterious thing, he and his friend begin to search their urban neighborhood looking for spring. In a vacant lot strewn with debris and an old abandoned car, they find a yellow crocus and a bird's nest holding four small, blue eggs. Finally, spring has become a meaningful concept for them.

Mud is another exciting phenomenon of nature—to children if not to their parents. Polly Chase Boyden's poem "Mud," which begins, "Mud is very nice to feel all squishy-squash between the toes!" is fun to read after the first heavy spring rain.[26] Charlotte Pomerantz's story *The Piggy in the Puddle* (P) is a rollicking rhyme that vividly details a baby pig's frolic in a mud puddle. When her family fails to persuade her to come out, they give up and join her—"so they all dove way down derry, and were very, very merry" in the middle of the "puddle, muddle puddle."

Animals

Children have a natural curiosity about the creatures in the natural world, from the tiniest bugs to the biggest elephants. They look at things with the intensity of a poet, the way Mary Ann Hoberman looks at insects in her collection of poems, *Bugs* (P-I). Each poem focuses on some special characteristic—for example, the sound of the beetle in "Click Beetle, Clack Beetle." The poems, a pleasure in themselves, cause us to examine carefully the creepy crawlers of the earth. Aileen Fisher's *When It Comes to Bugs* (P) presents a humorous look at the world of insects, often from the point of view of the creatures themselves.

Aileen Fisher, honored by the National Council of Teachers of English for her significant contribution to poetry for children, combines poetic vision with a true regard for nature. Her profound sense of wonder underlies the many story poems she writes for children, in which they see the natural world through her words. It is difficult to choose a favorite from the wealth she gives us, but *Listen, Rabbit* (P-I), from which the following verse is taken, stands out as one of the best:

> My heart went thump!
> And do you know why?
> 'Cause I hoped that maybe
> as time went by
> the rabbit and I
> (if he felt like me)
> could have each other
> for company.[27]

The young boy who watches the rabbit from a distance through an entire year yearns for companionship but understands the need for wild creatures to remain free. Each of Fisher's poems stresses communion with nature, its balance and integrity. Aileen Fisher collected 21 of her poems in *Rabbits, Rabbits* (P). This poem, "Early Spring," begins the book: "Rabbit,/with those ears you grow/you should be/the first to know/signs of Spring/before they show."[28]

Jim Arnosky's first books for children were informational nature guides, including *Secrets of a Wildlife Watcher* (P-I), *Drawing Life in Motion* (P-I), and *Drawing from Nature* (P-I). He then turned to books for younger children, first in *Watching Foxes* (N-P), then *Deer at the Brook* (N-P). Both contain realistic, full-color drawings and very simple text to help children make discoveries about their natural world.

Children who own pets learn something of the role of a parent, caring for the pet's physical needs, disciplining it, and showing it love and affection. Those who tame an animal from the wild often learn that it is better for it to

ACTIVITY: TEACHER TO STUDENT ===

NATURE IN POETRY (P-I) Collect poems, by Aileen Fisher and others, that help us see the wonders of the natural world. Choose your favorites and illustrate them with natural objects, such as pressed leaves, weeds, dried flowers, feathers, and sticks. Make a group booklet or classroom display that features book jackets, copies of the poems, and related art work.

---

return to its natural world. In both cases, children begin to put another's welfare above their own whims. They also learn to respect the creatures of their natural world.

Carol and Donald Carrick convey the pleasure and the pain of owning a dog in *Sleep Out, Lost in the Storm, The Accident, The Foundling, The Washout,* and *Ben and the Porcupine* (all P). Christopher and his dog, Bodger, romp through dramatic seascapes and storm scenes until one sad day Bodger is killed. *The Accident* occurs when Bodger is hit by a truck as he responds to Christopher's call. Christopher's anger, denial, and final acceptance follow a realistic course of grief. Christopher believes that loving another dog would be disloyal to Bodger, but he eventually accepts *The Foundling,* who needs his care. In *The Washout,* Ben—the new dog—and Christopher rescue Christopher's mother. In *Ben and the Porcupine,* Ben gets a snoutful of quills when he gets too close to a porcupine.

The magnificent scenes by Donald Carrick show not only the work of a fine artist but the work of a man who respects and observes nature closely. Children profit from seeing the natural world depicted in these sympathetic portraits as the backdrop for stories of pets.

Often the death of a pet is a child's first encounter with the loss of a loved one. Several books relate this experience and encourage children to express their feelings about their own pets. Miriam Cohen tells about *Jim's Dog Muffins* (P) who has died before the story begins. Jim's grief follows the normal stages be-

fore a happy memory of his dog leads to final acceptance. One day when he is eating pizza with his friend he muses, "Remember how I used to give Muffins the crust?" Jim begins to cry, but his tears are mixed with laughter as the two friends remember the good times they had with Muffins.

Mustard (P-I) by Charlotte Graeber was the family cat even before 8-year-old Alex was born. When the old cat begins to behave erratically, they take him to the veterinarian who confirms that Mustard is growing weak and urges them to keep him quiet and comfortable. One day when Mustard spots a dog, his natural instincts take over; he challenges the bigger animal and suffers a heart attack. Together the family buries their beloved pet under the lilac bush in the back yard. The story is sensitively and realistically told; the family's grief is real but not maudlin. Other books that deal with the death of a pet include *I'll Always Love You* (N-P) by Hans Wilhelm; *The Black Dog Who Went into the Woods* (P) by Edith Thacher Hurd; *Mrs. Huggins and Her Hen, Hannah* (P) by Lydia Dabcovich; and the classic *The Dead Bird* (P) by Margaret Wise Brown.

Lore Segal tells a hilarious spoof about a pet in *The Story of Mrs. Lovewright and Purrless Her Cat* (P-I). Mrs. Lovewright is a lonely widow who decides that she would like a cat to cuddle up at her feet and keep her warm at night. Of course the new pet does none of these things; in fact, he scratches, hisses, takes over the footstool and claims the center of the bed. Eventually the cat reluctantly and grudg-

TEACHING IDEA

PET SHOW (P)   Read Ezra Jack Keats's *Pet Show* (P) and plan an afternoon with students to show off their pets. Make it clear that each one is to be kept under the control of its owner at all times, lest there be dog fights, cat fights, lost turtles, or devoured birds. Encourage children who do not have pets to adopt one for the day—a cricket, cockroach, ant, or ladybug. Be sure to have a ribbon to be awarded for every pet—the smallest, the largest, most unusual, and other categories you and your students will create.

---

ingly allows his head to be scratched but never becomes the gentle companion his owner had envisioned. Animal lovers will understand this story of a pet taming its master. Paul Zelinsky's bright illustrations complement the humorous story.

THE CHILD'S AESTHETIC WORLD

As children's interests broaden, the aesthetic environment—music, dance, literature, and art—can add immeasurably to their overall sense of belonging. It is through literature that many children first encounter the cultural arts. Often the first lullabies ("Rock-a-Bye Baby") and the first games (Pat-a-Cake, This Little Piggy) are traditional songs of antiquity that appear in well-illustrated books. Moreover, through books children can be introduced to great works of art at an early age. Early and continued exposure to the arts lays a firm foundation on which children build an ever-spiraling appreciation for their aesthetic world.

Music

Music is an integral part of an aesthetic life. Almost from the time they hear their first lullaby, young children can hum or follow along with favorite melodies. Every culture is replete with songs of its people; many are illustrated and published in single-edition picture books—that is, a book in which a single rhyme or song is the basis for lavish illustration.

Margot Zemach illustrates some rollicking folk songs in her characteristically earthy and old-fashioned style. *Mommy, Buy Me a China Doll* (N-P) and *Hush Little Baby* (N-P), two cumulative songs, are augmented by Zemach's jovial interpretations. Aliki Brandenberg also illustrates familiar old songs in a charming style. Her rendition of *Hush Little Baby* (N-P) differs from Zemach's in that Aliki's family is more restrained, well-groomed, and younger than the roguish one Zemach portrays. Aliki's full-page scenes, filled with antiques of the period that give rise to the song, contain luxurious details. Similarly, in *Go Tell Aunt Rhody* (N-P), she preserves an image of the sentiment of the period in which the song originated. A patchwork quilt design on the endpapers alludes to an early American farm life setting. Tracey Campbell Pearson's *Old MacDonald Had a Farm* (N-P) is a visual romp through another traditional song.

Many Mother Goose songs appear in single-edition picture books. For example, Janina Domanska illustrated *I Saw a Ship A-Sailing* (N-P) in unique, stylized pictures. Stark lines and vivid colors reflect the movement and rhythm of the song. Susan Jeffers uses pastel shapes contrasted with bold lines to show a young girl's dreamlike vision in *All the Pretty Horses* (N-P). The flowing cadence and pensive mood of the song lulls sleepy heads to pleasant dreams when parents read it at bedtime; read aloud during the school day, it can soothe irritable, tired children.

Peter Spier has created several books for ''The Mother Goose Library,'' in which he illustrated well-loved songs and rhymes. One of them, *London Bridge Is Falling Down* (N-P), shows the famous old bridge amidst the magnificent panorama of its Thames river environs. Spier's precision and detail invite the child to explore new aspects of the song each time the favorite tune is sung. The entire song is repeated with the musical score at the end of the book, along with a history of the bridge.

Several musical compositions are skillfully transcribed into picture book format; as children visualize the scenes and learn the stories, they build a foundation for appreciation of the original musical scores. One of these, Sergei Prokofiev's *Peter and the Wolf* (P-I), a well-loved classic, is illustrated with full-color paintings by Jörg Müller. The menacing wolf and the forest creatures provide a vivid accompaniment to the recording of the music. Beni Montresor uses his experience as a theatrical set designer to create illustrations for several operas. His sets and costumes for Rossini's *Cinderella* (P-I), adapted by Montresor, and Mozart's *The Magic Flute* (P-I), adapted by Stephen Spender, give children the opportunity to visualize the elaborate spectacle of a production of these works. These books, of course, are not substitutes for the actual musical experiences children need. However, using them with recordings provides concrete visual images to strengthen appreciation of the music.

Anita Lobel illustrated two song books. One, written by b. p. Nichols, *Once: a Lullaby* (N-P), is an individual song with a strong repetitive pattern. The other, *Singing Bee* (P-I), is a comprehensive collection of familiar songs compiled by Jane Hart. Jane Yolen edited *The Lullaby Songbook* (N-P), which contains 15 of her favorite lullabies. Charles Mikolaycak's magnificent watercolors draw young eyes to many de-

tails while the ears listen for the sounds of the music.

Vera Williams celebrates the importance of music in our lives in *Something Special for Me* (P) and *Music, Music for Everyone* (P). Rosa, the child who first appeared in *A Chair for My Mother* (P), now helps to save money in the big jar again. In *Something Special for Me,* as the jar slowly fills, Mother says that the money will be spent on a birthday present for Rosa. More importantly, Rosa gets to pick it out. When they go shopping, Rosa tries on roller skates, dresses, and coats. She looks at camping equipment and thinks of sleeping bags and tents. But each time she is nearly ready to decide, she thinks of all the money in the jar and wonders if that item is really what she wants. After a long day she hears an accordion player, and decides that music *is* what she wants. In *Music, Music for Everyone,* Rosa plays her new accordion to help earn more money for the jar.

The Philharmonic Gets Dressed (P-I) by Karla Kuskin is a very funny yet informative look at an unusual topic in children's books. The story line is simple; the members of the New York Philharmonic Orchestra get dressed and go to work. What makes the book so intriguing are Marc Simont's cartoonlike illustrations that show a wide variety of sizes and shapes among the musicians who put on their socks, pants, shirts, and dresses in preparation for their performance.

Dance and Movement

Expressive movement is natural to children; they sway, tap their feet, and bounce, impelled by the pure joy of being. Music, stories, and poems invite movement. Who can sit still while singing the traditional rhymes Humpty Dumpty, Sing a Song of Sixpence, or Ring Around a Rosy?

Four children find delight in a summer night frolic in Janice May Udry's *The Moon Jumpers* (P). The magic of night compels a joyful romp that expresses their feelings and fancies. Elinor Horwitz evokes a similar mood in *When the Sky Is Like Lace* (P). The mystical splendor of a "bimulous" night brings out joy in dance and movement.

The structured movement that is ballet is shown in Jill Krementz's *A Very Young Dancer* (P-I), a photodocumentary biography of a young ballet student chosen to dance the role of Clara in "The Nutcracker." The strenuous work of the dancer is evident, as is the reward of the thrill and excitement of opening night. Through excellent black-and-white photographs, Krementz skillfully tells the story of the ballet within the story of a dancer learning her craft.

Rachel Isadora has written two stories about young ballet dancers. In *My Ballet Class* (N-P), she gives a simple explanation of the different dance steps and class exercises. The central character demonstrates the basic ballet positions as they practice their routines. In *Opening Night* (P), we see makeup, costumes, and the general excitement of the behind-the-scenes drama of a ballet production as a young ballerina appears in her first dance performance. Soft crayon and wash paintings convey the magical atmosphere of stage productions. A fanciful tale of a mouse who becomes a famous ballerina is told in Katharine Holabird's *Angelina Ballerina* (P).

Literature

A love for literature begins early if young children are given pleasurable book experiences. Children who read and are read to develop an intuitive awareness of the kinds of books they like. They also single out favorite characters and recognize similarities in illustrations. If authors and illustrators are talked about as real people, children will seek out other books by their favorites. Knowing books, and knowing about the people who create them, provides a solid beginning for a lifelong love of literature.

The names of some authors and illustrators are synonymous with good children's books; their work outlived the generation for whom it was written and has become classic because of its continued appeal. Children learn to associate a style of writing or illustrating with its creator when they encounter many works by the same person. Beatrix Potter is someone most children know through her miniature books with delicate illustrations of quaint and lovable animals. Although *The Tale of Peter Rabbit* (N-P) is the most famous, the tales of *Benjamin Bunny, Jemima Puddleduck, Mrs. Tiggy Winkle, Tom Kitten, Jeremy Fisher, Squirrel Nutkin* (all N-P), and others written by this shy Englishwoman nearly a century ago still appeal to children today.

Some of the tales of Beatrix Potter have recently been gathered in large editions. Although they are not in the small format that Potter preferred, they do retain her illustrations and her words. Children enjoy having *The Complete Adventures of Peter Rabbit, The Complete Adventures of Tom Kitten,* and *Mrs. Tittlemouse and Other Stories* (all N-P) together in one book.

There are several biographies available for readers who wish to find out more about the author of such special books. *Nothing Is Impossible: The Story of Beatrix Potter* (I), by Dorothy Aldis, is for older children who fondly remember the animal tales. Margaret Lane's *The Tale of Beatrix Potter* (adult) tells of Potter's early life and contains facsimiles of her original manuscripts. Judy Taylor, a children's book editor professionally involved in the world of Beatrix Potter for many years, has written an excellent biography, *Beatrix Potter: Artist, Storyteller and Countrywoman.* It is based on over 800 letters and papers and is filled with photographs, sketches and excerpts from Potter's letters. Taylor also traces the extraordinary publishing history of *The Tale of Peter Rabbit* from its appearance as a picture letter to the reoriginated editions in *That Naughty Rabbit: Beatrix Potter and Peter Rabbit. Beatrix Potter* and *That Naughty*

Rabbit, both adult books, contain a treasure of information that can be shared with children about an enchanting woman and a remarkable book.

Another English author whom children love is A. A. Milne, creator of *Winnie the Pooh* (I). Milne's books, discussed in detail in other sections of this book, warrant mention here for their classic appeal. Two poetry collections, *When We Were Very Young* (P) and *Now We Are Six* (P), appeal to children in the primary grades, while the subtle humor in *Winnie the Pooh* (I) and *The House at Pooh Corner* (I) makes these collections of stories more suitable for children in the intermediate grades.

Madeline (P), by Ludwig Bemelmans, is a perennial favorite. "In an old house in Paris/ that was covered with vines,/lived twelve little girls/in two straight lines./The smallest one was Madeline." Bemelmans's six books about the sprightly little girl who is a vexation to Miss Clavel were precursors to the non-sexist children's books of today. Madeline is one of the earliest derring-do females; her exploits continue in *Madeline's Rescue, Madeline and the Bad Hat, Madeline and the Gypsies, Madeline in London,* and *Madeline's Christmas* (all P).

A Frenchman, Jean DeBrunhoff, wrote *The Story of Babar* (P) in 1937; the story, concerning the life and mishaps of a lovable elephant family, continues in many books. Several publishers rejected DeBrunhoff's manuscripts about Babar because they were written in the present tense. Eventually published, they quickly became a hit and remain popular with children today, partially because of the sense of immediacy achieved by the use of the present tense. Children feel as if they are observing on-the-spot action in the lives of Babar, his wife Celeste, and their children.

Wanda Gág's *Millions of Cats* (N-P), written in 1928, was the first picture book published in America for children. The delightful rhythmic story of the little old man who brought home "hundreds of cats, thousands of cats, millions and billions and trillions of cats," followed by *Nothing at All* (P) in 1941, continues to be a favorite today.

The Velveteen Rabbit (P-I), written in 1922 by Margery Williams, also remains popular, with its tender story of the relationship between a stuffed animal and a child. The symbolic story concerning the question of what is real can be read on several levels of meaning and holds its rank among the best-loved books.

Art

Children see in their picture books some of the best products of artistic talent they may ever encounter. In fact, one critic claims that picture books are more a form of visual art than they are literature.[29]

Mitsumasa Anno is a superb artist whose talent is evident in *Anno's Journey* (P-I), a magnificent adventure of the imagination. The meticulous watercolor illustrations trace the wanderings of a man through the European countryside, where he meets a fascinating array of people absorbed in their work and play. Anno fills the pages with details and subtly includes many literary and historical figures one can search for amidst the bustling scenes.

John Goodall paints a similarly exquisite picture in *The Story of an English Village* (P-I) and *The Story of a Castle* (P-I). Shown from the same perspective over centuries, the countryside undergoes a gradual differentiation in architecture and life style. The artist skillfully uses half pages (which permit changes to parts of a field of view) to depict the continuous panorama of history; distant castle walls crumble and the interiors are transformed to meet changing needs. Both of these beautiful books are wordless; through their alluring illustrations, they evoke a mood of quiet contemplation. One does not glance casually at them, but pores over them time and again, appreciating the pure joy of discovery.

The art in picture books for children tells a story; it may evoke pensive moods or irrepres-

In *The Church Mice at Bay*, the new rector, here shown on his arrival, is not quite what the parishioners expected. (From *The Church Mice at Bay* by Graham Oakley.)

sible laughter. Graham Oakley achieves a superlative blend of text and pictures in *The Church Mouse* (P), which is one of a series. The church in the English village of Wortlethorpe is home to a large family of mice and their feline companion, Sampson. Each story is a riotous adventure in chaos, in which the extravagant illustrations add comedy to the droll, understated text. For example, in *The Church Mice at Bay* (P) the mice had hoped the vicar's summer replacement would be "a nice quiet young chap." The next page has only two words— "He wasn't"—but a picture that is a panorama of outlandish jumble; a car decorated with flowers, butterflies, and peace doves tears into the driveway leaving scattered pedestrians, shattered milk bottles, an overrun bicyclist, and startled mice in its wake.

The overall effect, the way the illustrations work with the words to tell a story, is of primary concern in picture books. Children are quick to judge and respond intuitively; they either like the pictures or they do not. The style, the medium used, and the images produced combine for an effect that can make a book acceptable or unacceptable to the reader.

As children become discriminating in their tastes, they begin to develop an aesthetic awareness. Understanding how the lines and colors work together to form pictures they like comes gradually to children given a great deal of exposure to art and illustrations of all kinds. As they learn to be sensitive to design and artistic effect, a study of techniques can add to their appreciation.

THE ART IN PICTURE BOOKS

The purpose of a picture book, indeed of any book, is to communicate meaning. Picture books are unique in that they use words and pictures in combination to tell a story; the two work closely together, with neither taking precedence. As with the verbal elements of the story, the individual pictures interrelate, creating a visual story that supports and extends the text. The storytelling quality of the art calls up mental images and sparks imaginative powers. Though one might expect that children do not remember their first books and that the quality of the art is irrelevant, early experiences take deep root, and beauty becomes a memorable part of a child's early experience.

Art in children's picture books involves the entire range of media, techniques, and styles used in art anywhere. The medium—the material used in the production of a work—may be watercolors, oils, acrylics, ink, pencil, charcoal, pastels, tissue paper, acetate sheets, or fabric. The technique might be painting, etching, wood and linoleum cuts, air brush, collage, and many other means. Finally, it is the individual artist's style, determined by the use made of the media, that evokes the mood. Since medium, technique, and style are intricately combined to produce the art, they are best discussed in that way.

Leo and Diane Dillon achieve with an air brush an iridescent quality in their Caldecott award-winning illustrations for Verna Aardema's *Why Mosquitoes Buzz in People's Ears* (P-I).

TEACHING IDEA

THE CREATORS OF PICTURE BOOKS (P-I) Children who repeatedly hear stories and view illustrations by the same artist grow to feel as if they know that person. Teachers and librarians can encourage children to learn about these people by making them the subjects of study.

An author and/or illustrator of the month soon becomes a popular attraction and consistently boosts circulation of the featured person's books. A bulletin board and a table with not only the books but realia associated with them, children's reviews of the books, projects based on books made by children, and photographs of the person draw attention to the creator. Children's favorite authors and illustrators can be featured, as well as others the teacher wants to introduce. Information about authors and illustrators can be obtained directly from their publishers, as well as from several books about authors:

Commire, ed., *Something About the Author* series
Holtze, ed., *The Fifth Book of Junior Authors and Illustrators*
Hopkins, *Books Are by People*
Hopkins, *More Books by More People*

One series presents authors and illustrators discussing their work; *Self-Portrait: Margot Zemach* (P-I) was the first. Others are available by Trina Schart Hyman and Erik Blegvad. In addition, several audiovisual packets present authors and illustrators describing how they work. Steven Kellogg's *The Island of the Skog* (P) is accompanied by a sound filmstrip (Weston Woods) in which Kellogg explains the creation of the book.

Holling Clancy Holling and Marguerite Henry are featured in two sound filmstrips ''The Story of a Book,'' part of the Literature for Children series (Pied Piper). Other companies, including Miller Brody (Random House) Weston Woods, and Spoken Arts, produce various materials in which authors and illustrators are featured.

Have your students write to living authors and illustrators. Letters can be sent to authors or illustrators in care of their publishers. (See Appendix F for addresses.)

Tom Feelings uses wet tissue paper and linseed oil with inks and tempera to obtain the delicate crackled-texture paintings in *Moja Means One* (P) and *Jambo Means Hello* (P).

Many types of illustrations and media can be models for children in creating their own books. Watercolors and pastels are relatively simple to use. Watercolor, a combination of powdered color, gum arabic, and glycerine, has a transparent look. Pastels, essentially soft, colored chalks, produce an opaque image. Peter Spier uses watercolors to compose meticulously detailed and aesthetically pleasing scenes with a touch of nostalgia. The exuberant pages of *Noah's Ark* (N-P) exemplify his art. Careful attention to the hundreds of small de-

ACTIVITY: TEACHER TO STUDENT

LEARN ABOUT YOUR FAVORITE AUTHOR OR ILLUSTRATOR (P-I)   Learn about the people who make your favorite books. Read all of their books, read articles written by or about them, and look at filmstrips and clippings about them.

Write a letter to your favorite authors or illustrators. Be sure to make your letter interesting by talking about their books and by telling them something about yourself. Authors receive many letters, so make yours one they will want to read and answer.

Make a collection of all the works of one person. Feature the person in an exhibit, in a notebook, or in a sales talk to your class.

---

tails Spier puts into his work will reward readers with the fullest delight. Adrienne Adams, Margot Zemach, Robert McCloskey, and William Steig are others who use watercolors imaginatively. Strong and vivid use of pastels is found in Nonny Hogrogian's purple heather and green fields in *Always Room for One More* (P), a Scottish folk song adapted by Sorche Nic Leodhas. Pen-and-ink line with crosshatching add distinction to the illustrations. Hogrogian visualizes the story almost as a shadow play rising out of the mist.

Oils and acrylics are oil- or resin-based combinations of color mixed with turpentine and other thinners and vehicles. These paints are usually opaque, with depth and dimension obtained from layering the colors. Few artists use oils for children's book illustration, although Nonny Hogrogian does in *One Fine Day* (N-P). Gouache and tempera or poster color are water based and usually have a white filler. Gerald McDermott uses gouache and black ink to create vivid, strong, stylized designs in *Arrow to the Sun: A Pueblo Indian Tale* (P-I). Blair Lent uses acrylic paints and gray pen-and-ink drawings in Arlene Mosel's *The Funny Little Woman* (P). The underground action in the story as the funny little woman goes into the world of the wicked *oni* appears in color; the change of seasons and the events occur-

ring at her home are shown in gray line drawings that convey the passage of time.

Woodcuts, linoleum cuts, cardboard cuts, and wood engravings all involve cutting the design into the various materials (areas not to be printed are cut away), applying color to the surface, and pressing this against the paper. Where the final composition is multicolored, separate woodcuts are usually made for each color.

Ed Emberley used woodcuts for the pictures in *Drummer Hoff* (N-P), first drawing the pictures on pine boards, then in conventional woodcut fashion, cutting away all the areas that were not to print. He used only the 3 primary colors, but he created the impression of 13:

> The drawings in *Drummer Hoff* are woodcuts. They were drawn on pine boards, all the white areas were cut away, ink was rolled on the remaining raised areas, and a set of prints was pulled on rice paper. . . . Although only three inks were employed—red, yellow, and blue— we were able to create the impression of thirteen distinct colors. This effect was accomplished by taking advantage of the fact that the inks with which most picture books are printed tend to be transparent. Therefore, by printing one ink over another, or "overprinting," a third color is made.[30]

TEACHING IDEA

THE WORK OF ONE ARTIST (P)   Marcia Brown has won the Caldecott Medal three times. She is an outstanding example of an artist who shapes her talent to meet the demands of the particular book she is illustrating. Her books do not look alike because she uses different media and art styles for each one. Collect several Marcia Brown books and compare the various media and styles she uses. Work with the art teacher to plan art projects in which children explore these various techniques.

The Three Billy Goats Gruff (by Perrault)—crayon and gouache drawings
Once a Mouse—bold and graceful woodcuts
Cinderella (by Perrault)—delicate pen line and colored crayon
Shadow (by Cendrars)—cut-paper figures of people and animals, wood blocks

Brown describes her work for *Shadow:*

> The text was a poem. Black, stark cut-paper figures for people and animals could unify its many episodes and avoid the individualization of character that would limit imagination. I used the deep violet-blue shadows I had seen at dusk in Africa to suggest actual shadows. I cut wood blocks and printed them in white on translucent paper to suggest memories, spirit-images, and ghosts. The round-headed Fang masks suggest that one newborn may be closest to his ancestors. A community consists of the ancestors, the living, and those yet unborn.
>
> When I had completed half the illustrations, I was forced to stop work for a year because of illness. I later worked out the method of blotting to suggest a land scarred by the history locked in its rocks. Fragments of blotted paper were pasted together to build up the landscapes I remembered.[31]

Cardboard cutouts, made from laminated cardboard (usually cut with a razor blade), are used to achieve unusual forms. Examples of this relatively uncommon graphic technique are found in Blair Lent's work for *John Tabor's Ride* (P) and Margaret Hodges's *The Wave* (P). Wood engraving, a form of woodcut in which cuts are made across the grain, generally in hardwood, is used for much finer detail. Lynd Ward used wood engraving for *The Biggest Bear* (P).

Photography has been questioned as an artistic technique by those who say it is more technical skill than art. The work of Tana Hoban in *Look Again* (P-I), however, shows that a combination of the artist's eye and the photographer's skill produces the true works of art found there.

Collage is a technique of cutting or tearing shapes from paper and fabric and arranging them to portray the characters and scenes in a story. Ezra Jack Keats used it so effectively that his work is consistently cited as an outstanding example of the technique. In *The Snowy Day* (N-P), his materials were scraps of wrapping paper, grass cloth, wallpaper, newspaper, and cotton.

When illustrating a picture book, artists make many choices in addition to the media and techniques they use. They must decide

TEACHING IDEA

SO MANY CATS! (P)   Artists see things differently from ordinary people; their visual imaginations are well developed. Collect several books that contain pictures of one animal. Compare them in terms of the nature of the animal or of how they complement the story. The following books feature cats and show a variety of visual interpretations:

Brett, *Annie and the Wild Animals* (P)
Brown, *Dick Whittington and His Cat* (P)
Brown, *Felice* (P)
Bryan, *The Cat's Purr* (P-I)
Carle, *Have You Seen My Cat?* (P)
Cauley, *The Three Little Kittens* (P)
dePaola, *The Kid's Cat Book* (P)
De Regniers, *So Many Cats* (P-I)
De Regniers, *This Big Cat and Other Cats I've Known* (P-I)
Gág, *Millions of Cats* (P)

Galdone, *King of the Cats* (P)
Keats, *Hi, Cat!* (P)
Keats, *Kitten for a Day* (P)
Kent, *The Fat Cat: A Danish Folktale* (P)
Perrault, *Puss in Boots*, illus. Brown (P)
Perrault, *Puss in Boots*, illus. Galdone (P)
Potter, *The Tale of Tom Kitten* (P)
Segal, *The Story of Mrs. Lovewright and Purrless Her Cat* (P)
Seuss, *The Cat in the Hat* (P)
Wolff, *Only the Cat Saw* (P)

Create a display of these books and encourage children to find others.

---

about color, style, and composition in their illustrations. They make choices about line, shape, placement on a page, the use of negative space, and texture. Book illustration is a part of all art; it can be judged as art and, as such, must go beyond the appeal of the literal to visual communication. Illustrations must not only be interesting and appealing but imaginative and dramatic as well.

A beautifully illustrated children's book is a work of art. From the first look at the jacket and the endpapers, it is apparent that a book has been illustrated with skill and care.

Endpapers In *Who's Counting?* (N), Nancy Tafuri places an animal's footprints across the endpapers to intrigue the reader; on the title page, she shows part of the running dog that left them. Nicki Weiss uses a textile-like design of tiny dots of color splashed with many replicas of the green stuffed hippopotamus who plays a major role in *Hank and Oogie* (P). The endpapers in the Grimm Brothers's *The Devil with the Three Golden Hairs* (P) by Nonny Hogrogian have a watermarked-style paper in a frame with a long, slinky tale looped around it.

Title Pages Title pages can be used to establish foreshadowing and set the mood of the story. Don Wood uses both the title page and the copyright page to establish the scene for *The Napping House* (P), *Heckedy Peg* (P), and *King Bidgood's in the Bathtub* (P), all written by Audrey Wood.

Composition Arranging the elements of art and text on a page requires an artist's eye. If the composition is awkward or unbalanced, if there is not enough space to set off the various parts of the picture, or if the illustration does not balance well with text, it detracts from the work. For some examples of graceful balance, look at Peter Parnall's work for Byrd Baylor's books: *Hawk, I'm Your Brother; Desert Voices;* and *The Other Way to Listen* (all P-I).

PROFILE

Leo and Diane Dillon

Working together since the early 1960s, Leo and Diane Dillon have blended their art so that even they do not know where one's contribution stops and the other's starts. The Dillons first met at the Parsons School of Design when they were assigned adjacent seats and had to share a drawing board. Leo was furious because he had hoped to have the drawing board to himself; furthermore, he had always been the best artist in his class and did not like the competition offered by Diane. They speak of their three years in school together at Parsons as a time of fierce competition with each other. Ultimately they decided to work together and to collaborate on everything, including marriage.

For a while, Leo worked as an art director for a magazine and Diane was the only woman artist in an advertising agency. In the early years of their joint career, the Dillons worked together on movie posters, book jackets, and magazine illustrations. Leo speaks of that time:

> It used to be that one of us would do the actual drawing and the other would make comments or draw a change on a tissue overlay. But now one of us can just pass the piece of art to the other, and he or she can erase what's wrong and redraw right on the original. Our egos aren't at stake anymore.[32]

It amazes many people that two artists can work on the same painting the way the

Texture Some illustrations invite touching to see if they are really on a smooth piece of paper. Molly Bang's cut paper shapes in *The Paper Crane* (P) look three dimensional. Garth Williams's rabbits in *The Rabbit's Wedding* (P) look so soft and fluffy that children will want to stroke them. Barbara Cooney achieves a diaphanous fabric texture with a thin wash of color for sunsets and hillsides in Donald Hall's *The Ox-Cart Man* (P).

The Caldecott Medal

Each year since 1938, the Caldecott Medal has been given to the illustrator of the most distinguished picture book for children published in the United States during that year. Named for Randolph Caldecott, the nineteenth-century British illustrator of books for childen, the award assures prestige for the illustrator and guarantees instant sales success. Honor books

Dillons do. Their successful collaboration earned them the Caldecott Medal for an unprecedented two consecutive years, 1976 and 1977. Discussing their work in the 1976 acceptance speech for *Why Mosquitoes Buzz in People's Ears*, by Verna Aardema, they say:

> The color was done in airbrush with frisket, which is a form of stencil. One area is done and then masked out, or covered, and the next area is done. The black areas are painted in last, then glazed with blue or purple. But as for who does what— sometimes even *we* aren't sure. Each illustration is passed back and forth between us several times before it is completed, and since we both work on every piece of art, the finished painting looks as if one artist has done it. Actually, with this method of working, we create a third artist. Together, we are able to create art we would not be able to do individually.[33]

The third artist the Dillons have created has rare talent.

The Dillons were at work on *Ashanti to Zulu*, by Margaret Musgrove, when they received the Caldecott Medal for *Mosquitoes*. In order to represent authentically the many African groups dealt with in the book, they did extensive research. They found that Africa is comprised of many peoples and customs and, in order to portray them accurately, needed pictures of, for example, the special blankets of the Sotho and the embroidered clothing of the Hausa. For every group the jewelry and even the style of hair had meaning. A Lozi barge, the last item, was tracked down by one of the editors at Dial Press. Leo Dillon is the first black artist to be named a Caldecott medalist.

Other books that the Dillons have collaborated on include *The People Could Fly* by Virginia Hamilton, *The Hundred Penny Box* by Sharon Bell Mathis, and *Happy Birthday Grampie, I Love You* by Susan Pearson.

receive almost as much attention. Selected by professionals who are elected by members of the Association for Library Services to Children of the American Library Association, the Caldecott Medal has become the hallmark by which we judge all picture books.

For many years there has been controversy surrounding the Caldecott award. Is the winning book appropriate for children? Do they even like the book? Is it truly distinguished or

did the committee give it to an illustrator who deserved the honor for the aggregate of his or her work? Is it really a picture book or merely an illustrated book?

Recently a new dispute has emerged. Anita Silvey, editor of *The Horn Book Magazine*, asks, "Could Randolph Caldecott Win the Caldecott Medal?" Indeed, the spirit of Caldecott's illustrations, the simple humor, the "liveliness, exuberance, movement, and economy" of his

TEACHING IDEA

THE CALDECOTT MEDAL (P-I)   Read aloud as many of the Caldecott winners as possible. A list of all previous winners and honor books can be found in Appendix A.

The following are some projects you can pursue:

1. Discuss the art medium used in each book: for example, collage, *The Snowy Day* (Ezra Jack Keats, 1962); cut paper, woodblocks, and blotting, *Shadow* (Blaise Cendrars, illus. Marcia Brown, 1982); woodcuts, *Once a Mouse* (Marcia Brown, 1961), *Drummer Hoff* (Barbara Emberley, illus. Ed Emberley, 1967), and *A Story, a Story* (Gail Haley, 1970); watercolor, *Sylvester and the Magic Pebble* (William Steig, 1969); airbrush, *Why Mosquitoes Buzz in People's Ears* (Verna Aardema, illus. Leo and Diane Dillon, 1975); pen and ink line drawings with acrylics, *The Funny Little Woman* (Arlene Mosel, illus. Blair Lent, 1972); oil paintings, *One Fine Day* (Nonny Hogrogian, 1971); gouache and ink, black line preseparations, *Arrow to the Sun: A Pueblo Indian Tale* (Gerald McDermott, 1974).
2. Prepare a bulletin board with book jackets from Caldecott Medal and Honor Books. Make an enlargement of the Caldecott Medal itself.
3. Compare the Honor Books and the Caldecott winner for a specific year to see if your students agree with the choice of the Caldecott Committee.
4. Focus on format and design elements of Caldecotts and Honor books—for instance, endpapers and title pages for *King Bidgood's in the Bathtub* (Audrey Wood, illus. Don Wood, 1985); and borders for *Little Red Riding Hood* (Grimm Brothers, illus. Trina Schart Hyman, 1983) and *A Chair for My Mother* (Vera Williams, 1982).
5. Compare the film version with the book version, such as *Why Mosquitoes Buzz in People's Ears* (Weston Woods.)
6. Have children choose a picture to reproduce from a preselected group of Caldecott winners. Choose the simplest media, such as watercolor, tempera, prints (potato or styrofoam instead of woodcuts), collage, pencil, or pen and ink. Work with the art teacher for this project.
7. Make a wall chart listing several Caldecott titles. Have students write their names beside books they have read.
8. Have a Caldecott mock election of the new picture books published this year. Children nominate and defend their choice for the "Name of the School" Award. Compare the students' choice with the Caldecott Committee choice when the official announcement is made.
9. Compare the illustrations in books by illustrators who have won the Caldecott Medal more than once: Marcia Brown, Chris Van Allsburg, Robert McCloskey, Barbara Cooney, Leo and Diane Dillon, Nonny Hogrogian.

---

drawings are missing in many recent winners of the award named for him.[34] There is masterful technique, elegant decoration, and elaborate embellishment, but do these designs complement the stories they are intended to illustrate? Do they extend the text and work with it to tell a complete story?

In the same magazine, Cynthia Rylant

raises a corresponding issue: Do these artistic masterpieces accompany a story worthy of such art? She takes offense at picture books with "extraordinary illustrations accompanied by depressingly empty language."[35] Rylant, the author of two Caldecott Honor books, decries the trend that allows good pictures to compensate for bad writing.

RECOMMENDED READING

Child's Inner World: Self-Concept

Henkes, Kevin. *All Alone.* New York: Greenwillow, 1981.

Hutchins, Pat. *Happy Birthday, Sam.* New York: Greenwillow, 1978.

Jonas, Ann. *When You Were a Baby.* New York: Greenwillow, 1982.

Kuklin, Susan. *Thinking Big: The Story of a Young Dwarf.* New York: Lothrop, Lee & Shephard, 1986.

Sharmat, Marjorie Weinman. *Twitchell the Wishful.* Illustrated by Janet Stevens. New York: Holiday House, 1981.

Child's Inner World: Fear, Feelings, Bedtime

Brandenberg, Aliki. *Feelings.* New York: Greenwillow, 1984.

Hoban, Russell. *Bedtime for Frances.* Illustrated by Garth Williams. New York: Harper & Row, 1960.

Howe, James. *There's a Monster under My Bed.* Illustrated by David Rose. New York: Atheneum, 1986.

Keller, Holly. *The Sleepy Sheep.* New York: Greenwillow, 1983.

Koide, Jan. *May We Sleep Here Tonight?* Illustrated by Yasuko Koide, New York: Atheneum, McElderry, 1983.

Lesser, Carolyn. *The Goodnight Circle.* Illustrated by Lorinda Bryan Cauley. San Diego: Harcourt Brace Jovanovich, 1984.

Stevenson, James. *We Can't Sleep.* New York: Greenwillow, 1982.

———. *What's under My Bed?* New York: Greenwillow, 1983.

Wells, Rosemary. *Goodnight, Fred.* New York: Dial, 1981.

Child's Inner World: Responsibility

dePaola, Tomie. *Marianna May and Nursey.* New York: Holiday House, 1983.

Hines, Anna Grossnickle. *Don't Worry, I'll Find You.* New York: Dutton, 1986.

Lobel, Anita. *The Straw Maid.* New York: Greenwillow, 1983.

Ness, Evaline. *Sam, Bangs and Moonshine.* New York: Holt, Rinehart & Winston, 1966.

Robins, Joan. *My Brother Will.* Illustrated by Marylin Hafner. New York: Greenwillow, 1986.

Child's Inner World: Imagination

Bodecker, N. M. *Carrot Holes and Frisbee Trees.* New York: Atheneum, McElderry, 1983.

Carrick, Carol. *Patrick's Dinosaurs.* Illustrated by Donald Carrick. New York: Clarion, 1983.

———. *What Happened to Patrick's Dinosaurs?* Illustrated by Donald Carrick. New York: Clarion, 1986.

Drescher, Henrik. *Simon's Book.* New York: Lothrop, Lee & Shephard, 1983.

Hines, Anna Grossnickle. *Bethany for Real.* New York: Greenwillow, 1985.

Mahy, Margaret. *The Dragon of an Ordinary Family.* Illustrated by Helen Oxenbury. New York: Watts, 1969.

Turkle, Brinton. *Do Not Open.* New York: Dutton, 1981.

Van Allsburg, Chris. *Ben's Dream.* Boston: Houghton Mifflin, 1982.

———. *The Wreck of the Zephyr.* Boston: Houghton Mifflin, 1983.

Child's Inner World: Humor

Marshall, James. *George and Martha Back in Town.* Boston: Houghton Mifflin, 1984.

Oakley, Graham. *The Church Mice in Action.* New York: Atheneum, 1983.

Rayner, Mary. *Garth Pig and the Ice Cream Lady.* New York: Atheneum, 1977.

Steig, William. *Doctor De Soto.* New York: Farrar, Straus & Giroux, 1982.

Stevenson, James. *Are We Almost There?* New York: Greenwillow, 1985.

———. *Could Be Worse!* New York: Greenwillow, 1977.

———. *That Dreadful Day.* New York: Greenwillow, 1985.

———. *When I Was Nine.* New York: Greenwillow, 1986.

Child's Inner World: Poetry

Brewton, Sara, and John E. Brewton, eds. *My Tang's Tungled and Other Ridiculous Situations.* Illustrated by Graham Booth. New York: Crowell, 1973.

Hoberman, Mary Ann. *I Like Old Clothes.* Illustrated by Jacqueline Chwast. New York: Knopf, 1976.

Holman, Felice. *The Song in My Head.* Illustrated by Jim Spanfeller. New York: Scribner's 1985.

Hopkins, Lee Bennett, comp. *By Myself.* Illustrated by Glo Coalson. New York: Crowell, 1980.

————, ed. *Me! A Book of Poems*. Illustrated by Talivaldis Stubis. New York: Seabury, 1970.

Kuskin, Karla. *Herbert Hated Being Small*. Boston: Houghton Mifflin, 1979.

Milne, A. A. *Now We Are Six*. Illustrated by Ernest H. Shepard. New York: Dutton, 1927.

Prelutsky, Jack. *The New Kid on the Block*. Illustrated by James Stevenson. New York: Greenwillow, 1984.

Russo, Susan. *The Moon's the North Wind's Cooky*. New York: Lothrop, Lee & Shepard, 1979.

Wallace, Daisy, ed. *Giant Poems*. New York: Holiday House, 1979.

Worth, Valerie. *All the Small Poems*. Illustrated by Natalie Babbitt. New York: Farrar, Straus & Giroux, 1987.

Child's Family World: Parents

Bunting, Eve. *The Mother's Day Mice*. Illustrated by Jan Brett. New York: Clarion, 1986.

Clifton, Lucille. *Amifika*. Illustrated by Thomas DiGrazia. New York: Dutton, 1977.

————. *Everett Anderson's Goodbye*. Illustrated by Ann Grifalconi. New York: H. Holt & Co., 1983.

Flack, Marjorie. *Ask Mr. Bear*. New York: Macmillan, 1932.

MacLachlan, Patricia. *Mama One, Mama Two*. Illustrated by Ruth Bornstein. New York: Harper & Row, 1982.

Schwartz, Amy. *Bea and Mr. Jones*. New York: Bradbury, 1982.

Scott, Ann Herbert. *Sam*. Illustrated by Symeon Shimin. New York: McGraw-Hill, 1967.

Thaler, Mike. *Owly*. Illustrated by David Wiesner. New York: Harper & Row, 1982.

Child's Family World: Family

Tompert, Ann. *Little Fox Goes to the End of the World*. New York: Crown, 1976.

Zolotow, Charlotte. *If You Listen*.

Illustrated by Marc Simont. New York: Harper & Row, 1980.

————. *Mr. Rabbit and the Lovely Present*. Illustrated by Maurice Sendak. New York: Harper & Row, 1962.

Child's Family World: Divorce

Dragonwagon, Crescent. *Always, Always*. Illustrated by Arieh Zeldich. New York: Macmillan, 1984.

Helmering, Doris Wild. *I Have Two Families*. Illustrated by Heidi Palmer. Nashville: Abingdon, 1981.

Lexau, Joan M. *Emily and the Klunky Baby and the Next-Door Dog*. Illustrated by Martha Alexander. New York: Dial, 1972.

Paris, Lena. *Mom Is Single*. Illustrated by Mark Christianson. Chicago: Children's Press, 1980.

Schuchman, Joan. *Two Places to Sleep*. Illustrated by Jim LaMarche. Minneapolis: Carolrhoda, 1979.

Sharmat, Marjorie Weinman. *Sometimes Mama and Papa Fight*. Illustrated by Kay Charao. New York: Harper & Row, 1980.

Child's Family World: New Baby

Burningham, John. *Avocado Baby*. New York: Crowell, 1982.

Edelman, Elaine. *I Love My Baby Sister (Most of the Time)*. Illustrated by Wendy Watson. New York: Lothrop, Lee & Shephard, 1984.

Galbraith, Kathryn Osebold. *Katie Did!* New York: Atheneum, 1982.

Jarrell, Mary. *The Knee Baby*. Illustrated by Symeon Shimin. New York: Farrar, Straus & Giroux, 1973.

Stevenson, James. *Worse Than Willy!* New York: Greenwillow, 1984.

Weiss, Nicki. *Chuckie*. New York: Greenwillow, 1982.

Wells, Rosemary. *Noisy Nora*. New York: Dial, 1973.

Child's Family World: Siblings

Clifton, Lucille. *My Brother Fine with Me*. Illustrated by Moneta Barnett. New York: Holt, Rinehart & Winston, 1975.

Hazen, Barbara Shook. *Why Couldn't I Be an Only Kid Like You, Wigger*. Illustrated by Leigh Grant. New York: Atheneum, 1975.

McPhail, David. *Sisters*. San Diego: Harcourt Brace Jovanovich, 1984.

Margolis, Richard J. *Secrets of a Small Brother*. Illustrated by Donald Carrick. New York: Macmillan, 1984.

Peterson, Jeanne Whitehouse. *I Have a Sister; My Sister Is Deaf*. Illustrated by Deborah Ray. New York: Harper & Row, 1977.

Pomerantz, Charlotte. *The Half-Birthday Party*. New York: Clarion, 1984.

Rice, Eve. *Oh, Lewis!* New York: Macmillan, 1974.

Sobol, Harriet. *My Brother Steven Is Retarded*. Illustrated by Patricia Agre. New York: Macmillan, 1977.

Steptoe, John. *Stevie*. New York: Harper & Row, 1969.

Stevenson, James. *Bored, Nothing to Do*. New York: Greenwillow, 1986.

Weiss, Nicki. *Princess Pearl*. New York: Greenwillow, 1986.

Wells, Rosemary. *Stanley and Rhoda*. New York: Dial, 1978.

Zolotow, Charlotte. *If It Weren't for You*. Illustrated by Ben Schecter. New York: Harper & Row, 1966.

Child's Family World: Grandparents

Brandenberg, Aliki. *The Two of Them*. New York: Greenwillow, 1979.

Brooks, Ron. *Timothy and Gramps*. New York: Bradbury, 1978.

Buckley, Helen. *Grandfather and I*. Illustrated by Paul Galdone. New York: Lothrop, Lee & Shephard, 1959.

————. *Grandmother and I*. Illustrated by Paul Galdone. New York: Lothrop, Lee & Shepard, 1961.

Burningham, John. *Grandpa*. New York: Crown. 1985.

Harranth, Wolf. *My Old Grandad*. Illustrated by Christina Oppermann-Dimov, translated by Peter Carter. Salem, N.H.: Merrimack, 1984.

Hedderwick, Mairi. *Katie Morag and the Two Grandmothers*. Boston: Little, Brown, 1986.

Henkes, Kevin. *Grandpa and Bo*. New York: Greenwillow, 1986.

Hurd, Edith Thacher. *I Dance in My Red Pajamas*. Illustrated by Emily Arnold McCully. New York: Harper & Row, 1982.

Lasky, Kathryn. *I Have Four Names for My Grandfather*. Photography by Christopher G. Knight. Boston: Little, Brown, 1976.

MacLachlan, Patricia. *Through Grandpa's Eyes*. Illustrated by Deborah Ray. New York: Harper & Row, 1979.

Rylant, Cynthia. *When I Was Young in the Mountains*. Illustrated by Diane Goode. New York: Dutton, 1982.

Child's Family World: Poetry

Ciardi, John. *You Read to Me, I'll Read to You*. Illustrated by Edward Gorey. New York: Harper & Row, 1962.

Greenfield, Eloise. *Honey, I Love and Other Love Poems*. Illustrated by Diane and Leo Dillon. New York: Crowell, 1978.

Griego, Margot C., Betsy L. Bucks, Sharon S. Gilbert, Laurel H. Kimball, eds. and trans. *Tortillitas Para Mama: And Other Nursery Rhymes, Spanish and English*. Illustrated by Barbara Cooney. New York: Holt, Rinehart & Winston, 1981.

Hall, Donald. *The Man Who Lived Alone*. Illustrated by Mary Azarian. Boston: Godine, 1984.

Hoberman, Mary Ann. *Yellow Butter Purple Jelly Red Jam Black Bread*. Illustrated by Chaya Burstein. New York: Viking, 1981.

Kennedy, X. J. *Brats*. Illustrated by James Watts. New York: Atheneum, McElderry, 1986.

Kuskin, Karla. *Dogs and Dragons, Trees and Dreams: A Collection of Poems*. New York: Harper & Row, 1980.

Prelutsky, Jack. *The Random House Book of Poetry for Children*. Illustrated by Arnold Lobel. New York: Random House, 1983.

Child's Social World: Friends

Alexander, Martha. *Move Over, Twerp*. New York: Dial, 1981.

Brandenberg, Aliki. *We Are Best Friends*. New York: Greenwillow, 1982.

Clifton, Lucille. *Everett Anderson's Friend*. Illustrated by Ann Grifalconi. New York: Holt, Rinehart & Winston, 1976.

Cohen, Miriam. *Best Friends*. Illustrated by Lillian Hoban. New York: Macmillan, 1971.

Kellogg, Steven. *Best Friends*. New York: Dial, 1986.

Steig, William. *Amos and Boris*. New York: Farrar, Straus & Giroux, 1971.

Vincent, Gabrielle. *Where Are You, Ernest and Celestine?* New York: Greenwillow, 1986.

Viorst, Judith. *Rosie and Michael*. Illustrated by Lorna Tomei. New York: Atheneum, 1974.

Weiss, Nicki. *Maude and Sally*. New York: Greenwillow, 1983.

Winthrop, Elizabeth. *Lizzie and Harold*. Illustrated by Martha Weston. New York: Lothrop, Lee & Shepard, 1986.

Child's Social World: School

Breinburg, Petronella. *Shawn Goes to School*. Illustrated by Errol Lloyd. New York: Crowell, 1974.

Brown, Tricia. *Someone Special, Just Like You*. Photography by Fran Ortiz. New York: Holt, Rinehart & Winston, 1984.

Cohen, Miriam. *Jim Meets the Thing*. Illustrated by Lillian Hoban. New York: Greenwillow, 1981.

———. *See You Tomorrow, Charles*. Illustrated by Lillian Hoban. New York: Greenwillow, 1983.

———. *Will I Have a Friend?* Illustrated by Lillian Hoban. New York: Macmillan, 1971.

Rabe, Berniece. *The Balancing Girl*. Illustrated by Lillian Hoban. New York: Dutton, 1981.

Watson, Clyde. *Hickory Stick Rag*. Illustrated by Wendy Watson. New York: Crowell, 1976.

Weiss, Leatie. *My Teacher Sleeps in School*. Illustrated by Ellen Weiss. New York: Warne, 1984.

Wolf, Bernard. *Don't Feel Sorry for Paul*. Philadelphia: Lippincott, 1974.

Child's Social World: Poetry

Livingston, Myra Cohn, ed. *I Like You—If You Like Me: Poems of Friendship*. New York: Atheneum, McElderry, 1987.

Merriam, Eve. *A Word or Two with You*. Illustrated by John Nez. New York: Atheneum, 1981.

Moore, Lilian. *Something New Begins*. New York: Atheneum, 1982.

Royds, Caroline. *Poems for Young Children*. Illustrated by Inga Moore, New York: Doubleday, 1986.

The Child's Natural World: Nature

Baylor, Byrd. *We Walk in Sandy Places*. Photography by Marilyn Schweitzer. New York: Scribner's, 1976.

Brinckloe, Julie. *Fireflies!* New York: Macmillan, 1985.

Hughes, Shirley. *Alfie's Feet*. New York: Lothrop, Lee & Shepard, 1982.

Hutchins, Pat. *The Wind Blew*. New York: Macmillan, 1974.

Kellogg, Steven. *The Mystery of the Missing Red Mitten*. New York: Dial, 1974.

Kurelek, William. *A Prairie Boy's Winter*. Boston: Houghton Mifflin, 1973.

Locker, Thomas. *The Mare on the Hill*. New York: Dial, 1985.

———. *Where the River Begins*. New York: Dial, 1984.

Ray, Deborah Kogan. *Fog Drift Morning*. New York: Harper & Row, 1983.

Rylant, Cynthia. *Night in the Country*. New York: Bradbury, 1986.

Scheffler, Ursel. *A Walk in the Rain*. Illustrated by Wlises Wensell. New York: Putnam's, 1986.

Skofield, James. *All Wet*. Illustrated by Diane Stanley. New York: Harper & Row, 1984.

Wildsmith, Brian. *Seasons*. New York: Oxford University Press, 1980.

Child's Natural World: Seasons

Arnosky, Jim. *Drawing Spring*. New York: Greenwillow, 1987.

Cole, Brock. *The Winter Wren*. New York: Farrar, Straus & Giroux, 1984.

Provensen, Alice, and Martin Provensen. *The Year at Maple Hill Farm*. New York: Atheneum, 1978.

Wolff, Ashley. *A Year of Beasts*. New York: Dutton, 1986.

———. *A Year of Birds*. New York: Dodd, Mead, 1984.

Child's Natural World: Animals

Freschet, Berniece. *Wood Duck Baby*. Illustrated by Jim Arnosky. New York: Putnam's, 1983.

George, Jean C. *The Grizzly Bear with the Golden Ears*. Illustrated by Tom Catania. New York: Harper & Row, 1982.

Hausherr, Rosmarie. *My First Kitten*. New York: Four Winds, 1985.

McNulty, Faith. *Mouse and Tim*. Illustrated by Marc Simont. New York: Harper & Row, 1978.

Provensen, Alice and Martin Prov-

ensen. *A Horse and a Hound, a Goat and a Gander*. New York: Atheneum, 1980.

———. *Our Animal Friends at Maple Hill Farm*. New York: Random House, 1984.

Child's Natural World: Poetry

Adams, Adrienne, ed. *Poetry of Earth*. New York: Scribner's, 1972.

Cole, William. *An Arkful of Animals: Poems for the Very Young*. Illustrated by Lynn Munsinger. Boston: Houghton Mifflin, 1978.

———. *A Book of Animal Poems*. Illustrated by Robert Andrew Parker. New York: Viking, 1973.

Fisher, Aileen. *Anybody Home?* Illustrated by Susan Bonners. New York: Crowell, 1980.

———. *Listen Rabbit*. Illustrated by Symeon Shimin. New York: Crowell, 1964.

———. *Out in the Dark and Daylight*. Illustrated by Gail Owens. New York: Harper & Row, 1980.

———. *Sing Little Mouse*. Illustrated by Symeon Shimin. New York: Crowell, 1969.

———. *When It Comes to Bugs*. Illustrated by Chris and Bruce Degen. New York: Harper & Row, 1986.

Frost, Robert. *Stopping by Woods on a Snowy Evening*. Illustrated by Susan Jeffers. New York: Dutton, 1978.

Hopkins, Lee Bennett, comp. *Dinosaurs*. Illustrated by Murray Tinkelman. San Diego: Harcourt Brace Jovanovich, 1987.

———, ed. *The Sea Is Calling Me*. Illustrated by Walter Gaffney-Kessell. San Diego: Harcourt Brace Jovanovich, 1986.

———, comp. *The Sky Is Full of Song*. Illustrated by Dirk Zimmer. New York: Harper & Row, 1983.

Worth, Valerie. *Small Poems Again*. Illustrated by Natalie Babbitt. New York: Farrar, Straus & Giroux, 1986.

Child's Aesthetic World: Art

Anno, Mitsumasa. *Anno's Britain*. New York: Philomel, 1982.

———. *Anno's U. S. A.* New York: Philomel, 1983.

Baskin, Leonard et al. *Hosie's Zoo*. Illustrated by Leonard Baskin. New York: Viking, 1981.

O'Kelley, Mattie Lou. *From the Hills of Georgia: An Autobiography in Painting*. Boston: Little, Brown, Atlantic, 1983.

Testa, Fulvio. *If You Look Around You*. New York: Dial, 1983.

———. *If You Take a Pencil*. New York: Dial, 1982.

Wildsmith, Brian. *Daisy*. New York: Pantheon, 1984.

———. *Give a Dog a Bone*. New York: Pantheon, 1985.

Zemach, Margot. *Margot Zemach: Self Portrait*. Reading, Mass: Addison-Wesley, 1978.

Child's Aesthetic World: Music

Hoffman, E. T. A. *Nutcracker*. Illustrated by Maurice Sendak. New York: Crown, 1984.

Isadora, Rachel. *Ben's Trumpet*. New York: Greenwillow, 1979.

Langstaff, John. *Frog Went a Courtin'*. Illustrated by Feodor Rojankovsky. New York: Harcourt Brace, 1955.

———. *Oh, A-Hunting We Will Go*. Illustrated by Nancy Winslow Parker. New York: Atheneum, 1974.

Lionni, Leo. *Geraldine the Music Mouse*. New York: Pantheon, 1979.

Quackenbush, Robert. *Clementine*. Philadelphia: Lippincott, 1974.

———. *Go Tell Aunt Rhody*. Philadelphia: Lippincott, 1973.

Spier, Peter. *The Erie Canal*. New York: Doubleday, 1970.

———. *The Star Spangled Banner*. New York: Doubleday, 1973.

Child's Aesthetic World: Dance and Movement

dePaola, Tomie. *Sing, Pierrot,*

Sing: A Picture Book in Mime. San Diego: Harcourt Brace Jovanovich, 1983.

Krementz, Jill. *A Very Young Dancer.* New York: Knopf, 1976.

Child's Aesthetic World: Literature

Andersen, Hans Christian. *The Emperor's New Clothes.* Illustrated by Nadine Bernard Westcott. Boston: Little, Brown, 1984.

————. *The Ugly Duckling.* Translated by Anne Stewart, illustrated by Monika Laimgruber. New York: Greenwillow, 1985.

Burningham, John. *Mr. Gumpy's Motor Car.* New York: Crowell, 1976.

Burton, Virginia Lee. *Mike Mulligan and His Steam Shovel.* Boston: Houghton Mifflin, 1939.

————. *The Little House.* Boston: Houghton Mifflin, 1942.

Duvoisin, Roger. *Petunia.* New York: Knopf, 1950.

Flack, Marjorie. *The Story About Ping.* Illustrated by Kurt Wiese. New York: Viking, 1933.

Piper, Watty. *The Little Engine That Could.* Illustrated by Ruth Sanderson. New York: Platt, 1976.

Potter, Beatrix. *Yours Affectionately, Peter Rabbit.* New York: Warne, 1984.

Provensen, Alice, and Martin Provensen. *The Glorious Flight: Across the Channel with Louis Bleriot July 25th, 1909.* New York: Viking, 1983.

Rey, Hans Augusto. *Curious George.* Boston: Houghton Mifflin, 1941.

Seuss, Dr. *The 500 Hats of Bartholomew Cubbins.* New York: Vanguard, 1938.

Child's Aesthetic World: Poetry

Hart, Jane, comp. *Singing Bee: A Collection of Children's Songs.* Illustrated by Anita Lobel. New York: Lothrop, Lee & Shephard, 1982.

Livingston, Myra Cohn. *Sea Songs.* Illustrated by Leonard Everett Fisher. New York: Holiday House, 1986.

————. *Sky Songs.* Illustrated by Leonard Everett Fisher. New York: Holiday House, 1984.

Longfellow, Henry Wadsworth. *Hiawatha.* Illustrated by Susan Jeffers. New York: Dial, 1983.

Milne, A. A. *Now We Are Six.* Illustrated by Ernest H. Shepard. New York: Dutton, 1927.

PROFESSIONAL REFERENCES

Brown, Marcia. "Caldecott Medal Acceptance." *Horn Book Magazine* 59, no. 4 (August 1983): 414–22.

Chukovsky, Kornei. *From Two to Five.* Edited and translated by Miriam Morton. Berkeley: University of California Press, 1963.

Cianciola, Patricia, ed. *Picture Books for Children.* Chicago: American Library Association, 1973.

Cullinan, Bernice E. "An Interview With Maurice Sendak." *Teaching Critical Reading and Thinking to Children and Adolescents.* Directed by Roy Allen, New York University's "Sunrise Semester." CBS, 1 May 1978.

Dillon, Leo. "Diane Dillon." *Horn Book Magazine* 53, no. 4 (August 1977): 415–21.

Dillon, Leo, and Diane Dillon. "Caldecott Medal Acceptance." *Horn Book Magazine* 52, no. 4 (August 1976): 373–77.

Kingman, Lee, ed. *Newbery and Caldecott Medal Books: 1966–1975.* Boston: Horn Book, 1975.

Marantz, Kenneth. "The Picture Book as Art Object: A Call for Balanced Reviewing." *Wilson Library Bulletin* 52, no. 2 (October 1977): 148–51.

Rylant, Cynthia. Letter to the Editor. *Horn Book Magazine* 62, no. 4 (July–August 1986): 387.

Silvey, Anita. "Could Randolph Caldecott Win the Caldecott Medal?" *Horn Book Magazine* 62, no. 4 (July–August 1986): 405.

Smith, Frank. *Comprehension and Learning: A Conceptual Framework for Teachers.* New York: Holt, Rinehart & Winston, 1975.

"The Story of a Book." Literature for Children series. Verdugo, Calif.: Pied Piper.

Taylor, Judy. *Beatrix Potter: Artist, Storyteller and Countrywoman.* New York: Warne, 1986.

————. *That Naughty Rabbit: Beatrix Potter and Peter Rabbit.* New York: Warne, 1987.

Van Allsburg, Chris. "Caldecott Medal Acceptance." *Horn Book Magazine* 62, no. 4 (July/August 1986): 420–24.

NOTES

1. Karla Kuskin, "Watch Out," in *Near the Window Tree* (New York: Harper & Row, 1975), 21.
2. Patricia Cianciola, ed., *Picture Books for Children* (Chicago: American Library Association, 1973), 1.
3. Frank Smith, *Comprehension and Learning: A Conceptual Framework for Teachers* (New York: Holt, Rinehart & Winston, 1975), 2.
4. Margaret Lane, *The Tale of Beatrix Potter* (New York: Penguin Books, 1946; reprint 1985), 56.
5. Felice Holman, "Leave Me Alone." in *At the Top of My*

Voice and Other Poems, illus. Edward Gorey (New York: Norton, 1970), 45.

6. A. A. Milne, "The End," in *Now We Are Six,* illus. Ernest H. Shepard (New York: Dutton, 1927), 102.

7. A. A. Milne, "Us Two," in *Now We Are Six,* 35.

8. Such objects are called transitional objects. For further information about the role of security symbols, see Simon A. Grolnich and Leonard Barkin, eds. *Between Reality and Fantasy* (New York: Aronson, 1978); D. W. Winnicott, "Transitional Objects and Transitional Phenomena," *International Journal of Psychoanalysis* 34. pt. 2 (1953): 89–97; Marion Milner, "Aspects of Symbolism in Comprehension of the Not-Self," *International Journal of Psychoanalysis,* 33, pt. 2 (1952): 181–95; and D. W. Winnicott, "The Location of Cultural Experience," *International Journal of Psychoanalysis,* 48 (1966): 368–72.

9. Kornei Chukovsky, *From Two to Five,* trans. and ed. Miriam Morton (Berkeley and Los Angeles: University of California Press, 1963), 119.

10. A. A. Milne, "Binker," in *Now We Are Six,* 17.

11. Chris Van Allsburg, "Caldecott Medal Acceptance," *Horn Book Magazine* 62, no. 4 (July–August 1986): 423.

12. Ibid., 423.

13. William Steig, *Farmer Palmer's Wagon Ride* (New York: Farrar, Straus & Giroux, 1974), n.p.

14. William Steig, *Newbery and Cal-decott Medal Books: 1966–1975,* ed. Lee Kingman (Boston: Horn Book, 1975), 219.

15. Maurice Sendak, interview with Justin Wintle in *The Pied Pipers.* Paddington, England, 1975.

16. Bernice E. Cullinan, "An Interview with Maurice Sendak," *Teaching Critical Reading and Thinking to Children and Adolescents,* Dir. Roy Allen, New York University's "Sunrise Semester." CBS, 1 May 1978. Another interview can be found in Jonathan Cott, "Maurice Sendak: King of all the Wild Things," in *Pipers at the Gates of Dawn: The Wisdom of Children's Literature* (New York: Random House, 1983), 40–84.

17. Cullinan, "An Interview with Maurice Sendak."

18. Kenneth Marantz, "The Picture Book: A Call for Balanced Reviewing," *Wilson Library Bulletin* 52, no. 2 (October 1977): 157.

19. Lucille Clifton, *Amifika,* illus. Thomas Di Grazia (New York: Dutton, 1977), n.p.

20. Jeannette Caines, *Daddy,* illus. Ronald Himler (New York: Harper & Row, 1977), 30–31.

21. Dorothy Aldis, "Little," in *All Together* (New York: Putnam's, 1952), 89.

22. Shel Silverstein, "For Sale," in *Where the Sidewalk Ends* (New York: Harper & Row, 1974), 52.

23. Tomie dePaola, *Now One Foot, Now the Other* (New York: Putnam, 1981), n.p.

24. Tomie dePaola, *Nana Upstairs and Nana Downstairs* (New York: Putnam, 1973), n.p.

25. Patricia Reilly Giff, *Today Was a Terrible Day,* illus. Susanna Natti (New York: Viking, 1982), 22.

26. Polly Chase Boyden, "Mud," in *The Arbuthnot Anthology of Children's Literature,* 4th ed., ed. Zena Sutherland et al. (New York: Lothrop, Lee & Shepard, 1976), 103.

27. Aileen Fisher, *Listen Rabbit,* illus. Symeon Shimin (New York: Crowell, 1964), n.p.

28. Aileen Fisher, "Early Spring," in *Rabbits, Rabbits,* illus. Gail Niemann (New York: Harper & Row, 1983), n.p.

29. Marantz, "The Picture Book."

30. Ed Emberley, "Caldecott Medal Acceptance," in *Newbery and Caldecott Medal Books: 1966–1975,* ed. Lee Kingman (Boston: Horn Book, 1975), 200.

31. Marcia Brown, "Caldecott Medal Acceptance," *Horn Book Magazine* 59, no. 4 (August 1983): 417.

32. Leo Dillon, "Diane Dillon," *Horn Book Magazine* 53, no. 4 (August 1977): 423.

33. Leo and Diane Dillon, "Caldecott Medal Acceptance," *Horn Book Magazine* 52, no. 4 (August 1976): 376.

34. Anita Silvey, "Could Randolph Caldecott Win the Caldecott Medal?," *Horn Book Magazine* 62, no. 4 (July–August 1986): 405.

35. Cynthia Rylant, letter to the editor, *Horn Book Magazine* 62, no. 4 (July–August 1986): 387.

CHILDREN'S BOOKS CITED

Aardema, Verna. *Why Mosquitoes Buzz in People's Ears: A West African Tale.* Illustrated by Leo and Diane Dillon. New York: Dial, 1975.

Aldis, Dorothy. *All Together.* New York: Putnam's, 1952.

———. *Nothing Is Impossible: The Story of Beatrix Potter.* Illustrated by Richard Cuffari. New York: Atheneum, 1969.

Alexander, Martha. *I'll Protect You from the Jungle Beasts.* New York: Dial, 1973.

———. *Nobody Asked Me if I Wanted*

a Baby Sister. New York: Dial, 1971.

———. *When the New Baby Comes, I'm Moving Out*. New York: Dial, 1981.

Allard, Harry. *Miss Nelson Has a Field Day*. Illustrated by James Marshall. Boston: Houghton Mifflin, 1985.

———. *Miss Nelson Is Back*. Illustrated by James Marshall. Boston: Houghton Mifflin, 1982.

———. *Miss Nelson Is Missing!* Illustrated by James Marshall. Boston: Houghton Mifflin, 1977.

———. *The Stupids Die*. Illustrated by James Marshall. Boston: Houghton Mifflin, 1981.

———. *The Stupids Have a Ball*. Illustrated by James Marshall. Boston: Houghton Mifflin, 1978.

———. *The Stupids Step Out*. Illustrated by James Marshall. Boston: Houghton Mifflin, 1974.

Allen, Jeffrey. *Nosey Mrs. Rat*. Illustrated by James Marshall. New York: Viking, Kestrel, 1987.

Ancona, George. *It's a Baby*. New York: Dutton, 1979.

Anno, Mitsumasa. *Anno's Journey*. New York: Putnam, 1978.

Arnosky, Jim. *Deer at the Brook*. New York: Lothrop, Lee & Shepard, 1986.

———. *Drawing from Nature*. New York: Lothrop, Lee & Shepard, 1982.

———. *Drawing Life in Motion*. New York: Lothrop, Lee & Shepard, 1985.

———. *Secrets of a Wildlife Watcher*. New York: Lothrop, Lee & Shepard, 1983.

———. *Watching Foxes*. New York: Lothrop, Lee & Shepard, 1985.

Aruego, José. *Look What I Can Do*. New York: Scribner's, 1971.

Asch, Frank. *Bear's Bargain*. Englewood Cliffs, N.J.: Prentice-Hall, 1985.

Bang, Molly. *The Paper Crane*. New York: Greenwillow, 1985.

———. *Ten, Nine, Eight*. New York: Greenwillow, 1983.

Bate, Lucy. *Little Rabbit's Loose Tooth*. Illustrated by Diane de Groat. New York: Crown, 1975.

Baylor, Byrd. *The Best Town in the World*. Illustrated by Ronald Himler. New York: Scribner's, 1983.

———. *The Desert Is Theirs*. Illustrated by Peter Parnall. New York: Scribner's 1975.

———. *Desert Voices*. Illustrated by Peter Parnall. New York: Scribner's, 1981.

———. *Hawk, I'm Your Brother*. Illustrated by Peter Parnall. New York: Scribner's, 1976.

———. *I'm in Charge of Celebrations*. Illustrated by Peter Parnall. New York: Scribner's, 1986.

———. *The Other Way to Listen*. Illustrated by Peter Parnall. New York: Scribner's, 1978.

Bemelmans, Ludwig. *Madeline*. 1939. Reprint. New York: Viking, 1962.

———. *Madeline and the Bad Hat*. New York: Viking, 1957.

———. *Madeline and the Gypsies*. New York: Viking, 1959.

———. *Madeline in London*. New York: Viking, 1961.

———. *Madeline's Rescue*. New York: Viking, 1953.

Blaine, Marge. *The Terrible Thing That Happened at Our House*. Illustrated by John. C. Wallner. New York: Macmillan, 1980.

Blegvad, Erik. *Self Portrait: Erik Blegvad*. Reading, Mass.: Addison-Wesley, 1979.

Boyden, Polly Chase. "Mud." In *Arbuthnot Anthology of Children's Literature*, 4th ed, 103. Edited by Zena Sutherland et al. New York: Lothrop, Lee & Shepard, 1976.

Brandenberg, Aliki. *Go Tell Aunt Rhody*. New York: Macmillan, 1974.

Brandenberg, Franz. *Aunt Nina and Her Nephews and Nieces*. Illustrated by Aliki. New York: Greenwillow, 1983.

———. *Aunt Nina's Visit*. Illustrated by Aliki Brandenberg. New York: Greenwillow, 1984.

———. *Otto Is Different*. Illustrated by James Stevenson. New York: Greenwillow, 1985.

Brett, Jan. *Annie and the Wild Animals*. Boston: Houghton Mifflin, 1985.

Briggs, Raymond. *The Snowman*. New York: Viking, 1978.

Brown, Marc. *Arthur's Tooth*. Boston: Atlantic, 1985.

Brown, Marcia. *Dick Whittington and His Cat*. New York: Scribner's, 1950.

———. *Felice*. New York: Scribner's, 1958.

———. *Once a Mouse*. New York: Scribner's, 1961.

Brown, Margaret Wise. *The Dead Bird*. Reading, Mass.: Addison-Wesley, 1958.

———. *Goodnight Moon*. Illustrated by Clement Hurd. New York: Harper & Row, 1947.

Browne, Anthony. *Gorilla*. New York: Knopf, 1985.

———. *Willy the Wimp*. New York: Knopf, 1985.

Bryan, Ashley. *The Cat's Purr*. New York: Atheneum, 1985.

Burningham, John. *Mr. Gumpy's Outing*. New York: Holt, Rinehart & Winston, 1971.

———. *Seasons*. New York: Bobbs, 1970.

Burton, Virginia Lee. *Katy and the Big Snow*. Boston: Houghton Mifflin, 1943.

Byars, Betsy. *Go and Hush the Baby*. Illustrated by Emily Arnold McCully. New York: Viking, 1971.

Caines, Jeannette. *Abby*. Illustrated by Steven Kellogg. New York: Harper & Row, 1973.

———. *Daddy*. Illustrated by Ronald Himler. New York: Harper & Row, 1977.

Cameron, Ann. *More Stories Julian Tells*. Illustrated by Ann Strugness. New York: Knopf, 1986.

———. *The Stories Julian Tells*. Illustrated by Ann Strugness. New York: Pantheon, 1981.

Carle, Eric. *Have You Seen My Cat?* New York: Watts, 1973.

Carrick, Carol. *The Accident*. Illustrated by Donald Carrick. New York: Clarion, 1976.

———. *Ben and the Porcupine*. Illustrated by Donald Carrick. New York: Clarion, 1981.

———. *The Climb*. Illustrated by Donald Carrick. New York: Clarion, 1984.

———. *Dark and Full of Secrets*. Illustrated by Donald Carrick. New York: Clarion, 1984.

———. *The Foundling*. Illustrated by Donald Carrick. New York: Clarion, 1986.

———. *Lost in the Storm*. Illustrated by Donald Carrick. New York: Clarion, 1974.

———. *Sleep Out*. Illustrated by Donald Carrick. New York: Clarion, 1973.

———. *The Washout*. Illustrated by Donald Carrick. New York: Clarion, 1978.

Cauley, Lorinda B. *The Three Little Kittens*. New York: Putnam's, 1982.

Cendrars, Blaise. *Shadow*. Translated and illustrated by Marcia Brown. New York: Scribner's, 1982.

Chorao, Kay. *The Baby's Bedtime Book*. New York: Dutton, 1984.

Clifton, Lucille. *Amifika*. Illustrated by Thomas Di Grazia. New York: Dutton, 1977.

———. *The Boy Who Didn't Believe in Spring*. Illustrated by Brinton Turkle. New York: Dutton, 1973.

———. *Everett Anderson's Nine Month Long*. Illustrated by Ann Grifalconi. New York: Holt, Rinehart & Winston, 1978.

———. *My Friend Jacob*. Illustrated by Thomas Di Grazia. New York: Dutton, 1980.

Coerr, Eleanor. *The Josefina Story Quilt*. Illustrated by Bruce Degen. New York: Harper & Row. 1986.

Cohen, Barbara. *Gooseberries to Oranges*. Illustrated by Beverly Brodsky. New York: Lothrop, Lee & Shepard, 1982.

Cohen, Miriam. *First Grade Takes a Test*. Illustrated by Lillian Hoban. New York: Greenwillow, 1980.

———. *Jim's Dog Muffins*. Illustrated by Lillian Hoban. New York: Greenwillow, 1984.

———. *Liar, Liar, Pants on Fire*. Illustrated by Lillian Hoban. New York: Greenwillow, 1985.

———. *Lost in the Museum*. Illustrated by Lillian Hoban. New York: Greenwillow, 1979.

———. *No Good in Art*. Illustrated by Lillian Hoban. New York: Greenwillow, 1980.

———. *Starring First Grade*. Illustrated by Lillian Hoban. New York: Greenwillow, 1985.

———. *When Will I Read?* Illustrated by Lillian Hoban. New York: Greenwillow, 1977.

Cole, Joanna. *The New Baby at Your House*. Photography by Hella Hammid. New York: Morrow, 1985.

Commire, Anne, ed. *Something about the Author*, Vols. 1–50. Detroit: Gale Research, 1971–1988.

Cooney, Barbara. *Miss Rumphius*. New York: Viking, 1982.

Cooney, Nancy. *The Wobbly Tooth*. New York: Putnam's, 1981.

Craft, Ruth. *The Winter Bear*. Illustrated by Erik Blegvad. New York: Atheneum, 1975.

Crowe, Robert L. *Clyde Monster*. Illustrated by Kay Chorao. New York: Dutton, 1976.

Dabcovich, Lydia. *Mrs. Huggins and Her Hen Hannah*. New York: Dutton, 1985.

De Brunhoff, Jean. *The Story of Babar*. New York: Random House, 1960.

De la Mare, Walter. *Molly Whuppie*. Illustrated by Errol Le Cain. New York: Farrar, Straus & Giroux, 1983.

Delton, Judy. *A Walk on a Snowy Night*. Illustrated by Ruth Rosner. New York: Harper & Row, 1982.

dePaola, Tomie. *The Cloud Book*. New York: Holiday House, 1975.

———. *Fin M'Coul: The Giant of Knockmany Hill*. New York: Holiday House, 1981.

———. *The Kid's Cat Book*. New York: Holiday House, 1979.

———. *The Mysterious Giant of Barletta*. San Diego: Harcourt Brace Jovanovich, 1984.

———. *Nana Upstairs and Nana Downstairs*. New York: Putnam's, 1973.

———. *Now One Foot, Now the Other*. New York: Putnam's, 1981.

———. *Oliver Button Is a Sissy*. San Diego: Harcourt Brace Jovanovich, 1979.

———. *Watch Out for the Chicken Feet in Your Soup*. Englewood Cliffs, N.J.: Prentice-Hall, 1974.

De Regniers, Beatrice Schenk. *Jack and the Beanstalk*. Illustrated by Anne Wilsdorf. New York: Atheneum, McElderry, 1985.

———. *So Many Cats*. Illustrated by Ellen Weiss. New York: Clarion, 1985.

———. *This Big Cat and Other Cats I've Known*. Illustrated by Alan Daniel. New York: Crown, 1985.

Domanska, Janina. *I Saw a Ship A-Sailing*. New York: Macmillan, 1972.

Douglass, Barbara. *Good as New*. Illustrated by Patience Brewster. New York: Lothrop, Lee & Shepard, 1982.

Dragonwagon, Crescent. *Jemima Remembers*. Illustrated by Troy Howell. New York: Macmillan, 1984.

Emberley, Barbara. *Drummer Hoff*. Illustrated by Ed Emberley. Englewood Cliffs, N.J.: Prentice-Hall, 1967.

Fair, Sylvia. *The Bedspread*. New York: Morrow, 1982.

Feelings, Tom and Muriel Feelings. *Jambo Means Hello: Swahili Alphabet Book*, New York: Dial, 1976.

———. *Moja Means One: Swahili Counting Book*. New York: Dial, 1976.

Field, Eugene. *Wynken, Blynken and Nod*. Illustrated by Barbara Cooney. New York: Hastings

House, 1980.

———. *Wynken, Blynken and Nod.* Illustrated by Susan Jeffers. New York: Dutton, 1982.

Fisher, Aileen. *I Like Weather.* Illustrated by Janina Domanska. New York: Crowell, 1963.

———. *Listen, Rabbit.* Illustrated by Symeon Shimin. New York: Crowell, 1964.

———. *Rabbits, Rabbits.* Illustrated by Gail Niemann. New York: Harper & Row, 1983.

———. *When It Comes to Bugs.* Illustrated by Chris and Bruce Degen. New York: Harper & Row, 1986.

Flournoy, Valerie. *The Patchwork Quilt.* Illustrated by Jerry Pinkney. New York: Dial, 1985.

Freeman, Don. *Corduroy.* New York: Viking, 1968.

———. *Dandelion.* New York: Viking, 1964.

———. *A Pocket for Corduroy.* New York: Viking, 1978.

Friedman, Ina R. *How My Parents Learned to Eat.* Illustrated by Allen Say. Boston: Houghton Mifflin, 1984.

Fritz, Jean. *The Good Giants and the Bad Pukwudgies.* Illustrated by Tomie dePaola. New York: Putnam's, 1982.

Gág, Wanda. *Millions of Cats.* New York: Coward, McCann & Geoghegan, 1928.

———. *Nothing at All.* New York: Coward, McCann & Geoghegan, 1941.

Galdone, Paul. *King of the Cats.* Boston: Houghton Mifflin, Clarion, 1985.

———. *The Three Sillies.* Boston: Houghton Mifflin, Clarion, 1981.

Giff, Patricia Reilly. *The Almost Awful Play.* Illustrated by Susanna Natti. New York: Viking, Kestrel, 1984.

———. *Happy Birthday, Ronald Morgan!* Illustrated by Susanna Natti. New York: Viking, Kestrel, 1986.

———. *Next Year I'll Be Special.* Illustrated by Marylin Hafner.

New York: Dutton, 1980.

———. *Today Was a Terrible Day.* Illustrated by Susanna Natti. New York: Viking, 1980.

———. *Watch Out, Ronald Morgan.* Illustrated by Susanna Natti. New York: Viking, Kestrel, 1985.

Goennel, Heidi. *Seasons.* Boston: Little, Brown, 1986.

Goodall, John. *The Story of a Castle.* New York: Atheneum, McElderry, 1986.

———. *The Story of an English Village.* Atheneum, 1979.

Graeber, Charlotte. *Mustard.* Illustrated by Donna Diamond. New York: Macmillan, 1982.

Greenfield, Eloise. *She Come Bringing Me that Little Baby Girl.* Illustrated by John Steptoe. Philadelphia: Lippincott, 1974.

Griffith, Helen V. *Georgia Music.* Illustrated by James Stevenson. New York: Greenwillow, 1986.

Grimm, Jakob, and Wilhelm Grimm. *The Devil with Three Golden Hairs.* Illustrated by Nonny Hogrogian. New York: Knopf, 1983.

———. *Little Red Riding Hood.* Illustrated by Trina Schart Hyman. New York: Holiday House, 1986.

Gundersheimer, Karen. *Happy Winter.* New York: Harper & Row, 1982.

Hader, Berta, and Elmer Hader. *The Big Snow.* New York: Macmillan, 1948.

Haley, Gail. *A Story, a Story.* New York: Atheneum, 1970.

Hall, Donald. *Ox-Cart Man.* Illustrated by Barbara Cooney. New York: Viking, 1979.

Hamilton, Virginia. *The People Could Fly.* Illustrated by Leo and Diane Dillon. New York: Knopf, 1985.

Hart, Jane, ed. *Singing Bee: A Collection of Favorite Children's Songs.* Illustrated by Anita Lobel. New York: Lothrop, Lee & Shepard, 1982.

Harvey, Brett. *Immigrant Girl: Becky of Eldridge Street.* Illustrated by

Deborah Kogan Ray. New York: Holiday House, 1987.

Herman, Emily. *Hubknuckles.* Illustrated by Deborah Kogan Ray. New York: Crown, 1985.

Hest, Amy. *The Crack-of-Dawn Walkers.* Illustrated by Amy Schwartz. New York: Macmillan, 1984.

Hoban, Lillian. *Arthur's Loose Tooth.* New York: Harper & Row, 1985.

Hoban, Russell. *A Baby Sister for Frances.* Illustrated by Lillian Hoban. New York: Harper & Row, 1964.

Hoban, Tana. *Look Again.* New York: Macmillan, 1971.

Hoberman, Mary Ann. *Bugs: Poems.* Illustrated by Victoria Chess. New York: Viking, 1976.

Hodges, Margaret. *The Wave.* Illustrated by Blair Lent. Boston: Houghton Mifflin, 1957.

Hogrogian, Nonny. *One Fine Day.* New York: Macmillan, 1971.

Holabird, Katharine. *Angelina Ballerina.* Illustrated by Helen Craig. New York: Potter, 1983.

Holland, Vicki. *We Are Having a Baby.* New York: Scribner's, 1972.

Holman, Felice. *At the Top of My Voice and Other Poems.* Illustrated by Edward Gorey. New York: Scribner's, 1976.

Holtze, Sally H., ed. *The Fifth Book of Junior Authors and Illustrators.* New York: H. W. Wilson, 1983.

Hopkins, Lee Bennett, ed. *And God Bless Me: Prayers, Lullabies and Dream Poems.* Illustrated by Patricia Henderson Lincoln. New York: Knopf, 1982.

———. *Best Friends.* Illustrated by James Watts. New York: Harper & Row, 1986.

———. *Books Are by People.* New York: Citation, 1969.

———. *Go to Bed! A Book of Bedtime Poems.* Illustrated by Rosekrans Hoffman. New York: Knopf, 1979.

———. *More Books by More People.* New York: Citation, 1974.

Horwitz, Elinor Lander. *When the Sky Is Like Lace*. Illustrated by Barbara Cooney. Philadelphia: Lippincott, 1975.

Howard, Jane R. *When I'm Sleepy*. Illustrated by Lynne Cherry. New York: Dutton, 1985.

Hughes, Shirley. *Alfie Gets in First*. New York: Lothrop, Lee & Shepard, 1982.

———. *Alfie Gives a Hand*. New York: Lothrop, Lee & Shepard, 1984.

———. *An Evening at Alfie's*. New York: Lothrop, Lee & Shepard, 1985.

Hurd, Edith Thatcher. *The Black Dog Who Went into the Woods*. Illustrated by Emily Arnold McCully. New York: Harper & Row, 1980.

Hutchins, Pat. *Don't Forget the Bacon*. New York: Greenwillow, 1976.

———. *The Doorbell Rang*. New York: Greenwillow, 1986.

———. *Titch*. New York: Macmillan, 1971.

———. *The Very Worst Monster*. New York: Greenwillow, 1985.

———. *You'll Soon Grow into Them, Titch*. New York: Greenwillow, 1983.

Hyman, Trina Schart. *Self Portrait: Trina Schart Hyman*. Reading, Mass.: Addison-Wesley, 1981.

Isadora, Rachel. *Max*. New York: Macmillan, 1976.

———. *My Ballet Class*. New York: Greenwillow, 1980.

———. *Opening Night*. New York: Greenwillow, 1984.

———. *Willaby*. New York: Macmillan, 1984.

Jacobs, Joseph. *Jack and the Beanstalk*. Illustrated by Lorinda B. Cauley. New York: Putnam's, 1983.

Jeffers, Susan. *All the Pretty Horses*. New York: Macmillan, 1974.

Johnston, Tony. *The Quilt Story*. Illustrated by Tomie dePaola. New York: Putnam's, 1985.

Jonas, Ann. *The Quilt*. New York: Greenwillow, 1984.

———. *The Trek*. New York: Greenwillow, 1985.

Jukes, Mavis. *Blackberries in the Dark*. Illustrated by Thomas B. Allen. New York: Knopf, 1985.

———. *Like Jake and Me*. Illustrated by Lloyd Bloom. New York: Knopf, 1984.

———. *No One Is going to Nashville*. Illustrated by Lloyd Bloom. New York: Knopf, 1983.

Kahl, Virgina. *The Duchess Bakes a Cake*. New York: Scribner's, 1955.

Keats, Ezra Jack. *Hi, Cat!* New York: Macmillan, 1970.

———. *Kitten for a Day*. New York: Watts, 1974.

———. *Pet Show*. New York: Macmillan, 1972.

———. *Peter's Chair*. New York: Harper & Row, 1967.

———. *The Snowy Day*. New York: Viking, 1962.

———. *Whistle for Willie*. New York: Viking, 1964.

Keller, Holly. *Geraldine's Blanket*. New York: Greenwillow, 1984.

———. *Too Big!* New York: Greenwillow, 1984.

Kellogg, Steven. *The Island of the Skog*. New York: Dial, 1973.

———. *The Mysterious Tadpole*. New York: Dial, 1977.

———. *Pinkerton, Behave!* New York: Dial, 1979.

———. *Ralph's Secret Weapon*. New York: Dial, 1983.

———. *A Rose for Pinkerton*. New York: Dial, 1981.

———. *Tallyho, Pinkerton!* New York: Dial, 1982.

Kent, Jack. *The Fat Cat: A Danish Folktale*. New York: Parents, 1974.

Kraus, Robert. *Leo the Late Bloomer*. Illustrated by José Aruego. New York: Windmill, 1971.

Krementz, Jill. *A Very Young Dancer*. New York: Knopf, 1976.

Kuskin, Karla. *Herbert Hated Being Small*. New York: Harper & Row, 1979.

———. *Near the Window Tree*. New York: Harper & Row, 1975.

———. *Night Again*. Boston: Little, Brown, Atlantic, 1981.

———. *The Philharmonic Gets Dressed*. Illustrated by Marc Simont. New York: Harper & Row, 1982.

———. *The Rose on My Cake*. New York: Harper & Row, 1964.

Lane, Margaret. *The Tale of Beatrix Potter: A Biography*. 2nd ed. New York: Warne, 1968.

Larrick, Nancy, comp. *When the Dark Comes Dancing*. Illustrated by John Wallner. New York: Philomel, 1983.

Lasky, Kathryn. *A Baby for Max*. Photographs by Christopher G. Knight. New York: Scribner's, 1984.

Laurence, Margaret. *The Olden Days Coat*. Illustrated by Muriel Wood. Toronto: McClelland, 1982.

Lent, Blair. *John Tabor's Ride*. Boston: Little, Brown, 1966.

Levinson, Riki. *I Go with My Family to Grandma's*. Illustrated by Diane Goode. New York: Dutton, 1985.

———. *Watch the Stars Come Out*. Illustrated by Diane Goode. New York: Dutton, 1985.

Lionni, Leo. *Alexander and the Wind-Up Mouse*. New York: Pantheon, 1967.

———. *Cornelius: A Fable*. New York: Pantheon, 1983.

Lobel, Arnold. *Giant John*. New York: Harper & Row, 1964.

McCloskey, Robert. *Blueberries for Sal*. New York: Viking, 1948.

———. *One Morning in Maine*. New York: Viking, 1952.

McCully, Emily Arnold. *First Snow*. New York: Harper & Row, 1985.

McDermott, Gerald. *Arrow to the Sun: A Pueblo Indian Tale*. New York: Viking, 1974.

MacLachlan, Patricia. *Seven Kisses in a Row*. Illustrated by Maria Pia Marrella. New York: Harper &

Row, 1983.

McPhail, David. *Emma's Pet.* New York: Dutton, 1985.

———. *Farm Morning.* San Diego: Harcourt Brace Jovanovich, 1985.

Mahy, Margaret. *Jam: A True Story.* Illustrated by Helen Craig. Boston: Little, Brown, Atlantic, 1986.

Marshall, James. *George and Martha.* Boston: Houghton Mifflin, 1972.

———. *Yummers.* Boston: Houghton Mifflin, 1973.

———. *Yummers Too: The Second Course.* Boston: Houghton Mifflin, 1986.

Martin, Bill, Jr, and John Archambault. *The Ghost-Eye Tree.* Illustrated by Ted Rand. New York: Holt, Rinehart & Winston, 1985.

———. *White Dynamite and Curly Kid.* Illustrated by Ted Rand. New York: Holt, Rinehart & Winston, 1986.

Martin, Charles E. *Island Winter.* New York: Greenwillow, 1984.

Mathis, Sharon Bell. *The Hundred Penny Box.* Illustrated by Leo and Diane Dillon. New York: Viking, 1975.

Mayer, Mercer. *There's a Nightmare in My Closet.* New York: Dial, 1968.

Milne, A. A. *The House at Pooh Corner.* Illustrated by Ernest H. Shepard. London: Dutton, 1928.

———. *Now We Are Six.* Illustrated by Ernest H. Shepard. London: Dutton, 1927.

———. *When We Were Very Young.* Illustrated by Ernest H. Shepard. London: Dutton, 1924.

———. *Winnie the Pooh.* Illustrated by Ernest H. Shepard. London: Dutton, 1926.

Montresor, Beni. *Cinderella.* New York: Knopf, 1965.

Mosel, Arlene. *The Funny Little Woman.* Illustrated by Blair Lent. New York: Dutton, 1972.

Musgrove, Margaret. *Ashanti to Zulu.* Illustrated by Leo and Diane Dillon. New York: Dial, 1976.

Ness, Evaline. *Sam, Bangs, and Moonshine.* New York: Holt, Rinehart & Winston, 1966.

Nichols, b. p. *Once: A Lullaby.* Illustrated by Anita Lobel. New York: Greenwillow, 1986.

Nic Leodhas, Sorche. *Always Room for One More.* Illustrated by Nonny Hogrogian. New York: Holt, Rinehart & Winston, 1965.

Oakley, Graham. *The Church Mice at Bay.* New York: Atheneum, 1979.

———. *The Church Mouse.* New York: Atheneum, 1972.

Odor, Ruth S. *Learning About Giants.* Chicago: Children's Press, 1981.

Ormerod, Jan. *Moonlight.* New York: Lothrop, Lee & Shepard, 1982.

———. *Sunshine.* New York: Lothrop, Lee & Shepard, 1981.

Oxenbury, Helen. *Pig Tale.* New York: Morrow, 1973.

Parish, Peggy. *Amelia Bedelia.* Illustrated by Fritz Siebel. New York: Harper & Row, 1963.

Pearson, Susan. *Happy Birthday Grampie, I Love You.* Illustrated by Leo and Diane Dillon. New York: Dial, 1987.

Pearson, Tracey Campbell. *Old MacDonald Had a Farm.* New York: Dial, 1984.

Perrault, Charles. *Cinderella.* Illustrated by Marcia Brown. New York: Scribner's, 1954.

———. *The Three Billy Goats Gruff.* Illustrated by Marcia Brown. New York: Harcourt Brace, 1957.

———. *Puss In Boots.* Illustrated by Marcia Brown. New York: Scribner's, 1952.

———. *Puss In Boots.* Illustrated by Paul Galdone. New York: Clarion, 1976.

Pomerantz, Charlotte. *All Asleep.* Illustrated by Nancy Tafuri. New York: Greenwillow, 1984.

———. *The Mango Tooth.* Illustrated by Marylin Hafner. New York: Greenwillow, 1977.

———. *The Piggy in the Puddle.* Il-

lustrated by James Marshall. New York: Macmillan, 1974.

Potter, Beatrix. *The Complete Adventures of Peter Rabbit.* New York: Warne, 1985.

———. *The Complete Adventures of Tom Kitten and His Friends.* New York: Warne, 1985.

———. *The Tale of Benjamin Bunny.* New York: Warne, 1904.

———. *The Tale of Jemima Puddleduck.* New York: Warne, 1908.

———. *The Tale of Mr. Jeremy Fisher.* New York: Warne, 1906.

———. *The Tale of Mrs. Tiggy Winkle.* New York: Warne, 1905.

———. *The Tale of Tom Kitten.* New York: Simon & Schuster, 1986.

———. *Mrs. Tittlemouse and Other Mouse Stories.* New York: Warne, 1985.

———. *The Tale of Peter Rabbit.* New York: Warne, 1902.

———. *The Tale of Squirrel Nutkin.* New York: Warne, 1903.

———. *The Tale of Tom Kitten.* New York: Warne, 1907.

Prokofiev, Sergei. *Peter and the Wolf.* Translated by Maria Carlson, illustrated by Charles Mikolaycak. New York: Penguin, 1986.

———. *Peter and the Wolf.* Translated by Loriot. Illustrated by Jörg Müller. New York: Knopf, 1986.

Provensen, Alice, and Martin Provensen. *The Year at Maple Hill Farm.* New York: Atheneum, 1978.

Quackenbush, Robert. *First Grade Jitters.* Philadelphia: Lippincott, 1982.

Radin, Ruth Yaffe. *A Winter Place.* Illustrated by Mattie Lou O'Kelley. Boston: Little, Brown, 1982.

Rayner, Mary. *Crocodarling.* New York: Bradbury, 1986.

———. *Mr. and Mrs. Pig's Evening Out.* New York: Atheneum, 1976.

Rogers, Fred. *The New Baby.* Photography by Jim Judkis. New York: Putnam's, 1985.

Rosenberg, Maxine B. *Being Adopted.* Photography by George Ancona. New York: Lothrop, Lee & Shepard, 1984.

———. *My Friend Leslie: The Story of a Handicapped Child.* Photography by George Ancona. New York: Lothrop, Lee & Shepard, 1983.

Roth, Susan, and Ruth Phang. *Patchwork Tales.* New York: Athenenum, 1984.

Rylant, Cynthia. *Miss Maggie.* Illustrated by Thomas Di Grazia. New York: Dutton, 1983.

———. *The Relatives Came.* Illustrated by Stephen Gammell. New York: Bradbury, 1985.

Segal, Lore. *The Story of Mrs. Lovewright and Purrless Her Cat.* Illustrated by Paul O. Zelinsky. New York: Knopf, 1985.

Sendak, Maurice. *In the Night Kitchen.* New York: Harper & Row, 1970.

———. *Maurice Sendak's Really Rosie.* New York: Harper & Row, 1975.

———. *Outside over There.* New York: Harper & Row, 1981.

———. *Where the Wild Things Are.* New York: Harper & Row, 1963.

———. *Maurice Sendak Fantasy Sketches.* Philadelphia: H. A. S. W. Rosenbach Foundation, 1970.

Seuss, Dr. *And to Think That I Saw It on Mulberry Street.* New York: Vanguard, 1937.

———. *The Cat in the Hat.* New York: Random House, 1957.

———. *Horton Hatches the Egg.* New York: Random House, 1940.

———. *The Lorax.* New York: Random House, 1971.

———. *Thidwick the Big-Hearted Moose.* New York: Random House, 1948.

———. *Yertle the Turtle and Other Stories.* New York: Random House, 1958.

Sharmat, Marjorie Weinman. *Attilla the Angry.* Illustrated by Lillian Hoban. New York: Holiday House, 1985.

———. *Bartholomew the Bossy.* Illustrated by Normand Chartier. New York: Macmillan, 1984.

———. *A Big Fat Enormous Lie.* Illustrated by David McPhail. New York: Dutton, 1978.

———. *Frizzy the Fearful.* Illustrated by John Wallner. New York: Holiday House, 1983.

———. *Gila Monsters Meet You at the Airport.* Illustrated by Byron Barton. New York: Macmillan, 1980.

———. *Grumley the Grouch.* Illustrated by Kay Chorao. New York: Holiday House, 1980.

———. *I'm Not Oscar's Friend Anymore.* Illustrated by Tony De Luna. New York: Dutton, 1975.

———. *I'm Terrific.* Illustrated by Kay Chorao. New York: Holiday House, 1977.

———. *Mooch the Messy.* Illustrated by Ben Shecter. New York: Harper & Row, 1976.

———. *Sasha the Silly.* Illustrated by Janet Stevens. New York: Holiday House, 1984.

Shulevitz, Uri. *Dawn.* New York: Farrar, Straus & Giroux, 1974.

Silverstein, Shel. *Where the Sidewalk Ends.* New York: Harper & Row, 1974.

Sobol, Hariet Langsam. *We Don't Look Like Our Mom and Dad.* Photography by Patricia Agre. New York: Coward-McCann, 1984.

Spender, Stephen. *The Magic Flute.* Illustrated by Beni Montresor. New York: Putnam's, 1966.

Spier, Peter. *Bored! Nothing to Do!* New York; Doubleday, 1978.

———. *Dreams.* New York: Doubleday, 1986.

———. *London Bridge Is Falling Down.* New York: Doubleday, 1967.

———. *Noah's Ark.* New York: Doubleday, 1977.

———. *Oh, Were They Ever Happy.* New York: Doubleday, 1978.

———. *Peter Spier's Rain.* New York: Doubleday, 1982.

Steig, William. *Abel's Island.* New York: Farrar, Straus & Giroux, 1976.

———. *The Amazing Bone.* New York: Farrar, Straus & Giroux, 1976.

———. *Doctor DeSoto.* New York: Scholastic, 1984.

———. *Farmer Palmer's Wagon Ride.* New York: Farrar, Straus & Giroux, 1974.

———. *Roland the Minstrel Pig.* New York: Harper & Row, 1968.

———. *Solomon the Rusty Nail.* New York: Farrar, Straus & Giroux, 1985.

———. *Sylvester and the Magic Pebble.* New York: Simon & Schuster, 1969.

Steptoe, John. *Stevie.* New York: Harper & Row, 1969.

Stevenson, Robert Louis. *The Moon.* Illustrated by Denise Saldutti. New York: Harper & Row, 1984.

Strand, Mark. *The Night Book.* Illustrated by William Pène DuBois. New York: Potter, Crown, 1985.

Sutherland, Zena, ed. *The Arbuthnot Anthology of Children's Literature.* New York: Lothrop, Lee & Shepard, 1976.

Szilagyi, Mary. *Thunderstorm.* New York: Bradbury, 1985.

Tafuri, Nancy. *Who's Counting?* New York: Greenwillow, 1986.

Tresselt, Alvin. *White Snow, Bright Snow.* Illustrated by Roger Duvoisin. New York: Lothrop, Lee & Shepard, 1947.

Turkle, Brinton. *The Sky Dog.* New York: Viking, 1969.

Udry, Janice May. *Let's Be Enemies.* Illustrated by Maurice Sendak. New York: Harper & Row, 1959.

———. *The Moon Jumpers.* Illustrated by Maurice Sendak. New York: Harper & Row, 1959.

Van Allsburg, Chris. *The Garden of Abdul Gasazi.* Boston: Houghton Mifflin, 1979.

———. *Jumanji*. Boston: Houghton Mifflin, 1981.

———. *The Polar Express*. Boston: Houghton Mifflin, 1985.

Viorst, Judith. *Alexander and the Terrible, Horrible, No Good, Very Bad Day*. Illustrated by Ray Cruz. New York: Atheneum, 1972.

———. *Alexander, Who Used to Be Rich Last Sunday*. Illustrated by Ray Cruz. New York: Atheneum, 1978.

———. *I'll Fix Anthony*. Illustrated by Arnold Lobel. New York: Harper & Row, 1969.

Waber, Bernard. *Ira Sleeps Over*. Boston: Houghton Mifflin, 1972.

———. *"You Look Ridiculous" Said the Rhinoceros to the Hippopotamous*. Boston: Houghton Mifflin, 1966.

Walter, Mildred Pitts. *My Mama Needs Me*. Illustrated by Pat Cummings. New York: Lothrop, Lee & Shepard, 1983.

Ward, Lynd. *The Biggest Bear*. Boston: Houghton Mifflin, 1952.

Weiss, Nicki. *Hank and Oogie*. New York: Greenwillow, 1982.

Wells, Rosemary. *Hazel's Amazing Mother*. New York: Dial, 1985.

———. *Peabody*. New York: Dutton, 1983.

———. *Timothy Goes to School*. New York: Dial, 1981.

Wilhelm, Hans. *I'll Always Love You*. New York: Crown, 1985.

Williams, Barbara. *Kevin's Grandma*. Illustrated by Kay Chorao. New York: Dutton, 1975.

Williams, Garth. *The Rabbit's Wedding*. New York: Harper & Row, 1958.

Williams, Margery. *The Velveteen Rabbit*. Illustrated by William Nicholson. 1922, Reprint. New York: Doubleday, 1958.

Williams, Vera B. *A Chair for My Mother*. New York: Greenwillow, 1982.

———. *Music, Music for Everyone*. New York: Greenwillow, 1984.

———. *Something Special for Me*. New York: Greenwillow, 1983.

Winter, Jeanette. *Hush Little Baby*. New York: Pantheon, 1984.

Winthrop, Elizabeth. *Katharine's Doll*. Illustrated by Marylin Hafner. New York: Dutton, 1983.

Wolff, Ashley. *Only the Cat Saw*. New York: Dodd, Mead, 1985.

Wood, Audrey. *Heckedy Peg*. Illustrated by Don Wood. San Diego: Harcourt Brace Jovanovich, 1987.

———. *King Bidgood's in the Bathtub*. Illustrated by Don Wood. San Diego: Harcourt Brace Jovanovich, 1985.

———. *The Napping House*. Illustrated by Don Wood. San Diego: Harcourt Brace Jovanovich, 1984.

Yolen, Jane. *The Giants' Farm*. Illustrated by Charles Mikolaycak. San Diego: Harcourt Brace Jovanovich, 1986.

———. *The Lullaby Songbook*. San Diego: Harcourt Brace Jovanovich, 1986.

Zemach, Harve. *Mommy, Buy Me a China Doll*. Illustrated by Margot Zemach. New York: Farrar, Straus & Giroux, 1975.

Zemach, Margot. *Hush, Little Baby*. New York: Dutton, 1976.

———. *Self Portrait: Margot Zemach*. Reading, Mass.: Addison-Wesley, 1978.

Zolotow, Charlotte. *I Know a Lady*. Illustrated by James Stevenson. New York: Penguin, 1986.

———. *My Grandson Lew*. Illustrated by William Pène DuBois. New York: Harper & Row, 1974.

———. *Someone New*. Illustrated by Erik Blegvad. New York: Harper & Row, 1978.

———. *The Song*. Illustrated by Nancy Tafuri. New York: Greenwillow, 1982.

5

Folklore

Invitation

If you are a dreamer, come in,
If you are a dreamer, a wisher, a liar,
A hope-er, a pray-er, a magic bean
    buyer . . .
If you're a pretender, come sit by my
    fire
For we have some flax-golden tales to
    spin.
Come in!
Come in![1]

Shel Silverstein

olklore, the body of literature that has no known authors, has been passed down through the generations by word of mouth and enhanced with variations bestowed by many storytellers. The legacy of this literature includes Mother Goose and nursery rhymes, folk tales, fables, myths, legends and tall tales, and folk songs. Each type is distinctive, but all echo the beliefs, customs, and eternal dreams that appeal to people across time.

ORIGINS OF FOLKLORE

Theories about the origin and function of folklore come from the work of social anthropologists, who study beliefs, celebrations, and ceremonies of primal societies. Ruth Sawyer, a well-known twentieth-century storyteller, draws upon collections of such materials in her description of the beginning of storytelling: "The first primitive efforts at conscious storytelling consisted of a simple chant, set to the rhythm of some daily tribal occupation such as grinding corn, paddling canoe or kayak, sharpening weapons for hunting or war, or ceremonial dancing."[2]

In addition to composing songs and tales about their daily work, their hunting, and their warfare, primal societies created stories about the world around them. Wonder and awe at the power of nature and speculation about the supernatural forces that might be at work behind it led to those tales we classify as myths. And as time passed and the tribes grew, so did the impulse to preserve the stories of their ancestors. Legends and hero tales of the mighty deeds of those who had gone before were passed from one generation to the next and became the cultural heritage.

The roots of folklore exist in all societies from all times. The story of civilization shows a continual quest to shape a harmonious balance between the physical world and the mortal's place in it. Through creative imagination, people transform outer reality into a vision of life that they control through analogy and metaphor. The lore they create is a rich source of literature for children.

At one time, common belief held that all folklore emerged from one prehistoric civilization. The Grimm brothers, who collected tales from all over Germany, held this view of singular origin, speculating that as people moved on to other geographic areas they took their stories with them. This theory would account for regional differences in some folk tales, such as the evolution of West Africa's trickster "Ananse the Spider" to "Anansi" in the Caribbean, and to "Aunt Nancy" in the southern United States. But as folklorists studied the tales of many diverse cultures, it became apparent that some stories must indeed have originated in a number of places. "The themes were . . . those concerning human beings everywhere and the stories were bound to be invented wherever communities developed,"[3] according to Joanna Cole.

John Bierhorst's collection, *The Monkey's Haircut and Other Stories Told by the Maya* (I),

LANDMARK

Illustrated Folktales

Folktales were handed down by word of mouth for generations and were among the first literature to be printed for children. The early collections appeared in voluminous tomes which seemed forbidding to the child who wanted to read them. The earliest illustrations for folktales were made in the late eighteenth century from crude woodcuts the printer had available, not necessarily ones designed for the particular tale with which they were used.

The most brilliant accomplishments in illustrated books for children occurred in the nineteenth century. At the beginning of the century, Thomas Bewick (1753–1828) perfected the use of woodcuts by developing the "white line" and using the end grain of the woodblock. Later, George Cruikshank (1792–1878) captured the magic of the sturdy folktales in his drawings for *Grimm's Fairy Tales* when they were translated into English in 1823. Cruikshank, noted for his animated fairies, gnomes, and elves, gave his figures a unique individuality despite their tiny size. *George Cruikshank's Fairy Library* was published in four volumes in 1853 and 1854, and contained "Puss in Boots," "Jack and the Beanstalk," and "Cinderella."

Three of the greatest names of the century, Walter Crane, Randolph Caldecott, and Kate Greenaway, made children's books a thing of beauty by adding color used with skill and imagination. Walter Crane (1845–1915) published *Sing a Song of Sixpence, The House That Jack Built,* and *The History of Cock Robin and Jenny Wren* in 1865 and 1866. Randolph Caldecott (1846–1886) began the work for which he is best remembered—lively action and animals that come to life on the page—in 1877 or 1878. *The Diverting History of John Gilpin* was his first, to be followed by 16 others, including *The Frog He Would A-Wooing Go, Hey Diddle Diddle and Baby-Bunting,* and *Three Jovial Huntsmen.* Kate Greenaway (1846–1901) is remembered for her portrayal of quaintly dressed children playing in flowered gardens. Her picture books include *A Day in a Child's Life* (1881), *Mother Goose* (1881), and *The Pied Piper of Hamelin,* retold by Robert Browning (1888). (See Chapter 12 for further discussion of these artists.)

Since the 1950s, renowned artists have chosen individual folktales as the text to illustrate in a single volume. Paul Galdone, Tomie dePaola, and Trina Schart Hyman are among the distinguished artists who have illustrated numerous folktales. These artists revived a trend initiated by nineteenth-century masters to make folklore accessible to young children. By putting folktales into a single edition format and making them come alive with spirited illustrations, these artists created a landmark in children's literature.

Mother Goose has raised countless generations of children. (From *Tomie dePaola's Mother Goose.*)

includes 22 of the nearly 1,000 Mayan tales that have been recorded since 1900. The primitive origin myths most certainly were told long before Christian missionaries arrived in the sixteenth century; other stories are unique variants of such European tales as "Hansel and Gretel." There is even a trickster rabbit whose tale resembles the tar baby story.

Today, social anthropologists believe that both theories about the origin of folk tales are correct: some did indeed spread among cultures, whereas others with similar themes appeared spontaneously in a number of separate places. Iona and Peter Opie, in *The Classic Fairy Tales*, note that no one theory "is likely to account satisfactorily for the origin of even a majority of the tales. Their wellsprings are almost certainly numerous, their ages likely to vary considerably, their meanings—if they ever had meanings—to be diverse."[4]

THE ROLE OF FOLKLORE

Children's thinking parallels the intuitive vision of life and simple explanation of the world of primal groups. This vision, not yet governed by logic, is structured first out of children's own awareness of themselves and next from perceptions of the world around them. Many psychologists believe that the emergence of emotions, thoughts, language, and literature in primal societies is analogous to that of individual human development.

In the same way that folklore explained the world to early people, it helps young children understand their own world today. Up to about the age of 7, children believe that magic accounts for the things they cannot understand; they attribute human characteristics to inanimate objects artlessly. André Favat explains:

> The characteristics of the child and the characteristics of the fairy tale permit a fairly clear observation: just as magic and animism suffuse the world of the fairy tale, so do they suffuse the

world of the child; just as a morality of constraint prevails in the fairy tale, so does it prevail in the moral system of the child; just as the fairy tale world and its hero become one in achieving his ends, so do children believe their world is one with them; and just as causal relations remain unexpressed in the fairy tale, so do they remain unexpressed in the child's communication.[5]

Innumerable interpretations are given to the role of folklore: according to Freud, fairy tale characters symbolize subconscious urges during a child's emotional development; Jung sees the mythical figures and conflicts as archetypes of racial memories. Bettelheim's views, much like Freud's, are that fairy tales tap deep unconscious wishes and desires—the wellsprings of repressed emotions. Bettelheim reasons that fairy tales help children deal with emotional insecurities by suggesting images—more easily dealt with—for their fantasies:

> It is here that fairytales have unequaled value, because they offer new dimensions to the child's imagination which would be impossible for him to discover as truly on his own. Even more important, the form and structure of fairy tales suggest images to the child by which he can structure his daydreams and with them give better direction to his life.[6]

According to Jung, the collective unconscious is a part of the mind from which come dream, fantasy, imagination and vision. Jung perceived this as a substratum of mind common to all people, and he attributes the commonality of the stories of diverse peoples to the universal nature of the unconscious. Whatever the explanation, it is clear that similar elements are found in the myths, legends, and folk tales of all people across time and place. The reappearing themes, or archetypes, are clearly visible in folklore. For example, the archetype of the hero's quest—slaying a dragon or winning a princess—is seen as the psychological expression of the normal process of maturing.

The good mother (fairy godmother), the bad mother (wicked stepmother or old witch), and the shadow (evil underside in every person) are vivid examples of archetypes familiar to us all.

Arthur Applebee explains children's fascination with stories from another perspective.[7] He sees children engaged in a search for meaning, a search for structures and patterns that will suggest order and consistency in the world around them. The patterns of meaning they find are transmitted by a range of social devices—stories among many others. Pleasure comes through mastery of the rules, a particularly important factor in highly patterned, stereotyped formula stories such as folk and fairy tales.

CRITERIA FOR SELECTING FOLKLORE

Because folklore is a part of culture, it is easily and readily published in a variety of forms. Unfortunately, there are many unimaginative and inferior editions that could, by their sheer number, overshadow the truly excellent ones that do exist. Therefore, one must look for certain qualities when evaluating books of folklore. Language is the primary criterion, for the old tales are best in pure form. Look for language that (1) retains the flavor of the oral form—with natural, easily spoken rhythms—and (2) maintains the dignity of the early retellings. Avoid simplified, controlled-vocabulary versions that dilute the stories to trite episodes.

Illustrated versions of folklore are abundant; they vary from slick cartoon drawings to the studied work of talented artists. Comic strips that portray Snow White as a simpering beauty queen or Zeus as a Superman hero destroy the authenticity of the ancient lore. Look for illustrations that (1) complement and extend the narrative and (2) portray the traditional character of the folk heroes and maintain the literary heritage of the tales.

MOTHER GOOSE AND NURSERY RHYMES

Mother Goose rhymes are the foundation of a rich literary heritage. The rhythm and rhyme of the language, the compact structure of the narratives, and the engaging characters all combine to produce the perfect model for young children who are learning language. There are phrases to chant, nonsense words to mimic, and alliterative repetitions to practice. Poet Walter De la Mare attests to their importance. Mother Goose rhymes, he declares,

> free the fancy, charm the tongue and ear, delight the inward eye, and many of them are tiny masterpieces of word craftsmanship. . . . Last, but not least, they are not only crammed with vivid little scenes and objects and living creatures, but, however fantastic and nonsensical they may be, they are a direct short cut into poetry itself.[8]

Mother Goose rhymes have come under attack many times through the years, but they have always survived the criticism and have continued to play an important role in the lives of children. As early as the seventeenth century, our stern forefathers considered many of the verses unfit for childish ears. Their adult perceptions saw brutality, dishonesty, and irresponsibility rather than silly whimsy and nonsensical fun. In more recent years, harsh criticism has been leveled at the apparent sexism in the verses. While some of these charges may indeed be valid from an adult perspective, we must remember that for young children the value is in the rhythm, rhyme, and fanciful language.

Origins

As is true of all folklore, there is no conclusive evidence about the exact origin of the Mother Goose rhymes or about the existence of an actual person with that name. Iona and Peter Opie, authors of two definitive works, *The Oxford Nursery Rhyme Book* and *The Oxford Dictionary of Nursery Rhymes*, display a healthy skepticism about the origin of the anonymous rhymes and the diverse referents ascribed to them:

> Much ingenuity has been exercised to show that certain nursery rhymes have had greater significance than is now apparent. They have been vested with mystic symbolism, linked with social and political events, and numerous attempts have been made to identify the nursery characters with real persons. It should be stated straightway that the bulk of these speculations are worthless. Fortunately the theories are so numerous they tend to cancel each other out.[9]

Some rhymes may have been composed to teach children to count, to learn the alphabet, or to say their prayers, while others—riddles, tongue twisters, proverbs, and nonsense— were simply for amusement.

The name "Mother Goose" seemingly was first associated with an actual collection of tales in 1697 with Charles Perrault's publication of *Histoires ou contes du temps passé, avec des moralities (Stories or tales of times past, with morals).* The frontispiece shows an old woman spinning and telling stories, and is labeled *"Contes de ma Mère l'Oye" (Tales of Mother Goose).* The exact origin of the name, like the authors of the verses, is lost in the past, but the vitality of the rhymes assures their appeal even today.

Characteristics

The dominant feature of this type of folklore is the powerful rhythm of the verses; the strong beat resounds in the ear and invites physical response. In the earliest days of a child's life, "Rock-a-bye baby" accompanies rocking in a chair. Long before meaning is attached to the sounds, the cadence of the language and bounce of an adult's knee undergird a child's developing rhythm. Northrop Frye emphasizes this physical aspect:

ACTIVITY: TEACHER TO STUDENT

OLD EDITIONS OF MOTHER GOOSE (P–I)   Every generation has enjoyed Mother Goose rhymes. Ask your parents and your grandparents if they remember their own Mother Goose books. Maybe they still have them and will let you borrow them. Go to the library and borrow some facsimiles of old Mother Goose books. See if you can find some of these:

Brooke, *Ring O' Roses*
Greenaway, *Mother Goose: Or, The Old Nursery Rhymes*
Rackham, *Mother Goose, Old Nursery Rhymes*

Rojankovsky, *The Tall Book of Mother Goose*
Smith, *The Jessie Willcox Smith Mother Goose.* (This is a compilation of the artist's work that appeared in magazines and books from 1888 to 1935.)

Compare the illustrations in some of these books with those by Tomie dePaola, Arnold Lobel, James Marshall, and other modern artists. What is different about them? What is the same?

Ideally, our literary education should begin, not with prose, but with such things as "this little pig went to market"—with verse rhythm reinforced by physical assault. The infant who gets bounced on somebody's knee to the rhythm of "Ride a Cock Horse" does not need a footnote telling him that Banbury Cross is twenty miles northeast of Oxford. He does not need the information that "cross" and "horse" make (at least in the pronunciation he is most likely to hear) not a rhyme but an assonance. He does not need the value judgment that the repetition of "horse" in the first two lines indicates a rather thick ear on the part of the composer. All he needs is to get bounced.[10]

Both adult and child know that toes are tweaked in "This little piggie went to market" and that hands are clapped for "Pat-a-cake, pat-a-cake, baker's man."

The pronounced beat of the Mother Goose rhymes reinforces the child's developing sense of physical rhythm. Even more crucial are the audible beat, stress, sound, and intonation patterns that establish themselves in memory and contribute to rhythm in the child's developing language. Who can chant

> Hickory, dickory, dock,
> The mouse ran up the clock.
> The clock struck one,
> The mouse ran down,
> Hickory, dickory, dock.

without some form of toe tapping, head nodding, or other physical accompaniment?

A second major characteristic of Mother Goose is the imaginative use of words and ideas. Nothing is too preposterous or ridiculous to form the content of a verse. Children delight in the images suggested by

> Hey diddle, diddle,
> The cat and the fiddle,
> The cow jumped over the moon;
> The little dog laughed
> To see such sport,
> And the dish ran away with the spoon.

The fanciful visions of "Three wise men of Gotham who went to sea in a bowl," and "There was an old woman tossed up in a basket, nineteen times as high as the moon," spark creativity and enrich the mythic springs of the developing imagination. Nothing is impossible, anything can happen in the young child's unfettered world, and the verses feed the fancy.

A third characteristic of Mother Goose rhymes is the compact structure. The scene is established quickly and the plot divulged at once. In four short lines we hear an entire story:

> Jack Sprat could eat no fat,
> His wife could eat no lean,
> And so between them both, you see,
> They licked the platter clean.

Undoubtedly, as in all folklore, the consolidation of action and the economy of words result from being said aloud for many generations before being set down in print. As they were passed from one teller to the next, they were honed to their present simplicity.

Another quality that accounts for the popularity and long life of Mother Goose verses is the wit and whimsy of the characters. Nonsense is so obvious that the child is in on the joke in

> Gregory Griggs, Gregory Griggs,
> Had twenty-seven different wigs.
> He wore them up, he wore them down,
> To please the people of the town;
> He wore them east, he wore them west,
> But he never could tell which he loved best.

The humor appeals to both children and the adults who share the verses with them. Surprise endings provide a clever resolution as in

> Peter, Peter, pumpkin eater,
> Had a wife and couldn't keep her;
> He put her in a pumpkin shell,
> And there he kept her very well.

Selecting Mother Goose Books

Because we share Mother Goose rhymes by reciting them, and their essence lies in the words, language is a crucial factor in selecting a collection. The verses should maintain the original poetic and robust vocabulary characteristic of them. Rewritten or abridged verses should be avoided, for the value lies in the quality and vigor of the language.

Most Mother Goose books are illustrated, so the quality of the art should also be considered. The normal function of illustrations—to help visualize the action and characters and to amplify and extend the text—is no simple task, according to the discerning Maurice Sendak:

> This elusive quality of the verses—that something more than meets the eye—partially explains the unique difficulty of illustrating Mother Goose. While it is true that the great children's literature is always underlaid with deeper shades of meanings which the perceptive illustrator must interpret, the Mother Goose rhymes stubbornly offer still further resistance. For a start, they have about them a certain blandness that betrays the unwary artist into banalities; the deceptively simple verse seems to slip just out of reach, leaving the illustrator with egg on his face. Another difficulty is related to that quality of the verses De La Mare described as "delighting the inward eye." Characteristic of the best imaginative writing, they evoke their own images, thus placing the artist in the embarrassing position of having to contend with Mother Goose the illustrator as well as the poet.[11]

Some illustrators develop an entire book around a single Mother Goose rhyme. Sendak, for example, creates a fanciful picture story around five simple lines in *Hector Protector and As I Went Over the Water* (N-P):

> Hector Protector was dressed all in green;
> Hector Protector was sent to the Queen.
> The Queen did not like him,
> No more did the King;
> So Hector Protector was sent back again.[12]

By playing with the ambiguity in the text, Sendak extends the boundaries of the rhyme in a book that invites careful perusal.

Paul Galdone, perhaps more than any other illustrator, was responsible for putting Mother Goose rhymes and folk tales into single-edition picture book format. Children raised with television like visual images and find the illustrated verses and stories appealing. Galdone's illustrations for *Three Little Kittens* (N-P) and *Little Bo-Peep* (N-P) are resplendent with lively, colorful characters and extended action. Children who already know the rhymes will proudly "read" the large, bold text.

Tracey Campbell Pearson has illustrated several nursery songs and rhymes in large, attractive picture book formats. The drawings in *Sing a Song of Sixpence* (N-P) extend the simple verse into an opportunity for storytelling beyond the rhyme. Children take delight in following the adventures of the young prince and princess who lure the birds into the pie and then watch with great pleasure as they fly off to wreak havoc on the stately palace. Pearson's drawings, filled with zany action and sunny color, create a riotous picture story.

Contemporary in mode and mischievous in spirit, the illustrations in Susan Jeffers's *Three Jovial Huntsmen: A Mother Goose Rhyme* (N) add to the delight of the verse. She captures in beautiful illustrations a less familiar rhyme:

> There were three jovial huntsmen,
> As I have heard men say,
> And they would go a-hunting
> Upon St. David's day.
> All the day they hunted,
> And nothing could they find,
> But a ship a-sailing,
> A-sailing with the wind.[13]

As the three huntsmen, clad in bright colors, amble through the wintry woods, they are unaware that they are surrounded by animals, which the artist has hidden in the muted line

A pocketful of rye;

Single Mother Goose rhymes offer a multitude of opportunities for the illustrator. Children delight, for example, in Tracey Campbell Pearson's *Sing a Song of Sixpence,* which shows the prince and princess wreaking havoc on the castle.

drawings of the woods. The ship "a-sailing with the wind" is a visual illusion made of sun and shadow. This book becomes a hide-and-seek game for children who readily spot the animals that are unseen by the gullible hunters.

Janet and Allan Ahlberg created an intriguing book that demands children's participation. Subtitled "An I Spy Story," *Each Peach Pear Plum* (N-P) is a visual game in which Mother Goose and folk tale characters are hidden among the illustrations. Verbal rhymes give a clue for the object of each search:

> "Tom Thumb in the cupboard
> I spy . . . Mother Hubbard.
> Cinderella on the stairs
> I spy . . . the three bears.[14]

Young children eagerly search the pictures for the familiar figures who peek out from beneath bushes, stairwells, and tree branches.

Collections of Mother Goose rhymes are more abundant than books based on the individual verses, but they vary in quality of selections and illustrations. Ideally, the illustrations extend the verses without overpowering them. An outstanding example—Marguerite de Angeli's *Book of Nursery and Mother Goose Rhymes* (N-P)—combines a comprehensive collection of verses with exquisite illustrations. The verses are a mixture of pathos, joy, and nonsense, and they retain the rhythmic language of the old versions. The adult reader and child viewer share a work of art as they look at spacious pages graced with finely crafted illustrations.

TEACHING IDEA

OLD MOTHER HUBBARD (N-P) Old Mother Hubbard who went to the cupboard to get her poor dog a bone has been presented as a full-length tale in several books. The cumulative story carries much appeal for its absurd situations and satisfactory resolution. Share these versions with children and encourage them to discuss the differences:

dePaola, *The Comic Adventures of Old Mother Hubbard and Her Dog*
Galdone, *Old Mother Hubbard and Her Dog*
Hawkins and Hawkins, *Old Mother Hubbard*
Ness, *Old Mother Hubbard and Her Dog*
Provensen and Provensen, *Old Mother Hubbard*

1. What is happening in the borders or in the background?
2. What kind of dog does each illustrator portray?
3. What does Mother Hubbard look like?
4. Are the verses the same? Do they include the same words?
5. Which illustrations do you like the best? Why?

ACTIVITY: TEACHER TO STUDENT

OLD MOTHER HUBBARD (N-P) After you have read several versions of "Old Mother Hubbard" and have looked at the illustrations, make a class mural of the rhyme. Decide first which verses to include and how they will be spaced. Write in the words before the illustrations are drawn.

Plan ahead by marking off equal spaces for scenes and rhymes so you can cut the mural into pages and bind them into a big book.

(See the enlarged book discussion in Chapter 3.)

De Angeli captures the whimsy of some verses and the tenderness of others.

In a totally different style, *Brian Wildsmith's Mother Goose* (N), with characteristic purple, blue, and fuschia geometric patterns, shows no timid shrinking from the cruelty in some verses. Wildsmith vividly portrays the malice of the farmer's wife, preparing to cut off the tails of the three blind mice, and the devilish excitement of Little Johnny Green who puts Pussy in the well. The bold designs and colors create a sophisticated version of the traditional verses.

Tomie dePaola celebrated his twentieth year of producing picture books with a lavish collection of over 200 traditional rhymes in *Tomie dePaola's Mother Goose* (N-P). His artwork is always distinctive, with clear, sharp colors, bold lines, and good use of white space. DePaola's characteristic figures are as familiar to children as the rhymes and verses they illustrate.

Arnold Lobel, another well-loved illustrator, also collected both familiar and less known rhymes in *The Random House Book of Mother Goose* (N-P). Lobel's comic figures are well-placed among over 300 traditional rhymes.

Nursery school and primary classrooms should have all of these standard Mother Goose collections for children to read, hold, share, and love. Other good collections, by such renowned illustrators as Michael Hague, James Marshall, Alice and Martin Provensen, Raymond Briggs, and Tasha Tudor, as well as many single-rhyme books, are listed in the "Recommended Reading" section at the end of this chapter and should be brought in to supplement these titles.

This illustration by Gustave Doré in 1872 is a famous version of the Little Red Riding Hood folktale. (From Iona and Peter Opie's *Classic Fairy Tales*.)

FOLK AND FAIRY TALES

Children and adults have shared and enjoyed the same literature for centuries. Folktales and songs have been handed down from one generation to the next, with each storyteller adding slight variations. Some Eastern stories appeared in print as early as the ninth century, but it was not until 1697, with the French publication of *Histoires ou contes du temps passé,* by Charles Perrault, that European folk tales appeared in book form. Among the tales included were "Sleeping Beauty," "Little Red Riding Hood," "Cinderella," and "Puss in Boots." During the course of the eighteenth century, La Fontaine's *Fables,* Countess d'Aulnoy's *Fairy Tales,* and Madame de Beaumont's *Beauty and the Beast* were published.

Toward the end of the eighteenth century, philologists began to examine folklore as a source of information about the customs and languages of different societies. In Germany, two brothers, Jakob and Wilhelm Grimm, traveled through the country asking people to tell the stories they remembered. The tales the brothers collected became the foundation of folklore as we know it today. Iona and Peter Opie, in their *Classic Fairy Tales*, discuss the accomplishment of the Brothers Grimm:

> Where the Grimms were remarkable was in what now seems to us most ordinary. The Grimms were the first substantial collectors to like folktales for their own sake; the first to write the tales down in the way ordinary people told them, and not attempt to improve them; and they were the first to realize that everything about the tales was of interest, even including the identity of the person who told the tales.[15]

The Grimms did eventually write both a German dictionary and a book of grammar, but they are remembered for retellings of the stories they heard. The two volumes of the first edition of *Kinder-und Hausmärchen* were published in 1812 and 1815, respectively.

Many of the tales collected by the Grimm brothers were translated into English in 1823. *German Popular Stories,* with pictures by the noted illustrator George Cruikshank, became an instant success and raised the respectability of the old tales among scholars and educators who had held them to be "an affront to the rational mind."[16]

PROFILE

Jakob and Wilhelm Grimm

Jakob Ludwig Carl Grimm (1785) and his brother Wilhelm Karl Grimm (1786) were born near Frankfurt, in the German state of Hesse. Their father, town clerk of Hanau, died when Jakob was 11, the oldest of 6 children. Jakob and Wilhelm studied law at Marburg University, where both became interested in the history of law and German folk poetry. Encouraged by their friends, Achim van Arnim and Clemens Brentano, who had published a collection of German folk songs in 1805, the Grimms began collecting folk stories the next year.

Wilhelm suffered from a heart condition and was not able to work full time, but the brothers collaborated in collecting folktales which they planned to publish as a history of German literature. Their friend von Arnim encouraged them to publish the stories they had already collected and their work, *Kinder-und Hausmärchen* (1812), was followed by a second volume three years later.

The relationship between the brothers was remarkably close from early childhood: they shared rooms as children and as university students. In later life, they lived in the same house and worked in adjacent studies. Wilhelm increasingly took responsibility for work on the folktales, while Jakob worked on studies of grammar. Wilhelm married Dortchen Wild, a neighbor from childhood, in 1825, but Jakob remained single. Dortchen had contributed some of the tales that were published in *Kinder-und Hausmärchen*. She and Wilhelm had three children.

The Grimm brothers began collecting their folktales by asking friends and neighbors. In fact, Dortchen's nursemaid, "Old Marie," told them "Little Red Cap," (a version of "Little Red Riding Hood") and "Little Briar Rose" (similar to "Sleeping Beauty"), and Dortchen herself told "Hansel and Gretel."

They collected local legends between 1816 and 1818 that they published as *Deutsche Sagen*, while Jakob devoted himself to Germanic philology and published his first volume of *Deutsche Grammatik* in 1819. Wilhelm died in 1859 and Jakob in 1863.

Scholars today argue about whether the Grimms diligently sought out folk sources or merely collected the stories from friends and family. Whatever the outcome of the scholarly debates, children's literature is enriched by their work.

Over the years, hundreds of translations of the stories have been published; many contain outstanding illustrations by respected artists. Walter Crane illustrated *Household Stories* in 1886, and Wanda Gág translated and illustrated *Tales from Grimm* in 1936. Of those published more recently, *The Juniper Tree and Other Tales from Grimm* (I), illustrated by Maurice Sendak, is one of the best. The translations by Randall Jarrell and Lore Segal retain the vigor and charm of the original language. Also noteworthy are *Popular Folk Tales: The Brothers Grimm* (I), translated by Brian Alderson and illustrated by Michael Foreman, and *Favorite Tales from Grimm* (I), retold by Nancy Garden and illustrated by Mercer Mayer.

Enthusiasm for collecting folklore spread around the world: Joseph Jacobs and Andrew Lang collected folk tales in England. Jacob's *Ardizzone's English Fairy Tales* includes some of the best-loved stories the world around. Lang's series, identified by color—*The Blue Fairy Book,* for example—have long served as the primary source of British tales. Norse scholars Peter Christian Asbjørnsen and Jorgen E. Moe collected most of the Scandinavian tales we have today. Asbjørnsen and Moe published a notable collection, *East O' the Sun and West O' the Moon* (I), during the 1840s. These tales were rendered into English by George Webbe Dasent in translations that retained the vitality of the spoken language. Many of the same tales appear in Ingri and Edgar Parin d'Aulaire's *East of the Sun and West of the Moon* (I), in which the illustrations echo Norwegian folk art.

Characteristics

Folk tales are story narratives in which heroes and heroines demonstrate cleverness, bravery, or other virtues to triumph over adversity. They have an artistic yet simple form attributable to their oral tradition. The plot lines are clean and direct: the first paragraph establishes characters and setting, the body develops the problem and moves toward the climax, the ending resolves the problem without complications.

There is little ambiguity in folk tales: the good are supremely good, the evil are outrageously evil, and justice prevails without compromise. The problem—that is, the conflict between good and evil—is identified early, and only incidents that build the problem or add complexity have survived oral transmission. The problem resolution is decisive, with little denouement; characters live happily ever after.

Characters in folk tales are delineated economically, with intentional stereotyping to quickly establish character traits. Subtleties are seldom found, since folk tales are concerned more with situation than character. The foolish, the wise, the wicked, or the virtuous immediately crystalize as characters who will perform in predictable ways. These little-developed characters are stock figures, either altogether good or altogether bad, who seldom change during a story. Names represent a group—Jack, for example, for any lad.

Themes in folk tales, obvious although not stated explicitly, express the values of the people who created them and reflect their philosophy of life. The language is direct, vivid vernacular uncluttered by awkward constructions or convolutions. Colloquialisms add to the flavor and reflect the heritage of the tale; they are tempered to the tongue, having been pruned and polished through centuries.

The setting of folk tales is geographically vague, leaving an impression of worlds complete in themselves. Stories occur at unidentified times in places defined by the minimal physical detail necessary to the events. Because children accept the idea that there was a different range of possibilities in the past, the stories are believable to them. Young children may know that giants do not live in today's world, but they readily accept the possibility that they lived at one time. A 6-year-old boy, asked when the events in "Little Red Riding Hood" happened, replied "A long time ago when I was a baby, they happened. There was witches and that, a long time ago."[17]

Fairy tales, like all folk tales, are structured by an unvarying sequence of episodes, but they are unique among folk tales in the deeply magical character of their events. In some, the action of the story is carried forward by the intervention of the wee people or a fairy godmother. Filled with enchantment, these stories nonetheless present a vision of life based on fundamental truths. Children see courage, hard work, and resourcefulness rewarded and the good living happily ever after. "Fairy tales," says Paul Hazard, "are like beautiful mirrors of water, so deep and crystal clear. In their depths we sense the mysterious experience of a thousand years."[18]

FOLKLORE IN THE CLASSROOM

Some children have at least a general acquaintance with the most familiar Mother Goose rhymes and folk tales. Unfortunately, many have never even heard "Humpty Dumpty" or "Baa Baa Black Sheep." Others may know nothing about Little Red Riding Hood or Goldilocks. Because traditional literature is the foundation on which all future literary understanding is built, it is of utmost importance to begin with the vast body of folklore if we are to give children the necessary tools to build their literary knowledge.

Children who do not know the significance of the wolf in folklore will not understand the meaning of the wolf-shaped bush in Anthony Browne's *Piggybook* (P-I). Neither will they know the reason for their classmates' "uh-ohs" when they see that the babysitter in Mary Rayner's *Mr. and Mrs. Pig's Evening Out* (P) is a

wolf. Modern references to folklore are countless and we shortchange children if we deny them the background information necessary to understand the contemporary books. Phrases from Aesop's fables are common; children need to know the meaning of "sour grapes" and "slow and steady wins the race." Mythology, too, has given us many key phrases that children should know, such as Pandora's box or the Midas touch.

There are many ways to teach children about folklore. The most important consideration is to immerse them in traditional stories until they begin to recognize similarities, see patterns, and make predictions. Children who have been exposed to the folklore of many cultures begin to see recurring themes in all of them. The values, hopes, fears, and beliefs of each culture are evidenced in its folklore; by knowing its stories we can begin to build a bridge of understanding about that society.

Children who have heard many folktales will tell you that they begin "once upon a time" and end "they lived happily ever after," the good people win, and the youngest son gets the princess. This response shows that children recognize the motifs, themes, and story conventions that are so plentiful in folklore. Awareness of these patterns develops through repeated experience and becomes the foundation for building a literary education.

Good teachers give children opportunities to discover recurring patterns; they do not *tell* them what to recognize. Understanding children's sense of story and knowing labels for conventions informs good teaching; but for the child being taught, it can in no way substitute for having the literary experience itself. By introducing folklore with its abundance of repeatable patterns, teachers can facilitate students' discovery of archetypes; as the children absorb them, the patterns become the structural framework for viewing all literature as one story.

DISCOVERING PATTERNS IN FOLKLORE

Teachers and librarians can help children recognize the patterns, or archetypes, in folklore if they provide both exposure to a wide array of stories and a structure on which the children can build their understanding.

Conventions

Conventions, literary devices that are the cornerstone in folktales, contribute to a child's sense of story. The story frame, the repeated use of the concept of three, and the formulaic pattern of the plot and characters are conventions that children identify early in their literary education. They recognize the story frames of "once upon a time" and "they lived happily ever after" and adopt them in the stories they tell.

Some tales open with variations of these story frames or markers; they contribute to children's ability to generalize the patterns. Anne Rose's retelling of an African tale, *Pot Full of Luck* (P), begins with "Back in the long ago." Others, including Anne Siberell's North American Indian story, *Whale in the Sky* (P), and Junko Morimoto's Japanese *The Inch Boy* (P) begin, simply, "Long ago. . . ." Virginia Tashjian titles her collection *Once There Was and Was Not: Armenian Tales* (I), after the beginning phrase common to many tales from Eastern Europe.

The use of the number *3* is one of the easiest folklore conventions for children to recognize. In addition to three main characters—three bears, three billy goats, three pigs—there are usually three events. In "Goldilocks and the Three Bears," there are three bears, of course, but there are also three more sets of three: bowls of porridge, chairs, and beds. Many folktales follow this pattern of three, whether the story involves adventures, tasks, magical objects, trials, or wishes. The number *7* appears frequently, too, as in "Snow White and the Seven Dwarfs," "The Seven Ravens," and "The Seven Swans."

Arthur N. Applebee examined stories children tell for their use of a formal opening or title, a formal closing, and a consistent past tense. He found that even 2-year-olds begin to set off their stories with frames and that, by age 5, nearly all children use at least one of these characteristics; nearly half of the stories are marked by the use of all three conventions. Children's expectations about stories and characters develop early.

Applebee asked 5-, 6-, and 7-year-olds about the nature of stories:

> "What happens in stories?" we asked Ernest: "They live happily ever after."—Who does?—"Poor people."
>
> The patterns of the stories are quickly sensed by children, just as they are by adults; even the characters have their appointed roles: "If you are reading a story about a rabbit, what is the rabbit usually like?"—"Fast."—What about a fox?—"Fast. He wants to eat someone."—What about a witch?—"Cook someone."—What about fairies?—"Fairies? They don't do nothing."—What are they usually like?—"Flying." (Stephen)
>
> And Charles in a similar vein: "What does a lion do in a story?"—"Kills people."—What about an elephant?—"He drinks water. He don't kill people. He just runs about."[19]

Such answers affirm the symbols and images built into myths and fairy tales; they bear little relation to the real nature of the animals involved, but then they were never intended to. These early expectations, coupled with children's intuitive grasp of the universal dreams of humankind, show the important position of folklore in a literary education.

Motifs

A motif is an element that has something distinctive about it; it may be a symbol, an image, a device—a thread that runs through a story to

Children develop a sense of story through the literary conventions that dominate folklore, and that sense is reinforced by the books they read.

accentuate the theme. Familiar motifs appear in stereotypic characters—gods, witches, fairies, noodleheads, or stepmothers.

Children learn to predict that these characters will behave in certain ways. Witches, of course, are evil; they try to eat children. Often it is a stepmother who becomes the witch, as in "Hansel and Gretel" and "Sleeping Beauty."

A second kind of motif—magical objects, spells, curses, or wishes—serves as a chief mechanism of some plots. Beans tossed carelessly out the window lead the way to a magical kingdom in "Jack and the Beanstalk." "The Magic Porridge Pot" and its variant, *Strega Nona* (P), hinge upon a secret ritual. In Tomie dePaola's Caldecott Honor book, Big Anthony disobeys the old woman, Strega Nona, and starts the magic pasta pot boiling. But unfortunately, he does not know how to stop it. The pasta boils and bubbles all over the house, out the door, and through the little town of Calabria. Strega Nona finally returns with the three magic kisses required to stop the pot. There is a satisfying denouement when Strega Nona hands Big Anthony a fork and says, "Start eating." DePaola combines folklore elements with his own imagination in this and other stories set in his grandmother's hometown of Calabria, Italy: *Big Anthony and the Magic Ring;*

TEACHING IDEA

"HANSEL AND GRETEL" (P)   Collect many different books of "Hansel and Gretel," and provide time for children to look at and read all of them. (See the Variants of Familiar Folktales chart on page 248.) Ask students to pay close attention to the illustrations of the stepmother and the witch. Do any of them give visual clues that the witch is indeed the stepmother? Are there verbal clues to substantiate this?

ACTIVITY: TEACHER TO STUDENT

"HANSEL AND GRETEL" (P)   Look at the way different artists have drawn the witch in "Hansel and Gretel." (See the table, "Variants of Familiar Folktales," on page 248.) Which is the scariest? What makes a witch look scary? Have any of the illustrators made the witch look like someone else in the story?

Write some words to describe a scary witch. Make a picture of a scary witch; be sure you follow your own description.

Big Anthony learned Strega Nona's chant for starting the magic pot but not for stopping it. His desperate measure fails to stem the flow of pasta. (From the book *Strega Nona* by Tomie dePaola.)

248–49 shows variants of other folk tales also suitable for this kind of investigation.

In some stories, the evil spell causes a transformation, and only love and kindness can return the frog, or donkey, or beast to its former state. "The Frog Prince," "The Donkey Prince," "The Seven Ravens," "The Six Swans," "Jorinda and Joringel," and "Beauty and the Beast" are all transformation tales. "The Hedgehog Boy," a less familiar transformation tale, is about a woman who wishes for a child "even if it looks like a hedgehog." In the way of enchantment, a son is born with ugly spiny quills. Unable to live with his father's revulsion, the boy goes to live alone in the forest. Years later a king, lost in the forest, appears at the hedgehog's door. As the hedgehog leads him home, the king promises to give the creature the first thing that greets them at the castle. Instead of the king's dog, which the king expected, the princess runs to greet her father. One year and a day later, the hedgehog comes to claim his reward. On their wedding night, the hedgehog sheds his prickly coat of fur and is transformed into a handsome young man. Jane Langton retells the Latvian variant of this story in *The Hedgehog Boy* (P-I). Ilse Plume's folk art illustrations integrate Lat-

Strega Nona's Magic Lessons; and *Merry Christmas, Strega Nona* (all P).

Sometimes the magical element in a story is a spell or enchantment. Both Snow White and Sleeping Beauty are victims of a witch's evil curse when they are put to sleep until a kiss from a handsome prince awakens them. There are many outstanding editions of both of these tales, and children will enjoy comparing both the language and the illustrations. The accompanying chart was worked out by a group of third grade students.[20] The list on pages

TEACHING IDEA

TRANSFORMATION TALES (P-I)   Transformation tales appear in the folklore of many cultures. Some of the most beautiful picture books produced in recent years tell these stories. Share these books and discuss the reasons for the transformations, the curses or spells, and restorations. Call special attention to the way the different artists depict the gradual changes. (All of the titles in the following list are at the P–I level).

Bang, *Dawn*, a Japanese tale
Cleaver, *The Enchanted Caribou*, an Eskimo tale
Cooper, *The Selkie Girl*, a Celtic tale
Gerstein, *The Seal Mother*, a Celtic tale

Goble, *Buffalo Woman*, a native American tale
Steptoe, *The Story of Jumping Mouse*, a native American tale
Yagawa, *The Crane Wife*, a Japanese tale

PROFILE

Tomie dePaola

Books have always been important to me. I remember way back in the early '40s when I was a young child, a poster (for Book Week, I imagine) of a ship made out of books. At least, I remember it that way, sailing off to "faraway places" with loads of book characters—Alice, Jo March, Robinson Crusoe, Puss-in-Boots, Cinderella, you name 'em—all around. I just can't imagine life without books.[21]

To see the world through the eyes of Tomie dePaola is to see a world of laughter, love, and hope. His ingenuity with words and illustrations places him at the forefront of the storytellers of the world.

A prolific creator of original stories, dePaola also recasts old tales, making them appeal to children of today as they have for countless years past. *The Clown of God* (P), a retelling of the ancient French legend of the juggler giving his final performance before the Lady and the Holy Child, is set in medieval Italy. *The Prince of the Dolomites* (P), an old Italian tale resembling the mythic creation stories, explains how the beautiful Dolomite mountains were changed from black peaks to glimmering pastels by the powerful force of love; a similar feeling of awe and wonder is conveyed in *The Lady of Guadalupe* (P). *Helga's Dowry* (P), from Scandinavian folklore, is a delightful story about how one troll maiden earns her dowry and the king's love at the same time. In *Tomie dePaola's Mother Goose* (N–P) and *Tomie dePaola's Favorite Nursery Tales* (N–P), he gives his own characteristic interpretations of many old favorites. In all of these retellings, Tomie dePaola acknowledges the influence of pre-Renaissance Italian masters on his art.

When asked if he fears running out of ideas, dePaola says, "Of course, I do. . . . But I have a trick. I always try to come up with new projects before I finish the one I'm working on. Sort of like sourdough bread, you take a little dough to start your new batch."[22]

Born in Meriden, Connecticut, and of Irish-Italian descent, he lives in New Hampshire in a nineteenth-century farmhouse.

vian designs into the overall compositions for this powerful transformation tale.

Children should be encouraged to make a chart of these transformation stories on which they list the former and transformed state, the evil character, the reason for the spell, and the vehicle for the restoration.

Another motif that also appears frequently is the noodlehead character—one who is pure-hearted but lacks good judgment. In Grimm's

VARIATION AND SIMILARITIES IN THREE VERSIONS OF "SLEEPING BEAUTY"

	Grimms/Hyman* Version (Germany, 1812)	Grimms/Le Cain* Version (Germany, 1812)	Perrault/Walker* Version (France, Nineteenth Century)
Name	Briar Rose	Thorn Rose	The Princess
Setting	Feast	Feast	Christening banquet
Characters	13 fairies	13 fairies	8 fairies
Prediction	Frog predicts daughter	Crab predicts daughter	No prediction
Onset of spell	15th birthday	15th birthday	16th birthday
Spell	Sleep 100 years	Sleep 100 years	Sleep 100 years
Action	All fall asleep	All fall asleep	Princess falls asleep (Good fairy puts others to sleep)
Obstacle	Thorny briar roses	Hedge of thorns	Briars and brambles
Ending	Lived in peace and joy until they died	Lived happily ever after	Married; at birth of their child princess no longer had memory of 100-year sleep.
Illustration quality	Powerful, sense of gloom, subtle carvings	Exquisite detail, foreboding darkness, tapestry borders, opulent, majestic	Romantic, dreamlike, bright color

*Illustrator.

Hans in Luck (P), Hans starts out with a bag of gold but ends with nothing after a series of bad trades. In *Noodlehead Stories from Around the World* (I), M. A. Jagendorf describes a noodlehead as a simple, blundering person who does not use good sense or learn from experience. Jagendorf includes stories of the noodlehead who loses because he tries to grab too much, has too much pride, or uses big words he does not understand.

"The Three Sillies" is a favorite noodlehead tale from English folklore that has been retold and illustrated with only slight variations by several artists. Children love the story of the young man whose sweetheart goes to the cellar to draw a jug of cider and sees an axe (or mallet) hanging from the ceiling. She wails because someday her future son might come down to the cellar and the axe will fall on his head. First her mother, then her father come down and they, too, begin to wail. Finally the young man

comes down to find the forgotten cider spilled all over the floor. He shuts off the spigot, pulls the axe from the ceiling, and vows to return only after he has found three bigger sillies than these. Of course he does, and so he returns and marries his sweet silly.

One of the sillies that this young man finds is a woman who is trying to get her cow to climb a ladder from the roof of her sod house. Getting the cow from the roof and the overflowing cider found in the English version of the noodlehead story are also found in Norwegian variants: *Turnabout* (P), by William Wiesner; *The Man Who Was Going to Mind the House* (P), by David McKee; and *The Man Who Kept House* (P) by Kathleen and Michael Hague.

Every cultural group has its noodlehead stories: the wise men of Gotham in England, the fools of Chelm in Poland, Juan Bobo in Puerto Rico, the Connemara man in Ireland, and the Montieri in Italy. Children enjoy the good-natured fun and laugh heartily at the silly blunders of noodlehead characters.

As children read widely, they soon begin to recognize these recurring patterns in the folklore of many countries. Characters, events, and resolutions appear over and over again, and students begin to make predictions and build their own conceptions of folkloric elements.

Trickery or outwitting another is an oft-played element in many tales. For example, a spider man is the trickster in African and Caribbean tales, as in Gail Haley's *A Story, A Story* (P-I). Anansi, the spider man, outwits the Sky God by accomplishing the three tasks he is assigned—the price he must pay for the Sky God's stories. Anansi is crafty and wise in other stories, such as Gerald McDermott's *Anansi the Spider* (P-I), in which he encounters trouble far from home. Using their special talents, Anansi's six sons save him and, when he is home again, he wants to give the moon to the son who rescued him. When he cannot decide which son deserves the prize, Nyame, the god of all things, takes the moon up into the sky, to hold it there to this day.

Trickery and cunning also appear in French and Swedish folk tales, as in Marcia Brown's *Stone Soup* (P) and in Harve Zemach's *Nail Soup* (P). In the first story, three soldiers trick an entire village into feeding them when they pretend to make soup from a stone. The soldiers ask for a piece of meat, a few potatoes and some vegetables to add to the stone—just for a bit of flavor. In the second story, an old man plays the same trick on an old woman as he makes magical soup from a nail, enriched, of course, by the bits of food she adds to the pot.

One of the criticisms of folk and fairy tales has been the passive role of many of the female characters.[23] In Walter De la Mare's retelling of *Mollie Whuppie* (P), however, we find a clever young girl who tricks the giant and wins not only a prince for herself but also one for each of her sisters.

The tales of Brer Rabbit are some of the best-known contributions to the world's rich collection of folklore. The wily rabbit's adventures, as we know them, take place in the rural South, but versions of these tales are told throughout the world. (From *Jump! The Adventures of Brer Rabbit*, illustrated by Barry Moser.)

The wiliest trickster of all times, Brer Rabbit, has traveled in one form or another in tales from Africa through Jamaica and to the rural South. While many of the tales were popularized by Joel Chandler Harris, the characters appear in many guises in stories told around the world. One of the most outstanding renditions of five of the tales is found in *Jump! The Adventures of Brer Rabbit* (I) and *Jump Again! More Adventures of Brer Rabbit* (I), both illustrated by Barry Moser. Moser's portrayal of Brer Rabbit and his friends is superb: spooky Brer Wolf, slinky Brer Fox, beak-faced Brer Terrapin, and the cigar-chewing rascal Brer Rabbit are shown in cameo portraits that reveal their inner traits. Other satisfying adaptations of these tales can be found in Virginia Hamilton's *The People Could Fly* (I), William Faulkner's *The Days When the Animals Talked* (I), Priscilla Jaquith's *Bo Rabbit Smart for True* (P-I), and Julius Lester's *Tales of Uncle Remus* (I), a new version of Brer Rabbit.

Themes

Themes, the central and dominating ideas in stories, evolve around topics of universal human concern. The struggle between good and evil is played out time and again in folklore. Hate, fear, and greed are contrasted with love, security, and generosity. The themes are usually developed through stereotyped characters that personify good and evil. The good are supremely good, and the bad are totally evil. For example, the bad fairy in Sleeping Beauty, the witch in Hansel and Gretel, and the stepmother in Snow White all represent evil. In each story, the evil one is destroyed and the virtuous one rewarded—satisfying endings to affirm that goodness prevails and evil is crushed. Such themes are reassuring to young children.

Evil characters appear in the folklore of all cultures, but none is so cruel as the witch Baba Yaga from Russia. There are many different stories about her, but in each she travels about in a mortar steered by a pestle—when she is not at home in her cottage, which is perched atop a pair of chicken legs. Around the cottage is a fence made from the bones and skulls of the children who had wandered too far into her forest. In each story, a young girl combines trickery with kindness to escape Baba Yaga's cruelty. *Bony Legs* (P) by Joanna Cole, *Anna and the Seven Swans* (P) by Maida Silverman, and *Baba Yaga* (P) by Ernest Small are all quite different Baba Yaga stories.

Baba Yaga appears also in the Russian versions of the Cinderella story, including *Vasilisa the Beautiful* (P) translated by Thomas P. Whitney and *Lovely Vassilisa* (P) retold by Barbara Cohen.

The theme of the struggle between good and evil is also shown as a contrast between surface appearance and the deeper qualities of goodness in transformation and enchantment tales. As we have seen, a curse is cast upon a handsome prince who must then live as a monstrous beast, frog, donkey—as in "Beauty and the Beast," "The Frog Prince," and "The Donkey Prince." The loathsome spell is broken by love—that of a beautiful princess who sees the goodness of the prince hidden beneath the gruesome exterior. In other stories, such as some versions of "Sleeping Beauty" and the Persephone myth, the entire world is under an evil spell, veiled and hidden from clear view until goodness prevails.

In one such story, adapted by Toni De Gerez from Finland's epic poem, the "Kalevala," *Louhi, Witch of North Farm* (P-I), plunges the world into darkness. When the sun and moon hide behind a tree to listen to the magical music of Vainamoinen, Louhi seizes the opportunity to steal their light by hiding them deep within a mountain. Barbara Cooney's magnificent paintings vivify the stark contrast between the somber wintry nights and the glorious day when Louhi is tricked into releasing the sun and moon to spread their light once again. This story contains many of the recurring patterns found in folklore. The more children read the traditional tales, the more they will discover the intricate threads and themes woven throughout them.

The search for happiness or lost identity in order to restore harmony to life is a recurring quest theme. In many stories, the hero succeeds only after a long journey, repeated trials, much suffering, and extended separation. In the Grimms' *The Seven Ravens* (P-I), a young girl travels far and faces difficult trials before she rescues her seven brothers. In *The Angry Moon* (P-I), by William Sleator, Lapin shoots a ladder of arrows to the sky and, with the help of three magic objects, rescues Lapowinsa from the moon, who had been holding her captive. In both stories, characteristically, the journey—from home through alienation, suffering, and trials—has a satisfying ending, with happiness restored.

A theme of courage, gallantry, and sacrifice is vividly treated in Margaret Hodges adaptation of *Saint George and the Dragon* (P-I). The story, adapted from Edmund Spenser's "Faerie Queene" and set in the days when "monsters and giants and fairy folk lived in England," tells of a young knight who had never yet faced a foe or tested his strength. Now he is sent by the Queen of the Fairies to face a deadly enemy, a dragon grim and horrible. The lovely young princess Una, veiled in sorrow, rides on a white donkey beside him; she is searching for a champion to face the terrible dragon who is laying waste to her land and frightening people from their homes. The dauntless courage of the Red Cross Knight helps him to slay the dragon, win the princess, and become the patron saint of England. Trina Schart Hyman won the Caldecott Medal for her illustrations of the grizzly battle, the bloodied but victorious knight, and the radiant Una. The tiffany-like paintings, framed with magnificent borders, represent some of Hyman's most distinguished art.

In Grimm's *The Twelve Dancing Princesses* (P-I), retold by Andrew Lang and illustrated by Adrienne Adams, the soldier must undergo many trials to discover where the princesses dance nightly. When he discovers the secret, with the help of a cloak of invisibility, he marries the eldest daughter and inherits the kingdom. In Tomie dePaola's *The Clown of God* (P-I), a juggler travels through a lifetime making people laugh, but when he grows old and in-

ept they taunt him. Desiring to present an offering to Mary and the baby Jesus, he gives his greatest and final performance. The theme of giving of oneself permeates the folk tale.

Types

There are many ways to look for patterns in folklore. In addition to conventions, motifs, and themes, some tales are distinguished by their structure. Two major types are *cumulative* tales and *pourquoi* tales.

Children recognize the cumulative pattern of some folk tales—such as the particularly conspicuous one of "This Is the House that Jack Built"—wherein each incident grows from the preceding one. Cumulative folk tales, characterized by their structure, are often called chain tales, since each part of the story is linked to the next. The initial incident reveals both central character and problem; each subsequent scene builds onto the original one. The accumulation continues to a climax and then unravels in reverse order or stops with an abrupt or surprise ending. "Henny Penny" and "The Old Woman and Her Pig" exemplify repetition and chaining. "The Gingerbread Boy" and its variant "Johnny Cake" illustrate the chain tale with a repetitive phrase—in this case, "Run, run as fast as you can. You can't catch me. I'm the Gingerbread man."

One Fine Day (P), by Nonny Hogrogian, and *Drummer Hoff* (P), by Barbara and Ed Emberley, are written in cumulative style. In *One Fine Day*, an old woman chops off the tail of a fox who has drunk her pail of milk. The fox begs the old woman to give back his tail, but she agrees to do so only if the fox gives back the milk. The story builds as the fox bargains for the milk. He goes to a cow, a field, a stream, and several other things before he is finally granted a request that unlocks all previous ones. "The Cat and the Mouse" in Joseph

PROFILE

Trina Schart Hyman

Trina Schart Hyman, born in Philadelphia, grew up in a rural area about 20 miles north of the city. The woman who owned a nearby farm was an artist who painted portraits; Trina at age 6 made one of her first drawings for this woman and submitted it to her timidly. She was encouraged and sus-

tained her early interest in art, went to art school in Philadelphia after high school graduation, and wandered through the art museum often. Hyman lived in Sweden and bicycled 2,800 miles around Sweden before she settled in Boston to raise her daughter Katrin. Hyman later moved to a farm in New Hampshire where she still lives.

Trina Schart Hyman's interest in folktales began very early. She describes her attachment to "Little Red Riding Hood" as a child.

She (my mother) read to me from the time I was a baby, and once, when I was three or four and she was reading my favorite story, the words on the page, her spoken words, and the scenes in my head fell together in a blinding flash. I could read! The story was *Little Red Riding Hood*, and it was so much a part of me that I actually became Little Red Riding Hood. My mother sewed me a red satin cape with a

Jacobs's *English Fairy Tales* (I) is a variant of the same story. *Drummer Hoff* is based on an English folk rhyme in which the story accumulates as additional people help to fire a cannon. The time-honed text, with illustrations that extend the content, combine several layers of meaning in the story. Jack Kent's *The Fat Cat: A Danish Folktale* (P) is another cumulative tale that children enjoy.

Pourquoi, or "why," tales explain certain traits or characteristics as well as customs and natural phenomena. Arlene Mosel's *Tikki Tikki*

Tembo (P) tells why all Chinese children are given short names. One day a small boy named Tikki tikki tembo-no sa rembo-chari bari ruchi-pip peri pembo fell into a well. His brother ran for help but because it took him so long to repeat the long name, the boy almost drowned. "And from that day to this the Chinese have always thought it wise to give all children little short names instead of great long names," the story concludes.

Ann Grifalconi brings new life to a West African story that explains why there is *The Vil-*

hood that I wore almost every day, and on those days, she would make me a "basket of goodies" to take to my grandmother's house. (My only grandmother lived in Rhode Island, three hundred miles away, but that didn't matter.) I'd take the basket and carefully negotiate the backyard, "going to Grandmother's house." My dog, Tippy, was the wolf. Whenever we met, which in a small backyard had to be fairly often, there was an intense confrontation. My father was the woodsman, and I greeted him when he came home each day with relief and joy. I was Little Red Riding Hood for a year or more.[24]

Trina Schart Hyman's version of *Little Red Riding Hood* (P), in full color reflects New England farmland, houses, and characters. Borders containing relevant side scenes frame the text on pages that face magnificent full-page paintings of the major events. The paintings of Little Red Riding Hood are self-

portraits of the artist as a child. The forest scenes and the wolf look mysterious and foreboding, to add just the right scariness to the tale.

Hyman won the Caldecott Medal and a New York Times Best Illustrated Book Award for *Saint George and the Dragon* (retold by Margaret Hodges). She also won a Caldecott Honor book award and the Golden Kite Award for *Little Red Riding Hood*. She received the Boston Globe–Horn Book Award for *King Stork*.

Trina Schart Hyman is noted for the quality of her illustrations for fantasy, nonfiction, picture books, historical fiction, realistic fiction, poetry and folklore. Her characters exude strength and vitality: beautiful princesses, wicked stepmothers, charming princes, and valiant knights wear their character on their faces and in their bearing.

lage of Round and Square Houses (P). A grandmother recalls that many years ago a volcano destroyed all but one round house and one square one in the Cameroon village of Tos. Thankful to be alive, the people interpreted this as a sign, so the men moved into the square house and the women and children moved into the round one. Grifalconi's art, which merited a Caldecott Honor award, dramatically shows the violent volcanic eruption. After the explosion, the strikingly modulated colors and textures slowly change from muted

ashy gray and brown monotones back to natural earth tones.

Verna Aardema's *Why Mosquitoes Buzz in People's Ears* (P) vivifies both the pourquoi and chain tale structure. In this Caldecott Medal winner, a mosquito sets off a chain of events that prevents the owl from waking the sun to begin a new day. Iguana, annoyed by the mosquito's buzzing, puts sticks in his ear. Frightened by the sight, python sends terror through the forest until a baby owl is accidentally killed. The mosquito is condemned for telling a lie and starting the whole unfortunate sequence. In spite of his chastisement, to this day he still whispers in people's ears.

Variants of Folk Tales

Although the origins of folk tales are clouded in prehistory, variants of some can be traced to many cultures. Marian Roalfe Cox uncovered an amazing number of variants of the Cinderella story. She gives brief excerpts and comparisons in *Cinderella: Three Hundred and Forty-Five Variants* (adult). In a foreword to this collection, Andrew Lang states, "The märchen [fairy tale] is a kaleidoscope: the incidents are the bits of coloured glass. Shaken, they fall into a variety of attractive forms; some forms are fitter than others, survive more powerfully, and are more widely spread."[25]

The more familiar version of "Cinderella," based on Perrault's tale, is a romantic rags-to-riches love story. This version has been illustrated in single-edition format by several noted artists; those by Marcia Brown, Susan Jeffers, and Errol LeCain are among the best. In contrast, the German version illustrated by Nonny Hogrogian takes on a macabre tone. In order to make their feet fit into the tiny glass slipper, one stepsister cuts off her toe and the other cuts off her heel. In the end they are blinded while their mother dances to her death in iron shoes.

In *Once Upon a Time: On the Nature of Fairy Tales*, Max Lüthi presents an insightful analysis of the many variants of "Sleeping Beauty."[26] Lüthi speaks of fairy tales as remnants of primal myths, playful descendants of an ancient, intuitive vision of life and the world. For example, Sleeping Beauty, mysteriously threatened and suffering a sleep similar to death but then awakened, parallels the story of death and resurrection. In much the same vein, the awakening of the sleeping maiden can represent the earth's awakening from winter to live and blossom anew when touched by the warmth of spring.

Lüthi shows that the story of Sleeping Beauty is more than an imaginatively stylized love story portraying a girl whose love breaks a spell. The princess is an image for the human spirit: the story portrays the endowment, peril, and redemption, not of just one girl but all of humankind. Sleeping Beauty's recovery symbolizes the human soul that, suffering repeated setbacks, is yet revived, healed, and redeemed. Human feelings, such as longing, grief, and joy, are expressed in the story. The fairy tale is a universe in miniature that not only reflects the wisdom of the ages but also presents that wisdom in an enchanting tale. Although such elaborate analysis is not for children, it informs a teacher's presentation.

The story of the little man who, for a cruel fee, helps the poor girl spin straw or flax into skeins of gold is a well-loved folk tale that has many variants in many countries. From Germany comes the best-known version, Grimm's *Rumpelstiltskin* (P), a tale in which the dwarf spins straw into gold. In the version from Suffolk, England, an impet (dwarf) spins five skeins of gold from flax in the story called *Tom Tit Tot* (P), retold by Evaline Ness. In Devonshire and Cornwall, England, the devil knits stockings, jackets, and other clothing for the Squire, as recounted in the tale *Duffy and the Devil* (P), retold by Harve Zemach. The corresponding character of Rumpelstiltskin is called Trit-a-Trot in Ireland and Whuppity Stoorie in Scotland.

"Jack and the Beanstalk" first appeared in Joseph Jacob's collection of English folk tales and has been illustrated by many contemporary artists (see the variant chart). Lorinda B. Cauley's beanstalk is a lush green forest that evokes a sense of danger and foreboding; her people are serious. In contrast, Paul Galdone's characters are oafish bunglers who create a more light-hearted story.

Arthur Rackham's gleeful Rumpelstiltskin celebrates the bargain he has made with the miller's daughter. (From *Grimm's Fairy Tales: Twenty Stories Illustrated by Arthur Rackham.*)

In one of Evaline Ness's artful woodcuts, the king watches the impet spin straw into gold in *Tom Tit Tot* by Evaline Ness.

Folk tales adapted by different cultural groups show corresponding differences in language and setting. Many Americanized versions of Old World tales are known as "Jack Tales," and revolve around a boy named Jack. One of the most familiar is a variant of "Jack and the Beanstalk" and is known as "Jack's Bean Tree," found in Richard Chase's *The Jack Tales* (I). *Jack and the Wonder Beans* (P-I) by James Still is another variant. Appalachian dialect permeates these versions of the familiar tale. For example, the giant's refrain in *Jack and the Wonder Beans* is "Fee, fie, chew tobacco, I smell the toes of a tadwhacker."

Gail Haley's *Jack and the Bean Tree* (P) is another Appalachian retelling, this time set within the context of a storyteller's tale. Family and neighbors gather round grandmother Poppyseed who gives a local flavor to her tales, such as a banty hen that lays the golden eggs and the giant that chants "Bein' he live or bein'/ he dead,/I'll have his bones/To eat with my pones."[27] Haley's illustrations are bold and energetic, painted on wood in brilliant colors that reflect the various intensities of light and shadow.

A parody of the Jack Tales is *Jim and the Beanstalk* (P-I) by Raymond Briggs. In this

TEACHING IDEA

COMPARING VARIANTS OF RUMPELSTILTSKIN (P-I) Students who read several versions of the Rumpelstiltskin story can compare the different names the little man is called, the chants and refrains used, and the price the dwarf demands for his services.

	Tom Tit Tot	Rumpelstiltskin	Duffy and the Devil
Names guessed	Bill, Ned, Mark, Sammle, Methusalem, Solomon, Zebedee, Tom Tit Tot	Timothy, Benjamin, Bandylegs, Hunchback, Crookshanks, John, Tom, Rumpelstiltskin	Does not tell
Chants or refrains	Nimmy, nimmy not My name is Tom Tit Tot and Well, that won't do no harm, if that don't do no good	Little goes my lady dream Rumpel-stilt-skin is my name	Tomorrow! Tomorrow! Tomorrow's the day! I'll take her! I'll take her I'll take her away! Let her weep, let her cry let her beg, let her pray— She'll never guess my name is . . . Tarraway.
Price	"You shall be mine"	First-born child	"I'll take you away"
Characterization	Impet	Gnome	Devil

version, the giant has grown old and has lost his appetite and his eyesight. Jim helps by getting him false teeth and glasses.

FABLES

The fable is a brief, didactic comment on the nature of human life that is presented in dramatic action to make the idea memorable. One factor that distinguishes the fable from other traditional literature forms is that it illustrates a moral, which is stated explicitly at the end. Many common sayings and phrases come from fables: "Better beans and bacon in peace than cakes and ale in fear," "Slow and steady wins

the race," "Sour grapes," and "Don't cry wolf." Such injunctions, explicitly stated as morals, are taught by allegory; animals or inanimate objects represent human traits in stories that clearly show the wisdom of the simple lessons.

Folklorist Joseph Jacobs relates the fable to the beast tales (in which characters are animals with human characteristics), which were used for satiric purposes and in some cases to teach a moral. In the single incident story typical of the fable, we are told not to be vain, not to be greedy and not to lie. Jacobs traces the origins of fables to both Greece and India. Reputedly, a Greek slave named Aesop used fables for political purposes, and though some doubt that he ever lived, his name has been associated with fables since ancient times. Early collections made in the East derive from the "Panchatantra" (Five Tantras, or Books), a famous collection from India known to English readers as the Fables of Bidpai and Jataka Tales. The Jatakas are stories of Buddha's prior lives as various animals—each tale told to illustrate a moral principle.

Rafe Martin and Ed Young combined their talents to produce a variant of a Jataka tale, *Foolish Rabbit's Big Mistake* (P). In this ancient ancestor of "Henny Penny" and "Chicken Little" who thought the sky was falling, a rabbit hears a thud beneath the nearby apple tree. Assuming the worst, he rushes off to warn the other animals that the earth is breaking up. Ed Young's magnificent paintings capture the intensity of the animals' fear. One stunning spread shows a close-up of the lion stopping the stampede of frightened animals with a powerful roar.

Steven Kellogg's *Chicken Little* (P) is a cheerful modern spoof of the same tale. Here the evil Foxy Loxy sits in his poultry truck while he awaits the inevitable parade of barnyard animals. Foxy Loxy even tosses the acorn that starts Chicken Little on her doomed chain of events. On the final page, a grandmotherly Chicken Little sits beneath a giant oak relating the story to her decendants.

A seventeenth-century French poet, Jean de La Fontaine, adapted many of Aesop's early fables into verse form. Several of these have

TEACHING IDEA

EXPLORING ONE FOLK TALE (I)   Students may enjoy one folk tale so much that they want to try various activities to extend their appreciation. Familiar folk tales are an excellent base for drama, art, and written and oral language experiences. "The Three Billy Goats Gruff" is a favorite for dramatization. Volunteers can play the roles of each of the billy goats and the troll. (There will be many requests for this part!) Scenery is minimal: the teacher's chair can serve as the bridge under which the troll hides. A narrator may tell the story, with characters speaking their lines, or children can play the scene with dialogue only.

Compare the well-done illustrations in the versions by Susan Blair, Marcia Brown, Paul Galdone, Janet Stevens, and William Stobbs (all N-P). Making judgments about illustrations is a particularly useful area in which to exercise discrimination. Ask which troll looks meanest, which is scariest, which one shows the fiercest battle between the third billy goat and the troll, which one shows best the size relationship between the smallest, middle-sized, and biggest billy goats. Children can then draw their impressions of the troll.

When language is the focus, children should be able to read the stories for themselves. Discuss the differences in the texts of the four versions. Ask how the troll is described, what words tell you about him, what words tell you what happened to him when he was pushed off the bridge, how each story ends. Point out that the phrase "Snip, Snap, Snout, this tale's told out" is a typical Norwegian ending.

Though engraver's tools of the time were relatively crude, Wenceslaus Hollar's 1665 engraving of the plight of the lion in Aesop's ''The Lion and the Mouse'' achieves a sense of the lion's strength and the intricacy of the net. (The Lion and the Mouse, engraving by W. Hollar for John Ogilby, *The Fables of Aesop.)*

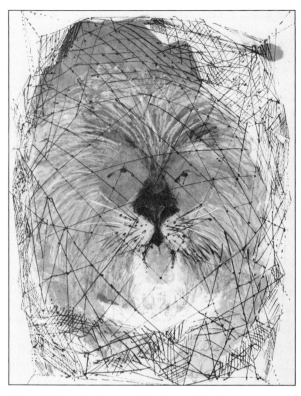

Brian Wildsmith's lion, in *The Lion and the Rat*, occupies almost all the space of the page to convey the strength of the trapped animal.

been beautifully illustrated by Brian Wildsmith. *The Lion and the Rat, The North Wind and the Sun*, and *The Rich Man and the Shoemaker* (all P) will enrich any fable collection.

Noted illustrators of children's books have chosen to interpret fables artistically, although there are only a few single editions. Marcia Brown's subtle yet powerful woodcuts enable *Once a Mouse* (P-I) to stand as a classic among illustrated fables. *The Hare and the Tortoise* (P) and *Three Aesop Fox Fables* (P-I) are illustrated by Paul Galdone in a flamboyant style that makes clear the subtle humor.

The theme of greed is treated in Marcia Sewall's retelling of La Fontaine's fable *The Cob-*

bler's Song (P). A poor cobbler lives happily in his basement home and sings all day long as he works. A rich man on the floor above is obsessed with his wealth. He cannot sleep at night for worrying about his money and cannot sleep in the daytime because of the cobbler's singing. Determined to give the cobbler something to worry about, the rich man gives him a bag of gold coins. His plot works because the cobbler, afraid of losing his newfound wealth, begins to worry and stops his singing. The cobbler's wife urges him to return the gold. She says, ''All the gold in the world is not worth as much to me as your happiness and one of your glad songs.''

Lorinda Bryan Cauley's *The Town Mouse and the Country Mouse* (P) is a new version of a classic fable. The two mice who visit each other decide that they each prefer their own homes. This fable illustrates the moral that it is better to eat simply in peace than to feast in fear.

There are several collections of fables. One of the most attractive, *Aesop's Fables* (I), is illustrated by Heidi Holder. Full-page paintings, delicately framed, convey the traditional mood of the stories. Arnold Lobel uses the fable form to point out modern human frailties in *Fables* (P-I), a Caldecott Medal book. He shows how vanity misfires and how social misfits are recognized.

Jack Kent illustrated two collections, *Jack Kent's Fables of Aesop* (P) and *More Fables of Aesop* (P), for younger children. There is very little evidence, however, that primary grade children understand the subtle abstractions on which the fables hinge. Because fables are very short and their language simple, many teachers mistakenly give fables to children who are too young to comprehend or fully appreciate them. Arlene Pillar, for instance, found that 7-year-olds often missed the point of widely used fables.[28] Since fables are constructed within the oblique perspective of satire, allegory, and symbolism, their intent may elude young children's literal understanding.

TEACHING IDEA

ALLUSIONS FROM FABLES (I-A)   Our language is replete with allusions to fables. Students enjoy looking for allusions, matching the morals to the fables, writing their own fables, and illustrating favorite ones. Compile a list of morals used as common sayings in our language, and encourage students to find the fable that illustrates the moral.

ACTIVITY: TEACHER TO STUDENT

FIND THE FABLES (I)   Match the following maxims with the fable.

_____1.   It's just sour grapes.
_____2.   You're a dog in the manger.
_____3.   Slow and steady wins the race.
_____4.   Are you crying wolf?
_____5.   Who will bell the cat?
_____6.   Don't bite the hand that feeds you.
_____7.   Better beans and bacon in peace than cakes and ale in fear.
_____8.   Vanity cometh before a fall.

a. The City Mouse and the Country Mouse
b. Belling the Tiger
c. The Fox and the Crow
d. The Dog in the Manger
e. The Boy Who Cried Wolf
f. The Fox and the Grapes
g. The Hare and the Tortoise
h. Once a Mouse

If you are especially interested in fables, extend the list of common sayings and search for their origins in folklore. Russian and Chinese proverbs are especially picturesque; search for some that have counterparts in our common sayings.

VARIANTS OF FAMILIAR FOLKTALES

Beauty and the Beast (originally recorded by Madame Le Prince De Beaumont)

Retold by Deborah Apy, illus. by Michael Hague
Retold by Anne Carter, illus. by Binette Schroeder
Illus. by Diane Goode
Retold and illus. by Warwick Hutton
Retold and illus. by Marianna Mayer

The Bremen Town Musicians (originally recorded by the Brothers Grimm)

Illus. by Paul Galdone
Illus. by Ilse Plume
Retold by Elizabeth Shub, illus. by Janina Domanska
(*The Traveling Musicians*) illus. by Hans Fischer

Cinderella (originally recorded by Charles Perrault and by the Brothers Grimm)

Illus. by Marcia Brown
Adapted by Amy Ehrlich, illus. by Susan Jeffers
Retold by C. S. Evans, illus. by Arthur Rackham
Trans. by John Fowles, illus. by Sheilah Beckett
Illus. by Paul Galdone
Illus. by Nonny Hogrogian
Illus. by Moira Kemp
Illus. by Errol Le Cain
Illus. by Otto Svend S.
Cinderella: From the Opera by Gioacchino Rossini, illus. by Beni Montresor
(*Moss Gown*) retold by William Hooks, illus. by Donald Carrick
(*Tattercoats*) retold by Flora Annie Steel, illus. by Diane Goode

The Frog Prince (originally recorded by the Brothers Grimm)

Illus. by Paul Galdone
Retold by Edith Tarcov, illus. by James Marshall
(*The Donkey Prince*) retold by M. Jean Craig, illus. by Barbara Cooney

The Gingerbread Boy

Retold and illus. by Paul Galdone
(*The Bun: A Tale from Russia*) retold and illus. by Marcia Brown
(*Johnny Cake*) retold and illus. by William Stobbs
(*Journey Cake, Ho!*) retold by Ruth Sawyer, illus. by Robert McCloskey

Goldilocks and the Three Bears

Retold and illus. by Jan Brett
Retold and illus. by Lorinda B. Cauley
Retold and illus. by Janet Stevens
Illus. by Bernadette Watts
(*The Three Bears*) retold and illus. by Paul Galdone
(*The Three Bears*) retold and illus. by Robert Southey
(*Deep in the Forest*—reversal of traditional tale) illus. by Brinton Turkle

Hansel and Gretel (originally recorded by the Brothers Grimm)

Illus. by Antonella Bolliger-Savelli
Illus. by Anthony Browne
Trans. by Elizabeth D. Crawford, illus. by Lisbeth Zwerger
Illus. by Paul Galdone
Retold by Ruth B. Gross, illus. by Margot Tomes
Illus. by Susan Jeffers
Retold by Rika Lesser, illus. by Paul O. Zelinsky
Illus. by Arnold Lobel
Trans. by Charles Scribner, Jr., illus. by Adrienne Adams

Illus. by John Wallner
(*Nibble Nibble Mousekin: A Tale of Hansel and Gretel*) illus. by Joan Walsh Anglund
(*Teeny Tiny and the Witch Woman*) retold by Barbara Walker, illus. by Michael Foreman

Henny Penny

Retold and illus. by Paul Galdone
Retold by Veronica S. Hutchinson, illus. by Leonard B. Lubin
Illus. by William Stobbs
(*Chicken Licken*) retold and illus. by Gavin Bishop
(*Chicken Licken*) retold by Kenneth McLeish, illus. by Jutta Ash
(*Chicken Little*) retold and illus. by Steven Kellogg
(*The Story of Chicken Licken*) retold and illus. by Jan Ormerod

Jack and the Beanstalk (originally recorded by Joseph Jacobs)

Illus. by Lorinda B. Cauley
Retold by Beatrice Schenk De Regniers, illus. by Anne Wilsdorf
Illus. by Paul Galdone
Illus. by Margery Gill
Illus. by William Stobbs
(*The History of Mother Twaddle and the Marvelous Achievement of Her Son Jack*) illus. by Paul Galdone
(*Jack and the Bean Tree*) retold and illus. by Gail Haley
(*Jack and the Wonder Beans*) retold by James Still, illus. by Margot Tomes
(*Jim and the Beanstalk*) by Raymond Briggs (parody)

Jorinda and Joringel (originally recorded by the Brothers Grimm)

Retold by Wanda Gág, illus. by Margot Tomes
Trans. by Elizabeth Shub, illus. by Adrienne Adams
Illus. by Bernadette Watts

VARIANTS OF FAMILIAR FOLKTALES *(continued)*

Little Red Hen

Retold and illus. by Janina
Domanska
Retold and illus. by Paul Galdone
Retold and illus. by Margot
Zemach

Little Red Riding Hood (originally
recorded by the Brothers Grimm
and by Charles Perrault)

Retold and illus. by Paul Galdone
Retold and illus. by John S.
Goodall
Retold and illus. by Trina Schart
Hyman
Illus. by William Stobbs
Illus. by Bernadette Watts
(The Gunniwolf) retold by
Wilhelmina Harper, illus. by
William Wiesner
(Little Red Cap) trans. by Elizabeth
D. Crawford, illus. by Lisbeth
Zwerger
(Red Riding Hood: Retold in Verse)
retold by Beatrice Schenk De
Regniers, illus. by Edward
Gorey
(Red Riding) retold by Jean Merrill,
illus. by Ronni Solbert (parody)

The Magic Porridge Pot

Retold and illus. by Paul Galdone
(Strega Nona) retold and illus. by
Tomie dePaola

Puss in Boots (originally recorded
by Charles Perrault)

Illus. by Marcia Brown
Illus. Lorinda Bryan Cauley
Illus. by Paul Galdone
Retold by Christopher Logue,
illus. by Nicola Bayley
Illus. by William Stobbs
Trans. by David Walser, illus. by
Jan Pienkowski

Rapunzel (originally recorded by
the Brothers Grimm)

Illus. by Jutta Ash
Illus. by Michael Hague
Illus. by Felix Hoffmann
Retold by Barbara Rogasky, illus.
by Trina Schart Hyman
Illus. by Bernadette Watts

Rumpelstiltskin (originally
recorded by the Brothers Grimm)

Illus. by Donna Diamond
Illus. by Paul Galdone
Illus. by William Stobbs
Retold by Edith Tarcov, illus. by
Edward Gorey
Illus. by John Wallner
Illus. by Paul O. Zelinsky
*(Duffy and the Devil: A Cornish Tale
Retold)* retold by Harve Zemach,
illus. by Margot Zemach
(Tom Tit Tot) retold and illus. by
Evaline Ness

The Shoemaker and the Elves
(originally recorded by the
Brothers Grimm)

Illus. by Adrienne Adams
Illus. by Cynthia and William
Birrer
(The Elves and the Shoemaker) illus.
by Katrin Brandt
(The Elves and the Shoemaker) illus.
by Paul Galdone
(The Elves and the Shoemaker) illus.
by Brinton Turkle

The Sleeping Beauty (originally
recorded by the Brothers Grimm
and by Charles Perrault)

Illus. by Warren Chappell
Retold by C. S. Evans, illus. by
Arthur Rackham
Illus. by Warwick Hutton
Illus. by Trina Schart Hyman
Illus. by Mercer Mayer
Illus. by David Walker
Trans. by David Walser, illus. by

Jan Pienkowski
(Briar Rose) illus. by Margery Gill
(Thorn Rose) illus. by Errol Le Cain

Snow White and Rose Red
(originally recorded by the
Brothers Grimm)

Trans. by Wayne Andrews, illus.
by Adrienne Adams
Illus. by Barbara Cooney
Illus. by John Wallner

**Snow White and the Seven
Dwarfs** (originally recorded by the
Brothers Grimm)

Trans. by Randall Jarrell, illus. by
Nancy Ekholm Burkert
Illus. by Wanda Gág
(Snow White) trans. by Anthea
Bell, illus. by Chihiro Iwasaki
(Snow White) trans. by Paul Heins
illus. by Trina Schart Hyman

The Three Billy Goats Gruff
(originally recorded by Peter
Christian Asbjørnsen and Jorgen
E. Moe)

Illus. by Susan Blair
Illus. by Marcia Brown
Illus. by Paul Galdone
Illus. by Janet Stevens
Illus. by William Stobbs

The Three Little Pigs (originally
recorded by Joseph Jacobs)

Illus. by Erik Blegvad
Illus. by Paul Galdone
Illus. by William Pène du Bois
Illus. by Edda Reinl

Tom Thumb (originally recorded
by the Brothers Grimm

Illus. by Felix Hoffmann
Trans. by Anthea Bell, illus. by
Otto Svend S.
Illus. by William Wiesner

MYTHS AND LEGENDS

Myths are symbolic stories created by the ancient peoples to explain their world. When the ancient Greeks, for instance, were frightened by and did not understand thunder, they created a story about a god that was angry and shook the heavens; when they did not understand how and why the sun moved, they invented a story about a god that drove a chariot across the sky. Pierre Grimal explains in his comprehensive *Larousse World Mythology* (I-A) that we humans lose our fear of things that we can identify and explain:

> Given a universe full of uncertainties and mysteries, the myth intervenes to introduce the human element: clouds in the sky, sunlight, storms at sea, all extra-human factors such as these lose much of their power to terrify as soon as they are given the sensibility, intentions, and motivations that every individual experiences daily.[29]

Myths comprise a sizable part of our literary heritage. They are exciting stories with well-defined characters, heroic action, challenging situations, and deep emotions. They offer readers magic, beauty, and strong visual images. They expand experience and transmit ancient values; from mythology we inherit language, symbols, customs, and law.

Creation and Nature Myths

Creation and nature myths describe both the origin of the earth and the phenomena that affect it. These are the tales that tell, for example, how the earth began and why the seasons change. Several books contain collections of creation myths from around the world. Penelope Farmer's *Beginnings: Creation Myths of the World* (I-A) and Maria Leach's *How the People Sang the Mountains Up: How and Why Stories* (I) bring together creation stories from many different cultures. Others focus on those stories from one society. Betty Baker, a resident of the American Southwest and a student of native American history, collected stories from the Papago and Pima Indians in her *At the Center of the World* (I).

Epics and Legends

Epics and legends, also known as hero tales, recount the courageous deeds of mortals as they struggle against each other or against gods and monsters. They reveal universal human emotions and portray the eternal struggle between good and evil.

Epics and legends contribute to an appreciation of world history and literature, to an understanding of national ideals of behavior, and to a knowledge of the valor, heroism, and nobility of humanity.

Hero tales include the stories of King Arthur and Robin Hood (discussed in Chapter 6), as well as the celebrated account of the Trojan War told in Homer's *Iliad* and *Odyssey*.

THE ROLE OF MYTH

Myths use symbolic expressions to explain the forces within human nature that we do not fully understand. Such descriptions of the unknown in human terms confer a sense of control through analogy and metaphor. Freudians see the myths as representations of sexual anxieties, jealousies, and psychic struggle between parents and children. Jungians call myths the memories of the human race that represent in each of us conflicts between the rational mind and the subconscious. Students do not read the myths for their deep levels of symbolic meaning, however. They read them because they are compelling stories of love, carnage, revenge, and mystery.

According to Northrop Frye, as folk tales, fables, songs, and legends develop, a special group of stories, the ones we call myths, crystallize at the center of the verbal culture. The stories are taken seriously because they express the meaning of beliefs and portray visions of destiny. The myths, unlike other stories, relate to each other and together build a mythology of an imaginative world. Literature throughout the ages echoes the themes of the ancient myths; certain motifs, or recurring patterns, are clearly identifiable. Frye traces the origins of all literature, and of the archetypal themes we may identify in it, back to one central story that explains

> how man once lived in a golden age or a garden of Eden or the Hesperides, or a happy island kingdom in the Atlantic, how that world was lost, and how we some day may be able to get it back again. . . . Literature is still doing the same job that mythology did earlier, but filling in its huge cloudy shapes with sharper light and deeper shadows.[30]

Exploring mythology through recurring themes and motifs leads to endless discoveries.

Elizabeth Cook states that the essence of a myth lies in its own concrete nature, not in the things it suggests to different readers, and not in its conjectural origins.[31] She says that a myth "is" everything that it has been and everything that it may become; it does not matter that the beautiful and evocative stories may be the product of unconscious misunderstanding and deliberate alteration.

Greek Mythology

The mythology that comes to us from the ancient Greeks is the most familiar and perhaps the most interesting. Myths are only tenuously related to historical fact and geographical location. They played an important role, however, in the lives of the ancients, and their influence permeates the art, music, and architecture of ancient Greece—in fact, all of Greek culture. Myths enrich historical study.

The ancient Greeks believed that gods and goddesses controlled the universe. Zeus, the chief god, was the most powerful. He ruled not only the weather, with its lightning and thunder, but also all the other gods who lived atop Mount Olympus as well as the mortals who lived around it. The chart below lists the Greek

The Greek Gods

Greek Name	Mythological Figure	Roman Name
Aphrodite	Goddess of love and beauty	Venus
Apollo	God of the sun and youth	Apollo
Ares	God of War	Mars
Artemis	Goddess of the moon and hunt	Diana
Athena	Goddess of wisdom	Minerva
Demeter	Goddess of agriculture	Ceres
Dionysus	God of the vine	Bacchus
Eros	God of love	Cupid
Hades	God of the underworld	Dis
Hephaestus	God of fire	Vulcan
Hera	Wife of Zeus, goddess of women and marriage	Juno
Hermes	Messenger of the gods	Mercury
Hestia	Goddess of home and hearth	Vesta
Kronos	God of time and agriculture	Saturn
Persephone	Goddess of spring	Prosperine
Poseidon	God of the sea	Neptune
Zeus	King of the gods, husband of Hera	Jupiter

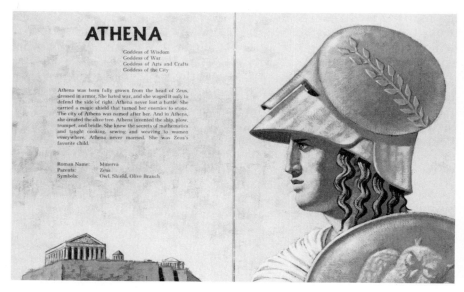

Mythology was created by ancient peoples to make sense of their world and forms the cornerstone of our literary heritage. There are many excellent books for young readers on the mythology of various cultures, such as Leonard Everett Fisher's *The Olympians: Great Gods and Goddesses of Ancient Greece,* shown here.

gods and goddesses, the functions and powers attributed to them, and the names later given to them by the Romans, who adopted the Greek deities as their own.

Leonard Everett Fisher's *The Olympians: Great Gods and Goddesses of Ancient Greece* (I) is an excellent introduction to 12 deities who dwelt on Mount Olympus. Brief narratives describe each one, including their parentage, symbols, and titles. Facing the narratives are Fisher's stunning full-color paintings of each hero.

The stories of Zeus's family are told in several comprehensive collections that provide a good introduction to the classic tales. Ingri and Edgar Parin d'Aulaire's *Book of Greek Myths* (I) has long been a standard resource. Colorful stone lithographs illustrate the stories and show the unique features of the gods and goddesses. A full-page family tree clarifies their relationships and delineates the relative impor-

tance of each. The text is clear and readable for intermediate grade students and the index provides page references and brief descriptions of each character.

Alice Low's *The Macmillan Book of Greek Gods and Heroes* (I) is a similar introduction to these exciting stories. She separates her book into sections: Mother Earth and Her Children, The Gods and Goddesses of Mount Olympus, Zeus and the Creation of Mankind, Triumphs of the Gods, The Heroes, and The Constellations. Students can read the text, which is complemented with many colorful illustrations, as one complete story or refer to the index to find specific tales. *Gods, Men and Monsters from the Greek Myths* (I-A) by Michael Gibson is a more complex text but one that is made equally intriguing by the many full-color paintings by Giovanni Caselli. Other books that give students an overview of the Greek myths include Bernard Evslin's *Heroes, Gods, and Monsters of*

Greek Myths (I-A), Roger Lancelyn Green's *Tales of the Greek Heroes* (I-A), and Olivia Coolidge's *Greek Myths* (I).

Greek myths are replete with wondrous monsters. Children are fascinated with these half-human, half-beast creatures who frightened early people and wreaked havoc on their lands. Just as young children delight in hearing tales of witches and giants, older students, too, love to read about Medusa, who grows hissing snakes on her head instead of hair, and Cerberus, the huge three-headed dog. The horrible one-eyed Cyclops appears in children's art whenever they are studying the myths. William Wise tells the stories of six of these creatures in *Monster Myths of Ancient Greece* (P-I). The Gorgons were three hideous monsters who turned into stone any mortals who looked at them. Their story is told by both Margaret Hodges and Ian Serraillier in two books, both titled *The Gorgon's Head* (I).

A good way for a beginner, whether teacher or student, to select versions of the myths is to turn to recognized translators who are good writers. These include Alfred J. Church, Penelope Farmer, Leon Garfield, Doris Gates, Roger Lancelyn Green, Charles Kingsley, Andrew Lang, Barbara Picard, Ian Serraillier, and Rex Warner, among others. Inclusion of the name of the translator or adapter on the title page of a book of myths or folklore is an indication that the book is an authentic version.

Myths are seldom appreciated fully until the later years of elementary school, and even then not by all students. The stories of King Midas, Pandora's Box, and Jason and the Golden Fleece are basic material for students' literary education. Good versions of the stories contain interesting language; the myths have a stately dignity that the language should reflect. Valid retellings do not change the myths from tales of grandeur into sentimental stories. Some retellers interpret characters and events in a unique mode, with variations that illustrate strikingly the effect that style of language can have. In myths, as in all folklore, much depends upon the telling.

Doris Gates wrote an outstanding series of books on the gods and goddesses of ancient Greece. Each is an interesting and highly readable narrative that captures the excitement and

ACTIVITY: TEACHER TO STUDENT

FASCINATING CREATURES (I–A)[32]   You have learned about many interesting creatures in your mythology reading. See how many of these creatures or monsters you can identify. Use any other reference books to help you. Include an illustration of each of these creatures. Organize your information in dictionary format: name, pronunciation, definition, and give a sentence using the word. Include the illustration.

Centaur	Griffin
Minotaur	Cerberus
Harpies	Pegasus
Chimaera	Sphinx
Hydra	Cyclops
Medusa	Unicorn

drama of the story and conveys a strong feeling for the brave and proud heroes whose exploits she recounts. *Mightiest of Mortals: Heracles; The Golden God: Apollo; Lord of the Sky: Zeus; Two Queens of Heaven: Aphrodite and Demeter;* and *The Warrior Goddess: Athena* (all I) are a fine addition to any collection of mythology.

Stories of individual heroes appear in many books. They tell of great adventures, tests, victories, and losses of the gods. They also feature the relationships between gods and mortals and show how life must be lived with morality and conscience.

Strong visual images appear in the stories about the master craftsman, Daedalus. Ian Serraillier, in *A Fall from the Sky: The Story of Daedalus* (I), and Penelope Farmer, in *Daedalus and Icarus* (I), present the story of the incarceration and escape of the craftsman and his son. The myth suggests that Apollo sought revenge and was angered when Icarus showed excessive pride and dared to emulate a god by flying close to the sun. Thus, the moral: excessive pride (called *hubris*) brings the wrath of the gods.

Theseus, Jason, and Hercules are heroes whose stories are told and retold. The archetypal journey—quest/test/cycle—appears in each

hero's tale. Ian Serraillier, in *Way of Danger: The Story of Theseus* (I) and *Clashing Rocks: The Story of Jason* (I), trace the exploits of these heroes. Bernard Evslin also details the story of *Jason and the Argonauts* (I-A). In this classic tale, Jason, in order to claim his rightful throne, must recover a ram's golden fleece that hangs from a tree guarded by a dragon that never sleeps. Evslin vividly describes the treacherous voyage through the Black Sea and across hostile land.

Hercules, also called Heracles, born to Alcmene, was sired by Zeus. Hercules demonstrates his prodigious strength by strangling two snakes that Hera, the jealous wife of Zeus, has maliciously placed in his cradle. His story is told in *The Labors of Hercules* (I), by Paul Hollander; *The Twelve Labors of Hercules* (I), by Robert Newman; and *Heracles the Strong* (I-A), by Ian Serraillier. The visual images of Hercules slaying a lion whose skin no weapon could pierce, killing a nine-headed Hydra, and cleaning the huge Augean stables in a single day will remain with the reader years after having read the stories.

Bernard Evslin selected only some of the many events associated with *Hercules* (I-A), but those he relates are dramatically told. This powerful narrative includes bold dialogue and

TEACHING IDEA

EXPLORING LITERARY COMPONENTS THROUGH MYTHOLOGY (I-A)[33]
Through the imaginative and exciting world of mythology, students can develop an understanding of myth as a literary form and enhance their knowledge of the components of narrative fiction. The nature of myths stimulates questions and leads to areas of thought beyond the tales themselves. The objectives of the following activities are to enable the student (1) to recognize plot structure and development in a hero tale, (2) to understand theme and develop an awareness of mood and its impact on theme, (3) to determine how characters are revealed, and (4) to identify and appreciate the recurring theme of creation.

ACTIVITY: TEACHER TO STUDENT

PLOT STRUCTURE AND DEVELOPMENT IN A HERO TALE (I-A)   The plot is the story's plan of action—the beginning, the middle, the climax, and the ending. It tells what the characters do and what happens to them. The plot of a hero tale is based upon a daring quest to accomplish a seemingly impossible goal and is complicated by the obstacles faced during the struggle to reach the goal.

Before you read *The Gorgon's Head* by Ian Serraillier, think about the following questions.

1. How does a person become a hero?
2. What kinds of physical, mental, and spiritual qualities might a hero have? Why might these qualities be necessary?
3. If you were to tell a story about a hero, what are some exciting and daring adventures you would tell? Who are your heroes today?

After reading *The Gorgon's Head*, discuss the following questions with someone who has read the book.

1. What did Perseus set out to prove?
2. What problems and dangers did he face before he accomplished his goal?
3. Why did Athena and Hermes help Perseus?
4. Did the people of his birthplace consider Perseus a hero from the time of his birth?
5. Could any man have accomplished such daring deeds if he had the same gifts as Perseus? Why or why not?
6. What is the climax? Why do you think so?

Choose one of these activities.

1. Rewrite the story of Perseus, the son of Zeus (king of the gods), from Zeus's point of view.
2. Write a dialogue between Danae and the king that shows how Perseus's mother was treated while he was away.

---

vivid description. The story of Hercules's birth and of Hera's early enmity toward him are followed by accounts of 6 of the 12 labors ascribed to him. Hercules's stature as a brave and gentle hero shines throughout the text.

Love stories interest people of all times; countless myths concern love between a god or goddess and a mortal. The unusual love story of Cupid (named Eros by the Greeks, but commonly known today by his Roman name) and Psyche is well known. Psyche, a mortal, incurs the wrath of Venus (Aphrodite) because she is declared the more beautiful. Venus, in a jealous rage, summons her son Cupid to destroy

ACTIVITY: TEACHER TO STUDENT

EROS (CUPID) AND PSYCHE (A)[34]   Read Edna Barth's *Cupid and Psyche* and choose one of the following activities:

1. Write an essay discussing the meaning of the story for you and give some interpretations others might have. (According to some, Psyche represents the human soul. The soul, or psyche, personified by Cupid, is condemned to wander the earth in misery and hardship. Faithful and true, as Psyche was, it eventually returns to heaven and is reunited with love eternal.)
2. Read "Orpheus and Eurydice" and "Echo and Narcissus" in *Mythology*, by Edith Hamilton, in order to compare other love stories with Cupid and Psyche's. Discuss the way love is portrayed in the three stories.
3. Psyche, as the representation of the human soul, provides the name for an entire branch of science. Use the dictionary to define the following words as they relate to the story of Cupid and Psyche: psychic, psychedelic, psychiatry, psychology, psychosis, psychosomatic, psychotherapy, cupid's bow, cupidity. Discuss why cupids, hearts, arrows, and love signs are symbols in the celebration of St. Valentine's Day.

Psyche by having her fall in love with a monster. Instead of following his mother's orders, Cupid falls in love with Psyche.

An Archetypal Theme in Mythology

Penelope Farmer, translator and interpreter of many myths, describes their purpose:

> Myths have seemed to me to point quite distinctly—yet without ever directly expressing it—to some kind of unity behind creation, not a static unity, but a forever shifting breathing one.
> . . . The acquisition by man of life or food or fire has to be paid for by the acceptance of death—the message is everywhere, quite unmistakable. To live is to die; to die is to live.[35]

This great archetypal theme appears again and again throughout all cultures. Children are familiar with the rebirth of flowers and trees in the spring. Most of them have buried a seed in the ground and watched for it to sprout, and some may have heard the quotation, "Unless a grain of wheat falls in the ground and dies it remains alone, but if it dies it brings forth much fruit." In image and symbol, these themes reappear under many guises, and children can recognize them through their study of myth.

There are many versions of the story of Persephone, goddess of springtime. In addition to those in collections, there are versions in individual picture-book format: *The Story of Persephone* (I) by Penelope Farmer, *Demeter and Persephone* (I) by Penelope Proddow, and *Persephone and the Springtime* (I) by Margaret Hodges. Hodges writes for the younger reader; for example, her version begins, "Everyone everywhere loves the springtime. The ancient Greeks said that spring was a beautiful young girl. Her name was Persephone and she always followed in the footsteps of her mother, Demeter, the earth goddess."[36] Penelope Farmer begins,

> She and the goddess of the corn harvest were more like sisters, like lovers even, than a mother and a daughter, wandering the hills together through a world which saw no winter, no au-

tumn, no death or decay, only spring and summer, birth and harvest. Wherever they wandered flowers sprang up, spring flowers for Persephone, summer flowers for the goddess Demeter.[37]

Proddow's version reads, "Now I will sing/ of golden-haired Demeter,/the awe-inspiring goddess,/and of her trim-ankled daughter,/Persephone,/who was frolicking in a grassy meadow."[38] Proddow's text is a translation of Hymn Number Two by Homer and is closest in style to the Greek original. It is complemented with illustrations by Barbara Cooney that capture the classic Greek style with its grace, balance, and dignity.

In the story, the beautiful Persephone, daughter of Demeter, the goddess of earth, is carried off by Hades, god of the underworld, to be his bride. Demeter searches everywhere for her daughter, and her grief causes winter to fall over the earth. Finally Persephone's return brings the springtime. It can be useful to children to consider why it was natural for pre-scientific societies to evolve stories such as Persephone's to explain their world.

The illustrations in several versions of Persephone range from somber, dark portrayals to paintings reminiscent of Greek vases. The black horses drawing Hades's fiery chariot, the fields filled with flowers, and the stark contrasts between beauty and the barren earth present strong visual images. The theme that life is carried out in an atmosphere of struggle rather than in a paradise is developed through contrasts in the illustrations. The most satisfying books are those in which the illustrations complement and extend both the theme and the mood of the story.

Mythology has given us a rich heritage of images, symbols, language, and art. Isaac Asimov explores the roots of hundreds of *Words*

TEACHING IDEA

CYCLE OF SEASONS IN MYTH AND FANTASY (I)   In helping students become more sensitive to the idea that all literature tells one story, ask them to consider other stories in which the seasons of the year mirror the theme. If they have read C. S. Lewis's *The Lion, The Witch, and the Wardrobe* (I), they will recall that the spell of the White Witch was that it always be winter but never Christmas; with Aslan came the spring. Mole, in Kenneth Grahame's *The Wind in the Willows* (I), illustrated by Ernest H. Shepard, emerges from his underground home to begin a new life during "spring cleaning." In Hans Christian Andersen's *Thumbelina* (P–I), illustrated by Susan Jeffers, the tiny creature spends a long sad winter underground before she is freed and carried off by her friend, the bird, to marry the fairy prince. Likewise, Andersen's duck in *The Ugly Duckling* (P–I), retold and illustrated by Lorinda Bryan Cauley, suffers through the winter before he is finally recognizable as a swan in the spring. And in *Charlotte's Web* (P–I), by E. B. White, Charlotte dies in the fall, but her children are hatched the following spring to bring new friends to lonely Wilbur. Through discussions of such stories, children can be encouraged to look for the interconnections between theme and mood and to begin to build a basis for recognizing recurring themes in all literature.

from the Myths (I), a handy reference for students interested in etymology. Penelope Proddow compiled a fascinating book, *Art Tells a Story: Greek and Roman Myths* (I-A), which is a collection of myths accompanied by photographs of art works that were inspired by the ancient stories.

Norse Mythology

The mythology of all cultures is replete with tales of bravery and courage. Origin, or creation, myths abound in all societies, as do tales of adventure. We have been focusing on tales from Greek mythology, and some of their Roman adaptations, but there are equally rich stories among other groups, most notably the Vikings.

The tales that grew from the cold, rugged climate of northern Europe are filled with exciting stories of man's struggles against the cruelty of nature and against the powerful gods and monsters who ruled the harsh land. Padraic Colum, an Irish poet and master storyteller, first published *The Children of Odin: The Book of Northern Myths* (I) in 1920; it remains

ACTIVITY: TEACHER TO STUDENT

PERSEPHONE (I)   *Before* you read the stories about Persephone, look at all of the illustrations and think about these questions:

1. How do the illustrations make you feel?
2. How do you think Persephone feels?
3. What would life be like in the setting shown?
4. What is happening to Persephone?
5. How does the mood of the story change?
6. How do the colors of the illustrations reflect the changes in mood of the story?

After you read the story discuss some of these questions:

1. Why didn't Persephone want to stay with Hades?
2. How did Demeter feel about children? How do you know?
3. What did Hecate mean by "Not even the owls know where to find her"? How does this make Demeter feel?
4. What words are used to describe Hades's underworld?
5. What natural occurrence does the story explain?

Choose activities from the following:

1. Pretend you are Demeter. Write a letter to Zeus explaining your feelings for your daughter. Tell him what you will do if he does not help you find her.
2. Write a scene between the river nymph and Demeter in which Demeter discovers that the nymph knows Persephone's whereabouts. Give a dramatic reading or performance of the scene.
3. Compose a song that tells of Demeter's sadness. Find a suitable melody and write the lyrics for it. Record it on a tape.
4. Prepare a brief act or pantomime to convey a strong emotion such as love, hate, anger, jealousy, or pain. Build it into a scene with Demeter, Persephone, and Zeus.

ACTIVITY: TEACHER TO STUDENT

WORDS FROM MYTHOLOGY (I–A)[39]   Some of our English words and names come from the names found in mythology. All of these words have come from mythology in some way. Use the information you have learned in your reading and your dictionary to help you find the definition of the word and how it is related to mythology (source).

Organize your findings in chart form using the following arrangement.

Word	Definition	Source

Words from mythology:

Atlas	Herculean	Lunatic
Cereal	Hygiene	Oceanography
Echo	Hypnotic	Martial
Floral	Iris	Mercurial
Museum	Geology	Furious
Gigantic	Jovial	Narcissism
Peony	Titanic	Phosphorus
Plutonium	Panic	Iridescent
The "Midas Touch"	Opening a "Pandora's Box"	

Do difficult English words look like "Greek" to you? Some of them may actually have come from the Greek language. There is an old saying: "Beware of Greeks bearing gifts." But the gifts brought to you by Greeks are valuable word treasures. Use these syllables, and add other parts to form English words. Write the English word that can be formed. What does the word mean?

Photo	Bio	Chrono
Auto	Tele	Mega
Mono	Phono	Graph
Psych	Gram	Thermo
Poly	Philo	Soph

available today to tell the magic and majesty of the Norse sagas. Olivia Coolidge's *Legends of the North* (I) is a well-written and lively account of the same stories. *Gods and Heroes from Viking Myth* (I) by Brian Branston, *The Faber Book of Northern Legends* by Kevin Crossley-Holland, and *Norse Gods and Giants* (I) by Ingri and Edgar Parin d'Aulaire are beautifully illustrated books that introduce children to the heroic tales of the Vikings.

AMERICAN LEGENDS AND TALL TALES

Legends are folk stories about real or imaginary people; they may have some basis in fact, but they are largely embroidered with fancy. It is difficult to tell where fact stops and imagination takes over because the stories come to us by way of all folklore—word of mouth. What may have started as a report of what nearly happened soon became an account of what *did* happen; many storytellers elaborated reports of a hero's exploits until the stories became full-blown legends. The result is an intricate interweaving of fact and fiction, with a grain of truth at the core.

Each country has its folk heroes who exemplify character traits its people value. American *tall tales* are a combination of history, myth, and fact. For example, Davy Crockett, Johnny Appleseed, and Daniel Boone were real people, but their stories have made them larger than life. They accomplished feats no mortal would dare. On the other hand, Paul Bunyan may be the creation of a Madison Avenue advertising agency. Mythic men, such as John Henry, Pecos Bill, and Mike Fink, vivify the Yankee work ethic, the brawn and muscle required to develop America. These folk heroes were created by people who needed idols and symbols of strength as they built a new country. Thus, their heroes are the mightiest, strongest, most daring lumberjacks, railroad

men, coal miners, riverboat drivers, and steelworkers possible.

Although tall tales gave early settlers symbols of strength, they also served another need, offsetting the harsh realities of an untamed land. The exaggerated humor and blatant lies in tall tales added zest to and lightened a life of hard labor.

Children love the exaggerated humor and lies that mark the tall tales. They laugh when Paul Bunyan's loggers tie bacon to their feet and skate across the huge griddle to grease it. The thought of Slewfoot Sue bouncing skyward every time her bustle hits the ground produces giggles. And when Pecos Bill falls out of the covered wagon, children can picture the abandoned infant scrambling toward the coyote mother who eventually raises him with the rest of the coyote pack. Paul Bunyan's folks could not rock his cradle fast enough so they put it in the ocean; the waves still pound because of the strength of Paul's kicking. Because the hero in tall tales is all-powerful, readers know that he will overcome any problem. The suspense is created, then, in *how* the problem will be solved.

There are very few single editions of tall tales, although two noted artists have each begun a series. Steven Kellogg retold *Paul Bunyan* (P-I) and *Pecos Bill* (P-I) and illustrated them with his characteristic humorous detailed drawings to portray the vigor of his heroes. Paul Bunyan and his blue ox Babe are shown with exaggerated strength and daring as they cut down trees and haul them from the forest.

Pecos Bill's adventures begin on the endpapers of the book. His family finds New England too crowded and so joins a wagon train headed west. Young Bill encounters huge bears and Texas-sized trout that look like whales. When he bounces off the back of the wagon, a family of coyotes adopts and raises him as one of its own. When Pecos Bill returns to live with humans, he is stronger and wilier than any man alive. He can wrestle rattlesnakes and long-

TEACHING IDEA

HERO TALES (I-A)   There are many different stories and variants about the adventures of the American tall tale heroes. Reading them aloud, telling them, and having children tell them are pleasurable ways to acquaint them with their own folk heroes. Children will look for the zaniest exaggerations and wildest portrayals of character, for it is one time that lying is condoned and the person who tells the most outlandish whopper is applauded.

ACTIVITY: TEACHER TO STUDENT

LEGITIMATE LIES OR SWAPPING WHOPPERS (I)   Read *Whoppers: Tall Tales and Other Lies Collected from American Folklore* by Alvin Schwartz. Form a group to explore tall tales. There are many things you can do to make your learning exciting. Choose some from the following:

1. Make a papier-mâché model of your hero. (Be certain the clothes are appropriate for the occupation.)
2. Draw pictures of your heroes. Place the pictures on a large map of the United States in the area where they lived.
3. Using a corrugated carton, create a diorama of one of your hero's wildest adventures.
4. Write a new adventure for your hero. (Remember to exaggerate wildly.) What would happen if your hero met another tall tale hero?
5. Have a contest to see who can tell the biggest whopper involving a folk hero.
6. Put the story of your character on slides and recite the story. Use a recording for background music.
7. Make up a ballad about your folk character. Sing it or say it as a group.
8. Although women do not appear as frequently as men in American folklore, some are becoming folk heroes. Select a famous woman, such as Harriet Tubman, Annie Christmas (longshorewoman), Annie Oakley, Sacajawea, Pocahontas, or Sally Ride, and create a tall tale about her.
9. Make up a game board using symbols associated with the various characters in tall tales.

horns and he outwits a gang of desperadoes. He tames a wild horse, Lightning, and marries Slewfoot Sue, who is just as robust as he is. Texas's claim of Pecos Bill is comically portrayed on the back cover of Kellogg's book: a rattlesnake, with a yellow rose clamped in its fangs, outlines the shape of the state of Texas.

Ariane Dewey writes for a younger audience than Kellogg in *Pecos Bill; Febold Feboldson; Gib Morgan, Oilman;* and *Lafitte the Pirate* (all P-I). Febold Feboldson was a farmer who overcame the hardships brought about by the weather. When the heat popped the corn and melted the sugar cane growing in the fields,

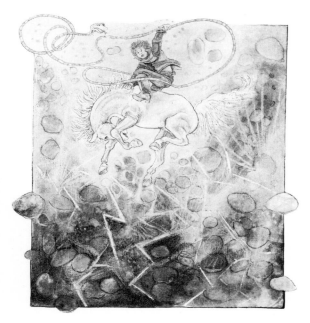

American folk heroes, such as Johnny Appleseed, Pecos Bill, and Annie Oakley vivify the Yankee work ethic. The stories were created or enhanced by people who needed idols and symbols of strength as they built a new country. (From *Pecos Bill*, retold and illustrated by Steven Kellogg.)

lore. Through careful research in language, superstition, and folk history, he has produced several books which delve into America's legendary past. *Whoppers: Tall Tales and Other Lies* (I), *Flapdoodle: Pure Nonsense from American Folklore* (I), and *Witcracks: Jokes and Jests from American Folklore* (I) are valuable resources for study and tremendously entertaining books to read for pure enjoyment.

FOLK SONGS AND WORK SONGS

Work songs, often developed as a diversion from boring work, capture the rhythm and spirit of the labor in which their creators were engaged. The songs sing of the values and the life-styles of the people who laid the railroads, dug the tunnels and canals, and toted the bales. In addition, ballads were used to inform and to persuade, to foster agreement and unify people.

Artemus Ward, in 1863, said, "Let me write the songs of a nashun and I don't care a cuss who goes to the legislator." The truth underlying this statement remains unchanged to this day. Civil rights marchers, led by Martin Luther King, Jr., singing "We Shall Overcome," were united in spirit and intent by the song's moving words. The power of the song and its singers focused our nation's attention on the march toward equality. Songs are powerful

this inventive pioneer made popcorn balls. Children will get a brief look at the American legendary heroes in these books.

Alvin Schwartz has contributed a wealth of material that enriches a study of American folk-

TEACHING IDEA

TRACING THE ORIGINS OF WORK SONGS (I) Glen Rounds illustrates a number of work songs and folk ballads that can serve as an adjunct to social studies courses. Use *Casey Jones: The Story of a Brave Engineer* (P-I) and *Sweet Betsy from Pike* (I). Each book reflects the regional flavor and occupational trappings of the group responsible for the origin of the song. Farmers, cowboys, railroad hands, and gold miners convey the spirit and the humor of the words. Ask your students to match songs with historic events. The rhythm of beating hoofs, pounding hammers, chugging trains, and lifting bales of cotton underlies the words from the world of work in which they grew.

ACTIVITY: TEACHER TO STUDENT

SONGFEST (I) For the people who were building our nation—digging canals, laying rails, working the mines—a popular pastime at the end of their hardworking day was to sit around campfires and spin yarns. During these times, and while they worked, they sang.

After reading and learning some of the famous folk songs, plan a songfest for your school. Accompany the singing with piano, guitar, or recordings. Make songbooks or songsheets with the words of each song so that everyone in the audience may join in. Before the introduction of each song, say a few words about the role it played in the lives of the people pioneering our nation. "Erie Canal," "Clementine," "Sixteen Tons," and "I've Been Workin' on the Railroad" are learned quickly.

persuasion in both shaping and preserving our cultural heritage.

Excellent single editions of nursery songs, folk songs, and patriotic songs are available. The best include guitar or piano musical scores, historical notes, and good illustrations coordinated with the text. Robert Quackenbush, Aliki, Glen Rounds, John Langstaff, and Peter Spier offer many excellent sources.

Traditional Songs

B. A. Botkin observed in *A Treasury of American Folklore* that singing folk songs is a functional activity; we sing them for self-gratification, for power, or for freedom.[40] We also sing them to lighten our labor, to fill our leisure time, to record events, and to voice praise or protest. Songs are used to teach young children to count or to say the ABCs and, most often, to soothe them and sing them to sleep.

John Langstaff's name is associated with high-quality editions of picture books containing a single folk song. One of his earliest books, *Frog Went A-Courtin'* (P), illustrated by Feodor Rojankovsky, received the Caldecott Medal in 1956. This old Scottish ballad details the courtship and eventually the arrangements and guest list for Mr. Frog and Miss Mousie's wedding. Langstaff and Rojankovsky later

combined their talents to present *Over in the Meadow* (P), a counting song. More recently, Langstaff worked with illustrator Nancy Winslow Parker to produce *Sweetly Sings the Donkey* (P) and *Oh, A-Hunting We Will Go* (P). The books serve well for beginning reading experiences because the verses follow a repetitive pattern that children recognize after hearing once or twice.

> Oh, a-hunting we will go,
> A-hunting we will go;
> We'll catch a mouse
> And put him in a house,
> And then we'll let him go!
>
> Oh, a-hunting we will go,
> A-hunting we will go;
> We'll catch a pig
> And put him in a wig
> And then we'll let him go!

In all 12 verses, only the last word in lines 3 and 4 vary. The words are predictable because of the rhyme, the rhythm of the language, and the match between the text and illustrations.

Peter Spier received a Caldecott Honor Book Award for his illustrations of another perennial favorite, *The Fox Went Out on a Chilly Night* (P). These traditional lyrics describe the father fox slipping quietly through the autumn night to get food for his cubs. Spier's illustrations place the setting for the nighttime adventures of the fox in the autumn countryside of a bucolic New England village with rolling hills and quaint barns and houses.

Other favorites of children include *I Know an Old Lady Who Swallowed a Fly* (P), by Nadine Westcott, and "The Three Blind Mice" found in John Ivimey's *Complete Version of Ye Three Blind Mice* (P). Versions of many of these old favorites are available in sound filmstrips from Weston Woods.

Individual songs in picture book format are still not plentiful, although one or two are published each year. Merle Peek recently added *Mary Wore Her Red Dress and Henry Wore His Green Sneakers* (P) and *Roll Over! A Counting Song* (P). Robert Quackenbush retold and illustrated *Pop! Goes the Weasel* (P) and *She'll Be Comin' 'round the Mountain* (P-I).

Collections of favorite songs, handsomely illustrated, enrich the store of materials we can draw upon for music and early reading programs. For example, Jane Hart compiled 125 songs in a splendid book, *Singing Bee! A Collection of Favorite Children's Songs* (P-I), beautifully illustrated by Anita Lobel. This very attractive book includes nursery rhymes, lullabies, and finger plays and cumulative, holiday, and activity songs with piano accompaniments and guitar chords for each selection. Lobel appropriately used historical settings and eighteenth-century garb for many of the traditional songs; she also expressed her interest in the theater by creating stage production settings around many songs.

Clyde Watson selected and Wendy Watson illustrated 21 rhythmic verses chosen from their previous books in *Father Fox's Feast of Songs* (P). Piano accompaniments and guitar chords for the simple, bouncy tunes make it possible for young musicians to play along with the singing.

Ashley Byran compiled and illustrated two volumes of black-American spirituals, *Walk Together Children* (P-I) and *I'm Going to Sing* (I). The spirituals, plantation melodies, and slave songs represent the concern and desire for freedom close to the heart of the songs' creators. Bryan's powerful woodcuts for illustrations and musical notation suggest the block-print style of early religious books and reflect the emotional fervor of the black-American spirituals. "Joshua Fit the Battle," "My Lord, What a Morning," and "Rise Up Shepherd and Follow" are among the many memorable songs.

THE BIBLE AS A FORM OF LITERATURE

One of the earliest forms of Western cultural literature is found in the Bible, and there are many reasons that forms of this traditional heritage should be a part of literary study. The universality of this body of literature is evident since the Bible is still the best-selling book in the world, it is printed in every language, it is known by all peoples, it is basic to all other literature, and it is a common denominator around the world.

Teachers and librarians distinguish between the use of biblical stories to teach a religious doctrine and the use of them to explore their literary content. In secular education, the literary content is stressed. From the obvious symbolism of the parables to the basic forms underlying all other literature, there is an abundant literary content to be explored. Northrop Frye contends that

> If we don't know the Bible and the central stories of Greek and Roman literature, we can still read books and see plays, but our knowledge of literature can't grow, just as our knowledge of mathematics can't grow if we don't learn the multiplication table.[41]

One approach to biblical stories amenable to public schools and libraries is to examine

ACTIVITY: TEACHER TO STUDENT

COMPARE VARIATIONS OF BIBLE STORIES (P-I)   Read several variations of the same Bible story. For example:

dePaola, *The Legend of Old Befana*
Mikolaycak, *Babushka: An Old Russian Folktale*
Robbins, *Baboushka and the Three Kings*

Discuss the categories on the chart and the components of each. Fill in the chart for one of the books read as a total group. Work in collaborative learning groups to complete the chart.

Read another similar story and complete the chart alone. Share it with the group.

NAME OF BOOK

	Baboushka and the Three Kings	Babushka: An Old Russian Folktale	The Legend of Old Befana	
Author				
Illustrator				
Name of Main Character				
Setting				
Characters				
Purpose of Main Character				
Ending				

how a contemporary author retells a Bible story. How does the author interpret the old tale, how is the character presented, how is the period portrayed, or how is the theme realized? Since the source of the tale is the Bible itself, early versions of each story are available for comparisons.

Some sections of the Bible reflect the oral tradition more dramatically than others: the use of lyric poetic forms, repetition, and the measured metric schemes were aids to memory before the stories were set down in writing. Al-though the verses may not rhyme in English, they probably did in Hebrew, and although the metric scheme may vary in English, it was measured and pronounced in Hebrew as a way of remembering.

From a literary perspective, the Bible contains myths, legends, fables, parables, short stories, essays, lyrics, epistles, sermons, orations, proverbs, history, biography, prophecy, and drama. The stories of Samson have even been called "tall tales." Teachers and librarians have a wealth of material from which to draw.

ACTIVITY: TEACHER TO STUDENT

COMPARE VERSIONS OF NOAH'S ARK (P-I-A)   Numerous versions of Noah's ark make comparisons easy and abundant. Peter Spier presents a seventeenth-century Dutch poem, "The Flood," in the front of his book, *Noah's Ark* (P-I-A), and then without further text presents the story in detailed watercolor drawings. The rewards and hard work associated with Noah's mission are clear. Spier masterfully presents contrasts of night and day, inner and outer views of the ark, joy and hardship connected with the voyage, and the humorous incidents, such as pushing a reluctant elephant down the ramp to leave the ark. In Isaac Bashevis Singer's *Why Noah Chose the Dove* (P-I-A), the animals compete for a place in the ark, and each one tells about his good points as a means of assuring a space. Nearly all of the text is the dialogue of the animals describing their own virtues while the dove remains silent until he is noticed by Noah.

Other versions to use for comparison include Gail Haley's *Noah's Ark*, Tomie dePaola's *Noah and the Ark*, Andrew Elborn's *Noah and the Ark and the Animals*, Nonny Hogrogian's *Noah's Ark*, Linda Yeatman's *Noah's Ark*, Jasper Diamond's *Noah's Ark*, and Gertrud Fusseneger's *Noah's Ark*.

RECOMMENDED READING

Mother Goose and Nursery Rhymes

Alderson, Brian, ed. *Cakes and Custard: Children's Rhymes.* New York: Morrow, 1975.

Briggs, Raymond. *The Mother Goose Treasury.* New York: Coward-McCann, 1966.

Hague, Michael. ed. *Mother Goose.* New York: Holt, Rinehart & Winston, 1984.

Hoguet, Susan Ramsey. *Solomon Grundy.* New York: Dutton, 1986.

Ivimey, John W. *The Complete Story of the Three Blind Mice.* Illustrated by Paul Galdone. New York: Clarion, 1987.

Jeffers, Susan. *If Wishes Were Horses: Mother Goose Rhymes.* New York: Dutton, 1979.

Marshall, James. *James Marshall's Mother Goose.* New York: Farrar, Straus & Giroux, 1979.

Oxenbury, Helen. *The Helen Oxenbury Nursery Story Book.* New York: Knopf, 1985.

Provensen, Alice, and Martin Provensen. *The Mother Goose Book.* New York: Random House, 1976.

Thompson, Pat, ed. *Rhymes Around the Day.* New York: Lothrop, Lee & Shepard, 1983.

Tripp, Wallace, comp. *Granpa' Grig Had a Pig and Other Rhymes Without Reason from Mother Goose.* Boston: Little, Brown, 1976.

Tudor, Tasha. *Mother Goose.* New York: McKay, 1944.

Folk and Fairy Tales: Collections

Baskin, Leonard, *Imps, Demons, Hobgoblins, Witches, Fairies and Elves.* New York: Pantheon, 1984.

Carle, Eric. *Eric Carle's Storybook: Seven Tales by the Brothers Grimm.* New York: Watts, 1976.

Cole, Joanna, ed. *Best Loved Folktales of the World.* Illustrated by Jill Karla Schwarz. New York: Doubleday, 1982.

Crossley-Holland, Kevin, and Susan Varley, trans. *The Fox and the Cat: Animal Tales from Grimm.* New York: Lothrop, Lee & Shepard, 1986.

Garner, Alan. *Alan Garner's Book of British Fairy Tales.* Illustrated by Derek Collard. New York: Delacorte, 1985.

Haviland, Virginia. *Favorite Fairy Tales Told Around the World.* Boston: Little, Brown, 1985.

———. *Fairy Tale Treasury.* Illustrated by Raymond Briggs. New

York: Coward, McCann & Geoghegan, 1972.

———. *Favorite Fairy Tales Told in Denmark.* Illustrated by Margot Zemach. Boston: Little Brown, 1971.

———. *Favorite Fairy Tales Told in Ireland.* Illustrated by Artur Marokvia. Boston: Little, Brown, 1961.

Martin, Eva, ed. *Canadian Fairy Tales.* Illustrated by Laszlo Gal. Toronto: Groundwood, 1984.

Folk and Fairy Tales: Single Tales

Bryan, Ashley. *The Dancing Granny.* Illustrated by Ashley Bryan. New York: Atheneum, 1977.

Dewey, Ariane. *The Thunder God's Son: A Peruvian Folktale.* New York: Greenwillow, 1981.

Domanska, Janina. *The Turnip.* New York: Macmillan, 1969.

Galdone, Joanna. *The Tailypo.* Illustrated by Paul Galdone. New York: Clarion, 1977.

Galdone, Paul. *The Monster and the Tailor.* New York: Clarion, 1982.

———. *The Teeny-Tiny Woman: A Ghost Story.* Boston: Houghton Mifflin, Clarion, 1984.

———. *The Three Little Pigs.* New York: Clarion, 1970.

———. *The Turtle and the Monkey.* New York: Clarion, 1982.

———. *What's in Fox's Sack?* New York: Clarion, 1982.

Grimm, Jakob, and Wilhelm Grimm. *Little Brother and Little Sister.* Illustrated by Barbara Cooney. New York: Doubleday, 1982.

———. *The Seven Ravens.* Translated by Elizabeth D. Crawford, illustrated by Lisbeth Zwerger. 1981. Reprint. Natick, Mass: Picture Book Studio, 1983.

———. *The Seven Ravens.* Illustrated by Felix Hoffmann. New York: Harcourt Brace, 1963.

———. *The Seven Ravens.* Trans lated by Wanda Gág, illustrated

by Margot Tomes. New York: Coward-McCann, 1982.

———. *The Twelve Dancing Princesses and Other Tales from Grimm.* Edited by Naomi Lewis, illustrated by Lidia Postma. New York: Dial, 1986.

———. *The Twelve Dancing Princesses.* Illustrated by Errol Le Cain. New York: Viking, 1978.

Hall, Amanda. *The Gossipy Wife: Adapted from a Russian Folk Tale.* New York: Bedrick Books, 1984.

Jacobs, Joseph. *Hereafterthis.* Illustrated by Paul Galdone. New York: McGraw-Hill, 1973.

Jameson, Cynthia. *The Clay Pot Boy.* Illustrated by Arnold Lobel. New York: Coward, McCann & Geoghegan, 1973.

McGovern, Ann. *Stone Soup.* Illustrated by Winslow Pinney Pels. New York: Scholastic, 1986.

Marshak, Samuel. *The Month Brothers: A Slavic Tale.* Translated by Thomas P. Whitney, illustrated by Diane Stanley. New York: Morrow, 1983.

Marshall, James. *Red Riding Hood.* Illustrated by James Marshall. New York: Dial, 1987.

Mayer, Marianna, ed. *Aladdin and the Enchanted Lamp.* Illustrated by Gerald McDermott. New York: Macmillan, 1985.

Shub, Elizabeth. *The Fisherman and His Wife.* Illustrated by Monika Laimgruber. New York: Greenwillow, 1979.

Shute, Linda. *Momotaro: The Peach Boy.* New York: Lothrop, Lee & Shepard, 1986.

Fables

Aesop. *The Lion and the Mouse.* Illustrated by Ed Young. New York: Doubleday, 1980.

———. *The Caldecott Aesop: Twenty Fables.* Illustrated by Randolph Caldecott. New York: Doubleday, 1978.

———. *The City Mouse and the Country Mouse.* Illustrated by

Jody Wheeler. New York: Putnam's, 1985.

———. *Favorite Animal Fables.* Illustrated by Betty Fraser. New York: Random House, 1984.

Bennett, Charles H. *Bennett's Fables: From Aesop and Others Translated into Human Nature.* Edited by Gerald Gottleib. New York: Viking, 1978.

Hague, Michael, ed. *Aesop's Fables.* New York: Holt, Rinehart & Winston, 1985.

Lorenz, Lee. *A Weekend in the Country.* Englewood Cliffs, N.J.: Prentice-Hall, 1985.

Wildsmith, Brian. *The Hare and the Tortoise.* New York: Oxford University Press, 1985.

Mythology

Baskin, Hosie. *A Book of Dragons.* Illustrated by Leonard Baskin. New York: Knopf, 1985.

D'Aulaire, Ingri, and Edgar Parin D'Aulaire. *Norse Gods and Giants.* New York: Doubleday, 1967.

———. *Book of Greek Myths.* New York: Doubleday, 1962.

Evslin, Bernard. *Greeks Bearing Gifts: The Epics of Achilles and Ulysses.* Illustrated by Lucy Martin Bitzer. New York: Four Winds, 1976.

Farmer, Penelope. *The Serpent's Teeth: The Story of Cadmus.* Illustrated by Chris Connor. New York: Harcourt Brace Jovanovich, 1972.

Gerstein, Mordicai. *Tales of Pan.* New York: Harper & Row, 1986.

Green, Roger Lancelyn. *The Tale of Thebes.* Illustrated by Jael Jordan. New York: Cambridge University Press, 1977.

Hamilton, Edith. *Mythology.* Illustrated by Steele Savage. Boston: Little, Brown, 1942.

McDermott, Gerald. *Daughter of Earth: A Roman Myth.* New York: Delacorte, 1984.

Pinsent, John. *Greek Mythology.* New York: Bedrick Books, 1983.

Proddow, Penelope. *Dionysus and the Pirates.* New York: Doubleday, 1970.

———. *Hermes, Lord of Robbers.* Illustrated by Barbara Cooney. New York: Doubleday, 1971.

Usher, Kerry. *Heroes, Gods and Emperors from Roman Mythology.* Illustrated by John Sibbuck. New York: Schocken Books, 1984.

Weil, Lisl. *Pandora's Box.* New York: Atheneum, 1986.

Legends and Tall Tales

Keats, Ezra Jack. *John Henry: An American Legend.* Edited by Anne Schwartz. New York: Knopf, 1987.

Rounds, Glen, comp. *Casey Jones: The Story of a Brave Engineer.* Chicago: Children's Press, 1968.

———. *Ol' Paul the Mighty Logger.* 1949. Reprint. New York: Holiday House, 1976.

Schwartz, Alvin, ed. *More Scary Stories to Tell in the Dark.* Illustrated by Stephen Gammell. Philadelphia: Lippincott, 1984.

Shepard, Esther. *Paul Bunyan.* Illustrated by Rockwell Kent. 1924. Reprint. San Diego: Harcourt Brace Jovanovich, 1985.

Stoutenburg, Adrien. *American Tall Tales.* Illustrated by Richard M. Powers. New York: Viking, 1966.

Folk Songs

Brandenberg, Aliki. *Go Tell Aunt Rhody.* New York: Macmillan, 1974.

Conover, Chris. *Six Little Ducks.* New York: Crowell, 1976.

Domanska, Janina. *Busy Monday Morning.* New York: Greenwillow, 1985.

———. *I Saw a Ship A-Sailing.* New York: Macmillan, 1972.

Larrick, Nancy, comp. *The Wheels of the Bus Go Round and Round: School Bus Songs and Chants.* Illustrated by Gene Holtan. Chicago: Children's Press, 1972.

Zemach, Margot. *Hush, Little Baby.* New York: Dutton, 1976.

———. *Mommy, Buy Me a China Doll.* New York: Farrar, Straus & Giroux, 1975.

Religious Stories

Bierhorst, John, trans. *Spirit Child: A Story of the Nativity.* Illustrated by Barbara Cooney. New York: Morrow, 1984.

Brodsky, Beverly. *The Golem: A Jewish Legend.* New York: Harper & Row, 1975.

———. *Jonah: An Old Testament Story.* New York: Harper & Row, 1977.

Chaikin, Miriam. *Joshua in the Promised Land.* Illustrated by David Frampton. New York: Clarion, 1982.

Cohen, Barbara. *I Am Joseph.* Illustrated by Charles Mikolaycak. Lothrop, Lee & Shepard, 1980.

dePaola, Tomie. *The Clown of God.* New York: Harcourt Brace, 1978.

———. *The Lady of Guadalupe.* New York: Holiday House, 1980.

———. *The Miracles of Jesus.* New York: Holiday House, 1987.

———. *The Parables of Jesus.* New York: Holiday House, 1987.

———. *The Prince of the Dolomites.* San Diego: Harcourt Brace Jovanovich, 1980.

———. *The Story of the Three Wise Kings.* New York: Putnam's, 1983.

Efron, Marshall, and Alfa B. Olsen. *Bible Stories You Can't Forget.* New York: Dell, 1979.

Evslin, Bernard. *Signs and Wonders: Tales from the Old Testament.* New York: Four Winds, 1982.

Fisher, Leonard Everett. *The Seven Days of Creation.* New York: Holiday House, 1981.

Freedman, Florence B. *Brothers: A Hebrew Legend.* Illustrated by Robert Andrew Parker. New York: Harper & Row, 1985.

Graham, Lorenz. *David He No Fear.* Illustrated by Ann Grifalconi. New York: Crowell, 1971.

———. *Every Man Heart Lay Down.* Illustrated by Colleen Browning. New York: Crowell, 1970.

———. *Hongry Catch the Foolish Boy.* Illustrated by James Brown, Jr. New York: Crowell, 1973.

———. *A Road down in the Sea.* Illustrated by Gregorio Prestopino. New York: Crowell, 1970.

Haubensak-Tallenbach, Margrit. *The Story of Noah's Ark.* New York: Crown, 1983.

Heine, Helme. *One Day in Paradise.* New York: Atheneum, McElderry, 1977.

Hogrogian, Nonny. *Noah's Ark.* New York: Knopf, 1986.

Hurd, Edith T. *Christmas Eve.* New York: Harper & Row, 1962.

Hutton, Warwick. *Jonah and the Great Fish.* New York: Atheneum, 1983.

———. *Noah's Ark.* New York: Atheneum, 1986.

Lindgren, Astrid. *Christmas in the Stable.* New York: Putnam's, 1979.

Pienkowski, Jan. *Christmas: The King James Version.* New York: Knopf, 1984.

Singer, Isaac Bashevis. *The Golem.* Illustrated by Uri Shulevitz. New York: Farrar, Straus & Giroux, 1982.

Spier, Peter. *The Book of Jonah.* New York: Doubleday, 1985.

———. *Noah's Ark.* New York: Doubleday, 1977.

Turner, Philip. *Brian Wildsmith's Illustrated Bible Stories.* New York: Watts, 1969.

Weil, Lisl. *Esther.* New York: Atheneum, 1980.

———. *The Very First Story Ever Told.* New York: Atheneum, 1976.

———. *The Story of the Wise Men and the Child.* New York: Atheneum, 1981.

Winthrop, Elizabeth. *A Child Is Born: The Christmas Story*. Illustrated by Charles Mikolaycak. New York: Holiday House, 1983.
———. *He Is Risen: The Easter Story*. Illustrated by Charles Mikolaycak. New York: Holiday House, 1985.

Poetry

Ciardi, John. *John J. Plenty and Fiddler Dan: A New Fable of The Grasshopper and the Ant*. Illustrated by Madeline Gekiere. Philadelphia: Lippincott, 1963.
Lobel, Arnold. *Whiskers and Rhymes*. New York: Greenwillow, 1985.
Plotz, Helen, ed. *As I Walked Out One Evening*. New York: Greenwillow, 1976.
———. *The Gift Outright: America to Her Poets*. New York: Greenwillow, 1977.

PROFESSIONAL REFERENCES

Applebee, Arthur N. "Children and Stories: Learning the Rules of the Game." *Language Arts* 56, no. 6 (September 1979): 641–46.
———. *The Child's Concept of Story*. Chicago: University of Chicago Press, 1978.
Bettleheim, Bruno. *The Uses of Enchantment: The Meaning and Importance of Fairy Tales*. New York: Knopf, 1976.
Botkin, B. A. *A Treasury of American Folklore*. New York: Bantam, 1981.
Carpenter, Humphrey, and Mari Prichard. *The Oxford Companion to Children's Literature*. New York: Oxford University Press, 1984–85.
Cook, Elizabeth. *The Ordinary and the Fabulous*. New York: Cambridge University Press, 1969.
Coxe, Marian Roalfe. *Cinderella: Three Hundred and Forty-Five Variants*. Published for the Folklore Society by David Nutt, 1893.
Favat, F. André. *Child and Tale: The Origins of Interest*. Urbana, Ill.: National Council of Teachers of English, 1977.
Frye, Northrop. *The Educated Imagination*. Bloomington: Indiana University Press, 1964.
———. *The Well-Tempered Critic*. Bloomington: Indiana University Press, 1963.
Grimal, Pierrre, ed. *Larousse World Mythology*. Secaucus, N.J.: Chartwell Books, 1965.
Hepler, Susan Ingrid. "Profile: Tomie de Paola: A Gift to Children." *Language Arts* 56, no. 3 (March 1979): 296–301.
Jung, Karl Gustav. *Man and His Symbols*. New York: Dell, 1964.
Lamme, Linda. "Song Picture Books: A Maturing Genre of Children's Literature." *Language Arts* 56, no. 4 (April 1979). 400–407.
Luthi, Max. *Once Upon a Time: On the Nature of Fairy Tales*. Edited by Lee Chadeayne and Paul Gottwald. New York: Ungar, 1970.
Sawyer, Ruth. *The Way of the Storyteller*. 1942. Reprint. New York: Viking, 1962.
Opie, Iona, and Peter Opie. *The Classic Fairy Tales*. New York: Oxford University Press, 1974.
———. *The Oxford Dictionary of Nursery Rhymes*. New York: Oxford University Press, 1951.
———. *The Oxford Nursery Rhyme Book*. New York: Oxford University Press, 1955.
Sendak, Maurice. "Mother Goose's Garnishings." *Book Week*, Fall Children's Issue. *Chicago Sun-Times*, 31 October 1965, 5, 38–40.

NOTES

1. Shel Silverstein, *Where the Sidewalk Ends* (New York: Harper & Row, 1974), 9.
2. Ruth Sawyer, *The Way of the Storyteller* (New York: Viking, 1962), 45–46.
3. Joanna Cole, ed., *Best-Loved Folktales of the World*, illus. Jill Karla Schwarz (Garden City, N. Y.: Doubleday, 1982), xix.
4. Iona Opie and Peter Opie, *Classic Fairy Tales* (London: Oxford University Press, 1974), 18.
5. F. André Favat, *Child and Tale: The Origins of Interest* (Urbana, Ill.: National Council of Teachers of English, 1977), 38, 50.
6. Bruno Bettelheim, *The Uses of Enchantment: The Meaning and Importance of Fairy Tales* (New York: Knopf, 1976), 6.
7. Arthur N. Applebee, "Children and Stories: Learning the Rules of the Game," *Language Arts* 56, no. 6 (September 1979): 645.
8. Walter De la Mare, quoted in William S. Baring-Gould and Cecil Baring-Gould, *The Annotated Mother Goose* (New York: Bramhall House, 1962), 21.
9. Iona Opie and Peter Opie, *The Oxford Dictionary of Nursery Rhymes* (London: Oxford University Press, 1951), 27.

10. Northrop Frye, *The Well-Tempered Critic* (Bloomington: Indiana University Press, 1963), 25.

11. Maurice Sendak. "Mother Goose's Garnishings," *Book Week,* Fall children's issue, *Chicago Sun Times,* 31 October 1965, 5, 38–40.

12. Mother Goose, "Hector Protector," in Maurice Sendak, *Hector Protector and As I Went Over the Water.* (New York: Harper & Row, 1965).

13. Susan Jeffers, *Three Jovial Huntsmen: A Mother Goose Rhyme* (New York: Bradbury, 1973), unpaged.

14. Janet and Allan Ahlberg, *Each Peach Pear Plum* (New York: Viking, 1979).

15. Iona Opie and Peter Opie, *Classic Fairy Tales,* 26.

16. Ibid., 25.

17. Arthur N. Applebee, *The Child's Concept of Story: Ages Two to Seventeen* (Chicago: University of Chicago Press, 1978), 44.

18. Paul Hazard, *Books Children and Men* (Boston: Horn Book, 1967), 157.

19. Arthur Applebee, "Where Does Cinderella Live?" in *The Cool Web: The Pattern of Children's Reading,* ed. Margaret Meek, Aidan Warlow, and Griselda Barton (New York: Atheneum, 1978), 54.

20. Cited in *The Web.,* Ohio State University (Winter 1978), 3–4.

21. Tomie dePaola, Harcourt Brace Jovanovich promotional material.

22. Ibid.

23. See, for example, Jack Zipes, "Kissing Off Snow White," *New York Times Book Review,* March 22, 1987, 34; also Nellie McCaslin, "Fairy Tales: To Be Trashed or Treasured?" in Insights and Viewpoints column, edited by William Waack, *Youth Theatre Journal* 2, no. 2 (Fall 1987): 34–35.

24. Trina Schart Hyman, *Self Portrait: Trina Schart Hyman* (Reading, Mass.: Addison-Wesley, 1981), unpaged.

25. Marian Roalfe Coxe, *Cinderella: Three Hundred and Forty-Five Variants* (Published for the Folklore Society by David Nutt, 1893), x.

26. Max Lüthi, *Once Upon a Time: On the Nature of Fairy Tales,* trans. Lee Chadeayne and Paul Gottwald (New York: Unger, 1970), 21–34.

27. Gail Haley, *Jack and the Bean Tree* (New York: Crown, 1986), unpaged.

28. Arlene M. Pillar, "Aspects of Moral Judgment in Response to Fables," in *Journal of Research and Development in Education* 16, no. 3 (Spring 1983): 37–46.

29. Pierre Grimal, ed. *Larousse World Mythology* (Secaucus, N.J.: Chartwell Books, 1965), 9.

30. Northrop Frye, *The Educated Imagination* (1964; reprint, Bloomington: Indiana University Press, 1970), 53, 57.

31. Elizabeth Cook, *The Ordinary and the Fabulous* (Cambridge: Cambridge University Press, 1969), 3.

32. This activity was contributed by Paula Baur, teacher, Worthington Hills Elementary School, Worthington, Ohio.

33. This teaching idea was contributed by Charlene Colbert-Manning, teacher, Orange, N.J.

34. This activity was contributed by Elizabeth Marcellaro, student, New York University.

35. Penelope Farmer, *Beginnings: Creation Myths of the World* (New York: Atheneum, 1979), 4.

36. Margaret Hodges, *Persephone and the Springtime,* illus. Arvis Stewart (Boston: Little, Brown, 1973), unpaged.

37. Penelope Farmer, *The Story of Persephone,* illus. Graham McCallum (New York: Morrow, 1973), unpaged.

38. Penelope Proddow, *Demeter and Persephone,* illus. Barbara Cooney (New York: Doubleday, 1972), unpaged.

39. Adapted from an activity created by Paula Baur.

40. B.A. Botkin, *A Treasury of American Folklore* (New York: Crown, 1944), 818–19.

41. Frye, *The Educated Imagination,* 70.

CHILDREN'S BOOKS CITED

Aardema, Verna. *Why Mosquitoes Buzz in People's Ears: A West African Tale.* Illustrated by Leo Dillon and Diane Dillon. New York: Dial, 1975.

Aesop. *Aesop's Fables.* Illustrated by Heidi Holder. New York: Viking, 1981.

———. "The Lion and the Mouse." In *The Fables of Aesop.* Adapted by John Ogilby, illustrated by Wenceslaus Hollar. London: Thomas Roycroft, 1665.

Ahlberg, Janet and Allan Ahlberg. *Each Peach Pear Plum.* New York: Viking, 1979.

Andersen, Hans Christian. *Thumbelina.* Retold by Amy Erlich, illustrated by Susan Jeffers. New York: Dial, 1979.

———. *The Ugly Duckling.* Retold and illustrated by Lorinda B. Cauley. New York: Harcourt Brace Jovanovich, 1979.

Asbjørnsen, Peter Christian & Jorgen E. Moe. *Three Billy Goats Gruff.* Illustrated by Susan Blair. New York: Holt, Rinehart & Winston, 1963.

———. *Three Billy Goats Gruff.* Illustrated by Marcia Brown. New York: Harcourt Brace Jovanovich, 1972.

———. *The Three Billy Goats Gruff:* Illustrated by Paul Galdone. New York: Clarion, 1981.

———. *Three Billy Goats Gruff.* Illustrated by Janet Stevens. San Diego: Harcourt Brace Jovanovich, 1987.

———. *The Three Billy Goats Gruff.* Illustrated by William Stobbs. New York: McGraw-Hill, 1968.

———. *East of the Sun and West of the Moon: Twenty-One Norwegian Folk Tales.* Illus. Ingri d'Aulaire and Edgar Parin d'Aulaire. New York: Viking, 1938.

Asimov, Isaac. *Words from the Myths.* Illustrated by William Barss. Boston: Houghton Mifflin, 1961.

Baker, Betty. *At the Center of the World: Based on Papago and Pima Myths..* Illustrated by Murray Tinkelman. New York: Macmillan, 1973.

Bang, Molly. *Dawn.* New York: Morrow, 1983.

Baring-Gould, William S. and Cecil Baring-Gould. *The Annotated Mother Goose: Nursery Rhymes Old and New.* Illustrated by Walter Crane, Randolph Caldecott, Kate Greenaway, Arthur Rackham, and Maxfield Parish. New York: Bramhall House, 1962.

Barth, Edna. *Cupid and Psyche.* New York: Clarion, 1976.

Bierhorst, John, ed. *The Monkey's Haircut: And Other Stories Told by the Maya.* Illustrated by Robert A. Parker. New York: Morrow, 1986.

Bishop, Gavin. *Chicken Licken.* New York: Oxford University Press, 1985.

Bolliger, Max. *Noah and the Rainbow: An Ancient Story.* Translated by Clyde Robert Bulla, illustrated by Helga Aichinger. New York: Crowell, 1972.

Branston, Brian. *Gods and Heroes from Viking Mythology.* Illustrated

by Giovanni Caselli. New York: Schocken Books, 1982.

Briggs, Raymond. *Jim and the Beanstalk.* New York: Coward-McCann, 1980.

Brooke, L. Leslie. *Ring O'Roses.* New York: Warne, 1923.

Brown, Marcia. *The Bun: A Tale from Russia.* New York: Harcourt Brace Jovanovich, 1972.

———. *Once a Mouse.* New York: Scribner's, 1961.

———. *Stone Soup.* New York: Scribner's, 1947.

Browne, Anthony, *Piggybook.* New York: Knopf, 1986.

Browning, Robert. *The Pied Piper of Hamelin.* Illustrated by Kate Greenaway. London: Routledge, 1888.

Bryan, Ashley. *I'm Going to Sing: Black American Spirituals, Volume II.* New York: Atheneum, 1982.

———. *Walk Together Children.* New York: Atheneum, 1974.

Caldecott, Randolph. *The Diverting History of John Gilpin.* London: Routledge, 1878.

———. *The Frog He Would A-Wooing Go.* London: Routledge, 1883.

———. *Hey Diddle Diddle.* London: Routledge, 1882.

———. *Three Jovial Huntsmen.* London: Routledge, 1880.

Cauley, Lorinda Bryan. *Goldilocks and the Three Bears.* New York: Putnam, 1981.

———. *The Town Mouse and the Country Mouse.* New York: Putnam, 1984.

Chase, Richard. *The Jack Tales.* Illustrated by Berkeley Williams. Boston: Houghton Mifflin, 1943.

Cleaver, Elizabeth. *The Enchanted Caribou.* New York: Atheneum, 1985.

Cohen, Barbara. *Lovely Vassilisa.* Illustrated by Anatoly Ivanov. New York: Atheneum, 1980.

Cole, Joanna. *Bony legs.* Illustrated by Dirk Zimmer. New York: Four Winds, 1983.

Colum, Padraic. *The Children of

Odin: the Book of Northern Myths.* New York: Macmillan, 1920.

Crane, Walter. *The History of Cock Robin and Jenny Wren.* London: Warne, 1865–66.

———. *The House That Jack Built.* London: Warne, 1865–66.

———. *Sing a Song of Sixpence.* London: Warne, 1865–66.

Coolidge, Olivia. *Greek Myths.* Illustrated by Edouard Sandoz. Boston: Houghton Mifflin, 1949.

———. *Legends of the North.* Illustrated by Edouard Sandoz. Boston: Houghton Mifflin, 1951.

Cooper, Susan, ed. *The Selkie Girl.* Illustrated by Warwick Hutton. New York: Atheneum, McElderry, 1986.

Craig, M. Jean. *The Donkey Prince.* Illustrated by Barbara Cooney. New York: Doubleday, 1977.

Crossley-Holland, Kevin. *The Faber Book of Northern Legends.* Illustrated by Alan Howard. New Yorker: Faber, 1983.

d'Aulaire, Ingri, and Edgar Parin d'Aulaire. *Book of Greek Myths.* New York: Doubleday, 1962.

———. *East of the Sun and West of the Moon.* New York: Doubleday, 1972.

———. *Norse Gods and Giants.* New York: Doubleday, 1967.

d'Aulnoy, Countess. *Fairy Tales.* 1697.

de Angeli, Marguerite. *Marguerite de Angeli's Book of Nursery and Mother Goose Rhymes.* New York: Doubleday, 1954.

De Beaumont, Madame Le Prince. *Beauty and the Beast.* Retold by Deborah Apy, illustrated by Michael Hague. New York: Holt, 1983.

———. *Beauty and the Beast.* Retold by Anne Carter, illustrated by Binette Shroeder. Crown, 1986.

———. *Beauty and the Beast.* Illustrated by Diane Goode. New York: Bradbury, 1978.

———. *Beauty and the Beast.* Retold and illustrated by Warwick Hutton. New York: Atheneum,

McElderry, 1985.

———. *Beauty and the Beast*. Retold and illustrated by Marianna Mayer. New York: Four Winds, 1978.

De Gerez, Toni. *Louhi, Witch of North Farm*. Illustrated by Barbara Cooney. New York: Viking, 1986.

De la Mare, Walter. *Molly Whuppie*. Illustrated by Errol Le Cain. New York: Farrar, Straus & Giroux, 1983.

dePaola, Tomie. *Big Anthony and the Magic Ring*. San Diego: Harcourt Brace Jovanovich, 1987.

———. *The Clown of God*. San Diego: Harcourt Brace Jovanovich, 1978.

———. *The Comic Adventures of Old Mother Hubbard and Her Dog*. San Diego: Harcourt Brace Jovanovich, 1981.

———. *Helga's Dowry*. New York: Harcourt Brace Jovanovich, 1977.

———. *The Lady of Guadalupe*. New York: Holiday House, 1980.

———. *The Legend of Old Befana*. San Diego: Harcourt Brace Jovanovich, 1980.

———. *Merry Christmas, Strega Nona*. San Diego: Harcourt Brace Jovanovich, 1986.

———. *Noah and the Ark*. New York: Harper & Row, 1983.

———*The Prince of the Dolomites*. San Diego: Harcourt Brace Jovanovich, 1980.

———. *Strega Nona*. Englewood Cliffs, N.J.: Prentice Hall, 1975.

———. *Strega Nona's Magic Lesson*. San Diego: Harcourt Brace Jovanovich, 1982.

———, ed. *Tomie dePoala's Favorite Nursery Tales*. New York: Putnam, 1986.

———. *Tomie dePaola's Mother Goose*. New York: Putnam's, 1985.

De Regniers, Beatrice Schenk. *Red Riding Hood: Retold in Verse*. Illustrated by Edward Gorey. New York: Atheneum, 1977.

Dewey, Ariane. *Febold Feboldson*. New York: Greenwillow, 1984.

———. *Gib Morgan, Oilman*. New York: Greenwillow, 1987

———. *Laffite, the Pirate*. New York: Greenwillow, 1985.

———. *Pecos Bill*. New York: Greenwillow, 1983.

Diamond, Jasper. *Noah's Ark*. Englewood Cliffs, N.J.: Prentice-Hall, 1983.

Domanska, Janina. *Little Red Hen*. New York: Macmillan, 1973.

Elborn, Andrew. *Noah and the Ark and the Animals*. Illustrated by Ivan Gantschev. Natick, Mass.: Picture Book Studio, 1984.

Emberley, Barbara. *Drummer Hoff*. Illustrated by Ed Emberley. Englewood Cliffs, N. J.: Prentice-Hall, 1967.

———. *The Story of Paul Bunyan*. Illustrated by Ed Emberley. Englewood Cliffs, N.J.: Prentice-Hall, 1963.

Evslin, Bernard. *Hercules*. Illustrated by Joseph A. Smith. New York: Morrow, 1984.

———. *Jason and the Argonauts*. Illustrated by Bert Dodson. New York: Morrow, 1986.

———, Dorothy Evslin, and Ned Hoopes. *Heroes, Gods, and Monsters of the Greek Myths*. Illustrated by William Hunter. New York: Four Winds, 1967.

Farmer, Penelope. *Beginnings: Creation Myths of the World*. New York: Atheneum, 1979.

———. *Daedalus and Icarus*. Illustrated by Chris Connor. New York: Harcourt Brace Jovanovich, 1971.

———. *The Story of Persephone*. Illustrated by Graham McCallum. New York: Morrow, 1973.

Faulkner, William. *The Days When The Animals Talked*. Chicago: Follett, 1977.

Fisher, Leonard Everett. *The Olympians: Great Gods and Goddesses of Ancient Greece*. New York: Holiday House, 1984.

Fussenegger, Gertrud. *Noah's Ark*. Illustrated by Annegert Fuschshuber. New York: Harper & Row, 1987.

Galdone, Paul. *Cinderella*. New York: McGraw-Hill, 1978.

———. *The Gingerbread Boy*. New York: Clarion, 1983.

———. *The Hare and the Tortoise*. New York: McGraw-Hill, 1962.

———. *Henny Penny*. New York: Clarion, 1984.

———. *Jack and the Beanstalk*. New York: Clarion, 1982.

———. *Little Bo-Peep*. New York: Clarion, 1986.

———. *The Little Red Hen*. New York: Clarion, 1985.

———. *Little Red Riding Hood*. New York: McGraw-Hill, 1974.

———. *The Magic Porridge Pot*. New York: Clarion, 1976.

———. *Old Mother Hubbard and Her Dog*. New York: McGraw-Hill, 1960.

———. *Rumpelstiltskin*. New York: Clarion, 1985.

———. *Three Aesop Fox Fables*. New York: Clarion, 1971.

———. *The Three Bears*. New York: Clarion, 1985.

———. *Three Little Kittens*. Boston: Clarion, 1986.

———. *The Three Little Pigs*. New York: Clarion, 1984.

Gates, Doris. *The Golden God: Apollo*. Illustrated by Constantine CoConis. New York: Penguin, 1983.

———. *Lord of the Sky: Zeus*. Illustrated by Robert Handville. New York: Penguin, 1982.

———. *Mightiest of Mortals: Heracles*. Illustrated by Richard Cuffari. New York: Penguin, 1984.

———. *Two Queens of Heaven: Aphrodite and Demeter*. Illustrated by Constantine CoConis. New York: Viking, 1983.

———. *The Warrior Goddess: Athena*. Illustrated by Don Bolognese. New York: Viking, 1972.

Gerstein, Mordicai. *The Seal Mother*. New York: Dial, 1986.

Gibson, Michael. *Gods, Men and Monsters from the Greek Myths*. Illustrated by Giovanni Caselli. New York: Hippocrene Books, 1978.

Goble, Paul. *Buffalo Woman.* New York: Bradbury, 1984.

Grahame, Kenneth. *The Wind in the Willows,* 75th ed. Illustrated by Ernest Shepard. New York: Scribner's, 1933.

Green, Roger Lancelyn *Tales of the Greek Heroes.* New York: Penguin, 1958.

Greenaway, Kate. *A Day in a Child's Life.* N.p., 1881.

————. *Kate Greenaway's Mother Goose.* Salem, N.H.: Merrimack, n.d.

————. *Mother Goose: Or, the Old Nursery Rhymes.* New York: Warne, 1882.

Grifalconi, Ann. *Village of Round and Square Houses.* Boston: Little, Brown, 1986.

Grimm, Jakob, and Wilhelm Grimm. *The Bremen Town Musicians.* Illustrated by Paul Galdone. New York: McGraw-Hill, 1968.

————. *The Bremen Town Musicians.* Retold by Elizabeth Shub, Illustrated by Janina Domanska. New York: Greenwillow, 1980.

————. *The Bremen Town Musicians.* Retold and illustrated by Ilse Plume. New York: Harper & Row, 1987.

————. *Cinderella.* Illustrated by Nonny Hogrogian. New York: Greenwillow, 1981.

————. *The Donkey Prince.* Illustrated by Barbara Cooney. New York: Doubleday, 1977.

————. *The Elves and the Shoemaker.* Illustrated by Katrin Brandt. Chicago: Follett, 1967.

————. *The Elves and the Shoemaker.* Illustrated by Paul Galdone. Boston: Houghton Mifflin, 1984.

————. *The Elves and the Shoemaker.* Retold by Freya Littledale, illustrated by Brinton Turkle. New York: Scholastic, 1975.

————. *Favorite Tales from Grimm.* Retold by Nancy Garden, illustrated by Mercer Mayer. New York: Four Winds, 1982.

————. *The Frog Prince.* Illustrated by Paul Galdone. New York: McGraw-Hill, 1975.

————. *The Frog Prince.* Retold by Edith Tarcov, illustrated by James Marshall. New York: Scholastic, 1987.

————. *German Popular Stories.* Illustrated by George Cruikshank. 1823.

————. *Grimm's Fairy Tales: Twenty Stories Illustrated by Arthur Rackham.* New York: Viking, 1973.

————. *Hans in Luck.* Illustrated by Felix Hoffmann. New York: Atheneum, 1975.

————. *Hansel and Gretel.* Illustrated by Antonella Bolliger-Savelli. New York: Oxford University Press, 1981.

————. *Hansel and Gretel.* Illustrated by Anthony Browne. New York: Watts, 1982.

————. *Hansel and Gretel.* Translated by Elizabeth D. Crawford, illustrated by Lisbeth Zwerger. New York: Morrow, 1980.

————. *Hansel and Gretel.* Illustrated by Paul Galdone. New York: McGraw-Hill, 1982.

————. *Hansel and Gretel.* Retold by Ruth B. Gross, illustrated by Margot Tomes. New York: Scholastic, 1974.

————. *Hansel and Gretel.* Illustrated by Susan Jeffers. New York: Dial, 1986.

————. *Hansel and Gretel.* Retold by Rika Lesser, illustrated by Paul O. Zelinsky. New York: Dodd, Mead, 1984.

————. *Hansel and Gretel.* Illustrated by Arnold Lobel. New York: Delacorte, 1971.

————. *Hansel and Gretel.* Translated by Charles Scribner, Jr., illustrated by Adrienne Adams. New York: Scribner's, 1975.

————. *Hansel and Gretel.* Illustrated by John Wallner. Englewood Cliffs, N.J.: Prentice-Hall, 1985.

————. *Household Stories of the Brothers Grimm.* 1886. Reprint. Translated by Lucy Crane, illustrated by Walter Crane. New York: McGraw-Hill, 1966.

————. *Household Tales.* Translated by Lucy Crane, illustrated by Walter Crane. Dover, 1886.

————. *Household Tales.* Introduction by Russell Hoban, illustrated by Mervyn Peake. New York: Schocken Books, 1979.

————. *Jorinda and Joringel.* Retold by Wanda Gág, illustrated by Margot Tomes. New York: Coward, McCann, Geoghegan, 1978.

————. *Jorinda and Joringel.* Translated by Elizabeth Shub, illustrated by Adrienne Adams. New York: Scribner's, 1968.

————. *Jorinda and Joringel.* Illustrated by Bernadette Watts. New York: World Books, 1970.

————. *The Juniper Tree and Other Tales from Grimm.* Edited by Lore Segal and Maurice Sendak, translated by Randall Jarrell, illustrated by Maurice Sendak. New York: Farrar, Straus & Giroux, 1976.

————. *Little Red Cap.* Translated by Elizabeth Crawford, illustrated by Lizbeth Zwerger. New York: Morrow, 1983.

————. *Little Red Riding Hood.* Retold and illustrated by John S. Goodall. New York: Atheneum, McElderry, 1988.

————. *Little Red Riding Hood.* Retold and illustrated by Trina Schart Hyman. New York: Holiday House, 1982.

————. *Nibble Nibble Mousekin: A Tale of Hansel and Gretel.* Retold and illustrated by Joan Walsh Anglund. San Diego: Harcourt Brace Jovanovich, 1977.

————. *Popular Folk Tales: The Brothers Grimm.* Translated by Brian Alderson, illustrated by Michael Foreman. New York: Doubleday, 1978.

————. *Rapunzel.* Illustrated by Jutta Ash. New York: Holt, Rinehart & Winston, 1982.

————. *Rapunzel.* Illustrated by Michael Hague. Mankato; Minn.: Creative Education, 1986.

————. *Rapunzel.* Edited and illustrated by Felix Hoffmann. New York: Harcourt Brace, 1961.

————. *Rapunzel*. Retold by Barbara Rogasky, illustrated by Trina Schart Hyman. New York: Holiday House, 1987.

————. *Rapunzel*. Illustrated by Bernadette Watts. New York: Crowell, 1975.

————. *Rumpelstiltskin*. Retold and illustrated by Donna Diamond. New York: Holiday House, 1983.

————. *Rumpelstiltskin*. Illustrated by Paul Galdone. New York: Clarion, 1985.

————. *Rumpelstiltskin*. Illustrated by William Stobbs. New York: Walck, 1970.

————. *Rumpelstiltskin*. Retold by Edith Tarcov, illustrated by Edward Gorey. New York: Four Winds, 1973.

————. *Rumpelstiltskin*. Illustrated by John Wallner. Englewood Cliffs, N.J.: Prentice-Hall, 1984.

————. *Rumpelstiltskin*. Illustrated by Paul O. Zelinsky. New York: Dutton, 1986.

————. *The Seven Ravens*. Illustrated by Lisbeth Zwerger. Natick, Mass.: Picture Book Studio, 1983.

————. *The Shoemaker and the Elves*. Illustrated by Adrienne Adams. New York: Scribner's, 1960.

————. *The Shoemaker and the Elves*. Retold and illustrated by Cynthia Birrer and William Birrer. New York: Lothrop, Lee & Shepard, 1983.

————. *The Sleeping Beauty*. Illustrated by Warwick Hutton. New York: Atheneum, McElderry, 1979.

————. *The Sleeping Beauty*. Retold and illustrated by Trina Schart Hyman. Boston: Little, Brown, 1977.

————. *The Sleeping Beauty*. Illustrated by Arthur Rackham. New York: Dover, 1920.

————. *Snow White*. Translated by Anthea Bell, illustrated by Chihiro Iwasaki. Natick, Mass.: Picture Book Studio, 1985.

————. *Snow White*. Translated by Paul Heins, illustrated by Trina Schart Hyman. Boston: Little, Brown, 1974.

————. *Snow White and Rose Red*. Translated by Wayne Andrews, illustrated by Adrienne Adams. New York: Scribner's, 1964.

————. *Snow White and Rose Red*. Illustrated by Barbara Cooney. New York: Delacorte, 1965.

————. *Snow White and Rose Red*. Illustrated by John Wallner. Englewood Cliffs, N.J.: Prentice-Hall, 1984.

————. *Snow White and the Seven Dwarfs*. Retold and illustrated by Wanda Gág. New York: Coward, McCann & Geoghegan, 1938.

————. *Snow White and the Seven Dwarfs*. Translated by Randall Jarrell, illustrated by Nancy Ekholm Burkert. New York. Farrar, Straus & Giroux, 1987.

————. *Tales From Grimm*. Illustrated by Wanda Gág. New York: Coward, McCann & Geoghegan, 1936.

————. *Teeny Tiny and the Witch-Woman*. Retold by Barbara Walker, illustrated by Michael Foreman. New York: Pantheon, 1975.

————. *Thorn Rose*. Illustrated by Errol Le Cain. New York: Penguin, 1978.

————. *Tom Thumb*. Translated by Anthea Bell, illustrated by Otto Svend. S. New York: Larousse, 1976.

————. *Thom Thumb*. Illustrated by Felix Hoffmann. New York: Atheneum, 1973.

————. *Tom Thumb*. Illustrated by William Wiesner. New York: Walck, 1974.

————. *The Traveling Musicians*. Illustrated by Hans Fischer. New York: Harcourt Brace, 1955.

————. *The Twelve Dancing Princesses*. Retold by Andrew Lang, illustrated by Adrienne Adams.

New York: H. Holt, 1980.

————. *The Twelve Dancing Princesses*. Retold and illustrated by Errol Le Cain. New York: Penguin, 1981.

Hague, Kathleen, and Michael Hague. *The Man Who Kept House*. San Diego, Harcourt Brace Jovanovich, 1981.

Haley, Gail. *Jack and the Bean Tree*. New York: Crown, 1986.

————. *Noah's Ark*. New York: Atheneum, 1971.

————. *A Story, a Story: An African Tale*. Illustrated by Gail Haley. New York: Atheneum, 1970.

Hamilton, Edith. *Mythology*. Boston: Little, Brown, 1942.

Hamilton, Virginia. *The People Could Fly*. Illustrated by Leo Dillon and Diane Dillon. New York: Knopf, 1985.

Harper, Wilhelmina. *The Gunniwolf*. Illustrated by William Wiesner. New York: Dutton, 1967.

Harris, Joel Chandler. *Jump! The Adventures of Brer Rabbit*. Adapted by Van Dyke Parks and Malcolm Jones, illustrated by Barry Moser. San Diego: Harcourt Brace Jovanovich, 1986.

————. *Jump Again! More Adventures of Brer Rabbit*. Adapted by Van Dyke Parks, illustrated by Barry Moser. San Diego: Harcourt Brace Jovanovich, 1987.

Hart, Jane, comp. *Singing Bee! A Collection of Favorite Children's Songs*. Illustrated by Anita Lobel. New York: Lothrop, Lee & Shepard, 1982.

Hawkins, Colin, and Jacqui Hawkins. *Old Mother Hubbard*. New York: Putnam's, 1985.

Hodges, Margaret. *The Gorgon's Head*. Illustrated by Charles Mikolaycak. Boston: Little, Brown, 1972.

————. *Persephone and the Springtime, A Greek Myth*. Illustrated by Arvis Stewart. Boston: Little, Brown, 1973.

————. *Saint George and the Dragon*. Illustrated by Trina Schart Hyman. Boston: Little, Brown, 1984.

Hogrogian, Nonny. *One Fine Day.* New York: Macmillan, 1971

———. *Noah's Ark.* New York: Knopf, 1986.

Hollander, Paul. *The Labors of Hercules.* Illustrated by Judith Ann Lawrence. New York: Putnam's, 1965.

Homer. *The Iliad of Homer.* Edited by Barbara Picard, illustrated by Joan Kiddell-Monroe. New York: Oxford University Press, 1960.

———. *The Odyssey.* Translated by Walter Shewring. New York: Oxford University Press, 1980.

Hutchinson, Veronica S. *Henny Penny.* Illustrated by Leonard B. Lubin. Boston: Little, Brown, 1976.

Ivimey, John W. *Complete Version of Ye Three Blind Mice.* Illustrated by Walton Courbould. New York: Warne, 1979.

Jacobs, Joseph. *Ardizzone's English Fairy Tales: Twelve Classic Tales from the Collection of Joseph Jacobs.* Illustrated by Edward Ardizzone. Bergenfield, N.J.: Deutsch, 1986.

———. *English Fairy Tales.* 1898. Reprint. Illustrated by John D. Batten. New York: Dover, 1967.

———. *The History of Mother Twaddle and the Marvelous Achievement of Her Son Jack.* Illustrated by Paul Galdone. New York: Clarion, 1974.

———. *Jack and the Bean Tree.* Retold by Gail Haley. New York: Crown, 1986.

———. *Jack and the Beanstalk.* Illustrated by Lorinda B. Cauley. New York: Putnam's, 1983.

———. *Jack and the Beanstalk.* Retold by Beatrice Schenk De Regniers, illustrated by Anne Wilsdorf. New York: Atheneum, McElderry, 1985.

———. *Jack and the Beanstalk.* Illustrated by Paul Galdone. New York: Clarion, 1982.

———. *Jack and the Beanstalk.* Illustrated by Margery Gill. New York: Walck, 1975.

———. *Jack and the Beanstalk.* Illustrated by William Stobbs. New York: Delacorte, 1969.

———. *The Three Little Pigs.* Illustrated by Erik Blegvad. New York: Atheneum, McElderry, 1980.

———. *The Three Little Pigs.* Illustrated by Paul Galdone. New York: Clarion, 1970.

———. *The Three Little Pigs.* Illustrated by William Pène du Bois. New York: Viking, 1962.

———. *The Three Little Pigs.* Illustrated by Edda Reinl. Natick, Mass.: Picture Book Studio, 1983.

Jagendorf, Moritz A. *Noodlehead Stories from Around the World.* Illustrated by Shane Miller. New York: Vanguard, 1957.

Jaquith, Priscilla. *Bo Rabbit Smart for True: Folktales from the Gullah.* Illustrated by Ed Young. New York: Putnam's, 1981.

Jeffers, Susan. *Three Jovial Huntsmen: A Mother Goose Rhyme.* Illustrated by Susan Jeffers. New York: Bradbury, 1973.

Kellogg, Steven. *Chicken Little.* New York: Morrow, 1985.

———. *Paul Bunyan.* New York: Morrow, 1974.

———. *Pecos Bill.* New York: Morrow, 1986.

Kent, Jack. *The Fat Cat: A Danish Folktale.* New York: Parent's, 1974.

———. *Jack Kent's Fables of Aesop.* New York: Parent's, 1972.

———. *More Fables of Aesop.* Retold and illustrated by Jack Kent. New York: Parent's, 1974.

La Fontaine, Jean *The Cobbler's Song.* Retold and illustrated by Marcia Sewall. New York: Dutton, 1982.

———. *The Lion and the Rat.* Illustrated by Brian Wildsmith. New York: Oxford University Press, 1963.

———. *The North Wind and the Sun.* Illustrated by Brian Wildsmith. New York: Oxford University Press, 1984.

———. *The Rich Man and the Shoemaker.* Illustrated by Brian Wildsmith. New York: Oxford University Press, 1965.

Langstaff, John. *Frog Went A-Courtin'.* Illustrated by Feodor Rojankovsky. San Diego: Harcourt Brace, Jovanovich 1972.

———. *Oh, A-Hunting We Will Go.* Illustrated by Nancy Winslow Parker. New York: Atheneum, McElderry, 1974.

———. *Over in the Meadow.* Illustrated by Feodor Rojankovsky. San Diego: Harcourt Brace Jovanovich, 1973.

———. *Sweetly Sings the Donkey: Animal Rounds for Children to Sing or Play on Recorders.* Illustrated by Nancy Winslow Parker. New York: Atheneum, McElderry, 1976.

Langton, Jane. *The Hedgehog Boy: A Latvian Folktale.* Illustrated by Ilse Plume. New York: Harper & Row, 1985.

Leach, Maria. *How the People Sang the Mountains Up: How and Why Stories.* New York: Viking, 1967.

Lester, Julius. *The Tales of Uncle Remus: The Adventures of Brer Rabbit.* Illustrated by Jerry Pinkney. New York: Dial, 1987.

Lewis, C.S. *The Lion, The Witch, and the Wardrobe.* Illustrated by Pauline Baynes. New York: Macmillan, 1968.

Lobel Arnold. *Fables.* New York: Harper & Row, 1980.

———. *The Random House Book of Mother Goose.* New York: Random House, 1986.

Low, Alice. *The Macmillan Book of Greek Gods and Heroes.* Illustrated by Arvis Stewart. New York: Macmillan, 1986.

McDermott, Gerald. *Anansi the Spider: A Tale from the Ashanti.* New York: Holt, Rinehart & Winston, 1972.

McKee, David. *The Man Who Was*

Going to Mind the House. New York: Abelard-Schuman, 1972.

McLeish, Kenneth, retel. *Chicken Licken*. Illustrated by Jutta Ash. New York: Bradbury, 1974.

Martin, Rafe. *Foolish Rabbit's Big Mistake*. Illustrated by Ed Young. New York: Putnam's, 1985.

Mayer, Marianna. *Twelve Dancing Princesses*. Illustrated by Gerald McDermott. New York: Morrow, 1987.

Merrill, Jean. *Red Riding*. Illustrated by Ronnie Solbert. New York: Pantheon, 1968.

Mikolaycak, Charles. *Babushka: An Old Russian Folktale*. New York: Holiday House, 1984.

Montresor, Beni. *Cinderella: From the Opera by Gioacchino Rossini*. New York: Knopf, 1965.

Morimoto, Junko. *The Inch Boy*. Illustrated by Junko Morimoto. New York: Viking, 1986.

Mosel, Arlene. *Tikki Tikki Tembo*. New York: Holt, Rinehart & Winston, 1968.

Ness, Evaline. *Old Mother Hubbard and Her Dog*. New York: Holt, Rinehart & Winston, 1972.

———. *Tom Tit Tot*. New York: Scribner's, 1965.

Newman, Robert. *The Twelve Labors of Hercules*. Illustrated by Charles Keeping. New York: Crowell, 1972.

Opie, Iona, and Peter Opie. *Classic Fairy Tales*. London: Oxford University Press, 1974.

Ormerod, Jan. *The Story of Chicken Licken*. New York: Lothrop, Lee & Shepard, 1986.

Pearson, Tracey Campbell. *Sing a Song of Sixpence*. New York: Dial, 1985.

Peek, Merle. *Mary Wore Her Red Dress and Henry Wore His Green Sneakers*. New York: Clarion, 1985.

———. *Roll Over! A Counting Song*. New York: Clarion, 1981.

Perrault, Charles. *Briar Rose*. Illustrated by Margery Gill. New York: Walck. 1972.

———. *Cinderella*. Illustrated by Marcia Brown. New York: Macmillan, 1981.

———. *Cinderella*. Edited by Amy Ehrlich, illustrated by Susan Jeffers. New York: Dial, 1985.

———. *Cinderella*. Retold by C.S. Evans, illustrated by Arthur Rackham. New York: Viking, 1972.

———. *Cinderella*. Translated by John Fowles, illustrated by Sheilah Beckett. Boston: Little, Brown, 1976.

———. *Cinderella*. Illustrated by Moira Kemp. London: Hamish Hamilton, 1981.

———. *Cinderella*. Illustrated by Errol Le Cain. New York : Bradbury, 1973.

———. *Cinderella*. Illustrated by Otto Svend S. New York: Larousse, 1978.

———. *Histoires Ou Contes Dutemps Passé, Avec Des Moralities* (Stories of Times Past, with Morals). 1697.

———. *Little Red Riding Hood*. Illustrated by William Stobbs. New York: Walck, 1973.

———. *Little Red Riding Hood*. Illustrated by Bernadette Watts. New York: Scholastic, 1971.

———. *Moss Gown*. Retold by William Hooks, illustrated by Donald Carrick. New York: Clarion, 1987.

———. *Puss in Boots*. Retold by Christopher Logue, illustrated by Nicola Bayley. New York: Greenwillow, 1977.

———. *Puss in Boots*. Retold and illustrated by Marcia Brown. New York: Scribner's, 1981.

———. *Puss in Boots*. Illustrated by Lorinda Bryan Cauley. San Diego. Harcourt Brace Jovanovich, 1986.

———. *Puss in Boots*. Illustrated by Paul Galdone. New York: Clarion, 1976.

———. *Puss in Boots*. Illustrated by William Stobbs. New York: McGraw-Hill, 1975.

———. *Puss in Boots*. Translated by David Walker, illustrated by Jan Pienkowski. New York: Crowell, 1978.

———, *The Sleeping Beauty*. Adapted and illustrated by Warren Chappell. New York: Schocken Books, 1982.

———. *The Sleeping Beauty*. Illustrated by Arthur Rackham. New York: Viking, 1972.

———. *The Sleeping Beauty*. Retold and illustrated by Mercer Mayer. New York: Macmillan, 1984.

———. *The Sleeping Beauty*. Translated and illustrated by David Walker. New York: Crowell, 1977.

———. *The Sleeping Beauty*. Translated by David Walker, illustrated by Jan Pienkowski. New York: Crowell, 1978.

———. *Thorn Rose*. Illustrated by Errol Le Cain. New York: Penguin, 1978.

Proddow, Penelope. *Art Tells a Story: Greek and Roman Myths*. New York: Doubleday, 1979.

———, trans. *Demeter and Persephone*. Illustrated by Barbara Cooney. New York: Doubleday, 1972.

Provensen, Alice, and Martin Provensen. *Old Mother Hubbard*. New York: Random House, 1982.

Pyle, Howard. *King Stork*. Illustrated by Trina Schart Hyman. Boston: Little, Brown, 1986.

Quackenbush, Robert. *Pop! Goes the Weasel and Yankee Doodle: New York in 1776 and Today, with Songs and Pictures*. Philadelphia: Lippincott, 1976.

———. *She'll Be Comin' 'round the Mountain*. Illustrated by Robert Quackenbush. Philadelphia: Lippincott, 1973.

Rackham, Arthur. *Mother Goose, Old Nursery Rhymes*. 1913. Reprint. New York: Viking, 1975.

Rayner, Mary. *Mr. and Mrs. Pig's Evening Out.* New York: Atheneum, 1979.

Robbins, Ruth. *Baboushka and the Three Kings.* Illustrated by Nicholas Sidjakov. Boston: Parnassus, 1960.

Rojankovsky, Feodor. *The Tall Book of Mother Goose.* New York: Harper & Row, 1942.

Rose, Anne. *Pot Full of Luck.* Illustrated by Margot Tomes. New York: Lothrop, Lee & Shepard, 1982.

Rounds, Glen. *Casey Jones: The Story of a Brave Engineer.* Chicago: Children's Press, 1968.

———. *Sweet Betsy from Pike.* Chicago Children's Press, 1973.

Sawyer, Ruth. *Journey Cake, Ho!* Illustrated by Robert McCloskey. New York: Viking, 1953.

Schwartz, Alvin. *Flapdoodle: Pure Nonsense from American Folklore.* Illustrated by John O'Brien. Philadelphia: Lippincott, 1980.

———. *Whoppers: Tall Tales and Other Lies Collected from American Folklore.* Philadelphia: Lippincott, 1975.

———. *Witcracks: Jokes and Jests from American Folklore.* Illustrated by Glen Rounds. New York: Harper & Row, 1973.

Sendak, Maurice. *Hector Protector and as I Went over the Water.* New York: Harper & Row, 1965.

Serraillier, Ian. *Clashing Rocks: The Story of Jason.* Illustrated by William Stobbs. New York: Walck, 1964.

———. *A Fall from the Sky: The Story of Daedalus.* Illustrated by William Stobbs. New York: Walck, 1966.

———. *The Gorgon's Head: The Story of Perseus.* Illustrated by William Stobbs. New York: Walck, 1962.

———. *Heracles the Strong.* Illustrated by Rocco Negri. New York: Walck, 1970.

———. *Way of Danger: The Story of Theseus.* Illustrated by William Stobbs. New York: Walck, 1963.

Siberell, Anne. *Whale in the Sky.* New York: Dutton, 1982.

Silverstein, Shel. *Where the Sidewalk Ends.* New York: Harper & Row, 1974.

Silverman, Maida. *Anna and the Seven Swans.* Edited by David Small. Morrow, 1984.

Singer, Isaac Bashevis. *Why Noah Chose the Dove.* Translated by Elizabeth Shub, illustrated by Eric Carle. New York: Farrar, Straus & Giroux, 1974.

Small, Ernest. *Baba Yaga.* Illustrated by Blair Lent. Boston: Houghton Mifflin, 1966.

Smith, Jessie Willcox. *The Jessie Willcox Smith Mother Goose.* Edited by Corey Nash. New York: Crown, Outlet, 1986.

Southey, Robert. *The Three Bears.* Illustrated by Kevin Scally. New York: Putnam's, 1984.

Spier, Peter. *Fox Went Out on a Chilly Night.* New York: Doubleday, 1961.

———. *Noah's Ark.* New York: Doubleday, 1977.

Steel, Flora Annie. *Tattercoats: An Old English Tale.* Illustrated by Diane Goode. New York: Bradbury, 1976.

Stobbs, William. *Johnny Cake.* New York: Viking, 1973.

Steptoe, John. *The Story of Jumping Mouse.* New York: Lothrop, Lee & Shepard, 1984.

Stevens, Janet. *Goldilocks and the Three Bears.* New York: Holiday House, 1986.

Sleator, William. *The Angry Moon.* Illustrated by Blair Lent. Boston: Little, Brown, 1970.

Still, James. *Jack and the Wonder Beans.* Illustrated by Margaret Tomes. New York: Putnam's, 1977.

Stobbs, William. *Henny Penny.* Chicago: Follett, 1970.

Tashjian, Virginia. *Once There Was and Was Not: Armenian Tales.* Illustrated by Nonny Hogrogian. Boston: Little, Brown, 1966.

Turkle, Brinton. *Deep in the Forest.* New York: Dutton, 1976.

Watson, Clyde. *Father Fox's Feast of Songs.* Illustrated by Wendy Watson. New York: Philomel, 1983.

Watts, Bernadette. *Goldilocks and the Three Bears.* New York: Holt, Rinehart & Winston, 1985.

Westcott, Nadine B. *I Know an Old Lady Who Swallowed a Fly.* Boston: Little, Brown, 1980.

White, E. B. *Charlotte's Web.* New York: Harper & Row, 1952.

Whitney, Thomas P. *Vasilisa the Beautiful.* New York: Macmillan, 1970.

Weisner, William. *Turnabout.* New York: Seabury, 1972.

Wilde, Oscar. *The Selfish Giant.* Illustrated by Lisbeth Zwerger. Natick, Mass.: Picture Book Studio, 1984.

Wildsmith, Brian. *Brian Wildsmith's Mother Goose.* New York: Oxford University Press, 1982.

———. *The Lion and the Rat.* New York: Watts, 1963.

Wise, William. *Monster Myths of Ancient Greece.* Illustrated by Jerry Pinkney. New York: Putnam's, 1981.

Yagawa, Sumiko. *The Crane Wife.* Translated by Katherine Paterson, illustrated by Suekichi Akaba. New York: Morrow, 1981.

Yeatman, Linda. *Noah's Ark.* Illustrated by Bob Gault. New York: Putnam, 1984.

Zemach, Harve. *Nail Soup.* Adapted from a text by Nils Djurklo, illustrated by Margot Zemach. Chicago: Follett, 1964.

———. *Duffy and the Devil: A Cornish Tale Retold.* Illustrated by Margot Zemach. New York: Farrar, Straus & Giroux, 1986.

Zemach, Margot. *The Little Red Hen: An Old Story.* New York: Farrar, Straus & Giroux, 1983.

6

Fantasy and Science Fiction

Dreams

Hold fast to dreams
For if dreams die
Life is a broken-winged bird
That cannot fly.

Hold fast to dreams
For when dreams go
Life is a barren field
Frozen with snow.[1]

Langston Hughes

*L*angston Hughes's admonition to hold fast to dreams is good advice—for without dreams and imagination, we cannot soar beyond our earthly limitations, and we cannot nurture our hopes and ideas. Fantasy opens doors to worlds of imagination not found in the real world. It enriches and illuminates children's lives because the stories deal with the great complexities of existence: the relativity of size, time, and space; good versus evil; the strength and courage of the individual; and self-integrity. Fantasy springs from myth and treats problems of the universe with a high seriousness reflective of its origins. Yet fantasy can also deal lightheartedly with capricious supernatural events, such as cars that fly through the air, as in *Chitty Chitty Bang Bang* (I) by Ian Fleming, or stuffed animals that talk, as in *Winnie the Pooh* (I) by A. A. Milne. The dividing line is not between fact and fiction; that line, as Lloyd Alexander shows, is very thin: "Some fiction claims to be true. We call it history. Some truth claims to be fiction. We call it literature."[2]

Fantasy is fiction that contains some element not found in the natural world; it hints of things magical. Size does not matter, time does not matter, place does not matter; the essence of life embodied in each being is what counts. Fantasy shows that there is more than one kind of reality and more than one level of truth. We judge the quality of fantasy by how thoroughly it convinces us of its reality: how long it haunts our memory and how deeply it moves us to new insights.

WHAT IS FANTASY?

Fantasy is imaginative fiction that deals with alternate realities, that suspends scientific explanations and natural laws; it is a search for a deeper reality and eternal truth.

Children respond to fantasy naturally. The rhythms of its language and the subtlety of its images appeal to readers with special sensibilities to things at once deep and high, elusive and visible. Fantasy invites wholehearted immersion in its compelling narratives. It is especially important because of the role it plays in the child's imaginative development. Fantasy forges links between language and images, making things unseen seen and making things unknown known. It helps the reader see beyond the concrete world to a world that could be. It helps children deal with what they unconsciously know and feel—those terrors and joys of childhood that are a part of the existential mysteries of life.

Children who never read fanciful stories have a difficult time considering the possibility of fantasy. They are bound to the literal, the practical, the ordinary. It may be that there is a critical period in which children need to know fantasy in order to be free to suspend disbelief and imagine a world they cannot see. Imagination educated by fantasy leads to visions of worlds beyond the one at hand. Herein lies the power of fantasy.

Great writers of fantasy—J. R. R. Tolkien, C. S. Lewis, Eleanor Cameron, Elizabeth Cook—themselves choose different words to describe the quality peculiar to fairy tale and fantasy. Tolkien uses the word *faerie* and takes care to specify that this word does not mean a small winged creature also called fairy; rather, it is a quality of feeling called *heart's desire*— that is, a yearning for a romantic, visionary world. C. S. Lewis describes this quality in terms of the response that certain imaginative works evoke in him. His term is *joy*, and in his autobiographical book *Surprised by Joy: The Shape of My Early Life* he tells of the aesthetic response called forth by such varied works as Beatrix Potter's *The Tale of Squirrel Nutkin*, Norse mythology, and George Macdonald's *Phantasies.* Lewis's joy is neither happiness nor pleasure; rather, he equates it with a Greek word that translates into "Oh, I desire too much."

Eleanor Cameron describes the response that fantasy evokes in her—in this case, while reading about the death of King Arthur:

> His death meant the passing of goodness and courage and idealism, the breaking up of the ring, the scattering of the great knights: all of that gone, perhaps forever. I remember now the almost unutterable poignancy I felt—sadness mixed with longing—yet a sense of exaltation, of having touched something very fine and powerful and strength-giving. For me, as a child, this was equal to the adult experience of Greek or Shakespearean tragedy.[3]

And Elizabeth Cook describes the quality unique to fantasy as "a sense of the strange, the numinous, the totally Other, of what lies quite beyond human personality and cannot be found in any human relationships."[4]

The terms we use to try to understand and embrace fantasy—a sense of faerie, heart's desire, joy, unutterable poignancy, a sense of the numinous—are more evocative than definitive. Our purpose as teachers, however, is to understand—rather than to analyze and define—enough aspects of the experience to enable us to start young readers on the path that will

E. B. White's *Charlotte's Web* is a classic animal fantasy. (Illustrated by Garth Williams.)

lead to a lifetime of delight. We speak with conviction if we have the experience firsthand.

Children move about comfortably in the world of fantasy if they have a secure grasp of what is real and what is make-believe. By about the second grade, children are quite capable of making these distinctions. It is not unusual for a group to become intensely involved in a discussion of what "could really happen." For instance, children break into spontaneous and heated argument about whether Santa Claus, elves, or the tooth fairy is real. Teachers aware of the level of development reflected in such discussions may lead children to new insights and help them see that, although fantasy is not true in a factual sense, it vivifies the truth.

Eventually, distinctions between fantasy and reality become unnecessary; children un-

LANDMARK

Fantasy: Charlotte's Web, *1952*

Whenever children are asked to name their favorite stories, *Charlotte's Web* (I) is always among their top choices. In a letter to readers, E. B. White describes his inspiration for the book:

> As for *Charlotte's Web,* I like animals and my barn is a very pleasant place to be, at all hours. One day when I was on my way to feed the pig, I began feeling sorry for the pig because, like most pigs, he was doomed to die. This made me sad. So I started thinking of ways to save a pig's life. I had been watching a big gray spider at her work and was impressed by how clever she was at weaving. Gradually I worked the spider into the story that you know, a story of friendship and salvation on a farm. Three years after I started writing it, it was published.[5]

In the story, Charlotte, a beautiful, large gray spider who lives in the doorway of Wilbur's pen is quite literate and turns out to be a true friend. Wilbur, a pig, is devastated when he finds out that he is to be butchered in the fall, but Charlotte promises to think of a way to save him. She does this by spinning words into her web above his pen. When farmer Zuckerman sees the words "radiant," "terrific," and "humble" spelled out in the spider's web above Wilbur's pen, he and everyone else decide that Wilbur is truly special and should not be subjected to the butcher's knife. Few people notice that it is Charlotte who is truly unusual, a subtle commentary on society's ways. The true story, however, is about friendship, and only a first-hand reading reveals the beauty of the language in which the story is told. *Charlotte's Web* has become the standard for all subsequent fantasies.

derstand the universal truth that transcends the artificial dichotomy. They are able to move on to that willing suspension of disbelief that imaginative literature evokes, and the wise teacher frees them to do so. A discussion that may have been necessary and desirable at an earlier point in a literary education hampers the appreciation of literature at a later time. Children move effectively in and out of fantasy if granted freedom from explanation—that is, if they are not asked to reconcile the fanciful events with the real world.

To accept the conventions of fantasy, then, becomes a basic rule of the game. The tacit acceptance of make-believe, necessary for the full enjoyment of literature, is illustrated in a scene from Edward Eager's *Half Magic* (I). The incident captures the child's attitude toward fantasizing. As the story opens, four children have just finished reading E. Nesbit's *The Enchanted Castle* (I):

> There was a contented silence when she closed the book, and then, after a little, it began to get discontented.
>
> Martha broke it, saying what they were all thinking. "Why don't things like that ever happen to *us?*"
>
> "Magic never happens, not really," said Mark, who was old enough to be sure about this.

"How do you know?" asked Katharine, who was nearly as old as Mark, but not nearly so sure about anything.

"Only in fairy stories."

"It *wasn't* a fairy story. There weren't any dragons or witches or poor woodcutters, just real children like us!"

They were all talking at once now.

"They *aren't* like us. We're never in the country for the summer, and walk down strange roads and find castles!"

"We never go to the seashore and meet mermaids and sand-fairies!"

"Or go to our uncle's, and there's a magic garden!"

"If the Nesbit children do stay in the city it's London, and *that's* interesting, and then they find phoenixes and magic carpets! Nothing like that ever happens here!"

"There's Mrs. Hudson's house," Jane said. "That's a *little* like a castle."

"There's the Miss Kings' garden."

"We could *pretend*. . . ."

It was Martha who said this, and the others turned on her.

"Beast!"

"Spoilsport!"

Because of course the only way pretending is any good is if you never say right out that that's what you're doing. Martha knew this perfectly well, but in her youth she sometimes forgot. So now Mark threw a pillow at her, and so did Jane and Katharine. . . .[6]

Fantasy readers, then, know that to say right out that it is pretending is to miss the whole point. If you have to explain—it's lost. Fantasies seldom reveal their ultimate secrets; they are suggestive and elusive.

The simplest fantasies are often humorous ones. In some, miniature worlds peopled by elves, trolls, and gnomes emphasize the dignity of every creature. In other stories, human nature is reflected through animal characters. In many fantasy stories, time past and time future meld into the present. The search for eternal truth becomes a hero's quest. Still others draw upon the legacy of stories from times gone by. Finally, some stories, called science fiction, speculate on what life could be like in other worlds and other times.

Criteria for Selecting Fantasy

As with all quality literature, good fantasy tells an interesting story, has well-developed characters, an engaging plot, and an identifiable theme. Authors manipulate these elements, particularly setting, character, and time, to create a fantasy world. For example, J. R. R. Tolkien begins *The Hobbit* (A) by describing the setting before introducing characters:

> In a hole in the ground there lived a hobbit. Not a nasty, dirty, wet hole, filled with the ends of worms and an oozy smell, nor yet a dry, bare, sandy hole with nothing in it to sit down on or to eat: it was a hobbit-hole, and that means comfort.[7]

We learn that the hobbit in this particular hobbit-hole is very well-to-do, and his name is Baggins. In a single page, Tolkien creates a make-believe world, introduces a major character that readers willingly follow, and hints of personality traits that lead to complications.

If the fantasy writer is successful, readers willingly suspend disbelief. They accept the writer's illusion of reality because it is convincing and the events are plausible within the fantasy world. Therefore, in selecting fantasy, we look for story elements that appeal to the imagination yet remain within the realm of the plot.

Characters are believable in good fantasy. Even if they become superheroes within the story, they are so carefully delineated that we accept their otherworldly powers. Robin McKinley establishes her character, foreshadows a problem, and alludes to the setting in the opening paragraph of *The Hero and the Crown* (A):

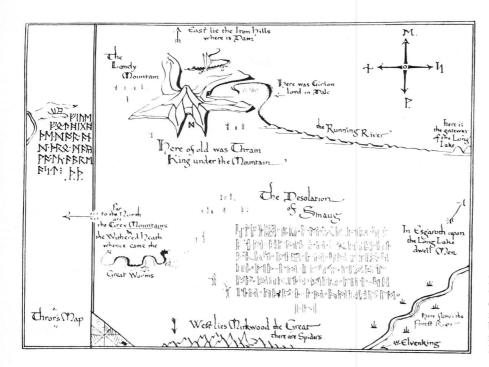

Runes on a map reinforce the setting, time, and otherworldliness of the fantasy *The Hobbit*. (Written by J. R. R. Tolkien, illustrated by Michael Hague.)

She could not remember a time when she had not known the story; she had grown up knowing it. She supposed someone must have told her it, sometime, but she could not remember the telling. She was beyond having to blink back tears when she thought of those things the story explained, but when she was feeling smaller and shabbier than usual in the large vivid City high in the Damarian Hills she still found herself brooding about them; and her brooding sometimes brought on a tight headachy feeling around her temples, a feeling like suppressed tears.[8]

We do not even find out the girl's name, Aerin, until the end of the first chapter, but we know a great deal about her by that time. Aerin's destiny leads her to battle with Maur, the Black Dragon; and we empathize with her because we have totally accepted her as a believable person; she acts within the constraints of the story.

The juxtaposition of the real and the unreal is deftly handled in high-quality fantasy. When authors manipulate time by slipping into the past or catapulting into the future, it is done artfully. Readers are jarred by an abrupt time slip; they also need careful preparation to switch between the real and the make-believe world. Jan Adkins achieves a masterful time slip in *A Storm Without Rain* (I–A). In this story, young John Swain Carter chooses to skip his grandfather's ninety-third birthday celebration by spending the day on Penikese Island in Massachusetts Bay. He had nothing against his grandfather—in fact, he had been named after him—but he knew very little about family history and had little in common with the old man. The day on the island changes his life because it proves to be a portal, a thin spot in time, through which he is transported to the year 1904 when his grandfather was exactly his own age. He gains a new perspective about his boisterous great-great-grandfather and John Carter Swain who was to become his grandfather. The two boys, age-mates joined across the generations, confront the problem of returning the time traveler to his own time. They also discuss the nature of time, which adds credibility to the plot.

In fantasy, as in other genres, a tale is all in the telling, and some of our finest writers choose humor as their form. Some writers use exaggeration, satire, and word play as the basis for their humor. For example, Norton Juster's *The Phantom Tollbooth* (I) is filled with word play and humorous satire; the entire plot hinges on untangling a clever word game. Other writers, such as James Howe, use understatement and witty dialogue. In the fourth book in the Bunnicula series, *Nighty Nightmare* (I), the Monroe family goes on an overnight camping trip, taking with them the naive puppy, Howie, and the overly imaginative and superstitious cat, Chester. When they meet up with backwoods natives—Bud and Spud and their dog called Dawg the Dog—strange things begin to happen. The animals are separated from their families, with the devilish Dawg as their leader, and before the night is over, it is a nightmare for all.

As with the selection of books in other genres, consider the developmental level of the child when choosing among the various levels of complexity in fantasy. Children must be able to understand the verbal word play, imagery, and subtle puns of the language. Similarly, they must understand the complex convolutions of a plot.

TYPES OF FANTASY

Light Fantasy

Although much fanciful literature deals with serious themes of self-determination through discovery, the struggle between good and evil, or questions of time and space, other fantasies are more lighthearted. Light fantasy uses the mask of comedy to reveal the absurd in the human condition. Word play, tongue-in-cheek humor, slapstick, and wit are the identifying characteristics of this kind of fantasy.

Pamela Travers created a fascinating character in *Mary Poppins* (I), the English nanny who flies across rooftops and dances with chimney sweeps. She convinces the Edwardian Mr. Banks to appreciate life and to see the beauty in the natural development of children.

Astrid Lindgren created the outrageous child who does everything all youngsters would like to do in *Pippi Longstocking* (I) and its sequels. When Pippi learns that her friends Tommy and Annika will have a Christmas vacation from school but that she will not because she does not go to school, she enrolls herself in the class. When the teacher asks her what seven and five are, Pippi replies, "Well, if you don't know that yourself, you needn't think I'm going to tell you." Pippi is fearless, independent, and outspoken—an alter ego for more timid humans.

Lindgren also created an endearing fantasy that echoes the author's Scandinavian background, landscape, and folklore in *Ronia, the Robber's Daughter* (I). Ronia, another fearless child, runs free, clambers over mountains, swims in the lakes, and makes friends with wild creatures. Ronia's father, a robber chieftain, is infuriated when a rival band of robbers sets up camp in his territory, across a perilous chasm. Birk, son of the rival chieftain, and Ronia meet as they wander through the wilderness; and they become inseparable friends. The children's friendship leads to an eventual resolution of their fathers' conflict.

Harmony, a rebellious 10-year-old in Dick King-Smith's *The Queen's Nose* (I), firmly decides that animals are nicer than people. So in her mind she turns everyone around her into animals: her mother becomes a tubby, fussy pouter pigeon; her father, a large, sleek, mustachioed sea lion, for instance. A very thoughtful uncle comes for a visit, so she immediately names him a silvertip grizzly bear, which she likes very much. When the silvertip grizzly has to leave, he gives Harmony an envelope with a clue in it that leads to another clue and another until she finds a British coin and even more clues. The coin bears a likeness of the queen and, when rubbed on the side where the queen's nose points, it makes wishes come true. Harmony foolishly wastes some of her wishes but finally gets a Labrador retriever puppy—the most important wish of all.

Sid Fleischman writes in a broad humorous style a story seasoned with trickery, wit, and hairbreadth escapes in *The Whipping Boy* (I–A), the 1987 Newbery winner. A king's arrogant and good-for-nothing son, Prince Roland—better known as Prince Brat—and a rat catcher's orphaned son, Jemmy, are drawn together when Jemmy is brought in to serve as the royal whipping boy. (Royalty can never be whipped, so Jemmy takes a beating each time Prince Brat misbehaves.) Prince Brat is furious with Jemmy for silently enduring his punishment so he behaves even more scandalously; he remains illiterate while the whipping boy learns to read and write. Prince Brat becomes bored with his life of self-indulgence and decides to run away; he forces Jemmy to go with him. The two runaways are captured by scoundrels who send a ransom note to the king. Since only Jemmy can write, he convinces the kidnappers that he is really the prince and his companion is actually an ignorant servant boy. Fleischman's story echoes the theme of Mark Twain's *The Prince and the Pauper* with clever dialogue and repartee on one level and the strength of courage, trust, and friendship on another.

Natalie Babbitt, a superb fantasy writer, crafts language and meaning on two levels: as she tells a story, she plays with language and pokes gentle fun at human foibles. In *Search for Delicious* (I), the prime minister is preparing a dictionary. When he reports his progress, the king is pleased with the first part: "affection-

ate" is your dog; "annoying" is a loose boot in a muddy place; "bulky" is a big bag of boxes, and "calamitous" is saying no to the king. The trouble arises with the word "delicious": the prime minister has defined "delicious" as fried fish, but the king does not care for fried fish. The general of the army says that, as far as he is concerned, "delicious" is a mug of beer. The queen says it is a Christmas pudding, but the king says nonsense, everybody knows the most delicious thing is an apple. Young Gaylen, an orphan raised by the prime minister, is sent out to poll the people of the kingdom to see what they think. Enter the villain, Hemlock, who uses the situation to try to overthrow the king by rushing ahead of Gaylen to warn the country folk that the king will outlaw all foods not chosen as the word for "delicious." Gaylen's quest changes from a search for delicious to an attempt to save the kingdom from the evil plot devised by Hemlock. An epilogue ties up all the loose ends established in the prologue in this tightly woven, mythic yet humorous adventure of derring-do.

Mary Rodgers created a clever fantasy device of having a mother and a daughter switch bodies in *Freaky Friday* (I). While Annabel is living in her mother's body, she must keep her mother's appointments but think and act as herself. One of the appointments is with Annabel's teachers to discuss her misbehavior in school. The hilarity of the situation carries an undercurrent of seriousness; Annabel begins to see herself as others see her. Rodgers's *Summer Switch* (I) uses the same device with a father and son. Boris's father goes off to a dreaded summer camp while Boris fulfills his father's duties. In *A Billion for Boris* (I), Annabel's friend and neighbor thinks his own mother needs help and redecorates their apartment which triggers a strange phenomenon: the television set now broadcasts the next day's news. Rodgers has a quick wit and a facile way with language; her stories zip along from one spirited episode to the next.

Small Worlds Close Up

Every cultural group has its traditional sprites, elves, trolls, hobbits, or leprechauns, which go unseen about houses and villages. Fantasies about toys or miniature beings highlight human emotions by displaying them in action on a miniscule scale. From Arriety in *The Borrowers* (I), by Mary Norton, to the Minnipins in *The Gammage Cup* (I), by Carol Kendall, the best and worst in human nature is magnified against a lilliputian backdrop where characters are memorable because of their size.

The soldier in Hans Christian Andersen's *Steadfast Tin Soldier* (P–I) appears all the more heroic because he is a tiny toy with no power over his own fate. Similarly, Andersen's *Thumbelina* (P–I) blossoms with dignity through her search for happiness. Respect for life, woven into the stories, says to small children that a person is a person no matter how small.

Mollie Hunter's fantasy stories are for younger children in *A Furl of Fairy Wind* (P). This collection of four short stories begins with "The Brownie." She opens with "There is nothing you can do if you have a Brownie in the house, except to leave him a bowl of hot porridge every night by the fire, with plenty of milk in it and a long-handled spoon to sup with."[9] The Brownie that lives at Bilbeg Farm is happy until newcomers move in who do not believe in Brownies. Because the new residents do not abide by the ancient rules, the Brownie is mischievious instead of helpful when he does not find his porridge; only after they learn their proper ways do things return to normal. Mollie Hunter's graceful story ends the way it begins—"There is nothing you can do if you have a Brownie in the house, except. . . ."[10]

Pod, Homily, and Arriety in Mary Norton's *The Borrowers* (I) live under the kitchen floor at Great-Aunt Sophy's and furnish their home with safety pins, postage stamps, and other items carelessly dropped by humans. Pod, the father, ventures out collecting whatever the family needs. Borrowing becomes dangerous and supplies run low for them when Aunt Sophy is bedridden, but they survive by their wits. Homily, Pod's wife, believes that humans exist solely to provide the things they need, but, she warns their daughter Arriety, it is dangerous to be seen by them. Despite her mother's warnings, Arriety makes friends with one of them—the boy who comes to stay at the old house. When the cook discovers the presence of the Borrowers and calls the rat catcher to exterminate them, it is the boy who silently helps them escape. So as not to offend their pride, the boy helps the Borrowers in ways unknown to them. Eventually, they are forced to find a new home, and their subsequent life is followed in *The Borrowers Afield* (I), *The Borrowers Aloft* (I), *The Borrowers Afloat* (I), and *The Borrowers Avenged* (I), in which the family continues its search for a peaceful and safe place to live.

Fantasy worlds inhabited by inanimate objects and fanciful creatures with human thought, language, and feelings become real to young children. Children's thinking goes

Fantasies about miniature lives display human emotions in microcosm. (From *The Borrowers*, written by Mary Norton and illustrated by Beth and Joe Krush.)

ACTIVITY: TEACHER TO STUDENT

DIORAMAS (P–I) Make a diorama of the Borrowers's home. Use the same kinds of items they use to furnish their house. Spools become tables, thimbles become bathtubs, and postage stamps become pictures for the walls. Use miniature dolls for Pod, Homily, and Arriety. See what else you can find around school that people drop carelessly, such as rubber bands and paper clips, that can be turned into useful items for the Borrowers.

---

through an animistic period when favorite toys and stuffed animals take on lives and personalities of their own. When they hear or read stories that meet their expectations—when toys come to life—their view of life (at that point) is confirmed.

A secret world-within-a-world where dolls live *Behind the Attic Wall* (I–A) is created in Sylvia Cassedy's novel of a lonely, belligerent girl. In a hypnotizing story with echoes from the halls of Victorian castles and mysterious characters, we meet Maggie, an incorrigible 12-year-old rebel who has been expelled from numerous boarding schools for "poor adjustment." The two elderly great-aunts who take her into their forbidding home provide little warmth and love for her, although visits by Uncle Morris bring her some joy and happiness. Maggie hears whispering voices behind the walls that gradually lead her to Miss Christabel and Timothy John, two dolls who welcome her into their strange, secret life. The contrast between the tenderness Maggie shows to Miss Christabel and Timothy John and her scathing response to humans around her is stark. She is accepted for herself by the dolls and responds with heartwarming tenderness.

Lynne Reid Banks devised an intriguing and immensely popular entry to miniature worlds in *The Indian in the Cupboard* and its sequel, *The Return of the Indian* (both I). Omri is not impressed with the secondhand plastic toy Indian that friend Patrick gives him for his birthday, but he is slightly intrigued with other gifts: a mysterious old cupboard and a key that happens to fit it. At bedtime he locks the toy Indian, Little Bear, in the cupboard and thinks he hears noises coming from it during the night. In the morning he opens the cupboard and to his astonishment finds the Indian alive. Little Bear demands a horse, a tepee, and later, a wife. When Omri shares the secret with Patrick, Patrick insists upon placing his own toy Indian alongside the others in the cupboard. Although the boys enjoy playing with the miniature Indians, Omri gradually realizes that he is responsible for their safety, so he sends the little people back to their own place and time.

In the sequel, *The Return of the Indian*, a year has passed. Patrick has moved away, Omri has won a prize for a story he wrote about the miniature people, and his mother wears the magic key on a necklace at Omri's request—to keep him from being tempted to bring the small people back to life. But loneliness causes him to try once more to glimpse into the lives of Little Bear and his wife, Bright Stars. This time, he finds Little Bear critically wounded in the French and Indian War and Bright Stars pleading, "Help us!" Patrick comes to visit bringing Boone, his toy Indian, along. The boys share more adventures with their beloved small people. Boone suggests that perhaps it is the key and not the cupboard that holds the magic and that the boys could travel across time if they use it in something larger. This turns out to be true as Patrick and then Omri are transported into Little Bear's world. It is all an exciting adventure believably told with gripping suspense.

Amy's Eyes (I) by Richard Kennedy is a very long but intriguing story; it has mystery, pathos, conflict between good and evil, magic, and romance. Amy is left in an orphanage by her widowed father; her only possession is the captain, a sailor doll. When Amy is 10, she accidentally sticks a needle into the doll's head and he magically comes to life. The captain grows so rapidly that Amy can no longer hide him and so he leaves her to seek his fortune at sea. Filled with loneliness and torn by despair, Amy herself withers into a doll when she never hears from him—his letters have been intercepted by a cruel matron at the orphanage. The captain does come to claim Amy, though, and takes her, in doll form, away to his ship to search for a treasure. A mysterious veiled woman insists on joining the crew to claim half of the treasure. The trip is disrupted by pirates, mutiny, and a shipwrecked sailor. Many other events happen in this action-packed novel, but there is a satisfying ending for all who are willing to take the journey.

In *The Return of the Twelves* (I–A), by Pauline Clarke, Max respects the dignity of the 12 toy soldiers he finds under a loose board in the attic of an old English home once occupied by the Brontës. He realizes the soldiers will be offended if he does not let them conduct their own affairs. Max's attitude toward the Twelves, like the attitude of the boy toward the Borrowers, underscores the importance of respecting the small and the weak.

When an American museum director wants to buy the soldiers, Max helps them escape to Haworth, which has now become the Brontë Museum. The Twelves devise a plan and are determined to carry it out: "[The] plan was bold and desperate, but if it worked it would enable

In *The Return of the Twelves*, by Pauline Clarke, 12 courageous and intrepid toy soldiers find an ingenious means of transport back to their museum home.

the noble Young Men to reenter their original home with the kind of dignity which befitted them, and completely . . . under their own steam."[11] The miniature soldiers make the journey on foot, as any self-respecting infantrymen would. Max realizes that they are beings in their own right and is tactful as he gives the courageous troops the means to leave the attic and travel through rough terrain to return to their home.

The importance of a name to creatures, however small, is shown in Tove Jansson's tales about the Moomins, little beings that inhabit the lands of Scandinavia. In *Tales from Moominvalley* (I), Snufkin meets a tiny "creep" during one of his long wanderings through the wilderness and asks his name. " 'I'm so small that I haven't got a name,' the creep [says] eagerly. 'As a matter of fact, nobody's even asked me about it before.' "[12] Snufkin accedes to the

A tiny ''creep'' explains how his recent acquisition of a name—Teety-woo—makes all the difference. Things no longer just happen; now they happen to Teety-woo, a creature with an identity. (Illustration from *Tales from Moominvalley* by Tove Jansson.)

creep's plea for a name, and thoughtfully selects ''Teety-woo'' as a good one for him because it has a light melodic beginning and a little sadness to round it off.

Teety-woo, ecstatic about being named, soon makes a name plate and begins truly living a real life rather than drifting around from one place to another. Having a name makes all

the difference to the little creep, for later, when he and Snufkin meet again, he says:

> Now I'm a person, and everything that happens *means* something. Because it doesn't only happen, it happens to *me,* Teety-woo. And Teety-woo may think this or think that about it, as the case may be—if you see what I mean?[13]

Once he has a name, everything about him takes on importance, so that even his feelings are worthy of consideration. The reader's satisfaction in this book and the others in the Moomin series comes from such respect for the small and from the brilliant language in which it is cast.

Russell Hoban's *The Mouse and His Child* (I) was relatively unnoticed immediately after its publication in 1967, but the significance of the book is now recognized. The story operates on several levels of meaning: at the surface, it is the story of a windup mouse father and son who are tossed onto a garbage dump. Manny Rat, the villain, rules the dump kingdom and threatens to take their innards for his spare parts collection. The mouse and his son not only want to avoid Manny Rat's plans for them, but desperately long to become self-winding and find a permanent home in a doll's house. Adventures, with narrow escapes from the enemy rat, include a bank robbery, battles between armies of shrews, and capture in the claws of a parrot.

On another level, the story explores the meaning of life, the hereafter, happiness, and hope. A label on a dog food can shows a dog carrying a can, which has on it the same label showing the dog carrying the can, and so on, ever smaller, seemingly endlessly. The phrase, ''beyond the last visible dog,'' which refers to this illusion, is used symbolically in the story to refer to the search for happiness and meaning in life—embodied in the mouse child's hopefulness and persistence.

Animal Fantasy

Children attribute human thought, feeling, and language to animals dressed like people. Actually, during this period of animistic thinking, anything may be invested with life in the child's mind and become an object upon which to project fantasies, hopes, and fears. Because books that extend and enrich such normal developmental tendencies strike a responsive chord in children, animal fantasy is a well-loved form. Like the folk tale, it becomes part of children's literary experiences before they make clear distinctions between fact and fancy.

Some of the most memorable characters from children's literature are created in animal fantasy. Wilbur, Peter Rabbit, Babar, and Winnie the Pooh call to mind many of the modern classics of this genre. Some animal fantasies for older readers create an allegorical world in which the human scene is replayed to amuse and, often, to instruct. *Watership Down* (A), by Richard Adams, an outstanding example, reflects human society allegorically in warrens of rabbits.

Animals that appear in *The Tale of Peter Rabbit* or *The Tale of Squirrel Nutkin* (both N–P) by Beatrix Potter have some human quality, as they know it, "writ small." Babar, created by Jean de Brunhoff in *The Story of Babar* (P), lives on in other adventures written by his son, Laurent de Brunhoff. Babar, a boxy gray elephant, encounters many of the same problems and joys in his family that humans encounter in their own. For example, Babar and his family find that a simple picnic leads to ants, wasps, and a smashed up car in *Babar Goes on a Picnic* (N–P). Flora loses the trail when *Babar Goes Skiing* (N–P), Pom falls out of the cherry tree in *Babar the Gardener* (N–P), and Alexander catches a big fish in *Babar at the Seashore* (N–P). Seeing the problems one step removed from human life gives young children a sense of perspective and helps them see the humor in ordinary mishaps.

A. A. Milne created a believable personality in the form of a stuffed animal, Winnie the Pooh. Winnie, the silly old bear, shines with the love and adoration that millions of children have bestowed upon him. Pooh, Piglet, Eeyore, Kanga, Roo, Tigger, Owl, and Rabbit romp through warm-hearted adventures in the 100 Aker Wood with their owner, Christopher Robin. These toy animals from the Milne nursery attained immortality in *Winnie the Pooh* (I) and *The House at Pooh Corner* (I). The two collections of stories are probably best understood by children above the third grade because of the subtle word play and innuendos, but they are excellent books to read aloud to younger chil-

Christopher Robin Milne's original nursery toys, on which the characters in A. A. Milne's Pooh stories were based, are on permanent display at the New York Public Library.

PROFILE

A. A. Milne

A. A. Milne with his son Christopher and Pooh, the models for Milne's four books

A. A. Milne established himself as an outstanding member of the London literary world when he was quite young. Editor of *Punch Magazine*, recognized as an adult novelist and playwright, he is remembered most of all for the four books he wrote for children. The first book, *When We Were Very Young*, published in 1924, was the result of a poem he gave his wife about their son Christopher Robin. His wife sent the poem, "Vespers," off to a magazine where it was published. Rose Fyleman, another poet and publisher of a children's magazine, read the poem and invited Milne to contribute more verses. Milne was reluctant, thinking it a foolish thing to do, but he complied. When the poems arrived, both the editor and illustrator encouraged him to publish them as a book, which he thought was equally foolish. *When We Were Very Young* was followed by the whimsical tales, *Winnie the Pooh* (1926), another book of poems, *Now We Are Six* (1927), and more stories in *The House at Pooh Corner* (1928).

Milne's ability to perceive the world through his son's eyes and to capture in a poetic voice his imaginative play are the distinguishing features of his work. Winnie the Pooh, Piglet, Eeyore, Kanga, Roo, Tigger, Owl, and Rabbit—all stuffed animals—were Christopher Robin's nursery companions; he imbued them with life while his father expressed that love and imagination as only a talented poet could do.

dren. (The actual stuffed toys, which belonged to Christopher Milne, are now displayed at the New York Public Library.) *Now We Are Six* (P–I) and *When We Were Very Young* (P–I), which are poetry collections by Milne, are enjoyed by very young children who delight in repeating parts of the verses spontaneously.

When we try to identify the basis of the appeal of Milne's menagerie, we note the strong characterization of Winnie the Pooh and each of the other animals. Eeyore's gloomy outlook as the eternal pessimist, Piglet's excitability and copycat tendencies, and Pooh's naive but loving nature endear them to the reader. In "In Which Eeyore Has a Birthday and Gets Two Presents," a deflated red balloon and an empty honey pot, birthday gifts from the two well-intentioned friends, are sources of great tongue-in-cheek hilarity.

Paddington is another lovable English bear whose name comes from the London train station where he is found after arriving there from

TEACHING IDEA

HAPPY BIRTHDAY, A. A. MILNE (January 18) Display the stuffed animals of the Milne characters (McCall's patterns). Create a bulletin board with prints from Milne books. Write "Happy Birthday" as Owl did in *Winnie the Pooh:* "*HIPY PAPY BTHUTHDTH THUTHDA BTHUTHDY.*"

---

darkest Peru. His stories, told by Michael Bond, appear in *A Bear Called Paddington* (I), *More About Paddington,* (I), *Paddington Takes to TV* (I), *Paddington at Large* (I), and many others. Paddington wears a deplorably shabby hat and a tag with a request, "Please take care of this bear." Children laugh at his clumsiness and bungling independence. Paddington behaves as if he were just another child in the Brown family with whom he lives; the incongruity of the resulting situations is the source of the fun.

A stuffed animal that has gained nearly the popularity of Pooh and Paddington, but who is more sentimental, is *The Velveteen Rabbit* (P–I). In Margery Williams's fine story, the rabbit, given to the boy for Christmas, is cast aside after a few hours of play. Another member of the nursery, the skin horse, explains to the rabbit about nursery magic and what it means to be real:

> "Real isn't how you are made," said the Skin Horse. "It's just a thing that happens to you. When a child loves you for a long, long time, not just to play with, but REALLY loves you, then you become Real."
>
> "Does it hurt?" asked the Rabbit.
>
> "Sometimes," said the Skin Horse, for he was always truthful. "When you are Real you don't mind being hurt."[14]

The boy eventually grows to love the rabbit, but the time comes when it must be burned because the boy has played with it while ill with scarlet fever. Providentially, a flower fairy turns the toy into a real rabbit, so that it is free to dwell with others of its kind. This gentle fantasy appeals to many, who are touched by its strong portrayal of the meaning and power of love.

The Wind in the Willows (I), by Kenneth Grahame, is one of the finest animal fantasies. Originally published in 1908, it has appeared in many editions over the years; two of the most notable are those illustrated by Ernest Shepard and by Arthur Rackham. Adrienne Adams illustrated the first chapter for a picture-book edition, *The River Bank* (P–I), and Beverly Gooding illustrated three others: *The Open Road, Wayfarers All,* and *Mole's Christmas: Or Home Sweet Home* (all P–I). These books intro-

Mole and Rat load the punt for a picnic in Kenneth Grahame's *The Wind in the Willows.* (Illustrated by Ernest Shepard.)

TEACHING IDEA

A SENSE OF PLACE   Children develop a sense of place when they visualize and concretize the setting of a story. The endpapers of *Winnie the Pooh*, illustrated by Ernest H. Shepard (I), show the map of the 100 Aker Wood. Project the map (use an opaque projector) onto a classroom wall to make, in effect, a mural on which children can, as you read the stories aloud, plot the routes the characters take.

ACTIVITY: TEACHER TO STUDENT

SAVORING MILNE'S LANGUAGE (P–I)   Listen to a reading of Milne's books.

Select some favorite verses to prepare for choral reading. Read the lines as a group several times. Discuss who is saying these lines? How should they be said (happy, sad, puzzled)? How can you show this feeling with your voice? Divide the lines so that some are read in unison by all speakers and others are read by a subgroup or by one speaker.

Dramatize the story "In Which Eeyore Has a Birthday and Gets Two Presents." (See Chapter 2 for directions for drama.)

Find phrases in Milne's work that have been adopted for wider use, such as "time for a little something," "a bear of very little brain," "hunting for heffalumps," "tracking woozles," "I do like a little bit of butter to my bread." List the occasions in which these phrases might be appropriate. Translate them into other ways to say the same thing.

---

duce the beloved animals to younger children who are not yet ready for the complete book. As with all great literature, however, presenting it to an audience too young to appreciate it can spoil for them the truly rich experience it embodies.

Kenneth Grahame's style is as smooth and poetic as the meanderings of the river where most of the action takes place. The story begins with Mole in the middle of spring cleaning, dusting, and whitewashing his little house.

> Spring was moving in the air above and in the earth below and around him, penetrating even his dark and lowly little house with its spirit of divine discontent and longing. It was small

wonder, then, that he suddenly flung down his brush on the floor, said "Bother!" and "O blow!" and also "Hang spring-cleaning!" and bolted out of the house without even waiting to put on his coat.[15]

Mole discovers the river:

> Never in his life had he seen a river before—this sleek, sinuous, full-bodied animal, chasing and chuckling, gripping things with a gurgle and leaving them with a laugh, to fling itself on fresh playmates that shook themselves free, and were caught and held again. All was a-shake and a-shiver—glints and gleams and sparkles, rustle and swirl, chatter and bubble. The Mole was bewitched, entranced, fascinated.[16]

When Mole meets Rat, he decides that life on the river bank is preferable to life in tunnels, and the two friends set up housekeeping together.

In succeeding chapters, Badger and Mr. Toad of Toad Hall enter the story, and the thread of plot winds in and about their fantastic adventures. The story is an idyllic evocation of human emotions from wanderlust to homesickness at Christmas time.

In the most poetic and most quoted chapter, "The Piper at the Gates of Dawn," Mole and Rat set out upon the river in search of lost Baby Otter. They find him asleep at the feet of Pan, the deity of forests and animals. The grandeur and power of love and awe, universal in appeal, stem from a scene where the animals are drawn in expectation to the sound of the pipes played by their god:

> Suddenly the Mole felt a great Awe fall upon him, an awe that turned his muscles to water, bowed his head, and rooted his feet to the ground. It was no panic terror—indeed he felt wonderfully at peace and happy—but it was an awe that smote and held him and, without seeing, he knew it could only mean that some august Presence was very, very near. With difficulty he turned to look for his friend, and saw him at his side cowed, stricken, and trembling violently. And still there was utter silence in the populous bird-haunted branches around them; and still the light grew and grew.
>
> Perhaps he would never have dared to raise his eyes, but that, though the piping was now hushed, the call and the summons seemed still dominant and imperious.[17]

The solemn strands are counterbalanced with hilarious comedy in the form of Toad's boastful songs in praise of himself, written in a mock-heroic style that is great fun.

George Selden chooses a busy urban subway station rather than an idyllic countryside for his animal fantasy, *Cricket in Times Square* (I). Chester Cricket makes lasting friends who eventually go with him to the country in *Tucker's Countryside* (I).

E. B. White's *Charlotte's Web* (P–I), a song in praise of barnyard creatures sung by a sensitive observer, tells of the friendship between Wilbur the pig and Charlotte the spider. It is a eulogy to all friendships and remains an all-time favorite for many children.

When Charlotte first speaks to Wilbur during the night, he can hardly wait until morning to find out who she is.

> "Attention, please!" he said in a loud, firm voice. "Will the party who addressed me at bedtime last night kindly make himself or herself known by giving an appropriate sign or signal."[18]

Charlotte eventually speaks to him, but after she describes the way she makes her living, Wilbur is not certain about her.

> Wilbur was merely suffering the doubts and fears that often go with finding a new friend. In good time he was to discover that he was mistaken about Charlotte. Underneath her rather bold and cruel exterior, she had a kind heart, and she was to prove loyal and true to the very end.[19]

Charlotte *is* loyal and true, and through her friendship and creative spinning of words in her spiderweb above Wilbur's pen she saves his life. Wilbur depends upon Charlotte's friendship, and although he is unable to save *her* life, he assures a place for her progeny.

This book is sometimes misused and overused. Very young children cannot understand some of the subtleties or appreciate the profound meaning inherent in the book. Experienced at an appropriate age, the story suggests images that last a lifetime.

Another pig has come along who nearly rivals Wilbur in spunk and personality. In Dick King-Smith's *Babe: The Gallant Pig* (I), Babe belongs to Farmer Hogget, a man of few words. He wins Babe by guessing his weight at a raffle and raises the pig with a bunch of collie puppies belonging to his sheepdog, Fly. Babe, plucky and bright, behaves as much like a dog as the puppies and one day asks his foster mother, "Why can't I learn to be a sheep-pig?" A sheep-pig is exactly what Babe becomes; Fly trains Babe to herd sheep and eventually Farmer Hogget enters Babe in the Grand Challenge Sheepdog Trials competition. The highly improbable events, told convincingly with zesty language, sparkle with word play and tongue-in-cheek humor. King-Smith, a British writer, tells of another marvelous pig in *Pigs Might Fly* (I) and a wonderful mouse in *Magnus Power-Mouse* (I).

Richard Adams's *Watership Down* (A), another animal fantasy, contains extended metaphor, imagery, and a delineation of the struggle between good and evil, suggesting that it is also an allegorical work. A visionary rabbit, Fiver, foresees his hillside home covered with blood. He persuades some of the rabbits to leave their warren and search for safety but their journey is filled with many trials, which test their ingenuity. When they arrive at Watership Down and find a measure of security, they must raid rival warrens to obtain female rabbits if they are to survive.

Richard Adams, an astute observer of nature, involves his reader in a true work of art. Only good readers in the upper elementary grades will persist through its 429 pages; for those who do, the involvement is complete. Reading it aloud will allow more children to relish its richness.

William Steig's books are subject to several levels of interpretation. In *Dominic* (I), a restless hound of that name packs his piccolo and collection of hats to set off in search of adventure—aiming only for wherever he gets and whatever he finds. William Steig spoofs the fairy tale tradition itself when Dominic meets the Doomsday Gang, an assortment of evil

foxes, weasels, and cats. Dominic nurses an ailing pig and inherits his treasure, provides music for fairy mice, and rescues a widow goose in distress. Finally, he finds a beautiful bride, Eleanor, sleeping in an enchanted garden. Dominic, the hero of many faces, changes moods and roles as he changes hats.

In a later story, *Abel's Island* (I), about Abel, an intrepid mouse, William Steig spoofs the Victorian novel. Abel and his lovely wife Amanda are caught in a torrential storm on a picnic, and when Amanda's scarf blows away, gallant Abel runs to rescue it. While chasing the scarf, Abel is swept away in a flood of water to a river island from which he cannot escape. During a year of isolation on the island, Abel learns to fend for himself and turns to sculpture and literature to create a pleasant and endurable life.

Abel's adjustment to the primitive life is not an easy one, for he is obviously a gentleman mouse of culture and refinement. The understated nature of William Steig's style is particularly well shown when, after a year of hardship, suffering, and emotional strain, Abel returns home to an empty house. He places Amanda's scarf on the table and, when she returns, says simply, "I've brought you back your scarf." This story of gallantry and commitment leaves many telling gaps for the adult reader, but the humor and pathos hold even young readers who miss the subtle parody.

Many of William Steig's books contain verses or magical incantations, and almost all contain marvelous lists of items, lists that are made humorous by the very disparity of the objects. For example, in *Sylvester and the Magic Pebble* (P), Sylvester's parents take alfalfa sandwiches, pickled oats, sassafras salad, and timothy compote with them on their picnic. In *Abel's Island*, Abel and Amanda enjoy delicate sandwiches of pot cheese and watercress, hard-boiled quail egg, onions, olives, black caviar, and bright champagne on their ill-fated picnic. Alert readers will notice the counterpart in

TEACHING IDEA

EXPLORING ONE AUTHOR'S WORK (I)[20]   William Steig's animal fantasies in picture-book format, because they are so manageable, provide a convenient way for intermediate grade students to trace theme, motif, and characterization. Shadings of human love and avarice are seen in the relationships between his animals. Amos the mouse and Boris the whale are the closest of friends in *Amos and Boris* (P), despite the fact that neither can long survive in the other's atmosphere. Violet, a most feminine little pig, develops a close friendship with a bone that talks and sings—and ultimately rescues her from a wolf—in *The Amazing Bone* (P). In *Caleb and Kate* (P), the principal characters display deep conjugal tenderness, and the title character in *Tiffky Doofky* (P) searches for the love of his life. *Doctor De Soto,* a mouse, is a dentist who dares to help a fox with a painful toothache although he endangers his own life. A panorama of human emotions is presented in animal disguise. As one child commented, "It's a way of getting us to think better about other people's feelings."

In *Farmer Palmer's Wagon Ride* (P), Farmer Palmer's thoughts of his wife and children give him the strength to continue on his ill-fated homeward journey.

"If I could only lay my own weary form on the dear, green ground and sleep like my friend Ebenezer," thought Farmer Palmer. But a vision of the beloved round faces and small sweet eyes of his wife and children gave him the heart to go on.[21]

In the space of an hour, all the books can be read or reread. Ask your students to compile a chart to compare the books. The chart in the following box, begun by fifth grade students, will give them a start. These students included *Abel's Island,* a longer novel.

Kenneth Grahame's *The Wind in the Willows* when Rat packs coldtonguecoldhamcoldbeefpickledgherkinssaladfrenchrollscresssandwichespottedmeatgingerbeerlemonadesodawater for his picnic.

Each of William Steig's books also deals with a journey away from or toward home and beloved persons or objects and, in some, with efforts to communicate with a beloved one. Sometimes the obstacle is distance; sometimes, a transformation that makes them unrecognizable and mute.

Robert O'Brien's *Mrs. Frisby and the Rats of NIMH* (I) is a story of a group of rats used for experimental purposes in the laboratories of NIMH. They are given DNA and steroid injections in tests to see if these substances raise intelligence. The injections are effective: the bright rats discover that they can now open their own cages. They do not use their newfound skill hastily, however, but carefully plot their escape from the building and plan their survival. In a parallel plot, which intersects the story of this highly intelligent rat society, Mrs. Frisby, a widowed mouse mother, is in danger of having her family home, in which her son is recuperating from pneumonia, destroyed by spring plowing of the garden where their home

TEACHING IDEA

THEMES, MOTIFS, LANGUAGE, AND CHARACTERS IN BOOKS BY WILLIAM STEIG (I)

Title	Characters	Themes	Motifs	Language Features
Roland, The Minstrel Pig	Villainous fox	Right prevails	Journey to find fame	Songs
Sylvester and the Magic Pebble	Burro family	Love conquers all	Transformation to pebble	Picnic list
Amos and Boris	Mouse and whale	Friends help	Journey for adventure	Supply list
The Amazing Bone	Naive child	Bone helps	Talking bone	Magic chant
Farmer Palmer's Wagon Ride	Pig and donkey	Ingenuity wins	Journey from home	Description
Caleb and Kate	Man and wife	Love prevails	Transformation	Dialogue
Tiffky Doofky	Boy and girl dogs	Trials of love	Search for love	Garbage
Abel's Island	Mouse	Happiness and home	Robinson Crusoe	Picnic list
Doctor De Soto	Mouse and fox	Outfox the fox	Small versus large	Fox's talk
Solomon, the Rusty Nail	Rabbit and cat	Perseverance	Transformation to rusty nail	Description

is located. Mrs. Frisby goes to the highly developed rat society to seek help. Through her conversations with them, the reader learns that her dead husband was one of the experimental rats. Although Mrs. Frisby goes to the rat society to seek aid for herself, she helps them by warning of their forthcoming extermination by the laboratory researchers. O'Brien's story leads to serious discussions about how our society deals with groups that differ from the dominant one.

After Robert O'Brien's death, his daughter, Jane Leslie Conly, wrote a smooth-seamed sequel, *Rasco and the Rats of NIMH* (I), that begins approximately three years later. Mrs. Frisby's son, Timothy, attends a school that is run by the superintelligent rats of NIMH. On his way to school, Timothy meets Rasco, a boastful city slicker rat who eventually becomes a true friend. When it appears that the community will be destroyed, Rasco's ingenuity leads to a resolution. The suspenseful episodic chapters, brightened by humor surrounding Rasco's mischief, make this an excellent book to read aloud. Readers do not mind the different authorship of the two books; in fact, they are excited to learn it is a father-daughter effort.

Bunnicula, (I) written by Deborah and James Howe, is narrated by Harold, the family watchdog, whose peaceful life with Chester, a well-read cat, is threatened by the entrance into the family of a pet rabbit. The rabbit, named Bunnicula because he's a bunny found at a Dracula movie, seems to have fangs and odd markings on his back that look like a cape. When Harold and Chester find white vegetables, drained dry with fang marks in them, they are certain that Bunnicula is a vampire bunny. James Howe continues the hilarious story of the three animals in *Howliday Inn, The Celery Stalks at Midnight,* and *Nighty-Nightmare* (all I).

A Rat's Tale (I–A) by Tor Seidler contains mystery, intrigue, and drama. Young Montague Mad-Rat lives very much in his own world in the sewers under New York City until a calamitous rainstorm sweeps him into the path of Isabel Moberly-Rat. Following this encounter, he searches her out again and finds that her less eccentric and more luxurious family faces a grave crisis—their home in abandoned piers will be turned into parking lots following an extermination campaign. Montague feels lonely and bewildered, unable to help, but his talents do help save the rat world from extinction. The strong writing and characterization reveals pathos, humor, and high tension in a strong addition to animal fantasy.

Fantasy as Mystery

Students in Donna Carrara's fourth grade class became excited about reading mysteries. Alfred Hitchcock, Donald Sobol, and Zilpha Snyder stories spread through the group like wildfire. The students even tried to write their own mysteries during their writing workshop. During a minilesson preceding writing time, the group talked about what makes a mystery story. This is the list of features they agreed upon; their teacher put them on a chart.

WHAT MAKES A MYSTERY STORY A MYSTERY STORY

1. Has clues.
2. Has a problem, something stolen, somebody killed.
3. Has police.
4. Bad guys and good guys.
5. Makes you wonder. (Suspense)
6. Has false leads.
7. Takes you off the track.
8. You find out who did it.[22]

By making the students aware of what they had picked up intuitively from their reading, their teacher was helping them recognize the characteristics of a genre. This not only made them more critical readers, but they also began to master the form in their writing.

As these students continue to grow as readers and writers, they will appreciate *The Illyrian Adventure* (A) by Lloyd Alexander. In this archeological mystery, a spunky 16-year-old girl, Vesper, goes with her guardian, a gentlemanly scholar who sounds very much like Lloyd Alexander himself, to clear up some details in her deceased father's research. The guardian is a reluctant participant in the investigations that Vesper undertakes; they become embroiled in the struggles between the king and the Illyrian guerillas. There are nicely intricate turns of the plot, clever dialogue from the witty Vesper and her less-than-enthusiastic guardian, and mysterious ruins and icons. In a sequel, *The Eldorado Adventure* (A), Vesper goes off to Central America with her guardian.

Diana Wynne Jones intrigues her readers in *Archer's Goon* (A) with an opening scene of a huge taciturn Goon sitting in the kitchen who has come to demand "2,000" from Howard's father. Howard and his little sister, Anthea— called Awful for very good reason—find out that it is not money but 2,000 words their father owes Archer. Tracking down who Archer is, why their father owes him any words at all, and why he will not write them leads into a maze of relationships and mysteries. The very clever plot evolves as the father writes episodes not only as they are happening but to make them happen through his words. Mystery, intrigue, and a writer's power all work together in this fascinating novel. Jones also wrote *Dogsbody* and *Howl's Moving Castle* (both A), which add to her growing body of fans.

John Christopher's trilogy, *Fireball, New Found Land*, and *Dragon Dance* (all A), follow an English boy, Simon, and his American cousin, Brad, as they are abruptly transported through a fireball from their contemporary world into a parallel world of Roman Britain. The fireball was a crossing point between their own world and one that lay on a different probability track—an *If* world. In *New Found Land*, they travel with the Roman gladiator Bos and centurion Curtius to the as-yet-undiscovered New World. During their adventures, they bargain with Algonquian Indians until they no longer have wampum to trade for food and set sail on a crudely made raft. They are rescued at sea by whale-hunting Vikings and live with them until they find they are marked for sacrifice and again must flee. In *Dragon Dance*, the boys and their Indian captors are in turn captured by the crew of a Chinese ship. When they are taken to the court of the Emperor, they claim to be ambassadors from the Roman people and are caught in a struggle for power over the boy ruler. The fast-paced narrative combines humor, mystery, and suspense.

Time Slip Fantasy

In some stories, time is the element that is carried beyond the world of everyday experience. The author, by using it symbolically, is making a statement about the meaning of time itself. Eleanor Cameron, in the title essay in *The Green and Burning Tree*, describes a globe of time, in which the past, present, and future are perceived as a whole. For writers like Cameron, past and future are present in time now. Cameron opens her essay with words from T. S. Eliot's "Burnt Norton":

> . . . say that the end precedes the beginning,
> And the end and the beginning were always
>   there
> Before the beginning and after the end.[23]

The implication of time being held still, coupled with the image of the green and burning tree from Welsh mythology (similar to the biblical image of Moses and the burning bush) suggest that in a timeless world of myth and magic, the ordinary laws of the natural world are set aside.

Authors of time fantasy invent a dazzling variety of devices to permit their characters to move in and out of conventional time. For example, Madeleine L'Engle in *A Wrinkle in Time* (I–A) moves her characters from the here and now to other parts of the universe by "tessering" or "wrinkling time." A conversation among Mrs. Whatsit, Mrs. Who, and Meg and Charles Wallace explains the fantastic phenomenon:

> "You see," Mrs. Whatsit said, "if a very small insect were to move from the section of skirt in Mrs. Who's right hand to that in her left, it would be quite a long walk for him if he had to walk straight across."
> Swiftly Mrs. Who brought her hands, still holding the skirt, together.
> "Now, you see," Mrs. Whatsit said, "he would be there, without that long trip. That is how we travel."[24]

Meg complains that she does not understand.

> "That is because you think of space only in three dimensions," Mrs. Whatsit told her. "We travel in the fifth dimension. This is something you can understand, Meg. Don't be afraid to try."[25]

Madeleine L'Engle's trilogy of space and time fantasies, *A Wrinkle in Time, A Wind in the Door*, and *A Swiftly Tilting Planet*, (I–A), is partially set in a place and a time that are within the conventional universe and partially in an imagined time and place.

C. S. Lewis chronicles the events in Narnia with human characters who move in and out of a fantasy universe existing beyond human constraints. Narnia stands in another time, so

Narnia is a world that exists in parallel with our own, but a traveler stepping into Narnia can live a lifetime there and then step back into our world without even a moment of our time having passed. (From C. S. Lewis's *The Lion, The Witch and the Wardrobe,* illustrated by Pauline Baynes.)

that one may live hundreds of years there and return to the ordinary world without any time having passed. In *The Lion, the Witch and the Wardrobe* (I), a skeptical Peter and Susan discuss Lucy's stories about Narnia with the professor:

> "Well, Sir, if things are real, they're there all the time."
> "Are they?" said the Professor; and Peter did not know quite what to say.
> "But there was not time," said Susan. "Lucy had had no time to have gone anywhere, even if there was such a place. She came running after us the very moment we were out of the

room. It was less than a minute, and she pretended to have been away for hours."
> "That is the very thing that makes her story so likely to be true," said the Professor. "If there really is a door in this house that leads to some other world (and I should warn you that this is a very strange house, and even I know very little about it)—if, I say, she had got into another world, I should not be at all surprised to find that that other world had a separate time of its own; so that however long you stayed there it would never take up any of *our* time."[26]

In other stories, fantastic journeys take place within dreams, as in *Through the Looking Glass* (I–A) by Lewis Carroll or in *Peter* (A) by Anne Holm. Frequently, either time or place, or both, are altered when the characters go through a particular door or follow a special path. The children in *The Lion, the Witch and the Wardrobe* go through the wardrobe, and the children in *A Walk Out of the World* (I), by Ruth Nichols, go down a slope through a certain stretch of woods.

The concept of the "eternal now" that fascinates Eleanor Cameron is developed in her own book, *The Court of the Stone Children* (I–A). The plot of the story, set in present-day San Francisco, centers on Nina's attempt to solve the mystery surrounding nineteenth-century Dominique, whose portrait hangs in the French Museum. Nina visits the museum's furnished rooms, to which Dominique's ghost returns for a time among the pieces that had once been part of her home. Together, the girls reconstruct the events of a scandal surrounding Dominique's father. When Nina is in the museum, particularly when she is in the rooms recreated from the furnishings of times gone by, she has what she calls her "Museum Feeling"—a sense of the continuity over time of these rooms, "with their massive pieces of furniture, carved, worn by thousands of hands, by innumerable brushings of cloth and flesh—all gone, gone long since."[27]

Another facet of the fused nature of time is evoked by a painting—"Time Is a River With-

TEACHING IDEA

WHO IS THE GHOST TO WHOM? (I–A)[28]   As children read a number of fantasies and accumulate a background of reading experience, they will enjoy discussing and comparing how the characters move back and forth in time and deciding who is the ghost to whom. After assembling a selection of books of time fantasy, have the class compile a chart that lists the title of the fantasy, the device for time travel, and the names of the ghost and the real person. If this is done as a mural or a bulletin board, all children can discuss and add to the chart as it grows. The chart might resemble the sample given here:

TIME FANTASIES AND GHOSTS

Title	Time Device	Who Is the Ghost?
The Court of the Stone Children (Cameron)	Dominique appears in Nina's time but they cannot touch	Nina is real; Dominique is ghost.
Peter (Holm)	In dreams, Peter goes back to time of his ancestors	Peter becomes someone else in the past
Tom's Midnight Garden (Pearce)	Tom is drawn into Hattie's childhood when she dreams of him	Tom is real; Hattie is a real woman. They meet as children in Hattie's dreams.
The Children of Green Knowe (Boston)	Tolly meets children from a painting	Tolly is real. Children from the painting lived at an earlier time.

out Banks," by Chagall—that Nina discovers in the museum. As the fairytale-like painting reappears in her dreams, she perceives that "if there are no banks, there is nothing for time to pass."[29] The time motif appears again in a friend's notebook, which is filled with quotations about the paradox of time, and in the faded landlady who gazes into mirrors, hoping that she might once again catch sight of the girl she used to be. Cameron says of time,

> In almost any fantasy of time travel, or of the mingling of different times, there inevitably arises the intriguing question of who, rightfully, is a ghost to whom, it being usually a matter of whose time the scene is being played in, though this is not invariably easy to decide— . . . the mood or feeling being often ambiguous or even wittily paradoxical.[30]

In *The Court of the Stone Children*, we recognize that Dominque knows she is a ghost to Nina. After the mystery of Dominique's father is solved, Nina realizes that the ghostly Dominique will not return to this time. In other novels, characters go back in time to live in the bodies and lives of people in ages past. For example, the title character in Holm's *Peter* lives the lives of his own ancestors. Much the same device is found in Madeleine L'Engle's *A Swiftly Tilting Planet*, where Charles Wallace, through his ability to kythe—that is, to understand the thoughts of another being—is able to live in and think with the minds of several persons in the past.

Lucy M. Boston weaves fantasies that lie just at the edge of reality. The transition from real to unreal is so subtle that the illusion is easy to believe. By the time fanciful elements

TEACHING IDEA

TIME TRAVEL: SLIPPING THE NET OF TIME (I–A)   Authors of time slip fantasies use creative devices to move their characters in and out of various time frames. Students increase their ability to read critically by comparing the techniques authors use. Collect several time slip fantasies for the comparisons, and compile the findings on a chart similar to the one below.

Title	Device for Time Slip
A Storm Without Rain (Adkins)	Grandfather's 93rd birthday
The Secret World of Polly Flint (Cresswell)	Time tunnel
The Root Cellar (Lunn)	Abandoned root cellar
Playing Beatie Bow (Park)	Child's game
Traveler in Time (Uttley)	Door
Building Blocks (Voigt)	Falling asleep inside construction of blocks
Jeremy Visick (Wiseman)	Gravestone, midnight wanderings

are drawn into the story in *The Children of Green Knowe* (I), readers are so intensely involved that they, too, almost see and hear the children in the painting playing hide and seek. We are never quite certain whether the fantasy elements are a part of the imagination or whether they are real. In this story, Toseland, called Tolly, comes to live with his great-grandmother, Mrs. Oldknow, at the intriguing ancient manor house called Green Knowe. They talk about the children in the painting who had lived at Green Knowe 400 years earlier. The presence of the children in the house and garden seems very possible.

Tolly discovers a key that opens a long-untouched toy box in which he finds objects the children in the painting are holding. His great-grandmother tells Tolly stories of how the children received the treasured objects. The love with which she speaks about the family brings a sense of those from the past into the present. When Tolly feels the children's presence, and Mrs. Oldknow shares his awareness

of them, there is a willing suspension of disbelief for readers, who also want it to be true. Alison Uttley's *Traveler in Time* (I) is also set in an old manor house in England that is steeped in history. Penelope, the protagonist, steps through a door and finds herself in an Elizabethan kitchen. During her visits she becomes involved with a plan to try to save Mary Queen of Scots.

David Wiseman's *Jeremy Visick* (I–A) is a gripping story in which Matthew becomes obsessed with the victims of a mine disaster in 1852. He first learned of Jeremy Visick, a child victim of that disaster, when he was doing a school history report and read the tombstones in the churchyard. Matthew roams through the past in a series of midnight rambles which alarm his parents very much. He meets Jeremy and is determined to rescue his skeleton from the mine shaft so it can be buried with the rest of his family. Matthew narrowly escapes death himself in a story that is spellbinding and believable.

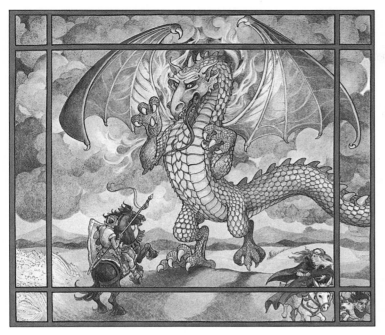

C-1 Trina Schart Hyman sets the story of *Saint George and the Dragon* in fourth-century England and so uses pre-Arthurian armor, dress, and weaponry. (Retold by Margaret Hodges. Boston: Little, Brown, 1984.)

C-2 Barbara Cooney pictures the Finnish Vainamoinen as he plays magical music to rescue the earth from darkness after the wicked witch Louhi steals the sun and moon from the sky. The Scandinavian motif is reflected in the sparseness of setting, the forest, and the clothing. (*Louhi: Witch of North Farm*, retold by Toni de Gerez. New York: Viking Kestrel, 1986.)

Interpretations of Folklore

Folklore reflects the values and cultural influences of its origins. In fact, noted critic Paul Hazard says that the tales are like beautiful mirrors of water, so deep and crystal clear that in their depths we sense the mysterious experiences of a thousand years. Contemporary artists interpret the ancient tales by presenting authentic images from the cultures in which the stories grew.

C-3 Maurice Sendak, the pre-eminent children's book illustrator, has developed joyous, heartrending pictures for this previously unknown tale by Wilhelm Grimm discovered in 1983. (*Dear Mili*. New York: Michael di Capua Books/Farrar, Straus & Giroux, 1988.)

C-4 In a free adaptation of the Japanese folktale of the crane wife, Molly Bang sets her version in a New England seaport village and uses Canada geese rather than cranes. This variant of a traditional folk theme is handsomely illustrated with delicate paintings framed with goose feathers as the background. (*Dawn*. New York: Morrow, 1983.)

Up she started; and when she saw the three bears on one side of the bed, she tumbled herself off the other, and ran to the window.

C-5 Jan Brett's faithful adaptation of Andrew Lang's version of *Goldilocks and the Three Bears* has elaborate, imaginative, and richly colored illustrations. The furry bears and Goldilocks are adorned in Scandinavian-style clothing as they move about the cottage filled with carved furniture and authentic folk art. (New York: Dodd, Mead, 1987.)

The people celebrated his return in the Dance of Life.

C-6 Patterns using rows and tassels symbolize the corn harvest in this native American tale. (*Arrow to the Sun* by Gerald McDermott. New York: Viking Press, 1974.)

C-7 Errol Le Cain's jewel-toned paintings and ornate gowns of peacock feathers bespeak the elegance of the French court in a retelling of Perrault's version of *Cinderella*. (New York: Puffin Books, 1972.)

C-8 Ed Young uses the Chinese concept of panel paintings, with a fish as the fairy godmother, for *Yeh-Shen*, the Chinese variant of the Cinderella story. (Retold by Ai-Ling Louie. New York: Philomel, 1982.)

C-9 Set in the South, this version portrays Cinderella's ballgown spun from the filmy strands of Spanish moss. Donald Carrick pictures the fairy godmother as the witch woman who protects the helpless. (*Moss Gown* by William Hooks. New York: Clarion Books, 1987.)

C-10 Moira Kemp uses a delicate palette to show the barefoot *Cinderella* befriending the birds and animals in a retelling of Perrault's version of the ancient tale. (London: Hamish Hamilton, 1981.)

C-11 Paul O. Zelinsky returns to paintings of the German Renaissance period to capture the ominous tones of the foreboding forest as the witch attempts to fatten Hansel. (*Hansel and Gretel*, retold by Rika Lesser. New York: Dodd, Mead, 1984.)

C-12 John Steptoe's exquisite illustrations were inspired by the ruins of an ancient city found in Zimbabwe and the flora and fauna of the region. His stunning paintings glow with the beauty, family love, and internal vision of the land and people of Africa. (*Mufaro's Beautiful Daughters*. New York: Lothrop, Lee & Shepard, 1987.)

C-13 From town to countryside and capture of the wolf, Charles Mikolaycak's illustrations are a perfect visual accompaniment to Prokofiev's delightful and imaginative musical tale. Peter's richly patterned peasant costume is portrayed with authentic detail. (*Peter and the Wolf*. New York: Viking Press, 1982.)

Janet Lunn centers her time slip fantasy, *The Root Cellar* (A), on 12-year-old Rose Larkin who had been raised by her cosmopolitan grandmother but is now forced to become a part of Aunt Nan's large, noisy family in Canada. Lonely and bewildered in a strange environment, Rose wanders into a long-abandoned root cellar and there discovers that she slips back to the time of the American Civil War. She meets Will Morrissay, who enlists in the Union Army, and Susan, a servant girl, who eventually accompanies her on an arduous trip to see Will. The root cellar serves well as a time slip device.

Several time slip fantasies focus on a central character who is going through a difficult adjustment period; loneliness, alienation, and deep thoughtfulness seem to be associated with time travel. In *The Secret World of Polly Flint* (I–A) by Helen Cresswell, Polly's poet-coalminer father is injured in a pit accident and confined to bed. Her mother must accompany him to a distant hospital so Polly is forced to live with stern Aunt Em. A strange old man tells Polly the legend of the village of Grimstone that disappeared to live secretly underground forever. Polly sees the children of Grimstone dance the maypole at dawn, and she meets the Porters, a family from Grimstone accidentally trapped in the modern world. In a courageous act, Polly helps the Porters return through the time tunnel to their own day and even dares to accompany them knowing that she might not return. When she does return, she finds her father recovered from his accident and her family able to go home. Strong characterization, lucid rhythmic prose, and subtle parallels between the Grimstone world and Polly's modern world will impel readers forward.

Playing Beatie Bow (I–A), by Ruth Park, was named the best children's book in Australia in 1981. In this story, 14-year-old Abigail is upset that her mother will take back her husband who had deserted her for another woman and that they will move her from Sydney to Nor-way. She watches children playing "Beatie Bow" and sees a waiflike girl who stays on the sidelines to watch but never play. The girl, named Beatie Bow, is from another time, but she does not understand how her name came to be used for the game modern children play. When Abigail accompanies her to her own time, a century earlier, a pattern emerges that answers troubling questions.

Other writers, such as Cynthia Voigt, manipulate time to explore conflicts between generations. For example, Brann is angry at his parents' incessant quarreling, so he retreats into a fortress his father, Kevin, had made from antique *Building Blocks* (I–A). Brann is also angry at his passive father, who blames all problems on fate. Upset and lonely, Brann crawls inside the fortress, falls asleep and slips back in time to his father's childhood. He meets Kevin in the midst of the Great Depression, a time when Kevin was dominated by fear of his abusive father. Brann gains respect for the plucky 10-year-old boy who would become his father and learns that real courage need not always be aggressive. He also learns that fate is possibilities, all the possibilities, even the impossible ones.

Quest Stories

Archetypal themes from folklore become vividly evident in quest fantasies. Here again is the misty outline of a story in which we search for the golden age or lose—and seek to regain—our identity. Victory in the battle between good and evil depends upon finding the missing heir, recognizing a prince or princess in disguise, or achieving utopia under the rule of a king whose coming has been foretold. Titles of popular contemporary fantasies reverberate with overtones of such a glorious kingdom—*The High King* (I–A), *The Lord of the Rings* (A), *The Grey King* (I–A), *The Once and Future King* (A)——or reflect the quest that must be undertaken before the golden time is ushered in—*Over Sea, Under Stone* (I–A); *The Farthest Shore* (I–A), *The Great and Terrible Quest* (A).

Many quest tales are structured within—in fact, draw explicitly upon—the framework of the Arthurian legends. In *Steel Magic* (I), by André Norton, three children who have ventured to an island "out of time" fight against powers that oppose the return of the age of Arthur using the "steel magic" in the knife, fork, and spoon in their picnic basket. In *The Dark Is Rising* (I–A), by Susan Cooper, Merlin—wizard of the Arthurian legend—appears in various incarnations across different periods of time to fight against the dark. In the final battle, the forces of light in every age join with those who fight against the dark.

Some characters simply experience altered consciousness as they go into times past. In the five volumes of Susan Cooper's series, *The Dark Is Rising*, the Old Ones, servants of the Light—immortals dedicated to keeping the world free of evil—are born with a special wisdom and power. Will Stanton, the last of the Old Ones, discovers his heritage on his eleventh birthday. In one scene, Will goes back into the historical time of an etching that depicts construction at an ancient Roman site in England. Many times within the story, Will communicates with the Old Ones, who have endured across the ages. Readers respond to the ancient struggle between light and dark, or good and evil, cast into a time slipped frame.

Quest stories that are most memorable describe characters' outer and inner struggles, and may involve Herculean journeys where overcoming obstacles vanquishes evil. Quests become a search for an inner, rather than an outer, enemy. Inner strength is required as characters are put to a variety of tests that ofttimes seem endless and unconquerable. It is the indomitable goodness of character that prevails.

Weaving legends from Arthurian days into the fabric of modern life, Susan Cooper dramatizes the risks of not standing up for what is right and just. The multilayered reality of her

Will Stanton, one of the "Old Ones," who, across the ages, work to protect the world from the ever-threatening forces of evil. (Illustration by Alan E. Cober from *The Dark Is Rising* by Susan Cooper.)

series *The Dark Is Rising* epitomizes tales dealing with the interconnection between visible and sensed reality. Although discussed as time fantasy, its subject may also be viewed as a quest. Susan Cooper bases the stories on English and Celtic myth, beginning with *Over Sea, Under Stone* and continuing with *The Dark Is Rising, Greenwitch* (I–A), *The Grey King* (I–A), and *Silver on the Tree* (I–A). The stories start realistically as Simon, Jane, and Barney Drew find an old manuscript with a maplike drawing through which they learn of a grail associated with King Arthur. Unlocking the inscription on the grail is a major problem, and the story becomes more complex as it reveals, in *The Dark Is Rising*, more about the struggle between the forces of light and dark. Will Stanton, seventh son of a seventh son, learns that he is called upon to carry the burden of power of the Old Ones, who fight across the centuries to ward off the powers of the Dark. Will also appears in *Greenwitch* where Jane becomes involved in a spring ritual of weaving a huge sacrificial figure (a greenwitch) from hazel, rowan, and hawthorne branches. This is cast into the sea to welcome summer and bring blessings of good crops and a good catch of fish to the small Cornwall village. The Dark in the village wears many faces and works through weak people to overpower the Light. In *The Grey King,* Will is sent to North Wales to recuperate from a serious illness and there continues his quest for the Signs that will finally overcome the Dark. Forces of evil appear in many forms: a wicked sheep owner, a chimerical fox, and the Grey King. Will meets Bran, an albino child who knows nothing of his origins. Together they find the golden harp, awaken the Six Sleepers of the past, and discover Bran's parentage: he is Arthur's son, the Pendragon, brought forward in time to the present when he is needed most. Clues from Celtic lore intrigue the reader already caught in a web woven of everday reality and mythic elements.

Finally, in *Silver on the Tree,* the story strands are braided dexterously as all the major characters are brought forward to the present for the ultimate confrontation with the Dark, embodiment of prejudice, hatred, and cruelty. In the memorable farewell of Bran to Arthur, human affection merges with the universal pain of being mortal.

Cooper's skillful manipulation of myth and reality is unparalleled. Based on ancient verses drawn from Arthurian legends, which foretell significant events, people, and places, the meaning of the myths is revealed gradually to Will Stanton and the reader.

Modern stories often echo symbolic meanings from Arthurian legends—a quest, an unacknowledged king, a Camelot. For example, Ged's inner and outer struggles with the evil shadow that would possess his soul—in Ursula Le Guin's *A Wizard of Earthsea* (I–A)—is both physical and emotional, as was King Arthur's quest. The idea of a high king in the Susan Cooper story also derives from the social structure of the sixth century A.D., when a loose confederation of nobles rallied under the banner of a high king in order to protect themselves against a common enemy. Even in fantasies where there is no direct connection with the Arthurian legends, such as C. S. Lewis's "Chronicles of Narnia," it seems entirely right that there be a medieval setting with the trappings of chivalry. Thus, the four children of Lewis's stories are destined to become kings and queens reigning from the four thrones in Cair Paravel when the golden age arrives in Narnia.

One of the key volumes in Lewis's "Chronicles," *The Magician's Nephew* (I), describes the creation of Narnia. In the "prequel" (introduction) to the six other volumes, young Digory Kirke and Polly Plummer gain entrance to other worlds with the help of three magic rings. In *The Magician's Nephew,* Digory, lonely and unhappy in his uncle's house, and with his mother seriously ill, seeks happiness and good fortune. Under the guidance of Aslan, he learns that life may be harsh before it is happy and that one must always be on guard against tyrants. Although few children enjoy all seven stories of the series equally (for, though great in conception, some are less than great in execution), many love and remember the passages describing Aslan singing Narnia into existence:

> The Lion was pacing to and fro about that empty land and singing his new song. It was softer and more lilting than the song by which he had called up the stars and the sun; a gentle, rippling music. And as he walked and sang the valley grew green with grass. It spread out from the Lion like a pool. It ran up the sides of the little hills like a wave. In a few minutes it was creeping up the lower slopes of the distant mountains, making that young world every moment softer. The light wind could now be heard ruffling the grass. The higher slopes grew dark with heather.[31]

As they read this, some children see the parallel with the opening chapters of Genesis, which Lewis, a distinguished scholar and theologian, intended. Some children will attend to the religious symbolism (which will be meaningful only if they discover it for themselves); others, who do not detect it, will still experience a sense of the numinous from the representation of a beneficent providence in the figure of Aslan. For students who would not appreciate the equation of Aslan with Christ, stressing the image could spoil the literary experience.

High fantasy—that is, fantasy that inhabits a secondary world created with high poetic seriousness—is most impressively realized in what we call *quest literature.* The finest authors of such works create whole worlds—with geographies, histories, languages, mythologies, and genealogies of their own. The names of the fantasy kingdoms—Narnia, Prydain, Middle Earth, Earthsea—have an irresistible allure that links them with the old names of Celtic and Saxon myths and legends. Of all fantasy, this type works the strongest enchantment. The Ring trilogy by J. R. R. Tolkien, the greatest for many readers, has inspired so devoted a following that we still see the legend "Frodo lives" on sidewalks and subway walls—attesting to nostalgia for a golden age.

June S. Terry says that children absorb quest tales "into the bloodstream," assimilating the values of human society past and present.[32] Values inherent in quest tales, shaped by generations of human experience, emerge consistently and are widely accepted. Because most children unconsciously learn from experience that goodness is generally rewarded and wickedness punished, quest tales affirm their knowledge. Further, fantasy readers learn a lesson common to most literature—that human nature has two sides and that life holds bitterness as well as happiness. Eternal hope is also conveyed in fantasy's almost always bouyant resolutions—offering the promise that, despite repeated setbacks, good fortune is ultimately assured.

In a study of the developmental levels of response to literature, intermediate grade students showed that they could draw generalizations about characters across literature, using quest stories as their examples.[33] For instance,

Eugene, a sixth grader, compared the shadow in Le Guin's *A Wizard of Earthsea* (A) to Sauron in Tolkien's *The Lord of the Rings* (A) and General Woundwort in Adams's *Watership Down* (A). "The shadow was only sneaky and sneaked around getting into people," Eugene said. "I like my evil to be more aggressive—like Sauron and General Woundwort. They line up their troops and go out after their enemies." Eighth grade students in the same study showed that they could interpret the metaphoric and symbolic meaning of the shadow. One explained, "The shadow represented the evil side of Ged, the other side of him. It was the world of shadow and death, the anti-Ged." Eighth graders were also able to generalize from the story to their own lives and talked about the underside of human nature. One student remarked, "I guess I have a shadow side, too, but I don't want to know about that right now." The developmental increments in students' understanding of literature were clearly based on the extent of their reading.

Lloyd Alexander's "Chronicles of Prydain" begin in *The Book of Three* (I—A), where readers meet memorable characters—the foundling Taran, an assistant pig-keeper; Princess Eilonwy of the red-gold hair; Gwydion, the good; and Arawn, Fflewddur Fflam, Gurgi, Dallben, and others. Five books catalogue Taran's quest, a quest that changes from story to story. First, he searches for Hen-Wen, the oracular pig in *The Book of Three*, then for the cauldron in *The Black Cauldron*, and later for the kidnapped Princess Eilonway in *The Castle of Llyr.* Finally, he sets out, in *Taran Wanderer*, to discover his identity, and in *The High King*, learns that greatness is not a matter of birth but of wisdom, humility, and responsible choice.

Taken together, the stories show an evolution of Taran's inner growth. In the final book, *The High King*, Taran, now a hero, finds that many of the things he sought seem insignificant, and his understanding of heroism has changed drastically; what he sought at the be-

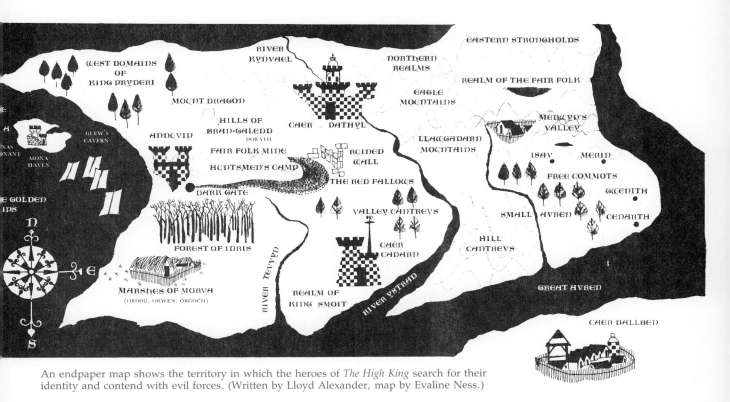

An endpaper map shows the territory in which the heroes of *The High King* search for their identity and contend with evil forces. (Written by Lloyd Alexander, map by Evaline Ness.)

ginning no longer interests him at the end. In this story of one seeking identity, Taran steadily progresses toward maturity in a quest as much internal as external. Throughout the chronicles, humor is sprinkled generously to lighten the seriousness of Taran's search and his struggles with evil along the way, which makes the series extremely popular with fifth and sixth graders. Each book can be read for the excitement, battles, mystery, and intrigue it contains, and for the thoughtful reader, subtle meanings are to be found in Taran's quest.

Lloyd Alexander created another quest of high adventure in the Westmark trilogy: *Westmark, The Kestrel*, and *The Beggar Queen* (all A). Theo, a printer's devil, is rescued by con artist Count Las Bombas and his dwarf, Musket, when royal inspectors kill Theo's master in a censorial raid on their print shop. Las Bombas, eager to leave town, shields Theo and in their travels adds a scruffy girl, Mickle, to their motley crew. Mickle, a spunky ragamuffin, has talents that enrich Las Bombas's repertoire of ways to steal. Meanwhile, the bereaved king and queen of Westmark mourn their lost daughter and rely on their sinister chief minister, Cabbarus, who secretly plots to take over the throne. Mystery, intrigue, superb characterization, tight plotting, and witty dialogue lead the way through battles, restoration of the long lost princess to her rightful throne, and the political evolution of Westmark.

Robin McKinley's *The Blue Sword* (A) introduces the mythical kingdom of Damar and its indomitable heroine, Harry, who is drawn to the Hillfolk, the last of the old Damarians. In a

TEACHING IDEA

THE NEWBERY MEDAL (I–A)   About one-fourth of the Newbery Medal winners have been from the fantasy genre, suggesting that some of our best writers use this literary form. Study the fantasies that have won this prestigious award to see if you can discern their qualities of excellence.

Displays Put up a poster of the Newbery Medal winners (available from the American Library Association). Fill a bulletin board with pictures of John Newbery, the Newbery Medal, and book jackets of the medal winners. Group the winners by genre (historical fiction, realistic fiction, fantasy), and add a title, such as "Take Your Pick of the Winners."

Activities Explain the Newbery Medal. Point out that it is given for literary quality rather than popularity. Survey the students and chart the winners they have read. Ask students to give a sales talk for the books they have read. Ask them to write brief annotations to display by the chart of winners; use these to encourage other students to read the books.

Plan a panel discussion with one group representing the criteria of literary quality and the other, popularity for book selection. Ask them to defend their positions and specific books by drawing upon examples that support their positions.

Collect several new books that are under consideration for the current Newbery Medal (ask your librarian for suggestions). Read as many as possible, discuss them as a group, and hold a mock election. Compare your results with the actual winner which is announced in mid-January

Some of the quest fantasies that have won the Newbery Award include *The High King* (I–A) by Lloyd Alexander, *The Grey King* (I–A) by Susan Cooper, and *The Hero and the Crown* (I–A) by Robin McKinley. Other fantasy books that have received the Newbery are *A Wrinkle in Time* (I–A) by Madeleine L'Engle, *The Twenty-One Balloons* (I–A) by William Péne du Bois, *Rabbit Hill* (I–A) by Robert Lawson, and *Hitty, Her First Hundred Years* (I–A) by Rachel Field.

---

prequel, *The Hero and the Crown* (A), which is set in an earlier time, we live among the Damarians and meet Aerin, the only child of the king of Damar who should be his rightful heir. A sense of mystery and legend permeates both stories of strong female characters who search for their destiny; they ultimately find that their destinies are intertwined. The links between Harry and Aerin lie beneath the surface, yet the

reader knows they exist. The mythical setting echoes traditional literature as young women go on a quest to explore their birthright.

A child who reads Tolkien's *The Hobbit* (I–A), can look forward to reading, as an adolescent, his complex, 1,300-page, multivolume *The Lord of the Rings* (A), to which *The Hobbit* is a prelude. Bilbo Baggins is the timid, insular hobbit that Gandalf the Wizard singles out as having the greatest potential for heroism and most capable of recovering the 13 dwarfs' long lost treasure from the dragon Smaug. Bilbo is understandably reluctant to undertake this quest, for it is much easier to live in his comfortable burrow, eating six meals a day. Discovering resources he did not know he had, this small, determined, self-sacrificing creature rises to the challenge of the personal and spiritual quest.

With the aid of Gollum's little gold ring, Bilbo attains the power of invisibility and the confidence to undertake more difficult tasks. Bilbo has no desire to be a hero and, in the final fierce battle of the Five Armies, uses the magic ring to protect his head from being chosen for a sweeping stroke by a goblin swordsman.

Upon his return to Hobbiton, Bilbo is considered somewhat strange by his neighbors, for he writes poetry and is often visited by dwarfs and wizards. Nonetheless, he remains very happy to the end of his days, which "were extraordinarily long." Tolkien's work has become the standard by which all other fantasies are judged; it is a touchstone in a literary education.

Literary Lore

All fantasy is rooted in folklore, a verity evident in some stories more than others. Mollie Hunter's fine novels acknowledge the "chain of communication through the centuries—the long, unbroken line of folk memory stretching . . . from Megalithic times to the present day."[34] So, too, do stories from Hans Christian Andersen, Jane Yolen, Natalie Babbitt, and Isaac Bashevis Singer.

We call *literary lore* those stories that have a haunting mythic quality and echo the sounds from storytellers' tongues of ages past. In *A Stranger Came Ashore* (I), Mollie Hunter captures on the very first page a timeless moment reflecting this quality:

> It was a while ago, in the days when they used to tell stories about creatures called the Selkie Folk. A stranger came ashore to an island at that time—a man who gave his name as Finn Learson—and there was a mystery about him which had to do with these selkie creatures. Or so some people say, anyway. . . .[35]

Haunting images of stories past return in the scene she sets and in the stories she tells.

Susan Cooper retells the Celtic legend of the seal maiden who is captured and wed by a mortal man in *The Selkie Girl* (P). Donallan captures the selkie on the one day in the year when she sheds her seal skin and is, for 24 hours, a young woman. The ending is foreshadowed in Old Thomas's prophecy when he tells Donallan how to capture the girl but warns him, "A wild creature will always go back to the wild, in the end." The beauty and bittersweet quality of an ancient legend is captured in Cooper's strongly cadenced prose and Warwick Hutton's translucent illustrations.

Mordicai Gerstein's *The Seal Mother* (P) gives a somewhat different version of the ancient legend. An old man tells the story of a fisherman who falls in love with a selkie, steals her skin, marries her, and has one son, Andrew. After seven years of promised bondage, she begs to return to the sea, but the fisherman has hidden her skin. Andrew finds it and gives it to his mother so that she can regain her seal form. She takes Andrew to meet his seal family and comes to him whenever he sings for her.

Bill Brittain draws upon ancient lore in the stories he produces for fantasy readers. *Devil's Donkey* (I) introduces the narrator, Stew Meat, a shortened form of Stewart Meade, who runs the general store and knows just about everything that happens in the town of Coven Tree. Stew has raised young Dan'l Pitt since he was orphaned and warns him about Old Magda the witch, although Dan'l doesn't much believe in witches. Dan'l even cut branches from the witch's Coven tree in defiance of local superstition. Even worse, he cut his ankle while

TEACHING IDEA

FANTASY (I–A) Fantasy contains elements not found in the natural world. Like the fairy tale, fantasy hints of things magical. Its themes affirm respect for life in all forms, the need for courage to combat obstacles, the importance of personal integrity, and the need for good to overcome evil. Universal truths spelled out in good fantasy help children grapple with the great mysteries of life.

Displays Display posters, such as "Live Your Fantasy: Read," or "Find Your Fantasy World in Books." Prepare an enchantment display with objects from books that hold special powers, such as a dragon egg for *Weird Henry Berg* (I) by Sarah Sargent, a key whistle for *Search for Delicious* (I) by Natalie Babbitt, and a toy grandfather clock for *Tom's Midnight Garden* (I) by Philippa Pearce.

Activities Show the filmstrip "Fantasy" (Pied Piper), or "Reading for the Fun of It: Fantasy" (Guidance Associates). Discuss concepts presented, and clarify children's definitions of the genre.

Ask students to group fantasies using books they have read to develop their categories. Compare their classification system with ones used by literary critics, such as animal fantasy, time slip fantasy, miniature worlds, and high fantasy.

Read aloud the first chapter from *The Cat Who Wished to Be a Man* (I–A) by Lloyd Alexander, *The Kelpie's Pearls* (I–A) by Mollie Hunter, and *Freaky Friday* (I–A) by Mary Rodgers. Ask the students to classify these.

Choose three or four books from the same category, or having the same kind of characters or theme, and give book talks on them showing that writers can develop the same idea or use similar characters in different ways. Post large sheets of paper with various headings, such as "Cats," "New Versions of Old Tales," or "Small Worlds," and ask students to list titles, characters or themes that are similar. For example:

chopping up the limbs, shed blood beneath the Coven tree, and thereby subjected himself to Old Magda's control. Dan'l pays dearly for his disregard of local superstition because Old Magda changes him into a donkey and it takes great strength for Dan'l to return to normal and leave the donkey world behind. *The Wish Giver* (I), a sequel to *Devil's Donkey*, is also narrated by the storekeeper who, along with three young people, visits a strange little man who sets up a booth at the church social. This funny little man gives them a magic card with a red spot in the center. They are to press their thumb on the spot and wish, wish, wish. What the little man does not tell them is that wishes sometimes bring more than one bargains for. A third book, *Dr. Dredd's Wagon of Wonders* (I), spins more tales with echoes of folklore in Coven Tree.

Rosemary Sutcliff, distinguished for her skillful historical fiction, draws upon the Arthurian legend in a trilogy beyond compare in *The Sword and the Circle: King Arthur and the Knights of the Round Table, The Light Beyond the*

CATS

Alexander, *The Cat Who Wished to Be a Man* (I–A)
Coatsworth, *The Cat Who Went to Heaven* (I)

MICE

Godden, *The Mousewife* (I)
Sharp, *Miss Bianca* (I)
Steig, *Abel's Island* (I)
White, *Stuart Little* (I)

SMALL WORLDS

Banks, *The Indian in the Cupboard* (I)
Cassedy, *Behind the Attic Wall* (I)
Norton, *The Borrowers* (I)

OVERCOMING EVIL

Cooper, *The Dark is Rising* (A)
Hunter, *A Stranger Came Ashore* (I–A)

Discuss the style of writing found in the best fantasies and compare it with the sounds of language in folklore. Recall literary conventions of folktales, such as beginnings and endings; the use of mystical numbers, such as 3, 7, or 12; and poetic imagery. Read aloud a few passages from various fantasies for comparisons of style. For example, use the underground scenes from the *The Hobbit* (I–A) by Tolkien and *The Weirdstone of Brisingamen* (I–A) by Alan Garner, or sections of Abel's life on *Abel's Island* (I) by William Steig.

Study one fantasy writer's work in depth.

Create a "Who am I?" game. Students write information on cards about a character they like and read it aloud to others who must guess the book it came from. "Where Am I?" can be an adaptation for famous settings in books, such as *The Borrowers* (I) by Mary Norton, *Abel's Island* (I) by Steig, and *Through the Looking Glass* (I–A) by Lewis Carroll.

Chart the characteristics of archetypal figures recurring in fantasy, such as wizards in *The Hobbit* (I–A) by Tolkien, *The Dark Is Rising* (A) by Susan Cooper, *A Wizard of Earthsea* (A) by Ursula Le Guin, *The Weirdstone of Brisingamen* (I–A) by Alan Garner, *Elidor* (A) by Alan Garner, and *The Once and Future King* (A) by T. H. White. What name do they use? What powers do they possess? What role do they play in the story?

Forest, and *The Road to Camlann* (all A). Stories from the Arthurian cycle, beginning with "The Coming of Arthur" through "The Last Battle" and "Avalon of the Apple Trees," are jewel toned in the telling and powerful in their impact. She gives coherence to the disparate narratives by interweaving allusions to Merlin, Morgan le Fay, and Sir Lancelot in the tales of King Arthur and his men. Sutcliff re-creates a sense of the times, using dignified and courtly prose. For example, in *The Road to Camlann,* she begins:

When the darkness crowds beyond the door, and the logs on the hearth burn clear red and fall in upon themselves, making caverns and ships and swords and dragons and strange faces in the heart of the fire, that is the time for story telling.

Come closer then, and listen.

The story of King Arthur is a long, long story, woven of many strands and many colours; and it falls naturally into three parts.[36]

This final book focuses on the love between Sir Lancelot, King Arthur's dearest friend and noblest knight, and Guenever, the Queen. It captures the sense of dread that permeates the scheming Mordred's plot to use that love to bring tragedy to all three at the end of their lives. The bittersweet characterization and the heart-rending theme resound in this epic and tragic story of the last years of Camelot.

Margaret Hodges's *Saint George andthe Dragon* (I–A), adapted from Edmund Spenser's *Faerie Queene*, is illustrated by Trina Schart Hyman and received the Caldecott Medal in 1985. Human describes how she decided to illustrate the book:

> [Hyman and Hodges] decided during lunch to put our George in his own, vague, pre-Arthurian time, and not in Mr. Spenser's Elizabethan period. We decided that perhaps I could use Spenser's bits about the little sailors and their voyage to bring in something Elizabethan. Or that maybe I should make a parallel to the main story in the borders of the pages, using Elizabethan children doing a George and the Dragon Mummers' play. I had already decided to make this book my own version of an illuminated manuscript, with decorative, lavishly illustrated page borders. Amazingly, it turned out that we agreed completely on how this book should look.[37]

Hyman's illustrations emphasize the romantic nature of this classic tale. In Tiffany-like pages, the heroic knight fights the dragon, rescues the dazzling princess, and becomes the patron saint of England.

Hans Christian Andersen was the first to use the classic fairy tale form to write stories of his own, which are often confused with the traditional ones because he emulates them so well. One of the most prolific writers of modern fantasy during his lifetime (1805–1875), Andersen worked as a cobbler in Denmark and was loved by the children who listened to his stories long before they were written down. *The Ugly Duckling*, said to be an autobiographical account in allegorical form, describes the indignities and heartaches Andersen suffered.

Many of Hans Christian Andersen's stories have been illustrated by outstanding artists and appear in picture-book format. *The Emperor's New Clothes* (P-I), illustrated by Virginia Lee Burton, Anne Rockwell, Janet Stevens, and Nadine Westcott, among others, strikes out at hypocrisy and pretentiousness. In this well-known story, two weavers tell the emperor that only wise men fit for high office can see the magic cloth they weave. No high official wants to admit that he cannot see the cloth and, thereby, to testify to his unfitness for the job. So each pretends to see the beautiful fabrics the two weavers describe. At a royal parade in which the emperor wears robes made of the nonexistent cloth, a small child exposes the hoax by calling out, in his innocence, that the emperor is, indeed, naked.

Andersen's *The Nightingale* (P-I), translated by Eva Le Gallienne and illustrated by Nancy Ekholm Burkert, is the story of a jeweled mechanical bird that so intrigues the emperor that he banishes the real nightingale despite its beautiful song. In a dramatic scene, the emperor realizes his mistake and asks to have the real nightingale returned, acknowledging that the beauties of nature are more precious than the most elaborate and lifelike objects made by man.

Following in the same tradition, Natalie Babbitt builds on the classic forms of literature to create fresh and original fantasies. In an artistically written literary tale, *Tuck Everlasting* (I), she presents the advantages and drawbacks of eternal life. The Tuck family, who had unwittingly drunk from a magic spring that gives everlasting life, remain forever the same age. Ten-year-old Winnie Foster discovers the magic spring and through it comes to know the Tucks. Pa Tuck tells Winnie about life as an immortal in the midst of a changing world. He describes life as a wheel: "But dying's part of the wheel, right there next to being born. You can't pick out the pieces you like and leave the rest. Being part of the whole thing, that's the

PROFILE

Natalie Babbitt

In *Tuck Everlasting,* Natalie Babbitt asks if the dream of an eternal life is really a blessing. For Tuck, who is explaining the cyclical nature of life to young Winnie Foster, there is no spoke on the wheel, for he has drunk from the spring granting everlasting life. Many of Natalie Babbitt's stories blur the line between fantasy and reality, leaving the reader to ponder the nature of truth.

Speaking about children and literature, Natalie Babbitt has said:

> I have the greatest respect for the intelligence, sensitivity, and imagination of young people. They are the true and unfettered audience, and as such deserve the best efforts of everyone who writes for them. Nothing can be good enough, but we can try.[38]

Natalie Babbitt grew up in Ohio. During her childhood, she spent many hours reading fairy tales and myths. She would often pretend that she was a librarian, stamping her books and checking them in and out to herself. She also liked to draw and, since her mother was an amateur landscape and portrait artist, had access to lots of paints, paper, and pencils. She studied art at Laurel School in Cleveland and at Smith College. Soon after graduation, she married Samuel Fisher Babbitt, who later became president of Kirkland College and now serves as an administrator at Brown University. The Babbitts have three children—Christopher, Tom, and Lucy—all now grown.

Natalie Babbitt collaborated on her first book with her husband, but then decided to write and illustrate on her own. In addition to the several books she has written, she has illustrated books of poems by Valerie Worth and the book jackets of her own novels. Told by a child interviewer how beautiful he thought the jacket illustration for *The Eyes of the Amaryllis,* she answered, "That's the nicest thing anyone ever said to me." Children's literature is enriched by Natalie Babbitt's work.

blessing."[39] The Tucks give Winnie a vial of the water to keep so that she can make a choice when she reaches womanhood. Bestowing the magical agent verifies the connection between this turn-of-the-century story and folklore traditions. Strong characterization, poetic prose, and careful plotting build a story that haunts the thoughtful reader.

Natalie Babbitt describes the demands of fantasy for the classic heroes and shows that their adventures are universal to all cultures; the hero's standard path of mythological adventure is separation, initiation, and return. In *Tuck Everlasting*, Winnie Foster, the real hero, follows that well-trodden path and achieves happiness. Fantasy raises important questions—to which Babbitt responds:

> For me, and for all writers devoted to fantasy as a means of exploring ideas, the total round of the hero's path is vitally important. Without it we cannot tell stories that satisfy us. And I think that as long as the basic, simple questions are asked, there will always be a place for us in the world of fiction. Fantasy will continue to answer those questions symbolically at some level and in some place that is always unexplained and yet universally understood. To carry on in that tradition, to take the hero through his round and bring him home again, over and over, is an ancient and honorable exercise that will never lose its vitality or its value.[40]

Natalie Babbitt's stories mirror the fundamental patterns of literary lore.

In his first book for children, *Zlateh the Goat* (I), Isaac Bashevis Singer, a masterful storyteller, retells seven middle-European Jewish tales of yesteryear that echo their heritage. Maurice Sendak's pictures enrich the book, and Weston Woods has re-created the title story as a beautiful film. Money is running low for Reuven and his family as Hanukkah nears. He decides to sell the beloved family goat, Zlateh, to the butcher. Aaron, the oldest son, is charged with the heartbreaking job of delivering the goat. A sudden blizzard causes them to lose their way, forcing Aaron and Zlateh to take refuge in a haystack:

> For three days Aaron and Zlateh stayed in the haystack. Aaron had always loved Zlateh, but in these three days he loved her more and more. She fed him with her milk and helped him keep warm. She comforted him with her patience. He

told her many stories, and she always cocked her ears and listened. When he patted her, she licked his hand and his face. Then she said "Maaaa," and he knew it meant, I love you too.[41]

Singer's re-creations of images from the folklore of the old country are embellished with sprightly wit. *Naftali the Storyteller and His Horse, Sus* (I-A), about a man very much like Singer himself, contains eight stories that echo traditional values and practices so meaningful during the Diaspora. "A Hanukkah Eve in Warsaw" is the story of a boy not yet 7 who, craving independence, leaves school to walk home alone. An assistant teacher had always accompanied him before, but the boy wants to boast to his friends that he is grown up enough to go alone. A sudden snowstorm causes him to lose his way, but his eventual return and the forgiveness that awaits him makes Hanukkah even sweeter. Follies of vanity, the vulnerability of being human, and faith in the ultimate goodness of life shine through Singer's stories.

Mollie Hunter's novels describe the struggle between good and evil in a manner that makes readers feel the author is speaking directly to them, for there is an immediacy and a timelessness in her tales. Folklore and legend reverberate in them, and they encompass the best of the old tales cast in the present. They carry a sense of continuity that what is has always been and evermore shall be. In *The Walking Stones* (I), the reader goes with Donald into a circle of stones that the ancient Druids had used for worship and feels the aura of the place and of the primordial rituals once performed there. In her *A Stranger Came Ashore* (I) Hunter sings the legends of the selkie folk (seals in human form) into life as she tells of unusual events in a village in the Shetland Isles. A young sailor, Finn Learson, washed ashore after a shipwreck on a stormy night, is not what he seems, but only 12-year-old Robbie Henderson senses the evil and mystery about him. Robbie's dying grandfather questions Finn Learson's identity, and with the help of his ravenlike schoolmaster, Yarl Corbie, Robbie learns the truth. Suspense works beneath the surface of routine occurences in the isolated village, where rumor, myth, and legend blend. When the tale is told, the author suggests that, although some may opt for conventional explanations of the events, those who see with the third eye and allow the imagination a life of its own will find more powerful symbols.

Mollie Hunter alludes to the factual base that underlies folklore; she shows the connections between the actual event and the fanciful tales that grow out of the repeated retelling of the stories. Her work vividly illustrates the idea that "all literature is but one story," for in it, fantasy, reality, and folklore intermix.

Two books, because they show their traditional parentage proudly, deserve special mention: Robin McKinley's *Beauty* (I-A), a loving rendition of the Beauty and the Beast tale; and Shirley Rousseau Murphy's *Silver Woven in My Hair* (I), an intermingling of several Cinderella tales. Beauty's father is a wealthy merchant who falls on hard times and moves his family to the country near a dark, forbidding forest. The father, who becomes lost in the woods, is saved by a gruesome monster who allows him to go free on condition that he hand over one of his daughters in his place. It is Beauty who willingly goes to the Beast to fulfill her father's bargain. After several months at the castle, Beauty begs to visit her family but is refused by the gentle Beast. In a fit of anger, Beauty faints, then returns to consciousness unaware that she is lying in the Beast's arms:

> My memory began to return. I had been unhappy because I was homesick. The Beast had said that he could not let me go home. Then I must have fainted. It occurred to me that the velvet my face rested on was heaving and subsiding gently, like someone breathing, and my

Echoes from folklore reverberate through a poetic retelling of the story of "Beauty and the Beast." (From *Beauty: A Retelling of the Story of Beauty and the Beast* by Robin McKinley.)

> fingers were wrapped around something that felt very much like the front of a coat. There was a weight across my shoulders that might have been an arm. I was leaning against the whatever-it-was, half sitting up. I turned my head a few inches, and caught a glimpse of lace, and beneath it a white bandage on a dark hand; and the rest of my mind and memory returned with a shock like a snowstorm through a window blown suddenly open.[42]

The terror of her early encounters with the Beast, the gradual recognition of his kindness and love for her, and the eventual release of the handsome prince from his imprisonment in the repulsive body of the Beast is played out in captivating prose.

LANDMARK

Science Fiction: Rise of the Genre

Science fiction has grown into a well-respected branch of literature. Jules Verne (1828–1905), a Frenchman, is recognized as the progenitor of the scientific adventure story. His publication of *20,000 Leagues Under the Sea* appeared in an English edition in 1869 and was followed by *Around the World in Eighty Days* in 1872. Verne focused his stories on technology and inventions without attempting to develop a society around them. Later, H. G. Wells included social concerns in his stories that created a detailed picture of a future society.[43]

The science fiction written after that often focused on the technological accomplishments of future times, with little emphasis of its impact on human beings. Much of it was a Buck Rogers type of comic strip farce, with little literary value, although it turned out to be prophetic in terms of technological advances. After World War II, however, writers focused on the consequences of advanced technology on society. The changes in human life-styles, sociological issues, famine, nuclear proliferation, and mind control all became fare for the science fiction writer.

Most early science fiction was published as short stories in magazines, *Amazing Stories* and later *Astounding Science Fiction* being two

Jules Verne's *20,000 Leagues Under the Sea* is regarded as the precursor of the scientific adventure. (Illustrated by Charles Molina.)

Literature study reveals numerous variants of the Cinderella theme; Murphy's *Silver Woven in My Hair* puts the rags-to-riches tale in a story set in the Middle Ages. Thursey, a kitchen maid in an inn in the village of Geis, comforts herself with the stories she collects and secretly records from wandering minstrels. One such story is played out in her own life. Her friend Gillie, the goatherd, is really the prince in disguise.

SCIENCE FICTION

Science fiction is similar to fantasy in that it is set in worlds that do not correspond to present

of the major sources. Prolific science fiction writer Isaac Asimov was influenced by these magazines. He recalls,

[When I was nine] while I was in charge of the magazine rack in my father's store, my fingers itched futilely after forbidden delights. Reams of fascinating blood and violence lay all about me and yet were kept from me by my father's stern notions about the degenerating influence of cheap literature. And there was no court of appeal, either. Then came a wonderful break. A science fiction magazine, *Amazing Stories*, passed under his eagle glance and received the august paternal nod. Science fiction, he decided, might improve my mind by interesting me in the achievements and potentialities of science. From then on I was hooked. I was a science fiction fan of the most confirmed variety.[44]

His science fiction novel *Pebble in the Sky* was published in 1950, the first of over 300 books he has written, many of which are science fiction.

Asimov, Robert Heinlein, and Ray Bradbury are some of the writers who have earned respect for the genre. The changes in science fiction are reflected in a statement of purpose by Ray Bradbury, who said,

I am writing large metaphors about my time, but not self-consciously—emotionally. I take in from my time, I digest it, and then I put it back out on paper in the form of a technological fairy tale of the near future. . . . Science fiction is a wonderful shorthand way of telling us the truth about the thing that is right in front of us.[45]

The rise of science fiction as a literary genre has greatly enriched the reading fare for today's young people.

realities. Yet it differs from fantasy in that the future realities it depicts are often based on extrapolation from scientific principles. In many books, the distinctions between fantasy and science fiction are blurred.

Science fiction is speculative fiction; it is based on scientific fact, set most often in the future, and deals with the impact of technology and science on humans, humanoids, or other creatures. Some of the best science fiction, however, especially stories by the masters that have lasted, have been about totally unscientific things such as faster-than-light travel, time travel, and teleportation. Highly respected science fiction writer Robert A. Heinlein defines it this way. In science fiction,

The author takes as his first postulate the real world as we know it, including all established facts and natural laws. The result can be extremely fantastic in content, but it is not fantasy; it is legitimate—and often very tightly reasoned—speculation about the possibilities of the real world.[46]

As some of the prophecies made by earlier science fiction writers came true, such as the atomic age and the computer revolution, science fiction attained credibility; it had long been considered merely sensationalist. Not only was the content more believable, but the quality of the writing and the seriousness of its themes improved. Early science fiction writers concentrated on bug-eyed Martians, ray guns, and space ships, to the neglect of strong characterization. Contemporary science fiction writers have grown more introspective, often dealing with the interaction of human beings and some aspect of science, technology, or the natural world that does not exist at the present time. In fact, they suggest hypotheses and ask probing questions about the future of humankind and the nature of the universe.

Science fiction as a genre has leaped beyond the boundaries of scientific fact; much of it is neither scientific nor fact. Some literary critics propose that we merely use the term "S. F." to allow for Science Fiction, Science Fantasy, Space Fantasy, or Speculative Fiction.[47] Science fiction enthusiasts, however, are not concerned with classification systems; they accept supersonic space travel, mind communication, and life on other planets without question. Kything, tesseracting, teleporting, and time warps are all taken for granted. They are interested in a crackling good story, notwithstanding our penchant for labels and categories. Perhaps only the atmosphere of scientific credibility distinguishes the genre.

Science fiction has developed a small but avid readership that continues to grow; the parallel popularity of film productions such as

Star Wars, Close Encounters of the Third Kind, E. T., The Dark Crystal, and *Star Trek* cannot be ignored. We can see loose connections between print and film characters: Luke Skywalker and Darth Vader arose from Buck Rogers and Flash Gordon, both cartoon strips; E. T. came from a play; and Mr. Spock, from a book of short stories entitled *The Voyage of the Space Beagle* by A. E. van Vogt. Although science fiction films still rely to some extent on special effects and gadgetry, science fiction writing concerns itself more with serious characterization and theme.

There was a time when we felt secure in believing that George Orwell's *1984* and Aldous Huxley's *Brave New World* were remote: the visions they present could only be found in books. Modern space travel has caused us to think that if some of the things prophesied have come to pass, so might others. Jules Verne, who wrote *20,000 Leagues Under the Sea* and who is considered the father of scientific science fiction, now reads like a historical novel rather than the science fiction it was when it was written. Yesterday's creative science fiction writers forecast many of today's scientific discoveries and tragedies.

The science fiction community has established its own awards to recognize outstanding writers. The Nebula Award, given for a short story, novelet, novella, or novel, is chosen by a vote of the membership of the Science Fiction Writers of America. The Hugo Award, given annually for excellence in science fiction, is named in honor of Hugo H. Gernsback, who is credited with the development of modern science fiction. Gernsback, an electrical engineer, in 1908 began publishing *Modern Electrics,* a magazine about radio. In 1911, however, he devoted a few pages to a serialized story which became popular, "Ralph 124C/41 + : A Romance of the Year 2660," a utopian vision about inventions and innovations of the future. In 1926, Gernsback began a magazine, *Amazing Stories,* with contributions from distinguished writers such as Edgar Allan Poe, Jules Verne, and H. G. Wells. By 1929, Gernsback had lost control of *Amazing Stories,* so he began another, called *Science Wonder Stories,* and coined the term, "science fiction." Many of today's science fiction writers first published in these magazines.

Criteria for Selecting Science Fiction

Critics of science fiction, as with other genres, do not always agree on what is required of high-quality literature. Generally, we expect that the elements of plot, style, theme, and characterization are fully developed, as in all good literature.

Science fiction most often adheres to natural law. It is based on scientific fact or hypothesis. If, however, a story is set on another planet or in another universe, the laws of that place are clearly defined and internally consistent. Isaac Asimov, noted science fiction writer, explained, "The best kind of sci-fi involves science. . . . Time travel is theoretically impossible but I wouldn't want to give it up as a plot gimmick."[48] A good writer will make a story sound plausible, or in other words, give it its own gravity.

In good science fiction, facts do not encumber the plot. Stories do not start sounding like Mr. Wizard, and some, on second look, are as inventive and as imaginative as fantasy stories. One of the differences between fantasy and science fiction is that the science in the story might work some time or some place. One of the flaws of early science fiction was that the reader tripped over beakers, wires, and monsters. Present-day science fiction themes lead readers to think about life and science, the possibilities of the future, alien invasions, and the thrill of exploration.

Finally, science fiction makes us consider the emotional, psychological, and mental effects of futuristic ideas, conflict, and change. It also helps us keep an open mind to consider unlimited possibilities and to raise questions about other forms of life. We are all carbon-based life. How about silicon-based life? How about life just beginning on one of the methane giants that are themselves small starlike planets? Science fiction deals in possibilities.

Some futurists say that the age when death will be obsolete is near; that "telebodies" or "telehumans" with electronic parts—quasi-humans who are maintained through telemonitoring—will be commonplace; that versatile and durable replacements for our fragile or deteriorated body parts will be readily available. Genetic intervention will make hereditary diseases obsolete and life-support suits will continuously monitor our internal body functions. Indeed, these ideas do not seem as far-fetched as they once did: much of what was once in the future is here with us today.

Michael Wood states that "Science fiction is a mirror in the house of intellect raised not by pride or passion or the urging of the gods but by the curiosity and the capacity for invention."[49] Gifted writers such as Isaac Asimov, Arthur C. Clarke, Robert Heinlein, H. M. Hoover, and John Christopher have harnessed this curiosity and capacity for invention to elevate science fiction to an art form dealing with serious themes.

A strong and oft-repeated theme is the effect of technological developments on human beings. For example, innovations in warfare, communications, and locomotion could shrink the world so that the behavior of one person might affect the lives of countless others. A science fiction writer, using this as a basis, might depict an individual or small group attempting to take power over the world.

In better science fiction, moral issues are not neglected. Stories set in worlds never known deal with problems we may someday face—the rights of extraterrestrials whose planets are colonized, the ethics of allocation of limited resources, the sharing of diminishing resources in a world of rapidly growing populations—and cause us to rethink the

Today's children have access to devices resembling some once found only in science fiction.

Robert Heinlein, dean of science fiction writers, illuminates the social implications of science and technology for life by critically examining the power and danger of modern technology. Heinlein was among the outstanding science fiction writers of the 1950s and 1960s who moved the genre to a place worthy of esteem. In an early work, *Farmer in the Sky (A)*, he re-creates the experience of taking off in a spaceship, the Bifrost:

> The Bifrost tilted over a little and the speaker said, "Minus three minutes!"
> And then "Minus one minute!" and another voice took up the count: "Fifty-nine Fifty-eight Fifty-seven."
> My heart started to pound so hard I could hardly hear it. But it went on: "Thirty-five Thirty-four. . . ."
> "And three."
> "And two. . . ."
> I never did hear them say "one" or "fire" or whatever they said. About then something fell on me and I thought I was licked. Once, exploring a cave with the fellows, a bank collapsed on me and I had to be dug out. It was like that—but nobody dug me out. My chest hurt. My ribs seemed about to break. I couldn't lift a finger. I gulped and couldn't get my breath. I wasn't scared, not really, because I knew we would take off with a high "g," but I was awfully uncomfortable. I managed to turn my head a little and saw that the sky was already purple. While I watched, it turned black and the stars came out, millions of stars. And yet the sun was still streaming in through the port.[50]

Using Science Fiction in the Classroom

Science fiction is easily adapted into a thematic approach since writers probe questions, such as a search for life on other worlds, eternal life, conflict of cultures, mind control, and life after a nuclear holocaust. Technological and societal developments include gene splicing, increasing the allowable radiation level in the air 100-fold, combining materials to make new ones, and newer roles for women. H. G. Wells, author of

choices and directions of our society. Science fiction, so appropriate for a changing world, is a literature about change and the attendant moral issues change brings.

There is much science fiction in a lighter vein that is filled with exciting adventure and humor. Some writers adhere strictly to the facts of science, whereas others take artistic license with them. Certainly, a child''s introduction to the genre should be through some of the lighter, suspenseful stories. Science fantasy, a blend of fantasy and science fiction, often set in other worlds and uncomplicated by elaborate scientific theories, provides a good entrée for beginning science fiction readers.

The War of the Worlds (1898) and considered the father of sociological science fiction, addressed some of these themes nearly a century ago.

Reader preference shows up markedly in science fiction. Those who like science fiction *love* it, and those who do not like it will hardly try it. In the research done by Cullinan, Harwood, and Galda, age and sex differences were apparent in how much children liked or did not like science fiction.[51] In that study, boys who chose science fiction as a favored genre far outnumbered the girls. Also, fourth grade boys chose the Narnia series, but the sixth and eighth grade boys were avowed science fiction readers. Fourth grade girls chose fairy tale-like fantasy, whereas sixth grade girls chose realistic, true-to-life stories, and eighth grade girls chose romance.

In a study reported by Constance A. Mellon, teenagers in eastern North Carolina did not differ markedly from the New York City students in the Cullinan and associates research.[52] Mellon reports that twice as many males read science fiction as did females. She also found differences in science fiction reading among students in various programs. Forty percent or more of students in gifted, college preparatory, and general studies programs claim to read science fiction compared to 20 percent or fewer in special education and Chapter I groups.

One of the best ways to introduce science fiction to young readers is through the short story. If they are going to like it, they find out quickly, and if not, they do not have to read an entire novel to make their judgment. Numerous good collections of short stories are available.

Isaac Asimov has compiled many collections of short stories. Along with Martin H. Greenberg and Charles G. Waugh, he has edited the following anthologies: *Young Witches and Warlocks, Young Mutants, Young Extraterrestrials, Young Monsters, Young Ghosts,* and *Young Star Travelers* (all A). Also, Sheila Williams and Cynthia Manson selected *Tales from Isaac Asimov's Science Fiction Magazine* (A), which includes an introduction and one short story by Asimov himself. In this story, "Potential," scientists Nadine and Basil are working on Multivac, a super computer, to identify a genetic pattern that can be modified to produce telepathy. After scanning millions of patterns, they find one that matches the new pattern Multivac has worked out as possessing telepathic potential. Immediately, Nadine wants to interview 15-year-old Roland Washman from Plainview, Iowa, who possesses this pattern, but Basil does some computerized investigation first. The research shows that Roland is a loner, not very bright in school, and that he works as a gardener's assistant in the summers. When Nadine and Basil go to Plainview, the gardener and Roland's parents are uncooperative. And when Roland finally does take their test, he does not perform well, so the scientists leave disappointed. The reader discovers, however, that Roland does have telepathic powers—with bees. All his life he had heard the bees thinking, and they could hear him. They pollinated his plants so that everything he touched grew beautifully.

The best science fiction short stories appear in two volumes of *The Science Fiction Hall of Fame* (A), edited by Robert Silverberg. In Volume 1, Silverberg selected 26 stories by the masters of science fiction that were published between 1934 and 1963. Stanley Weinbaum's "A Martian Odyssey," is an imaginative and lyrical presentation of Martian life forms, and Theodore Sturgeon's "Microcosmic God" is a god to his own universe inside his laboratory, where he has created a world of superbeings. Daniel Keyes's "Flowers for Algernon" is a touchingly beautiful story about Charlie, a mentally retarded boy who, as the result of some scientific experiments, becomes gradually smarter and smarter. Told through Charlie's journals, which move from illegible writing to brilliant essays, the story wrings the heart strings. Volume 2 contains 11 novellas, including H. G. Wells's "The Time Machine."

PROFILE

Isaac Asimov

Born in the Soviet Union in 1920, Isaac Asimov immigrated to the United States with his family when he was 3 years old. He attended public school in New York City, worked in his parents' store, and graduated from high school at age 15. From Columbia University he received a bachelor's degree (1939) and a master's degree (1941), both in chemistry.

During World War II he was a chemist in a Naval laboratory and also served in the armed forces. Asimov returned to Columbia University and received his Ph.D. in 1948.

He describes his early writing development this way:

I imagine there must be such a thing as a born writer; at least, I can't remember when I wasn't on fire to write. At the age of 12 (possibly earlier) I was filling a nickel notebook with endless penciled scrawlings, divided into chapters, and entitled "The Greenville Chums at College." In 1936, my father, observing my active scribblings, dug into the almost invisible family savings and bought me a second-hand typewriter. I promptly taught myself to touch-type and began a rambling fantasy-novel. (I don't remember the title, but I remember well that I saved paper by using both sides of the sheet, single spacing, and allowing no margins.)

TYPES OF SCIENCE FICTION

Mind Control

Several science fiction writers deal with themes of mind control, telepathy, ESP, and other forms of communication across time and space. One of the early examples is John Christopher's White Mountain trilogy. This trilogy about extraterrestial invaders of Earth appeals to today's readers in the upper elementary grades. *The White Mountains* (I-A), *The City of Gold and Lead* (I-A), and *The Pool of Fire* (I-A), a blend of science fiction and fantasy, are set in the twenty-first century in a world ruled by the Tripods, dreaded robots. When humans are 14, the Tripods implant steel caps in their skulls that keep them submissive, docile, and helpless. Will and his two friends learn that free people live in the White Mountains and make a hazardous journey to join them. Humane characters are pitted against hostile aliens in a

By June 1938, I had actually completed a story and carried it to the offices of *Astounding Science Fiction*. The editor, John W. Campbell, Jr., rejected the story at once but kindly and helpfully discussed with me, then and thereafter, all angles of the writing art. My father cooperated also by promptly finding the funds, somehow, to buy me a *spanking-new* typewriter.

I tried again and again and again—In October 1938, four months after my first submission and after a total of twelve rejections from various magazines, I made my first sale. It was a story entitled "Marooned Off Vesta," and was bought by *Amazing Stories*.[53]

The technological revolution during and after World War II brought literary acceptance to the science fiction genre and to Asimov as a writer. His first book, *Pebble in the Sky*, was published in 1950; by 1969 he had authored 100 books and in 1987 the total reached 375.

People usually ask after my writing habits, thinking, I suppose, there must be some carefully kept secret that accounts for my prolific production. Actually there isn't. I do all my own typing, but I type 90 words a minute and never slow down. The key characteristic is, I suppose, single-mindedness. I type every day, except when the typewriters are kept forcibly out of reach; I start early each day and continue typing till the number of typographical errors reaches an unacceptable concentration. I don't take vacations.[54]

Isaac Asimov writes for readers, and although some of his work has been adapted for television, the author contends, "Reading demands the most but it also offers the greatest rewards. On TV we see what everyone else sees—we are empty receptacles. In reading, you have to create it all—but it's yours alone."[55]

series of bizarre encounters. Christopher's narrative will impel readers to ponder the values of life and science.

Madeleine L'Engle's Wrinkle in Time trilogy (I–A) could be considered when discussing books about mind control. When Meg and Charles Wallace travel across time to rescue their father, they encounter the disembodied brain called 'It.' Meg and Charles Wallace must fight desperately to avoid being controlled by the powers of the oversize and powerful brain

that directs everyone and everything within its grasp.

Tomorrow's World

Sylvia Engdahl examines anthropological and sociological aspects of life in the future in her short stories and novels. One of the best, *Enchantress from the Stars* (A), is written from the perspective of the three central characters, each of whom is a member of one of three groups whose fortunes intertwine. Elana joins the Anthropological Service of the Federation of Planets, a group made up of the most advanced people in the universe. Georyn lives in primitive Andrecia, a world that still believes in enchanted forests and dragons. Jarel is one of the Imperialists invading Andrecia to place colonists on this rich virgin land.

Elana, only a First-Phase student at the Academy for Anthropological Service, does not qualify for a starship exploration to any of the Youngling planets. She tries to persuade her father, the Senior Agent, to allow her to join him when problems arise in Andrecia, especially since her bethrothed, Evrek, is a member of the crew. Failing to persuade her father, she stows away on the starship.

The Andrecians live on a beautiful Youngling planet but have advanced only to the stage of a feudal society and are in danger of being taken over by the Imperialists. The Imperialists, more advanced technologically, do not share the humanitarian values of the Federation. The power of love and faith are triumphant in Engdahl's examination of the interaction between cultures at different levels of development. This story and its sequel, *The Far Side of Evil* (A), raise significant questions that leave readers pondering their own society and its values.

In all of her work, Engdahl is suggesting hypotheses about humankind's future and the nature of the universe. She forces her characters (and her readers) to consider questions of individual commitment and ethical behavior. In the foreword to a collection of four of her stories, *Anywhere, Anywhen: Stories of Tomorrow* (A), Engdahl decries the tendency to assign books about the future automatically to the category of science fiction:

> Personally, I do not believe that the future is something that should be set apart and mentioned only in literature of one particular type,

directed to one specific audience. To me, past, present, and future are all parts of an unbroken thread, the thread of human experience. Almost everybody is interested in the future.[56]

Engdahl pinpoints the problematic nature of strict classifications; she focuses on the universality of human problems.

H. M. Hoover envisions an alien race that conquered Earth centuries ago in *The Delikon* (A). A violent revolution is brewing that will cast out the Delikon from Earth and their headquarters at Kelador. Varina, a young Delikon teacher, age 307, who has been restructured in human form to teach two human children, is torn between loyalties to her people and to the earthlings in her charge. When she and the two children go on a camping trip, they are caught between the battle lines of the revolutionaries and the Delikon. Varina, repelled by the brutality of war, wants to return to her native home, but when she finally reaches Kelador she finds the Delikon defeated and the last starship gone, stranding her on Earth. In a final touching scene, when Varina has run across a lawn and disappeared behind a hedge, the children call, "Are you coming back?" But, though Varina hears the question, she cannot answer, because she does not know. The larger questions of finding one's purpose and place in life are considered in this engrossing novel.

Hoover has contributed a sizable body of science fiction addressing sociological themes. In *The Shepherd Moon* (A), 13-year-old Merry Ambrose watches, in the forty-eighth century, for the rise of the five full moons circling the Earth: four of the moons were satellites built as space habitats. One, the Shepherd Moon, Terra II, was the first of the space satellites sent from Earth hundreds of years earlier. Mikel Goodman, the product of genetic engineering on Terra II, lands near Merry's home and initiates his plan to rule the Earth. His innocent appearance belies his malevolent amorality, and although he does not succeed in taking over the Earth, his questions cause Merry to become aware of many social problems on Earth. Hoover raises questions about the nature of the interaction between life on Earth and life in space.

Arthur C. Clarke, an internationally recognized scientist, sets *Dolphin Island* (I–A) in the twenty-first century and incorporates scientific conjecture based on research that has been done with dolphins. Johnny floats on a raft after his ship, the *Santa Anna*, is wrecked:

> Something jolted the raft, and he awoke with a start. For a moment he could hardly believe that he had been sleeping and that the sun was now almost overhead. Then the raft jerked again— and he saw why.
>
> Four dolphins, swimming side by side, were pushing the raft through the water. Already it was moving faster than a man could swim, and it was still gaining speed. Johnny stared in amazement at the animals splashing and snorting only inches away from him; was this another of their games?
>
> Even as he asked himself that question, he knew that the answer was No. The whole pattern of their behavior had changed completely; this was deliberate and purposeful. Playtime was over. He was in the center of a great pack of the animals, all now moving steadily in the same direction. There were scores, if not hundreds, ahead and behind, to right and left, as far as he could see. He felt that he was moving across the ocean in the midst of a military formation—a brigade of cavalry.[57]

The dolphins push Johnny to the waist-high water surrounding Dolphin Island, then leave. His new home and life on Dolphin Island provide fascinating reading for children.

Children also find it fascinating that dolphins communicate with each other, and they are intrigued by present-day scientists' efforts to communicate with dolphins.

Pamela Sargent tells of the young aboard a giant space ship (Ship), who must "seed" another planet with human life in *Earthseed* (A). Zoheret, the protagonist, spawned from Ship's genetic banks, had only lived within its protective climes: "Her earliest memory was of Ship's voice soothing her, though she could not recall why she had needed consolation. Ship had always been there, around her, watching and tending her."[58] Zoheret and her shipmates, taught that war and violence are evil, are sent into the Hollow (a natural, wild space within the ship) on a final survival training program before they become a planetary colony; there trouble erupts among them. They discover they have feelings of aggression and competition they never knew they had. Zoheret turns to Ship for help and inadvertently discovers a secret that Ship had kept: some adults are also on board. As the young people search for the deeper truths about Ship and "The Project," Ship decides that they are ready to be left on another planet and to make their own decisions while Ship travels on to produce other children and seed other planets. They must embark on their new life in a hostile world, wondering if they will be able to conquer the same instincts that destroyed their ancestors on Earth. The book probes important questions about the world of tomorrow.

Survival

Some writers' gloomy outlook of the future is apparent in the literature of survival. Although most nuclear scenarios are too all-encompassing and horrible to discuss, an entire body of books exists that show children surviving a nuclear war. Postnuclear holocaust books have proliferated.

But stories about survival are not limited to the horrors of life after a nuclear war. The problems of life as it is today—the overcrowding, the pollution, the extinction of animal and plant species, and the questions of an adequate food supply—provide science fiction writers with unlimited opportunites to project how humans will survive on Earth. Isaac Asimov writes,

> To put it bluntly, Earth is overfilled with us. We can reasonably call it overfilled because we are doing it damage. We are crowding into every corner of the planet in such numbers that we are leaving no room for other plants and animals. Hundreds and thousands of species may be driven into extinction, and life on Earth will lose much of its color and variety. We may even find out too late that some of the species that have vanished were very important to the web of life and that their loss will create problems for us.
>
> Then, too, all the billions of us are straining Earth's capacity to grow enough food, while our busy activities, whether industrial or biological, are pouring more poisons into the air, water and soil so that Earth is steadily becoming a less livable planet.[59]

Asimov and other science fiction writers propose that the new frontier lies in outer space. Still others propose that if we are stuck here on Earth, the new frontier might be what we could do to make Earth more livable.

Louise Lawrence unfolds the chilling story of the fate and evolution of three generations of one family after a nuclear holocaust in *Children of the Dust* (I-A). The novel, divided into three parts, shows nuclear missiles roaring toward Gloucestershire and the Cotswold Hills in England while Sarah and her family try to barricade themselves inside their home. Sarah watches all the members of her family die except for Catherine, a small sister, whom she takes to a safe house before going back to face her own death. Catherine is the only survivor, and in the second part, she is a mature woman living in a rebuilt rural community. Their father, who was away from home at the time of the bombing, has remarried, believing that none of his family has survived. One day, Catherine meets her young half-sister, Ophelia. In the third part of the book, Ophelia's son, Simon, returns to the farm settlement from the underground base when the technology they needed for survival fails. Simon is horrified to discover that the young people he meets are white-eyed and covered with a fine furry down. He finally realizes that they are strong, competent, and the hope of the new world.

Few have developed the nuclear holocaust theme more convincingly than Robert C. O'Brien in *Z for Zachariah* (I-A). A lone 16-year-old girl, Ann Burden, survives nuclear radiation

ACTIVITY: TEACHER TO STUDENT

A RACE OF THE FUTURE (A)   What do you think society will be like in the twenty-first century? Will it be one grand global village? Will there still be families as we know them? Assuming that technological advances continue, what will your community be like? To what will humanity have been reduced or elevated—or will it be unchanged?

With these questions in mind, draw upon examples from the science fiction you have read to describe the people who will be walking where you walk 1,000 years from now. Tell about their appearance, the things they do in their leisure time, and the things that make them happy and sad. You might bind your essays in an original book called "Future World."

ACTIVITY: TEACHER TO STUDENT

ON BEYOND ZACHARIAH (I–A)   When Ann Burden in Robert C. O'Brien's *Z for Zachariah* leaves her valley home, she carries with her the diary in which she records the terrifying days with Mr. Loomis. Now, finally free, Ann searches for the children she wants to teach. Write the daily entries in the diary that you think Ann would have written. You need to decide whether she realizes her goal or finds something else as satisfying.

Here is a sample written by a fifth grade student:

August 24. I have been walking for almost twenty days and have not found any life. Still, I have hope.

August 30. It is so hot in the safe-suit sometimes I want to take it off. Today I was walking and found a giant tree, an oak I think. I decided to climb it. I grabbed a branch and it broke off easily. It was dead, of course. I had forgotten. The tree may have been dead, but inside was something alive. Bugs, small but alive and if there are birds alive, I know what they are eating. I have more hope than ever.

September 3. Last night I had a dream. Not my usual dream of finding a valley, but a truly horrible dream. I dreamed Mr. Loomis was following me. I don't know how he could, because I have the safe-suit. Maybe he lied to me and could make another one. I don't know.

September 13. It is Friday the thirteenth. Believe it or not, it is my lucky day. I saw the birds, I actually saw the birds. I followed them five miles, I think. Now they are sleeping on a tree. I am going to watch them all the time so I don't lose them like Mr. Loomis did. They are flying west. I am very tired. I have not had my terrible dream again. I don't even think he could make another safe suit, even if he wanted to. I am very happy.

September 17. I followed the birds into another town. Too bad it is deserted and brown. In this town there is a library. I went inside and took three books. I would have taken more but they were too heavy. When I came out the birds were gone. I feel like crying. All my hopes and dreams are gone.

September 19. The birds are back!

May 3. I have not written for a long time and I don't think I will ever write again. I have found my valley, my kids. They were waiting for me just like in my dreams. Two days after I came, another wanderer came—without a safe-suit. He came from the west and was looking for others. He will stay with me and my kids. I am very, very happy.[60]

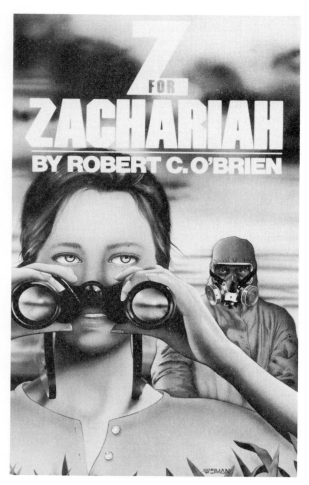

In *Z for Zachariah,* Ann Burden scans the horizon in her search for another living person in a world devastated by nuclear war. (Written by Robert C. O'Brien, cover illustration by Jon Weiman.)

that seemingly has destroyed all other human, animal, and vegetable life. Her desperation is recorded in her diary:

> At first when all the others went away, I hated being alone, and I watched the road all day and most of the night hoping that a car, *anybody,* would come over the hill from either direction. When I slept, I would dream that one came and

drove on past without knowing I was here; then I would wake up and run to the road looking for the taillights disappearing. Then the weeks went by and the radio stations went off, one by one. When the last one went off and stayed off, it came to me, finally, that nobody, no car, was ever going to come.[61]

When Ann's hope is gone that any other human lives, a man in a "safe-suit" walks into the valley. Delight and fear are mixed in Ann's relationship with the strangely aloof Mr. Loomis. She dreams of companionship but finds terror and eventually must hide when he threatens to kill her. There is no hope for mutual trust, making life in the valley intolerable; Ann steals the safe-suit and leaves the valley to go we know not where.

The story evokes a cry for decency essential to the survival of the last humans on earth. Ann, a vulnerable human being, looks for and hopes for the best in Mr. Loomis, but she does not find it. She refuses to compromise her dream, and escapes with the hope that she will find others alive in the world. Part of the beauty of Robert O'Brien's work is his sensitive and exquisite observation of details in things around us that we normally take for granted. Through Ann's words in a diary, O'Brien's perceptions shine strong.

A benefit of science fiction is the flexibility of imagination that it encourages. Reading science fiction aloud, a good way to entice students to read it independently, also engages the interests of those literal-minded students who disparage this genre. Some avid readers, so involved in the here-and-now, have little patience for reading about a make-believe future. These same children, of course, are the very ones who may some day turn science fiction into science fact. They are intuitive in perceiving relations, and, by exposure to science fiction, become more imaginative in approaching solutions to problems. Perhaps they are the ones who need it most.

ACTIVITY: TEACHER TO STUDENT

NUCLEAR POWER (I–A)   Early science fiction tended to emphasize the potential of nuclear power, whereas more recent works emphasize its destructive possibilities. Collect several books on this theme and compare the vision of the future they portray.

Chambers, *Out of Time*
Johnson and Johnson, *The Danger Quotient*
Lawrence, *Children of the Dust*
Strieber, *Wolf of Shadows*
Swindells, *Brother in the Land*

Activities Prepare a chart to list the positive and negative features of nuclear power as described in numerous books. For example,

Title	Positive	Negative
Wolf of Shadows	Animals help humans	Nuclear winter, no food

RECOMMENDED READING

Small Worlds Close Up

Bailey, Carolyn Sherwin. *Miss Hickory*. Illustrated by Ruth Gannett. 1946. Reprint. New York: Viking, 1962.

Clapp, Patricia. *King of the Dollhouse*. Illustrated by Judith Gwyn Brown. New York: Lothrop, Lee & Shepard, 1974.

Field, Rachael. *Hitty, Her First Hundred Years*. Illustrated by Dorothy P. Lathrop. New York: Macmillan, 1938.

Godden, Rumer. *The Doll's House*. Illustrated by Tasha Tudor. 1947. Reprint. New York: Viking, 1962.

———. *Impunity Jane*. Illustrated by Adrienne Adams. New York: Viking, 1954.

Krensky, Stephen. *A Troll in Passing*. New York: Atheneum, 1980.

Nixon, Joan Lowery. *The Gift*. Illustrated by Andrew Glass. New York: Macmillan, 1983.

Sleator, William. *Among the Dolls*. Illustrated by Trina Schart Hyman. New York: Dutton, 1975.

Animal Fantasy

Atwater, Richard, and Florence Atwater. *Mr. Popper's Penguins*. Illustrated by Robert Lawson. Boston: Little, Brown, 1938.

Bell, Clare. *Ratha's Creature*. New York: Atheneum, 1983.

———. *Tomorrow's Sphinx*. New York: Atheneum, 1986.

Cleary, Beverly. *The Mouse and the Motorcycle*. Illustrated by Louis Darling. New York: Morrow, 1965.

———. *Runaway Ralph*. Illustrated by Louis Darling. New York: Morrow, 1970.

Corbett, W. J. *The Song of Pentecost*. Illustrated by Martin Ursell. New York: Dutton, 1983.

Drury, Roger W. *The Champion of Merrimack County*. Illustrated by Fritz Wegner. Boston: Little, Brown, 1976.

Jarrell, Randall. *The Bat-Poet*. Illustrated by Maurice Sendak. New York: Macmillan, 1965.

Lawson, Robert. *Rabbit Hill*. New York: Viking, 1944.

———. *The Tough Winter*. New York: Viking, 1954.

Macaulay, David. *Baaa*. Illustrated by David Macaulay. Boston: Houghton Mifflin, 1985.

———. *Harry Cat's Pet Puppy*. Illustrated by Garth Williams. New York: Farrar, Straus & Giroux,

1974.

Stolz, Mary Slattery. *Quentin Corn*. Illustrated by Pamela Johnson. Boston: Godine, 1985.

Wangerin, Walter. *The Book of the Dun Cow*. New York: Harper & Row, 1978.

Fantasy as Mystery

Alcock, Vivien. *The Stonewalkers*. New York: Delacorte, 1983.

Bellairs, John. *The Figure in the Shadow*. New York: Dial, 1975.

Dexter, Catherine. *The Oracle Doll*. New York: Macmillan, 1985.

Dickinson, Peter. *Healer*. New York: Delacorte, 1985.

Fleischman, Paul. *Coming-and-Going Men: Four Tales*. Illustrated by Randy Gaul. New York: Harper & Row, 1985.

———. *Graven Images*. Illustrated by Andrew Glass. New York: Harper & Row, 1982.

———. *The Half-a-Moon Inn*. New York: Harper & Row, 1980.

Lively, Penelope. *Uninvited Ghosts and Other Stories*. Illustrated by John Lawrence. New York: Dutton, 1985.

Mahy, Margaret. *The Haunting*. New York: Atheneum, 1982.

Snyder, Zilpha. *The Witches of Worm*. New York: Atheneum, 1972.

Light Fantasy

Baker, Betty. *Seven Spells to Farewell*. New York: Macmillan, 1982.

Brittain, Bill. *Who Knew There'd Be Ghosts*. New York: Harper & Row, 1985.

Byars, Betsy. *The Computer Nut*. New York: Viking, 1984.

Dahl, Roald. *James and the Giant Peach*. Illustrated by Nancy Ekholm Burkert. New York: Knopf, 1961.

———. *Charlie and the Chocolate Factory*. Illustrated by Joseph Schindelman. New York: Knopf, 1964.

Konigsburg, E. L. *Up from Jericho Tel*. New York: Atheneum, 1986.

Pinkwater, Daniel. *The Snarkout Boys and the Avocado of Death*. New York: Lothrop, Lee & Shepard, 1982.

Time Slip Fantasy

Allan, Mabel Esther. *Romansgrove*. Illustrated by Gail Owens. New York: Atheneum, 1975.

Anderson, Margaret J. *In the Circle of Time*. New York, Knopf, 1979.

———. *In the Keep of Time*. New York: Knopf, 1977.

———. *The Mists of Time*. New York: Knopf, 1984.

Bond, Nancy. *A String in the Harp*. New York: Atheneum, McElderry, 1976.

Boston, Lucy M. *The Stones of Green Knowe*. Illustrated by Peter Boston. New York: Atheneum, 1976.

Curry, Jane Louise, *Poor Tom's Ghost*. New York: Atheneum, 1977.

Garner, Alan. *Red Shift*. New York: Macmillan, 1973.

Lively, Penelope. *The Ghost of Thomas Kempe*. Illustrated by Anthony Maitland. New York: Dutton, 1973.

———. *The Whispering Knights*. Illustrated by Gareth Floyd. New York: Dutton, 1976.

Mayne, William. *Earthfasts*. New York: Dutton, 1967.

Merrill, Jean. *The Pushcart War*. New York: Dell, 1978.

Ormondroyd, Edward. *All in Good Time*. Illustrated by Ruth Robbins. Boston: Parnassus, 1975.

———. *Time at the Top*. Illustrated by Peggie Bach. Boston: Parnassus, 1963.

Rodowsky, Colby. *The Gathering Room*. New York: Farrar, Straus & Giroux, 1981.

Wallin, Luke, *The Slavery Ghosts*. New York: Bradbury, 1983.

Wiseman, David. *Adam's Common*. Boston: Houghton Mifflin, 1984.

Quest Stories

Garner, Alan. *Elidor*. New York: Philomel, 1979.

———. *The Owl Service*. New York: Walck, 1968.

Hearne, Betsy. *Home*. Illustrated by Trina Schart Hyman. New York: Atheneum, 1979.

———. *South Star*. New York: Atheneum, 1977.

Jones, Diana Wynne. *The Spellcoats*. New York: Atheneum, 1979.

McKillip, Patricia A. *Harpist in the Wind*. New York: Atheneum, 1979.

———. *Heir of Sea and Fire*. New York: Atheneum, 1977.

———. *Riddle-Master of Hed*. New York: Atheneum, 1976.

Pierce, Meredith Ann. *The Darkangel*. Boston: Little, Brown, Atlantic, 1982.

———. *A Gathering of Gargoyles*. Boston: Little, Brown, Atlantic, 1984.

Yep, Laurence. *Dragon of the Lost Sea*. New York: Harper & Row, 1982.

———. *Dragon Steel*. New York: Harper & Row. 1985.

Literary Lore

Andersen, Hans Christian. *The Princess and the Pea*. Illustrated by Paul Galdone. New York: Seabury, 1978.

———. *The Fir Tree*. Illustrated by Nancy Eckholm Burkert. New York: Harper & Row, 1970.

Arkin, Alan. *The Lemming Condition*. Illustrated by Joan Sandin. New York: Harper & Row, 1976.

———. *The Clearing*. New York: Harper & Row, 1986.

Babbitt, Natalie. *The Devil's Storybook*. New York: Farrar, Straus & Giroux, 1974.

———. *The Devil's Other Storybook*. New York: Farrar, Straus & Giroux, 1987.

———. *Knee Knock Rise*. New York: Farrar, Straus & Giroux, 1970.

Godden, Rumer. *The Dragon of Og.* Illustrated by Pauline Baynes. New York: Viking, 1981.

Haley, Gail E. *Birdsong.* New York: Crown, 1984.

Hunter, Mollie. *The Wicked One.* New York: Harper & Row, 1977.

———. *The Knight of the Golden Plain.* Illustrated by Marc Simont. New York: Harper & Row, 1983.

McKinley, Robin. *The Door in the Hedge.* New York: Greenwillow, 1981.

———, ed. *Imaginary Lands.* New York: Greenwillow, 1986.

Maguire, Gregory. *The Dream Stealer.* New York: Harper & Row, 1983.

Nesbit, E. *The Deliverers of Their Country.* Illustrated by Lisbeth Zwerger. Picture Book Studio, Natick, Mass.: 1985.

O'Shea, Pat. *The Hounds of the Morrigan.* New York: Holiday House, 1986.

Science Fiction

Ames, Mildred. *Anna to the Infinite Power.* New York: Scribner's, 1981.

Christopher, John. *Empty World.* New York: Dutton, 1978.

Engdahl, Sylvia. *This Star Shall Abide.* New York: Atheneum, 1972.

———. *Doors of the Universe.* New York: Atheneum, 1981.

Heinlein, Robert A. *Have Space Suit, Will Travel.* New York: Scribner's, 1977.

———. *Tunnel in the Sky.* New York: Scribner's, 1955.

Hoover, H. M. *The Bell Tree.* New York: Viking, 1982.

———. *This Time of Darkness.* New York: Viking, 1980.

———. *Another Heaven, Another Earth.* New York: Viking, 1981.

———. *The Lost Star.* New York: Viking, 1979.

———. *Return to Earth.* New York: Viking, 1980.

Karl, Jean E. *The Turning Place: Stories of the Future Past.* New York: Dutton, 1976.

———. *But We Are Not of Earth.* New York: Dutton, 1981.

———. *Strange Tomorrow.* New York: Dutton, 1985.

Paton Walsh, Jill. *The Green Book.* Illustrated by Lloyd Bloom. New York: Farrar, Straus & Giroux, 1982.

Slote, Alfred. *My Robot Buddy.* New York: Harper & Row, 1975.

———. *The Trouble on Janus.* Philadelphia: Lippincott, 1985.

Townsend, John Rowe. *The Creatures.* Philadelphia: Lippincott, 1980.

Yolen, Jane H., comp. *Shape Shifters: Fantasy and Science Fiction Tales About Humans Who Can Change Their Shapes.* New York: Seabury, 1978.

———. Martin H. Greenberg, and

Charles G. Waugh, eds. *Dragons and Dreams: A Collection of New Fantasy and Science Fiction Stories.* New York: Harper & Row, 1986.

Poetry

Carroll, Lewis. *Poems of Lewis Carroll.* Edited by Myra Cohn Livingston. New York: Crowell, 1973.

Cole, William. *Poems of Magic and Spells.* Illustrated by Peggy Bacon. New York: Putnam, 1960.

Hopkins, Lee Bennett, comp. *A-Haunting We Will Go.* New York: Whitman, 1977.

Hughes, Ted. *Moon-Whales and Other Poems.* Illustrated by Leonard Baskin. New York: Viking, 1976.

Larrick, Nancy. *Bring Me All Your Dreams.* New York: M. Evans, 1980.

Prelutsky, Jack. *Nightmares: Poems to Trouble Your Sleep.* Illustrated by Arnold Lobel. New York: Greenwillow, 1976.

Wallace, Daisy, ed. *Monster Poems.* Illustrated by Kay Chorao. New York: Holiday House, 1976.

———. *Witch Poems.* Illustrated by Trina Schart Hyman. New York: Holiday House, 1976.

Silverstein, Shel. *A Light in the Attic.* New York: Harper & Row, 1981.

———. *Where the Sidewalk Ends.* New York: Harper & Row, 1974.

PROFESSIONAL REFERENCES

Cameron, Eleanor. *The Green and Burning Tree: On the Writing and Enjoyment of Children's Books.* 1962. Reprint. Boston: Little, Brown, 1969.

Cook, Elizabeth. *The Ordinary and the Fabulous.* New York: Cambridge University Press, 1969.

Cullinan, Bernice E., Kathy T. Harwood, and S. Lee Galda. "The

Reader and the Story: Comprehension and Response." In *Journal of Research and Development in Education* 16, no. 3 (Spring 1983): 29–38.

Egoff, Sheila A. *Thursday's Child: Trends and Patterns in Contemporary Children's Literature.* Chicago: American Library Association, 1981.

Hearne, Betsy, and Marilyn Kaye, eds. *Celebrating Children's Books: Essays on Children's Literature in Honor of Zena Sutherland.* New York: Lothrop, Lee & Shepard, 1981.

Heinlein, Robert. "Ray Guns and Rocket Ships." *Library Journal* 78 (July 1953): 1188.

Hunter, Mollie. *Talent Is Not*

Enough: Mollie Hunter on Writing for Children. New York: Harper & Row, 1976.

Hyman, Trina Schart. "Caldecott Acceptance Speech." *Horn Book Magazine* 61, no. 4 (July/August 1985): 415–16.

Kingman, Lee, ed. *Newbery and Caldecott Medal Books 1966–1975.* Boston: Horn Book, 1975.

Lewis, C. S. *Surprised by Joy: The*

Shape of My Early Life. New York: Harcourt Brace, 1966.

Macdonald, George. *Phantasies: A Faerie Romance for Men and Women.* 1858. Reprint. New York: Ballantine, 1970.

Nilsen, Alleen, and Ken L. Donelson. *Literature for Today's Young Adults,* 2nd ed. Glenview, Ill.: Scott, Foresman, 1985.

Terry, June S. "To Seek and to

Find: Quest Literature for Children." In *Children's Literature: Criticism and Response.* Edited by Mary Lou White. 139. Westerville, Ohio: Merrill, 1976.

Wood, Michael. "Coffee Break for Sisyphus: The Point of Science Fiction." *New York Review of Books* (2 October 1975): 3–4, 6–7.

NOTES

1. Langston Hughes, "Dreams," in *Don't You Turn Back: Poems by Langston Hughes,* ed. Lee Bennett Hopkins, illus. Ann Grifalconi (New York: Knopf, 1969), 44.
2. Lloyd Alexander, "The Grammar of Story," in *Celebrating Children's Books: Essays on Children's Literature in Honor of Zena Sutherland,* eds. Betsy Hearne and Marilyn Kaye (New York: Lothrop, Lee & Shepard, 1981), 3.
3. Eleanor Cameron, *The Green and Burning Tree* (Boston: Little, Brown, 1969), 3–4.
4. Elizabeth Cook, *The Ordinary and the Fabulous* (New York: Cambridge University Press, 1969), 5.
5. E. B. White, *Letter to Readers,* pamphlet from Children's Dept., Harper & Row, New York City.
6. Edward Eager, *Half Magic* (New York: Harcourt Brace, 1954), 8–9.
7. J. R. R. Tolkien, *The Hobbit* (Boston: Houghton Mifflin, 1938), 15.
8. Robin McKinley, *The Hero and the Crown* (New York: Greenwillow, 1984), 3.
9. Mollie Hunter, *The Furl of Fairy Wind: Four Stories,* illus. Stephen Gammell (New York: Harper & Row, 1977), 3.
10. Ibid., 15.

11. Pauline Clarke, *The Return of the Twelves* (New York: Coward, McCann & Geoghegan, 1963), 221–22.
12. Tove Jansson, *Tales from Moominvalley* (New York: Walck, 1964), 16.
13. Ibid., 21.
14. Margery Williams, *The Velveteen Rabbit* (New York: Doubleday, 1958), 17.
15. Kenneth Grahame, *The Wind in the Willows* (New York: Avon, 1965), 9.
16. Ibid., 11.
17. Ibid., 121.
18. E. B. White, *Charlotte's Web* (New York: Harper & Row, 1952), 34.
19. Ibid., 41.
20. Developed by Lillian Brightly, King's Road School, Madison, N.J., April 1981.
21. William Steig, *Farmer Palmer's Wagon Ride* (New York: Farrar, Straus & Giroux, 1974), unpaged.
22. Created by the fourth grade class taught by Donna Carrara, Montclair Kimberly Academy, Montclair, N.J., November 1986.
23. Eleanor Cameron, *The Green and Burning Tree: On the Writing and Enjoyment of Children's Books* (Boston: Little, Brown, 1969), 71. The poetry is from T. S. Eliot, "Burnt Norton," in *Collected Poems, 1909–1962*

(New York: Harcourt Brace Jovanovich, 1963).
24. Madeleine L'Engle, *A Wrinkle in Time* (New York: Farrar, Straus & Giroux, 1962), 75–76.
25. Ibid., 76.
26. C. S. Lewis, *The Lion, the Witch and the Wardrobe* (New York: Macmillan, 1951), 45–46.
27. Eleanor Cameron, *The Court of the Stone Children* (New York: Dutton, 1968), 5.
28. Developed by Margaret Anzul, Madison Elementary School, Madison, N.J., 1979.
29. Cameron, *Stone Children,* 30.
30. Cameron, *The Green and Burning Tree,* 90.
31. C. S. Lewis, *The Magician's Nephew,* illus. Pauline Baynes (New York: Macmillan, 1955), 92.
32. June S. Terry, "To Seek and to Find: Quest Literature for Children," in *Children's Literature: Criticism and Response,* ed. Mary Lou White (Columbus, Ohio: Merrill, 1976), 139.
33. Bernice E. Cullinan, Kathy T. Harwood, and S. Lee Galda, "The Reader and the Story: Comprehension and Response," in *Journal of Research and Development in Education* 16, no. 3 (Spring 1983): 29–38.
34. Mollie Hunter, *Talent is Not Enough* (New York: Harper & Row, 1976), 65.
35. Mollie Hunter, *A Stranger Came*

Ashore (New York: Harper & Row, 1975), 1.

36. Rosemary Sutcliff, *The Road to Camlann* (New York: Dutton, 1982), 7.

37. Trina Schart Hyman, "Caldecott Medal Acceptance," in *Horn Book Magazine* 61, no. 4 (July/August 1985): 415–16.

38. Natalie Babbitt, promotional material from Farrar, Straus & Giroux, New York City.

39. Natalie Babbitt, *Tuck Everlasting* (New York: Farrar, Straus & Giroux, 1975), 63.

40. Natalie Babbitt, "Fantasy and the Classic Hero," in *Innocence and Experience: Essays and Conversation on Children's Literature*, comps. Barbara Harrison and Gregory Maguire (New York: Lothrop, Lee & Shepard, 1987), 148–55.

41. Isaac Bashevis Singer, *Zlateh the Goat,* illus. Maurice Sendak (New York: Harper & Row, 1966), 86.

42. Robin McKinley, *Beauty: A Retelling of the Story of Beauty and the Beast* (New York: Harper & Row, 1978), 168.

43. Roland Green, "Modern Science Fiction and Fantasy," *Illinois Schools Journal,* 57 (Fall 1977), 46.

44. Isaac Asimov, "Isaac Asimov," pamphlet from Houghton Mifflin, Children's Book Dept., Boston.

45. Ray Bradbury, *Something About the Author,* Vol. 11, ed. Anne Commire (Detroit: Gale, 1978), 32.

46. Robert A. Heinlein, "Ray Guns and Rocket Ships," *Library Journal,* 78 (July 1953): 1188.

47. Sheila A. Egoff, *Thursday's Child: Trends and Patterns in Contemporary Children's Literature* (Chicago: American Library Association, 1981), 131.

48. Isaac Asimov quoted in Aileen Pace Nilsen and Kenneth L. Donelson, *Literature for Today's Young Adults* (Glenview, Ill.: Scott, Foresman, 1985), 177.

49. Michael Wood, "Coffee Break for Sisyphus: The Point of Science Fiction," *New York Review of Books* 2 (October 1975), 3–4, 6–7.

50. Robert Heinlein, *Farmer in the Sky* (New York: Scribner's, 1950), 33–34.

51. Cullinan, Harwood, and Galda, "The Reader and the Story," 36.

52. Constance A. Mellon, "Teenagers Do Read: What Rural Youth Say About Leisure Reading," *School Library Journal* 33, no. 6 (February 1987): 27–30.

53. Isaac Asimov, pamphlet from Houghton Mifflin, Boston.

54. Ibid.

55. Bernice E. Cullinan, "An Interview with Isaac Asimov," *Teaching Critical Reading and Thinking to Children and Adolescents,* taught by Bernice E. Cullinan, dir. Roy Allen, New York University's "Sunrise Semester," CBS, 8 May 1978.

56. Sylvia Engdahl, ed. *Anywhere, Anywhen: Stories of Tomorrow* (New York: Atheneum, 1976), viii.

57. Arthur C. Clarke, *Dolphin Island: A Story of People of the Sea* (New York: Holt, Rinehart & Winston, 1963), 30–31.

58. Paula Sargent, *Earthseed* (New York: Harper & Row, 1983), 4.

59. Isaac Asimov, Martin H. Greenberg, and Charles G. Waugh, eds., *Young Star Travelers* (New York: Harper & Row, 1986), xi.

60. Diane Litvak, student, Worthington Hills School, Worthington, Ohio.

61. Robert C. O'Brien, *Z for Zachariah* (New York: Atheneum, 1975), 5.

CHILDREN'S BOOKS CITED

Adams, Richard. *Watership Down.* New York: Macmillan, 1974.

Adkins, Jan. *A Storm Without Rain.* Illustrated by Jan Adkins. Boston: Little, Brown, 1983.

Alexander, Lloyd. *The Beggar Queen.* New York: Dutton, 1984.

———. *The Black Cauldron.* New York: Holt, Rinehart & Winston, 1965.

———. *The Book of Three.* New York: Holt, Rinehart & Winston, 1964.

———. *The Castle of Llyr.* New York: Holt, Rinehart & Winston, 1966.

———. *The Cat Who Wished to Be a Man.* New York: Dutton, 1973.

———. *The El Dorado Adventure.* New York: Dutton, 1987.

———. *The High King.* Illustrated by Evaline Ness. New York: Holt, Rinehart & Winston, 1968.

———. *The Illyrian Adventure.* New York: Dutton, 1986.

———. *The Kestrel.* New York: Dutton, 1982.

———. *Taran Wanderer.* New York: Holt, Rinehart & Winston, 1967.

———. *Westmark.* New York: Dutton, 1981.

Andersen, Hans Christian. *The Emperor's New Clothes.* Illustrated by Virginia Lee Burton. Boston: Houghton Mifflin, 1949.

———. *The Emperor's New Clothes.* Illustrated by Anne Rockwell. New York: Harper & Row, 1982.

———. *The Emperor's New Clothes.* Illustrated by Janet Stevens. New York: Holiday House, 1985.

———. *The Emperor's New Clothes.* Illustrated by Nadine B. Westcott. Boston: Little, Brown, 1984.

———. *The Nightingale.* Translated

by Eva Le Gallienne, illustrated by Nancy Eckholm Burkert. New York: Harper & Row, 1965.

———. *The Steadfast Tin Soldier*. Illustrated by Monika Laimgruber. New York: Atheneum, 1971.

———. *Thumbelina*. Illustrated by Susan Jeffers. New York: Dial, 1979.

———. *The Ugly Duckling*. Translated by Anne Stewart, illustrated by Monika Laimgruber. New York: Greenwillow, 1985.

Asimov, Isaac, Martin H. Greenberg, and Charles G. Waugh, eds. *Young Extraterrestrials*. New York: Harper & Row, 1984.

———. *Young Ghosts*. New York: Harper & Row, 1985.

———. *Young Monsters*. New York: Harper & Row, 1985.

———. *Young Mutants*. New York: Harper & Row, 1984.

———. *Young Star Travelers*. New York: Harper & Row, 1986.

———. *Young Witches and Warlocks*. New York: Harper & Row, 1987.

Babbitt, Natalie. *The Eyes of the Amaryllis*. New York: Farrar, Straus & Giroux, 1977.

———. *The Search for Delicious*. New York: Farrar, Straus & Giroux, 1969.

———. *Tuck Everlasting*. New York: Farrar, Straus & Giroux, 1975.

Banks, Lynne Reid. *The Indian in the Cupboard*. Illustrated by Brock Cole. New York: Doubleday, 1981.

———. *The Return of the Indian*. Illustrated by William Geldart. New York: Doubleday, 1986.

Bond, Michael. *A Bear Called Paddington*. Illustrated by Peggy Fortnum. Boston: Houghton Mifflin, 1958.

———. *More About Paddington*. Illustrated by Peggy Fortnum. Boston: Houghton Mifflin, 1962.

———. *Paddington at Large*. Illustrated by Peggy Fortnum. Boston: Houghton Mifflin, 1963.

———. *Paddington Takes to TV*. Illustrated by Ivar Wood. Boston: Houghton Mifflin, 1966.

Boston, Lucy M. *The Children of Green Knowe*. Illustrated by Peter Boston. New York: Harcourt Brace, 1955.

Brittain, Bill. *The Devil's Donkey*. New York: Harper & Row, 1981.

———. *The Wish Giver*. Illustrated by Andrew Glass. New York: Harper & Row, 1983.

———. *Dr. Dredd's Wagon of Wonders*. Illustrated by Andrew Glass. New York: Harper & Row, 1987.

Cameron, Eleanor. *The Court of the Stone Children*. New York: Dutton, 1973.

Carroll, Lewis. *Through the Looking Glass*. Illustrated by John Tenniel. New York: St. Martin's, 1977.

Cassedy, Sylvia. *Behind the Attic Wall*. New York: Crowell, 1983.

Chambers, Aidan, ed. *Out of Time*. New York: Harper & Row, 1985.

Christopher, John. *The City of Gold and Lead*. New York: Macmillan, 1967.

———. *Dragon Dance*. New York: Dutton, 1986.

———. *Fireball*. New York: Dutton, 1981.

———. *New Found Land*. New York: Dutton, 1983.

———. *The Pool of Fire*. New York: Macmillan, 1968.

———. *The White Mountains*. New York: Macmillan, 1967.

Clarke, Arthur C. *Dolphin Island: A Story of People of the Sea*. New York: Holt, Rinehart & Winston, 1963.

Clarke, Pauline. *The Return of the Twelves*. Illustrated by Bernarda Bryson. New York: Coward, 1963.

Coatsworth, Elizabeth. *The Cat Who Went to Heaven*. Illustrated by Lynd Ward. New York: Macmillan, 1967.

Conly, Jane Leslie. *Rasco and the Rats of NIMH*. Illustrated by Leonard B. Lubin. New York:

Harper & Row, 1986.

Cooper, Susan. *The Dark is Rising*. Illustrated by Alan E. Cober. New York: Atheneum, 1973.

———. *Greenwitch*. New York: Atheneum, 1974.

———. *The Grey King*. New York: Atheneum, 1975.

———. *Over Sea, Under Stone*. Illustrated by Marjorie Gill. New York: Harcourt Brace, 1966.

———. *The Selkie Girl*. Illustrated by Warwick Hutton. New York: Atheneum, McElderry, 1986.

———. *Silver on the Tree*. New York: Atheneum, McElderry, 1977.

Cresswell, Helen. *The Secret World of Polly Flint*. Illustrated by Shirley Felts. New York: Macmillan, 1984.

de Brunhoff, Jean. *The Story of Babar*. 1937. Reprint. New York: Random House, 1960.

de Brunhoff, Laurent. *Babar at the Seashore*. New York: Random House, 1969.

———. *Babar Goes on a Picnic*. New York: Random House, 1969.

———. *Babar Goes Skiing*. New York: Random House, 1969.

———. *Babar the Gardener*. New York: Random House, 1969.

Eager, Edward. *Half Magic*. Illustrated by N. M. Bodecker. New York: Harcourt Brace, 1954.

Engdahl, Sylvia, ed. *Anywhere, Anywhen: Stories of Tomorrow*. New York: Atheneum, 1976.

———. *Enchantress from the Stars*. New York: Atheneum, 1970.

———. *The Far Side of Evil*. Illustrated by Richard Cuffari. New York: Atheneum, 1971.

"Fantasy." Film by Pied Piper. Verdugo City, Calif.

Field, Rachel. *Hitty, Her First Hundred Years*. Illustrated by Dorothy P. Lathrop. New York: Macmillan, 1938.

Fleischman, Sid. *The Whipping Boy*. New York: Greenwillow, 1986.

Fleming, Ian. *Chitty Chitty Bang Bang*. 1964. Reprint. New York:

Scholastic, 1980.

Garner, Alan. *The Weirdstone of Brisingamen.* Philadelphia: Collins, 1960.

Gerstein, Mordicai. *The Seal Mother.* New York: Dial, 1986.

Godden, Rumer. *The Mousewife.* Illustrated by William Péne du Bois. New York: Viking, 1951.

Grahame, Kenneth. *Mole's Christmas: Or Home Sweet Home.* Illustrated by Beverly Gooding. Englewood Cliffs, N.J.: Prentice-Hall, 1983.

———. *The Open Road.* Illustrated by Beverly Gooding. New York: Scribner's, 1980.

———. *The River Bank: From "The Wind in the Willows."* Illustrated by Adrienne Adams. New York: Scribner's, 1977.

———. *Wayfarers All: From The Wind in the Willows.* Illustrated by Beverly Gooding. New York: Scribner's, 1981.

———. *The Wind in the Willows.* Illustrated by E. H. Shepard. 1908. Reprint. New York: Scribner's, 1940.

Heinlein, Robert. *Farmer in the Sky.* Illustrated by Clifford Geary. New York: Scribner's, 1950.

Hodges, Margaret. *Saint George and the Dragon: A Golden Legend Adapted by Margaret Hodges from Edmund Spenser's 'Faerie Queene.'* Illustrated by Trina Schart Hyman. Boston: Little, Brown, 1984.

Hoban, Russell. *The Mouse and His Child.* Illustrated by Lillian Hoban. New York: Harper & Row, 1967.

Holm, Anne. *Peter.* Translated by L. W. Kingsland. New York: Harcourt Brace Jovanovich, 1968.

Hoover, H. M. *The Delikon.* New York: Viking, 1977.

———. *The Shepherd Moon.* New York: Viking, 1984.

Howe, Deborah, and James Howe. *Bunnicula: A Rabbit Tale of Mystery.* Illustrated by Alan Daniel. New York: Atheneum, 1979.

Howe, James. *The Celery Stalks at Midnight.* Illustrated by Leslie Morrill. New York: Atheneum, 1983.

———. *Howliday Inn.* Illustrated by Lynn Munsinger. New York: Atheneum, 1982.

———. *Nighty Nightmare.* New York: Atheneum, 1987.

Hughes, Langston. "Dreams." In *Don't You Turn Back: Poems by Langston Hughes.* Edited by Lee Bennett Hopkins, illustrated by Ann Grifalconi. New York: Knopf, 1969.

Hunter, Mollie. *A Furl of Fairy Wind.* New York: Harper & Row, 1977.

———. *The Kelpie's Pearls.* Illustrated by Stephen Gammell. New York: Harper & Row, 1976.

———. *A Stranger Came Ashore.* New York: Harper & Row, 1975.

———. *The Walking Stones.* New York: Harper & Row, 1970.

Huxley, Aldous. *Brave New World.* New York: Harper & Row, 1932.

Jansson, Tove. *Tales from Moominvalley.* Translated by Thomas Warburton. New York: Walck, 1964.

Johnson, Annabel, and Edgar Johnson. *The Danger Quotient.* New York: Harper & Row, 1984.

Jones, Diana Wynne. *Archer's Goon.* New York: Greenwillow, 1983.

———. *Dogsbody.* New York: Greenwillow, 1977.

———. *Howl's Moving Castle.* New York: Greenwillow, 1986.

Juster, Norton. *The Phantom Tollbooth.* Illustrated by Jules Feiffer. New York: Random House, 1961.

Kendall, Carol. *The Gammage Cup.* 1959. Reprint, San Diego: Harcourt Brace Jovanovich, 1986.

Kennedy, Richard. *Amy's Eyes.* Illustrated by Richard Egielski. New York: Harper & Row, 1985.

King-Smith, Dick. *Babe: The Gallant Pig.* Illustrated by Mary Rayner. New York: Crown, 1985.

———. *Magnus Power-Mouse.* Illustrated by Mary Rayner. New York: Harper & Row, 1984.

———. *Pigs Might Fly.* Illustrated by Mary Rayner. New York: Viking, 1982.

———. *The Queen's Nose.* Illustrated by Jill Bennett. New York: Harper & Row, 1985.

Lawrence, Louise. *Children of the Dust.* New York: Harper & Row, 1985.

Lawson. Robert. *Rabbit Hill.* New York: Viking, 1944.

Le Guin, Ursula. *The Farthest Shore.* New York: Atheneum, 1972.

———. *A Wizard of Earthsea.* Illustrated by Ruth Robbins. Boston: Parnassus, 1968.

L'Engle, Madeleine. *A Swiftly Tilting Planet.* New York: Farrar, Straus & Giroux, 1977.

———. *A Wind in the Door.* New York: Farrar, Straus & Giroux, 1973.

———. *A Wrinkle in Time.* New York: Farrar, Straus & Giroux, 1962.

Lewis, C. S. *The Lion, The Witch, and the Wardrobe.* Illustrated by Pauline Baynes. New York: Macmillan, 1950.

———. *The Magician's Nephew.* Illustrated by Pauline Baynes. New York: Macmillan, 1955.

Lindgren, Astrid. *Pippi Longstocking.* Translated by Florence Lamborn, illustrated by Louis S. Glanzman. New York: Viking, 1950.

———. *Ronia, The Robber's Daughter.* New York: Viking, 1983.

Lovett, Margaret. *The Great and Terrible Quest.* New York: Holt, Rinehart & Winston, 1967.

Lunn, Janet. *The Root Cellar.* New York: Scribner's, 1983.

McKinley, Robin. *Beauty: A Retelling of the Story of Beauty and the Beast.* New York: Harper & Row, 1978.

———. *The Blue Sword.* New York: Greenwillow, 1982.

———. *The Hero and the Crown.*

New York: Greenwillow, 1984.

Milne, A. A. *The House at Pooh Corner.* Illustrated by Ernest H. Shepard. New York: Dutton, 1928.

―――. *Now We Are Six.* Illustrated by Ernest H. Shepard. New York: Dutton, 1927.

―――. *When We Were Very Young.* Illustrated by Ernest H. Shepard. New York: Dutton, 1924.

―――. *Winnie the Pooh.* Illustrated by Ernest H. Shepard. New York: Dutton, 1926.

Murphy, Shirley Rousseau. *Silver Woven in My Hair.* Illustrated by Alan Tiegreen. New York: Atheneum, 1977.

Nesbit, E. *The Enchanted Castle.* New York: Penguin, 1986.

Nichols, Ruth. *A Walk Out of the World.* Illustrated by Trina Schart Hyman. New York: Harcourt Brace Jovanovich, 1969.

Norton, Andre. *Steel Magic.* Illustrated by Robin Jacques. New York: Archway, 1978.

Norton, Mary. *The Borrowers.* Illustrated by Beth Krush and Joe Krush. New York: Harcourt Brace, 1953.

―――. *The Borrowers Afield.* Illustrated by Beth Krush and Joe Krush. New York: Harcourt Brace, 1955.

―――. *The Borrowers Afloat.* Illustrated by Beth Krush and Joe Krush. New York: Harcourt Brace, 1959.

―――. *The Borrowers Aloft.* Illustrated by Beth Krush and Joe Krush. New York: Harcourt Brace, 1961.

―――. *The Borrowers Avenged.* Illustrated by Beth Krush and Joe Krush. San Diego: Harcourt Brace Jovanovich, 1982.

O'Brien, Robert C. *Mrs. Frisby and the Rats of NIMH.* New York: Atheneum, 1971.

―――. *Z for Zachariah.* New York: Atheneum, 1975.

Orwell, George. *1984.* New York: Harcourt Brace, 1949.

Park, Ruth. *Playing Beatie Bow.* New York: Atheneum, 1982.

Pearce, Philippa A. *Tom's Midnight Garden.* Illustrated by Susan Einzig. Philadelphia: Lippincott, 1959.

Péne du Bois, William. *The Twenty-One Balloons.* New York: Viking, 1947.

Potter, Beatrix. *The Tale of Peter Rabbit.* New York: Warne, 1902.

―――. *The Tale of Squirrel Nutkin.* New York: Warne, 1903.

Raskin, Ellen. *The Westing Game.* New York: Dutton, 1978.

"Reading for the Fun of It: Fantasy." Film by Guidance Associates. Pleasantville, N.Y.

Rodgers, Mary. *A Billion for Boris.* New York: Harper & Row, 1974.

―――. *Freaky Friday.* New York: Harper & Row, 1972.

―――. *Summer Switch.* New York: Harper & Row, 1982.

Sargent, Sarah. *Earthseed.* New York: Harper & Row, 1987.

―――. *Weird Henry Berg.* New York: Crown, 1980.

Seidler, Tor. *A Rat's Tale.* Illustrated by Fred Marcellino. New York: Farrar, Straus & Giroux, 1986.

Selden, George. *The Cricket in Times Square.* Illustrated by Garth Williams. New York: Farrar, Straus & Giroux, 1960.

―――. *Tucker's Countryside.* Illustrated by Garth Williams. New York: Farrar, Straus & Giroux, 1969.

Sharp, Margery. *Miss Bianca.* Illustrated by Garth Williams. Boston: Little, Brown, 1962.

Silverberg, Robert, ed. *The Science Fiction Hall of Fame.* 1970. Reprint. New York: Avon, 1985.

Singer, Isaac Bashevis. *Naftali the Storyteller and His Horse, Sus, and Other Stories.* Illustrated by Margot Zemach. New York: Farrar, Straus & Giroux, 1976.

―――. *Zlateh the Goat and Other Stories.* Illustrated by Maurice Sendak. New York: Harper &

Row, 1984.

―――. *Zlateh the Goat.* Film by Weston Woods. Weston, Conn.

Steig, William. *Abel's Island.* New York: Farrar, Straus & Giroux, 1976.

―――. *The Amazing Bone.* New York: Farrar, Straus & Giroux, 1976.

―――. *Amos and Boris.* New York: Farrar, Straus & Giroux, 1971.

―――. *Caleb and Kate.* New York: Farrar, Straus & Giroux, 1977.

―――. *Doctor De Soto.* New York: Farrar, Straus & Giroux, 1982.

―――. *Dominic.* New York: Farrar, Straus & Giroux, 1972.

―――. *Farmer Palmer's Wagon Ride.* New York: Farrar, Straus & Giroux, 1974.

―――. *Roland the Minstrel Pig.* New York: Harper & Row, 1968.

―――. *Solomon the Rusty Nail.* New York: Farrar, Straus & Giroux, 1985.

―――. *Sylvester and the Magic Pebble.* Old Tappan, N.J.: Windmill Books, 1969.

―――. *Tiffky Doofky.* New York: Farrar, Straus & Giroux, 1979.

Strieber, Whitley. *Wolf of Shadows.* New York: Knopf, 1985.

Sutcliff, Rosemary. *The Light Beyond the Forest.* New York: Dutton, 1980.

―――. *The Road to Camlann.* New York: Dutton, 1982.

―――. *The Sword and the Circle: King Arthur and the Knights of the Round Table.* New York: Dutton, 1981.

Swindells, Robert. *Brothers in the Land.* New York: Holiday House, 1985.

Tolkien, J. R. R. *The Hobbit.* Boston: Houghton Mifflin, 1938.

―――. *The Lord of the Rings.* 1954. Reprint. Winchester, Mass., Allen & Unwin, 1979.

Travers, Pamela. *Mary Poppins.* Illustrated by Mary Shepard. San Diego: Harcourt Brace Jovanovich, 1981.

Twain, Mark. *The Prince and the*

Pauper. New York: Penguin, 1983.

Uttley, Alison. *A Traveler in Time*. Illustrated by Phyllis Bray. Winchester, Mass.: Faber, 1981.

Van Vogt, A. E. *The Voyage of the Space Beagle*. 1939. Reprint. New York: Simon & Schuster, 1950.

Verne, Jules. *Around the World in Eighty Days*. 1873. Reprint. New York: Dell, 1987.

———. *20,000 Leagues Under the Sea:* Illustrated by Charles Molina, 1869. Reprint. New York: Macmillan, 1962.

Voigt, Cynthia. *Building Blocks*. New York: Atheneum, 1984.

Wells, H. G. *The War of the Worlds*. New York: Random House, 1960.

White, E. B. *Charlotte's Web*. Illustrated by Garth Williams. New York: Harper & Row, 1952.

———. *Stuart Little*. Illustrated by Garth Williams. New York: Harper & Row, 1945.

White, Terrence H. *The Once and Future King, Part One: Sword in the Stone*. New York: Dell, 1963.

Williams, Margery. *The Velveteen Rabbit*. Illustrated by Michael Hague. New York: H. Holt, 1983.

———. *The Velveteen Rabbit*. Illustrated by William Nicholson. 1922. Reprint. New York: Doubleday, 1958.

———. *The Velveteen Rabbit*. Illustrated by Ilse Plume. San Diego: Harcourt Brace Jovanovich, 1987.

Williams, Sheila, and Cynthia Manson, eds. *Tales from Isaac Asimov's Science Fiction*. San Diego: Harcourt Brace Jovanovich, 1986.

Wiseman, David. *Jeremy Visick*. Boston: Houghton Mifflin, 1981.

7

Poetry and Verse

Inside a Poem

It doesn't always have to rhyme,
but there's the repeat of a beat, somewhere
an inner chime that makes you want to
tap your feet or swerve in a curve;
a lilt, a leap, a lightning-split;—
thunderstruck the consonants jut,
while the vowels open wide as waves in the noon-
      blue sea.

You hear with your heels, your eyes feel
what they never touched before:
fins on a bird, feathers on a deer;
taste all colors, inhale
memory and tomorrow and always the tang is
      today.[1]

Eve Merriam

WHAT IS POETRY?

oets themselves are the best source for a definition of poetry. Eve Merriam, for instance, captures the essence of poetry and reveals some of its characteristics as she describes what is *Inside a Poem* (I). She says poetry has a beat that repeats, words that chime, and images that we have not imagined before. Eleanor Farjeon gives a less tangible definition in her *Poems for Children*:

POETRY

What is Poetry? Who knows?
Not the rose, but the scent of the rose;
Not the sky, but the light in the sky;
Not the fly, but the gleam of the fly;
Not the sea, but the sound of the sea;
Not myself, but what makes me
See, hear, and feel something that prose
Cannot: and what it is, who knows?[2]

Actually, we can say more easily what poetry does than what it is; poetry eludes definition. We know that poetry can make us chuckle or laugh out loud. It can startle us with an unexpected turn of events or surprise us with its clarity. It can also bring a peacefulness and a sense of repose. Some poems express feelings that we did not even know we had until we read them; then we say, "Yes, that's just how it is." Poetry deals with truth—the essence of life and experience. Poetry, says Gregory Corso, is "the opposite of hypocrisy."[3]

Yet we need at least a provisional understanding of what poetry is. Most definitions focus on surface distinctions, such as elements, form, or the way it looks on a page, and many think that poetry is distinguished by the use of rhyme or meter. Indeed, children often remark, "It looks different." These are superficial distinctions, the most salient aspect of poetry being its highly charged, condensed, and concentrated language, which uses so few words to say so much. Poetry is filled with words artistically organized and pressurized in ways that call our attention to experiences we have not known or fully recognized. Poetry is a poet's intuition of truth.

Myra Cohn Livingston cites fellow poet May Swenson's distinction between poetry and other modes of expression:

Poetry doesn't tell; it shows. Prose tells.
Poetry is not philosophy; poetry makes things be, right now.
Not an idea, but a happening.
It is not music, but it sounds while showing.
It is mobile; it is a thing taking place—active, interactive, in a place.
It is not thought; it has to do with senses and muscles.
It is not dancing, but it moves while it remains.[4]

Although poetry's words can be familiar ones, they are carefully chosen and placed in such a way as to capture the imagination. The poetic experience is qualified by precise selection and

LANDMARK

Poetry: Songs of Childhood, *1902*

Walter De la Mare was an Englishman whose work epitomized poetry of and for childhood. His first collection of poetry for children, *Songs of Childhood* (P–I), was published in 1902, and was followed by *Peacock Pie, Come Hither,* and *Bells and Grass* (all P–I). Lillian Smith, noted critic of children's literature, praises his capacity to see the rarest charm of familiar in strangeness:

> His poetry is compounded of imagination, vision, and dream, into which beauty breaks through when we least expect it. His mastery of flexible and subtle rhythms is so deft that it is, perhaps, hardly realized. Yet it sweeps us into the mood of the poem almost unaware.[5]

His verses have a unique, nonsensical conception that leads children to transcend the literal and move easily into the world of dreams, with touches of nonsense, wonder about simple things, and the unearthly beauty of dreams. In the introduction to *Bells and Grass,* De la Mare wrote,

> I know well that only the rarest kind of best in anything can be good enough for the young. I know too that in later life it is just . . . possible now and again to recover fleetingly the intense delight, the untellable joy and happiness and fear and grief and pain of our early years, of an all but forgotten childhood. I have, in a flash, in a momentary glimpse, seen again a horse, an oak, a daisy, just as I saw them in those early years, as if with that heart, with those senses.[6]

This illustration from Walter De la Mare's *Peacock Pie* shows how inviting his poetry is for children.

ordering of words. Exceptional poets shape an ordinary, everyday experience into an emotional universal. As Northrop Frye says, ''The poet's job is not to tell you what happened, but what happens: not what did take place, but the kind of thing that always does take place.''[7]

WHAT DOES POETRY DO?

If literature is the lifeblood of the school curriculum, poetry is its heart. How is this so? Poetry makes us laugh, tells us stories, gives us something to think about, and helps us put our feelings into words. Poetry captures the essence of experience.

Poems Make Us Laugh

Whether you like slapstick or subtle puns, there are poems for your brand of humor. Edward Lear, father of nonsense, is remembered for his limericks in *The Complete Nonsense of Edward Lear*. For instance,

> There was a Young Lady of Turkey,
> Who wept when the weather was murky;
> When the day turned out fine,
> She ceased to repine,
> That capricious Young Lady of Turkey.[8]

Myra Cohn Livingston's collection about a ''goody-goody'' boy who does everything right is called *Higgledy-Piggledy* (P-I). The young narrator vents his true feelings at the close of each verse.

> Higgledy-Piggledy
>   always hits homers.
> He's great in the outfield;
>   he's fast at first base.
> He pitches a curve ball
>   and throws out all runners.
>
> (And I wish he'd stumble
> and fall on his face!)

> Higgledy-Piggledy
>   likes to eat liver.
> He drinks healthful juices
>   and passes up Cokes.
> He says that nutritious
>   old squash is delicious.
>
> (And one of these lunchtimes
> I hope that he chokes!)[9]

Poems Tell Stories

Think about stories from childhood that you first heard through poetry. Perhaps ''The Pied Piper of Hamelin,'' ''Casey at Bat,'' ''Hiawatha,'' or another rhyme story comes to mind. Henry Wadsworth Longfellow's ''Paul Revere's Ride,'' a classic narrative poem, is memorable in part from the galloping beat that echoes the sense of the story.

> Listen, my children, and you shall hear
> Of the midnight ride of Paul Revere,
> On the eighteenth of April, in Seventy-five;
> Hardly a man is now alive
> Who remembers that famous day and year.
>
> He said to his friend, ''If the British march
> By land or sea from the town tonight,
> Hang a lantern aloft in the belfry arch
> Of the North Church tower as a signal light,—
>
> One, if by land, and two, if by sea;
> And I on the opposite shore will be
> Ready to ride and spread the alarm
> Through every Middlesex village and farm,
> For the country-folk to be up and to arm.''[10]

Longfellow's traditional poem has been made more accessible in a picture-book format by Nancy Winslow Parker.

Poems Send Messages

Poems capture the essence of a situation, making a point or sending a message without a wasted word. They have been compared to tele-grams—brief and to the point. Lilian Moore, NCTE Poetry Award winner, illustrates this feature well in her poem "Foghorns," from *Something New Begins:*

> The foghorns moaned
>   in the bay last night
>   so sad
>   so deep
> I thought I heard the city
>   crying in its sleep.[11]

Poems Express Feelings

At times, poems express our feelings although we never thought to say it exactly that way until we read the poem. Whether we are experiencing joy, happiness, sadness, anger, jealousy, or loneliness, there is a poem that puts these emotions into words. Mary Ann Hoberman knows just how a younger brother makes us feel in *Yellow Butter Purple Jelly Red Jam Black Bread.*

> BROTHER
>
> I had a little brother
> And I brought him to my mother
> And I said I want another
> Little brother for a change.
>
> But she said don't be a bother
> So I took him to my father
> And I said this little bother
> Of a brother's very strange.
>
> But he said one little brother
> Is exactly like another
> And every little brother
> Misbehaves a bit, he said.
>
> So I took the little bother
> From my mother and my father
> And I put the little bother
> Of a brother back to bed.[12]

Other poets put feelings of remorse into words, such as Dorothy Aldis in *All Together:*

> BAD
>
> I've been bad and I'm in bed
> For the naughty things I said.
>
> I'm in bed. I wish I had
> Not said those things that were so bad.
>
> I wish that I'd been good instead.
> But I was bad. And I'm in bed.[13]

Whether or not poetry can work its magic depends upon the adults in a child's world. Paul Janeczko, poet and anthologist, encourages parents and teachers to expose children to poetry: "Poems aren't meant to be kept in a shoebox all banded together—they need to breathe, get out on the field and have a chance at bat."[14] The next section describes the environment for developing a love of poetry.

LEARNING CONDITIONS FOR DEVELOPING A LOVE OF POETRY

The conditions for learning language, as described in Chapter 3, apply equally well to learning to love poetry. If we want children to love poetry, we must surround them with it, expect them to love it, and give them opportunities to try out its magic in choral speaking, reading, and writing their own. We need to accept their approximations as they attempt to create their own poetic expressions. Finally, we need to give them feedback and continually provide models.

Immersion

Teachers who want to develop an appreciation for poetry in their students immerse them in it. They collect poems they and children like, read them aloud several times a day, put poems on charts for group reading, and sprinkle poetry throughout the curriculum. They do what Beatrice Schenk de Regniers suggests:

KEEP A POEM IN YOUR POCKET

Keep a poem in your pocket
and a picture in your head
and you'll never feel lonely
at night when you're in bed.

The little poem will sing to you
the little picture bring to you
a dozen dreams to dance to you
at night when you're in bed.

So—
Keep a picture in your pocket
and a poem in your head
and you'll never feel lonely
at night when you're in bed.[15]

Children in the Cypress-Fairbanks School District in Houston, Texas, benefit when their teachers respond to a questionnaire each fall from the district's language and reading coordinator, asking if they would like to receive the monthly newsletter "Poetry Supplement."[16] There are two requirements: teachers must (1) establish a personal (not team) poetry card file to keep poems at their fingertips for convenient use, and (2) return the form with their name and school. Each month, the "Poetry Supplement" contains 15 to 20 poems on a theme with suggested activities for each. Patricia Smith, the creator of the newsletter, explains, "I gather an assortment of poems intended to promote an appreciation of poetry and at the same time facilitate teaching the essential elements of speaking, listening, reading, and writing." The October 1986 issue of the "Poetry Supplement" contains such poems as "The Leaves Are Falling" by Jean Malloch; "Autumn Garden" and "On Halloween" by Aileen Fisher; "Echo" by Sara Asheron; "No One"

and "Empty House Song" by Lilian Moore, and "Wicked Witch Admires Herself" by X. J. Kennedy. Here is a sample poem and activity from this issue.

WICKED WITCH ADMIRES HERSELF

"Mirror, mirror on the wall,
Whose is the fairest face of all?
I'll come close, so you'll see me clearer—"

Pop! goes another magic mirror.[17]

Suggestion: Use a mirror attached to the wall or a chalked illustration of a mirror on the chalkboard. Recite the poem from memory and surreptitiously draw a crack in the mirror or illustration as you read line three. Encourage students to memorize the quatrain and then entertain others. Ask the students to think of other "sound" words (onomatopoeic examples) that could be substituted for "pop."

In the March issue of the "Poetry Supplement," many poems celebrate spring. Karla Kuskin's poem "Spring" is set off into solo parts for choral speakers or readers. Students are encouraged to predict from the context the meaning of the word "gamboling" and then to verify it with a dictionary. Mary Ann Hoberman's poem "How Many?" is suggested as a response-call experience. The teacher can print the last four lines of each stanza on charts, read the first two lines, and have the class read from the charts the final four lines of each stanza. They can ask students how many skunks are walking down the street, and they can discuss the cause-and-effect situation evident in the final stanza. Teachers who use the ideas in the newsletter are creating an environment that helps students develop a love of poetry.

Brewton's *Index to Poetry* is an extensive resource for locating poems on specific topics, and it is valuable for creating and enlarging a personal poetry file. Teachers who know and love poetry have the privileged task of passing on the beauty of language from one generation to the next.

Opportunity to Practice

We communicate expectations through body language, gestures, and how and what we say. Observe a teacher who loves poetry and one who does not read a poem aloud; the differences in behavior are startling. If teachers read poems in a spirited, enthusiastic manner, with a twinkle in the eye, children respond positively. If the reader is boring, children are bored.

Surround children with poetry, expect them to like it, and give them opportunities to practice its forms. Children who have the opportunity to hear and read lots of poetry will want to try to write it. In the introduction to *Dogs and Dragons, Trees and Dreams* (I), Karla Kuskin says,

> The poetry reader often becomes a poetry writer. What could be better? No imagination is freer than a child's, no eye is sharper. The conversation of young children is a constant reminder that they are natural poets. But fitting unrestrained thoughts into rigid forms can be discouraging and may cramp the eccentric voice that makes a child's work (any work) unique. Read rhymes to children, but encourage them, as they begin to write, to write without rhyming. To write any way at all. And to read everything, anything . . . more poetry.[18]

Creative teachers find many ways to involve children in poetry. One group noticed primary grades' interest in studying weather and asked, "Why not have poetic as well as meteorological reports?" The teachers assigned a poetry reporter to select a poem that best expressed the foggy, sunny, windy, or rainy day; the poems extended the meaning of the weather symbols attached to the classroom calendar.[19]

Poets themselves have good suggestions for aspiring poets. In her acceptance speech for the 1981 NCTE Award for Excellence in Poetry for Children, Eve Merriam encouraged children to

> Read a lot. Sit down with anthologies and decide which pleases you. Copy out your favorites in your own handwriting. Buy a notebook and jot down images and descriptions. Be specific; use all the senses. Use your whole body as you write. It might even help sometime to stand up and move with your words. Don't be afraid of copying a form or convention, especially in the beginning. And, to give yourself scope and flexibility, remember: It doesn't *always* have to rhyme.[20]

Approximations

Approximations are children's attempts to use a pattern modeled by an adult. We do not expect children (or anyone) to learn to master a skill or to display adult competence the first time they try it. Neither will children immediately master the art of writing poetry. Accept their approximations and praise what they do well. The following come from second grade children who had heard Mary Ann Hoberman's "A House Is a House for Me" (P), which begins

> A hill is a house for an ant, an ant.
> A hive is a house for a bee.
> A hole is a house for a mole or a mouse
> And a house is a house for me![21]

The children wrote individual lines instead of a long poem as Hoberman did. Their approximations show that her poetry stimulated their creativity.

> A book is a house for words.
> A piggy bank is a house for money.
> A shell is a house for a peanut.
> A mommy is a house for a baby.

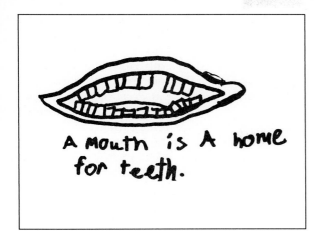

A mouth is a home for teeth.

A mailbox is a house for mail.
A refrigerator is a house for food.
A mouth is a house for teeth.
A cookie jar is a house for cookies.[22]

Feedback and Modeling

Children learn to use mature forms by hearing and seeing them used by others. When they are surrounded by the work of poets, they intuitively pick up some of the poets' techniques. Teachers who want students to experiment with poetry should choose strongly patterned verses as a frame for students to use in their own writing. They may read aloud numerous tongue twisters, alliterative poems, and parodies to give students the idea of what the poets are doing. For example, third grade teacher Kathy Grigoriadis read from *Puffin Book of Tongue Twisters* and *Faint Frogs Feeling Feverish* by Lilian Obligado in a unit study "All About Me" and had the students make up a tongue twister about themselves. She illustrated the tongue twister pattern with "Peter Piper picked a peck of pickled peppers." Children then used their own names as the basis for a similar patterned phrase. For example, David Loomis began his tongue twister "David Doomis drew ducks diving down to drink." Terry Watkins began

"Terry Tatkins tried to teach ten toads to trade tricycles and trucks."

Later, Kathy Grigoriadis read the parody "Cinderella dressed in yellow/went upstairs to kill her fellow" and encouraged her students to try the pattern for their own humorous verses. These are a couple of the verses from children in her third grade class:

Cinderella dressed in blue
Went downstairs to get a tattoo.
On the way, she got sued
And pretended she got the flue
Then she said, "A-a-a-a-chooo!"

CHERYL YEAM and **PAMELA LAHAR**

Cinderella dressed in blue,
In the kitchen cooking stew.
She accidentally tipped the pot,
And she shouted, "This is hot!"[23]

THOMAS FU

WHAT DO CHILDREN LIKE IN POETRY?

Children's responses to poetry depend heavily upon the way it is introduced to them. Certainly infants and toddlers respond to being bounced on a knee and hearing "Ride a little horsie up and down a hill. If you don't watch out, you'll take a little spill." During the early childhood years, they pick up jingles from media and readily commit them to memory. They sing songs as they play and will join in on refrains with delight. Poetry is the natural language of childhood.

Research on Poetry Preferences

Researchers have studied the kinds of poems children like as well as the kinds of poems teachers read to them. For example, in a national survey, Ann Terry studied the poetry preferences of students in the upper elementary grades and found that children like

1. Contemporary poems;
2. Poems they can understand;
3. Narrative poems;
4. Poems with rhyme, rhythm, and sound; and
5. Poems that relate to their personal experiences.[24]

She also found that children dislike poems that have much figurative language and imagery. They dislike highly abstract poems that do not make sense to them or do not relate to their own experiences. Haiku was consistently disliked. Girls like poetry more often than boys. Favorite poems were humorous and about familiar experiences or animals. John Ciardi's poem "Mummy Slept Late and Daddy Fixed Breakfast" in *You Read to Me, I'll Read to You* and limericks of all sorts were tops among the children's choices.

Amy McClure extended Terry's study and found that children respond much differently to poetry in a supportive literary environment.[25] Children responded more positively to a wider variety of poetry, showing that teachers' attitude makes a difference.

We hope that times have changed since Chow Loy Tom's 1973 national survey, which showed that teachers in the middle grades read neither poetry nor prose aloud more than once a month.[26] According to Tom, when they occasionally did read poetry, they chose poems such as "Paul Revere's Ride," "Fog," "Who Has Seen the Wind," and "The Daffodils"—all except "Fog" having been written before the turn of the century.

An encouraging sign about the increasing popularity of poetry comes from *Children's Choices*,[27] a national survey conducted annually by the International Reading Association and the Children's Book Council, which shows that children's preferences continue to reflect Terry's findings. Some of children's recent choices include Judith Viorst's *If I Were in Charge of the World and Other Worries* (P-I), Shel Silverstein's *The Missing Piece Meets the Big O* (I) and *A Light in the Attic* (I), Mary Ann Hoberman's *A House Is a House for Me* (P), Jack Prelutsky's *The Mean Old Mean Hyena* (I), and *Poem Stew* (I) selected by William Cole. The results are even more encouraging when we realize that these preferences surfaced in the midst of opportunities to choose hundreds of other picture books, novels, and nonfiction. Children continue to choose witty poems about things familiar to them as well as ones that puzzle and astonish them.

Children Like Humorous Poems

The natural appeal of humor is heightened when publishers put the light verse into well-illustrated editions. Numerous picture books filled with humorous verse and eye-catching art attract readers who may not have found them in dense anthologies. Jack Prelutsky has added to the wealth of humorous verse in picture-book formats. *Ride a Purple Pelican* (P) is illustrated by Garth Williams with full-page spreads. In this book, Prelutsky celebrates children, animals, and other creatures who live in scattered parts of the country. For example,

> Cincinnati Patty,
> smaller than a thumb,
> rode a mouse to Cleveland
> to feast upon a plum,
> she feasted for a minute,
> and that was her mistake,
> for Cincinnati Patty
> got a giant belly ache.[28]

Dennis Lee has also enriched the fare for humorous poetry readers. *Garbage Delight* and *Jelly Belly* (both P-I) are filled with funny and sometimes bizarre people and events. This, from *Jelly Belly*, echoes the lilt of a nursery rhyme:

Ride a purple pelican,
ride a silver stork,
ride them from Seattle
to the city of New York,
soar above the buildings,
bobble like a cork,
ride a purple pelican,
ride a silver stork.

Jack Prelutsky's *Ride a Purple Pelican* is a wonderfully colorful collection of poetry set across the country. (Illustrated by Garth Williams.)

There was an old lady
 Whose kitchen was bare,
So she called for the cat
 saying, "Time for some air!"

She sent him to buy her
 A packet of cheese.
But the cat hurried back
 With a basket of bees.

(More verses show inappropriate deliveries.)

She sent him to buy her
 A fine cup of tea.
But the cat waddled back
 With a dinosaur's knee.

The fridge was soon bulging,
And so was the shelf.
So she sent for a hot dog
And ate it herself.[29]

Fortunately, we have many poets who use humor as the mainstay of their verses: Shel Sil-verstein, William Cole, and X. J. Kennedy are among the best. Silverstein's *A Light in the Attic* (I) was on the New York Times Best Seller List for 180 weeks, longer than any other book since the list was begun. His collection *Where the Sidewalk Ends* (P–I) is credited with bringing more converts to poetry than any other vol-ume; for many it is the point at which they first become poetry lovers. When a teacher reads aloud from it, children who think they do not care for poetry may listen suspiciously at first, then cautiously ask to "see that book." *Where the Sidewalk Ends* contains verse and illustra-tions that tickle the reader in weird and ridicu-lous ways: for "Jumping Rope," a gangly girl is shown completely entangled in a jumping rope from head to foot. "Band-Aids" describes all the places a child needs band-aids, and the il-lustration shows head and torso covered with them. Silverstein shows no restraint in the sit-uations he mocks to make things laughable. He tells of a king whose mouth is stuck tight with peanut butter, gives a recipe for a hippopotamus sandwich, describes a dreadful situation in which someone eats a baby, and warns about the dangers of picking one's nose. Anything becomes the butt of Silverstein's humor, and he's on target about what makes children laugh.

In the gooey, smelly poem "Sarah Cynthia Sylvia Stout/Would Not Take the Garbage Out," Silverstein piles up the pits, the rinds, the crusts, and bones to show what happened to a girl who would not take the garbage out:

Sarah Cynthia Sylvia Stout
Would not take the garbage out!
She'd scour the pots and scrape the pans,
Candy the yams and spice the hams,
And though her daddy would scream and
  shout,
She simply would not take the garbage out.

And so it piled up to the ceilings:
Coffee grounds, potato peelings,
Brown bananas, rotten peas,
Chunks of sour cottage cheese. . . [30]

By the time you finish reading the graphic details of Sarah's overflowing garbage pail, students are gagging and groaning in mock horror. Despite their pretense of utter disgust, the comment heard most often is, "Read it again."

Although not as bizarre or graphic as Silverstein's work, *Beastly Boys and Ghastly Girls* (I), a collection by William Cole (of work from A. A. Milne, Hilaire Belloc, William Jay Smith, A. E. Housman, Ted Hughes, John Ciardi, Lewis Carroll, and James Whitcomb Riley, among others), also celebrates children's antics, mocking adult strictures with such advice as "put some mustard in your shoe," "spill broth on the tablecloth," "never stew your sister," and "beat him when he sneezes."

Other collections show Cole's zest for ridiculous situations, inane nonsense, and general, all-around silliness. *Oh, That's Ridiculous!* (P–I)

and *Oh, What Nonsense* (P–I) are appropriate for both younger and older children.

Children Like Involvement with Poetry

Movement and verse go together. From the earliest days, toddlers clap their hands to "Pat-a-cake, pat-a-cake" or stick out their toes to be tweaked for "This little piggy went to market." They will bounce through "Ride a cock horse to Banbury Cross" and play endless streams flowing through "London Bridge is falling down." The natural bent for movement as an accompaniment to words shows in numerous ways throughout life; much of it can be seen in response to poetry.

Movement and drama are a natural bridge to poetry. Nancy Larrick describes the effect of movement on poetry in workshops for teachers and librarians at Lehigh University.[31] A second grade teacher in one of the workshops demonstrated how poems from Larrick's *I Heard a Scream in the Street* (I–A) could be interpreted through dance. In another, a fourth grade group pretended they were taking a walk in the middle of the night as their room was darkened and the teacher played part of Dvorak's "New World Symphony" and read Aileen Fisher's *In the Middle of the Night* (P–I). These experiences heightened the enjoyment of poetry through involvement and led to "poetry happenings" in subsequent workshops. Dramatization, pantomime, puppets, and impromptu choral speaking extend children's involvement with poetry.

CRITERIA FOR SELECTING POETRY FOR CHILDREN

While some of the poetry of the past still speaks to today's children, there has been a wealth of excellent poetry written since the 1960s. Teachers need to search out new poems instead of relying, upon those they memorized

TEACHING IDEA

CHORAL SPEAKING   Paul Fleischman's poetry about birds in *I Am Phoenix: Poems for Two Voices* (I) is arranged in script form for choral speaking. The poems were written to be read aloud by two readers at once, one taking the left-hand part, the other taking the right-hand part. The poems should be read from top to bottom, the two parts meshing as in a musical duet. When both readers have lines at the same horizontal level, those lines are to be spoken simultaneously. This poem mourns the loss of the passenger pigeon.

THE PASSENGER PIGEON

We were counted not in	
	thousands
nor	
	millions
but in	
billions.	*billions.*
	We were numerous as the
stars	stars
	in the heavens
As grains of	
sand	
at the sea[32]	sand

in their own childhood. Keep the following in mind in selecting poetry.

Children like poems they can understand. Ones that refer to abstract and elusive subjects or depend upon an understanding of the distant past will elude them. Select poems geared to children's intellectual development and ones that fall within the parameters of their experience.

Research has repeatedly shown that children prefer humorous poems with strong rhythm and rhyme over free verse with abstract symbolism. They enjoy narrative poetry because it is based on their natural love of story. Choose poems to begin with that research has shown to be favorites: humorous poems and narrative poems.

We may not always know why a particular poem appeals to children but we do know

that the ones read aloud with enthusiasm are likely to become their favorites. A teacher's attitude toward a poem will influence the way it is received by children. Select poems that you like, too.

Poetry appeals to the emotions and intensifies them; it can make children happy or sad, proud or self-critical. Gradually expand children's experiences with poetry by exposing them to a broader range of forms.

Poetry enriches every school subject and every part of the school day. Select poems that can be integrated into every aspect of the curriculum.

David McCord notes, "poetry, like rain, should fall with elemental music, and poetry for children should catch the eye as well as the ear and the mind."[33] Though the criteria direct us to poems that catch eye, ear, and mind, only teachers with a developing love for poetry will catch the heart.

NCTE Award for Poetry for Children

Each year more than 60 awards are given for children's books. Until 1977, when the National Council of Teachers of English established the first award for poetry, all these awards were for prose work. The award, given annually from 1977 to 1982, is now given every three years. The NCTE Award for Poetry for Children is given to a poet for the entire body of work produced, not for individual poems or books. A national committee of professionals makes the selection.

The winners of the NCTE poetry award have been as follows:

1977   David McCord
1978   Aileen Fisher
1979   Karla Kuskin
1980   Myra Cohn Livingston
1981   Eve Merriam
1982   John Ciardi
1985   Lilian Moore
1988   Arnold Adoff

Seal of the National Council of Teachers of English Award for Poetry for Children, designed by Karla Kuskin.

Books by these poets carry the seal shown here.

Awards tell us what professionals in the field consider to be high-quality poetry. Newcomers can sharpen their own critical standards by reading poetry that experts consider outstanding. Study the works of the NCTE award–winning poets to discover the qualities of excellence that distinguish their poetry.

1978—Aileen Fisher Aileen Fisher says that she was lucky as a child: her father had a serious bout with pneumonia which caused him to give up his business in Iron River, Michigan, and move to the country. He bought 40 acres and built a big, square house on a high bank above a river; this is where Aileen grew up. She roamed the countryside with her brother and often followed the iced dirt roads that were cut by the loggers in the area. She has always loved the country.

After graduating from college and working in Chicago, she decided to get out of the city and subsequently settled in Colorado. She bought a 200-acre ranch outside Boulder in the Flagstaff Mountains and designed a comfortable cabin without electricity, central heat, or running water. She has since moved to the outskirts of Boulder, but she can still see deer on

Aileen Fisher

PROFILE

David McCord

David McCord was born near Greenwich Village in New York City. When he was 12 years old, he moved with his parents to a ranch on the Rogue River in Oregon where he learned about nature and wildlife. He studied the constellations and chose Orion as his favorite skymark. Although as a child he learned to shoot a rifle, McCord has never aimed at a living thing since he was 15 because his love of all life is far too deep.

McCord graduated from Harvard University, where he worked as an alumni editor and fund raiser for many years; he has written a history of Harvard, *In Sight of Sever*. The first honorary degree of Doctor of Humane Letters granted at Harvard was conferred on him, at the same ceremonies at which President John F. Kennedy received an LL.D.

Queen Elizabeth II of England invited David McCord to join the Royal Institute of Arts and Letters, and when she visited the United States during the bicentennial, he wrote a sestina in her honor.

Author or editor of nearly 50 books of poetry, essays, history, medicine, light verse, and verse for children, his work appears in more than 500 anthologies. Also an artist, he has had several one-man shows of watercolor landscapes. He lives in Boston and is a Boston Red Sox fan.

One of David McCord's teachers once told him never to let a day go by without looking on three beautiful things; he tries to live by that precept. Each day the sky, in all kinds of weather, is the first of the three.

McCord frequently talks with groups of children in elementary schools as a means of dispelling a misconception that once was his: "I learned when I was young that all poets had to be dead . . . . The fact that there were living poets never surfaced until high school."[34]

David McCord's books of poetry for children include *All Day Long, Away and Ago, Every Time I Climb a Tree, Far and Few, For Me to Say, The Star in the Pail, Take Sky*; there are many others. His collected poems for children, published in *One at a Time*, appeared in 1977, the year he was awarded the first National Council of Teachers of English Award for Poetry for Children.

PROFILE

Karla Kuskin

There's a line in *The Night Before Christmas* that will stay in my head forever because when I first learned it, I didn't understand all the words.

As dry leaves before the wild hurricane
  fly,
When they meet with an obstacle,
  mount to the sky,
So up to the housetop the coursers they
  flew,
With the sleigh full of toys, and St. Nicholas too.

I didn't know *hurricane;* I didn't know *ob-stacle;* I didn't know *coursers;* but I just loved the way they sounded.[35]

Karla Kuskin's fascination with words began in childhood when her parents and teachers read poetry to her and listened to her read aloud. Her love of language and poetry grew over the years, and she writes for children as a means of sharing her deep feeling with them.

Karla Kuskin illustrates her own books, extending the poetic images with visual ones. In *Near the Window Tree,* she wishes for three things: a chair, a book to read, and a tree to let the sun sift through. Opposite each poem in this book are capsule descriptions of how and why each was written. Her unique view, evident in all her work, is vividly expressed in *Any Me I Want to Be,* in which 30 animals and things describe themselves and their surroundings. The reader must guess the answer. In *Dogs and Dragons, Trees and Dreams* (I), she suggests ways to introduce children to poetry and to move them from readers and listeners of poetry to writers of poetry.

She writes of her work,

Instead of building a fence of formality around poetry I want to emphasize its accessibility, the sound, rhythm, humor, the inherent simplicity. Poetry can be as natural and effective a form of self-expression as singing or shouting.[36]

This belief enhances her style and won for her the 1979 NCTE Award for Poetry for Children.

Karla Kuskin is a native of New York City, where she lives with her husband. Their 2 children are grown.

the side of Flagstaff Mountain and finds raccoons, skunks, and even baby porcupines roaming in her yard.

Fisher says of herself,

> My pleasures in life are found through animals (especially dogs), mountain climbing, hiking, working with wood, unorthodox gardening, a few people in small doses, and reading. I like centrality in my life and peace and quiet, which means that I avoid commercialized excitement, cities, traffic, polluted air, noise, confusion, travel, crowds, and airports. For me early morning on a mountain trail is the height of bliss.[37]

1980—*Myra Cohn Livingston* Myra Cohn Livingston grew up in Omaha, Nebraska, and graduated from Sarah Lawrence College. Her first book of poetry, *Whispers and Other Poems*, written when she was 18 years old, reflects the quiet, idyllic sort of childhood world she knew. She says that she will probably never lose the curiosity of this childhood, the sense of wonder over the metaphysical universe, but that our world—her world—has changed. She recalls one day looking out her windows, down across the Santa Monica mountains to where the Pacific Ocean lies, only there wasn't any water—a thick brown-covered rise of smog obscured it from view.

Myra Cohn
Livingston

Livingston notes,

> Today's megalopolis has caused most of us to focus our attention on new sights and ideas, new wonders. Our global one-world necessarily changes my perspective, just as it alters that of the reader. We must all grapple with the effects of overcrowding, television, smog, pollution, multi-media encroachments on privacy, as well as more positive achievements in human interchange and scientific advances. To deny this, to wish to return to a sentimentalized past, is unrealistic. Yet there must be a balance between the eternal truths—what mankind has always experienced and will continue to—and contemporary realities. It is often the writer who attempts to achieve this balance.

She writes about her work,

> Trained as a traditionalist in poetry, I feel strongly about the importance of order imposed by fixed forms, meter and rhyme when I write about some things; yet free verse seems more suitable for other subjects. What comes to mind are two poems I have written about roller skating; the one in meter and rhyme about skilled, experienced skating; the other in free verse describing the attempts of a child just learning to skate. Accomplished, smooth skating calls for regularity of form; random movement, spills and false starts demand from me, as a poet, erratic lines and no rhyme. The force of what I wish to say shapes the form.[38]

1981—*Eve Merriam* Eve Merriam was born in Philadelphia and graduated from the University of Pennsylvania. She did graduate work at the University of Wisconsin and Columbia University. She lives in Manhattan and says, "I expect to be the last living inhabitant of Manhattan when everyone else has quit for sub or exurbia. The city in winter is my delight, as the ocean is in summer."[39]

Merriam won the Yale Younger Poets Prize, which was overseen by Archibald

Eve Merriam

John Ciardi

MacLeish. "He was my hero," she says of MacLeish. "I used to sleep with a copy of his *Conquistador* under my pillow." After graduation from college, Eve worked as a sales clerk in a department store and as a fashion copywriter at *Glamour* magazine. She published poetry and fiction regularly in the *Nation*, the *New Republic*, and the *New Yorker*. Several of her works have been produced as Broadway and off-Broadway musicals.

Merriam says of herself,

> I am fortunate in that my work is my main pleasure, and, while I find all forms of writing absorbing, I like poetry as the most immediate and richest form of communication. My favorite non-writing pursuits are frequenting public libraries and second-hand book stores, and travel travel travel. I also enjoy riding a bike, swimming (in temperate waters only!), and walking. In my dreams I am a proficient ice-skater—in real life, I am wobbly but willing.[40]

1982—John Ciardi John Ciardi (pronounced Char-dee) was born in Boston and received his Bachelor's degree from Tufts College and his Masters from the University of Michigan. He taught English at the University of Kansas City, Harvard University, and Rutgers University. He was poetry editor at *Saturday Review*

and director of the Bread Loaf Writers' Conference for many years.

Ciardi describes himself:

> I first began writing poems for children when my nephews were small. My first book, *The Reason for the Pelican*, came about as a way of playing games with them. At the time I had an apartment in the same house with them and their presence was all the motive there was for the poems. A few years later my own children provided me with the same motive and I wrote my next seven or eight books in the act of playing games with them. I think my most satisfying book in the course of this direct interplay was *I Met a Man*. I was asked to try a book based on first grade reading vocabulary. I knew nothing about school vocabularies but my daughter was then in kindergarten, and once I was supplied with the word list I found myself eager to write the first book she would read all the way through. My aim was to take the word list and to make reading as much fun as possible. My reward was that my daughter not only had fun but learned to read in the course of playing with *I Met a Man*. (Later I was scolded by her teacher for having "accelerated" her. It was, I may say, an easy scolding to brush off: Myra and I had obviously had more fun than her teacher was having.)[41]

John Ciardi died in 1986.

*1985—**Lilian Moore*** Lilian Moore lives on a farm near Kerhonkson, New York, and from her back door, you can see deer, an old apple orchard, and a pond. When her first book of poems was published, she was living in the city but laughs at the image of her as a "city person." She says, "I started out with a flower pot, then I had a window box, then I had a back yard, then I came here [to the farm]. So I've always wanted things that grow, and the light of the sky in the country."

Lilian Moore lived in the city for many years, however. She was a teacher and a reading specialist in the New York City schools where, she explains, "I found I had a gift for and a delight in helping children learn to read . . . . " She was editor of a paperback book club until she moved to the country. "I have had the best of both worlds," she continues. "I grew up in an exciting city, and now I live on this lovely farm. From time to time, Sam [her husband], ex-farmer, writes a children's book, and I, ex-city woman born and bred, drive the tractor."

In speaking about poetry, Lilian Moore states, "Poems should be like fireworks, packed carefully and artfully, ready to explode with unpredictable effects."[42] Her books include *Thinking of Shadows*, *I Feel the Same Way*, and *Something New Begins* (all I).

*1988—**Arnold Adoff*** Arnold Adoff is noted for his collections of black American poetry and for his distinctive style in his own poetry. He searches for a form that is unique to an individual poem, one that shapes it, holds it tight, and creates an inner tension that makes a whole shape out of the words. Adoff says that he wants a poem to "sprout roses and spit bullets," an ideal combination in his view.

Arnold Adoff was born in the East Bronx section of New York City. He received his B.A. degree from City College, was a history major at Columbia University, and studied writing under José Garcia Villa at the New School for Social Research. He was a teacher and a counselor for 12 years in New York City Public Schools in Harlem and the Upper West Side. He has also taught at New York University and Connecticut College and is currently visiting professor at Queens College.

Adoff is married to author Virginia Hamilton and resides in southwest Ohio. Their two children, Leigh and Jaime, are grown.

Adoff began collecting poetry for his classes in Harlem and the Upper West Side because he recognized the power of poetry to influence his students. As a youngster he was a voracious reader, devouring everything in the house and all he could carry home each week from several libraries.

Lilian Moore

Arnold Adoff

TEACHING IDEA

A YEAR OF POETRY From the list of poets who have received the NCTE Award for Poetry for Children, organize a "Poet of the Month" program to feature one of the award-winning poets.

Collect as many of their books as possible. Read aloud from their work work every day.

Arrange a bulletin board display with biographical material (available from their publishers) and book jackets from their books.

Encourage children to try writing poetry as they are inspired by the works of these outstanding poets.

Basic Collection of Poetry

The following list of poets and their works are ones that we believe to be basic to the elementary school curriculum. They are grouped according to the age group for whom they hold greatest interest, although designation should be considered flexible. Poetry, especially, appeals to a wide age range.

PRIMARY (P)

Bennett, *Days Are Where We Live, and Other Poems*
Bennett, *Roger Was a Razorfish and Other Poems*
Bodecker, *Snowman Sniffles and Other Verse*
Ciardi, *I Met a Man*
De la Mare, *Peacock Pie*
De la Mare, *Songs of Childhood*
Farjeon, *Poems for Children*
Field, *Taxis and Toadstools*
Fisher, *Out in the Dark and Daylight*
Greenfield, *Honey, I Love and Other Poems*
Greenfield, *Daydreamers*
Hoberman, *Yellow Butter Purple Jelly Red Jam Black Bread*
Holman, *At the Top of My Voice and Other Poems*
Hopkins, *A Song in Stone*
Hopkins, *Surprises*
Lear, *The Owl and the Pussy Cat*
Lee, *Jelly Belly*
Lee, *Garbage Delight*
Livingston, *A Song I Sang to You*
McCord, *All Small*

Milne, *Now We Are Six*
Milne, *When We Were Very Young*
Prelutsky, *Ride a Purple Pelican*
Richards, *Tirra Lirra*
Worth, *Small Poems*

INTERMEDIATE (I)

Adoff, *Sports Pages*
Benet and Benet, *A Book of Americans*
Ciardi, *Doodle Soup*
Cole, *Poem Stew*
Holman, *The Song in My Head*
Hopkins, *Moments: Poems About the Seasons*
Hopkins, *To Look at Anything*
Hopkins, *Side by Side: Poems to Read Together*
Kennedy, *Knock at a Star: A Child's Introduction to Poetry*
Kuskin, *Dogs and Dragons, Trees and Dreams*
Larrick, *On City Streets*
Larrick, *Piping down the Valleys Wild: Poetry for the Young of All Ages*
Lear, *The Complete Nonsense of Edward Lear*
Livingston, *I Like You, If You Like Me: Poems of Friendship*
Livingston, *Sky Songs*
Livingston, *Worlds I Know and Other Poems*
Merriam, *A Word or Two with You: New Rhymes for Young Readers*
McCord, *One at a Time*
Moore, *Something New Begins*
Moore, *Think of Shadows*
Silverstein, *A Light in the Attic*

Silverstein, *Where the Sidewalk Ends*
Stevenson, *A Child's Garden of Verses*
Willard, *A Visit to William Blake's Inn: Poems for Innocent and Experienced Travelers*
Worth, *Small Poems Again*

ADVANCED (A)

Dunning, Leuders, and Smith, *Reflections on a Gift of Watermelon Pickle and Other Modern Verse*
Fleischman, *I Am Phoenix: Poems for Two Voices*
Frost, *A Swinger of Birches*
Hopkins, *Don't You Turn Back: Poems by Langston Hughes*
Hopkins, *Voyages: Poems by Walt Whitman*
Hughes, *Season Songs*
Hughes, *Under the North Star*
Janeczko, *Don't Forget to Fly*
Janeczko, *Going Over to Your Place: Poems for Each Other*
Janeczko, *Pocket Poems: Selected for a Journey*
Janeczko, *Poetspeak: In Their Work, About Their Work*
Longfellow, *Paul Revere's Ride*
Plotz, *Saturday's Children: Poems of Work*
Sandburg, *Rainbows Are Made*

Anthologies and Collections

To provide variety in poetry and yet hold collections to a manageable size, teachers and librarians need anthologies. Poems are also sometimes easier to locate and select in these collections than when shelved individually by author.

Three types of anthologies have proven particularly useful in the classroom: the specialized anthology, with work by several poets on one subject; the generalized anthology, with works by many poets on many subjects; and the anthology of the work of only one poet.

Specialized anthologies are gaining in popularity. The spate of books of poems and verses on holidays, monsters, dinosaurs, fairies, and other special topics bears witness to this. Noted anthologist Nancy Larrick brings the visions of some fine poets to *Bring Me All of Your Dreams* (I-A). This collection includes works from such well-known poets as Langston Hughes, Walter De la Mare, e.e. cummings, and Carl Sandburg, as well as from lesser known poets—all bound together by the filament of dreams. The organization of the book is enhanced by an index of first lines, an index of poets and poems, and a biographic section, "Meet the Poets."

Humor is the strand that ties together David Kherdian's collection *If Dragon Flies Made Honey* (P-I). The lively poems by Jack Kerouac, Ruth Krauss, and William Carlos Williams take on hilarity with José Aruego and Ariane Dewey's exuberant illustrations. Although at first glance the book appears to be for the very young, its subleties make it equally appealing to more mature children as well.

The classic generalized anthology, May Hill Arbuthnot's *Time for Poetry*, now incorporated into *The Arbuthnot Anthology of Children's Literature*, is a complete volume with verse on many subjects. Best-loved poems of childhood include those about people, animals, adventures, games, jokes, magic and make-believe, wind and water, holidays and seasons, and wisdom and beauty. The anthology is essential for any teacher who considers poetry central to children's lives.

A Flock of Words: An Anthology of Poetry for Children and Others (I-A), an additional fine resource, began as David MacKay's personal poetry collection made while he was a teacher. In his teaching, MacKay used poems clipped from newspapers and magazines and was a pioneer in encouraging children to emulate the work of great poets by examining closely the many ways poets use evocative language.

A most beautiful book, one of today's classics, *Reflections on a Gift of Watermelon Pickle and Other Modern Verse* (I–A) was compiled by Stephen Dunning, Edward Lueders, and Hugh Smith. The compilers began with 1,200 poems considered good, and, by testing them with students, gradually refined the collection to 114 poems. The broad spectrum of poetic statements, on subjects from a bud to a steamshovel, to advice to travelers, or arithmetic, is augmented with dramatic black-and-white photographs. A brief section of interpretive comments and questions concerning some of the poems is appended. Dunning, Lueders, and Smith used the same process of field-testing poems to produce another excellent anthology, *Some Haystacks Don't Even Have any Needles: And Other Complete Modern Poems* (A).

David McCord's *One at a Time* (all ages) is an anthology comprised solely of his work. An impressive volume, it is a collection of most of his poetry. McCord's wit and thoughtful perception sing in the music of his words. *One at a Time*, more than any other single volume, is

a key to cultivating poetic taste—to produce children who will read poetry for pleasure.

When you find a poem that delights you and your students, look for others by the same poet; you may be surprised to find an entire anthology devoted to your favorite poet. Brewton's *Index to Poetry* will hasten the search. Every classroom needs several specialized, generalized, and individualized anthologies of poetry. Teachers who know and love poems can do justice to the privileged task of passing on the beauty of language from one generation to the next.

Although we have included some good anthologies in the lengthy list above, there are some more anthologists you should know. In addition to Nancy Larrick, Lee Bennett Hop-

ACTIVITY: TEACHER TO STUDENT

APPRECIATING NARRATIVE POEMS (I-A)   The best way to appreciate the unfolding of the plot in narrative poetry is to read it aloud. Do not be concerned about vocabulary that is unfamiliar. Unfamiliar words can usually be understood from context—the way they are used in a line or sentence.

Choose some poems to read from the following:

1. *The Pied Piper of Hamelin* by Robert Browning, illustrated by C. Walter Hodges. This story is fun to tape-record dramatically. Pay special attention to the lines:

> Great rats, small rats, lean rats, brawny rats,
> Brown rats, black rats, grey rats, tawny rats.

Recite them slowly and dramatically to paint a vivid and memorable picture.

Write what you think of the story's moral, summed up in the statement, "So, Willy, let's keep our promise to all men—especially pipers"? Locate the edition that Kate Greenaway illustrated and compare her pictures with those of Hodges. In what way does this narrative poem document the dramatic conflict between greed and honor?

2. *Hiawatha* by Henry Wadsworth Longfellow, illustrated by Susan Jeffers. Read Susan Jeffer's introduction to discover what this poem meant to her as a child and how she prepared to illustrate it. How did she maintain the poem's epic quality yet concentrate only on the section about Hiawatha's boyhood? Discuss what Jeffers conveys in the endpapers and title pages to retain the

kins, Jill Bennett, and William Cole, look for the following collections:

Bober, *Let's Pretend: Poems of Flight and Fancy*
Cole, *A New Treasury of Children's Poetry: Old Favorites and New Discoveries*
De Regniers, *So Many Cats!*
Downey and Robertson, *The New Wind Has Wings: Poems from Canada*
Hall, *The Oxford Book of Children's Verse in America*
Prelutsky, *The Random House Book of Poetry*

FORMS OF POETRY

It is evident to the beginning reader that poetry comes in many forms. Poems look different; the visual form, which reflects the pattern, affects the way the poem is to be read and con-

tributes to meaning. Poetic patterns are clearly defined, although poets manipulate the conventional patterns as often as they manipulate word meanings.

The discussion in this section and the one that follows ("Elements of Poetry") is intended to provide a basic understanding of these elements for teachers so they may be better informed when sharing poetry with children. In no way do we intend for these to be taught to children sequentially, element by element or form by form. Instead, through the illustrative activities, children can construct meaningful experiences for themselves. Children will enjoy poetry without consciously noticing form, but when they begin to write poetry, they will recognize and use some of its conventions.

---

essence of the poem. How does Jeffers show Wenonah's spirit watching over Hiawatha as he grows? Compare this version with the one illustrated by Errol LeCain.

3. *The Highwayman* by Alfred Noyes. The ominous tone of this narrative is set forth in the first stanza:

The wind was a torrent of darkness among the gusty trees,
The moon was a ghostly galleon tossed upon cloudy seas,
The road was a ribbon of moonlight over the purple moor,
And the highwayman came riding—riding—riding—
The highwayman came riding, up to the old inn-door.

Some questions to think about after reading are:

How does Noyes make us sympathetic to Bess and to the outlaw, who is really nothing more than a thief?
Can you find similarities here to the infamous outlaws Bonnie and Clyde?
How does the illustrator's use of pastel shades of blue, indigo, and violet influence the poem's mood?
What events have you seen reported in the news that concern love, betrayal, and death? How could they be described in poetic verse?

Adapt this idea for younger students through selection of poems and level of activity.

In poetry, perhaps more than in any other area, children need to discover. Instead of starting with definitions of poetic forms and moving to illustrations of them, it is best to expose children to many examples of a form and allow them to deduce the commonalities. Reading many poems in the same form gives children a feel for and a sense of it in use.

The true expression of real feelings is far more important than form in creative writing. Myra Cohn Livingston, in *When You Are Alone/It Keeps You Capone*, describes the relation between technical aspects and creative ideas in children's poetry writing:

> One encourages expression, true and meaningful expression (as distinguished from factual statement); reads poetry, introduces forms, and speaks about the elements and tools of poetry and how meaning is to be found in poetry, so that each child will, we hope, find a form that best expresses his own thoughts and feelings.[43]

Knowing about the many possibilities of poetic form, however, *can* help in selecting poetry for children.

Poetry as Story: Narrative Poems

A narrative poem tells a story. A book-length narrative poem is called an epic, but most story poems for children are relatively short and relate one or more episodes. Children like narrative poems best; they appeal to their natural love of story.

Narrative poetry sets a story—with characters, plot, and theme, like any other story—into a poetic framework, which can make even a humble story memorable. A. A. Milne, Aileen Fisher, Henry Wadsworth Longfellow, and Rosemary and Stephen Vincent Benét are known for their narrative poems.

Milne's work is collected in *When We Were Very Young* (P) and *Now We Are Six* (P). "Sneezles," "Binker," and "Forgiven," all in *Now We Are Six*, are favorites, but "Bad Sir Brian Botany" is even more popular.

Sir Brian had a battleaxe with great big knobs
  on;
He went among the villagers and blipped them
  on the head.
On Wednesday and on Saturday, but mostly
  on the latter day,
He called at all the cottages, and this is what
  he said:
"I am Sir Brian!" (ting-ling)
  "I am Sir Brian!" (rat-tat)
"I am Sir Brian, as bold as a lion—
  Take that!—and that—and that!"[44]

Aileen Fisher's narrative poems focus on nature and often appear in picture-book formats. *Listen Rabbit; Going Barefoot; Like Nothing at All; Anybody Home?; Where Does Everyone Go?;* and *Sing, Little Mouse* (all P) celebrate the beauty of the natural world and its animals. Fisher describes "ears standing rabbit tall," a child going barefoot "like kittens and dogs,/bears and beetles/and hoppity frogs," and seeing something that was "hunchy, bunchy,/and halfway tall"—a pile of leaves that looked "like nothing at all" but instead was a rabbit, fawn, grouse, or weasel. Fisher invites us to look at "the small grass house/of a mother mouse/in a velvety blouse." She wonders where everyone goes in the fall and if it could be "that someone/their uncle knew/had a singing mouse./Do you think it's true?" Whatever Fisher examines with a poet's eye draws children in to look more closely, too.

When poetry is read aloud, the words can truly sing, and the musical quality of the verse can be fully savored; narrative poetry is most appreciated in oral presentations. This form of poetry usually describes a single event and tells a tale in the figurative language of adventure. Listening to story poems helps children develop a sensitivity to the charm of the spoken word and the tune of verse.

With increasing frequency, beautifully illustrated, single editions of narrative poems are available. No longer need we settle for the simple, dull, and standard verses of textbooks.

Limericks

Limericks, a form of light verse, have five lines and a rhyme scheme of a a b b a. The first, second, and fifth lines have three feet, the third and fourth, two feet (in poetic meter).

Limericks appeal to children because they poke fun and have a definite rhythm and rhyme. Edward Lear (1812–1888) is given credit for making the limerick popular, although he did not create it. His *Book of Nonsense* (I) was published in 1846 and is still popular today. Part of the lasting appeal of limericks lies in their tendency to lampoon and spoof those who take themselves too seriously.

Edward Lear's association with the limerick form is insoluble; a typical Lear effort is:

> There was an Old Lady whose folly,
> Induced her to sit in a holly;
> Whereon by a thorn,
> her dress being torn,
> She quickly became melancholy.[45]

Learning Lear's work is essential to an exploration of the limerick. *The Complete Nonsense of Edward Lear* (I) and *Whizz!* (P) are required reading. In *Whizz!* the "old man in a tree who was horribly bored by a bee" is portrayed by Janina Domanska as crossing a bridge. Characters from other limericks are added in cumulative fashion until the entire bridge collapses and everyone falls into the river.

Myra Cohn Livingston provides a sense of the man and his times as well as his works in *How Pleasant to Know Mr. Lear* (I) and *A Learical Lexicon* (I). In the first book, she provides biographical facts and quotes from Lear's letters, along with his sketches and limericks, culled from primary sources. In the second, she presents in alphabetical order a sampling of the outlandish words and made-up spellings that Lear used in his poems, journals, and letters to friends.

Limericks are devoured by the many students who enjoy this brand of humor. Some limericks are in the stream of folklore, where original authorship is lost. One such is:

> A flea and a fly in a flue
> Were imprisoned, so what could they do?
> Said the fly, "Let us flee."
> Said the flea, "Let us fly."
> So they flew through a flaw in the flue.[46]

Children laugh at the nonsense primarily because the verses break the conventions of language; limericks encapsulate a joyful absurdity.

TEACHING IDEA

WRITING LIMERICKS (I) Limericks are fun to write, although, of course, not all children will want to write them. When children do enjoy writing, it is usually about themselves—their thoughts and their feelings—although, they enjoy writing about real and/or imaginary animals or pets.

Those who want to try limericks should know the rhyme scheme—a a b b a—and that the third and fourth lines are shorter than the rest. Before asking children to set out on their own, it is good to read several limericks aloud and to have them create one as a group. Come prepared with three or four starting sentences and let children choose a favorite. You might find it helpful to prepare a simple list of rhyming words.

Concrete Poems

Concrete poetry uses the appearance of the verse lines on the page to suggest or imitate the poet's subject. Concrete verses do not use words alone to make a statement; instead they use the appearance of the thing described as well. Children call them shape (or picture) poems. The actual physical form of the words is used to depict the subject, so that the whole becomes an ideogrammatic statement; the work illustrates itself as the shapes of words and lines take form.

Myra Cohn Livingston's *O Sliver of Liver and Other Poems* (I) has some fine concrete poems. Children take delight in deciphering the poetic architecture of her "Winter Tree" and of Shel Silverstein's funny giraffe poem in *Where the Sidewalk Ends*.

Statements of Mood and Feeling: Lyric Poetry

Lyric poetry offers a direct and intense outpouring of thoughts and feelings. Any subjective, emotional poem can be called lyric, but most are songlike and expressive of a single mood. As its Greek name indicates, a lyric was originally sung to the accompaniment of a lyre. Lyrics have a melodic quality to this day.

Eleanor Farjeon's "The Night Will Never Stay" is a good example.

> The night will never stay,
> The night will still go by,
> Though with a million stars
> You pin it to the sky;
> Though you bind it with the blowing wind
> And buckle it with the moon,
> The night will slip away
> Like a sorrow or a tune.[47]

TEACHING IDEA

CONCRETE POETRY[48] Children are fascinated by concrete poetry. To heighten interest and understanding, draw the concrete poems in this chapter on large sheets of paper or charts. Search for other concrete poems to display in large print. Post them around the classroom.

Read the poems aloud with students joining in on the reading. Discuss the language used, the meaning of the poem, and the shape the poem has taken.

Give students an opportunity to create their own concrete poems. Experiencing concrete poems and seeing some that their peers have created, such as the examples here,[49] make most children eager to write their own.

A SEEING POEM

A SEEING POEM HAPPENS WHEN WORDS TAKE A SHAPE THAT HELPS THEM TO TURN ON A LIGHT IN SOMEONE'S MIND

Winter Tree

Be patient, bare branches—if you wait

long enough

you will bring forth a

leaf

and

another

and

another

and maybe even

a
lemon

Robert Froman's "A Seeing Poem" cleverly illuminates the concrete poetry format and invites readers to turn on the lightbulbs in their own minds. (From Froman's *Seeing Things: A Book of Poems.*)

The lemon brought forth by this winter tree is an unexpected delight for young readers. ("Winter Tree" from *O Sliver of Liver and Other Poems* by Myra Cohn Livingston, drawings by Iris Van Rynbach.)

Many of Christina Rossetti's poems are lyrics. Her "Who Has Seen the Wind?" leaves the question drifting in the mind.

Who has seen the wind?
Neither I nor you:
But when the leaves hang trembling,
The wind is passing through.

Who has seen the wind?
Neither you nor I:
But when the trees bow down their heads,
The wind is passing by.[50]

Nearly all children's poems can be called lyrical in the sense that they have a singing quality and are personal expressions of feeling.

Older students, with a richer understanding of symbolism, have a better appreciation for this type of poetry. Lyric poems above all others are not a one-time thing; they are for reading many times over. That children must come to trust their own feelings and learn that there is no right interpretation when it comes to poetry is particularly the case with the lyrical mode.

Haiku and Cinquain

The word *haiku* means "beginning." It generally refers to nature, a particular event happening at the moment, and an attendant emotion or feeling, often of the most fragile and evanescent kind.

This Japanese verse form consists of three lines and 17 syllables: the first line containing 5 syllables; the second line, 7; and the third, 5. A haiku usually focuses on an image that suggests a thought or emotion, as in the following examples.

> Take the butterfly:
> Nature works to produce him.
> Why doesn't he last?

> All these skyscrapers!
> What will man do about them
> When they have to go?[51]

Poets who master the haiku form sometimes stretch its boundaries by varying the five-seven-five syllable count while maintaining the essence of its meaning. Issa, a noted Japanese poet, demonstrates the beauty of haiku in these variations.

> Where can he be going
> In the rain,
> This snail?

> Little knowing
> The tree will soon be cut down,
> Birds are building their nests in it.[52]

Although haiku is a favorite with teachers, Ann Terry's study of children's preferences in poetry shows that it is *not* always a favorite with children—a signal for teachers to handle with care. Myra Cohn Livingston, noted children's poet, deplores the fact that haiku is given the status of a game by many teachers. She recommends that teachers who want to know the essence of haiku read *Wind in My Hand, The Story of Issa* (I), by Hanako Fukuda. Collections of haiku by Issa and others in *Don't Tell the Scarecrow* (P–I) provide excellent examples for children.

The haiku form is both abstract and tightly constructed. Ann Atwood, collector and author, in *Haiku: The Mood of Earth* (I–A), explains:

> The haiku form itself, bound within the limitations of approximately seventeen syllables, is paradoxical in nature. It is both simple and profound, constrictive and expansive, meticulously descriptive and yet wholly suggestive. And it is the very limitations of haiku that demand the discipline necessary to all art. For with this meagre allowance of words, the poet must not be tempted to stop at the right word, but must enlarge his search until the *only* word is within his grasp.[53]

Atwood's work has features that should make haiku interesting to students. First, she parallels the words with magnificent color photographs to extend the images. She does with photography what haiku does with words; detailed close-ups of each subject contrasted with a long-distance shot help reveal the essence of her poem. Second, she refers to concrete things students can identify, such as a sea creature's shell, the "hand" of a leaf, and a piece of driftwood. (An excellent sound filmstrip, which extends the function of the book's photographs, is also available.)

Atwood's several books illustrate her belief that seeing and feeling are fused in haiku po-

Looking straight ahead
going some definite Where——
the geese goose-stepping.

Ann Atwood fuses seeing
and feeling in her haiku
poetry and photography.
(From her *Fly with the Wind,
Flow with the Water.*)

etry and haiku photography. Teachers should look at *Haiku-Vision: In Poetry and Photographs; My Own Rhythm: An Approach to Haiku; Haiku: The Mood of Earth;* and *Fly with the Wind, Flow with the Water* (all I–A). The photographs in each are especially exciting for the counterpoint they provide.

A *cinquain* consists of five unrhymed lines that are usually made up of two, four, six, eight, and two syllables, in that order. A sim-plified variation that has five lines of one, two, three, four, and one word is manipulated eas-ily by children in the intermediate grades. The pattern can be as follows:

Line 1: One word, the title, usually a noun
Line 2: Two words describing the title
Line 3: Three words that show action
Line 4: Four words that show feeling or emotion
Line 5: One word, a synonym for the title

ACTIVITY: TEACHER TO STUDENT

DESIGNING A HAIKU CARD (I–A)   Plan an outing with some classmates. Col-lect bits and pieces of nature such as a smooth stone, a grasshopper, a flow-erless branch, a cocoon, an abandoned nest, a colorful leaf. Arrange these specimens on a table in the poetry corner of your classroom. Take a quick-developing snapshop of your favorite and mount it on a piece of construction paper. You might want to write a haiku to accompany the picture. Give the card to someone special.

The cinquain and other verse forms, such as the diamante, are useful when children begin writing their own poetry, and although they should not be compelled to adhere to a rigid structure, children sometimes find a set pattern helpful.

A sixth grade boy using the original cinquain syllable count to convey his father's injunction on the subject of poetry produced the following.

> Poem
> Read it good son
> It's educational
> People everywhere having fun
> Writing.[54]

Haiku and the cinquain are probably the most abstract poetry that children will experience. Since their symbolism and imagery are elusive for many children, they need to have wide exposure to other forms before they meet these.

Ballads and Sonnets

A ballad is a story told in verse and is usually meant to be sung. There are *folk ballads* and *literary ballads*. Folk ballads have no known author; they are composed anonymously and transmitted orally. "John Henry" is a well-known folk ballad. Literary ballads are composed by known writers who are imitating folk ballads. Billy Joel, Bruce Springsteen, Paul Simon, Harry Chapin, and Dan Fogelberg, for example, write contemporary literary ballads.

Here are some lines from Bruce Springsteen's "My Hometown."

> I was eight years old and running with a dime in my hand.
> Into the bus stop to pick up a paper for my old man.
> I'd sit on his lap in that big old Buick
> And steer as we drove through town.

> He'd tousle my hair, said, "Son, take a good look around.
> This is your home town."[55]

Ballads are relatively short narrative poems that are adapted for singing or give the effect of a song. Usually written in stanzas, ballads are characterized by lyricism and a story line relating a single incident or subject.

Generally speaking, ballads sing of heroic deeds and of murder, unrequited love, and feuds. Carl Sandburg's *The American Songbag* (A) is a classic collection of the ballads of railroad builders, lumberjacks, and cowboys. Use of dialogue in the telling of the story and repetition in the refrains characterize this form.

One teacher used ballads by contemporary songwriters to introduce his jaded junior high-school students to poetry. He played Simon and Garfunkel songs—"I Am a Rock" and "Sounds of Silence"—in his classroom to make the statement that poetry is song. Gradually, he exposed students to the words of songs written as poetry and eventually discussed the metaphoric statements the poem-songs make.

Helen Plotz presents 150 ballads in *As I Walked Out One Evening: A Book of Ballads* (A) that tell of love, death, work, war, and fairy folk. She cites individual authors, although many of the pieces are folksongs, changed by the singer as they are passed along. In the introduction, Plotz discusses origins, characteristics, and types of ballads:

> Ballads are elemental, stark, outspoken. Words are simple, direct, few. Ballads tell of faithfulness and faithlessness, of revenge, jealousy and murder, of transcending love and blinding hate. The story is stripped to the bare bone—there is no probing, no explanation. Often we must guess at what went before and this very spareness gives tremendous force to the climax.[56]

Plotz includes traditional ballads that tell of supernatural happenings: the changeling child, the demon lover, and the young man enticed

TEACHING IDEA

RECITING CONTEMPORARY BALLADS (A)   Older students love the ballads of
Billy Joel, John Denver, and other contemporary troubadours. Billy Joel's song
"Just the Way You Are" is a poem that has been set to music.

Don't go changing to try and please me
You never let me down before
Don't imagine you're too familiar
And I don't see you anymore

I would not leave you in times of trouble
We never could have come this far
I took the good times, I'll take the bad times
I'll take you just the way you are.[57]

Encourage your students to read the words with, and then without, thinking of the music. Have them form groups to plan reciting contemporary ballads
as dramatic readings, with the lines of the lyrics divided for the various male
and female voice parts.

---

by the Queen of Elfland. She also describes the
broadside, a ballad that tells about a political
happening, a murder, or another sensational
event. Some broadsides still exist in the folk
songs of today, although political ballads seldom outlive their day; "The Wearin' o' the
Green" and "Yankee Doodle," however, are
two that did. Her collection enriches the study
of past and present, providing material for
happy songfests.

Unlike ancient poetic forms that became archaic, such as the rondeau and the triolet, sonnets continue to be well known. Sonnets are
lyric poems of 14 lines, usually written in
rhymed iambic pentameter and expressing a
single idea or theme. They follow two models:
the Petrarchan, an eight-line stanza followed
by a six-line stanza; and the Shakespearean,
three four-line stanzas followed by a rhyming
couplet. Perennial themes for sonnets—love,
friendship, time, and the meaning of life—are
skillfully expressed within the rigidity of the
rhyme scheme and meter. The lineage of some
of our most famous sonneteers, W. H. Auden,
Louise Bogan, John Berryman, and Edna St.
Vincent Millay, can be traced to Wordsworth,

Shelley, and Keats. Helen Plotz, foremost anthologist, has collected 130 poems in *This Powerful Rhyme: A Book of Sonnets* (A). The title
comes from Shakespeare's sonnet that begins
"Not marble, nor the gilded monuments/Of
princes, shall outlive this pow'rful rhyme."

The lure of this fragile form is as durable as
Circe's enchantment. Phyllis McGinley's "Good
Humor Man" seems up to the minute with this
classical form as she likens the ice cream man
to the Pied Piper:

So, long ago, in some such shrill procession
Perhaps the Hamelin children gave pursuit
To one who wore a red-and-yellow fashion
Instead of white, but made upon his flute
The selfsame promise plain to every comer:
Unending sweets, imperishable summer.[58]

Students nurtured on poetry can make
meaningful experiences from linguistically
complex adult forms such as ballads and sonnets. Like Wordsworth's "Michael," building
stone by stone, students building poem by
poem can reach a gratifying eminence, for poetry once possessed is forever a wellspring
of joy.

Free Verse

Free verse is unrhymed verse that has either no metrical pattern or an irregular pattern. The arrangement on the page, the essence of the subject, and the density of thought distinguish free verse. Teachers often encourage children to write in free verse when they are experimenting with poetry; it helps children avoid some of the difficulties of trying to rhyme.

Ted Kooser's "Treehouse" in Paul Janeczko's *Pocket Poems* is free verse.

> Whose kite was this?
> It must have caught here
> summers ago. Winters
> have tugged it apart.
> Here is its tail,
> this piece of knotted rope
> still blowing.[59]

"Snow," by Nan Fry, is also in *Pocket Poems*.

> drifting we wake
> to a world of no angles
> no edges
>
> mysterious loaves
> huddle
> in front of each house
>
> an old VW
> is a rising bun
> an upended egg
>
> everywhere the plumpness of doves
> the hospitable hollows
> the scooped-out insides of waves[60]

THE ELEMENTS OF POETRY

Poets manipulate the elements of sound, rhythm, and meaning to distinguish their work from prose. Sound and rhythm are more pronounced and meaning is more condensed in poetry. Together they create an impact more powerful than any found in prose.

Words as Sound

Although poetry need not rhyme, most research in children's preferences indicates that children prefer rhyme. Rhyme is not as fashionable with adults as it once was, but children enjoy reciting it. It sticks better in the mind and lingers longer on the tongue. Generation after generation repeats the same jump rope jingles and rhyming street games. In more sophisticated poetry, the sound echoes the sense.

Of all the elements of poetry, sound offers the most pleasure to children. The choice and arrangement of sounds make the music of poetry and, at the same time, serve to reinforce meaning. Alliteration, assonance, onomatopoeia, and rhyme are among the language resources of sound.

Poets' ears are tuned to the repetition of consonants, vowels, syllables, words, phrases, and lines, separately and in combination. Anything may be repeated to achieve effect. *Alliteration* refers to the repetition of the initial consonant sounds of words at close intervals, such as "thin spaghettis softly scream/and curdle quarts of quiet cream,"[61] or "Timothy Tompkins had turnips and tea./The turnips were tiny./He ate at least three."[62]

Rhoda W. Bacmeister uses *assonance*, the repetition of vowel sounds at close intervals, and alliteration in the verses of "Galoshes":

> Susie's galoshes
> Make splishes and sploshes
> And slooshes and sloshes,
> As Susie steps slowly
> Along in the slush.[63]

Repetition is like meeting an old friend again; children find it reassuring. Repetition of words underscores meaning, establishes a sound pattern, and is a source of humor in many nursery rhymes, as in Janina Domanska's version of "If All the Seas Were One Sea":

If all the seas were one sea,
What a *great* sea that would be!
If all the trees were one tree,
What a *great* tree that would be!
And if all the axes were one axe,
What a *great* axe that would be!
And if all the men were one man,
What a *great* man that would be!
And if the *great* man took the *great* axe,
And cut down the *great* tree,
And let it fall into the *great* sea,
What a splish-splash that would be![64]

Onomatopoeia is the creation of a word from natural sounds associated with the thing or action designated, or the use of such words. For example, the word "murmur" resembles somewhat the sound of murmuring. Other words that sound like what they mean are bang, snap, and hiss. Shel Silverstein plays with onomatopoeia in "The Fourth":

> Oh
> CRASH!
> my
> BASH
> it's
> BANG!
> the
> ZANG!
> Fourth
> WHOOSH!
> of
> BAROOOM!
> July
> WHEW![65]

Onomatopoeia in combination with other sound resources can achieve poetic effect to light up any child's eyes.

An example of end rhyme—in which the rhyming words are at the ends of lines—is Dennis Lee's popular "I Eat Kids Yum Yum!"

A child went out one day.
She only went to play.

A mighty monster came along
And sang its mighty monster song:

"I EAT KIDS YUM YUM!
I STUFF THEM DOWN MY TUM.
I ONLY LEAVE THE TEETH AND CLOTHES.
(I SPECIALLY LIKE THE TOES.)"

The child was not amused.
She stood there and refused.
Then with a skip and a little twirl
She sang the song of a hungry girl:

"I EAT MONSTERS BURP!
THEY MAKE ME SQUEAL AND SLURP.
IT'S TIME TO CHOMP AND TAKE A
    CHEW—
AND WHAT I'LL CHEW IS YOU!"

The monster ran like that!
It didn't stop to chat.
(The child went skipping home again
And ate her brother's model train.)[66]

When rhyme spills over from the end of one line to the beginning of the next it is called *runover*. David McCord gives us a beautiful example of this (together with end rhyme) in his "Runover Rhyme":

Down by the pool still fishing,
Wishing for fish, I fail
Praying for birds not present,
Pheasant or grouse or quail.

Up in the woods, his hammer
Stammering, I can't see
The woodpecker, find the cunning
Sunning old owl in the tree.

Over the field such raucous
Talk as the crows talk on!
Nothing around me slumbers;
Numbers of birds have gone.

Even the leaves hang listless,
Lasting through days we lose,
Empty of what is wanted,
Haunted by what we choose.[67]

If children are provided with many opportunities to experience a variety of rhyme schemes, the chances are that they will then come to see how the use of rhyme can add to and enhance the meaning of a poem.

Words as Rhythm

Rhythm is everywhere in life; think of ocean waves, the tick of a clock, hoofbeats, one's pulse. In poetry, rhythm refers to recurrences of syllables and accents, in the rise and fall of words spoken or read. All good poetry is rhythmical, just as other forms of high art are. The rhythm in painting, sculpture, and other visual arts is seen in the repetition of line, form, or color. Rhythm in dance is apparent in the flow of the body movements and the graceful flow of motion. In music it is evident in the beat. Well-written prose has rhythm, too, although it is less evident or regular than in poetry.

Rhythm is usually manifest in poetry as accented and unaccented syllables are alternated. It is what Eve Merriam calls "the repeat of a beat . . . an inner chime that makes you want to tap your feet or swerve in a curve."[68]

The rhythm in poetry is most often metrical. Meter is ordered rhythm, in which certain syllables are regularly stressed or accented in a more or less fixed pattern. "Meter" means "measure," and metrical language in poetry can be measured. The meter in poetry can run from that of tightly structured verse patterns to loosely defined free verse. Whatever it is, rhythm helps to create and then reinforce a poem's meaning. In *Circus* (N–P), Jack Prelutsky adjusts his rhythms to the subject:

> Over and over the tumblers tumble
> with never a fumble
> with never a stumble,
> top over bottom and back over top
> flop-flippy-floppity-flippity-flop.

But the tumblers pass and are followed by the elephants, whose plodding walk echoes in the new rhythm:

> Here come the elephants, ten feet high,
> elephants, elephants, heads in the sky.
> Eleven great elephants intertwined,
> one little elephant close behind.[69]

and the rhythm plods along in the way elephants walk. Here is an example of how Karla Kuskin uses rhythm to echo the meaning of a poem.

"Eletelephony" by Laura E. Richards establishes a clear rhythm as the narrator becomes hopelessly tongue-tied. (From *The Random House Book of Poetry for Children*, selected by Jack Prelutsky and illustrated by Arnold Lobel.)

Eletelephony

Once there was an elephant,
Who tried to use the telephant—
No! no! I mean an elephone
Who tried to use the telephone—
(Dear me! I am not certain quite
That even now I've got it right.)

Howe'er it was, he got his trunk
Entangled in the telephunk;
The more he tried to get it free,
The louder buzzed the telephee—
(I fear I'd better drop the song
Of elephop and telephong!)

Laura E. Richards

WHERE WOULD YOU BE?

Where would you be on a night like this
With the wind so dark and howling?
Close to the light
Wrapped warm and tight
Or there where the cats are prowling?

Where would you wish you on such a night
When the twisting trees are tossed?
Safe in a chair
In the lamp-lit air
Or out where the moon is lost?

Where would you be when the white waves
    roar
On the tumbling storm-torn sea?
Tucked inside
Where it's calm and dry
Or searching for stars in the furious sky
Whipped by the whine of the gale's wild cry
Out in the night with me?[70]

David McCord captures the rhythmic chant of children's playground behavior in "Bananas and Cream":

Bananas and cream,
Bananas and cream:
All we could say was
Bananas and cream.

We couldn't say fruit,
We wouldn't say cow,
We didn't say sugar—
We don't say it now.

Bananas and cream,
Bananas and cream,
All we could shout was
Bananas and cream.

We didn't say why,
We didn't say how;
We forgot it was fruit,
We forgot the old cow;
We *never* said sugar,
We only said *WOW!*

Bananas and cream,
Bananas and cream;
All that we want is
Bananas and cream!

We didn't say dish,
We didn't say spoon;
We said not tomorrow,
But NOW and HOW SOON

Bananas and cream,
Bananas and cream?
We yelled for bananas,
Bananas and scream![71]

When Robert Louis Stevenson writes

Faster than fairies, faster than witches,
Bridges and houses, hedges and ditches;
And charging along like troops in a battle
All through the meadows the horses and
    cattle.[72]

he is using a rapid rhythm that suggests the view "From a Railway Carriage."

Word order, too, contributes to the rhythm of poetry. Arranging words is central to the making of a poem. Teachers, and perhaps some special students, should be aware of the ways poets manipulate syntax to make poetry distinctive from prose. One noticeable feature of poetic language is the way it varies from the straight declarative sentence. In Stevenson's "Where Go the Boats?" the poet states:

Dark brown is the river
    Golden is the sand.
It flows along forever,
    With trees on either hand.[73]

The literal meaning of the poem could probably be communicated in this way:

The river is dark brown,
    The sand is gold.
The river keeps on flowing forever,
    With trees on both sides.

But the reader immediately recognizes that much is lost. Retaining most of Stevenson's words but rearranging the word order totally distorts the visual image. Poets manipulate syntax until they find an order and rhythm pleasing to them and one that communicates more than the literal message. For children, the inverted sentence order used for poetic effect can at first interfere with meaning; however, they grow in their ability to comprehend in-

TEACHING IDEA

PARALLEL POEMS (I–A)   Having students write poems as homework is a sure-fire way to make them dislike poetry. None of us would want to be told to go home and write a poem tonight, as if the creative spark could be ignited on request. The ability to write poetry that is not doggerel develops gradually; some never achieve it.

Students can be eased into poetry writing when they perceive it as fun and not as assigned work. Sometimes it can be done collaboratively, with two or three students working together; sometimes it can be done by using an established poet's work as a guide. Here it is suggested that students experiment with writing parallel poems—poems that have a subject and a style similar to an existing poem used as a model. Before sending them out on their own, you may want to begin with a whole-class collaboration. A poetry worksheet can be used to brainstorm for descriptive words about the subject and related words that rhyme with these. Preliminary planning eases poetic expression of ideas.

ACTIVITY: TEACHER TO STUDENT

SPINNING OFF WITH SPECIES AND SEEDS (I–A)   Read David McCord's "Glowworm" in *One at a Time* that begins with the line "Never talk down to a glowworm." Work with one or two other students to write a parallel poem (a poem that has a subject and a form like McCord's) about a bumblebee, gypsy moth, mosquito, or firefly. Try to use the pattern of the opening line. For example, you could begin, "Never light up with a firefly."

Or read David McCord's "Pumpkin Seeds" (in *One at a Time*) to spark poems about apple seeds, avocado seeds, or peach pits. Ask yourself and your writing partners what kind of imaginary special thing could grow from your seed. What word would you substitute for "pumpkin" in the opening lines, "There is a man who says he may/Have on the market any day/A pumpkin of tremendous size"?[74] Or accept Shel Silverstein's poem "The Toucan" (in *Where the Sidewalk Ends*) as an invitation to continue writing with the same rhythm and shape. Continue adding clever verses about this broad-billed bird.

Once you begin, you will find many poems to parallel.

verted sentences as they hear poetry read aloud.

Words as Meaning: Imagery

Poetry often carries many layers of meaning and, as in other literature, is subject to many different interpretations. I. A. Richards demonstrates in *Practical Criticism* that the level of sophistication and experience in reading poetry affect the meaning the reader obtains. The meaning children create is directly proportionate to what experience has prepared them to understand.

One teacher read William Jay Smith's "The Toaster"[75] to children of varying levels of development and asked them to draw a picture of what the poem was about. The poem describes the toaster as a "silver-scaled dragon who sits at my elbow and toasts my bread." Children in the concrete operations stage interpreted the poem as an actual dragon and drew fiery-

mouthed dragons showing that they unde stood the poem at the literal, concrete level Older children, above the fourth grade, drew pictures of toasters that resembled dragons, suggesting that they understood the figurative language Smith used in the poem.

Not all poems have hidden meanings that can be recognized only by those who can ferret out the relationship between symbols and details about the poet's view of life. It is true that some poems bear subtle messages; however, most are descriptions of character, expressions of emotions, or accounts of events. We chance losing our students if we continually send them searching for hidden messages. It is perfectly acceptable to assert, as Alice did, after reading "Jabberwocky": "Somehow it seems to fill my head with ideas, only I don't know exactly what they are."

Among the poetic devices used to convey meaning are figurative language, imagery, and denotation and connotation. Through them

Children often appreciate creative efforts of their peers as much as those of adults.

more is meant than meets
eft unsaid is often as impor-
ut down on the page.

language produces a meaning
e literal one of the words used. In
urative language is used frequently
ts meaning in unique ways. Meta-
mile, and personification make the lan-
of poetry different from that of prose. As
s create vivid experiences, they use lan-
uage metaphorically; they help us to see or
feel things in new ways. It is not enough just
to have the idea; poets must also have the
words. Carl Sandburg says, "The right words,
the special and particular words for the purpose in view, these must come. For out of
them the poem is made."[76] The special and
particular words often involve figurative language.

Children need experience in using and understanding figurative language before they
can fully appreciate the poetry that relies on it.
How they will understand this use of language
in a poem depends upon their background.
Young children understand the comparisons
made on a physical plane but not at a psychological one. Bushes that look like popcorn balls
and cars that look like big, fat raisins are more
likely to be meaningful to these children than a
prison guard's heart of stone. Young children
interpret such a prison guard's heart as being
physically of stone. When they are more mature, they recognize that the comparison refers
to a psychological state.

Once children gain some understanding of
how figurative language contributes to meaning, poetry assumes a deeper dimension. Recognizing contrast, comparison, and exaggeration on a psychological plane affords children
richer interpretations.

Arnold Adoff, in *Sports Pages*, makes a simple comparison in his "My Knee Is Only
Sprained":

My knee is only sprained,
         is only swollen,
and
the doctor says I will be
                    fine.
         I'll play again.

He says this as he
sits on his padded
leather chair that
can swivel 360 de
         grees.
Oh
         why can't knees?

Still.   We do not make the Six O'Clock News
                    with this old story, often told, of
                         pain and frustration and fear.

Still.
         I must sit on this bench and be as
still as this brace demands;
         as
still as the other spectators behind me in
                              the stands.
I have been told: next season,
                    next y e ar. [77]

ACTIVITY: TEACHER TO STUDENT

PORTRAITS IN PERSONIFICATION (I–A)   Collect poems in which personification is used. (You may want to work in groups.) When you have found several
poems, read them aloud to each other. Draw or paint what you think the
personified object would look like if you could see it. Compare the different
interpretations and select several for a classroom bulletin board. Be sure to
include a copy of the poem that inspired the pictures.

More complex comparisons can be made using the devices of metaphor and simile, which compare one thing to another or view something in terms of something else. The comparison in a *simile* is stated and uses the words "like" or "as" to draw the comparison. A comparison in a *metaphor* is inferred; something is stated as something else.

Eve Merriam makes a comparison unmistakable by entitling her equation of morning with a new sheet of paper, "Metaphor":

Morning is
a new sheet of paper
for you to write on.

Whatever you want to say,
all day
until night
folds it up
and files it away.

The bright words and the dark words
are gone
until dawn
and a new day
to write on.[78]

Personification refers to the representation of a thing or abstraction as a person. When we say "Fortune smiled on us" or "If the weather permits," we are giving human qualities to an idea like fortune or a force of nature like the weather. Poets often give human feelings or thoughts to plants and animals. Hilda Conkling uses personification to make the ideas more vivid or unusual in "Dandelion":

O little soldier with the golden helmet,
What are you guarding on my lawn?
You with your green gun
And your yellow beard,
Why do you stand so stiff?
There is only the grass to fight![79]

Langston Hughes's "April Rain Song" employs personification:

Let the rain kiss you.
Let the rain beat upon your head with silver
   liquid drops.
Let the rain sing you a lullaby.[80]

Poets create imagery through the use of words in ways that arrest our senses; we can imagine that we almost see, taste, touch, smell, or hear what they describe. Little escapes the poet's vision; nothing limits the speculations upon what he sees. In just such speculation, Robert Frost makes a seemingly commonplace incident memorable:

DUST OF SNOW

The way a crow
Shook down on me
The dust of snow
From a hemlock tree

Has given my heart
A change of mood
And saved some part
Of a day I had rued.[81]

Ted Hughes's uncompromising imagery in "Moon Whales" evokes an emotion solitary and existential:

They plough through the moon stuff
Just under the surface
Lifting the moon's skin
Like a muscle
But so slowly it seems like a lasting mountain
Breathing so rarely it seems like a volcano
Leaving a hole blasted in the moon's
   skin . . .[82]

Denotation refers to the literal or dictionary definition of a word or phrase. *Connotation* refers to the suggested meaning associated with the literal one—the overtones of meaning. Connotations can vary with the individual person. Water, for instance, may have connotations of refreshment, cooling, beauty, pleasure, or cleansing, depending on which of its many

TEACHING IDEA

THINGS TO DO (ALL AGES) Poetry can be regarded as an oral art form and can often be appreciated most when it is spoken or read aloud. Long before children learn to read and long after they are reading alone, they should hear poetry read. The primary purpose in sharing poetry with children is to extend their understanding and increase their pleasure and enjoyment of it. Some guidelines for reading poetry aloud include

1. Read it silently first, to grasp its meaning for yourself.
2. Read it aloud to yourself several times to determine where pauses will affect the sense. Thus, you will not necessarily stop at the end of a line, but carry over from one to the next to complete the thought. Poets use punctuation purposefully to guide our reading.
3. Listen to recordings of poets reading their own work to gain a feeling for phrasing.
4. Read with expressiveness appropriate to the poem. The content determines the tone.
5. Read poems in a natural, not sing-song or stagelike, voice.
6. Give children time to enjoy the words of the poem. In poetry's condensed language every word can carry much meaning.
7. Read the same poem aloud to the class more than once.
8. Invite children to join in so they can savor the words, too.

---

aspects you are thinking of and where you have enjoyed water the most. But it might also arouse feelings of terror in a person who has been in danger of drowning.

Poetry makes use of both denotative and connotative meaning, saying what it means but saying much more. Connotation enriches meaning. Sometimes the sounds of words combine with their connotations to make a very pleasing pattern.

"Reflections on a Gift of Watermelon Pickle Received from a Friend Called Felicity," by John Tobias, carries both denotative and connotative meanings, with several possibilities for interpretation. Trying to arrive at consensual validation of "one right meaning," as with most poems, is counterproductive.

During that summer
When unicorns were still possible;
When the purpose of knees
Was to be skinned;

When shiny horse chestnuts
  (Hollowed out
  Fitted with straws
  Crammed with tobacco
  Stolen from butts
  In family ashtrays)
Were puffed in green lizard silence
While straddling thick branches
Far above and away
From the softening effects
Of civilization;

During that summer—
Which may never have been at all;
But which has become more real
Than the one that was—
Watermelons ruled.

Thick pink imperial slices
Melting frigidly on sun-parched tongues
Dribbling from chins;
Leaving the best part,
The black bullet seeds,
To be spit out in rapid fire

ACTIVITY: TEACHER TO STUDENT

A POETRY PAGEANT (P–I)   Poetry is fun when you share it with your friends. One way to do that is through choral speaking. Select some of your favorite poems and divide them into parts as music is divided for singing by a chorus. Use the natural rhythm of the language and the swinging cadence of the lines to help in dividing the poem into parts. Blend high and low voices to emphasize poetic sounds just as instruments are used in an orchestra. You can have solos, duets, boys alone, girls alone, boys and girls together, and whatever other variations the poem suggests. You can find some poems about unusual and imaginative animals that are especially good for choral speaking in X. J. Kennedy's *The Phantom Ice Cream Man: More Nonsense Verse*; Mary Ann Hoberman's *The Raucous Auk*; Jack Prelutsky's *The Pack Rat's Day and Other Poems*; and William Cole's *An Arkful of Animals*.

Rehearse until your production is polished. You might want to make simple animal costumes or face masks. Take a troupe of "troubadors" around the school, dropping into classrooms for about 10 minutes to share your interpretations.

Against the wall
Against the wind
Against each other;

And when the ammunition was spent,
There was always another bite:
It was a summer of limitless bites,
Of hungers quickly felt
And quickly forgotten
With the next careless gorging.

The bites are fewer now.
Each one is savored lingeringly,
Swallowed reluctantly.

But in a jar put up by Felicity,
The summer which maybe never was
Has been captured and preserved.
And when we unscrew the lid
And slice off a piece
And let it linger on our tongue:
Unicorns become possible again.[83]

The sensory images evoked by the phrases "green lizard silence," "thick pink imperial slices," or "sun-parched tongues" paint pictures in the mind's eye as vivid as any that a painter creates on canvas. Tobias helps us imagine a time when unicorns were still possible.

Understanding poetry is a long and continual process built only upon experiences that are both wide and broad. Children develop better understanding the more they internalize poetry. They profit little from verbal definitions and descriptions. It is firsthand experience of listening to, reading, writing, and discussing poetry that contributes the most to fostering their love of it. Children who live with poetry in their homes and in their schools turn to poems again and again for pleasure.

Close attention to children's comments can supply a basis for thought-provoking questions that will lead children to discover the substance of poetry for themselves. The object is to develop a child's liking for the music of words; detailed analysis divests poetry of its splendor. Misconceptions may be of greater value than

TEACHING IDEA

A POETRY FESTIVAL (ALL AGES)   A poetry festival celebrates the primacy of poetry in our lives. It is an undertaking limited only by the wingspan of our imaginations. Children should participate in planning every step; brainstorm with them to determine what different attractions and exhibits they want to have.

An entire school day might be set aside to celebrate the many faces of poetry. Select a site that is spacious. Some teachers use the entire school, but you may want to begin with the gymnasium or playground. Mark off areas for game booths and exhibits. The entrance can be a large archway decorated with poetry book jackets. Would you like a yellow brick road leading up to it?

Invitations made by children can be sent out. They could contain favorite poems accompanied by original drawings. A good choice for the invitations might be "How to Eat a Poem," by Eve Merriam:

> Don't be polite.
> Bite in.
> Pick it up with your fingers and lick the juice that may run down your chin.
> It is ready and ripe now, whenever you are.[84]

To this can be added the invitation, such as "Come join us for a Poetry Festival," with date, time, and place added. Among the attractions you might have the following booths:

Recordings: Listen to poets reading their own work.

Meet a Poet: Invite local poets to talk to students

Food for Thought: Taste "watermelon pickles," "bananas and cream," "rice pudding," or "chicken soup with rice."

Balloon Game: Put poems inside balloons and use them in a dart throw.

Graffiti Wall: Cover a wall with craft paper. Let aspiring poets write their words on the wall.

Show Time: Entertainers perform poems. *When I First Came to this Land,* by Oscar Brand (P–A); *Sweet Betsy from Pike,* by Robert A. Parker (P); *Mommy, Buy Me a China Doll,* by Harve Zemach (N–P); and *The Star-Spangled Banner,* by Peter Spier (P–I).

---

the explanation that destroys it. The magic that the words exercise on the imagination, more valuable than accuracy at beginning stages, leaves a telling mark. Appropriate discussions of poetry take children back to the poem, not away from it and into discussions of values, moral judgments, or personal opinion.

Poetry is valuable for the full realization of life. Only by hard work can we participate in the imaginative experience of others—and thereby get to know our own better. The more readers participate, the more they themselves create, and the more personal and enjoyable the experience of poetry becomes. The rewards are more than worth the effort.

Teachers can help children trust their own feelings about poetry, to free their thinking about it so that it becomes as flexible as it can

TEACHING IDEA

CHILD-MADE BOOKS OF POEMS (P–I)[85]   In a writing center or poetry corner, have a variety of poems written out. Let students choose the poems they like, and encourage them to illustrate the poems using watercolors, pastels, crayons, markers, or collage. Students may group their collections by topic—such as nature, seasons, or holidays—by author, or by theme.

Poems can be put into an anthology that becomes part of the classroom library or is taken home to share with family members. The anthologies can also contain original poems by the children. Make copies of all the poems and illustrations so children have a complete set of their classmates' work. Put a table of contents and a dedication page in the book. The books can be bound (see Chapter 2) or tied with ribbons.

---

be. They can help children not to think in a predictable manner.

Experience with the fun of verse is all children need to develop discrimination. Teachers can use the special pleasure inherent in poetry to extend the imagination, contribute new sensations, and enhance past experiences. This is most readily achieved by teachers whose enthusiasm shows, who read good poetry aloud in such a way as to show the value and worth they themselves place in it. It is a most important first step toward making a love of poetry catching.

RECOMMENDED READING

Narrative Poems

Browning, Robert. *The Pied Piper of Hamelin*. Illustrated by Kate Greenaway. London: Warne, 1888.

Clifton, Lucille. *Some of the Days of Everett Anderson*. Illustrated by Evaline Ness. New York: H. Holt, 1970.

———. *Everett Anderson's Friend*. Illustrated by Ann Grifalconi. New York: H. Holt, 1976.

———. *Everett Anderson's Year*. Illustrated by Ann Grifalconi. New York: H. Holt, 1974.

Lear, Edward. *The Owl and the Pussycat*. Illustrated by Janet Stevens. New York: Holiday House, 1983.

———. *The Scroobius Pip*. Illustrated by Nancy Ekholm Burkert. New York: Harper & Row, 1987.

Moore, Clement Clarke. *The Night Before Christmas*. Illustrated by Tomie dePaola. New York: Holiday House, 1980.

Nash, Ogden. *Custard and Company: Poems by Ogden Nash*. Illustrated by Quentin Blake. Boston: Little, Brown, 1980.

Parker, Elinor. *One Hundred More Story Poems*. Illustrated by Peter Spier. New York: Crowell, 1960.

Prelutsky, Jack. *Rolling Harvey Down the Hill*. Illustrated by Victoria Chess. New York: Greenwillow, 1980.

Riley, James Whitcomb. *Little Orphant Annie*. Illustrated by Diane Stanley. New York: Putnam's, 1983.

Limericks

Bodecker, N. M. *A Person from Britain Whose Head Was the Shape of a Mitten and Other Limericks*. New York: Atheneum, 1980.

Brewton, Sara, and John Brewton. *Laughable Limericks*. Illustrated by Ingrid Fitz. New York: Crowell, 1965.

Livingston, Myra Cohn. *A Lollygag*

of Limericks. New York: Atheneum, 1978.

Lobel, Arnold. *The Book of Pigericks*. New York: Harper & Row, 1983.

Concrete Poems

Finlay, Ian Hamilton. *Poems to Hear and See*. New York: Macmillan, 1971.

Froman, Robert. *Seeing Things: A Book of Poems*. Illustrated by Ray Barber. New York: Crowell, 1974.

———. *Street Poems*. New York: Dutton, 1971.

Merriam, Eve. *Out Loud*. Illustrated by Harriet Sherman. New York: Atheneum, 1973.

Pilon, Barbara A. *Concrete Is Not Always Hard*. Boston: Xerox Education Publications, 1972.

Rimanelli, Giose, and Paul Pinsleur. *Poems Make Pictures, Pictures Make Poems*. Illustrated by Ronni Solbert. New York: Pantheon, 1972.

Lyric Poetry

Behn, Harry. *Crickets and Bullfrogs and Whispers of Thunder*. San Diego: Harcourt Brace Jovanovich, 1984.

Blake, William. *Songs of Innocence*. Illustrated by Ellen Raskin. 1789. Reprint. New York: Doubleday, 1966.

De la Mare, Walter. *Come Hither*. Illustrated by Alec Buckels. New York: Knopf, 1923.

Forrester, Victoria. *A Latch Against the Wind*. New York: Atheneum, 1985.

Haiku

Kherdian, David. *Country Cat, City Cat*. Illustrated by Nonny Hogrogian. New York: Scholastic, 1978.

Lewis, Richard, ed. *In a Spring Garden*. Illustrated by Ezra Jack Keats. New York: Dial, 1964.

Ballads

Benet, Stephen Vincent. *The Ballad of William Sycamore (1790–1871)*. Illustrated by Brinton Turkle. Boston: Little, Brown, 1972.

Coleridge, Samuel Taylor. *The Rime of the Ancient Mariner*. Illustrated by C. Walter Hodges. New York: Coward-McCann, 1971.

Pomerantz, Charlotte. *The Ballad of the Long-Tailed Rat*. Illustrated by Marian Parry. New York: Macmillan, 1975.

Thayer, Ernest Lawrence. *Casey at the Bat: A Ballad of the Republic, Sung in the Year 1888*. Illustrated by Walter Tripp. New York: Putnam's, 1980.

Free Verse

Adoff, Arnold. *All the Colors of the Race*. Illustrated by John Steptoe. New York: Lothrop, Lee & Shepard, 1982.

Turner, Anne Warren. *Street Talk*. Illustrated by Catherine Stock. Boston: Houghton Mifflin, 1986.

Worth, Valerie. *More Small Poems*. Illustrated by Natalie Babbitt. New York: Farrar, Straus & Giroux, 1976.

———. *Small Poems*. Illustrated by Natalie Babbitt. New York: Farrar, Straus & Giroux, 1972.

———. *Still More Small Poems*. Illustrated by Natalie Babbitt. New York: Farrar, Straus & Giroux, 1978.

Collections

Abercrombie, Barbara Mattes, ed. *The Other Side of a Poem*. Illustrated by Harry Bertschmann. New York: Harper & Row, 1977.

Bennett, Jill, comp. *Tiny Tim: Verses for Children*. Illustrated by Helen Oxenbury. New York: Delacorte, 1981.

Blishen, Edward. *The Oxford Book of Poetry for Young Children*. Illustrated by Brain Wildsmith. New York: Watts, 1963.

Cole, William. *Good Dog Poems*. Illustrated by Ruth Sanderson. New York: Scribner's, 1981.

Corrin, Sara, and Stephen Corrin, comps. *Once upon a Rhyme: One Hundred One Poems for Young Children*. Illustrated by Jill Bennett. Winchester, Mass.: Faber, 1982.

Ferris, Helen, comp. *Favorite Poems Old and New*. Illustrated by Leonard Weisgard. New York: Doubleday, 1957.

Frank, Josette. *More Poems to Read to the Very Young*. New York: Random House, 1968.

———. *Poems to Read to the Very Young*. New York: Random House, 1961.

Kherdian, David, ed. *Poems Here and Now*. Illustrated by Nonny Hogrogian. New York: Greenwillow, 1976.

Livingston, Myra Cohn, ed. *Why Am I Grown So Cold? Poems of the Unknowable*. New York: Atheneum, 1982.

Molloy, Paul. *Beach Glass and Other Poems*. New York: Four Winds, 1970.

Prelutsky, Jack. *The New Kid on the Block*. Illustrated by James Stevenson. New York: Greenwillow, 1984.

Royds, Caroline, ed. *Poems for Young Children*. Illustrated by Inga Moore. New York: Doubleday, 1986.

Sandburg, Carl. *The Sandburg Treasury: Prose and Poetry for Young People*. Illustrated by Paul Bacon. New York: Harcourt Brace Jovanovich, 1970.

Strickland, Dorothy S., ed. *Listen, Children*. Illustrated by Leo Dillon and Diane Dillon. New York: Bantam, 1982.

Untermeyer, Louis, comp. *The Golden Treasury of Poetry*. Illustrated by Joan Walsh Anglund. New York: Golden Press, 1959.

Humorous Poems

Adoff, Arnold. *Eats.* Illustrated by Susan Russo. New York: Lothrop, Lee & Shepard, 1979.

Bodecker, N. M. *Hurry, Hurry, Mary Dear! And Other Nonsense Poems.* Atheneum, McElderry, 1976.

———. *Let's Marry Said the Cherry and Other Nonsense Poems.* New York: Atheneum, 1974.

———. *Pigeon Cubes and Other Verse.* New York: Atheneum, McElderry, 1982.

Brewton, Sara, John E. Brewton and G. Meredith Blackburn III, eds. *My Tang's Tungled And Other Ridiculous Situations.* Illustrated by Graham Booth. New York: Crowell, 1973.

Ciardi, John. *Fast and Slow: Poems for Advanced Children of Beginning Parents.* Illustrated by Becky Garver. Boston: Houghton Mifflin, 1975.

———. *The Man Who Sang the Sillies.* Illustrated by Edward Gorey. Philadelphia: Lippincott, 1961.

———. *The Reason for the Pelican.* Philadelphia: Lippincott, 1959.

Cole, William. ed. *An Arkful of Animals: Poems for the Very Young.* Illustrated by Lynn Munsinger. Boston: Houghton Mifflin, 1978.

———. *A Boy Named Mary Jane, And Other Silly Verse.* Illustrated by George MacLain. New York: Avon, 1979.

———. *Give Up?* Illustrated by Mike Cole. New York: Avon, 1981.

———. *Monster Knock Knocks.* Illustrated by Mike Thaler. New York: Simon & Schuster, 1988.

———. *Oh, Such Foolishness!* Illustrated by Tomie dePaola. Philadelphia: Lippincott, 1978.

Farber, Norma. *Never Say Ugh to a Bug.* Illustrated by José Aruego. New York: Greenwillow, 1979.

Hoberman, Mary Ann. *I Like Old Clothes.* Illustrated by Jacqueline Chwast. New York: Knopf, 1976.

———. *Nuts to You and Nuts to Me.* New York: Knopf, 1974.

Jacobs, Leland B., comp. *Funny Bone Ticklers in Verse and Rhyme.* Illustrated by Edward Malsberg. Easton, Md.: Garrard, 1973.

———. *Poetry for Chuckles and Grins.* Illustrated by Tomie dePaola. Easton, Md.: Garrard, 1968.

Kennedy, X. J. *One Winter Night in August and Other Nonsense Jingles.* Illustrated by David McPhail. New York: Atheneum, 1975.

Kuskin, Karla. *Alexander Soames: His Poems.* New York: Harper & Row, 1962.

Lear, Edward. *The Pelican Chorus and the Quangle Wangle's Hat.* Illustrated by Kevin W. Maddison. New York: Viking, 1981.

———. *The Pobble Who Has No Toes.* Illustrated by Kevin W. Maddison. New York: Viking, 1978.

Livingston, Myra Cohn, ed. *Speak Roughly to Your Little Boy: A Collection of Parodies and Burlesques, Together with the Original Poems, Chosen and Annotated for Young People.* Illustrated by Joseph Low. New York: Harcourt Brace Jovanovich, 1971.

———. *What a Wonderful Bird the Frog Are: An Assortment of Humorous Poetry and Verse.* New York: Harcourt Brace Jovanovich, 1973.

Merriam, Eve. *Blackberry Ink.* Illustrated by Hans Wilhelm. New York: Morrow, 1985.

———. *New Rhymes for Young Readers.* New York: Atheneum, 1981.

Nash, Ogden. *The Moon Is Shining Bright as Day: An Anthology of Good-Humored Verse.* Illustrated by Rose Shirvanian. Philadelphia: Lippincott, 1953.

Prelutsky, Jack. *The Baby Uggs Are Hatching.* Illustrated by James Stevenson. New York: Greenwillow, 1982.

———. *The Snopp on the Sidewalk and Other Poems.* New York: Greenwillow, 1977.

———. *Toucans Two and Other Poems.* Illustrated by José Aruego. New York: Macmillan, 1970.

———. *Zoo Doings: Animal Poems.* Illustrated by Paul O. Zelinsky. New York: Greenwillow, 1983.

Roethke, Theodore. *Dirty Dinky and Other Creatures: Poems for Children.* Edited by Beatrice Roethke and Stephen Lushington. New York: Doubleday, 1973.

Tripp, Wallace, comp. *A Great Big Ugly Man Came Up and Tied His Horse to Me: A Book of Nonsense Verse.* Boston: Little, Brown, 1973.

———. *Marguerite Go Wash Your Feet.* Boston: Houghton Mifflin, 1985.

Nature Poems

Bramblett, Ella, ed. *Shoots of Green: Poems for Young Gardeners.* New York: Crowell, 1968.

Cole, William. *Dinosaurs and Beasts of Yore.* Philadelphia: Collins, 1979.

———. *The Poetry of Horses.* New York: Scribner's, 1979.

Fisher, Aileen. *Out in the Dark and Daylight.* Illustrated by Gail Owens. New York: Harper & Row, 1980.

Frost, Robert. *Stopping by Woods on a Snowy Evening.* Illustrated by Susan Jeffers. New York: Dutton, 1978.

Hopkins, Lee Bennett. *Dinosaurs.* Illustrated by Murray Tinkelman. San Diego: Harcourt Brace Jovanovich, 1987.

———. *The Sky Is Full of Song.* Illustrated by Dirk Zimmer. New York: Harper & Row, 1983.

Livingston, Myra Cohn. *Circle of Seasons.* Illustrated by Leonard

Everett Fisher. New York: Holiday House, 1982.

———. *Sea Songs*. Illustrated by Leonard Everett Fisher. New York: Holiday House, 1986.

Russo, Susan. *The Moon's the North Wind's Cooky*. New York: Lothrop, Lee & Shepard, 1979.

Ryder, Joanne. *Inside Turtle's Shell and Other Poems of the Field*. Illustrated by Susan Bonners. New York: Macmillan, 1985.

Child's World

Adoff, Arnold. *Make a Circle, Keep Us in: Poems for a Good Day*. Illustrated by Arnold Himler. New York: Delacorte, 1975.

———. *Ma nDa la*. Illustrated by Emily McCully. New York: Harper & Row, 1971.

———. *Big Sister Tells Me That I'm Black*. Illustrated by Lorenzo Lynch. New York: H. Holt, 1976.

———. *I Am the Running Girl*. Illustrated by Ronald Himler. New York: Harper & Row, 1979.

———. *Black Is Brown Is Tan*. Illustrated by Emily McCully. New York: Harper & Row, 1973.

———. *Today We Are Brother and Sister*. Illustrated by Glo Coalson. New York: Lothrop, Lee & Shephard, 1981.

Brooks, Gwendolyn. *Bronzeville Boys and Girls*. Illustrated by Ronni Solbert. New York: Harper & Row, 1956.

Bryan, Ashley, ed. *I Greet the Dawn: Poems by Paul Laurence Dunbar*. New York: Atheneum, 1978.

Giovanni, Nikki. *Spin A Soft Black Song*. Illustrated by George Martins. New York: Farrar, Straus & Giroux, 1987.

Griego, Margot C., et al. *Tortillitas Para Mama: And Other Spanish Nursery Rhymes*. Illustrated by Barbara Cooney. New York: H. Holt, 1981.

Hoberman, Mary Ann. *The Cozy Book*. Illustrated by Tony Chen. New York: Viking, 1982.

Hopkins, Lee Bennett, comp. *Best Friends*. Illustrated by James Watts. New York: Harper & Row, 1986.

———. *Circus, Circus*. Illustrated by John O'Brien. New York: Knopf, 1982.

———. *Click, Rumble, Roar: Poems about Machines*. Photography by Anna Held Audette. New York: Crowell, 1987.

———. *Elves, Fairies and Gnomes*. Illustrated by Rosekrans Hoffman. New York: Knopf, 1980.

———. *Morning Noon and Nighttime, Too*. New York: Harper & Row, 1980.

———. *Munching: Poems About Eating*. Illustrated by Nelle Davis. Boston: Little, Brown, 1985.

Kennedy, X. J. *The Forgetful Wishing Well: Poems for Young People*. Illustrated by Monica Incisa. New York: Atheneum, McElderry, 1985.

Kuskin, Karla. *Any Me I Want to Be*. New York: Harper & Row, 1972.

Larrick, Nancy. *When the Dark Comes Dancing*. Illustrated by John Wallner. New York: Philomel, 1983.

Livingston, Myra Cohn. *No Way of Knowing: Dallas Poems*. New York: Atheneum, McElderry, 1980.

Merriam, Eve. *Finding a Poem*. Illustrated by Seymour Chwast.

New York: Atheneum, 1970.

Millay, Edna St. Vincent. *Edna St. Vincent Millay's Poems Selected for Young People*. New York: Harper & Row, 1979.

O'Neill, Mary. *Hailstones and Halibut Bones*. Illustrated by John Wallner. New York: Doubleday, 1989.

———. *People I'd Like to Keep*. Illustrated by Paul Galdone. New York: Doubleday, 1964.

Pomerantz, Charlotte. *If I Had a Paka: Poems in Eleven Languages*. Illustrated by Nancy Tafuri. New York: Greenwillow, 1982.

———. *The Tamarindo Puppy*. Illustrated by Byron Barton. New York: Greenwillow, 1980.

Prelutsky, Jack. *Circus*. Illustrated by Arnold Lobel. New York: Macmillan, 1974.

Rylant, Cynthia. *Waiting to Waltz: A Childhood*. Illustrated by Stephen Gammell. New York: Bradbury, 1984.

Starbird, Kaye. *The Covered Bridge House and Other Poems*. New York: Four Winds, 1979.

Wallace, Daisy, ed. *Fairy Poems*. Illustrated by Trina Schart Hyman. New York: Holiday House, 1980.

———. *Ghost Poems*. Illustrated by Tomie dePaola. New York: Holiday House, 1979.

———. *Witch Poems*. Illustrated by Trina Schart Hyman. New York: Holiday House, 1976.

Zolotow, Charlotte. *Everything Glistens and Everything Sings: New and Selected Poems*. Illustrated by Margot Tomes. San Diego: Harcourt Brace Jovanovich, 1987.

PROFESSIONAL REFERENCES

Arbuthnot, May Hill, et al. *The Arbuthnot Anthology of Children's Literature*, 4th ed. Edited by Zena Sutherland. Glenview, Ill.: Scott, Foresman, 1976.

———, and Shelton L. Root, Jr., comps. *Time For Poetry: Third General Edition*. Illustrated by Arthur Paul. Glenview, Ill.: Scott, Foresman, 1968.

Barron, Pamela Petrick, and Jennifer Q. Burley, eds. *Jump over the Moon: Selected Professional Readings*. New York: Holt, Rinehart & Winston, 1984.

Brewton, John E., G. Meredith Blackburn III, and Lorraine A. Blackburn, comps. *Index to Poetry for Children and Young People 1970–1975*. New York: H. W. Wilson, 1978.

Fisher, Carol J., and Margaret A. Natarella. "Young Children's Preferences in Poetry: A National Survey of First, Second and Third Graders." *Research in the Teaching of English* 16, no. 4 (December 1982): 339–54.

Frye, Northrop. *The Educated Imagination*. Bloomington: Indiana University Press, 1964.

Glazer, Joan. "Profile: Lilian Moore." *Language Arts* 62, no. 6, (October 1985): 647–52.

Harris, Karen. "Children's Choices: A Theme Issue." *Louisiana Library Association* 49, no. 2 (Fall 1986): 65–66.

Hopkins, Lee Bennett. "David McCord." In *Books Are by People*. New York: Citation Press, 1969.

———. *Pass the Poetry, Please!* New York: Harper & Row, 1987.

———. "Profile: Aileen Fisher." In *Language Arts* 55, no. 7 (October 1978): 868–72.

Livingston, Myra Cohn. *When You're Alone/It Keeps You Capone: An Approach To Creative Writing with Children*. New York: Atheneum, 1973.

McClure, Amy A. "Children's Response to Poetry in a Supportive Literary Context." Ph.D. diss., Ohio State University, 1984.

Richards, Ivor A. *Practical Criticism: A Study of Literary Judgment*. New York: Harcourt Brace, 1956.

Smith, Dorothy, and Eva Andrews, comps. *Subject Index to Poetry for Children and Young People: 1957–1975*. Chicago: American Library Association, 1975.

Smith, Patricia. "Poetry Supplement." Cypress-Fairbanks School District, Houston, Texas, 1986.

Terry, Ann. *Children's Poetry Preferences: A National Survey of the Upper Elementary Grades*. Urbana, Ill.: National Council of Teachers of English, 1974.

Tom, Chow Loy. "Paul Revere Rides Ahead: Poems Teachers Read to Pupils in the Middle Grades." *Library Quarterly* 43 (January 1973): 27–38.

Woodburn, Mary Stuart. "Poetry with a Smile." In *Early Years* 16, no. 7 (March 1986): 35–38.

NOTES

1. Eve Merriam, "Inside a Poem," in *It Doesn't Always Have to Rhyme*, illus. Malcolm Spooner (New York: Atheneum, 1964), 3.
2. Eleanor Farjeon, "Poetry," *Poems for Children* (Philadelphia: Lippincott, 1951), 58.
3. Gregory Corso, *Poetspeak*, ed. Paul Janeczko (New York: Bradbury, 1983), 11.
4. May Swenson, "Notes on Poetry," in Myra Cohn Livingston, *When You Are Alone/It Keeps You Capone: An Approach to Creative Writing with Children* (New York: Atheneum, 1973), 237.
5. Lillian H. Smith, *The Unreluctant Years: A Critical Approach to Children's Literature* (1953; reprint, New York: Viking, Compass, 1967), 111.
6. Walter De la Mare, *Bells and Grass* (New York: Viking, 1942), 9.
7. Northrop Frye, *The Educated Imagination* (Bloomington: Indiana University Press, 1964), 63.
8. Edward Lear, *The Complete Nonsense of Edward Lear*, collected and introduced by Holbrook Jackson (New York: Dover, 1951), 23.
9. Myra Cohn Livingston, *Higgledy-Piggledy*, illus. Peter Sis (New York: Atheneum, McElderry, 1986), 7–8.
10. Henry Wadsworth Longfellow, *Paul Revere's Ride*, illus. Nancy Winslow Parker (New York: Greenwillow, 1985), 9–11.
11. Lilian Moore, "Foghorns," *Something New Begins* (New York: Atheneum, 1982), 34.
12. Mary Ann Hoberman, "Brother," in *Yellow Butter Purple Jelly Red Jam Black Bread*, illus. Chaya Burstein (New York: Viking, 1981), 28.
13. Dorothy Aldis, "Bad," *All Together: A Child's Treasury of Verse*, illus. Helen D. Jameson, Marjorie Flack, and Margaret Freeman (1925; reprint, New York: Putnam's, 1952), 109.
14. Paul Janeczko, promotional material, Bradbury Press, New York City.
15. Beatrice Schenk de Regniers, "Keep a Poem in Your Pocket," in *The Random House Book of Poetry*, sel. Jack Prelutsky, illus. Arnold Lobel (New York: Random House, 1983), 226.
16. Patricia Smith, Language and Reading Coordinator, *Poetry Supplement*, Cypress-Fairbanks School District, Houston.
17. X. J. Kennedy, "Wicked Witch Admires Herself," in *The Phantom Ice Cream Man: More Nonsense Verse*, illus. David McPhail (New York: Atheneum, 1979), 26.
18. Karla Kuskin, *Dogs and Dragons, Trees and Dreams* (New York: Harper & Row, 1980), introduction.
19. Barbara Holland Baskin, Karen H. Harris, and Colleen C. Salley, "Making the Poetry Connection," in *The Reading Teacher* 30, no. 3 (December 1976): 259–65.
20. Eve Merriam, *Pass the Poetry*,

Please! ed. Lee Bennett Hopkins (New York: Harper & Row, 1987), 113.

21. Mary Ann Hoberman, *A House Is a House for Me*, illus. Betty Fraser (New York: Viking, 1978), unpaged.

22. Shelly Lagumis, second grade classroom, 1987–88, Mastic-Shirley School, Long Island, New York.

23. Katherine Grigoriadis, third grade class, 1986–87, Highgate Public School, Markham, Ontario.

24. Ann Terry, *Children's Poetry Preferences: A National Survey of Upper Elementary Grades* (Urbana, Ill.: National Council of Teachers of English, 1974), 47–53.

25. Amy A. McClure, "Children's Response to Poetry in a Supportive Literary Context," Ph.D. diss., Ohio State University, 1984.

26. Chow Loy Tom, "Paul Revere Rides Ahead: Poems Teachers Read to Pupils in the Middle Grades," *Library Quarterly* 43 (January 1973): 27–38.

27. *Children's Choices*, (Newark, Del.: International Reading Association/Children's Book Council, 1974 to present).

28. Jack Prelutsky, "Cincinnati Patty," in *Ride a Purple Pelican*, illus. Garth Williams (New York: Greenwillow, 1986), 56.

29. Dennis Lee. "There Was an Old Lady," in *Jelly Belly*, illus. Juan Wyngaard (New York: Bedrick Books, 1985), 14–15.

30. Shel Silverstein, "Sarah Cynthia Sylvia Stout/Would Not Take the Garbage Out," in *Where the Sidewalk Ends* (New York: Harper & Row, 1974), 70–71.

31. Nancy Larrick, "Poetry in the Story Hour," in *Jump Over the Moon: Selected Professional Readings*, eds. Pamela Petrick Barron and Jennifer Q. Burley (New York: Holt, Rinehart &

Winston, 1984), 102–11.

32. Paul Fleischman, "The Passenger Pigeon," in *I Am Phoenix: Poems for Two Voices*, illus. Ken Nutt (New York: Harper & Row, 1985), 17.

33. Lee Bennett Hopkins, "David McCord," in *Books Are by People* (New York: Citation Press, 1969), 169.

34. David McCord, "Acceptance Speech for the NCTE Award for Poetry for Children," NCTE national meeting, New York City, November 29, 1977.

35. Alvina Treut Burrows, "Profile: Karla Kuskin," *Language Arts* 56, no. 8 (November-December 1979): 935–37.

36. Karla Kuskin, promotional material, Harper & Row, New York City.

37. Lee Bennett Hopkins, "Profile: Aileen Fisher," *Language Arts* 55, no. 7 (October 1978): 868–72.

38. Myra Cohn Livingston, promotional material, Atheneum, New York City, 1980.

39. Anne Commire, ed., "Eve Merriam," in *Something About the Author*, vol. 3 (Detroit: Gale Research, 1972), 128–29; and vol. 40 (1984), 141–49.

40. Ibid., vol. 3, 129.

41. Anne Commire, ed., "John Ciardi," in *Something About the Author*, vol. 1 (Detroit: Gale Research, 1971), 59–61.

42. Joan Glazer, "Profile: Lilian Moore," *Language Arts* 62, no. 6 (October 1985): 647–52.

43. Livingston, *When You're Alone/ It Keeps You Capone*, 5.

44. A. A. Milne, "Bad Sir Brian Botany," in *Now We Are Six*, illus. E. H. Shepard (New York: Dutton, 1955), 94.

45. Edward Lear, *The Complete Nonsense Book* (New York: Dodd, Mead, 1958), 31.

46. Louis Untermeyer, comp., *Golden Treasury of Poetry*, illus. Joan Walsh Anglund (New York: Golden Press, 1963), 241.

47. Eleanor Farjeon, "The Night Will Never Stay," in *Poems for Children* (Philadelphia: Lippincott, 1951), 11.

48. Developed by Leslie Serling, teacher, Public School 11, 1987–88, Manhattan, N.Y.

49. Nancy, age 12, wrote the poem on chairs, and Stephanie, also age 12, wrote the poem on snakes. Both were students at Worthington Hills School in Worthington, Ohio.

50. Christina Rossetti, "Who Has Seen the Wind? in *The Scott, Foresman Anthology of Children's Literature*, eds. Zena Sutherland and Myra Cohn Livingston (Glenview, Ill.: Scott, Foresman, 1984), 134.

51. David McCord, "Haiku," in *One at a Time*, illus. Henry B. Kane (Boston: Little, Brown, 1986), 482–83.

52. Issa et al., *Don't Tell the Scarecrow and Other Japanese Poems*, illus. Talivaldis Stubis (New York: Four Winds, 1969), unpaged.

53. Ann Atwood, *Haiku: The Mood of Earth* (New York: Scribner's, 1971), unpaged.

54. Adam, age 12, Worthington Hills School, Worthington, Ohio.

55. Bruce Springsteen, "My Hometown," BMI Record Company, New York, 1984.

56. Helen Plotz, *As I Walked Out One Evening: A Book of Ballads* (New York: Greenwillow, 1976), xiii.

57. Billy Joel, "Just the Way You Are," in *The Stranger* (New York: Bradley Publications, 1977), 28.

58. Phyllis McGinley, "Good Humor Man," in *This Powerful Rhyme: A Book of Sonnets*, sel. Helen Plotz (New York: Greenwillow, 1979), 28.

59. Ted Kooser, "Treehouse," in *Pocket Poems*, comp. Paul Janeczko (New York: Bradbury Press, 1985), 26.

60. Nan Fry, "Snow," in *Pocket Poems*, 61.

61. Jack Prelutsky, "The Ghostly Grocer of Grumble Grove," in *Ghost Poems*, ed. Daisy Wallace, illus. Tomie dePaola (New York: Holiday House, 1979), 12.

62. Karla Kuskin, "The Meal," in *Alexander Soames: His Poems* (New York: Harper & Row, 1962), unpaged.

63. Rhoda Bacmeister, "Galoshes," in *Time for Poetry*, comp. May Hill Arbuthnot (Glenview, Ill.: Scott, Foresman, 1952), 146.

64. Janina Domanska, *If All the Seas Were One Sea* (New York: Macmillan, 1987), unpaged.

65. Silverstein, "The Fourth," in *Where the Sidewalk Ends*, 15.

66. Dennis Lee, "I Eat Kids Yum Yum!" in *Garbage Delight*, illus. Frank Newfield (Boston: Houghton Mifflin, 1977), 37.

67. McCord, "Runover Rhyme," in *One at a Time*, 410.

68. Eve Merriam, "Inside a Poem," in *It Doesn't Always Have to Rhyme*, 3.

69. Jack Prelutsky, *Circus*, illus. Arnold Lobel (New York: Macmillan, 1974), unpaged.

70. Karla Kuskin, "Where Would You Be?" in *Dogs and Dragons, Trees and Dreams*, 11.

71. McCord, "Bananas and Cream," in *One at a Time*, 129.

72. Robert Louis Stevenson, "From a Railway Carriage," in *A Child's Garden of Verses*, illus. Jessie Willcox Smith (New York: Scribner's, 1905), 45.

73. Stevenson, "Where Go the Boats," in *A Child's Garden of Verses*, 16.

74. McCord, "Pumpkin Seeds," in *One at a Time*, 218.

75. Terry, *Children's Poetry Preferences*. "The Toaster" is in William Jay Smith's *Laughing Time*, illus. Juliet Kepes (Boston: Little, Brown, 1955), 20.

76. Carl Sandburg, "Short Talk on Poetry," in *Early Moon* (New York: Harcourt Brace, 1958), 19.

77. Arnold Adoff, "My Knee Is Only Sprained," in *Sports Pages*, illus. Steve Kuzma (Philadelphia: Lippincott, 1986), 20.

78. Eve Merriam, "Metaphor," in *It Doesn't Always Have to Rhyme*, 27.

79. Hilda Conkling, "Dandelion,"

in *Shoots of Green: Poems for Young Gardeners*, ed. Ella Bramblett (New York: Crowell, 1968), 26.

80. Langston Hughes, "April Rain Song," in *The Dream Keeper* (New York: Knopf, 1932), 8.

81. Robert Frost, "Dust of Snow," in *You Come Too: Favorite Poems for Young Readers*, illus. Thomas W. Nason (New York: H. Holt, 1959), 80.

82. Ted Hughes, "Moon Whales," in *Moon Whales and Other Moon Poems* (New York: Viking, 1976), 1.

83. John Tobias, "Reflections on a Gift of Watermelon Pickle Received from a Friend Called Felicity," in *Reflections on a Gift of Watermelon Pickle and Other Modern Verse*, comp. Stephen Dunning et al. (Glenview, Ill.: Scott, Foresman, 1966), 142–43.

84. Merriam, "How to Eat a Poem," in *It Doesn't Always Have to Rhyme*, 79.

85. Developed by Leslie Serling, Public School 11, 1987, Manhattan, N.Y.

CHILDREN'S BOOKS CITED

Adoff, Arnold. *Sports Pages*. Illustrated by Steve Kuzma. Philadelphia: Lippincott, 1986.

Aldis, Dorothy. *All Together: A Child's Treasury of Verse*. Illus. Helen D. Jameson, Marjorie Flack, and Margaret Freeman. 1925. Reprint. New York: Putnam's, 1952.

Atwood, Ann. *Fly with the Wind, Flow with the Water*. New York: Scribner's, 1971.

———. *Haiku: The Mood of Earth*. New York: Scribner's, 1971.

———. *Haiku-Vision in Poetry and Photography*. New York: Scribner's, 1977.

———. *My Own Rhythm: An Ap-*

proach to Haiku. New York: Scribner's, 1973.

Bacmeister, Rhoda W. "Galoshes." In *The Arbuthnot Anthology of Children's Literature*, 4th ed. Edited by Zena Sutherland et al. New York: Lothrop, Lee & Shepard, 1976.

Benet, Rosemary, and Stephen Vincent Benet. *A Book of Americans*. New York: H. Holt, 1933.

Bennett, Jill, comp. *Days Are Where We Live, and Other Poems*. Illustrated by Maureen Roffey. New York: Lothrop, Lee & Shepard, 1981.

———. *Roger Was a Razor Fish; And Other Poems*. Illustrated by Mau-

reen Roffey. New York: Lothrop, Lee & Shepard, 1981.

Bober, Natalie, comp. *Let's Pretend: Poems of Flight and Fancy*. Illustrated by Bill Bell. New York: Viking, 1986.

Bodecker, N. M. *Snowman Sniffles and Other Verse*. New York: Atheneum, McElderry, 1983.

Brand, Oscar. *When I First Came to This Land*. New York: Putnam's, 1974.

Browning, Robert. *The Pied Piper of Hamelin*. Illustrated by C. Walter Hodges. New York: Coward, 1971.

———. *The Pied Piper of Hamelin*. Illustrated by Kate Greenaway.

London: Warne, 1888.

Ciardi, John. *Doodle Soup*. Illustrated by Merle Nacht. Boston: Houghton Mifflin, 1985.

———. *I Met a Man*. Boston: Houghton Mifflin, 1961.

———. *You Read to Me, I'll Read to You*. Illustrated by Edward Gorey. Philadelphia: Lippincott, 1961.

Cohen, Mark. *Puffin Book of Tongue Twisters*. Toronto: Penguin, 1983.

Cole, Joanna, comp. *A New Treasury of Children's Poetry: Old Favorites and New Discoveries*. Illustrated by Judith Gwyn Brown. New York: Doubleday, 1984.

Cole, William, comp. *An Arkful of Animals*. Boston: Houghton Mifflin, 1978.

———. *Beastly Boys and Ghastly Girls*. Illustrated by Tomi Ungerer. New York: Putnam, 1964.

———. *Oh, That's Ridiculous!* Illustrated by Tomi Ungerer. New York: Viking, 1972.

———. *Oh, What Nonsense!* Illustrated by Tomi Ungerer. New York: Viking, 1966.

———. *Poem Stew*. Illustrated by Karen Ann Weinhaus. New York: Harper & Row, 1983.

Conkling, Hilda. "Dandelion." In *Shoots of Green: Poems for Young ____* ʒ. Edited by Ella Bramew York: Crowell, 1968.

.re, Walter. *Bells and Grass.* York: Viking, 1942.

. *Come Hither*. Illustrated by Alec Buckels. New York: Knopf, 1923.

———. *Peacock Pie*. 1920 Reprint. Winchester, Mass.: Faber, 1980.

———. *Songs of Childhood*. Illustrated by Estella Canziani. New York: Garland, 1976.

De Regniers, Beatrice Schenk. *So Many Cats*. Illustrated by Ellen Weiss. Boston: Clarion, 1985.

Domanska, Janina. *If All the Seas Were One Sea*. New York: Macmillan, 1971.

Downie, Mary Alice, and Barbara Robertson, comps. *The New Wind Has Wings: Poems from Canada*. Illustrated by Elizabeth Cleaver. New York: Oxford University Press, 1985.

Dunning, Stephen, et al. *Reflections on a Gift of Watermelon Pickle and Other Modern Verse*. New York: Lothrop, Lee & Shephard, 1966.

———. *Some Haystacks Don't Even Have Any Needles: And Other Complete Modern Poems*. New York: Lothrop, Lee & Shepard, 1969.

Farjeon, Eleanor. *Poems for Children*. Philadelphia: Lippincott, 1951.

Field, Rachel. *Taxis and Toadstools*. New York: Doubleday, 1926.

Fisher, Aileen. *Anybody Home?* Illustrated by Susan Bonners. New York: Crowell, 1980.

———. *Going Barefoot*. Illustrated by Adrienne Adams. New York: Crowell, 1960.

———. *In the Middle of the Night*. Illustrated by Adrienne Adams. New York: Crowell, 1965.

———. *Like Nothing at All*. Illustrated by Leonard Weisgard. New York: Crowell, 1962.

———. *Listen, Rabbit*. Illustrated by Symeon Shimin. New York: Crowell, 1964.

———. *Out in the Dark and Daylight*. Illustrated by Gail Owens. New York: Harper & Row, 1980.

———. *Sing, Little Mouse*. Illustrated by Symeon Shimin. New York: Crowell, 1969.

———. *Where Does Everyone Go?* Illustrated by Adrienne Adams. New York: Crowell, 1961.

Fleischman, Paul. *I Am Phoenix: Poems for Two Voices*. Illustrated by Ken Nutt. New York: Harper & Row, 1985.

Froman, Robert. *Seeing Things: A Book of Poems*. Illustratd by Ray Barber. New York: Crowell, 1974.

Frost, Robert. *Robert Frost's Poems*. Edited by Louis Untermeyer. New York: Washington Square Press, 1960.

———. *A Swinger of Birches*. Illustrated by Susan Jeffers. Owings Mills, Md.: Stemmer, 1982.

———. *You Come Too: Favorite Poems for Young Readers*. Illustrated by Thomas Nason. New York: Holt, Rinehart & Winston, 1959.

Fukuda, Hanako, *Wind in My Hand, The Story of Issa*. Edited by Mark Taylor. Illustrated by Lydia Cooney. Chicago: Golden Gate, 1970.

Greenfield, Eloise. *Honey, I Love and Other Love Poems*. Illustrated by Diane Dillon and Leo Dillon. New York: Crowell, 1972.

Hall, Donald, ed. *The Oxford Book of Children's Verse in America*. New York: Oxford University Press, 1985.

Hoberman, Mary Ann. *A House Is a House for Me*. Illustrated by Betty Fraser. New York: Viking, 1978.

———. *The Raucous Auk: A Menagerie of Poems*. Illustrated by Joseph Low. New York: Viking, 1973.

———. *Yellow Butter Purple Jelly Red Jam Black Bread*. Illustrated by Chaya Burstein. New York: Viking, 1981.

Holman, Felice. *At the Top of My Voice and Other Poems*. Illustrated by Edward Gorey. New York: Scribner's, 1970.

———. *The Song in My Head*. Illustrated by Jim Spanfeller. New York: Scribner's, 1985.

Hopkins, Lee Bennett, comp. *Surprises*. Illustrated by Megan Lloyd. New York: Harper & Row, 1984.

———. *To Look at Any Thing*. Photography by John Earl. New York: Harcourt Brace Jovanovich, 1978.

———. *Moments: Poems About the Seasons*. Illustrated by Michael Hague. San Diego: Harcourt Brace Jovanovich, 1980.

———. *Side by Side: Poems to Read Together*. Illustrated by Hilary Knight. New York: Simon & Schuster, 1988.

————. *A Song in Stone: City Poems.* Photography by Anna Held Audette. New York: Crowell, 1983.

————. *Voyages: Poems by Walt Whitman.* Illustrated by Charles Mikolaycak. San Diego: Harcourt Brace Jovanovich, 1988.

Hughes, Langston. *Don't You Turn Back.* Edited by Lee Bennett Hopkins. Illustrated by Ann Grifalconi. New York: Knopf, 1969.

Hughes, Ted. *Moon Whales and Other Moon Poems.* Illustrated by Leonard Baskin. New York: Viking, 1976.

————. *Season Songs.* Illustrated by Leonard Baskin. New York: Viking, 1975.

————. *Under the North Star.* Illustrated by Leonard Baskin. New York: Viking, 1981.

Issa, et al. *Don't Tell the Scarecrow.* Illustrated by Talivaldis Stubis. New York: Scholastic, 1969.

Janeczko, Paul B., comp. *Don't Forget to Fly.* New York: Bradbury, 1981.

————. *Going Over to Your Place: Poems for Each Other.* New York: Bradbury, 1987.

————. *Pocket Poems: Selected for a Journey.* New York: Bradbury, 1985.

————. *Poetspeak: In Their Work, About Their Work.* New York: Bradbury, 1983.

Joel, Billy. *The Stranger.* New York: Bradley Publications, 1977.

Kennedy, X. J. *The Phantom Ice Cream Man: More Nonsense Verse.* Illustrated by David McPhail. New York: Atheneum, 1979.

———— and Dorothy Kennedy, *Knock at a Star: A Child's Introduction to Poetry.* Illustrated by Karen Ann Weinhaus. Boston: Little, Brown, 1982.

Kherdian, David, comp. *If Dragon Flies Made Honey.* Illustrated by José Aruego and Ariane Dewey. New York: Greenwillow, 1977.

Kuskin, Karla. *Dogs and Dragons, Trees and Dreams.* New York: Harper & Row, 1980.

————. *Near the Window Tree.* New York: Harper & Row, 1975.

Larrick, Nancy, ed. *Bring Me All of Your Dreams.* Photography by Larry Mulvehill. Philadelphia: Evans, 1980.

————. *I Heard a Scream in the Street: Poetry by Young People in the City.* Philadelphia: Evans, 1970.

————. *On City Streets.* Philadelphia: Evans, 1968.

————. *Piping Down the Valleys Wild.* Illustrated by Ellen Raskin. New York: Delacorte, 1986 (1968).

Lear, Edward. *The Book of Nonsense.* 1846. Reprint. New York: Garland, 1976.

————. *The Complete Nonsense Book.* 1912. Reprint. New York: Dodd, Mead, 1958.

————. *The Complete Nonsense of Edward Lear.* Edited by Holbrook Jackson. New York: Dover, 1951.

————. *How Pleasant to Know Mr. Lear!* Edited and compiled by Myra Cohn Livingston. New York: Holiday House, 1982.

————. *A Learical Lexicon from the Works of Edward Lear.* Compiled by Myra Cohn Livingston. Illustrated by Joseph Low. New York: Atheneum, McElderry, 1985.

————. *The Owl and the Pussycat.* Illustrated by Lorinda Bryan Cauley. New York: Putnam's, 1986.

————. *Whizz!* Illustrated by Janina Domanska. New York: Macmillan, 1973.

Lee, Dennis. *Jelly Belly.* Illustrated by Juan Wijngaard. New York: Harper & Row, 1985.

————. *Garbage Delight.* Illustrated by Frank Newfield. Boston: Houghton Mifflin, 1977.

Livingston, Myra Cohn. *Higgledy-Piggledy: Verse and Pictures.* Illustrated by Peter Sis. New York: Atheneum, McElderry, 1986.

————. *I Like You, If You Like Me: Poems of Friendship.* New York: Atheneum, McElderry, 1987.

————. *O Sliver of Liver and Other Poems.* Illustrated by Iris Van Rynbach. New York: Atheneum, 1979.

————. *Sky Songs.* Illustrated by Leonard Everett Fisher. New York: Holiday House, 1984.

————. *A Song I Sang to You.* Illustrated by Margot Tomes. San Diego: Harcourt Brace Jovanovich, 1984.

————. *Whispers and Other Poems.* Illustrated by Jacqueline Chwast. New York: Harcourt Brace, 1958.

————. *Worlds I Know and Other Poems.* Illustrated by Tim Arnold. New York: Atheneum, 1985.

Longfellow, Henry Wadsworth. *Hiawatha.* Illustrated by Susan Jeffers. New York: Dial, 1983.

————. *Hiawatha's Childhood.* Illustrated by Errol Le Cain. New York: Farrar, Straus & Giroux, 1984.

————. *Paul Revere's Ride.* Illustrated by Nancy Winslow Parker. New York: Greenwillow, 1985.

McCord, David. *All Day Long.* Illustrated by Henry B. Kane. Boston: Little, Brown, 1966.

————. *All Small.* Illustrated by Madelaine Gill Linden. Boston: Little, Brown, 1986.

————. *Away and Ago.* Illustrated by Leslie Morrill. Boston: Little, Brown, 1952.

————. *Every Time I Climb a Tree.* Boston: Little, Brown, 1967.

————. *Far and Few, Rhymes of Never Was and Always Is.* Illustrated by Henry B. Kane. Boston: Little, Brown, 1952.

————. *For Me to Say.* Illustrated by Henry B. Kane. Boston; Little, Brown, 1970.

————. *The Star in the Pail.* Illustrated by Marc Simont. Boston: Little, Brown, 1975.

————. *One at a Time.* Illustrated by Henry B. Kane. Boston: Little, Brown, 1986.

————. *Take Sky.* Illustrated by Henry B. Kane. Boston: Little, Brown, 1962.

MacKay, David. *A Flock of Words:*

An Anthology of Poetry for Children and Others. Illustrated by Margery Gill. New York: Harcourt Brace Jovanovich, 1969.

Merriam, Eve. *It Doesn't Always Have to Rhyme.* Illustrated by Malcolm Spooner. New York: Atheneum, 1964.

———. *A Word or Two with You: New Rhymes for Young Readers.* Illustrated by John Nez. New York: Atheneum, 1981.

Milne, A. A. *Now We Are Six.* Illustrated by E. H. Shepard. 1927. Reprint. New York: Dutton, 1955.

———. *When We Were Very Young.* Illustrated by E. H. Shepard. 1924. Reprint. New York: Dutton, 1955.

Moore, Lilian. *Something New Begins.* Illustrated by Mary Jane Dunton. New York: Atheneum, 1982.

———. *Think of Shadows.* Illustrated by Deborah Robinson. New York: Atheneum, 1980.

Obligado, Lilian. *Faint Frogs Feeling Feverish And Other Terrifically Tantalizing Tongue Twisters.* New York: Viking, 1983.

Parker, Robert Andrew. *Sweet Betsy from Pike.* New York: Viking, 1978.

Plotz, Helen, comp. *As I Walked out One Evening: A Book of Ballads.* New York: Greenwillow, 1976.

———. *Saturday's Children: Poems of Work.* New York: Greenwillow, 1982.

———. *This Powerful Rhyme: A Book of Sonnets.* New York: Greenwillow, 1979.

Prelutsky, Jack. *Circus.* Illustrated by Arnold Lobel. New York: Macmillan, 1974.

———. *The Mean Old Mean Hyena.* Illustrated by Arnold Lobel. New York: Greenwillow, 1978.

———. *The Pack Rat's Day and Other Poems.* Illustrated by Margaret Bloy Graham. New York: Macmillan, 1974.

———. *The Random House Book of Poetry.* Illustrated by Arnold Lobel. New York: Random House, 1983.

———. *Ride a Purple Pelican.* Illustrated by Garth Williams. New York: Greenwillow, 1986.

Richards, Laura. *Tirra Lirra: Rhymes Old and New.* Illustrated by Marguerite Davis. Boston: Little, Brown, 1955.

Rosetti, Christina. "Who Has Seen the Wind?" In *The Arbuthnot Anthology of Children's Literature,* 4th ed. Edited by Zena Sutherland. 1961. Reprint. Glenview, Ill.: Scott, Foresman, 1976.

Sandburg, Carl, ed. *American Songbag.* New York: Harcourt, 1927.

———. *Early Moon.* Illustrated by James Daugherty. 1930. Reprint. New York: Harcourt Brace, 1958.

———. *Rainbows Are Made.* Edited by Lee Bennett Hopkins, illustrated by Fritz Eichenberg. San Diego: Harcourt Brace Jovanovich, 1982.

Silverstein, Shel. *A Light in the Attic.* New York: Harper & Row, 1981.

———. *The Missing Piece Meets the Big O.* New York: Harper & Row, 1981.

———. *Where the Sidewalk Ends.* New York: Harper & Row, 1974.

Smith, William Jay. "The Toaster." In *Laughing Time.* Illustrated by Fernando Krahn. New York: Dell, 1986.

Spier, Peter. *The Star-Spangled Banner.* New York: Doubleday, 1973.

Stevenson, Robert Lewis. *A Child's Garden of Verses.* Illustrated by Brian Wildsmith. New York: Watts, 1966.

———. *A Child's Garden of Verses.* Illustrated by Jessie Willcox Smith. New York: Scribner's, n.d.

Viorst, Judith. *If I Were in Charge of the World and Other Worries: Poems for Children and Their Parents.* Illustrated by Lynne Cherry. New York: Atheneum, 1982.

Willard, Nancy. *A Visit to William Blake's Inn: Poems for Innocent and Experienced Travelers.* Illustrated by Alice Provensen and Martin Provensen. San Diego: Harcourt Brace Jovanovich, 1981.

Worth, Valerie. *Small Poems Again.* Illustrated by Natalie Babbitt. New York: Farrar, Straus & Giroux, 1985.

Zemach, Harve. *Mommy, Buy Me a China Doll.* New York: Farrar, Straus & Giroux, 1975.

8

Realistic Fiction

Reflections

On this street
of windowed stores
see,
in the glass
shadow people meet
and pass
and glide to
secret places.

Ghostly mothers
hold
the hands of dim gray children,
scold
them silently
and melt away.

And
now and then,
before
the window mirror
of a store,
phantom faces
stop
and window shop.[1]

Lilian Moore

s a story a window through which we see the world, or a mirror in which we see ourselves? For most of us, it is both window and mirror, endlessly expanding our experience beyond a life lived in one time and one place.

Eleven-year-old Christine, discussing what made Judy Blume's books seem so real, said, "Her books are about life the way it really is—not fairy tale endings. Her books don't have happy endings; they're just like real life. Some have sad endings and some just sort of stop and you know things will go on just the way they are. That's the same way it really is." Christine's reading of the works of this author has left her with the mirror concept of literature. Evan, another child discussing realistic books, said, "I really don't like to tell people, but I pretend I am the person in the book not only while I'm reading it but for a long time after. If it's rainy or boring, I go to my room and I just play that I'm Margaret or Harriet." (Margaret is the protagonist of *Are You There, God? It's Me, Margaret* (I), by Judy Blume; and Harriet is the title character of *Harriet the Spy* (I), by Louise Fitzhugh.) Thus, Evan experiences literature as a window.

Realistic fiction has a strong sense of actuality; its plausible stories seem to be reports of what is happening or what could happen anywhere. Such stories are both mirrors and windows of life; they cause us to reflect on life and they show us lives that may not be attainable by us in reality. They allow us many ex-periences in the safety and security of our own lives: we can sail around the world without fear of shipwreck or suffer blindness without loss of sight, while still probing the emotions of the moment. We can also rehearse experiences we might someday have: we can fall in love, find or lose a friend, or go on an exciting journey. While reading, we unconsciously participate in a story, all the while composing similar stories to deal with our own wishes and fears. We draw analogies between stories we read and stories that, in effect, we tell ourselves. This premeditation of experiences through the stories helps prepare us for reality, creating expectations and models that influence our reactions to real events.

National surveys and librarians' reports have repeatedly shown that intermediate-grade students choose realistic stories far more than any other type. Perhaps children at this age, searching for an identity and looking for a yardstick against which to measure themselves, turn to realistic fiction to help them define the person they want to become.

No definition of realism is *simple,* and to say that realism is fiction that could happen in the real world—as opposed to fantasy, which could not—is *simplistic.* Every work of fiction, like the stories we tell ourselves, is part fantasy and part reality. As we create the myth we call reality, we selectively remember and reshape events of our past and present; the same thing happens in books.

The realistic books we discuss—which have contemporary settings, as distinct from

LANDMARK

Realistic Fiction: Little Women, *1868*

Louisa May Alcott's (1832–1888) *Little Women*, considered a prototype of American family stories, cannot be considered apart from her family. Its strength lies in the masterly characterization of the four girls, particularly Jo March, who has become the universal girl in literature. In many ways, the story of the March family is the story of the Alcotts themselves. The impact of the story rests in the verisimilitude to reality described in the

minute details of everyday happenings of rather uneventful family life. As Cornelia Meigs and her colleagues note,

> It is remarkable that in an age when reticence was the fashion in life and in books, Louisa Alcott had the insight to realize that what girls wanted was truth and warmth and that she had the courage to let them share the intimacy of life in her own home.[2]

What is remarkable is that this was the first time an author presented a story of ordinary family life. Beth, Jo, Meg, and Amy, four teenage girls in a warm, loving family, struggle with poverty and social conventions of the day. They are sustained by an abiding affection for each other and find pleasure in simple things by making their own fun. Alcott said of the story, "We really lived most of it, and if [the book] succeeds, that will be the reason [for the success]."[3] *Little Women* set the standard by which subsequent family stories are judged.

fiction set in the historical past or in the future—touch upon nearly every facet of life that students see reported in the newspapers and on television. The best of them illuminate life, whereas the news merely reports it. Good literature presents social and personal concerns in a fully human context, not as sensationalistic news items. Children who read widely, testing and tasting from alternative life-styles, have

many opportunities to try out roles vicariously through realistic books.

Realistic books today do not ask young people to believe in a perfectly run world. When headlines proclaim that some schools are more dangerous than the streets, harsh reality strikes close. Children know that the world is not entirely safe. Good literature does not resolve complex problems with easy answers.

There is no such thing as a "no pain, no re-morse" abortion, and good literature does not pretend there is. Literature reflects the society that creates it, and as our world changes, so do children's books.

On the other hand, most young people do not live in a world full of fear and hatred. Their lives revolve around school and family, and although their concerns are very real to them, most are temporal. Friendship, sibling rivalry, and school issues suffuse their lives, and books that deal with these relationships speak to children and adolescents in a reassuring way. When the adults in their lives minimize what is important to children, they turn to books to find that they are not alone. They can laugh at the turmoil in fictional lives and at the same time internalize the values in the stories.

Realistic books serve children in countless ways, one of which shows that, although values and norms may change from generation to generation, basic emotions do not. Realistic fiction, serving up new experiences, can be a factor in helping children mature. To be sure, this does not deny the roles of fantasy, biography, or poetry as conveyers of truth; we need them all.

CRITERIA FOR SELECTING REALISTIC FICTION

Realistic fiction portrays the real world in all its dimensions; it shows the humorous, the sensitive, the thoughtful, and the painful sides of life. Consequently, more controversy surrounds realistic fiction than any other genre. By its very nature, it deals with the vast range of sensitive topics prevalent in today's world. "The raw materials of story," says Lloyd Alexander, "are the raw materials of all human cultures. Story deals with the same questions as theology, philosophy, psychology. It is concerned with polarities: love and hate, birth and death, joy and sorrow, loss and recovery."[4]

Life's raw materials, questions, and polarities appear most starkly in realistic fiction. Here we sometimes find explicit language, earthy dialogue, and unseemly behavior. Some adults prefer to shield children from books that deal with subjects that are too mature. Others believe that they can benefit from reading and having a safe experience once removed from reality. Both positions have merit. Individual parents and communities will interpret the standards of what they believe to be suitable for their children. When we, as teachers, select realistic fiction, we should look for books that (1) deal with topics the child can understand, and (2) contain language and episodes that are in keeping with a community's standards.

Authors of realistic stories choose as a *setting* a time and place that actually does or could possibly exist. In some stories, the setting is almost irrelevant; in others, it is of primary importance. When judging setting in realistic fiction, we should expect (1) credibility or authenticity in time and place and (2) logical connections between the time and events of the story.

The *point of view* from which a story is told influences everything else in the story: the author selects a narrator who will selectively report and shape events in the telling. Many realistic fiction novels are told through the voice of the central character who reports events in a first-person narrative, solely from one point of view. Omniscient narrators can reveal the thoughts and inner feelings of several characters. They can move about in time and space to report events from an unbiased position. This third-person form is the one most widely used in books for children.

Other forms also exist. In Paul Zindel's *The Pigman* (A), the two main characters alternate telling the story, while in Alice Childress's *A Hero Ain't Nothin' but a Sandwich* (A), different characters tell each chapter. S. E. Hinton completed writing *Rumble Fish* (A) from the point of view of one character but then decided the story had to be told through a different character's eyes. She ultimately rewrote the entire story to tell it from another voice. When selecting realistic fiction, read to see if the point of view (1) gives a perspective that is believable and that enriches the story; and (2) is clear, arises naturally in the telling, and is consistent through the story plan the author chose.

Characters in realistic fiction are like human beings we know; they are circumscribed by the natural powers of a real person in a real world. We may learn about them from what they do or say, what others say about them or to them, or by what the narrator reveals about their thoughts and actions. Character development—that is, how a character changes during a story—can reasonably be expected in good fiction. For realistic fiction, then, we should look for characters that (1) are credible and authentic, (2) are well delineated, and (3) show change or development during the story.

Plot revolves around the character, problem, and resolution. It is the series of events that lead to the logical outcome of the story. Children are plot readers; they want something to happen and for it to happen fast. Richard Peck originally used the first 10 pages of a novel to set the mood, introduce characters, and establish the scene. He says that he cannot do that anymore, however, because children raised on television will not stick with a book for 10 pages; he has to start the action on page 1.[5] Most often, the plot structure is a straightforward chronology, but sometimes authors use a flashback, cyclical, or convoluted plot. Very young children cannot follow complex plot manipulations, so when selecting realistic fiction, look for (l) plot structures that can be understood by the children most interested in the story content and (2) fast-paced action that moves toward the resolution of the problem.

Theme, sometimes called the main idea of a story, is the message the author wants to convey. Often a theme is the reason authors write in the first place: a story allows them to say what they want to say. Readers gain a sense of the way authors view life through the themes of their stories. Themes in good literature are seldom stated explicitly; they are subtle and permeate the entire story. There is seldom only one interpretation of a theme. More often, there are as many realizations of a theme as there are readers—each one internalizing the theme in an individual way. When selecting realistic fiction, look for books that have worthwhile themes (1) woven intrinsically into the story and (2) that children can understand and mull over long after they have read the book.

A tale is all in the telling, so *style* is an important criterion for all literature. Style is the way the author writes; it involves sentence patterns, rhythms, imagery, and word choice. In realistic fiction, style can easily become pedestrian when an author tries to capture the current lingo of teenagers in the dialogue. This, in turn, dates the book very quickly. Often, teenagers in books are much more facile, glib, and witty than their counterparts in the real world. When selecting literature, look for books with a language style that (1) engages the reader and (2) has a rhythmic, melodic quality that is appropriate to the subject matter and the reader.

James Cross Giblin, editor and author of children's books, looks for writers who portray reality authentically but in a way that is appropriate to its audience.[6] He feels that almost any subject can be presented to children if it is dealt with sensitively and honestly. He expects an author to portray both sides of a conflict and to depict characters as multidimensional, not as one-sided personalities. He finds that writers who care deeply about a subject convey their ideas with emotion and thoughtfulness. Writers who write from personal experience evince a spirit that extends beyond their particular topic to help children develop a perspective of their own. Giblin says that violence comes in many forms. For example, a superficial treatment of a subject does violence to one's feelings, just as desecration of the environment does violence to one's sense of the aesthetic. As our society becomes increasingly complex, thoughtful writers are more important than ever.

Modern realistic books are different from realistic books of the past because their readers are different. Today's social and psychological environment impinges upon young people in ways that their literature also reflects. Jacqueline Peters summarizes part of the life-style of the present generation of children.

> It watched mom and dad staying in bed on Sunday morning instead of attending church; it sat for hours in front of a television set watching the make-believe world come to life. It read magazine covers which announced that God was dead. It found stacks of *Playboy* under dad's bed. It saw the inhabitants of the earth being beaten, lynched, robbed, murdered and bombed.[7]

Whether or not we agree with this, realistic books cannot avoid dealing with urgent issues. We can expect, however, that they not offend our personal sense of what is proper.

We cannot deny that young readers carry a world in their heads that is different from ours. For those who think that some of the harshness in realistic books is burdensome for children, La Rochefoucauld's observation may be pertinent: "We *all* have sufficient strength to endure the misfortunes of others." When children read about this kind of reality, they are shielded by the fact that the misfortune befalls a character in a book. The veil of fiction protects them, although the situations do reflect real life. Children intuitively distance themselves from scenes they find emotionally distressing; they push away books that hurt too much.

To give children only problem books is just as unrealistic as it is to shield them from all problems. Children need to read about happy families, ideal friendships, and safe, exciting adventures. Even amidst trouble there should be hope and optimism. Life can be dreary, but more often it is fun.

We should select books that are relevant but not relentlessly so—grim reality in books should be relieved by wit and humor. Since taboos are now infrequent, the content and language of books cover a wide spectrum, and almost any subject in adult novels may appear in children's books. Hence, if you want to be sure that books you select conform to community standards of taste, you need to read them before introducing them to your students.

THE REALISTIC BOOK AS MIRROR

Literature mirrors our perception of life; we see in stories reflections of our own values, disappointments, and dreams. We view both our inner and outer worlds in those created by perceptive writers. We create the images for the worlds the author describes.

Of Growing Up

Children unabashedly ask for books "about someone just like me." The balance between the book and the reader does not hinge upon age, time, or place, however, but upon the validity of the emotions presented. Feelings must ring true in the reader's view; they are more important than surface actuality. When children read books that show others searching for self, they find that they are not alone. They learn that life will be what they make of it.

Because our society has few of the formalized rites of passage of primal societies, the way is less clear for our preadolescents; they must mark their own paths. Books that portray a character struggling toward adulthood allow such readers to see themselves reflected and provide a rehearsal for real life.

Cynthia Voigt introduces the memorable Tillerman family, who shape their own destiny, in *Homecoming* (I–A) and follows them and their acquaintances in several books. The story opens in a shopping mall where Dicey and her three younger siblings have been abandoned by their mother. Dicey knows that they will be split up and placed in foster homes if they wait for the police to come, so the 13-year-old girl decides that they must go to their great-aunt Cilla's. They set out along the highway and follow the coast toward southern Connecticut. With only 10 dollars they manage to buy enough food to keep going. After many days they arrive, only to find that Aunt Cilla has died. After a brief stay with a cousin, who tells them that they have a maternal grandmother, they set out again. Another lengthy journey takes them to her home in Maryland, where she greets them with these heart-stopping words: "I know who you are, and you can't stay here."

They do stay, however, and *Dicey's Song* (I–A) winner of the 1983 Newbery Award, is the story of Gram's adjustment to the children, and theirs to her. Dicey has been so protective of her brothers and sister that she has difficulty relinquishing to her grandmother the role as surrogate mother. Dicey matures as she learns how to make friends and how to forgive those who have neglected her; in a touching final episode she accepts her mother's mental illness and eventual death and puts away the secret dream that would bring her back to them well and happy. The theme of reaching out, holding on, and letting go is woven throughout the story.

A boy who appears briefly in *Dicey's Song* is featured in *A Solitary Blue* (A). Jeff's mother left home when he was 7; her cryptic note explained that starving children and an endangered ecology demanded her time and energies. Left alone with his distant but kind

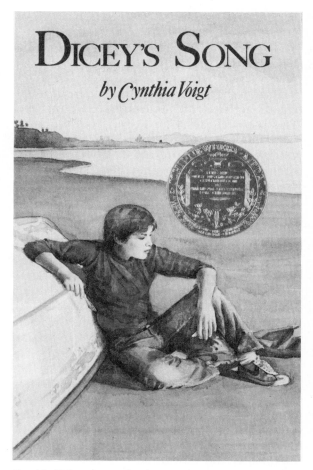

Cynthia Voigt weaves the themes of reaching out, holding on, and letting go throughout her Newbery Award–winning *Dicey's Song*. (Cover illustration by James Shefcik.)

father, Jeff conjures up in his mind the image of a wonderful humanitarian mother. A visit to her home some years later strengthens the image as he is completely taken in by her charm. But once again she betrays him and the pain and hurt sends Jeff into a deep depression. The gentle understanding of his father, as well as his growing friendship with Dicey Tillerman, lead Jeff to accept his mother for what she is—a selfish child who could not deal with motherhood—as well as to see his father as the one who truly loves him.

The Runner (A) goes back one generation in the Tillerman family to follow Bullet, Dicey's uncle. Bullet struggled to accept his bitter, taciturn father and was dismayed by his mother's (Gram's) silent submission to her husband. This book reveals a great deal about the Tillerman emotions and shows the evolution of Gram's need to isolate herself from the hurt of caring. Voigt continues the Tillermans' story in *Came a Stranger* and *Sons from Afar* (both A).

Realistic books mirror critical periods when young people make major decisions about their lives; we call the process growing up. Eleanor Cameron's series about a young girl growing up was written in reverse order, starting when Julia, the central character, was an adolescent and working back in subsequent books to her younger years. *A Room Made of Windows* (I), shows Julia Redfern as a self-centered and sensitive adolescent who is determined to become a writer to fulfill her late father's dream. The room that she eventually calls her own at the top of a rambling old house gives her a feeling of special privilege, but she is shaken by the death of a friend—an old man who shared her writer's zeal—and by the threat of her mother's remarriage. The slow but positive change in Julia as she grows more responsive to the needs of others is believable. *Julia and the Hand of God* (I) begins with her eleventh birthday when Uncle Hugh presents her with a richly bound volume of blank pages for her to fill— her "Book of Strangenesses." *That Julia Redfern* (I) and *Julia's Magic* (I) are set even earlier in Julia's life; they show her as an irrepressible scamp who is strongly influenced by her father's writing ambition.

Bette Greene shows a young black girl grappling with the feelings of first love in *Philip Hall Likes Me. I Reckon Maybe.* (I). Eleven-year-old Beth is the second-best arithmetic student, the second-best speller, and the second-best reader in her class. Philip Hall is first, but Beth wonders, Is he number one only because I let him be? Am I afraid he wouldn't like me if I were best? Though she considers such thoughts preposterous, they gnaw at her, and eventually she has the courage to test them.

Beth fluctuates between loving and hating Philip Hall. She wins and then lets him win; she does his work for him while he plays the guitar for her. When they prepare to enter their calves in the same 4-H Club contest, Philip tries to dissuade her, and Beth clarifies her feelings:

> The dumb bum! Where in the good book is it written that a girl's calf can't be in the same contest with a boy's calf? Well, Mister Philip Hall, for too long I've worried that you wouldn't like me if I became the number-one best student, ran faster in the relay race, or took the blue ribbon for calf-raising. . . . Well, I reckon I'm still worried, but with a difference. Now I'm worried that I might not win and that would give you entirely too much satisfaction.[8]

Although Beth's determination wavers, she eventually enters the calf in the contest. When she takes the blue ribbon, Philip admits that losing is a hard thing to get used to. He is able to accept it after pouting awhile and finally admits, "Sometimes I reckon I likes you, Beth Lambert."[9] Beth's innocence and heartwarming ambivalence toward a boy are captured as authentic feelings. Beth's story continues in *Get on Out of Here, Philip Hall.* (I–A)

Many readers outside the Appalachian setting of Virginia Hamilton's *M. C. Higgins the Great* (I–A) find that the emotions ring true as an adolescent makes decisions about his life. The finely crafted story centers on 13-year-old M. C., the oldest son, and is told from a perspective of respect for the culture's diversity and richness.

M. C.'s family has lived for three generations on Sarah's Mountain, now scarred by strip-mining bulldozers that leave a spoil heap of uprooted trees and earth plastered together by rain hanging like a huge boil over his home.

A 40-foot pole in the front yard stands in contrast to the spoil heap. M. C. climbs the pole to sit and look at the Ohio River Valley and avoid the chore of caring for the younger children. Sitting atop the pole, he rises above his environment literally and figuratively. The pole is associated with freedom, escape from problems, and a finer life:

> Forty feet up, he was truly higher than everything on the outcropping. Higher than the house and higher than the trees. Straight out from Sarah's Mountain, he could see everything in a spectacular view. He occasionally saw people clearly walking the hill paths nine miles away. Thinking they were absolutely alone, they had no inkling his eyes were upon them.[10]

It is from atop the pole that M. C. sees two strangers enter the hill country. One is a Chicago "dude" whom M. C. thinks will make his mother a country-and-western singing star. The other is Lurhetta Outlaw, at first just a stranger, but eventually a girl who inspires M. C. to take charge of his life, to see that he has choices and is responsible for determining his own future.

For many adolescents, the message of our culture is to stand up for what they believe and to take pride in being different; Robert Cormier's *The Chocolate War* (A) shows that in some cases a person who stands up for his beliefs may stand alone. In this novel, Jerry refuses to participate in a fund-raising school sale of chocolate bars being led by the powerful school gang leader, Archie. Each morning, the tension mounts as students report their sales for the preceding day, and Jerry continues to report "None." The pressure for Jerry to participate grows and, with it, his resolve to act according to his beliefs. Archie, who sees Jerry's refusal as a personal affront, joins with Brother Leon,

power-hungry headmaster of the school, to break Jerry's resistance, and between them they give Jerry a physical and psychological beating. The poster Jerry keeps in his locker, "Do I dare disturb the universe?" symbolizes his dare to question the stifling atmosphere of the school and to stand against the tyranny of peer pressure.

A sequel, *Beyond the Chocolate War* (A), fleshes out pivotal characters and follows logically from the first story. The opening sentence, "Ray Bannister started to build the guillotine the day Jerry Renault returned to Monument," establishes the tension as we read to discover how these two seemingly disparate events are connected. Cormier makes it clear that life will not be easy for Jerry as he returns to his hometown and subsequently his high school, Trinity. The principle that evil exists because it is tolerated is vividly played out in dramatic terms by adolescents who are told in no uncertain terms that they have a choice. Jerry is one of the few who has the courage to make the choice to stand up against evil; others accept a fatalistic attitude that becomes a self-fulfilling prophecy. As with most of Cormier's books, this one lingers in the mind long after the reading; his works are among the best realistic fiction being written for teenagers today.

Sometimes we can take charge of our own lives only after a traumatic experience that forces us to look closely at the forces that shape our motivation. Cynthia Rylant tells a gripping story of a boy's blind loyalty to an itinerant preacher in her Newbery Honor book, *A Fine White Dust* (I–A). Pete tells his own story as a flashback, an explanation for the shattered ceramic cross he ponders as the book begins. At 13, Pete looks back over his early fascination with church, a fascination that culminated the summer before with the arrival in the small North Carolina town of the Preacher Man.

From the first tent revival meeting, Pete was under the spell of the smooth-talking

James W. Carson. After only a week, he accepted the man's invitation to go with him into the world to save the souls of thousands of people. Pete would meet him after the last revival, after he had packed and left a note for his parents and told his best friend Rufus of his plans. Pete went to the highway where he was to meet the Preacher Man; he waited until 1 a.m. and then slowly started home. "I was a half-block down the street when somebody rose up out of some bushes, and my body gave one big jerk of fear and hope. Preacher, I thought. 'I'll walk you home, Pete' "[11] It was Rufus, his old friend, who waited for him, and came to lead him back. Rylant writes eloquently of the pain of rejection. Pete's emotions run the full range from blind devotion to raging hate. The loyal friendship of Rufus and the quiet, accepting love of his parents help him finally to wipe his hands clean of the fine white dust of the shattered ceramic cross he had broken in anger the night he was betrayed.

Paula Danziger's novels incorporate themes of growing up, becoming one's own person, developing friendships, and getting along in a family, all written in a breezy style with lots of humor and engaging dialogue. Thirteen-year-old Marcy, in *The Cat Ate My Gymsuit* (I–A), hates her father, hates school, and hates being fat. Most of all, she dislikes herself and is always giving excuses, such as the one in the title, to her gym teacher because she does not want to be seen in a gymsuit. Life begins to change when Ms. Finney, the English teacher, shows her class that learning is exciting and that they *can* like themselves and each other. When Ms. Finney is fired because of her unconventional teaching methods, Marcy and her friends protest; they in turn are suspended. Marcy's tyrannical father refuses to believe that Ms. Finney should not have been fired, but her mother finally goes to the hearing to support Ms. Finney. Danziger's deft plotting and skillful writing gracefully interweave Marcy's growth toward maturity, family conflict, and an important social issue. *There's a Bat in Bunk Five* (I–A), is a sequel in which Marcy serves as a junior counselor at a summer camp that Ms. Finney and her husband run. Marcy continues to grow up as she takes more responsibility for her life and her decisions; she also learns that not all problems can be solved. Danziger's ability to touch the pulse of teenagers' concerns makes her books extremely popular with readers.

Of Peer Relations

You may remember reading books as a child that pictured friendships as idyllic relationships of loyalty and noble sacrifice. Not so books today. A wide range of relationships among peers is explored, with some characters noble, some loyal, but most simply human—warts and all.

Because teens and preteens value acceptance by their friends, they are highly susceptible to peer pressure. Their literature reflects

ACTIVITY: TEACHER TO STUDENT

OBSERVE AND DESCRIBE PEOPLE (I)   Keep a journal similar to Harriet's that you carry with you every place you go. Describe the people you see and speculate about what they are like, what their lives are like, and what they like or don't like to do. Be sure to include your feelings about them. Put a star next to the entries that you might not say out loud. Think about why you would not say these things in public.

Intrepid Harriet runs into some problems on her "spy route," a means of practicing her writing craft. (From *Harriet the Spy*, written and illustrated by Louise Fitzhugh.)

their vulnerability and their strengths. Louise Fitzhugh, in *Harriet the Spy* (I), was one of the earliest novelists to sketch the full dimensions of childhood, with its unbecoming parts and its passions. Harriet M. Welsch's passion is to become a writer, and in order to practice her craft, she routinely records her observations in a journal. Here she is riding on the subway with her friend Sport:

"What are you writing?" Sport asked.

"I'm taking notes on all those people who are sitting over there."

"Why?"

"Aw, Sport"—Harriet was exasperated—"because I've *seen* them and I want to *remember* them." She turned back to her book and continued her notes: MAN WITH ROLLED WHITE SOCKS, FAT LEGS. WOMAN WITH ONE CROSS-EYE AND A LONG NOSE. HORRIBLE LOOKING LITTLE BOY AND A FAT BLONDE MOTHER WHO KEEPS WIPING HIS NOSE OFF.[12]

Harriet writes her frankest opinions in her notebook, and many are not complimentary to her classmates. One horrible day her notebook is missing and terror strikes her heart:

When she got back to where they had started she saw the whole class— . . . all sitting around a bench while Janie Gibbs read to them from the notebook. Harriet descended upon them with a scream that was supposed to frighten Janie so much she would drop the book. But Janie didn't frighten easily. She just stopped reading and looked up calmly. The others looked up too. She looked at all their eyes and suddenly Harriet M. Welsch was afraid. They just looked and looked, and their eyes were the meanest eyes she had even seen.[13]

The mean eyes are only the beginning of Harriet's classmates' retaliation; they refuse to speak to her, spill ink on her, steal her tomato sandwich, and shove her around. The resolution of Harriet's problems with her peers is tinged with a little heartache but is relieved by wit and humor. She has embarked on the voyage of growing up to become the person she wants to be even though the trip is not an easy one.

Understandably, a number of realistic books dealing with peer relations are set in school or revolve around a school-related problem. Writers who excel in capturing the spirit of an elementary classroom include Johanna Hurwitz, Robert Burch, Barthe De-Clements, Patricia Reilly Giff, Barbara Park, and Jamie Gilson. Johanna Hurwitz is one of the finest writers of realistic fiction to emerge in recent years; her work has the appeal of Judy Blume and Beverly Cleary and is accessible to the same audience. In one of Hurwitz's books, Lucas Cott has the reputation of being the *Class Clown* (P–I) in his third grade room. He writes his initials on his desk, fiddles with a drinking straw as if it were a cigarette, and continually plays to his audience of peers to get a laugh. He reads the note his teacher sends home to his mother about him but has trouble with the word "obstreperous." When he asks Cricket Kaufman, the smartest girl in his class, what the word is, she tells him that it's a kind of doctor that a lady goes to when she's having a baby. Eventually, Lucas decides to turn over a new leaf and become the perfect student, but it is not as easy as he thinks. When the third grade puts on a minicircus at the end of the year, his teacher gives him the opportunity to play the part of a real clown, a role he no longer wants to fulfill. Lucas desperately wants to be the ringmaster and because of a classmate's illness, he gets his wish. His final report card carries an *S* for Satisfactory in Conduct—a rating he had never received before.

In *The Adventures of Ali Baba Bernstein* (P–I), Hurwitz describes how a name change leads to unexpected adventures.

> David Bernstein was eight years, five months, and seventeen days old when he chose his new name.
> There were already four Davids in David Bernstein's third-grade class. Every time his teacher, Mrs. Booxbaum, called, "David," all four boys answered. David didn't like that one bit. He wished he had an exciting name like one of the explorers he learned about in social studies—Vasco Da Gama. Once he found two unusual names on a program his parents brought

home from a concert—Zubin Mehta and Wolfgang Amadeus Mozart. Now those were names with pizzazz!

David Bernstein might have gone along forever being just another David if it had not been for the book report that his teacher assigned.

"I will give extra credit for fat books," Mrs. Booxbaum told the class.[14]

David asked his mother for the fattest book she knew and she told him she guessed it was the New York City telephone book. David

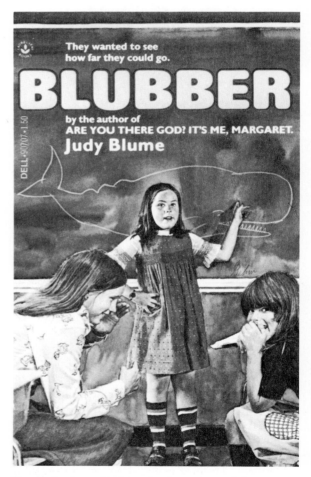

Pleasingly plump Linda's school report on whales includes a description of "blubber," a nickname with which she then becomes tagged. (From *Blubber* by Judy Blume.)

PROFILE

Judy Blume

School isn't as boring as it used to be. Wendy and Caroline made copies of their *How To Have Fun With Blubber* list and on Monday morning they passed them out.

We made Linda say, *I am Blubber, the smelly whale of class 206.* We made her say it before she could use the toilet in the Girls' Room, before she could get a drink at the fountain, before she ate her lunch and before she got on the bus to go home. It was easy to get her to do it. I think she would have done anything we said. There are some people who just make you want to see how far you can go.[15]

The things Judy Blume remembers, such as being afraid of thunderstorms or wanting a first bra, are the concerns of many children today, and she captures these experiences in stories that fast become children's favorites. In a letter to her readers, Judy Blume says:

Most of you want to know where I get my ideas. That's a scary question because I'm

not sure. Ideas seem to come from everywhere. In *Blubber* I drew heavily on an incident that took place in my daughter's classroom. The idea for *Deenie* came from a woman whose daughter had scoliosis. I wrote *It's Not the End of the World* because I knew many families who were suffering the pains of divorce. Since that time I have experienced divorce myself and while it wasn't easy, it wasn't the end of the world for any of us. The idea for the book *Tales of a Fourth Grade Nothing* came from a news article about a real toddler who actually swallowed a pet turtle. I based the character of Fudge on my son, Larry, when he was that age.[16]

Blume's ideas have become a dozen books that children adore. She is high on their list of best-loved authors because her books deal with first experiences that carry strong personal and emotional meaning. Her readers often ask, "How do you know all our secrets?"

It's because I remember just about everything from third grade on, and many things that happened before that. I can tell you exactly what I was wearing on the spring day that one of my kindergarten classmates stepped on my little finger while I was sketching on the floor. And how embarrassing it was when I cried in front of the whole class.

Blume fans are delighted that she has begun a new trilogy, *Just As Long As We're Together* (I), about best friends who can accommodate a third girl in their circle.

Judy Blume was a very quiet little girl who lived an exciting life inside her head. Blume's two children are now grown; she lives in New York City.

started to read it and found it boring, but he also found 17 David Bernsteins listed. He decided two things: he would change his name, and he would find a new book to read. The librarian gave him *The Arabian Nights* and soon he decided, "From now on, I want to be called Ali Baba Bernstein." The plot moves quickly through a series of escapades until his ninth birthday when he invites the 17 David Bernsteins to his party.

Robert Burch sets *King Kong and Other Poets* (I) in a sixth grade class where Andy and his classmates hardly notice the new girl—shy, colorless Marilyn—until she wins a newspaper contest for one of her poems. The class elects her as the "poet laureate," and she begins to reveal bits of her life through her poems, although she is still an enigma. She lives in an elegant resort but dresses in faded nondescript clothes and resists any overtures of friendship. Andy reaches out to her in quiet ways until he gains her trust and learns what causes her to be so somber. He eventually discovers that her mother has died and her father has had a nervous breakdown. Sessions on writing and sharing poetry in class ring with humor and authentic dialogue. This vignette of a brief friendship between two sixth graders will strike a responsive chord in writing process classrooms and ones in which children wonder about befriending a classmate who somehow seems different and aloof.

Barthe DeClement's *Nothing's Fair in Fifth Grade* (I) received more awards chosen by children than any other book the year it was published. With authentic classroom dialogue, Jenny tells the story that focuses on Elsie, a new girl in class, and their relationship with her. Classmates whisper, "Gross. Ugly. Ugh!" when overweight Elsie enters the room. When someone starts stealing food from lunch boxes and money from students' desks, it is clear that Elsie is the culprit. Jenny wants to help Elsie, but she does not want to jeopardize her own popularity, especially with Sharon and Diane,

her two best friends. When the three friends plan a slumber party and include Elsie, they begin to gain some insight into Elsie's problem. Elsie's mother, who favors her other daughter and is embarrassed by Elsie's size, shows little love for Elsie. Gradually Elsie takes some responsibility for her own diet as she realizes the reasons she is overeating. Some of the same characters appear in *Sixth Grade Can Really Kill You* (I), which is about a learning disabled girl.

Jamie Gilson speaks with clarity about Sam Mott, who is in the sixth grade but reads at a second grade level in *Do Bananas Chew Gum?* (I), and Hobie Hanson, who goes with his class on three days of Outdoor Education in *4B Goes Wild* (I). Hobie Hanson was also the narrator in *Thirteen Ways to Sink a Sub* and *Hobie Hanson, You're Weird* (both I).

Suzy Kline introduced *Herbie Jones* (P–I) in a book that quickly became a favorite of students in the IRA/CBC Children's Choices Project. Herbie appears again in *What's the Matter with Herbie Jones?* (P–I), which contains as many trials, tribulations, and laughs.

All of these books hold great appeal for middle grade students who are rapidly developing both their reading and their social skills. They offer humor and satisfaction as well as reassurance that boys and girls are not alone in their feelings. The books can be read quickly and with ease; they form a solid foundation for more complex stories and relationships that students will encounter as they near adolescence.

Nancy Bond's *A Place to Come Back To* (I–A) continues a story begun in *The Best of Enemies* (I–A). Charlotte, age 12 in the first book and now an adolescent, does not understand why she is always paired with Andy, while Andy's sister Kath is matched up with the more attractive Oliver. Charlotte grows in her realization that she cares deeply for Oliver and she suffers with him as he must face the death of his beloved great uncle with whom he has made his home. The uncle leaves the house to Oliver in his will and this, as well as the village of Concord, become his "place to come back to." Oliver must leave Concord and his familiar home to stay with his mother and her new husband, but his plans for the future revolve about the place to come back to.

Walter Dean Myers portrays merrymaking coupled with a sense of responsibility among peers in *The Young Landlords* (A). Fifteen-year-old Paul and a group of his Harlem friends, organized into a spur-of-the-moment "action group," complain to the owner of a run-down apartment building on their street:

> "You got forty-eight hours to give us some action," Gloria said, "or we'll be down here with our picket signs. And you can smile all you want to, but we'll see who'll be smiling in the end."
>
> "Who is the spokesman for your group?" Mr. Harley asked. . . . "Well, who's the oldest?"[17]

Paul discovers that he is the oldest and must serve as the contact person for the Action Group.

> So I gave him my name and address, although I knew I didn't want to. But as soon as everybody else found out that I was the oldest, they jumped right on my case.
>
> "Go on and give it to him," Omar said. "He can't do nothing."
>
> "Now, sir, do you have a dollar?" Mr. Harley said to me.
>
> "A dollar?"
>
> "Surely, if you're really interested in the building and the improvements you're suggesting, you won't mind investing a dollar?"[18]

Paul learns that by giving the owner a dollar, his group has just purchased the building, and the problems of improving it are now theirs. They discover that answers are a lot easier to come by when you stand across the street from the problem and—even harder to accept—that

A 16-year-old fashion model struggles with the temptations of glamour and fame as she solidifies her own values. (From *Crystal* by Walter Dean Myers. Cover illustration by Darryl Zudek.)

there are not good answers to every problem. They learn to make do the best they can.

In a subplot to the learning-to-be-landlords theme, Myers tells a story of peer loyalty: when a friend of the group is falsely accused of theft, all work actively to prove his innocence. The bittersweet story told from Paul's point of view in modern teenage language shows a boy on his way to manhood, learning to be loyal, learning to be responsible, and learning to accept his parents.

Richard Peck explores the feelings of two teenagers who must come to grips with the suicide of their friend, Trav Kirby, in *Remembering the Good Times* (A). Close companions since they were 12, the three shared many happy times despite their differences. Buck, the narrator, lives in a trailer with his father, a construction worker. Kate lives with her great-grandmother, Polly, in an old house in an orchard. Trav's family is well-to-do. In addition, he is a fine student who writes poetry and worries about his SATs. Four years after Trav's suicide, Buck and Kate look back and blame themselves: why hadn't they seen the signs that seem all too obvious to them in retrospect? Why hadn't their friendship been enough to save Trav from the burden of perfectionism? Peck's novel raises as many questions as it answers, which is in keeping with our understanding of the growing incidence of teenage suicide. The probing novel reflects the anguish

---

PROFILE

Beverly Cleary

Beverly Cleary has an unusual ability to see life from another person's point of view. She also has the ability to see humor in the ordinary events and lives of ordinary people. She has used that ability to write about Ramona and Beezus Quimby, Henry Huggins, Leigh Botts, and even an intrepid mouse, Ralph S. Mouse, who likes to ride motorcycles.

Beverly Cleary was born in McMinnville, Oregon, and until she was old enough to go to school, lived on a farm in Yamhill. Yamhill, Oregon, was so small it had no library.

Her mother arranged with the state library to send books to Yamhill and served as the librarian in a lodge room upstairs over a bank. It was there that Cleary learned to love books.

When her family moved to Portland, she attended elementary school but found herself in the low reading group. By the third grade she had conquered reading, but she has always had a special sympathy for children with reading problems. She spent much of her childhood either with books or on her way to and from the public library. Her school librarian suggested that she should write for boys and girls when she grew up. The idea appealed to her, and she decided that someday she would write the books she longed to read but was unable to find on the library shelves—funny stories about her neighborhood and the children she knew.

After graduation from junior college in Ontario, California, and the University of California at Berkeley, Cleary entered the School of Librarianship at the University of Washington, Seattle. There she specialized in library work with children. She was Children's Librarian in Yakima, Washington, until she married and moved to California. During World War II, she was Post Librarian at the Oakland Army Hospital. The Clearys

of close friends who cannot intercede in tragedy.

Bruce Brooks gets into the skin and thoughts of two teenage boys in *The Moves Make the Man* (A). Jerome, the narrator, is articulate and obsessed with playing basketball. He is the only black student in the newly integrated junior high school in a Southern town. There Jerome meets Bix, a white boy, who be-

comes his student on the basketball court where they meet night after night to shoot baskets. Bix becomes a reasonable basketball player, but he refuses to learn the moves that Jerome has mastered and has tried to teach him. One day, Bix challenges his stepfather to a basketball match; if Bix wins he can visit his mother who is in a mental institution. Bix wins the bet and visits his mother, but the visit has

now live near Carmel, California, and are the parents of twins, now grown. Her autobiography, *A Girl from Yamhill: A Memoir*, will delight her fans.

Beverly Cleary wrote her first book, *Henry Huggins,* after she heard several young library visitors complain that there were no books about ordinary children like themselves. Most books she saw as a child had characters who lived in foreign countries and had adventures that could never happen to any child she knew. Most of the children were uninterestingly well-behaved. Henry Huggins is a composite of the boys she knew as a child. She said, "I didn't know how to write so I just wrote as I had told stories."[19]

Many of Cleary's stories stem from her own childhood memories. For example, Ramona Quimby's experiences are autobiographical. Beverly Cleary explains, "I had the same feelings but I didn't do the same things" that Ramona does.

When students ask Beverly Cleary where she gets her ideas for her books, she replies, "From my own experience and from the world around me." When they ask her for writing tips, she tells them, "Read widely and when the time comes for you to write, you will find your own way of writing and will not need tips to guide you."

"I think about a book long before I begin to write," says Cleary. "And I don't begin with Page 1. If I have characters vividly in mind, and several incidents, I just start writing." The actual writing process for a book—including the extensive editing the author particularly enjoys—takes about six months. She plans carefully and is willing to rework her drafts rigorously to attain a freshness and accuracy of detail.

Beverly Cleary's ability to see life from another's point of view has served her well as a writer. She won the Newbery Award for *Dear Mr. Henshaw,* the most distinguished contribution to literature for children in 1983. Several of the Ramona books have been named Newbery Honor Books, American Library Association Notable Books, and selected by children in several statewide competitions. *Ramona Forever* was selected by children all over America as a Children's Choice Award in 1985. Because of Ramona's popularity, PBS has made three Ramona books into a 10-part video. Cleary served as story consultant and approved all of the scripts.

tragic repercussions for him. Jerome reaches out to try to help his friend, but there is a limit to how far his help can extend. Brooks's writing is intense; the basketball scenes alone are all-consuming.

Of Families

Contemporary children's books present a varied picture of family life and probe new dimensions of realism. Not only are traditional families portrayed, but also communal, one-parent, and extended families, as well as families headed by divorced or separated parents, and children living alone without a family. Although Louisa May Alcott's classic *Little Women* (I–A) has Jo express the conventional view when she says "families are the most beautiful things in all the world," Jo's own daring in stepping out of her traditional role signaled changes to come in children's books.

Although there have always been books like Sydney Taylor's *All-of-a-Kind Family* (I)—a nostalgic account of a Jewish family in New York in the 1930s, in which each member stays in culturally assigned roles—books about non-

---

 PROFILE

Lois Lowry

Lois Lowry's mother was a teacher who read to her and her brother and sister from their earliest days. When Lois was 3½ years old, she spent the summer with her grandparents in Philadelphia. Her grandfather, who liked antiques and nineteenth-century literature, put her to bed on the first night and read to her from his favorite poem, "Thanatopsis."

Somewhat awed by the huge mahogany four-poster bed and anxious to please her grandfather, when asked if she liked the poem, she lied and said yes. After that, he read "Thanatopsis" to her every night for what began to seem an interminable summer. Gradually, Lois joined in saying the words with her grandfather as he read, and they both discovered that she was learning every word of the ponderous poem by heart. One night when her grandparents were entertaining dinner guests, her grandfather asked her to come downstairs to recite the poem. Sleepy eyed and in her pink nightgown, Lois stood before the astonished group with her eyes clenched tight shut and recited "To him who in the love of Nature holds communion with her visible forms . . ." and on to the lengthy end of Thanatopsis.

Lois majored in writing at Brown University and in American Literature at the University of Southern Maine where she has also done graduate work. She is the mother

traditional households appear with increasing frequency, answering the child's need to see life as it really is. Modern readers find both mirrors and windows in the wealth of family stories today.

Traditional families still exist, of course, and none are so endearing as the Quimbys and the Krupniks. Beverly Cleary first introduced Beezus Quimby in her series about Henry Huggens (I). Soon *Beezus and Ramona* (I) appeared, and then the pesky younger sister starred in her own book in *Ramona the Pest* (P–I), followed by *Ramona the Brave* (P–I). *Ramona and*

Her Mother, Ramona and Her Father, Ramona Quimby, Age Eight, and *Ramona Forever* (all P–I) follow the growth pangs of the adorable girl who has progressed to the third grade in *Ramona Quimby, Age Eight* and *Ramona Forever*.

Ramona's family has undergone changes, too. When her mother went back to work while her father began college, Ramona and her sister Beezus didn't like the new ways of doing things in the family. In *Ramona Forever*, her favorite Aunt Bea marries and moves away, her pet cat Picky Picky dies, her father has trouble finding a teaching job, and she gets a new baby

of four grown-up children and now divides her time between Boston and New Hampshire.

She had been writing for adults when editor Melanie Kroupa asked her if she had ever considered writing for children. In response, she wrote *A Summer to Die*, which won the International Reading Association Children's Book Award. *A Summer to Die* was based on her own experiences, and although every detail in the book may not be actual, the emotions are authentic. The book was written in 1976 in Falmouth, Maine, but in 1983 she was driving down a dirt road in New Hampshire when she saw the very house she had described in that earlier book. She said, "I have to have that house," and indeed, she now owns the house that loomed so vividly in her imagination. She has loved it since the moment she saw it.

Lois explains, "The pervasive theme in my life which is reflected in my books is the inevitability of change and loss in human experience. I believe in the probability of

growth through change and loss but I know the necessity of close human relationships to make that growth possible."[20] She has developed that theme creatively in a variety of books.

Autumn Street, also autobiographical, could well reflect the tree-lined street where her grandfather took her for daily walks as a child. This, like her other earlier books, is somber, but as her own life brightened in happiness, so did her books. Lois Lowry says that *Anastasia Krupnik* is probably a combination of her two daughters. One incident in *Anastasia Again*, in which Anastasia answers her father's fan mail, was based on an actual incident—one of Lois's daughters answered her mail and not in a way Lois would have wanted it answered. She, like Anastasia's father, had to write to explain to startled fans.

sister. Ramona faces life with an intensity that causes problems to loom large to her although they may seem humorous to children just a few years older.

Ramona's fans will be delighted to discover *Beverly Cleary's Ramona: Behind the Scenes of a Television Show*. Readers will meet not only a real-live version of Ramona but also the people who re-created the magic of Klickitat Street.

Lois Lowry creates a memorable look at families through her introduction of *Anastasia Krupnik* and its sequels (all I). Anastasia is 10 years old when the series begins. Her mother is an artist; her father, a professor of literature and a poet. Anastasia is articulate, opinionated, and bright. She makes lists of things she loves and things she hates but items often move from one list to the other. One thing she is certain she will hate is babies after her parents inform her that there will soon be a new baby in the family. She is deeply offended that her parents have decided to have a baby without consulting her. In *Anastasia Again!* she is upset that they have decided to move to the suburbs, again as Anastasia would say, "without consulting me, for pete's sake!" Anastasia is made lovable by her quick wit and naive, immoderate zest as she barrels through life. She gets her first job in *Anastasia at Your Service*, buys a plaster bust of Freud and talks to him in *Anastasia, Ask Your Analyst* and has other adventures in *Anastasia on Her Own, Anastasia Has the Answers*, and *Anastasia's Chosen Career*.

Betsy Byars, noted for her ability to treat serious themes with the light touch of humor, often describes unusual families. She has shown some children caught in difficult family situations and others as members of close-knit extended family groups. In *The Glory Girl* (I), Anna is the only one in a family of gospel singers who cannot carry a tune. Her father, cold and domineering Mr. Glory, behaves much differently off-stage than he does in front of an audience. He drives a dilapidated old school bus to travel between shows, while Anna cringes in the back seats trying to avoid notice.

She considers herself a family misfit and sympathizes with Uncle Newt who has been pardoned from prison and needs to stay with the family. One night, some roguish boys force the family bus off the road to crash into a flooding stream. Through Anna's quick wit and Uncle Newt's heroism the family is saved. Before Uncle Newt leaves to start a new life for himself, he praises Anna's thoughtfulness and kindness; this adds a boost to her self-esteem.

Byars's *The Not-Just-Anybody Family* (I) is made up of three children—Junior, Vern, and Maggie—and their grandfather, Pap Blossom. The children's mother is away on a rodeo circuit so it is up to Vern and Maggie to solve the family's problems, particularly, getting Junior out of the hospital and Pap out of jail. Junior breaks both legs when he jumps from the barn roof in an attempt to fly with wings made out of wire, old sheets, and staples, and Pap is arrested when his truck dumps over 2,000 soda cans in the middle of the street. A hysterically funny jailbreak ensues—Vern breaks *into* jail to be with his grandfather—and a series of rib-tickling scenes takes place with Junior's hospital roommate, Ralph. The plot is filled with cliff-hangers and slapstick action that includes the family dog's escapades as he tries to find Pap.

The Blossoms appear again in *The Blossoms Meet the Vulture Lady* (I) and in *The Blossoms and the Green Phantom* (I), where Junior's inventiveness and Pap's bad luck lead to more trouble spiced with hilarity. Junior creates and launches a helium-filled conglomeration made of air mattresses and trash bags, which sails through the air for a short distance before collapsing on top of a neighbor's chicken house, and Pap falls unceremoniously into a garbage dumpster and cannot get out. Alternating chapters focus on Pap's unfortunate circumstance and Junior's delight and then despair at the launching of the Green Phantom. Witty Ralph, who shared Junior's hospital room, and the faithful dog, Mud, are both back to enliven the Blossom family. The series continues in *A Blossom Promise* (I).

PROFILE

Betsy Byars

Unlike many writers, Betsy Byars had no childhood aspirations of becoming an author. Although she has always been an avid reader, she says that she spent too much time enjoying herself ever to pursue anything seriously. It was not until she became a homemaker with time on her hands that she thought of writing. Her first efforts were humorous articles for popular magazines, such as *Look, TV Guide,* and *Saturday Evening Post.* She turned to writing for children when her own four youngsters were growing up.

In addition to being her most severe critics, her children provided endless material from things that happened in school and with their friends. *The Midnight Fox* is her favorite among her books because, she explains, "It is very personal. A great deal of my own children and their activities went into it, and a great deal of myself. It came closer to what I was trying to do than any of my other books."[21] *Summer of the Swans* grew from an experience she had when she worked with mentally retarded children.

Byars describes herself as a wife and mother. She remembers that she had just thrown a load of laundry in the washing machine when she received the phone call telling her that she had won the Newbery Medal. It was "a startling experience" because "at that point in life I was not what you would think of as a professional-type writer. I knew very little about the publishing business; I had never been in an editor's office. I didn't even know any other writers." She still has no set rules for writing and, in fact, writes the way she does many other things— "fast, without patterns, and with great hope and determination."[22]

Byars thoroughly enjoys life. She believes that the world is an exciting and lively place and that children are very bright and individualistic. In her stories, she explores the many challenges facing today's young people and tries to develop her characters so they meet their world with humor, compassion, and understanding.

A native of North Carolina, Betsy Byars now lives in Clemson, South Carolina. She does most of her writing in the winter; her summers are spent sharing her husband's hobby of gliding.

Katherine Paterson portrays another family bound in love but fraught with tensions in *Come Sing, Jimmy Jo* (I). Born into an Appalachian family of country and western singers, 11-year-old James is destined to become a part of the family musical act. He enjoys playing the guitar and singing for his grandmother but is terrified at the thought of performing in front of other people. Despite his fears, James is tricked into singing with the family group and inadvertently leads them to big-time stardom. James is uncomfortable when they change his name to Jimmy Jo and he hates the publicity that fame brings. A man who claims he is James's real father appears, and although he finally accepts the truth of that claim, James realizes that the loving man he has always known as his father is the one he still loves. The dialogue filled with the authentic language of Appalachian dialect and colloquialisms rings just as true as the emotions of a child caught within the bonds of family love and loyalties. Both the tale and the telling are superb.

Paterson also explores the love within a family in *Park's Quest* (I–A). Young Parkington Waddell Broughton V wants to find his father's name on the Vietnam Memorial. His search takes him not only to the monument, but to the grandfather and uncle he has never met. Park pictures himself as a knight in King Arthur's court and imagines that his grandfather will claim him as heir. Park's quest leads to revelations about his family and himself.

Virginia Hamilton weaves an absorbing story around Orson Welles's 1938 Halloween broadcast of "War of the Worlds" in *Willie Bea and the Time the Martians Landed* (I–A). Willie Bea Mills is a part of a large extended black family living in rural Ohio when Orson Welles makes the ill-fated broadcast that frightened

TEACHING IDEA

FATHER-DAUGHTER RELATIONSHIPS (A)[23] In many novels, daughters do not know their fathers as parents, mentors, or persons. The daughters may feel incomplete, that a piece of the puzzle of their adolescent identities is missing. Each teenager feels compelled to find that missing piece so she can be a complete person and a unique personality. In novels about fathers and sons, the sons often go on a physical quest to identify themselves with their fathers. The daughters' odysseys usually describe an inner, introspective quest.

The following activities help the students to recognize the traditional structure of these contemporary novels and to recognize how literature can be pertinent to their own lives.

1. In the following books, how does each teenager express her sadness at not knowing her father? What language, imagery, and metaphor are used to express each girl's sad feelings?

   A Little Love: Sheema—feeling of emptiness inside herself
   In Summer Light: Kate—artistic terms, light and dark colors
   Moonlight Man: Catherine—light/dark; moonlight/daylight
   Rear-View Mirrors: Olivia—mirrors, light/dark reflections
   Midnight Hour Encores: Sib—music terms, light/dark tones

2. Each of the books just listed has a physical aspect of the girl journeying to get to know her father that moves the events of the story along and helps to provide action for the plot. Describe the physical journey or quest each girl undertakes.

millions of people throughout the United States. Aunt Leah, highly dramatic and glamorous, is convinced that Martians have landed in New Jersey and she persuades others to believe her when she brings the news to the Mills family. Their reactions vary from Aunt Lu, who is ready to jump down the well and get it over with, to a neighboring farmer, who is ready to shoot anything that steps on his land. All in all, the chaos is good fun, believable, and riotous as any family reunion is with lively kinfolk.

Fathers Fathers have received increasing attention in books for children and adolescents.

Where they had been ignored in earlier years, they are now recognized as viable literary characters; their relationships, especially with daughters, are never simple.

Paula Fox's *The Moonlight Man* (A) is the story of 15-year-old Catherine as she comes to terms with the pain of her parents' divorce 12 years earlier. Catherine's father, an alcoholic but an irrepressible charmer, remains an elusive force in her life. Their separation has increased her desire to renew their relationship. Her father promises an extended vacation together, which after many delays finally comes to pass when he rents a cottage by the sea in Nova Scotia. During the month they have

(Sheema, car trip; Kate, travel home; Catherine, journey to a remote beach area; Olivia, symbolic bicycle trip; Sib, a cross-country pilgrimage)

How was this journey related to the inner emotional journey to find her father, to find out who she really was? How was this journey part of her growing up so she could feel a sense of wholeness, of being ready to get on with her own life?

Ask five students to form a collaborative learning group, have them discuss the similarities and differences among the five novels, and have each member select one of the novels to write about.

3. Each book is really a modern fairy tale in the tradition of Snow White and Sleeping Beauty. Each main character is in a state of isolation or suspension of activity (lethargy), cut off from the usual teenage group scene and activities. It is as if this self-imposed isolation is giving her a chance to find herself so that she will then be ready to go on and enjoy regular relationships. Each girl is unable to reach out to love anyone else until she resolves the conflict within herself. The importance of mirrors and appearance as a reflection of one's inner self is an important image (motif) in these books just as they are in Snow White, Sleeping Beauty, and other fairy tales. The journey or quest as a means of growing up, also an important element of fairy tales, is a vital part of each story.

Ask students to try to write a traditional fairy tale based on any one of these five books.

together, Catherine begins to see through the shadows and mirage of the man who stays hidden behind them. She realizes that he is not only hiding from her but also from himself and, through his excessive drinking, is escaping from reason and obligation. He had spoken deprecatingly of her neat, orderly mother as a "daylight person" and Catherine gradually comes to know that he is "a moonlight man." She realizes that she can accept him as he is and pity him, but once and for all, in her own mind, her parents' divorce is final.

In Summer Light (A) is Zibby Oneal's story of a father-daughter relationship that changes over the years. As a small child, Kate had adored her father, a famous artist. Now, at 17, she believes him to be self-centered and cruel, needing all the attention and affection in the family. She aches when he denigrates her own attempts at painting, something that has once again become very important to her. Her father's criticism drives Kate away from her art, leaving an empty space in her life. A young graduate student, Ian, who has been sent to catalogue her father's paintings, helps her see herself and her father in a clearer light, a summer light. Kate believes she is in love with Ian, but he wisely leaves without her at the end of his summer's work. The gift he leaves behind is his belief in her and in her ability to paint. The images Oneal creates with words reflect the canvases both Kate and her father paint. In freeing herself to pick up a paintbrush once again, Kate is free to understand her father. She no longer needs his approval of her work and is able to be sympathetic to his fear that he can no longer produce masterpieces like those that had made him famous earlier. She has grown up and gained some mature insights.

Olivia, in *Rear-View Mirrors* (I–A) by Paul Fleischman, grew up acquainted with her father only by report. He was like a distant land known only through travelers' tales. Olivia's parents, divorced when she was hardly 8

months old, did not communicate, one living in California, the other in New Hampshire. Olivia is surprised, then, when her father sends her an airline ticket and a telegram-style message, "Come if you can," asking her to visit him the summer of her junior year in high school. A year later she is on her way back to his little New Hampshire village after he has been killed by lightning while replacing shingles up on his roof in a storm. For Olivia, the road to his village is "lined with . . . rear-view mirrors," in which she beholds the summer that she had spent with him; she reflects upon the memory of images created as she learned to see the world through her father's eyes. Their summer together, filled with intense, witty, and sometimes sarcastic, verbal one-up-manship, gave her a rare legacy—the ability to see the world in a totally new way. Olivia's return trip, a pilgrimage in honor of her father and what he has taught her, revolves around a 70-mile, day-long bicycle race with time. The trip, an annual ritual for her father, is one she must now complete as she fulfills her legacy. Her physical ride is a rite of passage: she cycles through a storm, bathes in a river, helps a stranger, and completes the journey with a new wheel she finds in a junkyard.

On the surface, *Midnight Hour Encores* (A) by Bruce Brooks seems to be about finding the mother who abandoned Sib at birth. She and Taxi, the loving father who raised her, journey by van to California, ostensibly to meet Sib's mother and to participate in a music competition. But it is really her father, a distant, self-controlled, highly disciplined musician, that Sib is getting to know. As her father explains the 1960s era and the motives of both her parents, Sib understands she was not so much abandoned by her mother as she was chosen by her father and that he wants her to understand him. He explains that she is the most important part of his life; he has shared her life and now, in an old VW van reliving the 1960s, she is sharing his life. Sib and her mother will become friends, but in her "midnight hour encore" it is a time for beginnings, and Sib goes back to her father with a new understanding of who she is and of their relationship. She is able to forgo the music competition she came to California to seek.

A Little Love (A) by Virginia Hamilton tells the story of Sheema, a black teenager being raised by her loving grandparents, her mother having died in childbirth and her father having deserted her. Sheema feels abandoned, alone, lost and "empty"—her own word. Despite the love of her elderly grandparents and her caring boyfriend, Forrest, Sheema fantasizes that her father really is waiting for her and will protect her against the vagaries of adult life. Forrest keeps asking how Sheema can miss someone so much, someone she has never known, but he helps her to go in search of him. At the end of their car trip to find him, Sheema is released from her belief that her father will rescue her from the hard decisions of life; she realizes that finding meaning in her life has to come from herself, not others.

Mothers Fictional mothers run the full range of character just as they do in real life. From the quiet, supportive mother in Cynthia Rylant's *A Fine White Dust* to the selfish one in Cynthia Voigt's *A Solitary Blue,* authors show that not all women are equally suited to motherhood. Elisabet McHugh wrote a wonderful series that encompasses a warm, loving family extended by adoption and marriage. In *Raising a Mother Isn't Easy* (I) 10-year-old Karen describes her life as a Korean child adopted by a single woman who is a veterinarian. Convinced that her loving but disorganized mother needs help, she decides to find a husband for her. Instead of a new father, however, Mom announces that she is bringing home another child. *Karen's Sister* (I) tells of the arrival of 5-

year-old Meghan, also Korean, whose charm is matched only by her stubborn determination. Finally, in *Karen and Vicki* (I), when Karen is 12, her mother does get married, to a widower with three children. Karen's relationship with her older stepsister is tenuous at first, but slowly they all become a loving, happy family as they look forward to the birth of a new baby. All three books focus on the positive, accepting attitudes of the family members as they share laughter and love.

Lois Lowry does a fine job of characterization and unfolding character development of a girl and her child-mother in *Rabble Starkey* (I–A). Eleven-year-old Rabble, named Parable Starkey at birth, lives with her mother Sweet Hosanna above the garage of the family her mother serves as housekeeper. Sweet Ho had run off with a truck driver when she was 14 years old and returned home with a baby and no husband soon after. Rabble grows up in a supportive rural community with no father, but with good relationships with her mother and grandmother. Rabble longs for stability and finds strength in herself as her family is drawn intimately into the lives of the employer's family. Lowry's deft touches of humor lighten a story of tension, pain, and growing up. Teachers will enjoy Rabble's manipulation of family trees and the thesaurus as she crafts her writing for school assignments.

Siblings Children growing up in the same home must learn to share possessions, space, and parents or guardians. Stories of the idyllic relationships portrayed in *Little Women* or *Little House on the Prairie* are seldom found in today's books. More often, sibling rivalry or learning to accept stepsisters, stepbrothers, or wards in foster homes is treated in contemporary novels.

The intensity of a child's demand for attention in competition with a sibling can be seen in this child's letter to the editor of *Highlights for Children*, a children's magazine. A translation of the letter follows.

Dear Editor:

More attention, please! I have both a younger brother and sister. One night when my Mom was sitting on my bed, and I was telling her about the pottery I had made that afternoon at school, my sister came in at least 8 times telling my mother about her tooth hurting and she doesn't even have any loose teeth! And my Mom was nice as ever, fine with me! Then I went in my sister's room to ask my mother when we were going to get Leabra's Blooming Rose (a new fish for my tank) and believe it or not, she said, "Go in your room." I, by then, was on the verge of tears. I may not be very smart but I'm not crazy! I know the rules of this house! And one of them is to be fair, if that's fair I'm a Siamese fighting fish (or Batal!)!

I thought everyone needed some ATTENTION at least once in a while? Please answer me.
Elizabeth
Age 8

Katherine Paterson has won the Newbery Award twice, once for *Bridge to Terabithia* (I) and once for *Jacob Have I Loved* (A). In *Jacob Have I Loved*, Paterson probes the deep and compelling feelings that permeate the life of a twin. Louise, who tells the story, lives in the shadow of her beautiful, selfish twin sister, Caroline, who is given every advantage by the family and favored by all who know them. Louise feels she is deprived of schooling, friends, and even her mother who pampers Caroline while she takes Louise for granted. Their dotty grandmother recognizes Louise's resentment and taunts her with the biblical phrase, "Jacob have I loved but Esau have I hated." Louise's anger and hurt pervade the text.

> I longed for the day when they would have to notice me, give me all the attention and concern

that was my due. In my wildest daydreams there was a scene taken from the dreams of Joseph. Joseph dreamed that one day all his brothers and his parents as well would bow down to him. I tried to imagine Caroline bowing down to me. At first, of course, she laughingly refused, but then a giant hand descended from the sky and shoved her to her knees. Her face grew dark. "Oh, Wheeze," she began to apologize. "Call me no longer Wheeze, but Sara Louise," I said grandly, smiling in the darkness, casting off the nickname she had diminished me with since we were two.[24]

Louise's resentment toward her sister abates only as she matures and prepares for a life Caroline cannot touch. A tone of reconciliation emanates from the closing scenes as Louise, now a midwife, fights to save the weaker one of a set of twins.

In another complicated family, *The Animal, the Vegetable, and John D. Jones* (I), by Betsy Byars, Clara and Deanie look forward to spending a vacation with their divorced father until they learn that he has invited a woman friend and her conceited son, John D., to join them. Sixth grader Clara has always had to compete for her father's attention with Deanie, who is two years older, two years smarter, and two years funnier than she, but now the situation is even worse. The woman friend is bad enough, but her son is intolerable. Just as unwilling a participant, John D. prefers his own company to that of any girls; he labels one "The Animal" and the other "The Vegetable." John D. chooses to stay aloof, observing what he considers ridiculous behavior and writing a chapter for his book, called "Simple Ways to Get What You Want." The three young people keep their distance until a near-tragedy strikes—Clara falls asleep on a flimsy plastic raft and is swept out to sea. Only then do they begin to pull together and reveal their true feelings about each other. In typical Byars fashion, the witty dialogue and wry humor brighten a tense situation.

Books about children in foster homes depict adults ranging from child molesters to all-loving parent figures. Children are portrayed as victims of child abuse, abandonment, alcoholism, neglect, and a whole range of society's ills. The children themselves are often cynical, bitter, disillusioned, and despondent but sometimes courageous and strong.

The interaction between foster parents and homeless children reveals a mixture of motivations and human conflicts. For some foster children, the memories of the natural parents may be rightfully idealized, whereas for others, the memories are haunting nightmares.

Katherine Paterson tells about a self-proclaimed genius in *The Great Gilly Hopkins* (I) who is determined to hate Maime Trotter as much as she has hated all of her other foster parents. She believes her stay with Maime is only temporary, to be ended when her beautiful mother, Courtney (a flower child gone to seed) comes to get her.

Gilly scorns the fat, illiterate Maime as well as the strange 7-year-old William Ernest who lives with them, and she wonders what it is that Mr. Randolph, the blind black man who lives next door, wants. Slowly and reluctantly, Gilly learns to love these people.

Eventually, Gilly's grandmother takes Gilly home with her. Gilly, unhappy there, is convinced by Maime Trotter to stay, because her grandmother, lonely all the years since her daughter Courtney disappeared, needs her. In a bittersweet ending, Gilly recognizes the responsibilities of love.

Betsy Byars paints a vivid description of three foster children with bitter memories who come to live with Mr. and Mrs. Mason in *The Pinballs* (I). First to arrive is Harvey, who has two broken legs—acquired when his drunken father ran over him in his haste to get to his poker game. Next is Thomas J., left on the doorstep of 82-year-old twins who kept him for six years, then gave him up when they were incapacitated. Finally there is Carlie, a scrappy, television-addicted girl who fought pitched battles with her most recent stepfather. On her arrival, Carlie heads for the television set, saying "Don't talk to me when 'Young and Restless' is on." When Mrs. Mason protests that she just wants to welcome her, Carlie snaps back, "Welcome me during the commercial."

The three children gradually learn to respect themselves and each other. Carlie confers the name "pinballs" on them because they get knocked around by others and cannot help what happens to them. But they come to realize that they do have some control over their lives; the book ends hopefully as the three children resolve that they will no longer be pinballs.

ACTIVITY: TEACHER TO STUDENT

"MEET THE CHARACTER" RADIO SCRIPT (I)   Interview Carlie and Gilly on a radio talk show. Needed are someone to play the announcer, MC, Carlie, and Gilly. Others can write book commercials for the station breaks. They can be advertisements for the books *The Pinballs,* by Betsy Byars, and *The Great Gilly Hopkins,* by Katherine Paterson. Use the following script as a model for the interview, filling in the blanks, of course.

ANNOUNCER: Hello folks! Welcome to "Meet the Character." Today's special guests are Gilly Hopkins and Carlie, who come directly to us from Katherine Paterson and Betsy Byars. Now, let's give a warm welcome to our genial MC, _____.

MC: Well, I'm certainly happy to be here. Today we're going to chat with two unusual young women. By the time the show is over, you'll know more about foster homes and what it feels like to live in them. Both of our guests have spent most of their lives in foster homes and have strong feelings about them. But, first, a word from our sponsor.

ANNOUNCER: (book commercial)

MC: Let's begin with you, Carlie. Tell us a little about the circumstances under which you were placed in a foster home. How did you feel about your foster parents?

CARLIE: _____.

MC: Gilly, I understand that you were in about four or five homes before you got to Maime Trotter's. Did you ever think any of those places were permanent, or were they all temporary?

GILLY: _____.

MC: Carlie, we know you called yourself and the other foster children "pinballs." What do you mean by that? Do you think you have any control over what happens to you now?

CARLIE: _____.

MC: Gilly, we know for a fact that you think you're brilliant and that you said that you are too clever and too hard to manage. What do you think Maime Trotter thought about you when you first arrived? How does she feel now that you're living with your grandmother?

GILLY: _____.

MC: Here's a question for both of you. You both had foster brothers that you had mixed feelings about when you first met. What are they doing and how do you feel about them now?

GILLY: _____.

CARLIE: _____.

MC: What hopes do you two girls have for the future? I know, Carlie, that you want to be a nurse.

CARLIE: _____.

GILLY: _____.

MC: Well, our time is almost up. What advice do you have for the foster children who might be listening to us today?

CARLIE: _____.

GILLY: _____.

MC: We'd like to thank you both for being our guests.

Of Personal Integrity

Young people are engaged in a process of trying to find out who they are, what they like and do not like, and what they will and will not do. They are passionately preoccupied with themselves and may look to literature for solutions to or escape from their preoccupations. They enter into books in ways they cannot with television, making it a more personal and creative experience.

When students want to understand themselves, they create images of themselves behaving nobly and are left with important memories. Stories that hinge upon the personal integrity of a character draw readers instinctively into grappling with envisaged tests of their own mettle.

One of the most sensitive and gripping stories published in recent years is Paula Fox's *One-Eyed Cat* (I–A), which merited a Newbery Honor Book Award. When Ned Wallis receives an air rifle for his eleventh birthday from his Uncle Hilary, Ned's father, a minister, forbids him to use it and immediately packs it away in the attic. Temptation to hold the gun just once to see how it feels is too strong; Ned sneaks into the attic while his parents sleep and takes it out into the dark of night. Suddenly something moves across a shadow and before he can think, Ned feels his finger squeezing the trigger. Frozen in time and space he waits, but there is only dark now where before there had been shadow, silence where there had been a quick "whoosh." Slowly returning up the path he glances toward the house and sees a face pressed against the window. Did someone hear or see what he had done? Ned returns the gun to the attic and goes to his room with guilt gnawing his very being. For weeks he goes about in a daze wondering, worrying.

Ned feels safe with Mr. Scully, an elderly neighbor, for whom he does small chores. One day, a scraggly cat appears at Mr. Scully's woodshed; it shakes its head constantly as though it cannot see. Dried blood and a small hole where an eye should have been confirm what Ned has known all along: "He had disobeyed his father and he had shot at something that was alive. He knew it was that cat." Ned and Mr. Scully feed the cat through the autumn until Mr. Scully suffers a stroke. Ned visits Mr. Scully and one day has the courage to blurt out, "Oh, Mr. Scully—. It was me that shot the cat." Although he cannot speak, Mr. Scully reaches out feebly to press Ned's hand.

> Ned walked to the library. He raised the hand Mr. Scully had touched and looked at it as though it could talk. Finally, he had spoken to another person about shooting the cat. Mr. Scully had been unable to speak. Yet he had pressed that hand. He wouldn't have done that if he had thought Ned was truly bad. But he must have had a thought about Ned. Still, he'd tried to comfort him. He had understood that Ned was suffering. What *would* he have said? He hadn't ever had to lie to Mr. Scully the way he had at home—except by leaving out a few things he knew about that cat. Mr. Scully was going to die; he was leaving Ned perched on the top rung of a ladder built out of lies; the ladder was leaning against nothing.[25]

Paula Fox's storytelling ability and rich imagery turns a single incident in a child's life into a compelling narrative. She creates a stark contrast between Ned's inability to speak about an important event and the intense interior monologues which show that guilt is consuming him. Ned's ability to come to terms with the truth is a step toward self-determination and taking control of his own life.

Words by Heart (I–A), by Ouida Sebestyen, sketches another kind of integrity in her story of Lena, a 12-year-old girl with an exceptional capacity for memorizing beautiful literary passages as well as the words of her father. Lena knows that her only competition in a Scriptures-quoting contest will be Winslow Starnes, recognized champion in her town, but she is determined to outstrip him in the face of obvious favoritism from the judge. When it is clear that Lena cannot be denied as the winner, the judge hesitantly hands her the prize he holds wrapped in his hand.

> "You win the prize, Miss Lena." He handed it out abruptly. "I wish it could have been just what you wanted, because you deserve. . . ." Then he sat down as if *his* memory had failed *him* too.
>
> Lena held it in her trembling hand and said, "Thank you, Mr. Kelsey." She unwrapped the paper.
>
> Inside was a tie, a blue bow tie with a little celluloid hook at the back that was supposed to fit over a collar button. A boy's prize.[26]

Lena rejects the prize that was obviously meant for Winslow Starnes, but she worries that her father is disappointed by her haughty act. It is Papa, disappointed in his ambition to become a preacher, who has taught Lena to love beautiful words and to aspire to live by them, and who sustains her by his resolute faith. Through her father's example, she learns to love her enemies even in the face of shattering loss and maintains the integrity he modeled for her:

> She knew, with a heavy sinking, how Papa would answer, whom he would quote. Love your enemies and do good to those who hate you. Give to them that asketh thee. The words that had been so beautiful to say, so easy, turned to stone. No one had told her, not Papa, not the preacher, that they could change like that when they had to be lived, and crush her with their weight.[27]

Ouida Sebestyen wraps her story in poetry and vivifies the clear distinction between saying beautiful words and living them.

Gary Paulsen writes of adolescents coming to terms with the persons they will become. In *Tracker* (A), 13-year-old John is hunting alone for the first time; his grandfather who had always accompanied him is terminally ill with cancer. John grieves as he tracks a beautiful doe, but although he levels the gun's sight on her, he cannot bring himself to pull the trigger. Instead, he follows slowly, gaining her trust so that he can touch the warm flesh that surges with life, leading him to understand the interplay of life and death.

Dogsong (A), which received a Newbery Honor Award, is another story of an adolescent's rites of passage. Russel resents the growing deprecation of his Eskimo culture and is drawn to the old man, Oogruk, who retains the natural ways of his people. Instead of using modern machines to hunt seal and caribou, Oogruk keeps a good dogsled team and carefully tends to the old-fashioned weapons that hang on his walls. Oogruk becomes a model for Russel as he shares the stories and songs of the old ways. Russel gains confidence in himself as he learns to master the dog team in preparation for his solitary quest toward the north to find his "song." The hardships he faces on the icy, barren landscape and fear of the wild animals would have overwhelmed him if he had not learned well from Oogruk's teachings. He discovers his own strength and the wisdom of the old ways as he grows toward maturity.

Paulsen also received a 1988 Newbery Honor Book award for *Hatchet* (A), a survival story interlaced with a coming-of-age theme. A young boy survives a plane crash in the wilderness and learns to fend for himself with only the hatchet his mother had given him. He comes to grips with his bitterness at his parents' divorce and his mother's interest in another man.

Suzanne Newton's *An End to Perfect* and its sequel, *A Place Between* (both I–A), follow 12-year-old Arden who believes that her life in Haverlee, a small town in North Carolina, is "perfect." She has parents who love her, a best friend, DorJo, who makes ordinary games exciting, and a big brother, Hill, who teases her affectionately. Arden's perfect life begins to erode when Hill decides to leave Haverlee and live with their grandparents so that he can go to a better high school in a large city. Then DorJo has problems with her own mother and seeks refuge with Arden's family. Arden is pleased because DorJo fills the empty chair left by her brother and tries to keep her with them even when DorJo's mother comes to take her home. In A *Place Between,* Arden's grandfather dies and her parents move to live with the widowed grandmother. Desperate to hold onto the life she once knew in Haverlee, Arden schemes to return. In a bittersweet, "You can't go home again" ending, Arden faces up to the changes in her life and determines to be true to herself as she finds a place in a new world.

Of Physical Disabilities

Physical impairments range from minimal muscular dysfunction to total paralysis, with as many causes as there are limitations on the disabled person's ability to move about. Orthopedic problems are central or peripheral elements in children's books more frequently than any other type of disability.

Physically disabled children have dreams and aspirations like any child; overprotection and patronage, no matter how well intended, can destroy these. In *Let the Balloon Go* (I), Ivan Southall tells a story about John, who is 12 years old, has cerebral palsy, and wants more than anything to swim and climb and play like other boys. His anxious mother, though, constantly reminds him of what he can*not* do, such as ride a bike, chop wood, get into fights. On a rare day in which he is briefly left alone, John decides to build a tree house. His progress is slow and clumsy, but with the help of a ladder he drags to the tree, he persists until he reaches the topmost branches. He sits there exhilarated. He is strong, free, a boy like any other. But neighbors notice him, assume that he is stranded, and form a rescue party. The constable climbs the tree, but gets stuck before he reaches John. The boy defies orders to stay where he is and begins the dangerous descent

With fierce determination, John struggles against his cerebral palsy to climb to the top of a tree, where he will feel strong and free. (From *Let the Balloon Go* by Ivan Southall. Illustrated by Jon Weiman.)

unaided; he slips and struggles but reaches the constable, whom he frees, then continues with faltering and unsteady progress. He slips near the bottom and falls with a scream.

John awakens in his bed, and his mother confirms that he really climbed the tree—and got down unaided. His parents at last realize that John needs to take risks and needs to be free to try. He likens his release to a balloon, which is not really a balloon until someone cuts the string.

Disability need not prevent participation.

Bernard Wolf's *Don't Feel Sorry for Paul* (I) describes a heroic child's adjustment to the use of artificial limbs. Born with incomplete hands and feet, Paul wears prostheses—artificial body parts. Clear black-and-white photographs show Paul getting himself ready for and participating in many activities with his family and friends. He rides a horse, attends public school, helps his mother prepare dinner, wrestles with his sisters, and rides a bike. Wolf gives factual information about Paul's regular visits to the Institute of Rehabilitation Medicine for examination and adjustment of the prosthetic devices. The honest, objective book is neither patronizing nor pallid.

Cynthia Voigt presents a powerful fictional account of dealing with a physical handicap in *Izzy, Willy-Nilly* (A). A young girl loses her legs in a car accident and has to deal with her friend's embarrassment and sympathy. In addition, she must face her mother's anger and refusal to deal with the situation as well as her own emotions. Voigt is a strong writer.

Deafness and Hearing Impairment Deafness is an invisible disability; there are no obvious signs, and as a result, misunderstandings are frequent. Because the deaf look like everybody else, they are expected to cope with the environment normally. When this does not happen, strange inferences are made—most often about their intellectual abilities.

The deaf and hearing impaired communicate with the help of hearing aids, lip reading, and sign language. They express themselves through speech, writing, and sign language. Because speaking depends so heavily upon hearing, the age at which the hearing loss occurs correlates highly with the normalcy of the deaf person's speech: the earlier the age at which the loss occurred, the greater the divergence from normal speech.

The deaf person has language and knows what he wants to say; the difficulty arises in enunciation, for which he has had no models. It is a great accomplishment for the deaf to communicate freely with hearing people. Helen Keller once said that her most fervent wish was to be able to speak to another person without an interpreter; she accomplished this by working against multiple odds. Her autobiography describes the steps along the way and the role books played in her progress.

Books for children reflect the misunderstandings that vex the deaf and hearing impaired. In Veronica Robinson's *David in Silence* (I), the neighborhood boys distrust David because they can neither understand his imperfect speech nor make him understand what they say. They tease and mock him, and one child suggests that David is only pretending to be deaf. One day David misinterprets their shouts of contempt as an invitation to play with them. The boys turn on him, and frightened, he flees, loses his way, and when he is unable to make anyone understand him, panics. One child who had tried to befriend David finds him and helps him return home. Gradually, the other boys learn to respect David, and in turn, he learns to respect himself.

In Barbara Corcoran's *A Dance to Still Music* (I–A), Margaret's sense of isolation imposed by her deafness is compounded when she moves from Maine to Florida with her self-centered mother. Fearful of meeting new people, and yet resentful of the idea that she should attend a school for the deaf, 14-year-old Margaret starts to hitchhike back north to her former home. Along the way, when she finds an injured fawn and stops to care for it, she meets Josie, an older woman who persuades the girl to stay with her. Josie listens as Margaret haltingly expresses her fears of ridicule and convinces her that she can learn to overcome the social and emotional ramifications of her disability. They notify Margaret's mother who willingly turns over the responsibility for her to Josie. In the final scene, Margaret joins a training program—a hopeful note that she has stopped running and is going to face her disability.

Bernard Wolf's *Anna's Silent World* (P–I) is a photodocumentary about a 6-year-old deaf child. Anna leads a happy life as she plays with her friends and joins in many activities. Her deafness is explained, and lip reading and her hearing aid are described.

Jeanne Whitehouse Peterson drew on her own experiences with a younger sister to tell the story of *I Have a Sister. My Sister Is Deaf* (P). In a simple conversational style, she tells about the many things her sister can do and some that she cannot. The sisters talk to each other with their hands, their eyes, their faces, as well as with their mouths. She explains that although her sister's ears do not hurt, sometimes her feelings are hurt when people do not understand her or make fun of her. This loving report is a good introduction to deafness, one in which it is viewed not as a handicap but as a straightforward fact of life.

Visual Impairment Visually disabled children range from those who are totally blind and read braille to those who are visually impaired and read large print or with the aid of special magnifying lenses or optical monoculars. An *opticon* translates printed material into electrical patterns that can be read aloud or with the fingers. Tape recorded stories also allow blind children to experience the same literature as their sighted peers. Such tapes are available commercially and at libraries, but of course, you can make your own. In one school, a talking-books project has students recording their favorite stories on cassette tapes and sending them to blind children at the local hospital. Other students become readers who keep a regular schedule visiting hospitalized people, including those who are blind.

Outstanding stories and poems are collected in an annual braille publication called *Expectations* that is provided without charge to blind children in grades 3 through 6 throughout the United States.[28]

The literature curriculum for blind and partially sighted children is the same as for children with normal vision; only the materials and techniques differ. Like the rest of us, blind children need special role models, and although many accounts of Helen Keller's life are romanticized, children should certainly know her inspirational story. Several biographies of Helen Keller and of her teacher, Anne Sullivan Macy, tell the story well. *The Story of My Life* (I–A) is Helen Keller's own account and is supplemented, in some editions, with notes, letters, and documents by Anne Sullivan and others involved in her education.

The Helen Keller Story (I), by Catherine Owens Peare, is a biography that shows children a

Blind and partially sighted children have the same curriculum as sighted children; the materials and techniques are the only things that differ.

Jimmy's new guide dog, Leader, helps him adjust to his blindness, providing him with a feeling of independence and a renewed sense of his own worth. (From *Follow My Leader* by James B. Garfield. Illustrated by Robert Greiner.)

warm, loving human being who happened to be deaf and blind. Helen Keller always gave the greatest credit to her beloved teacher, Anne Sullivan, who, nearly blind herself, came to the rebellious and uncommunicative 6-year-old Helen and, with tremendous dedication and determination, opened the doors of the world to her.

Laura Bridgman was a mature resident at the Perkins Institute for the Blind when Anne Sullivan was a student there. Many of the methods developed to teach the blind and deaf Laura Bridgman were adapted by Anne Sullivan in her work with Helen Keller. Edith Hunter tells the story in *Child of the Silent Night: The Story of Laura Bridgman* (I).

Fiction portraying the blind coping with their disability offers many fine stories. Children who read James Garfield's *Follow My Leader* (I) will not forget the baseball game that

turns into tragedy for 11-year-old Jimmy when one of his friends finds a firecracker. Despite warnings from the other boys to leave it alone, Mike hurls the firecracker, which explodes in Jimmy's face. Blinded by the accident, Jimmy refuses to speak to Mike; his bitterness grows until he hates himself, Mike, and the whole world. As he slowly adjusts to moving about with his new guide dog, Leader, he gradually accepts his blindness and, in a moving scene, comes to terms with Mike.

Jean Little's story, *From Anna* (I), is based on the life of the blind author. Anna is awkward and clumsy and the brunt of her family's scorn because she cannot do anything right. Her brothers and sisters tease her unmercifully and call her Awkward Anna when she stumbles and drops things. As World War II becomes inevitable, the family leaves their native Germany to settle in Canada. There, a doctor finally discovers that her problems are due to extremely poor vision and prescribes glasses

PROFILE

Jean Little

Jean Little is a person who has not allowed a disability to become a handicap. Born with very limited eyesight, she nonetheless developed an early love for language and books. Her earliest memories include being read to by her mother—in fact, one of her first spoken words was "book-a."

As she grew she made up her own stories and, at the age of 10, wrote her first book. When she was 15 her father had a collection of her poems printed. Jean Little has always preferred stories about true-to-life people in a realistic context; even as a child she didn't "like fairy tales or legends much because the people weren't real enough." Her stories are about real people, often chil-

dren, who successfully cope with problems. Mental retardation, cerebral palsy, blindness, and even broken bones—all affect the lives of her characters but do not handicap them.

Although she wanted to be a writer, she thought authors "lived in garrets and starved," and to avoid that fate, she became a teacher. It was only after she met Virginia Sorensen—who "looked well-nourished"— that she took the chance. The result of that first effort—winner of the 1961 Canadian Children's Book Award—was *Mine for Keeps*, a realistic story about a girl with cerebral palsy. She drew upon her own painful experiences when she wrote *From Anna*, a story about a young girl who suffers teasing and ostracism because of her poor eyesight.

A Canadian, she was born in Taiwan, where her parents were serving as medical missionaries. Her family returned to Canada when she was 7 years old, and after one year in a special class, she attended regular school, though she was never able to see what was written on the blackboard. She received a Bachelor's degree in English language and literature from the University of Toronto. She likes to travel, but "what my life is really all about is writing. It's a terrible way to make a living but I wouldn't do anything else. I get to live so many extra lives this way."[29] Jean Little tells her own story in an autobiography, *Little by Little*.

and a special school for Anna. The family still considers her a problem, but Anna's self-image grows as she learns to cope with poor vision.

Bernard Wolf's *Connie's New Eyes* (I), a photographic essay, opens when Alison begins

raising a seeing eye dog as a part of a 4-H Club project. Her strong devotion to the dog is evident in the way she cares for and trains her, but she knows that at the end of a year the dog must be taken to Seeing Eye, Inc., for further training. A blind young teacher, Connie, then assumes ownership and learns to work with the dog, who will become her guide. Connie's story focuses on her independence, enhanced by the arrival of the dog, and her ability to succeed in a career.

In *Goldengrove* (A), by Jill Paton Walsh, young Madge Fielding reads regularly to a blind professor. One day, as she reads to him from Milton's *Paradise Lost,* the meaning of the verses overwhelms her, and she weeps at the words that describe the plight of her blind listener. Madge asks the professor how he can bear to hear words that echo his loss. His answer aptly portrays a role of literature in life:

> It puts things outside me. Makes them into objects external to the mind. . . . Another man's pain, against which to measure one's own. A scream to put against one's own silence. It helps me to grasp how much of what I am is blindness and how much is me.[30]

Literature provides a measuring stick for some; a portrait of another's life dominated by a disability for the rest. It enables all of us to share another's distress and celebrate the unconquerable joy in life.

THE REALISTIC BOOK AS WINDOW

An author invites us to look through a window, and we respond, to see the world through another's eyes. Literature gives us many windows from which to view the world: through some, we see landscape—a countryside, a skyline, the sea—through others, we see bustling activity or quiet contemplation; sometimes the view is stormy and sorrowful. Literature's windows on the world look upon the full range of human experience, including our joys and sorrows, our virtues and vices.

On Laughter

To reflect the world, realistic books must present all its dimensions. From the plethora of problem books in the 1980s, it would seem that we live in *only* a problem world, all grimness and sordid facts. As we know, the real world has both laughter and tears, both happiness and sadness; children's books reflect them all. A world made up of all problems and no joy is just as unrealistic as the Panglossian vision of the happily-ever-after world we gave children a generation ago, when so many books displayed the happy-ending syndrome.

Beverly Cleary has remarked, that if children only viewed life as they see it in their books, they would forget how to laugh. As we have seen, when children are given choices about the types of books they want to read, they choose humorous books more often than any other type from the ones available. In the annual field test of newly published books, the "Children's Choices," sponsored by the International Reading Association and the Children's Book Council, humorous books repeatedly top the list. Dianne Monson studied children's responses to humorous situations in literature to characterize the types of humor found in the selections. She categorized five types: (1) character humor, (2) humor of surprise, (3) humor of the impossible, (4) humor of words, and (5) humor of a ridiculous situation.[31] Each of these types can be found in contemporary fiction.

Beverly Cleary is a master of humorous situations. Children howl when *Ramona Quimby, Age Eight* (P–I) cracks what she *thinks* is a hard-boiled egg over her head in the school cafeteria. They smother giggles but share her horror when she throws up in school.

> And then she knew that the most terrible, horrible, dreadful, awful thing that could happen was going to happen. Please, God, don't let me. . . . Ramona prayed too late.
> The terrible, horrible, dreadful, awful thing happened. Ramona threw up. She threw up right there on the floor in front of everyone.[32]

Judy Blume, too, brings giggles from the reader when Fudge, Peter's younger brother, swallows his pet turtle in *Tales of a Fourth Grade Nothing* (P–I) and when Fudge gets an unsuspecting visiting illustrator to paint a picture of the school principal in a school assembly in *Superfudge* (P–I).

Robert Burch builds character humor in *Ida Early Comes Over the Mountain* and the sequel *Christmas with Ida Early* (both I). Ida Early comes to the Sutton family to care for the four children after their mother has died. She shocks crusty Aunt Earnestine when she twirls her sweater above her head and flings it across the room to land neatly on the hatrack. Ida is also good at yodeling, flinging dishes across the room to set the table, and telling stories about her former exploits that include falling off a mustang. The tall, gangly Ida dresses in bizarre clothes and behaves outrageously, but she brings much-needed laughter back into the Sutton home and into readers' lives.

Johanna Hurwitz has a light touch of gentle humor in her books about Aldo Sossi, who was introduced in *Much Ado about Aldo* (P–I) and stars in *Aldo Applesauce* and *Aldo Ice Cream* (both I). Aldo hates the nickname "Aldo Applesauce" that his classmates give him but finally decides that at least people know his name. In *Aldo Ice Cream*, he tries to find a job so he can buy his sister a birthday gift, but he finds that there are not too many jobs for a boy his age. He decides that his best chance is to win the prize offered for the worst looking sneakers. He wins the sneaker contest and with a little extra money from his mother buys an ice cream freezer (on sale).

Helen Cresswell's British humor crosses the Atlantic with few problems in the Bagthorpe saga. The Bagthorpe family first appears in *Ordinary Jack*, then in *Absolute Zero, Bagthorpes Unlimited, Bagthorpes vs. the World,* and *Bagthorpes Abroad* (all I–A). This wacky, hilarious, ludicrous family is a source of delight. Characterization is so strong that readers know exactly how each member of the zany family will react to every crisis. In *Bagthorpes Unlimited*, Grandma prepares a list of the family's most prized possessions, totally worthless things to anyone else, instructing any robber to leave them alone. She gives the exact location of the items and, of course, in due time, the items are stolen. Grandma is so unnerved by this catastrophe that she wants her nearest and

ACTIVITY: TEACHER TO STUDENT

AN AUTHOR INTERVIEW (I–A) Plan with your class to invite an author whose books you enjoy. Before the visit, discuss questions you might ask, such as,

Were there experiences in your own life that led you to write this book?
Did you think you were going to be a writer when you were our age?
Do you have a special place to write?
When do you write?
What are you working on now?

Record the interview so that you can enjoy it again; then share it with others. Names and addresses of authors are available from publishers, who will discuss arrangements with you. If it is not possible to have an author visit, you might consider a phone call. The telephone company can help arrange for a conference call so that everyone can take part in Dial-an-Author programs.

dearest close by. This brings some unwanted relatives into the house whom the Bagthorpe children try to drive away by insidious means, such as placing maggots in a box of chocolate candy. Each member of the family is gifted and feels that it is his duty to "add strings to his bow." Father is a television script writer, Mother writes the "Agony Column" for the local newspaper, and each child has his own talents to perfect. Grandma is unquestioningly the ruler of the family, while Grandpa remains hazily in the background using his hearing aid to be selectively deaf. All the children are precocious, except for Ordinary Jack, who is eclipsed by his outgoing, gregarious family.

In Ellen Raskin's *The Westing Game* (I), Turtle Wexler is one of 16 rather strange people who are invited to the reading of Sam Westing's will. The group is divided into eight pairs, given different sets of clues, and $10,000 per team. All the partners have to do is find the answer—but no one knows the question. The teams play the Westing Game through one hilarious escapade after another. Competition is strong and alliances are soon made (though no one trusts anyone else) and disasters ensue as they try to outwit each other. Readers are as much in the dark as the participants until the very end. The zany word play and intrigue in the puzzle-knotted, word-twisting plot show off Ellen Raskin's special brand of ingenuity.

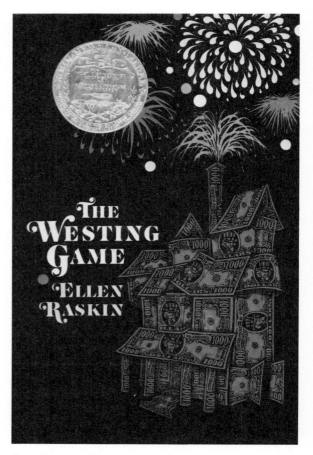

Sam Westing's house seems to be made of money when he plays a zany game with his heirs. (From *The Westing Game* by Ellen Raskin.)

On Courage

Although many realistic novels are problem laden, and critics who read them cry out, "Please deliver me from yet another book with the cracked ceiling syndrome," realism contains stories of courage in which people are not beaten down by life, but transform it into something splendid through inner strength. If we are to examine life adequately through realistic literature, we need to share the inspirational books with our students as well as the dismal ones. In a day when we have few he-

roes in real life, it can be good to look to literature for lives to emulate.

Discussing *The Third Eye* (I–A), Mollie Hunter declared that "courage needs witness," and her uplifting theme is vivified in this book. The gripping story is a fitting testament to her belief that courageous acts should be recognized. We first meet Jinty on her way to give evidence to the Procurator Fiscal, an attorney or judge taking pretrial testimony. Through a series of flashbacks, we find the reason for her appearance: she was the last person to see the

ACTIVITY: TEACHER TO STUDENT

THE WESTING GAME **GAME (I)**   Make a board game for Ellen Raskin's *The Westing Game.* Go through the book and write the clues on game cards—for example, "FRUITED PURPLE WAVES FOR SEA" (p. 44) and "SKIES AM SHINING BROTHER" (p. 82). Draw a twisting path that runs around the board and is divided into spaces. You might ornament this with a picture of a rolled up will at the start and the Westing house at the end. Put the clues on the board at various spaces. Some clues can turn out to be dead ends, while others lead to the solution of the story's puzzle. Make a set of markers to represent the characters and use a spinner to determine how far each one moves on a turn. Make up rules, such as dead-end clues require the player to go back three spaces; valid clues allow the player to skip ahead three spaces. The winner is the first player to reach the Westing house.

Earl of Ballinford alive. The earl, wealthy land-owner and acknowledged lord of the village, lived under the Ballinford doom—a prophetic curse that meant an oldest son would never outlive his father. The earl lived and died courageously as he tried to change the pattern that had cursed his family for generations. Jinty recognizes the brand of courage the earl portrays but aches that it is such a lonely one.

Jinty's story involves much more: her two sisters display a certain kind of courage as they defy parental rules in order to shape the lives they choose to live. Jinty's mother, seemingly hardened and determined to raise her three daughters according to her unbending standards, personifies the courage of endurance.

In the midst of conflict and tension, Jinty herself characterizes yet another kind of courage, the quiet kind that causes her to see and to know strengths and weaknesses of those around her and to acknowledge their humanness.

Hunter uses rich, vivid language in *The Third Eye* as she describes Jinty's visit to Toby, a lonely blind boy, through the fence that surrounds his yard. He begs Jinty to bring flowers so he can see them in his mind's eye. Jinty tries to describe the colors to him:

"Jaggedy-hot" for "red." That was easy. "A sunny day that's still cold." That was easy, too, for "yellow." But what could she say for "purple"?

"It's like a taste," she decided eventually. "You think it's going to be jaggedy-hot, like red; but when you do taste it, it slides away into something smoother, and really cold."

Toby laughed at this, and fanned his hand across his eyes as if to make himself see purple, stuck out his tongue as if he were tasting it.[33]

A different kind of courage is shown by Betsy Byars when 11-year-old *Cracker Jackson* (I) receives an anonymous note warning him to "Keep away, Cracker, or he'll hurt you." The only person who called him Cracker was Alma, his former babysitter. Now Alma is married and has a child of her own, but Jackson has reason to believe she is being abused by her husband. Jackson promises Alma not to involve his mother, so he turns to his friend Goat, the class clown, to help him rescue Alma. At a critical moment, Alma backs down from seeking help and returns to her husband. Jackson's mother finally becomes aware of the heavy burden he is carrying; she intervenes, not in time to save Alma one more beating, but in time to save her life and to relieve Jackson from the tremendous responsibility he has shouldered. Despite the serious theme, the story is sprinkled with humor. In one particularly funny scene, Jackson and Goat, armed with pillows, try to drive a car to rescue Alma.

Vera and Bill Cleaver document courage in a different setting in *Where the Lilies Bloom* (I–A) and its sequel, *Trial Valley* (I–A). Mary Call Luther lives in the Great Smoky Mountains, where people are free, proud, and achingly poor. She is a plucky girl who uses all of her resources to maintain the raw dignity and independence of her problem-plagued family. One of Mary Call's heartaches is her 18-year-old sister, Devola, who is "cloudy in the head." Another is Roy Luther, her father, who is desperately ill from "worms in the chest." Ima Dean and Romey, a younger sister and brother, complete her family; their mother is long dead.

The family survives by collecting medicinal herbs from the mountain slopes and selling them at the general store. Roy Luther dies, and Mary Call keeps a promise to her father, when she and Romey drag his body to the top of the mountain to bury him so that officials and nosy neighbors will not send the children to the county home. She keeps another promise to hold the family together and never take charity.

> And I get scared and I think, but how am I going to do this? Who will show me how and who will help me?
> And then I get madder and I say to myself, Aw, quit your bellyaching. There's a way; all you have to do is find it.[34]

Mary Call finds the way but it tests her mettle and courage every step along the mountain paths she climbs.

Pity can diminish its object, but true compassion requires courage even as it ennobles and strengthens. Through literature, children can see models of many kinds of emotional response. During childhood, when values are crystallizing, fiction with windows on compassion is imperative.

Jill Paton Walsh, noted English writer, balances two stories against each other in *Unleaving* (A), a story that takes its inspiration from Gerard Manley Hopkins's poem "Spring and Fall." The reader first meets Gran as she makes her way downstairs falteringly to join her daughter, son-in-law, and their three children for tea. In the second paragraph, the reader meets Madge in a school uniform, traveling alone on a night train to Goldengrove, the scene of Gran's tea party.

Before long, the reader learns that Madge inherited Goldengrove, but Madge's story and Gran's story continue until we discover eventually that the stories are one, separated only by time. The muted, interlacing stories center the narrative on one consciousness while avoiding a first-person narration.

After the tea party, the children beg their grandmother to take them to the beach, and although the others protest, she agrees.

> "I'll take them this time," says Gran, getting up from her chair, both hands down on the chair arms to raise herself. . . . "I can manage," says Gran. "I had a rest this afternoon. I can get down the path if I take my time, you know. . . ." Their voices, as they descend the cliff path, fade; and left behind in the peace among the crumbs and jam and unwashed teacups—someone has licked the cream spoon cloudy clean—the grownups smile and sigh.[35]

Back again with schoolgirl Madge as she is summoned to the headmistress's study, we find that arrangements are being made for a university professor to take a reading party to Goldengrove for the summer. When the professor and his wife arrive, Madge is there to greet them.

> "You must be Madge Fielding," says Mrs. Tregeagle. "This is Molly. Say hello, Molly."

Madge stoops toward the child, hands held out, and smiling. ''Hello, Molly,'' she says.

The child looks up. Its face is very ruddy, with almond-shaped pale blue eyes, and hardly any lashes. It smiles, and as it does so the smile fills with spittle, which overflows and oozes down its chin. The eyes swim inward into a squint. Madge sickens for an instant, then realizes, then covers up and steadies her smile. Forcing herself, she bends and picks up the child, staggered at its solidity and weight.[36]

There is another Tregeagle child, Patrick, who is Madge's age; he observes her revulsion at meeting Molly and hates her for it. Later, Madge shows compassion for Molly but, eventually, far greater compassion is asked of her for Patrick.

The professor and the reading party discuss profound philosophical questions related to moral and ethical issues. The students staunchly defend their logic as long as their discussions remain in the abstract, but when a tragedy strikes, their profound statements seem hollow. They are unable to make the link between their scholarly talk and compassion when Patrick desperately needs it. Madge, who feels herself an outsider in the lofty discussions, is the only one able to help ease his pain.

Natalie Babbitt fuses fantasy and realism with skill in several books, each more enchanting than the last. In *The Eyes of the Amaryllis* (I)—a story of faith, love, and compassion—she makes us believe in Geneva's search for a sign from the sea and in the vision of a man who walks the shore unseen by others. She also makes us feel the compassion of Geneva's 11-year-old granddaughter, Jenny, and helps us to see through her eyes and her hopes the possibility of life and death overlapping, of past and present intermingling. Jenny believes and sees with her grandmother; she respects the woman's sturdy dignity and independence that even her father ignores.

On Survival

Readers build expectations about literature and about the world by accumulating experience in both. They explore life and plumb its depths through firsthand, but also virtual, experiences. Not many children have the opportunity—or would want—to live alone on a frozen tundra, or beneath the ground in a subway. They can have these and much more as virtual experiences through books. Heroism lies on the horizon of expectations in literature and in life.

Physical survival is an oft-played theme in children's books. Most often, characters struggle against the elements of nature, but in some cases, too much civilization puts lives in peril.

In Felice Holman's *Slake's Limbo* (I), a street gang taunts and chases 13-year-old Aremis Slake through the alleys and junkyards of his neighborhood. He expects to be beaten, as always, but this time he escapes into a subway. Once there he discovers, in the wall of the subway tunnel, a hole that becomes his refuge for 121 days.

Slake's survival depends upon his wit and cunning; his heroism lies in the tenacious determination through which he overcomes the terror and the desperation that bind him to his dark molelike subsistence. His routine of scavenging for food soon becomes easy, but eventually he knows that he must return to the outside. ''He turned and started up the stairs and out of the subway. Slake did not know exactly where he was going, but the general direction was up.''[37] Though afraid, he was going to face life.

In Brock Cole's story, *The Goats* (I–A), two children who are victimized by fellow campers run away into the wilderness. They develop self-esteem through their survival efforts and create a deep and abiding friendship.

Jean George's *Julie of the Wolves* (I–A), winner of the 1973 Newbery Award, is an example of realistic fiction that can be read at several levels of meaning. It is a story of a girl's search for identity, a journey from a safe home through danger and hardship toward maturity, a commentary about the destruction of nature and earlier ways of life, a fight for individualism, initiation rites and loss of innocence, and an adventure story about wolves.

Julie, the English name for the Eskimo girl Miyax, is the heroine; all other characters are known through their relationship with her. Kapugen, Miyax's father, does not enter the story in person until the final pages, and yet his power and guiding influence are felt throughout the story. Amaroq, untamed leader of the wolf pack, becomes a father figure for Miyax, and his cub, named Kapu by the girl, becomes something close to a brother. Miyax's devotion to her father is seen in several ways: in her frequent references to things he taught her; in her naming of the young son of Amaroq, Kapu, a shortened form of her father's name; in the changes in her life when she hears that Kapugen is lost forever; and in the overwhelming gratitude she experiences when she believes he may still be alive.

The story engages the reader from the outset, with Miyax's desperate situation clearly stated:

> She was frightened, not so much of the wolves, . . . but because of her desperate predicament. Miyax was lost. She had been lost without food for many sleeps . . . and . . . the very life in her body . . . depended upon these wolves for survival. She must somehow tell him [the wolf] that she was starving and ask him for food.[38]

The novel is divided into three sequences: the present, the past, and the present once again. Part I chronicles Miyax's strategy as she learns the ways of the wolves in order to gain entry to their world and obtain food. Part II presents Miyax's memories of the days following her mother's death, endless days spent with her father learning the Eskimo ways. In this part Miyax's reasons for running away become evident. The present resumes in Part III,

Julie, a courageous girl alone in the Alaskan tundra, insinuates herself into a wolf pack in order to survive. (From *Julie of the Wolves* by Jean Craighead George. Pictures by John Schoenherr.)

when the wolf pack moves on and Miyax is left alone on the tundra.

Various devices heighten the drama. Dramatic foreshadowing concerning Miyax's father establishes the importance of a father figure for Miyax. There are hints about a white house in San Francisco that seem to reflect an unexpressed dream of finding friends, a home, and a family in a gussak (white man's) world. After an unknown and uncaring pilot shoots Miyax's beloved wolf-father, Amaroq, the gussak world comes to symbolize killing, guns, and other horrors. The small caribou bone replica that Miyax carves in the image of Amaroq and the golden plover she rescues now become far more meaningful to her.

The author's use of Eskimo words and traditions establishes an authentic tone. Time is measured by the number of ''sleeps'' and by

PROFILE

Jean Craighead George

Jean George was born in Washington, D.C., into a family of naturalists and ecologists. She spent her childhood summers on a family farm in Pennsylvania and graduated from Pennsylvania State University. She has written many books, all of which show her profound respect for nature and her deep understanding of the reciprocal relationship between the human world and the natural world.

George's writing career started in the third grade. She was sent to the board to do a math problem and because she could not cope with it wrote a poem instead. Her teacher encouraged her literary talents and she went on to major in English and science in college. Early in her career, Jean was a member of the White House press corps and a reporter for the International News Service and the *Washington Post*. She has written widely for magazines and newspapers and has traveled extensively on research projects.

Over the years, George, mother of three children, has kept hundreds of pets, not counting the numerous cats and dogs, in her home in Chappaqua, New York. She says, "Most of these wild animals depart in autumn when the sun changes their behavior and they feel the urge to migrate or go off alone. While they are with us, however, they become characters in my books, articles, and stories."

Jean George's standards for accurate science and impeccable details of nature in her stories are due to the careful research she undertakes prior to writing. She lives the conditions she ascribes to her character so that the survival techniques they use are ones she has actually tried. One of her early books, *My Side of the Mountain* (I), is the story of a boy who goes into the woods for a year to live in a tree house he shapes inside a hollow tree. His survival techniques are truly ingenious.

Jean George's inspiration for *Julie of the Wolves* evolved from two specific events during a summer she spent studying wolves at the Arctic Research Laboratory of Barrow, Alaska:

> One was a small girl walking the vast and lonesome tundra outside of Barrow; the other was a magnificent alpha male wolf, leader of a pack in Mt. McKinley National Park. . . . They haunted me for a year or more as did the words of one of the scientists at the lab: "If there ever was any doubt in my mind that a man could live with the wolves, it is gone now. The wolves are truly gentlemen, highly social and affectionate."[39]

The Newbery Award citation by the Association for Library Service to Children states, "Jean George, a naturalist, understands the pain of growing up and demonstrates a profound reverence for life—for humanity and nature together."

ACTIVITY: TEACHER TO STUDENT

DWELLERS OF THE TUNDRA (I–A)   After you have read Jean George's *Julie of the Wolves* and *Water Sky* (both I-A) study wolves and the habits of the Alpha leader. The author's description of the relationships within the wolf pack may lead you to wonder about control and leadership in other animal families.

Investigate the hunting laws in your state and trace the legislation on endangered species.

Study the geography of the Arctic tundra and make a map to trace Miyax's journey. You may want to use some of the following books:

Barry, *The Kingdom of Wolves*. (A)
Berrill, *Wonders of the World of Wolves* (I)
George, *The Wounded Wolf* (P–I)
Houston, *Wolf Run: A Caribou Eskimo Tale* (I)
Jenness, *Dwellers of the Tundra: Life in an Alaskan Eskimo Village* (I)
Pringle, *Wolfman: Exploring the World of Wolves* (I)
Steiner, *Biography of a Wolf* (I)

the signs in nature Miyax reads. The behavior of the wolves and the means that Miyax uses to establish communication with them are described graphically.

Perplexing questions remain in the reader's mind long after the book has been read. Julie's father had become a hunter in a gussak world. Was it actually he who shot the wolves? Did Julie leave her Eskimo ways behind and accept the changes that her father had accepted?

Survival is just one of the elements in another story Jean George sets in Alaska. In *Water Sky* (I–A), Lincoln goes to Barrow, Alaska, to search for his beloved Uncle Jack. He thought Vincent Ologak, an Eskimo whaling captain, could tell him where his uncle was, for Vincent was the person Uncle Jack planned to see when he went to Alaska to help save the bowhead whale from extinction. But Vincent Ologak will not give him a straight answer. Lincoln almost forgets his original goal when he gets caught up in the excitement of traditional Eskimo whale hunting. His fascination with learning about the Eskimo culture and the

teachings of old Vincent Ologak lead Lincoln ultimately to question his own identity. Jean George combines the search for self with an exciting survival theme.

Jean George has written over a dozen novels that pit human against nature. From the frozen Alaskan tundra to the Colorado Rocky Mountains to the Catskill Mountains of New York, her characters learn respect for the environment. Deep in the Florida Everglades, the Seminole Indians listen to *The Talking Earth* (I–A). Billie Wind scoffed at the beliefs of her tribe when she returned from the white man's school at the Kennedy Space Center. When she speaks derisively of these ideas and is recognized as a doubter, they send her to serve penance in the wilderness. She avoids having three white heron feathers waved over her, the symbol of safe journey, as she leaves to spend the assigned one night and two days in the swampy Lake Okeechobee. Billie Wind's journey lasts more than three months after she is caught in a swamp fire and must hide in an ancient cave. There she rescues a baby otter and finds trappings of her tribes' ancient rituals. Before her return, she learns to communicate with a panther and a turtle, endures a hurricane, carves out a boat from a fallen cypress tree, and befriends a young boy who is on his own rite of passage looking for a name of which he can be proud. Billie Wind gains respect for the ancient Seminole ways, not by accepting them unquestioningly but by seeing them proven to her in times of trial. Her own courage and battle for survival are uplifting.

On Aging

Our society is gradually according more respect to older people. Once content to shunt the elderly to rocking chairs and retirement centers, we are now beginning to rediscover the vast resources the elderly constitute and realize the personal value of continuing an active, contributing life.

An unusual story by the award-winning Australian author Patricia Wrightson, *A Little Fear* (I), tells of the fierce drive for independence by old Mrs. Tucker. When she learns that she has inherited a small cottage in the swamp flats, she steals away from the nursing home to live out her days there with her dog Hector. A Njimbin, a small ancient gnome, who has lived in the swamp for all time, resents the intrusion and begins a battle of wits as he tries to drive the old woman away. Pathos pervades this story as the reader cheers for Mrs. Tucker's success. In the end it is not the victory she had hoped for, but "This cottage had given her back a great deal: the dignity of independence in her own home; the right to risk breaking her leg in a fall from a stepladder; the freedom to choose her own undershirts and her own company."[40]

Janni Howker wrote five short stories in *Badger on the Barge and Other Stories* (I–A). In each tale, a lonely young person is drawn to a cranky, independent older one. Each story stands alone, but together they form a unifying picture of friendship among the generations and hope for people who care about others. The final story in the collection deals with Liz, an adolescent unhappy with her role as chief cook and bottle washer for her biker father and brother, and Sally Beck, a 91-year-old woman who works in a topiary garden. Liz wanders into the park to sketch some of the trees and shrubs shaped into dramatic forms and to escape yet another of her father's bike trial competitions. Sally Beck frightens her when suddenly she stands over Liz's shoulder draped in a huge coat and wellingtons with a face that looked like a crumpled brown paper bag. The unlikely pair share a cup of tea, and as they talk, Sally Beck tells Liz about her life. As a young girl, Sally disguised herself as Jack Beck, a boy, for several years and served as an apprentice to the old gardener in the topiary garden. After a few years, her masquerade was revealed due to the escapades of Liddy, a maid from the Hall, and a laborer from one of the estate's farms. Liddy blamed her untimely pregnancy on Jack Beck and so Sally was forced to admit that she was a girl, after all. The old gardener never quite forgave her deception, but he allowed her to stay on to work in the gardens. As Liz listens to Sally's story, she gains a sense of her own self worth.

Children often see their families in conflict over the problem of what to do with grandparents who no longer can care for themselves. Norma Fox Mazer creates a thought-provoking story about aging in *A Figure of Speech* (I). A harsh, insensitive atmosphere pervades the Pennoyer's home where Grandfather Carl lives in the basement, out of the way of the rest of the family. Gradually Grandpa is being divested of his independence: he is not allowed to cross streets alone, and is told "at eighty-three nobody expects you to be a hundred percent" and "if you move out of your basement apartment you'll be upstairs with all of us watching you." Only 13-year-old Jenny, herself feeling unwanted, is compassionate toward her grandfather, who is considered a burden by everyone else and referred to as an "old guy" and a "senior citizen," which makes him feel like a "figure of speech." When Jenny's older brother brings his new wife home, they move into the basement apartment and Grandpa is forced to share a room with the teenage son, a situation that leads to further tension in the uncaring family.

Grandpa finally tires of living as a fourth-class citizen and returns to his former home to salvage his dignity. Unknown to her parents, Jenny goes with him to share his final days. After his death, the family persists in platitude and cliché: Grandpa "didn't suffer a bit"; "it's a real comfort to us that he went so easily." The devastating cruelty and indifference of this family stimulate important discussions among readers.

Stephanie S. Tolan tells a similar story in *Grandpa — and Me* (I), although here the grandfather remains an important member of the family. Kerry, narrator of the story, is at first embarrassed by her grandfather's senile behavior. She becomes increasingly distressed when her parents discuss the possibility of putting him in a nursing home. "Does *he* have a choice?" she asks when they talk about the alternatives. Grandpa's alertness is intermittent: he lives in the past but then returns to lucid moments in the present. Near the end of the summer when it becomes obvious that a solution must be found, Grandpa goes through his personal belongings, sorting and distributing mementos to his family. He speaks to Kerry as if she were his older sister, but Kerry knows that although he is talking crazy, he isn't. One morning he leaves the house, and walks into the neighborhood swimming pool and drowns. Kerry goes to his room where she finds the bed has been made and the remaining items from his closet neatly labeled with the names of those who are to receive them. Grandpa had, after all, made his own choice about his future.

After the Rain (A) by Norma Fox Mazer, a 1988 Newbery Honor Book, relates an adolescent's resistance to spending time with her cranky, irascible grandfather. At first she spends time with him because she has promised her parents to do so, but gradually she goes to him out of her own need to be with him during his final days. Her reflections on her actions and motives, set down in her journal, chronicle the change from a self-centered child to a caring young adult.

Alzheimer's disease is a deteriorating condition most often found in the older population; people with Alzheimer's are increasingly forgetful—often not recognizing those closest to them—and progressively helpless. Richard Graber's story, *Doc* (I–A), focuses on Brad's grandfather, an outstanding medical doctor. Doc is increasingly irrational, forgetful, and often confused. Brad does not want to accept the changes he sees in his grandfather because he has been a model and good friend throughout his life. At the scene of a car crash, Doc's sharp mind returns; he uses his medical skills and makes his grandson proud and happy. The exertion, however, takes its toll, and Doc dies. Brad's pride in his grandfather and his love for him live on.

Gaffer Samson's Luck (I) by Jill Paton Walsh is a touching story of a friendship between young James and a very old man, Gaffer Samson. It is also James's struggle for acceptance in a new community where clannish children reject a stranger and belligerently close him out. After numerous rebuffs, James realizes that his only friends are Angey, a ragged part-Gipsy girl ostracized by the village children, and Gaffer Samson, a sick and aging neighbor. Gaffer's luck is a stone charm that has lain buried for seven years; he begs James to look for it but the boy searches in vain. Then after a week of rain the land is drowned in floodwater and the air, sky, and water fuse seamlessly on the horizon. James's search is dramatically rewarded

ACTIVITY: TEACHER TO STUDENT

COMPARING STORIES ABOUT AGING (I)   Both Stephanie Tolan in *Grandpa— and Me* and Norma Mazer in *A Figure of Speech* and *After the Rain* tell stories about an aging grandfather from the point of view of a granddaughter who has a special relationship with him. Discuss why the authors chose compassionate girls as their narrators. Also answer the following questions.

1. What alternate ways of caring for the aging parent did each family explore? Was the person about whom the decisions were being made involved in the decision process? What do you think the grandfathers would have chosen for themselves?
2. Which author evokes the grandfather's feelings most vividly? (Read aloud the parts of the stories that support your choice.)
3. Can you imagine how a fiercely independent person feels when he is treated like a small child and given rules to follow? Describe the reactions of the three men in these stories and try to guess how your own grandparents would cope with similar treatment.
4. You might also pretend that you are Jenny, Kerry or Rachel and write a eulogy for your grandfather. Try to capture the loving and sensitive part of his nature while avoiding clichés. Include tranquil recollections that involve other members of your family so that the eulogy has a direct impact upon them.

and in the dark of night, he faces the belligerent village gang. Gaffer's belief in him gives him faith in himself as well as the courage to face his tormentors and to determine what his own role will be in the new village.

On Death

The death of a family member or a friend is something no one wishes to experience but something all of us do at some time in our lives. Children begin to discover that people and animals are not immortal as soon as a beloved pet dies, grandparents grow old, or children themselves fall ill.

Children may first encounter death through the loss of a beloved pet. In *Whiskers, Once and Always* (P–I), Doris Orgel uses a flashback technique to explain why Becky hit her friend Jason, an atypical act for this sensitive young girl. Gradually the reason for Becky's behavior unfolds. One night while her mother was preparing dinner, her beloved cat, Whiskers, slipped out of the apartment. Later a neighbor brought Whiskers back, wrapped in a towel; he had found her lying beside the garbage cans. Despite loving care and medical attention, Whiskers died. As Becky is sharing the bitter news with friends at school, Jason overhears part of the story and says, "I thought it was your mom, or somebody—." Shocked by the implication that Whiskers was not important and unwilling to face the fact that her mother could ever die, Becky strikes out at him.

Katherine Paterson's *Bridge to Terabithia* (I) contains the unexpected and shocking death of a child. Jess is in the fifth grade and not very happy. He does not get along with his older sisters or his mother. His father is not often at home and he has no really close friends. When Leslie moves in next door, Jess's world changes. The two create the magic kingdom of Terabithia, and Leslie's knowledge and imagination expand Jess's world and his self-confidence.

The story is full of small meaningful events, school encounters, and the growth of the strong friendship between Leslie and Jess. The magic kingdom of Terabithia lies across a gully that they reach by swinging on a rope. When they are in Terabithia, they are its king and queen and rule their imaginary subjects with royal dignity and grace. One day, crossing to Terabithia alone over a rain-swollen creek, Leslie falls, is knocked unconscious, and drowns. Jess's world ends that day, too.

Jess cannot accept Leslie's death. He returns to the place Terabithia had once been, taking her dog, one of their subjects.

> He landed upstream from Terabithia. If it was still Terabithia. . . . They went into the castle stronghold. It was dark and damp, but there was no evidence there to suggest that the queen had died. He felt the need to do some-

---

PROFILE

Katherine Paterson

I never meant to hurt them. I just wanted—what had she wanted? A home—but Trotter had tried to give her that. Permanence—Trotter had wanted to give her that as well. No, what she wanted was something Trotter had no power over. To stop being a "foster child," the quotation marks dragging the phrase down, almost drowning it. To be real without any quotation marks. To belong and to possess. To be herself, to be the swan, to be the ugly duckling no longer—Cap O' Rushes, her disguise thrown off—Cinderella with both slippers on her feet—Snow White beyond the dwarfs—Galadriel Hopkins, come into her own.[41]

Galadriel, called Gilly, wants to be with her mother despite the fact that Maime Trotter provides her with a loving home. Katherine Paterson expresses Gilly's longing in literary allusions from folklore that conjure images that help readers visualize inner feelings. Her alternation of short terse sentences and long complex ones heightens tension and expands the dramatic action. Like the protagonist

thing fitting. But Leslie was not here to tell him what it was. . . .

"C'mon, Prince Terrien," he said quite loudly. "We must make a funeral wreath for the queen."[42]

While Jess works a pine bough and flowers into a symbolic offering, a bird hops close to him.

"It's a sign from the Spirits," Jess said quietly. "We made a worthy offering."

He walked slowly, as part of a great procession, though only the puppy could be seen, slowly forward carrying the queen's wreath to the sacred grove. He forced himself deep into the dark center of the grove and, kneeling, laid the wreath upon the thick carpet of golden needles.

"Father, into Thy hands I commend her spirit." He knew Leslie would have liked those words. They had the ring of the sacred grove in them.

The solemn procession wound its way through the sacred grove homeward to the castle. Like a single bird across a stormcloud sky, a tiny peace winged its way through the chaos inside his body.[43]

in her *The Master Puppeteer,* she is a master of her craft, her memorable stories are marked with imagery evoked by vivid language and with a believability that derives from her use of many characters and incidents drawn from life.

In her acceptance speech for the 1977 National Book Award, Katherine Paterson said:

I don't write for children. . . . I write for myself and then look in the catalog to see how old I am. But it's not true that I simply write for myself. I do write for children. For my own four children and for others who are faced with the question of whether they dare to become adult, responsible for their own lives and the lives of others. . . . I want to become a spy like Joshua and Caleb. . . .

I have crossed the river and tangled with a few giants but I want to go back and say to those who are hesitating, Don't be afraid to cross over. The promised land is worth possessing and we are not alone. I want to be a spy for hope.[44]

Readers take strength from her dramatic stories, rich with feeling, to face heartache in their own lives.

Winner of the 1977 National Book Award and the 1978 and 1981 Newbery Medals, Katherine Paterson was born in China, the daughter of American missionary parents from the American South. She attended schools in China, Virginia, North Carolina, West Virginia, and Tennessee. In fact, she went to 13 different schools during her first 18 years. As a young woman, she lived in Japan for four years, but now lives with her minister husband and their four children in Vermont.

Eventually Jess finds strength in himself, and as a tribute to Leslie's life, the kingdom of Terabithia continues.

Three fifth grade girls, discussing this story, appreciated the sense of hope evident in the ending: "Only at one little part it made you sad. But the very ending I loved because it made you feel, like, happy again."[45] Another response to the ending: "If you feel sad about something, you shouldn't try to forget it, but you should try to get over it as much as you can so you can enjoy things, because life shouldn't be something where you can't enjoy anything."[46] All three felt that the story showed them that one could, and should, get over the death of a friend and that Jess was a good model of how they might react if they were in similar circumstances.

In Constance Greene's *Beat the Turtle Drum* (I), 13-year-old Kate and her 11-year-old sister, Joss, are having a wonderful summer. Joss's savings and a birthday check from her grandmother allow her to rent a horse for a week, fulfilling a cherished dream. The horse, Prince, is delivered on her birthday. Joss is supremely happy, and because of her love for her sister, so is Kate.

The birthday week is filled with joy, and at its end, Kate and Joss are picnicking in a favorite tree. Prince is grazing peacefully below when Joss falls, breaks her neck, and dies instantly. There are foreshadowings of the tragic event, especially Ian Serraillier's poem at the beginning of the book, but the suddenness and terrible finality of Joss's death shock the reader.

Ann, a young reader of *Beat the Turtle Drum,* said of the story: "In . . . just one second the whole thing shifts, like very instantly. The whole book changes and everybody's personality changes completely."[47]

Ann was explicit about her use of this story as a "practice" session in experiencing life:

When I wasn't reading, I was thinking what it would be like if that really happened, because

In the moment before a profound tragedy, Kate and her younger sister Joss sit in a tree observing the horse Joss has rented with her birthday money. (From Constance Greene's *Beat the Turtle Drum.* Illustrated by Donna Diamond.)

it's such a big thing that happened, . . . like if it happened to me or something. Like if I had a sister, or if my mother died or something, how that would affect me.[48]

Ann's comments reveal the role this story can play in a child's life.

A sister's lingering death from leukemia and the problems of growing up are mingled in Lois Lowry's *A Summer to Die* (A). The story is told by Meg, 13, who shares a room with her older sister Molly, prettier and neater than Meg. From Meg's perspective, Molly did everything right; she always knew what to say, she was full of fun and enthusiasm, and she was gorgeous. She acquired a figure and boyfriends the same year that Meg was given her outgrown winter coat.

Then Molly falls sick. At first problems are minor, but then terrible test results foretell that she would never come home from the hospital. During the summer that Molly slowly dies, Meg begins to mature and discover her strengths. The warmth of a close family and good friends help sustain Meg through the traumatic summer. She grows in the knowledge that her world must change and that those she loves may not always be with her.

Sue Alexander's *Nadia the Willful* (P–I) is a far more powerful story than its slender size and picture-book format suggest. Nadia's favorite brother, Hamed, is the only one who can calm her temper when it flares and tease her back to civility. One day he rides a white stallion across the desert sands to search for new grazing ground for the sheep and does not return. Grief spreads throughout the clan as they finally realize that the desert has claimed his life. Nadia's father, Tarik, decrees "From this day forward, let no one utter Hamed's name. Punishment shall be swift for those who would remind me of what I have lost." At first, Nadia obeys her father's painful command but one day, outside his hearing, she blurts out the rules for a game Hamed had taught her. Another day, she tells Hamed's stories to the women who sit at their looms. Her mother warns her of Tarik's decree, but Nadia cries, "I will speak of my brother! I will!" Gradually, others begin to speak Hamed's name secretly to Nadia. One day, the youngest shepherd calls into a tent asking Nadia to come see Hamed's black lamb but Tarik comes forth instead of Nadia. The young shepherd is ordered to leave while Tarik sits alone staring into the desert. Nadia can stand it no longer and goes to face her father. "You will not rob me of my brother Hamed! I will not let you!" She helps

her father to understand the need to talk about Hamed and that Hamed can live again—in the hearts of all who remember him. The enduring message is emphatic in its simplicity.

Patricia Hermes deals with the heartbreaking effects of death in *You Shouldn't Have to Say Good-bye* (I). Sarah is 13 when her lawyer mother is subjected to a series of medical tests and trips to the hospital with the ultimate diagnosis that she has cancer. Her father is attentive but distracted by his own heartache. When she tells Sarah the diagnosis, her mother is painfully truthful. "It's melanoma, a terrible kind of cancer, too advanced to do anything. It's spread to my kidneys—everywhere. They say I'm not going to get better. . . ."

Sarah and her best friend, Robin, are gymnasts; Robin always tests the limits of personal safety in gymnastics and other daredevil pranks, whereas Sarah is more cautious. Robin confides to Sarah that her mother has agoraphobia—fear of open or public places—and as the two friends practice hard for their gymnastics show, neither is certain that her mother will be in the audience. Sarah is the first to spot her mother, in a wheelchair. Robin's mother is also there, clinging desperately to her husband's hand. The girls receive a standing ovation and spill tears of joy because their parents shared the experience with them.

The final chapters of Sarah's home life are devastating. Her mother continues to weaken, and dies in the close circle of her family on Christmas Eve. She left a legacy for Sarah, a journal she had been writing for a long time. It contained all of the things she wanted Sarah to know, books she hoped she would read and thoughts she wanted to share. Among other things, she wrote, "The hardest and most important thing that anyone must do is to let go. When I am gone, you must let go of me. Not stop loving me. Not stop remembering me. But keep what I've given you. Keep what's important to you, and let go of the rest. And go on."[49]

Acceptance of what life deals out is a theme realized in literature in many ways. Jean Little develops it in *Mama's Going to Buy You a Mockingbird* (I–A), the story of 11-year-old Jeremy's struggle to accept the worsening illness and eventual death of his father. Jeremy's Dad, a teacher, had a special relationship with his son and helped him to see life beyond its surface level. He encouraged Jeremy to be open to a friendship with Tess, a girl he had taught but one the other children thought was strange. He also give Jeremy a small, polished stone owl as a special memento of an experience the two of them had shared. Tess proves worthy of the praise his father had used as she helps Jeremy ward off pity from his teachers and classmates. In an act of love, Jeremy gives his father's small stone owl to his mother on Christmas morning. He is able to do this because he has grown strong in the knowledge that what his father left him is something that will never die.

Deborah Gould captures a sensitive means of accepting a loved one's death in *Grandpa's Slide Show* (P–I). Watching the slide show grandfather used to show his family makes the young boys realize the strong family memories they share. They find that they can talk about the memories and support each other and their grandmother.

On Caring

Though we share the earth with other creatures, in our preoccupation with our dominion of it we often fail to think about the balance of nature and the contribution animals make to it. Children find it easy to love animals—whether wild creatures or pets—and respond to stories about them.

Jean George's *Julie of the Wolves* (I–A) provides a vivid picture of the complex structure of a wolf pack. It is only by observing and imitating the wolves' actions that Julie gets them to accept her into their group and, so, survives on the frozen Alaskan tundra.

Children have a special affinity for animals—creatures that neither scold nor pass judgment. Unquestioning loyalty and devotion from an animal can sometimes help a child progress toward maturity. Children who devote themselves to nurturing and caring for an animal begin to recognize another's needs—the first step toward compassion.

Realistic animal stories often involve a child who grows in understanding and caring. In Betsy Byars's *The Midnight Fox* (I), 9-year-old Tom dreads the two months he must spend at his Aunt Millie's farm while his parents vacation in Europe. His parents are outdoorsy people who cannot understand Tom's fear of animals or his distaste for farm life. His mother enthusiastically describes the fun he will have climbing trees, watching the cows and horses, and gathering eggs, but Tom only imagines being attacked by an angry chicken if he goes near the hen house. Unhappily settled on the farm, Tom mopes and gets in everyone's way. The only bright spot in his day is the walk to the mailbox where there is often a letter from Petie, a friend who shares his misery. The outlook for the summer is dismal until the day he sees a black fox. The fox's black fur is tipped with white, "as if it were midnight and the moon were shining on her fur, frosting it." Tom is enchanted and sits quietly watching the fox until it bounds away.

During the next few weeks, Tom tracks the fox, awed by its grace and poise. One day she appears with her cub and Tom watches as the two romp and play, unaware that they are watched. Caught up in observing the fox, Tom forgets his misery until Aunt Millie informs her husband that a fox has taken her turkey. Tom, stunned, begins to sense that tragedy for his fox is near. Compassion for the animal and understanding of the need for balance between freedom and responsibility create conflict for the sensitive child.

Although wild animals are within the experience of relatively few children, pets are im-

Tom learns much about himself when he tracks a fox, then saves her and her cub from destruction. (From *The Midnight Fox* by Betsy Byars.)

portant to many. Wilson Rawls's *Where the Red Fern Grows* (I–A), an autobiographical account, tells about Billy Colman, who lives in the Arkansas mountains during the Great Depression. In a family with scarcely enough money for food, Billy has to scrimp and save for two years before he accumulates the 50 dollars needed to purchase the two coon hounds he wants. Billy dreams of the day he can start training the coon hounds, which he had to have because, "there I was sitting right in the middle of the finest hunting country in the world" and so no other kind of dog would do. Billy's faithful training of the two dogs is repaid when they win the gold cup in the annual coon hunting contest. But their training works against the dogs when they refuse to give up the chase for a savage bobcat. Billy's grief as he buries his beloved dogs where the red fern grows is shared by child and adult readers.

Dogs are the subject of many books for children in stories full of adventure, excitement, and often pathos. Meindert DeJong's *Hurry Home, Candy* (I) describes, from the point of view of a dog, its lonely search for security. Repeatedly beaten with brooms, the dog grows increasingly fearful of humans. Sep-

arated from his owners, he searches for a new home, but the images of brooms continually plague him and prevent his finding refuge. Eventually he finds a home with a man who senses the dog's fear. This story draws forth empathy.

Two memorable classics center upon a dog's search for security. Eric Knight's *Lassie Come Home* (I), well known to children through television and movies, is an account of a perilous journey a beloved collie takes to return to his master. Sheila Burnford's *The Incredible Journey* (I) is a story about a young Labrador retriever, an old bull terrier, and a Siamese cat who make a similar, 250-mile journey to their home. Starvation, always threatening, recedes into the background when the three encounter a bobcat, a bear, a tribe of Indians, storms, dangerous terrain, and other seemingly insurmountable obstacles. Children find the animals' shared responsibility and concern believable.

Several authors write about horses with a deep sense of compassion. In the forefront is Marguerite Henry, who thoroughly researches the stories of actual animals and events to bring dramatic reality to her writing. In *King of*

TEACHING IDEA

WILD ANIMALS IN LITERATURE (I) Read Betsy Byars's *The Midnight Fox* (I) aloud to your students, and encourage them to read similar stories on their own, such as Keith Robertson's *In Search of a Sandhill Crane* (I), Lee Kingman's *The Year of the Raccoon* (I–A), and Betsy Byars's *The House of Wings* (I). Discuss the books and compare the protagonists' attitudes and feelings before and after their encounters with the animals. Discuss how animals sometimes help people discover something about themselves.

the Wind (I), she traces the life of the beautiful horse, Sham, from a small stable in Morocco to France and then to England. A white spot on the horse's foot symbolizes speed, and the mark of the wheat ear on his chest, misfortune. Orphaned at birth, Sham is raised by a mute boy, Agba, whose devotion to the horse endures through bitter trials. Sham and Agba survive and, at the close of the story, Sham's quality, recognized at his birth by Agba, is acknowledged by the Earl of Godolphin.

Marguerite Henry fills her stories with a sense of caring and appreciation for animals, as *Misty of Chincoteague* (I); *Stormy, Misty's Foal* (I); and *Sea Star, Orphan of Chincoteague* (I), based in fact, bear out. The first story begins as a shipwreck leaves a cargo of Spanish horses floundering in a stormy sea. A few of the horses reach Assateague Island, where they survive and live for hundreds of years. The other two stories follow the Chincoteague line to the present. The island of Chincoteague, just off the coast of Virginia and Maryland, is today the scene of an annual Pony Penning Day, in which the wild descendants of those first Spanish horses are herded across a channel from their island refuge.

Some children are fearful of animals; they may have been frightened by an animal or never had the opportunity to be around one. Jean Little writes sensitively of a boy who is afraid of dogs in *Different Dragons* (I). Young

Ben Tucker must stay with Aunt Rose while his parents are away for the weekend. He dreads the forced visit because his aunt has a big Labrador Retriever, Gully, and he does not want to be near the dog. When he arrives, a neighbor girl, Hana Uchida, is playing with the dog in the yard, so now he is torn by two problems: he must not allow the dog to get near him, and he cannot reveal his fear of the dog in front of the girl. Aunt Rose, actively involved in church and community affairs, goes about her business leaving Ben and Gully alone. Ben explores the old family home and finds an attic door that he feels compelled to investigate. Hana comes over and, in an attempt to impress her with his courage, Ben climbs to the attic door and dares her to come, too. They are trapped there for several hours and would not have been found if it were not for the mournful sounds from Gully. In the end, Ben and Gully become friends, and he wonders why he had ever been frightened of such a loving creature. Ben's father explains that we each have "different dragons" that we fear, sometimes without reason.

Jean Little also wrote a story about how a dog helps a girl adjust to a new community in *Lost and Found* (P–I). Lucy's family moves to a new town just before school opens. On a walk around the new neighborhood, she finds a fluffy white dog that reminds her of a mop, and she loves him instantly. The dog seems to be lost and when she tries to figure out his name, her mother says, "What's the trouble?" The dog begins to jump and whirl around excitedly. It seems that his name is "Trouble." Lucy and Nan, a neighbor girl who wants to be a detective and volunteers to work on this case, search for Trouble's owner. Ultimately, Lucy finds Trouble's owner and faces up to a decision—not one she makes easily but one that is in Trouble's best interests.

Cynthia Rylant wrote 12 short stories in which an animal enriches someone's life in *Every Living Thing* (I). In one, Leo, who is labeled "slower than the rest," finds a box turtle that he names Charlie. During Fire Prevention Week, Leo takes Charlie to school and in a heartwarming way explains the effects of forest fires on animals. He explains that some animals might run fast enough to escape but, he says, "It isn't fair for the slow ones." For the first time, Leo wins a prize at school and the victory makes him feel "fast." In another story, a retired school teacher receives a dog that leads her back into the world of children. Each brief story captures the pathos in human lives and the small but significant difference that an animal can make.

Chester Aaron spins a gripping tale that shows the positive effects that caring for an animal can have on a person's life in *Duchess* (I–A). Thirteen-year-old Martin's parents and a juvenile judge agree that the boy should leave his New York home to live on Uncle Lee's California sheep ranch. They hope life on the ranch will remove him from the gang environment which had led to his trouble. Martin intends to outsmart both the judge and his parents by running away from the ranch, but as he is leaving, he finds an abandoned puppy that needs his care. Uncle Lee, proud of his prize-winning Border Collie, Princess, keeps only pedigreed dogs to guard his sheep; he would have discarded the mongrel pup. Martin cares for the dog he names Duchess and, once he gets involved in training her as a sheep dog,

learns that he and the misbegotten dog can be successful. When Martin's family comes for a holiday, his brother George gets lost in a blizzard on a skiing trip. Even though it is the day before the Grand National Sheep Dog Trials in which Duchess is entered, the two dogs lead the rescue team across the ice and snow to George. Both exhausted, Martin and Duchess enter the national trials, and although they do not win first prize, they receive the heartfelt acclaim of the audience. The owner of the first-prize winner also recognizes their noble performance and thrusts the first place trophy upon them. One of the particpants at the sheep dog trials says, "If there was a dry eye in the stands it had to be on a bloody stone statue." That expression applies equally well to the readers of this book.

On Mental and Emotional Disabilities

Disabled characters appear with increasing frequency in children's books: the trend has been from nearly absolute neglect, to an occasional secondary character, to the present realistic distribution of disabled characters reflective of their incidence in our population. Changes in the overall field of children's literature brought about an opening of the floodgates to children's books concerned with problems— among them, every manner of disability. Once the early taboos were broken, during the 1960s, almost any subject was suitable for children's books; authors were not only freed to write about the full range of human concerns, but encouraged to focus on problem novels.

The movement toward greater flexibility in subject also led to variety in problem resolution. In today's novels, disabled characters do not always recover or improve, and sometimes they die. Attitudes toward the disabled of those around them do not always improve, often remaining narrow and cruel. Happy endings are no longer taken for granted in children's books.

Neither do devoted attempts to teach, train, or help a disabled character always result in progress, as they would have two decades ago. For example, in Vera and Bill Cleaver's *Me Too* (I–A), Lydia works unflaggingly with her retarded twin, Lorna, to teach her to do simple tasks. Lydia hopes to make her twin acceptable to their father, who cannot bear to stay in their home and face the continual disappointment that Lorna represents. Despite Lydia's valiant efforts, her retarded sister does not respond, and Lydia must learn to accept the things she cannot change.

Though the jacket illustration of *Me Too* shows no differences between twins Lorna and Lydia, Lorna is severely retarded. (From *Me Too* by Vera and Bill Cleaver.)

Early novels with disabled characters often contained episodes of miraculous cures, but the trend is toward gradual improvement and partial resolution of problems, or totally open-ended novels. A character's progress results from training programs, therapy, rehabilitation programs, or schools, rather than from the actions of some *deus ex machina.* Moral strength and personal determination, however, continue to be attributes of the characters who succeed.

Teachers will find several selection aids for books portraying the disabled. Barbara H. Baskin and Karen H. Harris, in *Notes from a Different Drummer* and *More Notes from a Different Drummer*, provide excellent guidance for those seeking works on visual, intellectual, and orthopedic impairment, and emotional dysfunction. *The Bookfinder*, by Sharon Spredemann Dreyer, a three-volume reference citing books with a variety of themes, is also a valuable resource for book selection about the disabled. An informational book, *What If You Couldn't . . .?* (I), by Janet Kamien, gives teachers valuable insights into special needs. The author asks readers to imagine that they are the disabled person in an attempt to foster acceptance and satisfy curiosity. Learning disabilities, emotional disturbances, auditory and visual impairments, and physical disabilities are covered.

Sarah Bonnett Stein writes two books in one in *About Handicaps* (P). One story, for the primary age group, is printed in bold type and illustrated with photographs. Joe has cerebral palsy, and the way he does many things frightens Matthew, who apes and mocks him. As Matthew learns about the things Joe can do— and about a man with an artificial arm—he loses some of his fear about disabilities. The parallel story, for adults, runs alongside the primary one. In this story, we find much more information about Joe's handicap and Matthew's fears of it.

Stories about the disabled child are sometimes told from the point of view of a sibling. Harriet Sobol has a younger sister tell the story in *My Brother Steven Is Retarded* (P); Jeanne Whitehouse Peterson has an older sister tell *I Have a Sister. My Sister Is Deaf* (P). In Sobol's book, many of Beth's concerns about Steven revolve around her own feelings: embarrassment when others stare, happiness when Steven laughs. She worries about what he will do when he grows up and says longingly, "I hope he will be happy." Peterson's narrator emphasizes all the positive and joyous things her deaf sister can do and subtly counterbalances them with the special considerations she requires. The positive tone makes the limitations seem minimal for a child who is spontaneous, active, and wholesome. It is evident that she is loved.

Mental Retardation Mentally retarded characters appear in children's books less often than blind or emotionally disturbed ones, or those with orthopedic problems, but more often than the deaf or speech impaired. Mental retardation was among the first special-needs topics to appear in children's books when the prohibitions began to crumble in the late 1960s and early 1970s.

The Newbery Medal, given for Betsy Byars's *Summer of the Swans* (I–A), recognized the literary merit of a book that deals with retardation. Although this portrayal is a compassionate one, Charlie, the retarded child, appears essentially as a catalyst for his sister Sara's emotional growth. In the story, 14-year-old Sara finds Charlie to be just one more problem than she can handle during a summer of personal trauma. Concerned about her appearance, she cries in fits of self-pity about big feet and skinny legs. She loves Charlie but readily admits that he is a bother to her. Sara quickly forgets her self-preoccupation when Charlie disappears. Charlie, lost three blocks from home, is unable to ask for help. He is described

Mute Charlie wears the watch that is both a connection to and a shelter from the world around him. (From *Summer of the Swans* by Betsy Byars. Illustrated by Ted CoConis.)

as having huge blank spaces in his life that he can never fill. Her very real fright and subsequent relief on finding him cause her to reflect on the relative importance of people and events in her life. Sara is a volatile teenager who copes with more than the normal share of problems, but her wholesome acceptance and love for her retarded brother make her a memorable character. Sara's love and sense of responsibility for Charlie help her to clarify her personal values and sense of self.

Welcome Home, Jellybean (I–A), by Marlene Fanta Shyer, is told by 12-year-old Neil. The return home of his sister Geraldine, who is a year older than he, after she lived for years in institutions for the retarded, brings problems Neil and his parents can hardly bear. His father moves out, inviting Neil to go with him. The episode that precipitates his father's move is the discovery that the keys of his piano are sticky:

> "What from? What are they sticky from?" my father said.
> . . . I figured applesauce, but it didn't matter; we both knew that they were sticky from Gerri, that it was Gerri who had messed up the piano, that it was Gerri, again and again, who was fouling things up, snafuing everything.[50]

Gerri spoils more than the piano keys: she interrupts Neil's long-awaited chance to perform at school and is the cause for a petition to evict the family from their apartment. Finally, Neil, too, decides he has had enough and agrees to join his father. As he leaves the apartment, Gerri calls out Neil's name, evidence of the slow but steady progress she is making. When Neil reaches his father's waiting car, he is torn and can go no farther:

> "Neil, what's the matter?" my father asked. I couldn't say it; it just jammed up in my throat like old rags, that not everybody can have perfect pitch, that even though Gerri would always be strange/different/funny/weird, she was the way she was, and she was my sister.[51]

Neil's story sensitively portrays, without sentimentality, a family's problems with a mentally retarded child. The honest confrontation of personal and familial torment that devastates the family shocks the reader, but the eternal strength of love and compassion inspire as well.

Casey, the 12-year-old girl in Sue Ellen Bridger's *All Together Now* (I–A), spends the summer with her grandparents while her mother works two jobs and her father is overseas in the Korean War. Casey's name, too much like a boy's to suit her grandmother, works to her advantage in developing a friendship with Dwayne Pickens, a man in his thirties with the mind of a 12-year-old. Casey hears Dwayne at play in a solitary baseball game before she meets him; he fills all positions and announces each play:

> "And here's the pitch. Robinson *bunts!* Holy cow!" Dwayne dashed to the plate, picked up the ball with his bare hand, turned and made a throwing motion toward first base, although he still held the ball in his hand. He raced off toward first himself.
> "Garagiola's off with the mask! He grabs the ball and fires it to first! Is it in time?"
> At first base, Dwayne toed the bag and then snared the ball from its invisible flight with a flick of his gloved wrist.
> "They've got him. Garagiola throws out Robinson on a beau-ti-ful play! And that's all for the Dodgers! In the top of the ninth, it's three up and three down!"[52]

Dwayne thinks Casey is a boy, and, so that he will let her play baseball with him, she tells him no different. Several subplots intricately undergird the story of the friendship between Casey and Dwayne, but the sympathetic portrayal of a retarded adult is paramount. Capitalizing upon a minor incident, Dwayne's brother attempts to institutionalize him, although he has always moved freely and with acceptance throughout their small village. Despite Dwayne's innocence, the villagers' unfounded fears and ignorance prevent them from resisting his brother's plan. Many stand silently by.

Books that portray mentally retarded characters are meant for readers who want a better understanding of the disability. Obviously, complexities of plot, theme, and language make most such books inaccessible to many mentally retarded children themselves. Retarded children, however, should not be denied the joys of fine books. If they are able to speak and to understand others, resourceful teachers can design literature programs that are realistic and effective in maximizing their responses. The child's mental age should be used as a guide for selecting books. Because mentally retarded children go through the same developmental stages as all children, although more slowly, the methods, techniques, and materials should correspond to that slower developmental rate and more limited cognitive capacity. All children grow through carefully sequenced experiences appropriately matched to their learning characteristics.

Dorothy Butler tells the story of the important part played by books in the early development of her severely disabled granddaughter in *Cushla and Her Books* (adult). Although Cushla's problems were more physical than mental, her development was slow; the influence of books on her cognitive and language abilities was significant.

The teacher's role is crucial, for most literary experiences will need to be shared. Mentally retarded children delight in being read to, and colorful illustrations and film versions of stories intrigue them. Filmstrips or recordings of stories make it possible for all children to share in the bounties of literature. Once teachers sensitive to the unique needs of retarded children become aware of the many fine books suitable for the retarded, designing learning activities for them can become a joyful task.

Emotional Disturbance Emotional disturbance is often poorly understood, misdiagnosed, and feared. This is understandable because it is such a complex syndrome, with bizarre and idiosyncratic manifestations. Some children who are emotionally disturbed cannot control their actions and require protection and a great deal of tolerance. Any situation may lead to hysteria or acting out of hostile impulses.

John Neufeld portrays erratic behavior (and the lack of understanding about it) in *Lisa, Bright and Dark* (A). In his novel, only Lisa's teenage friends recognize that she is becoming more emotionally disturbed each day. Lisa herself thinks she is losing her mind and pleads with her parents to listen to her; they are too preoccupied to take her seriously. Lisa's friends try to persuade a number of adults to seek help for her but find no one willing to take the necessary steps or to heed the warning signs. Some days are very bright for Lisa, but others are abysmally dark; the story ends on a very dark note.

Marilyn Sachs portrays an emotionally disturbed mother in *The Bears' House* (I), although the focus is the effect on her daughter, Fran Ellen, who is nearly 10 years old, sucks her thumb, and smells bad. Fran Ellen's greatest joy is playing with a miniature dollhouse at school, where she moves the three bears about, puts Goldilocks to sleep in baby bear's bed, and endlessly replays the story. It is the only time she feels at ease:

> I'm me in the Bears' House.
> The door is open, naturally, and I go up the stairs and stand by the bed. She opens her eyes.
> "Move over!" I tell her, and she says," Yes, ma'am"
> "You sure are some pushy, good-for-nothing," I tell her.
> "What kind of nerve you got, anyway, pushing yourself in here where you weren't invited and eating up a family's food and breaking their furniture and messing up their beds!"
> "Yes, ma'am," says Goldilocks. She gets out of the bed, and I get in. But I go on telling her what I think of her, and all she can say is, "Yes, ma'am," and suck her thumb.
> "Thumb sucker," I tell her.
> Then we both suck our thumbs together for a while, and I get over being mad at her.[53]

Fran Ellen immerses herself in the fantasy play to escape the harshness of her real life. In the well-ordered, snug family of the bears, she finds all the things she wants—love, admiration, attention. In her own life, Fran Ellen faces unrelenting burdens with a wraithlike mother, no father, and four siblings who try to survive alone. The mother's devastating withdrawal is echoed in Fran Ellen's escape to a fantasy world.

Fran Ellen's House (I), a sequel to *The Bears' House*, opens with Fran Ellen deeply involved in fantasy play with the Bear family in the dollhouse. She reassures Baby Bear, who is crying, that she will get everything shipshape in a

Fran Ellen idealizes life in her bears' dollhouse as a way to make sense of and stabilize her own family's troubled life. (From *Fran Ellen's House* by Marilyn Sachs.)

jiffy. In the same way, Fran Ellen tries to reassure her own fragile family that everything will soon be shipshape again. The family is together after having been apart for more than two years while Mama was sick and the five children were separated to live in various foster homes. Now 12½, Fran Ellen has a difficult time adjusting to the reality that her once-adoring 3-year-old sister, Flora, wants to return to the foster family she lived with during the separation. Her nearly 8-year-old sister, Felice, shows little interest in the doll's house and pushes away Flora who tags along after her. As the family tries to stabilize itself, Fran Ellen finds escape in her beloved doll's house. Marilyn Sachs masterfully reflects the problems in Fran Ellen's real world with those she plays out for the Bear family in the dollhouse world.

Learning Disabilities

Specific learning disabilities suffer from lack of definition and clarification in schools as well as in children's books. "Neurological impairment," a frequent designation, seems to be an umbrella term for many different types of behavior; typically, children with reading problems, motor problems, visual problems, and others are called "learning disabled."

The lack of clarity of definition spills over into literature, and there are few books of literary quality that accurately portray a learning-disabled character. Doris Buchanan Smith gives the most adequate portrayal of a learning-disabled child in *Kelly's Creek* (I). Kelly knows that he is not like other 9-year-old children: he does not read, write, or draw circles the way they do. He is not successful in school, but he achieves great success in studying the marsh life at a nearby creek. Phillip, a college student in biology who is studying the marsh, befriends Kelly. In fact, Phillip is Kelly's only friend; they share a common love for the marsh. When Kelly is at the creek, he is competent, agile, and relaxed, but in school he is tense and uncoordinated. After a bad report card from school, Kelly is forbidden to go to the marsh or to see Phillip, the only sources of happiness he knows. Kelly's dejection and his joy are shown in hauntingly beautiful illustrations, especially those set in the marshlands.

Kelly's parents typify well-intentioned adults whose decisions can deny a child the most meaningful part of his life.

Lynn Hall's book, *Just One Friend* (I–A), about a learning-disabled student being mainstreamed and her fear of a regular classroom, is powerful reading.

RECOMMENDED READING

Growing Up

Byars, Betsy. *The Night Swimmers.* Illustrated by Troy Howell. New York: Delacorte, 1980.

Carrick, Carol. *What a Wimp!* Illustrated by Donald Carrick. New York: Clarion, 1983.

Cleaver, Vera. *Sugar Blue.* Illustrated by Eric Nones. New York: Lothrop, Lee & Shepard, 1984.

———. *Sweetly Sings the Donkey.* Philadelphia: Lippincott, 1985.

———, and Bill Cleaver. *Hazel Rye.* Philadelphia: Lippincott, 1983.

Fox, Paula. *How Many Miles to Babylon?* Illustrated by Paul Giavanopoulos. New York: Bradbury, 1980.

Hunter, Mollie. *Cat, Herself.* New York: Harper & Row, 1986.

———. *Hold on to Love.* New York: Harper & Row, 1984.

MacLachlan, Patricia. *Arthur for the Very First Time.* Illustrated by Lloyd Bloom. New York: Harper & Row, 1980.

Mark, Jan. *Handles.* New York: Atheneum, 1985.

Rylant, Cynthia. *A Blue-Eyed Daisy.* New York: Bradbury, 1985.

Peer Relations

Garden, Nancy. *Peace, O River.* New York: Farrar, Straus & Giroux, 1986.

Giff, Patricia Reilly. *Have You Seen Hyacinth Macaw?* New York: Delacorte, 1981.

Greene, Constance C. *A Girl Called Al.* Illustrated by Byron Barton. New York: Viking, 1969.

———. *Just Plain Al.* New York: Viking, 1986.

———. *Isabelle Shows Her Stuff.* New York: Viking, 1984.

Hinton, S. E. *The Outsiders.* New York: Viking, 1967

———. *Tex.* New York: Dell, 1986.

———. *That Was Then, This Is Now.* New York: Viking, 1971.

Howe, James, *A Night Without Stars.* New York: Atheneum, 1983.

Hurwitz, Johanna. *Yellow Blue Jay.* New York: Morrow, 1986.

Levoy, Myron. *Pictures of Adam.* New York: Harper & Row, 1986.

Little, Jean. *Kate.* New York: Harper & Row, 1971.

———. *Look Through My Window.* Illustrated by Joan Sandin. New York: Harper & Row, 1970.

Myers, Walter Dean. *Fast Sam, Cool Clyde and Stuff.* New York: Viking, 1975.

Townsend, John Rowe. *Tom Tiddler's Ground.* Philadelphia: Lippincott, 1986.

Families

Adler, Carole S. *The Shell Lady's Daughter.* New York: Coward-McCann, 1983.

Alcock, Vivien. *The Cuckoo Sister.* New York: Delacorte, 1986.

Bauer, Marion Dane. *Foster Child.* New York: Seabury, 1977.

Bawden, Nina. *The Finding.* New York: Lothrop, Lee & Shepard, 1985.

Blume, Judy. *It's Not the End of the World.* New York: Bradbury, 1972.

Byars, Betsy. *The Cartoonist.* Illustrated by Richard Cuffari. New York: Viking, 1978.

Conrad, Pam. *Holding Me Here.* New York: Harper & Row, 1986.

Danziger, Paula. *The Divorce Express.* New York: Delacorte, 1982.

Fox, Paula. *Blowfish Live in the Sea.* New York: Bradbury, 1970.

Hahn, Mary Downing. *Wait Till Helen Comes: A Ghost Story.* Boston: Houghton Mifflin, Clarion, 1986.

Hamilton, Virginia. *Sweet Whispers, Brother Rush.* New York: Philomel, 1982.

Haugen, Tormod. *The Night Birds.* Translated by Sheila La Farge. New York: Delacorte, 1982.

Hurwitz, Johanna. *Baseball Fever.* Illustrated by Ray Cruz. New York: Morrow, 1981.

———. *Hurricane Elaine.* New York: Morrow, 1986.

Krementz, Jill. *How It Feels to Be*

Adopted. New York: Knopf, 1982.

LeShan, Eda. *Grandparents: A Special Kind of Love.* Illustrated by Tricia Taggert. New York: Macmillan, 1984.

Lowry, Lois. *The One-Hundreth Thing About Caroline.* Boston: Houghton Mifflin, 1983.

————. *Switcharound.* Boston: Houghton Mifflin, 1985.

McDonnell, Christine. *Count Me in.* New York: Viking, Kestrel, 1986.

Mahy, Margaret. *The Catalogue of the Universe.* New York: Atheneum, McElderry, 1986.

Mark, Jan. *Trouble Half-Way.* Illustrated by David Parkins. New York: Atheneum, 1986.

Pearce, Philippa. *The Way to Sattin Shore.* Illustrated by Charlotte Voake. New York: Greenwillow, 1984.

Peck, Richard. *Father Figure.* New York: Viking, 1978.

Porte, Barbara Ann. *The Kidnapping of Aunt Elizabeth.* New York: Greenwillow, 1985.

Rodowsky, Colby. *H, My Name Is Henley.* New York: Farrar, Straus & Giroux, 1982.

————. *Julie's Daughter.* New York: Farrar, Straus & Giroux, 1985.

Sebestyen, Ouida. *IOU's.* Boston: Little, Brown, Atlantic, 1982.

Snyder, Zilpha Keatley. *Blair's Nightmare.* New York: Atheneum, 1984.

Personal Integrity

Bess, Clayton. *Story for a Black Night.* Boston: Houghton Mifflin, 1982.

Branscum, Robbie. *The Adventures of Johnny May.* New York: Harper & Row, 1984.

Bridgers, Sue Ellen. *Home Before Dark.* New York: Knopf, 1976.

Burch, Robert. *Queenie Peavy.* Illustrated by Jerry Lazare. New York: Viking, 1966.

Cormier, Robert. *The Bumblebee Flies Anyway.* New York: Knopf, 1983.

Fitzhugh, Louise. *Nobody's Family Is Going to Change.* New York: Farrar, Straus & Giroux, 1974.

Lawrence, Louise. *The Dram Road.* New York: Harper & Row, 1983.

Paulsen, Gary. *Dancing Carl.* New York: Bradbury, 1983.

Physical Disabilities

Brighton, Catherine. *My Hands, My World.* New York: Macmillan, 1984.

Butler, Beverly. *Light a Single Candle.* New York: Archway, 1970.

Fanshawe, Elizabeth. *Rachel.* Illustrated by Michael Charlton. New York: Merrimack, 1983.

Fassler, Joan. *Howie Helps Himself.* Illustrated by Joe Lasker. Niles, Ill.: Whitman, 1975.

Hermann, Helen, and Bill Hermann. *Jenny's Magic Wand.* Photography by Don Purdue. New York: Watts, 1988.

Konigsburg, E. L. *Father's Arcane Daughter.* New York: Atheneum, 1976.

McGraw, Eloise. *The Seventeenth Swap.* New York: Atheneum, McElderry, 1986.

Neimark, Anne E. *A Deaf Child Listened: Thomas Gallaudet, Pioneer in American Education.* New York: Morrow, 1983.

Newton, Suzanne. *I Will Call It Georgie's Blues.* New York: Viking, 1983.

Rosenberg, Maxine B. *My Friend Leslie: The Story of a Handicapped Child.* Photography by George Ancona. New York: Lothrop, Lee & Shepard, 1983.

Rabe, Berniece. *The Balancing Girl.* Illustrated by Lillian Hoban. New York: Dutton, 1981.

Roy, Ron. *Move Over, Wheelchairs Coming Through!* Photography by Rosemarie Hausherr. New York: Clarion, 1985.

Slepian, Jan. *The Alfred Summer.* New York: Macmillan, 1986.

————. *Lester's Turn.* New York: Macmillan, 1981.

Walker, Lou Ann. *Amy: The Story of a Deaf Child.* Photography by Michael Abramson. New York: Lodestar, 1985.

Laughter

Hurwitz, Johanna. *Rip-Roaring Russell.* Illustrated by Lillian Hoban. New York: Morrow, 1983.

————. *Russell Rides Again.* Illustrated by Lillian Hoban. New York: Morrow, 1985.

————. *Super Duper Teddy.* New York: Morrow, 1980.

Konigsburg, E. L. *From the Mixed-Up Files of Mrs. Basil E. Frankweiler.* New York: Atheneum, 1967.

Levitin, Sonia. *The Mark of Conte.* Illustrated by Bill Negron. New York: Atheneum, 1976.

McDonnell, Christine. *Don't Be Mad, Ivy.* New York: Dial, 1981.

————. *Lucky Charms and Birthday Wishes.* New York: Viking, 1984.

————. *Toad Food and Measle Soup.* New York: Dial, 1982.

Park, Barbara. *Skinnybones.* New York: Knopf, 1982.

Pinkwater, Manus. *Alan Mendelsohn, the Boy from Mars.* New York: Dutton, 1979.

Robertson, Keith. *Henry Reed, Inc.* Illustrated by Robert McCloskey. New York: Viking, 1958.

————. *Henry Reed's Think Tank.* New York: Viking, 1986.

Robinson, Barbara. *The Best Christmas Pageant Ever.* Illustrated by Judith Gwyn Brown. New York: Harper & Row, 1972.

Steiner, Barbara. *Oliver Dibbs and the Dinosaur Cause.* New York: Macmillan, 1986.

Courage

Armstrong, William. *Sounder.* Illustrated by James Barkley. New York: Harper & Row, 1969.

Bauer, Marion Dane. *On My*

Honor. New York: Clarion, 1986.

Bawden, Nina. *Kept in the Dark*. New York: Lothrop, Lee & Shepard, 1982.

Estes, Eleanor. *The Hundred Dresses*. Illustrated by Louis Slobodkin. New York: Harcourt Brace, 1944.

Howker, Janni. *The Nature of the Beast*. New York: Greenwillow, 1985.

L'Engle, Madeleine. *A Ring of Endless Light*. New York: Farrar, Straus & Giroux, 1980.

Naylor, Phyllis Reynolds. *The Keeper*. New York: Atheneum, 1986.

Slote, Alfred. *Hang Tough, Paul Mather*. Philadelphia: Lippincott, 1973.

Sperry, Armstrong. *Call It Courage*. New York: Macmillan, 1940.

Taylor, Mildred. *Roll of Thunder, Hear My Cry*. New York: Dial, 1976.

Voigt, Cynthia. *Jackaroo*. New York: Atheneum, 1985.

Survival

Houston, James. *Black Diamonds: A Search for Arctic Treasure*. New York: Atheneum, 1982.

———. *The Falcon Bow: An Arctic Legend*. New York: Atheneum, 1986.

———. *Frozen Fire*. New York: Atheneum, 1977.

———. *Ice Swords: An Undersea Adventure*. New York: Atheneum, 1985.

———. *Wolf Run: A Caribou Eskimo Tale*. New York: Harcourt Brace Jovanovich, 1971.

Mayhar, Ardath. *Medicine Walk*. New York: Atheneum, 1985.

O'Dell, Scott. *Island of the Blue Dolphins*. Boston: Houghton Mifflin, 1960.

———. *Zia*. Boston: Houghton Mifflin, 1976.

Taylor, Theodore. *The Cay*. New York: Doubleday, 1969.

Aging

Burch, Robert. *Two That Were Tough*. Illustrated by Richard Cuffari. New York: Viking, 1976.

Cleaver, Vera, and Bill Cleaver. *Queen of Hearts*. Philadelphia: Lippincott, 1978.

Farber, Norma. *How Does It Feel to Be Old?* Illustrated by Trina Schart Hyman. New York: Dutton, 1979.

Hurd, Edith Thatcher. *I Dance in My Red Pajamas*. Illustrated by Emily Arnold McCully. New York: Harper & Row, 1982.

Mathis, Sharon Bell. *The Hundred Penny Box*. Illustrated by Leo Dillon and Diane Dillon. New York: Viking, 1975.

Pevsner, Stella. *Keep Stompin' Till the Music Stops*. New York: Seabury, 1977.

Wartski, Maureen Crane. *A Boat to Nowhere*. Illustrated by Dick Teicher. Philadelphia: Westminster Press, 1980.

Death

Dixon, Paige. *May I Cross Your Golden River?* New York: Atheneum, 1975.

———. *Skipper*. New York: Atheneum, 1979.

Greenberg, Jan. *A Season in Between*. New York: Farrar, Straus & Giroux, 1980.

Heide, Florence Parry. *Growing Anyway Up*. Philadelphia: Lippincott, 1976.

Holland, Isabelle. *Of Love and Death and Other Journeys*. Philadelphia: Lippincott, 1975.

Lee, Virginia. *The Magic Moth*. Illustrated by Richard Cuffari. New York: Clarion, 1972.

Lorentzen, Karin. *Lanky Longlegs*. Illustrated by Jan Ormerod. New York: Atheneum, McElderry, 1983.

MacLachlan, Patricia. *Cassie Binegar*. New York: Harper & Row, 1982.

Oneal, Zibby. *A Formal Feeling*.

New York: Viking, 1982.

Smith, Doris Buchanan. *Return to Bitter Creek*. New York: Viking, Kestrel, 1986.

———. *A Taste of Blackberries*. Illustrated by Charles Robinson. New York: Crowell, 1973.

Caring (Animals)

Aaron, Chester, *Spill*. New York: Atheneum, 1977.

Carrick, Carol. *Stay Away from Simon*. Illustrated by Donald Carrick. New York: Clarion, 1985.

Eckert, Allan. *Incident at Hawk's Hill*. Illustrated by John Schoenherr. Boston: Little, Brown, 1971.

George, Jean Craighead. *The Cry of the Crow*. New York: Harper & Row, 1980.

Holland, Isabelle. *Alan and the Animal Kingdom*. Philadelphia: Lippincott, 1977.

———. *A Horse Named Peaceable*. New York: Lothrop, Lee & Shepard, 1982.

Thiele, Colin. *Storm Boy*. Illustrated by John Schoenherr. New York: Harper & Row, 1978.

Mental and Emotional Disabilities

Albert, Louise. *But I'm Ready to Go*. New York: Bradbury, 1976.

Baldwin, Anne Norris. *A Little Time*. New York: Viking, 1978.

Brown, Roy. *Find Debbie!* New York: Seabury, 1976.

Brown, Tricia. *Someone Special, Just Like You*. Photography by Fran Oritz. New York: Holt, Rinehart & Winston, 1982.

Cassedy, Sylvia. *M. E. and Morton*. New York: Crowell, 1987.

Garrigue, Sheila. *Between Friends*. New York: Bradbury, 1978.

Hunt, Irene. *The Everlasting Hills*. New York: Scribner's, 1985.

Little, Jean. *Take Wing*. Illustrated by Jerry Lazare. Boston: Little, Brown, 1968.

McKillip, Patricia A. *The Night Gift.* Illustrated by Kathy McKillip. New York: Atheneum, 1976.

Sorensen, Virginia. *Miracles on Maple Hill.* Illustrated by Beth Krush and Joe Krush. New York: Harcourt Brace, 1956.

Poetry

Adoff, Arnold, ed. *Black Out Loud: An Anthology of Modern Poems by Black Americans.* Illustrated by Alvin Hollingsworth. New York: Macmillan, 1970.

———. *I Am the Darker Brother: An Anthology of Modern Poems by Negro Americans.* Illustrated by Benny Andrews. New York: Macmillan, 1968.

Brooks, Gwendolyn. *Bronzeville Boys and Girls.* Illustrated by Ronni Solbert. New York: Harper & Row, 1956.

Cole, William, ed. *Beastly Boys and Ghastly Girls.* Illustrated by Tomi Ungerer. New York: Putnam, 1964.

———. *Oh, How Silly!* Illustrated by Tomi Ungerer. New York: Viking, 1970.

———. *Oh, Such Foolishness!* Illustrated by Tomie dePaola. Philadelphia: Lippincott, 1978.

———. *Oh, That's Ridiculous!* Illustrated by Tomi Ungerer. New York: Viking, 1972.

de Regniers, Beatrice Schenk. *So Many Cats.* Illustrated by Ellen Weiss. New York: Clarion, 1986.

Hopkins, Lee Bennett. *A Dog's Life.* Illustrated by Linda Rochester Richards. San Diego: Harcourt Brace Jovanovich, 1983.

Hughes, Langston. *The Dream Keeper and Other Poems.* Illustrated by Helen Sewell. New York: Knopf, 1932.

Larrick, Nancy comp. *Crazy to Be Alive in Such a Strange World: Poems About People.* New York: Evans, 1979.

Livingston, Myra Cohn, ed. *I Like You, If You Like Me.* New York: Atheneum, McElderry, 1987.

———. *What a Wonderful Bird the Frog Are: An Assortment of Humorous Poetry and Verse.* New York: Harcourt Brace Jovanovich, 1973.

MacKay, David. *A Flock of Words.* Illustrated by Margery Gill. New York: Harcourt Brace Jovanovich, 1969.

Merriam, Eve. *Jamboree: Rhymes for All Times.* Illustrated by Walter Gaffney-Kessell. New York: Dell, 1984.

———. *Rainbow Writing.* New York: Atheneum, 1976.

Molloy, Paul. ed. *Beach Glass and Other Poems.* New York: Four Winds, 1970.

Nash, Ogden, ed. *The Moon Is Shining Bright As Day: An Anthology of Good-Humored Verse.* Illustrated by Rose Shirvanian. Philadelphia: Lippincott, 1953.

O'Neill, Mary. *People I'd Like to Keep.* Illustrated by Paul Galdone. New York: Doubleday, 1964.

Viorst, Judith. *If I Were in Charge of the World and Other Worries.* Illustrated by Lynne Cherry. New York: Atheneum, 1981.

PROFESSIONAL REFERENCES

Butler, Dorothy. *Cushla and Her Books.* Boston: Horn Book, 1980.

Baskin, Barbara H., and Karen H. Harris. *Notes from a Different Drummer: A Guide to Juvenile Fiction Portraying the Handicapped.* New York: Bowker, 1977.

———. *More Notes from a Different Drummer: A Guide to Juvenile Fiction Portraying the Handicapped.* New York: Bowker, 1984.

Commire, Anne, ed. *Something About the Author.* Vols. 1–50. Detroit: Gale Research, 1971–1988.

De Montreville, Doris, and Elizabeth D. Crawford, eds. "Jean Little." In *Fourth Book of Junior Authors and Illustrators.* New York: Wilson, 1978, 228–29.

Dreyer, Sharon S. *Bookfinder: A Guide to Children's Literature about the Needs and Problems of Youth Aged 2 to 15,* 3 vols. Circle Pines, Minn.: American Guidance, 1981.

Hopkins, Lee Bennett. *More Books by More People.* New York: Citation Press, 1974.

Hunter, Mollie. *Talent Is Not Enough: Mollie Hunter on Writing for Children.* New York: Harper & Row, 1976.

Kalagian, Betty. *Expectations.* Los Angeles: Braille Institute Press, 1988.

Kamien, Janet. *What If You Couldn't . . . ? A Book About Special Needs.* Illustrated by Signe Hensen. New York: Scribner's, 1979.

Meeks, Margaret, Aidan Warlow, and Griselda Barton. *The Cool Web: The Patterns of Children's Reading.* New York: Atheneum, 1977.

Monson, Dianne L. "Children's Responses to Humorous Situations in Literature." Ph.D. diss., University of Minnesota, 1966.

Peters, Jacqueline. "Life Styles of Today and Tomorrow: A Scenario." *National Association of Women Deans and Counselors Journal* 36, no. 3 (Spring 1973): 103.

Townsend, John Rowe. "It Takes More Than Pot and the Pill." *The New York Times Book Review,* 9 November 1969, 2.

Weiss, M. Jerry, ed. "Jean Greenlaw: An interview with Mollie Hunter" In *From Writers to Students,* 44–48. Newark, Del: International Reading Association, 1979.

NOTES

1. Lilian Moore, "Reflections," in *Something New Begins* (New York: Atheneum, 1982), 33.
2. Cornelia Meigs, Anne Thaxter Eaton, Elizabeth Nesbitt, and Ruth Hill Viguers, *A Critical History of Children's Literature,* rev. ed. (New York: Macmillan, 1969), 212.
3. Ibid.
4. Lloyd Alexander, "The Grammar of Story," in *Celebrating Children's Books,* eds. Betsy Hearne and Marilyn Kaye (New York: Lothrop, Lee & Shepard, 1981), 11.
5. Richard Peck, "An Interview with Richard Peck," from *Teaching Critical Reading to Children and Adolescents,* taught by Bernice E. Cullinan, dir. Roy Allen, New York University's "Sunrise Semester," CBS, 9 February 1978.
6. James Cross Giblin, "Trends in Children's Publishing," Highlights Foundation Writers Workshop, lecture, 23 July 1987, Chautauqua, N.Y.
7. Jacqueline Peters, "Life Styles of Today and Tomorrow: A Scenario," *National Association of Women Deans and Counselors Journal* 36, no. 3 (Spring 1973): 103.
8. Bette Greene, *Philip Hall Likes Me. I Reckon Maybe* (New York: Dial, 1974), 118–19.
9. Ibid., 135.
10. Virginia Hamilton, *M. C. Higgins, the Great* (New York: Macmillan, 1974), 26.
11. Cynthia Rylant, *A Fine White Dust* (New York: Bradbury, 1986), 81.
12. Louise Fitzhugh, *Harriet the Spy* (New York: Harper & Row, 1964), 10–11.
13. Ibid., 180.
14. Johanna Hurwitz, *The Adventures of Ali Baba Bernstein,* illus. Gail Owens (New York: Morrow, 1985), 1–2.
15. Judy Blume, *Blubber* (New York: Bradbury, 1974), 89.
16. Judy Blume, promotional material, Bradbury Press, New York City.
17. Walter Dean Myers, *The Young Landlords* (New York: Viking, 1979), 8.
18. Ibid., 9.
19. Celia Herron, "Cleary Thinks Books Should Be Fun." *Christian Science Monitor,* 14 May 1982; and Beverly Cleary, Promotional Material, Morrow, New York City.
20. Lois Lowry, "Writing Fiction," Highlights Foundation Writers Workshop, lecture, 17 July 1986, Chautauqua, N.Y.
21. Lee Bennett Hopkins, "Betsy Byars," in *More Books by More People* (New York: Citation Press, 1974), 70.
22. Ibid., 71, 69.
23. Teaching idea adapted from Diane Person, Librarian, Brooklyn Polytechnic Institute, N.Y.
24. Katherine Paterson, *Jacob Have I Loved* (New York: Crowell, 1980), 34.
25. Paula Fox, *One-Eyed Cat* (New York: Bradbury, 1984), 188–89.
26. Ouida Sebestyen, *Words by Heart* (Boston: Little, Brown, 1979), 14–15.
27. Ibid., 148.
28. For further information, write to Braille Institute Press, Braille Institute of America, Inc., 741 North Vermont Avenue, Los Angeles, Calif., 90029.
29. Doris De Montreville and Elizabeth D. Crawford, eds., *Fourth Book of Junior Authors and Illustrators* (New York: Wilson, 1978), 228, 229.
30. Jill Paton Walsh, *Goldengrove* (New York: Farrar, Straus & Giroux, 1972), 80.
31. Dianne Monson, "Children's Responses to Humorous Situations in Literature" (Ph.D. diss., University of Minnesota, 1966).
32. Beverly Cleary, *Ramona Quimby, Age Eight,* illus. Alan Tiegreen (New York: Morrow, 1981), 115.
33. Mollie Hunter, *The Third Eye* (New York: Harper & Row, 1979), 67.
34. Vera Cleaver and Bill Cleaver, *Where the Lilies Bloom* (Philadelphia: Lippincott, 1969), 15.
35. Jill Paton Walsh, *Unleaving* (New York: Farrar, Straus & Giroux, 1976), 9.
36. Ibid., 24.
37. Felice Holman, *Slake's Limbo* (New York: Scribner's, 1974), 117.
38. Jean Craighead George, *Julie of the Wolves* (New York: Harper & Row, 1972), 5–6.
39. Jean Craighead George, promotional material, Harper & Row, New York City.
40. Patricia Wrightson, *A Little Fear* (New York: Atheneum, McElderry, 1983), 109.
41. Katherine Paterson, *The Great Gilly Hopkins* (New York: Crowell, 1978), 124.
42. Katherine Paterson, *Bridge to Terabithia* (New York: Crowell, 1977), 119.
43. Ibid., 120.
44. Katherine Paterson, promotional material, Crowell, New York City.
45. S. Lee Galda, "Three Children Reading Stories: Response to Literature in Preadolescents" (Ph.D. diss., New York University, 1980), 111.
46. Ibid., p. 75.

47. Galda, "Three Children Reading Stories," 103.
48. Ibid., 109.
49. Patricia Hermes, *You Shouldn't Have to Say Goodbye* (San Diego: Harcourt Brace Jovanovich, 1982), 115.
50. Marlene Fanta Shyer, *Welcome Home, Jellybean* (New York: Scribner's 1978), 111.
51. Ibid., 77.
52. Sue Ellen Bridgers, *All Together Now* (New York: Knopf, 1979), 16.
53. Marilyn Sachs, *The Bears' House* (New York: Dutton, 1987), 29–30.

CHILDREN'S BOOKS CITED

Aaron, Chester. *Duchess*. Philadelphia: Lippincott, 1982.

Alcott, Louisa May. *Little Women*. 1868. Reprint. Illustrated by Jessie Willcox Smith. Boston: Little, Brown, 1968.

Alexander, Sue. *Nadia the Willful*. Illustrated by Lloyd Bloom. New York: Pantheon, 1983.

Babbitt, Natalie. *The Eyes of the Amaryllis*. New York: Farrar, Straus & Giroux, 1977.

Barry, Scott. *The Kingdom of Wolves*. New York: Putnam, 1979.

Berrill, Jacquelyn. *Wonders of the World of Wolves*. New York: Dodd, Mead, 1970.

Blume, Judy. *Are You There God? It's Me, Margaret*. New York: Bradbury, 1970.

———. *Blubber*. New York: Dell, 1986.

———. *Deenie*. New York: Dell, 1986.

———. *It's Not the End of the World*. New York: Dell, 1987.

———. *Just as Long as We're Together*. New York: Orchard Books, 1987.

———. *Tales of a Fourth Grade Nothing*. Illustrated by Ray Doty. New York: Dell, 1986.

Bond, Nancy. *The Best of Enemies*. New York: Atheneum, McElderry, 1978.

———. *A Place to Come Back to*. New York: Atheneum, McElderry, 1984.

Bridgers, Sue Ellen. *All Together Now*. New York: Knopf, 1979.

Brooks, Bruce. *Midnight Hour Encores*. New York: Harper & Row, 1986.

———. *The Moves Make the Man*. New York: Harper & Row, 1987.

Burch, Robert. *Christmas with Ida Early*. New York: Penguin, 1985.

———. *Ida Early Comes Over the Mountain*. New York: Viking, 1980.

———. *King Kong and Other Poets*. New York: Viking, 1986.

Burnford, Sheila. *The Incredible Journey*. Illustrated by Carl Burger. Boston: Little, Brown, 1961.

Byars, Betsy. *The Animal, the Vegetable, and John D. Jones*. Illustrated by Ruth Sanderson. New York: Delacorte, 1982.

———. *A Blossom Promise*. Illustrated by Jacqueline Rogers. New York: Delacorte, 1988.

———. *The Blossoms and the Green Phantom*. Illustrated by Jacqueline Rogers. New York: Delacorte, 1987.

———. *The Blossoms Meet the Vulture Lady*. Illustrated by Jacqueline Rogers. New York: Delacorte, 1986.

———. *Cracker Jackson*. New York: Puffin, 1986.

———. *The Glory Girl*. New York: Viking, 1983.

———. *The House of Wings*. Illustrated by Daniel Schwartz. New York: Puffin, 1982.

———. *The Midnight Fox*. Illustrated by Ann Grifalconi. New York: Avon, 1975.

———. *The Not-Just-Anybody-Family*. Illustrated by Jacqueline Rogers. New York: Delacorte, 1986.

———. *The Pinballs*. New York: Harper & Row, 1987.

———. *Summer of the Swans*. Illustrated by Ted CoConis. New York: Avon, 1980.

Cameron, Eleanor. *Julia and the Hand of God*. Illustrated by Gail Owens. New York: Dutton, 1977.

———. *Julia's Magic*. Illustrated by Gail Owens. New York: Dutton, 1984.

———. *A Room Made of Windows*. Boston: Little, Brown, 1971.

———. *That Julia Redfern*. New York: Dutton, 1982.

Childress, Alice. *A Hero Ain't Nothin' but a Sandwich*. New York: Avon, 1982.

Cleary, Beverly. *Beezus and Ramona*. Illustrated by Louis Darling. New York: Dell, 1979.

———. *Dear Mr. Henshaw*. Illustrated by Paul O. Zelinsky. New York: Morrow, 1983.

———. *A Girl from Yamhill: A Memoir*. New York: Morrow, 1988.

———. *Henry Huggins*. Illustrated by Louis Darling. New York: Dell, 1979.

———. *Ramona Forever*. Illustrated by Alan Tiegreen. New York: Dell, 1985.

———. *Ramona Quimby, Age Eight*. Illustrated by Alan Tiegreen. New York: Morrow, 1981.

———. *Ramona and Her Father*. Illustrated by Alan Tiegreen. New York: Morrow, 1977.

———. *Ramona and Her Mother*. New York: Morrow, 1979.

———. *Ramona the Brave*. Illustrated by Alan Tiegreen. New York: Dell, 1981.

_____. *Ramona the Pest.* Illustrated by Louis Darling. New York: Dell, 1982.

Cleary's Ramona series can be found on videotape by Lorimar. See Elaine Scott for the book about this series.

Cleaver, Vera, and Bill Cleaver. *Me Too.* Philadelphia: Lippincott, 1973.

_____. *Trial Valley.* Philadelphia: Lippincott, 1987.

_____. *Where the Lilies Bloom.* Illustrated by James Spanfeller. Philadelphia: Lippincott, 1969.

Cole, Brock. *The Goats.* New York: Farrar, Straus & Giroux, 1987.

Corcoran, Barbara. *A Dance to Still Music.* New York: Atheneum, 1974.

Cormier, Robert. *Beyond the Chocolate War.* New York: Knopf, 1985.

_____. *The Chocolate War.* New York: Dell, 1986.

Cresswell, Helen. *Absolute Zero: Being the Second Part of the Bagthorpe Saga.* New York: Penguin, 1987.

_____. *Bagthorpes Abroad: Being the Fifth Part of the Bagthorpe Saga.* New York: Macmillan, 1984.

_____. *Bagthorpes Unlimited: Being the Third Part of the Bagthorpe Saga.* New York: Avon, 1985.

_____. *Bagthorpes vs. the World: Being the Fourth Part of the Bagthorpe Saga.* New York: Penguin, 1987.

_____. *Ordinary Jack: Being the First Part of the Bagthorpe Saga.* New York: Penguin, 1987.

Danziger, Paula. *The Cat Ate My Gymsuit.* New York: Delacorte, 1974.

_____. *There's a Bat in Bunk Five.* New York: Dell, 1986.

De Clements, Barthe. *Nothing's Fair in Fifth Grade.* New York: Viking, 1981.

_____. *Sixth Grade Can Really Kill You.* New York: Viking, 1985.

De Jong, Meindert. *Hurry Home,*

Candy. Illustrated by Maurice Sendak. New York: Harper & Row, 1958.

Fitzhugh, Louise. *Harriet the Spy.* New York: Harper & Row, 1964.

Fleischman, Paul. *Rear-View Mirrors.* New York: Harper & Row, 1986.

Fox, Paula. *The Moonlight Man.* New York: Bradbury, 1986.

_____. *One-Eyed Cat.* New York: Bradbury, 1984.

Garfield, James B. *Follow My Leader.* Illustrated by Robert Greiner. New York: Viking, 1957.

George, Jean Craighead. *Julie of the Wolves.* Illustrated by John Schoenherr. New York: Harper & Row, 1972.

_____. *My Side of the Mountain.* New York: Dutton, 1975.

_____. *The Talking Earth.* New York: Harper & Row. 1987.

_____. *Water Sky.* New York: Harper & Row, 1987.

_____. *The Wounded Wolf.* Illustrated by John Schoenherr. New York: Harper & Row, 1978.

Gilson, Jamie. *Do Bananas Chew Gum?* New York: Lothrop, Lee & Shepard, 1980.

_____. *4-B Goes Wild.* Illustrated by Linda S. Edwards. New York: Lothrop, Lee & Shepard, 1983.

_____. *Hobie Hanson, You're Weird.* New York: Lothrop, Lee & Shepard, 1987.

_____. *Thirteen Ways to Sink a Sub.* New York: Lothrop, Lee & Shepard, 1982.

Gould, Deborah. *Grandpa's Slide Show.* New York: Lothrop, Lee & Shepard, 1987.

Graber, Richard. *Doc.* New York: Harper & Row, 1986.

Greene, Bette. *Get on Out of Here, Philip Hall.* New York: Dial, 1981.

_____. *Philip Hall Likes Me. I Reckon Maybe.* New York: Dial, 1974.

Greene, Constance C. *Beat the Tur-*

tle Drum. Illustrated by Donna Diamond. New York: Viking, 1976.

Hall, Lynn. *Just One Friend.* New York: Macmillan, 1985.

Hamilton, Virgina. *Willie Bea and the Time the Martians Landed.* New York: Greenwillow, 1983.

_____. *A Little Love.* New York: Philomel, 1984.

_____. *M. C. Higgins, the Great.* New York: Macmillan, 1987.

Henry, Marguerite. *King of the Wind.* Illustrated by Wesley Dennis. New York: Macmillan, 1948.

_____. *Misty of Chincoteague.* Illustrated by Wesley Dennis. New York: Macmillan, 1947.

_____. *Sea Star, Orphan of Chincoteague.* Illustrated by Wesley Dennis. New York: Macmillan, 1949.

_____. *Stormy: Misty's Foal.* Illustrated by Wesley Dennis. New York: Macmillan, 1963.

Hermes, Patricia. *You Shouldn't Have to Say Good-Bye.* San Diego: Harcourt Brace Jovanovich, 1982.

Hinton, S. E. *Rumble Fish.* New York: Delacorte, 1975.

Holman, Felice. *Slake's Limbo.* New York: Scribner's, 1974.

Howker, Janni. *Badger on the Barge and Other Stories.* New York: Greenwillow, 1985..

Hunter, Edith F. *Child of the Silent Night: The Story of Laura Bridgman.* Illustrated by Bea Holmes. Boston: Houghton Mifflin, 1963.

Hunter, Mollie. *The Third Eye.* New York: Harper & Row, 1979.

Hurwitz, Johanna. *The Adventures of Ali Baba Bernstein.* Illustrated by Gail Owens. New York: Scholastic, 1987.

_____. *Aldo Applesauce.* Illustrated by John Wallner. New York: Morrow, 1979.

_____. *Aldo Ice Cream.* Illustrated by John Wallner. New York: Morrow, 1981.

_____. *Class Clown.* Illustrated by Sheila Hamanaka. New York:

Morrow, 1987.

————. *Much Ado About Aldo.* Illustrated by John Wallner. New York: Morrow, 1978.

Jenness, Aylette. *Dwellers of the Tundra: Life in an Alaskan Eskimo Village.* New York: Macmillan, 1970.

Keller, Helen. *The Story of My Life.* New York: Doubleday, 1954.

Kingman, Lee. *The Year of the Raccoon.* Boston: Houghton Mifflin, 1966.

Kline, Suzy. *Herbie Jones.* Illustrated by Richard Williams. New York: Putnam's, 1985.

————. *What's the Matter with Herbie Jones?* Illustrated by Richard Williams. New York: Putnam's, 1986.

Knight, Eric. *Lassie Come Home.* Illustrated by Marguerite Kirmse. 1940. Reprint. New York: Holt, Rinehart & Winston, 1978.

Little, Jean. *Different Dragons.* New York: Viking, 1987.

————. *From Anna.* Illustrated by Joan Sandin. New York: Harper & Row, 1972.

————. *Little by Little: A Writer's Education.* New York: Viking, 1987.

————. *Lost and Found.* New York: Viking, 1986.

————. *Mama's Going to Buy You a Mockingbird.* New York: Viking, 1985.

————. *Mine for Keeps.* Illustrated by Lewis Parker. Boston: Little, Brown, 1962.

Lowry, Lois. *Anastasia Again!* Illustrated by Diane De Groat. Boston: Houghton Mifffln, 1981.

————. *Anastasia, Ask Your Analyst.* Boston: Houghton Mifflin, 1984.

————. *Anastasia at Your Service.* Illustrated by Diane De Groat. Boston: Houghton Mifflin, 1982.

————. *Anastasia Has the Answers.* Boston: Houghton Mifflin, 1985.

————. *Anastasia Krupnik.* Boston: Houghton Mifflin, 1979.

————. *Anastasia on Her Own.* Boston: Houghton Mifflin, 1985.

————. *Anastasia's Chosen Career.* Boston: Houghton Mifflin, 1987.

————. *Autumn Street.* Boston: Houghton Mifflin, 1980.

————. *Rabble Starkey.* Boston: Houghton Mifflin, 1987.

————. *A Summer to Die.* Illustrated by Jenni Oliver. Boston: Houghton Mifflin, 1977.

Mazer, Norma Fox. *After the Rain.* New York: Morrow, 1987.

————. *A Figure of Speech.* New York: Delacorte, 1973.

McHugh, Elisabet. *Karen and Vicki.* New York: Greenwillow, 1984.

————. *Karen's Sister.* New York: Greenwillow, 1983.

————. *Raising a Mother Isn't Easy.* New York: Greenwillow, 1983.

Moore, Lilian. "Reflections." In *Something New Begins.* New York: Atheneum, 1982.

Myers, Walter Dean. *Crystal.* New York: Viking, Kestrel, 1987.

————. *The Young Landlords.* Illustrated by Diane De Groat. New York: Viking, 1979.

Neufeld, John. *Lisa, Bright and Dark.* Chatham, N.Y.: Phillips, 1969.

Newton, Suzanne. *An End to Perfect.* New York: Viking, 1984.

————. *A Place Between.* New York: Viking, 1986.

Oneal, Zibby. *In Summer Light.* New York: Viking, 1985.

Orgel, Doris. *Whiskers: Once and Always.* Illustrated by Carol Newsom. New York: Viking, 1986.

Paterson, Katherine. *Bridge to Terabitha.* New York: Crowell, 1977.

————. *Come Sing, Jimmy Jo.* New York: Dutton, 1985.

————. *The Great Gilly Hopkins.* New York: Crowell, 1978.

————. *Jacob Have I Loved.* New York: Crowell, 1980.

————. *The Master Puppeteer.* Illustrated by Haru Wells. New York: Crowell, 1976.

————. *Park's Quest.* New York: Dutton, 1988.

Paton Walsh, Jill. *Gaffer Samson's Luck.* Illustrated by Brock Cole. New York: Farrar, Straus & Giroux, 1984.

————. *Goldengrove.* New York: Farrar, Straus & Giroux, 1972.

————. *Unleaving.* New York: Farrar, Straus & Giroux, 1976.

Paulsen, Gary. *Dogsong.* New York: Bradbury, 1985.

————. *Hatchet.* New York: Bradbury, 1987.

————. *Tracker.* New York: Bradbury, 1984.

Peare, Catherine Owens. *The Helen Keller Story.* New York: Crowell, 1959.

Peck, Richard. *Remembering the Good Times.* New York: Delacorte, 1985.

Peterson, Jeanne Whitehouse. *I Have a Sister. My Sister Is Deaf.* Illustrated by Deborah Ray. New York: Harper & Row, 1977.

Pringle, Laurence. *Wolfman: Exploring the World of Wolves.* New York: Scribner's, 1983.

Raskin, Ellen. *The Westing Game.* New York: Dutton, 1978.

Rawls, Wilson. *Where the Red Fern Grows: The Story of Two Dogs and a Boy.* New York: Doubleday, 1961.

Robertson, Keith. *In Search of a Sandhill Crane.* Illustrated by Richard Cuffari. New York: Viking, 1973.

Robinson, Veronica. *David in Silence.* Illustrated by Victor Ambrus. Philadelphia: Lippincott, 1965.

Rodowsky, Colby. *H, My Name Is Henley.* New York: Farrar, Straus & Giroux, 1982.

Rylant, Cynthia. *Every Living Thing.* Illustrated by S. D. Schindler. New York: Bradbury, 1985.

————. *A Fine White Dust.* New York: Bradbury, 1986.

Sachs, Marilyn. *The Bears' House.* Illustrated by Louis Glanzman. New York: Dutton, 1987.

————. *Fran Ellen's House*. New York: Dutton, 1987.

Scott, Elaine. *Beverly Cleary's Ramona: Behind the Scenes of a Television Show*. Photography by Margaret Miller. New York: Dell, 1988.

Sebestyen, Ouida. *Words by Heart*. Boston: Little, Brown, 1979

Shyer, Marlene Fanta. *Welcome Home, Jellybean*. New York: Scribner's, 1978.

Smith, Doris Buchanan. *Kelly's Creek*. Illustrated by Alan Tiegreen. New York: Crowell, 1975.

Sobol, Harriet Langsman. *My Brother Steven Is Retarded*. Photography by Patricia Agre. New York: Macmillan, 1977.

Southall, Ivan. *Let the Balloon Go*. Illustrated by Jon Weiman. New York: Bradbury, 1985.

Steiner, Barbara. *Biography of a Wolf*. Illustrated by Kiyo Komoda. New York: Putnam, 1973.

Taylor, Sidney. *All-of-a-Kind Family*. Illustrated by Helen John. Chicago: Follett, 1951.

Tolan, Stephanie. *Grandpa and Me*. New York: Scribner's, 1978.

Voigt, Cynthia. *Came a Stranger*. New York: Atheneum, 1987.

————. *Dicey's Song*. New York: Atheneum, 1982.

————. *Homecoming*. New York: Atheneum, 1981.

————. *Izzy, Willy-Nilly*. New York: Atheneum, 1986.

————. *A Solitary Blue*. New York: Atheneum, 1983.

————. *Sons from Afar*. New York: Atheneum, 1987.

————. *The Runner*. New York: Atheneum, 1985.

Wolf, Bernard. *Anna's Silent World*. Philadelphia: Lippincott, 1977.

————. *Connie's New Eyes*. Philadelphia: Lippincott, 1976.

————. *Don't Feel Sorry for Paul*. Philadelphia: Lippincott, 1974.

Wrightson, Patricia. *A Little Fear*. New York: Atheneum, McElderry, 1983.

Zindel, Paul, *The Pigman*. New York: Harper & Row, 1968.

9

Historical Fiction and Biography

Ancient History

I hope the old Romans
Had painful abdomens.

I hope that the Greeks
Had toothache for weeks.

I hope that the Arabs
Were bitten by scarabs.

I hope that the Vandals
Had thorns in their sandals.

I hope that the Persians
Had gout in all versions.

I hope that the Medes
Were kicked by their steeds.

They started the fuss
And left it to us![1]

Arthur Guiterman

458

In the poem that opens this chapter, Arthur Guiterman expresses the feelings of many students who are bored with the study of history. They may memorize names of kings and dates of battles, but the names and numbers are isolated, the people merely shadows, the events disconnected.

History is made by people—what they do, what they say, and what they are—people with strengths and weaknesses who experience victories and defeats. Authors of books set in the past want children to know historical figures as human beings who have shortcomings as well as strengths. Historical events affected the common people perhaps even more than they did kings and battle leaders; the way the common folk responded to traumatic events shows adaptability and gives modern children a sense of reality of times past. Today's children have a hard time imagining life without computers, video technology, rapid transportation, and modern communication. They fully expect problems to be solved in the 30 minutes of a TV sitcom. When they read good historical fiction, they can imagine themselves living in another time and place. They can speculate as to how they would have reacted and how they would have felt. They can read about ordinary people acting heroically. By doing so, they begin to build an understanding of the impact one person can have on history.

There are several ways to incorporate historical fiction and biography into the social studies curriculum. One fifth grade teacher be-gins a study of the Revolutionary War period by asking students to brainstorm "facts" about George Washington, Betsy Ross, and Paul Revere. He writes the offered information and misinformation on charts, which are referred to frequently during the study. Inevitably, there are conflicting reports, and the students revise their original statements as they locate additional information.

Another teacher works with her third grade children to develop a study plan for a unit on early settlers in America. She fills the room with many sources of information, including books, records, films, realia, and pictures. The students spend several days exploring the material and making suggestions about topics that interest them, and the teacher then writes these on the chalkboard. The list might include the Pilgrims, Plymouth Rock, the Mayflower, the first Thanksgiving, and witch trials. The group organizes the ideas into reasonably logical categories, and students then choose topics they want to pursue, identify sources of information, and begin the research for the study. Examining the past in this way helps students begin to understand human behavior, the ways that people and societies interact, the concept of humans as social beings, and the values that make people human.

One teacher reluctantly decided to try using trade books instead of the social studies text for the study of the American Revolution. Students were asked to read one novel, one biography, and one informational book on that historical period. In addition, they read an

LANDMARK

Historical Fiction: Little House in the Big Woods, *1932*

Laura Ingalls Wilder (1867–1957) wrote a series of books about pioneer life in the 1870s and 1880s based on her memories and family records. The stories have become the best-loved historical fiction today. It was not until Laura was an adult that her daughter, Rose, convinced her to write down the stories from her childhood. Reluctant at first, believing that no one would be interested in the simple life of a pioneer family, Laura finally bought a student composition notebook and began to write about her early years. The books are based on her own life; not even the names are changed: Pa and Ma Ingalls and their four little girls: Mary, Laura, Carrie, and Grace. The stories begin with *Little House in the Big Woods*, set in the Wisconsin forests in the 1870s, when Laura was 4 years old. They continue through the family's other little houses on the Kansas Prairie to a dugout in Minnesota and finally to DeSmet in the Dakota Territory.

These stories are notable for their portrayal of a time in America's past and the importance of family unity in meeting physical hardships. The strength of the closely knit

The series of Little House books helps young readers understand the hardships and adventures of frontier life. (From *Little House on the Prairie* by Laura Ingalls Wilder, illustrated by Garth Williams.)

pioneer family provided not only security but also the courage and moral fiber to build a new nation.

encyclopedia account of one of the events described in the novel. The students then critically examined the presentations in the various sources. The teacher modeled the process, and they worked in collaborative learning groups to discuss their findings. The group concluded that no single book could have given them the basis for understanding they gained from their wide reading. Even more exciting, the children begged their teacher to use the same approach for the next social studies unit.

The books discussed in this chapter show that history is created by people, that people living now are tied to those who lived in the past through a common humanity, and that human conditions of the past shape our lives today. By relating trade books to topics in the social studies, we enrich children's understanding with a wealth of material that far exceeds the limited view of any single text. Historical fiction and biographies are read for insights into the panoply of history; they are a lively and fascinating way to transmit the story of the past to the guardians of the future.

Historical fiction, though set in a time prior to the one in which we live, is like contemporary realism in that it relates human experiences in the natural world. In essence, a historical novel is an imaginative story anchored by some historical event. Historical biography tells primarily the life story of an actual person, with the times in which he or she lived in a secondary role. Reading about one person brings the wide scope of history to a focus in a single life, showing the interaction between that person and events.

When do contemporary events become history? Unlike the condition "antique," which takes decades to achieve, the classification "historical" does not have a formal basis in time. Hence, it is difficult to tell where to draw the line, because what may seem contemporary to us will be historical to our younger students.

Historical fiction and biography are grounded in facts but are not restricted by them. An author may use historical records to document events, but the facts merely serve as a framework for the story.

The best historical stories come from good storytellers who are well acquainted with the facts. Two works exemplifying this combination of historical knowledge and storytelling ability are books by Esther Forbes and by two brothers—James Lincoln Collier, a writer, and Christopher Collier, a historian. While researching information for an adult biography of Paul Revere, Esther Forbes became intrigued with stories of the young apprentices who lived in eighteenth-century Boston. She told their story in *Johnny Tremain* (I-A), maintaining a level of historical accuracy like that of the biography. The Colliers combined their talents to produce a bittersweet story of a family caught

between loyalty to the English crown and desire for independence in *my brother Sam is dead* (I-A).

CRITERIA FOR SELECTING HISTORICAL BOOKS AND BIOGRAPHIES

Many books that present historical facts do not qualify as literature. To do so, historical fiction and biography must meet the criteria for *all* literature—they must tell an engaging story, have well-developed characters, and evolve themes—while, in addition, evoking a historical setting through a well-structured plot. Basic themes, such as comradeship, loyalty, treachery, love and hate, revenge, and the struggle between good and evil, run through historical fiction and biography.

Historical fiction and biography should be consistent with historical evidence. The story, though imaginative, must remain within the limits of the historical background chosen, avoiding distortion and anachronism.

Setting is a crucial element in evaluating historical fiction, since it is this feature that distinguishes it most dramatically from other literary forms. Details of setting must be spelled out so clearly that readers can create a mental image of the time and place in which the events occur. These elements are integral to the plot of historical fiction; they determine characters' beliefs and actions. The setting must also be authentic and consistent with historical and geographical evidence. In *Censoring Reality: An Examination of Books on South Africa*, Beverley Naidoo describes an informational book that quotes a meagerly paid miner saying that he goes home to visit his family every weekend. The location of the mines and his home are 2,000 miles apart, a distance that would make weekly visits impossible. Therefore, in evaluating historical books, we look for settings that are (1) integral to the story and (2) authentic in historical and geographical detail.

Language should be in keeping with the period and the place, particularly in dialogue. A problem arises in the case of words of the past that would be understood today by few readers. This can be dealt with by synthesizing language that has the right sound for a period but is understandable to contemporary readers. Rosemary Sutcliff explains how she works the language into her writing:

> I try to catch the rhythm of a tongue, the tune that it plays on the ear, Welsh or Gaelic as opposed to Anglo-Saxon, the sensible workmanlike language which one feels the Latin of the ordinary Roman citizen would have translated into. It is extraordinary what can be done by the changing or transposing of a single word, or by using a perfectly usual one in a slightly unusual way: "I beg your pardon" changed into "I ask your pardon." . . . This is not done by any set rule of thumb; I simply play it by ear as I go along.[2]

When evaluating language in books of historical fiction and biography, therefore, look for (1) authentic speech patterns that sound right for the time period and (2) dialogue that rings true to the characters.

Characters in historical fiction should *believe* and *behave* in ways that are in keeping with the times in which they live. Authors who attribute contemporary values to historical figures run the risk of creating an anachronism, mistakenly placing something in a historical period. When actual historical figures appear in historical fiction, careful writers do not attribute dialogue to them unless there is some documentary evidence or record of what they said. Therefore, in evaluating characterization in historical fiction, we look for persons who (1) behave according to the standards and mores of the time and (2) speak and believe in ways that are appropriate to the period.

History is filled with a tremendous amount of *raw material* for exciting plots and themes. Yet it is the abundance of historical facts that

may overburden a story. In *Talent Is Not Enough*, Mollie Hunter, noted writer of historical fiction and other books, says that the facts of the past are needed to create a book, but it is the author's sense of history and knowledge of people's dreams, realities, and passions that recreate some part of the past as a living link in the chain of human experience. None of the facts of the historical situation, she continues, may be relevant except that they serve the main function of source material—which is to yield a theme that has universal application and appeal.[3]

Historical fiction writer Elizabeth Janet Gray Vining adds,

> It's absolutely essential to subordinate research to the story. You have to do your research, live with it, assimilate it, and then write your story about life in the past as if it happened to you. . . .
>
> The most difficult thing in writing about the past is to get the climate of thought of the past. It's easy enough to pick up costumes, customs, and events, but people thought differently, entirely differently, in the past period from the way they think now. It's the hardest thing to pick up the thought, express it in your book, and make modern people accept it.[4]

Therefore, in evaluating historical fiction, we look for books that (1) blend factual background as subordinate to the story and (2) contain a theme with universal application and appeal.

Historical fiction and biography should also reflect the *values* of the period: portraying the sexes as equal, for example, in a story set in Victorian times would be inconsistent with the "father knows best" customs that prevailed.

Good historical books show no *revisionism;* that is, they do not rewrite history to suit present ways of thinking. For example, Paula Fox, though the attitudes are offensive to her (and probably to her readers), has characters express racist ones in *The Slave Dancer* (I-A) in order to

---

LANDMARK

Biography: And Then What Happened, Paul Revere? 1974

Jean Fritz believes that we make history dull by presenting our national heroes as frozen statues immersed in stale facts and images that emasculate our past:

> Sometimes it seems to me that we have forced our heroes to play the children's own game of Statues. We have twirled them about, called *time,* and then told them to hold their positions. Whatever stance they happen to assume is the one they must perpetuate.[5]

She believes that the stereotyped impressions carry over into adulthood and rob us of a sense of the full force of a person's character.

Jean Fritz's biographies about Revolutionary War heroes present a refreshing view. Her biographies are tinged with humor, one of the most effective ways of bringing a deeper understanding of a person from the past. She presents the foibles as well as the good deeds through character-revealing incidents and anecdotes.

In *And Then What Happened, Paul Revere?* she chronicles the true events on the night of April 18, 1775; they differ from the romanticized version set forth in "Paul Revere's Ride" by Henry Wadsworth Longfellow. Paul Revere had set up the system of signal lanterns in the steeple of North Church and arranged for his horse in Charlestown across the river. When Revere mounted his horse, another courier, William Dawes, was halfway to Lexington by the Brookline road. In Lexington, Dr. Samuel Prescott, a young physician from Concord, said goodnight to his sweetheart and mounted his horse to return home. At the edge of town, he fell in with two horsemen, who turned out to be Revere and Dawes on their way to Concord with the news of the British march. The three proceeded on the Concord road, awakening each house along the way. About halfway to Concord, they were accosted by four British officers. On a shout from Prescott, the threesome split and rode off in different directions. Prescott jumped his horse over a stone wall and escaped to carry the news to Concord. Dawes fell off his horse but remounted and rode on to alert other towns, and Revere was captured by the British. Jean Fritz describes the ride to Lexington with hilarious and harrowing detail. Her approach to historical biography has made it accessible to younger children. Her touches of humor have made biography appealing to a wide range of readers. Jean Fritz's work is a landmark because it changed the way historical figures are described.

---

reflect accurately the temper of the times during slavery.

Finally, noteworthy historical novels do not *overgeneralize;* they do not lead the reader to believe, for example, that all native Americans are like the one portrayed in this story. Each character is unique, just as each of us is, and while the novelist focuses on one person in a group, it is clear that it *is* only a person, and not a stereotype. Therefore, in evaluating historical fiction and biography, look for (1) values and attitudes that are consistent with the time period and (2) stories that avoid generalization, including stereotypes of gender or of ethnic or racial groups.

PREHISTORIC TIMES

Prehistoric times, the ancient period before written records were kept, are wrapped in the shrouds of antiquity. Scientists theorize about the daily life and culture of ancient peoples by observing fragments of life and making inferences from bits of pottery, weapons, or scraps of bone. Authors draw from the findings of archaeologists, anthropologists, and paleontologists to create vivid tales of life as it might have been.

Many novels of prehistoric times are set in distant lands around the Mediterranean Sea or in ancient Britain, but William O. Steele creates his picture of prehistoric life on the North American continent. *The Magic Amulet* (I-A) is a story about Tragg, a child of an early nomadic band that roamed what is now the southeastern United States. Tragg knows that tribal code requires that any member who becomes a burden to the tribe must be left behind, and yet he fearfully resents being abandoned. His leg, swollen and feverish from a gash made by a saber-tooth tiger, prevents him from walking; but he is determined to live. In the deserted camp, Tragg finds his uncle's bracelet, a magic amulet, which gives him strength and hope. He vows that he will recover and find a new family band to join. The amulet plays a far more powerful role in his life than he had imagined.

Ann Turnbull creates a picture of what she believes family life was like in the late Ice Age, 25,000 years ago, in *Maroo of the Winter Caves* (I-A). Maroo's family traveled across the plains to spend the warm summer months by the sea, and during the winter, they found shelter in mountain caves. This summer is especially happy because Mother gives birth to a new baby, there is plenty of food, and there is a new puppy to tame. Life changes drastically, however, as the family begins the return trip to the winter caves. One day, when father fails to return from the hunt, Maroo and her brother find him lying at the foot of a cliff, dead from a fall. Grandmother makes a difficult decision: when she is aware that the family will not be able to reach the winter caves before the blizzards come, she sends Maroo and her brother on a shortcut across the mountains in search of help. The children's hunger and hardship as they journey through bitter, stinging cold gives readers a sense of what life must have been like in the Ice Age.

In *Time of the Bison* (I), Ann Turner tells the story of an 11-year-old called Scar Boy by the people in his clan of primitive cave dwellers. He was given his name after he took a bad fall that left him with lacerations on his face. Scar Boy did not like his unfortunate name but knew that he could earn a new one only by performing an act of courage or an unusual deed, according to the tradition of his clan. One night he dreams of a horse, a great stallion with strong muscles and wide dark eyes. The next morning he scrapes clay from the river bank to shape a statue of his dream horse. His family is astounded by his skill as a sculptor and suffers hardships to take him to the Painter of Caves in a distant clan. The Painter of Caves recognizes the boy's talent, agrees to take him as an apprentice, and foresees a time when Scar Boy will be called "Animal Shaper," a far more appealing and honorable name. This unusual story shows that a boy is rewarded for artistic talent, not the usual killing of bison or feats of physical endurance.

The best fiction about prehistoric people does more than re-create possible settings and events of the past. It engages itself with themes basic to all persons everywhere—the will to survive, the need for courage and honor, the

ACTIVITY: TEACHER TO STUDENT

TIME LINES AND MAPS (I)   Gather information to make a classroom time-line mural to help show more clearly the possible times various groups of prehistoric peoples might have existed. The time line can be constructed so that the dates of eras run across the top and the titles of stories set in the various periods appear along the bottom. In some cases, of course, you may need to infer when the story takes place.

Make a series of world maps—one for each story read. On each map, locate the setting of the story, either stated or implied, and fill in the location of other prehistoric peoples known to exist at the time. Julian May's *Before the Indians* is a good reference work for the project. Maps show the locations of tribes known to have existed in North and South America and also provide illustrations of artifacts and plant and animal life that you could use to decorate your maps.

See also Walter Oleksy's *Treasures of the Land: Archaeology Today in America;* Harry Behn's *The Faraway Lurs;* T. A. Dyer's *A Way of His Own;* Shirley Glubok's *Art and Archaeology;* and Bruce Porell's *Digging the Past.*

growth of understanding, the development of compassion.

Rosemary Sutcliff, an artist whose novels of ancient Britain are masterful evocations of their time, provides sensitive insights into the human spirit. In *Warrior Scarlet* (A), Drem One-Arm, crippled since birth, spends all his years in the Boys' House training and struggling to learn a warrior's skills in spite of his handicap. He fails his wolf-slaying task and is not permitted to complete the initiation ceremonies. Instead, he is considered dead and is banished to live with the shepherd people in the hill country. Toward the end of the famine winter that follows, the wolf that Drem failed to kill returns to attack an aged shepherd, and this time Drem is triumphant. He returns to wear the warrior scarlet of his tribe, but with an understanding of the vicissitudes experienced by those who live different lives.

Sutcliff is distinguished among historical fiction writers for her ability to recreate an au-thentic picture of life in early Britain. She writes knowledgeably about people and places in a way that fills in many of the missing pieces of ancient Britain during the years it was occupied by Norsemen, and later by Romans, Normans, and Saxons. The ring of authenticity is not the sole distinguishing feature of Sutcliff's work: each story reverberates with an eternal truth and lasting theme. Sutcliff's heroes live and die for values and principles that we hold today. Her stories reveal the eternal struggle between light—that which we value—and darkness—the forces that work to destroy it. Sutcliff's characters fight relentlessly for good and face the blackness of despair in their enemies. Although we do not discuss the comprehensive span of her work, it is central to those who study the early Britain historical time periods.

Mollie Hunter's *The Stronghold* (A) is a historical novel about a young man whose vision far exceeds that of his contemporaries. The story takes place in the days when Roman slave raiders often descended on the Orkney Islands; a young man stands guard:

> Reluctantly Coll turned his gaze from the settlement, and once more braced his sinewy frame to meet the cold sea wind whistling over the headland. The movement woke pain in his crippled leg, and he endured it with gritted teeth and tightened grip on the long stem of the bronze warning trumpet in his right hand. The pain passed. His fingers relaxed, and his face regained its normal appearance of spare, bony strength.[6]

Coll understandably hates the Roman soldiers; one of them pulled him, as a baby, from his mother and threw him against some rocks, crushing his hipbone. Coll's strength and ingenuity pervade this story of a physically disabled young man in ancient times who successfully designs a fortress that will protect his people.

ANCIENT TIMES

Stories of ancient times focus on life in the Mediterranean civilizations. Children are fascinated by the pyramids and mummies of an-

---

PROFILE

Mollie Hunter

The first light of literature on a young mind does more than illumine. A touch of glory descends, and that mind can never be truly dark again.[7]

Such is the belief of Mollie Hunter, who has brought touches of glory to innumerable young minds. Historical fact and legend mingle in her tales; her gift for bringing the spell of the past into modern stories is unmatched.

Mollie Hunter knows that things are not always what they seem and convinces readers to listen with an inner ear and to see, as one title has it, with *The Third Eye.* Her talent brings to the surface the secret hopes and emotions that nourish life and creative work: "I don't say that I am wedded to my craft, that I'm steeped in my craft, that I'm involved in it. I *am* my work.[8] While facts have their place, Mollie Hunter has her fictions, which are far more convincing.

She grew up in the highlands of Scotland with an aura of myth and legend permeating her days. The visionary Coll in *The Stronghold,* who plans and builds an impregnable fortress for his people despite his physical handicap, could have been created by a Mollie Hunter imagination only. So, too, could it only have been a Mollie Hunter who

cient Egypt and by the ruins and myths of ancient Greece and Rome. Viewing museum treasures, such as those from the tomb of Tutankhamen, can heighten this interest.

Mara, Daughter of the Nile (A), by Eloise Jarvis McGraw, is a romance in which a slave girl is instrumental in protecting a pharoah and winning the love of a lord. Children who discover the mysteries of ancient Egypt through books will find labyrinths to probe and set their minds imagining. Many fine books tell them what the great Sphinx might say if only it would speak.

Jill Paton Walsh links three short stories by their connection to the Athenian hero, Themistokles, in *Children of the Fox* (I-A). Three fictional narrators give first-person accounts of their roles in real events during the time of the Persian Wars when the relationship between Athens and Sparta was changing. Aster, the first narrator, helps the Greek general Themistokles defeat the Persian ships at Salamis. Demeas, the second narrator, runs to Sparta to deliver a message to the leader who is rebuilding the walls of Athens without Spartan consent. In the final story, a young princess saves

described, in *The Walking Stones,* the relationship between Donald and the Bodach, believers in each generation who pass on the torch of legend to their heirs.

When asked why many of her books are set in historical times, Mollie Hunter replied:

> I'm interested in the past, and it just so happens that the past is all around me in the circumstances in which I live; there are reminders of it, for instance, in the form of old buildings. And, I've always been curious about what happened before I was born, and I've done a lot of research to find out. But I also have the sense of all the people who lived before me and I like to try to recreate their lives . . . . And I just like the sensation of wandering back into the past. It's like a country that I have come to know. I like walking through the past and coming back into my own time with a good story to tell.[9]

Mollie Hunter's Scottish brogue and lilting laughter ring through her speech; chatting with her is like catching a sunbeam. Her powerful convictions about the goodness of people permeate her writing and life. "If there is a message" in her writing, she says, "it is that the most powerful force on earth is the capacity of human beings to reach out, to be warm, responsive to one another—to love."[10]

It is no wonder that Mollie Hunter's books are popular with young people; they evoke response in readers because of her ability to share love. Her peers have acclaimed her status as an exceptional writer by awarding her the Carnegie Medal (counterpart of the Newbery Medal) for *The Stronghold* and by inviting her to give the Arbuthnot Lecture in 1975. An outgrowth of the lecture series is a book of essays, entitled *Talent Is Not Enough,* which explores her strong beliefs about the craft and passion of writing.

Themistokle's life by helping him escape from the Athenians and Spartans who have accused him of bribery. Paton Walsh is meticulous in her research, using it to undergird her story rather than overpower it.

Some stories of the ancient Olympic athletes merge with mythology, whereas other authors attempt to retain a more factual base for their work. Shirley Glubok and Alfred Tamarin describe an imaginary Olympiad of the 5th century B.C. in *Olympic Games in Ancient Greece* (I-A). Anecdotal and historical material enrich their account of the origins of games still played today. Photographs of sculpture and pottery show athletes developing their skills. In another book, Stephen Krensky uses photographs from the exhibit "The Search for Alexander" to portray 13 years in which Alexander the Great built his empire in *Conqueror and Hero: The Search for Alexander* (I-A). Krensky provides line drawings, a map of the Greek world at the time of Alexander, and an interesting story about this Greek hero.

The Bronze Bow (I-A) by Elizabeth Speare is the story of Daniel Bar Jamin's journey from bitter hatred to acceptance and understanding of love. Consumed with a passion to avenge the heartless killing of his parents by driving the Romans out of Israel, he fights them ruthlessly and with a vindictiveness that causes him to ignore his comrades' needs. The title, based on a biblical verse referring to a bow that no man could bend with his strength alone, symbolizes Daniel's submission to a greater power. Daniel finally recognizes his need for help and accepts the greater power of love over hate. The theme of love conquering hate, which is realized repeatedly in great literature, would make a powerful theme unit study.

Chelsea Quinn Yarbro wrote more than 20 books for adults before she began writing for a younger audience in *Locadio's Apprentice* (I-A). In this riveting novel, set in Pompeii during the reign of Emperor Vespasian, 14-year-old Enecus desperately hopes to become a doctor's ap-

prentice. Enecus works in his parents' thermopolium, an open-air restaurant, but his family does not have enough money to afford an apprenticeship for him. A kind doctor, Locadio Priscus, recognizes the boy's talents, however, and accepts a minimal sum to pay for his training. In the early days with Locadio, Enecus finds life disappointing; the work is difficult and menial. Later he faces blood and suffering and survives with little sleep after long hours of work. As Enecus learns to practice the healing skills, the giant volcano Vesuvius rumbles threateningly in the background. While Enecus struggles to master his chosen profession, he inevitably is faced with a catastrophe that puts his skills and his spirit to the ultimate test.

In *Four Horses for Tishtry* (I-A), Yarbro tells the story of Tishtry, a slave girl in ancient Rome who passionately hopes to buy freedom for her family and herself. Tishtry is a stunt rider who dares to perform acts others cannot do, but her master keeps her away from the finer arenas of the Roman empire. Finally she gets to try her skills in the larger cities, but greater rewards bring greater risks. She is pushed to try flashier and more dangerous stunts which test her skill; finally she must face the jealousy of competitors who would endanger her life.

Rosemary Sutcliff, one of the best historical fiction writers, sets two stories in ancient Britain. One, *Frontier Wolf* (A), is set in the fourth century when Alexios, a Centurion, is sent to take charge of a frontier outpost. Alexios's mission is a punishment, and his leadership at the outpost is questioned by the Frontier Wolves, a band of native Britons, who feel they know far more than their young leader.

In *Song for a Dark Queen* (A), Sutcliff tells Boudicca's (Boadicea's) story through an old harpist who recalls her life and the fate of her people, the Iceni, during the time of the Roman occupation of Britain. Lady Boudicca is left motherless at age 4, forced to marry a man she scorns, and angry and bitter when her father is killed in battle. Boudicca is remembered as the warrior queen, defeated in a final battle and choosing her own death. The historical detail is integrated smoothly in a superb story of Roman Britain.

THE MIDDLE AGES

The dissolution of the Roman Empire signaled the beginning of that part of the medieval period sometimes referred to as the Dark Ages. There is little recorded history of these times, which were marked primarily by the battles of the "barbarian" tribes that swept across Europe. Shadowy figures have life breathed into them in novels set in this period—novels that blend fact and legend, as here:

> On a summer night in the year 408 a flaming red comet appeared over Europe striking terror into the hearts of all who saw it; a menacing omen, a flaming red comet shaped like a tremendous eagle with a sword in its talons.
>
> In that year, when the walls of Rome were cracking before the onslaught of the Goths led by King Alaric; when the Vandals were invading Hispania led by King Gunderic; when Roman Britain was fighting a losing war against the terrible barbarian pirates, the Saxons—on a summer night of that year was Atilla born.[11]

These words occur near the closing of the stirring saga *The White Stag* (I), by Kate Seredy, a haunting retelling of the legend of the founding of the Hungarian nation, unique in literature for children. It opens in an uncharted land of the East, filled with echoes of the Biblical stories of the beginning of human history. Legend touches history as the bloody armies of Attila the Hun push back the borders of the Roman Empire. One group of the many comprising the great Hun migrations has been seeking a "promised land." When the group's wanderings lead it to the sheer, seemingly impassable walls of the Carpathian Mountains, the White Stag of Hungarian mythology appears in a wintry storm and leads it through a mountain pass into the land promised to the fathers.

Kate Seredy grew up in Hungary before World War I and came to the United States after the war to continue her career as an artist and illustrator. Her drawings for *The White Stag* have great strength and sweep; they are entirely in keeping with the poetic majesty of the tale. Reading this Newbery Award winner aloud makes manifest the poetic beauty of its language.

Elaine Konigsburg combines biography, historical fiction, and fantasy in a clever twist in *A Proud Taste for Scarlet and Miniver* (I-A). Eleanor of Aquitaine is waiting in Heaven for Henry II. She has done some things on Earth for which she was sent to Hell, but due to the help of friends in high places, Eleanor was later admitted to Heaven. Henry, though, who had preceded her in death, is still waiting to be admitted to Heaven. Henry's mother, Matilda-Empress, Abbot Suger, and William the Marshal tell portions of Eleanor's story, each in a distinctive voice. These vignettes are interspersed among sections told by Eleanor herself. Lively and witty Eleanor of Aquitaine is credited with helping establish the concept of trial by jury, the English Common Laws, unifying the monetary system, and encouraging poets and musicians to romanticize the legend of King Arthur. In addition to enjoying the clever repartee, readers will gain some insight into the complexities of French and English history and how these characters' lives intertwined. Compare this book to Eleanor of Aquitaine's biography, *Queen Eleanor* described later.

Adam of the Road (A), Elizabeth Janet Gray Vining's Newbery Award winner, is set in thirteenth-century England. Adam with his minstrel father, Roger, and his faithful cocker spaniel, Nick, are on their way to the Fair of St. Giles. Thieves steal Nick, and as Adam chases them to save his dog, he is separated

ACTIVITIES: TEACHER TO STUDENT

MIDDLE AGES (I-A)   After reading many books on the subject, show what you have learned about the Middle Ages by doing one of the following projects.

Heraldry   Make a banner, shield, or coat of arms using paper, fabric, or wood. Find illustrative designs in reference books and use them as models to create your own distinguishing marks of honor.

Castles   Build a replica of a medieval castle or cathedral from balsa wood, sugar cubes, or blocks. Use David Macaulay's *Castle* (I-A) and *Cathedral: The Story of Its Construction* (I-A) and John Goodall's, *The Story of a Castle* (P-I-A) for models and detailed designs.

Clothing and Customs   Make clothing for dolls or miniature figures in the fashions of medieval times. Use Joe Lasker's *Merry Ever After* (P-I) for ideas about the dress of nobility and serfs. Re-enact a wedding celebration such as Lasker describes. Design clothing for knights and their ladies, serfs, and noblemen to show how one's position determined dress.

Stained Glass   Make small replicas of stained-glass windows and decorative panels from cellophane or plastic.

Scrolls   Make a scroll or proclamation using Old English lettering.

Chess   Out of clay, pâpier-maché, or wood, make a chess board and its pieces, which are like a feudal population—king, queen, knights, pawns (serfs), and so on. Research the origin of the game of chess. Have a chess tournament in your class.

DISTINGUISH HISTORY AND LEGEND (I-A)   Select one of the many stories about the Middle Ages and do research using fiction and nonfiction to separate history from legend.

Read Marguerite de Angeli's *The Door in the Wall* (I-A), Elizabeth J. Gray's *Adam of the Road*, (A), Rosemary Sutcliff's *Knight's Fee*, (A), or another book set in medieval times. Compare events and characters with corresponding ones in history textbooks and reference books. Read Jay Williams's *The Sword of King Arthur* (I), Clyde Robert Bulla's *The Sword in the Tree* (P-I), Howard Pyle's *The Story of King Arthur and His Knights* (I-A), and other books about King Arthur and compare the different authors' visions of him.

Research (and report on) a topic, such as barbarians, serfs, knights, ladies of the court, Crusades, guilds, or apprentices. Find out about customs, and dramatize a scene of everyday life that might have occurred in medieval times.

Read the play "Camelot," by Alan Jay Lerner and Federick Lowe, and listen to the recording of that Broadway musical. Use the musical background for special effects while you enact the play in readers' theatre style—each actor reading aloud one character's part from a script.

Macaulay's detailed drawings and clear text provide
explicit information on the building of a medieval castle.
(From *Castle* by David Macaulay.)

from his father. During nearly a year while
Adam continues to hunt for his dog and his
father, he meets many strangers—jugglers,
minstrels, plowmen, and nobles—who try to
convince him that their life is best. Fully cog-
nizant of his alternatives, Adam chooses to be
a minstrel and is completely happy when he is
reunited with his beloved father and his dog.

Fourteenth-century England is the backdrop for Marguerite de Angeli's *The Door in the
Wall* (I-A), a magnificent Newbery Award–
winning story about a crippled boy. Robin's father has gone off to fight in the Scottish wars
and his mother is in service as a lady-in-wait-
ing to the queen. Robin is waiting to be taken

as a page to Sir Peter de Lindsay when he is
stricken by the crippling plague. Brother Luke
rescues Robin and takes him to the monastery
to nurse him back to health. There, Brother
Luke also teaches the now-crippled boy to walk
with crutches, to read, to write, to swim, and
most important of all, to have patience. Brother
Luke continually reminds Robin that whenever
there is an obstacle—a wall—there is someplace, a door in the wall, where one can go beyond the problem. Robin learns to search for
and work for the doors in the walls that face
him. Eventually Robin reports as a page to Sir
Peter, who assures him that there are many
ways to serve one's king. During a siege, Robin
swims across an icy river to seek help and becomes Sir Robin for his valiant deeds. The castles, churches, monasteries, and pageantry of
the medieval period are shown in stark contrast to the bitterness of life among the common folk. As readers enjoy a gripping story,
they will be learning a great deal about life in
medieval England.

John Goodall produced two picture books
that visually convey the changes from medieval
times to the present. In *The Story of an English
Village* (P-I-A), he shows the growth from a
medieval clearing to the urban congestion of
the present day. Using the same vantage point
for perspective, Goodall captures the scene approximately every hundred years in half-page
inserts that ingeniously alter the scene and un-
roll the pageantry of history. In the early
pages, peasants haul logs on ancient wagons
while the beginnings of a castle take shape on
the top of a hill. Interior scenes show changes
in the social patterns of living as the exterior
ones reveal the addition of more houses, horse-
drawn carriages, and eventually automobiles.
The castle, the church, the market cross, and
one house survive to some extent down
through the centuries in this beautiful book
without words. In *The Story of a Castle* (P-I-A),
Goodall shows the step-by-step construction of

a castle in the same artful manner. Full-page spreads of colorful detail with half-page inserts follow the laborious and treacherous work involving the years and the hundreds of people required to build a castle.

Three excellent picture books appropriate for older students that illuminate life in medieval days are *A Medieval Feast* by Aliki, and *Merry Ever After* and *A Tournament of Knights* (all P-I) by Joe Lasker. Aliki's *A Medieval Feast* shows the weeks of preparation and bustle in a manor house as the nobility and their serfs prepare for a festive visit from the king and queen and their entourage. They hunt, harvest, fish, clean, and bake in preparation for the banquet, which is elegant beyond words. Aliki's jewel-toned paintings go far beyond the text to provide a sense of the times.

Lasker's *Merry Ever After* has as a subtitle *The Story of Two Medieval Weddings.* One wedding is for peasants; the other, for nobility. Anne and Gilbert, born to noblemen, are betrothed by their fathers when Anne is 10 and Gilbert is 11 years old. The marriage will take place when Anne is 15, but she will not see Gilbert until the wedding day. During the intervening five years, many people work on arrangements for the two families as the major event comes near. In glorious splendor, Anne and Gilbert are wed in a cathedral.

On the very same day, in one of the lord's distant villages, another marriage takes place. Martha and Simon's betrothal and wedding are much simpler. Martha's father, a blacksmith, tells the other serfs he is ready to give his daughter in marriage. Simon's father, a plowman, is interested after he checks the size of the dowry that will accompany her. Martha and Simon have always known each other and do not question their fathers' choices.

In *A Tournament of Knights*, readers learn the background and ignoble conditions that surrounded medieval tournaments. Baron Orlando announces the tournament to honor his son, Lord Justin, who has just been made a knight. Sir Rolf's father, a poor nobleman without land, can only give his son advice—questionable at that. He tells Rolf to fight for profit first and later, after he has wealth and power, to fight for honor and chivalry. Rolf challenges Justin in hopes of winning his fortune; Justin must accept the challenge to defend his honor. The games of the tournament culminate in Rolf's challenge to Justin and their battle. Although Justin finally unseats Rolf and wins, he knows that Rolf was the better man and that his victory was due to luck. Lasker's full-color illustrations extend the text and visually describe the medieval pageantry.

Biography

The study of the medieval period is enriched by two biographies, one of Eleanor of Aquitaine, the other of Leonardo da Vinci. *Queen Eleanor: Independent Spirit of the Medieval World* (I-A) by Polly Schoyer Brooks captures the spirit of power, intelligence, and grandeur of a truly remarkable woman. This woman was the wife of two kings, mother of two others, grandmother of an emperor, and great-grandmother of a saint. In addition, she arranged marriages for her children who were not in the direct line of succession that also produced a number of other rulers. Eleanor had strengths other than her dynasty, though: she led reforms, negotiated with religious and political leaders, and brought an appreciation of the arts into her court. Her influence helped establish the ideals of romantic love; her chivalrous court became the standard for social conduct throughout Europe. Brooks separates legend from fact in this enchanting life story of a fascinating woman.

Leonardo da Vinci: The Artist, Inventor, Scientist in Three-Dimensional Movable Pictures (P-I-A) by Alice and Martin Provensen pushes the boundaries of pop-up books to their highest ideals. The Provensens' art and skillful paper engineering combine to provide an artistic look at this creator's life and work. The Provensens include reproductions of some of da Vinci's work, including the *Mona Lisa* as it stood on the easel. As you pull the tab to bring the painting forward, da Vinci faces you, brush in hand, as if you caught him in the midst of work. This unusual biography calls for repeated viewing.

EXPLORATIONS

Whether in real life or in books, explorations of the unknown, where the explorers find danger and mystery, mesmerize. Accounts of the navigators of the earlier world are as intriguing to today's children as travels to the moon or to Mars. Explorers of the past and those of the present need the same kind of courage and willingness to face the unknown.

Vikings

The cadences of an ancient saga permeate Erik Haugaard's novel, *Hakon of Rogen's Saga* (I), and its sequel, *A Slave's Tale* (I). In the first person, Hakon tells of his exile and his struggle to regain the birthright stolen by a cruel uncle. Helga, a slave girl, continues the story of the harsh but heroic Viking people from *her* point of view in *A Slave's Tale*. Themes of slavery of the mind and slavery of power are interwoven in both stories. Haugaard states that he has not blunted his pen in writing for young people and asks to be judged by adult standards; even when judged by the highest standards, he succeeds. Readers savor the metaphorical language: disasters lurk behind each day; pride makes a poor shield. Images of the Vikings crystallize in such prose.

In *Leif the Unlucky* (I-A), Haugaard writes with vivid detail about the last survivors of an abandoned Norwegian colony set in early fifteenth-century Greenland. A small band of farmers whose lives are endangered by frozen lands dream of returning to Norway, but they have no ships or wood to build them. Instead, they fight among themselves for possession of an island that grows more ice bound each year. Leif recognizes that the old men of the village have given up hope so he brings together a group of young people to fight off another group led by the bloodthirsty Egil. The dramatic struggle can only lead to tragedy which, indeed, it does. Although the story carries a sense of gloom and the inevitable, it is suspenseful and conveys the drama of the hardships the Vikings endured.

Henry Treece, another English writer steeped in the history of the Norse, writes convincingly about an eighth-century man, Harald Sigurdson, in a trilogy: *Viking's Dawn, The Road to Miklagard,* and *Viking's Sunset* (all I-A). The daring sea chases, plunderings, and burial at sea keep modern readers excited about Viking lore.

Tales of the Vikings often tell about coastal raids to conquer new lands as well as the never-ending struggle for power among themselves. Leif Erickson's life, representative of the Viking explorer, is the basis of Ingri and Edgar Parin d'Aulaire's picture biography *Leif the Lucky* (P-I). The d'Aulaires' excellent stone lithography illustrations convey the strength and valor of a man who roamed the seas hundreds of years ago.

In Clyde Robert Bulla's *Viking Adventure* (P-I), a follow-up of Leif Erickson's exploration to Vineland is described as it might have occurred. Sigurd, a young Norwegian boy, hears from his father stories of the distant Vineland discovered by Leif and to which his father dreams of returning. Sigurd fulfills his father's dreams by making the journey—one in which human treacheries prove to be as great as those from the uncharted seas. Adroitly, Bulla establishes strong characterization to build high tension in the plot. One third grade class, after reading the story, became enamored of Viking lore and produced several projects, including a journal of Sigurd's journey, a model of his ship, and a map of the route taken.

ACTIVITY: TEACHER TO STUDENT

NORSE MYTHS (I)   The Norse myths, a part of the Viking culture, provided models of strength and power for their hearers, just as the sagas of valorous deeds also inspired some to strike out for far-off lands. The stories about the powerful gods and men of the Vikings, as told in the Norse myths and sagas, are subtle integrations of literature and history.

Reading Ingri and Edgar Parin d'Aulaire's *Norse Gods and Giants* (I-A) is a good way to begin a study of Norse mythology as a part of a study of the Vikings. As you read the myths, examine the illustrations and the endpapers, which illustrate the nine Norse worlds.

Identify the major Norse gods and tell which domains they ruled. In what ways are Greek gods similar or different? Identify story threads, and the ideas of a cycle of life and death and of the relatedness of fertility and seasons, which appear in both Greek and Norse myths.

Most of the names of the days of the week derive from Norse gods— Tuesday is named for Tiu; Wednesday, Odin; Thursday, Thor; and Friday, Freya. Research the stories of these gods and their characteristics. Find other allusions in our language to the Norse myths.

Dramatize and read in chorus a Viking saga. What events do the sagas tell about that were later verified by archaeological findings?

Use these sources in investigating Norse myths:

Ingri and Edgar Parin d'Aulaire, *Norse Gods and Giants* (I-A)
Margaret Hodges, *Baldur and the Mistletoe: A Myth of the Vikings* (I)
Cynthia King, *In the Morning of Time: The Story of the Norse God Baldur* (I)
Ann Pyk, *The Hammer of Thunder* (P-I)

Scandinavian folklore, especially the sagas, provides additional insights concerning the Viking age and, combined with other sources, supplements and modifies interpretations made by archaeologists and historians. In *The Vinlanders' Saga* (I), Barbara Schiller rewrites a saga dealing with the discovery and exploration of North America 500 years before Christopher Columbus. She cautions that though the facts of history in the saga may not be accurate, the humanity of history can be heard in the voices of the Vikings and seen through their eyes. That Scandinavian folklore embodied much authentic history is borne out by the records kept by Icelandic scribes, which verifies the idea that much history is reflected in the literature of a culture.

Columbus and After

From the early fifteenth to the mid-sixteenth centuries, adventurers from many European countries actively explored the world, with the Portuguese, Spanish, and English dominating the seas. In many schools, Christopher Columbus's discovery of America in 1492 is parroted as fact but most books today provide a broader historical perspective. Frances FitzGerald, in

America Revised: History Schoolbooks in the Twentieth Century (adult), comments on some of the changes in viewpoint:

> Poor Columbus! He is a minor character now, a walk-on in the middle of American History. Even those books that have not replaced his picture with a Mayan temple or an Iroquois mask do not credit him with discovering America—even for the Europeans. The Vikings, they say, preceded him to the New World, and . . . having lost or forgotten their maps, simply neglected to cross the ocean again for five hundred years.[12]

Ellen Pugh, in *Brave His Soul* (I-A), presents the theory that a Welsh prince, Madog, came to North America in 1170, over three centuries before Columbus. She also discusses evidence that the Mandan Indians were possibly the first discoverers of America. Books such as this, which present conflicting reports, get children to question, not to accept uncritically, what they find in books. Authors recognize that they can give children their perceptions of the truth without closing the doors of their readers' minds to alternate explanations.

Scott O'Dell has written numerous historical fiction stories about the explorers of the New World. In *The King's Fifth* (I-A), 15-year-old Esteban sails with Admiral Alarcon as a cartographer, carrying supplies for Coronado. The expedition goes astray and Esteban's small

TEACHING IDEA

EVALUATING FACTS IN HISTORICAL FICTION (I)   Any report or account, and certainly those constituting historical fiction or historical biography, is of necessity an interpretation. Children need to learn that what they read in historical books is only one person's view of what happened, rather than an incontrovertible account. One way to make this evident is to compare books that present divergent views of the same person or event.

ACTIVITY: TEACHER TO STUDENT

COMPARE FACTS IN FICTION (I)   Read several books about Christopher Columbus and the discovery of America: *Columbus* (P-I), by Ingri and Edgar Parin d'Aulaire; *The Columbus Story* (P-I), by Alice Dalgleish; and *Following Columbus: The Voyage of the Niña II* (I), by Robert F. Marx. Discuss the following:

How does each author describe the discovery of America?
What points differ in the presentations?
What documentation does each author provide?
What would you tell a younger child who asked you who discovered America?

Role-play a discussion between two people in which one person is convinced that Columbus *did* discover America and the other person is convinced that he *did not*.

band is put ashore to find Coronado's camp. His group undertakes a dangerous journey searching for the fabled gold of Cibola; later Esteban is charged with stealing a fifth share of the gold which rightfully is due to the King of Spain. Esteban tells the story as flashback while he sits in prison awaiting trial; these scenes are interwoven with ones from the courtroom. Esteban is given a three-year sentence or an offer of escape if he will return to search for the fabled gold. His choice to remain in prison gives a sense of the ominous nature of his journey.

O'Dell writes with vigor about the Spanish conquest of the Mayan kingdom in a trilogy: *The Captive, The Feathered Serpent,* and *The Amethyst Ring* (all I-A). The story, set in the sixteenth century, begins when Julian Escobar, a young seminarian, is forced to accompany his lord on an expedition to claim a land grant in the New World. Julian narrates the tale, which shows that he is horrified with the slavery and exploitation of the natives, yet he is unable to intervene. Furthermore, he cannot bring his message from his church to them. Unable to stand up to the authority of Don Luis, yet loved by the people, Julian is mistaken for the god Kukulcan by the Mayans, Aztecs, and Incas. The power and adulation go to his head as Julian dreams of restoring the ancient Mayan structures and bringing Christianity to people still practicing human sacrifice. The story of corruption, conquest, greed, and struggle for power continues in the sequels. Today's readers learn that modern problems have an ancient past.

Biography

Despite revisions of long-held beliefs, there are some books that treat Columbus's voyages in time-honored fashion. For example, Ronald Syme's comprehensive *Columbus: Finder of the New World* (I) chronicles the mutiny, starvation, and exhaustion plaguing Columbus's voyages.

Shortly after returning from his fourth voyage, Columbus died, but left long instructions, maps, and charts of the seas for others to use. Themes of courage and sacrifice permeate this adulatory biography.

Robert Meredith and E. Brooks Smith edited original source material for *The Quest of Columbus* (I) and based their biography on Columbus's son's detailed journals. The tone is understandably laudatory. *The High Voyage* (I), by Olga Litowinsky, recounts the explorer's fourth and final voyage to the New World; it, too, is based on the biography by Columbus's son, Fernando.

Gian Paolo Ceserani's *Christopher Columbus* (I) is an informative, well-written biography that chronicles the many travels of the famous explorer. Interesting facts about his life are intermingled with accounts of his travels. Exquisite color paintings by Piero Ventura feature minute details within full-page spreads.

Cesarani records the adventures of *Marco Polo* (I) in another book illustrated by Ventura.

The explorer's many travels are chronicled in Gian Paolo Ceserani's *Christopher Columbus,* which is beautifully illustrated by Piero Ventura.

The text is informative and straightforward as it describes Polo's explorations and discoveries of new lands. It explains why he spent so much time in China with his father and uncle at the court of Kublai Khan and concludes with his return to Venice and his imprisonment.

THE NEW WORLD

Immigrants began sailing to America in the late sixteenth century, some seeking adventure and financial gain, some escaping religious persecution, some hoping to convert the natives, and some seeking political freedom. Economic and social conditions made the New World attractive to people who were willing to sacrifice the known for the possibilities of a promising unknown. The settlements by the English at Roanoke, Jamestown, Plymouth, and Boston are vivid settings for stories based on early colonial life.

COLONIAL LIFE

Roanoke and Jamestown

One of the most fascinating mysteries in American history centers around the lost colony of Roanoke. John White led a small group to America and established the colony at Roanoke in 1587. When he returned to England for supplies, the rest—men, women, and children—stayed on in Roanoke, building the settlement. Delayed by three years because all English ships were in use against the Spanish Armada, he finally returned to find that the colony had disappeared; no trace of its people was ever found. Archaeologists have uncovered groundworks they believe could have been built by the lost colonists. Sonia Levitin, in *Roanoke: A Novel of the Lost Colony* (I-A), embroiders the historical record with her imaginative story of one of the young men who stayed to build the community.

Jean Lee Latham's *This Dear-Bought Land* (I-A) conveys some of the hardship and personal sacrifice of establishing a colony in America. The story begins in England in 1606 and describes young David Warren's attempts to sail with Captain John Smith. David, 15 and small for his age, wants to carry on his family's tradition as a blustering sea dog, but Smith disparagingly decrees that the difficult journey is not for women and children.

Elizabeth Campbell chronicles the story of Jamestown in *Jamestown: The Beginning* (I). Written from the points of view of the settlers, the ship's crew, the American Indians, and the

ACTIVITIES: TEACHER TO STUDENT

ROANOKE AND JAMESTOWN (I-A)   Dramatize the scene between David Warren and John Smith—two of the characters of Jean Lee Latham's *This Dear-Bought Land* (I-A)—in which David pleads with Captain Smith to allow him to go with him to America. Shift the scene to three years later, when David, who has decided to stay in Jamestown rather than return to England, says goodbye to Captain Smith, who, wounded, is returning to England.

Also, research information about Roanoke and Jamestown, and find out what roles were played by John White, Virginia Dare, John Smith, John Rolfe, and Pocahontas.

Write your version of what may have happened to Roanoke.

captain of the expedition, the author, using documented sources, conveys the suspense of the journey and the joy and thankfulness at the long-awaited sighting of land.

Master storyteller Clyde Robert Bulla tells about Amanda Freebold and her brother and sister, Jemmy and Meg, in *A Lion to Guard Us* (P–I). In 1609, young Amanda is forced to work as a servant for crotchety Miss Trippett as she fills in for her mother who is dreadfully ill after their father has gone to Jamestown to build houses for the colonists. Jemmy and Meg beg Amanda to tell them the story of how their father took the brass door knocker shaped as a lion's head from their own front door and gave it to them before he left. The impoverished children's mother dies and, fearful about their future, the children find a way to go to America where they are reunited with their father. The symbolic meaning of the brass doorknocker serves to give the children courage in their journey.

Biography

Jean Fritz is noted for her meticulous research in the historical and biographical novels she writes. *The Double Life of Pocahontas* (I) meets her highest standards with its maps, informational notes, bibliography, and index. In 1607, Pocahontas was 11 years old and happy in the knowledge that her father, Chief Powhatan, favored her most. On April 26 of that year, when the English settlers reached the Chesapeake Bay, 27-year-old John Smith was among them. Fritz describes the quarrelsome relationships among the Jamestown colonists and the varied friendships with Chief Powhatan and his tribe. When Pocahontas intercedes to save Captain John Smith's life, he is adopted by the tribe and Pocahontas grows to love her adopted brother. She travels freely between the white world and the Indian world, fully accepted by both. But then there is trouble. Pocahontas is kidnapped by the settlers and forced to live solely in their world. Later, she marries John

Rolfe and returns with him to live in England. Fritz shows the turmoil that surrounds Pocahontas and the Jamestown colonists between 1607 and 1622. The conflict of cultures and the uneasy truce forces Pocahontas to sacrifice one world to live in another.

New England and New York

Patricia Clapp uses a diary format to tell the story of the early settlers through the eyes of a young girl in *Constance: A Story of Early Plymouth* (I–A). Constance, the daughter of Stephen Hopkins, is not as enthusiastic as her father about the promise of the new land. An opinionated girl, she expresses her distaste for certain people freely. Her insights breathe life into the people who appear in her diary, which continues until 1626.

In Margaret Hodges's book about Constance's father, *Hopkins of the Mayflower: Portrait of a Dissenter* (I–A), the character of Hopkins is a composite of Elizabethan men who sought profit and adventure in the New World. Because the last sections of this book overlap the

The story of the Pilgrims' struggles at Plymouth, how they were aided by the natives, and how settlers and Indians came together to give thanks for the bountiful harvest forms the cornerstone of our cultural heritage. (From *The Pilgrims of Plimoth* by Marcia Sewall.)

TEACHING IDEA

SETTLERS AT PLYMOUTH AND THE FIRST THANKSGIVING (P-I)   Stories of the early settlers who faced countless obstacles but joined together with the local Indians in Thanksgiving at their first harvest celebration have become legends. Collect several different accounts of the Pilgrims and the first Thanksgiving as the basis for a vivid lesson in critical reading. Include the following:

Anderson, *The First Thanksgiving Feast* (P-I)
Barth, *Turkeys, Pilgrims, and Indian Corn: The Story of Thanksgiving Symbols.* (I)
Clapp, *Constance: A Story of Early Plymouth* (I-A)
Dalgleish, *The Thanksgiving Story* (P-I)

Fritz, *Who's That Stepping on Plymouth Rock?* (P-I)
Sewall, *The Pilgrims of Plimoth* (P-I)
Voight, *Massasoit: Friend of the Pilgrims* (P-I)
Wyndham, *A Holiday Book: Thanksgiving* (I)

Have the students compare versions to see how the stories about the Pilgrims and the first Thanksgiving vary.

Fact or Fiction? List all of the facts (or purported facts) about Pilgrims and the first Thanksgiving and give the sources.

Are there discrepancies in the reports? What differences are there? How do the
   versions vary?
What is reported as factual? What is reported as fiction?
What documentation do the authors provide for their facts?
What are the qualifications of the author? What sources were used? Check additional
   references provided to verify accounts.
List the facts that have the strongest support.
Discuss how and why the stories vary.

Write to the National Park Service for brochures about Plimoth Plantation.

---

years described in *Constance,* they can serve for interesting comparisons.

Jean Fritz takes an unusual approach in *Who's That Stepping on Plymouth Rock?* (P-I), which is, in effect, a biography of the rock. She tells of the number of times Plymouth Rock has been moved, and the discussions that have arisen about its prominence in history; she adds a touch of humor to a subject that has long been treated with reverence.

Squanto: Friend of the Pilgrims (P-I) by Clyde Robert Bulla is a biography that young readers can enjoy. Bulla's relaxed style and natural sto-

rytelling bent serve him well as he describes Squanto's life and his encounters with the early settlers. Some readers are surprised to learn that Squanto had lived and studied in England—a far different person from the stereotypic deerskin and feathers Indian often pictured with the early settlers at the first Thanksgiving feast.

Eilis Dillon writes sensitively of young Andrew's adventures as he travels from Yorkshire to the New World in *The Seekers* (I-A). Andrew had not planned to leave Yorkshire, but he learns that the girl he hopes to marry, Rebecca, is sailing for America with her father, so he persuades his friend Edward to join him in following her. Andrew finds that the hazardous voyage and the difficult adjustment to life among the "Saints," the Puritans who had founded Boston a decade earlier to follow their strict religion, was not the adventure he imagined. Life in New England was grim, plagued by problems with the Indians and the puritanical lifestyle of the colonists. Andrew and Rebecca are torn by the question of whether to stay or to return home, but they eventually decide to return to Yorkshire. Dillon paints a picture of life of the early settlers that is grim and unyielding.

By 1692, the early settlers were well established in their new communities and were stern guardians of the religious views, pious behavior, and moral standards. In Salem, Massachusetts, several young girls were titillated by colorful tales recounted by a Barbadian slave, Tituba. The girls interpreted these tales according to the rigid Puritanical beliefs, and though they may have started as innocent storytelling, they ultimately caused the death of 20 people convicted in the infamous Salem witch trials.

Patricia Clapp uses a first-person narrator in *Witches' Children* (A) to bring a sense of im-mediacy and a personal view to the terrifying events in Salem. Mary Warren, an adolescent bound in service to a Salem family, is only mildly interested in the tales and fortune-telling she hears Tituba spinning for her and her friends. However, Mary is aware that Abigail Williams, a member of the audience, is craftily pushing Tituba to wilder extremes for her own excitement and subtle purposes. Mary tells the story of mass hysteria and witch trials from her own point of view, a literary device that makes it all seem more possible and comprehensible.

In Elizabeth Speare's *The Witch of Blackbird Pond* (I-A), winner of the 1959 Newbery Award, Kit befriends an old woman living outside the village and discovers the principle of guilt by association when she is accused, together with the old woman, of being a witch.

Leonard Everett Fisher's *The Warlock of Westfall* (I-A) adds another perspective on the witchcraft hysteria that swept Massachusetts in 1692. In the story, Samuel Swift, a lonely, eccentric bachelor in his late seventies, is accused, tried, and hanged; Westfall was close enough to Salem Village to be infected by its hysteria. Ann Petry, in *Tituba of Salem Village* (I-A), relates the dramatic Salem story from the point of view of Tituba, the slave woman ac-

ACTIVITY: TEACHER TO STUDENT

WITCH HUNTS (A) The witchcraft trials in Salem Village in 1692 have been reported in fiction and nonfiction. Compare the books and identify points on which they differ.

You may want to draw some tentative conclusions about the causes and outcomes of the witchcraft trials. Also, describe the commonly held view of witches, and look for modern cases that resemble witchcraft trials. What has the term "witch hunt" come to mean in our language?

You might also discuss the events of 1692 from the perspectives of people involved: Tituba, Reverend Parris, Cotton Mather. Dramatize one of the trials in which the young girls accuse Tituba of witchery.

cused of witchcraft because of her innocent storytelling.

Marion Starkey's books, *The Devil in Massachusetts* (A), *The Visionary Girls* (A), and *The Tall Man from Boston* (A), are based on careful research of the historical record and show meticulous attention to detail. The third of these books focuses on an incident in which Tituba charges a "tall man from Boston" with devil dealing. The terrified villagers need someone to fit Tituba's hysterical description and fall upon John Alden, son of Myles Standish's famous friend.

Another story that portrays life at the time of the witchtrials yet is not connected to them is *Mercy Short* (A), by Norma Farber. Seventeen-year-old Mercy has been captured by the Indians, given birth to a child who died, and marched to Quebec and is now ransomed to Cotton Mather's Boston church. Mather prays exhaustingly for forgiveness of her sins and asks her to keep a diary so that he might know more precisely what demons he must exorcise. Her diary entries span December 1691 to March 1692, but they do not provide Reverend Mather with the documentation he needs. Instead, we read about her personal anguish over her lost child, her parents, and her questions about the rightness of the beliefs she holds. She weighs the values of Indian life, such as kindness to children, appreciation of nature, and the freedom to celebrate with joy against the dour, stark, and punitive values of her religious community.

Nathaniel Hawthorne was born in Salem, Massachusetts, a descendant of a judge in the celebrated witchcraft trials. His heritage accounts for his interest in writing two fictional accounts of the era. *The Scarlet Letter* and *Young Goodman Brown* (both adult) vividly portray the repressive atmosphere that prevailed among the early New England people so devoutly concerned with their religious life.

Peter Stuyvesant is one of the more colorful characters among the early settlers of New York. Robert Quackenbush describes him in *Old Silver Leg Takes Over! A Story of Peter Stuyvesant* (P-I), and Arnold Lobel portrays him in *On the Day Peter Stuyvesant Sailed into Town* (P-I). Both books depend heavily on illustration to add significant detail, but both can extend young readers' understanding of the Dutch settlement that became New York. The text in both books is simple but informative, with a touch of humor and hyperbole apropos of Peter Stuyvesant. Lobel's final drawing shocks the reader with the full-page spread of what the small village of New Amsterdam was to become: New York City with all the glare and bustle.

The Colonial Frontier

Accounts of the adventures and dangers surrounding the early settlers of the original 13 colonies appear frequently. Alice Dalgliesh's *The Courage of Sarah Noble,* illustrated by Leonard Weisgard (P-I), vividly describes the experiences of an eight-year-old girl who goes with her father to establish a new home on the Connecticut frontier. Indians help the colonists in this and other stories, including Elizabeth Yates's *Carolina's Courage,* illustrated by Nora S. Unwin (P-I), in which a doll given to young Carolina assures safe travel through Indian territory. Anne Colver's *Bread and Butter Indian* and *Bread and Butter Journey,* both illustrated by Garth Williams (and both P-I), tell of the friendship between a white girl and an Indian in the New Hampshire wilderness. Jean Fritz tells about a lonely girl's resentment of her family's move to the Pennsylvania frontier in *The Cabin Faced West,* illustrated by Feodor Rojankovsky (P-I).

THE REVOLUTIONARY WAR PERIOD

Neither the beginning nor the end of the American Revolution is clearly marked in time, nor is the story clearly told. Some colonists resented paying taxes to England when they were not represented in the English Parliament. Many, however, remained loyal to King George III and fully disapproved of the rebellious leaders who agitated for the independence of the colonies.

Fiction set in this period frequently involves divided loyalties in colonial families or communities. Authors often tell the story through the eyes of a child or an adolescent character who supports the rebels but whose parents remain loyal to Britain.

James Lincoln Collier and Christopher Collier tell of one family caught in conflicting loyalties in *my brother Sam is dead* (I-A). The father, a Connecticut tavern-keeper, thinks the colonists have a few legitimate complaints against England but nothing serious enough to cause bloodshed. Twelve-year-old Tim idolizes his brother Sam, who reports in detail on his debates when he comes home from college. Tim

The bitter ending of a tale of divided loyalties is revealed in the title of this book about the American Revolution. (Illustration from *my brother Sam is dead* by Karl W. Stuecklen. Written by James Lincoln Collier and Christopher Collier.)

ACTIVITIES: TEACHER TO STUDENT

LITERARY ANALYSIS (I-A)   After you finish reading *my brother Sam is dead*, (I-A) by James L. Collier and Christopher Collier, use the following questions to rethink and discuss some of the important parts:

1. What did the title suggest before you read the story? What does it reveal about who is telling the story? Where in the story do you begin to realize the full significance of the title?
2. What clues do you find in the first four pages of historic events that set the scene for the story? For example, "went on up to Concord" (p. 2); "the Minute Men hid in the fields" (p. 2); "somebody signalled them from some church steeple in Boston" (p. 4).
3. When do you discover there is family conflict? For example, Sam's father corrects him when he speaks of "lobster backs" (p. 4); and his father's comments: "I will not have treason spoken in my house," and "Nobody wants rebellion except fools and hotheads" (p. 6).
4. How does the conflict become a central theme in the story? How is the conflict affecting Tim when he says: "It made me nervous to listen to Sam argue with Father" (p. 7); and "It seemed to me that everybody was to blame, and I decided that I wasn't going to be on anybody's side any more: neither one of them was right" (p. 167)?
5. Compare this book with Esther Forbes's *Johnny Tremain* (I-A).

begs for Sam's stories, savoring the clever "telling points" Sam makes against his opponents. Conflict begins when Sam arrives home wearing a rebel uniform, and it increases in intensity as the family becomes enmeshed in the struggle between loyalists and rebels. Sam is accused of stealing cattle, and an ironic turn of events leads to the bitter outcome foretold in the title.

Esther Forbes's classic story *Johnny Tremain* (I-A) describes the life of an apprentice to silversmith Paul Revere. Injured when he disobeys safety procedures, Johnny must learn to overcome not only his disability but also his strong, independent spirit. The frenzied activities in Boston are carefully described as actual historical figures, including John Adams and Benjamin Franklin, lead the fight for independence.

The Colliers also collaborated on a trilogy that includes *Jump Ship to Freedom, War Comes to Willy Freeman,* and *Who Is Carrie?* (all I-A). Dan Arabus tells the story, beginning in 1787, of his flight from slavery and his unscrupulous owner, Captain Ivers. Dan runs away after a frightening sea voyage and is protected by a Quaker on his way to the Constitutional Convention in Philadelphia. Dan carries the proposal that becomes known as the fugitive slave law to the convention. In *War Comes to Willy Freeman,* a thirteen-year-old free black girl, Wilhelmina Freeman, is caught up in the Revolutionary War. After her father is killed right before her eyes and her mother disappears, Willy flees down the Connecticut coast to relatives, the Arabus family. The family does not trust their unprincipled master, Captain Ivers, who they fear will sell Willy back into slavery. She disguises herself as a boy and escapes from the Ivers house to go to New York. There she works for Black Sam Fraunces for nearly two years until she learns that her mother is critically ill and dying. Risking Ivers's wrath, she returns to participate in a trial in which her uncle sues for his freedom and wins. The final

book is an attempt to find out *Who Is Carrie?*, a young black girl who works in Fraunces Tavern in New York. As in all of the Colliers's work, the historical incidents are based on authentic records. They are meticulous in providing accurate details of the period, including the trial, Fraunces Tavern, the language, and geography.

War seems exciting and glamorous to some young people before they know the cruelties and suffering it brings. Avi describes such a young boy, 13-year-old Jonathan, in *The Fighting Ground* (I-A), a riveting novel that takes

Young Jonathan experiences in one day the events that transform him from an idealistic boy to a young man who grasps the realities of war and respects those who feel they must fight. (From *The Fighting Ground* by Avi.)

place in a single day. On April 3, 1778, at 9:58 in the morning, Jonathan first heard the bell from a tavern calling the men to arms. He wanted to join the fight against the British, their German-speaking Hessian allies, and the Tories, American traitors who sided with the British. By 11:00 a.m., a corporal says to Jonathan, "You said you could shoot. Get a musket from the tavern. You're needed." Jonathan is proud to obey but by 4:30 in the afternoon, he is begging to be released from the senseless killing. By 10:30 at night, Jonathan returns home, happy to be alive and understanding more about his father, himself, and his feelings about war. Avi received the Scott O'Dell Award for Historical Fiction for this tightly structured masterpiece.

Scott O'Dell based his story of *Sarah Bishop* (I-A) on the experiences of an actual person by that name who lived during the Revolutionary War period. Sarah lived in fear after her father, who did not hide his sympathy for the British, was tarred and feathered by zealous patriots. After her brother died on a British prison ship, she was falsely arrested. Sarah hides out in the Connecticut wilderness where she struggles to stay alive. Her return to civilization is more an inner battle than a physical one, however, as she recognizes how different she is from her compatriots.

Early Thunder (I), by Jean Fritz, is the story of 14-year-old Daniel, who shares his father's loyalist viewpoint at first but gradually moves toward sympathy with the rebels. His change in allegiance leads to a family confrontation.

Such stories, by presenting political issues of the Revolution in terms of family and personal conflicts, engage the reader's emotions. Readers' identification with the fictional characters helps clarify motives of historical figures and gives meaning to the choices that had to be made.

Robert Newton Peck's stories, set near Fort Ticonderoga, are about Ethan Allen and the Green Mountain Boys. *Hang for Treason* (A), set in 1745, depicts in earthy language some of the conflict and unrest that led to the Revolutionary War. In *Rabbits and Redcoats* (A), Peck shows romantic notions of war evaporating in the midst of battle. Two teenaged boys who have sneaked into the ranks of the Vermont revolutionaries so they can brag that they fought with Ethan, learn that battles are not glamorous and that honor and dignity depend upon more than fighting.

A briefer book dealing with the Revolutionary period is Patricia Gauch's *This Time, Tempe Wick?* (P-I), which gives a humorous account of American soldiers encamped in New Jersey who confiscate food and horses from farmers. When Tempe Wick learns that her horse Bonny may be one of them, she hides it in her bedroom. The author's note adds authenticity to the story, for there *was* a Bonny, and her hoofprints remain on the bedroom floor to this day. Tempe's creative resolution of the problem adds a spark of life to history.

Legends of the Revolution

Legends from the American Revolutionary period are abundant; the national pride and desire to create a legacy gave rise to stories that were quickly embellished. Many of the legends are distortions and exaggerations of actual events. Tracing the origins of the stories, separating fact and fiction, adds adventure and mystery to the study of history.

Fiction says that Betsy Ross made the first flag; fact says that nobody knows who made it. According to legend, George Washington asked Betsy Ross, a seamstress in Philadelphia, to make a flag with 13 stars and stripes to represent the 13 colonies. Supposedly, he sketched six-pointed stars, but she suggested five-pointed ones. There is no historical evidence to support the story; Betsy Ross's grandson, William J. Canby, first told it at a meeting of the Philadelphia Historical Society in 1870, almost a century after the supposed event.

Fiction says that George Washington chopped down a cherry tree when he was 6 years old and, admitting to the offense, said "I cannot tell a lie." Fact says there is no historical truth to the tale. The story first appeared in a biography of George Washington by Parson Mason Locke Weems who credited George not with cutting down the tree but only with cutting through the bark. Biographies of George Washington help to separate the fiction that has been embroidered into the facts. Genevieve Foster's *George Washington's World* (I), and Robin McKown's *Washington's America* (I) are comprehensive biographies that clarify fact and fiction. McKown states that the cherry tree story is the most popular fanciful tale told about Washington, and true or not, the cherry tree story lives on as a part of American folklore.

Fiction says that Paul Revere took a midnight ride to warn that the British were coming. Fact says that one other man set out with him to warn the colonists, that on the way they picked up a third messenger, and that Revere was captured by a British patrol in Lexington. Largely because Henry Wadsworth Longfellow's poem does not mention William Dawes or Samuel Prescott, they have been dropped from the popular historical record of the event.

Jean Poindexter Colby, in *Lexington and Concord, 1775* (I), discusses how the facts about the past can become distorted:

What one writer said might have happened on one day, the next writer said *did* happen on that day. In this way incidents that did not occur became "facts," and people appeared or disappeared on the scene at the will of the historians,

ACTIVITY: TEACHER TO STUDENT

DISPEL THE MYTHS (I-A)   Read several different accounts of a historical legend to discover any differences. Identify statements based on opinion. Look carefully for documentation and for statements that seem direct and factual but are not.

Check for authenticity of an account by asking yourself the following questions:

1. How did the story first get started; when and where was it first told?
2. What documentation or sources does the author provide?
3. What do you think happened? What evidence supports your position?
4. Do any words make it seem that the author is not certain about the truthfulness of the story? For example, are phrases such as "some people say" or "there is a story that" used?
5. Does the author make up dialogue for imagined meetings between historical figures? (There may be justification for created dialogue; discuss possible reasons.)

The following reference books can be useful in tracing some of the stories:

Tom Burnham, *Dictionary of Misinformation (I-A)*.
L. Ethan Ellis, *Forty Million School Books Can't Be Wrong: Myths in American History* (I).
Robert Myers et al., *Celebrations: The Complete Book of American Holidays* (I-A).

essayists, or—in one important instance—a poet. Henry Wadsworth Longfellow, for example, took the events and the characters that appealed to him and made a narrative poem of them. His "Paul Revere's Ride" has been the favorite source of information on the subject for one hundred years even though he omitted such an important man as William Dawes, and had Paul Revere spreading the alarm of the British march in Concord in spite of the fact that he never got there. There are many other historical errors in it but it is still published for children and taken as truth, presumably.[13]

Students need to read Longfellow's poem in conjunction with the many other—and more authentic—reports about the important events of 1775 and 1776.

Biography

Biographies about the people involved in the American Revolution give a serious view of their beliefs, sometimes a humorous glimpse of their foibles, and, ideally, a feeling that they were real people with blood in their veins.

Jean Fritz decries the way we turn people from our past into stone statues to revere. She prefers to enter their world, match their words to their actions, follow the criss-cross of their public and private lives, and accept them finally as friends. Fritz feels that a picture that shows a believable human being is preferable to one that idealizes the subject as a saint.[14]

She contends that humor is one of the most effective ways to appreciate the past and to see historical figures as fully human. Instead of stale facts about leaders of the American Revolution, she presents affectionate and well-informed biographical narratives. Each of her titles is a question: *Why Don't You Get a Horse, Sam Adams?; What's the Big Idea, Ben Franklin?; And Then What Happened, Paul Revere?; Where Was Patrick Henry on the 29th of May?; Will You Sign Here, John Hancock?;* and *Can't You Make*

Sam Adams envisions how posterity may see him should he fail to learn to ride a horse. (From *Why Don't You Get a Horse, Sam Adams?* by Jean Fritz, illustrated by Trina Schart Hyman.)

Them Behave, King George? (all P-I). Their brevity, humanizing personal insights, and humorous illustrations make these biographical narratives favorites. Share them among a group, with readers assigned one book, describing and explaining it to the others, or presenting their subject in creative impersonation. In *Why Don't You Get a Horse, Sam Adams?* (P-I), for example, Fritz pokes fun at Adams's refusal to ride a horse. Adams finally relents, however, so that his historical image remains untarnished, and he appears in sculptured representations not on foot but mounted like his contemporaries.

Traitor: The Case of Benedict Arnold (I-A) is another excellent biography by Jean Fritz. Benedict Arnold's life is presented in an objective way; he is not judged by the author—she leaves that up to the reader. Fritz chronicles his life and shows his deeds in the bright light of a detached observer; they speak for themselves to show an egotist who believed that his talents were not recognized. Fritz provides a thorough

PROFILE

Jean Fritz

Jean Fritz was 5 years old when she announced to her father that she was going to be a writer; she would write about America. At the time, she was living in China, where her parents were missionaries, and spent a good deal of her time defending her country to a neighbor boy who said derogatory things about George Washington.

For her, America represented an ideal, a place where everything was perfect. As an only child, she spent a lot of time with books and "learned early that words could get me where I wanted to go, which was simply some place else but most especially America."[15] As soon as she could write, she composed stories about children doing all the American things she dreamed of doing—exploding firecrackers on the Fourth of July and going to grandmother's house for Thanksgiving.

After she moved to the United States, she continued to pursue her fascination with America. She says that *The Cabin Faced West*, although ostensibly written about her great-great-grandmother's pioneer girlhood, was really her attempt to establish her roots as an American. She has written about other periods in American history, but her favorite is the Revolutionary era.

Fritz bemoans the dull way in which history is usually taught. She believes that stale facts and images should be replaced with studies that show historical characters as real people and that humorous anecdotes help children relate to history much better than cold dates. Her series of biographies of Revolutionary-era personalities presents fresh insights into the lives of people too often placed on pedestals, beyond understanding and caring.

Fritz lives in Dobbs Ferry, New York, where she takes an active interest in today's national and international concerns. "I join groups, write letters, make phone calls, and have on occasion demonstrated; in short, my life . . . is caught up in the special agonies of the times."[16] She describes her own childhood in China in *Homesick: My Own Story* (I-A) and her visit as an adult in *China Homecoming* (I-A).

Jean Fritz's deep love for and pride in America enrich yesterday's history and that of tomorrow.

section of notes and bibliography to document her sources.

Deborah Sampson, using the name Robert Shurtliff, served for a year and a half as a soldier in the Continental Army. Her masquerade went undiscovered until she was hospitalized for a fever. Patricia Clapp wrote *I'm Deborah Sampson: A Soldier in the War of the Revolution* (I-A) in a lively first-person account of the contribution of this woman. Ann McGovern tells the same story in *The Secret Soldier: The Story of Deborah Sampson* (I). After Deborah Sampson's identity was disclosed, she left the Continental Army but continued to defy convention by traveling and lecturing—unbecoming behavior for a woman of her day. Her story is also told in Cora Cheney's *The Incredible Deborah* (I). Comparing these different approaches to Deborah Sampson's story can provide an excellent experience in critical reading.

Samuel Adams failed at nearly everything he tried, except being a politician; in this role, he excelled. He was elected to a number of minor offices in Boston and to the Boston Assembly in 1765. Words were his best weapon: he wrote under at least 25 different pen names to spread his ideas and stormed around Boston talking to everyone about the injustice of English treatment of the colonists. Fayette Richardson writes about Adams's early life in *Sam Adams: The Boy Who Became Father of the American Revolution* (P-I), and Margaret Green provides another view in *Radical of the Revolution: Samuel Adams* (I-A).

Benjamin Franklin, with his continuing leadership role in the establishment of the new nation, is a favorite subject for biographers. Jeannette Eaton, in *That Lively Man, Ben Franklin* (I), describes his life from an apprenticeship to a printer through political engagements and involvement with the drafting of the Declaration of Independence. James Daugherty writes about a similar period in *Poor Richard* (I)), but also includes Franklin's experiences in London and his role as an inventor, scientist, and pa-

triot. Aliki wrote and illustrated a colorful picture book that describes *The Many Lives of Benjamin Franklin* (P-I). Humorous anecdotes and lively vignettes capture the spirit of this multi-talented man.

George Washington and the Birth of Our Nation (I-A) by Milton Meltzer puts the man in the context of his times, a victim of both ignorance and prejudice. Instead of idealizing a legend, Meltzer paints a realistic picture of George Washington and the world in which he lived. Washington's strength as a leader still shines, although his attitude toward slavery represents the common thought of his day. Meltzer provides documentation in the form of a bibliographic essay, index, reproductions of historic art, manuscript pages, and maps.

Meltzer also captures the spirit of the people involved in the revolution in *The American Revolutionaries: A History in Their Own Words* (I-A). In this carefully researched book, he collects documents from diaries, letters, and other primary sources to show a glimpse of the personal and private lives of people caught up in the American Revolution. In his well-balanced and scholarly approach, Meltzer incorporates various points of view. When he includes a description of a brutal Indian attack, he follows with an account of Colonel George Clark's butchery of the Indian captives. Letters from husbands on the front line to their wives at home, women who accompanied the troops, and blacks who fought with the army are included in this direct account of the people of this era.

Many books are available on the Constitution, but one is illustrative. *If You Were There When They Signed the Constitution* (A) by Elizabeth Levy gives a detailed account of what happened before, during, and after that notable event. This well-researched book helps students to understand the personalities and the reasoning of the signers.

Rhoda Blumberg's *The Incredible Journey of Lewis and Clark* (I-A) is one of the outstanding

Great explorations form the milestones of American history, and one of the most remarkable adventures was Lewis and Clark's expedition to chart the lands of the Louisiana Purchase. (From *The Incredible Journey of Lewis and Clark* by Rhoda Blumberg.)

examples of nonfiction. Filled with excellent photographs and told in a gripping narrative style, Blumberg's book helps us to know these explorers and the bitter conditions they encountered. The Indian girl, Sacajewa, who helped them through treacherous country, played a major part in helping them map the territories that were so important to the growth of America.

AMERICAN INDIANS

The history of America is incomplete without chapters on its native inhabitants, American Indians. Often their story was told by white men who characterized them in stereotyped ways— as ferocious savages, or as downtrodden people who suffer nobly. Although many books perpetuate this teepee-and-feathers image, a growing number now give more accurate portrayals of the native American's culture and a more objective picture of the 300-year clash between the white and American Indian cultures.

Stories for younger children often present a simple view of the interaction between whites and Indians. For example, in Anne Colver's *Bread and Butter Indian* (P-I), young Barbara meets an Indian while she plays in the forest near her family cabin. One day as she has a tea party with her doll Ariminta, she notices an Indian watching her and offers him some of her bread with butter and sugar, instead of running away as her parents had warned her to do. The Indian bows gratefully to thank Barbara for the food then slips away silently through the trees leaving her unharmed. Barbara continues to take bread and butter to her Indian unbeknownst to her parents, although Aunt Dossy shares her secret. One day another Indian comes, however, and takes Barbara back to his village against her wishes. Terrified and alone, she fears she will never see her parents again. In the middle of the night, her old Indian friend helps her to slip away from the tent and guides her home. The story is continued in *Bread and Butter Journey* (P-I).

Scott O'Dell received the Newbery Award for *Island of the Blue Dolphin* (I-A), a story based on fact about a courageous Indian girl, Karana, who lived on an island off the coast of California for 18 years. Karana's village is plundered, and her people plan to leave to search for a more hospitable home. When everyone is aboard and the small canoes are pulling away from shore, Karana sees that her small brother, Ramo, has been left behind. She jumps from the boat and swims back to the small island to care for him. A wild dog pack, led by the ferocious Rontu, roams the island. The dogs attack, and Ramo is killed. Karana has lost everything she cares about: her father, her people, and the brother she sacrificed herself to save. The theme of forgiveness, acceptance, and courage pervade Karana's story as she makes a life for herself and eventually tames Rontu. In a sequel, *Zia* (I-A), Karana's niece, describes Karana's last days in a Spanish mission.

Jamake Highwater's Ghost Horse Cycle of the Northern Plains Indians begins with *Legend Days* (A). Amana's people suffer from the dwindling herds of buffalo and the invasions by white traders, settlers, soldiers, and government restrictions. When she is sent away to escape the smallpox spreading through her village, she gains a vision that gives her the power and song of the fox. She is given status and rank because of her gift. But when her elderly husband is trampled by buffalo, the men hold her responsible. Abandoned and unable to care for herself, she is desolate. Only the symbolic appearance of a fox gives her any hope of survival.

In contrast to this grim story is Elizabeth George Speare's compelling novel about a faltering friendship of a white boy and an Indian boy in the 1700s, entitled *The Sign of the Beaver* (I-A). Thirteen-year-old Matt's father leaves him behind to guard the log cabin they had built in the Maine wilderness while he returns to Massachusetts to bring the rest of the family.

Alone in the wilderness, Matt tries to survive by hunting, but a renegade tramp who asks for shelter steals his gun. Matt has few other resources for finding food in the forest. When he meets proud, resourceful Attean, grandson of the chief of the Beaver Clan, he is dubious about the relationship. Attean makes it obvious that he has been encouraged against his will to meet Matt. The friendship flourishes, however, as Matt teaches Attean to read and Attean teaches Matt how to fish, hunt, and survive in the forest. Matt's respect for the Indian culture grows as he learns more about it.

Within recent decades we have developed a new consciousness about American Indians and about the differences between their concepts and those of the early settlers. The native American believed, for example, that the land belonged to all, while the European settlers, of course, brought with them the idea of individual ownership. Staking their claims to lands that the American Indians had roamed freely for hundreds of years set the stage for conflict—from grisly battles, in which hundreds were killed, to inner conflicts, in which individuals who had come to know each other as friends had to choose between friendship and loyalty to their own people. Several stories, based on true accounts, describe the turmoil of such people caught between two cultures. In *Betrayed* (A), by Virginia Driving Hawk Sneve, three Sioux Indian boys are beset with a moral dilemma: Should they rescue women and children captives despite the broken promises of the Indian agent? In *Indian Captive: The Story of Mary Jemison* (I-A), by Lois Lenski, a woman tries to escape her Seneca Indian captors but finally chooses to remain with them.

William O. Steele, in *The Man with the Silver Eyes* (I-A), tells of Talatu, an 11-year-old Cherokee who hates all whites. Sent to live with Benjamin Shinn, a "silver-eyed" Quaker, Talatu grudgingly comes to respect the peace-loving man even as he endures his fate in noble Cherokee tradition. When Shinn is mortally wounded in an attempt to save Talatu's life, the boy learns that Shinn is his natural father.

Evelyn Sibley Lampman conveys a native American point of view in *Squaw Man's Son* (A), in which Billy Morrison's Modoc Indian mother is sent back to her people by his white father. When his father marries a white woman, who treats Billy with contempt, Billy runs away to live with the Modocs, but finds that they will not accept him. The struggle between the Indians and whites is reflected in conflict both between groups and in the personal life of one boy.

Conrad Richter's *The Light in the Forest* (I-A) is the story of True Son, kidnapped when he is 4 years old and raised by an Indian chief. When a treaty releases all prisoners, True Son must return to his white home, where he finds the ways of the white people intolerable. He returns to his Indian tribe, but when he refuses to participate in an ambush, he is banished. Values clash for True Son, caught between two cultures. A sequel, *A Country of Strangers* (I-A), tells a comparable story of Stone Girl, who attempts to return to a white community after living with her Indian family.

Scott O'Dell's *Sing Down the Moon* (I-A) vividly describes the "Long Walk"—an actual event—of the forced resettlement of the Navajo from Canyon de Chelly to Fort Sumner, New Mexico—300 miles away. O'Dell relates the story through the eyes of Bright Morning, a courageous Navajo woman who wants to escape the disease, poverty, and spiritlessness of the resettlement and return with her husband to the peace of their home in the canyon.

Biography

Blue Jacket: War Chief of the Shawnees (I-A) by Allan Eckert is the story of a white boy captured by the Shawnee Indians in the year 1771. The Shawnees, living in the land now called West

A somber cover reflects the tragic nature of Scott O'Dell's story of the forced resettlement of thousands of Navajo to Fort Sumner, New Mexico. (From *Sing Down the Moon* by Scott O'Dell.)

Virginia which at that time was part of the American frontier, did not kill the boy. Instead, they adopted him into the tribe and gave him the name "Blue Jacket" for the color of the shirt he was wearing at the time of his capture. Blue Jacket learned the Shawnee ways quickly and became recognized as an excellent fighter. The Shawnee nation honored him as they made him their War Chief.

Some Indian tribes were decimated by the whites' appropriation of their territory. Theodora Kroeber details the disappearance of one

ACTIVITY: TEACHER TO STUDENT

INTEGRATING LITERATURE AND THE ARTS (I-A)[17]   After you read Scott O'Dell's *Sing Down the Moon*, choose from the following activities.

Art   Make a large mural showing Canyon de Chelly and the "trail of tears" the Navajo were forced to take to the desolate site of Fort Sumner, or make a diorama of Canyon de Chelly showing the home sites and pastures contrasted with the barren landscape of Fort Sumner.

Written Language   Make a crossword puzzle using words from the story: mesa (p. 3), goading (p. 11), hogan (p. 19), hobble (p. 25), haggle (p. 25), omen (p. 37), baile (p. 39), tethered (p. 47), tortillas (p. 57), sheathed (p. 59), mottled (p. 63), piñon (p. 97), pillaged (p. 136).

Drama   Dramatize a scene from the novel, such as when Tall Boy is taken away to prison, when Bright Morning and Nehana run away, the womanhood ceremony, when the Long Knives come, when the Navajo are forced from the canyon, the Long Walk. Pantomime scenes after listening to a recording of the story.

---

such tribe—the Yana Indians—in *Ishi: Last of His Tribe* (A). The author's husband was curator of the Museum of Anthropology and Ethnology at the University of California when Ishi was found wandering near the ruins of his native village. The Kroebers recorded Ishi's memories of the life of his people and pieced together fragments of tribal history. A sequel, *Ishi in Two Worlds: A Biography of the Last Wild Indian in North America* (A), further recounts the history of the Yana and documents in photographs a way of life now extinct. Ishi served as a consultant to the museum staff and added immeasurably to knowledge about the Yana Indians.

CIVIL WAR

Slavery was a part of American history until the Emancipation Proclamation. Many chapters of American history are grim, but those involving slavery and the Civil War are among the most so; the war was a long, savage contest, costly not the least in human lives. Books about this period offer students accounts of the turmoil and tragedy of the bloody period and of its reverberations still felt today.

The years immediately before the Civil War, although a bleak period in American history, are marked with acts of heroism. Jean Fritz's *Brady* (I-A) tells of a young boy who, because he cannot keep a secret, has not been told by his parents about their activities with the underground railroad. When his father is injured, Brady shows that he can be trusted and carries out the plan for moving a refugee slave to the next haven of safety, courageously driving a wagon, with its hidden human cargo, through a countryside dangerously populated with slave hunters.

Novels set in the Civil War period focus on the horrors of war, especially that of countryman fighting countryman, and, in some cases, brother against brother. Books set in this period do not paint an exciting picture or romanticize the battles; instead, they focus on injury and death, divided loyalties, and, frequently, the anguish of those who wanted no involvement in the war.

Irene Hunt's *Across Five Aprils* (I-A) describes the tragic involvement of Matthew Creighton's family, which has loved ones on both the Confederate and Union sides. In April 1861, Matthew's 9-year-old son Jethro, too young to join either army, thinks that war is exciting and wonderful. One by one Jethro's brothers and a beloved schoolmaster join the Union Army, but his favorite brother, Bill, feels he must join the Confederates. Jethro experiences the war through letters from his brothers and teacher as well as newspaper accounts but mostly by word of mouth. News spreads through the county quickly as neighbors share news of disasters, battles, and lost sons. Jethro's enthusiasm for war changes to hatred for the cruelty and senseless loss of lives. Hunt paces the story deftly by using the critical five Aprils of the title to structure the novel. She also catches the language of Civil War years in the dialogue of her characters.

Any children born in the antebellum South grew up accepting slavery as a way of life; those born in the North questioned the practice. In Patricia Clapp's novel, *The Tamarack Tree: A Novel of the Siege of Vicksburg* (A), a British girl brings the somewhat objective view of an outsider. Orphaned at age 13, Rosemary Leigh comes from England in 1859 to live with an older brother, Derek, in Vicksburg, Mississippi. She enjoys the Southern hospitality afforded by Derek's position in their uncle's law firm but a gnawing discontent grows as she becomes aware that the gracious hospitality rests on the institution of slavery. Torn between personal loyalty to her Southern friends and her moral conviction that slavery is wrong, she becomes more uneasy as the tensions heighten. She is unwilling to leave her brother, though, and eventually finds herself trapped in a blockaded city. As a means of maintaining her sanity, she jots down her thoughts and memories

TEACHING IDEA

ACROSS FIVE APRILS (I-A)   Viewing the issues involved in the Civil War from the perspective of one family gives students an awareness of the complexities that were involved. Because the issues in *Across Five Aprils* (I-A), by Irene Hunt, are indeed complex, it is advisable to read and discuss the first four chapters before proceeding to the last half of the story. Also, at this stage, students are developing a historical perspective and need help putting events into chronological order; a timeline of events in the Civil War or a timeline of American history that includes the Civil War can help students create a coherent time frame.

Your class could use this book as a framework for the study of the Civil War, since it begins with the original causes and continues until the death of Abraham Lincoln. The historical background, however, should not be allowed to obscure the vivid character development.

The book also provides an excellent background for discussion of how suffering can change people, as seen in the attitudes of Tom and Eb; the effects of rumor and prejudice, as experienced by Bill's family when he runs away to join the Southern forces; and how the innocent—for example, the father, Matt Creighton—may suffer for the positions others take.

ACTIVITY: TEACHER TO STUDENT

HISTORY THROUGH LITERATURE (I-A)   Read Irene Hunt's *Across Five Aprils* (I-A) and choose one of the following activities.

1. Prepare a bulletin board or a large mural divided to represent the five Aprils covered in the novel. Illustrate each section with pictures and note news events and family events from the story, as begun here:

April 1861	April 1862	April 1863	April 1864	April 1865
War begins	Father ill	Eb deserts Yankee army	Turning point of war	War ends; Lincoln shot

2. Select words and phrases from the story that are no longer used in conversation. Write the words or phrases and their meanings on cards; put the cards on a bulletin board labeled "Old Time Talk." If there is a modern counterpart, write it next to the old one in a different color. Some examples from the book are "bedded" (p. 8), "spent" and "tol'able" (p. 20), "put one's hand in the fire" (p. 25), "take by the britches" (p. 44), "passel" (p. 168). When the list is long enough, say five or six items, make a word-matching game. For example,

1. _____ allow (p. 15)   a. food
2. _____ grub (p. 163)   b. remember
3. _____ mind (p. 131)   c. improve handwriting
4. _____ feathering (p. 9)   d. agree, suppose
5. _____ write a better hand (p. 132)   e. softly rising

3. News of the war, carried mainly by word of mouth, made the war seem much closer than do the ones reported on radio and television. Dramatize a modern newscast about a distant battle and then give an eyewitness report about Jethro's visit to the army camp.

4. Re-enact the scene in which Shad brings the news that the Confederates have fired on Fort Sumter or the scene in which Bill asks John to tell his mother that he was not at Pittsburg Landing (so that she will know he was not involved in Tom's death). Continue the scene as John goes to Mrs. Creighton to carry the message Bill asks him to relay.

on the backs of leftover wallpaper. By using this literary device, the author brings a sense of immediacy and poignancy to the siege of Vicksburg. War is not just distant battles that happen to someone someplace, it is the crippling and suffering of friends. Patricia Clapp, one of our well-respected historical fiction writers, appends a bibliography to indicate the sources of her careful research for this novel.

Good historical fiction is based on historical fact. A writer often uses an authentic historical incident or condition as the backdrop for an invented character and the way the condition impinged upon him or her. Patricia Beatty uses the effect of the Civil War on Southern mill workers as the background for *Turn Homeward, Hannalee* (I-A). It is historical fact that Northern soldiers burned Southern textile mills and sent their workers away from their homes as traitors. Twelve-year-old Hannalee Reed and her younger brother, Jem, work 13-hour days in one of the Georgia textile mills making gray cloth for Confederate Army uniforms. When the Northern soldiers burn their mill, the children are sent North, but Hannalee vows to return home. In the North, the children are separated and forced to accept menial jobs or be imprisoned. Eventually, Hannalee disguises herself as a boy, tracks down Jem, and begins the journey homeward. They slip through the lines and witness a battle in which the Confederate Army is defeated. Near the war's end, they reach their impoverished family after a treacherous journey. Patricia Beatty provides a comprehensive note to distinguish what is fact and what is fiction in this stirring novel.

Janet Hickman explores conflicting loyalties within a pacifist community at the time of the Civil War in *Zoar Blue* (I-A). Remote but prosperous Zoar, Ohio, was a farming community founded by the German Separatists whose beliefs refused any participation in war. Thirteen-year-old Barbara Hoff and 17-year-old John Keffer question the Separatist principles and shake the parochial community from within. Barbara runs away to find a relative in Pennsylvania, and John enlists in the Union Army; both see the tragedies wrought by war. They both return to Zoar but with much different perceptions of themselves and their lives. Hickman adds an author's note that explains which characters are based on actual people who lived in Zoar and which ones she invented to tell this thoughtful story.

Biography

History could be written as a series of biographies since it is often the influence of one person who shapes historical events; biographies also show the human element in abstract and complex issues.

Lincoln: A Photobiography (I-A) by Russell Freedman, was awarded the 1988 Newbery Medal for its distinction in literary quality. Since the Newbery is seldom given to a book of nonfiction, the award was doubly notable. Freedman selects telling photographs to chronicle Abraham Lincoln's life. A series of four, taken during his four years in office, shows the visible signs of aging in the face of a man deeply concerned about his country and its people. Freedman uses the technique of showing his readers what is important rather than telling them. In a closing chapter, he explains that the contents of Lincoln's pockets were emptied and placed in a box on the morning Lincoln died. The box was wrapped in brown paper and tied with a string. Robert Lincoln later gave the box to his daughter, who presented it to the Library of Congress in 1937. The box was labeled "Do Not Open," and so remained sealed until 1976. Freedman lists the contents:

> The morning he died, Lincoln had in his pockets a pair of small spectacles folded into a silver case; a small velvet eyeglass cleaner; a large linen handkerchief with *A. Lincoln* stitched

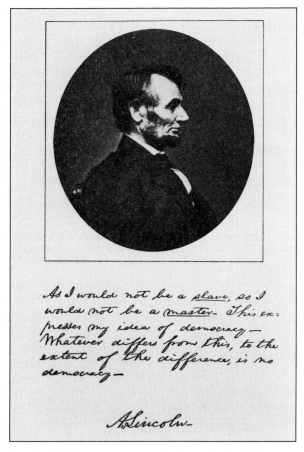

As I would not be a *slave*, so I would not be a *master*. This expresses my idea of democracy — Whatever differs from this, to the extent of the difference, is no democracy —

A. Lincoln

Russell Freedman captures Abraham Lincoln's life in a collection of revealing photographs. (From *Lincoln: A Photobiography*.)

in red; an ivory pocketknife trimmed with silver; and a brown leather wallet lined with purple silk. The wallet contained a Confederate five-dollar bill bearing the likeness of Jefferson Davis and eight newspaper clippings that Lincoln had cut out and saved. All the clippings praised him. As president, he had been denounced, ridiculed, and damned by a legion of critics. When he saw an article that complimented him, he often kept it.

One clipping found in Lincoln's wallet quotes the British reformer John Bright. Shortly before the presidential election of 1864, Bright wrote to the American newspaper publisher Horace Greeley and said:

"All those who believe that Slavery weakens America's power and tarnishes your good name throughout the world, and who regard the restoration of your Union as a thing to be desired . . . are heartily longing for the reelection of Mr. Lincoln. . . . They think they have observed in his career a grand simplicity of purpose and a patriotism which knows no change and does not falter."[18]

There are many comprehensive biographies for the student who wants to learn more about Lincoln and the Civil War. Carl Sandburg's multivolume tome is the definitive work; the first 27 chapters of Sandburg's *Abraham Lincoln: The Prairie Years* (A) are reprinted in *Abe Lincoln Grows Up* (A), which is usually appreciated most by elementary students if it is read aloud by the teacher. James Daugherty's *Abraham Lincoln* (I-A) is a lusty account of the man and his concerns. During the war years, Lincoln kept himself informed on every battle, troop movement, and military decision, and often criticized his generals severely. Daugherty's book reveals Lincoln's deep concerns about the causes of the war and his even deeper concern that the North would not win. F. N. Monjo's *Me and Willie and Pa* (P-I) is a refreshing and unusual biography of Lincoln, not a staid account of his greatness but a child's-eye view written as if told by Lincoln's son Tad. Personal glimpses into the Lincoln household are conveyed through Tad's naive comments.

Robert E. Lee's biography enriches a study of the Civil War. Paxton Davis's *Three Days: With Robert E. Lee at Gettysburg* (A) is a narrative of the battle of Gettysburg as it might have been seen by Lee and by an enlisted Confederate solider. Using interior monologues as a literary device to reveal Lee's thoughts and feelings, the author unfolds the confusion, uncertainty, and frustration facing the commander of the Confederate Army as he attempted to retaliate for each Union Army movement. Readers are more likely to understand the broad scope and the specific minute-by-minute drama of the battle from reading this in connection with Bruce Catton's *The Battle of Gettysburg* (A).

Harriet Beecher Stowe's *Uncle Tom's Cabin* (A) was one of the books that sparked abolitionist sentiments—one of the factors that led to the Civil War. The genteel daughter of a New England clergyman and married to a minister, Harriet Beecher Stowe vowed in her anger over the Fugitive Slave Act: "I will write something. I will if I live!" Despite her lack of firsthand knowledge of slavery, she kept her vow, writing a story that influenced thousands. *Uncle Tom's Cabin*, first serialized in an antislavery weekly, sold 300,000 copies after it was published in book form in March, 1852. *Woman Against Slavery: The Story of Harriet Beecher Stowe* (I), by John Anthony Scott, is a well-documented story of the life and beliefs of the author of *Uncle Tom's Cabin*. Students of literature need to know about this occasion, on which a book had obvious and direct impact upon the course of history.

Frances Cavanah gives an account of the man whose life and memoirs were used as a basis for Harriet Beecher Stowe's novel in *The Truth About the Man Behind the Book That Sparked the War Between the States* (I-A). It is exciting to trace the course of real lives reflected in literature and to see the interplay between literature and history.

Julius Lester uses first-person narratives in *To Be a Slave* (I-A), edited verbatim transcripts of accounts by blacks who escaped from the antebellum South. The transcripts were made by workers in the Federal Writers' Project interested in preserving a record of black speech patterns and language. Julius Lester also uses interviews, footnotes to history (such as bills of sale for slaves, letters, marriage registers), and primary sources for six stories about slaves and freedmen in *Long Journey Home* (I-A). He tells the stories of minor figures because he feels that they are the true movers of history, while the famous exist as symbols of their actions. The stories are dramatic, sometimes bitter, always poignant.

Historical biography can personalize the impact of social conditions on individual lives, making facts come alive by focusing on feelings. Elizabeth Yates accomplishes this by tracing the life an an African prince from his capture by slave traders, through his years of bondage, to his death as a free man in *Amos Fortune: Free Man* (I). For Elizabeth Yates, the story began with two tombstones—those of Amos Fortune and his wife—in the ancient churchyard of her New England village. Although, traditionally, the man's tombstone was higher, Fortune's and his wife's were of the same size. Curiosity about a man who would choose such a striking symbol of equality led her on a search through wills, official documents, indenture papers, and other historical records. She found that Amos Fortune had been sold into slavery in 1725 and after working more than 40 years was able to buy his own freedom when he was 60 years old. He also bought the freedom of at least four other slaves whose lives touched his own. Readers sense compassion and respect for a man who lived nobly.

A clear image of the turbulent times is portrayed in a biography of an outstanding writer. Louisa May Alcott (1832–1888), author of *Little Women* (A), was not an ordinary woman of her times; she was strong and independent, quite opposite from the prevailing role women were supposed to play during the Victorian era. Cornelia Meigs valued Alcott's spirit and portrayed it well in *Invincible Louisa* (I-A), her biography that merited the Newbery Award in 1934. When Meigs accepted the Newbery Award for *Invincible Louisa*, she accepted it for both Alcott and herself. Meigs captures Louisa's own complex feelings about her success and the combative yet loving relationship between Louisa and her father, Transcendentalist Bronson Alcott.

TEACHING IDEA

AMOS FORTUNE: FREE MAN (I)   Because of the beauty of the language and the strength of the images it evokes, Elizabeth Yates's *Amos Fortune: Free Man* (I), begs to be read aloud. Use some of the following questions to extend your students' appreciation of Amos Fortune's story.

1. What visual images are suggested by the words used to establish the setting (for example, "no lingering of daylight," "snuffing out of the sun," "people were gathering for their mystic dance that would welcome in the time of herbage, the time for the planting of corn")?
2. Monadnock means "mountain that stands alone." What significance does the mountain have for Amos Fortune?
3. What does the sentence "He had won his way to equality by work well done and a life well lived" mean to you?
4. What should an obituary about Amos Fortune include?

ACTIVITY: TEACHER TO STUDENT

STUDY THE PAST THROUGH TOMBSTONES (I)   The tombstones in an old cemetery often contain interesting information. Visit a cemetery in your area to see what the tombstones reveal about the past. Are there many deaths in one year, which might indicate a plague or other disaster? Are women buried with infants, suggesting death at childbirth? Do the men tend to have had several wives? Can you tell when there was a war? Did people die young?

Survey the first names that were popular during a period. Look for family names that are still represented in your community. Did any of the people buried here achieve historical significance? Make a rubbing of a symbol or inscription on a tombstone that carries historical significance by placing a sheet of paper on the stone and rubbing the paper lightly with pencil, charcoal, crayon, or chalk.

LIFE ON THE FRONTIER: THE PIONEERS

Frontier life required great physical strength and an unlikely counterpart: the ability to endure loneliness. Pioneer families worked hard by necessity, providing their own food, clothing, shelter, and entertainment. Of the many good historical novels describing families who endure the hardships of frontier living and find abiding satisfaction in their lives, one series of books stands out above all others—the "Little House" series by Laura Ingalls Wilder. These autobiographical stories convey the strong feelings of love and companionship in a family facing danger and difficulties. Starting with *Little*

ACTIVITY: TEACHER TO STUDENT

APPRECIATING PIONEER LIFE (I)   After reading the Little House books, invite your parents to school to share what you have learned about pioneer living. When they arrive, give them a copy of the newspaper from Plum Creek, Minnesota, which you have published. The paper could use events from the books, such as when grasshoppers covered the land and destroyed the Ingalls's crops, or when there was a flood, drought, or blizzard. Report the disaster in front-page stories and headlines. Here is a sample from a fourth grade class:

PLUM CREEK GAZETTE

GRASSHOPPERS COVER EARTH: CROPS DESTROYED

The Charles Ingalls farm was one of many hit by grasshoppers this week when swarms of the hungry insects devoured their crops.

(continued on page 2)

Weather forecast

Hot and dry.

Letters to the Editor

Dear Editor,
The grasshoppers were the last straw.
I'm pulling out and going back East to civilization.

Personal: Mrs. Oleson entertained in honor of Nellie's birthday.

Help Wanted: Barn raising, Saturday. Food for all workers.

Treat parent visitors to a pioneer luncheon. Use *The Little House Cookbook,* (I) by Barbara Walker and illustrated by Garth Williams, which gives recipes for bread, pancake men, and starling pie, as well as pioneer methods for churning butter, drying blackberries, and making ice cream.

Entertain your guests with square dancing. Learn one of the square dances that Laura watched at Grandpa's house. Use recordings for music and instructions by a caller.

Re-create an evening in Laura's home: Pa's fiddle music can be recaptured with recordings. *The Laura Ingalls Wilder Song Book,* (I) edited by Eugenia Garson and Herbert Haufrecht and illustrated by Garth Williams, contains the music and words for many of the songs the family sang. *On the Banks of Plum Creek* includes "Captain Jinks" (p. 338) and "Weevily Wheat" (p. 336). Learn the words to the songs that Pa played on his fiddle and have a songfest.

House in the Big Woods (P-I) and continuing through seven more books about Laura, Pa, Ma, Mary, Carrie, and Grace, these stories have been loved by generations of children who imagine themselves romping behind a covered wagon with Laura.

Some children who have seen the televised series "Little House on the Prairie" may think they know the story and so will not want to read the books. Such ideas will be set aside after they hear the beautiful language and share some of the warm fireside scenes with Laura and her books.

The sense of isolation permeates the opening paragraph of the first book in the series:

> The great, dark trees of the Big Woods stood all around the house, and beyond them were other trees and beyond them were more trees. As far as a man could go to the north in a day, or a week, or a whole month, there was nothing but woods. There were no houses. There were no roads. There were no people. There were only trees and the wild animals who had their homes among them.[19]

Laura shows how she feels about her life as she describes what she does. She is glad that her world is the way it is, that her father and mother are there, that the warmth of love fills her home. The family saga continues in *Little House on the Prairie, On the Banks of Plum Creek, By the Shores of Silver Lake, The Long Winter, Little Town on the Prairie,* and *These Happy Golden Years* (all I). The eighth book, *The First Four Years* (I) found as a manuscript among Mrs. Wilder's effects after her death at the age of 90, ends the sensitive chronicles of this pioneer family on the wild prairies of the American West in the 1870s and 1880s.

Themes of loneliness, hardship, and acceptance of what life deals out are threaded through many excellent novels about the pioneers and their struggle to tame a wild land. Among the best is the 58-page Newbery Award winner by Patricia MacLachlan, *Sarah, Plain*

Sarah, Plain and Tall, by Patricia MacLachlan, weaves a simple story of love and family that transcends the loneliness and hardship of living on the frontier.

and Tall (P-I-A). Anna and Caleb live with Papa in a small sod house on the prairie of the Nebraska frontier. Momma died the morning after Caleb was born and Anna has served as surrogate mother and housekeeper despite her tender years. Caleb often asks Anna about their mother and begs her to sing him the songs their mother sang. He says, "Maybe . . . if you remember the songs, then I might remember her, too." Both children are surprised when Papa announces that he has put an advertisement in the newspaper for help. Anna thinks he means a housekeeper but Papa says slowly, "Not a housekeeper. . . . A wife." Caleb stared at Papa. "A wife? You mean a mother?" . . . "That, too," said Papa. After Papa reads aloud the letter he has received in response to his advertisement for a mail-order bride, Caleb is smiling and Anna says, "Ask her if she sings." More letters are exchanged until a final one arrives, saying, "I will come by train. I will wear a yellow bonnet. I am plain and tall. (signed) Sarah." Sarah is a proud independent woman who desperately misses her home by the sea in Maine. Papa is a quiet gentle man who waits patiently for those he loves. Caleb and Anna fear that Sarah is leaving them the day she takes the horses and wagon from the homestead. When she returns Anna voices her fear, but Sarah says "I will always miss my old home, but the truth of it is I would miss you more." The beauty of MacLachlan's spare prose and the simplicity of naive love make this a book to treasure.

Prairie Songs (I-A) by Pamela Conrad is another story set in the same period and in the same Nebraska region as *Sarah, Plain and Tall.* The young narrator, Louisa, and her younger brother, shy, quiet Lester, love their prairie home, the vast sky, and the prairie flowers they pick. They are drawn, though, to the new doctor and his beautiful but tragically frail wife who move into a neighboring sod house. Mrs. Berryman, from New York, fascinates Louisa with her clothes, manners, and especially the books she brings to the frontier. Mrs. Berryman teaches Louisa from her books and passes on to her a love of literature and poetry. Lester comes for lessons, too, but seldom speaks. Gradually, loneliness, primitive surroundings, and a stillborn child eat into Mrs. Berryman's sanity. She disintegrates into madness and dies of the cold as she wanders off into the freezing prairie winter. There are several themes operating in this multilayered story. First, Louisa's love of the prairie beauty stands in stark contrast to Mrs. Berryman's hatred of it. Second is the theme of acceptance of what life deals out to us. And third is that to force human beings into molds they have not chosen is charged with potential tragedy.

Two excellent picture books enlarge our scope of understanding about life on the prairie frontier. Ann Turner's *Dakota Dugout* (P-I-A), illustrated by Ronald Himler, is an evocative recollection of what it was like to live in a sod house on the Dakota prairie a century ago. Life changed as material comforts were added, but the nostalgic final comment rings true: "Sometimes the things we start with are best." *My Prairie Year: Based on the Diary of Elenore Plaisted* (P-I-A), by Brett Harvey and illustrated by Deborah Kogan Ray, is told through 9-year-old Elenore's eyes. Her family moves from Lincoln, Maine, to the Dakota Territory in 1889, and as Elenore explains "life on the prairie was different from life back home . . . in every way." There are no close neighbors, no playmates, and no household help, so the three children help with washing, ironing, and gardening. Sundays are different: "glorious," Elenore writes, "no work and no lessons. . . . We were free to run wild on the prairie." After a year, a younger sister asks if they would ever go home, and their mother replies quietly, "We are home." Soft paintings capture the rich gold prairie grasses waving against a clear blue sky. Both of these stories offer new dimensions in appreciating the pleasures and problems of nineteenth-century homesteaders.

Other notable stories of the pioneers deserve mention. Carol Ryrie Brink based her story *Caddie Woodlawn* (I-A), illustrated by Trina Schart Hyman, on her tomboy grandmother's life in the 1860 Wisconsin wilderness, while Ann Nolan Clark describes a young girl's adjustment to the Minnesota wilderness in *All This Wild Land* (I). Willa Cather wrote several pioneer stories for adults; her biography is told in Ruth Franchere's *Willa: The Story of Willa Cather's Growing Up* (I). The true story of the Sager family of seven children who, after the deaths of their parents, made the long, hard journey on the Oregon Trail to a new life beyond the Rocky Mountains, is told in several books, including Anna Rutgers Van der Loeff's *Oregon at Last!* (I); Neta L. Frazier's *Stout-Hearted Seven* (I); and Honore Morrow's *On to*

The adjustments to the solitude and the hard work of pioneer life on the prairie are told through the eyes of a 9-year-old. (From *My Prairie Year: Based on the Diary of Elenore Plaisted* by Brett Harvey, illustrated by Deborah Kogan Ray.)

Oregon (I). Evelyn Sibley Lampman tells about a young girl orphaned on the Oregon Trail in *Bargain Bride* (I-A).

Biography

Children who become Laura Ingalls Wilder fans will want to know more about her life and how her books reflected her life. Their curiosity can be satisfied in Gwenda Blair's book, *Laura Ingalls Wilder* (P-I). This biography is based largely upon incidents described in the Little House books. It gives the basic facts of her life as a child in a pioneer family and as an adult who turned to writing when she was 60 years old. Children will want to compare the facts of Laura's life as described here with those described in their beloved books.

Laura Ingalls Wilder: Growing Up in the Little House (I) by Patricia Reilly Giff begins with the 63-year-old Laura deciding to write down the stories that her daughter Rose loved to hear—the stories about Pa and Ma Ingalls in the olden days when Laura was a child. Rose, a journalist, lived far away from the Missouri farm where her parents lived, but she had encouraged her mother to record the stories for her and her child. Giff writes lovingly of Laura as she weaves bits from the Little House books themselves into the account of the elderly woman writing them. This biography extends our appreciation for one of the most notable writers for children of the twentieth century.

IMMIGRANTS

The story of America is the story of immigration. Thousands of immigrants came from distant lands dreaming of freedom and hoping to seek a better life. Their stories are our stories repeated at family gatherings where young children gather around the older members asking them to "tell us what it was like back in the olden days." Historical fiction contains a wealth of immigrant stories.

Kathryn Lasky tells a poignant tale of 13-year-old Rachel, who ignores her parents' wishes and persuades her great-grandmother to tell her of her escape from Czarist Russia. Rachel slips upstairs each day to see Nana Sashie, her great-grandmother, for each installment of *The Night Journey* (I-A), which is what she considers the heartwrenching story she hears. Bit by bit, Nana Sashie tells of what she went through as a child: there were persecutions and pogroms that she and her family endured before their escape and the treachery they faced during it. Near the end of the story, Nana Sashie dies and Rachel thinks with horror what she would have missed if she had not pressed her to share her stories. Rachel reflects on the way time marches on and how her afternoons with Nana Sashie were a detour in time. She says, "It was time out of line, but time laced with the bright filaments of memory that in turn linked two people at the opposite ends of life for a vital moment in each one's existence."[20]

Margery Evernden's *The Dream Keeper* (I-A) is a parallel story that makes connections between Jewish immigrants and their great grandchildren; it provides an excellent comparison for Lasky's *The Night Journey*. Both stories share the Russian origins and frame the historical events in the midst of the ongoing life of a contemporary family, but they differ in the way they reveal the past. In *The Dream Keeper*, Young Becka listens to some tapes that reveal her dying great-grandmother Bobe's dramatic family saga. There were six children in Bobe's family, but they were separated—one went to the Russian army, several went to America, and one died. The rich legacy of spiritual strength and appreciation for music that Becka inherits from her family deserves to be passed along to others.

Many books describe the conditions in another country that led families to immigrate to America, and others focus on the difficulties and hardships endured during immigration. Few, however, deal with the arduous circumstances that immigrants faced after their arrival. Judie Angell's *One-Way to Ansonia* (A) is an exception. Sixteen-year-old Rose is buying a ticket at Grand Central Station in 1899 as the story begins. Her destination is determined by the amount of money she has; she buys a ticket that takes her as far away from New York as she can afford to go. In flashbacks, we learn why she is anxious to leave the teeming city. Rose was 10 years old in 1893 when her father welcomed his five children at Ellis Island. He announced that they were a surprise for the widow he was marrying that very day. His bride says, "A surprise they are . . . . Moshe's children, . . . you'll have to live somewhere else." Life on New York's Lower East Side is not easy for penniless children, but they occasionally find unforeseen kindness. Rose goes to night school and reads books loaned to her by a teacher. At age 16, she is determined to make a better life for herself, her child, and her husband and, therefore, buys the ticket to the unknown Connecticut town, Ansonia.

Immigrant life is sensitively portrayed in Marietta Moskin's *Waiting for Mama* (I-A). Because there was only enough money to pay passage for part of the family to come to America, Mama stayed behind. The family works hard to earn the money for Mama to join them. Becky, too young to work, finds a way to help by sewing with her 10-year-old sister late at night. An immigrant family's life was not easy, but hardship drew its members close together.

Bette Bao Lord sprinkles with humor the story of her own immigration to the United States in 1947 in *The Year of the Boar and Jackie Robinson* (I). In China in the House of Wong, a girl called Sixth Cousin, otherwise known as Bandit, observes closely the day her mother receives a letter that makes her smile and her grandparents cry. The letter from her father means that they will go to America. Bandit believes that she should have an American name, so she chooses one that her grandfather bestows upon her, Shirley Temple Wong. Shirley's adjustment to the strange houses, customs, and language is slow and difficult, although she undertakes it with a spirited heart. Finally, her classmates discover her talent for stickball and they all become caught up in the World Series. The Brooklyn Dodgers were the champions of the National League and Jackie Robinson was voted "The Rookie of the Year." The Yankees beat the Dodgers to become the World Champions, but the comaradarie of cheering and playing together helps Shirley feel part of her new country. When Jackie Robinson visits her Brooklyn school, she is chosen to present him with a huge golden key.

Biography

David Kherdian tells a major segment of his mother's life in *The Road from Home* and continues it in *Finding Home* (both I-A). Veron Dumehjian was born to a prosperous Armenian family that lived in the Armenian section in Azizya, Turkey. Her childhood was filled with sunlight until the Turkish government decided in 1915 to evict the Armenians; then the shadows of dark clouds hung over her. Veron and her family were deported amidst many injustices; eventually she came to America as a "mail-order bride." *Finding Home* follows Veron into that rushed marriage within weeks of her arrival and shows her chafing under the constraints of living in a close-knit Armenian family.

Isaac Bashevis Singer: The Story of a Storyteller (A) is written by Paul Kresh, who also wrote Singer's biography for adults. Kresh interviewed Singer frequently and spent a great deal of time with him, so the view of his life is warm and personal. Singer was the son of a scholarly and impractical rabbi in Poland. He lived in several Polish towns before coming to New York to join his older brother, who was a dear friend and mentor, the author Joshua Singer. A balance of personal and literary information makes this good reading for Singer's fans as well as for prospective writers.

Jean Fritz says that parts of *Homesick: My Own Story* (I) are fictionalized, though all of the events are true. She says, "Strictly speaking, I have to call this book fiction, but it does not feel like fiction to me. It is my story, told as truly as I can tell it." The story covers her childhood in China in the 1920s and her early months in America. The daughter of missionaries, Jean felt strong loyalties to America during her days in China. She refused to sing the British national anthem and stoutly defended George Washington to her classmates. Upon her arrival in America, Jean stood at the front railing of the ship, dressed in a navy skirt, white blouse, and silk stockings and feeling every bit as proud as Columbus or Balboa. Caught up with the moment, she shouted "This is my land, my native land." Her return trip to China many years later is told in *China Homecoming* (I-A).

World War I

There is a paucity of books set in World War I, although two excellent novels bring some measure of understanding to young readers. Margaret Rostkowski's *After the Dancing Days* (I-A) is a beautifully told story of a 13-year-old girl's growing awareness that the war is not over for

Thirteen-year-old Annie grows to realize that the crippled soldiers returning from fighting in the Great War must now struggle to overcome their injuries and find new lives for themselves. (From *After the Dancing Days* by Margaret Rostkowski, cover art by Ted Lewin.)

its maimed and crippled veterans. Annie watches for her father, a doctor in the army, to return to their small town in Kansas at the end of the war. Several badly scarred and injured veterans precede him from the train, and Annie turns away in horror at their appearance. Her father chooses to work at St. John's Hospital, where the soldiers are treated, rather than return to his former position. One day, Annie accompanies him there where she meets Andrew who is so horribly scarred from burns that she cannot bear to look at him. Andrew recognizes her revulsion and walks away in shame. Annie's mother believes that everyone should put the war behind them and go on to happier things in life; she forbids Annie to go to St. John's again. The fact that her own brother, Annie's Uncle Paul, was killed in the war is something she would like to suppress. When her mother takes her own parents away for a month, Annie goes to St. John's each day, knowing it to be against her mother's wishes. She reads to Andrew and others and begins to have a sense that these young men are normal human beings with needs like anyone else. In a traumatic scene, she faces her mother about the older woman's insensitivity and gradually helps her to see the young veterans as real people. This is a powerful story of a young girl's growth in humanity.

Rudolf Frank's *No Hero for the Kaiser* (A), an antiwar novel, was first published in 1931 by a World War I veteran and burned publicly by the Nazis in 1933 for its indictment of militarism. Jan, a Polish boy, is alone. His mother is dead, his father has been conscripted to fight the Germans, and his Uncle Peter is killed in a battle between the Russians and Germans on September 14, 1914, Jan's fourteenth birthday. Caught in the crossfire between warring troops, Jan's village is destroyed. When the Germans move on in pursuit of the Russians, they take Jan with them. He lives for two years with the German army troop that adopted him and learns the cruelties of war from the inside.

Biography

A Spy for Freedom: The Story of Sarah Aaronsohn (A), by Ida Cowen and Irene Gunther, is a fictionalized biography of a woman who worked in the Jewish intelligence network during World War I. As an adolescent, she had lived in the Turkish-owned part of Palestine. During the war she left her husband to report Turkish activities to the British military. When she was caught as a spy, she killed herself rather than chance breaking down under torture and revealing anything to the enemy. The authors provide the original sources and interview data they used to write their story.

THE GREAT DEPRESSION

Stories of the depression years portray America in times of trouble. The beginning of the period is generally recognized as the stock market crash of 1929. Stories of ruined businessmen jumping from skyscrapers filled the headlines of daily newspapers. Stories for children describe the grim effect of living in poverty. Harry Mazer's *Cave Under the City* (I-A), shows what poverty was like in an urban area. Twelve-year-old Tolley and his little brother Bubber take to the streets of New York when their father leaves to look for work and their mother is hospitalized with tuberculosis. The boys rummage through garbage cans, do odd jobs, steal, and beg. Life is hard for two boys on their own, but eventually the family reunites, and life promises to be better. This is a good book to compare with Felice Holman's *Slake's Limbo,* another story of a child who lives alone in the vast city.

Crystal Thrasher sets her Great Depression story in a southern Indiana city after a move out of the hill country in *A Taste of Daylight* (A). Told through the eyes of 17-year-old Seely, the move does not improve the family's lot. Seely and her younger brother, Robert, must work at low-paying jobs to get the basic necessities of food and water, which could have been obtained more easily in the country. The end of the story expresses hope: Seely leaves to live with an older sister so she can go to school, and Robert works for the man who will become his stepfather.

Mildred D. Taylor's trilogy of Cassie Logan in *The Song of the Trees* (I); *Roll of Thunder, Hear My Cry* (I-A); and *Let the Circle Be Unbroken* (I-

A) show rural poverty and prevailing racism. One episode revolves around the distribution of textbooks in a rural black school in Mississippi in the 1930s. Cassie's little brother, a proud first grade student who is already reading and anxious to have his own book, is heartsick when the teacher gives him a book with soiled covers and marred pages. He hesitantly asks his teacher for another, pointing out that his is dirty:

> "Dirty!" Miss Crocker echoed, appalled by such temerity. . . . "Dirty! And just who do you think you are, Clayton Chester? Here the county is giving us these wonderful books during these hard times and you're going to stand there and tell me the book's too dirty? Now you take that book or get nothing at all!"[21]

Clayton tries to explain, but then overcome with anger, throws the tattered book to the floor and stamps madly on it. When Cassie receives her own book, she sees immediately the cause of his fury. Stamped inside the cover is a chart showing the race of the 12 previous owners and the condition of the book each year. During the first eleven years the book had been issued to a "white," but only when the condition of the book had descended to "very poor," was it issued to a "nigra." Cassie is well aware of the consequences when she also returns her book and gets in line behind her brother to feel the sting of the teacher's switch.

Cassie Logan evinces personal integrity and maturity often in the story: she trounces a snippy white girl who humiliates her; she refuses to continue a friendship with one who is instrumental in getting her mother fired from her teaching job; she helps prevent a lynching; and she grieves for a friend when he is jailed. Cassie's love for her family, their land and their trees rings throughout her story. Her quiet dignity nurtured by an upright, proud, and independent family, attests to the strength of the human spirit.

PROFILE

Mildred Taylor

> By the time I entered high school, I was confident that I would one day be a writer. . . . Once I had made up my mind to write, I had no doubts about doing it. It was just something that would one day be. I had always been taught that I would achieve anything I set my mind to.[22]

In a talk cosponsored by the International Reading Association and the Children's Book Council, Mildred Taylor described her childhood memories of vibrant countryside and the vitality of black community life, with its revivals and courtings, prayer meetings and picnics. Where there was beauty, however, there was also insufferable hatred and bigotry. She and her sister attended local schools, and she recalls how each book was marked, not only with previous owners' names, but with their race as well. Even as a child she sensed some wrong, so she scratched out the information.

As a child, Taylor wondered why the history books contained no stories about blacks, when the stories from her own family's past were filled with heroic men and women who fought against oppression and indignities with valor. Her desire to tell the story of strong black families facing difficulties heroically and with integrity led her to write *Song of the Trees; Roll of Thunder, Hear My Cry,* winner of the 1977 Newbery Medal and 1977 National Book Award; *Let the Circle Be Unbroken; Gold Cadillac* (I); and *The Friendship* (I).

She decries the depiction of black ghettos only as slums. The ghetto in which she grew up was not a slum, and she has no recollection of fatherless families; rather, she remembers the protective presence of strong adults—somewhat like the Logans' protection of Cassie and her brothers in the *Roll of Thunder* series.

From her Peace Corps experience in Ethiopia, Taylor learned the price independence exacts from the individual. Although her writing carries powerful themes about survival in a hostile society, Taylor's messages radiate rather than pummel:

> It is my hope that to the children who read my books, the Logans will provide those heroes missing from the schoolbooks of my childhood; Black men, women, and children of whom they can be proud.[23]

Throughout, the strength and importance of the family is central. She credits her father, a master storyteller, with having a powerful influence on her life. Her values and principles were shaped in a wholesome and loving family with strong and sensitive parents. Pride in one's heritage is a universal theme meaningful for all readers.

In another story, *The Friendship* (I), Taylor again uses Cassie Logan as the narrator to relate a dramatic confrontation between a black man and a white man. Set in Mississippi during the Great Depression, the story revolves around Mr. Tom Bee, an old black man, and Mr. John Wallace, the white storekeeper. Tom had saved John's life as a young man and John had promised that they would always be friends. Now, years later, John insists that Tom call him "Mister" and shoots him when Tom defiantly calls him by his first name. Taylor's strong style and sense of drama heighten the impact of difficult race relations and the miseries of poverty.

Three excellent picture books convey the feelings and images of the depression: *Shaker Lane* (P-I) by Alice and Martin Provensen, *In Coal Country* (P-I) by Judith Hendershot, and *When I Was Young in the Mountains* (P-I) by Cynthia Rylant. In the Provensons' story, a Shaker meeting house had once stood at the corner of *Shaker Lane,* but only a few stones remained as the Herkimer sisters sell off bits of their farm in order to live. Assorted houses, shacks, and trailers crop up along Shaker Lane until the county land agent announced, "A reservoir is to be built. Most of you folks will have to move." The scenes change as the reservoir fills spaces once inhabited by people of the depression.

In Coal Country is a personal narrative of a girl whose father is a coal miner in a small Ohio mining town. When he comes home from the mines she can see only the whites of his eyes smiling at her. Evocative illustrations convey the love and the poverty vividly.

When I Was Young in the Mountains, another personal narrative, is a poetic accounting of all the good times of a mountain family. Grandfather comes home covered with the black dust of the coal mine, but his lips are clean and he uses them to kiss the top of the child's head. Swimming in the creek, pumping water from a well, and taking a bath in an old washtub are memories strung like pearls on a chain. The story closes, "I never wanted to go anywhere else in the world, for I was in the mountains. And that was always enough."

WORLD WAR II

The years 1936 to 1946 encompassed Adolph Hitler's climb to power in Germany and Japanese military activity in the Pacific. The Second World War brought to vivid awareness the potential of man's inhumanity, particularly to man. The horrors of the period were so unthinkable that it was several decades before the story was told in books for young people.

Santayana's admonition that those who do not know the past are condemned to repeat it is adequate cause for attending to the tragedy, and the books describing Hitler's reign of terror, with its effects ultimately on all people, are a good place to begin. Many emphasize—some in small ways, some in great ways—that in the midst of inhumanity there can be humaneness. Eric Kimmel, in an article about the importance of writing stories about the Holocaust for juvenile fiction, echoes Santayana: "If the Holocaust remains incomprehensible, it will be forgotten. And if it is forgotten, it is certain to recur."[24]

Despite their grimness, some books are affirmative: young people work in underground movements, strive against terrible odds, plan escapes, and struggle for survival. Some show heroic Jewish resistance, in which characters fight back or live with dignity and hope in the face of a monstrous future. There are some teachers who will agonize over the place of literature in teaching about the Holocaust. Valid questions for them to consider are: Is mass murder a suitable subject for a children's novel? What is the place of an account of it in the school curriculum? What are the possible consequences of not informing young people about one of the most bitter lessons of history?

The European Theater

Books about World War II remind us of the tragedies wrought by war—families were decimated, and 6 million Jews were sent to gas chambers. The scar on humanity cannot be erased, nor should we let new generations bypass these parts of our history lest its tragedies become possible again. Two picture books rivet our attention on the inhumanities children suffered at the hands of thoughtless adults. Roberto Innocenti adapted and illustrated *Rose Blanche* (I-A), which recalls "The White Rose," an organization of young Germans who protested the war. The symbol of a white rose suggests the innocence of children trapped in a meaningless and dehumanizing war. A small girl, Rose Blanche, watches tanks and trucks rumble through her small German village without understanding their horror. One day, she sees the mayor grab a child who leaps from a truck; he calls an armed soldier who forces the child back. Rose follows the truck to a barbed wire enclosure where children tell her they are hungry. She hands them a piece of bread. The story then shifts to the third person and in the final days of the war, Rose Blanche makes her final trip to the abandoned camp. There she is killed by soldiers who "saw the enemy everywhere."

Chana Byers Abells's *The Children We Remember* (I-A) is a photo essay with a simple text recalling life before the Nazis and then after they came. The startling, unforgettable photographs are from the Yad Vashem Archives in Jerusalem. The power of the understated text and the stark photographs tell of death and loss but also of courage and endurance.

Goodnight Mr. Tom (I-A), by Michelle Magorian, won the International Reading Association Children's Book Award for the best book from a promising new writer. In this tender story set during the bombings in London, Willie, a pale, frightened child, is thrust upon old Tom who lives quietly in his English village. Willie cringes when Tom picks up the poker to stir the fire; it is obvious that Willie has been an abused child. Tom nurses Willie's physical bruises and emotional scars back to a shaky health. Just as the boy is beginning to trust "Mr. Tom," a telegram informs them that Willie's mother is ill and wants him back. When Tom does not hear from Willie, he goes to London and finds that Willie's mentally ill mother has locked him in a closet with a little sister who died in his arms. Tom takes Willie to the hospital, attends to him himself, and when aware that the officials will not release Willie to him, picks the child up and takes him out of the hospital. Magorian's story keeps readers riveted.

Judith Kerr's three novels, *When Hitler Stole Pink Rabbit* (I), *The Other Way Round* (I-A), and *A Small Person Far Away* (A), chronicle a life that could be the author's own from days as a refugee from Germany to the present. Anna, daughter of an affluent Jewish journalist, is forced to leave Berlin because her father's views are not acceptable to the Nazis. The family goes first to Switzerland and then to England, and with each move, Anna's resentment grows as life becomes more degrading.

Consciousness of their ethnic backgrounds and traditions, slight in most of the Jewish characters in the refugee novels, is not much greater in the novels laid in Germany or the occupied countries. One exception to this appears in Hans Richter's *Friedrich* (I), a story of a friendship between two German boys, one Jewish. The boys see no differences between themselves except in religious practice. As the diabolic plan of Nazi persecution slowly unfolds, Friedrich and his family find themselves denied even simple dignities, and in a bitter ending, Friedrich is forbidden entrance to a bomb shelter during an air raid. Ultimately, his resulting death must seem to him a refuge from the unrelenting hatred.

In striking contrast to the accounts of hatred, death, and betrayal are the stories of those who had the courage to reach out to others across lines of nationality or self-interest. In Jaap ter Haar's *Boris* (I-A), a young boy lives in Leningrad while it is under siege by German troops. His father was killed when his truck carrying food to Leningrad's starving people broke through the ice of Lake Ladoga. Boris and his friend, Nadia, trying to supplement their meager daily ration of watery soup, are digging for potatoes in a barren field in the "no-man's land" between the German and Russian lines when Nadia collapses. A German soldier takes them back to the Russian lines behind a white flag. The soldiers temporarily lay aside their differences in compassion for the children, and a Russian, speaking to the German soldier through his interpreter, says, "'Tell them they are free to go back, Ivan Petrovitch.' He hesitated, as if searching for words. 'Say to them that we are grateful; it would be shameful if we, in the brutality of war, should forget all humanity.'"[25]

Uri Orlev describes his childhood experiences hiding in the Warsaw ghetto in *Island on Bird Street* (I-A). Eleven-year-old Alex is resourceful; he builds a secret hideout in the cellar of a bombed-out building as he eludes the Nazis who would shoot him on sight. His father had told him to wait there for his return, "even if it took a whole year." Alex spends his time foraging for food and wistfully watching children play in the schoolyard across the way. His lonely desperation gnaws at the reader's heart.

In T. Degens's *Transport 7-41-R* (I-A), another gripping story, a 13-year-old German girl is traveling illegally aboard a crowded cattle car carrying refugees home to Cologne. Observing with distaste the callousness and inconsiderateness of the motley group of passengers, she tries to remain aloof. Eventually, however, she is drawn to an elderly couple, the Lauritzens, who seem especially vulnerable to the brutishness of the group. She learns that Mr. Lauritzen is trying to fulfill a pledge to his critically ill wife that she will be buried near the cathedral in Cologne. When Mrs. Lauritzen quietly dies while still aboard the train, both the girl and Mr. Lauritzen know that the others will throw the body, in its cumbersome wheelchair, off the train if they discover her death. As the transport is delayed time and time again, keeping the secret of Mrs. Lauritzen's death and fulfilling the promise to her become less realistic. The dedication of the nameless girl to the elderly couple is a touching story, believably told through gradual interweaving of detail.

Degens writes a compelling novel in *The Visit* (I-A), which includes a mystery and dark secrets. Kate Hoffman discovers a diary written by her long-dead aunt, for whom she was named, four decades after it had been written. The diary was written in the summer of 1943 when the original Kate and her sister, Sylvia, were active participants in Hitler's Youth Movement. Kate tries to understand the implications in the diary that suggest that Sylvia was responsible for Kate's death. The family secrecy heightens Kate's curiosity about her Aunt Kate but when she confronts her parents, she learns that it was true that Aunt Sylvia had, indeed, caused her sister's death.

Biography

Stories of Jews forced into hiding show strong and courageous individuals who, although living under terrifying stress, maintained hope for eventual freedom. *Anne Frank: The Diary of a Young Girl* (I-A) is the actual journal of this sensitive girl who, with her family, hid in a secret annex of an office building in Amsterdam for two years. The firsthand chronicles of the fear, hunger, and indignities of their hidden existence are chilling. Only Anne's father survived the Frank's subsequent imprisonment in a concentration camp. Anne's diary was found in 1946.

Johanna Reiss wrote *The Upstairs Room* (I-A), an autobiographical account of her escape to freedom, primarily for her own daughters, but readers everywhere learn about persecution from reading it. Ten-year-old Annie and her older sister expect to be hidden in the upstairs room of the Dutch farm home for only a few weeks, but the weeks stretch into more than two years. Usually the girls are free to move about the farm, but at one point Nazi soldiers make their headquarters in the front of the house and the girls are required to stay in bed day and night to avoid discovery. A sequel, *The Journey Back* (I-A), follows the girls as they make difficult adjustments after the war.

Aranka Siegal bases *Upon the Head of the Goat: A Childhood in Hungary, 1939–1944* (I-A) on her personal memories of the persecution of Hungarian Jews under German occupation. Using Piri Davidowitz as her narrator, Siegal describes the small pleasures in her life before the Nazis came to her town. Piri observes subtle and then not-so-subtle changes as restric-

tions appear and freedoms disappear. Eventually, they must share living quarters with many others, and in a final shocking scene, the remaining members of her family are herded onto a train headed for a work camp no one has heard of—Auschwitz. In the sequel, *Grace in the Wilderness: After the Liberation, 1945–1948* (A), Piri describes her and her sister's postwar recovery in Sweden. Through painful memories of the concentration camp, Piri details the misery of the past as she tries to adjust to the present.

Ruth Minsky Sender, now a grandmother, begins her first-person account of her experiences as a survivor of the Nazi concentration camps in *The Cage* (A) by giving her identification number. Forced to live inside the barbed-wire cage that is the Lodz ghetto in Nazi-occupied Poland, Riva's family fights for survival for five years. When Riva is too malnourished to stand, her brothers give up their bread ration so that she might have a tangerine and some vitamins. From the Lodz ghetto, they are

ACTIVITY: TEACHER TO STUDENT

THE IMPACT OF WORLD WAR II (A) The death camps in Europe and the atomic bombs in Japan stand as haunting evidence of the extent of man's capability for inhumanity to man. As you read books on these subjects, keep in mind the following questions and suggestions.

Discussion   How is it possible that a nation that produced great scientists and artists also allowed Dachau, Auschwitz, and Buchenwald? What comparisons can you draw between the death camps in Europe and the bombing of Hiroshima?[26]

Research   Read eyewitness reports of survivors, examine photodocumentaries and view filmed documentaries of the war-scarred world. (Your local newspaper or library may have files of the war-years issues of newspapers.)

Drama   Conduct a ''You Are There'' program of the bombing of Pearl Harbor, the bombing of Hiroshima, the Battle of the Bulge, D-Day at Normandy Beach, the Nuremberg trials, the discovery of a Nazi war criminal living in the United States, or an hour in the heart of the Warsaw ghetto.

Writing   Write an essay on what you think we should have learned from World War II. Write an opinion on the treatment of war criminals. Write a diary entry as if you had been caught in the midst of a battle area.

taken to Auschwitz where she is separated from her brothers. From Auschwitz she goes to a slave labor camp in Germany where a daring act of kindness saves her life. A kind guard shelters her until the advancing Russian army releases the prisoners who are "too weak, too numb to move."

The increase in the number of personal narratives about experiences during World War II suggest that the distance of time makes it possible for some to speak about events that were unspeakable from a closer vantage point. Modern readers can select from a plethora of riches in books about World War II.

Barbara Gehrts, in *Don't Say a Word* (A), begins her story in 1940 when Anna's prosperous family is intact and living relatively safely on the outskirts of Berlin. Her father is a high-ranking staff officer in the Luftwaffe, although he is unalterably opposed to Hitler's regime. Before the story's end, Anna's Jewish friends—the Schmidkes family—commit suicide, her first love is killed on the Russian front, her father is arrested by the Gestapo and later shot for treason, her brother dies from an infection contracted during military training, their home is destroyed, and her mother is a broken woman. An afterword by the author startles us: "The events of the story are not made up."

Several books show that every German child was involved in some way in the German Youth Corps. Often without being aware that Hitler's motives were as corrupt as they were, children were involved in sports events and charitable fund drives sponsored by the corps. Hans Richter gives a riveting first-person account of the years before and during the Hitler regime in *I Was There* (I-A). Heinz, Gunther, and the young narrator take part in events that have more far-reaching implications than they realize. The first-person narration gives a solid ring of authority.

Ilse Koehn describes her childhood in *Mischling, Second Degree* (I-A), which is the label Hitler gave children who had any particle of Jewish blood in them. Ilse participated actively in the Hitler youth movement during her early years. Ilse's mother was half-Jewish, but in order to protect Ilse from Hitler's wrath, her family kept the secret even from her.

In an excellent work of nonfiction, Milton Meltzer collects first-person narratives growing out of the Holocaust in *Never to Forget* (A). Letters, diaries, memoirs, eyewitness reports, and autobiographies are excerpted and woven into the fabric of history. Jewish ideals—"Live and die with dignity," and "Not by force but by the strength of the spirit"—emanate from the personal reports.

Two biographies of Hannah Senesh (Szenes) bring added insight to the understanding of World War II and the people who played central roles. Linda Atkinson describes the conditions that existed in Europe when, on March 13, 1944, four young Jews parachuted into Yugoslavia. *In Kindling Flame: The Story of Hannah Senesh, 1921–1944* (I-A), details the life of one of those parachutists. All had escaped from Hitler's Europe to safety in Palestine, now they were returning "to gather information for the British about German defenses, to establish escape routes for captured Allied airmen and to rescue as many Jews as they could." Hannah had grown up in a wealthy, cultured Jewish family and was aware of no prejudice as a child. When Hannah graduated from high school in 1939, she was committed to an active Zionist role and decided to emigrate to Palestine rather than go to college. She worked in Israel in kibbutzim until 1943 when she began to work more actively to help her family and other Jews who were still trapped in Europe. She was 22 years old when she parachuted into Yugoslavia, but three months later she was captured. Five months after that, following brutal treatment, she was executed as the last official act of a Nazi official preparing to retreat from the advancing Russian Army. Photographs, excerpts from Hannah's diary, family correspondence, and recollections of her

PROFILE

Milton Meltzer

To forget what we know would not be human.

To remember it is to think of what being human means. The Holocaust was a measure of man's dimensions. One can think of the power of evil it demonstrated—and of those people who treated others as less than human, as bacteria. Or of the power of good—and of those people who held out a hand to others.

By nature, man is neither good nor evil. He has both possibilities. And the freedom to realize the one or the other.[27]

Milton Meltzer followed the path to the terror and grief of the Nazi era through eyewitness accounts—letters, diaries, journals, and memoirs. However inadequate words are, he says, language is all we have to reach across barriers to understanding. Letting history speak for itself characterizes all his work and provides accuracy and authenticity normally found only in primary sources. His technique brings a sense of immediacy to the past and recreates a feeling of the time.

Meltzer's more than 45 books reveal his love of the American story and his respect for the struggles of our forebears. He portrays turn-of-the-century working-class life in *Bread and Roses* and the hardships of the depression in *Brother Can You Spare a Dime?*, *Poverty in America*, and in *Violins and Shovels*, the story of government-supported, depression-era WPA projects.

Milton Meltzer believes that young people are interested in the past and that it is best discovered through letters, memoirs, journals, and other original documents. He feels it is unnecessary to fabricate stories about historical events since the truth itself is inherently intriguing. One need only read the letters and poems in *Never to Forget: The Jews of the Holocaust* to recognize the validity of his belief.

The son of hard-working immigrant parents, Milton Meltzer was born in Worcester, Massachusetts, and studied to be a journalist. He and his wife, who have two grown daughters, live in New York City, where he devotes himself to scholarly research and writing. Meltzer tells his own story in *Starting from Home: A Writer's Beginnings*, recalling with affection a teacher who introduced him to the great works of literature.

companions are used to chronicle her life. Maxine Schur also tells Hannah's story in *Hannah Szenes: A Song of Light* (I-A), a briefer cataloguing of detail and background information. Some of Hannah's poetry and diary entries are included along with the narrative.

Albert Marrin paints an unforgettable portrait of *Hitler* (I-A) in a book that shows the costs of tyranny to the German nation and to the world. Hitler rose from a penniless tramp to wield more power than any other man in history. He shaped a strong army from the remnants of a crushed nation and committed murder on a scale that is beyond human belief. Hitler's lust for power was insatiable. As Germany's new chancellor, he stood listening to the storm troopers bellow: "The rickety bones of the world are shivering with fear,/But to us this fear means a great victory/For today Germany belongs to us, tomorrow the whole world." Hitler took the strong words to heart and was on his way to making them come true. The legacy he left is a divided Germany, a walled city of Berlin, and the hatred of the world.

The Pacific Theater

Despite the fact that American armed forces fought for four years in the Pacific, there are fewer children's and adolescent novels set in this theater than the European scene.

One novel set in the Pacific during the war—*The House of Sixty Fathers* (I), by Meindert DeJong—tells the story of Tien Pao, son of Chinese refugees, who is swept by floodwaters into Japanese-held territory. During his efforts to make his way through enemy land to find his parents, he meets an American pilot. They eventually reach an American air base, where an entire company of GIs adopts Tien Pao and thereby become his "sixty fathers."

Hiroshima No Pika (I-A) is Toshi Maruki's picture-book version of what happened to one family who was in Hiroshima the day the atom bomb was dropped. Seven-year-old Mii and her parents are at the breakfast table when the relentless destruction begins. After the first blinding flash, Mii's mother carries her father and drags her to the river. There they are surrounded by wounded and dead neighbors. The aftermath of the bomb is as vicious as the original destruction. Burned bodies and heaps of rubble in a burning city surround them. Mii's father dies of radiation burns and Mii herself is permanently retarded. This heart-wrenching depiction of the results of war is powerful; it is a picture book not meant for young readers.

Eleanor Coerr's *Sadako and the Thousand Paper Cranes* (P-I) describes lingering death from radiation. Sadako was only 2 years old when the atomic bomb was dropped on her home city, Hiroshima; when she was 12, she was stricken with leukemia. Restricted to bed, Sadako folded paper cranes because legend says the crane lives for 1,000 years and that sick persons who fold 1,000 of them and keep them at their side will be granted long life. Sadako was able to fold only 644 before her death, but her classmates folded 356 more so that 1,000 paper cranes could be buried with her. Coerr tells how, in Japan, the death of Sadako came to symbolize the death of all children killed by the bomb, and how children collected money to erect a powerful monument, inscribed at the base of which is the plea for all children: "This is our cry, this is our prayer; peace in the world."

Stories written from the perspective of people who were on opposite sides of battle present a sympathetic view of the so-called enemy. Yoko Kawashima Watkins tells her own autobiographical story about life after World War II in *So Far from the Bamboo Grove* (I-A). Yoko, who is Japanese, lived with her parents and an older brother and sister near a bamboo grove in Korea in 1945 when her story begins. Her father, a Japanese government official, worked in Manchuria, so she had grown up in the ancient town 50 miles from the Manchurian border. The Koreans bitterly resented Japanese rule, so Yoko's family was in grave danger. The story of her escape with her mother and sister, separated from their father and brother, is harrowing. The three women are humiliated and brutalized. Even when the two girls are in Japan adjusting to their mother's death, they are poverty stricken and ostracized by schoolmates.

War Echoes in America

Some stories of the World War II period are not set in the European or Pacific theater. In Janet Hickman's *The Stones* (I), Garrett McKay's father is missing in action. When Garrett and his friends discover that Jack Tramp, a village recluse who has often borne the brunt of childish pranks, is actually named Adolph—like Hitler—their pranks become more serious. The characters and events in Hickman's novel ring true in this story about the perniciousness of anger and hatred disguised as patriotism

Farewell to Manzanar (I-A), by Jeanne Wakatsuki Houston and James Houston, begins when Jeanne Wakatsuki is 7 years old and is taken with her family to a relocation camp, Manzanar. Release from the camp is nearly as traumatic as the incarceration for, in the process, the family is broken up. The whole experience leaves those subjected to it with a pervasive sense of unworthiness that plagues their lives long after.

Yoshiko Uchida's *Journey to Topaz* (I) describes the life of Japanese-Americans who, following the attack on Pearl Harbor, were shunted by the thousands to internment camps, despite lifelong loyalty to America. The FBI arrests the father as an enemy alien and places the rest of the family in an evacuation center, where they live in converted horse stables. Uchida continues her story in *Journey Home* (I-A). This book shows what life was like as the shreds of their family return from the internment camp and try to reconstruct a life for themselves.

Thousands of children were evacuated from their homes during World War II. Sheila Garrigue describes her own experiences when *All the Children Were Sent Away* (I-A) and in the sequel *The Eternal Spring of Mr. Ito* (I-A). Sara, an English child, came to stay with an uncle and aunt in Vancouver, Canada, during the bombings in Britain. With the bombings of Pearl Harbor and Hong Kong, anti-Japanese feeling runs high in their West Coast community. Sara is upset by the way her uncle's family treats Mr. Ito, the wise and gentle Japanese gardener, and she secretly pays a visit to his family in their dismal internment camp home. Unable to tolerate life in the internment camp, Mr. Ito spends his last days hiding in a cliffside cave. Sara's compassion does bring about small changes, but the persecution and prejudice against the Japanese is strong.

RECOMMENDED READING

Prehistoric

Anderson, Margaret J. *Light in the Mountain.* New York: Knopf, 1982.

Baker, Betty. *Walk the World's Rim.* New York: Harper & Row, 1965.

Barringer, D. Moreau. *And the Waters Prevailed.* Illustrated by P. A. Hutchinson. New York: Dutton, 1956.

Bato, Joseph. *The Sorcerer.* Edited by Katherine Fair Donnelly. New York: McKay, 1976.

Baumann, Hans. *The Caves of the Great Hunters,* rev. ed. New York: Pantheon, 1962.

———. *In the Land of Ur: The Discovery of Ancient Mesopotamia.* Translated by Stella Humphries. New York: Pantheon, 1969.

Kjelgaard, James. *Fire Hunter.* New York: Holiday House, 1951.

Osborne, Chester. *The Memory*

String. New York: Atheneum, 1984.

Sutcliff, Rosemary. *Sun Horse, Moon Horse*. Illustrated by Shirley Felts. New York: Dutton, 1978.

Ancient Times

Aliki (Brandenberg). *Mummies Made in Egypt*. New York: Crowell, 1979.

Glubok, Shirley, and Alfred Tamarin. *The Mummy of Ramose: The Life and Death of an Ancient Egyptian Nobleman*. New York: Harper & Row, 1978.

Hodges, Margaret. *The Avenger*. New York: Scribner's, 1982.

Lasker, Joe. *The Great Alexander the Great*. New York: Viking, 1983.

Macaulay, David. *Pyramid*. Boston: Houghton Mifflin, 1975.

Picard, Barbara L. *The Iliad of Homer*. Illustrated by Joan Kiddell-Monroe. New York: Oxford University Press, 1960.

Middle Ages

Goodall, John S. *The Story of a Castle*. New York: Atheneum, McElderry, 1986.

———. *The Story of a Main Street*. New York: Atheneum, McElderry, 1987.

Hodges, Margaret. *Knight Prisoner: The Tale of Sir Thomas Malory and His King Arthur*. Illustrated by Don Bolognese and Elaine Raphael. New York: Farrar, Straus & Giroux, 1976.

Mallory, Sir Thomas. *King Arthur and His Knights of the Round Table*. Illustrated by Florian. Edited by Sidney Lanier and Howard Pyle. Putnam, 1950.

Paton Walsh, Jill. *A Parcel of Patterns*. New York: Farrar, Straus & Giroux, 1983.

Schnurnberger, Lynn Edelman. *Kings, Queens, Knights and Jesters: Making Medieval Costumes*. Illustrated by Alan Robert Showe. Photography by Barbara Brooks

and Pamela Hart. New York: Harper & Row, 1978.

Sutcliff, Rosemary. *Bonnie Dundee*. New York: Dutton, 1984.

———. *The Sword and the Circle*. New York: Dutton, 1981.

Turner, Ann. *The Way Home*. New York: Crown, 1982.

Explorations

Barth, Edna. *Balder and the Mistletoe: A Story for the Winter Holidays*. Illustrated by Richard Cuffari. New York: Clarion, 1979.

Clements, Bruce. *Prison Window, Jerusalem Blue*. New York: Farrar, Straus & Giroux, 1977.

Syme, Ronald. *Magellan: First Around the World*. Illustrated by William Stobbs. New York: Morrow, 1953.

New World

Campbell, Elizabeth. *Jamestown: The Beginning*. Illustrated by William S. Bock. Boston: Little, Brown, 1974.

Hooks, William H. *The Legend of the White Doe*. Illustrated by Dennis Nolan. New York: Macmillan, 1988.

Jackson, Shirley. *The Witchcraft of Salem Village*. Illustrated by Lili Rethi. New York: Random House, 1956.

Monjo, F. N. *The House on Stink Alley: A Story About the Pilgrims in Holland*. Illustrated by Robert Quackenbush. New York: Dell, 1980.

Spier, Peter. *The Legend of New Amsterdam*. New York: Doubleday, 1979.

Revolutionary War

Avi. *Night Journeys*. New York: Pantheon, 1979.

Bourne, Miriam Ann. *Uncle George Washington and Harriot's Guitar*. Illustrated by Elise Primavera. New York: Coward, McCann & Geoghegan, 1983.

D'Aulaire, Ingri, and Edgar Parin

D'Aulaire. *Benjamin Franklin*. New York: Doubleday, 1950.

Davis, Burke. *Black Heroes of the American Revolution*. New York: Harcourt Brace Jovanovich, 1976.

———. *George Washington and the American Revolution*. New York: Random House, 1975.

DePauw, Linda Grant. *Founding Mothers: Women of America in the Revolutionary Era*. Illustrated by Michael McCurdy. Boston: Houghton Mifflin, 1975.

Edwards, Sally. *George Midgett's War*. New York: Scribner's, 1985.

Finlayson, Ann. *Rebecca's War*. New York: Warne, 1972.

Fritz, Jean. *Stonewall*. Illustrated by Stephen Gammell. New York: Putnam's, 1979.

Lawrence, Mildred. *Touchmark*. New York: Harcourt Brace Jovanovich, 1975.

Lawson, Robert. *Ben and Me*. Boston: Little, Brown, 1951.

———. *Mr. Revere and I*. Boston: Little, Brown, 1953.

Peck, Robert Newton. *Fawn: A Novel*. Boston: Little, Brown, 1975.

American Indians

Bealer, Alex. *Only the Names Remain: The Cherokees and the Trail of Tears*. Illustrated by William S. Bock. Boston: Little, Brown, 1972.

Bierhorst, John, ed. *Songs of the Chippewa*. Illustrated by Joe Servello. New York: Farrar, Straus & Giroux, 1974.

Bulla, Clyde Robert. *Squanto: Friend of the White Men*. Illustrated by Peter Burchard. New York: Crowell, 1954.

Fritz, Jean. *Make Way for Sam Houston*. Illustrated by Elise Primavera. New York: Putnam's, 1986.

Glubok, Shirley. *The Art of the North American Indian*. New York: Harper & Row, 1964.

Goble, Paul. *The Girl Who Loved Wild Horses*. New York: Bradbury, 1978.

Harris, Christie. *Mouse Woman and the Muddleheads.* Illustrated by Douglas Tait. New York: Atheneum, 1979.

Highwater, Jamake. *Anpao: An American Indian Odyssey.* Illustrated by Fritz Scholder. Philadelphia: Lippincott, 1977.

Jones, Weyman. *Edge of Two Worlds.* New York: Dial, 1968.

McDermott, Gerald. *Arrow to the Sun.* New York: Viking, 1974.

Malatesta, Anne, and Ronald Friedland. *The White Kikuyu: Louis S. B. Leakey.* New York: McGraw-Hill, 1978.

Parrish, Thomas. *The American Flag.* New York: Simon & Schuster, 1973.

Sleator, William. *The Angry Moon.* Illustrated by Blair Lent. Boston: Little, Brown, 1981.

Speare, Elizabeth George. *Calico Captive.* Boston: Houghton Mifflin, 1957.

Supree, Burton, and Ann Ross. *Bear's Heart: Scenes from the Life of a Cheyenne Artist of One Hundred Years Ago with Pictures by Himself.* Philadelphia: Lippincott, 1977.

Wolkstein, Diane. *Squirrel's Song: A Hopi Indian Tale.* Illustrated by Lillian Hoban. New York: Knopf, 1976.

Wood, Nancy. *War Cry on a Prayer Feather: Prose and Poetry of the Ute Indians.* New York: Doubleday, 1979.

Civil War

Beatty, Patricia. *Charley Skedaddle.* New York: Morrow, 1987.

Hiser, Berniece T. *The Adventure of Charlie and His Wheat-Straw Hat: A Memorat.* Illustrated by Mary Szilagyi. New York: Dodd, Mead, 1986.

Kassen, Lou. *Listen for Rachel.* New York: Atheneum, McElderry, 1986.

Keith, Harold. *Rifles for Watie.* New York: Crowell, 1957.

Petry, Ann. *Harriet Tubman: Conductor on the Underground Railroad.* New York: Crowell, 1955.

Wisler, G. Clifton. *Thunder on the Tennessee.* New York: Dutton, 1983.

Pioneers

Anderson, Joan. *Christmas on the Prairie.* Photography by George Ancona. New York: Clarion, 1985.

————. *Pioneer Children of Appalachia.* Illustrated by George Ancona. New York: Clarion, 1986.

Blos, Joan. *A Gathering of Days: A New England Girl's Journal, 1830–32.* New York: Scribner's, 1979.

Bohner, Charles. *Bold Journey: West with Lewis and Clark.* Boston: Houghton Mifflin, 1985.

Fisher, Leonard Everett. *The Schools.* New York: Holiday House, 1983.

Harvey, Brett. *Cassie's Journey: Going West in the 1860s.* Illustrated by Deborah Kogan Ray. New York: Holiday House, 1988.

Hoople, Cheryl G. *As I Saw It: Women Who Lived the American Adventure.* New York: Dial, 1978.

Lasky, Kathryn. *Beyond the Divide.* New York: Macmillan, 1983.

Levitin, Sonia. *The No-Return Trail.* New York: Harcourt Brace Jovanovich, 1978.

O'Dell, Scott. *Streams to the River, River to the Sea: A Novel of Sacagawea.* Boston: Houghton Mifflin, 1986.

Pellowski, Anne. *First Farm in the Valley: Anna's Story.* Illustrated by Wendy Watson. New York: Philomel, 1982.

Stewart, Elinore Pruitt. *Letters of a Woman Homesteader.* Illustrated by N. C. Wyeth. Boston: Houghton Mifflin, 1982.

Talbot, Charlene Joy. *The Sodbuster Venture.* New York: Atheneum, 1982.

Turner, Ann. *Third Girl from the Left.* New York: Macmillan, 1986.

Yolen, Jane. H. *The Gift of Sarah Barker.* New York: Viking, 1981.

Immigrants and the Depression

Aaron, Chester. *Lackawanna.* Philadelphia: Lippincott, 1986.

Anderson, Margaret. *The Journey of the Shadow Bairns.* New York: Knopf, 1980.

Avi. *Shadrach's Crossing.* New York: Pantheon, 1983.

Bess, Clayton. *Tracks.* Boston: Houghton Mifflin, 1986.

Burch, Robert. *Ida Early Comes over the Mountain.* New York: Viking, 1980.

Cameron, Eleanor. *Julia and the Hand of God.* Illustrated by Gail Owens. New York: Dutton, 1977.

————. *A Room Made of Windows.* Boston: Little, Brown, 1971.

Cleaver, Vera and Bill Cleaver. *Dust of the Earth.* Philadelphia: Lippincott, 1975.

Fahrmann, Willi. *The Long Journey of Lukas B.* Translated by Anthea Bell. New York: Bradbury, 1985.

Fisher, Leonard Everett. *Ellis Island: Gateway to the New World.* New York: Holiday House, 1986.

Freedman, Russell. *Immigrant Kids.* New York: Dutton, 1980.

Gates, Doris. *Blue Willow.* Illustrated by Paul Lantz. New York: Viking, 1940.

Kherdian, David. *The Road from Home: The Story of an Armenian Girl.* New York: Greenwillow, 1979.

Kurelek, William. *They Sought a New World: The Story of European Immigration to North America.* Edited by Margaret S. Engelhart. Cheektowaga, N.Y.: Tundra Books, 1985.

Langford, Sondra Gordon. *Red Bird of Ireland.* New York: Atheneum, McElderry, 1983.

Lenski, Lois. *Strawberry Girl.* Philadelphia: Lippincott, 1945.

Taylor, Sydney. *All-of-a-Kind Family.* Illustrated by Helen John. Chicago: Follett, 1951.

World War II

Baer, Frank. *Max's Gang.* Translated by Ivanka Roberts. Boston: Little, Brown, 1983.

Bauer, Marion Dane. *Rain of Fire.* New York: Clarion, 1983.

Bawden, Nina. *Carrie's War.* Illustrated by Colleen Browning. Philadelphia: Lippincott, 1973.

Benchley, Nathaniel. *Bright Candles: A Novel of the Danish Resistance.* New York: Harper & Row, 1974.

Fife, Dale. *North of Danger.* Illustrated by Haakon Soether. New York: Dutton, 1978.

Hautzig, Esther. *The Endless Steppe: Growing up in Siberia.* New York: Crowell, 1968.

Kerr, M. E. *Gentlehands.* New York: Harper & Row, 1978.

Lowry, Lois. *Autumn Street.* Boston: Houghton Mifflin, 1980.

Magorian, Michelle. *Back Home.* New York: Harper & Row, 1984.

Matsubara, Hisako. *Cranes at Dusk.* Translated by Leila Vennewitz. New York: Dial, 1985.

Mattingley, Christobel. *The Angel with a Mouth Organ.* Illustrated by Astra Lacis. New York: Holiday House, 1986.

———. *The Miracle Tree.* Illustrated by Marianne Yamaguchi. San Diego: Harcourt Brace Jovano-vich, Gulliver, 1986.

Moskin, Marietta. *I Am Rosemarie.* New York: Day, 1972.

Rogasky, Barbara. *Smoke and Ashes: The Story of the Holocaust.* New York: Holiday House, 1988.

Streatfield, Noel. *When the Sirens Wailed.* Illustrated by Judith Gwyn Brown. New York: Random House, 1976.

Vinke, Herman. *The Short Life of Sophie Scholl.* Translated by Hedwig Pachter. New York: Harper & Row, 1984.

Poetry

Benet, Rosemary, and Steven Vincent Benet. *A Book of Americans.* Illustrated by Charles Child. New York: Holt, Rinehart & Winston, 1961.

Brand, Oscar. *Songs of '76: A Folksinger's History of the Revolution.* New York: Evans, 1973.

———. *When I First Came to This Land.* Illustrated by Doris Burn. New York: Putnam, 1974.

Brewton, Sara, and John E. Brewton, eds. *America Forever New: A Book of Poems.* Illustrated by Ann Grifalconi. New York: Crowell, 1968.

Cole, William, ed. *Rough Men, Tough Men: Poems of Action and Adventure.* Illustrated by Enrico Arno. New York: Viking, 1969.

Hine, Al, ed. *This Land is Mine: An Anthology of American Verse.* Illustrated by Leonard Vosburgh. Philadelphia: Lippincott, 1965.

Hopkins, Lee Bennett, ed. *Beat the Drum, Independence Day Has Come.* Illustrated by Tomie de-Paola. New York: Harcourt Brace Jovanovich, 1976.

Key, Frances Scott. *The Star-Spangled Banner.* Illustrated by Paul Galdone. New York: Crowell, 1966.

———. *The Star-Spangled Banner.* Illustrated by Peter Spier. New York: Doubleday, 1973.

Kraske, Robert. *America the Beautiful: Stories of Patriotic Songs.* New York: Garrard, 1972.

Lewis, Claudia. *Long Ago in Oregon.* New York: Harper & Row, 1987.

Merriam, Eve. *Finding a Poem.* Illustrated by Seymour Chwast. New York: Atheneum, 1970.

———. *Independent Voices.* Illustrated by Arvis Stewart. New York: Atheneum, 1968.

Untermeyer, Louis. *The Golden Treasury of Poetry.* Illustrated by Joan Walsh Anglund. New York: Golden Press, 1959.

PROFESSIONAL REFERENCES

Alpenfels, Ethel J. *Man on the Move: An Introduction to Anthropology.* Filmstrip. New York: Random House, Miller Brody.

Browne, C. A. *The Story of Our National Ballads.* Edited by William Heaps. New York: Crowell, 1960.

Commire, Anne, ed. *Something About the Author.* Vols. 1–50. Detroit: Gale Research, 1971–1988.

De Montreville, Doris, and Donna Hill, eds. *Third Book of Junior Authors.* New York: Wilson, 1972.

FitzGerald, Frances. *America Revised: History Schoolbooks in the Twentieth Century.* Boston: Little, Brown, 1979.

Fritz, Jean. "George Washington, My Father, and Walt Disney." *Horn Book Magazine* 52, no. 2 (April 1976): 191–98.

Greenlaw, M. Jean. "An Interview With Mollie Hunter." in *From Writers to Students.* Edited by M. Jerry Weiss. Newark, Del.: International Reading Association, 1979.

Haviland, Virginia, ed. *Children and Literature: Views and Reviews.* Glenview, Ill.: Scott, Foresman, 1973.

Hickman, Janet. "Profile: The Person Behind the Book—Mollie Hunter." *Language Arts* 56, no. 3 (March 1979): 302.

Hopkins, Lee Bennett, ed. *More Books by More People.* New York: Citation Press, 1974.

Hunter, Mollie. *Talent Is Not Enough.* New York: Harper & Row, 1976.

Kimmel, Eric. "Confronting the Ovens: The Holocaust and Juvenile Fiction." *Horn Book Magazine*

53, no. 1 (February 1977): 84–91.

Naidoo, Beverly. *Censoring Reality: An Examination of Books on South Africa*. London: ILEA Centre for Anti-Racist Education, 1984.

Vining, Elizabeth Gray. *Profiles in Literature*. Philadelphia: Temple University Press, 1969.

Weiss, M. Jerry, ed. *From Writers to Students*. Newark: Del.: International Reading Association, 1979.

NOTES

1. Arthur Guiterman, "Ancient History," in *The Arbuthnot Anthology of Children's Literature*, 4th ed., ed. Zena Sutherland et al. (New York: Lothrop, Lee & Shepard, 1976), 7.
2. Rosemary Sutcliff, "History Is People," in *Children and Literature: Views and Reviews*, ed. Virginia Haviland (Glenview, Ill.: Scott, Foresman, 1973), 307–8.
3. Mollie Hunter, *Talent Is Not Enough: Mollie Hunter on Writing for Children* (New York: Harper & Row, 1976), 40–41.
4. Elizabeth Janet Gray Vining, "Profiles in Literature" (Philadelphia: Temple University Press, 1969), video.
5. Jean Fritz, "George Washington, My Father, and Walt Disney," *Horn Book Magazine* 52, no. 2 (April 1976): 191.
6. Mollie Hunter, The *Stronghold* (New York: Harper & Row, 1974), 2.
7. Hunter, *Talent Is Not Enough*, 18.
8. Janet Hickman, "Profile: The Person Behind the Book—Mollie Hunter," *Language Arts* 56,

no. 3 (March 1979): 302.

9. M. Jean Greenlaw, "An Interview with Mollie Hunter," in *From Writers to Students*, ed. M. Jerry Weiss (Newark, Del.: International Reading Association, 1979), 45.
10. Ibid., 46.
11. Kate Seredy, *The White Stag* (New York: Viking, 1937), 67.
12. Frances FitzGerald, *America Revised: History Schoolbooks in the Twentieth Century* (Boston: Little, Brown, 1979), 8–9.
13. Jean Poindexter Colby, *Lexington and Concord, 1775* (New York: Hastings House, 1975), 87–88.
14. Fritz, "George Washington, My Father, and Walt Disney," 191–98.
15. Doris DeMontreville and Donna Hill, eds. *The Third Book of Junior Authors* (New York: Wilson, 1972), 95.
16. Lee Bennett Hopkins, "Jean Fritz," in *More Books by More People* (New York: Citation Press, 1974), 177.
17. Adapted from a plan by Diane R. Confer, Kane Public Schools, Kane, Pa.

18. Russell Freedman, *Lincoln: A Photobiography* (New York: Clarion, 1987), 130.
19. Laura Ingalls Wilder, *Little House in the Big Woods* (New York: Harper & Row, 1953), 1–2.
20. Kathryn Lasky, *The Night Journey*, illus. Trina Schart Hyman (New York: Warne, 1981), 150.
21. Mildred D. Taylor, *Roll of Thunder, Hear My Cry* (New York: Dial, 1976), 23.
22. Mildred D. Taylor, promotional material, Dial Publishers, New York City.
23. Ibid.
24. Eric A. Kimmel, "Confronting the Ovens: The Holocaust and Juvenile Fiction," *Horn Book Magazine* 53, no. 1 (February 1977): 84.
25. Jaap ter Haar, *Boris* (New York: Delacorte, 1966), 66.
26. Idea adapted from Erika Hess Merems, *The Holocaust Years: Society on Trial, Teacher's Guide* (New York: Bantam, 1978), 6.
27. Milton Meltzer, *Never to Forget: The Jews of the Holocaust* (New York: Harper & Row, 1976), 191.

CHILDREN'S BOOKS CITED

Abells, Chana Byars. *The Children We Remember*. New York: Greenwillow, 1986.

Alcott, Louisa May. *Little Women*. New York: Macmillan, 1986.

Aliki (Brandenberg). *A Medieval Feast*. New York: Crowell, 1983.

———. *The Many Lives of Benjamin Franklin*. Englewood Cliffs, N.J.: Prentice-Hall, 1977.

Anderson, Joan. *The First Thanksgiving Feast*. Illustrated by George Ancona. New York: Clarion, 1984.

Angell, Judie. *One-Way to Ansonia*. New York: Bradbury, 1985.

Atkinson, Linda. *In Kindling Flame: The Story of Hannah Sanesh, 1921–1944*. New York: Lothrop, Lee & Shepard, 1984.

Avi. *The Fighting Ground*. Philadelphia: Lippincott, 1984.

Barth, Edna. *Turkeys, Pilgrims, and Indian Corn: The Story of the Thanksgiving Symbols*. Illustrated by Ursula Arndt. New York: Seabury, 1975.

Beatty, Patricia. *Turn Homeward, Hannalee*. New York: Morrow, 1984.

Behn, Harry. *The Faraway Lurs*. Boston: Hall, 1981.

Blair, Gwenda. *Laura Ingalls Wilder*.

Illustrated by Thomas B. Allen. New York: Putnam's, 1981.

Blumberg, Rhoda. *The Incredible Journey of Lewis and Clark.* New York: Lothrop, Lee & Shepard, 1987.

Brink, Carol Ryrie. *Caddie Woodlawn.* Illustrated by Trina Schart Hyman. New York: Macmillan, 1973.

Brooks, Polly Schoyer. *Queen Eleanor: Independent Spirit of the Medieval World.* Philadelphia: Lippincott, 1983.

Bulla, Clyde Robert. *A Lion to Guard Us.* Illustrated by Michele Chessare. New York: Crowell, 1981.

———. *Squanto: Friend of the Pilgrims.* Illustrated by Peter Burchard. New York: Scholastic, 1971.

———. *The Sword in the Tree.* Illustrated by Paul Galdone. New York: Crowell, 1956.

———. *Viking Adventure.* Illustrated by Douglas Gorsline. New York: Crowell, 1963.

Burnam, Tom. *Dictionary of Misinformation.* New York: Crowell, 1975.

Campbell, Elizabeth A. *Jamestown: The Beginning.* Illustrated by William Sauts Bock. Boston: Little, Brown, 1974.

Catton, Bruce. *The Battle of Gettysburg.* New York: American Heritage, 1963.

Caudill, Rebecca. *Tree of Freedom.* Illustrated by Dorothy Morse. New York: Viking, 1949.

Cavanah, Frances. *The Truth About The Man Behind the Book That Sparked the War Between the States.* Philadelphia: Westminster, 1975.

Cesarani, Gian Paolo. *Christopher Columbus.* Illustrated by Piero Ventura. New York: Random House, 1979.

———. *Marco Polo.* Illustrated by Piero Ventura. New York: Putnam's, 1982.

Cheney, Cora. *The Incredible Deborah: A Story Based on the Life of Deborah Sampson.* New York: Scribner's, 1967.

Clapp, Patricia. *Constance: A Story of Early Plymouth.* New York: Viking, Penguin, 1986.

———. *I'm Deborah Sampson: A Soldier in the War of the Revolution.* New York: Lothrop, Lee & Shepard, 1977.

———. *The Tamarack Tree: A Novel of the Siege of Vicksburg.* New York: Lothrop, Lee & Shepard, 1986.

———. *Witches' Children: A Story of Salem.* New York: Lothrop, Lee & Shepard, 1982.

Clark, Ann Nolan. *All This Wild Land.* New York: Viking, 1976.

Coerr, Eleanor. *Sadako and the Thousand Paper Cranes.* Illustrated by Ronald Himler. New York: Putnam's, 1977.

Colby, Jean Poindexter. *Lexington and Concord 1775: What Really Happened.* Photography by Barbara Cooney. New York: Hastings House, 1975.

Collier, James Lincoln, and Christopher Collier. *my brother Sam is dead.* New York: Scholastic, 1974.

———. *War Comes to Willy Freeman.* New York: Delacorte, 1983.

———. *Who is Carrie?* New York: Delacorte, 1984.

Colver, Anne. *Bread and Butter Indian.* Illustrated by Garth Williams. New York: Holt, Rinehart & Winston, 1964.

———. *Bread and Butter Journey.* Illustrated by Garth Williams. New York: Holt, Rinehart & Winston, 1970.

Conrad, Pamela. *Prairie Songs.* New York: Harper & Row, 1985.

Cowen, Ida, and Irene Gunther. *A Spy for Freedom: The Story of Sarah Aaronsohn.* New York: Lodestar, 1984.

Dalgleish, Alice. *The Columbus Story.* Illustrated by Leo Politi. New York: Scribner's, 1955.

———. *The Courage of Sarah Noble.* Illustrated by Leonard Weisgard. New York: Macmillan, 1986.

———. *The Thanksgiving Story.* Illustrated by Helen Sewell. New York: Macmillan, 1985.

Daugherty, James. *Abraham Lincoln.* New York: Viking, 1943.

———. *Poor Richard.* New York: Viking, 1964.

D'Aulaire, Ingri, and Edgar Parin D'Aulaire. *Columbus.* New York: Doubleday, 1955.

———. *Leif the Lucky.* New York: Doubleday, 1941.

———. *Norse Gods and Giants.* New York: Doubleday, 1967.

Davis, Paxton. *Three Days with Robert E. Lee at Gettysburg.* New York: Atheneum, 1980.

De Angeli, Marguerite. *The Door in the Wall.* New York: Doubleday, 1949.

Degens, T. *Transport 7-41-R.* New York: Viking, 1974.

———. *The Visit.* New York: Viking, 1982.

De Jong, Meindert. *The House of Sixty Fathers.* Illustrated by Maurice Sendak. New York: Harper & Row, 1956.

Dillon, Eilis. *The Seekers.* New York: Scribner's, 1986.

Dyer, T. A. *A Way of His Own.* Boston: Houghton Mifflin, 1981.

Eaton, Jeanette. *That Lively Man, Ben Franklin.* Illustrated by Henry Pitz. New York: Morrow, 1948.

Eckert, Allan W. *Blue Jacket: War Chief of the Shawnees.* Boston: Little, Brown, 1969.

Ellis, L. Ethan. *Forty Million Schoolbooks Can't Be Wrong: Myths in American History.* New York: Macmillan, 1975.

Evernden, Margery. *The Dream Keeper.* New York: Lothrop, Lee & Shepard, 1985.

Farber, Norma. *Mercy Short.* New York: Dutton, 1982.

Fisher, Leonard. *The Warlock of Westfall.* New York: Doubleday, 1974.

Forbes, Esther. *Johnny Tremain.* Illustrated by Lynd Ward. Boston: Houghton Mifflin, 1946.

Foster, Genevieve. *George Washington's World.* New York: Scribner's, 1949.

Fox, Paula. *The Slave Dancer.* Illustrated by Eros Keith. New York: Bradbury, 1973.

Franchere, Ruth. *Willa: The Story of Willa Cather's Growing Up.* New York: Crowell, 1958.

Frank, Anne. *Anne Frank: The Diary of a Young Girl*, rev. ed. Translated by B. M. Mooyart. New York: Doubleday, 1967.

Frank, Rudolf. *No Hero for the Kaiser.* Illustrated by Klaus Steffins, translated by Patricia Crampton. New York: Lothrop, Lee & Shepard, 1986.

Frazier, Neta L. *Stout-Hearted Seven.* New York: Harcourt Brace Jovanovich, 1973.

Freedman, Russell. *Lincoln: A Photobiography.* New York: Clarion, 1987.

Fritz, Jean. *And Then What Happened, Paul Revere?* Illustrated by Margot Tomes. New York: Coward, McCann & Geoghegan, 1973.

———. *Brady.* Illustrated by Lynd Ward. New York: Coward, McCann & Geoghegan, 1960.

———. *The Cabin Faced West.* Illustrated by Feodor Rojankovsky. New York: Coward, McCann & Geoghegan, 1958.

———. *Can't You Make Them Behave, King George?* Illustrated by Tomie dePaola. New York: Coward, McCann & Geoghegan, 1977.

———. *China Homecoming.* Photography by Michael Fritz. New York: Putnam's, 1985.

———. *The Double Life of Pocohontas.* Illustrated by Ed Young. New York: Putnam's, 1983.

———. *Early Thunder.* Illustrated by Lynd Ward. New York: Coward, McCann & Geoghegan, 1967.

———. *Homesick: My Own Story.* Illustrated by Margot Tomes. New York: Putnam's, 1982.

———. *Traitor: The Case of Benedict Arnold.* New York: Putnam 1981.

———. *What's the Big Idea, Ben Franklin?* Illustrated by Margot Tomes. New York: Coward, McCann & Geoghegan, 1976.

———. *Where Was Patrick Henry on the 29th of May?* Illustrated by Margot Tomes. New York: Putnam's, 1975.

———. *Who's That Stepping on Plymouth Rock?* Illustrated by J. B. Handelsman. New York: Coward, McCann & Geoghegan, 1975.

———. *Why Don't You Get a Horse, Sam Adams?* Illustrated by Trina Schart Hyman. New York: Coward, McCann & Geoghegan, 1974.

———. *Will You Sign Here, John Hancock?* Illustrated by Trina Schart Hyman. New York: Coward, McCann & Geoghegan, 1976.

Garrigue, Sheila. *All the Children Were Sent Away.* New York: Bradbury, 1976.

———. *The Eternal Spring of Mr. Ito.* New York: Bradbury, 1985.

Garson, Eugenia, and Herbert Haufrecht. *The Laura Ingalls Wilder Songbook.* Illustrated by Garth Williams. New York: Harper & Row, 1968.

Gauch, Patricia Lee. *This Time, Tempe Wick?* Illustrated by Margot Tomes. New York: Coward, McCann & Geoghegan, 1974.

Gehrts, Barbara. *Don't Say a Word.* Translated by Elizabeth D. Crawford. New York: Atheneumn, McElderry, 1986.

Giff, Patricia Reilly. *Laura Ingalls Wilder: Growing Up in the Little House.* Illustrated by Eileen McKeating. New York: Viking, 1987.

Glubok, Shirley. *Art and Archaeology.* New York: Harper & Row, n.d.

———, and Alfred Tamarin. *Olympic Games in Ancient Greece.* New York: Harper & Row 1984.

Goodall, John S. *The Story of a Castle.* New York: Atheneum, McElderry, 1986.

———. *Story of an English Village.* New York: Atheneum, McElderry, 1979.

Green, Margaret. *Radical of the Revolution: Samuel Adams.* New York: Messner, 1971.

Guiterman, Arthur. "Ancient History." In *The Arbuthnot Anthology of Children's Literature*, 4th ed. Edited by Zena Sutherland et al. New York: Lothrop, Lee & Shepard, 1976.

Haar, Jaap Ter. *Boris.* New York: Delacorte, 1970.

Harvey, Brett. *My Prairie Year: Based on the Diary of Elenore Plaisted.* Illustrated by Deborah Kogan Ray. New York: Holiday House, 1986.

Haugaard, Erik Christian. *Hakon of Rogen's Saga.* Illustrated by Leo Dillon and Diane Dillon. Boston: Houghton Mifflin, 1963.

———. *Leif the Unlucky.* Boston: Houghton Mifflin, 1982.

———. *A Slave's Tale.* Illustrated by Leo Dillon and Diane Dillon. Boston: Houghton Mifflin, 1965.

Hendershot, Judith. *In Coal Country.* Edited by Frances Foster, illustrated by Thomas B. Allen. New York: Knopf, 1987.

Hickman, Janet. *The Stones.* Illustrated by Richard Cuffari. New York: Macmillan, 1976.

———. *Zoar Blue.* New York: Macmillan, 1978.

Highwater, Jamake. *Legend Days.* New York: Harper & Row, 1984.

Hodges, Margaret. *Baldur and the Mistletoe: A Myth of the Vikings.* Boston: Little, Brown, 1974.

———. *Hopkins of the Mayflower: Portrait of a Dissenter.* New York: Farrar, Straus & Giroux, 1972

Holman, Felice. *Slake's Limbo.* New York: Dell, 1986.

Houston, Jeanne Wakatsuki, and James D. Houston. *Farewell to Manzanar.* Boston: Houghton Mifflin, 1973.

Hunt, Irene. *Across Five Aprils.* Chicago: Follett, 1964.

Hunter, Mollie. *The Stronghold.* New York: Harper & Row, 1974.

———. *The Third Eye.* New York: Harper & Row, 1979.

———. *The Walking Stones.* New York: Harper & Row, 1970.

———. *You Never Knew Her As I Did!* New York: Harper, & Row, 1981.

Innocenti, Roberto. *Rose Blanche.* Mankato, Minn.: Creative Education, 1985.

Kerr, Judith. *The Other Way Round.* New York: Coward, McCann & Geoghegan, 1975.

———. *A Small Person Far Away.* New York: Coward, McCann & Geoghegan, 1979.

———. *When Hitler Stole Pink Rabbit.* New York: Coward, McCann & Geoghegan, 1972.

Kherdian, David. *Finding Home.* New York: Greenwillow, 1981.

———. *The Road from Home.* New York: Greenwillow, 1979.

King, Cynthia. *In the Morning of Time: The Story of the Norse God Baldur.* New York: Four Winds, 1970.

Koehn, Ilse. *Mischling, Second Degree.* New York: Greenwillow, 1977.

Konigsburg, E. L. *A Proud Taste for Scarlet and Miniver.* New York: Atheneum, 1973.

Krensky, Stephen. *Conqueror and Hero: The Search for Alexander.* Boston: Little, Brown, 1981.

Kresh, Paul. *Isaac Bashevis Singer: The Story of a Storyteller.* Illustrated by Penrod Scofield. New York: Lodestar, 1984.

Kroeber, Theodora. *Ishi in Two Worlds: A Biography of the Last Wild Indian in North America.* Berkeley: University of California Press, 1961.

———. *Ishi: Last of His Tribe.* Boston: Parnassus, 1964.

Lampman, Evelyn Sibley. *Bargain Bride.* New York: Atheneum, 1977.

———. *Squaw Man's Son.* New York: Atheneum, 1978.

Lasker, Joe. *Merry Ever After: The Story of Two Medieval Weddings.* New York: Viking, 1976.

———. *A Tournament of Knights.* New York: Crowell, 1986.

Lasky, Kathryn. *The Night Journey.* Illustrated by Trina Schart Hyman. New York: Warne, 1981.

Latham, Jean Lee. *This Dear-Bought Land.* Illustrated by Jacob Landau. New York: Harper & Row, 1957.

Lenski, Lois. *Indian Captive: The Story of Mary Jemison.* Philadelphia: Lippincott, 1941.

Lester, Julius. *Long Journey Home: Stories from Black History.* New York: Dial, 1972.

———. ed. *To Be a Slave.* New York: Dial, 1968.

Levitin, Sonia. *Roanoke: A Novel of the Lost Colony.* New York: Atheneum, 1973.

Levy, Elizabeth. *If You Were There When They Signed the Constitution.* Illustrated by Richard Rosenblum. New York: Scholastic, 1987.

Litowinsky, Olga. *The High Voyage.* New York: Viking, 1977.

Lobel, Arnold. *On the Day Peter Stuyvesant Sailed into Town.* New York: Harper & Row, 1971.

Longfellow, Henry Wadsworth. *Paul Revere's Ride.* Illustrated by Nancy Winslow Parker. New York: Greenwillow, 1985.

Lord, Bette Bao. *In the Year of the Boar and Jackie Robinson.* Illustrated by Marc Simont. New York: Harper & Row, 1984.

Macaulay, David. *Castle.* Boston: Houghton Mifflin, 1977.

———. *Cathedral: The Story of Its Construction.* Boston: Houghton Mifflin, 1973.

McGovern, Ann. *The Secret Soldier: The Story of Deborah Sampson.* Illustrated by Ann Grifalconi. New York: Scholastic, 1975.

McGraw, Eloise Jarvis. *Mara, Daughter of the Nile.* New York: Viking, Penguin, 1985.

McKown, Robin. *Washington's America.* New York: Grosset & Dunlap, 1961.

MacLachlan, Patricia. *Sarah, Plain and Tall.* New York: Harper & Row, 1985.

Magorian, Michelle. *Good Night, Mr. Tom.* New York: Harper & Row, 1982.

Marrin, Albert. *Hitler.* New York: Macmillan, 1987.

Maruki, Toshi. *Hiroshima No Pika.* New York: Lothrop, Lee & Shepard, 1982.

Marx, Robert F. *Following Columbus: The Voyage of the Niña II.* New York: World, 1964.

May, Julian. *Before the Indians.* Illustrated by Simeon Shimin. New York: Holiday House, 1969.

Mazer, Harry. *Cave Under the City.* New York: Crowell, 1986.

Meigs, Cornelia. *Invincible Louisa: The Story of the Author of Little Women.* Boston: Little, Brown, 1933.

Meltzer, Milton. *The American Revolutionaries: A History in Their Own Words.* New York: Crowell, 1987.

———. *Bread and Roses: The Struggle of American Labor.* New York: Mentor Books, 1977.

———. *Brother Can You Spare a Dime?* New York: Knopf, 1969.

———. *George Washington and the Birth of Our Nation.* New York: Watts, 1986.

———. *Never to Forget—The Jews of the Holocaust.* New York: Harper & Row, 1976.

———. *Poverty in America.* New York: Morrow, 1986.

———. *Starting from Home: A Writer's Beginnings.* New York: Viking, 1988.

———. *Violins and Shovels: The WPA Arts Project.* New York: Delacorte, 1976.

Meredith, Robert, and E. Brooks Smith, eds. *The Quest of Columbus: An Exact Account of the Discovery of America Being the History*

Written by Ferdinand Columbus. Illustrated by Leonard Everett Fisher. Boston: Little, Brown, 1966.

Monjo, F. N. *Me and Willie and Pa.* Illustrated by Douglas Gorsline. New York: Simon & Schuster, 1973.

Morrow, Honore. *On to Oregon.* Illustrated by Edward Shenton. New York: Morrow, 1946.

Moskin, Marietta. *Waiting for Mama.* Illustrated by Richard Lebenson. New York: Coward, McCann & Geoghegan, 1975.

Myers, Robert J. *Celebrations: The Complete Book of American Holidays.* Illustrated by Bill Greer. New York: Doubleday, 1972.

O'Dell, Scott. *The Amethyst Ring.* Boston: Houghton Mifflin, 1983.

———. *The Captive.* Boston: Houghton Mifflin, 1979.

———. *The Feathered Serpent.* Boston: Houghton Mifflin, 1981.

———. *Island of the Blue Dolphin.* Boston: Houghton Mifflin, 1960.

———. *The King's Fifth.* Illustrated by Samuel Bryant. Boston: Houghton Mifflin, 1966.

———. *Sarah Bishop.* Boston: Houghton Mifflin, 1980.

———. *Sing Down the Moon.* Boston: Houghton Mifflin, 1970.

———. *Zia.* Illustrated by Ted Lewin. Boston: Houghton Mifflin, 1976.

Oleksy, Walter. *Treasures of the Land: Archaeology Today in America.* New York: Messner, 1981.

Orlev, Uri. *Island on Bird Street.* Boston: Houghton Mifflin, 1984.

Paton Walsh, Jill. *Children of the Fox.* Illustrated by Robin Eaton. New York: Farrar, Straus & Giroux, 1978.

Peck, Robert Newton. *Hang for Treason.* New York: Doubleday, 1976.

———. *Rabbits and Redcoats.* Illustrated by Laura Lydecker. New York: Walker, 1976.

Petry, Ann. *Tituba of Salem Village.* New York: Crowell, 1964.

Porell, Bruce. *Digging the Past.* Illustrated by Bruce Elliot. New York: Harper & Row, 1979.

Provensen, Alice, and Martin Provensen. *Leonardo Da Vinci: The Artist, Inventor, Scientist in Three-Dimensional Movable Pictures.* New York: Viking, 1984.

———. *Shaker Lane.* New York: Viking, 1987.

Pugh, Ellen. *Brave His Soul.* New York: Dodd, Mead, 1970.

Pyk, Ann. *The Hammer of Thunder.* New York: Putnam, 1972.

Pyle, Howard. *The Story of King Arthur and His Knights.* New York: Scribner's, 1954.

Quackenbush, Robert. *Old Silver Leg Takes Over: A Story of Peter Stuyvesant.* Englewood Cliffs, N.J.: Prentice-Hall, 1986.

Reiss, Johanna. *The Journey Back.* New York: Crowell, 1976.

———. *The Upstairs Room.* New York: Crowell, 1972.

Richardson, Fayette. *Sam Adams: The Boy Who Became Father of the American Revolution.* New York: Crown, 1975.

Richter, Conrad. *A Country of Strangers.* New York: Knopf, 1966.

———. *The Light in the Forest.* New York: Knopf, 1953.

Richter, Hans Peter. *I Was There.* Translated by Edite Kroll. New York: Viking, Penguin, 1987.

———. *Friedrich.* Translated by Edite Kroll. New York: Holt, Rinehart & Winston, 1970.

Rostkowski, Margaret. *After the Dancing Days.* New York: Harper & Row, 1986.

Rylant, Cynthia. *When I Was Young in the Mountains.* Illustrated by Diane Goode. New York: Dutton, 1985.

Sandburg, Carl. *Abe Lincoln Grows Up.* Illustrated by James Daugherty. New York: Harcourt Brace, 1956.

Schiller, Barbara. *The Vinlanders' Saga.* Illustrated by William Bock. New York: Holt, Rinehart

& Winston, 1966.

Schur, Maxine. *Hannah Szenes—A Song of Light.* Illustrated by Donna Ruff. Philadelphia: Jewish Publications, 1986.

Scott, John Anthony. *Woman Against Slavery: The Story of Harriet Beecher Stowe.* New York: Crowell, 1978.

Sender, Ruth Minsky. *The Cage.* New York: Macmillan, 1986.

Seredy, Kate. *The White Stag.* New York: Viking, 1937.

Sewall, Marcia. *The Pilgrims of Plimoth.* New York: Atheneum, 1986.

Siegal, Aranka. *Grace in the Wilderness: After the Liberation, 1945–1948.* New York: Farrar, Straus & Giroux, 1985.

———. *Upon the Head of the Goat: A Childhood in Hungary, 1939–1944.* New York: Farrar, Straus & Giroux, 1981.

Sneve, Virginia Driving Hawk. *Betrayed.* Illustrated by Chief Oren Lyons. New York: Holiday House, 1974.

Speare, Elizabeth George. *The Bronze Bow.* Boston: Houghton Mifflin, 1961.

———. *The Sign of the Beaver.* Boston: Houghton Mifflin, 1983.

———. *The Witch of Blackbird Pond.* Boston: Houghton Mifflin, 1958.

Starkey, Marion L. *The Devil in Massachusetts: A Modern Inquiry into the Salem Witch Trials.* New York: Knopf, 1949.

———. *The Tall Man from Boston.* Illustrated by Charles Mikolaycak. New York: Crown, 1975.

———. *The Visionary Girls: Witchcraft in Salem Village.* Boston: Little, Brown, 1973.

Steele, William O. *The Magic Amulet.* New York: Harcourt Brace Jovanovich, 1979.

———. *The Man with the Silver Eyes.* New York: Harcourt Brace Jovanovich, 1976.

Stowe, Harriet Beecher. *Uncle Tom's Cabin.* 1852. Reprint. New York: Dutton, 1972.

Sutcliff, Rosemary. *Frontier Wolf.* New York: Dutton, 1981.

———. *Knight's Fee.* Illustrated by Charles Keeping. New York: Walck, 1960.

———. *Song for a Dark Queen.* New York: Crowell, 1979.

———. *Warrior Scarlet.* Illustrated by Charles Keeping. New York: Walck, 1958.

Syme, Ronald. *Columbus: Finder of the New World:* Illustrated by William Stobbs. New York: Morrow, 1952.

Taylor, Mildred D. *Gold Cadillac.* New York: Dial, 1987.

———. *The Friendship.* Illustrated by Max Ginsburg. New York: Dial, 1987.

———. *Let the Circle Be Unbroken.* New York: Dial, 1981.

———. *Roll of Thunder, Hear My Cry.* New York: Dial, 1976.

———. *Song of the Trees.* Illustrated by Jerry Pinkney. New York: Dial, 1975.

Thrasher, Crystal. *A Taste of Daylight.* New York: Atheneum, McElderry, 1984.

Treece, Henry. *The Road to Miklagard.* Illustrated by Christine Price. Chatham, N.Y.: Phillips, 1957.

———. *Viking's Dawn.* Chatham, N.Y.: Phillips, 1956.

———. *Viking's Sunset.* New York: Criterion, 1961.

Turnbull, Ann Warren. *Maroo of the Winter Caves.* New York: Clarion, 1984.

Turner, Ann. *Dakota Dugout.* Illustrated by Ronald Himler. New York: Macmillan, 1985.

———. *Time of the Bison.* Illustrated by Beth Peck. New York: Macmillan, 1987.

Uchida, Yoshiko. *Journey Home.* Illustrated by Charles Robinson. New York: Atheneum, 1978.

———. *Journey to Topaz.* Illustrated by Donald Carrick. New York: Scribner's, 1971.

Van der Loeff, Anna Rutgers. *Oregon at Last!* New York: Morrow, 1962.

Vining, Elizabeth Janet Gray. *Adam of the Road.* New York: Viking, 1942.

Voight, Virginia. *Massasoit: Friend of the Pilgrims.* Illustrated by Cary. New York: Garrard, 1971.

Walker, Barbara. *The Little House Cookbook.* Illustrated by Garth Williams. New York: Harper & Row, 1979.

Watkins, Yoko Kawashima. *So Far from the Bamboo Grove.* New York: Lothrop, Lee & Shepard, 1986.

Wilder, Laura Ingalls. *By the Shores of Silver Lake.* Illustrated by Garth Williams. New York: Harper & Row, 1953.

———. *The First Four Years.* Illustrated by Garth Williams. New York: Harper & Row, 1971.

———. *Little House in the Big Woods.* Illustrated by Garth Williams. New York: Harper & Row, 1953.

———. *Little House on the Prairie.* Illustrated by Garth Williams. New York: Harper & Row, 1953.

———. *Little Town on the Prairie.* Illustrated by Garth Williams. New York: Harper & Row, 1953.

———. *The Long Winter.* Illustrated by Garth Williams. New York: Harper & Row, 1953.

———. *On the Banks of Plum Creek.* Illustrated by Garth Williams. New York: Harper & Row, 1953.

———. *These Happy Golden Years.* Illustrated by Garth Williams. New York: Harper & Row, 1953.

Williams, Jay. *The Sword of King Arthur.* New York: Crowell, 1966.

Wyndham, Lee. *A Holiday Book: Thanksgiving.* Illustrated by Hazel Hoecker. New York: Garrard, 1963.

Yarbro, Chelsea Quinn. *Four Horses for Tishtry.* New York: Harper & Row, 1985.

———. *Locadio's Apprentice.* New York: Harper & Row, 1984.

Yates, Elizabeth. *Amos Fortune: Free Man.* Illustrated by Nora Unwin. New York: Dutton, 1950.

———. *Carolina's Courage.* New York: Dutton, 1964.

10

Nonfiction

Buffalo Dusk

The buffaloes are gone.
And those who saw the buffaloes are gone.
Those who saw the buffaloes by thousands and how they pawed the
    prairie sod into dust with their hoofs, their great heads down pawing
    on in a great pageant of dusk,
Those who saw the buffaloes are gone.
And the buffaloes are gone.[1]

Carl Sandburg

arl Sandburg's poem, "Buffalo Dusk," reminds us that poetry is a powerful way of knowing. The images he creates stir a haunting feeling of loss. When children read informational books about the buffalo in addition to the poem, both types of literature can enhance their understanding. The term *nonfiction* describes books of information and fact.

The elementary school curriculum is comprised of areas of knowledge divided into specific subjects, such as mathematics, science, and social studies. Children are taught all of these as separate disciplines but must learn to

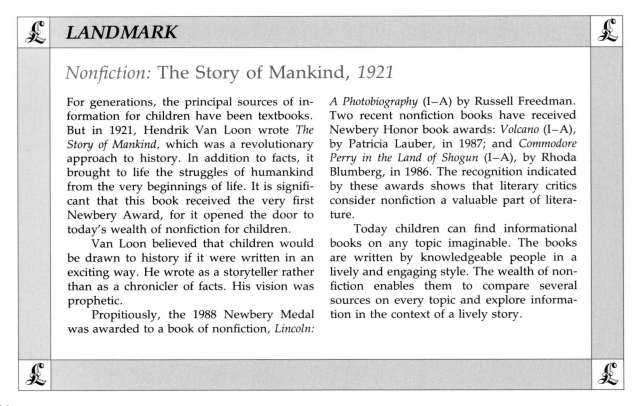

LANDMARK

Nonfiction: The Story of Mankind, *1921*

For generations, the principal sources of information for children have been textbooks. But in 1921, Hendrik Van Loon wrote *The Story of Mankind,* which was a revolutionary approach to history. In addition to facts, it brought to life the struggles of humankind from the very beginnings of life. It is significant that this book received the very first Newbery Award, for it opened the door to today's wealth of nonfiction for children.

Van Loon believed that children would be drawn to history if it were written in an exciting way. He wrote as a storyteller rather than as a chronicler of facts. His vision was prophetic.

Propitiously, the 1988 Newbery Medal was awarded to a book of nonfiction, *Lincoln:*

A Photobiography (I–A) by Russell Freedman. Two recent nonfiction books have received Newbery Honor book awards: *Volcano* (I–A), by Patricia Lauber, in 1987; and *Commodore Perry in the Land of Shogun* (I–A), by Rhoda Blumberg, in 1986. The recognition indicated by these awards shows that literary critics consider nonfiction a valuable part of literature.

Today children can find informational books on any topic imaginable. The books are written by knowledgeable people in a lively and engaging style. The wealth of nonfiction enables them to compare several sources on every topic and explore information in the context of a lively story.

integrate them to make sense of the world. Learning, then, is more than the laying on of discrete areas of information; it requires an active response from students, an interpretation or reconstruction of new information in relation to what they already know. Instead of teaching a body of facts for memorization, our goal is to help students learn to think. Teachers fashion learning activities that cut across the curriculum and that draw upon books of fiction, nonfiction, and poetry in ways that encourage in children an active search for meaning.

Nonfiction (or informational) books are distinguished from fiction by their emphasis. Both may tell a story and both may include fact. In fiction, however, the story is uppermost, with facts sometimes used to support it; whereas in nonfiction, the facts are uppermost, with storytelling perhaps used as an expressive technique.

Sixty to 70 percent of most library collections in elementary schools and in the children's sections of public libraries are nonfiction; fiction makes up the smallest part—a surprise to most people. Nonfiction writers complain, justifiably, that their work—even though numbers are on their side—receives less attention than fiction. In many good schools the entire curriculum is taught with informational books rather than textbooks. The form of nonfiction now being published has a direct appeal to the young reader. Instead of forbidding, dense texts, we find spacious pages with color illustrations and brief paragraphs. Writers select topics that interest children rather than choosing topics from a school curriculum outline. Further, the number of nonfiction books for very young children is increasing tremendously; it is appealing, attractive, and abundant.

Because there are too many nonfiction trade books to permit review of them in any comprehensive way, what follows is a mere sampling of the great range and variety of informational books available; selections are given for the primary, intermediate, and advanced grade levels.

LEARNING FROM TRADE BOOKS

Even though the typical school day is segmented according to subjects, we know that learning is not similarly compartmentalized; children do not learn reading in reading class alone, science in science class alone, or history in social studies alone. Children learn best to think, read, write, speak, and listen when instruction in all curriculum areas is integrated— when, for example, a teacher exploring plant life in a science lesson grasps the opportunity to relate "phototropism" to other words with the prefix "photo." This kind of integration in instruction parallels the way children actually learn—not facts in isolation, but rather parts of a meaningful whole.

Reading for information is related to other language uses; it is part of the scheme of the total language system. Children do read to learn in assigned textbooks, but they read to learn with enthusiasm and excitement in specialized trade books of quality. Compared to a textbook, a trade book can reveal the point of view of the author more directly, focus on an individual or a topic with a sharper light, and present specialized information that often gives readers a fuller understanding. For example, a textbook may mention that Marie Curie discovered radium, but Mollie Keller's biography, *Marie Curie* (A), gives a far more intimate and revealing picture of the woman and her work. Or, while a textbook may barely mention that some plants open only during the day or that birds seem to know when to migrate, Seymour Simon's *The Secret Clocks: Time Sense of Living Things* (I) probes these phenomena thoroughly.

When young children read *Eat the Fruit, Plant the Seed* (P), by Millicent E. Selsam and Jerome Wexler, they learn how to plant fruit seeds that grow into interesting house plants.

Eat the Fruit, Plant the Seed explains to primary grade children how they can grow plants from the fruit they eat. (Written by Millicent E. Selsam and Jerome Wexler.)

Photographs show the various stages of growth, and the text details the best growing conditions. The limited number of seeds discussed allows full explication for the beginning gardener. When intermediate grade students read Millicent E. Selsam's *How Animals Live Together* (I), they learn how scientists observe the social life of the animal world and about the problems associated with observing animals in their natural habitats. Behavior of animals in captivity is often uncharacteristic.

A Frog's Body (P–I), by Joanna Cole, offers simply related facts and clear photographs and diagrams. Because the bullfrog's organs are similar to those of human beings, readers learn by analogy about their own bodies. The magnificent photographs capture for study aspects of a frog's body and behavior that would be difficult to reproduce in real life.

It is probable that you remember, from your elementary school textbooks, not more than some isolated fragments. It is equally probable that you remember much more associated with some special project that you may have had to research and develop for a presentation, a science fair, or a demonstration. We learn when our emotions are involved, we

learn when we are actively engaged, and we learn when we pursue our own—rather than someone else's—interests. We remember facts when they are integrated into our conception of reality, and we most often learn and retain them when they are part of a meaningful experience. Dorothy Gardner stresses the interdependence of our intellectual and emotional life. She states:

> The basis of learning is emotion. . . . There is no intellectual interest which does not spring from the need to satisfy feelings. . . . Not only is learning fostered by the need to satisfy feelings but feelings themselves are relieved and helped by learning. For work to be creative, feeling as well as intellect is involved. Any education must always take into account education of the emotions.[2]

We all learn by fitting new information into a coherent frame or schema in a process of assimilation and accommodation that is described by Piaget. Nonfiction makes information available to children in ways that facilitate the creation of meaningful category systems and critical schemata. When children seek out information for themselves, identify what is relevant, and use it for meaningful goals, they become more efficient at storing and retrieving facts. The especially fine informational books published today illuminate their path. Furthermore, there are trade books on virtually any topic and for almost any level of understanding, and this rich and vast array of materials generates an interest and excitement that encourages students to grow.

CRITERIA FOR EVALUATING NONFICTION

Each year, a committee of subject area specialists and children's literature specialists selects the outstanding examples of books in their discipline. The work, coordinated by the Children's Book Council,[3] involves the National

Science Teachers Association, the National Council of Social Studies, the International Reading Association, and the National Council of Teachers of English. The committee states their criteria for science books in three areas: the book must be accurate and readable and its format and illustrations must be pleasing. Above all, information in a book selected for the list of Outstanding Science Trade Books for Children must be consistent with current scientific knowledge. In areas where scientists differ, a book should present different points of view, and information should not be distorted by personal biases or values. Facts and theories must be clearly distinguished, generalizations supported by facts, and significant facts not omitted. If experiments are a feature of a book, the committee considers whether they lead to an understanding of basic principles. Moreover, experiments must be appropriate for the reader's age group and be both feasible and safe. The committee eschews anthropomorphized animals and plants. It also has a bias against books that are racist, sexist, or extol violence.[4] The following discussion expands on these criteria and gives examples as they apply to informational books in related areas.

Integrity

Integrity in nonfiction is shown by authors who are honest with their readers. They reveal their point of view and let the reader know how their interest in the topic motivates them. They inculcate a questioning attitude in their readers and reveal the sources of their own research.

Are facts and theories clearly distinguished? Highly qualified writers state clearly and succinctly what is known and what is conjectured; they do not mislead by stating as fact what is still a theory or hypothesis. Careful writers use qualifying phrases when they are tentative about the information. For example, some use "many scientists believe," "Dinosaurs probably could not run fast," and "The evidence to date suggests," to indicate that experts in the field are not certain about all things. Good writers describe the changing status of information about a topic:

> For a long time scientists thought *Apatosaurus* was too heavy to walk on land and assumed that it was a water dweller. However, recent bone studies prove that its legs could have supported its weight. It was probably a plains and forest dweller, and it probably traveled in herds.[5]

Are animals and plants anthropomorphized? Good nonfiction writers stay away from attributing human traits to plants or animals (called *anthropomorphism*), such as "The little bird cried real tears because it was homesick" or "The flower asked the sky for a drink of water." The problem in this area arises most often when writers try to disguise information by slipping it into a fictional story; they do not clearly distinguish their work as fiction or nonfiction. Talking animals, such as in White's *Charlotte's Web,* or sacrificing trees, such as in Silverstein's *The Giving Tree,* which are integral to fantasy, are not accepted in nonfiction.

Are differing views presented? Nonfiction writers with integrity acknowledge other opinions of value; they recognize that their views may vary from what is generally accepted. For example, in *Death Is Natural* (I), Laurence Pringle states,

> Although human bodies decay after death, some people believe that there is a soul, or spirit, that lives on afterward. . . . Some people believe there is no life after death. An afterlife is not the sort of idea that scientists can prove or disprove. However, scientists do agree on two facts about death. First, it is inevitable. . . . Second, death is necessary.[6]

Are generalizations supported with facts? Good writers use specific facts to support broad generalizations: for example,

Young pigs can almost be seen growing right before your eyes. It has been scientifically proved that pigs grow more rapidly than any other farm animal; 400 pounds of feed produces 100 pounds of body weight. By the time the piglets are weaned, they have increased their weight more than ten times, to about 35 pounds. In just six months those youngsters that weighed 3 pounds at birth will increase their weight by about seven thousand percent, to 220 pounds. If left to grow to adulthood, an average pig will weigh about 800 pounds, the record weight being 1,904 pounds.[7]

Is the author qualified to write on this topic? Authors' qualifications to write about a subject are often provided on the book jacket; in other cases, authors acknowledge expert advisors or consultants who reviewed their work prior to publication: for example, "The author wishes to thank Dr. John H. Ostrom, Professor of Geology, Division of Vertebrate Paleontology, Peabody Museum of Natural History, Yale University, for reading and suggesting changes in the manuscript of this book."[8]

Tone

The tone of a nonfiction work is judged by its substance or its objective. The tone reveals the significance, the heart, the core, or the meaningfulness of an author's work.

Milton Meltzer, an outstanding biographer and historian, objects to the way most nonfiction is judged by reviewers. He decries the fact that critics look at how much information a book contains and how accurate or up-to-date it is but rarely compare it with other books on the same subject. Meltzer believes that critics must look at more than mere facts in a work of nonfiction and must ask,

What literary distinction, if any, does the book have? And here I do not mean the striking choice of word or image but the personal style

revealed. I ask whether the writer's personal voice is heard in the book. In the writer who cares, there is a pressure of feeling which emerges in the rhythm of the sentences, in the choice of details, in the color of the language. Style in this sense is not a trick of rhetoric or a decorative daub; it is a quality of vision. It cannot be separated from the author's character because the tone of voice in which the book is written expresses how a human being thinks and feels. If the writer is indifferent, bored, stupid, or mechanical, it will show in the work.[9]

A book's literary value, therefore, depends in large part on how much the author gives of himself or herself. Laurence Pringle acknowledges that his passions enter his work.

When I'm writing, I write about my values and feelings. Many people ask what nonfiction has to do with feelings. If you want feelings, they would say, turn to fiction. But I don't think that has to be true. In some ways my goals and values are much the same as a teacher's. The majority of teachers are trying to give kids a bigger picture of the world and a better understanding of how it works. In that sense, teaching and good nonfiction writing are the same.[10]

Content

Is the book well organized? A flip test can often reveal how well a book is arranged. What are the contents of the book? Are there additional features such as a subject and an author index, a bibliography for further reading, and appendices with further information? Are the pages well designed or do they appear crowded?

Is the text clearly structured? The structure of a text depicts the relationships among the ideas in the passage. It shows how the author has organized ideas to convey the information. Careful, logical development of concepts is essential. Ideas should flow from the simple to the complex in clear order. The text also needs strong transitions to guide the reader from one idea to the next. Readers find it difficult to follow and to recall texts that jump from one topic to another without logical links.

Is the book comprehensible to the intended audience? The concepts and vocabulary need to be within a reasonable range of difficulty for the primary readers. Look for a descriptive style that presents the information in a clear and simple manner. Responsible writers respect their readers and know that children, no matter what their age, can understand important scientific terms and concepts if they are presented clearly and defined in the context.

Nonfiction books should be as appealing in layout and design as fiction books are. For example, Patricia Lauber's book, *Volcano: The Eruption and Healing of Mount St. Helens* (I–A) is a well designed and visually appealing book. Spacious pages contain clear photographs that illustrate the text aligned beside them. The magnificent photographs carry explanatory notes that highlight the information the author intends to convey. Diagrams and maps, provided where necessary, extend the information about volcanoes that cannot be shown in actual photographs. By turning the pages, however, the reader can see exactly what Mount St. Helens looked like before, during, and after the series of explosions during the spring of 1980. Lauber also shows the effect of the eruption on plant, animal, and human life in the area. *Volcano* is one of the few nonfiction books to receive a Newbery Honor Book Award.

Books of nonfiction are changing in appearance. Whereas they once had few illustrations, they are now profusely illustrated. Award-winning editor James Giblin notes that children today, accustomed to the visual stimulation of television, want graphics—particularly photographs—in their books.[11] This has led to a greatly increased number of photo essays. Giblin was the editor for Russell Freedman's *Lincoln: A Photobiography,* winner of the 1988 Newbery Award.

LEARNING TO READ CRITICALLY

Critical reading and thinking are basic to learning for a lifetime. The schemata we develop as we learn to read, and read to learn, influence all subsequent knowledge. Thinking readers, called critical readers, evaluate new information in light of what they already know, compare many sources instead of accepting only one point of view, and make judgments about what they read. They can discriminate fact from opinion. The goal of education—to develop informed, thinking, participating citizens—requires such readers.

The habit of reading critically, then, is invaluable. The child who believes that anything found in print is the truth, the whole truth, is at a disadvantage relative to the one who has learned to check sources, compare reports, and evaluate. Children do not question what they read when they are given one textbook, which is held up as embodying the final and complete truth on its subject. They do learn to question and evaluate as they read if we encourage them to make comparisons among different sources—often nonfiction trade books.

We can engender unquestioning respect for the authority of the textbook by the way we respond to students' questions. Replies such as "Look it up in the book," or "What does the book say?" may inadvertently teach students to pay abject homage to textbooks in general.

Developmental differences in children's ability to think critically are not so much a matter of kind as of degree. Long before they turn to information found in books, very young children can make comparisons: they can deal with ideas such as who is taller, which coat is warmer, which cookie is bigger. Listening to stories or looking at books, young children can attend to detail and make comparisons. For example, when looking at the photographs in the portfolios by Jorg Müller, *The Changing City* (P–I–A) and *The Changing Countryside* (P–I–A), they can observe that parts of the landscape such as mountains and rivers may remain the same from one decade to the next, and other parts, such as a new highway, are very different. Older children will make many more inferences about what causes the changes in the landscape when a country road becomes a main road with gas stations, shops, restaurants, and motels and later is replaced as a thoroughfare by a super highway. Students who are even more mature will draw implications from the scenes about ecology, the quality of life, and the need for planning.

Verify Information

Children of all ages can verify information found in books by checking it against observations made in real life, as, for example, when a forgotten peanut butter sandwich turns up covered with green mold while the class is reading about fungi in Lucia Anderson's *The Smallest Life Around Us* (P–I). Young children can hypothesize about the causes of mold; experiment with different conditions that promote or retard it; see that it grows on bread, lemons, or grass; and learn about useful molds that help make cheese or bread.

Children can also make evaluative decisions—about what they do and do not like—although the bases for their judgments differ. Young children pressed for their reasons draw from an egocentric base and offer subjective, affective reasons: "Just because I like it." Intermediate grade students might say they like a book "Because it's good"; whereas older students evaluate in terms of the object itself: "It's good because it is well written and has clear illustrations." Each evaluative decision is developmentally appropriate.

Compare Sources

Primary grade children compared and evaluated two books about popcorn—*The Popcorn Book* (P), by Tomie dePaola, and *Popcorn* (P), by Millicent E. Selsam. Both books tell about varieties of corn and where and when popcorn was discovered. They differ markedly, however, in style of presentation, illustrations, and amount and kind of information given. Selsam's book contains striking color and black-and-white photographs, whereas dePaola's book is illustrated with humorous and whimsical cartoon-like drawings. Selsam devotes a major part of her discussion to germinating seeds, planting and growing corn, the properties of corn plants, and pollenization. DePaola devotes more of his book to the popping process; he has one character read from an encyclopedia some interesting facts about popcorn: how much is eaten each year, which cities are the top popcorn-eating cities, and funny stories about popcorn (such as the popcorn blizzard in the Midwest). After the books had been read aloud, children in one group said, "*The Popcorn Book* is more fun but the other one tells you more stuff"; "If you want to know about growing popcorn, you should read *Popcorn* because it tells you what to do."

The children also found a discrepancy between the two books concerning when popcorn was first found. DePaola says, "In a bat cave in New Mexico, archeologists found some popped corn that was 5,600 years old." Selsam says, "Scientists do know that people who lived in caves in New Mexico 2,000 years ago did pop corn, because popped kernels of that age were found there in a cave named Bat Cave." DePaola also states, "and 1,000-year-old popcorn kernels were found in Peru that could still be popped." Selsam adds, "There were also unpopped kernels in the cave, and the scientists studying the corn were able to pop some of these 2,000-year-old kernels." When the children discussed which was right, one said, "Well, I think she's [Selsam] right because we have a lot of other books by both of them and hers are all science books and his are mostly funny books." In further evaluation one child said, "Hers is more like a real science book but his tells you real stuff in a funnier way."

These remarks of children show how natural it is for them to make comparisons. They also illustrate the usefulness of informational books in the curriculum to foster growth in critical reading and thinking.

Students in advanced grades deal with topics, compare sources, and use more complex skills than do younger students. Older children can understand chronology and profit from the study of archaeology and early constructions. Gian Paolo Ceserani's *Grand Constructions* (I–A), illustrated by Piero Ventura, is a good place to start. The large format and magnificent illustrations—paintings done from unusual perspectives—appeal visually and give the reader a sense of the time periods in which the grand constructions were made. The first, Stonehenge, is an intricate and puzzling pattern of enormous stones that archaeologists believe were used as a sophisticated calendar by people thousands of years ago. Ceserani and Ventura also portray the symbolism and the majesty of the Gothic cathedral from the thirteenth century. They explain that the architectural principle of the ogive, or Gothic arch, allowed architects to build cathedrals of incredible heights.

Comparing books on early constructions provides excellent practice in critical reading. For example, Olivier Dunrea's *Skara Brae: The Story of a Prehistoric Village* (I) traces a stone village in the Orkney Islands from its earliest construction, around 3500 B.C., through various stages of building. The architectural diagrams, site plans and layouts, and artifacts provide a wealth of comparative information. Students could prepare a timeline to show the discoveries of ancient structures that occurred in various periods and in various parts of the world. David Macaulay's works, *Cathedral* (I–A), *Castle* (I–A), and *Mill* (I–A), contain architectural drawings and details for various stages of each construction. Enrich the comparison with Sheila Sancha's *The Luttrell Village: Country Life in the Middle Ages*, W. John Hackwell's *Digging to the Past: Excavations in Ancient Lands*, and

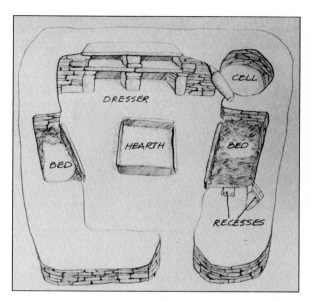

Children can develop critical-reading skills by comparing what various books say about a selected topic. For example, archaeologists are beginning to piece together the information they have collected about prehistoric life by using a wide range of methods. This illustration of a primitive stone house is from a book about an ancient village in the Orkney Islands. (From *Skara Brae: The Story of a Prehistoric Village* by Olivier Dunrea.)

Jonathan Rutland's *See Inside a Roman Town* (all A). *Walls, Defenses Throughout History* (I–A) by James Cross Giblin and *The Great Wall of China* (I) by Leonard Everett Fisher add another dimension to the comparisons and critical evaluations.

Compare with Experience

Adolescent readers will evaluate the author's statements in light of their own experience. They can also compare one book with others and decide which they prefer and why.

Many books encourage the reader to adopt a critical stance based on observing, collecting, and analyzing data, drawing conclusions, making inferences, and testing hypotheses. In *The Secret Clocks: Time Sense of Living Things* (I), Seymour Simon suggests,

PROFILE

Seymour Simon

The sun is far away from Earth and its moon. A spaceship that could travel to the moon in a few days would take more than a year to come close to the sun.

The sun is an average-size star. There is nothing very special about it, except for the fact that it is our star. Life on Earth depends upon the heat and light of the sun.[12]

A rare combination of talent and knowledge of children, science, and teaching, Seymour Simon is a believer in the hands-on approach of leading children to discover their world. For example, he used the appeal of making paper airplanes to teach the concepts of aerodynamics in *The Paper Airplane Book*. The diagrams explain thrust, lift, gravity, and how movable wing surfaces, like flaps, affect flight.

The author of over 100 books, Simon builds on a generation of teaching experience. He knows what readers are interested in and how to relate science to their interests. He involves the child as scientist as well as reader by providing projects, experiments, and things to observe in many books.

Pets in a Jar and *Look to the Night Sky* are among many of his works named "outstanding science trade books for children" by the National Science Teachers Association. The practical activities that he provides for children to try on their own lead to greater understanding because they make the children active participants in the learning process. Simon knows, and shows that he knows, that children learn by doing.

Simon's writing interests have expanded in at least two directions. He initiated the popular *Einstein Anderson: Science Sleuth* series, which solves mysteries through the application of a scientific fact. Further, he has produced a number of books on the sun, moon, stars and planets. Simon received the New York Academy of Science's Science Children's Book Award for *Icebergs and Glaciers* in 1988.

Seymour Simon was born in New York City, where he attended school and later taught. He lives in suburban Long Island with his wife. Their two sons are grown. A full-time writer and scholar, he takes time out for tennis and for talks with teachers and students.

During the summer or during the warmer months of spring and fall, you can do a simple experiment to demonstrate the time sense of bees. Spread out some honey or syrup on a piece of blue paper. Place the paper outdoors each morning at the same time in the same spot. Bees can see blue, yellow, blue-green, and ultraviolet (a color you cannot see). The honey on the paper will attract the bees by its odor. . . . After you are sure that the bees are showing up on schedule, place the same color sheet in the same spot but without any honey smeared on it. Start observing an hour earlier than the regular feeding time and continue for an hour later than the regular time. Record the number of bees that come in fifteen-minute blocks of time. Use a bar graph to show your results. [He gives a sample graph.] Keep setting the paper each day at the same time until the bees stop showing up. . . . How do your results compare with those shown on the graph? For how many days did your bees continue to show up at the correct time? Try the same experiment at different seasons or at different times of the day to see if that makes any difference in the results you get.[13]

Simon involves readers as scientists—having them check information by conducting experiments and observing, interpreting, and comparing their results with his.

ORGANIZING INTEGRATED UNITS

There are numerous ways to approach a unit of study with informational books. Much depends upon the children in your group—their developmental level, their interests, and their background in the area of study.

One of the major things a teacher must know is how to locate books on a subject. Several avenues are open: the card catalog and librarians in school and public libraries can lead you to books on your topic. There are also specific reference sources that list books by subject—for example, *Subject Guide to Children's Books in Print* and *Children's Catalog* are updated each year. Other valuable resources include *The*

Elementary School Library Collection and *Index to Children's Poetry*. In addition, professional organizations in several disciplines publish annual lists of outstanding books for children. "Notable Children's Trade Books in the Field of Social Studies" appears in the April issue of the journal *Social Education*, "Outstanding Science Trade Books for Children" appears in the March issue of *Science and Children*, and "Children's Choices" appears in the October issue of *The Reading Teacher*. Many of the specialized lists are available from the Children's Book Council.

As you locate books, many different ways of organizing a study become evident. One, favored by some teachers, is "creating a web of possibilities," which shows the relationships among various parts of a topic.[14] Another, called semantic mapping, helps students see how words, books, or topics are related to one another. In *Semantic Mapping: Classroom Applications*, Joan E. Heimlich and Susan D. Pittelman explain why this organizational method has gained popularity.

Comprehension, no longer viewed as simply getting meaning from the printed page, is . . . an active process in which students integrate prior knowledge with text information to create new knowledge. . . . Skilled readers actively call into play and integrate the knowledge and experiences stored in their memories with the words on the printed page. . . . In fact, research has shown that background knowledge about a topic, particularly understanding of key vocabulary, is a better predictor of text comprehension than is any measure of reading ability or achievement.[15]

Teachers have found that semantic mapping helps students activate and retrieve prior knowledge related to a topic. They have also found that it is an effective way to organize a unit of study. The units in this chapter—one each for the primary, intermediate, and advanced levels—are developed around a topic in this fashion. Each unit is illustrative, not prescriptive. Your students' curiosity and interests lead the way.

The primary grades unit is based on children's enduring interest in animals. Pets, dinosaurs, zoo animals, farm animals, and wildlife are suggested as a way of cataloguing books and activities in the web that is presented in this section. Each of these subtopics could be expanded into an entire unit of study; there are many excellent books in each area. The intermediate grades unit, on wildlife management, grew from a group of student scientists, who, interested in ecology, were outraged when an antipollution law failed to be enacted. They began to write to their community's representatives, and on the assumption that they might be more convincing if they knew their facts, they researched their topic. The unit is, in effect, a trace of their steps along the way. The advanced grades unit, on space, was sparked by a single child's interest in the subject. Working with a children's librarian, we tracked down hundreds of beautiful books to pursue this interesting topic.

THE PRIMARY GRADES UNIT: ANIMALS

A child's fascination with animals begins early and often endures throughout a lifetime. Reasons for the abiding affection may be associated with the fact that some animals are small and cuddly, need protection and care, respond to attention, and are not judgmental. We can build upon children's interest in animals to achieve three purposes: (1) to increase their understanding of all living things, (2) to teach them to read widely, and (3) to teach them to compare sources.

Pets

Pets are a favorite topic in early childhood classrooms; children talk about them, write about them, read about them, and listen to sto-

ries about them. Rosemarie Hausherr's book, *My First Kitten* (P), is a good introduction to responsible pet ownership. In a photodocumentary, 7-year-old Adam tells in a first-person narrative the story of choosing his very own pet. In the hills of northern Vermont, Adam's family has a dog, ducks, and two goslings, but the old dog belongs to his father, and the fluffy goslings belong to his sister. Adam wants his own pet. When Adam hears that a neighbor has kittens for adoption, he convinces his parents that he would take good care of one, so they take him to pick one out. Three of the kittens are black and white but the fourth one has beautiful orange stripes. Adam announces, "That's the one I want, the little tiger, and that's what I'll call it." Adam's father shows him how to hold his kitten properly; when it comes to treatment, he suggests, "Think how you would like to be treated." Adam keeps his kitten from being lonely at night, housebreaks him, and takes him to the veterinarian to keep him healthy. Information about pet care is worked into the story naturally, and a final page is filled with what parents should know about adopting a kitten.

Guinea pigs are popular pets. Colleen Stanley Bare shows that *Guinea Pigs Don't Read Books* (N–P), but she also shows a lot of other things they do. In large, full-color photographs, she shows that guinea pigs chew apples and carrots, stare, listen, sniff, and make sounds. She also shows many types of guinea pigs whose fur coats differ markedly: some have long shaggy fur, others are sleek and shiny. Guinea pigs, Bare points out, are not pigs; they do not eat like pigs, walk like pigs, sound like pigs, or even look like baby pigs. "Guinea pigs like to be held and hugged. They are gentle and calm and lovable. Guinea pigs may not read books, but they can be your friends." The magnificent color photographs convey their appeal.

Alvin and Virginia Silverstein's *Guinea Pigs* (P–I) gives more information in a straightforward way. Three sections, all indexed, describe the origins of guinea pigs, guinea pigs as pets, and guinea pigs in the laboratory. In the section on guinea pigs as pets, the Silversteins suggest ways to check for a healthy animal and the kinds of homes a child can prepare for them. Unlike many other pets, guinea pigs can be kept in cardboard houses, although, they warn, the boxes need to be replaced often since guinea pigs love to gnaw on things and will chew at the doorway and windows until the walls are eaten away and the house comes tumbling down. Outdoor hutches must be sturdier to protect the guinea pigs from other animals, such as cats or dogs, that can injure them.

Joanna Cole has written a number of excellent books about animals that often become pets, such as *A Horse's Body, A Dog's Body, A Cat's Body,* and *My Puppy Is Born* (all P). Working with photographer Jerome Wexler, Cole presents accurate information involving the birth process, growth patterns, and characteristics of each animal in a spare, clearly written text. The treatment of sensitive topics is tasteful without omitting facts or misleading readers. Wexler uses both color and black-and-white photographs to attain a sense of intimacy and warmth with the subject yet maintaining clarity and artistic perspective. The same author-photographer team collaborated on *A Chick Hatches, A Bird's Body, A Snake's Body, An Insect's Body,* and *A Frog's Body* (all P).

Some animals serve both as pets and as working partners with their masters. For example, guide dogs have long led their blind or partially sighted owners across busy streets and around obstacles. Three books show dogs in other helping roles. *Cindy: A Hearing Ear Dog* (P–I), by Patricia Curtis, encompasses the selection, training, and transition-to-owner period that a hearing ear dog undergoes. Cindy, chosen from the dog pound because she was alert, friendly, and medium sized, was trained to obey commands; she would bark when there was a knock at the door, the telephone rang, or the alarm clock went off. She also barked when the teakettle on the stove began to sing or when the oven timer buzzed. After several weeks of training, Cindy was ready for her new owner, a deaf teenager named Jennifer. Cindy had learned how to respond to one person and now she must be transferred to Jennifer. Jennifer stayed at the hearing ear dog training college and took over Cindy's care and feeding. Gradually Cindy began to accept Jennifer as her owner. The next step was to teach Cindy to tell Jennifer instead of the trainers when the dog heard the sounds she had learned to respond to. Eventually this happened and the girl and dog were sent home together. The author provides additional information about hearing ear dogs and an index.

George Ancona's photo essay, *Sheep Dog,* depicts another role dogs play to serve humankind, herding sheep. Sheep are jeopardized by predatory animals, such as the coyote, that attack both lambs and adult sheep. Losing the sheep to coyotes causes the owner financial hardship and heartache; therefore, training sheep dogs to protect and herd the flock is a needed activity. Ancona features some of the breeds that are good sheep dogs and describes the Livestock Dog Project at Hampshire College in Amherst, Massachusetts, where much of the research on sheep dogs has been conducted. A bibliography of sources is provided. Dorothy Hinshaw Patent provides simpler information for younger students about one dog in *Maggie, A Sheep Dog* (P). Excellent photographs and a sparsely written text follow Maggie in her work on a sheep ranch.

Hamsters, appealing pets for many children, are described in Heiderose Fischer-Nagel's *Inside the Burrow: The Life of the Golden Hamster* (P). Color photographs by Heiderose and Andreas Fischer-Nagel give a close-up view of many of the hamster's activities that are normally conducted outside human view. Through ingenious photography, they show

TEACHING IDEA

DINOSAUR PROJECTS (P)[16]   As a part of the writing process program, kindergarten teacher Jeanne McPadden made numerous books about dinosaurs available to her students. As students looked through the books and shared with each other interesting facts about dinosaurs, some of their information began to show up in their writing. Below is a copy of one of her students' books about dinosaurs.

The interest in dinosaurs led another classroom, taught by Jane Maisel and Scarlote West, to the following activities:[17]

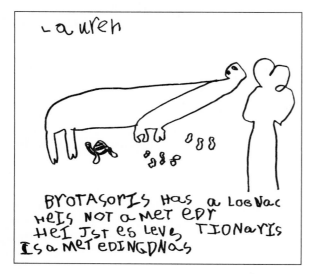

(Brontosaurus has a long neck. He is not a meat eater. He just eats leaves. Tyrannosaurus is a meat-eating dinosaur.)

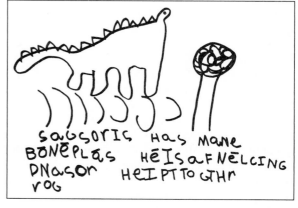

(Stegosaurus has many bony plates. He is a funny looking dinosaur. He is put together wrong.)

hamsters' sleeping, storage, and bathroom areas, all connected by tunnels. They also show the birth sequence and subsequent phases of the growth and development of the baby hamsters. The clear, impersonal text includes information on general behavior patterns of the species and tips on pet care.

Prehistoric Animals: Dinosaurs

Nearly all children are interested in dinosaurs at some point in their educational careers. Often this interest starts early and is lasting.

Books serve as a rich and continuing source of information for children interested in the names, characteristics, habitats, and other interesting facts about the ancient beasts.

Aliki has written and illustrated some of the best books for the youngest dinosaur enthusiasts. *My Visit to the Dinosaurs, Fossils Tell of Long Ago, Dinosaurs Are Different,* and *Digging up Dinosaurs* (all P) provide a wealth of information for primary grade children. In *Dinosaurs Are Different,* she gives the classification of two major orders, saurischian and ornithischian, and four suborders of ornithopoda, cer-

Sculpting dinosaurs from clay
Reading books about dinosaurs
Making a dinosaur museum in one section of the classroom
Writing about dinosaurs
Painting pictures about dinosaurs

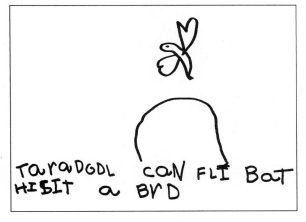

(Pterodactyl can fly but he isn't a bird.)

(Dinosaurs lived a long time ago.)

atopsia, stegosauria, and ankylosauria. Young children are not overwhelmed by the lengthy names; they speak and write the complicated words with seeming ease. In *Digging up Dinosaurs*, Aliki begins with a survey of dinosaur exhibits in a museum and then explains how the fossils came to be exhibited. She shows scientists and archaeologists excavating, labeling, preserving, and packing fossil remains. She shows how museum workers assemble and mount the huge dinosaur skeletons and the great care they take to assure the preservation of the bones and the accuracy of the exhibits.

Aliki maintains a child's perspective not only for the vantage point of her drawings but for the kind of questions a child would want answered.

Gail Gibbons uses bold colors to catalog the most familiar creatures in *Dinosaurs* (P). Children know the animals so well that they have no trouble reading the long, complicated dinosaur names. This attractive book adds to the wealth of information for young children.

Seymour Simon, a dependable science writer, has written two books about dinosaurs—*The Smallest Dinosaurs* and *The Largest*

One of the very biggest of all dinosaurs was Brachiosaurus. It stood about 40 feet tall and was 80 feet long. Brachiosaurus liked eating water plants, too.

BRACHIOSAURUS
BRAK · e · o · sore · us

Gail Gibbons's bold drawings and simple text are especially good for young children who want to read about *Dinosaurs.*

Dinosaurs (both P)—that present a scientific attitude and provide a sound factual base. The facts show that some small species existed and may have been the ancestors or relatives of today's birds. In a section from *The Largest Dinosaurs,* entitled "How Sauropods Lived," Simon states:

> Scientists are not exactly sure how sauropods lived. That's because no one has ever seen a real sauropod. The last sauropods died many years before people lived on Earth. But the sauropods left clues to what they were like. Some of the clues are *fossils.* Bones that change to rock are called fossils. Other clues are tracks in mud that hardened into rock. Scientists have also found hardened sauropod eggs and nests.[18]

Simon describes six of the biggest and best-known sauropods, plus a lightweight giant, and two recently discovered sauropods nick-

named Supersaurus and Ultrasaurus. He explains how scientists use clues to help them understand how dinosaurs lived and to help solve the mystery of their disappearance.

Helen Roney Sattler is an expert on dinosaurs and paleontology. Her books include *Dinosaurs of North America; The Illustrated Dinosaur Dictionary; Baby Dinosaurs; and Pterosaurs, the Flying Reptiles* (all I). Although the books are more appropriate for the intermediate grades, students in the primary grades learn from their illustrations, labels, and succinct explanations. Just about everything there is to know about dinosaurs can be found in *The Illustrated Dinosaur Dictionary.* Scientists have known about dinosaurs for only a little more than 150 years, and paleontologists make new discoveries and develop new hypotheses every year. Over 300 kinds of dinosaurs that have been discovered all over the world and named are listed in Sattler's comprehensive book. Spacious pages with clear black and white line drawings accompanying each entry make this a very useful book for all ages. *Dinosaurs of North America* describes the 80 different types of dinosaurs that once inhabited this continent. Organizing the text by time periods in which the dinosaurs lived—the Triassic, the Jurassic, and the Cretaceous periods—the author explains the physical characteristics, eating habits, habitats, and locations of the dinosaurs discovered in North America. She further discusses the mystery of their extinction and explains some of the hypotheses about their disappearance. Sattler also deals with the *Pterosaurs, the Flying Reptiles* (I), the less familiar contemporaries of the dinosaurs. The pterosaurs lived in many parts of the world for about 120 million years; they differed remarkably from the modern reptile species. Their wings, some spanning 40 to 50 feet, were attached in batlike fashion to their small bodies. Sattler's descriptions of their possible appearance and behavior, based on scientific discoveries, are cogent and clearly stated.

Laurence Pringle's first book, *Dinosaurs and Their World* (I), was based on his favorite subject. Although he has written many other books about nature, ecology, and environmental problems, he returned to dinosaurs for his thirtieth book, *Dinosaurs and People: Fossils, Facts, and Fantasies* (I). Pringle explains,

> *Dinosaur* is a magic word. Soon after children learn to say their own names, they proudly pronounce the names of some dinosaurs: *Stegosaurus, Brontosaurus,* and especially *Tyrannosaurus rex.* Long after childhood, people are still fascinated by the word dinosaur. There is nothing make-believe about these creatures. Dinosaurs really existed, and some of them resembled terrifying dragons or monsters.[19]

Pringle gives a brief history of some of the pioneers in paleontology and describes some of their big discoveries. Although Pringle's books are more appropriate at the intermediate grades, they can be read aloud or used as reference material for primary grade students.

Russell Freedman's books, *Dinosaurs and Their Young* and *They Lived with the Dinosaurs* (both P), are written for a primary grade audience. In *Dinosaurs and Their Young*, he tells about the discovery of the fossil skeleton of a baby dinosaur in Montana in 1978. Previously, scientists had thought that adult dinosaurs buried their eggs and then deserted them, but the discovery of the nest of baby duckbill dinosaur fossils and the skull of an adult duckbill nearby caused scientists to conjecture that at least duckbilled dinosaurs cared for their young. Freedman's language indicates the tentative nature of the information. For example,

> Full-grown duckbills were probably strong enough to fight off many of their enemies. They could bite hard with their beaks. And they could lash out with their powerful tails. But when big enemies like *Tyrannosaurus* came along, the duckbills had to run for their lives. They could probably run as fast as 30 miles an hour. . . . Duckbills seem to have had a keen sense of smell.[20]

Zoo Animals

For children, a trip to a zoo is one of the highlights of their year. The visit to the zoo is one of the most memorable experiences of childhood. Most zoos care for animals in areas as close to their natural habitat as possible so children see them roaming in open areas rather than standing inside cages.

A Children's Zoo (N–P) by Tana Hoban presents an engaging view of 11 popular zoo animals through color photographs and three descriptive words. Spacious black pages contain the three descriptors and the animal's name in bold white letters, whereas the facing page frames in white a large photograph of the animal. For example, ''big/smooth/swims Hippopotamus,'' and ''strong/shaggy/roars Lion,''

Tana Hoban's *A Children's Zoo* combines a color photograph with three words to inform the youngest readers about each of the zoo animals she presents. This panda is "black," "white," and "furry."

Francine ("Penny") Patterson chronicles a project to teach sign language to her gorilla Koko. Over several months, Koko signed how much she wanted a kitten, and so she received one. (From *Koko's Kitten*, photographs by Ronald Cohn.)

and "gray/wrinkled/trumpets Elephant," are some of the entries. The final page contains a chart listing where the animals come from, where they live, and what they eat.

Jack Denton Scott wrote and Ozzie Sweet took the photographs for *City of Birds and Beasts: Behind the Scenes at the Bronx Zoo* (P–I). This informative book gives an overview of the numerous activities that occur in a typical day in a large metropolitan zoo. It also provides a personal view of the people who work in a zoo and shows how their skill and dedication are necessary to keep the animals healthy and happy. Scott uses the time of day to organize his report, sometimes switching from three-minute to half-hour segments. The clock schedule provides the sense of urgency when staff members rush off to rescue an escaped hummingbird, start a parade, or meet a feeding schedule. Teachers could use this book as an excellent read-aloud for a group studying the zoo.

Close to the Wild: Siberian Tigers in a Zoo (P–I) by Thomas Cajacob and Teresa Burton also gives a behind-the-scenes look at beautiful animals living in a natural habitat zoo, the Minnesota Zoo. In clear informative prose, the authors describe the size of the tigers, their behavior, and the care they require. For example,

> Of the big cats—lions, tigers, leopards, jaguars, and cheetahs—tigers are the biggest, and the Siberian tiger is the biggest of all. A full-grown male can weigh as much as 600 pounds (270 kg), though 400 pounds (180 kg) is the average, and measure over 13 feet from its head to the tip of its tail. Females tend to be smaller and usually weigh under 300 pounds (135 kg).[21]

TEACHING IDEA

COMMUNICATING WITH ANIMALS (P–I)   Several attempts by scientists to teach animals to communicate with humans have been reasonably successful. Students interested in this topic will find numerous books for their research.

Koko's Kitten (I) by Francine Patterson, illustrated with photographs by Ronald H. Cohn. Koko, a gorilla, has lived at the Gorilla Foundation since 1972 and has learned to communicate through American Sign Language. When asked what she wanted for a gift, she signed that she wanted a cat. When offered a choice of three, she chose a tabby kitten.

The Story of Nim: The Chimp Who Learned Language (P–I) by Anna Michel, illustrated with photographs by Susan Kuklin and Herbert S. Terrace. This is a documentary of Nim's training, written by a staff member who worked with him.

Books on the same topic for older students include *The Gorilla Signs Love* (A) by Barbara Brenner.

Jane Goodall's research efforts to study chimpanzees' methods of communication and their family structures in the wild have captured adults' imaginations for years. Children can read about Goodall's work in the following:

Jane Goodall: Living Chimp Style (P–I) by Mary Virginia Fox, illustrated by Nona Hengen. Goodall's childhood, her first job in Africa, her observations of chimpanzees, and her lifelong interest in animal behavior are detailed.

My Life with the Chimpanzees (I) by Jane Goodall. The author chronicles for children her decades of research with chimpanzees in the wild.

Activities   Read several books about animals that have been trained to communicate. Compare the ways they learned, the amount of effort required to train them, and the level of success achieved.

Cajacob's color photographs, carefully placed in relationship to the accompanying text, are magnificent studies of the animals. Technical words, highlighted in the text, are defined in a glossary.

Farm Animals

Children enjoy learning about farm animals, especially if they are able to visit a farm and see some of the animals in real life. They learn how farm animals contribute to the production of food and recognize their role in the food chain. Some farm animals, especially horses, become pets.

Joanna Cole, an excellent animal writer whose work appeals to the primary grade students, has written several books about animals, some of them farm animals. Working with photographer Jerome Wexler, she wrote *A Chick Hatches* (P), in which she introduces the day-by-day development of a chick embryo

PROFILE

Laurence Pringle

Laurence Pringle was born in Rochester, New York, and took his Bachelor of Science degree from Cornell University, and his Masters of Science degree from the University of Massachusetts, majoring in wildlife biology. He also did further graduate work at Syracuse University. He taught science in high school and edited a children's science magazine before beginning his writing career and has served as writer-in-residence at Kean College in New Jersey. He is active in environmental and nature organizations and travels widely, taking photographs and doing research for his books.

Pringle's first book, published in 1968, was *Dinosaurs and Their World*. He endures the hardships of writing to communicate his appreciation and concern for the natural world. He has written over 50 books for young people that convey his concern for the biological and environmental subjects that intrigue him. He has also published articles in numerous magazines, including *Highlights for Children, Ranger Rick,* and *Audubon*.

In 1983, Pringle won the Eva L. Gordon Award for Children's Science Literature from the American Nature Study Society. The award is given to an author whose books exemplify "high standards of accuracy, readability, sensitivity to interrelationships, timeliness and joyousness while they extend either directly or subtly an invitation to the child to become involved." His contributions to the literature of natural history have helped many children discover, enjoy, and understand the world of nature.

When he is doing research, he explains, he is particularly interested in finding out about people who are looking for solutions to problems.

I'm especially looking for real people who are solving, or attempting to solve, real problems. It adds a personal touch. Whenever possible I like to have a name and a face to connect with my story. Once when I was doing some research on a book about dinosaurs, I learned about a woman in Poland, a paleontologist, who had led some important expeditions. It was a treasure to be able to use her in my book, because it helped to destroy the notion that notable scientists are almost always male.

Pringle says of his work:

If there is a single thread that runs through all of my books—including the controversial and gloomy ones like the one on nuclear war—I think it is a thread of hopefulness. It is important to offer children some hope for solving our problems.[22]

The Pringle family resides in the New York Hudson River valley.

ACTIVITIES: TEACHER TO STUDENT

ANIMALS (P)

Create a model of a dinosaur museum, a zoo, or a farm. Place models of the various
animals in their appropriate habitats.

Read aloud familiar folktales that contain animals (see Chapter 5). Discuss why the
animals are portrayed as they are, for instance, fox as sly, wolf as vicious, chicken
as naive, eagle as powerful, and so on.

Compare Hans-Heinrich Isenbart's *A Duckling Is Born* with Robert McCloskey's *Make
Way for Ducklings*. How do nonfiction and fiction differ in portrayal?

Make a mural of a farm or a zoo. Work collaboratively in groups to plan and create
the mural with different types of animals in separate areas.

Make a chart of the ways animals help us. Some categories might be "Give Us Food,"
"Companionship," "Transportation," "Guide Blind/Deaf," "Give Us Clothing." List
the animals that do each.

Take a survey of the pets people have. Create a graph to show the results. An
example is shown below.

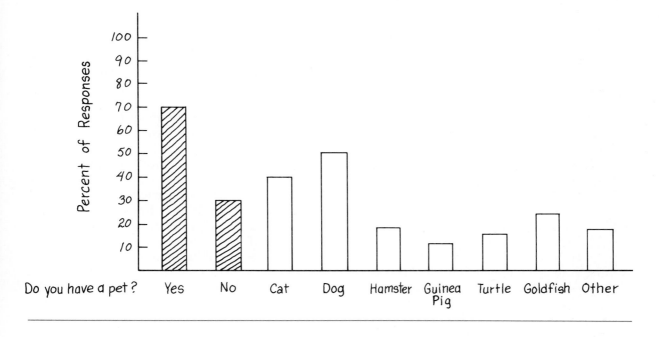

within an egg. In as simple prose as possible,
along with excellent photographs in color and
black and white, she describes clearly the development of a chick from fertilization through
the three-week incubation. The growth of the
fetus, the cracking of the shell, and the emergence of the chick that soon dries off and becomes fluffy yellow are shown in natural

progression. This book can be compared to Millicent Selsam's *Egg to Chick*, illustrated by Barbara Wolff.

Hans-Heinrich Isenbart has written three excellent books about farm animals. *Baby Animals on the Farm* (P), illustrated with photographs by Ruth Rau, presents color photographs and a slender text about each of several domestic animals. Notes on the animals are appended. *Birth of a Foal* (P), illustrated with photographs by Thomas David, gives a summary of the equine reproduction cycle, diagrams of the development of the fetus, the passage through the birth canal, and scenes from the foal's early life. *A Duckling Is Born* (P), illustrated with photographs by Othmar Baumli, follows the development of the duckling embryo from fertilization through incubation and hatching. The photographs, integrated with the text, give a clear picture of the beginnings of a duckling's life.

Wildlife

Wildlife is especially appealing to youngsters. Animals who fend for themselves, getting food and avoiding danger, seem especially vulnerable and deserving of admiration from children. If you go to the lake to feed the ducks, toss acorns to squirrels at the park, or feed the birds in winter, you will have a willing helper in any child. Books that look at wildlife are among the most beautiful and the most plentiful.

A child's joyous occupation on a summer evening is to catch glowing *Fireflies!* (P), sensitively described by Julie Brinckloe. In this story, as in real life, a young boy and his friends take great pleasure in capturing an entire glass jar full of the harmless insects. The boy takes the jar filled with the fireflies to his room where their glow slowly diminishes until they fall to the bottom of the jar. He realizes that the fireflies will die if he keeps them entrapped so he finally sets them free to fly away and glow in the night sky. The mixture of pleasure and sadness expressed on the child's face shows the conflict he faces. The theme that we need to set something free in order to keep it appears often in children's books about wildlife. *Fireflies* (I) by Sylvia A. Johnson is a good book for comparison. Rather than an artistic interpretation, this book has detailed full-color photographs of actual fireflies. Johnson also describes the firefly's physical characteristics, habitats, and reproductive cycle.

Berniece Freschet's books present wildlife creatures in their natural habitat and often show their life cycle. In *Raccoon Baby* (P), she describes three raccoon cubs from their birth in the spring until their first winter hibernation. Jim Arnosky, an artist and naturalist, sketched soft, realistic pencil drawings alternating with pages of earth tones to show the development of the cubs. In *Bear Mouse* (P–I), illustrated by Donald Carrick, Freschet follows the growth and development of the wild mouse who hibernates in the winter.

Hide and Seek (P), follows the life cycle, habits, and predators in the life of 12 animals. Brilliant color photographs show how these animals blend in with the environment to camouflage themselves from dangerous creatures. The major hazards for harvest mice, for example, are the automated harvesting machines that destroy their homes and put hay into wired bales rather than into haystacks, which had been a haven for mice. Each animal's different habitat is described.

Owl Lake (P) by Tejima is a large format book with magnificent woodcut illustrations by a master Japanese craftsman and two-time winner of the graphics arts award at the international children's book fair in Bologna, Italy. A simple text graces each page, which is filled with huge nocturnal scenes of the rare eagle owl at a lake. As the sun sets, the colors change from golden to dark blue. It is then that the owls come out. Father owl hunts across the

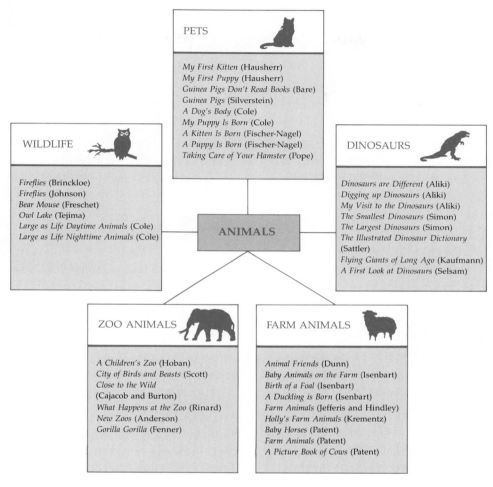

PETS

My First Kitten (Hausherr)
My First Puppy (Hausherr)
Guinea Pigs Don't Read Books (Bare)
Guinea Pigs (Silverstein)
A Dog's Body (Cole)
My Puppy Is Born (Cole)
A Kitten Is Born (Fischer-Nagel)
A Puppy Is Born (Fischer-Nagel)
Taking Care of Your Hamster (Pope)

WILDLIFE

Fireflies (Brinckloe)
Fireflies (Johnson)
Bear Mouse (Freschet)
Owl Lake (Tejima)
Large as Life Daytime Animals (Cole)
Large as Life Nighttime Animals (Cole)

DINOSAURS

Dinosaurs are Different (Aliki)
Digging up Dinosaurs (Aliki)
My Visit to the Dinosaurs (Aliki)
The Smallest Dinosaurs (Simon)
The Largest Dinosaurs (Simon)
The Illustrated Dinosaur Dictionary (Sattler)
Flying Giants of Long Ago (Kaufmann)
A First Look at Dinosaurs (Selsam)

ANIMALS

ZOO ANIMALS

A Children's Zoo (Hoban)
City of Birds and Beasts (Scott)
Close to the Wild (Cajacob and Burton)
What Happens at the Zoo (Rinard)
New Zoos (Anderson)
Gorilla Gorilla (Fenner)

FARM ANIMALS

Animal Friends (Dunn)
Baby Animals on the Farm (Isenbart)
Birth of a Foal (Isenbart)
A Duckling is Born (Isenbart)
Farm Animals (Jefferis and Hindley)
Holly's Farm Animals (Krementz)
Baby Horses (Patent)
Farm Animals (Patent)
A Picture Book of Cows (Patent)

Activities

Create a model farm, zoo, or dinosaur museum or diorama.
Make a wall mural of animals on a farm or in a zoo.
Read aloud animal folktales.

Compare books on similar topics.
Make a chart of how animals help us.
Take a survey of types of pets.
Have a pet show.

lake until he captures a fish by clutching it in his claws. He takes it back to share with the family. As the stars fade away, the sky brightens from black to blue. It is then that the owls go to sleep. The beauty of the illustrations conveys the quiet message that eagle owls sleep during the day, hunt at night, and sometimes catch fish for their food.

SWOOSH go his wings

SWOOSH SWOOSH...

...faster and faster until

he sees the fish swimming right beneath him.

Tejima's woodcut illustrations grace his story of *Owl Lake*, which uses a narrative to inform the young reader about the nocturnal life of the rare eagle owl.

THE INTERMEDIATE GRADES UNIT: WILDLIFE MANAGEMENT

Wildlife management is the careful study of species, development of the natural environments that nurture the species, and protection of endangered species. Since the 1970s, many people have become concerned about the environment and the natural wildlife that inhabits it. The study here is categorized into four parts: discovering nature's secrets, wildlife refuges, endangered species, and life cycle studies.

By reading about the potential and real dangers to plant and animal life, students learn that anything we do in our environment affects all else that lives in it. This kind of understanding is basic to a study of endangered species.

One of the greatest advantages in using the unit study approach is that you can find material for students whatever their reading level. The wealth of beautiful books on a multitude of topics at many reading levels delights the intellect as well as the eye.

Discovering Nature's Secrets

A large group of environmentalists and naturalists stress the interdependence of all living things. They lobby for protection of wetlands, forests, lakes, wildlife, and natural resources. They also are alert to the effects of overdevelopment on water supplies, pollution levels, and drainage systems. They believe that young people who are informed about the beauties of nature will be more likely to protect them.

Jean Craighead George, a naturalist and a writer, has produced a number of outstanding nature books for children. One group, *One Day in the Prairie, One Day in the Desert*, and *One Day in the Alpine Tundra* (all I), describes the plants and animals on a typical day in each environment. In *One Day in the Prairie*, for example, she begins with sunrise at 6:55 a.m. on September 28 in southwestern Oklahoma. A herd of buffalo moves restlessly sensing a distant storm. Killdeer and scissor-tailed flycatchers fly about through the prairie grasses. At

Jean Craighead George's *One Day in the Prairie* combines information about animals and ecology in her suspenseful narrative of life on the Oklahoma prairie.

7:15 a.m., the buffalo send out an odor of fear that can drive them to panic and stampede. At 7:40 a.m., a young amateur photographer, Henry Rush, jumps out of his father's pickup truck and calls back, "Pick me up at five fifteen. I'll wait for you by the sign." The board on the post reads "Prairie Wildlife Refuge." Henry's goal for the day is to get a picture of a prairie dog doing a back flip, a silent shriek of danger prairie dogs use to attract the attention of animals who live close to the ground. As the day passes, Henry watches a prairie dog he calls Red Dog; he is unaware that the buffalo continue to grow more restless due to the growing storm. At 4:45 p.m., when the sky is ominous, Red Dog does his back flip just as the herd of

buffalo stampedes and Henry lies directly in its path. Jean George includes aspects of ecology, information about the animals, and descriptions of the grasses that grow on the prairie, all held together by the narrative flow of watching an amateur photographer at work.

Molly McLaughlin begins *Earthworms, Dirt, and Rotten Leaves* (I) with the question, "Why would anyone want to have anything to do with earthworms?" She notes that they are not very big, and they are certainly not pretty. They live in the dirt and eat dead leaves. McLaughlin convinces us that we are indeed interested in earthworms as we learn the difference between looking and observing. She gives us a guide for observing, shows us how to do some experiments and gives us the methods of documentation. Sections on the anatomy and characteristics of earthworms demonstrate the principle of adaptation and lead to a discussion of the ecological background on food chains. By the time she asks the question "Earthworms: Who needs 'em?" we know about the connections and relationships among plants and animals and other parts of the environment. McLaughlin writes in an informal, appealing style based on solid scientific information. She piques curiosity and involves readers in the scientific method based on careful observation, experimentation, and documentation.

Wildlife Refuges

The history of wildlife conservation is a rather brief one. Before the turn of the century, most people looked upon nature as an endless storehouse of raw materials to be used. Wild animals were often viewed as a threat and were killed for food, fur, profit, or sport. Birds were especially vulnerable because their ornamental feathers were used to adorn hats.

Wilderness and wildlife conservation movements evolved separately, and today the official wilderness system and the National Wildlife Refuge system are different political entities, but they serve similar objectives. Both have made efforts to protect wildlife habitats from the ax, plow, or gun; whether it is called "wilderness" or "refuge" is not relevant here. Most wilderness areas are so inaccessible that they serve as *de facto* wildlife refuges. John Muir, one of the pioneers of the American conservation movement, was able to arouse widespread attention to the beauties of nature and the threats to its shrinking wilderness. In 1892, with the help of friends, he founded the Sierra Club, a national conservation organization. About the same time, Audubon Societies, named for the famous painter John James Audubon, were formed to fight for the protection of birds. In 1903, President Theodore Roosevelt created the first game preserve by setting aside a three-acre site, Pelican Island in Florida, to protect birds from hunters. Such sanctuaries eventually became known as national wildlife refuges.

The system for refuge acquisition evolved as private gain competed with public good and naturalists for the acquisition of land. Groups still lobby in Congress for rights to cut timber or drill for oil in the limited wildlands remaining.

Noel Grove gives a comprehensive picture of the current situation in wildlife management in *Wildlands for Wildlife: America's National Refuges* (I–A). Filled with spectacular photographs by Bates Littlehales and a sensitive personal narrative by Grove, the book provides a thought-provoking look at what Grove calls "a scattering of arks," comparing the wildlife refuges to Noah's ark as a means of saving the animals. Grove traveled to refuges on the East and West Coasts, in the Eastern woodlands, on the prairies, and in the interior West and Alaska.

Grove illustrates in a vignette the general public's seeming disregard for nature and lack of ability to see the beauty in nature. At Sabine Refuge on the Louisiana coast, he walked along a trail through the freshwater marsh when he met a man in a plaid shirt, trailed by his wife and child, who said, "They told us we could see alligators and everything out here."

> It was midmorning, when many creatures have either gone into hiding till dusk or flown to distant feeding grounds. Patience, however, and a sharp eye will reveal those that remain. Plaid Shirt trudged unseeing near a full-grown nutria that quietly climbed ashore among the reeds and began grooming itself. A group of northern shoveler ducks sweeping their broad bills through the water, straining plankton, rated a glance, as did a dabbling family of coots. Hurrying past a statue-still egret he failed to see its lightning thrust at a fish, and he walked within fifteen feet of a seventeen foot gator lying still as a log.
>
> When I caught up with him later, waiting morosely while the woman and boy read a placard about marsh habitat, I asked him if he'd seen anything. He lifted his shoulders in a disappointed shrug: "Bunch'a ducks."[23]

Grove calls Alaska "a world apart" and describes the reasons:

> We've been given another chance. The refuges elsewhere in the U.S. were mostly salvaged from land badly eroded, heavily logged, drained dry, or seriously overgrazed. We brought back wildlife where it had been obliterated, or defended the few that somehow had survived. In Alaska the refuges were started before despoliation gained a foothold. Habitats are being preserved, not restored; populations of creatures that use them are being protected, not rebuilt.[24]

Wildlands for Wildlife is appropriate for all ages; the color photographs will be a treat for even the young child.

Endangered Species

An *endangered species* is wildlife officially designated by the U.S. Fish and Wildlife Service as having its continued existence threatened over its *entire range* because its habitat is threatened with destruction, drastic modification, or severe curtailment, or because of overexploitation, disease, predation, or other factors. A *threatened species* is wildlife officially designated as having its continued existence threatened in a *localized area*, such as a state, province, or lesser area for any of the same reasons. Once a species is given the protection and benefits of modern wildlife management, it often replenishes in surprising numbers. Technically, many species, such as the Eastern bluebird and the barn owl, are rapidly diminishing but are still abundant enough that they have not yet been officially recognized as threatened.

Caroline Arnold, in *Saving the Peregrine Falcon* (I), describes attempts to protect a species that is endangered because of the high levels of chemical contaminants in its food supply.* Scientists and conservationists have built up the peregrine population by captive breeding, rescuing eggs that would not hatch naturally, and hatching them in incubators. The chicks are returned to the nests of wild parents to increase the numbers of peregrine falcons.

*Before people were aware of the widespread effects of DDT, they sprayed it on hedges, crops, marshes, streams, orchards, and lawns to kill insects; it also killed birds.

Faith McNulty draws readers into the drama of an ornithologist's attempts to breed and hatch a whooping crane. (From *Peeping in the Shell: A Whooping Crane Is Hatched*, illustrated by Irene Brady.)

TEACHING IDEAS

ANALYZE THE PROBLEM OF ENDANGERED SPECIES (I)   As part of the study of endangered species, have students take positions concerning which factors they see as most significant in causing extinction. Have them examine the source material cited in this chapter for evidence to support their views.

PREDICT THE FUTURE FOR ENDANGERED SPECIES (I)   On the basis of their readings, have students hypothesize about the future of an endangered species. Ask them to predict how soon the species will become extinct if no action is taken and have them evaluate the effectiveness of present and proposed plans for protection.

GENERALIZE FROM FINDINGS (I)   After students have completed individual studies and shared their information, the class can formulate principles based on the findings, generalizing across species and predicting possible results and solutions. One prediction that might arise is that humans will become an endangered species. Whether or not students make that prediction, you might want to use it as a topic for a pro-or-con essay or a debate.

The Crocodile and the Crane: Surviving in a Crowded World describes the captive breeding efforts at St. Catherine's Wildlife Survival Center. (Written by Judy Cutchins and Ginny Johnston.)

The "wattle" of red, warty skin and white feathers makes this crane species easy to identify.

Faith McNulty tells a fascinating story about breeding a whooping crane and hatching its egg in *Peeping in the Shell: A Whooping Crane Is Hatched* (I). Tex, a whooping crane raised by a zookeeper and thereby imprinted to a human, refused to mate with male cranes when she grew up. George Archibald, an ornithologist, was determined to get Tex to hatch a chick and he practically lived with the crane until he could perform artificial insemination. Some funny scenes describe the "courting" behavior when George participated in a mating dance with the crane. When the egg was close to hatching, Faith McNulty flew to Wisconsin to observe firsthand this momentous occasion. She provides a tension-filled, minute-by-minute account of the tiny crane peeping in the shell and finally emerging after a strenuous battle with the shell. This very personal account helps us to realize the patience and dedication it takes to assure the life of one small wild creature.

Captive breeding of six species is described in *The Crocodile and the Crane: Surviving in a Crowded World* (I–A) by Judy Cutchins and Ginny Johnston. Cutchins and Johnston, staff members at the Fernbank Science Center in Atlanta, describe their work in wildlife conservation. Captive breeding, a new and important trend in preserving endangered species from extinction, requires extensive knowledge of the species and endless patience. Hutchins and Johnston describe the care required in saving the eggs of African wattled cranes at the St. Catherine's Island Wildlife Survival Center.

One morning . . . in the spring, the center's bird expert and his assistant quietly approached the yard of one wattled crane pair. The men stood outside the fence watching as the female crane probed for food in the wet soil. Her whole body shook as she plunged her beak into the swampy water, searching hungrily for plants.

That morning, the two men had an important job to do, and a difficult one. Wattled cranes normally lay a clutch of only two eggs each spring. The mother crane had just laid her second egg in the nest. The scientists had to

killer whale (*Orcinus orca*) 30 ft.

The color pattern varies among individual killer whales.

Helen Roney Sattler's
Whales, The Nomads of the Sea
is an excellent resource for
students interested in these
migratory animals.
(Illustrated by Jean Day
Zallinger.)

take the two eggs from the nest quickly, upsetting the parent cranes as little as possible. Although this seems like a cruel thing to do, it is an important captive breeding method. If the eggs are removed from the nest soon after they are laid, the female will be tricked and will lay two more eggs. This method is called "double-clutching." The number of eggs laid by one female crane is doubled from two to four. The "stolen" eggs are then placed in a heated container called an incubator, where they will hatch. Double-clutching can quickly increase the captive population of an endangered bird species.[25]

This book also shows how conservationists keep five other rare animals alive: a Grevy's zebra, an African cheetah, a Morelet crocodile, a golden lion tamarin, and an Arabian oryx.

Sevengill: The Shark and Me (I–A) by Don C. Reed is a firsthand account by a diver at a marine park in California. Reed, an active conservationist, works with the broadhead seven-gilled sharks in the aquarium. He tells in a dramatic way and with obvious affection how he cares for the unusual creatures. His personal narrative is authoritative and engaging.

Helen Roney Sattler tells how much is known about *Sharks, the Super Fish* (I–A), but she also describes what is still not known about them. When most of us think of sharks, we think of "*Jaws*," but there are many different types ranging from the dwarf shark, which is about six inches long, to the whale shark that is about 60 feet long. Sattler provides a comprehensive glossary of the specific species and families with a drawing for each. The main body of the book is devoted to descriptions of shark characteristics. A list of sharks, organized by families, and a list of books for further reading make this an outstanding resource. Sattler also produced an excellent book in *Whales, The Nomads of the Sea* (I), a comprehensive guide to a group that includes the world's largest animal and what may be the most intelligent and most playful of animals as well. All whales are nomadic; they migrate with the seasons. They visit every ocean and sea on earth; some even venture into freshwater rivers and

ACTIVITIES: TEACHER TO STUDENT

IDENTIFY THE MAJOR CAUSES OF EXTINCTION OF VARIOUS ANIMALS (I)
Organize the causes of extinction into categories, such as humans killing for food, sport, profit, and commercial reasons; environmental and pollution causes; loss of habitat. With this end in mind, do the following:

1. Analyze the process by which whooping cranes nearly became extinct and the steps taken to replenish and protect them.
2. Choose one endangered species, research its present status, analyze the major causes of extinction, and propose steps to ensure continuation and to reverse the downward trend in the species' population.

GATHER INFORMATION FOR GENERALIZATIONS (I)
1. Find out what has been done to preserve endangered species. (For example, in the case of the whooping cranes, nesting places were found and protected, eggs were placed with sandhill cranes for hatching and raising the young, wildlife preserves were established, and people were alerted to their scarcity.)
2. Learn as much as possible about the natural habitat, mating, and life patterns of one endangered species.
3. Generalize from the case of the whooping cranes to determine what needs to be done to protect the species you study. (For example, hunters must pass a bird-identification course and carry radios tuned to a station that warns of approaching whoopers.)
4. What might have been done to save the seal mink or the passenger pigeon?

Children who have read about wanton destruction of wildlife often become active in efforts to stop it.

PREPARE A CLASSROOM NEWSPAPER OR NEWS RELEASE (I)   Set up writing teams and choose one area for each to research and report. Some teams may choose to write about the poachers, looters, and unsportsmanlike hunters who rob us of natural wildlife beauty. Research some of the famous cases such as the "deer shiners" in North Dakota who blind deer at night with powerful spotlights to make bagging them easier; the alligator thieves in Florida and Georgia who use baited hooks to snare the alligators, then shoot them through the eyes; or the hawk and eagle killers in Pennsylvania who use long-range rifles with telescopic sights; and others who hunt down animals from helicopters. Along the Maine coast and in Long Island Sound, between New York and Connecticut, licensed lobstermen are allotted a limited catch of lobsters, but poachers set illegal traps and steal lobsters from the regulated ones.

Find out what measures are taken to control illegal killing and thefts in your area. Write your findings as a news story about an issue that causes local concern. You can distribute it as a flyer to fellow townspeople at the library or post office.

WRITE LETTERS TO ORGANIZATIONS THAT SUPPORT PROTECTION OF WILDLIFE (I)   The National Wildlife Federation, the International Wildlife Society, the Audubon Society, the Sierra Club, the Wilderness Society, and others provide guidelines and suggestions for projects you can carry out in your locale. Ask for materials to display and for things you can do to help wildlife conservation.

Write letters to the editor of newspapers pleading the cause of wildlife conservation in your area. Describe cases in which people make changes in the natural environment that unintentionally become traps for birds, fish, and other animals. Describe any positive changes that have helped conserve wildlife.

Visit a game preserve, a bird sanctuary, or a wildlife refuge, and write an account of your visit for the school newspaper.

RESEARCH THE PRESENT STATUS OF A SPECIES (I)   Find out how many whales, seals, or other endangered species now exist, how many have been killed in the last year, and the cause of their death. Describe the conditions needed for the species to remain alive, the current laws intended to protect them, and the legislation needed to assure survival. Search for reports of wildlife conservation.

Research the history of your area to find out what wildlife inhabited it 50, 100, and 200 years ago. Describe the changes in the environment that caused the wildlife to leave or reduced or increased their number. Make predictions about the status of wildlife 10, 50, and 100 years from now if trends continue. Outline a list of steps that must be taken if your children are to see a living specimen of the wildlife.

DEVELOP A POSTER CAMPAIGN (I)   Make posters calling attention to wildlife that needs protection. Much of the credit of the success of saving the whooping crane is attributed to the widespread poster campaign that alerted people along the migration path and around possible nesting grounds to be on the lookout for the diminishing species. (Several of those alerted by posters were partially responsible for the eventual tracking; there is no telling how many hunters' bullets the campaign averted from the rare birds.)

Select one from the following list of the world's rarest animals to be the subject of your poster campaign: California condor (fewer than 30, all in captivity in southern California), giant panda (fewer than 1,000, in Tibet and China), monkey-eating eagle (about 40, in the Philippine Islands), Kakapo (fewer than 100, in New Zealand), great Indian rhinoceros (about 500, in India and Nepal), mountain gorilla (about 400, in equatorial Africa), blue whale (fewer than 2,000), and the whooping crane (a few hundred in the U.S. and Canada).

Design and construct a model billboard alerting your community to the need for action on a conservation issue, and see if a local billboard or sign company will erect it, or if wildlife societies will use it to support a campaign.

---

lakes. Still, most people have never seen one of these amazing mammals in the wild.

Research Efforts

The science of wildlife management is making progress partially due to the extensive research into animal behavior. For example, for years naturalists have been camping out in duck blinds watching the natural movements, nesting sites, and migration patterns of water fowl.

Hope Ryden, a naturalist, writer, and photographer, used talents in all three areas to produce a book about *America's Bald Eagle* (A), our national symbol. She describes the appearance, mating, nesting, breeding, and migration patterns in the life cycle of the bald eagle. As with many naturalists who specialize in a particular species, she is an ardent admirer of the eagle and stresses the importance of the 1973 Endangered Species Act which protects them. Ryden also describes some of the conservation programs, such as hacking and raptor rehabilitation centers, that increase the numbers of our national bird.

Dorothy Hinshaw Patent focuses on the same bird in *Where the Bald Eagles Gather* (I). The site of the gathering each fall is Montana's Glacier National Park, where the salmon spawn and the eagles feed upon them. Subsequently, the eagles continue their southward migration and eventually return to Alaska and the Northwest Territories for breeding. Scientists gather information about the eagles by visually and electronically tagging them to track them in their flight patterns.

In *America's Endangered Birds: Programs and People Working to Save Them* (I–A), Robert M. McClung reminds us that in 1875 a hunter shot the last recorded Labrador duck. In 1914, the last passenger pigeon died in a cage in the Cincinnati Zoo, and the last Carolina parakeet died in captivity. In 1932, the last heath hen died in Martha's Vineyard. The grievous knowledge that we will never again see these species causes us to wonder how many more will go into oblivion in the near future.

McClung describes the programs and people working to help endangered wildlife. He traces the historical background of some en-

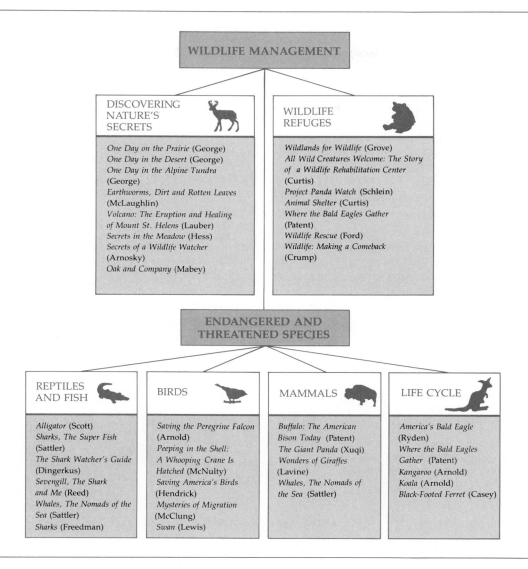

WILDLIFE MANAGEMENT

DISCOVERING NATURE'S SECRETS

One Day on the Prairie (George)
One Day in the Desert (George)
One Day in the Alpine Tundra (George)
Earthworms, Dirt and Rotten Leaves (McLaughlin)
Volcano: The Eruption and Healing of Mount St. Helens (Lauber)
Secrets in the Meadow (Hess)
Secrets of a Wildlife Watcher (Arnosky)
Oak and Company (Mabey)

WILDLIFE REFUGES

Wildlands for Wildlife (Grove)
All Wild Creatures Welcome: The Story of a Wildlife Rehabilitation Center (Curtis)
Project Panda Watch (Schlein)
Animal Shelter (Curtis)
Where the Bald Eagles Gather (Patent)
Wildlife Rescue (Ford)
Wildlife: Making a Comeback (Crump)

ENDANGERED AND THREATENED SPECIES

REPTILES AND FISH

Alligator (Scott)
Sharks, The Super Fish (Sattler)
The Shark Watcher's Guide (Dingerkus)
Sevengill, The Shark and Me (Reed)
Whales, The Nomads of the Sea (Sattler)
Sharks (Freedman)

BIRDS

Saving the Peregrine Falcon (Arnold)
Peeping in the Shell: A Whooping Crane Is Hatched (McNulty)
Saving America's Birds (Hendrick)
Mysteries of Migration (McClung)
Swan (Lewis)

MAMMALS

Buffalo: The American Bison Today (Patent)
The Giant Panda (Xuqi)
Wonders of Giraffes (Lavine)
Whales, The Nomads of the Sea (Sattler)

LIFE CYCLE

America's Bald Eagle (Ryden)
Where the Bald Eagles Gather (Patent)
Kangaroo (Arnold)
Koala (Arnold)
Black-Footed Ferret (Casey)

dangered birds and attempts to explain how and why their numbers dwindled. The whooping crane, the bald eagle, the brown pelican, the California condor, Kirtland's warbler, and the ivory-billed woodpecker are among the threatened birds he studies. Maps showing the range and area of concentration of the disappearing species, the role of pesticides in their death, new developments in research, and programs to save them make this book a rare gem for students of conservation. The enormity of the problem is presented without sensationalism.

Conservationists have tried various methods to save the whooping crane. One group, in an effort to raise some cranes in captivity, "stole" a few eggs from the nests each year. Another group, believing the chicks would have a better chance if they hatched in the wild, placed whooper eggs in sandhill cranes' nests in a reasonably successful experiment, reported by Roderick C. Drewien with Ernie Kuyt in "Teamwork Helps the Whooping Crane."[26] Sandhill cranes, more plentiful than whoopers, serve as satisfactory foster parents while the whoopers are young, but amazingly, the whoopers return to their own kind during adolescence. The whooping crane population has slightly increased, and because millions support the efforts to conserve them, the whooping crane has become a symbol for conservationists everywhere.

THE ADVANCED GRADES UNIT: SPACE

Space, the term children use, is a part of the field of astronomy. It is the study of celestial bodies, their size, their composition, and their patterns of movement. Astronomy includes the study of the earth in relation to other planets, the related science of physics, and the activities of the space program and the astronauts. The following unit is divided into segments on the space program, telescopes, planets, and mysteries, moons, and meteors.

The Space Program

Sally Ride answers many questions that children ask about travel in outer space in *To Space and Back* (I–A). In an oversized book with magnificent color photographs, she describes lift-off, weightlessness, eating, sleeping, and even going to the bathroom. In a personal narrative

Sally Ride describes for her young audience what life is like in the space shuttle. (From *To Space and Back* by Sally Ride and Susan Okie.)

My calculator floats within easy reach on the flight deck.

TEACHING IDEA

COMPARING SOURCES (A)   Collect information on a current issue or event dealing with the space program, paying special attention to reports found in the media (especially newspapers and magazines) and in government publications, scientific journals, and first-person accounts in diaries, journals, or letters. File the articles and pictures by type of report, legislative action, activity, and so forth.

Have your students examine the information in the file and do the following:

1. Identify contradictory reports and phrases that indicate personal opinion is being expressed—such as "in my view," "it seemed to me," "some people say."
2. List and compare the facts as given in the media, scientific journals, government documents, and personal reports. Determine which facts are verifiable, which are assumptions, and whether the assumptions follow logically from the facts.
3. Examine the perspective of each source and determine how that perspective might have influenced the presentation of the issue.
4. If information is given about the writer's authority in the area under discussion, evaluate it.

This kind of exercise gives students practice in the critical thinking skills of distinguishing between fact and opinion, verification, logic, identifying bias, and evaluating.

---

style, she gives her reactions to events but adds general information to make the discussion interesting to all readers. For example, in her description of weightlessness, she says:

> During my first day in space, I had to learn how to move around. I started out trying to "swim" through the air, but that didn't work at all; air isn't dense, the way water is, and I felt silly dog-paddling in the air, going nowhere. Before long I discovered that I had to push off from one of the walls if I wanted to get across the room. At first I would push off a little too hard and crash into the opposite wall, but I soon learned to wind my way around with very gentle pushes. . . . In weightlessness the slightest touch can start an astronaut's body floating across the room or drifting over in a slow-motion somersault. The only way to stop moving

is to take hold of something that's anchored in place.[27]

Ride also describes rendezvous with satellites already in space and some of the scientific experiments. For example,

> Inside the space shuttle, astronauts perform experiments exploring ways to make new substances—medicines, metals, or crystals—in weightlessness. We also record data about our own bodies to help scientists understand the effects of weightlessness. Before astronauts can set out on a two-year trip to Mars, scientists must be able to predict what will happen to people who stay in space that long.[28]

The commanding photographs were taken by Sally Ride and the other astronauts.

ACTIVITY: TEACHER TO STUDENT

ANALYZE AND EVALUATE MEDIA REPORTS (A)   When an issue about space is in the news, obtain newspapers from different parts of the country, or different newspapers from one city, or three magazines of the same date. This might be arranged through a newsstand or by phoning or writing to friends or relatives in different parts of the country. Then:

1. Note the number of space travel issues that make headlines compared with other front-page news items.
2. Compare what issues are presented in the editorials of the different newspapers.
3. Look at ads about jobs and housing to see if they are located near space centers.
4. Identify any "slanting" in presenting the material. Distinguish between editorial, hidden persuasion, and objective reporting. Do articles that are supposedly objective reports contain editorializing or disguised persuasion?

Don Dwiggins uses some of the same photographs on a smaller scale in *Flying the Space Shuttles* (I–A). His writing style is also more formal and objective than personal and subjective. He writes of weightlessness:

> Riding in orbit at about 17,500 miles an hour, the pull of gravity is nearly balanced by what is called centrifugal force. The slight difference is called microgravity. You are in a condition of weightlessness. If you bend down to pick up something, you may end up doing somersaults. So you'll use portable handholds with suction cups.
>
> Even eating is different in space. Your fork and spoon will drift off the table if you aren't careful. Crumbs will float upward, a danger if you inhale them. And spilled water doesn't drip down. It, too, floats up, in tiny balls that stick to the wall and spread like glue.[29]

Dwiggins briefly describes some of the experiments conducted on shuttle flights. One, suggested by a student, involved a box of bees to find out if bees built their honeycombs in zero gravity the same way they do on Earth. The experiment showed they could. He also describes experiments to make insulin and to separate biological materials, such as egg albumin, using their surface electrical charges in zero gravity. Such work will lead to manufacturing pure medical products in space.

Franklyn M. Branley, Astronomer Emeritus and former chairman of the American Museum-Hayden Planetarium, gives an even more objective view of space exploration in *From Sputnik to Space Shuttles: Into the New Space Age* (I–A). He explains how satellites and shuttles are pushed into space and the work shuttles do and how they do it. He sketches the 30-year history since Sputnik and describes efforts for manned space stations.

> In 1973 Skylab, America's first manned space station, was put into a 300-mile orbit. Two years earlier the Russians had launched their first Salyut station. In 1979 Skylab moved closer to Earth. It entered our atmosphere and burned up. Salyut 7 is still in orbit, and the Russians continue to use it.[30]

Branley uses both color and black and white photographs. He mentions the Challenger explosion in a photo caption, although it is not discussed in the text.

TEACHING IDEA

PRESENTING WHAT YOU HAVE LEARNED (A)   After your students have researched in the library and in the community various space explorations and
proposed explorations, have them present their findings. Other students can
take notes for a class discussion, for debating issues, or as a basis for research
reports. Committees may be formed. This will give students practice in oral
presentation, listening, note-taking, evaluation, and cooperative group work.

Plan a space fair at which students will share the results of their research
and other work during the study. Plan exhibits, demonstrations, debates, discussions, and presentations. Groups studying different aspects of the topic can
decide the best way to share their findings with others. For example, those
who study other possibilities of life in outer space can set up a demonstration
booth to show how those life forms might look. Brainstorm with your students
for other possible exhibits.

Telescopes, Stars, Looking at the Sky

Wendy Saul, in *Science Fare,* an excellent book
on science materials, says,

> To most children, astronomy is virtually synon-
> ymous with owning a telescope. So they talk
> their parents into plunking down $50 or $60, no
> small sum to be sure, on a nicely packaged item
> from their local toy supermarket, and set out to
> explore the night sky. The evening starts out
> well; the moon is an impressive sight through
> one of these instruments, and expectations
> build. Next the child turns to a star, any star.
> Surprisingly the dot on the sky looks slightly
> bigger, and considerably blurrier, through the
> new telescope. At random they try star after
> star, with no effect.[31]

Saul goes on to explain that the children actually have two problems that make the satis-
factions of astronomy inaccessible. First, they
have no roadmap of the sky or a conceptualization of the differences between planets and
stars, and second, their equipment is simply
inadequate.

Seymour Simon's work is exemplary in its
presentation of information which breeds a
sense of wonder. In *The Sun* (P–I–A), his one-

hundredth book, he explains that the sun is a
medium-sized star. The reason it appears bigger and brighter than other stars is that it is so
much closer to us. "The sun is about 93 million
miles away from Earth. The next closest star is
about 25 million million miles away. Although
scientists can see countless stars through telescopes, the sun is the only star that they can
study closely."[32]

Simon writes with a sense of authority: he
uses facts well and casts them in language simple enough for young readers to comprehend;
his comparisons are understandable. For instance,

> The sun is large compared to Earth. If the sun
> were hollow it could hold 1.3 million Earths.
> Think of this: If Earth were the size of a golf
> ball, then the sun would be a globe about fifteen
> feet across. In fact, the sun is nearly 600 times
> bigger than all the planets in the Solar System
> put together.[33]

The clarity of information is equalled by
the splendor of the color photographs and
diagrams which add to comprehension and
wonder. *Stars* (P–I–A) is an equally outstanding work.

An earlier book by Seymour Simon, *Look to the Night Sky: An Introduction to Star Watching* (I–A), is the road map to the sky Wendy Saul described as necessary for understanding astronomy. Seymour Simon gives the road map and in comprehensible prose explains many facts along the way.

> You may be able to pick out a group of stars that seems to form a pattern. These patterns of stars are called *constellations*. You may see a few bright stars in the night sky that don't twinkle as the others do. These are probably not stars but planets such as Mars, Jupiter, Saturn, Mercury, and the brightest of all, Venus.[34]

The book helps aspiring astronomers pick out planets, stars, and constellations. It also explains how the constellations got their names, which stars are easiest to find, and how the constellations change with the seasons. Clearly labeled diagrams help with understanding.

Planets

Patricia Lauber explores the planets of our solar system, highlighting the prominent features of each in *Journey to the Planets* (I–A). Starting with Earth, the planet seen from space that looks like a beautiful big blue marble, she moves her discussion to the center of the solar system and then back out to the dark worlds of Uranus, Neptune, and Pluto. When theories dominate, Lauber distinguishes between them and fact and explains the state of knowledge clearly.

> Billions of years ago, a vast cloud of gas and dust was floating in space. It was dark and cold and spread very thin. Then something happened, and the particles of gas and dust began to draw closer together. The cloud kept growing smaller and more dense. Slow-moving whirlpools developed within it. They caused the giant cloud to break up into smaller clouds. One of these was to become our solar system.

> As our cloud went on contracting, it rotated faster and flattened into a disk. More and more gas and dust were drawn into the center of the disk, which became hotter and hotter. At last the heat and pressure were so great that atoms began to fuse. The center of the disk glowed with nuclear fires, and a new star was born.

> In some such way, astronomers think, our sun came into being. Much of what happened remains a mystery, but astronomers are sure that new stars form in clouds of gas and dust. Through telescopes they can see such clouds glowing with the light of newborn stars.[35]

Lauber presents technical information with clarity and simplicity.

Roy Gallant is a member of the faculty at the American Museum-Hayden Planetarium; a fellow of the Royal Astronomical Society, London; and director of the Southworth Planetarium, University of Southern Maine. In *The Planets: Exploring the Solar System* (A), he gives a comprehensive description of our solar system, its nine known planets with about 45 moons circling them, the millions of rock-metal fragments called asteroids and meteoroids, and billions of "dirty snowballs" of ice and dust that we call comets. Each chapter opens with a chart containing information of how the planet is represented in mythology, its symbol, diameter, mass, density, distance from the sun, rotation, revolution, speed in orbit, inclination, gravity, and moons. Appendices, glossary, and an index make this a very helpful resource in a study of the planets.

Seymour Simon has produced a number of outstanding books on the planets. *Jupiter, Saturn, Uranus,* and *Mars* (all I–A) are illustrative of his work. Each book presents scientific knowledge in comprehensible language and uses large-scale photographs in color to help readers see what can be seen through powerful telescopes. Jupiter's atmospheric average ranges about 250 degrees below zero; it is more than double the weight of any other planet,

Seymour Simon's series of books on the planets provide comprehensive information with large colorful illustrations. (From *Uranus.*)

and has 16 moons. Saturn has a 150,000-mile ring system and has more than 20 moons. Both books have an appealing format and brilliant photographs that look like huge fireworks displays.

Mysteries, Moons, and Meteors

Franklyn Branley asks the question that intrigues us in *Is There Life in Outer Space?* (I–A).

Written in an engaging style, he tells what investigations have shown about the two most likely candidates for life: the moon and Mars. He also explains what is known about other planets that makes it unlikely that they sustain life. Clearly explaining that his statements are conjecture, he describes what kind of life he thinks might exist in other galaxies.

In *Mysteries of the Universe* (A), Franklyn Branley covers some of the questions that

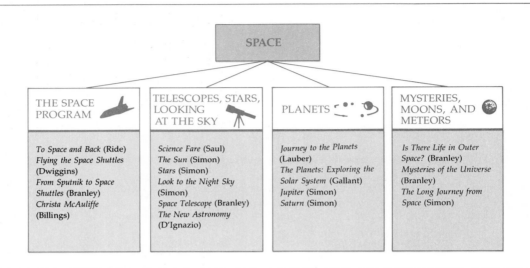

remain unanswered in scientists' exploration of outer space. He distinguishes between fact and theory in his discussion. When he asks a question, such as "What are supernovas?" he gives enough background information for the reader to understand the nature of the question and as much of the answer as is known. His information is authoritative and arranged logically. Bibliographies and a complete index add to the book's usefulness.

Seymour Simon's *The Long Journey from Space* and *The Long View into Space* (both I–A)

are other large-format books that have visual as well as informational appeal. Simon describes earlier beliefs about comets in the past and tells what we now know about them. He explains what comets and meteors are, how they travel, and how they behave when they enter the earth's atmosphere. He describes some of the particular comets and meteors that have been studied and shows examples of them in the large, excellent photographs.

RECOMMENDED READING

Animals

Aliki (Brandenberg). *Dinosaur Bones*. New York: Harper & Row, 1988.

Branley, Franklyn Mansfield. *Dinosaurs, Asteroids, and Superstars: Why the Dinosaurs Disappeared*. Illustrated by Jean Zallinger. New York: Crowell, 1982.

Busch, Phyllis S. *The Seven Sleepers:*

The Story of Hibernation. Illustrated by Wayne Trimm. New York: Macmillan, 1985.

Carter, Anne. *Molly in Danger*. Illustrated by John Butler. New York: Crown, 1987.

Cobb, Vicki. *The Monsters Who Died*. Illustrated by Greg Wenzel. New York: Coward, McCann & Geoghegan, 1983.

Fischer-Nagel, Heiderose, and Andreas Fischer-Nagel. *Life of a Honeybee*. Minneapolis: Carolrhoda, 1985.

———. *Life of a Ladybug*. Minneapolis: Carolrhoda, 1985.

———. *Season of the White Stork*. Minneapolis: Carolrhoda, 1985.

Florian, Douglas. *Discovering Frogs*. New York: Scribner's, 1986.

Foster, Sally. *A Pup Grows Up.* New York: Dodd, Mead, 1984.

Freedman, Russell. *Farm Babies.* New York: Holiday House, 1981.

Gibbons, Gail. *Farming.* New York: Holiday House, 1988.

Isenbart, Hans Heinrich. *Baby Animals on the Farm.* Illustrated by Ruth Rau. New York: Putnam's, 1984.

Johnston, Ginny, and Judy Cutchins. *Andy Bear: A Polar Cub Grows up at the Zoo.* Photography by Constance Noble. New York: Morrow, 1985.

Knight, David C. *"Dinosaurs" That Swam and Flew.* Illustrated by Lee J. Ames. Englewood Cliffs, N.J.: Prentice-Hall, 1985.

Lauber, Patricia. *Dinosaurs Walked Here.* New York: Bradbury, 1987.

McClung, Robert. *Gorilla.* Illustrated by Irene Brady. New York: Morrow, 1983.

———. *Rajpur: Last of the Bengal Tigers.* Illustrated by Irene Brady. New York: Morrow, 1982.

Mannetti, William. *Dinosaurs in your Back Yard.* New York: Atheneum, 1982.

Patent, Dorothy Hinshaw. *Mosquitoes.* New York: Holiday House, 1986.

———. *The Sheep Book.* Photography by William Muñoz. New York: Dodd, Mead, 1985.

Pope, Joyce. *Do Animals Dream? Children's Questions About Animals Most Often Asked of the Natural History Museum.* New York: Viking, 1986.

———. *Taking Care of Your Cat.* New York: Watts, 1986.

Pringle, Laurence. *Animals at Play.* San Diego: Harcourt Brace Jovanovich, 1985.

Rojankovsky, Feodor. *Animals on the Farm.* New York: Knopf, 1967.

Selsam, Millicent E. *Benny's Animals and How He Put Them in Order.* Illustrated by Arnold Lobel. New York: Harper & Row, 1966.

———. *Egg to Chick,* rev. ed. Illustrated by Barbara Wolff. New York: Harper & Row, 1970.

———, and Joyce Hunt. *A First Look at Kangaroos, Koalas, and Other Animals with Pouches.* Illustrated by Harriet Springer. New York: Walker, 1985.

Simon, Seymour. *101 Questions and Answers About Dangerous Animals.* Illustrated by Ellen Friedman. New York: Macmillan, 1985.

Wildlife Management

Bonners, Susan. *A Penguin Year.* New York: Delacorte, 1981.

Bowman, Margret. *Blue-Footed Booby: Bird of the Galapagos.* Adapted by Nicholas Millhouse. New York: Walker, 1986.

Brady, Irene. *Wild Mouse.* New York: Scribner's, 1976.

Coldrey, Jennifer, and Karen Goldie-Morrison, eds. *Hide and Seek.* New York: Oxford Scientific Films, Putnam's, 1986.

Cook, David. *Environment.* New York: Crown, 1985.

Curtis, Patricia. *Animal Rights: Stories of People Who Defend the Rights of Animals.* New York: Four Winds, 1980.

Featherly, Jay. *Wild Horses of the American West.* Minneapolis: Carolrhoda, 1986.

Graham, Ada, and Frank Graham. *Careers in Conservation.* Illustrated by Drake Jordon. New York: Sierra Club, Scribner's, 1980.

———. *The Changing Desert.* Illustrated by Robert Shetterly. New York: Sierra Club, Scribner's, 1981.

Hisock, Bruce. *Tundra, the Artic Land.* New York: Atheneum, 1986.

Hirschi, Ron. *One Day on Pika's Peak.* Photography by Galen Burell. New York: Dodd, Mead, 1986.

Hurd, Edith Thatcher. *The Mother Owl.* Illustrated by Clement Hurd. Boston: Little, Brown, 1974.

———. *The Mother Whale.* Illustrated by Clement Hurd. Boston: Little, Brown, 1973.

McClung, Robert. *Peeper, First Voice of Spring.* Illustrated by Carol Lerner. New York: Morrow, 1977.

———. *Vanishing Wildlife of Latin America.* Illustrated by George Founds. New York: Morrow, 1981.

McDearmon, Kay. *Giant Pandas.* New York: Dodd, Mead, 1986.

Malnig, Anita. *Where the Waves Break: Life at the Edge of the Sea.* Illustrated by Jeff Rothman, Alex Kerstitch and Franklin H. Barnwell. Minneapolis: Carolrhoda, 1985.

Minta, Kathryn A. *The Digging Badger.* New York: Dodd, Mead, 1985.

Newton, James R. *A Forest Is Reborn.* Illustrated by Susan Bonners. New York: Crowell, 1982.

Place, Marian Templeton. *Mount St. Helens: A Sleeping Volcano Awakes.* New York: Dodd, Mead, 1981.

Powzyk, Joyce. *Wallaby Creek.* New York: Lothrop, Lee & Shepard, 1985.

Rahn, Joan Elma. *Animals That Changed History.* New York: Atheneum, 1986.

Rogers, Jean. *Goodbye, My Island.* Illustrated by Rie Muñoz. New York: Greenwillow, 1983.

Rue, Leonard Lee, III, and William Owen. *Meet the Moose.* New York: Dodd, Mead, 1985.

Ryden, Hope. *The Beaver.* New York: Putnam's, 1986.

Scott, Jack Denton. *Moose.* Photography by Ozzie Sweet. New York: Putnam's, 1981.

Smith, Elizabeth Simpson. *A Dolphin Goes to School: The Story of Squirt, a Trained Dolphin.* Illustrated by Ted Lewin. New York: Morrow, 1986.

Steiner, Barbara. *Biography of a Polar Bear.* Illustrated by Steve Tamara. New York: Putnam's, 1972.

Stuart, Gene. S. *Wildlife Alert: The Struggle to Survive*. Washington, D.C.: National Geographic, 1980.

Van Wormer, Joe. *Eagles*. New York: Lodestar, 1985.

Wakefield, Pat, and Larry Carrara. *A Moose for Jessica*. Illustrated by Larry Carrara. New York: Dutton, 1988.

Weinstock, Edward B. *Wilderness War: The Struggle to Preserve America's Wildlands*. New York: Messner, 1982.

Williams, Terry Tempest. *Between Cattails*. Illustrated by Peter Parnall. New York: Scribner's, 1985.

Zipco, Stephen J. *Toxic Threat: How Hazardous Substances Poison Our Lives*. New York: Messner, 1986.

Space

Asimov, Isaac. *Asimov's Guide to Haley's Comet*. New York: Walker, 1985.

Ballard, Robert D. *Exploring Our Living Planet*. Washington, D.C.: National Geographic, 1983.

Billings, Charlene W. *Space Station: Bold New Step Beyond Earth*. New York: Dodd, Mead, 1986.

Branley, Franklyn Mansfield. *Comets*. Illustrated by Giulio Maestro. New York: Crowell, 1984.

———. *Journey into a Black Hole*. Illustrated by Marc Simont. New York: Crowell, 1986.

———. *What the Moon Is Like*. Illustrated by True Kelley. New York: Crowell, 1986.

Gallant, Roy A. *The Macmillan Book of Astronomy*. Illustrated by Ron Miller, Don Dixon, Davis Meltzer, and Brian Sullivan. New York: Macmillan, 1986.

Hansen, Rosanna, and Robert A. Bell. *My First Book of Space*. New York: Messner, 1986.

Jespersen, James, and Jane Fitz-Randolph. *From Quarks to Quasars: A Tour of the Universe*. New York: Atheneum, 1987.

McPhee, Penelope, and Raymond McPhee. *Your Future in Space: The U.S. Space Camp Training Program*. New York: Crown, 1986.

Maurer, Richard. *The Nova Space Explorer's Guide: Where to Go and What to See*. New York: Clarkson Potter, 1985.

O'Conner, Karen. *Sally Ride and the New Astronauts: Scientists in Space*. New York: Watts, 1983.

Simon, Seymour. *Earth, Our Planet in Space*. New York: Four Winds, 1984.

White, Jack R. *Satellites of Today and Tomorrow*. New York: Dodd, Mead, 1985.

Zisfein, Melvin B. *Flight: A Panorama of Aviation*. Illustrated by Robert Andrew Parker. New York: Pantheon, 1981.

Poetry

Amon, Aline, ed. *The Earth Is Sore: Native Americans on Nature*. New York: Atheneum, 1981.

Brewton, Sara, and John E. Brewton, comps. *Of Quarks, Quasars, and other Quirks: Quizzical Poems for the Supersonic Age*. Illustrated by Quentin Blake. New York: Crowell, 1977.

Cole, William. *An Arkful of Animals*. Illustrated by Lynn Munsinger. Boston: Houghton Mifflin, 1978.

———, comp. *The Poetry of Horses*. New York: Scribner's, 1979.

Fisher, Aileen. *Out in the Dark and Daylight*. Illustrated by Gail Owens. New York: Harper & Row, 1980.

Hopkins, Lee Bennett, comp. *Dinosaurs*. Illustrated by Murray Tinkelman. San Diego: Harcourt Brace Jovanovich, 1987.

———. *Moments: Poems About the Seasons*. Illustrated by Michael Hague. San Diego: Harcourt Brace Jovanovich, 1980.

Hughes, Ted. *Moon Whales and Other Poems*. Illustrated by Leonard Baskin. New York: Viking, 1976.

Kuskin, Karla. *Dogs and Dragons, Trees and Dreams*. New York: Harper & Row, 1980.

Livingston, Myra Cohn. *Earth Songs*. Illustrated by Leonard Everett Fisher. New York: Holiday House, 1986.

McCord, David. *One at a Time*. Illustrated by Henry B. Kane. Boston: Little, Brown, 1980.

Prelutsky, Jack. *Zoo Doings*. Illustrated by Paul O. Zelinsky. New York: Greenwillow, 1983.

PROFESSIONAL REFERENCES

Brewton, John E., and Sara W. Brewton, eds. *Index to Poetry for Children and Young People, 1976–1981*. New York, Wilson, 1983.

Children's Catalog. New York: Wilson, annual.

Fitzgerald, Sheila, and Bernice E. Cullinan. "Speakout: Readability Formulas Play Too Dominant a Role!" In *Instructor* 94, no. 8 (April 1985): 18.

Gardner, Dorothy. "Emotions: A Basis for Learning." In *Feelings and Learning*. Washington, D.C.: Association for Childhood Education International, 1965.

Heimlich, Joan E., and Susan D. Pittelman. *Semantic Mapping: Classroom Applications*. Newark, Del.: International Reading Association, 1986.

McPadden, Jeanne. "Dinosaurs Unit." P.S. 321, District 15, Brooklyn, New York, 1986.

Maisel, Jane, and Scarlote West. "Four and FIve Year Olds." An Interview with Jane Maisel and Scarlote West. Edited by Bernice Cullinan. Friends Seminary, New York, 1987.

Meltzer, Milton. "Where Do All the Prizes Go? The Case For Nonfiction." *Horn Book Magazine* 52, no. 1 (February 1976): 17–23.

Meyer, Bonnie J., and G. Elizabeth Rice. "The Structure of Text." In *Handbook of Reading Research,* Edited by P. David Pearson, 319–51. New York: Longman, 1984.

"Outstanding Science Trade Books For Children in 1986." In *Science and Children.* New York: Joint Committee of the Children's Book Council and the National Science Teachers Association: March 1987.

Pringle, Laurence. "Pringle: The Thread of Hopefulness . . . Runs Through All My Books." In *Highlights for Children* Writers Workshop Chautauqua, N.Y. July 12–19, 1986.

Saul, E. Wendy. "Living Proof: What Helen Keller, Marilyn Monroe, and Marie Curie Have in Common." In *School Library Journal* 33, no. 2, (October 1986): 103–108.

NOTES

1. Carl Sandburg, "Buffalo Dusk," in *Rainbows Are Made,* ed. Lee Bennett Hopkins (San Diego: Harcourt Brace Jovanovich, 1982), 26.

2. Dorothy Gardner, "Emotions: A Basis for Learning," in *Feelings and Learning* (Washington, D.C.: Association for Childhood Education International, 1965), 34.

3. Children's Book Council, 67 Irving Place, New York, N.Y. 10003.

4. *Outstanding Science Trade Books for Children in 1986* (New York: Children's Book Council and the National Science Teachers Association Book Review Committee, 1987).

5. Helen Roney Sattler, *The Illustrated Dinosaur Dictionary* (New York: Lothrop, Lee & Shepard, 1983), 48.

6. Laurence Pringle, *Death Is Natural* (New York: Four Winds, 1977), 12.

7. Jack Denton Scott, *The Book of the Pig,* photos. Ozzie Sweet (New York: Putnam's, 1981), 29.

8. Laurence Pringle, *Dinosaurs and People: Fossils, Facts, and Fantasies* (New York: Harcourt Brace Jovanovich, 1978), copyright page.

9. Milton Meltzer, "Where Do All the Prizes Go?: The Case for Nonfiction," *Horn Book Magazine* 52, no. 1 (February 1976): 21–22.

10. Laurence Pringle, *Highlights for Children* Writers Workshop, Chautauqua, N.Y. (July 12–19, 1986), 26.

11. James Cross Giblin, *Highlights for Children* Writers Workshop, Chautauqua, N.Y. (July 12–19, 1986), 14.

12. Seymour Simon, *The Long View into Space* (New York: Crown, 1979), unpaged.

13. Seymour Simon, *The Secret Clocks: Time Sense of Living Things,* illus. Jan Brett (New York: Viking, 1979), 55–56.

14. The concept of webbing, developed in England, was popularized in America by Charlotte S. Huck. A quarterly, *The Web,* is published by Ohio State University, Charlotte S. Huck and Janet Hickman, eds. (200 Ramseyer Hall, 29 West Woodruff, Columbus, Ohio 43210). See also Donna E. Norton, "Using a Webbing Process to Develop Children's Literature Units," *Language Arts* 59, no. 4 (April 1982): 348–56.

15. Joan E. Heimlich and Susan D. Pittelman, *Semantic Mapping: Classroom Applications* (Newark, Del.: International Reading Association, 1986).

16. Jeanne McPadden, Kindergarten teacher, P.S. 321, District 15, Brooklyn, N.Y., *"Lauren's Dinosaur Book."*

17. Jane Maisel and Scarlote West, Primary Teachers, Friends Seminary, 222 E. 16th Street, New York, N.Y.

18. Seymour Simon, *The Largest Dinosaurs,* illus. Pamela Carroll (New York: Macmillan, 1986), 6.

19. Laurence Pringle, *Dinosaurs and People: Fossils, Facts, and Fantasies,* 7.

20. Russell Freedman, *Dinosaurs and Their Young,* illus. Leslie Morrill (New York: Holiday House, 1983), 28–29.

21. Thomas Cacajob and Teresa Burton, *Close to the Wild: Siberian Tigers in a Zoo* (Minneapolis: Carolrhoda, 1985), 5.

22. Laurence Pringle, Lecture, *Highlights for Children* Writer's Workshop, Chautauqua, N.Y., July 18, 1986.

23. Noel Grove, *Wildlands for Wildlife: America's National Refuges* (Washington, D.C.: National Geographic Society, 1984), 15–18.

24. Ibid., 182.

25. Judy Cutchins and Ginny Johnston, *The Crocodile and the Crane: Surviving in a Crowded World* (New York: Morrow, 1986), 18.

26. Roderick C. Drewien and Ernie Kuyt, "Teamwork Helps the Whooping Crane," *National Geographic* (May 1979): 680–92.

27. Sally Ride and Susan Okie, *To Space and Back* (New York: Lothrop, Lee & Shepard, 1986), 29–31.

28. Ibid., 59.

29. Don Dwiggins, *Flying the Space Shuttles* (New York: Dodd, Mead, 1985), 14.

30. Franklyn M. Branley, *From Sputnik to Space Shuttles: Into the New Space Age* (New York: Crowell, 1986), 44.

31. Wendy Saul with Alan R. Newman, *Science Fare: An Illustrated Guide and Catalog of Toys, Books, and Activities for Kids*, intro. Isaac Asimov (New York: Harper & Row, 1986), 222.

32. Seymour Simon, *The Sun* (New York: Morrow, 1986), unpaged.

33. Ibid.

34. Seymour Simon, *Look to the Night Sky: An Introduction to Star Watching* (New York: Viking, 1977), 2.

35. Patricia Lauber, *Journey to the Planets* (New York: Crown, 1982), 15.

CHILDREN'S BOOKS CITED

Aliki (Brandenberg). *Fossils Tell of Long Ago*. New York: Crowell, 1972.

———. *Digging up Dinosaurs*. New York: Crowell, 1981.

———. *Dinosaur Bones*. New York: Harper & Row, 1988.

———. *Dinosaurs Are Different*. New York: Crowell, 1985.

———. *My Visit to the Dinosaurs*. New York: Harper & Row, 1985.

Ancona, George. *Sheep Dog*. New York: Lothrop, Lee & Shepard, 1985.

Anderson, Lucia. *The Smallest Life Around Us*. Illustrated by Leigh Grant. New York: Crown, 1978.

Anderson, Madelyn Klein. *New Zoos*. New York: Watts, 1987.

Arnold, Caroline. *Kangaroo*. Photography by Richard R. Hewett. New York: Morrow, 1987.

———. *Koala*. Photography by Richard R. Hewett. New York: Morrow, 1987.

———. *Saving the Peregrine Falcon*. Illustrated by Richard R. Hewett. Minneapolis: Carolrhoda, 1985.

Arnosky, Jim. *Secrets of a Wildlife Watcher*. New York: Lothrop, Lee & Shepard, 1983.

Bare, Colleen Stanley. *Guinea Pigs Don't Read Books*. New York: Dodd, Mead, 1985.

Billings, Charlene W. *Christa McAuliffe: Pioneer Space Teacher*. Hillside, N.J.: Enslow, 1986.

Blumberg, Rhoda. *Commodore Perry in the Land of the Shogun*. New York: Lothrop, Lee & Shepard, 1985.

Branley, Franklyn Mansfield. *From Sputnik to Space Shuttles: Into the New Space Age*. New York: Crowell, 1986.

———. *Is There Life in Outer Space?* Illustrated by Don Madden. New York; Crowell, 1984.

———. *Mysteries of the Universe*. Illustrated by Sally J. Bensusen. New York: Lodestar, 1984.

———. *Space Telescope*. Illustrated by Giulio Maestro. New York: Crowell, 1985.

Brenner, Barbara. *The Gorilla Signs Love*. New York: Lothrop, Lee & Shepard, 1984.

Brinkloe, Julie. *Fireflies!* New York: Macmillan, 1985.

Cajacob, Thomas, and Theresa Burton. *Close to the Wild: Siberian Tigers in a Zoo*. Minneapolis: Carolrhoda, 1986.

Casey, Denise. *Black-Footed Ferret*. Photography by Jim W. Clark. New York: Dodd, Mead, 1985.

Ceserani, Gian Paolo. *Grand Constructions*. Illustrated by Piero Ventura. New York: Putnam's, 1983.

Cole, Joanna. *A Bird's Body*. Photography by Jerome Wexler. New York: Morrow, 1983.

———. *A Cat's Body*. Photography by Jerome Wexler. New York: Morrow, 1982.

———. *A Chick Hatches*. Photography by Jerome Wexler. New York: Morrow, 1976.

———. *A Dog's Body*. Photography by Jim Monteith and Ann Monteith. New York: Morrow, 1986.

———. *A Frog's Body*. Photography by Jerome Wexler. New York: Morrow, 1980.

———. *A Horse's Body*. Photography by Jerome Wexler. New York: Morrow, 1981.

———. *An Insect's Body*. Photography by Jerome Wexler. New York: Morrow, 1984.

———. *Large as Life Daytime Animals*. Illustrated by Kenneth Lilly. New York: Knopf, 1985.

———. *Large as Life Nighttime Animals*. Illustrated by Kenneth Lilly. New York: Knopf, 1985.

———. *My Puppy Is Born*. Photography by Jerome Wexler. New York: Morrow, 1973.

———. *A Snake's Body*. Photography by Jerome Wexler. New York: Morrow, 1981.

Crump, Donald J. *Wildlife: Making a Comeback*. Washington, D.C.: National Geographic, 1987.

Curtis, Patricia. *All Wild Creatures Welcome: The Story of a Wildlife*

Rehabilitation Center. Photography by David Cupp. New York: Lodestar, 1985.

_____. *Animal Shelter*. Photography by David Cupp. New York: Lodestar, 1984.

_____. *Cindy: A Hearing Ear Dog*. Photography by David Cupp. New York: Dutton, 1981.

Cutchins, Judy, and Ginny Johnston. *The Crocodile and the Crane: Surviving in a Crowded World*. New York: Morrow, 1986.

dePaola, Tomie. *The Popcorn Book*. New York: Holiday House, 1978.

D'Ignazio, Fred. *The New Astronomy: Probing the Secrets of Space*. New York: Watts, 1982.

Dingerkus, Guido. *The Shark Watcher's Guide*. Illustrated by Dietrich Burkel. New York: Messner, 1985.

Dunn, Phoebe. *Animal Friends*. New York: Random House, 1985.

Dunrea, Olivier. *Skara Brae: The Story of a Prehistoric Village*. New York: Holiday House, 1986.

Dwiggins, Don. *Flying the Space Shuttles*. New York: Dodd, Mead, 1985.

Fenner, Carol. *Gorilla Gorilla*. Illustrated by Symeon Shimin. New York: Random House, 1973.

Fischer-Nagel, Heiderose, and Andreas Fischer-Nagel. *Inside the Burrow: The Life of the Golden Hamster*. Minneapolis: Carolrhoda, 1986.

_____. *A Kitten Is Born*. New York: Putnam's, 1983.

_____. *A Puppy Is Born*. Translated by Andrea Mernan. New York: Putnam's, 1985.

Fisher, Leonard Everett. *The Great Wall of China*. New York: Macmillan, 1986.

Ford, Barbara. *Wildlife Rescue*. Edited by Kathleen Tucker, illustrated by Steve Ross. New York: Whitman, 1987.

Fox, Mary Virginia. *Jane Goodall: Living Chimp Style*. Illustrated by Nona Hengen. Minneapolis: Dillon, 1981.

Freedman, Russell. *Dinosaurs and Their Young*. Illustrated by Leslie Morrill. New York: Holiday House, 1983.

_____. *Farm Babies*. New York: Holiday House, 1982.

_____. *Lincoln: A Photobiography*. New York: Clarion, 1987.

_____. *Sharks*. New York: Holiday House, 1985.

_____. *They Lived with the Dinosaurs*. New York: Holiday House, 1980.

Freschet, Berniece. *Bear Mouse*. Illustrated by Donald Carrick. New York: Scribner's, 1973.

_____. *Raccoon Baby*. Illustrated by Jim Arnosky. New York: Putnam's, 1984.

Gallant, Roy A. *The Planets: Exploring the Solar System*. New York: Four Winds, 1982.

George, Jean Craighead. *One Day in the Alpine Tundra*. Illustrated by Walter Gaffney Kessell. New York: Crowell, 1984.

_____. *One Day in the Desert*. Illustrated by Fred Brenner. New York: Crowell, 1983.

_____. *One Day in the Prairie*. Illustrated by Bob Marstall. New York: Crowell, 1986.

Gibbons, Gail. *Dinosaurs*. New York: Holiday House, 1987.

Giblin, James Cross. *Walls: Defenses Throughout History*. Illustrated by Anthony Kramer. Boston: Little, Brown, 1984.

Goodall, Jane. *My Life with the Chimpanzees*. New York: Pocket Books, Minstrel, 1988.

Grove, Noel. *Wildlands for Wildlife: America's National Refuges*. Photography by Bates Littlehales. Washington, D.C.: National Geographic Society, 1984.

Hackwell, W. John. *Digging to the Past: Excavations in Ancient Lands*. New York: Scribner's, 1986.

Hausherr, Rosemarie. *My First Kitten*. New York: Macmillan, 1985.

_____. *My First Puppy*. New York: Four Winds, 1986.

Hendrick, Paula. *Saving America's Birds*. New York: Lothrop, Lee & Shepard, 1982.

Hess, Lilo. *Secrets in the Meadow*. New York: Scribner's, 1986.

Hoban, Tana. *A Children's Zoo*. New York: Greenwillow, 1985.

Isenbart, Hans-Heinrich. *Baby Animals on the Farm*. Translated by Elizabeth D. Crawford, photography by Ruth Rau. New York: Putnam's, 1984.

_____. *Birth of a Foal*. Photography by Thomas David. Minneapolis: Carolrhoda, 1986.

_____. *A Duckling Is Born*. Translated by Catherine Edwards Sadler, photography by Othmar Baumli. New York: Putnam's, 1981.

Johnson, Sylvia A. *Fireflies*. Illustrated by Satoshi Kuribayashi. Minneapolis: Lerner, 1986.

Jefferis, Tony, and Judy Hundley. *Farm Animals*. New York: Watts, 1982.

Kaufmann, John. *Flying Giants of Long Ago*. New York: Crowell, 1984.

Keller, Mollie. *Marie Curie*. New York: Watts, 1982.

Krementz, Jill. *Holly's Farm Animals*. New York: Random House, 1987.

Lauber, Patricia. *Dinosaurs Walked Here and Other Stories Fossils Tell*. New York: Bradbury, 1987.

_____. *Journey to the Planets*. New York: Crown, 1982.

_____. *Volcano: The Eruption and Healing of Mount St. Helens*. New York: Bradbury, 1986.

Lavine, Sigmund A. *Wonders of Giraffes*. New York: Dodd, Mead, 1986.

Lewis, Naomi. *Swan*. Illustrated by Deborah King. New York: Lothrop, Lee & Shepard, 1986.

Mabey, Richard. *Oak and Company*. Illustrated by Clare Roberts. New York: Greenwillow, 1982.

Macaulay, David. *Castle*. Boston: Houghton Mifflin, 1977.

———. *Cathedral*. Boston: Houghton Mifflin, 1973.

———. *Mill*. Boston: Houghton Mifflin, 1983.

McCloskey, Robert. *Make Way for Ducklings*. New York: Viking, 1941.

McClung, Robert M. *America's Endangered Birds: Programs and People Working to Save Them*. Illustrated by George Founds. New York: Morrow, 1979.

———. *Mysteries of Migration*. New York: Garrard, 1983.

McLaughlin, Molly. *Earthworms, Dirt and Rotten Leaves: An Exploration in Ecology*. Illustrated by Robert Shetterly. New York: Atheneum, 1986.

McNulty, Faith. *Peeping in the Shell: A Whooping Crane Is Hatched*. Illustrated by Irene Brady. New York: Harper & Row, 1986.

Michel, Anna. *The Story of Nim: The Chimp Who Learned Language*. Photography by Susan Kuklin and Herbert S. Terrace. New York: Knopf, 1980.

Morris, Sean, and David Thompson, eds. *Hide and Seek*. Photography by George Bernard. New York: Oxford Scientific Films, Putnam's, 1982.

Müller, Jörg. *The Changing City*. New York: Atheneum, 1977.

———. *The Changing Countryside*. New York: Atheneum, 1977.

Patent, Dorothy Hinshaw. *Baby Horses*. Photography by William Muñoz. New York: Dodd, Mead, 1985.

———. *Buffalo: The American Bison Today*. Photography by William Muñoz. New York: Clarion, 1986.

———. *Farm Animals*. Illustrated by William Muñoz. New York: Holiday House, 1984.

———. *Maggie, A Sheep Dog*. Photography by William Muñoz. New York: Dodd, Mead, 1986.

———. *A Picture Book of Cows*. Illustrated by William Muñoz. New York: Holiday House, 1982.

———. *Where the Bald Eagles Gather*. Photography by William Muñoz. New York: Clarion, 1984.

Patterson, Francine. *Koko's Kitten*. Illustrated by Ronald H. Cohn. New York: Scholastic, 1985.

Pope, Joyce. *Taking Care of Your Hamster*. New York: Watts, 1986.

Pringle, Laurence. *Death is Natural*. New York: Four Winds, 1977.

———. *Dinosaurs and People: Fossils, Facts, and Fantasies*. New York: Harcourt Brace Jovanovich, 1978.

———. *Dinosaurs and Their World*. New York: Harcourt Brace Jovanovich, 1968.

Reed, Don C. *Sevengill: The Shark and Me*. Illustrated by Pamela Ford Johnson. New York: Knopf, 1986.

Ride, Sally, and Susan Okie. *To Space and Back*. New York: Lothrop, Lee & Shepard, 1986.

Rinard, Judith E. *What Happens at the Zoo*. Washington D.C.: National Geographic, 1984.

Rojankovsky, Feodor *Animals on the Farm*. New York: Knopf, 1967.

Rutland, Jonathan. *See Inside a Roman Town*, rev. ed. Edited by R. J. Unstead. New York: Warick, Watts, 1986.

Ryden, Hope. *America's Bald Eagle*. New York: Putnam's, 1985.

Sancha, Sheila. *The Luttrell Village: Country Life in the Middle Ages*. New York: Crowell, 1983.

Sattler, Helen Roney. *Baby Dinosaurs*. Illustrated by Jean D. Zallinger. New York: Lothrop, Lee & Shepard, 1984.

———. *Dinosaurs of North America*. Illustrated by Anthony Rao. New York: Lothrop, Lee & Shepard, 1981.

———. *The Illustrated Dinosaur Dictionary*. Edited by John H. Ostrom, illustrated by Pamela Carol, Anthony Rao, and Christopher Santoro. New York: Lothrop, Lee & Shepard, 1983.

———. *Pterosaurs, the Flying Reptiles*. Illustrated by Christopher Santoro. New York: Lothrop, Lee & Shepard, 1985.

———. *Sharks, the Super Fish*. Illustrated by Jean Day Zallinger. New York: Lothrop, Lee & Shepard, 1986.

———. *Whales, the Nomads of the Sea*. Illustrated by Jean Day Zallinger. New York: Lothrop, Lee & Shepard, 1987.

Saul, Wendy, and Alan R. Newman. *Science Fare: An Illustrated Guide and Catalog of Toys, Books, and Activities for Kids*. Introduction by Isaac Asimov. New York: Harper & Row, 1986.

Schlein, Miriam. *Project Panda Watch*. Illustrated by Robert Shetterly. New York: Atheneum, 1984.

Scott, Jack Denton. *Alligator*. Photography by Ozzie Sweet. New York: Putnam's, 1984.

———. *The Book of the Pig*. Photography by Ozzie Sweet. New York: Putnam's, 1981.

———. *City of Birds and Beasts: Behind the Scenes at the Bronx Zoo*. Photography by Ozzie Sweet. New York: Putnam's, 1978.

Selsam, Millicent E. *Eat the Fruit, Plant the Seed*. Photography by Jerome Wexler. New York: Morrow, 1980.

———, and Joyce Hunt. *A First Look at Dinosaurs*. Illustrated by Harriet Springer. New York: Walker, 1982.

———. *How Animals Live Together*. New York: Morrow, 1979.

———. *Popcorn*. Illustrated by Jerome Wexler. New York: Morrow, 1976.

Silverstein, Alvin, and Virginia Silverstein. *Guinea Pigs*. Photography by Roger Kerkham. New York: Lothrop, Lee & Shepard, 1972.

Simon, Seymour. *Einstein Anderson: Science Sleuth*. New York: Viking, 1980.

———. *Icebergs and Glaciers*. New, York: Morrow, 1987.

———. *Jupiter*. New York: Morrow, 1985.

———. *The Largest Dinosaurs*. Illustrated by Pamela Carroll. New York: Macmillan, 1986.

———. *The Long Journey from Space*. New York: Crown, 1982.

———. *The Long View into Space*. New York: Crown, 1979.

———. *Look to the Night Sky: An Introduction to Star Watching*. New York: Viking, 1977.

———. *Mars*. New York: Morrow, 1987.

———. *The Paper Airplane Book*. Illustrated by Byron Barton. New York: Viking, 1971.

———. *Pets in a Jar: Collecting and Caring for Small Animals*. Illustrated by Betty Fraser. New York: Viking, 1975.

———. *Saturn*. New York: Morrow, 1985.

———. *The Secret Clocks: Time Sense of Living Things*. Illustrated by Jan Brett. New York: Viking, 1979.

———. *The Smallest Dinosaurs*. Illustrated by Anthony Rao. New York: Crown, 1982.

———. *Stars*. New York: Morrow, 1986.

———. *The Sun*. New York: Morrow, 1986.

———. *Uranus*. New York: Morrow, 1987.

Tejima, Keizaburo. *Owl Lake*. New York: Philomel, 1987.

Van Loon, Hendrik. *The Story of Mankind*. New York: Liveright, 1921.

Xuqi, Jin, and Markus Kappler. *The Giant Panda*. Translated by Noel Simon. New York: Putnam's, 1986.

THE
WORLD
OF
CHILDREN'S
BOOKS

PART III

11

Literature of Many Cultures

Saying Yes

"Are you Chinese?"
"Yes."

"American?"
"Yes."

"*Really* Chinese?"
"No . . . not quite."

"*Really* American?"
"Well, actually, you see . . ."

But I would rather say
yes

Not neither-nor,
not maybe,
but both, and not only

The homes I've had,
the ways I am

I'd rather say it
twice,
yes[1]

Diana Chang

574

The image of a melting pot once used to characterize the United States when millions of immigrants came from various lands and supposedly were homogenized into Americans is no longer accurate. Although the melting pot may have described the situation during periods when many newcomers wanted to discard traces of their former culture, the term no longer represents the mix of distinct cultural groups now living in the United States. Rudine Sims Bishop says, "Contrary to popular belief, the people of the United States have not been homogenized in a melting pot. While we all share some common experiences, many of the diverse groups that make up the country maintain distinctive cultural traditions and experiences. It is a multicultural society."[2] The image of a salad bowl or a hearty stew in which diverse elements blend together but each retains its distinctive flavorings is a more appropriate metaphor. Each group blends with the larger society, when such is demanded for the common good, but preserves its own cultural traditions in the home and community in the multicultural society we live in today.

A multicultural society requires a multicultural literature. But what is multicultural literature? Ruth Carlson says that it is literature about a racial or ethnic group that is culturally or socially different from the white majority in the United States.[3] Multicultural literature reflects the values and mores of a specific cultural group rather than the general prevailing values of the majority.

It is important to have multicultural literature in schools and libraries because stories do shape readers' views of their world and of themselves. If some children never see themselves in books, then that absence subtly tells them that they are not important enough to appear in books. Even more harmful are the negative or stereotypic images of an ethnic group in children's books; they not only damage the children of that ethnic group but give others a distorted and unfortunate view of self-importance. Children's literature that accurately reflects cultural values can be a potent force in the socialization, acculturation, and personal and moral development of children.

A recent study of children's picture books that present pluralistic, balanced racial and ethnic images of children shows that they are in short supply.[4] Fewer such books are being published today than were published in the 1960s and 1970s. Leslie Edmonds compared two samples of picture books by mainstream publishers between 1928 and 1974 and between 1980 and 1984, taking into account the race of major characters and the positive or negative treatment of various racial groups. In the 1928–1974 grouping, 57 percent of the books featured major characters who were white; 27 percent presented a racial mix of main characters; 7 percent were black; 5 percent, Asian; 2 percent, native American; and 2 percent, Hispanic. Positive traits such as kindness outnumbered negative traits such as meanness by about five to one for all groups. In the later sample (1980–1984), Edmonds found that books about native

LANDMARK

Multicultural Books: Call Me Charley, *1945;* Bright April, *1946*

Prior to World War II, most books for children totally ignored racial and ethnic minorities. Even those that did include any minorities often did so through blatant stereotyping and exaggerated dialect. Seldom were different racial groups shown interacting in any way. *Call Me Charley* and *Bright April* (both I) openly explore racial prejudice and discrimination.

Jesse Jackson was the first black writer to openly describe discrimination in *Call Me Charley*. Charley is the only black child in a

white school where he is not welcomed but tolerated. He is bitterly disappointed when he is excluded from the class play but he patiently accepts his lot.

Marguerite De Angeli was the first white writer to integrate black and white characters and to show the effects of prejudice. *Bright April* confronts discrimination in a member of her Brownie Scout troop. Although considered inadequate by today's standards, these books do focus—for the first time—on a black child's difficulties in a white society.

Americans were being published at about the same level, but there were fewer books being published about other groups. Blacks are still presented most frequently with more variety and less stereotyping. There are not yet strong images of Asian characters or cultures other than Chinese and Japanese, and Hispanics continue to receive very meager coverage.

A MULTICULTURAL HERITAGE OF CHILDREN'S LITERATURE

In approaching the study of multicultural children's literature, we reflect upon its origins where many contributed and many received. The roots of all literature, certainly, lie in folklore, the ancient stories told since humans first learned to speak. According to Thackeray, many of the stories have been narrated, almost in their present shape, for thousands of years. "The very same tale has been heard by the Northmen Vikings, as they lay on their shields

on deck; and by the Arabs, couched under the stars in the Syrian plains, when the flocks were gathered in, and the mares were picketed by the tents."[5]

Children's books, however, are a recent development in the history of humankind. The sources of early American children's books are explored in Chapter 12, "The History of Children's Literature." In this chapter, we examine books that portray characters from the largest minority groups in the U.S.; namely, Asian-Americans, black Americans, Hispanic Americans, Jewish Americans, and native Americans. Finally, we develop a teaching unit on "Living Together in a World of Peace" to illustrate the array of international literature for children.

Today the cultural exchange of contemporary books among nations is a common occurrence due to the ease of international travel. Moreover, many authors of American children's books live in England, Australia, Japan, and elsewhere. Publishers the world over meet at the annual Frankfurt Book Fair, the Jerusa-

Schoolchildren learn that their multiethnic friends all share the same needs and feelings, and multicultural literature echoes these common bonds.

lem Book Fair, and the Bologna Book Fair which specializes in children's books. Publishers meet at the fairs to buy manuscripts and arrange for copublication of the same book in several languages. Thus, children in several countries read the very same books written in their native languages.

Paul Hazard, renowned French literary critic of the early 1900s, described the world republic of childhood in *Books, Children and Men*. He recalled the day as a child that he escaped with two boys his own age from his dull hometown to travel all over France through the pages of a beautiful book. Another time, led by Don Quixote and Sancho, he saw the plains of Castile, white-hot in the sun, with dusty roads and inns full of adventure. He lived in *Uncle Tom's Cabin* and cultivated sugar cane with slaves as companions. Like Baron Munchausen, he fastened a rope to the crescent moon so he could glide to earth, and the rope being too short he cut it above him to attach it to the end that was hanging under his feet.

Yes, children's books keep alive a sense of nationality; but they also keep alive a sense of humanity. They describe their native land lovingly, but they also describe faraway lands where unknown brothers live. They understand the essential quality of their own race; but each of them is a messenger that goes beyond mountains and rivers, beyond the seas, to the very ends of the world in search of new friendships. Every country gives and every country receives—innumerable are the exchanges—and so it comes about that in our first impressionable years the universal republic of childhood is born.[6]

Children's literature is richer because of this international exchange of books.

ASIAN-AMERICANS

A smaller number of high-quality books deal with Asian-Americans than with some of the other ethnic groups, although the excellent folklore and the works of a few outstanding writers are changing the situation rapidly.[7] The following books identify some of the most outstanding sources and will lead to other works by the same writers.

Folklore

Variants of the same folktale appeared in many different countries, causing some scholars to believe that similar human needs gave rise to them. One such fairy tale, *Yeh-Shen: A Cinderella Story from China* (P-I), retold by Ai-Ling Louie and illustrated by Ed Young, dates back to the T'ang Dynasty (A.D. 618–907). In this version, Yeh-Shen's only friend is a fish that comes to the water's edge to talk to her, but one day her jealous stepmother disguises herself as Yeh-Shen and stabs the fish. Yeh-Shen learns, however, that even the bones of her fish are filled with a powerful spirit, and whenever she is in serious need, she must kneel before them and let them know her heart's desire. The fish bones function as the fairy godmother in this ancient and beloved tale.

Catherine Edwards Sadler compiled two collections, *Heaven's Reward: Fairy Tales from China* and *Treasure Mountain: Folktales from Southern China* (both P-I). Sadler explains that fairy tales have served as the literature of the scholarly, tools of the socially rebellious, a means of expression for the oppressed, and a vehicle to rally and inspire the masses. She also shows that they reflect differing philosophies since they come from varying historical periods. In *Treasure Mountain*, she explains that many tales of the common folk (folktales) reflect their response to hardship and oppression while others are used to entertain and inspire hope.

Jeanne M. Lee retold and illustrated *Toad Is the Uncle of Heaven: A Vietnamese Folk Tale* (P). The opening page explains that in Vietnam, when you wish to show respect to someone, you call that person "Uncle." Because of a dev-

astating drought, Toad sees that his body will soon dry up, and so he sets out to seek an audience with the King of Heaven, the one who makes rain. Along the way he is joined by a swarm of bees, a rooster, and a tiger who also want the rain. Each time the King of Heaven orders the lowly Toad out of the court, his animal friends come to the rescue. The King of Heaven is so impressed with Toad and his friends, he calls him "Uncle Toad" and sends the much-needed rain.

Yoshiko Uchida retold *The Two Foolish Cats* (P), which was suggested by a Japanese folktale. While hunting for food, two cats, the large one called Big Daizo, and the small one called Little Suki, come upon two rice cakes.

> "Look!" Little Suki shouted. And because he was faster, he got to the rice cakes first.
> "I'll take the big one," he said, "because I'm small and skinny and need more food to grow on."
> "Oh no you don't!" Big Daizo hissed. "I should have the biggest rice cake because I need more food than you do. Give it to me at once!"

The two cats finally go to wise old monkey of the mountain to settle their dispute.

> "Ah *hah*, ha *hah*," the monkey said. "I can soon fix that." And he quickly took a bite from the larger rice cake.
> "Now," he said, "they should both be equal." But he had eaten too much, and now the smaller rice cake was heavier.
> "Ah *hah*, ha *hah*, I can soon fix that," the old monkey said. And this time he took a bite from the smaller rice cake. But of course he had again eaten too much.

While the two foolish cats watch the monkey eat up both rice cakes trying to make them equal, they are chagrined and slink home.

> And ever since that day, the two cats never quarreled again, but lived peacefully together at the edge of the dark pine forest.[8]

Yoshiko Uchida also retells a number of Japanese folktales in *Samurai of Gold Hill; The Sea of Gold and Other Tales from Japan;* and *The Magic Listening Cap: More Folktales from Japan* (all I).

One Japanese folktale, *The Funny Little Woman* (P), retold by Arlene Mosel and illustrated by Blair Lent, won the Caldecott Award in 1973. It tells of how a rice dumpling rolled down into the underearth, land of the wicked Oni. When the funny little woman who made the dumpling chases after it, the wicked Oni capture her and keep her to make dumplings for them. Through her wit and sense of humor, she figures out a way to escape.

The Crane Wife (P-I), retold by Sumiko Yagawa, translated by Katherine Paterson, and illustrated by Suekichi Akaba, is perhaps Japan's most beloved folktale. Yohei, a poor young peasant, finds a wounded crane and tenderly cares for it. That night a beautiful young woman comes to his door. " 'I beg you, sir,' she said in a voice both delicate and refined, 'please allow me to become your wife.' " Because Yohei is poor and his wife wants to help earn money, she asks for a loom but she begs him never to look upon her while she is weaving. Tonkara is the sound of the loom.

> Tonkara tonkara. For three days and three nights the sound of the loom continued. Without stopping either to eat or drink, the young woman went on weaving and weaving. Finally, on the fourth day, she came out. To Yohei she seemed strangely thin and completely exhausted, as without a word, she held out to him a bolt of material.

Things go well until Yohei becomes greedy and presses his wife to weave even more fabric for him to sell. He waits impatiently for her to finish and finally peeks into the room.

> What Yohei saw was not human. It was a crane, smeared with blood, for with its beak it had plucked out its own feathers to place them in the loom. At the sight Yohei collapsed into a deep faint.

When Yohei awakens, he finds a bolt of fabric and hears his wife's delicate voice, but she is gone, never to return.

> "I had hoped," the voice said sorrowfully, "that you would be able to honor my entreaty. But because you looked upon me in my suffering, I can no longer tarry in the human world. I am the crane that you saved on the snowy path. I fell in love with your gentle, simple heart, and trusting it alone, I came to live by your side. I pray that your life will be long and that you will always be happy."[9]

Every year thousands of Japanese see some version of this story as a play, movie, or opera in addition to reading it aloud to their children. It is a treasured bit of their cultural heritage.

Poetry

The brief nonrhyming haiku of Issa, Basho, and Kikaku are among the best-known works of Japanese poets. Harry Behn translated many of the delicate verses in *Cricket Songs* and *More Cricket Songs* (both I-A).[10] The words whisper about the marvels of nature, laugh at incongruity, or shout about the excitement of beauty.

> Back in my home town
> even the flies aren't afraid
> to bite a big man.
>
> ISSA

> The waves are so cold
> a rocking gull can scarcely
> fold itself to sleep.
>
> BASHO

> Who can stay indoors
> on such a day with the sun
> dazzling on new snow!
>
> KIKAKU

Don't Tell the Scarecrow (I-A), a collection edited by Issa, Yayu, Kikaku, and others and illustrated by Talivaldis Stubis, contains haiku from a wider range of poets.[11]

An umbrella and a raincoat
Are walking and talking together.

BUSON

Don't tell the scarecrow
But someone is stealing the beans!

YAYU

The harvest moon is so bright!
My shadow walks home with me.

SODO

Richard Lewis collected haiku verses that follow a day of spring from an early-morning admonition, to a careless grasshopper, to the glowing goodnight of a firefly in *In a Spring Garden* (I-A).[12] Ezra Jack Keats illustrated the collection in collage and delicate gouache color.

Grasshopper,
Do not trample to pieces
The pearls of bright dew.

ISSA

The moon in the water
Turned a somersault
And floated away.

RYOTA

A giant firefly:
that way, this way, that way, this—
and it passes by.

ISSA

According to Virginia Olsen Baron, collector and adaptor of *Sunset in a Spider Web: Sijo Poetry of Ancient Korea* (I-A), the sijo is one of the most popular and earliest poetic forms found in Korean literature.[13] The sijo is written in three lines with approximately 44 syllables, but because they are awkwardly long in English, they are presented in six lines instead of the traditional three. The first line usually states the theme, the second elaborates on it, and the third line is a twist on the theme or a resolution; sometimes called an antitheme. The following can be found in *Sunset in a Spider Web:*

When a shadow appeared on the water,
I looked up to see a monk crossing the bridge.
Stay, I said, so I could ask
Where he was going.

But, pointing at white clouds, he moved on,
Answering without words.

ANONYMOUS

Ten years it took
To build my little cottage.
Now the cool wind inhabits half of it
And the rest is filled with moonlight.

There is no place left for the mountain and the stream
So I guess they will have to stay outside.

SONG SOON

Fiction

Picture Books Taro Yashima first published *Crow Boy* (P-I) in 1955 and *Umbrella* (P) in 1958; more than 30 years later, their story and art retain their original distinctiveness. *Crow Boy* is the story of a shy child named Chibi who hid underneath the building on the first day of school. Chibi was afraid of the teacher and could not learn; he was afraid of the children and could not make friends. Steadfastly, year after year, Chibi came trudging to school until finally the group was in the sixth grade. That year, a new teacher, Mr. Isobe, often took the class to the hilltop behind the school. He was pleased to learn that Chibi knew where the wild grapes grew. He liked Chibi's drawings and hung Chibi's handwriting up on the wall. He spent time talking with Chibi when no one was around. When Chibi appeared on the stage for the talent show, people were shocked. They were even more disbelieving when Mr. Isobe announced that Chibi was going to imitate the voices of crows. The sounds Chibi made imitated crows from the far and lonely place where Chibi lived. When Mr. Isobe explained how Chibi had learned those calls leaving for school at dawn and arriving home at sunset every day for six long years, his classmates cried knowing that they had been wrong to Chibi all these years. Soon after came graduation day and Chibi was the only one in the class honored for perfect attendance through all the six years. No one called him Chibi anymore; now they called him "Crow Boy." Other books by Yashima include *Youngest One* (P) and *Momo's Kitten* (P). See also *How My Parents Learned to Eat*, by Ina Friedman, which is discussed in Chapter 4.

Novels Yoshiko Uchida writes about a refreshing child, 11-year-old Rinko, who tells in a spirited fashion about her life as a Japanese in California during the Great Depression in *A Jar of Dreams*, *The Best Bad Thing*, and *The Happiest Ending* (all I). In the first book, Rinko is afraid that Aunt Waka, her mother's sister who is coming to visit from Japan, will be dreary. When they pick her up at the ship, Rinko says,

> I sat in the back seat of the car with Mama and Aunt Waka, and they talked and laughed and cried all the way home. Mama told her about our new home laundry, but mostly they talked about how things were when they were growing up in Japan.
>
> I watched Aunt Waka out of the corner of my eye, trying not to stare at her. So far she didn't sound like she'd be such a bleak, sorrowful presence, but it was still too early to tell. When we were almost home, Aunt Waka turned to me and asked if I was healthier now, and I told her I was.
>
> "I drink two extra glasses of milk every day," I said, sounding like a five-year-old and feeling like a stupid ninny.
>
> But Aunt Waka just said, "That's good, Rinko. I brought you more medicine for your knee aches too." and she reached out and patted my knees.

> I wished Mama hadn't written Aunt Waka every single detail of my life.
>
> "I guess I get those because I'm trying to grow too fast," I explained.
>
> "Like a noodle," Aunt Waka said.
>
> Suddenly we both laughed. And that was when I thought maybe Aunt Waka was going to be an OK person after all.[14]

Aunt Waka is more than just okay because she helps the entire family stand up against discrimination and, in the process, feel stronger about themselves.

Uchida draws upon her own life experiences as she writes for children.

> Some of the experiences of Rinko in *A Jar of Dreams* and its sequels *The Best Bad Thing* and *The Happiest Ending* are similar to a few of the experiences in my own life. Many of the things that happen to Rinko were experienced by my Japanese American friends, but her feelings of alienation and rejection are based upon my own memories. I remember feeling different and I gave those feelings to Rinko.[15]

She expresses how these basic feelings are universal: "I know that any child can feel alienated, not just Asian Americans. Through Rinko, I help children link up with the feelings of one child in a minority group. I had Rinko express how she felt about speaking up in class." Rinko says:

> I don't know why I can't speak up in class. I certainly can make myself heard when I'm at home. And when I'm having conversations with people inside my head, I'm always speaking up, telling them exactly what I think in a loud, firm voice. But at school it's different. If you feel like a big nothing and don't like who you are, naturally you don't speak up in a loud, firm voice. You don't talk to other people either, unless they talk to you first.[16]

Yoshiko Uchida has also written *Journey to Topaz* and *Journey Home* (both I-A), which together comprise the moving story of Yuki Sakane and her family as they are uprooted from their California home and sent to a desert

PROFILE

Yoshiko Uchida

Yoshiko Uchida was born in Alameda, California, and grew up in Berkeley. Her parents were first-generation immigrants from Japan (called Issei). Her father had come first to work in the United States; then her mother came a few years later. She says of her parents,

> My mother came from Japan to marry my father, a man with whom she had only corresponded. Their marriage was a successful one. I remember them both as strong, sensitive, and loving people. Rinko's parents, [in *A Jar of Dreams*], had the same kind of marriage arranged by a go-between which was the accepted tradition of that time.[17]

Uchida values her Japanese and American cultural heritage. As a college student she was forced to go to a relocation camp with her family. As a result, she explains, "I received my college diploma from the mailman in Tanforan. My sister and I volunteered to teach the children at the camp. We had practically no supplies but we had eager, enthusiastic children who wanted to learn."

All of Yoshiko Uchida's books have been about Japan and its children or about Japanese Americans because, as she says, "I felt I could make the best contribution in this area." Many of her early books contained Japanese folktales, such as *The Dancing Kettle*, *The Magic Listening Cap*, and *Samurai of Gold Hill* (all P–I).

Yoshiko Uchida received the University of Oregon's Distinguished Service Award for "having made a significant contribution to the cultural development of society . . . and . . . [helping] to bring about a greater understanding of the Japanese American culture." She also received the California Commonwealth Club Medal for *Samurai of Gold Hill* (1972) and *A Jar of Dreams* (1982).

When asked what her major goal is in the work she does, she replied:

> I hope my books are meaningful to all children. I try to stress the positive aspects of life that I want children to value and cherish. I hope they can be caring human beings who don't think in terms of labels—foreigners or Asians or whatever—but think of people as human beings. If that comes across, then I've accomplished my purpose.

Yoshiko Uchida's books reflect and help achieve multicultural understanding.

concentration camp (called a relocation camp) during World War II. She describes the tragic herding of innocent people with a sorrowful sense of injustice yet does not become bitter.

Uchida also draws upon her own life experiences as she writes books for older readers. During World War II, she and her family were placed in a relocation camp because they were Japanese American. She says:

> On the day that Pearl Harbor was bombed by Japan, I was studying for my final exams in the library at the University of California. When I returned home, FBI men were in the living room watching everything my family did. My father, along with other leaders of the Japanese community, had been taken for questioning and was being held at the Immigration Detention Quarters. He was later sent to an Army Prisoner of War camp in Montana. My mother, my older sister, and I had ten days to pack in preparation for our "removal" from Berkeley. We were forced to sell most of our possessions at a tremendous loss. We were taken, along with thousands of other Japanese Americans, to a temporary "relocation camp" at Tanforan, an abandoned racetrack. My father was eventually released from the camp in Montana and joined us in Tanforan, where we lived in a 10' by 20' horse stall. Later we were all transferred to Topaz, a square mile area in the middle of the Utah desert, which housed eight thousand internees.[18]

Lawrence Yep has contributed a sizable amount of literature with Asian American characters. In *Sea Glass* (I-A), Craig Chin, an awkward Chinese American, moves from Chinatown to Concepcion and is faced with a conflict between cultures. Torn between keeping his Chinese culture and adopting the language and behaviors of his American neighbors, Craig is distressed. His agemates think of him as a foreigner and the older Chinese think of him as an American. He also tries to live up to his father's expectations of making him an all-American boy and a basketball star. Craig eventually

meets Uncle Quail who understands his confusion; he tells Craig to observe the world around him and to learn from it but also to listen to his inner desires and act upon those.

In *Dragonwings* (I-A), Yep tells how Moon Shadow Lee leaves China to join his father in San Francisco's Chinatown. After a few years of living in the Chinese community, Moon Shadow and his father move to a stable behind Miss Whitlaw's boarding house. Moon Shadow learns to read and write English and in turn teaches Miss Whitlaw and her niece about Chinese dragons. A solid friendship develops between the Whitlaws and the Lees. Moon Shadow's father dreams of building a flying machine; he rents a barn that serves as a home and a place to work. When Dragonwings, the flying machine, is completed, Moon Shadow's father makes a short but successful flight. Yep's other books include *Child of the Owl, Mountain Light,* and *The Serpent's Children* (all I-A).

So Far from the Bamboo Grove (I-A), by Yoko Kawashima Watkins, is an autobiographical account of 11-year-old Yoko's escape from Korea to Japan with her mother and sister at the end of World War II. Although Yoko had lived in northeastern Korea all her life, Yoko was not Korean. Yoko's family was Japanese; her father, a Japanese government official working in Manchuria, traveled to their Korean village 50 miles from the Manchurian border as often as he could. For most of World War II, Korea was not at war. The shadow of war, however, had been creeping across their peaceful village, and it breaks through in 1945 when warning of a communist attack comes. All of a sudden, Yoko, her mother, and sister Ko are fleeing to Seoul where they hoped to make connections to Japan. They spend a long arduous time as refugees in Seoul before they can get to Kyoto, and even when they arrive, they find a war-weary city. Yoko enrolls in school but must find paper and pencils from wastepaper baskets with help from a friendly custodian. Yoko,

Ko, and their mother live in the train station and it is there that mother dies. The harsh cruelty of war rings through this story gently told by a survivor.

On a lighter note, Elisabet McHugh's series—*Raising a Mother Isn't Easy, Karen's Sister,* and *Karen and Vicki* (all I)—begins with 11-year-old Karen, an adopted Korean orphan, trying to get her mother organized.

Nonfiction

Nonfiction is seldom selected as literary prize winners, but *Commodore Perry in the Land of the Shogun* (I-A) received a Newbery Honor Book Award in 1986 for its distinguished literary quality. Rhoda Blumberg describes the engaging story of Matthew Perry's expedition to open Japan to American trade and whaling ports. The significance of the diplomatic achievement is foreshadowed in text and numerous illustrations that were selected from museum collections. The opening paragraphs give a sense of the storytelling character of the informational report.

> If monsters had descended upon Japan the effect could not have been more terrifying.
> People in the fishing village of Shimoda were the first to spot four huge hulks, two streaming smoke, on the ocean's surface approaching the shore. "Giant dragons puffing smoke," cried some. "Alien ships of fire," cried others. According to a folktale, smoke above water was made by the breath of clams. Only a child would believe that. Perhaps enemies knew how to push erupting volcanoes toward the Japanese homeland. Surely something horrible was happening on this day, Friday, July 8, 1853.[19]

Blumberg's work illustrates the best of informational sources available for a study of the beginnings of Asian American relations.

Milton Meltzer, also an award-winning informational writer, traces the history of the Chinese in the United States in *The Chinese Americans* (I-A). He opens with a famous photograph taken on May 10, 1869, at Promontory Point, Utah, when the Chinese construction crews of the Central Pacific Railroad coming from the west and the Irish construction crews of the Union Pacific Railroad coming from the east completed the first railroad to span the North American continent. This photograph, showing the last railroad tie and rail in place, and the last spike—the golden spike—rammed home, has something missing. In fact, Meltzer asks, "What's wrong with this picture?" It is clear that there are no Chinese people in the picture, yet, he writes, "No group of workers did more to build that railroad than the Chinese. Their bone, their muscle, their nerve, their sweat, their skill made an impossible dream come true."[20] Even a century later, when America celebrated the anniversary of the completion of the railroad, the U.S. Secretary of Transportation spoke, representing himself and the president, and never mentioned the Chinese American workers. Meltzer traces the history of those missing Chinese Americans and describes many other contributions they made in the development of America.

Behind Barbed Wire: The Imprisonment of Japanese Americans During World War II (A) by Daniel S. Davis gives a chilling factual account of some of America's darkest days. Within two months after the December 7, 1941, bombing of Pearl Harbor, President Franklin Roosevelt signed Executive Order 9066 giving permission for the evacuation of the West Coast and the creation of "relocation" camps for those of Japanese ancestry. By June 1942, 120,000 Japanese Americans were behind barbed wire. Most of the camps were in isolated, windswept locations that were ripped by dust storms or sagging in mud. Hastily prepared barracks or converted horse stables housed people who were forced to leave their possessions and friends behind.

The legacy of the evacuation and the camps is not really measurable, but their costs are. The army spent $90 million to build and to guard the concentration camps. The WRA spent over $160 million to keep 120,000 people locked up. The inmates had done nothing to justify their imprisonment other than to be born of Japanese ancestry in a nation that was at war with Japan. The costs to the evacuees will never be known. The $400 million estimate of property losses does not take into account the fact that land values had multiplied.

And dollar values cannot be placed on the broken hopes and shattered dreams of the Japanese American victims of the evacuation. Nor can they be applied to the flawed integrity of an entire nation that betrayed its own people.[21]

Biography

Quang Nhuong Huynh speaks lovingly of *The Land I Lost: Adventures of a Boy in Vietnam* (I) in a collection of biographical essays featuring scenes from his childhood in the central highlands. The author describes his life in the small hamlet of 50 bamboo houses. The village, surrounded by a jungle on one side and a river on the other, was in close proximity to many animals, some life threatening, others friendly. His father, like most of the villagers, was a farmer and a hunter, depending upon the season. But he also had a college education, so in the evenings he helped to teach other children in the hamlet. Huynh recalls,

> I went to the lowlands to study for a while because I wanted to follow my father as a teacher when I grew up. I always planned to return to my hamlet to live the rest of my life there. But war disrupted my dreams. The land I love was lost to me forever. These stories are my memories.[22]

Some of his fondest memories center on the family's water buffalo, Tank, so named because when he hit another male during a fight, he

Quang Nhuong Huynh reminisces about his youth in essays of life in the central highlands of Vietnam. (From *The Land I Lost: Adventures of a Boy in Vietnam*, illustrated by Vo-Dinh Mai.)

struck as heavily as a tank. Tank does collide head on with other young bulls who trespass on his territory or challenge his authority, but he also is gentle enough to allow children to ride astride his broad back. Tank overpowers a vicious tiger, helps catch eels and a huge white catfish, and continually serves as the village protector. The final essay is called "Sorrow."

> One day when I was in the field with the herd, fierce fighting between the French forces and the Resistance led by Ho Chi Minh erupted

ACTIVITY: TEACHER TO STUDENT

THE SAME, YET DIFFERENT (I-A)[23]   Read the books set in the various countries to see what is similar and what is different among them and from your own life. Discuss customs of dress, food, entertainment, language, and beliefs that may differ for each country. Discuss feelings, relationships, and attitudes that may be similar across many countries. Use some of the following to probe specific areas.

1. Rewrite one of the stories making yourself the main character. How would the story change? Why? Is the change critical to the idea of the story?
2. Write a story about one of the characters in the book in your home or neighborhood. Do you think he or she would be happy, comfortable? Why or why not?
3. Divide the class into groups and have them research the different foods, costumes, holidays, and traditions of the various countries in the books. Have an international fair.
4. If you could live in one of these countries with the main character as your friend, which would it be? Why?
5. Create a new adventure for one of the characters in his/her native land. Illustrate and bind the children's books.
6. Choose two of the books listed. After you've read them, make a list of how the character is like you and how he or she is different from you. Have you experienced some of the same things that these children have? When? How?
7. Compare the various places described in the stories. How are they different? The same?

---

in our hamlet. The battle was so close that I tried to run away and find shelter in the river nearby. I led Tank and the rest of the herd toward the river, but suddenly I noticed that Tank was lagging behind and limping. I ran back and saw that Tank had been hit by a stray bullet which had passed through his chest. . . .

We buried Tank in the graveyard where we buried all the dead of our family, and every Lunar New Year my father burned incense in front of all the tombs, including Tank's.[24]

Two authors, Fritz and Lord, present biographical fiction based on fact about their childhood experiences in a strange land. Jean Fritz's

Homesick: My Own Story and *China Homecoming* (both I), cited in Chapter 9, tell the story of an American in China. Because Fritz's parents were missionaries, she grew up in China, but she longed to be an American. In *China Homecoming*, Jean returns to China as an adult; she finds that she cares for people and places she was anxious to leave as a child. *In the Year of the Boar and Jackie Robinson* by Bette Bao Lord, also discussed in Chapter 9, tells about a young Chinese girl who comes to live in Brooklyn, New York. Shirley Temple Wong, the name she gives to herself, provides another perspective on multicultural understanding; she views

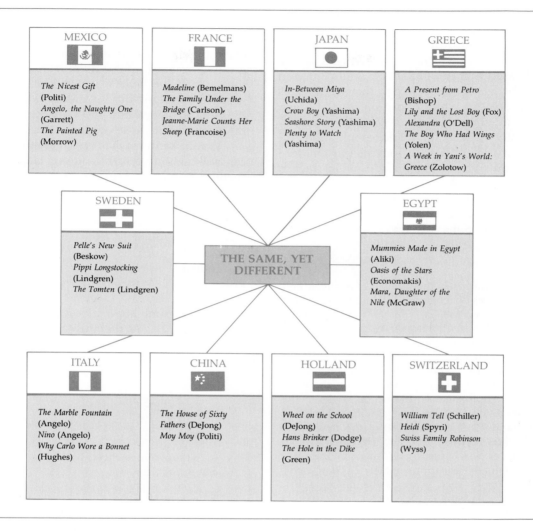

MEXICO

The Nicest Gift
(Politi)
Angelo, the Naughty One
(Garrett)
The Painted Pig
(Morrow)

FRANCE

Madeline (Bemelmans)
The Family Under the
Bridge (Carlson)
Jeanne-Marie Counts Her
Sheep (Francoise)

JAPAN

In-Between Miya
(Uchida)
Crow Boy (Yashima)
Seashore Story (Yashima)
Plenty to Watch
(Yashima)

GREECE

A Present from Petro
(Bishop)
Lily and the Lost Boy (Fox)
Alexandra (O'Dell)
The Boy Who Had Wings
(Yolen)
A Week in Yani's World:
Greece (Zolotow)

SWEDEN

Pelle's New Suit
(Beskow)
Pippi Longstocking
(Lindgren)
The Tomten (Lindgren)

**THE SAME, YET
DIFFERENT**

EGYPT

Mummies Made in Egypt
(Aliki)
Oasis of the Stars
(Economakis)
Mara, Daughter of the
Nile (McGraw)

ITALY

The Marble Fountain
(Angelo)
Nino (Angelo)
Why Carlo Wore a Bonnet
(Hughes)

CHINA

The House of Sixty
Fathers (DeJong)
Moy Moy (Politi)

HOLLAND

Wheel on the School
(DeJong)
Hans Brinker (Dodge)
The Hole in the Dike
(Green)

SWITZERLAND

William Tell (Schiller)
Heidi (Spyri)
Swiss Family Robinson
(Wyss)

American behavior from her Chinese background and begins to become acculturated when she joins the ranks of Brooklyn Dodgers fans.

See also *Isamu Noguchi: The Life of a Sculptor* (I–A) by T. Tobias. Born to a Japanese father and an American mother, Noguchi was conscious of being only half Japanese. After coming to the U.S., he felt displaced and alone; his feelings are depicted in his work.

BLACK AMERICANS

Nancy Larrick's article, "The All-White World of Children's Books," in the September 11, 1965, issue of the *Saturday Review* is generally credited with calling attention to the omission of blacks in children's literature. Larrick pointed to the hurtful effects on black children who never see themselves in books, but she also stressed that the impact on white children is probably even worse. When the only images children see are white ones, she said, "There seems little chance of developing the humility so urgently needed for world cooperation, instead of world conflict, as long as our children are brought up on gentle doses of racism through their books." During the 1970s, there was an increase in the number of books with black characters, but the 1980s saw a steady decline. Rudine Sims Bishop assessed the situation:

> Since the mid-70's, the number of available children's books dealing with Black life has declined steadily. *The Black Experience in Children's Books*, a comprehensive bibliography published about every five years that lists in-print children's books about Blacks, reflects some dramatic statistics: the 1974 edition listed approximately 950 titles, but the 1984 edition cites only about 450 books. Approximately 100 of the books in this latest edition are titles newly published between 1979 and 1984, and only 80 of the new books published between 1980 and 1983—an average of 20 per year—focus on American Blacks. If publishers release approximately 2,000 new children's books each year, as the bibliography's compiler, Barbara Rollock, notes, only about 1 per cent of the children's books published in the first half of the 80's focused on [the] Black experience in the United States.[25]

Even though the percentages are small, many fine books in every genre reflect the heritage and contemporary experiences of black Americans. The folklore, poetry, fiction (including picture books and novels), informational books and biographies will help children from all racial and ethnic groups appreciate the contributions of black Americans.

Folklore

Folktales provide a window on the collective experiences, dreams, and values that a cultural group possesses. Called a "mirror of a people," they reflect the beliefs, rituals, and songs of a group's heritage. Black-American folklore has its roots in Africa and the Carribean; many of the tales reflect those origins.

Verna Aardema has retold numerous African folktales in colorful, lilting language that retains the sound of drumbeats and the rhythm of native dances. She captures the rhythm of the teller's voice by representing the sounds with unusual words. For example, she describes an animal moving through the grass with words such as "wasawusu, wasawusu, wasawusu," "mek, mek, mek," or "krik, krik, krik" in *Why Mosquitoes Buzz in People's Ears* (P). In another, she captures the rhythm and rhyme in a cumulative tale, *Bringing the Rain to Kapiti Plain* (P). A repetitive refrain describes the starving cattle on the barren Kapiti Plain which suffers a drought.

> These are the cows,
> all hungry and dry,
> Who mooed for the rain
> to fall from the sky;
> To green-up the grass,
> all brown and dead,
> That needed the rain
> from the cloud overhead—
> The big, black cloud,
> all heavy with rain,
> That shadowed the ground
> on Kapiti Plain.[26]

The plain grows verdant green after Ki-pat pierces the rain cloud with an eagle feather to bring down the rain to Kapiti Plain. The story rings of the oral tradition with the rhythm and cadence of West African storytelling.

Animals play an important role in many African tales. In Aardema's *Oh, Kojo! How Could You!* (P), a lonely woman asks the supernatural for a son; her wish is granted, but she is told that, after some foolish acts, he will eventually prove to be wise. Kojo is outwitted three times by Ananse—spelled Anansi in other stories—the spider trickster. The last time, when he returns a captured dove to her kingdom, he receives a magic ring as a reward. The jealous Ananse wheedles his beautiful niece into stealing the ring, although Kojo retrieves it with the help of a cat. "In Ashantiland, in the old days, whenever mischief was done, people would always say: "It isn't one thing. It isn't two things. It's Ananse!""

What's So Funny, Ketu? A Nuer Tale (P) is Aardema's story of how Ketu helps a snake and receives a reward of a magic gift; he'll be able to hear animals think. But he must not tell anyone about his gift or he will die. When the cow refuses to let Ketu's wife milk her, Ketu roars with laughter at the cow's impudent thoughts. But his wife thinks he is laughing at her and she refuses to be appeased. Only luck and magic help Ketu resolve the dilemma.

Like Aardema's other retellings, *The Vingananee and the Tree Toad, Who's in Rabbit's House, Why Mosquitoes Buzz in People's Ears,* and *Bimwilli and the Zimwi* (all P) show the close association between animals and people. The retellings also contain rhythm, repetition, and onomatopoeia reflective of the African storyteller's voice.

Ashley Bryan retells and illustrates both African and West Indian folktales, including *The Ox of the Wonderful Horns and Other African Folktales, The Adventures of Aku, The Dancing Granny,* and *Lion and the Ostrich Chicks* (P-I-A). A collection of Nigerian folktales, *Beat the Story Drum, Pum-Pum* (P-I-A), contains a story about "Hen and Frog," which is reminiscent of the little red hen who asked for help, got none, and said, "Then I'll do it myself." In this version, Hen, worried about a coming storm, builds a house and gathers corn, all the while beseeching Frog to help her. Frog, however, refuses to help and is content to lie about although he seeks Hen's shelter once the storm

hits. When he has been washed out of his hole by torrents of rain, he asks Hen if he may lie on her bed:

> "No!" said Hen. "Uh-uh!
> You didn't help me make the hut,
> Hands on your hips.
> You didn't help me gather wood,
> Pursed your lips.
> You didn't help me pick the corn,
> Rolled your eyes.
> You didn't help me make the bed,
> An' it ain't your size!"[27]

In Bryan's lyrical retelling of a West Indian pourquoi tale, *The Cat's Purr* (P), Cat and Rat were once the best of friends. "Uh-huh, uh-huh, they really were!" sings the West Indian storyteller's voice. When Cat receives a tiny drum from his uncle with instructions to stroke it gently and never let anyone else play with it, Rat becomes jealous and craftily figures out a way to get his hands on the drum. In the struggle over the drum, Rat shoves it into Cat's mouth and he inadvertently swallows it. The story explains that the tiny drum stuck in the cat's throat is the reason that if we stroke cats gently, even today, they will purr "purrum, purrum."

Bryan also catches the rhythms of black-American spirituals in *Walk Together Children* and *I'm Going to Sing* (both P-I). He explains that the African had come from societies with ancient musical traditions where song and dance were interwoven with daily life, and music was an integral part of all social functions. Under the cruelties and deprivations of slavery, the Africans used their musical heritage as a vital resource for survival.

An outstanding collection of black-American folktales, *The People Could Fly* (I-A), retold by Virginia Hamilton and illustrated by Leo and Diane Dillon, includes animal tales, fanciful tales, tales of the supernatural, and tales of freedom. In the introduction, Hamilton explains that

Black-American folktales give us a glimpse of how the peoples wrenched from their homelands tried to retain their cultures and make sense of the new one into which they were forced. (From *The People Could Fly*, collected by Virginia Hamilton and illustrated by Leo and Diane Dillon.)

Folktales take us back to the very beginnings of people's lives, to their hopes and their defeats. American black folktales originated with peoples, most of whom long ago were brought from Africa to this country against their will. These peoples were torn from their individual cultures as they left the past, their families and their social groups, and their languages and customs behind.[28]

Black slaves brought their art of storytelling with them and created in America even more subtle tales to counter racial oppression. The tellers created towering beings as well as animal figures who personified their experiences of defeat, triumph, and hope. The familiar theme of the weak overpowering the strong through wit and humor was always appealing and showed up in many stories. Hamilton reminds us that the folktales were once a creative way for an oppressed people to express their fears and hopes to one another. "The Riddle Tale of Freedom" shows how a slave and a slaveowner would exchange riddles. If the slaveowner could not figure out the answer, he must give the slave his freedom. Hamilton includes a typical slave riddle in the notes.

> Was twelve pear hangin high
> An twelve pear hangin low.
> Twelve king come ridin by.
> Each he took a pear,
> An how many leave hangin there?
> > Answer: Begin with, there were twenty-four pears.
> > A man called Each took one pear.
> > That left twenty-three pears hangin there.[29]

The tales, created out of sorrow, were shaped by people full of love and hope; they celebrate the human spirit. Author's notes follow each tale to describe its origins and motifs. Variants of Bruh (also known as Brer) Rabbit, the legendary John de Conquer, and the Tailypo are included, but there are also slave tales from Hamilton's ancestors. The Dillons' exquisite art appears in full color on the cover and in textured monochrome paintings throughout.

See Tacquith's *Bo Rabbit Smart for True*, Keats's *John Henry*, Guy's *Mother Crocodile*, McDermott's *Anansi the Spider*, Steptoe's *Mufaro's Beautiful Daughters*, and Haley's *A Story, A Story* (all P-I) for other excellent individual tales. Collections by Harold Courlander, particularly *The Cow-Tail Switch and Other West African Stories* (P-I), by Courlander and George Herzog, provide further sources. Julius Lester retold several of the Brer Rabbit stories in *The Tales of Uncle Remus: The Adventures of Brer Rabbit* (P-I). See especially Joel Harris's *Jump:*

The Adventures of Brer Rabbit and *Jump Again! More Adventures of Brer Rabbit*, both wonderfully illustrated by Barry Moser (and both P-I).

Poetry

The black experience has been interpreted by a number of talented poets, namely Gwendolyn Brooks, Ashley Bryan, Lucille Clifton, Arnold Adoff, Langston Hughes, Paul Laurence Dunbar, Eloise Greenfield, Nikki Giovanni, and others.

Gwendolyn Brooks received the Pulitzer Prize for poetry in 1950 for *Annie Allen* (I-A) a collection of poems about black life in Chicago. She is best known in the children's book world for *Bronzeville Boys and Girls* (I-A), which contains poems such as "Cynthia in the Snow," "Rudolph Is Tired of the City," "Michael is Afraid of the Storm," "Eldora, Who is Rich," "Beulah at Church," "Robert, Who Is Often a Stranger to Himself," and "Eunice in the Evening." For Cynthia, the snow "Sushes, it hushes" and "whitely whirs away,/To be/ Some otherwhere."

Ashley Bryan says that reading aloud from the poems of the black-American poets greatly influences the prose of stories he writes. Whenever he is asked to share his African tales, he reads aloud first from the black-American poets to demonstrate the vocal play he carries over into the stories. Bryan edited and illustrated a collection of poetry by Paul Laurence Dunbar, *I Greet the Dawn* (A).

Lucille Clifton, named Poet Laureate of Maryland (in 1979), writes both stories and poetry for children and adults. She introduced a lovable child in *Some of the Days of Everett Anderson* (P) in 1970 and has followed his life in several books through to *Everett Anderson's Goodbye* (P), in which his father dies. Clifton says, "Interestingly enough, I don't think of 'Everett Anderson' as poetry, because it doesn't take as much out of me [to write it]. I think it's very good verse, and I think it's useful. It's a way to get kids into poetry, to head them towards poetry. But I don't think it's poetry."[30] Despite Clifton's distinction between poetry and lyrical prose, her work has much to offer as a positive image of black Americans.

Eloise Greenfield's first collection of poems, *Honey, I Love and Other Love Poems* (P-I-A), attracted widespread attention for its joyous sounds and thoughts of love and courage. She captures the child's voice when speaking of her love for her cousin from the South:

> I love
> I love a lot of things, a whole lot of things
> Like
> My cousin comes to visit and you know he's
> from the South
> 'Cause every word he says just kind of slides
> out of his mouth
> I like the way he whistles and I like the way he
> walks
> But honey, let me tell you that I LOVE the way
> he talks
> I love the way my cousin talks[31]

Arnold Adoff has frequently written and collected poetry about the black experience. His story poem, *Black Is Brown Is Tan* (P), celebrates the joys of being alive and promotes an awareness of the color variations in an interracial family.

> Black is brown is tan
> is girl is boy
> is nose is face
> is all the colors
> of the race[32]

Adoff's words capture in lilting rhythms a family playing together and loving each other. In *Ma nDa La* (P-I), Adoff sings another story poem in praise of the African earth which produces corn for the family. It soon becomes apparent that "Ma nDa La" means "Mom and Dad sing" as they go about their work. Adoff's story poems (P-I) include *Big Sister Tells Me That I'm Black*, *All the Colors of the Race*, *Today We Are Brother and Sister*, and *Outside/Inside Poems*. The newest collections of poems he has written include *Eats*, about all kinds of good food, and *Sports Pages*, about the victories and pains of playing sports. Arnold Adoff has edited five anthologies of black-American poetry, including *The Poetry of Black America*, *Celebrations*, *I Am the Darker Brother*, *Black Out Loud*, and *My Black Me* (P-I-A).

For excellent poetry for older students, see the work of Langston Hughes, Paul Laurence Dunbar, and Nikki Giovanni.

Fiction

Picture Books Lucille Clifton presents a loving image of black children in her books. They are irrepressible, enthusiastic, and strong. In fact, feeling good about being black is one of the themes that runs through Clifton's work. Families are supportive, proud of their heritage, and aware of the ties that bind generations together. *Amifika* (P), a winsome child, fears he'll be tossed out as his mother cleans house in preparation for his father's homecoming from the army. He runs away to hide in the yard and falls asleep behind a tree but awakens in his father's strong arms. Clifton's *Good, Says Jerome* (P), told in rhythmic verse, identifies some of the things that can be frightening for a child, such as moving. *My Brother Fine with Me* (P), by Clifton, is narrated by Johnetta.

> My brother Baggy, he gonna run away. He say he tired of Mama and Daddy always telling him what to do. He say he a Black man, a warrior. And he can make it by hisself. So he gonna run away. I help him get his stuff together.

Baggy tells Johnetta that she can come with him but she declines.

> "That's O.K.," I say to Baggy. I don't want to run away 'cause I like it home O. K. The only

problem I got at home is him and if he be gone it be fine with me. But I don't tell him that.[33]

Johnetta is delighted that she will be the only child after he leaves. When he is gone, however, she misses him and is happy to find that he has only run away to the front steps.

Clifton's *All Us Come Cross the Water* (P) is a search for Afro-American heritage and roots. In it Ujamaa seeks and finds the answer to the question "Where did we come from?"

Clifton includes interracial friendships in her books. The books just mentioned contain only black characters, but in others she includes both black and white. For example, King Shabazz, *The Boy Who Didn't Believe in Spring* (P), is black while his good friend, Tony Polito, is Italian American; in *My Friend Jacob* (P), Sam is black and Jacob, a retarded teenager, is white. In the interracial friendships, the children depend upon each other, but it is clear that the black child takes the leadership role.

Eloise Greenfield, whose poetry we have just seen, is another outstanding black writer who has written more than a dozen books, many of them picture books. Greenfield, according to Rudine Sims Bishop, tries

> through her books, to sustain children by (1) giving them a love of the arts, (2) encouraging them to hold positive attitudes towards themselves, (3) presenting them with alternative methods for coping with the negative aspects of their lives, (4) giving them an appreciation for the contributions of their elders, (5) providing true knowledge of Black (African and American) heritage, (6) allowing them to fall in love with Black heroes, (7) reflecting and reinforcing positive aspects of their lives, and (8) sharing her own love of words.[34]

Among Greenfield's books are *She Come Bringing Me That Little Baby Girl*, *Me and Neesie*, *First Pink Light*, and *Africa Dream (all P-I)*. With her mother, Lessie Jones Little, she wrote *I Can Do It By Myself* (P) (a picture book) and *Childtimes:*

A Three-Generation Memoir (P-I) (an autobiography, not a picture book). In a foreword in *Childtimes*, the authors state,

> This book is about family. Kinsfolk touching across the centuries, walking with one hand clasping the hands of those who have gone before, the other hand reaching back for those who will come after. This book, most of all, is about black people struggling, not just to stay alive, but to live, to give of their talents, whether to many or to few. Through all of their pain and grief, and even their mistakes, black people have kept on going, had some good times, given a lot of love to one another, and never stopped trying to help their children get on board the freedom train.[35]

Sharon Bell Mathis has produced some notable work, primarily *The Hundred Penny Box* (P-I), which is the touching story of an old woman and a young child. Although the story is longer than the usual picture book, it is filled with sensitive misty brown and white paintings by Leo and Diane Dillon that extend the tenderness of the story. Great-great Aunt Dew had raised Michael's father when he was orphaned and now she has come to live with them. She keeps a treasured box filled with a penny dated in each year of her long life; a penny becomes the impetus for a story when Michael slips in to visit her. She recalls events of a particular year as she turns each penny over in her hands. Michael's mother is not patient with Aunt Dew and wants to get rid of the box, but Michael fights to protect it, hoping to add the next penny. The gentle communication between the child and the elderly woman is heartwarming, while the tension between them and the mother intensifies the story.

John Steptoe's *Stevie* (P) captured the attention of the children's book world when it was published in 1969. At the time, Steptoe was only 19 years old—17 when he wrote and illustrated it. In the story, Robert complains about Stevie, a boy his mother babysits each day.

> I used to get so mad at my mother when I came home after school.
> "Momma, can't you watch him and tell him to leave my stuff alone?"
> Then he used to like to get up on my bed to look out the window and leave his dirty footprints all over my bed. And my momma never said nothin' to him.

One Saturday Stevie's mother and father come to pick him up like always but they said they were moving away and Stevie wouldn't come back anymore. Robert enjoys his privacy for a little while but then begins to remember the fun he and Stevie used to have; he misses him. The story ends with Robert's melancholy thoughts.

> He was a nice little guy.
> He was kinda like a little brother.
> Little Stevie.[36]

John Steptoe has continued to grow as an artist and writer; he has made a significant contribution to children's literature. He received a Caldecott Honor Book Award for *Mufaro's Beautiful Daughters* in 1988.

Novels Virginia Hamilton is one of the most distinguished and prolific writers in the field today. She was the first black writer to win the John Newbery Award and her honors include the National Book Award, the Coretta Scott King Award, the Boston Globe-Horn Book Award, and the International Board on Books for Young People (IBBY) Honor List, among others. She has contributed a sizable body of work that ranges from fantasy, mystery, realistic fiction, and historical fiction to biographical works. In her first book, *Zeely* (I), 11-year-old Elizabeth (Geeder) Perry sees a portrait of a beautiful Watusi queen and fantasizes that neighbor Zeely Tayber, 6½ feet-tall, is also a Watusi queen. Geeder sees the beautiful Zeely walking at night and frightens her brother with stories about night travelers. Zeely herself helps Geeder understand the difference between dreams and reality, and leads her to an even greater understanding of herself and the beauty of being what you are. In *The House of Dies Drear* and *The Mystery of Drear House* (both I-A), a black professor and his family live in a house that was once a station on the Underground Railway. Movable wall panels, secret tunnels, and a fabulous treasure in this home of a long-dead abolitionist, Dies Drear, lead to mystery, intrigue, and a test of loyalties. The rightful ownership of a priceless treasure is finally decided in a suspenseful and tightly drawn plot.

TEACHING IDEA

BLACK-AMERICAN HISTORY MAKERS[37]   To increase ethnic and racial group awareness and understanding, have students select and read the biographies of black Americans who have made significant contributions to history. After students select the black American they would like to represent, plan a "Living Pictures" presentation in which they pretend to be their subject and tell about that person's life to another class or to a school assembly.

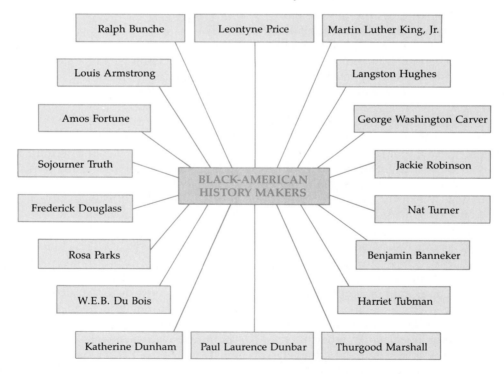

Note: This idea could be used with other racial and ethnic groups.

Some books by Virginia Hamilton, namely *M. C. Higgins, The Great; Willie Bea and the Time the Martians Landed;* and *A Little Love* (all I-A), are discussed in Chapter 8. Her other realistic books include *Arilla Sun Down* (I-A), *The Planet of Junior Brown* (I-A), and *Junius over Far* (A). Her fantasy novels include *Justice and Her Brothers, Dustland,* and *The Gathering* (all I-A). *The Time Ago Tales of Jahdu* (P-I) and *Sweet Whispers, Brother Rush* (A) contain a story within a story, combining reality and fantasy. Hamilton's strong graphic writing describes the real world and the fanciful world with equal clarity.

The black-American heritage includes strong cross-generational ties. Grandmothers, grandfathers, aunts, uncles, and cousins play an important role in children's lives. *The Times They Used to Be* (I-A) by Lucille Clifton stresses the continuity that runs through the generations of a black family. It begins, "Mama, Mama, tell us about when you was a girl," and Mama tells about her life. The memorable experiences when she was 12 years old include her friend Tassie's first menstrual period and reaction that "sin done broke all out in my body." The strength of family love is ever apparent.

Walter Dean Myers conveys the strengths of the extended black family and the love among its members and friends in his books. He most often chooses teenagers as central character and sprinkles the dialogue with the humor they toss about. He also often deals with the theme of growing up, but he marks his work with a healthy dose of love and laughter. *Fast Sam, Cool Clyde, and Stuff* (I-A) are three boys who make up the 116th Street Good People—along with Gloria, Binky, Cap, Maria, and Debbie who all hang out together. The issues the teenagers face and the discussions they have are realistic, tinged with pathos but softened with humor. Myers's *The Young Landlords* (A) is discussed in Chapter 8. Myers continues to focus on positive aspects of black teenage experience in *It Ain't All for*

Nothin', Hoops, Motown and Didi, Won't Know Till I Get There, The Legend of Tarik, The Nicholas Factor, and *Crystal,* (all A). *The Young Landlords* and *The Legend of Tarik* were named ALA Best Books for Young Adults. *The Young Landlords* and *Motown and Didi* both received the Coretta Scott King Award.

Nonfiction and Biography

Many of the same black writers cited previously have produced nonfiction and biographies. For example, Eloise Greenfield has written three biographies: *Paul Robeson, Rosa Parks,* and *Mary McLeod Bethune* (P-I). Virginia Hamilton has contributed some notable biographical literature about black leaders. They include *W.E.B. Du Bois: A Biography; Paul Robeson: The Life and Times of a Free Black Man;* and *The Writings of W.E.B. Du Bois* (all A).

Julius Lester comments in the opening pages of *To Be a Slave* (I-A) that one of the greatest overlooked sources for information concerning slavery has been the words of those who were slaves. During the first half of the nineteenth century, abolitionists took down the stories of thousands of blacks who escaped from the South; the narratives of exslaves became a literary genre even before the Civil War. But after the Civil War, interest in the slave narratives dwindled and was not revived until the 1930s when workers on the Federal Writers' Project interviewed those exslaves still alive. Lester selected from both the nineteenth-century slave narratives and the oral history taken down by the Federal Writers' Project to convey in the words of black Americans how it feels to be a slave. In one excerpt, a former slave describes the slave auction:

> My brothers and sisters were bid off first, and one by one, while my mother, paralyzed with grief, held me by the hand. Her turn came and she was bought by Isaac Riley of Montgomery County. Then I was offered. . . . My mother,

half distracted with the thought of parting forever from all her children, pushed through the
crowd while the bidding for me was going on,
to the spot where Riley was standing. She fell at
his feet, and clung to his knees, entreating him
in tones that a mother could only command, to
buy her baby as well as herself, and spare to her
one, at least, of her little ones. . . . This man
disengage[ed] himself from her with . . . violent blows and kicks. . . . I must have been
then between five and six years old.[38]

The dehumanizing effects of slavery ring out
on every page. Lester extends the documentary
of black history in *Long Journey Home* (I-A) by
telling stories of ordinary people; the stories
are based on historical fact. Lester believes that
the lives of the common people comprise the
essence of black history and need to have their
stories told along with those of the heroes.
That is what he has done.

James Haskins, now a professor of English,
has taught nearly every grade level from elementary school through college. Haskins has
written over 50 books, including *Black Theater in
America; Street Gangs, Yesterday and Today;* and,
with Kathleen Benson, *The Sixties Reader* (all A).
His experiences, some described in *Diary of a
Harlem Schoolteacher* (A), have given him a
sense of the topics and an approach that appeal
to young readers. He writes in a candid, forth-
right style, objective, yet dramatic. For example, the opening lines of *Black Music in America:
A History Through Its People* (A) begin,

> They came in chains, brought to the New World
> as slaves. They did not immigrate, seeking
> greater opportunity, like others who came to
> America. They were seized from their villages
> and homes and not allowed to take any posses-
> sions with them—no favorite piece of clothing
> or kitchen utensil or handmade musical instru-
> ment. But they did have their songs, and they
> would re-create their instruments and their mu-
> sic to keep their hearts and souls alive through
> nearly two hundred fifty years of slavery in the
> New World.[39]

Haskins takes a historical perspective on black
music in America, showing that its development was a matter of overcoming obstacles as
much as it was of creating new musical forms.
He describes the type of music that dominated
each period and gives vignettes of the musicians who brought it to life.

James Haskins has also written a number
of biographies about black Americans as well
as many informational books on topics in the
social sciences and the performing arts. Haskins's biographies most often feature black
leaders in religion, politics, music, or sports,
such as *The Life and Death of Martin Luther King*
(I-A), *Fighting Shirley Chisholm* (A), *Katherine
Dunham* (I-A), and *From Lew Alcindor to Kareem
Abdul-Jabbar* (I-A). Haskins probes thoughtfully
into the lives of his subjects, detailing their
hardships as well as their successes. In a biography of the first black astronaut, *Space Challenger: The Story of Guion Bluford* (I-A), which
Haskins coauthored with Kathleen Benson, we
learn that Bluford was told by a high school
guidance counselor that he was not college material. Bluford has gone on to distinguish himself as an astronaut and a scientist.

HISPANIC AMERICANS

According to the U.S. Census Bureau, 17 million people of Spanish origin live in America
today, and the Hispanic population is growing
more rapidly than any other minority group.
The census prediction is that Hispanics will replace blacks as the country's biggest minority
by the end of the decade. By the year 2000, the
Hispanic population will have increased 60 percent, more than double the 29 percent expected
for blacks. Among the Hispanics, Mexicans
outnumber all others: of the 17 million, about
10 million are Mexican; 3 million are Puerto Rican; about 1 million, Cuban; and 3 million,
other origins, including Caribbean and Central
and South American. Milton Meltzer, in *The*

Hispanic Americans (A), reminds us that this ethnic group is quite diverse:

> Although they have much in common [in the Spanish language], Hispanics differ in many ways too. To lump all Hispanics together and insist that they are exactly alike would be foolish. Each Hispanic group has its own identity, and each Hispanic person feels the importance of the differences between groups. A Puerto Rican does not like to be mistaken for a Cuban, just as someone from the South does not like to be called a Yankee.[40]

The number of books for children portraying Hispanic characters stands in stark contrast to the numbers of Hispanics in the population. According to the study conducted by Edmonds, only 2 percent of all children's books published represent the Hispanic culture.[41] Considering the numbers of Hispanic American children who need to see themselves represented in books, there is a dearth of books available.

Despite the limited number of books, standards for selection are not lowered. Gilda Baeza, in *Library Services for Hispanic Children* (adult), edited by Adela Artola Allen, cites the criteria used in a border city, the El Paso, Texas, Public Library, to evaluate materials for children. In addition to criteria that specify compliance with the library's mission, goals, accuracy, and timeliness of the material, the list of guidelines includes:

1. Language. Materials should reflect the language standards set by local usage. In the case of translated works, the quality of the translation is noted.
2. Characterization, illustrations, and story development. Only materials portraying positive images of Hispanics are accepted. Material must be presented in a nonsexist, nonracist manner. Illustrations, settings, and characters are to be presented in a way that a Hispanic child can relate to positively.
3. Value system. Materials should incorporate Hispanic values. For example, books on sex educa-

tion, treatment of the elderly, and social etiquette are more closely evaluated than others. Any item that violates the value system is rejected.[42]

The books discussed here include the best books in English about Hispanic Americans; reviews by Hispanic Americans were used to verify the accuracy and authenticity of the portrayal of Hispanic culture.

Folklore

Traditional folk tales and nursery rhymes have been crafted over centuries in verbal patterns and rhythms that can be easily remembered. Each culture has its own unique style of rendering folk tales and nursery rhymes that should be apparent in the retelling. One collection that retains the melodies of the Hispanic origins is *Tortillitas para Mama and Other Nursery Rhymes: Spanish and English* (N-P) by Margot C. Griego and others, illustrated by Barbara Cooney. This bilingual book contains 13 well-known Hispanic nursery rhymes which are passed along from one generation to the next. "Little Frog Tail" ("Colita de Rana"), "The Chicks" ("Los Pollitos"), and "Lullaby" ("Arrullo") are among the favorite lilting rhymes.

Isabel Schon, Professor of Library Science at Arizona State University, has published numerous books on Hispanic literature for children and young adults. In one collection, *Doña Blanca and Other Hispanic Nursery Rhymes and Games* (P-I), she provides both Spanish and English translations of 18 well-known Hispanic verses and games. Some of the favorites include "La Cucaracha," "A la rueda de San Miguel," and "Matarile-Rile-Ro."

Verna Aardema retold a Mexican folktale, *The Riddle of the Drum: A Tale from Tizapan, Mexico* (P-I). The King of Tizapan decided that whoever married his beautiful daughter would have to prove himself worthy so he asked a wizard to make a very special drum; potential suitors must guess what the drumhead is made of. Prince Tuzan from a nearby land hears about the riddle of the drum so he sets out to try to win the princess. On his way he meets Corrin Corran, the runner; Tirin Tiran, the archer; Oyin Oyan, the hearer; Soplin Soplan, the blower; and Comin Coman, the eater. Fortunately, he invites the various talented friends to join him in his quest because the king sets additional trials after Prince Tuzan guesses correctly that the drumhead is made from the wings of fleas. It takes the magical talents of all to help the prince win the hand of the princess.

Pura Belpre, born and educated in Puerto Rico, retells Puerto Rican folklore and historical legends, some in collections, as *Once in Puerto Rico* (I), and some in single editions, as *The Rainbow-Colored Horse* (P-I). The stories in *Once in Puerto Rico* tell, in legendary form, the early history of many places on the beautiful island. For example, one story tells the legend behind "The Chapel on Cristo Street." In 1753 during the Feast of Saint Peter and Saint Paul, two young men raced their horses from the wall overlooking the harbor up the steep hill toward the center door of the church of Saint Thomas of Aquino and reached the goal at the same time. On their way down the hill they decided to race their horses to the starting point and see which one would first reach the wall. One of the riders, Baltazar Montañez, lost control of his mount halfway down the hill and the maddened beast plunged over the wall. Miraculously, the rider was saved although the horse was killed instantly on the rocks below. The chapel was built on the very spot where the horse had leaped over the wall. They call it the Chapel of the Christ of Good Health.

In the single tale, *The Rainbow-Colored Horse*, a farmer finds that his fields of maize are being trampled. The two older sons try to solve the problem but cannot. It is the youngest son, Pio, who uses his ingenuity to surprise the rainbow-colored horse who is trampling the field and to extract three favors for his kindness. The three favors help Pio win the hand of wealthy Don Nicanor's daughter in marriage. Don Nicanor sets difficult trials that Pio must conquer, but with the help of the rainbow-colored horse, he succeeds.

Religion is an important part of life in Mexico; it shows up in their folklore and in their family celebrations. Tomie dePaola retold and illustrated the story of Mexico's patron saint, *The Lady of Guadalupe* (P-I), who appeared to Juan Diego in 1531. Before the white men came across the sea from Spain, Juan Diego, an Indian, was called "He-who-speaks-like-an-eagle." He lived simply with his wife in the village of Tolpetlac, planted his corn, and paid his taxes to the great Aztec Empire. When the Spaniards came in 1519, the couple converted to Catholicism and obtained their Christian names. One winter, Maria Lucia, his wife, became ill and died, but Juan Diego continued to

Religion is an integral part of Mexican folklore. Tomie dePaola retells and illustrates the story of *The Lady of Guadalupe*, the patron saint of Mexico.

worship despite his grief. On December 9, 1531, Juan put on his tilma (a cloak) and set out for prayer services. When he neared the hill of Tepeyac, he saw a vision, a beautiful lady dressed in what looked like the robes of an Aztec princess. The lady asked Juan to carry a message to the bishop of Mexico: she wanted a church built in her honor on this exact spot so she could show her love to all his people, the Indians.

Juan carried the message to the bishop but was forced to wait and return another day. Twice Juan returned to the hill and twice more he saw the lady. The third time, the lady asked him to cut roses from the hillside, and although no roses had ever grown there before, Juan now found beautiful fresh roses. The lady arranged the roses in Juan's tilma and he hurried back to the bishop. As Juan spilled the roses out in front of the bishop and the monks, they all stared at his tilma. His rough cactus-fiber tilma had been transformed; it now carried a painting of the lady just as he had seen her at the foot of Tepeyac. The bishop begged forgiveness for doubting Juan, hung the tilma over the altar, and began planning for the church exactly as the lady had requested. In the space of a few days, an adobe church was built on the site but many years later, a great church was built there with the painting of the lady hung over the altar. An author's note explains that Juan Diego's tilma was made of ayate, a coarse fabric woven from cactus fiber. Even though it is over 400 years old, the tilma still shows no signs of deterioration. Ayate usually deteriorates in 10 years or so. Nor have the colors of the portrait faded. To this day, Mexican Indians say to newborn children, "May God be as good to you as he was to Juan Diego."

Susana Martinez-Ostos illustrated six Mexican folktales and one riddle in *Why Corn Is Golden: Stories About Plants* (P-I) collected by Vivien Blackmore. The title story explains that long ago a curious man wanted to know where

the sun lived. His wife, knowing that the Sun was a god and highly respected, cautioned him against asking such foolish questions. The man ignored her warnings and turned himself into a sparrow and later an eagle who tried to fly to the place where the Sun rises. When he arrived the Sun wasn't there any longer, because he had gone off to warm the young seeds. The man resolved to wait for the Sun where he sleeps and this time found the end of the earth and the beginning of the sea. He hid behind a tree to watch the Sun spilling gold into the water and the sea swallowing it up. Knowing that he could not carry the heavy gold, he asked some dwarves to help him. The dwarves, however, were really sun rays who warmed the roots of plants and fruits, helping them to grow. When the greedy man tried to take all the gold for himself, he was turned into a buzzard who flew away ashamed. The dwarves took half the gold to the buzzard's wife and carefully put the rest into some roots that were growing in their cave at the center of the earth. It so happened that the roots were corn roots, and the gold flowed upward. This is why the corn is as golden as the Sun in the sky. The magnificent illustrations and large-sized format make this a spectacular book.

Poetry

Toni de Gerez adapted poems of the ancient Toltecs of Mexico in *My Song Is a Piece of Jade: Poems of Ancient Mexico in English and Spanish* (I-A). This anthology includes fragments of poems originally composed in the Nahuatl language in honor of gods of ancient Mexico. During the pre-Christian era, the people spent days and nights at magical ceremonies where the poems were sung to a background of drums and flute music. The song poems, presented in both Spanish and English, make it clear that to be a Toltec is "to be a wise man, to be an artist." The images evoked in the graphic poems sing of the green, dark jade world and of the yellow pumpkins that were as round and as heavy as drums and as gold as the sunrise. One ear of corn was all that a man could carry. The poems celebrate Toltec life and give guidance to the young: "You are a gift/you are a precious stone/Be just/Be strong . . . Be careful/Do not make fun of your elders/ of the sick/of beggars." This collection of sacred songs is distinctive in tone; you can almost hear the sound of the storyteller's voice, the sound of the drumbeats, and the tinkle of the flute ring through the language.

> What is my song?
> It is a piece of jade
> I can cut into it
> it is my song.
>
> Look!
>
> I am making a necklace
> with beads of jade
>
> it is my song
> it is jade. . . [43]

The two final poems, "My Son" and "My Daughter," celebrate the children who will inherit the jade necklace of the song. A glossary provides the meanings of unfamiliar words.

Para Chiquitines (P-I) by Jiminez Holguin and colleagues is a collection of 15 songs, 22 poems, and 21 finger plays that have been sung and recited in Spanish-speaking homes for generations. A glossary presents an English translation of each selection.

Fiction

Picture books In *Yagua Days* (P) by Martel Cruz, Adan, a Puerto Rican born in New York, thinks that rainy days are no fun. When he goes with his parents to Puerto Rico, he discovers the kinds of things children do there on rainy days. His mail carrier had told him about "yagua days," and Adan finds out what that means. When the grass is slick with rain, he uses a yagua, a large palm leaf, to slide down the grassy hills, over a ledge, and into the river. Back home, Adan tells the mail carrier about his own "yagua days" and the things he saw in Puerto Rico. A glossary provides an English translation for the many Spanish words used in the happy report of a visit to Puerto Rico. This book was chosen as a Notable Trade Book in the Field of Social Studies, a Reading Rainbow Review Book, and a runner-up for the Council on Interracial Books for Children Award.

Santiago (P), by Pura Belpre, is an engaging young boy transplanted into New York City from his beloved Puerto Rico. Symeon Shimin's illustrations make Santiago look as if he will speak from the page when he is telling his friends at his new school about his life in Puerto Rico and his pet hen, Selina. Santiago has both a loving mother and an understanding teacher because they make it possible for Santiago to bring his classmates to his home to look at pictures of Selina. The pride shines in Santiago's face as classmates look at his pictures and learn about his Puerto Rican homeland. The experience raises Santiago's self-concept as it should for any fortunate child who reads his story.

Novels Barbara Brenner describes a rare pre-Columbian Mexican treasure that is missing in *Mystery of the Plumed Serpent* (I). Twins, Michael and Elena Garcia, who live in New York City with their mother and grandmother, become involved in tracking down the golden snake. Legends about pre-Columbian history woven into the modern-day story of a smuggling ring enrich the excitement and intrigue. Grandma Garcia reads the Spanish newspaper in this urban setting of a Spanish community.

Nicholasa Mohr vividly portrays the everyday richness of a close-knit Puerto Rican community in New York that *Felita* (I) loves. Nine-year-old Felita knows everybody on her block and meets her girl friends to play. Every day is filled with exciting things to do. Felita is upset when her parents move to a "better neighborhood" and she refuses to go outside. She begs her mother to move back to their old neighborhood but her mother answers:

> "Felita, this neighborhood has better schools. You and your brothers will get a good education. But yes, we will visit the old neighborhood. After all, Abuelita, your grandmother, still lives there, and your Tio Jorge too. Besides, we will have our friends come to our new home. Please try to understand, honey."

When Felita does venture out to play, the children are nice to her until an adult calls them over and speaks to them. Then they turn on Felita as she is trying to make her way back to her front door.

> Thelma quickly stepped in front of me, blocking my way. "Why did you move here?"
> "Why don't you stay with your own kind?" Mary Beth stood next to Thelma.
> "Yeah, there's none of your kind here and we don't want you." As I tried to get by them the other three girls ran up the stoop and formed a line across the building entrance.
> I turned toward the grown-ups. Some were smiling. Others looked angry.
> "She should stay in her own place, right, Mama?"
> "Can't you answer? No speak the English no more?" The grown-ups laughed.[44]

After several more unpleasant incidents in which Felita's family is subjected to acts of violence, her family does move back to their old neighborhood. Felita confides in her grandmother about the problems she had, and Abuelita helps her understand something about prejudice, encourages her to develop inner strength, and to be proud of her Puerto Rican heritage. Abuelita promises that one day she will take Felita to Puerto Rico so she can show her the beautiful island. Life is still not smooth for Felita, however. Gigi, her best friend, gets the starring role in the class play while Felita gets to paint scenery. Weeks of avoiding Gigi and pouting about their friendship takes its toll on Felita. Again, it is through a special talk with Abuelita that Felita understands herself and her feelings about Gigi. Abuelita's death forces yet another step in Felita's growing up process; her grandmother's influence would remain with her forever.

Going Home (I-A), the sequel in which Felita is now 11 years old and excited about her forthcoming trip to Puerto Rico, shows that discrimination comes in many forms. Felita's mother watches her like a hawk now that boys are trying to get her attention, and petty jealousies arise among her girl friends to complicate her life. When Felita gets to Puerto Rico, some welcome her openly but others turn on her, calling her a "gringa" and "Miss Nuyorican" because she was born in New York and, according to them, not a true Puerto Rican. Felita grows in understanding of herself and realizes that she is truly going home when she is headed back to New York. Mohr has a good ear for natural dialogue and a strong sense of preteens' relationships.

Nonfiction

George Ancona is noted for excellent photographic essays in several fields. In *Bananas: From Manolo to Margie* (P-I), he follows the process of growing, harvesting, and transporting bananas from the plantation in Honduras to their purchase in a city store. The final photograph shows Margie eating a banana, but the story focuses on Manolo Perez and his family. His father works on the banana plantation that is owned by a large fruit company and his mother works as a packer. The book concludes with a glossary of Spanish words and a list of the vitamins and minerals in bananas.

Fran Ortiz took the photographs for Tricia Brown's book, *Hello, Amigos!* (P). This appealing book follows a Mexican-American child, Frankie Valdez, through a day, his birthday, in the Mission district of San Francisco. Frankie is an engaging child whose exuberance sparkles from the photographs of him bouncing off to school, peeking out the school bus window, and writing at his desk. When his class plays kickball, his teacher lets him serve first because it is his birthday. After school, Frankie does his homework and goes to the boy's club while anxiously awaiting time for the birthday party to start. His mother and father invite family and friends to join them for enchiladas, frijoles refritos, arroz, tortillas, and guacamole amidst family singing and fun before the long-awaited birthday cake with seven candles. Frankie gets to break a piñata, and later he and his father walk to their church to light a candle and count their blessings. A glossary of Spanish words is appended.

Milton Meltzer, historian and biographer, has studied various immigrant cultural groups in their struggle for freedom and justice. In *The Hispanic Americans* (A), he traces the roots of the many Hispanic people living in the United States. After giving a brief history of the first settlers, Meltzer focuses on individual families and neighborhood groups. The vignettes of the Vinas from the Dominican Republic, Rodolfo de León from Cuba, and Ernesto Galarza, Pascual Jiminez Martinez, and Bernardo Vega from Mexico give a personal view of real people and their lives. Meltzer includes a poem that Rodolfo "Corky" Gonzales wrote to describe his feelings:

> La Raza!
> Mejicano!
> Espanol!
> Latino!
> Hispano!
> Or whatever I call myself,
> I look the same
> I feel the same
> I cry
> and
> Sing the same
> I am the masses of my people and
> I refuse to be absorbed. . . .
> The odds are great
> but my spirit is strong

> My faith unbreakable
> My blood is pure
> I am Aztec Prince and Christian Christ
> I SHALL ENDURE!
> I WILL ENDURE![45]

Biography

Elizabeth Borten de Treviño had to fill in around the few facts that are known about the seventeenth-century painter, Velázquez, and his talented black assistant in *I, Juan de Pareja* (A). In an afterword, Treviño explains,

> Whenever one tells a story about personages who actually lived, it becomes necessary to hang many invented incidents, characters, and events upon the thin thread of truth which has come down to us. The threads of the lives of Velázquez and Pareja are weak and broken; very little, for certain, is known about them.[46]

Treviño knew that Velázquez, the Spanish court painter in the first half of the seventeenth century, had a black slave standing by his side handing him brushes and grinding his colors. There is evidence, too, that Velázquez had inherited the slave, Juan de Pareja, from relatives in Seville and had later granted Pareja his freedom. She also knew that Pareja became an accomplished artist in his own right because his canvases hang in several European museums. While it is true that slaves were not allowed to practice the arts in Spain, Treviño hypothesizes how it might have come about that Pareja learned to paint and became a close companion and friend to Velázquez. The story of the two men who began as slave and master and ended as equals and friends is a fascinating one. Treviño also wrote *Juarez, Man of Law* (A), about another Hispanic leader.

JEWISH AMERICANS

Looking for books with Jewish characters is not as much a problem as finding some that truly embody Jewish values. Frequently, Jewish educational groups will identify books for Jewish children, but upon examination, the books contain only a superficial reflection of Jewish values. Some that do reflect Jewish values present them in a heavy-handed didactic manner, which causes the books to have limited appeal for the average reader. The most effective books for the general public use a subtle approach in which the values permeate the entire story and theme. Marcia Posner, leading authority in Jewish children's literature, points out that there are different readerships for even the most didactic books.

> In the world of Jewish books there is more than one marketplace—which is as it should be, because the book that fits one type of marketplace may not be right for another. Traditional Jews have their own standards for the books they will allow into their homes, schools, and libraries; and libraries in Reform synagogues will usually not want books suitable for traditional Jews. Children's books for the Traditional (Orthodox) Jewish marketplace (from right-wing Orthodox to Modern Orthodox) must represent their beliefs. . . . On the other hand, because the books frequently deal with subjects not found elsewhere, and because of their increasing attractiveness, the books are often purchased and/ or read by those outside the Orthodox community.[47]

Posner, who conducted her doctoral research on identifying Jewish values and assessing the level of their presence in children's literature, has continued to research the area and has written a number of useful guides, namely *Jewish Children's Books: How to Choose Them-How to Use Them*, and *Selected Jewish Children's Books*. She stresses that one key to Jewish survival is continuity with the Jewish past; books can make these connections for many. Some of the criteria Posner uses to select books are:

1. Is Jewish ritual behavior displayed? (everyday, on holidays, for life-cycle events—in the home and in the synagogue)

2. Is involvement in Jewish education evident?
3. Is the responsibility of one Jew for another demonstrated?
4. Is the sense of being a unique people shown?
5. Are the religious and secular roles of Israel recognized?
6. Are the effects of Jewish ethical teachings shown?
7. Do the characters care for the poor, the sick, the elderly?
8. Do they show concern for social justice?[48]

Posner cites a number of other ways Jewish identity can be displayed. She also makes it clear that Jewish content alone does not necessarily make a good book; it must also meet the accepted standards of good literature in general.

Folklore

A rich body of Jewish folklore has been handed down to children by their parents, grandparents, and rabbis. Many tales revolve around religious holidays and treat serious themes, while other lighter stories are tinged with an ironic sense of humor—actually laughing at oneself. Nobel Prize–winner Isaac Bashevis Singer is one of the most valued contemporary writers. He writes original stories and retells versions of Eastern European folklore. Singer did not believe that he could write for children, but editor Elizabeth Shub convinced him to try. He was 62 years old when his first collection of children's stories appeared in *Zlateh the Goat and Other Stories* (I), illustrated by Maurice Sendak; this is discussed in Chapter 6.

The importance of stories is underscored in "Naftali the Storyteller and His Horse, Sus," which appears in Singer's *Stories for Children* (I-A) and as a single edition by the same name. Naftali always loved stories and wanted to be a bookseller when he grew up. One day he speaks with Reb Zebulun, an itinerant bookseller. Reb Zebulun tells him,

> "When a day passes, it is no longer there. What remains of it? Nothing more than a story. If

PROFILE

Isaac Bashevis Singer

Isaac Bashevis Singer, the son and grandson of rabbis, was born in Radzymin, Poland, in 1904. Although he was a student at the Rabbinical Seminary in Warsaw, he chose not to become a rabbi and went to work as a journalist for the Yiddish press in Poland after completion of his studies. He immigrated to America in 1935. He has been a prolific writer: journalist, memoirist, children's storyteller, and novelist. Although he originally wrote in Hebrew, Singer long ago adopted Yiddish as his medium of expression. He

personally supervises the translation of his works into English.

Singer has been the recipient of many literary awards. In 1978 he was awarded the Nobel Prize for Literature; in 1980 he received the Medal of Honor for Literature given by the National Arts Club in New York; in 1970 he received a National Book Award in Children's Literature for *A Day of Pleasure;* and in 1974, another National Book Award in fiction, for *A Crown of Feathers*.

Singer's works have been translated into numerous languages. When asked if he would take a guess about why people all over the world appreciate what he writes, he said: "The guess is that there is a kinship between souls. Souls are either close to one another or far from one another. There are people who, when they read me, they like what I say." Discussing the appeal of literature across national borders, Singer explains,

It seems that to enjoy a book you don't really have to go there and to know the land and the people, because human beings, although they are different, also have many things in common. And through this you get a notion which writer

stories weren't told or books weren't written, man would live like the beasts, only for the day."

Reb Zebulun said, "Today we live, but by tomorrow today will be a story. The whole world, all human life, is one long story."[49]

Naftali does become a bookseller and storyteller, traveling with his horse, Sus, from one village to another. After many years, he travels

to Reb Falik's estate, for he has heard that Reb Falik loved books and stories. At Reb Falik's, Naftali stands admiring an ancient oak tree that has put down deep roots; he, too, longs to settle down himself and he knows that Sus is weary from traveling. Reb Falik understands Naftali's wishes and builds him a home and a print shop and a stable for Sus. Naftali spends

says the truth and which writer is fabricating. . . .

When I sit down to write a story, I will write the kind of stories which I write. It's true that since I know the Jewish people best and since I know the Yiddish language best, so my heroes, the people of my stories, are always Jewish and speak Yiddish. I am at home with these people.[50]

Isaac Bashevis Singer did not begin writing for children until he was well over 60 years old. He had, of course, been writing all his life so the transition was not a difficult one for him. Once he started, he found it very rewarding. He says,

There are five hundred reasons why I began to write for children, but to save time I'll mention only ten of them.

1. Children read books, not reviews. They don't give a hoot about the critics.
2. Children don't read to find their identity.
3. They don't read to free themselves of guilt, to quench their thirst for rebellion, or to get rid of alienation.
4. They have no use for psychology.
5. They detest sociology.
6. They don't try to understand Kafka or *Finnegans Wake*.
7. They still believe in God, the family, angels, devils, witches, goblins, logic, clarity, punctuation, and other such obsolete stuff.
8. They love interesting stories, not commentary, guides, or footnotes.
9. When a book is boring, they yawn openly, without shame or fear of authority.
10. They don't expect their beloved writer to redeem humanity. Young as they are, they know that it is not in his power. Only the adults have such childish illusions.[51]

Children's literature is richer since Isaac Bashevis Singer began to write for children.

the rest of his days writing and printing books. Both he and Sus are buried under the ancient oak tree.

Poetry

Poems for Jewish Holidays (P-I-A) is the only recent book to focus on Jewish poetry. There are 16 poems, selected by Myra Cohn Livingston, that celebrate Jewish holy days. Twelve contemporary authors contributed to the collection which contains three poems for Rosh Hashanah and Yom Kippur, two for Hanukkah, Passover, and Shabbat, and one for each of seven other holidays. Valerie Worth captures the effect of sounding the Ram's horn, the Shofar, calling people to prayer.

Zlateh the Goat and Other Stories contains seven middle-European Jewish tales that echo the Jewish heritage. (Written by Isaac Bashevis Singer and illustrated by Maurice Sendak.)

HOLY DAYS

Suddenly, in the
Midst of everything
New—paved cities,
Calm suburban
Gardens, endless
Acres of corn—

There rise these
Palms, these deserts,
These bitter herbs:

These ancient days
Called up by the
Ram's echoing horn.[52]

Carol Adler uses the traditional chant of the Sabbath (Shabbat) in

HAVDALAH

"A good week," we sing
at the end of Shabbat.

"A week as bright as
candlelight, as
sweet as spice
and sweeter than wine!

"A good week!" we sing
as we light the candles
sniff the spice box
and lifting the wine cup
take a sip.

Can you see the light
dancing on your fingertips?

Can you feel inside
another week
ready to begin?[53]

A body of traditional poetry for children celebrates Jewish holidays. One poem song that is included in *Poems for Jewish Holidays*, "An Only Kid," makes the point that eternity is everlasting. The cumulative rhyme begins

An only kid! An only kid!
My father bought for two zuzim *had gadya*.
Then came the cat
And ate the kid
My father bought for two zuzim *had gadya*.[54]

The same verses are included in Marilyn Hirsh's book *One Little Goat: A Passover Song* (P). Another traditional participation poem with gestures, "Who Knows One?" proceeds around the table at Passover. Each person responds to a question and adds the next number and stanza with all repeating all stanzas that preceded plus the current stanza before going on to the next.

> Q. "One, One, who knows what is One?"
> A. "I know what is One: One God, of Heaven and Earth."
>
> Q. "Two, two, who knows what is two?"
> A. "I know what is two: Two tablets of the law."
> All: "One God, of Heaven and Earth."
> "Two tablets of the law."[55]

As Yiddish literature flowered during the 1920s, it included both stories and poetry for children. In Israel these poems continue to be translated into Hebrew where poetry is much more popular with adults and children than it is in the U.S.

One haunting anthology echoes the horrors of the Holocaust. . . . *I Never Saw Another Butterfly* (I) is a collection of poems written by children in the Theresienstadt Concentration Camp between 1942 and 1944. The children's poetry reflected the hunger, dirt, and disease they faced but also the spirit of courage and optimism they maintained.

Fiction

Picture Books *Mrs. Moskowitz and the Sabbath Candlesticks* (P) by Amy Schwartz shows how Jewish traditions add meaning to life. Mrs. Moskowitz misses her old house and wanders aimlessly around her new apartment unwilling to unpack or to settle in. She says to her cat, "You call this a home, Fred? . . . This apartment will never be a home." When her son comes by that evening, he brings a package she had left behind in the basement of the old house. Hesitantly Mrs. Moskowitz opens the box and unwraps her Sabbath candlesticks; the tarnished candlesticks bring back memories of happier times. The importance of the candle-

sticks spur Mrs. Moskowitz to action: they must be polished; they must have a special tablecloth beneath them; a challah must be baked. The candlesticks become the focal point in preparing for the Sabbath when the family gathers to worship. An author's note explains the meaning of the traditions cited.

Barbara Cohen's work also shows an understanding of Jewish life and values. In *Molly's Pilgrim* (P), Molly, a recent Jewish immigrant from Russia, comes home from school with an assignment of making a Pilgrim doll. Her mother asks, "What's a Pilgrim?"

> "Pilgrims came to this country from the other side," I said.
> "Like us," Mama said.
> That was true. "They came for religious freedom," I added. "They came so they could worship as they pleased."[56]

Mama volunteers to make the doll and dresses it as she herself dressed before leaving Russia to seek religious freedom. Molly fears that the doll does not look like the Pilgrim woman in the picture in her reading book, but she takes the doll to school. After scornful remarks from classmates, an understanding teacher explains. "Listen to me, all of you. Molly's mother *is* a Pilgrim. She's a modern Pilgrim. She came here, just like the Pilgrims long ago, so she could worship in her own way, in peace and freedom." The teacher goes on to explain that the Pilgrims in New England got the idea for their Thanksgiving from the Jewish harvest holiday of Sukkos (Succoth).

Gooseberries to Oranges (P-I), also by Barbara Cohen, is the true story of a little girl born in Eastern Europe who came to live in America when she was 8 years old. Told as a reminiscence, the personal narrative describes Fanny in the little village of Rohatyn; she and Aunt Rebecca often ate gooseberries right off the bushes and sucked brown pears from trees in front of Aunt Rebecca's house. But winter came, and war. Finally, Papa, who had already come to America, sent a ticket for Fanny to come, too. On board ship, Fanny watches a man eating an orange, something she had never seen before. After passing the Statue of Liberty and spending time in an Ellis Island hospital, Fanny is finally claimed by her Papa. One day, she earns two nickels delivering coats for a neighbor. When Papa insists that she keep the nickels for herself, she puts one under her pillow to save. With the other she buys two bright, round, large oranges. Peeling the orange, pulling apart the sections, sucking each section until it was dry, and chewing and swallowing the rest tasted like heaven. "If at that very moment a gate had opened, and on the other side of the gate were the wild gooseberries and little brown pears of Rohatyn, I would not have walked through that gate. I was already home."[57]

Novels Eth Clifford's gentle story, *The Remembering Box* (P-I), is about Joshua and his Grandma Goldina who spend the Sabbath together each week. Grandma Goldina had refused to move in with Joshua's family because she preferred her own quiet apartment to the hustle and bustle of a big family. When Joshua is 5 years old he begins spending time with Grandma Goldina, partially as a way to check on her, but he also tremendously enjoys their time together. Grandma would often open her "remembering box," a big trunk, filled with treasures from the past. Each item led to a story which Grandma would tell with loving detail. There are photographs, a willow branch, ribbons, a stocking *knippel* which served as a bank for savings, and a silver bell. Joshua polishes the Sabbath candlesticks each week and gradually, as the years pass, takes more responsibility for their time together. One Sabbath evening when Joshua is 10, Grandma gives him his own "remembering box" with each of the treasures he has grown to love. They talk quietly about each treasure and its story while Grandma Goldina slips into a quiet sleep not to awaken. Joshua lights the candles, says "Shabbat Shalom," and goes to telephone his father. This is a gentle and tender story of a special relationship between a grandmother and her grandchild.

The Night Journey (I-A) by Kathryn Lasky is a touching story within a story about a young girl's relationship with her great-grandmother, Nana Sashie. Rachel's Americanized mother and grandmother are not very interested in the stories that Nana Sashie tells about her early life, but Rachel finds them fascinating. She slips upstairs each evening to listen to Nana Sashie tell about her agonizing escape from persecution of the Jews in Czarist Russia in 1900. Sashie was 9 years old when her family found they must leave Russia. The only way they could leave was to masquerade as itinerant Purim players, an idea that Sashie proposes herself. They make their way to the border hiding under chicken crates and bribe the dangerous border guards. Alternating chapters focus on Rachel's current school life and her family's modern concerns. The urgency of Rachel's visits with Nana Sashie is made clear when she realizes that her great-grandmother could have died without telling her poignant story.

See also *The Island on Bird Street* by Uri Orlev, *I Am Rosemarie* by Marietta Moskin, *Monday in Odessa* by Eileen Bluestone Sherman, *The Return* by Sonia Levitin, and *Falasha No More: An Ethiopian Jewish Child Comes Home* by Arlene Kushner.

Nonfiction

Many nonfiction books deal with the meaning of Jewish holidays, while others discuss historical origins, immigration, and the Holocaust. One, an excellent compendium of Judaica, *The Jewish Kid's Catalog* (I-A) by Chaya Burstein, is a miscellany of Jewish customs, history, language, holidays, crafts, recipes, beliefs, literature, music, songs, dances, folklore, genealogy, and landmarks. Other books focus on a specific topic, a person, or a historical period.

Miriam Chaikin, one of the foremost Jewish writers for children, explains the meaning of Jewish holidays in a laudable series. *Light Another Candle: The Story and Meaning of Hanukkah* (P-I) describes the historical background of Hanukkah, stressing the importance of the holiday as a struggle for religious freedom. It also shows how Jews have fought oppression in order to celebrate Hanukkah even in the most dire circumstances. *Make Noise, Make Merry: The Story and Meaning of Purim; Shake a Palm Branch: The Story and Meaning of Sukkot; Ask Me Another Question: The Story and Meaning of Passover;* and *Sound the Shofar: The Story and Meaning of Rosh Hashanah* (all P-I) are other titles in the series. Jewish life-cycle events are described and explained in Malka Drucker's *Celebrating Life: Jewish Rites of Passage* (I-A).

Milton Meltzer has contributed a significant body of informational literature on the history of Jews. In *Remember the Days* (A) he gives a short history of the Jews in America from 1654 to the present. The first permanent community of Jews in what is now the United States began on September 1, 1654, when 23 Jewish passengers aboard the *Saint Charles* sailed into New Amsterdam (New York) harbor. Like the Pilgrims who had landed at Plymouth Rock 34 years earlier, they were seeking freedom from persecution. In *World of Our Fathers* (A), Meltzer concentrates on the Jews from Eastern Europe, where over half of the Jews in the world lived in the year 1800. "The true beginnings of Eastern European Jewry," Meltzer writes of their history, "have been clouded by myth and legend. It is known that there were Jewish settlements in Europe as far back as the time of the Second Temple (70 C.E.). But the centers of Jewish life were in Babylonia, Egypt, and Palestine."[58] *Taking Root: Jewish Immigrants in America; The Jewish Americans: A History in Their Own Words, 1650–1950;* and *Never to Forget: The Jews of the Holocaust* (all A) are some of

Meltzer's other works. *Never to Forget* is the most poignant. Instead of chronicling the bitter facts of the Holocaust, Meltzer gives us eyewitness accounts through the letters, diaries, journals, and memoirs of those who experienced the terror and grief. Meltzer asks,

> How could it have happened?
> It did not occur in a vacuum. It was the logical outcome of certain conditions of life. Given the antihuman nature of Nazi beliefs, the crime of the Holocaust could be expected. We see that now. That it happened once, unbelievable as it seems, means it could happen again. Hitler made it a possibility for anyone. Neither the Jews nor any other group on earth can feel safe from that crime in the future.[59]

That is the reason underlying Meltzer's title: we must never forget, lest it should happen again.

See also *The Young Reader's Encyclopedia of Jewish History* (I-A), edited by Ilana Shamir and Shlomo Shavit, for an excellent reference book.

Biography

Many of the biographies about Jewish leaders focus on the time of the Holocaust in Germany and its aftermath around the world. Two superior examples by Aranka Siegal, include *Upon the Head of a Goat*, which is based upon the author's memories of childhood in Hungary, 1939–1944; and *Grace in the Wilderness: After the Liberation*, 1945–1948, which chronicles her postwar recuperation in Sweden. (Both books are discussed in Chapter 9)

Two other biographies narrate the life of Hannah Senesh, who was born into a wealthy Jewish family in Hungary in 1921. She was a young poet living in relative safety in Palestine when she volunteered to parachute into Yugoslavia to gather information about the German troops and to try to rescue victims of the Holocaust. Her story is told in the book *In Kindling Flame: The Story of Hannah Senesh, 1921–1944,*

TEACHING IDEA

BOOK DISCUSSION[60]   Have your students read *Once I Was a Plum Tree,* by Johanna Hurwitz. The themes in this book are assimilation, alienation, and Jewish identity. Briefly, Gerry Flamm feels foolish and left out when she must stay home for the High Holy Days and not go any further than her front steps. She is frustrated and confused by her assimilated family's ambivalence toward their Jewishness. New neighbors, refugees from the Holocaust, teach her about Jewish customs and values, helping Gerry to learn the meaning of her Jewish identity and its importance to her.

Second-generation American Jews were often so eager to become "fully American" that they disdained the European ways of their parents—which were also Jewish ways. When the old traditions faded, they frequently were not replaced by new Jewish traditions but by traditions borrowed from their Christian neighbors. Gerry could have drawn away from her past. Instead, she met a *shaliach,* a "messenger." Had the family next door not escaped, Hitler would have murdered them for being Jewish. Having escaped, they rescued another Jewish soul.

The following are questions and activities that the students can pursue:

1. Why do you think Gerry's family did not belong to a synagogue or send Gerry to Hebrew school? Did Gerry enjoy staying out of school on Jewish holidays without having to go to synagogue? Why, or why not?
2. Explore the ways in which you are Jewish. What do you do, or believe, as a result of Jewish teachings and traditions?
3. Describe your childhood to your children. Discuss the values your parents taught you or exemplified. Discuss the values of your current home.
4. Does your family go to the synagogue? Does it observe the holidays? Why?
5. Are Christian holidays a problem in your home? How do you handle the problem? Read *There's No Such Thing As a Chanukah Bush, Sandy Goldstein* by Susan Sussman.

by Linda Atkinson, and in *Hanah Szenes: A Song of Light* by Maxine Schur. Many of her poems are included.

There are also many new biographies other than those of the Holocaust survivors. For example, Natalie Bober wrote an outstanding study of an artist in *Breaking Tradition: The Story of Louise Nevelson* (A). Louise Berliawsky came with her family from a Russian shtetl to a New England seacoast town; an inspiring teacher helped her develop her interests. After her marriage and a move to New York, Louise Nevelson continued to grow as an artist, developing a personal statement in her art. While in her eighties, she was acknowledged as one of the major artists in the United States. For further biographies, see the work of one publisher (the Lodestar imprint of Dutton) that has developed a series including *Isaac Bashevis Singer: The Story of a Storyteller* by Paul Kresh, *A Spy for Freedom: The Story of Sarah Aaronsohn* by Ida Cowen and Irene Gunther, *I Lift My Lamp:*

Emma Lazarus and the Statue of Liberty by Nancy Smiler Levinson, *Justice Felix Frankfurter: A Justice for All the People* by David Gross, *Daughter of My People: Henrietta Szold and Hadassah* by Hazel Krantz, and *An American Rhapsody: The Story of George Gershwin* by Paul Kresh.

NATIVE AMERICANS

The history of America is incomplete without chapters on its native inhabitants, American Indians. Often their story was told by white men who characterized them in stereotyped ways— as ferocious savages, or as downtrodden people who suffer nobly. Although some books perpetuate this tepee-and-feathers image, a growing number now give more accurate portrayals of the native American's culture and a more objective picture of the 300-year clash between the white and American Indian cultures.

The native American experience has been interpreted in literature for children by members of various tribal groups, anthropologists, folklorists, and others who have lived among native Americans. This literature is another link in the chain of universal understanding, and it rings true to its culture, with accurate detail.

Folklore

Anpao: An American Indian Odyssey (I-A), by Jamake Highwater, is a folk history chronicle of the Indians of America. It combines numerous tales passed down through generations, sometimes borrowed by one tribe from another, into a continuous life journey of one hero. The book illustrates a way of knowing history through literature.

When asked about the myths and legends that are its basis, Highwater said: "That is something I would like to discuss but you're using the *wrong words*. They are *not* myths and legends, they are an alternate way of viewing

reality." He further explains his point in the storyteller's farewell in *Anpao*:

> You may have noticed that I am disinclined to refer to "myths" and "legends" when I talk about *Anpao*. This is because these words express the dominant society's disregard for the beliefs of other peoples, just as I would be expressing a nonchalant superiority were I to speak to Christians of their "Jesus myths." *Anpao* is not concerned with myths but with a reality which seems to have escaped the experience of non-Indians.[61]

Highwater's perspective is undergirded by a Blackfoot-Cherokee heritage and a study of cultural anthropology, comparative literature, and music. The old tales are neither curiosities nor naive fiction; they are alternate visions of the world and reveal an alternate process of history. Indeed, the stories

> exist as the river of memory of a people, surging with their images and their rich meanings from one place to another, from one generation to the next—the tellers and the told so intermingled in time and space that no one can separate them.[62]

Tales, chants, poetry, and song can serve as a bridge to understanding American Indian culture. John Bierhorst, a folklorist, compiled several volumes showing how, in their lore, American Indians pay tribute to the beauty of nature, the power of spirits, and the role of the supernatural. In 1899, Edward Curtis, a photohistorian who realized that the Indian culture might soon disappear, saved the remnants of a vanishing race through photographs and transcriptions. Nine of the tales Curtis preserved appear in *The Girl Who Married a Ghost and Other Tales from the North American Indian* (I-A), edited by John Bierhorst.

We can also learn about American Indian culture from the chants and songs that they believe possess the power to make things happen. For example, their songs describing the

ACTIVITY: TEACHER TO STUDENT

ANPAO: AN AMERICAN INDIAN ODYSSEY (A) In order to recapture the spirit of Indian lore, share parts of *Anpao* through dramatic reading or storytelling. Trace variants of the tales in the folklore of other tribes and cultures. For example, look at *The Angry Moon* by William Sleator, *The Girl Who Loved Wild Horses* by Paul Goble, and *The Naked Bear: Folktales of the Iroquois* by John Bierhorst.

American Indians believe in the wholeness of experience, the interdependence of man and nature, the importance of the quest for love, and the search for one's destiny. During the Westward Expansion, how did the basic beliefs of settlers and natives make conflict inevitable?

Discuss some of the ideas that are uniquely Indian, such as their concepts of time (measured by suns, moons, and seasons) and space, a "contrary" (a person who does and says everything in reverse—as with Oapna in *Anpao*), the river of stars, the relationship with one's horse, the ownership of land, and the meaning of fences.

beautiful dawn are sung with the aim of making the dawn come again, and a song about a horse is both a tribute to it and a means of investing it with the strength about which the song sings.

Ritual occasions—such as daybreak, hunts, festivals, and times of initiation—have their special sounds and rhythms. In *The Trees Stand Shining: Poetry of the North American Indians* (P-I), Hettie Jones explains that the songs show the American Indians' view of their world, their land, and their lives. The song-poems include prayers, stories, lullabies, and war chants.

Within recent decades we have developed a new consciousness about American Indians and about the differences between their concepts and those of the early settlers. The native American believed, for example, that the land belonged to all, whereas the European settlers, of course, brought with them the idea of individual ownership. Staking their claims to lands that the American Indians had roamed freely for hundreds of years set the stage for conflict—from grisly battles, in which hundreds were killed, to inner conflicts in which individuals who had come to know each other as friends had to choose between friendship and loyalty to the violently opposed groups.

The folklore of native Americans is voluminous; it is as varied as the languages and life-styles of many tribal groups, but like all folklore, the tales share commonalities. Many stories explain the how and why of natural phenomena and stress the close association between people and nature; others are creation myths, transformation tales, trickster tales, and sacred legends. Ravens, eagles, wolves, bears, and buffalo often appear in the tales. Storytelling is deeply rooted in the culture and ceremonial life of the native American; they hold storytellers in high regard.

The Whale in the Sky (P-I), retold and illustrated by Anne Siberell, is from the Northwest Coast Indians. The story, symbolically told on a totem pole, explains why Thunderbird sits ever watchful at the top of the totem pole. Below him, Whale, Raven, Salmon, and Frog hold their positions because of the events of one fateful day. An author's note shows the tools totem pole carvers used and the mixtures they used to make their colors. Siberell's strong simple woodcuts used for illustration were inspired by the totem pole carvings of the Northwest Coast tribes in this authentic retelling.

Paul Goble has retold, adapted, and illustrated numerous native American legends. Some are from a particular Indian group, but for others he synthesized elements from many tribes. Among his books are *Buffalo Woman* (P-I), a transformation tale about an Indian brave's quest to rejoin his buffalo wife and child; *Star Boy* (P-I), a Blackfoot Indian legend about a badly scarred brave who visits his Grandfather, the Sun, to save his people; and *The Girl Who Loved Wild Horses* (P-I), a girl who travels with wild horses until she "surely had become one of them" at last. Goble's artistic interpretation of *The Girl Who Loved Wild Horses* earned the Caldecott Award in 1979.

Paul Goble explains in *Death of the Iron Horse* (P-I) that there are many trains wrecked by Indian people in the pages of fiction, but it really happened only once. On August 7, 1867, a Union Pacific freight train was derailed by the Cheyenne. Goble's book is loosely based on that incident, but it is mainly a story of Indian courage against the steam locomotive, a frightening and unknown invention of the white man. The young Indian braves who cut the railroad ties and lift the tracks of the iron horse are trying to protect the women and children as their fathers had done. Goble's brilliant paintings tell the story as the Cheyenne might have told it.

John Bierhorst, one of the foremost native American folklorists, collected 16 tales in *The Naked Bear: Folktales of the Iroquois* (I). The Iroquois roamed the Catskill Mountains in upper New York State along the shores of Lake Ontario, but sent war parties over a territory stretching from Montreal to present-day Chi-

cago and as far south as the Carolinas. The Five Nations of the Iroquois—the Mohawk, Oneida, Onondaga, Cayuga, and Seneca—commanded the respect of the outside world. Of the five original nations, all but the Cayuga continue to hold tribal lands in New York State. Lewis Henry Morgan, the most important of the early writers on the Iroquois, said the Five Nations exerted greater political influence than any other American Indian group except for the Aztecs and the Incas. Arthur Parker, the eminent Iroquois specialist of the early 1900s, believed that the Iroquois were the "Indian of Indians," and declared that their folktales were the "classics" of all the unwritten literature of the native American. Bierhorst says:

> Whether Iroquois folktales are the "classics" of American Indian lore, as Parker imagined, it is certainly true that in no other body of Indian tales are there so many happy endings or such a modern sense of evil punished and virtue rewarded. The reason, perhaps, is that the Iroquois have been carefully absorbing European influences for more than three hundred years. Nevertheless, the plots and even the minor incidents are thoroughly grounded in Indian tradition.[63]

Bierhorst has also edited or compiled *The Mythology of North America* (A), *The Ring in the Prairie: A Shawnee Legend* (I), *A Cry from the Earth: Music of the North American Indians* (I-A), *Doctor Coyote* (I), and *The Sacred Path: Spells, Prayers, and Power Songs of the American Indians* (I-A).

Elizabeth Cleaver tells an Inuit Indian transformation tale in *The Enchanted Caribou* (P-I). Tyya, a young woman, loves to wander about the northland, but one day she is lost in a dense fog. Etosack rescues her and takes her to his home, a tent made from caribou skins, where he and his two brothers live. When the three brothers go off to hunt caribou, they warn Tyya not to allow anyone into the tent. She forgets to follow their warning, however, and allows an old woman, who is a shaman,

The Enchanted Caribou, an Inuit Indian transformation tale, tells why hunters should not shoot a white caribou. (Written and illustrated by Elizabeth Cleaver.)

into the tent. The old woman combs Tyya's hair and turns her into a white caribou who trots across the tundra to join the herd. When the brothers return, Etosack is unhappy because he has fallen in love with Tyya. That night Etosack has a dream. In the dream his dead grandmother who had also been a shaman speaks to him.

> Do what I tell you and you will have her back. In the morning take a feather, the bone and sinew of a caribou, a stone, and the doll that Tyya made. Then go out and look for the white caribou. When you find it, throw these things on its back and you will see what happens.[64]

Etosack does as his grandmother bids, and when he sees the white caribou he tosses the magical objects onto its back. Instantly the caribou changes back into Tyya. Etosack invites Tyya to his tent where they lived together happily. "And ever since," the story concludes,

"when hunters meet a white caribou they treat it kindly and do not kill it, for it might be enchanted."

Cleaver illustrated the story with black and white drawings that approximate the look of a shadow theater. At the close of the book she gives instructions for making shadow puppets and a theater. Shadow theater is ideal for showing dreams, visions, and magical happenings like a human turning into an animal.

Tomie dePaola retold and illustrated a Comanche story, *The Legend of the Bluebonnets* (P), that explains why bluebonnets blossom in Texas each spring. Long ago during a great drought, the legend goes, the Comanche prayed to the Great Spirits asking them to send the rain. The land was dying, and the people were dying. Among the few people left was a child, called She-Who-Is-Alone. Her parents and her grandparents were only shadowy memories, but she had a doll made from buckskin by her mother. It wore the bright blue feathers from a blue jay brought home by her father. She loved her doll dearly. It was the only thing she had left from the distant days when her parents had lived.

One day the shaman returned from the hilltop. He had heard the words of the Great Spirits, "The people have become selfish. For years, they have taken from the Earth without giving anything back." He told them that when the sacrifice was made, the draught and famine would cease. All the Comanche people returned to their tepees to think about what the Great Spirits had said, for indeed, they had become selfish. All, that is, except She-Who-Is-Alone. She took her beloved doll and went to the hilltop where the Great Spirits had spoken. She built a fire and thrust her beloved doll into its flames. She thought of her parents and her grandparents and all the people who had died from the great famine. She prayed while the fire burned the last shreds of her doll into glowing embers. When the ashes cooled, she scooped them up and scattered them to the winds, and then she slept.

When the morning sun awoke her, she looked out across the hills and valleys, and wherever the ashes had fallen, the ground was covered with flowers—beautiful flowers—as blue as the feathers from her doll. And then the rains came and the land began to live again. From that day on, the Comanche people called her by another name, One-Who-Loved-Her-People-Dearly. They loved her for the sacrifice she made. Every Spring, the Great Spirits remember the sacrifice of a little girl and fill the hills and valleys of that land, now called Texas, with the beautiful bluebonnets, even to this very day. DePaola's full-color illustrations add to the beauty of the legend.

Christie Harris, another noted folklorist, retells native American tales, most often focusing on the Tlinglit, Haida, and Kwakiutl Indians of the Northwest coast. *Once Upon a Totem, Once More Upon a Totem, Mouse Woman and the Van-*

ished Princesses, and *The Trouble with Princesses* (all I-A) are among her works.

The Story of Jumping Mouse (P-I), retold and illustrated by John Steptoe, is from the Indians of the Great Plains. A young mouse listens with great interest to the stories of the old ones as they tell about the far-off land. He longs to go there and one morning sets off before the sun has risen, but soon he comes to a river. Magic Frog helps him cross the river and gives him the gift of a name, Jumping Mouse, and the ability to jump far. In his travels, Jumping Mouse meets a shaggy bison who cannot see; he gives him his own gift of sight. He meets a wolf who cannot smell; he gives him his own gift of smell. Each animal leads him closer until he is in the far-off land, but he wonders how he will manage. As he sits weeping, Magic Frog comes to him again and says, "Don't cry, Jumping Mouse. Your unselfish spirit has brought you great hardship, but it is that same spirit of hope and compassion that has brought you to the far-off land." Magic Frog encourages Jumping Mouse to jump higher and higher and then says, "Jumping Mouse, I give you a new name. . . . You are now called Eagle, and you will live in the far-off land forever." Steptoe's soft black and white paintings merited a Caldecott Honor Book Award.

Poetry

Byrd Baylor's lyric prose celebrates the lifestyle and beliefs of the Southwest Indians. She collected favorites in *And It Is Still That Way: Legends Told by Arizona Indian Children* (I); shows petraglyphs on Southwest canyon walls in *Before You Came This Way* (P-I), and in *The Other Way to Listen* (P-I) tells how an old man teaches a young girl how to listen to nature.

The Trees Stand Shining: Poetry of the North American Indians (P-I), collected by Hettie Jones and illustrated by Robert Andrew Parker, is an impressionistic collage of songs, chants, and lullabies; they mirror the climates of the heart

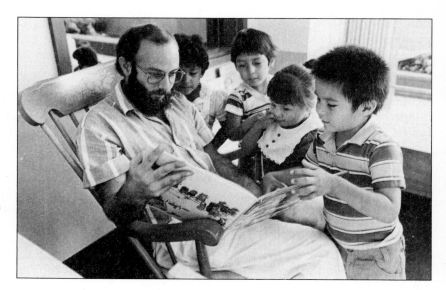

The lyric poetry that is collected from the oral histories of the Indian nations reinforces the heritage of young Indians and allows non-Indians to experience and appreciate these cultures. Young Pueblo Indians share a story on the Santa Clara Pueblo, New Mexico.

as well as the natural world. They express a reverence for creation, nature, and beauty and bespeak a communion with animals and the earth. This one is from the Teton Sioux.

> The old men
> Say
> The earth
> Only
> Endures,
> You spoke
> Truly,
> You are right.[65]

John Bierhorst included the words, music, and dance steps in his collection of native American songs of love, prayer, magic, dreams, and greeting in *A Cry from the Earth: Music of the North American Indians* (P-I-A). There is a Hopi flute song, a Hopi sleep song, a Cherokee lullaby, and a Kwakiutl cradlesong. Bierhorst explains how native Americans believed that songs held magical powers; they could help bring the rain, win a battle, or chase away bad spirits.

Nancy Wood has known the Indians at Taos Pueblo in the Rio Grande Valley of New

Mexico for many years. She has studied their art, their beliefs, and their way of life. In *Many Winters* (I-A), she wrote down what they passed on to her, not always in their exact words but in the expression of a life that is richly and fully lived. The final poem expresses a belief about living:

> Hold on to what is good
> even if it is
> a handful of earth.
> Hold on to what you believe
> even if it is
> a tree which stands by itself.
> Hold on to what you must do
> even if it is
> a long way from here.
> Hold on to life even when
> it is easier letting go.
> Hold on to my hand even when
> I have gone away from you.[66]

In a fourth grade classroom, the students read many different types of poetry, including native American poetry. They tried to write in the same vein. Here is one sample of a child's response.

ACTIVITY: TEACHER TO STUDENT

NORTH AMERICAN INDIANS (I)[67]   Read some of the books and poetry suggested in the web and try to imagine what life was like as an Indian before the white settlers and what it is like now. Here are some suggestions to help you:

Take a trip to the Museum of the American Indian.
Discuss the art and content of some of Paul Goble's books.
Make a totem pole from boxes or styrofoam.
Make masks, discuss their purpose and use.
Create a miniature replica of an Indian village.
Write journal entries for an Indian child.
Write Indian poetry.
Make corn cakes.
Plant corn.
Weave some Indian designs.
Sing Indian songs and chants.
Dance Indian ceremonial dances.

NORTH
AMERICAN INDIANS

FICTION AND
FOLKLORE

The Story of Jumping Mouse
(Steptoe)
A Country of Strangers (Richter)
The Gift of the Sacred Dog
(Goble)
The Great Race (Goble)
People of the Short Blue Corn
(Courlander)
Sing Down the Moon (O'Dell)
The Girl Who Loved Wild Horses
(Goble)
Arrow to the Sun (McDermott)
Doctor Coyote (Bierhorst)
In My Mother's House (Clark)
Raven's Cry (Harris)
They Dance in the Sky (Monroe
and Williamson)
Kiviok's Magic Journey (Houston)
Three Fools and a Horse (Baker)

POETRY

The Trees Stand Shining (Jones)
Whirlwind Is a Ghost Dancing
(Belting)
Before You Came This Way
(Baylor)
When Clay Sings (Baylor)
Songs of the Dream People
(Houston)
Many Winters (Wood)
Hiawatha's Childhood
(Longfellow)
The Sacred Path (Bierhorst)
In the Trail of the Wind
(Bierhorst)
I Breathe a New Song (Lewis)

INFORMATION AND
BIOGRAPHY

Children of the Wild West
(Freedman)
Cowboys of the Wild West
(Freedman)
Indian Chiefs (Freedman)
*American Indians Today: Issues
and Conflicts* (Harlan)
The Double Life of Pocahontas
(Fritz)
North American Indians
(Gorsline)
*Happily May I Walk: American
Indians and Alaska Natives Today*
(Hirschfelder)
Ishi: Last of His Tribe (Kroeber)
Indians (Tunis)
First Came the Indians (Wheeler)

THE DESERT

The sound of a coyote
howling breaks the stillness
of the night in the desert. . . .
Pitter . . . Patter . . .
But what's that?
Pit . . . Pat . . . Pit . . . Pat . . .
Oh, yes. It's my good friend
the rain.

DANIEL POLER[68]

Fiction

Picture Books *Where the Buffaloes Begin* (P), by Olaf Baker, first appeared in *St. Nicholas Magazine* in 1915, but Stephen Gammell's art gave it renewed life. Little Wolf hears the legend of his tribe and is drawn to the shores of the silvery lake where buffalo are created. He sees them rise from the misty waters and sweep across the prairie, gleaming in the moonlight. The immensity of the buffalo in their roaring stampede is overwhelming; Little Wolf shouts for joy and joins the thundering herd. As they near his village he sees an enemy tribe about to attack and turns the buffalo to ride over the enemy and save his people. Gammell's illustrations suggest the mythic origins of the story; they convey both strength of the mighty buffalo and the sense of isolation and sweep of the prairie.

Novels Anego, a Chippewa Indian, was the only Indian in the northern Minnesota school in *A Brown Bird Singing* (I), by Frances Wosmek; most of the people in the community were Scandinavian. Anego's mother died when Anego was very small, and her father, Hamigeesek, who needed to move with the rest to hunt and gather the wild rice, had left her with his white friend until he could come to claim her.

> As time passed, her mother's face and the music of her words faded. Nothing was left but a feeling that was soft, warm, and trembling to escape. It was like a brown bird she had once held in her hands. The bird had flown away, but she had always remembered it. Even now, just thinking about the bird brought back the soft, warm feeling. It reminded her to be brave and not to be afraid.

Anego knew that the brown bird and her mother's songs were a part of her life before her mother had died and her father had brought her to live with the Veselkas. She knew that Hamigeesek would return, but she had grown used to her new family and wanted nothing to change. When the day of Hamigeesek's arrival is upon them, Anego runs aimlessly through the forest until she loses her way. Hamigeesek finds her thrashing through the forest and assures her that the choice will be hers. He then coaxes a small brown bird into his hands by giving bird calls and slips it into Anego's hands.

> "Remember?" he asked her, smiling.
> Anego held out her hand and took the bird from Hamigeesek. She curled her fingers around it. She felt it, soft and warm, trembling to escape. She felt the quick little heartbeat inside its small feathered breast. She felt Hamigeesek's kind, smiling face looking down at her.
> All at once she remembered. She remembered her mother's warm, brown, smiling face. She remembered the music of her mother's Chippewa words, telling her to be brave and not afraid. She remembered the face, every detail. It had been filled with love.

When she releases the bird, she puts her hand into Hamigeesek's, feeling a great pride. "It's a good sign," said Hamigeesek, turning to look back over his shoulder. "The brown bird is singing."[69]

Nonfiction and Biography

Russell Freedman wrote the stories of six western *Indian Chiefs* (A), namely Sitting Bull of the Hunkpapa Sioux, Red Cloud of the Oglala

Russell Freedman chronicles the lives of six Western *Indian Chiefs* and the struggles their peoples faced in the white encroachment of their lands.

Sioux, Joseph of the Nez Percé, Quanah Parker of the Comanche, Satanta of the Kiowa, and Washakie of the Shoshoni. The story of the courageous native Americans who led the resistance to whites taking over their western lands is a tragic one. They had roamed the country freely and did not understand why that should change. For example, Sitting Bull insisted that his people should be able to live freely in the Black Hills and the Powder River country, as promised by the Treaty of Fort Laramie. He said, "The Great Spirit made me an Indian, but not a reservation Indian, and I don't intend to become one!" Freedman lightens the story of broken treaties and deadly battles with touches of humor. For example, while fleeing from the army in 1877, the Nez Percé

paced themselves to stay two days ahead of General Howard; they began to call him "General Day-After-Tomorrow."

The native American way of life ended as a result of encroachments, reprisals, and broken treaties, but the legendary heroes leave a rich heritage. Freedman's human-interest approach to his subjects gives us a better understanding of the Indian chiefs as real human beings. The photographs he includes from numerous university and national archival collections are excellent.

LIVING TOGETHER IN A WORLD OF PEACE

The General Assembly of the United Nations proclaimed their fortieth year, 1985, as the International Year of Peace. Specific goals within the proclamation center on people practicing tolerance and living together in peace. They state that all people need to continue their positive action aimed at the prevention of war, and the removal of threats to peace—including the nuclear threat. They also state that we must respect the principle of nonuse of force, work toward the peaceful settlement of disputes, and maintain outer space for peaceful uses. Further, we need to develop a world where all people can exercise human rights and fundamental freedoms; it would be a world where discrimination and apartheid are eliminated. Safeguarding peace and preserving the future of humankind are inextricably linked.

A chapter on multicultural literature is incomplete without a section addressing a world of peace. The goals of multicultural education include people of many backgrounds living together peaceably. If we understand the people of many nations, we can no longer place them on different sides in times of conflict; war strategy teaches that anonymous masses of strangers are easier to kill than real people we know as individuals who have dreams and feelings much like our own. Children can know people of other lands through literature; they can recognize similarities between themselves and others and can understand the universal nature of humankind.

The stories of our past must be told over and over again to each new generation of children. Although some of us remember the tragedies of the Holocaust and the bombing of Hiroshima, for children today it is ancient history. And while it may seem incongruous to teach children about war in the name of peace, peace educators believe that we must warn children of the dangers of war by telling them about our past wars if we are to educate them to live in a world of peace. One group states:

> [Children] have to be told the lessons of maturity long before they are mature. But slogans can't be relied upon to spread the meaning of the maturity a peaceful mankind will require. The poetry and drama of individual experience, the fragile wonder of individual discovery, the mysterious resolve of those willing and able to stand alone—all this has to be continually renewed, or even born for the first time, in the young.[70]

Literature is one of the most compelling ways to share the poetry and drama of individual experience. The fragile wonder of individual discovery is cast in first-person accounts by authors who write with passion—a plea to save the world from war. In these stories the common enemy is war itself and although they show man's inhumanity to man, there are individual acts of humanity and courage. When we read the words of survivors or victims, the sound of authenticity rings in their thoughts.

The Holocaust

The Holocaust refers to the Nazi extermination of 6 million Jews during World War II. Though it may be difficult to believe that such an inhumane act could happen, the facts stand stark and clear. *The Diary of a Young Girl* (I-A) by

Anne Frank was one of the earliest pieces of literature to surface following World War II. The diary contains the actual words that 13-year-old Anne, a Jewish girl, wrote during the two years she and her family were hiding in an old Amsterdam warehouse. The innocent and honest introspection of a young girl caught up in survival has moments of pathos and shows an abiding sweetness of a loving girl.

Anna Steenmeijer worked with Anne Frank's father, Otto Frank, to edit *A Tribute to Anne Frank* (I-A) which explains how the diary was found, what happened to Anne when she and the others were captured, and how Anne's handwriting was authenticated. The book contains photographs of Anne and other writings by her. It also presents a historical background with a chronology from 1919 to 1942, when the Frank family went into hiding, and the numbers of victims who died in 15 concentration camps. For older readers, Ernest Schnabel's *Anne Frank: A Portrait of Courage* (A), based on interviews with 42 people who knew Anne, provides information about Anne's experiences in Auschwitz and Bergen-Belsen extermination camps and her death.

The Children We Remember (P-I-A) by Chana Byers Abells is a gripping photo-essay about children who lived and died during the Holocaust. The spare text and stark photographs, culled from the Archives of Yad Vashem, the Holocaust Martyrs' and Heroes' Remembrance Authority in Jerusalem, weave a story of tragic death and loss but also show courage and endurance. With a simple phrase and a powerful photo on each page, the text states simply, "Before the Nazis . . . some children lived in towns like this, went to schools like this, prayed in synagogues like this, played with their friends, or sat alone." Then the Nazis came, and they closed Jewish stores and schools, burned synagogues, took away homes, and forced Jews to live in the streets. A photograph of a Nazi soldier shooting a woman and her child chills the blood, and the

They made the Jews
sew patches
on their clothes.

As they read *The Children We Remember,* children and adults alike feel the loss of the Jewish children who fell victim to the Holocaust. (Written by Chana Byers Abells.)

innocent faces of children who were killed wrench the heart. But the book turns toward a note of hopefulness at the end, stressing that some children survived. "The children who survived are grown now. Some have children of their own. They live in towns like yours, go to schools like yours, play with their friends, or sit alone. . . . Just like the children we remember."

My Brother's Keeper: The Holocaust Through the Eyes of an Artist (I-A), by Israel Bernbaum, is an unusual book in that the illustrations are five huge paintings placed at chapter openings with enlarged sections of the paintings interspersed through the text. With a chilling sense of horror, you discover actual black and white photographs of the very same scenes placed alongside the artist's paintings. Bernbaum, an artist, painted the five large canvases known as "Warsaw Ghetto 1943" using photographs

taken from General Stroop's records as the basis for his work. He then adds a brief, stark history of the rise of Nazism and describes the various scenes the paintings represent. Bernbaum raises questions that hang unanswered, such as "Who killed six million Jews? Who murdered five million non-Jews? Who were the people who kept silent while they watched the slaughter?" The disturbing theme that permeates Bernbaum's work concerns indifference. He asks where all the people were who could have helped, but the question remains unanswered. He makes a strong case for the fact that we must be our brother's keeper.

Roberto Innocenti presents a haunting story of how a child experiences war without really understanding it in *Rose Blanche* (P-I-A), an oversized picture book with stunning art. Rose tells her own story in the first half of the book, expressing a child's bewildered response to the gradual encroachment of tanks, soldiers, and barbed wire enclosures in their small German village. Rose watches a young boy try to escape from Nazi soldiers but he is stopped, held at gunpoint, and forced to return to the truck loaded with victims for a concentration camp. Rose wanders through the forest near her village and finds hungry children and adults cringing behind barbed wire enclosures. She shares her meager ration of food with them. One day when Rose returns to share food again, the entire concentration camp is destroyed. Soldiers patrolling the area see enemies everywhere. There was a shot. The grim ending of a child's life underscores the cold-heartedness and senselessness of war.

The Nuclear Threat and Hiroshima

The bombing of Hiroshima showed the unfathomable power of an atom bomb and foreshadowed the even greater destruction from nuclear warfare. Toshi Maruki helps us see the tragic effects of the bombing in the lives of one family in *Hiroshima No Pika* (P-I-A). Mii was 7 years old having a breakfast of country fresh sweet potatoes with her parents.

> Then it happened. A sudden, terrible light flashed all around. The light was bright orange—then white, like thousands of lightning bolts all striking at once. Violent shock waves followed, and buildings trembled and began to collapse. Moments before the Flash, United States Air Force bomber *Enola Gay* had flown over the city and released a top-secret explosive. The explosive was an atomic bomb, which had been given the name "Little Boy" by the B-29's crew.
>
> "Little Boy" fell on Hiroshima at 8:15 on the morning of August 6, 1945.

Fire engulfed the city, bodies floated in the rivers, mothers tried to feed babies who were dead in their arms. Mii watched a swallow try to fly but its wings had been burned off. Three days later another atomic bomb was dropped on the city of Nagasaki to inflict the same kind of desolation. Mii never grew after that day. Although many years have passed, she is still the same size as a 7-year-old. Shards of glass still work their way out of her scalp. Her father died from the effects of radiation.

> Every year on August 6 the people of Hiroshima inscribe the names of loved ones who died because of the bomb on lanterns. The lanterns are lit and set adrift on the seven rivers that flow through Hiroshima. The rivers flow slowly to the sea, carrying the lanterns in memory of those who died.[71]

Mii prepares a lantern in memory of her father and the swallow. She says, "It can't happen again, if no one drops the bomb."

Maruki's paintings spare no quarter in their portrayal of the tragedy. Fire sweeps across pages, chasing Mii and her parents. Burned bodies lie in heaps. Parents reach out for children who are not there. Despite the horror they depict, the paintings are beautiful and capture some of the tenderness expressed within a family and among a group of desperately injured people.

Whitley Strieber foretells a ghastly but intriguing story of a conjectured aftermath of a nuclear holocaust in *Wolf of Shadows* (I-A). The story, told from the viewpoint of the wolf, opens;

> He was a giant of his kind; he had been the biggest of his litter and he had stayed much larger than the other wolves. He was black and had pale eyes, and from an early age he made the others uneasy. He was never accepted, and was driven to live at the edge of the pack. Because he was dark and spent his life hanging back in the forest, he was Wolf of Shadows.[72]

Wolf of Shadows, sitting alone on a hillside, watches a series of brilliant white flashes as a huge light mushrooms upward in the sky and knows that there is cause for alarm. When ashen clouds block out the sun and an icy black rain comes, washing away the smells of all living things, he knows it is time to leave the area. It gets colder, then colder still. Nuclear winter has begun. As snow and sleet fall, a desperate human mother and her daughter join Wolf of Shadows as he leads his wolf pack south to escape the desolate, frozen wasteland that was once the United States. The woman was an animal ethologist who had escaped from a Minnesota town, managing to keep one of her children alive. Threatened by savage dog packs, lack of food, and freezing weather, the wolf pack and two humans make the grim journey toward a place where life can be reborn. During the journey, humans and wolves understand that they must depend upon each other for survival, and bonds of love and respect grow among them. Strieber presents the horrors of nuclear war in a novel where compassion and concern among humans and animals can still survive.

D-1 Edward Lear, whose profession was botanical and zoological drawings, illustrated his *Book of Nonsense* to amuse the children of his patron, the Earl of Derby. Note the exaggerated heads and caricatures of his birdlike characters. (London: N.p., 1870.)

There was an Old Man of the Hague, whose ideas were excessively vague;
He built a balloon to examine the moon,
That deluded Old Man of the Hague.

D-2 Walter Crane believed that children prefer well-defined forms and bright, frank colors, so he used black outline with flat, brilliant, and delicate colors. He attributed these characteristics to the influence of Japanese prints. (*An Alphabet of Old Friends*. New York: Routledge, 1874.)

The History of Children's Literature

Tracing the development of illustrations in children's books reflects the corollary improvements in printing techniques and methods of color reproduction. Progressing from the early simplicity of wood-cut block printing to the contemporary technology of the graphic arts industry, children's book illustration has become a fine art.

Goosey, goosey, gander,
Where shall I wander?
Up stairs, down stairs,
And in my lady's chamber:
There I met an old man,
Would not say his prayers;
Take him by the left leg,
Throw him down the stairs.

D-3 Kate Greenaway drew children wearing clothing modeled largely but not exclusively from the high-waisted dresses and jackets, buttoned breeches, and smocks of the late eighteenth century. Her characters engaged in idyllic play in sunlit gardens and Queen Anne cottages. (*Mother Goose*. New York: Routledge, 1881.)

D-4 Randolph Caldecott conveyed a sense of delight in movement and energy in his illustrations. His art brought boisterous characters and an easy playfulness to children's picture books. The Caldecott Award is named in his honor. (*Hey Diddle Diddle and Baby Bunting*. New York: Routledge, 1882.)

D-6 Beatrix Potter's meticulous handling of detail conveys the essence of animal nature despite the anthropomorphic functions of her characters. She worked from live models. (*The Tale of Two Bad Mice*. London: Warne, 1904.)

D-5 Richard Doyle is noted for his creatures of fairyland, which include large-eyed and fat-bellied elves. He used a fine quill pen and clear porcelain colors that he transferred to engravings. (*The Princess Nobody* by Andrew Lang. London: Longmans, Green, 1884.)

D-7 Edmund Dulac's paintings are reminiscent of Persian and Indian book illumination. He excelled in nocturnal scenes and shadowy figures who stand out against deep blue or violet backgrounds. (*Stories from Hans Anderson*. London: N.p., 1912.)

D-8 L. Leslie Brooke has sometimes been described as a twentieth-century successor to Randolph Caldecott for the verve and action captured in his illustrations. He is notable for his lively portrayal of anthropomorphic animals. (*Stories from The Golden Goose Book*. London: Warne, 1904.)

D-9 Ernest H. Shepard has been called the last of the great Victorian illustrators. His art conveys a sense of movement and earthy humor. (*Wind in the Willows* by Kenneth Grahame. New York: Scribner's, 1908.)

D-10 Theodor Seuss Geisel (Dr. Seuss) was a cartoonist and an animator before he illustrated children's books. His cartoonlike figures and objects are exaggerated to convey an impression of great movement and emotion. (*And to Think That I Saw It on Mulberry Street*. New York: Vanguard Press, 1937.)

D-11 The simplicity of Jean De Brunhoff's illustrations and his imaginative use of white space give them a childlike appeal. He miniaturizes lovable elephants and portrays Babar in family settings to add to the warmth of his stories. (*Babar and His Children*. New York: Random House, 1966.)

D-12 The dreamlike nature of Ezra Jack Keats's pictures feature a child exploring his environment. The intense colors of Peter's suit stand in vivid contrast to the snow-covered city streets. (*The Snowy Day*. New York: Viking Press, 1962.)

D-13 Maurice Sendak's work illustrates superb draftsmanship and mastery of styles as he explores the realms of the unconscious. *In the Night Kitchen* is based on Sendak's childhood memories of life in New York. He is among the major artists of the twentieth century. (New York: Harper & Row, 1970.)

D-14 Mitsumasa Anno, an outstanding Japanese artist, illustrates panoramas with meticulous attention to detail. His line and watercolor paintings portray European architecture authentically. He includes subtle allusions to scenes and characters from biblical and traditional nursery stories. (*Anno's Italy*. New York: Philomel, 1978.)

Peace Education

Novels that make a strong statement against war and informational books that present decidedly antiwar messages can be used in peace education programs. Readers learn about individual acts of courage and the resolve to stand alone to prevent acts of war.

No Hero for the Kaiser (I-A) by Rudolf Frank, first published in 1931, had been reprinted several times by 1933 when Hitler came to power in Germany. Rudolf Frank was arrested in March 1933 and his book was burned with other "un-German" works on May 10, 1933. The book is the story of 14-year-old Jan Kubitzky, a Polish boy who is adopted, along with his dog, by a German artillery battery after German and Russian troops had devastated his village. Jan has an uncanny ability to read the landscape for signs that would show him "where a man might be hidden, disturbing the peace of nature," and he speaks Polish which is an advantage for the German troops. Jan and his dog save the soldiers more than once and are eventually transferred to the even more dangerous Western front. Jan learns about war firsthand both on the battlefield and in the field hospital where men, previously enemies, find unity in suffering. He learns that the African soldiers are fighting because they had been promised the return of the skull of Sultan Mkwawa of the protectorate of German East Africa, an issue actually addressed in the Treaty of Versailles.

Although the soldiers treat Jan kindly, he gradually realizes that war is a gigantic lie that begins with deception through language. "Going into the field" does not mean farming but preparing to kill, and "uniforms" do not mean equality but signify rank and status. Finally he realizes that words such as peace, freedom, and fatherland mean to the Europeans what the skull of Mkwawa means to the Africans. (It is clear why the original title of the book was "The Skull of Sultan Mkwawa.") Jan distinguishes himself through his service, and the Germans decide to make him a citizen. They also plan to use him as propaganda, like a German Joan of Arc, to pump up the spirits of their sagging troops. On the day Jan is to be honored, he realizes he is to become sort of "a skull of Mkwawa," glorifying war and trying to make sense out of senseless shallow deeds. He does not come forth for the honor; instead, he disappears forever with his dog.

The Wave (A) by Morton Rhue is based on a true incident that occurred in a high school history class in Palo Alto, California, in 1969. The incident was so terrifying that for three years afterward no one talked about it. *The Wave* recreates one of the most frightening events ever experienced in a classroom, a situation that grew out of hand. The story describes how Ben Ross, the history teacher, shows a film about Adolph Hitler, trying to help his students understand how the Nazis came to power in Germany and how the world stood by silently to allow them to kill 11 million people. When his students ask questions he cannot answer and his explanations seem unconvincing, he proposes an experiment in which he tries to re-create what life might have been like in Nazi Germany.

Ross starts the experiment by probing the meaning and the power of "Strength Through Discipline" by involving students in highly formalized procedures for classroom conduct. When they respond positively and choose to maintain the highly structured procedures on their own initiative, Ross shows them that they have become a community, developing a bond between people who work and struggle together for a common goal. The experiment continues to grow as Ross chooses a symbol for their community, a circle with the outline of a wave inside it. Since a wave is a pattern of change; it has movement, direction, and impact. Ross tells his students, "From now on,

TEACHING IDEA

LIVING TOGETHER IN A WORLD OF PEACE[73]   Read aloud one of the books from each category in the web. Ask students to write in their journals and reflect on what the books mean to them. Discuss in small groups some of the shared meanings before choosing from the projects below.

Strategies to Use When Talking About Peace

Discuss war toys; have students write to major toy manufacturers expressing their feelings about war toys.

Learn about the goals and work of the United Nations: take a class trip, write for informational material, collect for UNICEF.

Plan a day devoted to peace; put on plays, dances, sing songs, write poems, read books about peace.

Call a radio station and ask a disc jockey to play an hour of peace songs (or more, if possible).

Subscribe to peace letters and magazines; display them in the classroom.

Learn about the work of peace organizations. For example:

Children's Campaign for Nuclear Disarmament
R.D. 1, Box 550
Plainfield, Vt. 05667   (802) 454-7119
(This is a national organization for grade school children. It educates and activates young children against nuclear weapons.)

Educators for Social Responsibility
275 Riverside Drive, Room 207
New York, N.Y. 10025   (212) 666-0056
(This is a national organization of teachers and administrators. They work on peace curricula and assess educational materials on the arms race.)

Greenpeace, USA
2007 R Street, NW.
Washington, D.C. 20009   (202) 462-1177
(This is an international organization based on ecology. It has four main campaigns: wildlife conservation, ocean ecology, toxic waste, and disarmament.)

Become well informed about issues that relate to peace. Start a scrapbook of articles in the news related to peace.

Make a peace quilt. Children design the quilt and work on sections with embroidery, fabric crayons, or other techniques. Raffle the quilt off and donate profits to a peace charity.

Biography study. Read biographies of people of peace. Role-play an event in their lives that demonstrated their stand for peace.

Music. Sing anti-war songs and songs about ecology.

Write letters to the president, to the Soviet premier, and to your congressmen about concerns you have relating to peace.

Above all, work on peaceful means of living on a daily basis in the classroom—talking, not fighting; feeling compassion for other people; sharing. Role-play peaceful ways to solve problems.

Read aloud books on peace and have many available for students to read at their leisure.

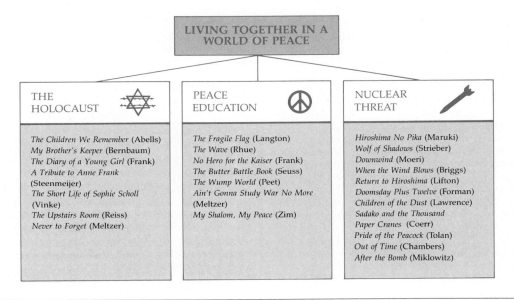

LIVING TOGETHER IN A WORLD OF PEACE

THE HOLOCAUST	PEACE EDUCATION	NUCLEAR THREAT
The Children We Remember (Abells) *My Brother's Keeper* (Bernbaum) *The Diary of a Young Girl* (Frank) *A Tribute to Anne Frank* (Steenmeijer) *The Short Life of Sophie Scholl* (Vinke) *The Upstairs Room* (Reiss) *Never to Forget* (Meltzer)	*The Fragile Flag* (Langton) *The Wave* (Rhue) *No Hero for the Kaiser* (Frank) *The Butter Battle Book* (Seuss) *The Wump World* (Peet) *Ain't Gonna Study War No More* (Meltzer) *My Shalom, My Peace* (Zim)	*Hiroshima No Pika* (Maruki) *Wolf of Shadows* (Strieber) *Downwind* (Moeri) *When the Wind Blows* (Briggs) *Return to Hiroshima* (Lifton) *Doomsday Plus Twelve* (Forman) *Children of the Dust* (Lawrence) *Sadako and the Thousand Paper Cranes* (Coerr) *Pride of the Peacock* (Tolan) *Out of Time* (Chambers) *After the Bomb* (Miklowitz)

our community, our movement will be known as The Wave."

Ross's students respond even more enthusiastically about belonging to a special group and begin to exercise their power among their peers, especially when a third command, "Action," is added to their charges. The spirited response by the students leads to some questionable uses of their power and, even more pernicious, Ross begins to enjoy the control he exercises. Finally, in a dramatic ending, Ross again shows the film about Adolph Hitler and helps his students see that they behaved as the young people in Germany behaved. Ross says to them,

If history repeats itself, you will all want to deny what happened to you in The Wave. But, if our experiment has been successful—and I think you can see that it has—you will have learned that we are all responsible for our own actions, and that you must always question what you do rather than blindly follow a leader, and that for the rest of your lives, you will never, ever allow a group's will to usurp your individual rights.[74]

The Wave is a chilling account, showing that the unspeakable tragedies of Nazism could happen again unless we have the courage to question and stand up for human rights.

RECOMMENDED READING

Asian-Americans

Bang, Molly Garrett. *Tye May and the Magic Brush.* New York: Greenwillow, 1981.

Clark, Ann Nolan. *To Stand Against the Wind.* New York: Viking, 1978.

Cox, David. *Ayu and the Perfect Moon.* London: Bodley Head, 1984.

Demi. *A Chinese Zoo: Fables and Proverbs.* San Diego, Harcourt Brace Jovanovich, 1987.

————. *Dragon Kites and Dragonflies: A Collection of Chinese Nursery Rhymes.* San Diego: Harcourt Brace Jovanovich, 1986.

Friedman, Ina R. *How My Parents Learned to Eat.* Illustrated by Allen Say. Boston: Houghton Mifflin, 1984.

Greaves, Margaret. *Once There Were No Pandas: A Chinese Legend.* Illustrated by Beverly Gooding. New York: Dutton, 1985.

Ishii, Momoko. *The Tongue-Cut Sparrow.* Illustrated by Suekichi Akaba, translated by Katherine Paterson. New York: Lodestar, Dutton, 1987.

Lee, Jeannie M. *Ba' Nam.* New York: Holt, 1987.

————, retel. *Legend of the Li River: An Ancient Chinese Tale.* Boston: Holt, Rinehart & Winston, 1983.

Lewis, Richard, ed. *Miracles: Poems by Children of the English Speaking World.* New York: Simon & Shuster, 1984.

————. *There Are Two Lives: Poems By Children of Japan.* Translated by Haruna Kimura. New York: Simon & Schuster, 1970.

————. *The Way of Silence: The Prose and Poetry of Basho.* Photography by Helen Buttfield. New York: Dial, 1970.

Liyi, He, trans. *The Spring of the Butterflies and Other Folktales of China's Minority Peoples.* Edited by Neil Philip, illustrated by Pan Aiqing and Li Zhao. New York: Lothrop, Lee & Shepard, 1986.

McLean, Virginia. *Chasing the Moon to China.* Memphis, Tenn.: Redbird, 1987.

Myers, Walter Dean. *The Golden Serpent.* Illustrated by Alice and Martin Provensen. New York: Viking, 1980.

Namioka, Lensey. *Valley of the Broken Cherry Trees.* New York: Delacorte, 1980.

Wallace, Ian. *Chin Chiang and the Dragon's Dance.* New York: Atheneum, McElderry, 1984.

Williams, Jay. *Everyone Knows What a Dragon Looks Like.* Illustrated by Mercer Mayer. New York: Four Winds, 1976.

Wolkstein, Diane. *The Magic Wings: A Tale from China.* New York: Dutton, Unicorn, 1983.

————. *White Wave: A Chinese Tale.* Illustrated by Ed Young. New York: Crowell, 1979.

Yolen, Jane. *The Emperor and the Kite.* Illustrated by Ed Young. New York: Putnam's, 1988.

Black Americans

Aardema, Verna. *Bringing the Rain to Kapiti Plain: A Nandi Tale.* Illustrated by Beatriz Vidal. New York: Dial, 1981.

Adoff, Arnold. *Malcolm X.* New York: Crowell, 1970.

Bang, Molly Garrett. *Wiley and the Hairy Man.* New York: Macmillan, 1976.

Bess, Clayton. *Story for a Black Night.* Boston: Houghton Mifflin, 1982.

Bryan, Ashley. *The Cat's Purr.* New York: Atheneum, 1985.

Carew, Jan. *Children of the Sun.* Illustrated by Leo and Diane Dillon. Boston: Little, Brown, 1980.

Courlander, Harold. *The Crest and the Hide: And Other African Stories of Heroes, Chiefs, Bards, Hunters, Sorcerers, and Common People.* Illustrated by Monica Vachula. New York: Coward, McCann & Geoghegan, 1982.

Davis, Ossie. *Langston: A Play.* New York: Delacorte, 1982.

De Trevino, Elizabeth Borton. *I, Juan de Pareja.* New York: Farrar, Straus & Giroux, 1965.

Feelings, Muriel. *Jambo Means Hello: Swahili Alphabet Book.* Illustrated by Tom Feelings. New York: Dial, 1974.

————. *Moja Means One: Swahili Counting Book.* Illustrated by Tom Feelings. New York: Dial, 1971.

Flournoy, Valerie. *The Patchwork Quilt.* Illustrated by Jerry Pinkney. New York: Dial, 1985.

Giovanni, Nikki. *Ego-Tripping and Other Poems for Young People.* Illustrated by George Ford. Westport, Conn.: Lawrence Hill, 1974.

————. *Spin a Soft Black Song,* rev. ed. Illustrated by George Martins. New York: Hill & Wang, 1985.

————. *Vacation Time.* Illustrated by Marisabina Russo. New York: Morrow, 1981.

Greenfield, Eloise. *Daydreamers.* Illustrated by Tom Feelings. New York: Dial, 1985.

————. *Sister.* Illustrated by Moneta Barnett. New York: Harper & Row, 1987.

Grifalconi, Ann. *The Village of Round and Square Houses.* Boston: Little, Brown, 1986.

Hamilton, Virginia. *The Magical Adventures of Pretty Pearl.* New York: Harper & Row, 1983.

Harris, Joel Chandler. *The Complete Tales of Uncle Remus.* Compiled by Richard Chase, illustrated by Arthur Frost et al. Boston: Houghton Mifflin, 1955.

Haskins, James. *Black Music in*

America: A History Through its People. New York: Crowell, 1987.

Katz, William Loren. *Black Indians: A Hidden History*. New York: Atheneum, 1986.

Lewin, Hugh. *Jafta: The Town*. Illustrated by Lisa Kopper. New York: Carolrhoda, 1984.

McDermott, Gerald. *Anansi the Spider: A Tale from the Ashanti*. New York: H. Holt, 1972.

Meltzer, Milton, ed. *The Black Americans: A History in Their Own Words, 1619–1983*. New York: Crowell, 1984.

Musgrove, Margaret. *Ashanti to Zulu: African Traditions*. Illustrated by Leo and Diane Dillon. New York: Dial, 1976.

Myers, Walter Dean. *The Outside Shot*. New York: Delacorte, 1984.

Naidoo, Beverly. *Journey to Jo'Burg: A South African Story*. Illustrated by Eric Velasquez. Philadelphia: Lippincott, 1986.

Rees, Ennis. *Brer Rabbit and His Tricks*. Illustrated by Edward Gorey. Glenview, Ill.: Scott Foresman, 1967.

———. *More of Brer Rabbit's Tricks*. Illustrated by Edward Gorey. Glenview, Ill.: Scott, Foresman, 1968.

Rose, Ann. *Pot Full of Luck*. Illustrated by Margot Tomes. New York: Lothrop, Lee & Shepard, 1982.

Strickland, Dorothy S., ed. *Listen Children: An Anthology of Black Literature*. Foreward by Coretta Scott King, illustrated by Leo and Diane Dillon. New York: Bantam Books, 1982.

Taylor, Mildred D. *The Friendship*. Illustrated by Max Ginsburg. New York: Dial, 1987.

———. *Let the Circle Be Unbroken*. New York: Dial, 1981.

———. *Roll of Thunder, Hear My Cry*. Illustrated by Jerry Pinkney. New York: Dial, 1976.

———. *The Song of the Trees*. Illustrated by Jerry Pinkney, New York: Dial, 1975.

Walter, Mildred Pitts. *Brother to the Wind*. Illustrated by Leo and Diane Dillon. New York: Lothrop, Lee & Shepard, 1985.

———. *Justin and the Best Biscuits in the World*. New York: Lothrop, Lee & Shepard, 1986.

———. *Trouble's Child*. New York: Lothrop, Lee & Shepard, 1985.

———. *Ty's One Man Band*. Illustrated by Margot Tomes. New York: Four Winds, 1987.

Weik, Mary Hays. *The Jazz Man*. Illustrated by Ann Grifalconi. New York: Atheneum, 1966.

Yarbrough, Camille. *Cornrows*. Illustrated by Carole Bayard. New York: Coward, McCann & Geoghegan, 1979.

Yates, Elizabeth. *Amos Fortune: Free Man*. Illustrated by Nora S. Unwin. New York: Dutton, 1950.

Hispanic Americans

Aardema, Verna, trans. *The Riddle of the Drum: A Tale from Tizapan, Mexico*. Illustrated by Tony Chen. New York: Four Winds, 1979.

Belpre, Pura. *The Dance of the Animals: A Puerto Rican Folk Tale*. Illustrated by Paul Galdone. New York: Warne, 1972.

———. *Once in Puerto Rico*. Illustrated by Christine Price. New York: Warne, 1973.

Bierhorst, John, ed. *Black Rainbow: Legends of the Incas and Myths of Peru*. New York: Farrar, Straus & Giroux, 1976.

———. *The Hungry Woman: Myths and Legends of the Aztecs*. New York: Morrow, 1984.

———. *The Monkey's Haircut and Other Stories Told by the Maya*. Illustrated by Robert Andrew Parker. New York: Morrow, 1986.

———. *Spirit Child: A Story of the Nativity*. Illustrated by Barbara Cooney. New York: Morrow, 1984.

Clark, Ann Nolan. *Paco's Miracle*. Illustrated by Agnes Tait. New York: Farrar, Straus & Giroux, 1962.

———. *Year Walk*. New York: Viking, 1975.

De Messieres, Nicole. *Reina the Galgo*. New York: Dutton, 1981.

Dewey, Ariane. *The Thunder God's Son: A Peruvian Folktale*. New York: Greenwillow, 1981.

Erdoes, Richard, and Alfonso Ortiz, eds. *American Indian Myths and Legends*. New York: Pantheon, 1984.

Ets, Marie Hall, and Aurora Labastida. *Nine Days to Christmas: A Story of Mexico*. New York: Viking, 1959.

Gemming, Elizabeth. *Lost City in the Clouds: The Discovery of Machu Picchu*. Illustrated by Mike Eagle. New York: Putnam's, 1980.

Griego y Miestas, José, and Rudolfo A. Anaya. *Cuentos: Tales from the Hispanic Southwest*. Illustrated by Jaime Valdez. Santa Fe, NM.: Museum of New Mexico, 1980.

Hall, Lynn. *Danza!* New York: Scribner's, 1981.

Hinojosa, Francisco, ed. *The Old Lady Who Ate People*. Illustrated by Leonel Maciel. Boston: Little, Brown, 1984.

Jagendorf, M.A., and R.S. Boggs. *The King of the Mountains: A Treasury of Latin American Folk Stories*. New York: Vanguard, 1960.

Krumgold, Joseph. *. . . And Now Miguel*. Illustrated by Jean Charlot. New York: Crowell, 1953.

Kurtycz, Marcos, and Ana Garcia Kobeh. *Tigers and Opossums: Animal Legends*. Boston: Little, Brown, 1984.

Mangurian, David. *Children of the Incas*. New York: Macmillan, 1979.

Meyer, Carolyn, and Charles Gallenkamp. *The Mystery of the Ancient Maya*. New York: Atheneum, 1985.

Millard, Anne. *The Incas*. Illustrated by Richard Hook. New York: Warwick, 1980.

O'Dell, Scott. *Carlota*. Boston: Houghton Mifflin, 1981.

Perl, Lila, and Alma Flor Ada. *Piñatas and Paper Flowers/Piñatas y flores de papel: Holidays of the Americas in English and Spanish.* New York: Clarion, 1983.

Politi, Leo. *Lito and the Clown.* New York: Scribner's, 1964.

———. *Pedro, the Angel of Olvera Street.* New York: Scribner's 1946.

———. *Song of the Swallows.* New York: Scribner's, 1949.

Singer, Julia. *We All Came from Puerto Rico.* New York: Atheneum, 1977.

Stein, Conrad R. *Enchantment of the World: Mexico.* Chicago: Childrens Press, 1984.

Jewish Americans

Aranow, Sara. *Seven Days of Creation: Bible Stories in Rhyme.* Brooklyn, N.Y: Hermon, 1985.

Hirsh, Marilyn. *Could Anything Be Worse? A Yiddish Tale.* New York: Holiday House, 1974.

———. *Joseph Who Loved the Sabbath.* Illustrated by Devis Grebu. New York: Viking, 1986.

Kimmel, Eric A. *The Chanukkah Tree.* Illustrated by Giora Carmi. New York: Holiday House, 1988.

Lasky, Kathryn. *Pageant.* New York: Four Winds, 1986.

Lepon, Shoshana. *Ten Tests of Abraham.* New York: Judaica Press, 1986.

Levitin, Sonia. *Journey to America.* Illustrated by Charles Robinson. New York: Atheneum, 1970.

Mani-Leib. *Tsingl Yingl Khvat.* Translated by Jerry Shandler, illustrated by El Lissitzky. Mt. Kisco, N.Y.: Moyer Bell, 1987.

Sendak, Philip. *In Grandpa's House.* Translated by Seymour Barofsky, illustrated by Maurice Sendak. New York: Harper & Row, 1985.

Warshawski, M. *Oif'n Pripichek/On the Little Hearth.* Illustrated by Gabriel Lisowski. New York: Holt, Rinehart & Winston, 1987.

Zemach, Margot. *It Could Always Be Worse.* New York: Farrar, Straus & Giroux, 1976.

Native Americans

Aliki. *Corn is Maize: The Gift of the Indians.* New York: Crowell, 1976.

Amon, Aline. *The Earth is Sore: Native Americans on Nature.* New York: Atheneum, 1981.

Ashabranner, Brent. *To Live in Two Worlds: American Indian Youth Today.* Photography by Paul Conklin. New York: Dodd, Mead, 1984.

———. *Morning Star, Black Sun: The Northern Cheyenne Indians and America's Energy Crisis.* Photography by Paul Conklin. New York: Dodd, Mead, 1982.

Baker, Betty. *And Me, Coyote!* Illustrated by Maria Horvath. New York: Macmillan, 1982.

———. *Rat is Dead and Ant is Sad.* Illustrated by Mamoru Funai. New York: Harper & Row, 1981.

Baylor, Byrd. *The Desert is Theirs.* Illustrated by Peter Parnall. New York: Scribner's, 1975.

———. *God on Every Mountain.* Illustrated by Carol Brown. New York: Scribner's, 1981.

———. *Hawk, I'm Your Brother.* Illustrated by Peter Parnall. New York: Scribner's, 1976.

———. *Moonsong.* Illustrated by Ronald Himler. New York: Scribner's, 1982.

———. *They Put on Masks.* Illustrated by Jerry Ingram. New York: Scribner's, 1974.

Bierhorst, John, ed. *Songs of the Chippewa.* Illustrated by Joe Servello. New York: Farrar, Straus & Giroux, 1974.

Belting, Natalie. *Our Fathers Had Powerful Songs.* New York: Dutton, 1974.

Brown, Marion Marsh. *Homeward the Arrow's Flight.* Nashville: Abingdon, 1980.

Bulla, Clyde Robert. *Squanto: Friend of the Pilgrims.* Illustrated by Peter Burchard. Harper & Row, 1954.

———, and Michael Syson. *Conquista!* Illustrated by Ronald Himler. New York: Crowell, 1978.

Cleaver, Elizabeth. *The Fire Stealer.* New York: Oxford University Press, 1979.

Coatsworth, Emerson, and David Coatsworth, comps. *The Adventures of Nanabush: Ojibway Indian Stories.* Illustrated by Francis Kagige. New York: Atheneum, 1980.

Curry, Jane Louise, retel. *Back in the Beforetime: Tales of the California Indians.* Illustrated by James Watts. New York: Atheneum, McElderry, 1987.

D'Aulaire, Ingri, and Edwar Parin. *Pocahontas.* New York: Doubleday, 1949.

De Leeuw, Adele. *Maria Tallchief: American Ballerina.* Champaign, Ill.: Garrard, 1971.

Eastman, Charles A. *Indian Boyhood.* Illustrated by E. L. Blumenschein. 1902. Reprint. Williamstown, Mass.: Corner House, 1975.

Erdoes, Richard, ed. *The Sound of Flutes and Other Indian Legends.* Illustrated by Paul Goble. New York: Pantheon, 1976.

Fall, Thomas. *Jim Thorpe.* Illustrated by John Gretzer. New York: Crowell, 1970.

George, Jean Craighead. *The Talking Earth.* New York: Harper & Row, 1983.

Grant, Matthew G. *Squanto: The Indian Who Saved the Pilgrims.* Illustrated by John Nelson and Harold Henriksen. Philadelphia: Publications Associates, 1974.

Grinnell, George Bird. *The Whistling Skeleton: American Indian Tales of the Supernatural.* Edited by John Bierhorst, illustrated by Robert Andrew Parker. New York: Four Winds, 1982.

Haseley, Dennis. *The Sacred One.* Illustrated by Deborah Howland. New York: Warne, 1983.

Highwater, Jamake. *Anpao: An*

American Indian Odyssey. Illustrated by Fritz Scholder. Philadelphia: Lippincott, 1977.

———. *The Ceremony of Innocence.* New York: Harper & Row, 1985.

———. *I Wear the Morning Star.* New York: Harper & Row, 1986.

———. *Legend Days.* New York: Harper & Row, 1984.

Hodges, Margaret. *The Fire Bringer: A Paiute Indian Legend.* Illustrated by Peter Parnall. Boston: Little, Brown, 1972.

Marrin, Albert. *War Clouds in the West: Indians and Cavalrymen, 1860–1890.* New York: Atheneum, 1984.

Miles, Miska. *Annie and the Old One.* Illustrated by Peter Parnall. Boston: Little, Brown, 1971.

Mowat, Farley. *Lost in the Barrens.* Illustrated by Charles Greer. Toronto: McClelland & Stewart, 1984.

O'Dell, Scott. *Streams to the River, River to the Sea: A Novel of Sacagawea.* Boston: Houghton Mifflin, 1986.

Paige, Harry O. *Johnny Stands: The Story of a Sioux Indian.* New York: Warne, 1982.

Robinson, Gail. *Raven the Trickster: Legends of the North American Indians.* Illustrated by Joanna Troughton. New York: Atheneum, 1982.

Schweitzer, Byrd Baylor. *One Small Blue Bead.* Illustrated by Symeon Shimin. New York: Macmillan, 1965.

Seeger, Pete. *Abiyoyo.* Illustrated by Michael Hays. New York: Macmillan, 1986.

Sneve, Virginia Driving Hawk. *High Elk's Treasure.* Illustrated by Oren Lyons. New York: Holiday House, 1972.

———. *Jimmy Yellow Hawk.* Illustrated by Oren Lyons. New York: Holiday House, 1972.

———. *When Thunder Spoke.* New York: Holiday House, 1974.

Speare, Elizabeth George. *The Sign of the Beaver.* Boston: Houghton Mifflin, 1983.

Tobias, Tobi. *Maria Tallchief.* Illustrated by Michael Hampshire. New York: Crowell, 1970.

Toye, William. *The Loon's Necklace.* Illustrated by Elizabeth Cleaver. New York: Oxford University Press, 1977.

Living Together in a World of Peace

Armstrong, Louise. *How to Turn War into Peace.* New York: Harcourt Brace Jovanovich, 1979.

Chaikin, Miriam. *A Nightmare in History: The Holocaust 1933–1945.* New York: Clarion, 1987.

Cheney, Glenn Alan. *Mohandas Gandhi.* New York: Watts, 1983.

Cooney, Robert, and Helen Michalowski, eds. *The Power of the People.* Philadelphia: New Society Publishers, 1987.

Finkelstein, Norman H. *Remember Not to Forget: A Memory of the Holocaust.* Illustrated by Lois and Lars Hokanson. New York: Watts, 1985.

Fitzgerald, Merni. *The Peace Corps Today.* New York: Dodd, Mead, 1986.

Gay, Kathlyn. *Changing Families: Meeting Today's Challenges.* Hillside, N.J.: Enslow, 1987.

Georgiou, Constantine. *Rani, Queen of the Jungle.* Englewood Cliffs, N.J.: Prentice-Hall, 1971.

Gerstein, Mordicai. *The Mountains of Tibet.* New York: Harper & Row, 1987.

Giff, Patricia Reilly. *Mother Teresa: Sister to the Poor.* Illustrated by Ted Lewin. New York: Viking, 1986.

Hirsh, Marilyn. *Leela and the Watermelon.* New York: Crown, 1974.

International Physicians for the Prevention of Nuclear War. *Peace: A Dream Unfolding.* San Francisco: Sierra Club Books, 1987.

Larsen, Peter. *The United Nations at Work Throughout the World.* New York: Lothrop, Lee & Shepard, 1971.

Lobel, Anita. *Potatoes, Potatoes.* New York: Harper & Row, 1967.

Pringle, Laurence P. *Nuclear War: From Hiroshima to Nuclear Winter.* Hillside, N.J.: Enslow, 1985.

Romanova, Natalia. *Once There Was a Tree.* Illustrated by Gennady Spirin. New York: Dial, 1985.

Smith, Samantha. *Journey to the Soviet Union.* Boston: Little, Brown, 1985.

Sweeney, Duane. *The Peace Catalog.* Seattle: Press for Peace, 1984.

Zim, Jacob, ed. *My Shalom, My Peace.* New York: McGraw-Hill, 1974.

PROFESSIONAL REFERENCES

Allen, Adela Artola, ed. *Library Services for Hispanic Children: A Guide for Public and School Librarians.* Phoenix: Oryx Press, 1987.

Beilke, Patricia, and Frank J. Sciara. *Selecting Materials for and About Hispanic and East Asian Children and Young People.* Hamden, Conn.: The Shoe String Press, Library Professional Publication, 1986.

Bishop, Rudine Sims. "Extending Multicultural Understanding Through Children's Books," in *Children's Literature in the Reading Program.* Edited by Bernice E. Cullinan. Newark, Del.: International Reading Association, 1987: 60–67.

———. "Profile: Lucille Clifton." *Language Arts* 59, no. 2 (February 1982): 160–67.

———. *Shadow and Substance: Afro-American Experience in Contemporary Children's Fiction.* Urbana, Ill.: National Council of Teachers of English, 1982.

Burns, Allan F. "Mexican Myths and Stories as Children's Literature." In *Children's Literature*, Vol. 15. *Annual of the Modern Language Association Division on Children's Literature and the Children's Literature Association.* New Haven, Conn.: Yale University Press, 1987.

Carlson, Ruth Kearney. *Emerging Humanity: Multi-Ethnic Literature for Children and Adolescents.* Dubuque, Iowa: Brown, 1972.

Council on Interracial Books for Children (CIBC). *Human (and Anti-Human) Values in Children's Books.* New York Council on Interracial Books for Children, 1976.

Davis, Enid. *A Comprehensive Guide to Children's Literature with a Jewish Theme.* New York: Schocken, 1981.

Elleman, Barbara, ed. *Children's Books of International Interest*, 3rd. ed. Chicago: American Library Association, 1984.

Hurlimann, Bettina. *Three Centuries of Children's Books in Europe.* New York: Oxford University Press, 1967.

Larrick, Nancy. "The All-White World of Children's Books." *Saturday Review* (September 11, 1965): 63–65.

Monson, Dianne L., ed. *Adventuring with Books: A Booklist for Pre-K—Grade 6.* Urbana, Ill.: National Council of Teachers of English, 1985.

Posner, Marcia. "The Broad Range of Jewish Children's Books." *A. B. Bookman's Weekly* 79, no. 12 (March 23, 1987): 1225–33.

———. *Jewish Children's Books: How to Choose Them, How to Use Them.* New York: Haddassah, Department of Jewish Education, 1986.

———, comp. *Selected Jewish Children's Books.* New York: JWB Jewish Book Council, 1984.

Rollock, Barbara, ed. *The Black Experience in Children's Books.* New York: New York Public Library, 1984.

———. *Black Authors and Illustrators of Children's Books: A Biographical Dictionary.* New York: Garland Press, 1988.

NOTES

1. Diana Chang, "Saying Yes," from *Asian-American Heritage: An Anthology of Prose and Poetry,* ed. David Hsin-Fu Wand (New York: Washington Square Press, 1974).

2. Rudine Sims Bishop, "Extending Multicultural Understanding Through Children's Books," in *Children's Literature in the Reading Program,* ed. Bernice E. Cullinan (Newark, Del.: International Reading Association, 1987), 60–67.

3. Ruth Kearney Carlson, *Emerging Humanity: Multi-Ethnic Literature for Children and Adolescents* (Dubuque, Iowa: Brown, 1972).

4. Leslie Edmonds, "The Treatment of Race in Picture Books for Young Children," *Book Research Quarterly* 2, no. 3 (Fall 1986): 30–41.

5. Quoted by Caroline M. Hewins, "The History of Children's Books (1888)," in *Children and Literature: Views and Reviews,* ed. Virginia Haviland (Glenview, Ill.: Scott, Foresman, 1973), 30–32.

6. Paul Hazard, *Books, Children and Men,* trans. Marguerite Mitchell (Boston: Horn Book, 1967), 146.

7. Elaine M. Aoki, "Are You Chinese? Are You Japanese? Or Are You Just a Mixed-up Kid?" *The Reading Teacher* 34, no. 4 (January 1981): 382–85.

8. Yoshiko Uchida, *The Two Foolish Cats,* illus. Margot Zemach (New York: Atheneum, McElderry, 1987), unpaged.

9. Sumiko Yagawa, *The Crane Wife,* trans. Katherine Paterson, illus. Suekichi Akaba (New York: Morrow, 1981), unpaged.

10. Harry Behn, trans., *Cricket Songs: A Japanese Haiku* (New York: Harcourt Brace Jovanovich, 1964), unpaged, and *More Cricket Songs: Japanese Haiku* (New York: Harcourt Brace Jovanovich, 1971), unpaged.

11. Issa, Yayu, Kikaku et al., eds., *Don't Tell the Scarecrow: And Other Japanese Poems,* illus. Talivaldis Stubis (New York: Four Winds, 1969), unpaged.

12. Richard Lewis, ed., *In a Spring Garden,* illus. Ezra Jack Keats (New York: Dial, 1965), unpaged.

13. Virginia Olsen Baron, ed., *Sunset in a Spider Web: Sijo Poetry of Ancient Korea* (New York: Holt, Rinehart & Winston, 1974), unpaged.

14. Yoshiko Uchida, *A Jar of Dreams* (New York: Atheneum, McElderry, 1982), 51–52.

15. Quotations taken from author's interview with Yoshiko Uchida (September 25, 1985).

16. Uchida, *A Jar of Dreams,* 41.

17. Quotations taken from author's interview with Yoshiko Uchida (September 25, 1985).

18. Ibid.

19. Rhoda Blumberg, *Commodore Perry in the Land of the Shogun* (New York: Lothrop, Lee & Shepard, 1985), 13.

20. Milton Meltzer, *The Chinese Americans* (New York: Crowell, 1980), 2.

21. Daniel S. Davis, *Behind Barbed Wire: The Imprisonment of Japanese Americans During World War II* (New York: Dutton,

1982), 140.

22. Quang Nhuong Huynh, *The Land I Lost: The Adventures of a Boy in Vietnam* (New York: Harper & Row, 1982), xi.

23. Activity developed by Domenica Mazzochi, teacher, New York City Public School System.

24. Huynh, *Land I Lost,* 127.

25. Rudine Sims Bishop, "Children's Books About Blacks: A Mid-Eighties Status Report," *Children's Literature Review,* 8 (Detroit: Gale Research, 1985): 9–14.

26. Verna Aardema, *Bringing the Rain to Kapiti Plain,* illus. Beatriz Vidal (New York: Dial, 1981), unpaged.

27. Ashley Bryan, *Beat the Story Drum, Pum-Pum* (New York: Atheneum, 1980), 10.

28. Virginia Hamilton, *The People Could Fly,* illus. Leo and Diane Dillon (New York: Knopf, 1985), ix.

29. Ibid., 159.

30. Rudine Sims Bishop, "Profile: Lucille Clifton," *Language Arts* 59, no. 2 (February 1982): 160–67, 163.

31. Eloise Greenfield, *Honey I Love and Other Love Poems,* illus. Leo and Diane Dillon (New York: Viking, 1972), unpaged.

32. Arnold Adoff, *Black Is Brown Is Tan,* illus. Emily McCully (New York: Harper & Row, 1973), 4.

33. Lucille Clifton, *My Brother Fine with Me,* illus. Moneta Barnett (New York: Holt, Rinehart & Winston, 1975), unpaged.

34. Rudine Sims Bishop, *Shadow and Substance: Afro-American Experience in Contemporary Children's Fiction* (Urbana, Ill.: National Council of Teachers of English, 1982), 83.

35. Eloise Greenfield and Lessie Jones Little, *Childtimes: A Three-Generation Memoir* (New York: Crowell, 1979), ix.

36. John Steptoe, *Stevie* (New York: Harper & Row, 1969), unpaged.

37. Teaching idea developed by Muriel Clarkston, Chicago Public Schools.

38. Julius Lester, *To Be a Slave,* illus. Tom Feelings (New York: Dial, 1968), 48–49.

39. James Haskins, *Black Music in America: A History Through Its People* (New York: Crowell, 1987), 1.

40. Milton Meltzer, *The Hispanic Americans,* photos. Morrie Camhi and Catherine Noren (New York: Crowell, 1982), 12.

41. Edmonds, "The Treatment of Race in Picture Books for Young Children," 30–41.

42. Gilda Baeza, "The Evolution of Educational and Public Library Services to Spanish-Speaking Children," *Library Services for Hispanic Children,* ed. Adela Artola Allen (Phoenix: Oryx Press, 1987), 3–11.

43. Toni de Gerez, ad., "My Song," *My Song is a Piece of Jade: Poems of Ancient Mexico in English and Spanish,* illus. William Stark (Boston: Little, Brown, 1984), 6.

44. Nicholosa Mohr, *Felita,* illus. Ray Cruz (New York: Dial, 1979), 30–31, 35.

45. Meltzer, *The Hispanic Americans,* 81–82.

46. Elizabeth Borten de Trevino, *I, Juan de Pareja* (New York: Farrar, Straus & Giroux, 1965), 177.

47. Marcia Posner, "The Broad Range of Jewish Children's Books," in *A. B. Bookman's Weekly* 79, no. 12 (March 23, 1987): 1225–1233.

48. Marcia Posner, *Jewish Books: How to Choose Them, How to Use Them* (New York: Haddassah, Department of Jewish Education, 1986), 10.

49. Isaac Bashevis Singer, *Stories for Children* (New York: Farrar, Straus & Giroux, 1984), 173.

50. Laurie Colwin, "I. B. Singer, Storyteller," *The New York Times Book Review,* 7 (July 23, 1978): 1, 23.

51. Isaac Bashevis Singer, Farrar Straus & Giroux, promotional material, New York City.

52. Valerie Worth, "Holy Days," *Poems for Jewish Children,* ed. Myra Cohn Livingston, illus. Lloyd Bloom (New York: Holiday House, 1986), 5.

53. Carol Adler, "Havdalah," in ibid., p. 31.

54. Traditional from the Haggadah, in ibid., p. 18–20.

55. Marilyn Hirsh, *One Little Goat: A Passover Song* (New York: Holiday House, 1979), unpaged.

56. Barbara Cohen, *Molly's Pilgrim,* illus. Michael Deraney (New York: Lothrop, Lee & Shepard, 1983), unpaged.

57. Barbara Cohen, *Gooseberries to Oranges,* illus. Beverly Brodsky (New York: Lothrop, Lee & Shepard, 1982), unpaged.

58. Milton Meltzer, *World of Our Fathers: The Jews of Eastern Europe* (New York: Farrar, Straus & Giroux, 1974), 5–6.

59. Milton Meltzer, *Never to Forget: The Jews of the Holocaust* (New York: Harper & Row, 1976), xvi.

60. Adapted from an activity developed by Marcia Posner in *Jewish Children's Books,* 24.

61. Jamake Highwater, *Anpao: An American Indian Odyssey* (Philadelphia: Lippincott, 1977), 242.

62. Ibid., 239.

63. John Bierhorst, ed., *The Naked Bear: Folktales of the Iroquois,* illus. Dirk Zimmer (New York: Morrow, 1987), xiv.

64. Elizabeth Cleaver, *The Enchanted Caribou* (New York: Oxford University Press, 1985), unpaged.

65. Hettie Jones, sel., *The Trees Stand Shining,* illus. Robert Andrew Parker (New York:

Dial, 1971), unpaged.
66. Nancy Wood, *Many Winters,* illus. Frank Howell (New York: Doubleday, 1974), 78.
67. Activities adapted from those by Corie Adjmi, graduate student, New York University.
68. Daniel Poler, "The Desert," student at Friends Seminary, New York City. Contributed by teacher Linda Chu and stu-

dent teacher Inky Inkung.
69. Frances Wosmek, *A Brown Bird Singing* (New York: Lothrop, Lee & Shepard, 1986), 3–4, 119–20.
70. Manas, May 5, 1976.
71. Toshi Maruki, *Hiroshima No Pika* (New York: Lothrop, Lee & Shepard, 1980), unpaged.
72. Whitley Strieber, *Wolf of Shadows* (New York: Knopf, 1985), 3.

73. Developed by Lucy Rubin, teacher, P.S. 3, Manhattan, New York City Public Schools.
74. Morton Rhue, *The Wave: The Classroom Experiment That Went Too Far* (New York: Dell, 1981), 140.

CHILDREN'S BOOKS CITED

Asian-Americans

Baron, Virginia Olsen, ed. *Sunset in a Spider Web: Sijo Poetry of Ancient Korea.* Translated by Chung Seuk Park, illustrated by Minja Park Kim. New York: Holt, Rinehart & Winston, 1974.

Behn, Harry, trans. *Cricket Songs: Japanese Haiku.* New York: Harcourt Brace Jovanovich, 1964.

———. *More Cricket Songs: Japanese Haiku.* New York: Harcourt Brace Jovanovich, 1971.

Blumberg, Rhoda. *Commodore Perry in the Land of the Shogun.* New York: Lothrop, Lee & Shepard, 1985.

Chang, Diana. "Saying Yes." In *Asian-American Heritage: An Anthology of Prose and Poetry.* Edited by David Hsin-Fu Wand. New York: Washington Square Press, 1974.

Davis, Daniel S. *Behind Barbed Wire: The Imprisonment of Japanese Americans During World War II.* New York: Dutton, 1982.

DeJong, Meindert. *The House of Sixty Fathers.* Illustrated by Maurice Sendak. 1956. Reprint. New York: Harper & Row, 1987.

Fritz, Jean. *China Homecoming.* New York: Putnam's, 1985.

———. *Homesick: My Own Story.* Illustrated by Margot Tomes. New York: Putnam's, 1982.

Issa, Yayu, Kikaku et al., eds.

Don't Tell the Scarecrow: And Other Japanese Poems. Illustrated by Talivaldis Stubis. New York: Four Winds, 1969.

Lee, Jeanne M. *Toad Is the Uncle of Heaven: A Vietnamese Folk Tale.* New York: Holt, Rinehart & Winston, 1985.

Lewis, Richard, ed. *In a Spring Garden.* Illustrated by Ezra Jack Keats. New York: Dial, 1965.

Lord, Bette Bao. *In the Year of the Boar and Jackie Robinson.* Illustrated by Marc Simont. New York: Harper & Row, 1984.

Louie, Ai-Ling. *Yeh-Shen: A Cinderella Story from China.* Illustrated by Ed Young. New York: Philomel, 1982.

McHugh, Elisabet. *Karen and Vicki.* New York: Greenwillow, 1984.

———. *Karen's Sister.* New York: Greenwillow, 1983.

———. *Raising a Mother Isn't Easy.* New York: Greenwillow, 1983.

Meltzer, Milton. *The Chinese Americans.* New York: Crowell, 1980.

Mosel, Arlene. *The Funny Little Woman.* Illustrated by Blair Lent. New York: Dutton, 1972.

Nhuong Huynh, Quang. *The Land I Lost: Adventures of a Boy in Vietnam.* Illustrated by Vo-Dinh Mai. New York: Harper & Row, 1982.

Politi, Leo. *Moy Moy.* New York: Scribner's, 1960.

Sadler, Catherine Edwards. *Heav-

en's Reward: Fairy Tales from China.* Illustrated by Cheng Mung Yun. New York: Atheneum, 1985.

———. *Treasure Mountain: Folktales from Southern China.* Illustrated by Cheng Mung Yun. New York: Atheneum, 1982.

Tobias, Tobi. *Isamu Noguchi: The Life of a Sculptor.* New York: Crowell, 1973.

Uchida, Yoshiko. *The Best Bad Thing.* New York: Atheneum, McElderry, 1983.

———. *The Dancing Kettle and Other Japanese Folktales.* New York: Harcourt Brace, 1949.

———. *The Happiest Ending.* New York: Atheneum, McElderry, 1985.

———. *In-Between Miya.* Berkeley, Calif.: Creative Arts Books, 1967.

———. *A Jar of Dreams.* New York: Atheneum, McElderry, 1981.

———. *Journey Home.* New York: Atheneum, McElderry, 1978.

———. *Journey to Topaz.* Berkeley, Calif.: Creative Arts, 1985.

———. *The Magic Listening Cap: More Folktales from Japan.* New York: Harcourt Brace Jovanovich, 1965.

———. *Samurai of Gold Hill.* Berkeley, Calif.: Creative Arts, 1985.

———. *The Sea of Gold and Other Tales from Japan.* New York: Scribner's, 1965.

―――. *The Two Foolish Cats*. Illustrated by Margot Zemach. New York: Atheneum, McElderry, 1987.

Watkins, Yoko Kawashima. *So Far from the Bamboo Grove*. New York: Lothrop, Lee & Shepard, 1986.

Yagawa, Sumiko. *The Crane Wife*. Translated by Katherine Paterson, illustrated by Suekichi Akaba. New York: Morrow, 1981.

Yashima, Taro. *Crow Boy*. New York: Viking, 1955.

―――. *Momo's Kitten*. New York: Penguin, 1977.

―――. *Seashore Story*. New York: Viking, 1967.

―――. *Plenty to Watch*. New York: Viking, 1954.

―――. *Umbrella*. New York: Penguin, 1977.

―――. *Youngest One*. New York: Viking, 1962.

Yep, Laurence. *Child of the Owl*. New York: Harper & Row, 1977.

―――. *Dragonwings*. New York: Harper & Row, 1975.

―――. *Mountain Light*. New York: Harper & Row, 1985.

―――. *Sea Glass*. New York: Harper & Row, 1979.

―――. *The Serpent's Children*. New York: Harper & Row, 1984.

Black Americans

Aardema, Verna. *Bimwili and the Zimwi*. Illustrated by Susan Meddaugh. New York: Dial, 1985.

―――. *Bringing the Rain to Kapiti Plain*. Illustrated by Beatiz Vidal. New York: Dial, 1981.

―――. *Oh, Kojo! How Could You!* Illustrated by Marc Brown. New York: Dial, 1984.

―――. *The Vingananee and the Tree Toad*. Illustrated by Ellen Weiss. New York: Warne, 1983.

―――. *What's So Funny, Ketu? A Nuer Tale*. Illustrated by Marc Brown. New York: Dial, 1982.

―――. *Who's in Rabbit's House?* Illustrated by Leo and Diane Dillon. New York: Dial, 1977.

―――. *Why Mosquitoes Buzz in People's Ears*. Illustrated by Leo and Diane Dillon. New York: Dial, 1975.

Adoff, Arnold. *All the Colors of the Race*. Illustrated by John Steptoe. New York: Lothrop, Lee & Shepard, 1982.

―――. *Big Sister Tells Me That I'm Black*. New York: Holt, Rinehart & Winston, 1976.

―――. *Black Is Brown Is Tan*. New York: Harper & Row, 1973.

―――. *Black Out Loud*. Illustrated by Alvin Hollingsworth. New York: Macmillan, 1970.

―――. *Celebrations: A New Anthology of Black American Poetry*. Chicago: Follett, 1977.

―――. *I Am the Darker Brother*. New York: Macmillan, 1968.

―――. *Ma nDa La*. Illustrated by Emily McCully. New York: Harper & Row, 1971.

―――. *My Black Me*. New York: Dutton, 1974.

―――. *Outside/Inside Poems*. New York: Lothrop, Lee & Shepard, 1981.

―――. *The Poetry of Black America*. New York: Harper & Row, 1973.

―――. *Sports Pages*. Illustrated by Steve Kuzma. Philadelphia: Lippincott, 1986.

―――. *Today We Are Brother and Sister*. New York: Lothrop, Lee & Shepard, 1981.

Brooks, Gwendolyn. *Annie Allen*. New York: Harper & Row, 1949.

―――. *Bronzeville Boys and Girls*. Illustrated by Ronni Solbert. New York: Harper & Row, 1956.

Bryan, Ashley. *The Adventures of Aku*. New York: Atheneum, 1976.

―――. *Beat the Story Drum, Pum-Pum*. New York: Atheneum, 1980.

―――. *The Dancing Granny*. New York: Atheneum, 1977.

―――. *I'm Going to Sing: Black American Spirituals*. Vol. 2. New York: Atheneum, 1982.

―――. *Lion and the Ostrich Chicks*. New York: Atheneum, 1986.

―――. *The Ox of the Wonderful Horns and Other African Folktales*. New York: Atheneum, 1971.

―――. *Walk Together Children: Black American Spirituals*. Vol. 1. New York: Atheneum, 1974.

―――, ed. *I Greet the Dawn: Poems By Paul Laurence Dunbar*. New York: Atheneum, 1978.

Clark, Margaret G. *Benjamin Banneker: Astronomer and Scientist*. New York: Garrard, 1971.

Clifton, Lucille. *All Us Come Cross the Water*. Illustrated by John Steptoe. New York: Holt, Rinehart & Winston, 1973.

―――. *Amifika*. Illustrated by Thomas Di Grazia. New York: Dutton, 1977.

―――. *The Boy Who Didn't Believe in Spring*. Illustrated by Brinton Turkle. New York: Dutton, 1978.

―――. *Everett Anderson's Goodbye*. Illustrated by Ann Grifalconi. New York: Holt, Rinehart & Winston, 1983.

―――. *Good, Says Jerome*. Illustrated by Stephanie Douglas. New York: Dutton, 1973.

―――. *My Brother Fine with Me*. Illustrated by Moneta Barnett. New York: Holt, Rinehart & Winston, 1975.

―――. *My Friend Jacob*. Illustrated by Thomas Di Grazia. New York: Dutton, 1980.

―――. *Some of the Days of Everett Anderson*. Illustrated by Evaline Ness. New York: Holt, Rinehart & Winston, 1970.

―――. *The Times They Used to Be*. Illustrated by Susan Jeschke. New York: Holt, Rinehart & Winston, 1974.

Collier, James Lincoln. *Louis Armstrong: An American Success Story*. New York: Macmillan, 1985.

Cornell, Jean G. *Ralph Bunche: Champion of Peace*. New York:

Garrard, 1976.

Courlander, Harold, and George Herzog. *The Cow-Tail Switch and Other West African Stories*. Illustrated by Madye Lee Chastain. New York: Holt, Rinehart & Winston, 1986.

Fenderson, Lewis H. *Thurgood Marshall: Fighter for Justice*. New York: McGraw-Hill, 1969.

Greenfield, Eloise. *Africa Dream*. New York: Harper & Row, 1977.

———. *First Pink Light*. New York: Crowell, 1976.

———. *Honey I Love and Other Love Poems*. Illustrated by Leo and Diane Dillon. New York: Crowell, 1978.

———. *Mary McLeod Bethune*. New York: Crowell, 1977.

———. *Me and Neesie*. New York: Harper & Row, 1984.

———. *Paul Robeson*. New York: Crowell, 1975.

———. *Rosa Parks*. New York: Crowell, 1973.

———. *She Come Bringing Me That Little Baby Girl*. Philadelphia: Lippincott, 1974.

———, and Lessie Jones Little. *Childtimes: A Three Generation Memoir*. New York: Crowell, 1979.

Guy, Rosa. *Mother Crocodile*. Illustrated by John Steptoe. New York: Delacorte, 1981.

Haley, Gail. *A Story, A Story*. New York: Atheneum, 1970.

Hamilton, Virginia. *Arilla Sun Down*. New York: Greenwillow, 1976.

———. *Dustland*. New York: Greenwillow, 1980.

———. *The Gathering*. New York: Greenwillow, 1980.

———. *The House of Dies Drear*. New York: Macmillan, 1968.

———. *Junius Over Far*. New York: Harper & Row, 1985.

———. *Justice and Her Brothers*. New York: Greenwillow, 1978.

———. *A Little Love*. New York: Philomel, 1984.

———. *M. C. Higgins the Great*. New York: Macmillan, 1974.

———. *The Mystery of Drear House*. New York: Greenwillow, 1987.

———. *Paul Robeson: The Life and Times of a Free Black Man*. New York: Harper & Row, 1974.

———. *The People Could Fly: American Black Folktales*. Illustrated by Leo and Diane Dillon. New York: Knopf, 1985.

———. *The Planet of Junior Brown*. New York: Macmillan, 1971.

———. *Sweet Whispers, Brother Rush*. New York: Putnam's 1982.

———. *The Time-Ago Tales of Jahdu*. Illustrated by Nonny Hogrogian. New York: Macmillan, 1969.

———. *W. E. B. Dubois: A Biography*. New York: Crowell, 1972.

———. *Willie Bea and the Time the Martians Landed*. New York: Greenwillow, 1983.

———. *The Writings of W. E. B. Dubois*. New York: Crowell, 1975.

———. *Zeely*. New York: Macmillan, 1967.

Harris, Joel. *Jump: The Adventures of Brer Rabbit*. Edited by Van D. Parks and Malcolm Jones, illustrated by Barry Moser. San Diego: Harcourt Brace Jovanovich, 1986.

———. *Jump Again! More Adventures of Brer Rabbit*. Adapted and illustrated by Barry Moser. San Diego: Harcourt Brace Jovanovich, 1987.

Haskins, James. *Black Music in America: A History Through its People*. New York: Crowell, 1987.

———. *Black Theater in America*. New York: Crowell, 1982.

———. *Diana Ross: Star Supreme*. Illustrated by Jim Spence. New York: Viking, 1985.

———. *Diary of a Harlem Schoolteacher*. New York: Grove Press, 1969.

———. *Fighting Shirley Chisholm*. New York: Dial, 1975.

———. *From Lew Alcindor to Ka-reem Abdul-Jabbar*. New York: Lothrop, Lee & Shepard, 1979.

———. *Katherine Dunham*. New York: Putnam's, 1982.

———. *The Life and Death of Martin Luther King, Jr.* New York: Lothrop, Lee & Shepard, 1977.

———. *Street Gangs, Yesterday and Today*. New York: Hastings House, 1977.

———, and Kathleen Benson. *The Sixties Reader*. New York: Viking, 1986.

———. *Space Challenger: The Story of Guion Bluford*. Minneapolis: Carolrhoda, 1984.

Jaquith, Priscilla. *Bo Rabbit Smart For True: Folktales from the Gullah*. Illustrated by Ed Young. New York: Philomel, 1981.

Keats, Ezra Jack. *John Henry: An American Legend*. New York: Pantheon, 1965.

Lester, Julius. *Long Journey Home: Stories from Black History*. New York: Dial, 1972.

———. *The Tales of Uncle Remus: The Adventures of Brer Rabbit*. Illustrated by Jerry Pinkney. New York: Dial, 1987.

———. *To Be a Slave*. Illustrated by Tom Feelings. New York: Dial, 1968.

McDermott, Gerald. *Anansi the Spider: A Tale from the Ashanti*. New York: Holt, Rinehart & Winston, 1972.

McKissack, Patricia. *Paul Laurence Dunbar: A Poet to Remember*. Chicago: Children's Press, 1984.

Mathis, Sharon Bell. *The Hundred Penny Box*. New York: Viking, 1975.

Meltzer, Milton. *Mary McLeod Bethune: Voice of Black Hope*. Illustrated by Stephen Marchesi. New York: Viking, 1987.

Myers, Walter Dean. *Crystal*. New York: Viking, 1987.

———. *Fast Sam, Cool Clyde and Stuff*. New York: Viking, 1975.

———. *Hoops*. New York: Delacorte, 1981.

————. *It Ain't All for Nothin'*. New York: Avon, 1979.

————. *The Legend of Tarik*. New York: Scholastic, 1982.

————. *Motown and Didi*. New York: Viking, 1984.

————. *The Nicholas Factor*. New York: Viking, 1983.

————. *Won't Know Till I Get There*. New York: Viking, 1982.

————. *The Young Landlords*. New York: Viking, 1979.

Patterson, Lillie. *Frederick Douglass: Freedom Fighter*. New York: Garrard, 1965.

Steptoe, John. *Mufaro's Beautiful Daughters*. New York: Greenwillow, 1987.

————. *Stevie*. New York: Harper & Row, 1969.

Walker, Alice. *Langston Hughes, American Poet*. New York: Crowell, 1974.

Williams, Sylvia. *Leontyne Price: Opera Superstar*. Chicago: Childrens Press, 1984.

Yates, Elizabeth. *Amos Fortune: Free Man*. Illustrated by Nora S. Unwin. New York: Dutton, 1967.

Hispanic Americans

Aardema, Verna. *The Riddle of the Drum: A Tale from Tizapan, Mexico*. Illustrated by Tony Chen. New York: Four Winds, 1979.

Ancona, George. *Bananas: From Manolo to Margie*. New York: Clarion, 1982.

Belpre, Pura. *Once in Puerto Rico*. Illustrated by Christine Price. New York: Warne, 1973.

————. *The Rainbow-Colored Horse*. Illustrated by Antonio Martorell. New York: Warne, 1978.

————. *Santiago*. Illustrated by Symeon Shimin. New York: Warne, 1969.

Blackmore, Vivian, retel. *Why Corn Is Golden: Stories About Plants*. Illustrated by Susana Martinez-Ostos. Boston: Little, Brown, 1984.

Brenner, Barbara. *Mystery of the Plumed Serpent*. Illustrated by Blanche Sims. New York: Knopf, 1981.

Brown, Tricia. *Hello Amigos!* Photography by Fran Oritz. New York: Holt, Rinehart & Winston, 1986.

Cruz, Martel. *Yagua Days*. Illustrated by Jerry Pinkney. New York: Dial, 1987.

de Gerez, Toni, trans. *My Song Is a Piece of Jade: Poems of Ancient Mexico in English and Spanish*. Illustrated by William Stark. Boston: Little, Brown, 1984.

dePaola, Tomie. *The Lady of Guadalupe*. New York: Holiday House, 1980.

de Treviño, Elizabeth Borten. *I, Juan de Pareja*. New York: Farrar, Straus & Giroux, 1965.

————. *Juarez, Man of Law*. New York: Farrar, Straus & Giroux, 1974.

Griego, Margot C, et al. *Tortillitas Para Mama and Other Spanish Nursery Rhymes*. Illustrated by Barbara Cooney. New York: Holt, Rinehart & Winston, 1981.

Holguin, Jiminez, Emma Morales Puncel and Conchita Morales Puncel. *Para chiquitines*. New York: Bowker, 1969.

Meltzer, Milton. *The Hispanic Americans*. Photography by Morrie Camhi and Catherine Noren. New York: Crowell, 1982.

Mohr, Nicholasa. *Felita*. Illustrated by Ray Cruz. New York: Dial, 1979.

————. *Going Home*. New York: Dial, 1986.

Morrow, Elizabeth. *The Painted Pig*. New York: Knopf, 1930.

Politi, Leo. *The Nicest Gift*. New York: Scribner's, 1973.

Schon, Isabel, ed. *Doña Blanca and Other Hispanic Nursery Rhymes and Games*. Minneapolis: Denison, 1983.

Jewish Americans

Atkinson, Linda. *In Kindling Flame: The Story of Hannah Senesh, 1921–1944*. New York: Lothrop, Lee & Shepard, 1985.

Bober, Natalie. *Breaking Tradition: The Story of Louise Nevelson*. New York: Atheneum, 1984.

Burstein, Chaya. *The Jewish Kid's Catalog*. Philadelphia: Jewish Publication Society, 1983.

Chaikin, Miriam. *Ask Another Question: The Story and Meaning of Passover*. Illustrated by Marvin Friedman. New York: Clarion, 1985.

————. *Light Another Candle: The Story and Meaning of Hanukkah*. Illustrated by Demi. New York: Clarion, 1981.

————. *Make Noise, Make Merry: The Story and Meaning of Purim*. Illustrated by Demi. New York: Clarion, 1983.

————. *Shake a Palm Branch: The Story and Meaning of Sukkot*. Illustrated by Marvin Freidman. New York: Clarion, 1984.

————. *Sound the Shofar: The Story and Meaning of Rosh Hashanah*. Illustrated by Erika Weihs. New York: Clarion, 1986.

Clifford, Eth. *The Remembering Box*. Illustrated by Donna Diamond. Boston: Houghton Mifflin, 1985.

Cohen, Barbara. *Gooseberries to Oranges*. Illustrated by Beverly Brodsky. New York: Lothrop, Lee & Shepard, 1982.

————. *Molly's Pilgrim*. Illustrated by Michael J. Deraney. New York: Lothrop, Lee & Shepard, 1983.

Cowen, Ida, and Irene Gunther. *A Spy for Freedom: The Story of Sarah Aaronsohn*. New York: Dutton, Lodestar, 1985.

Drucker, Malka. *Celebrating Life: Jewish Rites of Passage*. New York: Holiday House, 1984.

Gross, David. *Justice Felix Frankfurter: A Justice for All the People*.

New York: Dutton, Lodestar, 1987.

Hirsh, Marilyn. *One Little Goat: A Passover Song.* New York: Holiday House, 1979.

Hurwitz, Johanna. *Once I Was a Plum Tree.* Illustrated by Ingrid Fetz. New York: Morrow, 1980.

. . . I Never Saw Another Butterfly: Children's Drawings and Poems from Terezin Concentration Camp 1942–1944. Translated by Lew Goldberg and Hana Volavkova. New York: Schocken Books, 1978.

Krantz, Hazel. *Daughter of My People: Henrietta Szold and Hadassah.* New York: Dutton, Lodestar, 1987.

Kresh, Paul. *An American Rhapsody: The Story of George Gershwin.* New York: Dutton, Lodestar, 1987.

———. *Isaac Bashevis Singer: The Story of a Storyteller.* New York: Dutton, Lodestar, 1984.

Kushner, Arlene. *Falasha No More: An Ethiopian Jewish Child Comes Home.* Illustrated by Amy Kalina. New York: Shapolsky Steimatzky, 1986.

Lasky, Kathryn. *The Night Journey.* Illustrated by Trina Schart Hyman. New York: Warne, 1981.

Levinson, Nancy Smiler. *I Lift My Lamp: Emma Lazarus and the Statue of Liberty.* New York: Dutton, Lodestar, 1985.

Levitin, Sonia. *The Return.* New York: Atheneum, 1987.

Livingston, Myra Cohn, ed. *Poems for Jewish Holidays.* Illustrated by Lloyd Bloom. New York: Holiday House, 1986.

Meltzer, Milton. *Never to Forget: The Jews of the Holocaust.* New York: Harper & Row, 1976.

———. *Remember the Days: A Short History of the Jewish American.* New York: Doubleday, 1974.

———. *Taking Root: Jewish Immigrants in America.* New York: Farrar, Straus & Giroux, 1976.

———. *World of Our Fathers: The Jews of Eastern Europe.* New York:

Farrar, Straus & Giroux, 1974.

———, ed. *The Jewish Americans: A History in Their Own Words, 1650–1950.* New York: Crowell, 1982.

Moskin, Marietta. *I Am Rosemarie.* New York: Day, 1972.

Orlev, Uri. *The Island on Bird Street.* Translated by Hillel Halkin. Houghton Mifflin, 1984.

Shamir, Ilana, and Shlomo Shavit. *The Young Reader's Encyclopedia of Jewish History.* New York: Viking, Kestrel, 1987.

Schur, Maxine. *Hannah Szenes—A Song of Light.* Philadelphia: Jewish Publication Society, 1985.

Schwartz, Amy. *Mrs. Moskowitz and the Sabbath Candlesticks.* Philadelphia: Jewish Publication Society, 1983.

Sherman, Eileen Bluestone. *Monday in Odessa.* Philadelphia: Jewish Publication Society, 1986.

Siegal, Aranka. *Grace in the Wilderness: After the Liberation, 1945–1948.* New York: Farrar, Straus & Giroux, 1985.

———. *Upon the Head of a Goat: A Childhood in Hungary, 1939–1944.* New York: Farrar, Straus & Giroux, 1981.

Singer, Isaac Bashevis. *A Crown of Feathers.* New York: Farrar, Straus, & Giroux, 1973.

———. *A Day of Pleasure: Stories of a Boy Growing up in Warsaw.* Photography by Roman Vishniac. New York: Farrar, Straus & Giroux, 1969.

———. *Naftali the Storyteller and His Horse, Sus, and Other Stories.* Illustrated by Margot Zemach. New York: Farrar, Straus & Giroux, 1976.

———. *Stories for Children.* New York: Farrar, Straus & Giroux, 1984.

———. *Zlateh the Goat and Other Stories.* Illustrated by Maurice Sendak. New York: Harper & Row, 1984.

Sussman, Susan. *There's No Such Thing as a Chanukah Bush, Sandy Goldstein.* Niles, Ill.: Whit-

man, 1983.

Native Americans

Baker, Betty. *Three Fools and a Horse.* Illustrated by Glen Rounds. New York: Macmillan, 1975.

Baker, Olaf. *Where the Buffaloes Begin.* Illustrated by Stephen Gammell. New York: Warne, 1981.

Baylor, Byrd. *And It Is Still That Way: Legends Told by Arizona Indian Children.* New York: Scribner's, 1976.

——— *Before You Came This Way.* Illustrated by Tom Bahti. New York: Dutton, 1969.

———. *The Other Way to Listen.* Illustrated by Peter Parnell. New York: Scribner's, 1978.

———. *When Clay Sings.* Illustrated by Tom Bahti. New York: Scribner's, 1972.

Belting, Natalia. *Whirlwind Is a Ghost Dancing.* Illustrated by Leo and Diane Dillon. New York: Dutton, 1974.

Bierhorst, John. *The Mythology of North America.* New York: Morrow, 1985.

———. *The Ring in the Prairie: A Shawnee Legend.* Illustrated by Leo and Diane Dillon. New York: Dial, 1970.

———, ed. *A Cry from the Earth: Music of the North American Indians.* New York: Four Winds, 1979.

———. *Doctor Coyote: A Native American Aesop's Fables.* Illustrated by Wendy Watson. New York: Macmillan, 1987.

———. *The Girl Who Married a Ghost and Other Tales from the North American Indian.* Photography by Edward Curtis. New York: Four Winds, 1977.

———. *In the Trail of the Wind: American Indian Poems and Ritual Orations.* New York: Farrar, Straus & Giroux, 1971.

———. *The Naked Bear: Folktales of the Iroquois.* Illustrated by Dirk Zimmer. New York: Morrow,

1987.

————. *The Sacred Path: Spells, Prayers and Power Songs of the American Indians*. New York: Morrow, 1983.

Clark, Ann Nolan. *In My Mother's House*. Illustrated by Velino Herrera. New York: Viking, 1969.

Cleaver, Elizabeth. *The Enchanted Caribou*. New York: Oxford University Press, 1985.

Courlander, Harold. *People of the Short Blue Corn: Tales and Legends of the Hopi Indians*. Illustrated by Enrico Arno. New York: Harcourt Brace Jovanovich, 1970.

dePaola, Tomie. *The Legend of the Bluebonnets*. New York: Putnam's, 1983.

Freedman, Russell. *Children of the Wild West*. New York: Clarion, 1983.

————. *Cowboys of the Wild West*. New York: Clarion, 1985.

————. *Indian Chiefs*. New York: Holiday House, 1987.

Fritz, Jean. *The Double Life of Pocahontas*. Illustrated by Ed Young. New York: Putnam's, 1983.

Goble, Paul. *Buffalo Woman*. New York: Bradbury, 1984.

————. *Death of the Iron Horse*. New York: Bradbury, 1987.

————. *The Gift of the Sacred Dog*. New York: Bradbury, 1980.

————. *The Girl Who Loved Wild Horses*. New York: Bradbury, 1978.

————. *The Great Race of the Birds and Animals*. New York: Bradbury, 1985.

————. *Star Boy*. New York: Bradbury, 1983.

Gorsline, Douglas. *North American Indians*. New York: Random House, 1978.

Harlan, Judith. *American Indians Today: Issues and Conflicts*. New York: Watts, 1987.

Harris, Christie. *Mouse Woman and the Vanished Princesses*. Illustrated by Douglas Tait. New York: Atheneum, 1976.

————. *Once More Upon a Totem*. Illustrated by Douglas Tait. New York: Atheneum, 1973.

————. *Once Upon a Totem*. Illustrated by John Frazer Mills. New York: Atheneum, 1963.

————. *Raven's Cry*. Illustrated by Bill Reid. New York: Atheneum, 1966.

————. *The Trouble with Princesses*. Illustrated by Douglas Tait. New York: Atheneum, 1980.

Highwater, Jamake. *Anpao: An American Indian Odyssey*. Illustrated by Fritz Scholder. Philadelphia: Lippincott, 1977.

Hirschfelder, Arlene. *Happily May I Walk: American Indians and Alaska Natives Today*. New York: Scribner's, 1986.

Houston, James. *Kiviok's Magic Journey*. New York: Atheneum, McElderry, 1973,

————. *Songs of the Dream People: Chants and Images from the Indians and Eskimos of North America*. New York: Atheneum, McElderry, 1972.

Jones, Hettie, ed. *The Trees Stand Shining: Poetry of the North American Indians*. Illustrated by Robert Andrew Parker. New York: Dial, 1971.

Kroeber, Theodora. *Ishi: Last of His Tribe*. Illustrated by Ruth Robbins. Boston: Parnassus, 1964.

Lewis, Richard. *I Breathe a New Song: Poems of the Eskimo*. Illustrated by Oonark. New York: Simon & Schuster, 1971.

Longfellow, Henry Wadsworth. *Hiawatha's Childhood*. Illustrated by Errol LeCain. New York: Farrar, Straus & Giroux, 1984.

McDermott, Gerald. *Arrow to the Sun: A Pueblo Indian Tale*. New York: Viking, 1974.

Monroe, Jean Guard, and Ray A. Williamson. *They Dance in the Sky: Native American Star Myths*. Illustrated by Edgar Stewart. Boston: Houghton Mifflin, 1987.

O'Dell, Scott. *Sing Down the Moon*. Boston: Houghton Mifflin, 1970.

Richter, Conrad. *A Country of Strangers*. New York: Knopf, 1966.

Siberell, Anne. *The Whale in the Sky*. New York: Dutton, 1982.

Sleator, William. *The Angry Moon*. Illustrated by Blair Lent. Boston: Little, Brown, 1970.

Steptoe, John. *The Story of Jumping Mouse*. New York: Lothrop, Lee & Shepard, 1984.

Tunis, Edwin. *Indians*, rev. ed. New York: Harper & Row, 1978.

Wheeler, M. J. *First Came the Indians*. Illustrated by James Houston. New York: Atheneum, McElderry, 1983.

Wood, Nancy. *Many Winters*. Illustrated by Frank Howell. New York: Doubleday, 1974.

Wosmek, Frances. *A Brown Bird Singing*. New York: Lothrop, Lee & Shepard, 1986.

Living Together in a World of Peace

Abells, Chana Byers. *The Children We Remember*. New York: Greenwillow, 1986.

Aliki. *Mummies Made in Egypt*. New York: Harper & Row, 1985.

Angelo, Valenti. *The Marble Fountain*. New York: Viking, 1951.

————. *Nino*. New York: Viking, 1938.

Bemelmans, Ludwig. *Madeline*. New York: Viking, 1939.

Bernbaum, Israel. *My Brother's Keeper: The Holocaust Through the Eyes of an Artist*. New York: Putnam's, 1985.

Beskow, Elsa. *Pelle's New Suit*. New York: Harper & Row, 1929.

Bishop, Claire. *A Present from Petro*. New York: Viking, 1961.

Briggs, Raymond. *When the Wind Blows*. New York: Schocken Books, 1982.

Carlson, Natalie Savage. *The Family Under the Bridge*. Illustrated by Garth Williams. New York: Harper & Row, 1958.

Chambers, Aidan, ed. *Out of Time*. New York: Harper & Row, 1985.

Coerr, Eleanor B. *Sadako and the Thousand Paper Cranes*. New York: Putnam's, 1977.

De Angeli, Marguerite. *Bright April*. New York: Doubleday, 1946.

DeJong, Meindert. *Wheel on the School*. Illustrated by Maurice Sendak. New York: Harper & Row, 1954.

Dodge, Mary Mapes. *Hans Brinker; or, The Silver Skates*. New York: Penguin, 1985.

Economakis, Olga. *Oasis of the Stars*. New York: Coward-McCann, 1965.

Forman, James D. *Doomsday Plus Twelve*. New York: Scribner's, 1984.

Fox, Paula. *Lily and the Lost Boy*. New York: Orchard Books, 1987.

Françoise. *Jeanne-Marie Counts Her Sheep*. New York: Scribner's, 1951.

Frank, Anne. *The Diary of a Young Girl*. New York: Doubleday, 1967.

Frank, Rudolf. *No Hero for the Kaiser*. Translated by Patricia Crampton, illustrated by Klaus Steffens. New York: Lothrop, Lee & Shepard, 1986.

Friedman, Ina. *How My Parents Learned to Eat*. Illustrated by Allen Say. Boston: Houghton Mifflin, 1984.

Garrett, Helen. *Angelo, the Naughty One*. Illustrated by Leo Politi. New York: Viking, 1944.

Green, Norma. *The Hole in the Dike*. Illustrated by Eric Carle. New York: Crowell, 1975.

Greenfield, Eloise, and Lessie Jones Little. *I Can Do It by Myself*. Illustrated by Carole Byard. New York: Crowell, 1978.

Hughes, Madeline. *Why Carlo Wore a Bonnet*. New York: Lothrop, Lee & Shepard, 1965.

Innocenti, Roberto. *Rose Blanche*. Mankato,Minn.: Creative Education, 1985.

Jackson, Jesse. *Call Me Charley*. Illustrated by Doris Spiegel. New York: Harper & Row, 1945.

Langton, Jane. *The Fragile Flag*. New York: Harper & Row, 1984.

Lawrence, Louise. *Children of the Dust*. New York: Harper & Row, 1985.

Lifton, Betty Jean. *Return to Hiroshima*. New York: Atheneum, 1970.

Lindgren, Astrid. *Pippi Longstocking*. New York: Penguin, 1977.

———. *The Tomten*. Illustrated by Harald Wiberg. New York: Coward-McCann, 1979.

McGraw, Eloise Jarvis. *Mara, Daughter of the Nile*. New York: Penguin, 1985.

Maruki, Toshi. *Hiroshima No Pika*. New York: Lothrop, Lee & Shepard, 1980.

Meltzer, Milton. *Ain't Gonna Study War No More: The Story of America's Peace Seekers*. New York: Harper & Row, 1985.

Miklowitz, Gloria D. *After the Bomb*. New York: Scholastic, 1985.

Moeri, Louise. *Downwind*. New York: Dutton, 1984.

O'Dell, Scott. *Alexandra*. Boston: Houghton Mifflin, 1984.

Peet, Bill. *The Wump World*. Boston: Houghton Mifflin, 1970.

Reiss, Johanna. *The Upstairs Room*. New York: Crowell, 1972.

Rhue, Morton. *The Wave: The Classroom Experiment That Went Too Far*. New York: Dell, 1981.

Schiller, Freidrich von. *William Tell*. Morristown, N.J.: Silver Burdett, 1984.

Schnabel, Ernest. *Anne Frank: A Portrait of Courage*. Translated by Richard and Clara Winston. New York: Harcourt Brace, 1958.

Seignobosc, Françoise. *Jean-Marie Counts Her Sheep*. New York: Scribner's, 1951.

Seuss, Dr. *The Butter Battle Book*. New York: Random House, 1984.

Spyri, Johanna. *Heidi*. Illustrated by Greta Elgaard. 1884. Reprint. New York: Macmillan, 1962.

Steenmeijer, Anna S., ed. *A Tribute to Anne Frank*. New York: Doubleday, 1971.

Strieber, Whitley. *Wolf of Shadows*. New York: Knopf, 1985.

Tolan, Stephanie, S. *Pride of the Peacock*. New York: Scribner's, 1985.

Vinke, Hermann. *The Short Life of Sophie Scholl*. New York: Harper & Row, 1984.

Von Schiller, Freidrich. *William Tell*. Morristown, N.J.: Silver, 1984.

Wyss, Johann. *Swiss Family Robinson*. New York: Penguin, 1986.

Yolen, Jane. *The Boy Who Had Wings*. New York: Crowell, 1974.

Zim, Jacob, ed. *My Shalom, My Peace*. New York: McGraw-Hill, 1974.

Zolotow, Charlotte. *A Week in Yani's World: Greece*. Photography by Donald Getsug. New York: Macmillan, 1969.

12

The History of Children's Literature

"Does the road wind up hill all the
   way?"
        "Yes, to the very end."
"Will the day's journey take the whole
   long day?"
        "From morn to night, my
           friend."[1]

C. G. Rosetti

osetti's poem suggests images of a long journey that could be applied to the study of children's literature. The more we learn, it seems, the more there is to learn. If we read from "morn to night," we find still more new books and old books that invite reading. The study of the history of children's literature is a long journey, one that deserves a book unto itself. It is not, however, an uphill journey. The pleasures found along the way reward the traveler in full measure.

A few hours spent in the children's section at a local bookstore or public library can bring home some of the considerable changes that have occurred in children's books since you were a child. More striking is the vast transformation that has taken place since the first children's books were published, nearly four centuries ago.

What can account for these tremendous changes? Primary among several factors is the way adults regard children. In some ancient and primal societies, there was a definite age—usually marked by a ceremony, a rite of passage—at which the child passed into adulthood. From our perspective, it seems that this often occurred quite early. Other societies viewed children as happy, unthinking creatures, not deserving of special consideration.

Historically, in our own society, children were regarded as miniature adults; little distinction was made between occupations and recreations for children and those for adults,

and no special learning materials were provided for children. However, children eventually came to be viewed as seeking, learning individuals, developmentally distinct from adults, with unique perceptions of the world and with different needs and abilities. Only then was there a demand for books that children could call their own.

Our society now recognizes childhood as a distinct and very special phase of life. Much time and effort are devoted to the education of children. Childhood and adolescence extend over a longer period than in any other culture, and most people have very definite ideas about what is suitable for children, both for their work and for their play.

Our society depends, and knows that it depends, on the success of the educational system. We have a formal plan of education, a concept of what it means to be educated, and an awareness of its importance. This is a time of scientific child study. The wide-ranging disciplines of psychology devote considerable attention to the problems of childhood; and the findings are transmitted to parents and teachers by the mass media and professional or popular literature. Recent emphasis upon the primacy of reading in cognitive development has provided the impetus for a continuing expansion of the realm of children's books.

The prevailing perception of childhood is itself a part of the social, ethical, philosophic, and aesthetic forces of the given time, all of which also leave their mark on children's books. Books do not exist in a vacuum; they are shaped by the world around them. Henry Steele Commager states it succinctly:

> We have in literature not only a continuous record of childhood, but a continuous record of society as a whole, and—what is more important—of the ideals and standards that society wishes to inculcate into each new generation.[2]

In early colonial days, when children were viewed as miniature adults, books for children were of a practical, religious nature. Later, as our young nation attempted to promote the merits of our democracy, children's books tended to focus on the glories of the nation. Gillian Avery points out that authors are surprisingly likely to dance to the tune of their age:

> The heroes of the children's story show the qualities that the elders of any given time have considered desirable, attractive, or interesting in the young. Sometimes they have wanted the obedient, diligent, miniature adult, sometimes the evangelical child, or perhaps they have had a penchant for sprightly mischief, or sought to inculcate self-knowledge and independence. The surprise lies not in the swings of fashion in the pattern child, but in the unanimity of opinion at any given time about his qualities.[3]

This should not be surprising, however, since authors write from the world in which they live—the world they know. How else could we account for the rash of books about national heroes during wars, or the increase in books about blacks during the Civil Rights movement, or those about liberated females since the rise of the women's movement? Although some authors may write about whatever is currently fashionable, lasting trends represent generally accepted customs of conduct. By depicting characters and circumstances that mirror society, authors leave for posterity pictures of the prevailing social codes that allow us to look into the world of their times.

Thus, in evaluating children's books of the past, we must be careful to remember the social climate in which they were written and should not assess them according to today's values and standards; rather, we must examine them in terms of the social milieu in which they grew. In light of the current feelings concerning racial equality, we can look at earlier literature for children and see that black characters were stereotyped and narrowly depicted. Similarly, female characters in children's books published prior to 1970 seldom have the broad range of roles characteristic of females today. Although we need to weigh these considerations when sharing books with children, literary judgments of books of the past cannot be made in the context of current social knowledge and attitudes.

THE COLONIAL PERIOD

Religious and Moral Instruction

To have a clear perspective on American children's literature of the colonial period, it is necessary to recall the literary and social conditions in Europe at that time. The Gutenberg Bible, the first book to be printed with movable type, appeared only about 200 years before the Pilgrims settled in New England in 1620. At that time, bookmaking was still a slow and costly process, and the Bible and other religious books were the chief products of the printer's craft. The English novel was not to appear for nearly 100 years after the Pilgrims landed and would not be a well-developed genre until the 1800s. Prior to that time, books for pleasure reading were virtually nonexistent; most books were meant to inform. Further, there were few distinctions between books for children and books for adults.

During the 1600s, people experienced literature largely as an oral tradition—through folk

---

THE COLONIAL PERIOD

1636 *Youth's Behavior*
1646 *Milk for Babes* (John Cotton)
1650
 1658 *Orbis sensualium pictus* (John Amos Comenius)
 1665 *All the Principal Nations of the World* (Henry Winstanly)
 1672 *A Token for Children* (James Janeway)
1675
 1678 *Pilgrim's Progress* (John Bunyan)
 1690 *The New England Primer* (Benjamin Harris)
1700
 1702 *A Token for the Children of New England* (Cotton Mather)
 1715 *Divine & Moral Songs for Children* (Isaac Watts)
1725
 1740 Chapbooks
 1744 *A Little Pretty Pocketbook* (John Newbery)
1750
 1765 *The Renowned History of Little Goody Two Shoes* (Oliver Goldsmith)
 1769 Battledores
 1783 *Webster's Blue-Backed Speller* (Noah Webster)

---

tales and fables, Bible stories, ballads, epics, romances, and the performances of wandering players and minstrels. Slight distinction was made between forms of recreation appropriate for adults and those for children. Books were scarce and relatively expensive and so were available primarily to a small, wealthy class of which few early colonists were members. In addition, living conditions were harsh for the general population, with everyone, including children, working long hours. During the dark winter months, even light to read by was a luxury.

The values held by the colonists reflected their desire to be obedient to the will of God and to cast off the wages of original sin in order to redeem the soul. These values were transmitted to children primarily through direct instruction by adults. The few books that were available for colonial children, therefore, were moralistic, didactic, and riddled with sanctions. Through books of catechism and lists of duties, children were instructed to live deeply spiritual lives, to obey their parents, to prepare for death, and to avoid incurring the wrath of God. Having been born in sin, they could be saved only by cleansing themselves through piety.

John Cotton's *Milk for Babes, Drawn out of the Breasts of Both Testaments, Chiefly for the Spiritual Nourishment of Boston Babes in either England, but may be of like use for any Children* (1646) was a catechism for children. Explicit questions such as "How did God make you?" were to be memorized with the answer "I was conceived in sin and born in iniquity." James Janeway's *A Token for Children. Being An Exact Account of the Conversion, Holy and Exemplary Lives, and Joyful Deaths of several Young Children* (1672) was popular both in England and in the colonies. Cotton Mather's American edition of the same book, *A Token for the Children of New England, or Some Examples of Children in Whom the Fear of God was Remarkably Budding Before they Died*, was first published in Boston in 1702. The preface of the 1749 edition reads,

> You may now hear (my dear Lambs) what other good Children have done, and remember how they wept and prayed by themselves; how earnestly they cried out for an Interest in the Lord Jesus Christ. . . . Do you do as these Children did? Did you ever see your miserable state by Nature? Did you ever get by yourself and weep for sin?[4]

The Puritans regarded human nature as inherently sinful. According to their doctrine, children were born naturally depraved; religion led to salvation, and children were taught to read for the primary purpose of reading the Bi-

[107]

A

T O K E N

F O R T H E

C H I L D R E N

O F

N EW-E N G L A N D.

*I*F *the Children of* New-England *should not with an Early* Piety, *set themselves to* Know *and* Serve *the Lord* JESUS CHRIST, *the* GOD of *their* Fathers, *they will be condemned, not only by the* Examples *of pious* Children *in other Parts of the World, the publish'd and printed Accounts whereof have been brought over hither; but there have been* Exemplary Children *in the Midst of New-England itself, that will rise up against them for their Condemnation. It would be a very profitable Thing to our* Children, *and*

[108]

highly acceptable to all the godly Parents *of the* Children, *if, in Imitation of the excellent* JANE-WAY's Token *for* Children, *there were made a true Collection of notable Things, exemplified in the* Lives *and* Deaths *of many among us, whose* Childhood *hath been signalized for what is virtuous and laudable.*

In the Church-History *of* New-England *is to be found the* Lives *of many eminent* Persons, *among whose* Eminencies, *not the least was,* Their fearing of the Lord *from their* Youth, *and their being* loved *by the Lord when they were* Children.

But among the many other Instances, *of a* Childhood *and* Youth *delivered from* Vanity *by* serious Religion, *which* New-England *has afforded, these few have particularly been preserved.*

Cotton Mather's foreword to the New England edition of Janeway's *A Token for the Children of New England,* which presented stories of pious children held up as models to the reader. (From *Yankee Doodle's Literary Sampler of Prose, Poetry & Pictures.* Selected from the Rare Book Collections of the Library of Congress and introduced by Virginia Haviland and Margaret N. Coughlan.)

ble. The average life expectancy was not long, and the mortality rate among infants and children was very high. The Puritans are criticized for their grim concentration on deathbed scenes, but indeed, sickness and death were an ever-present part of their lives.

The funeral elegy was a popular form of literature for children. It gloomily detailed the death of a young person who had given wise counsel from dying lips, as in Benjamin Colman's *A Devout Contemplation On the Meaning of Divine Providence, in the Early Death of Pious and Lovely Children. Preached upon the Sudden and Lamented Death of Mrs. Elizabeth Wainwright. Who Departed this Life, April the 8th, 1714. Having just compleated the Fourteenth Year of Her Age.* The first of many of its kind to come, this book contained an address to the mournful relatives of the deceased, an address to the children of the town, and the sermon at her funeral. Similar in kind was *A Legacy for Children, being Some of the Last Expressions, and Dying Sayings, of Hannah Hill, Junr. Of the City of Philadelphia, in the Province of Pennsilvania in America, Aged*

Eleven Years and near Three Months, published in 1717. The preface to this sentimental account of the death of a young Quaker states that it was published at the "ardent desire of the deceased." Hannah took several days to die and used the time to give moral advice to her family and friends. Children were taught to be in constant preparation for death and warned that it could come at any moment.

Books from this period affirm the Puritan ethic and the role of religious guidance in children's lives. The concern for children's souls and the search for salvation appear grim and dreary to us today, but the images of fire and brimstone rife in these books were frighteningly real for Puritan children.

In contrast to this threatening picture is the work of Isaac Watts. Somewhat more subtle in his moralizing, Watts states in the preface to *Divine and Moral Songs for Children,* published in England in 1715, that his work is intended to "give the minds of children a relish for virtue and religion." Some of Watts's hymns are still sung today, notably "Joy to the World," "O God, Our Help in Ages Past," and "Hush, My Dear, Lie Still and Slumber."

Generally, damnation lay everywhere for the colonial child 300 years ago; preachers warned of the lurking dangers of a sin-filled life, with death a constant companion. Children who were trying to get to heaven faced the twin threats of impending death and a fall from grace. They and their elders feared Satan, who actively sought their souls. Working for salvation was a full-time job mirrored in books, religious organizations, and daily life.

Hornbooks, first used around 1550, were small wooden paddles. Lesson sheets were attached to the paddles and covered with a sheet of transparent horn—made from hammered cow's horns—and fastened with small strips of brass. They were used to teach the alphabet (in upper and lower case) and often contained a list of syllables and vowels, the Lord's Prayer, or short verses. "In Adam's fall we sinned all"

The simple text of horn books was mounted on a wooden paddle covered with a sheet of hammered cow's horn—hence the name. (Facsimile of a horn book reproduced by *The Horn Book.*)

began one such alphabet verse. These instructional materials were aimed at combining the learning of skills with religious salvation—the ultimate goal.

Secular Tales: Chapbooks and Battledores

Chapbooks, crudely printed little books that were sold for a few cents by peddlers—or chapmen—contained poorly retold stories. Despite their quality, the wide circulation of chapbooks created a readership for later books published for children. Perhaps even more important, they preserved many fairy tales and nursery rhymes for later and better retellings.

The earnest spiritual leaders of the Puritans were dismayed by the sale of chapbooks. Cotton Mather decried the "foolish Songs and Ballads, which the Hawkers and Peddlars carry into all parts of the Countrey." He urged the publication of "Compositions full of Piety, and such as may have a Tendency to advance Truth and Goodness."[5]

Battledores, of folded cardboard, contained some of the same material found on hornbooks. The cover was embellished with crude woodcuts of animals, while the inside was filled with alphabets, numerals, and simple reading lessons. They were intended "to instruct and amuse" and contained only vague religious references. Battledores were prevalent in the mid-1700s, and their popularity continued well into the 1800s.

Books for Formal Education

Typical colonial schools were "dame schools," conducted in private homes, with children attending to their lessons while the teacher carried on her household duties. The curriculum included reading, writing, spelling, arithmetic, prayers, hymns, and catechism read from hornbooks, the Bible, and a few other books. One of the first compulsory education laws was the Education Act of 1647 in Massachusetts, commonly known as the Old Deluder Satan Act. Its authors believed that if the children could read the Bible, they wouldn't be fooled

Battledores, made of heavy, folded cardboard, offered alphabets, simple pictures, and religious precepts. (From *Yankee Doodle's Literary Sampler of Prose, Poetry & Pictures.* Selected from the Rare Book Collections of the Library of Congress and introduced by Virginia Haviland and Margaret N. Coughlan.)

A dame school in session. Lessons consisted largely of recitation of Bible verses and syllabaries.

by the Devil. It required schools for towns with more than 100 households. Many of these were carried on simultaneously with the dame schools.

The New England Primer, often called the most important book for children in the eighteenth century, provided religious education in language children could understand. First published in London as *The Protestant Tutor* or *The Royal Primer,* its author, Benjamin Harris, was sent to the pillory in 1681 for printing the book, which was one of the first to depart from traditional religious catechism. Harris escaped to Boston where he reissued the book as *The New England Primer,* in 1690, its first printing in America. Pictures in the *Primer* were crude woodcuts, but they held children's attention with their gruesomely detailed accounts of burnings and other punishments.

There were numerous editions of the *Primer,* and although the subject matter varied, all editions had certain features in common, including the alphabet in couplets of admonitory sentences, the catechism, and various hymns and prayers. A. S. W. Rosenbach says that "a woodcut of the burning of John Rogers, retained from *The Protestant Tutor,* the violently anti-Catholic forerunner of *The New England Primer,* was rarely omitted, and was usually accompanied by the verses of Advice to his Children."[6] Children were expected to learn it "up and down, backward and forward" until they had memorized it word for word.

George Fox, founder of the Society of Friends in England, wrote a primer called *Instructions for Right-Spelling and Plain Directions for Reading and Writing True English. With several delightful things very Useful and Necessary, both for Young and Old, to Read and Learn.* The first American edition of this text appeared in 1702, and the second was printed by Benjamin Franklin in 1737. This book contained sections designated "The Marks of a true Christian; the Catechism; the Names which the children of God are call'd by; Proverbs, tables of Numeration, Multiplication, etc.; A ready Way to

This is a page from one version of *The New England Primer,* showing a portion of the alphabet with biblical and other rhymes as mnemonic devices.

reckon what one's daily Expenditure comes unto in a whole year; and Proper Names in Scripture, with their signification in English, and other useful information."

Major sections of the books the colonists gave their children were filled with directives for manners and morals. Any child who followed all of these today would be considered priggish indeed. Typical of some of the rules for table manners are the following:

Grease not thy fingers or napkin more than necessity requires. Lean not they elbow on the table, or on the back of the chair. Stuff not thy mouth so as to fill thy cheeks, be content with smaller mouthfuls. Smell not of thy meat nor put it to thy nose, turn it not the other side upward to view it upon thy plate. Gnaw not bones at the table but clean them with thy knife (unless they be very small ones) and hold them not with a whole hand, but with two fingers.[7]

The authors of these behavior manuals tried to anticipate all situations where guidance might be required. One such compendium of rules included

> I. Twenty Mixt Precepts. II. One Hundred and Sixty Three Rules for Childrens Behaviour. III. Good Advice for the Ordering of their Lives; With a Baptismal Covenant. IV. Eight wholesome Cautions. V. A short, plain, & Scriptural Catechism. VI. Principles of the Christian Religion. VII. Eleven short Exhortations. VIII. Good Thoughts for Children, a compendious Body of Divinity; An Alphabet of useful Copies; and Cyprian's Twelve Absurdities.[8]

Treatises on manners and morals, popular since the beginnings of Western civilization, were circulated in manuscript form even before printed books were available. Codes of behavior differed for girls and boys; separate sets of instructions were written. *School of Good Manners*, written for boys in 1685 by Eleazer Moody, contains the following directives:

> When in Company, If thou canst not avoid Yawning, shut thy mouth with thine hand or handkerchief before it, turning thy face aside. Spit not in the Room, but in the Corner, and rub it with thy Foot, or rather go out and do it abroad. If thy Superior be relating a Story, say not I have heard it before, but attend to it as if it were to thee altogether new; Seem not to question the Truth of it; If he tell it not right, snigger not, nor endeavor to help him out or add to his Relation.[9]

Children's behavior and manners were of great importance to the prim and unbending writers of the colonial period. It was recommended that children live well in order to die well, so nearly every book intended for other purposes also included instructions on proper behavior, with large doses of humility and correct manners. The didactic nature of books for children during this period established a trend that was to influence children's literature for years to come.

CHANGING IDEAS OF EDUCATION

Throughout the seventeenth and eighteenth centuries, while the American colonists were wresting a living from an untamed country and winning their political independence, there were some in Europe whose thoughts were moving away from the stern Puritan morality toward a child-centered system of education. The forerunners were Comenius, Locke, and Rousseau.

John Amos Comenius, a Moravian educational reformer and theologian, believed in a uniform system of education for all children and wrote a compendium of the information he believed every child should know. His *Orbis sensualium pictus (Illustrated World of the Senses)* appeared in 1658 and is particularly noteworthy because it was the first textbook in which pictures were as important as the text.

A stronger and more lasting influence came from John Locke, the English philosopher whose *Some Thoughts Concerning Education* (c.

Comenius.

John Amos Comenius, a mid-seventeenth-century reformer, believed all children should have the same curriculum.

1690) set forth the view that when an infant comes into the world his mind is a "tabula rasa"—a blank slate—upon which we can write what we choose. Accordingly, the impressions made upon the child are most important. Locke's precept, "The light of reason is the candle of the Lord," caused him to view self-control and self-discipline as the ultimate goals of all education. He believed that children should be treated as rational creatures, that their curiosity was an expression of an appetite for knowledge. His view of childhood as a time of special significance, as well as his stress on human reason, had widespread influence throughout the eighteenth century.

Locke's work held many implications for early childhood training. Fire-and-brimstone preachers interpreted his philosophy (however mistakenly) to say that children should be brought up with strict discipline and that they should learn to bury their desires and endure privation even from the cradle. People had believed children had demonic natures, and Locke held out the promise of change through the careful use of rewards and punishments. He believed the strongest of these incentives to be esteem and disgrace.

Fifty years later, French philosopher Jean-Jacques Rousseau startled the world with a view of the inner-directed nature of child growth. Here, too, were implications for the education of the child. In *Emile* (1762), Rousseau set forth the idea that the child is born with an innate sense of right and wrong that is only warped and distorted by the efforts of parents and teachers. Left to follow his natural impulses, the child, like the "noble savage," would develop and grow into an adulthood superior to that imposed by civilization.

Rousseau brightened the view of childhood by denying the idea of original sin and by deeming childhood important in its own right. His cry against the established educational practices led to a revision in thinking about how children learn. Still debated today is one of the primary principles of his theory of natural education: "Do not teach but let the child instruct himself through experience." He held that we should allow children to follow their natural inclinations and take our lead from their questions. Another maxim, "Nature wants children to be children before they are men," embodied an affirmation of the importance of childhood and countered the miniature-adult notion prevalent for so long. He sowed the seeds for the ensuing developmental stance that was to lead to the scientific study of children.

Locke and Rousseau, alike in their positions that childhood is a special time, differed dramatically in their views of how the child learns. Locke's emphasis on the importance of training, discipline, and reason foretold the assertions of modern behavioral psychologists, who believe that the child's behavior is molded primarily by rewards and punishments. Rousseau's views, on the other hand, prefigured those of developmental psychologists, who assert that the child's growth is primarily the result of the development of innate abilities and personal discovery of the world.

THE NATIONAL PERIOD

At the beginning of the nineteenth century, the "good godly" books of the Puritans were still widespread with characters who were noble, virtuous, and strongly religious. Reproving tones were used to describe "rough house and knock about" characters; the exemplary child was never guilty of rudeness or improper thoughts. Child characters were continually admonished to exercise moral judgment and, whenever they strayed from the path of righteousness, were ultimately punished.

Moral Instruction in the Guise of Entertainment

The child portrayed in books was polite, diligent, dutiful, and prudent. The young were expected to be well-informed and, to that end, to seek information doggedly. Questions by children, such as "Pray Papa, what is a camel?" would trigger a flow of factual information from the all-knowing adult. Parents, teachers, and ministers were unquestioned as ultimate sources of information and as translators of God's prescriptions for behavior.

Fairy tales and other imaginative literature were held in disfavor through most of the early 1800s. Belief in magical powers and the idea of receiving anything through means other than hard work and persistence were frowned upon. Few people wanted their children to waste time on frivolous stories, and it was widely believed that fairy tales were dangerous and corrupting influences on the child.

In spite of this earnest regard for instilling in children the fundamentals of moral and righteous living, there emerged early in the nineteenth century a belief that these same ideas could be made more palatable by presenting them in the guise of entertainment. Children had already taken for their own several books that had been written for adults, but in the early 1800s there began to appear a new type of book: stories expressly for enjoyment by children.

Books Originating in Europe

Many of the books read by American children were first published in Europe, then brought to the New World. A few of these, in addition to the textbooks and books of religious and moral instruction, were epics and ballads, as well as narrative accounts of explorations and stories of adventure. Several books (in particular *Pilgrim's Progress, Robinson Crusoe, Gulliver's Travels*, and *The Swiss Family Robinson*), although not for children, were widely read by them. Despite the somber, moralistic tone of some of these, children no doubt relished them for their departure from the rigid lessons of their textbooks.

In 1678, John Bunyan, who spent much of his life in jail for preaching against the accepted

---

THE NATIONAL PERIOD

1775
   1779 *The American Primer*
   1780 New edition, *New England Primer*
   1782 New edition, *New England Primer*
   1783 *The History of Sanford and Merton* (Thomas Day)
   1786 *Hymns in Prose* (Anna Barbauld and Dr. John Aiken)
   1786 "History of the Robins" in *Fabulous Histories* (Sarah Trimmer)
   1796 *Parent's Assistant* (Maria Edgeworth)
   1797 *The American Accountant*
1800
   1801 *Moral Tales, Early Lessons* (Maria Edgeworth)
   1818 *The History of the Fairchild Family*, Part I (Mary Martha Sherwood)
   1822 *Peter Parley's History of the United States* (Samuel and Charles Goodrich)
1825
   1827 *Tales of Peter Parley About America* (Samuel and Charles Goodrich)
   1834 *Rollo Learning to Talk* (Jacob Abbott)
   1834 McGuffey's *Eclectic Readers*
1850
   1858 *Rollo in Rome, Rollo's Tour in Europe* (Jacob Abbott)

---

religious beliefs of his day, wrote *Pilgrim's Progress*, one of the epics. The story, of a Christian who travels from the land of destruction to the New Jerusalem, contains long theological dialogues but was enjoyed by children, who undoubtedly skipped the theology and savored the adventure.

In 1719, Daniel Defoe wrote for adults *The Wonderful Life, and surprizing adventures of the renouned hero, Robinson Crusoe: Who Lived Twenty-eight Years on an Uninhabited Island, Which he afterwards colonised*, but it, too, was soon adopted by children. *Robinson Crusoe* contains many of the elements that we look for in children's literature today. For example, a hero, cast away on a remote island, is pitted against seemingly insurmountable odds and, through bravery, hard work, and the faith and trust of a valued friend, survives.

Jonathan Swift's *Gulliver's Travels*, written in 1726, combines fantasy and adventure in a story originally penned as a scathing social satire. Gulliver's voyage to the land of the Lilliputians, Brobdingnagians, and others interests children today.

Johann David Wyss used Defoe's survival theme in his *Swiss Family Robinson*, which was published in Switzerland in 1812. This story of a shipwrecked family is filled with pious and pedantic overtones, but the adventure and excitement also emerge to hold young readers' attention even today.

These forerunners of the modern adventure story provided the basis for many stories that followed. It was not until the middle of the nineteenth century that educational thought caught up with Defoe, and people began to believe that children were not harmed by reading books that entertained as well as informed. True, these stories, too, were filled with righteous morality, but adventure was acceptable if the hero worked hard to reach his goal.

In addition to the adult books that children adopted from mainstream literature, other stories written specifically for young people became popular, and many undoubtedly made their way to America. Although the stern work ethic that prevailed well into the 1800s condemned such frivolity, many children did have access to fairy tales and other books published abroad, including Charles Perrault's *Histoires ou contes du temps passé avec moralités (Stories or Tales of Times Past with Morals)* and *Contes de ma Mère l'Oye (Tales of Mother Goose)*, which included Sleeping Beauty, Little Red Riding Hood, Blue Beard, Puss in Boots, Cinderella, and Tom Thumb.

In 1744, a London businessman, John Newbery, undertook a venture that was to affect children not only in England but in the United States and Canada as well. Newbery

Title page from *The History of Little Goody Two Shoes*, attributed to Oliver Goldsmith. After much privation Goody Two Shoes acquired "learning and wisdom," which she passed on to others.

Goody Twoshoes.

THE
HISTORY
OF LITTLE
GOODY TWOSHOES;
OTHERWISE CALLED
Mrs. *Margery Twoshoes.*
WITH
The Means by which she acquired her Learning and Wisdom, and in Consequence thereof her Estate.
Set forth at large for the Benefit of those,
Who from a State of Rags and Care,
And having Shoes but half a Pair,
Their Fortune and their Fame would fix,
And gallop in their Coach and Six.
See the original Manuscript in the VATICAN at ROME, and the Cuts by MICHAEL ANGELO; illustrated with the Comments of our great modern Criticks.

THE FIRST *WORCESTER* EDITION.

PRINTED at WORCESTER, *Massachusetts.*
By ISAIAH THOMAS,
And SOLD, Wholesale and Retail, at his Book Store. MDCCLXXXVII.

was an English merchant who perhaps saw in the popularity of Perrault's tales a potential market. He opened The Bible and Sun, originally called The Bible and Crown, a London shop where he offered for sale, along with a variety of medicines, the first book that, though intended for instruction, was specifically designed to entertain children. *A Little Pretty Pocket-Book: Intended for the Instruction and Amusement of Little Master Tommy and Pretty Miss Polly* was a new attempt to teach children the use of the alphabet by way of diversion, and included rhymed directions and morals, games, fables, proverbs, rules of behavior, poems, and a rhyming alphabet. This publication and Newbery's bookshop earned him a place in children's literature matched by no other. In 1765, he published *The Renowned History of Little Goody Two Shoes.* Attributed to Oliver Goldsmith, the bittersweet story tells of Margery Meanwell, an orphan who is taken in by a virtuous clergyman and his wife. When they buy her new shoes, she is so overcome with gratitude that she cries out, "Two shoes, Madam, see my two shoes"—and thus her name. ("Goody," an archaic, polite term for a woman of humble social standing—a "Goodwoman"—was often used as a title preceding a surname.) Margery, forced to leave the house of the clergyman, persists in learning to read and goes from house to house teaching other children. Her virtue and goodness spill forth from the pages, and even today "Little Goody Two Shoes" connotes a saintly, pious, albeit saccharine child.

F. J. Harvey Darton, noted historian of children's books, places Newbery's deeds in context.

> It is no good pretending that John Newbery was consistent, or had any reasoned theory of infant psychology, or was an apostle of this or that school of educational thought. He was simply an active and benevolent tradesman, who was the first to see that, in his line of business, children's books deserved special attention and development. He produced almost nothing original that has passed into the nursery library to live for ever. Even his most famous juvenile publication, *Goody Two-Shoes*, is utterly dead. His personality and his friendships—what he was and what he did, in fact—have endured longer than any of his wares. He prospered, and his books proved by success that they met a want.[10]

In the late eighteenth and early nineteenth century, England was in a state of social and religious upheaval. Life was influenced by the American War of Independence, the French Revolution, the theories of John Locke and Jean-Jacques Rousseau, the splintering of religious groups, and the beginnings of the industrial revolution. It is not surprising that people were concerned about the education of children in such tumultuous times. Neither is it surprising that their concern was manifested by preaching and teaching morals and manners to the young in an attempt to preserve the remnants of life as they knew it. The combined forces led to a rise in children's book publishing, building on a market that John Newbery had clearly established. Some publishers commissioned authors to write expressly for children; many of these writers were women. According to Margaret Hodges and Susan Steinfirst,

> The books that the women turned out were primarily didactic or moralistic, with intent clearly to educate and inculcate morality by example. These women were educators at heart—educational theorists whose own philosophies were derived from those of Jean Jacques Rousseau. The women theorists diverged from Rousseau in varying degrees. Those who remained closest to his philosophies omitted, as he had done, any reference to religion. Other women writers of the period, while adhering to Rousseau's basic tenets, continued to link morality with religion in their works for children.[11]

Three of the most important women writers during this period were Sarah Kirby Trimmer (1741–1810), Anna Laetitia Aiken Barbauld (1743–1825), and Maria Edgeworth (1767–1849). These women were a product of their times who wanted their books to be enjoyed and at the same time to teach children acceptable modes of behavior. Mrs. Trimmer, mother of 12 children, published her most popular book, *Fabulous Histories*, in 1786. This book was published frequently in the next century under the title *The History of the Robins*. In it, she presented a series of what she called "fables" about a robin family to teach about a human family. A conscientious and sympathetic "Mrs. Benson" teaches her two children, 11-year-old Harriet and 6-year-old Frederick, to care about the robins who came to their breakfast table. The father robin addresses his children Robin, Dicky, Flapsy, and Pecksy:

> You must be sensible, my dear young ones, that from the time you left the egg-shell, till the present instant, both your mother and I have nourished you with the tenderest love. We have taught you all the arts of life which are necessary to procure you subsistence, and preserve you from danger. We have shewn [sic] you a variety of characters in the different classes of birds, and pointed out those which are to be imitated, and those which are to be shunned. You must now shift for yourselves; but before we part, let me repeat my admonition, to use industry, avoid contention, cultivate peace, and be contented with your condition. Let none of your own species excel you in any amiable quality, for want of your endeavours to equal the best; and do your duty in every relation of life, as we have done ours by you. Prefer a calm retirement to the gay scenes of levity and dissipation, for there is the greatest degree of happiness to be found. You, Robin, I would advise, on account of your infirmity, to attach yourself to Mr. Benson's family, where you have been so kindly cherished.[12]

Anna Laetitia Aiken had published her first volume of adult poems in 1773 before her marriage to Reverend Rochemont Barbauld in 1774. The newly married couple began teaching at a boy's school in Palgrave and adopted her nephew Charles, the son of her brother John. During her stay in Palgrave, Mrs. Barbauld wrote *Easy Lessons for Children* and *Hymns in Prose*, which were created for young Charles and her other students. She published *Hymns in Prose for Children* in 1786. She did not consider it proper to lower poetry to the "capacities of children" and, therefore, wrote the 12 hymns in prose that were "intended to be committed to memory, and recited." Barbauld expressed her conviction that all was for the best in the best of all possible worlds. In Hymn VIII, she writes,

> See where stands the cottage of the labourer, covered with warm thatch; the mother is spinning at the door; the young children sport before her on the grass; the elder ones learn to labour, and are obedient; the father worketh to provide them food: either he tilleth the ground, or he gathereth in the corn, or shaketh his ripe apples from the tree: his children run to meet him when he cometh home, and his wife prepareth the wholesome meal.[13]

Maria Edgeworth, the eldest daughter in a large Irish family, knew the likes and dislikes of children at first hand. Her mother died a few years after her birth; her father, Richard Lovell Edgeworth, remarried three times and fathered 21 children, 18 of whom survived infancy. "To amuse the ever expanding Edgeworth brood," Bette Goldstone explains,

> Maria wrote "wee, wee stories" to amuse and instruct her brothers and sisters. Usually these tales were written on a slate; only after they won the approval of the household and suitable corrections were made, did they get copied out in ink. Probably no author, past or present, has had such an excellent opportunity to consistently judge the reaction of the prospective juvenile audience.[14]

Edgeworth is acknowledged as a skillful raconteur; "one of the most natural story-tellers who ever wrote English," says F. J. Harvey Darton, "and the best of the women writers of this period."

Maria Edgeworth . . . had the essential humanity which Rousseau at his best inspired. She wanted her children to be natural; and if her conception of nature was Irish, full of exceptions and even failures, so much the better. Her characters never became abstractions: they had to work out their own salvation as human beings, not in a groove.[15]

Maria Edgeworth's most famous story, though perhaps not her best, is *The Purple Jar.* The story first appeared in *The Parent's Assistant* in 1796 and was later reissued in 1801. Rosamond craved a glowing purple jar in an apothecary's window, but her mother suggested a new pair of shoes instead.

"Well, which would you rather have, that jar, or a pair of shoes? I will buy either for you."
"Dear mamma, thank you—but if you could buy both?"
"No, not both."
"Then the jar, if you please."
"But I should tell you, that in that case I shall not give you another pair of shoes this month."

Her mother hopes reason will prevail and suggests the higher value of frugality, but Rosamond persists in wanting the purple jar. When Rosamond discovers sadly that the jar is not actually purple but merely contains colored water with a disagreeable smell, she bursts into tears.

"And so I am disappointed, indeed. I wish I had believed you at once. Now I had much rather have the shoes for I shall not be able to walk all this month; even walking home that little way hurt me exceedingly. Mamma, I will give you the flower-pot [jar] back again, and that purple stuff and all, if you'll only give me the shoes."

"No, Rosamond, you must abide by your own choice, and now the best thing you can possibly do is to bear your disappointment with good humour."
"I will bear it as well as I can," said Rosamond, wiping her eyes, and she began slowly and sorrowfully to fill the vase with flowers.[16]

Rosamond suffers every day with shoes that grow more shabby until at last she cannot run, dance, jump, or walk in them. Her mother could not take her on walks, and her father could not take her with him on an outing to see a glasshouse because of her worn-out shoes. Her closing remark shows that although she is remorseful and repentant, she still recognizes her fallibility in the future: "O mamma," . . . "how I wish that I had chosen the shoes! They would have been of so much more use to me than that jar: however, I am sure—no not quite sure, but I hope I shall be wiser another time."

Darton believes that last paragraph is almost an epitome of Edgeworth's books for children. The story appeals because of the excellence of the narrative; we want to find out what happens despite the oppressive certainty that a calamity with a vivid moral will befall the injudicious little girl. We dislike the mother although we know she is right, and we loathe rectitude accordingly. In the end, however, we know that Rosamond is a real child.[17]

Thomas Day (1748–1789), a contemporary of the didactic English women writers, was a fervent follower of Rousseau in his books, *The History of Sandford and Merton* (three volumes, 1783, 1786, 1789) and *The History of Little Jack* (1788). Harry Sandford, a farmer's son, is a bright, well-informed little boy although he seems to be an insufferable prig to the modern reader. Tommy Merton, from a wealthy family, is a spoiled brat, illiterate and high handed. Harry rescues the inept Tommy from a snake, the two boys become friends, and they become students of Mr. Barlow. Harry is receptive to his teacher's guidance, but Tommy is reluctant to learn. Throughout the stories, contrasts are drawn between the eager learner and the recalcitrant simpleton who gradually learns to mend his ways from the consistent good example.

Books Originating in America

In America, while religious leaders continued to influence many writers who instructed the young in ways to lead proper and virtuous lives, other books were produced that were intended to imbue a feeling of patriotism. After the Revolutionary War, Americans, struggling to become a united nation, were eager to show that they were no longer a part of England. In trying to develop a sense of pride in their country, authors extolled the virtues of the new land to such an extent that many books were tainted with provincialism, and their case was often overstated; Americans were more fortunate than others, and people across the sea were to be pitied because they were strange and different.

Adventures of travel on the American frontier and courageous stories of daring battles with the Indians became a part of the reading material for young people. Most of these books retained the didacticism of the earlier "teach and preach" books but added lessons on history and geography as well as recitations on the new American "work hard and make good" ethic.

The American Sunday school movement grew along the same lines as those laid down by Mrs. Trimmer and her contemporaries. Between 1825 and 1850, Samuel Griswold Goodrich, who believed in the power of books to guide children along the right path, collaborated with other writers, including Nathaniel Hawthorne, to produce the Peter Parley books. These books combined history, geography, and science with themes of truth and moral conduct. The Peter Parley character was a venerable older gentleman who answered—in *Tales of Peter Parley About America* (1827) and in more than 100 titles that followed—the many questions children put to him. Although some books were designed as texts, most were what were then called "toy books," which were books intended for out-of-school hours. They were simple, well illustrated, clearly printed, and inexpensive. Despite the wide approval for the information and codes of conduct in the books, the slight story frames were often criticized as contrivances that made children imaginative and indolent.[18] Nevertheless, the Peter Parley books were the first of a new kind of literature for children—series books. Jonathan Cott estimates Goodrich's place in the history of children's literature.

> Samuel Griswold Goodrich (1793–1860) is perhaps the best-known and most influential figure in nineteenth-century American children's literature. Goodrich's Peter Parley books (about 116 of them) sold 7 million copies—not including the thousands of imitations and pirate copies printed and sold in the United States and England. Illustrated with wood engravings, they were generally nationalistic but occasionally tolerant utilitarian schoolbooks written in the compendious and moronic style that has served as the model for generations of first-grade primers: "Here I am! My name is Peter Parley! I am an old man. I am very gray and lame. But I have seen a great many things, and had a great many adventures, and I love to talk about them. . . . And do you know that the very place where Boston stands was once covered with woods, and that in those woods lived many Indians? Did you ever see an Indian? Here is a picture of some Indians."[19]

The 1800s saw a deluge of series books, which children eagerly devoured as an alternative to their textbooks. Jacob Abbott wrote a series of books about a young boy who gratefully and eagerly learns all that he can about his world while remaining ever mindful of his supposedly superior American heritage. The series, *Rollo's Tour in Europe*, reads much like a travelogue, with wise Uncle George serving as guide and mentor to young Rollo. Endless de-

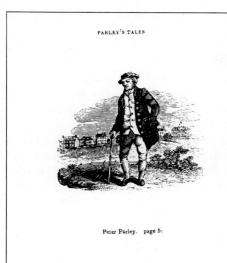

PARLEY'S TALES

Peter Parley.   page 5:

THE
TALES
OF
PETER PARLEY.

——

HERE I am. My name is Peter
Parley. I am an old man. I am
very grey and lame. But I have
seen a great many things, and had
a great many adventures in my time,
and I love to talk about them. I
love to tell stories to children, and
very often they come to my house,
and they get around me, and I tell

Opening of *The Tales of Peter Parley About America,* stories of travel and adventure with a wise mentor that also offered lessons on geography and manners. (From *Yankee Doodle's Literary Sampler of Prose, Poetry & Pictures.* Selected from the Rare Book Collections of the Library of Congress and introduced by Virginia Haviland and Margaret N. Coughlan.)

scriptions of the geography and history of each place they visit are interspersed with frequent injunctions about responsibility, thriftiness, manners, and morals. Abbott, mindful of ways of encouraging sales, would conclude each book with a device aimed at provoking interest in the next. *Rollo in Paris* (1854), for example, concludes with Rollo's receiving an invitation to Switzerland (and an implied new adventure—in the next book). Rollo eventually returns to America, joyous and proud of his country, "with the satisfied consciousness of hailing from a land superior to those inhabited by foreigners."[20] The democratic form of government was still budding, and authors felt obliged to tell readers they were very lucky to live in America.

Books for General Instruction

The New England Primer continued to be a popular textbook for children during the first half of the 1800s. It was revised several times, with additions and deletions reflecting the changing American values. Three successive editions show the shifting attitudes toward the English crown in these couplets for the letter *K*:

(pre-1776)
Our King the good
No man of Blood

. . . .

(1780)
The king should be good
No man of blood

. . . .

(1782)
Kings should be good
Not men of Blood

In later editions (1784, 1786) the king is omitted altogether, and a new verse is substituted.[21]

The period immediately following the American Revolution saw a great increase in the production of new textbooks intended to develop a purely American education. Books were marked by practicality, with Noah Webster pointing the way with his spelling book—"a book from which American children could really learn how to spell." After various changes of title it was eventually known as *The Elementary Spelling Book* or, more popularly, as "The Blue-Backed Speller;" it sold more than 80 million copies during the nineteenth century.

A concern that children learn through understanding resulted in the publication of reading textbooks that were whole-word based instead of alphabet based, so that understanding word concepts, rather than reading by spelling and rote memorization, was the basis of acquiring information. Arithmetic books gradually began to concentrate on practical problems, often dealing with agricultural and industrial concerns of the new nation. The pride Americans felt in their new country, evident in the provincialism of content and topics, which often dealt with only "American" spelling, "American" mathematics, and American history, was mirrored in such titles as: *The American Primer* (1779) and *The American Accountant: Being a Plain, Practical and Systematic Compendium of Federal Arithmetic* (1797). The famous *History of the United States of America* (1822) was one of the abovementioned Peter Parley books by Goodrich.

The textbook was the primary tool of education in early nineteenth-century America. Because school attendance was sporadic, at best, and children most often learned their lessons at home, the textbook was the one constant in a pupil's educational experience. Even where schools existed, teachers changed frequently and families were continually on the move to new territories. Difficulties in reaching distant schools, especially in bad weather, and the need for children to help their families with the daily chores of survival often precluded school attendance. Yet students always knew where they were in their studies: they had completed the Primer or were halfway through Webster; textbooks marked pupils' progress. In addition, the method of study was always the same: students memorized the lessons and then recited them to the teacher or parent.

The United States was 60 years old before the first system of public education was established—in Massachusetts, under the leadership of Horace Mann. As the young country expanded westward, organized public education was slow to follow, so that decades would pass before all children had access to schools.

McGuffey's *Eclectic Readers*, first appearing in 1834, were considered a landmark. These were a series of books of increasing difficulty and were filled with good stories by many authors as well as a wide range of information. They provided a national literature and a national curriculum for a people who sought stability, a common culture, and continuity in their rapidly changing lives.

In the early nineteenth century the work of a Swiss educator, Johann Heinrich Pestalozzi, had an immediate and far-reaching reform influence on American education. New textbooks appeared based on the concept that the child learns best through his own ability to observe and understand.

Pestalozzian theory also led to the inductive method, based on a progression of learning from simple facts to more complex ones, with questions to lead the student to an understanding of rules and definitions. Today we accept these as common-sense approaches that also have a basis in research. By contrasting these innovations with those that had preceded them, in which children learned to read by memorizing meaningless syllables and learned to spell long lists of difficult and seldom-used words, we see the child-centered approach in its true significance.

The Need for Fantasy

Children had little time for childhood in mid–nineteenth-century America. The social conditions of the time dictated that many young people work, often in truly horrible circumstances. The industrial revolution brought with it the necessity for a plentiful supply of cheap labor; and so women, children, and immigrants were enticed to the cities to lives that were filled with unremitting drudgery. Ruth Holland describes those lives in *Mill Child: The Story of Child Labor in America:*

> Twelve hours a day, six days a week, the children fed the endless, ravening hunger of the machines. Machines which were never tired, never sleepy, never sick. Nothing could stop the swift shuttles as they hurled themselves across the looms. And the children raced to keep up. Anyone who couldn't keep up was out. Out of a job. If the machines went faster, hands went faster. And eyes. The mechanical mouths were not choosy about what they ate. They would just as soon munch on a strand of hair as a silk thread from the bobbins.
>   Little girls must not bend too closely over their work. A lock of hair could easily get caught in the whirring wheels. It took just a moment for the machine to pull the hair and a piece of scalp from a child's head. It was not an uncommon accident.[22]

Out of the thinking of a society that tolerated such conditions—and, indeed, often took pride in justifying them—grew a literature that served both as a fantasy escape from the harsh workaday world and a justification of the work ethic.

Around this time, two books that heralded changes to come were published in England. In 1806, Charles and Mary Lamb offered children *Tales from Shakespeare,* which was immediately successful and remains in circulation today. Two years later, Charles Lamb produced *The Adventures of Ulysses,* which has been called a classic in its own right. Other rich and imaginative literary works were published as the century began: Washington Irving's *The Sketch Book of Geoffrey Crayon* (1819–20), which included "The Legend of Sleepy Hollow" and "Rip Van Winkle"—two stories set in the Catskill region—helped begin an American treasury of legends.

CLOSE OF THE CENTURY: A MOVE TOWARD REALISM

The desire to instruct children in the work ethic was nowhere more evident than in the series Horatio Alger began in 1868. The humble characters who reaped generous rewards for hard work and conscientiousness epitomized the virtues of the day and had so strong an impact that the name of Horatio Alger still invokes this ethic. Alger was a prolific author, turning out more than 100 stories in which the male characters acquire power and wealth through fortitude, dauntless courage, and the exercise of impeccable morality. The stories were dramatic—snatching a baby from a burning building or a damsel from the heels of a runaway horse were all in a day's work for the Alger hero—and children read them avidly. Alger broke literary tradition—for example, by setting *Ragged Dick* (1868) in a New York slum rather than in the customary rural surroundings. Subtitled "Street Life in New York with the Boot Blacks," *Ragged Dick,* like all the other books in the series, traces a poor boy's achievement of wealth and respectability.

Mass-produced series books that appeared during the middle of the nineteenth century set a trend that continues today. *Rollo Learning to Talk* (1834) by Jacob Abbott, *Boys of '76* (1876) by Charles C. Coffin, and *The Young Buglers* (1880) by George Henty signaled a torrent of such books to follow. However, the "Immortal Four"—Martha Farquharson [Finley], Horatio

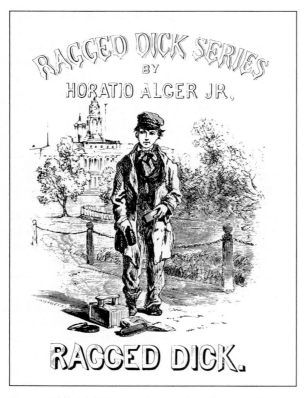

Cover of *Ragged Dick*, one of many formula stories by Horatio Alger, Jr., with the theme that hard work and exemplary behavior will be rewarded with success.

From the mid-nineteenth century, the Elsie Dinsmore stories captured the imaginations of young ladies and extolled the feminine virtues. (From *Elsie Dinsmore,* written by Martha Finley.)

Alger, Jr., William Taylor Adams (who wrote under the name Oliver Optic), and Charles Austin Fosdick (who wrote under the name Harry Castlemon)—win the prize for productivity, in which it was quantity, not quality, that counted.

While books for boys, filled with thrills of travel and adventure, urged them to strive and succeed, those for girls urged their readers to practice the tamer virtues of kindness, sympathy, and piety. Martha Farquharson [Finley] epitomized melodrama in the Elsie Dinsmore stories, wherein tears and prayers were called forth regularly. Young girls devoured these stories and eagerly followed Elsie throughout her lifetime. (Unlike many children's series book characters, Elsie grew old—somewhat more quickly than her audience—leaving the secure world of childhood and quickly passing through the traditional roles of girlhood, wifehood, motherhood, and, to continue the tears, widowhood.)

Elsie Dinsmore's sentimental righteousness made the stories enormously popular throughout the last half of the 1800s. In a typical episode, Elsie's father asks her to sing for his friends during a Sunday afternoon tea. Although Elsie shows unremitting respect toward her father, her strict piety will not allow her to sing on the Sabbath:

> Elsie sat with her little hands folded in her lap, the tears streaming down from her downcast eyes over her pale cheeks. She was trembling, but though there was no stubbornness in her countenance, the expression meek and humble, she made no movement toward obeying her father's order.[23]

Elsie remains sitting, unable to bring herself to sing, until she faints, whereupon her forgiving father carries her gently to her room. Elsie Dinsmore is one link in the chain of tearful, saintly girls that includes Little Goody Two Shoes, Rosamond (of *The Purple Jar*), and the somewhat later *Sara Crewe*, written by Frances Hodgson Burnett in 1888.

Gradually a new type of literature appeared in which characters were more human. Priggishness gave way to devilment as boys— but not yet girls—were portrayed more realistically. Thomas Bailey Aldrich's semiautobiographical *The Story of a Bad Boy* (1870) acknowledges tricks, pranks, and mischievous behavior in a "boys will be boys" spirit:

> It was a custom observed from time immemorial for the towns-boys to have a bonfire on the Square on the midnight before the Fourth. I did n't ask the Captain's leave to attend this ceremony, for I had a general idea that he would n't give it. If the Captain, I reasoned, does n't forbid me, I break no orders by going. Now this was a specious line of argument, and the mishaps that befell me in consequence of adopting it were richly deserved.[24]

THE MOVE TOWARD REALISM

1719 *Robinson Crusoe* (Daniel Defoe)	1877 *Black Beauty* (Anna Sewell)
1807 *Tales from Shakespeare* (Charles and Mary Lamb)	1880 *The Peterkin Papers* (Lucretia P. Hale)
1812 *The Swiss Family Robinson* (Johann Wyss)	1880 *The Five Little Peppers and How They Grew* (Margaret Sidney)
1825	1883 *Treasure Island* (Robert Louis Stevenson)
1826 *The Last of the Mohicans* (James Fenimore Cooper)	1884 *Heidi* (Johanna Spyri)
1843 *A Christmas Carol* (Charles Dickens)	1886 *Little Lord Fauntleroy* (Frances Hodgson Burnett)
1850	1888 *Sara Crewe* (Frances Hodgson Burnett)
1856 *The Daisy Chain* (Charlotte Yonge)	**1900**
1865 *Hans Brinker; or, The Silver Skates* (Mary Mapes Dodge)	1903 *Rebecca of Sunnybrook Farm* (Kate Douglas Wiggin)
1867 *Elsie Dinsmore* (Martha Farquharson Finley)	1908 *Anne of Green Gables* (Lucy M. Montgomery)
1868 *Little Women* (Louisa May Alcott)	1911 *The Secret Garden* (Frances Hodgson Burnett)
1868 *Ragged Dick* (Horatio Alger, Jr.)	1912 *Pollyanna* (Eleanor Porter)
1870 *The Story of a Bad Boy* (Thomas Bailey Aldrich)	
1875	
1876 *The Adventures of Tom Sawyer* (Mark Twain)	

This book began an era of "bad boy literature" that peaked in Mark Twain's *The Adventures of Huckleberry Finn* 14 years later, but continues even now.

The last half of the nineteenth century brought a surge of inexpensive, aesthetically poor, mass-produced books written according to a formula and printed on spongy, poor quality paper. These series books—unlike those, such as The Peter Parley books, of the early part of the century—had no literary distinction or originality to recommend them. Children, however, devoured them with the same uncritical enthusiasm of readers of today's series books. The so-called Immortal Four were responsible for this bumper crop of fast-moving adventures. Finley, Alger, Adams, and Fosdick all used a variety of pseudonyms under which they ground out hundreds of books. This wave of fast-paced, cheap, and extremely popular books provoked objections that recall Mrs. Trimmer's distaste for *Robinson Crusoe*, but as entertainment they gained much popularity with children.

Building on the success of Horatio Alger and the Elsie Dinsmore stories, other writers produced quantities of fast-moving adventure stories. To turn the growing demand to account, Edward Stratemeyer, an enterprising writer, developed a scheme that was to turn into a vast syndicate responsible for the mass publication of millions of tawdry juvenile books—some available even today. With this development, children no longer had to read books under an adult's Sunday supervision and with clean hands; inexpensive production had made books dispensable.

After working for pulp magazines, Stratemeyer wrote *Under Dewey at Manilla* shortly after the Spanish-American War. He enjoyed writing war stories and began several series with America's wars as background. As Stratemeyer's syndicate grew, he limited his participation to outlining the stories and hiring hack writers to do the actual writing, producing in this way the Colonial Boys series, the Mexican War series, and the Pan American series. He continued with other series—including those of the Rover Boys, the Motor Boys, Tom Swift, the Hardy Boys, and the Bobbsey Twins—using the pseudonyms Arthur Winfield, Clarence Young, Victor Appleton, Franklin W. Dixon, and Laura Lee Hope, respectively. Stratemeyer produced 68 different series under 46 pseudonyms. At his death in 1935, his daughter, Harriet Stratemeyer Adams, took over the massive operation, which is still producing books.

Harriet Stratemeyer Adams continued the family tradition by writing, under the pen name Carolyn Keene, Nancy Drew stories—more than 80 of them! The Nancy Drew series and the Hardy Boys series, another Stratemeyer creation, are the best-selling of all series books and have been translated into Spanish, French, German, Italian, Danish, Finnish, Norwegian, Swedish, and Icelandic. Despite bitter criticism from literary critics, Stratemeyer's books, like Enid Blyton's cozy stories of children in rural England, continue to sell amazingly well.

Girls were given an alternative to the melodrama of Elsie Dinsmore when Louisa May Alcott wrote *Little Women* in 1868. Although considered too worldly by fundamentalist leaders, *Little Women* has been called the century's most significant piece of fiction. Alcott's substantial work focused on the homespun virtues of the wholesome American family.

Girls also found pleasure in a series of family stories by Margaret Sidney (pseudonym of Harriet M. Lothrop). *The Five Little Peppers and How They Grew* (1880) begins a series—filled with touching sentimentality—about a widowed mother and her brave struggles to raise her children. Embedded in the idyllic family life portrayed is the idea that generosity, humility, and proper manners earn rewards, whereas the contrary warrant atonement.

The turn of the century brought a new surge of stories for children. Although moral overtones were not forgotten, most books now

PROFILE

Louisa May Alcott

Louisa May Alcott grew up in what she described as "genteel poverty." Her father was Bronson Alcott, a visionary whose educational and social views were well in advance of his times, and their neighbors were outstanding minds of the day—Emerson, Thoreau, Hawthorne. Rich in books and ideas, Louisa's life and writings reflect many of the time's popular literary and social movements. Magazine stories and cheap novels in the gothic style inspired by Mary Shelley's *Frankenstein* were great popular favorites, and Louisa began her life's work of rescuing her beloved family from chronic poverty by scribbling these potboilers for the ever-hungry publishers.

She was deeply affected by—and involved in—the social issues of her day, emancipation of the slaves being the greatest of these. Louisa spent several months as a nurse during the Civil War caring for wounded soldiers in an army hospital, where conditions were deplorable. With her own health impaired, Louisa returned home from this exhausting experience to produce her first serious book, *Hospital Sketches* (c. 1866). Its instant popularity was an inspiration to continue writing serious fiction. Her astute publisher, Thomas Niles, encouraged her to do "something for girls." *Little Women* (1868) was the result. In its pages and in those of the several novels and dozens of short stories that followed, readers can glimpse much of popular culture of the times.

Louisa herself was an avid reader, and through Jo (in *Little Women*) we see the influence of *Pilgrim's Progress* and the work of Charles Dickens. We also hear the story of Rosamond (of *The Purple Jar*) retold and find occasional references to the very popular novels of "dear Miss Yonge," one of Alcott's predecessors in writing the American family story.

A succession of novels followed *Little Women*, namely, *An Old-Fashioned Girl* (1869), *Little Men* (1871), *Work* (1873), *Eight Cousins* (1874), *Rose in Bloom* (1876), *Under the Lilacs* (1877), *Jack and Jill* (1879), and *Jo's Boys* (1886). All of these are still widely read. Alcott's short stories have also been reissued: *Glimpses of Louisa* appeared in 1968 to celebrate the centenary of *Little Women*, as did *An Old-Fashioned Thanksgiving*, which was reissued in picture-book format.

Interested readers can find additional information in such sources as "Louisa May Alcott and the American Family Story" in *A Critical History of Children's Literature*, by Cornelia Meigs et al.; *Bronson Alcott: His Life and Philosophy*, by F. B. Sanborn and W. T. A. Harris; and Meigs's *Invincible Louisa*.

contained humor, adventure, and spirit—and enough connection with rough-and-tumble to provide a firm ground for the even more true-to-life stories that were to follow. Dora V. Smith describes *The Children's Catalog* of 1909 as being "filled with stories of vigorous battles on land and sea, in which American boys took on Indians, foreign invaders, phantom vessels, grizzlies, or their brothers on one side or other of the Mason-Dixon line."[25]

Boys were reading George Grinnell's *Jack Among the Indians* (1900); Henry H. Clark's *Joe Bentley, Naval Cadet* (1899); Everett T. Tomlinson's *Boy Soldiers of 1812* (1895); and George Henty's *Under Drake's Flag* (1883) and *With Kitchener in the Soudan* (1903). Girls' stories retained their emphasis on the quieter virtues of home and family. Among the favorites were Kate Douglas Wiggin's *Rebecca of Sunnybrook Farm* (1903), Lucy M. Montgomery's *Anne of Green Gables (1908),* and Frances Hodgson Burnett's three books, *Little Lord Fauntleroy* (1886), *Sara Crewe* (1888), and *The Secret Garden* (1911). One story, *Pollyanna* (1912), by Eleanor Porter became so well-loved that the character's name still symbolizes an ever-joyful optimistic disposition.

As interest in other peoples grew and provincialism waned, authors began to write about children in lands beyond the American shores. Mary Mapes Dodge wrote *Hans Brinker; or, The Silver Skates* (1865), which, though ostensibly to teach American children about life in far-off Holland, was enjoyed most for its exciting story. The drama of the skating race and the picture of the poor family combine to offer a tale of courage and adventure more lasting than the pallid geography lesson. Similarly, Johanna Spyri wrote *Heidi* (1884) to give a glimpse of life in Switzerland, but children loved it for its portrayal of a young girl's relationship with her grandfather.

There is a tendency to regard the books of yesteryear as "quaint" and to laugh at the simple virtues and life-styles pictured in them.

Perhaps we should, rather, applaud those writers of the past without whom our vision of former days would be so much poorer. Moreover, those books from the recent and distant past that have become classics help us to recognize the universal—as opposed to simple timeliness—in children's books.

CHILDREN'S LITERATURE ESTABLISHED

The Beginnings of Fantasy

Once upon a time, before there was fantasy as we know it, there was folklore. From what began as the oral tradition of folklore and then was invested with the convoluted morals and manners of the seventeenth and eighteenth centuries, there finally emerged a literature with the sole purpose of delighting the fancy. But not until the middle of the nineteenth century, with the publication of *Alice in Wonderland* (1865), by Lewis Carroll, did children have fantasy they could call their own.

One of Rudyard Kipling's drawings for his *Just So Stories,* fanciful tales of how animals acquired their distinctive characteristics. (Illustration from "The Elephant's Child," by Rudyard Kipling, from *Rudyard Kipling's Verse: Definitive Edition.)*

Fairy tales came in and out of favor through the 200 years of American history. Told to children and adults long before writing was invented, the ethereal tales, tough as shoe leather in their ability to survive, reappear time and again. Puritan children, their minds filled with Biblical stories, heard few of them. Even though the tales had, by their time, been written down, Victorian children, too, heard few of them, for morality and the seriousness of life were the keynotes of their time, and fairy tales were considered frivolous.

Surviving in oral form and in underground chapbooks sold by peddlers, fairy tales burst forth sporadically into the legitimate marketplace. In *Contes de ma Mère l'Oye* (1697), Charles Perrault wrote down the tales told in the French court, but more than 30 years passed before his collection was translated into English (1729), and another 50 years before there was an American edition (1785). Although the Grimm Brothers' *Household Tales* (*Kinder- und Hausmärchen*, 1812) was translated into English in 1823 (by Edgar Taylor), children rarely saw the stories again because of the conservatism of educational thought of the time.

Hans Christian Andersen is credited with the literary fairy tale, which first appeared in

---

THE BEGINNINGS OF FANTASY

1484 *Aesop's Fables* (printed by Caxton)	1867 *Ting-a-Ling* (Frank Stockton)
1697 Perrault's *Contes de ma Mère l'Oye*	1871 *At the Back of the North Wind* (George Macdonald)
1725	
1726 *Gulliver's Travels* (Jonathan Swift)	**1875**
1729 English translation, *Tales of Mother Goose*	1881 *Uncle Remus* stories (Joel Chandler Harris)
1775	1883 *The Merry Adventures of Robin Hood* (Howard Pyle)
1785 First American edition, *Tales of Mother Goose*	1889 *The Blue Fairy Book* (Andrew Lang)
1800	1891 *Pinocchio* (C. Collodi)
1808 *The Adventures of Ulysses* (Charles and Mary Lamb)	1894 *The Jungle Book* (Rudyard Kipling)
	1899 *The Story of the Treasure Seekers* (E. Nesbit)
1812 *Kinder- und Hausmärchen* (Jakob and Wilhelm Grimm)	**1900**
1819 "Rip Van Winkle," "Legend of Sleepy Hollow" in *The Sketch Book* (Washington Irving)	1900 *The Wizard of Oz* (L. Frank Baum)
	1902 *The Tale of Peter Rabbit* (Beatrix Potter)
	1904 *Peter Pan* (James M. Barrie)
1823 Grimms' *Popular Stories* translated	1906 *The Fairy Ring* (Kate Douglas Wiggin)
1825	1908 *The Wind in the Willows* (Kenneth Grahame)
1835 *Fairy Tales* (Hans Christian Andersen)	
1850	1911 *Peter and Wendy* (James M. Barrie)
1856 *Heroes* (Charles Kingsley)	1920 *The Story of Dr. Dolittle* (Hugh Lofting)
1863 *The Water Babies* (Charles Kingsley)	
1864 *Journey to the Center of the Earth* (Jules Verne)	**1925**
	1926 *Winnie-the-Pooh* (A. A. Milne)
1865 *Alice in Wonderland* (Lewis Carroll)	1934 *Mary Poppins* (Pamela Travers)

his *Fairy Tales* (1835), translated into English by Mary Howitt in 1846. Andersen adapted basic folk tale themes, adding his own fanciful elaborations, including a strong measure of pathos and melancholy. His work shows clear connections between folklore and fantasy.

Despite repeated attempts by well-intentioned adults to subvert them, fanciful stories survived and eventually blossomed in full glory near the end of the 1800s. In 1863, Charles Kingsley, a clergyman and scientist, wrote one of the earliest fanciful tales—*The Water Babies*, which was grounded in science and laced with the stern moral lessons of his day. In the story (written for Kingsley's son), Tom, a chimney sweep, is carried off into a world under the water, where he becomes a Water Baby. The not-so-subtle lessons evident in the names of characters—such as stern Mrs. Bedonebyasyoudid, loving Mrs. Doasyouwouldbedoneby, and powerful Mother Carey—show that, even though fantasy had emerged, it did so still laden with the moral lessons of its predecessor forms. The story reflects Kingsley's view that redemption can be attained through love and compassion as well as punishment, and the mixture of fact and fancy attempts a reconciliation of the seemingly conflicting views of science and faith. Through this period, fantasy continued to be burdened with heavy moral lessons; it was as if children needed to be given a dose of goodness with every taste of imagination.

Although *Gulliver's Travels* (1726) and *The Water Babies* (1863) preceded them, *Alice's Adventures in Wonderland* (1865) and *Through the Looking Glass* (1871), by Charles Dodgson (pseudonym, Lewis Carroll), are recognized as the first significant works of fantasy for children. Dodgson, cleric and mathematics professor who took up the pen name to avoid identification with his books, often told stories to the three Liddell girls, daughters of a minister friend at Christ Church, Oxford. On an afternoon boat ride, his favorite, Alice, asked for a story with nonsense. The story she heard became the world-famous one after he wrote it for her the following Christmas.

The curious, complicated kind of nonsense Alice Liddell loved intrigues readers who become curioser and curioser along with Alice, who, when she saw a white rabbit with pink eyes check his pocket watch, muttering "I shall be too late,"

> ran across the field after it and was just in time to see him pop down a large rabbit hole under the hedge. In another moment down went Alice after it never once considering how in the world she was to get out again.[26]

Thus begins the story of memorable madness read by generations of children and adults alike. The story is filled with subtleties that poke fun at English social customs of the time; the satiric meaning often eludes modern readers, but the cleverness of the story holds them.

George Macdonald, a personal friend of Dodgson, read *Alice* to his own children while it was still in manuscript form. Macdonald's writing moved toward more symbolic, religious allegorical fantasy—a forerunner of C. S. Lew-

The tea party, drawn by John Tenniel for Lewis Carroll's *Alice's Adventures in Wonderland* and *Through the Looking Glass*. Carroll and Tenniel conferred frequently during the preparation of the drawings.

is's "Narnia" series to come later. In *At the Back of the North Wind* (1871), Macdonald presents a story of allegorical search and wearisome trials before joy, a theme that reverberates throughout literature. One night little Diamond, a child with divine powers, who was named after old Diamond, a horse above whose stall he sleeps, hears a voice from a knothole his mother had stuffed with paper: "What do you mean, little boy—closing up my window?"[27] In this way Diamond meets the North Wind, who is to take him on magical journeys through sea storms and great cathedrals. He walks on ice to the Back of the North Wind, where he feels the disturbing awareness that, although nothing went wrong there, neither was anything quite right.

Diamond's family becomes poor and they take up the hansom cab business in London, but fortunately they are able to buy old Diamond to pull the cab. When his father is ill, Diamond takes over. Many times during his busy life, the North Wind comes to him in different guises—as an old woman, a beautiful young woman, or a terrible one—but each time he recognizes her. Later, Diamond is taken into a household as a page and is given the religious instruction whose basis he had known intuitively. Through all he longs to be with the North Wind, and at last the weary child finds his way there—through death—to eternal happiness.

American children received their first fantasy from English writers. One of these was E. Nesbit, who delighted children with the series *The Story of the Treasure Seekers* (1899), which featured the six mischievous Bastable children who had an unmistakable propensity for getting into trouble. The mixture of realism and fantasy in their chaotic adventures laid the foundations for many stories to come, notable among them P. L. Travers's *Mary Poppins* (1934).

A classic story-play by J. M. Barrie, *Peter Pan* (1904), loved by adults and children every-

Arthur Rackham's illustrations of *Peter Pan* (1906) are wondrous in their imagination and detail. (Written by J. M. Barrie.)

where, takes us to Never-Never Land to meet Peter Pan, a boy who refuses to grow up, and Tinker Bell, a fairy who loses her shadow. Wendy, John, and Michael—proper children with proper parents—are taken by Peter Pan to Never-Never Land, where they encounter a ticking crocodile, lost boys, redskins, and Captain Hook and his pirates. The children begin to forget their parents in the time-held-still place, but a story Wendy tells convinces her brothers and the lost boys that they should return to reality in order to continue the serious business of growing up. A tense moment in the play occurs when Tinker Bell seems certain to die. Only one thing will save her—the belief, by children, in fairies. And, when Peter Pan asks the audience, "Do you believe in fairies?" the usually tremendous roar of "Yes. Yes. We do!" assures Tinker Bell's life for yet another generation.

The truth in fantasy is so strong that it continues to permeate our culture in the form of film (*Pinocchio*, *The Wizard of Oz*, *Mary Poppins*), opera (*Cinderella*), ballet (Grimm's *Sleeping Beauty*, *The Nutcracker*), Broadway shows (*Peter Pan*), and continual interpretations and retellings by talented illustrators and storytellers (Andersen's *Thumbelina* as retold by Amy Erhlich and illustrated by Susan Jeffers).

Fantasy is durable and universal, for it transcends time and place across the generations. Timeless in its appeal, it rises from the depths of folklore, deeply ingraining itself in human lives, forever feeding the imagination.

Poetry

In the day of literature for children, poetry is just dawning. And although great poetry is written much less often than prose, what does exist would seem capable of enduring through the ages. Taste and fashion in poetry change less rapidly than in the case of prose stories, particularly realistic ones. Outstanding poetry from days gone by comes alive for each succeeding generation. Poetry's history, which meshes with that of all literature, is indistinguishable at times from the history of adult poetry, for children often appropriate works that were intended for adults.

Three hundred years ago young children had poetic forms and lilting songs to delight the ear in the verses of Mother Goose; a great deal of doggerel and sentimental stanzas existed as well. Riddles and traditional rhymes were also plentiful, but of actual poetry written for children there was little until the middle of the nineteenth century.

In children's poetry, as in all other literary forms, there were the rare exceptions of truly

great works that became pieces of lasting attraction. William Blake, who lived near the edge of London in relentless poverty from birth to the end of his days, was one of the first to capture the spirit of childhood in verse. Barely noticed in his lifetime, his *Songs of Innocence* (1789) and *Songs of Experience* (1794) were eventually recognized as the masterpieces they truly are. Although not written for children, the poems in *Songs of Innocence* had, in their portrayal of the human mind before the restraints of reason and maturity set in, a childlike quality. In the introduction, Blake says:

> Piping down the valleys wild,
> Piping songs of pleasant glee,
> On a cloud I saw a child,
> And he laughing said to me.
> Pipe a song about a Lamb.[28]

Critics believe that Blake was himself, in a spiritual sense, a happy child on a cloud singing the songs. He was expressing the innocent ecstasy of joy without shadow or reflection. Blake's poems, which show the child as refreshingly curious and responding intuitively to unfathomable beauty, are a benchmark for all subsequent poetry of this kind.

Ann and Jane Taylor, daughters of a British engraver, began writing verses when they were very young. Ann, the elder, won a puzzle contest sponsored by publishers Harvey and Darton, and began to contribute to their magazine; Jane soon followed her sister's lead. When Ann was 22 and Jane 21, the two published *Original Poems for Infant Minds by Several Young Persons* (1804). (Adelaide O'Keefe and their 17-year-old brother, Isaac, also contributed to the volume.) Among their memorable verses, brightened with childlike spirit despite an intent to teach a lesson, and read and memorized avidly by children through the centuries to follow, are "Twinkle, Twinkle, Little Star," by Jane Taylor, and "Welcome, welcome little stranger, to this busy world of care," by Ann Taylor. Their poems were rare exceptions

POETRY

1789	*Songs of Innocence* (William Blake)
1800	
1804	*Original Poems for Infant Minds* (Ann and Jane Taylor)
1823	*A Visit from St. Nicholas* (Clement Moore)
1825	
1834	*Mary's Lamb* (Sara Josepha Hale)
1845	*The New England Boy's Song About Thanksgiving Day* (*Over the River and through the Woods*) (Lydia Maria Child)
1846	*A Book of Nonsense* (Edward Lear)
1850	
1872	*Sing-Song* (Christina Rossetti)
1875	
1875	*Childhood Songs* (Lucy Larcom, illus. Winslow Homer)
1881	*Sketches and Scraps* (Laura E. Richards)
1885	*A Child's Garden of Verses* (Robert Louis Stevenson)

1888	*Casey at the Bat* (Ernest L. Thayer)
1888	*The Pied Piper of Hamelin* (Robert Browning, illus. Kate Greenaway)
1891	*Rhymes of Childhood* (James Whitcomb Riley)
1896	*The Bad Child's Book of Beasts* (Hilaire Belloc)
1900	
1903	*Johnny Crow's Garden* (L. Leslie Brooke)
1913	*Peacock Pie* (Walter De la Mare)
1924	*The Pointed People* (Rachel Field)
1924	*When We Were Very Young* (A. A. Milne)
1925	
1925	*All Together* (Dorothy Aldis)
1926	*Taxis and Toadstools* (Rachel Field)
1930	*Early Moon* (Carl Sandburg)
1933	*A Book of Americans* (Rosemary and Stephen Vincent Benét)

among the somber lessons of their time that were taught in biblical verses and hymns, most of which, sentimental and sermonlike, are now forgotten.

Many early stories and poems became so commonly known and so widespread it is difficult to remember they are not from Mother Goose or folklore: "Mary Had a Little Lamb" (1830), for example, by Sarah Josepha Hale; "Cradle Hymn" (1715), by Isaac Watts, which began, "Hush thee, my dear, lie still and slumber"; "The Three Bears" (1834–37), by Robert Southey; and " 'Will you walk into my parlor!' said the Spider to the Fly" in *Fireside Verses* (1799–1888), by Mary Howitt.

Most nineteenth-century poets still had a strong desire to teach a lesson, but some went beyond the moralistic verses. Some of the early English poets were able to portray life from the perspective of children and to sing the pleasures of childhood as children saw them. Among these—some of whom continued the tradition begun by William Blake and added to the poetic tradition we draw upon today— were William Roscoe, *The Butterfly's Ball* (1806); Edward Lear, *A Book of Nonsense* (1846); Robert Louis Stevenson, *A Child's Garden of Verses* (1885); A. A. Milne, *When We Were Very Young* (1924) and *Now We Are Six* (1927); William Allingham, *In Fairyland* (1870), in which "The Fairies" begins, "Up the airy mountain, Down the rushy glen"; and William Brighty Rands, "Wonderful World" (1870), which begins "Great, wide, beautiful, wonderful World, With the wonderful water round you curled."

An American, Clement Moore, produced a work, *A Visit from St. Nicholas* (1823), that would keep the magic of Christmas in our

Richard Doyle's fantastical illustrations complement William Allingham's imaginative poetry for children. (From Allingham's *In Fairyland*—1870)

hearts. Written for his children, it appeared anonymously in the Troy (N.Y.) *Sentinel* on December 23, 1823; it was one of the rarities in its complete freedom from the didacticism so prevalent at the time. Children's delight in the visions his words called forth caused them to take it for their own and, as an owner's right, to rename it "The Night Before Christmas," which it shall forever remain. Moore's call

> To the top of the porch, to the top of the wall!
> Now, dash away, dash away, dash away all![29]

might have been signaling the beginning of the boundless visions future poets would paint.

Illustration

It may be true, as some educators claim, that the pictures children see in their minds are better than any an illustrator can make. Still there is no doubt that book illustration has developed into a fine art through the establishment of publishing specifically for children. Illustrations can carry great importance, because the art in children's books may be the only art they ever see; certainly it is the first they see and has a lasting impact upon the development of a taste for beauty.

John Amos Comenius can be credited with developing the first picture book. *Orbis sensualium pictus,* or "The World in Pictures," was published in 1658 and was filled with pictures and words as a way for children to learn about their world.

Illustrated books can be considered to have begun with the artless (and often anonymous) woodcuts of children's eighteenth-century catechism pages. The printer used any woodcuts he had; not necessarily ones that went with the story. Among the earliest outstanding work is that by George Cruikshank (1792–1878). In Cruikshank's day, the artist was limited because the final say was always the engraver's. Despite the restrictions, his delicate artistry showed a feeling for the magic of the folktale and the ephemeral qualities of the fairies so prevalent in children's stories and poems. Cruikshank illustrated *Grimm's Fairy Tales* (1823) in a luxuriant style that extended the

George Cruikshank's artistry brought to life the simple folk, the giants, and the sprites of the classic fairy tales. (From *The History of Jack and the Beanstalk* by Cruikshank.)

fancy of the tenacious tales; his interpretations were so enchanting they were republished in Germany with the original text. Cruikshank came into his own with fairy art, and *George Cruikshank's Fairy Library* (1853–54), published in four volumes, contains some of his most memorable work.

At first artists merely lightened the text with decoration or with incidental illustrations that filled gaps in the page or emphasized crucial moments in the story. Because of technical limitations they seldom achieved a perfect match between their picture images and the author's literary images.

Full-fledged illustrations—by Walter Crane, John Tenniel, Kate Greenaway, and Randolph Caldecott—soon followed, however. Walter

Crane, the son of a portrait painter, abhorred the cheap, crudely illustrated books for children of his day. Apprenticed to a wood engraver, he would wander at lunch time to the offices of *Punch*, a popular magazine of high quality. Despite the venture's high financial risk, publisher Frederick Warne brought out Walter Crane's first nursery picture books— *Sing a Song of Sixpence, The House that Jack Built, Dame Trot and Her Comical Cat,* and *The History of Cock Robin and Jenny Wren*—in 1865–66, launching Crane's productive career.

John Tenniel left his artistic mark on Lewis Carroll's *Alice's Adventures in Wonderland* (1865) and *Through the Looking Glass* (1871). His mark is so substantial that we find it difficult to think of Alice except in the ways Tenniel envisioned

Walter Crane helped to establish the high standards for illustrated children's books. (From Crane's *Sixpenny Picture Toy Book*—1868.)

her. Tenniel had worked on *Punch* and was recommended by George Macdonald, noted fantasy writer, as an illustrator for Carroll's books.

Kate Greenaway, born in London in 1846, is noted for renditions of prim, well-groomed children surrounded by the bouquets and garden scenes from her childhood; her name identifies a line of quaint Victorian-style children's dresses today. *Under the Window* (1878), which was her first picture book, was followed by a long and distinguished line of books marked with her unique style and charm. The Greena-

way Medal, the English counterpart of our Caldecott Medal for distinguished illustration, is named in her honor.

Randolph Caldecott, like Kate Greenaway, born in 1846, was interested in art very early but was not encouraged to pursue it. He worked in a bank for 10 years but, in 1872, decided to return to the work he loved so much. His work appeared in several magazines both in England and the United States, but the turning point in his career was *The Diverting History of John Gilpin* (1878), a picture book that immor-

 PROFILE

Kate Greenaway

O ring the bells! O ring the bells!
  We bid you, sirs, good morning;
Give thanks, we pray,—our flowers are gay.
  And fair for your adorning.

UNDER THE WINDOW

Kate Greenaway has few peers when it comes to conveying the beauty of children and the world in rose-colored images.

Born in London on March 17, 1846, the daughter of Elizabeth Jones and John Greenaway, Kate was devoted to her father, a prominent wood-engraver and draftsman, and delighted in those times when her father brought his wood blocks home to complete an engraving job. His work was a source of inspiration to her.

When Kate Greenaway was 2 years old she went to live on an aunt's farm in Nottinghamshire, where she learned firsthand a love for nature—hedgerows, apple blossoms, and especially the lovely flowers in gardens surrounding her home. She described standing under an apple tree and looking at the sky through the white blossoms as going into another country. Most of her early education was conducted at home, where she took French lessons and music instruction. Recognizing their daughter's artis-

talized him in the field of children's literature, and that was followed by 16 others. A scene from *John Gilpin* appears on the Caldecott Medal.

Gradually, illustrations became more integral to the text than the early decorative panels, and the storyteller's word conjoined with the illustrator's line to produce books of lasting impression. No longer were artists a bridge between wonderland and reality; rather, they were interpreters and partners in the storytelling itself. With the spread of literacy in the nineteenth century, the distribution of books expanded, and publishers sought more than a frontispiece or sporadic illustration. In the 1860s, Edmund Evans, who joined with Walter Crane in criticizing the poor quality of art in children's books, introduced the use of color, and in the 1880s, the development of photoengraving processes finally freed artists from the tyranny of the hand-engraved (and distorting) translation of their art. Illustrations in children's books were boosted in their evolution into distinct style and design.

tic gift, the Greenaways enrolled Kate in art classes, where she won her first prize at the age of 12.

Starting in 1871, at the age of 25, Kate produced a number of "toy books" and other illustrated collections. In 1878, Edmund Evans, friend of Kate's father, published her first important work, *Under the Window,* a collection of about 50 drawings with quaint verses. It was in this book that Kate developed the fresh, highly original style that was to become her hallmark. Evans was chided for printing a large first edition of 20,000 copies, but the book sold out before he had time to reprint another edition. Within the next few years, more than 70,000 copies were sold. *Under the Window* and many other Greenaway titles continue to be reprinted.

The Birthday Book for Children, published in 1880, is special even today. In addition to 350 miniature black-and-white illustrations and 12 in color, there are month-by-month verses and space to record birth dates.

Kate Greenaway's watercolor drawings and portraits are marked by children attired in charmingly adapted eighteenth-century smocks and frocks, bonnets and breeches, ribbons and aprons. The term "Greenaway costumes" was quickly attached to the designs she fashioned and remains a distinctive label to this day. Characterized by elegance, delicacy, and grace, children from Greenaway's brush reflect her vision of childhood as a time of happy innocence. This has widespread appeal, whether in the scores of Christmas and Valentine cards she created or the numerous books of verse she illustrated. During the years of Britain's industrial revolution, Kate hewed to the pre-Raphaelite injunction to venerate the simple and poetic in nature.

For the unique impression of childhood her illustrations have left on the minds and hearts of readers, Kate Greenaway's name has a place in children's literature not easily matched.

Kate Greenaway is known for her finely styled children and the Victorian garden settings of her works. (From *Marigold Garden* by Kate Greenaway.)

In the early 1900s, Arthur Rackham and Beatrix Potter, unique in their own ways, gave form to fictitious characters who became memorable because of the rare talent they reflect. Edmund Dulac contributed outstanding interpretations of old favorites, such as his classic painting for "The Princess and the Pea."

Picture books as we know them today emerged around the turn of the century, when many of today's classic illustrations were published. Some of these were W. W. Denslow's pictures in Baum's *Wizard of Oz* (1900), Charles Robinson's for Rand's *Lilliput Lyrics* (1899), and L. Leslie Brooke's in *The Golden Goose Book* (1905). These earn them a place beside Cruikshank, Crane, Tenniel, Potter, Rackham, Greenaway, and Caldecott as outstanding illustrators of early children's books.

During the period of the Second World War, many talented European artists came to work and live in America. Ingri and Edgar Parin d'Aulaire (*Abraham Lincoln*, 1939), Ludwig Bemelmans (*Madeline*, 1939), and Roger Duvoisin (*White Snow, Bright Snow,* by Alvin Tresselt, 1947) are a few such artists.

The golden age of the picture book (1950 to today) has attracted many skilled artists to the field of children's books. Leonard Weisgard, Marcia Brown, and Maurice Sendak are among those whose work typifies the changing styles of the period. Comparing an early Weisgard (*The Little Island* by MacDonald, 1946) with a later one (*Where Does the Butterfly Go When It*

ILLUSTRATORS

1823	*German Popular Stories* (George Cruikshank)
1850	
1860	Color printing
1867	*Sing a Song of Sixpence* (Walter Crane)
1872	*Alice In Wonderland* (John Tenniel)
1875	
1878	*Under the Window* (Kate Greenaway)
1878	*The Diverting History of John Gilpin* (Randolph Caldecott)
1880	Photoengraving process developed
1885	*A Child's Garden of Verses* (Jessie Willcox Smith)
1894	*The Jungle Book* (Rudyard Kipling)
1900	
1902	*The Tale of Peter Rabbit* (Beatrix Potter)
1906	*Peter Pan in Kensington Gardens* (Arthur Rackham)
1907	*Johnny Crow's Garden* (L. Leslie Brooke)
1925	
1939	*Madeline* (Ludwig Bemelmans)
1939	*Abraham Lincoln* (Ingri and Edgar d'Aulaire)
1947	*White Snow, Bright Snow* (Roger Duvoisin)
1956	*Kenny's Window* (Maurice Sendak)

Rains? by Garelick, 1970) will give some idea of the range of the changing art styles as well as the growth of an artist. Compare Marcia Brown's early art in Perrault's *Cinderella* (1954) with her work in *Once a Mouse* (1961) and later in *Shadow* (1982) to see how she adapts the art to a story but also how she has developed as an artist. Sendak's work began as cartoonlike drawings in Krauss's *A Very Special House* (1953) and developed into elaborate art in *Outside Over There* (1981).

The best of today's illustrators show remarkable ability to tap and share their own childhood. Some modern artists use old methods, sometimes called revivalist techniques; others spark the reader's imagination with stark black and white photographs or the full array of color and technique made possible by today's technology. Maurice Sendak credits artists of the past with influencing the growth of his own singular style, particularly evident in *Where the Wild Things Are* (1963), *In the Night Kitchen* (1970), and *Outside Over There* (1981). For all illustrators, the cultural legacy that is art's is glimpsed in countless proof sheets.

Magazines

Many of the early magazines for children were Sunday school periodicals filled with religious writings, sayings, and anecdotes. There was *The Encourager* (Methodist), *The Children's Magazine* (Episcopal), *The Juvenile Instructor* (Mormon), and *Catholic Youth's Magazine*. Even secular ones such as *Frank Leslie's Chatterbox* (1879–86) advertised that it intended to "improve the mind, diffuse knowledge," and provide good, healthy, and interesting literature for the young. Each sketch promised to convey a moral or some useful information in only the purest tone and language. Despite an avowed "immense circulation," *Chatterbox* lasted only seven years.

Some prestigious children's magazines had excellent writers contributing to them. Notable

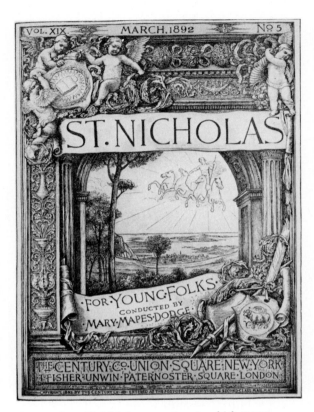

A cover from *St. Nicholas* magazine, in which many authors who subsequently became noted in the field of children's books were first published. (From *Yankee Doodle's Literary Sampler of Prose, Poetry & Pictures.* Introduced by Virginia Haviland and Margaret N. Coughlan.)

among them was Frank Stockton, a frequent contributor to and later associate editor of *St. Nicholas*, which ended 70 years of publication in 1943. Another editor of *St. Nicholas*, Mary Mapes Dodge, best known for her *Hans Brinker*, actively sought established writers and artists to contribute to the magazine. The creative leadership of these two accounted for the primary position the magazine maintained for three-quarters of a century and the standards of excellence it set for the entire children's publishing world. Work by Arthur Rackham, Frances Hodgson Burnett, Howard Pyle, Rudyard Kipling, and Laura E. Richards often graced its pages. Dodge intended to make the periodical a child's pleasure ground with no sermonizing, no spinning out of facts, and no rattling of dry bones; under her guidance, this goal was achieved. Many of the short stories were reprinted as books, and anthologies of its articles were published; some of the serialized novels remain classics today. Frances Hodgson Burnett's *Sara Crewe* (1888); Frank Stockton's *America's Birthday Party* (1876); Susan Coolidge's *What Katy Did* (1872); Louisa May Alcott's *Jo's Boys* (1873), *An Old-Fashioned Girl* (1870), and *Eight Cousins* (1875); Rudyard Kipling's *The Jungle Book* (1894); and Lucretia P. Hale's *The Peterkin Papers* (1880) first appeared in the pages of *St. Nicholas*.

The *Youth's Companion* (1827–1929) survived longer than any other magazine in America; in 1929 it merged with *The American Boy*, which ceased publication in 1941. From the beginning, editorial policy demanded that its content remain seemly; parents could give the weekly magazine to their children without fear of introducing them to any untoward subject. In addition to the enticement of a distinguished list of contributors—Sarah Orne Jewett, Jack London, Theodore Roosevelt, Henry Wadsworth

---

MAGAZINES

1826–1834	*Juvenile Miscellany*
1827–1929	*The Youth's Companion*
1850	
1865–1873	*Our Young Folks*
1867–1870	*Riverside Magazine for Young People*
1873–1943	*St. Nicholas*
1875	
1875–1893	*Wide Awake*
1879–1895	*Harper's Young People*
1879–1886	*Frank Leslie's Chatterbox*
1900	
1911 to present	*Boy's Life*
1917–1979	*American Girl*

Longfellow, Alfred Lord Tennyson, James M. Barrie, H. G. Wells, and Oliver Wendell Holmes, among others—the editors offered various premiums to its readers.

The pioneer children's magazine (the first published in America), *The Juvenile Miscellany* (1826–34) was edited by Lydia Maria Child and became an immediate success. Lydia Maria Francis (later Mrs. Child) was a former teacher who wanted children to learn to read with material they could enjoy but found very little that answered this requirement. *The Juvenile Miscellany* filled the void, but when Lydia Maria Child spoke out with a tongue of flame against slavery, sales dropped so drastically that the magazine stopped publication in 1834. Sarah Josepha Hale's "Mary Had a Little Lamb" first appeared in this magazine.

Children's magazines have always been an important part of children's reading material; the fresh surprise of each issue brings a special pleasure. Some of the most popular magazines today center on nature and the environment with *Ranger Rick's Nature Magazine*, *National Geographic World*, and *Current Science* exemplifying the best. The flagship magazine, *Highlights for Children* (founded in 1946), contains stories, poems, games, informational articles, and hidden pictures. This excellent general magazine has more than 2.5 million subscribers. *Cricket Magazine* includes some of the best literature, often the published work of established authors. *Cobblestone*, *Penny Power*, *Sesame Street*, and *The Electric Company* promise a bright future for young magazine readers.

TRENDS IN CHILDREN'S LITERATURE

Children's literature continues to grow and develop as a field of study. Teachers have discovered that using children's books in the classroom enriches their curriculum. Librarians have found that more children—and younger children—are visiting libraries to participate in story hours, summer reading programs, after school programs, author visits, and other special events. New organizations have been founded to pursue literary criticism (such as Children's Literature Association and Children's Literature Assembly of the National Council of Teachers of English); others focus on using literature in the classroom (Special Interest Group on Using Literature in the Classroom of International Reading Association, Committee on Trade Books in the Classroom of the National Council of Teachers of English, and Notable Trade Books in the Language Arts). New professional journals have been founded to promote the use of literature (*The New Advocate, The Lion and the Unicorn, Bookbird*, and *Children's Literature in Education*). Parent study groups interested in children's books are cropping up in various parts of the country. Television programs include numerous productions based on children's books (Reading Rainbow). In general, there is a rebirth of enthusiasm for children's books.

The growing enthusiasm for children's books has created new markets and increased production. Whereas there were approximately 2,000 books published annually in 1960, there were 3,000 in 1970, and 4,000 in 1980. Children's books mean business—big business—for publishers, booksellers, and agents.

Books for the Very Young

Part of the increase in children's book publishing is due to the greater numbers of children being born and the younger ages at which children are being introduced to books. Studies of the effect of reading aloud to young children have convinced parents that they need to make books available to children from their earliest days. Publishers have responded by creating new lines of books for infants, toddlers, and preschoolers. Toy books with pop-up designs, plastic bathtub books, cloth books, board books, and many other types spill from booksellers shelves. Young upwardly mobile parents with two incomes, anxious to educate

their children early, have the money to buy books for their babies.

Cassette recordings of the author or someone reading aloud often accompany a book; these are packaged to sell as a unit. Books are also packaged with toys: in one series there are books with puzzles, chalkboards, clocks, wall charts, recordings, and a soft pillow with a story in its folds.

Nonfiction

Nonfiction aimed at transmitting information to readers has changed in format, design, and audience. In the early 1970s, the genre was represented by books filled with dense text and few illustrations. It was geared to the upper elementary school reader and paralleled school curricula. Today, nonfiction appears in beautiful books with spacious pages brimming with color illustrations. Nonfiction is available for the youngest child in the form of board books, pop-up books, and unique formats. Nonfiction writers no longer use school curricula as a guide; they discover topics of interest to them and make them appealing to the curious minds of children. Space travel, planets, dinosaurs, computers, social problems, and international relations are all treated by today's nonfiction writers. As a result, there are more books on a wider variety of topics, more attractive books, and more books for younger children than in the past. Nonfiction has been recognized as true literature in that it has been chosen as Newbery Honor books in 1986 and 1987; in 1988 a nonfiction book won the Newbery Award.

Series Books

There has always been a market for books in a series but it, too, is growing. Once youngsters have read and enjoyed one book, they are eager to have another like it. The *Sweet Valley High* series, *Sweet Dreams, Apple Romance*, and others have enjoyed tremendous success. Preteen and teenage readers respond to the books much as their parents and grandparents did to *The Bobbsey Twins, Nancy Drew,* and the *Hardy Boys.* Books that offer alternate paths for reading, such as the "Choose Your Own Adventure" series, reached a responsive audience. First developed by Edward Packard and Ray Montgomery, they have now been imitated for every age group and developed in every genre. Children read each book several times—until they have exhausted each of the alternate routes to the end of the story.

Paperbacks

A sizeable part of the increase in children's books publishing and sales is due to the widespread use of paperbacks. Teachers and librarians found that students *like* to read paperbacks even more than they like to read hardcover books. Distribution in discount stores, drugstores, grocery stores, and airports has made paperbacks widely accessible. Studies of adolescents' reading preferences show that they prefer the small size and softer cover of a paperback over a hardcover book. The fact that a paperback will fit into a jeans pocket does not go unnoticed by adolescents who are concerned about convenience and not appearing too bookish to their peers.

Censorship

Censorship is the removal or banning of books, films, or magazines that are harmful or unacceptable according to the views of the censor. For those who believe that education involves exposure to a variety of ideas, opinions, and value systems, any type of censorship is inappropriate. Book banning, particularly in the public schools, has become an increasingly important problem. The number of cases that end in litigation has increased yearly; censorship

cases erupt in communities from Maine to California and from Florida to Michigan. Books in elementary, junior high, and high schools are challenged and defended. Library books have often been the center of the controversies, but textbooks are also coming under the fire of censors. Church Hill, Tennessee; Mobile County, Alabama; Wasco Union School Board, California; Anderson Union High School District, California; Columbia County, Maryland; Panama City, Florida; Westmoreland County, Pennsylvania; Hawkins County, Tennessee; Baileyville School, Maine; and others too numerous to mention reach the courts in lawsuits intended to remove books from library shelves or classroom use.

Some of the most frequently banned books include *Huckleberry Finn* (Mark Twain); *Go Ask Alice* (Anonymous); *Are You There, God? It's Me, Margaret; Deenie; Then Again, Maybe I Won't* (Judy Blume); *The Chocolate War* (Robert Cormier); and *Catcher in the Rye* (J. D. Salinger).

In addition to the censorship that becomes public, there is often hidden censorship—or the quiet removal of books from circulation by teachers, administrators, or librarians who fear they may be a problem. The result is the same: choice is limited.

The American Library Association, the National Council of Teachers of English, and the International Reading Association have taken a position against censorship. Each organization has free materials to help with censorship problems.

Multiethnic Literature

Multiethnic literature contains works by authors from all of the different racial and ethnic groups represented in our society. Although children's literature has been dominated by Anglo-Saxon writers and illustrators, the scene is changing—albeit slowly. There are still groups of children who cannot see themselves reflected in books, but there is some progress.

Chapter 11 describes literature by and about five ethnic minorities.

The Future

It is clear from the voluminous body of children's literature that the field has attracted talented writers and illustrators. Creative people have a way of continuing to change their world, so we can rest assured that innovations will always be a part of the children's book world. If the number of books published continues to increase, as it probably will, selection may become difficult because of the sheer volume. Recognizing what is good literature and why it is good has been the goal of this text.

Our job as teachers, librarians, and parents is to select from the vast array of books—past, present, and future—the best there is to offer. As poet Walter De la Mare stated, "Only the rarest kind of best is good enough for children."

PROFESSIONAL REFERENCES

Amies, Marion. "Amusing and Instructive Conversations: The literary genre and its relevance to home education." *History of Education*, 14 (June 1985): 87–99.

Avery, Gillian. "Fashions in Children's Fiction." *Children's Literature in Education*, no. 12 (September 1973): 10–19.

Arnold, Arnold. *Pictures and Stories from Forgotten Children's Books*. New York: Dover, 1969.

Bingham, Jane, and Grayce Scholt. *Fifteen Centuries of Children's Literature: An Annotated Chronology of British and American Works in Historical Context*. Westport, Conn.: Greenwood Press, 1980.

Church, Robert L. *Education in the United States: An Interpretive History*. New York: The Free Press, 1976.

Clark, Isabel C. *Maria Edgeworth: Her Family and Friends*. London: Hutchinson, 1949.

Clarke-Stewart, Alison, Susan Friedman, and Joanne Koch. *Child Development: A Topical Approach*. New York: Wiley, 1985.

Cleverley, John, and D. C. Phillips. *Visions of Childhood: From Locke to Spock*. New York: Teachers College Press, 1986.

Cremin, Lawrence A. *American Education: The Colonial Experience 1607–1783*. New York: Harper & Row, 1970.

Darton, F. J. Harvey. *Children's Books in England*, 3rd ed. Edited by Brian Alderson. New York: Cambridge University Press, 1982.

Demers, Patricia, and Gordon Moyles. *From Instruction to Delight: An Anthology of Children's Literature to 1850*. New York: Oxford University Press, 1982.

Fisher, Margery. *Who's Who in Children's Books: A Treasury of the Familiar Characters of Childhood*. New York: Holt, Rinehart & Winston, 1975.

Goldstone, Bette P. *Lessons to Be Learned: A Study of Eighteenth Century English Didactic Children's Literature*. New York: Lang, 1984.

Greven, Philip J., Jr. *Child-Rearing Concepts 1628–1861: Historical Sources*. Itasca, Ill.: Peacock, 1973.

Haviland, Virginia, and Margaret N. Coughlan, eds. *Yankee Doodle Sampler of Prose, Poetry, and Pictures*. New York: Crowell, 1974.

Humm, Rosamond Olmstead. *Children in America: A Study of Images and Attitudes*. Atlanta, Ga.: The High Museum of Art, 1978.

Jordon, Alice M. *From Rollo to Tom Sawyer, and Other Papers*. Illustrated by Nora S. Unwin. Boston: Horn Book, 1948.

Kaestle, Carl F., and Maris A. Vinovskis. "History: Transitions to and from the Family, from Apron Strings to ABCs: Parents, Children and Schooling in Nineteenth-Century Massachusetts," *American Journal of Sociology*, 84 (Supplement 1978), s. 38.

Kuhn, Anne L. *The Mother's Role in Childhood Education: New England Concepts 1830–1860*. New Haven, Conn.: Yale University Press, 1947.

Lantz, Everett D. *Educational Leaders*. Laramie, Wyo.: Center for Research, Service and Publication, University of Wyoming, 1971.

Locke, John. *Some Thoughts Concerning Education*. London: n.p., 1693.

Lystad, Mary. *From Dr. Mather to Dr. Seuss: 200 Years of American Books for Children*. Cambridge, Mass.: Schenkman Books, 1980.

McLean, Ruari, ed. *The Reminiscences of Edmund Evans: Wood Engraver and Colour Printer 1826–1905*. New York: Oxford University Press, 1967.

Meigs, Cornelia, et al. *A Critical History of Children's Literature: A Survey of Children's Books in English*. Illustrated by Vera Bock. New York: Macmillan, 1969.

Meyer, Adolphe E. *An Educational History of the American People*, 2nd ed. New York: McGraw-Hill, 1967.

Morgan Library, The J. Pierpont. *Early Children's Books and Their Illustrations*. Boston: Godine, 1975.

National Institute of Education. *Early American Textbooks 1775–1900*. Washington, D.C.: Alvina Treut Burrows Institute, 1978.

————. *Rare Books on Education: Fifteenth to Eighteenth Century. A Catalog of the Titles Held by the Educational Research Library*. Washington, D.C.: U.S. Department of Health, Education, and Welfare, 1976.

Newby, P. H. *Maria Edgeworth*. London: Swallow, 1950.

Perilstein, Bette L. *An Historical Study of Five Late Eighteenth Century English Didactic Children's Books*. Ph.D. diss., Temple University, Philadelphia, 1982.

Pickering, Samuel F., Jr. *John Locke and Children's Books in Eighteenth Century England*. Knoxville, Tenn.: University of Tennessee Press, 1981.

Pulliam, John D. *History of Education in America*, 4th ed. Columbus, Ohio: Merrill, 1987.

Rippa, S. Alexander. *Education in a Free Society: An American History*. 5th ed. New York: Longman, 1984.

Rosenbach, Abraham S. W. *Early American Textbooks*. Millwood, N.Y.: Kraus Reprint Co., 1966.

Rousseau, John Jacques. *Emile*. Paris: n.p., 1762. Reprint.

Sanborn, F. B., and W. T. A. Harris. *Bronson Alcott: His Life and Philosophy*. (2 vols.) Boston: Ticknor, 1893.

Smith, Dora V. *Fifty Years of Children's Books*. Urbana, Ill.: National Council of Teachers of English, 1963.

Smith, Elva S. *The History of Children's Literature*, rev. ed. Edited by Margaret Hodges and Susan Steinfirst. Chicago: American Library Association, 1980.

Zigler, Edward F., and Matia Finn-Stevenson. *Children: Development and Social Issues*. Lexington, Mass.: Heath, 1987.

NOTES

1. Christina G. Rosetti, poem in *Our Own Gazette* 5, no. 52 (April 1888), 1.
2. Henry Steele Commager, in Cornelia Meigs et al., *A Critical History of Children's Literature* (New York: Macmillan, 1969), xvi–xvii.
3. Gillian Avery, "Fashions in Children's Fiction," *Children's Literature in Education*, 12 (September 1973): 10.
4. A. S. W. Rosenbach, *Early American Children's Books* (1933; rpt. Millwood, N.Y.: Kraus Reprint Co., 1966), 19.
5. Cotton Mather's diary.
6. Rosenbach, *Early American Children's Books*, 19.
7. Ibid., xxxix.
8. Ibid., 21.
9. Ibid., 22.
10. F. J. Harvey Darton, *Children's Books in England*, 3rd ed, revised by Brian Alderson (London: Cambridge University Press, 1982), 4–5.
11. Margaret Hodges and Susan Steinfirst, *Elva S. Smith's The History of Children's Literature* (Chicago: American Library Association, 1980), 97.
12. Patricia Demers and Gordon Moyles, eds., *From Instruction to Delight: An Anthology of Children's Literature to 1850* (Toronto: Oxford University Press, 1982), 190.
13. Ibid., 188.
14. Bette P. Goldstone, *Lessons to Be Learned: A Study of Eighteenth Century English Didactic Children's Literature*, American University Studies Series 14, vol. 7 (New York: Lang, 1984), 48.
15. Darton, *Children's Books in England*, 142, 143.
16. Maria Edgeworth, *The Purple Jar*, in Demers and Moyles, *From Instruction to Delight*, 144–45.
17. Darton, *Children's Books in England*, 41.
18. For a full discussion, see Henry J. Perkinson, "American Textbooks and Educational Change" in National Institute of Education, *Early American Textbooks 1775–1900* (Washington, D.C.: Alvina Treut Burrows Institute, 1978).
19. Jonathan Cott, *Pipers at the Gates of Dawn: The Wisdom of Children's Literature* (New York: Random House, 1983), 48–49.
20. Alice Jordan, *From Rollo to Tom Sawyer, and Other Papers* (Boston: Horn Book, 1948), 76.
21. Rosenbach, *Early American Children's Books*, 42–43.
22. Ruth Holland, *Mill Child: The Story of Child Labor in America* (New York: Macmillan, 1970), 16–17.
23. Martha Farquharson [Finley], *Elsie Dinsmore*, cited in Virginia Haviland and Margaret N. Coughlan, comps., *Yankee Doodle Sampler of Prose, Poetry and Pictures* (New York: Crowell, 1974), 233.
24. Thomas Bailey Aldrich, *The Story of a Bad Boy* (1870), cited in Haviland and Coughlan,

Yankee Doodle Sampler, 346–47.
25. Dora V. Smith, *Fifty Years of Children's Books* (Urbana, Ill.: National Council of Teachers of English, 1963), 3.
26. Lewis Carroll, *The Annotated Alice: Alice's Adventures in Wonderland and Through the Looking Glass*, ed. Martin Gardner, illus. John Tenniel (New York: Macmillan, 1960), 25–26.
27. George Macdonald, *At the Back of the North Wind* (London, 1871; rpt. New York: Macmillan, 1964), 4.
28. William Blake, *Works* (London: Oxford University Press, 1925), 65.
29. Clement Clarke Moore, *A Visit from St. Nicholas*, illus. T. C. Boyd (1823; rpt. New York: Simon and Schuster, 1971).

CHILDREN'S BOOKS CITED

Abbott, Jacob. *Rollo in Paris.* Boston: Reynolds, 1854.
———. *Rollo in Rome.* 1858.
———. *Rollo Learning to Talk.* 1834.
———. *Rollo's Tour of Europe.* 1858.
Adams, William T. *Oliver Optic* series. Boston: Brown, Bazin & Co., 1854–94.
Aesop. *Aesop's Fables.* Edited by Anne Terry White. New York: Random House, 1964.
Alcott, Louisa May. *Eight Cousins.* New York: Western, Golden Press, 1977.
———. *Glimpses of Louisa: A Centennial Sampling of the Best Short Stories of Louisa May Alcott.* Boston: Little, Brown, 1968.
———. *Hospital Sketches.* 1866.
———. *Jack and Jill.* 1879. Reprint. New York: Grosset, 1971.
———. *Jo's Boys.* 1886. Reprint. New York: Grosset, 1971.
———. *Little Men.* 1871. Reprint. New York: Macmillan, 1963.
———. *Little Women.* New York: Macmillan, 1962.
———. *An Old-Fashioned Girl.* 1869. Reprint. New York: Grosset, 1971.
———. *An Old-Fashioned Thanksgiving.* Illustrated by Holly Johnson. 1870. Reprint. Philadelphia: Lippincott, 1974.
———. *Rose in Bloom.* 1876. Reprint. New York: Grosset, 1971.
———. *Under the Lilacs.* 1877. Reprint. New York: Grosset, 1971.
———. *Work.* 1873.
Aldis, Dorothy. *All Together: A Child's Treasury of Verse.* 1925. New York: Putnam's, 1952.

Aldrich, Thomas Bailey. *The Story of a Bad Boy.* 1870. Reprint. New York: Garland, 1976.
Alger, Horatio. *Ragged Dick.* 1868.
Allingham, William. *In Fairyland.* Illustrated by Richard Doyle. London: Longmans, Green & Co., 1870.
The American Accountant: Being a Plain, Practical and Systematic Compendium of Federal Arithmetic. 1797.
American Boy magazine. 1929–41.
American Girl magazine. 1917–79.
The American Primer. 1779.
Andersen, Hans Christian. *Fairy Tales.* Illustrated by Lawrence B. Smith. 1835. Reprint. New York: Macmillan, 1963.
———. *Thumbelina.* Retold by Amy Erhlich, illustrated by Susan Jeffers. 1836. New York: Dial, 1979.
Apple Romance series. New York: Scholastic.
Appleton, Victor. *Tom Swift* series. 1910. Reprint. New York: Grosset, 1977.
Barbauld, Mrs. Anna. *Easy Lessons for Children.* c. 1786.
———. *Hymns in Prose for Children.* London: N.p., c. 1786.
———, and Dr. Aiken. *Evenings at Home.* 1786.
Barrie, James M. *Peter Pan.* Illustrated by Jan Omerod. New York: Viking, 1988.
———. *Peter Pan.* Edited by Eleanor Graham, illustrated by Nora S. Unwin. New York: Scribner's, 1950.
———. *Peter and Wendy.* 1911.
———. *Peter Pan in Kensington Gardens.* Illustrated by Arthur Rackham. 1906. Reprint. Cutchogue, N.Y.: Buccaneer Books, 1981.
Baum, L. Frank. *The Wizard of Oz.* 1900. Reprint. New York: Macmillan, 1970.
Belloc, Hilaire. *The Bad Child's Book of Beasts.* Illustrated by Wallace Tripp. 1896. Reprint. Jaffrey, N.H.: Sparhawk, 1982.
Bemelmans, Ludwig. *Madeline.* New York: Viking, 1939.
Benet, Rosemary, and Stephen Vincent Benet. *A Book of Americans.* Illustrated by Charles Child. New York: Holt, Rinehart & Winston, 1952.
Blake, William. *Songs of Experience.* 1794.
———. *Songs of Innocence.* Illustrated by Ellen Raskin. 1789. Reprint. New York: Doubleday, 1966.
Blume, Judy. *Are You There, God? It's Me, Margaret.* New York: Bradbury, 1970.
———. *Deenie.* New York: Bradbury, 1973.
———. *Then Again, Maybe I Won't.* New York: Bradbury, 1971.
Boy's Life magazine. 1911–present.
Brooke, L. Leslie. *The Golden Goose Book.* 1905. Reprint. New York: Warne, 1977.
———. *Johnny Crow's Garden.* 1903. Reprint. New York: Watts, 1967.
Brown, Marcia. *Once a Mouse.* 1961. Reprint. New York: Scribner's, 1982.
———. *Shadow.* New York: Scribner's, 1982.

Browning, Robert. *The Pied Piper of Hamelin.* Illustrated by Kate Greenaway. 1888. Reprint. New York: Coward-McCann, 1971.

Buccaneer magazine. 1981–present.

Bunyan, John. *Pilgrim's Progress.* 1678. Reprint. New York: Dodd, Mead, 1979.

Burnett, Frances Hodgson. *Little Lord Fauntleroy.* 1886. Reprint. New York: Garland, 1976.

———. *Sara Crewe*, rev. as *The Little Princess.* 1888. Reprint. Philadelphia: Lippincott, 1963.

———. *The Secret Garden.* Illustrated by Tasha Tudor. 1911. Reprint. Philadelphia: Lippincott, 1962.

Caldecott, Randolph. *The Diverting History of John Gilpin,* available as *Randolph Caldecott's John Gilpin and Other Stories.* 1878. Reprint. New York: Warne, 1978.

Carroll, Lewis. *Alice's Adventures in Wonderland* and *Through the Looking Glass.* Illustrated by John Tenniel. 1865. Reprint. New York: Macmillan, 1963.

———. *The Annotated Alice: Alice's Adventures in Wonderland and Through the Looking Glass.* Edited by Martin Gardner. New York: New American Library, 1960.

Catholic Youth's Magazine. 1857–61.

Chatterbox magazine. 1866–1946.

Child, Lydia Maria. *The New England Boy's Song About Thanksgiving Day or over the River and Through the Woods.* Illustrated by Brinton Turkle. 1845. Reprint. New York: Coward-McCann, 1974.

The Children's Magazine. 1911–14.

Clark, Henry H. *Joe Bentley, Naval Cadet.* 1899.

Cobblestone: The History Magazine for Young People. 20 Grove Street, Peterborough, N.H., 03458. 1980–present.

Coffin, Charles C. *Boys of '76.* 1876.

Collodi, C. *The Adventures of Pinocchio.* Illustrated by Naiad Einsel. 1891. Reprint. New York: Macmillan, 1963.

Colman, Benjamin. *A Devout Contemplation on the Meaning of Divine Providence, in the Early Death of Pious and Lovely Children. Preached upon the Sudden and Lamented Death of Mrs. Elizabeth Wainwright, Who Departed this Life, April the 8th, 1714. Having Just compleated the Fourteenth Year of Her Age.* 1714.

Comenius, John Amos. *Orbis sensualium pictus.* 1658.

Coolidge, Susan. *What Katy Did.* 1872. Reprint. New York: Dent, 1977.

Cooper, James Fenimore. *The Last of the Mohicans.* Illustrated by N. C. Wyeth. 1826. Reprint. New York: Scribner's, 1919.

Cormier, Robert. *The Chocolate War.* New York: Pantheon, 1974.

Cotton, John. *Milk for Babes, Drawn out of the Breasts of Both Testaments, Chiefly for Spiritual Nourishment of Boston Babes in either England, but may be of like use for any Children.* 1646.

Crane, Walter. *Dame Trot and Her Comical Cat.* c. 1865.

———. *The History of Cock Robin and Jenny Wren.* c. 1866.

———. *The House That Jack Built.* c. 1865.

———. *Sing a Song of Sixpence.* 1867.

———. *Sixpenny Picture Toy Book.* 1868.

Cricket. Literary magazine. P.O. Box 2670, Boulder, CO. 80321. 1973–present.

Cruikshank, George. *George Cruikshank's Fairy Library.* (4 vols.) 1853–1854.

———. *The History of Jack and the Beanstalk.* London: Bogue, 1853.

Current Science. 1927–present.

D'Aulaire, Ingri, and Edgar Parin d'Aulaire. *Abraham Lincoln.* 1939. Reprint. New York: Doubleday, 1957.

Day, Thomas. *The History of Little Jack.* 1788.

———. *The History of Sandford and Merton.* 1783. Reprint. New York: Garland, 1977.

Defoe, Daniel. *Robinson Crusoe.* Illustrated by N. C. Wyeth. 1719. Reprint. New York: Scribner's, 1920.

De la Mare, Walter. *Come Hither.* Illustrated by Warren Chappell. New York: Knopf, 1957.

———. *Peacock Pie.* Illustrated by Barbara Cooney. 1913. Reprint. New York: Knopf, 1961.

Dickens, Charles. *A Christmas Carol.* Illustrated by Arthur Rackham. 1843. Reprint. Philadelphia: Lippincott, 1952.

Dixon, Franklin W. *Hardy Boys* series. New York: Grosset.

Dodge, Mary Mapes. *Hans Brinker; Or, The Silver Skates.* Illustrated by Hilda Van Stockum. 1865. Reprint. Philadelphia: Collins, 1975.

Edgeworth, Maria. *Early Lessons.* 1801.

———. *Moral Tales.* 1801.

———. *Parent's Assistant.* 1796.

The Electric Company magazine. 1974–present.

The Encourager magazine. 1866–1946.

Field, Rachel. *Taxis and Toadstools.* 1926.

———. *The Pointed People.* 1924.

Finley, Martha. *Elsie Dinsmore.* Edited by Alison Lurie and Justin G. Schiller. 1867. Reprint. New York: Garland, 1981.

Fox, George. *Instructions for Right-Spelling and Plain Directions for Reading and Writing True English. With several delightful things very Useful and Necessary, both for Young and Old, to Read and Learn.* 1702.

Frank Leslie's Chatterbox magazine. 1879–86.

Garelick, May. *Where Does the Butterfly Go When It Rains?* Illustrated by Leonard Weisgard. Reading, Mass.: Addison-Wesley, 1961.

Goldsmith, Oliver. *The Renowned History of Little Goody Two Shoes.* Illustrated by Alice Woodward. 1765. Reprint. New York: Macmillan, 1924.

Goodrich, Samuel G. *Peter Parley's History of the United States of America.* 1822.

———, and Charles Goodrich. *Tales of Peter Parley About America.* 1827. Reprint. New York: Garland, 1976.

Grahame, Kenneth. *The Wind in the Willows.* Illustrated by Ernest H. Shepard. New York: Scribner's, 1908.

Greenaway, Kate. *The Birthday Book for Children.* London: Warne, 1880.

———. *Marigold Garden.* London: Routledge, 1885.

———. *Under the Window.* London: Warne, 1878.

Grimm, Jakob, and Wilhelm Grimm. *German Popular Stories.* Illustrated by George Cruikshank. 1823.

———. *Grimm's Fairy Tales.* Illustrated by George Cruikshank. 1820. Reprint. San Diego: Green Tiger, 1977.

———. *Kinder-und Hausmarchen.* Translated by Lucy Crane, illustrated by Walter Crane. 1812. Reprint. New York: McGraw-Hill, 1966.

———. *The Sleeping Beauty.* Illustrated by Trina Schart Hyman. Boston: Little, Brown, 1977.

Grinnell, George. *Jack Among the Indians.* 1900.

Hale, Lucretia. *The Peterkin Papers.* 1880. Reprint. Boston: Houghton Mifflin, 1960.

Hale, Sarah Josepha. *Mary's Lamb.* 1834.

Harper's Young People magazine. 1875–93.

Harris, Benjamin. *The New England Primer.* 1683.

———. *The Protestant Tutor.* c. 1681.

Harris, Joel Chandler. *Uncle Remus*

Stories. 1881. Reprint. New York: Schocken, 1966.

Henty, George. *Under Drake's Flag.* 1883.

———. *With Kitchener in the Soudan: A Story of Atbara and Omdurman.* London: Blackie, 1903.

———. *The Young Buglers.* 1880.

Highlights for Children. 2300 West Fifth Ave., P.O. Box 269, Columbus, Ohio 43272-0002. 1946– present.

Hoffmann, E. T. *The Nutcracker.* Translated by Ralph Manheim, illustrated by Maurice Sendak. New York: Crown, 1984.

Holland, Ruth. *Mill Child: The Story of Child Labor in America.* New York: Macmillan, 1970.

Hope, Laura Lee. *Bobbsey Twins* series. New York: Grosset, 1904– present.

Howitt, Mary. *Fireside Verses.* c. 1871.

Irving, Washington. *The Sketch-Book of Geoffrey Crayon (Rip Van Winkle and the Legend of Sleepy Hollow).* Illustrated by Arthur Rackham. 1819. Reprint. London: Heinemann, 1928.

Janeway, James. *A Token for Children: Being An Exact Account of the Conversion, Holy and Exemplary Lives, and Joyful Deaths of several Young Children.* 1672. Reprint. New York: Garland, 1976.

The Juvenile Instructor magazine. 1866–?

Juvenile Miscellany magazine. 1826– 34.

Keene, Carolyn. *Nancy Drew* series. c. 1890–present.

Kingsley, Charles. *Heroes.* Illustrated by Vera Brock. 1856. Reprint. New York: Macmillan, 1954.

———. *The Water Babies.* Illustrated by Harold Jones. 1863. Reprint. New York: Watts, 1961.

Kipling, Rudyard. *The Jungle Book.* Illustrated by Robert Shore. 1894. Reprint. New York: Macmillan, 1964.

———. *Just So Stories.* Illustrated by Michael Foreman. New York: Viking, 1988.

———. *Rudyard Kipling's Verse: Definitive Edition.* New York: Doubleday, 1956.

Krauss, Ruth. *A Very Special House.* Illustrated by Maurice Sendak. New York: Harper & Row, 1953.

Lamb, Charles. *The Adventures of Ulysses.* 1808.

———, and Mary Lamb. *Tales from Shakespeare.* Illustrated by Richard M. Powers. 1806. Reprint. New York: Macmillan, 1963.

Lang, Andrew. *The Blue Fairy Book.* Edited by Brian Alderson. Illustrated by John Lawrence. 1889. Reprint. New York: Viking, 1978.

Larcom, Lucy. *Childhood Songs.* Illustrated by Winslow Homer. Boston: Houghton, 1874.

Lear, Edward. *A Book of Nonsense.* 1846. Reprint. New York: Garland, 1976.

A Legacy for Children, being Some of the Last Expressions, and Dying Sayings, of Hannah Hill, Junr. Of the City of Philadelphia, in the Province of Pennsilvania, in America, Aged Eleven Years and near Three Months. Philadelphia: Bradford, 1717.

Lofting, Hugh. *The Story of Dr. Dolittle.* 1920. Reprint. Philadelphia: Lippincott, 1967.

MacDonald, Golden. *The Little Island.* Illustrated by Leonard Weisgard. 1946. Reprint. New York: Doubleday, 1971.

Macdonald, George. *At the Back of the North Wind.* Illustrated by Ernest H. Shephard. 1871. Reprint. New York: Macmillan, 1964.

McGuffey, William H. *McGuffey's Eclectic Readers.* 1837. Reprint. Milford, Mich.: Mott Media, 1982.

Mather, Cotton. *A Token for the Children of New England, or Some Examples of Children in Whom the Fear of God was Remarkably Bud-*

ding Before they Died. 1702.

Meigs, Cornelia. *Invincible Louisa.* Boston: Little, Brown, 1968.

Milne, A. A. *Now We Are Six.* Illustrated by Ernest H. Shepard. New York: Dutton, 1927.

———. *When We Were Very Young.* Illustrated by Ernest H. Shepard. New York: Dutton, 1924.

———. *Winnie the Pooh.* Illustrated by Ernest H. Shepard. New York: Dutton, 1926.

Montgomery, Lucy M. *Anne of Green Gables.* 1908. Reprint. New York: Bantam, 1976.

Moody, Eleazer. *School of Good Manners.* 1685. Reprint. New London, Conn.: T. Green, 1715.

Moore, Clement Clarke. *A Visit from St. Nicholas.* Illustrated by T. C. Boyd. 1823. Reprint. New York: Simon & Schuster, 1971.

National Geographic World magazine. 1975–present.

Nesbit, Edith. *The Story of the Treasure Seekers.* 1899. Reprint. New York: Penguin, 1986.

Newbery, John. *A Little Pretty Pocket Book: Intended for the Instruction and Amusement of Little Master Tommy and Pretty Miss Polly.* 1744. Reprint. New York: Harcourt Brace, 1967.

Our Young Folks magazine. 1865–73.

Pascal, Francine. *Sweet Valley High* series. New York: Bantam.

Penny Power magazine. 1980–present

Perrault, Charles. *Cinderella.* Illustrated by Marcia Brown. New York: Scribner's, 1954.

———. *Contes de ma Mère l'Oye (Tales of Mother Goose).* 1697.

———. *Histoires ou contes du temps passe avec moralities (Stories of Long Ago with Morals).* 1697.

Porter, Eleanor. *Pollyanna.* 1912.

Potter, Beatrix. *The Tale of Peter Rabbit.* London: Warne, 1902.

Pyle, Howard. *The Merry Adventures of Robin Hood.* 1883. Reprint. New York: Scribner's, 1946.

Rands, William Brighty. *Lilliput Lyrics.* Edited by R. Brimley Johnson, illustrated by Charles Robinson. London: J. Lane, 1899.

Ranger Rick's Nature Magazine. 1967–present.

Richards, Laura E. *Sketches and Scraps.* 1881.

Riley, James Whitcomb. *Rhymes of Childhood.* 1891. Reprint. Great Neck, N.Y.: Core Collection Books, 1976.

Riverside Magazine for Young People magazine. 1867–70.

Roscoe, William. *The Butterfly's Ball.* 1807.

Rossetti, Christina. *Sing-Song.* Illustrated by Marguerite Davis. 1872. Reprint. New York: Macmillan, 1924.

St. Nicholas magazine. 1873–1943.

Salinger, J. D. *Catcher in the Rye.* Boston: Little, Brown, 1951.

Sandburg, Carl. *Early Moon.* Illustrated by James Daugherty. New York: Harcourt, 1930.

Sendak, Maurice. *In the Night Kitchen.* New York: Harper & Row, 1970.

———. *Kenny's Window.* New York: Harper & Row, 1956.

———. *Outside Over There.* New York: Harper & Row, 1981.

———. *Where the Wild Things Are.* New York: Harper & Row, 1963.

Sesame Street magazine. 1971–present

Sewell, Anna. *Black Beauty.* Illustrated by John Groth. 1877. Reprint. New York: Macmillan, 1962.

Shelley, Mary. *Frankenstein.* Edited by Alice and Joel Schick. New York: Delacorte, 1980.

Sherwood, Mary Martha. *The History of the Fairchild Family,* Part I. 1818.

Sidney, Margaret. *The Five Little Peppers and How They Grew.* 1880. Reprint. New York: Lothrop, Lee & Shephard, 1976.

Spyri, Johanna. *Heidi.* Illustrated by Greta Elgaard. 1884. Reprint. New York: Macmillan, 1962.

Stevenson, Robert Louis. *A Child's Garden of Verses.* Illustrated by Michael Foreman. 1885. Reprint. New York: Delacorte, 1985.

———. *Treasure Island.* Illustrated by N. C. Wyeth. 1883. Reprint. New York: Scribner's, 1981.

Stockton, Frank R. *Ting-a-Ling.* Illustrated by E. B. Bensell. New York: Scribner's, 1867.

Stratemeyer, Edward. *Under Dewey at Manilla.* 1898.

Sweet Dreams series. New York: Bantam.

Swift, Jonathan. *Gulliver's Travels.* Illustrated by Arthur Rackham. 1726. Reprint. New York: Dutton, 1952.

Taylor, Ann, and Jane Taylor. *Original Poems for Infant Minds.* 1804. Reprint. New York: Garland, 1977.

Thayer, Ernest L. *Casey at the Bat.* Illustrated by Wallace Tripp. 1888. Reprint. New York: Coward-McCann, 1978.

Tomlinson, Everett T. *Boy Soldiers of 1812.* 1895.

Travers, Pamela L. *Mary Poppins.* Illustrated by Mary Shephard. 1934. Reprint. New York: Harcourt Brace Jovanovich, 1972.

Tresselt, Alvin. *White Snow, Bright Snow.* Illustrated by Roger Duvoisin. New York: Lothrop, Lee & Shepard, 1947.

Trimmer, Sarah. *Fabulous Histories.* 1786. Reprint. New York: Garland, 1976.

Twain, Mark. *The Adventures of Huckleberry Finn.* 1888. Reprint. New York: Penguin, 1986.

———. *The Adventures of Tom Sawyer.* 1876. Reprint. New York: Penguin, 1983.

Verne, Jules. *Journey to the Center of the Earth.* 1864. Reprint. New York: Dodd, Mead, 1979.

Watts, Isaac. *Divine and Moral Songs for Children.* 1715.

Webster, Noah. *The Elementary Spelling Book (Webster's Blue-Backed Speller)*. 1783.

Wide Awake magazine. 1875–93.

Wiggin, Kate Douglas. *The Fairy Ring*. N.p.: McClure, 1906.

———. *Rebecca of Sunnybrook Farm*. Illustrated by Lawrence B. Smith. 1903. Reprint. New York: Macmillan, 1962.

Winfield, Arthur. *Rover Boy* series. 1899.

Winstanly, Henry. *All the Principal Nations of the World*. 1665.

Wyss, Johann. *The Swiss Family Robinson*. Illustrated by Lynd Ward. 1812. Reprint. New York: Grosset, 1949.

Yonge, Charlotte. *The Daisy Chain*. 1856. Reprint. New York: Garland, 1977.

Young, Clarence. *Motor Boys* series. 1899.

Youth's Behavior magazine. 1636–?

The Youth's Companion magazine. 1827–1929.

Children's Book Awards

THE JOHN NEWBERY MEDAL

The John Newbery Medal, named for an eighteenth-century British publisher and bookseller, the first to publish books for children, is given annually for the most distinguished contribution to literature for children published in the United States in the year preceding the award.

Selection of the award winner is made by a committee of the Association for Library Services for Children of the American Library Association.

The list below gives the title, author, and publisher of winners and of runners-up (honor books) since the inception of the award in 1922.

1922
The Story of Mankind by Hendrik Willem van Loon, Liveright
Honor Books: *The Great Quest* by Charles Hawes, Little, Brown; *Cedric the Forester* by Bernard Marshall, Appleton; *The Old Tobacco Shop* by William Bowen, Macmillan; *The Golden Fleece and the Heroes Who Lived Before Achilles* by Padraic Colum, Macmillan; *Windy Hill* by Cornelia Meigs, Macmillan

1923
The Voyages of Doctor Dolittle by Hugh Lofting, Lippincott
Honor Books: No record

1924
The Dark Frigate by Charles Hawes, Little, Brown, Atlantic,
Honor Books: No record

1925
Tales from Silver Lands by Charles Finger, Doubleday
Honor Books: *Nicholas* by Anne Carroll Moore, Putnam's; *Dream Coach* by Anne Parrish, Macmillan

1926
Shen of the Sea by Arthur Bowie Chrisman, Dutton
Honor Book: *Voyagers* by Padraic Colum, Macmillan

1927
Smoky, The Cowhorse by Will James, Scribner's
Honor Books: No record

1928
Gayneck, The Story of a Pigeon by Dhan Gopal Mukerji, Dutton
Honor Books: *The Wonder Smith and His Son* by Ella Young, Longmans; *Downright Dencey* by Caroline Snedeker, Doubleday

1929
The Trumpeter of Krakow by Eric P. Kelly, Macmillan
Honor Books: *Pigtail of Ah Lee Ben Loo* by John Benett, Longmans; *Million of Cats* by Wanda Gág, Coward-McCann; *The Boy Who Was* by Grace Hallock, Dutton; *Clearing Weather* by Cornelia Meigs, Little, Brown; *Runaway Papoose* by Grace Moon,

Doubleday; *Tod of the Fens* by Elinor Whitney, Macmillan

1930

Hitty, Her First Hundred Years by Rachel Field, Macmillan
Honor Books: *Daughter of the Seine* by Jeanette Eaton, Harper & Row; *Pran of Albania* by Elizabeth Miller, Doubleday; *Jumping-Off Place* by Marian Hurd McNeely, Longmans; *Tangle-Coated Horse and Other Tales* by Ella Young, Longmans; *Vaino* by Julia Davis Adams, Dutton; *Little Blacknose* by Hildegarde Swift, Harcourt Brace

1931

The Cat Who Went to Heaven by Elizabeth Coatsworth, Macmillan
Honor Books: *Floating Island* by Anne Parrish, Harper & Row; *The Dark Star of Itza* by Alida Malkus, Harcourt Brace; *Queer Person* by Ralph Hubbard, Doubleday; *Mountains Are Free* by Julia Davis Adams, Dutton; *Spice and the Devil's Cave* by Agnes Hewes, Knopf; *Meggy Macintosh* by Elizabeth Janet Gray, Doubleday; *Garram the Hunter* by Herbert Best, Doubleday; *Ood-Le-Uk the Wanderer* by Alice Lide and Margaret Johansen, Little, Brown

1932

Waterless Mountain by Laura Adams Armer, Longmans
Honor Books: *The Fairy Circus* by Dorothy P. Lathrop, Macmillan; *Calico Bush* by Rachel Field, Macmillan; *Boy of the South Seas* by Eunice Tietjens, Coward-McCann; *Out of the Flame* by Eloise Lownsbery, Longmans; *Jane's Island* by Marjorie Allee, Houghton-Mifflin; *Truce of the Wolf and Other Tales of Old Italy* by Mary Gould Davis, Harcourt Brace

1933

Young Fu of the Upper Yangtze by Elizabeth Foreman Lewis, Winston

Honor Books: *Swift Rivers* by Cornelia Meigs, Little, Brown; *The Railroad to Freedom* by Hildegarde Swift, Harcourt Brace; *Children of the Soil* by Nora Burglon, Doubleday

1934

Invincible Louisa by Cornelia Meigs, Little, Brown
Honor Books: *The Forgotten Daughter* by Caroline Snedeker, Doubleday; *Swords of Steel* by Elsie Singmaster, Houghton Mifflin; *ABC Bunny* by Wanda Gág, Coward-McCann; *Winged Girl of Knossos* by Erik Berry, Appleton; *New Land* by Sarah Schmidt, McBride; *Big Tree of Bunlahy* by Padraic Colum, Macmillan; *Glory of the Seas* by Agnes Hewes, Knopf; *Apprentice of Florence* by Ann Kyle, Houghton Mifflin

1935

Dobry by Monica Shannon, Viking
Honor Books: *Pageant of Chinese History* by Elizabeth Seeger, Longmans; *Davy Crockett* by Constance Rourke, Harcourt Brace; *Day on Skates* by Hilda Van Stockum, Harper & Row

1936

Caddie Woodlawn by Carol Ryrie Brink, Macmillan
Honor Books: *Honk, the Moose* by Phil Stong, Dodd, Mead; *The Good Master* by Kate Seredy, Viking; *Young Walter Scott* by Elizabeth Janet Gray, Viking; *All Sail Set* by Armstrong Sperry, Winston

1937

Roller Skates by Ruth Sawyer, Viking
Honor Books: *Phoebe Fairchild: Her Book* by Lois Lenski, Stokes; *Whistler's Van* by Idwal Jones, Viking; *Golden Basket* by Ludwig Bemelmans, Viking; *Winterbound* by Margery Bianco, Viking; *Audubon* by Constance Rourke, Harcourt Brace; *The Codfish Musket* by Agnes Hewes, Doubleday

1938

The White Stag by Kate Seredy, Viking

Honor Books: *Pecos Bill* by James Cloyd Bowman, Little, Brown; *Bright Island* by Mabel Robinson, Random House; *On the Banks of Plum Creek* by Laura Ingalls Wilder, Harper & Row

1939
Thimble Summer by Elizabeth Enright, Rinehart
Honor Books: *Nino* by Valenti Angelo, Viking; *Mr. Popper's Penguins* by Richard and Florence Atwater, Little, Brown; *"Hello the Boat!"* by Phyllis Crawford, Holt; *Leader by Destiny: George Washington, Man and Patriot* by Jeanette Eaton, Harcourt Brace; *Penn* by Elizabeth Janet Gray, Viking

1940
Daniel Boone by James Daugherty, Viking
Honor Books: *The Singing Tree* by Kate Seredy, Viking; *Runner of the Mountain Tops* by Mabel Robinson, Random House; *By the Shores of Silver Lake* by Laura Ingalls Wilder, Harper & Row; *Boy with a Pack* by Stephen W. Meader, Harcourt Brace

1941
Call It Courage by Armstrong Sperry, Macmillan
Honor Books: *Blue Willow* by Doris Gates, Viking; *Young Mac of Fort Vancouver* by Mary Jane Carr, Crowell; *The Long Winter* by Laura Ingalls Wilder, Harper & Row; *Nansen* by Anna Gertrude Hall, Viking

1942
The Matchlock Gun by Walter D. Edmonds, Dodd
Honor Books: *Little Town on the Prairie* by Laura Ingalls Wilder, Harper & Row; *George Washington's World* by Genevieve Foster, Scribner's; *Indian Captive: The Story of Mary Jemison* by Lois Lenski, Lippincott; *Down Ryton Water* by Eva Roe Gaggin, Viking

1943
Adam of the Road by Elizabeth Janet Gray, Viking
Honor Books: *The Middle Moffat* by Eleanor Estes, Harcourt Brace; *Have You Seen Tom Thumb?* by Mabel Leigh Hunt, Lippincott

1944
Johnny Tremain by Esther Forbes, Houghton Mifflin
Honor Books: *These Happy Golden Years* by Laura Ingalls Wilder, Harper & Row; *Fog Magic* by Julia Sauer, Viking; *Rufus M.* by Eleanor Estes, Harcourt Brace; *Mountain Born* by Elizabeth Yates, Coward-McCann

1945
Rabbit Hill by Robert Lawson, Viking
Honor Books: *The Hundred Dresses* by Eleanor Estes, Harcourt Brace; *The Silver Pencil* by Alice Dalgliesh, Scribner's; *Abraham Lincoln's World* by Genevieve Foster, Scribner's; *Lone Journey: The Life of Roger Williams* by Jeanette Eaton, Harcourt Brace

1946
Strawberry Girl by Lois Lenski, Lippincott
Honor Books: *Justin Morgan Had a Horse* by Marguerite Henry, Rand; *The Moved-Outers* by Florence Crannel Means, Houghton Mifflin; *Bhimsa, the Dancing Bear* by Christine Weston, Scribner's; *New Found World* by Katherine Shippen, Viking

1947
Miss Hickory by Carolyn Sherwin Bailey, Viking
Honor Books: *Wonderful Year* by Nancy Barnes, Messner; *Big Tree* by Mary and Conrad Buff, Viking; *The Heavenly Tenants* by William Maxwell, Harper & Row; *The Avion My Uncle Flew* by Cyrus Fisher, Appleton; *The Hidden Treasure of Glaston* by Eleanore Jewett, Viking

1948
The Twenty-One Balloons by William Pène du Bois, Viking
Honor Books: *Pancakes-Paris* by Claire Huchet Bishop, Viking; *Li Lun, Lad of Courage* by Carolyn Treffinger, Abingdon; *The Quaint and Curious Quest of Johnny Longfoot* by Catherine Besterman, Bobbs; *The Cow-Tail Switch, and Other West African Stories* by Harold Courlander, Holt; *Misty of Chincoteague* by Marguerite Henry, Rand

1949
King of the Wind by Marguerite Henry, Rand
Honor Books: *Seabird* by Holling C. Holling, Houghton Mifflin; *Daughter of the Mountains* by Louise Rankin, Viking; *My Father's Dragon* by Ruth S. Gannett, Random House; *Story of the Negro* by Arna Bontemps, Knopf

1950
The Door in the Wall by Marguerite de Angeli, Doubleday
Honor Books: *Tree of Freedom* by Rebecca Caudill, Viking; *The Blue Cat of Castle Town* by Catherine Coblentz, Longmans; *Kildee House* by Rutherford Montgomery, Doubleday; *George Washington* by

Genevieve Foster, Scribner's; *Song of the Pines* by Walter and Marion Havighurst, Winston

1951

Amos Fortune, Free Man by Elizabeth Yates, Aladdin
Honor Books: *Better Known as Johnny Appleseed* by Mabel Leigh Hunt, Lippincott; *Ghandi, Fighter Without a Sword* by Jeanette Eaton, Morrow; *Abraham Lincoln, Friend of the People* by Clara Ingram Judson, Follett; *The Story of Appleby Capple* by Anne Parrish, Harper & Row

1952

Ginger Pye by Eleanor Estes, Harcourt Brace
Honor Books: *Americans Before Columbus* by Elizabeth Baity, Viking; *Minn of the Mississippi* by Holling C. Holling, Houghton Mifflin; *The Defender* by Nicholas Kalashnikoff, Scribner's; *The Light at Tern Rock* by Julia Sauer, Viking; *The Apple and the Arrow* by Mary and Conrad Buff, Houghton Mifflin

1953

Secret of the Andes by Ann Nolan Clark, Viking
Honor Books: *Charlotte's Web* by E. B. White, Harper & Row; *Moccasin Trail* by Eloise McGraw, Coward-McCann; *Red Sails to Capri* by Ann Weil, Viking; *The Bears on Hemlock Mountain* by Alice Dalgliesh, Scribner's; *Birthdays of Freedom*, Vol. 1, by Genevieve Foster, Scribner's

1954

. . . and now Miguel by Joseph Krumgold, Crowell
Honor Books: *All Alone* by Claire Huchet Bishop, Viking; *Shadrach* by Meindert DeJong, Harper & Row; *Hurry Home, Candy* by Meindert DeJong, Harper & Row; *Theodore Roosevelt, Fighting Patriot* by Clara Ingram Judson, Follett; *Magic Maize* by Mary and Conrad Buff, Houghton Mifflin

1955

The Wheel on the School by Meindert DeJong, Harper & Row
Honor Books: *The Courage of Sarah Noble* by Alice Dalgliesh, Scribner's; *Banner in the Sky* by James Ullman, Lippincott

1956

Carry on, Mr. Bowditch by Jean Lee Latham, Houghton Mifflin
Honor Books: *The Secret River* by Marjorie Kinnan Rawlings, Scribner's; *The Golden Name Day* by Jennie Linquist, Harper & Row; *Men, Microscopes, and Living Things* by Katherine Shippen, Viking

1957

Miracles on Maple Hill by Virginia Sorensen, Harcourt Brace
Honor Books: *Old Yeller* by Fred Gipson, Harper & Row; *The House of Sixty Fathers* by Meindert DeJong, Harper & Row; *Mr. Justice Holmes* by Clara Ingram Judson, Follet; *The Corn Grows Ripe* by Dorothy Rhoads, Viking; *Black Fox of Lorne* by Marguerite de Angeli, Doubleday

1958

Rifles for Watie by Harold Keith, Crowell
Honor Books: *The Horsecatcher* by Mari Sandoz, Westminster; *Gone-Away Lake* by Elizabeth Enright, Harcourt Brace; *The Great Wheel* by Robert Lawson, Viking; *Tom Paine, Freedom's Apostle* by Leo Gurko, Crowell

1959

The Witch of Blackbird Pond by Elizabeth George Speare, Houghton Mifflin
Honor Books: *The Family Under the Bridge* by Natalie Savage Carlson, Harper & Row; *Along Came a Dog* by Meindert DeJong, Harper & Row; *Chucaro: Wild Pony of the Pampa* by Francis Kalnay, Harcourt Brace; *The Perilous Road* by William O. Steele, Harcourt Brace

1960

Onion John by Joseph Krumgold, Crowell
Honor Books: *My Side of the Mountain* by Jean George, Dutton: *America Is Born* by Gerald W. Johnson, Morrow; *The Gammage Cup* by Carol Kendall, Harcourt Brace

1961

Island of the Blue Dolphins by Scott O'Dell, Houghton Mifflin
Honor Books: *America Moves Forward* by Gerald W. Johnson, Morrow; *Old Ramon* by Jack Schaefer, Houghton Mifflin; *The Cricket in Times Square* by George Selden, Farrar, Straus & Giroux

1962

The Bronze Bow by Elizabeth George Speare, Houghton Mifflin
Honor Books: *Frontier Living* by Edwin Tunis, World; *The Golden Goblet* by Eloise McGraw, Coward-

McCann; *Belling the Tiger* by Mary Stolz, Harper & Row

1963

A Wrinkle in Time by Madeleine L'Engle, Farrar, Straus & Giroux

Honor Books: *Thistle and Thyme* by Sorche Nic Leodhas, Holt; *Men of Athens* by Olivia Coolidge, Houghton Mifflin

1964

It's Like This, Cat by Emily Cheney Neville, Harper & Row

Honor Books: *Rascal* by Sterling North, Dutton; *The Loner* by Ester Wier, McKay

1965

Shadow of a Bull by Maia Wojciechowska, Atheneum

Honor Books: *Across Five Aprils* by Irene Hunt, Follett

1966

I, Juan de Pareja by Elizabeth Borten de Treviño, Farrar, Straus & Giroux

Honor Books: *The Black Cauldron* by Lloyd Alexander, Holt; *The Animal Family* by Randall Jarrell, Pantheon; *The Noonday Friends* by Mary Stolz, Harper & Row

1967

Up a Road Slowly by Irene Hunt, Follett

Honor Books: *The King's Fifth* by Scott O'Dell, Houghton Mifflin; *Zlateh the Goat and Other Stories* by Isaac Bashevis Singer, Harper & Row; *The Jazz Man* by Mary H. Weik, Atheneum

1968

From the Mixed-Up Files of Mrs. Basil E. Frankweiler by E. L. Konigsburg, Atheneum

Honor Books: *Jennifer, Hecate, Macbeth, William McKinley, and Me, Elizabeth* by E. L. Konigsburg, Atheneum; *The Black Pearl* by Scott O'Dell, Houghton Mifflin; *The Fearsome Inn* by Isaac Bashevis Singer, Scribner's; *The Egypt Game* by Zilpha Keatley Snyder, Atheneum

1969

The High King by Lloyd Alexander, Holt

Honor Books: *To Be a Slave* by Julius Lester, Dial; *When Shlemiel Went to Warsaw and Other Stories* by Isaac Bashevis Singer, Farrar, Straus & Giroux

1970

Sounder by William H. Armstrong, Harper & Row

Honor Books: *Our Eddie* by Sulamith Ish-Kishor, Pantheon; *The Many Ways of Seeing: An Introduction to the Pleasures of Art* by Janet Gaylord Moore, World; *Journey Outside* by Mary Q. Steele, Viking

1971

Summer of the Swans by Betsy Byars, Viking

Honor Books: *Kneeknock Rise* by Natalie Babbitt, Farrar Straus & Giroux; *Enchantress from the Stars* by Sylvia Louise Engdahl, Atheneum; *Sing Down the Moon* by Scott O'Dell, Houghton Mifflin

1972

Mrs. Frisby and the Rats of NIMH by Robert C. O'Brien, Atheneum

Honor Books: *Incident at Hawk's Hill* by Allan W. Eckert, Little, Brown; *The Planet of Junior Brown* by Virginia Hamilton, Macmillan; *The Tombs of Atuan* by Ursula K. Le Guin, Atheneum; *Annie and the Old One* by Miska Miles, Little, Atlantic; *The Headless Cupid* by Zilpha Keatley Snyder, Atheneum

1973

Julie of the Wolves by Jean Craighead George, Harper & Row

Honor Books: *Frog and Toad Together* by Arnold Lobel, Harper & Row; *The Upstairs Room* by Johanna Reiss, Crowell; *The Witches of Worm* by Zilpha Keatley Snyder, Atheneum

1974

The Slave Dancer by Paula Fox, Bradbury

Honor Book: *The Dark Is Rising* by Susan Cooper, Atheneum, McElderry

1975

M. C. Higgins, The Great by Virginia Hamilton, Macmillan

Honor Books: *Figgs & Phantoms* by Ellen Raskin, Dutton; *my brother Sam is dead* by James Lincoln Collier & Christopher Collier, Four Winds; *The Perilous Gard* by Elizabeth Marie Pope, Houghton Mifflin; *Philip Hall Likes Me. I Reckon Maybe* by Bette Greene, Dial

1976

The Grey King by Susan Cooper, Atheneum, McElderry

Honor Books: *The Hundred Penny Box* by Sharon Bell Mathis, Viking; *Dragonwings* by Lawrence Yep, Harper & Row

1977
Roll of Thunder, Hear My Cry by Mildred D. Taylor, Dial
Honor Books: *Abel's Island* by William Steig, Farrar Straus & Giroux; *A String in the Harp* by Nancy Bond, Atheneum, McElderry

1978
Bridge to Terabithia by Katherine Paterson, Crowell
Honor Books: *Ramona and Her Father* by Beverly Cleary, Morrow; *Anpao: An American Indian Odyssey* by Jamake Highwater, Lippincott

1979
The Westing Game by Ellen Raskin, Dutton
Honor Book: *The Great Gilly Hopkins* by Katherine Paterson, Crowell

1980
A Gathering of Days: A New England Girl's Journal, 1830–32 by Joan Blos, Scribner's
Honor Book: *The Road from Home: The Story of an Armenian Girl* by David Kherdian, Greenwillow

1981
Jacob Have I Loved by Katherine Paterson, Crowell
Honor Books: *The Fledgling* by Jane Langton, Harper & Row; *A Ring of Endless Light* by Madeleine L'Engle, Farrar, Straus & Giroux

1982
A Visit to William Blake's Inn: Poems for Innocent and Experienced Travelers by Nancy Willard, Harcourt Brace Jovanovich
Honor Books: *Ramona Quimby, Age 8* by Beverly Cleary, Morrow; *Upon the Head of the Goat: A Childhood in Hungary, 1939–1944* by Aranka Siegel, Farrar, Straus & Giroux

1983
Dicey's Song by Cynthia Voigt, Atheneum
Honor Books: *The Blue Sword* by Robin McKinley, Greenwillow; *Dr. De Soto* by William Steig, Farrar, Straus & Giroux; *Graven Images* by Paul Fleischman, Harper & Row; *Homesick: My Own Story* by Jean Fritz, Putnam's; *Sweet Whispers, Brother Rush* by Virginia Hamilton, Philomel

1984
Dear Mr. Henshaw by Beverly Cleary, Morrow
Honor Books: *The Wish Giver: Three Tales of Coven Tree* by Bill Brittain, Harper & Row; *A Solitary Blue* by Cynthia Voigt, Atheneum; *The Sign of the Beaver* by Elizabeth George Speare, Houghton Mifflin; *Sugaring Time* by Kathryn Lasky, Macmillan

1985
The Hero and the Crown by Robin McKinley, Greenwillow
Honor Books: *The Moves Make the Man* by Bruce Brooks, Harper & Row; *One-Eyed Cat* by Paula Fox, Bradbury; *Like Jake and Me* by Mavis Jukes, Knopf

1986
Sarah, Plain and Tall by Patricia MacLachlan, Harper & Row
Honor Books: *Commodore Perry in the Land of Shogun* by Rhoda Blumberg, Lothrop, Lee & Shepard; *Dogsong* by Gary Paulsen, Bradbury

1987
The Whipping Boy by Sid Fleischman, Greenwillow
Honor Books: *On My Honor* by Marion Dane Bauer, Clarion; *A Fine White Dust* by Cynthia Rylant, Bradbury; *Volcano* by Patricia Lauber, Bradbury.

1988
Lincoln: A Photobiography by Russell Freedman, Clarion
Honor Books: *Hatchet* by Gary Paulsen, Bradbury; *After the Rain* by Norma Fox Mazer, Morrow

THE RANDOLPH CALDECOTT MEDAL

The Randolph Caldecott Medal, named for a nineteenth-century British illustrator of books for children, is given annually for the most distinguished picture book for children published in the United States in the year preceding the award.

Selection of the award winner is made by a committee of the Association for Library Services for Children of the American Library Association.

The list below gives the title, illustrator, author, and publisher of winners and runners-up (honor books) since inception of the award in 1938. Where two names are given, the illustrator is listed first, followed by the text's author in parentheses. Where only one name is given, the book was written and illustrated by the same person.

1938
Animals of the Bible by Dorothy P. Lathrop (Helen Dean Fish), Lippincott

Honor Books: *Seven Simeons* by Boris Artzybasheff, Viking; *Four and Twenty Blackbirds* by Robert Lawson (Helen Dean Fish), Lippincott

1939
Mei Li by Thomas Handforth, Doubleday
Honor Books: *The Forest Pool* by Laura Adams Armer, Longmans; *Wee Gillis* by Robert Lawson (Munro Leaf), Viking; *Snow White and the Seven Dwarfs* by Wanda Gág, Coward; *Barkis* by Clare Newberry, Harper & Row; *Andy and the Lion* by James Daugherty, Viking

1940
Abraham Lincoln by Ingri and Edgar Parin d'Aulaire, Doubleday
Honor Books: *Cock-a-Doodle Doo . . .* by Berta and Elmer Hader, Macmillan; *Madeline* by Ludwig Bemelmans, Viking; *The Ageless Story*, by Lauren Ford, Dodd, Mead

1941
They Were Strong and Good by Robert Lawson, Viking
Honor Book: *April's Kittens* by Clare Newberry, Harper & Row

1942
Make Way for Ducklings by Robert McCloskey, Viking
Honor Books: *An American ABC* by Maud and Miska Petersham, Macmillan; *In My Mother's House* by Velino Herrera (Ann Nolan Clark), Viking; *Paddle-to-the-Sea* by Holling C. Holling, Houghton Mifflin; *Nothing at All* by Wanda Gág, Coward-McCann

1943
The Little House by Virginia Lee Burton, Houghton Mifflin
Honor Books: *Dash and Dart* by Mary and Conrad Buff, Viking; *Marshmallow* by Clare Newberry, Harper & Row

1944
Many Moons by Louis Slobodkin (James Thurber), Harcourt Brace
Honor Books: *Small Rain: Verses from the Bible* by Elizabeth Orton Jones (selected by Jessie Orton Jones), Viking; *Pierre Pigeon* by Arnold E. Bare (Lee Kingman), Houghton Mifflin; *The Mighty Hunter* by Berta and Elmer Hader, Macmillan; *A Child's Good Night Book* by Jean Charlot (Margaret Wise Brown), Scott, Foresman; *Good Luck Horse* by Plao Chan (Chin-Yi Chan), Whittlesey

1945
Prayer for a Child by Elizabeth Orton Jones (Rachel Field), Macmillan
Honor Books: *Mother Goose* by Tasha Tudor, Walck; *In the Forest* by Marie Hall Ets, Viking; *Yonie Wondernose* by Marguerite de Angeli, Doubleday; *The Christmas Anna Angel* by Kate Seredy (Ruth Sawyer), Viking

1946
The Rooster Crows . . . (traditional Mother Goose) by Maud and Miska Petersham, Macmillan
Honor Books: *Little Lost Lamb* by Leonard Weisgard (Golden MacDonald), Doubleday; *Sing Mother Goose* by Marjorie Torrey (Opal Wheeler), Dutton; *My Mother Is the Most Beautiful Woman in the World* by Ruth Gannett (Becky Reyher), Lothrop, Lee & Shepard; *You Can Write Chinese* by Kurt Wiese, Viking

1947
The Little Island by Leonard Weisgard (Golden MacDonald), Doubleday
Honor Books: *Rain Drop Splash* by Leonard Weisgard (Alvin Tresselt), Lothrop, Lee & Shepard; *Boats on the River* by Jay Hyde Barnum (Marjorie Flack), Viking; *Timothy Turtle* by Tony Palazzo (Al Graham), Viking; *Pedro, the Angel of Olvera Street* by Leo Politi, Scribner's; *Sing in Praise: A Collection of the Best Loved Hymns* by Marjorie Torrey (Opal Wheeler), Dutton

1948
White Snow, Bright Snow by Roger Duvoisin (Alvin Tresselt), Lothrop, Lee & Shepard
Honor Books: *Stone Soup* by Marcia Brown, Scribner's; *McElligot's Pool* by Dr. Seuss, Random House; *Bambino the Clown* by George Schreiber, Viking; *Roger and the Fox* by Hildegard Woodward (Lavinia Davis), Doubleday; *Song of Robin Hood* by Virginia Lee Burton (edited by Anne Malcolmson), Houghton Mifflin

1949
The Big Snow by Berta and Elmer Hader, Macmillan
Honor Books: *Blueberries for Sal* by Robert McCloskey, Viking; *All Around the Town* by Helen Stone (Phyllis McGinley), Lippincott; *Juanita* by Leo Politi, Scribner's; *Fish in the Air* by Kurt Wiese, Viking

1950
Song of the Swallows by Leo Politi, Scribner's
Honor Books: *America's Ethan Allen* by Lynd Ward, (Stewart Holbrook), Houghton Mifflin; *The Wild*

Birthday Cake by Hildegard Woodward (Lavinia Davis), Doubleday; *The Happy Day* by Marc Simont (Ruth Krauss), Harper & Row; *Bartholomew and the Oobleck* by Dr. Seuss, Random House; *Henry Fisherman* by Marcia Brown, Scribner's

1951

The Egg Tree by Katherine Milhous, Scribner's
Honor Books: *Dick Whittington and His Cat* by Marcia Brown, Scribner's; *The Two Reds* by Nicholas Mordvinoff (William Lipkind), Harcourt Brace; *If I Ran the Zoo* by Dr. Seuss, Random House; *The Most Wonderful Doll in the World* by Helen Stone (Phyllis McGinley), Lippincott; *T-Bone, The Baby Sitter* by Clare Newberry, Harper & Row

1952

Finders Keepers by Nicholas Mordvinoff (William Lipkind), Harcourt Brace
Honor Books: *Mr. T. W. Anthony Woo* by Marie Hall Ets, Viking; *Skipper John's Cook* by Marcia Brown, Scribner's; *All Falling Down* by Margaret Bloy Graham (Gene Zion), Harper & Row; *Bear Party* by William Pène du Bois, Viking; *Feather Mountain* by Elizabeth Olds, Houghton Mifflin

1953

The Biggest Bear by Lynd Ward, Houghton Mifflin
Honor Books: *Puss in Boots* retold and illustrated by Marcia Brown (Charles Perrault), Scribner's; *One Morning in Maine* by Robert McCloskey, Viking; *Ape in a Cape* by Fritz Eichenberg, Harcourt Brace; *The Storm Book* by Margaret Bloy Graham (Charlotte Zolotow), Harper & Row; *Five Little Monkeys* by Juliet Kepes, Houghton Mifflin

1954

Madeline's Rescue by Ludwig Bemelmans, Viking
Honor Books: *Journey Cake, Ho!* by Robert McCloskey (Ruth Sawyer), Viking; *When Will the World Be Mine?* by Jean Charlot (Miriam Schlein), Scott, Foresman; *The Steadfast Tin Soldier* by Marcia Brown (Hans Christian Andersen), Scribner's; *A Very Special House* by Maurice Sendak (Ruth Krauss), Harper & Row; *Green Eyes* by A. Birnbaum, Capitol

1955

Cinderella, or the Little Glass Slipper retold and illustrated by Marcia Brown (Charles Perrault), Scribner's
Honor Books: *Book of Nursery and Mother Goose Rhymes* by Marguerite de Angeli, Doubleday; *Wheel on the Chimney* by Tibor Gergely (Margaret Wise Brown), Lippincott; *The Thanksgiving Story* by Helen Sewell (Alice Dalgliesh), Scribner's

1956

Frog Went A-Courtin' by Feodor Rojankovsky (John Langstaff), Harcourt Brace
Honor Books: *Play with Me* by Marie Hall Ets, Viking; *Crow Boy* by Taro Yashima, Viking

1957

A Tree Is Nice by Marc Simont (Janice May Udry), Harper & Row
Honor Books: *Mr. Penny's Race Horse* by Marie Hall Ets, Viking; *1 Is One* by Tasha Tudor, Walck; *Anatole* by Paul Galdone (Eve Titus), McGraw-Hill; *Gillespie and the Guards* by James Daugherty (Benjamin Elkin), Viking; *Lion* by William Pène du Bois, Viking

1958

Time of Wonder by Robert McCloskey, Viking
Honor Books: *Fly High, Fly Low* by Don Freeman, Viking; *Anatole and the Cat* by Paul Galdone (Eve Titus), McGraw-Hill

1959

Chanticleer and the Fox adapted and illustrated by Barbara Cooney, (Chaucer,) Crowell
Honor Books: *The House That Jack Built* by Antonio Frasconi, Harcourt Brace; *What Do You Say, Dear?* by Maurice Sendak (Sesyle Joslin), Scott, Foresman; *Umbrella* by Taro Yashima, Viking

1960

Nine Days to Christmas by Marie Hall Ets (Aurora Labastida, Marie Hall Ets), Viking
Honor Books: *Houses from the Sea* by Adrienne Adams (Alice E. Goudey), Scribner's; *The Moon Jumpers* by Maurice Sendak (Janice May Udry), Harper & Row

1961

Baboushka and the Three Kings by Nicholas Sidjakov (Ruth Robbins), Parnassus
Honor Book: *Inch by Inch* by Leo Lionni, Obolensky

1962

Once a Mouse . . . by Marcia Brown, Scribner's
Honor Books: *Fox Went Out on a Chilly Night* by Peter Spier, Doubleday; *Little Bear's Visit* by Maurice Sendak (Else Holmelund Minarik), Harper & Row; *The Day We Saw the Sun Come Up* by Adrienne Adams (Alice E. Goudey), Scribner's

1963

The Snowy Day by Ezra Jack Keats, Viking

Honor Books: *The Sun Is a Golden Earring* by Bernarda Bryson (Natalia M. Belting), Holt; *Mr. Rabbit and the Lovely Present* by Maurice Sendak (Charlotte Zolotow), Harper & Row

1964

Where the Wild Things Are by Maurice Sendak, Harper & Row

Honor Books: *Swimmy* by Leo Lionni, Pantheon; *All in the Morning Early* by Evaline Ness (Sorche Nic Leodhas), Holt; *Mother Goose and Nursery Rhymes* Philip Reed, Atheneum

1965

May I Bring a Friend? by Beni Montresor (Beatrice Schenk De Regniers), Atheneum

Honor Books: *Rain Makes Applesauce* by Marvin Bileck, (Julian Scheer), Holiday House; *The Wave* by Blair Lent (Margaret Hodges), Houghton Mifflin; *A Pocketful of Cricket* by Evaline Ness (Rebecca Caudill), Holt

1966

Always Room for One More by Nonny Hogrogian (Sorche Nic Leodhas), Holt

Honor Books: *Hide and Seek Fog* by Roger Duvoisin (Alvin Tresselt), Lothrop, Lee & Shepard; *Just Me* by Marie Hall Ets, Viking; *Tom Tit Tot* by Evaline Ness,

1967

Sam, Bangs and Moonshine by Evaline Ness, Holt

Honor Book: *One Wide River to Cross* by Ed Emberley (Barbara Emberley), Prentice-Hall

1968

Drummer Hoff by Ed Emberley (Barbara Emberley), Prentice-Hall

Honor Books: *Frederick* by Leo Lionni, Pantheon; *Seashore Story* by Taro Yashima, Viking; *The Emperor and the Kite* by Ed Young (Jane Yolen), World

1969

The Fool of the World and the Flying Ship by Uri Shulevitz (Arthur Ransome), Farrar, Straus & Giroux

Honor Book: *Why the Sun and the Moon Live in the Sky* by Blair Lent (Elphinstone Dayrell), Houghton Mifflin

1970

Sylvester and the Magic Pebble by William Steig, Windmill

Honor Books: *Goggles!* by Ezra Jack Keats, Macmillan; *Alexander and the Wind-Up Mouse* by Leo Lionni, Pantheon; *Pop Corn and Ma Goodness* by Robert Andrew Parker (Edna Mitchell Preston), Viking; *Thy Friend, Obadiah* by Brinton Turkle, Viking; *The Judge* by Margot Zemach (Harve Zemach), Farrar, Straus & Giroux

1971

A Story—A Story by Gail E. Haley, Atheneum

Honor Books: *The Angry Moon* by Blair Lent (William Sleator), Little, Atlantic; *Frog and Toad Are Friends* by Arnold Lobel, Harper & Row; *In the Night Kitchen* by Maurice Sendak, Harper & Row

1972

One Fine Day by Nonny Hogrogian, Macmillan

Honor Books: *If All the Seas Were One Sea*, by Janina Domanska, Macmillan; *Moja Means One: Swahili Counting Book* by Tom Feelings (Muriel Feelings), Dial; *Hildilid's Night* by Arnold Lobel (Cheli Durán Ryan), Macmillan

1973

The Funny Little Woman by Blair Lent (retold by Arlene Mosel), Dutton

Honor Books: *Anansi the Spider* adapted and illustrated by Gerald McDermott, Holt; *Hosie's Alphabet* by Leonard Baskin (Hosea, Tobias and Lisa Baskin), Viking; *Snow White and the Seven Dwarfs* by Nancy Ekholm Burkert (translated by Randall Jarrell) Farrar, Straus & Giroux; *When Clay Sings* by Tom Bahti (Byrd Baylor), Scribner's

1974

Duffy and the Devil by Margot Zemach (Harve Zemach), Farrar, Straus & Giroux

Honor Books: *Three Jovial Huntsmen* by Susan Jeffers, Bradbury; *Cathedral: The Story of Its Construction* by David Macaulay, Houghton Mifflin

1975

Arrow to the Sun retold and illustrated by Gerald McDermott, Viking

Honor Book: *Jambo Means Hello* by Tom Feelings (Muriel Feelings), Dial

1976

Why Mosquitoes Buzz in People's Ears by Leo and Diane Dillon (retold by Verna Aardema), Dial

Honor Books: *The Desert Is Theirs* by Peter Parnall (Byrd Baylor), Scribner's; *Strega Nona* retold and illustrated by Tomie dePaola, Prentice-Hall

1977

Ashanti to Zulu: African Traditions by Leo and Diane Dillon (Margaret Musgrove), Dial

Honor Books: *The Amazing Bone* by William Steig, Farrar, Straus & Giroux; *The Contest* retold and illustrated by Nonny Hogrogian, Greenwillow; *Fish for Supper* by M. B. Goffstein, Dial; *The Golem* by Beverly Brodsky McDermott, Lippincott; *Hawk, I'm Your Brother* by Peter Parnall (Byrd Baylor), Scribner's

1978

Noah's Ark by Peter Spier, Doubleday

Honor Books: *Castle* by David Macaulay, Houghton Mifflin; *It Could Always Be Worse* by Margot Zemach, Farrar, Straus & Giroux

1979

The Girl Who Loved Wild Horses by Paul Goble, Bradbury

Honor Books: *Freight Train* by Donald Crews, Greenwillow; *The Way to Start a Day* by Peter Parnall (Byrd Baylor), Scribner's

1980

Ox-Cart Man by Barbara Cooney (Donald Hall), Viking

Honor Books: *Ben's Trumpet* by Rachel Isadora, Greenwillow; *The Treasure* by Uri Shulevitz, Farrar, Straus & Giroux; *The Garden of Abdul Gasazi* by Chris Van Allsburg, Houghton Mifflin

1981

Fables by Arnold Lobel, Harper & Row

Honor Books: *The Bremen-Town Musicians* by Ilse Plume, Doubleday; *The Grey Lady and the Strawberry Snatcher* by Molly Bang, Four Winds; *Mice Twice* by Joseph Low, Atheneum, McElderry; *Truck* by Donald Crews, Greenwillow

1982

Jumanji by Chris Van Allsburg, Houghton Mifflin

Honor Books: *On Market Street* by Anita Lobel (Arnold Lobel), Greenwillow, *Outside Over There* by Maurice Sendak, Harper & Row; *A Visit to William Blake's Inn: Poems for Innocent and Experienced Travelers* by Alice and Martin Provensen (Nancy Willard), Harcourt Brace Jovanovich; *Where the Buffaloes Begin* by Stephen Gammell (Olaf Baker), Warne

1983

Shadow by Marcia Brown (Blaise Cendrars), Scribner's

Honor Books: *A Chair for My Mother* by Vera B. Williams, Greenwillow; *When I was Young in the Mountains* by Diane Goode (Cynthia Rylant), Dutton

1984

The Glorious Flight: Across the Channel with Louis Blériot by Alice and Martin Provensen, Viking

Honor Books: *Little Red Riding Hood* retold and illustrated by Trina Schart Hyman, Holiday House; *Ten, Nine, Eight* by Molly Bang, Greenwillow

1985

Saint George and the Dragon by Trina Schart Hyman (retold by Margaret Hodges), Little, Brown

Honor Books: *Hansel and Gretel* by Paul O. Zelinsky (retold by Rika Lesser), Dodd, Mead; *Have You Seen My Duckling?* by Nancy Tafuri, Greenwillow; *The Story of Jumping Mouse* retold and illustrated by John Steptoe, Lothrop, Lee & Shepard

1986

The Polar Express by Chris Van Allsburg, Houghton Mifflin

Honor Books: *The Relatives Came* by Stephen Gammell (Cynthia Rylant), Bradbury; *King Bidgood's in the Bathtub* by Don Wood (Audrey Wood), Harcourt Brace Jovanovich

1987

Hey, Al by Richard Egielski (Arthur Yorinks), Farrar, Straus & Giroux

Honor Books: *The Village of Round and Square Houses* by Ann Grifalconi, Little, Brown; *Alphabatics* by Suse MacDonald, Bradbury; *Rumpelstiltskin* by Paul O. Zelinsky, Dutton

1988

Owl Moon by John Schoenherr (Jane Yolen), Philomel

Honor Book: *Mufaro's Beautiful Daughters* by John Steptoe, Lothrop, Lee & Shepard

BOSTON GLOBE-HORN BOOK AWARDS

This award has been presented annually in the fall since 1967 by *The Boston Globe* and *The Horn Book Magazine*. Through 1975, two awards were given, one for outstanding text and one for outstanding illustration; in 1976, the award categories were changed to outstanding fiction or poetry, outstanding nonfiction, and outstanding illustration. A monetary gift is awarded to the winner in each category.

1967
Text: *The Little Fishes* by Erik Christian Haugaard, Houghton Mifflin
Illustration: *London Bridge Is Falling Down!* illustrated by Peter Spier, Doubleday

1968
Text: *The Spring Rider* by John Lawson, Crowell
Illustration: *Tikki Tikki Tembo* by Arlene Mosel, illustrated by Blair Lent, Holt

1969
Text: *A Wizard of Earthsea* by Ursula K. Le Guin, Houghton Mifflin, Parnassus
Illustration: *The Adventures of Paddy Pork* by John S. Goodall, Harcourt Brace Jovanovich

1970
Text: *The Intruder* by John Rowe Townsend, Lippincott
Illustration: *Hi, Cat!* by Ezra Jack Keats, Macmillan

1971
Text: *A Room Made of Windows* by Eleanor Cameron, Little, Brown, Atlantic
Illustration: *If I Built a Village* by Kazue Mizumura, Crowell

1972
Text: *Tristan and Iseult* by Rosemary Sutcliff, Dutton
Illustration: *Mr. Gumpy's Outing* by John Burningham, Holt

1973
Text: *The Dark Is Rising* by Susan Cooper, Atheneum, McElderry
Illustration: *King Stork* by Trina Schart Hyman, Little, Brown

1974
Text: *M. C. Higgins, the Great* by Virginia Hamilton, Macmillan
Illustration: *Jambo Means Hello* by Muriel Feelings, illustrated by Tom Feelings, Dial

1975
Text: *Transport 7-41-R* by T. Degens, Viking
Illustration: *Anno's Alphabet* by Mitsumasa Anno, Crowell

1976
Fiction: *Unleaving* by Jill Paton Walsh, Farrar, Straus & Giroux
Nonfiction: *Voyaging to Cathay: Americans in the China Trade* by Alfred Tamarin and Shirley Glubok, Viking
Illustration: *Thirteen* by Remy Charlip and Jerry Joyner, Four Winds

1977
Fiction: *Child of the Owl* by Laurence Yep, Harper & Row
Nonfiction: *Chance, Luck and Destiny* by Peter Dickinson, Little, Brown, Atlantic
Illustration: *Granfa' Grig Had a Pig and Other Rhymes Without Reason from Mother Goose* by Wallace Tripp, Little, Brown

1978
Fiction: *The Westing Game* by Ellen Raskin, Dutton
Nonfiction: *Mischling, Second Degree: My Childhood in Nazi Germany* by Ilse Koehn, Greenwillow
Illustration: *Anno's Journey* by Mitsumasa Anno, Philomel

1979
Fiction: *Humbug Mountain* by Sid Fleischman, Little, Brown, Atlantic
Nonfiction: *The Road from Home: The Story of an Armenian Girl* by David Kherdian, Greenwillow
Illustration: *The Snowman* by Raymond Briggs, Random House

1980
Fiction: *Conrad's War* by Andrew Davies, Crown
Nonfiction: *Building: The Fight Against Gravity* by Mario Salvadori, Atheneum, McElderry
Illustration: *The Garden of Abdul Gasazi* by Chris Van Allsburg, Houghton Mifflin

1981
Fiction: *The Leaving* by Lynn Hall, Scribner's
Nonfiction: *The Weaver's Gift* by Kathryn Lasky, Warne
Illustration: *Outside Over There* by Maurice Sendak, Harper & Row

1982
Fiction: *Playing Beatie Bow* by Ruth Park, Atheneum
Nonfiction: *Upon the Head of the Goat: A Childhood in Hungry 1939–1944* by Aranka Siegal, Farrar, Straus & Giroux
Illustration: *A Visit to William Blake's Inn: Poems for

Innocent and Experienced Travelers by Nancy Willard, illustrated by Alice and Martin Provensen, Harcourt Brace Jovanovich

1983
Fiction: *Sweet Whispers, Brother Rush* by Virginia Hamilton, Philomel
Nonfiction: *Behind Barbed Wire: The Imprisonment of Japanese Americans During World War II* by Daniel S. Davis, Dutton
Illustration: *A Chair for My Mother* by Vera B. Williams, Greenwillow

1984
Fiction: *A Little Fear* by Patricia Wrightson, Atheneum, McElderry
Nonfiction: *The Double Life of Pocahontas* by Jean Fritz, Putnam's
Illustration: *Jonah and the Great Fish* retold and illustrated by Warwick Hutton, Atheneum, McElderry

1985
Fiction: *The Moves Make the Man* by Bruce Brooks, Harper & Row
Nonfiction: *Commodore Perry in the Land of the Shogun* by Rhoda Blumberg, Lothrop, Lee & Shepard
Illustration: *Mama Don't Allow* by Thacher Hurd, Harper & Row
Special Award: *1, 2, 3,* by Tana Hoban, Greenwillow

1986
Fiction: *In Summer Light* by Zibby Oneal, Viking
Nonfiction: *Auks, Rocks and the Odd Dinosaur: Inside Stories from the Smithsonian's Museum of Natural History* by Peggy Thomsen, Crowell
Illustration: *The Paper Crane* by Molly Bang, Greenwillow

1987
Fiction: *Rabble Starkey* by Lois Lowry, Houghton Mifflin
Nonfiction: *The Pilgrims of Plimoth* by Marcia Sewall, Atheneum
Illustration: *Mufaro's Beautiful Daughters* by John Steptoe, Lothrop, Lee & Shepard

1988
Fiction: *The Friendship* by Mildred Taylor, Dial
Nonfiction: *Anthony Burns: The Defeat and Triumph of a Fugitive Slave* by Virginia Hamilton, Knopf
Illustration: *The Boy of the Three-Year Nap* by Diane Snyder, Houghton Mifflin

THE LAURA INGALLS WILDER AWARD

The Laura Ingalls Wilder Award, named for its first winner, the author of the Little House books, is given to an author or illustrator whose books, published in the United States, have made a substantial and lasting contribution to literature for children. Until 1980, the award was given every five years; now it is awarded every three years. Selection of the award winner is made by the Association for Library Services for Children of the American Library Association. The winners since inception of the award in 1954 are as follows:

1954
Laura Ingalls Wilder

1960
Clara Ingram Judson

1965
Ruth Sawyer

1970
E. B. White

1975
Beverly Cleary

1980
Theodor S. Geisel (Dr. Seuss)

1983
Maurice Sendak

1986
Jean Fritz

THE NATIONAL COUNCIL OF TEACHERS OF ENGLISH AWARD FOR EXCELLENCE IN POETRY FOR CHILDREN

Sponsored by the National Council of Teachers of English, the award was given annually from 1977 to 1982 to a living American poet in recognition of an aggregate body of work for children ages 3–13. Currently, the award is presented every three years. A citation is given to the poet and a medallion design of the seal is available for use on the dust jacket of all the poet's books.

1977
David McCord

1978
Aileen Fisher

1979
Karla Kuskin

1980
Myra Cohn Livingston

1981
Eve Merriam

1982
John Ciardi

1985
Lilian Moore

1988
Arnold Adoff

THE HANS CHRISTIAN ANDERSEN AWARD

This award has been given biennially since 1956 by the International Board on Books for Young People to one author and one illustrator (since 1966) in recognition of his or her entire body of work. A medal is presented to the recipient.

1956
Eleanor Farjeon (Great Britain)

1958
Astrid Lindgren (Sweden)

1960
Erich Kästner (Germany)

1962
Meindert DeJong (U.S.A.)

1964
René Guillot (France)

1966
Author: Tove Jansson (Finland)
Illustrator: Alois Carigiet (Switzerland)

1968
Authors: James Krüss (Germany)
José Maria Sanchez-Silva (Spain)
Illustrator: Jiri Trnka (Czechoslovakia)

1970
Author: Gianni Rodari (Italy)
Illustrator: Maurice Sendak (U.S.A.)

1972
Author: Scott O'Dell (U.S.A.)
Illustrator: lb Spang Olsen (Denmark)

1974
Author: Maria Gripe (Sweden)
Illustrator: Farshid Mesghali (Iran)

1976
Author: Cecil Bødker (Denmark)
Illustrator: Tatjana Mawrina (U.S.S.R.)

1978
Author: Paula Fox (U.S.A.)
Illustrator: Svend Otto S. (Denmark)

1980
Author: Bohumil Ríha (Czechoslovakia)
Illustrator: Suekichi Akaba (Japan)

1982
Author: Lygia Bojunga Nunes (Brazil)
Illustrator: Zbigniew Rychlicki (Poland)

1984
Author: Christine Nöstlinger (Austria)
Illustrator: Mitsumasa Anno (Japan)

1986
Author: Patricia Wrightson (Australia)
Illustrator: Robert Ingpen (Australia)

1988
Author: Annie M. G. Schmidt (Holland)
Illustrator: Dusan Kallay (Czechoslovakia)

INTERNATIONAL READING ASSOCIATION (IRA) CHILDREN'S BOOK AWARD

The IRA award, sponsored by the Institute for Reading Research and administered by the IRA, is presented annually for a children's book (published in the year preceding the award) by an author who shows unusual promise. Books originating in any country are eligible. For a book written in a language other than English, the IRA first determines if the book warrants an English translation and, if so, then extends to it an additional year of eligibility.

The list below gives title, author, and publisher of winners since inception of the award in 1975. Since 1987, the award has been presented for both picture books and novels.

1975
Transport 7-41-R by T. Degens, Viking

1976
Dragonwings by Lawrence Yep, Harper & Row

1977
A String in the Harp by Nancy Bond, Atheneum

1978
A Summer to Die by Lois Lowry, Houghton Mifflin

1979
Reserved for Mark Anthony Crowder by Alison Smith, Dutton

1980
Words by Heart by Ouida Sebestyen, Little, Brown

1981
My Own Private Sky by Delores Beckman, Dutton

1982
Goodnight Mister Tom by Michelle Magorian, Kestrel, Great Britain; Harper & Row, U.S.A.

1983
The Darkangel by Meredith Pierce, Little, Brown, Atlantic

1984
Ratha's Creature by Clare Bell, Atheneum, McElderry

1985
Badger on the Barge by Janni Howker, MacRae, Great Britain; Greenwillow, U.S.A.

1986
Prairie Songs by Pam Conrad, Harper & Row

1987
Picture Book: *The Line Up Book* by Marisabina Russo, Greenwillow
Novel: *After the Dancing Days* by Margaret I. Rostkowski, Harper & Row

1988
Picture Book: *The Third-Story Cat* by Leslie Baker, Little, Brown
Novel: *The Ruby in the Smoke* by Philip Pullman, Knopf

THE EZRA JACK KEATS NEW ILLUSTRATOR AWARD

Cosponsored by the U.S. Board on Books for Young People (U.S. National Section of IBBY) and the United Nations Children's Fund (UNICEF), this award is given biennially to a promising new artist. It recognizes graphic and technical prowess, the relationship of illustration with text, storytelling quality, and appeal to children. Funded by the Ezra Jack Keats Foundation, the recipient receives a monetary award and a medallion.

1986
Felipe Daválos (Mexico)

1988
Barbara Reid (Canada)

THE EZRA JACK KEATS NEW WRITER AWARD

This award, first presented in 1985 and 1986, is given biennially to a promising new writer. It honors work done in the tradition of Ezra Jack Keats: appeal to young children, storytelling quality, relation between text and illustration, positive reflection of families, and the multicultural nature of the world. The award is presented at the Early Childhood Resource and Information Center of the New York Public Library. Funded by the Ezra Jack Keats Foundation, the recipient receives a monetary award and a medallion.

1985
Valerie Flournoy, *The Patchwork Quilt*, illustrated by Jerry Pinkney, Dial

1987

Juanita Havill, *Jamaica's Find*, illustrated by Anne Sibley O'Brien, Houghton Mifflin

OTHER AWARDS

There are approximately 125 different awards given for children's books, each with its own unique selection process and criteria. Some are chosen by adults and some by children; some are international, some state or regional. A comprehensive listing of the various award winners is provided in *Children's Books: Awards and Prizes,* published by the Children's Book Council. This publication is updated periodically.

Book Selection Aids

A to Zoo: Subject Access to Children's Picture Books, 2nd ed., compiled by Carolyn Lima, Bowker, 1986. 706 pages. Approximately 8,600 picture books grouped by topic, author, and title under 600 subject headings.

Accept Me As I Am: Best Books of Juvenile Nonfiction on Impairments and Disabilities by Joan Brest Friedberg, June B. Mullins, and Adelaide Weir Sukiennik, Bowker, 1985. 363 pages. Annotated lists grouped according to specific physical, sensory, cognitive-behavioral, and multiple-severe conditions. Biographies, memoirs, and histories included.

Adventuring with Books: A Booklist for Pre-K–Grade 6, edited by Dianne L. Monson, National Council of Teachers of English, 1985. 395 pages. A list of books selected for their merit and their potential for use in the classroom and at home. Approximately 1700 new books are annotated and several hundred from previous editions are listed by genre. New editions are prepared periodically.

Anatomy of Wonder: A Critical Guide to Science Fiction, 3rd ed., edited by Neil Barron, Bowker, 1987. 880 pages. Summaries and evaluations of 2,000 adult and juvenile science fiction titles published through 1986.

Best Books for Children: Preschool Through the Middle Grades, 3rd ed., edited by John T. Gillespie and Christine B. Gilbert, Bowker, 1985. 595 pages. A listing of 11,000 books arranged alphabetically by author under 500 subject headings.

The Best in Children's Books: The University of Chicago Guide to Children's Literature: 1979–1984, edited by Zena Sutherland, University of Chicago Press, 1986. 522 pages. Selected reviews from the Bulletin of the Center for Children's Books listed alphabetically by author. Previous editions cover 1966–1972 and 1973–1978. Indexes include title, developmental values, curricular use, reading level, type of literature, and subject.

Beyond Fact: Nonfiction for Children and Young People, edited by Jo Carr, American Library Association, 1982. 236 pages. Articles on qualities of good nonfiction and lists of titles.

Bibliography of Books for Children , rev. ed., edited by Sylvia Sunderlin, Association for Childhood Education International, 1983. Criteria for selecting books for children and annotated list of books that qualify.

The Black Experience in Children's Books, rev. ed., compiled by Barbara Rollock, New York Public Library, 1984. Annotated bibliography of books about black life in America, Africa, the Caribbean, and England.

The Bookfinder: A Guide to Children's Literature about the Needs and Problems of Youth Aged 2 and Up, edited by Sharon Spredemann Dreyer, American Guidance Service, Vol. 1, 1977; Vol. 2, 1981; Vol. 3, 1985. Reviews of children's and adolescent books that identify the problem or need touched upon. A subject index with headings, such as courage, death, and friendship, lists relevant titles. The cumulative index in Volume 3 includes the earlier volumes.

Books, Children and Men by Paul Hazard, translated by Marguerite Mitchell, Horn Book, 1944. (5th rev. ed., 1985.) An enlightened discussion of children's literature among the literatures of the world. Hazard, a distinguished French scholar, establishes basic criteria which underly quality literature for children.

Books for the Gifted Child by Barbara H. Baskin and Karen H. Harris, Bowker, 1980. 263 pages. Critical annotations of books judged stimulating for gifted children.

Books for You: A Booklist for Senior High Students, edited by Donald R. Gallo, National Council of Teachers of English, 1985. 364 pages. Lively annotations of young adult books grouped by categories, such as careers and jobs, computers and microprocessors, ethnic experiences, and drama and theater.

Books to Help Children Cope with Separation and Loss, 2nd ed., compiled by Joanne E. Bernstein, Bowker, 1983. 439 pages. Discussions of bibliotherapy and annotated lists of books grouped by categories, such as adoption, divorce, and disabilities.

Building A Children's Literature Collection: A Suggested Basic Reference Collection for Academic Libraries and a Suggested Basic Collection of Children's Books, 3rd ed., by Harriet B. Quimby and Margaret Mary Kimmel, *Choice* Magazine, 1986. 45 pages. Materials to support the study of children's literature at all levels including reference and children's books.

Children's Books: Awards and Prizes, compiled and edited by the Children's Book Council, 1986. 257 pages. A comprehensive list of honors awarded to children's books. Awards chosen by adults and children are grouped by state, national, and international designations.

Children's Books in Print, Bowker, Annual. A comprehensive index of all children's books in print at time of publication. Author, title, and illustrator indexes give pertinent publishing information. A directory of publishers and addresses is appended.

Children's Books of International Interest, 3rd ed., edited by Barbara Elleman, American Library Association, 1984. Books published in the U.S. that incorporate universal themes or depict the American way of life.

Children's Catalog, 15th ed., Wilson, 1986. 1,298 pages. A comprehensive catalog classified by Dewey Decimal System with nonfiction, fiction, short stories, and easy books. Five year cumulations and annual supplements available.

Children's Literature Review, edited by Ann Block and Carolyn Riley, Gale Research. Since 1976 new volumes added periodically. Articles about authors and topics of interest with excerpts from reviews of the works of each author.

A Comprehensive Guide to Children's Literature with a Jewish Theme by Enid Davis, Schocken, 1981. Fiction and nonfiction related to Judaism arranged in subject categories.

Elementary School Library Collection, 14th ed., edited by Lois Winkel, Bro-Dart Foundation, 1984. Comprehensive bibliography of 13,000 print and nonprint materials for school media collections. Dewey Decimal subject classification, age level, and brief annotations.

The Family Story-Telling Handbook by Anne Pellowski, illustrated by Lynn Sweat, Macmillan, 1987. 150 pages. A guide to using stories, anecdotes, rhymes, handkerchiefs, paper, and other objects to enrich family traditions. Line drawings appear alongside scripts for the storyteller to make it clear how objects and stories relate.

Fantasy for Children: An Annotated Checklist and Reference Guide, 2nd ed., by Ruth Nadelman Lynn, Bowker, 1983. 444 pages. Comprehensive list of over 2,000 recommended fantasy titles, extensive bibliography of criticism and professional readings. Entries include bibliographic data, reading level, annotations, major awards won, and review citations.

Fiction for Youth, 2nd ed., edited by Lillian L. Shapiro, Neal-Schuman, 1986. A guide to recommended titles for junior high grades. Arranged alphabetically by author with a title and subject index, directory of publishers, bibliography of out-of-print titles that are worth seeking out.

Fiction, Folklore, Fantasy & Poetry for Children, 1876–1985, Bowker, 1986. 2,563 pages, 2 volumes. Entries cite 133,000 titles, pages, bibliographic data, ISBNs, LC numbers, pseudonyms, primary illustrator dates, series, grade levels, award notations. Author, title, illustrator, and award indexes. Essays by Lillian Gerhardt and Barbara Rollock.

For Reading Out Loud! by Margaret Mary Kimmel and Elizabeth Segel, Delacorte, 1983. A guide to selecting books for sharing with young people and techniques for sharing them. Subject, title, author index.

Her Way: A Guide to Biographies of Women for Young People, 2nd ed., by Mary Ellen Siegal, American Library Association, 1984. Single and collective biographies of 1,000 notable women in history.

Hey, Miss! You Got a Book for Me? A Model Multicultural Resource Collection, rev. ed., by Joanna F. Chambers, Austin Bilingual Language Editions, 1981. Annotated guide to media and books for multicultural education.

A Hispanic Heritage: A Guide to Juvenile Books about Hispanic Peoples and Cultures by Isabel Schon, Scarecrow Press, 1980. Critical reviews of books that portray Hispanic cultures grouped by countries.

Index to Collective Biographies for Young Readers: Elementary and Junior High School Level, 3rd ed., edited by Judith Silverman, Bowker, 1979. 405 pages. Cross referenced listing of 7,000 notable figures in 900 collective biographies.

Indian Children's Books by Hap Gilliland, Montana Council for Indian Education, 1980. Brief reviews of more than 1,650 books about Native Americans.

Jewish Children's Books: How to Choose Them, How to Use Them by Marcia Posner, Hadassah, 1986. 48 pages. Summaries, themes, discussion guides, questions and activities, and further resources are given for more than thirty books.

Let's Read Together: Books for Family Enjoyment, 4th ed., edited by the Association for Library Service to Children, American Library Association, 1981. 124 pages. Annotated lists of books for reading aloud grouped by interest and age levels.

Library Services for Hispanic Children: A Guide for Public and School Librarians, edited by Adela Artola Allen, Oryx Press, 1987. 201 pages. Articles on professional issues related to library service for Hispanic children. Annotated bibliographies of children's books in English about Hispanics, recent noteworthy children's books in Spanish, computer software, and resources about Hispanic culture for librarians.

Mexico and Its Literature for Children and Adolescents, compiled by Isabel Schon, Arizona State University, 1977. Annotated guide to Mexican children's books with biographical information about their authors.

Michele Landsberg's Guide to Children's Books: With a Treasury of More Than 350 Great Children's Books by Michele Landsberg, Penguin, 1985. 272 pages. A book-loving Canadian's journey through children's literature with commentary on reasons for loving and/or detesting specific books. Annotated list and chapters about various genres.

More Notes from a Different Drummer: A Guide to Juvenile Fiction Portraying the Disabled by Barbara H. Baskin and Karen H. Harris, Bowker, 1984. 495 pages. Extends *Notes from a Different Drummer*. Discusses criteria for selection of 450 books about the disabled and provides a comprehensive annotated guide of fiction for a readership ranging from infants to adolescents.

A Multimedia Approach to Children's Literature: A Selective List of Films (and Videocassettes), Filmstrips, and Recordings Based on Children's Books, 3rd ed., edited by Mary Alice Hunt, American Library Association, 1983. 182 pages. Annotations of books with recommended media based upon them.

Museum of Science and Industry Basic List of Children's Science Books, edited by Bernice Richter, Chicago Museum of Science & Industry. First edition covers 1973–1984 + update. A bibliography of science trade literature from the Chicago museum of Science and Industry's Kresge Library and its annual Children's Book Fair. Rates books, has author and title index, and tells which science magazine reviewed the book. Published in conjunction with the ALA.

Newbery and Caldecott Medalists and Honor Book Winners: Bibliographies and Resource Material through 1977 by James W. Roginski, Libraries Unlimited, 1982. A comprehensive listing of source material on Newbery and Caldecott medalists and honor book winners.

Notes from a Different Drummer: A Guide to Juvenile Fiction Portraying the Handicapped by Barbara H. Baskin and Karen H. Harris, Bowker, 1977. Criteria for selection of books about the disabled with critical reviews of 400+ books with disabled characters.

Opening Doors for Preschool Children and Their Parents, 2nd ed., Preschool Services and Parent Education

Committee, Association for Library Service to Children, American Library Association, 1981. 98 pages. An annotated list of books for adult caregivers of preschool children, and books and nonprint materials for preschool children.

A Parent's Guide to Children's Reading, rev. 5th ed., by Nancy Larrick, Bantam, 1982. 271 pages. Chapters on the joys and importance of introducing children to books, the effect on language development, the influence of television, the role of poetry, and reading instruction.

Popular Reading for Children: A Collection of Booklist Columns, compiled by Barbara Elleman, American Library Association, 1981. Updated periodically. Bibliographies and round up titles from *Booklist* which focus on specific topics and genres, such as mysteries, sports, and time-slip fantasy.

The Read-Aloud Handbook, 2nd ed., by Jim Trelease, Viking, 1985. An enthusiastic argument for why we should read to children, techniques for reading aloud, and a treasury of over 300 hundred books that worked well for the author.

Reading Ladders for Human Relations, 6th ed., edited by Eileen Tway, National Council of Teachers of English, 1981. Discusses the role of reading in developing children's self and social awareness and provides annotated bibliographies grouped by theme.

Reference Books for Young Readers: Bowker Buying Guides, Shirley A. Fitzgibbons, Brent Allison, Rebecca L. Thomas et al., consultants. Bowker, 1987. 560 pages. Ratings of 20 encyclopedias, 203 dictionaries, 34 atlases and a chapter on computerized references. Evaluations include scope, currency, clarity, graphics, bibliographies, cross-referencing, indexing, grade level, and price.

Storytelling: Art and Technique, 2nd ed., by Augusta Baker and Ellin Greene, Bowker, 1987. Two masters of storytelling give practical advice on how to select, prepare, and tell stories. Recommended stories are included.

Selected Jewish Children's Books, compiled by Marcia Posner, Jewish Book Council, 1984. 34 pages. Annotated list of books containing Jewish content and values categorized by topic and age levels.

Selecting Materials for and About Hispanic and East Asian Children and Young People by Patricia F. Beilke and Frank J. Sciara, Library Professional Publications, 1986. 178 pages. Chapters on selection of materials, staff development, backgrounds of Hispanic and East Asian children and young people in the U.S., and guidelines for selecting culturally relevant materials. Some children's book titles are discussed in the text.

The Story Vine by Anne Pellowski, illustrated by Lynn Sweat, Macmillan, 1984. A source book of unusual and easy-to-tell stories from around the world. An internationally known storyteller shares some of her secrets about telling stories, some with string, objects, and musical or visual effects.

Subject Guide to Children's Books in Print, Bowker, Annual. Over 40,000 titles grouped under 7,100 subject categories. An indispensable reference for finding picture books, fiction, and nonfiction on specific topics.

Subject Index to Poetry for Children and Young People, compiled by Violet Sell, Core Collection Books, 1982. 1,035 pages. An index of poetry organized by subject with a code for title and author.

Your Reading: A Booklist for Jr. High and Middle School Students, edited by Jane Christensen, National Council of Teachers of English, 1983. An annotated list of over 3,000 fiction and nonfiction books recommended for junior high and middle school students, arranged by subject. Author and title indexes.

Books About Authors and Illustrators

The Art of Leo and Diane Dillon, edited by Byron Preiss, Ballantine Books, 1981. Introductory critical essay with 120 illustrations, including 48 color plates of the Dillons's art. The Dillons comment on the meaning, context, and techniques used in each painting.

The Art of Nancy Ekholm Burkert, edited by David Larkin, Harper & Row, 1977. 50 pages. Full-page color spreads of 40 Burkert paintings with an interpretive essay by Michael Danoff.

Authors of Books for Young People, 2nd ed., edited by Martha E. Ward and Dorothy Marquant, Scarecrow Press, 1971. 579 pages. (Supplement to the Second Edition, 1979. 308 pages.) Biographical information about authors including publications.

Books are by People: Interviews with 104 Authors and Illustrators of Books for Young Children by Lee Bennett Hopkins, Citation Press, 1969. (Companion volume: *More Books by More People.* Citation Press, 1974.) Conversations between Hopkins and his talented friends.

Boy: Tales of Childhood by Roald Dahl, Puffin, Viking, 1984. 176 pages. An autobiography that describes the origins of one author's ideas.

Carl Larsson by the Brooklyn Museum and the National Museum in Stockholm with the support of the Swedish Institute in Stockholm, The Brooklyn Museum, 1982. 96 pages. A catalog of Carl Larsson's paintings with commentary by Sarah Faunce, Gorel Cavalli-Bjorkman, Ulf Hard af Segerstad, and Madeleine von Heland. Chronology and selected bibliography.

Caldecott Medal Books: 1938–1957 by Bertha Mahony Miller and Elinor Whitney Field, Horn Book, 1958. Artists' acceptance speeches and biographical articles of the Caldecott Medal winners.

Celebrating Children's Books, edited by Betsy Hearne and Marilyn Kaye, Lothrop, Lee & Shepard, 1981. Writings about their craft by some of the foremost authors writing for children today. The essays appear in this collection in honor of Zena Sutherland.

From Writers to Students: The Pleasures and Pains of Writing, edited by Jerry Weiss, International Reading Association, 1979. 113 pages. Interviews about their work with 19 top-notch authors who reveal the inside story on their writing. Includes Judy Blume, Mollie Hunter, Milton Meltzer, Mary Rodgers, Laurence Yep, and others.

Horn Book Reflections, edited by Elinor Whitney Field, Horn Book, 1969. Essays, selected from 18 years of the *Horn Book Magazine*, 1949–1966, represent the reflections of authors and illustrators as they comment upon their craft.

Illustrators of Books for Young People, 2nd ed., edited by Martha E. Ward and Dorothy A. Marquant, Scarecrow Press, 1975. 223 pages. Biographical information about illustrators. Bibliographies and references to further sources are included.

Illustrators of Children's Books, 1744–1945, edited by Bertha E. Mahony, Louise Payson Latimer, and Beulah Folmsbee, Horn Book, 1947. 527 pages.

Illustrators of Children's Books, 1946–1956, edited by Bertha Mahony Miller, Ruth Hill Viguers, and Marcia Dalphin, Horn Book, 1958. 229 pages.

Illustrators of Children's Books, 1957–1966, edited by Lee Kingman, Joanna Foster, and Ruth Giles Lontoft, Horn Book, 1968. 295 pages.

Illustrators of Children's Books, 1967–1976, edited by Lee Kingman, Grace Allen Hogarth, and Harriet Quimby, Horn Book, 1978. 290 pages.

Illustrators of Children's Books, 1977–1986, edited by Lee Kingman, Horn Book, 1987. All volumes contain biographical sketches of illustrators during the period covered by each volume. The artists' techniques and point of view, trends in illustration and bibliographies are included.

Little by Little: A Writer's Education by Jean Little, Viking, 1987. 233 pages. Jean Little's life story.

Newbery and Caldecott Medal Books: 1956–1965, edited by Lee Kingman, Horn Book, 1965. 300 pages. Acceptance papers, biographical notes and evaluative essays by Elizabeth H. Gross, Carolyn Horovitz, and Norma R. Fryatt.

Newbery and Caldecott Medal Books: 1966–1975, edited by Lee Kingman, Horn Book, 1975. Acceptance papers, biographies of the award winners, and evaluative articles by John Rowe Townsend, Barbara Bader, and Elizabeth Johnson.

Newbery and Caldecott Medal Books, Vol. 5, 1976–1985, edited by Lee Kingman, Horn Book, 1987. Compiles the winning speeches, biographies, book notes. Essays by Barbara Bader, Ethel L. Heins, and Zena Sutherland.

Newbery Medal Books: 1922–1955, edited by Bertha Mahony Miller and Elinor Whitney Field, Horn Book, 1955. Acceptance papers and biographical sketches, plus notes on and excerpts from Newbery award winning books.

Oxford Companion to Children's Literature, compiled by Humphrey Carpenter and Mari Prichard, Oxford University Press, 1984. Included are nearly 2,000 entries, more than 900 of which are biographical sketches of authors, illustrators, printers, and publishers. Other entries cover traditional materials such as fairy tales and folklore; characters from books, cartoons, comic strips, radio, and television; and genres such as school stories, dime novels, and science fiction. Plot summaries for major works of fiction and their publishing history are given.

Pipers at the Gates of Dawn: The Wisdom of Children's Literature by Jonathan Cott. Random House, 1983. 327 pages. A noted historian and critic of children's literature reflects upon his encounters with six extraordinary creators of children's literature—Dr. Seuss, Maurice Sendak, William Steig, Astrid Lindgren, Chinua Achebe, P. L. Travers—and with Iona and Peter Opie, scholars of children's lore, games, and language.

Reflections on Literature for Children, edited by Francelia Butler and Richard Rotert, Library Professional Publications, 1984. Selections from Children's Literature Annual. Critical reviews, essays, and biographical pieces by and about notable children's authors and illustrators.

Secret Gardens by Humphrey Carpenter, Houghton Mifflin, 1985. A book about the authors who wrote during the so-called Golden Age of Children's Literature in the late 19th and early 20th century.

Self-Portrait: Erik Blegvad, written and illustrated by Erik Blegvad, Addison-Wesley, 1979. 32 pages. Blegvad discusses himself, his life, and his work.

Self-Portrait: Trina Schart Hyman, written and illustrated by Trina Schart Hyman, Addison-Wesley, 1981. 32 pages. Hyman describes her life, friends, and family and their reflections in her painting.

Self-Portrait: Margot Zemach, written and illustrated by Margot Zemach, Addison-Wesley, 1978. 32 pages. Zemach talks about her life, her family, and her work.

A Sense of Story: Essays on Contemporary Writers for Children by John Rowe Townsend, Horn Book, 1973. 216 pages. Critical essays on nineteen notable authors and their works, including Joan Aiken, L. M. Boston, H. F. Brinsmead, John Christopher, Helen Cresswell, Meindert DeJong, Eleanor Estes, Madeleine L'Engle, Andre Norton, Scott O'Dell,

Philippa Pearce, and Rosemary Sutcliff. Seven others are updated in *A Sounding of Storytellers*.

Something About the Author, edited by Anne Commire, Gale Research, 50 volumes in print with periodic additions. Biographical information, photographs, publication records, honors and awards received, and quotations from and about thousands of authors and illustrators of children's books.

A Sounding of Storytellers: New and Revised Essays on Contemporary Writers for Children by John Rowe Townsend. Lippincott, 1979. 218 pages. Fourteen essays about contemporary writers; seven are about writers who were not in *A Sense of Story:* Nina Bawden, Vera and Bill Cleaver, Peter Dickinson, Virginia Hamilton, E. L. Konigsburg, Penelope Lively, and Jill Paton Walsh. The other seven, included in the earlier book, are Paula Fox, Leon Garfield, Alan Garner, William Mayne, K. M. Peyton, Ivan Southall, and Patricia Wrightson.

Starting from Home: A Writer's Beginnings by Milton Meltzer, Viking, 1988. Meltzer's life story.

Twentieth-Century Children's Writers, 2nd ed., edited by Daniel Kirkpatrick, St. Martin's Press, 1983. 1,500 pages. More than 700 entries, critical essays, and bibliographies of contemporary writers and illustrators, including William Steig, Maurice Sendak, Nikki Giovanni, and Isaac Bashevis Singer.

Ways of the Illustrator: Visual Communication in Children's Literature by Joseph H. Schwarz, American Library Association, 1982. 202 pages. An informed presentation of the role of illustration in communicating meaning in picture books. The relationship between the text and illustration, the use of style and technique, and the effect on the child's aesthetic experience are discussed and illustrated with examples.

Written for Children: An Outline of English-Language Children's Literature, 3rd rev. ed., by John Rowe Townsend. Lippincott, 1987. 364 pages. An account of the development of children's books in the United States, England, Canada, and Australia.

Periodicals About Children's Literature

Bookbird: International Periodical on Literature for Children and Young People. Published quarterly by Forlaget ARNIS, Bergensvej 5, 6230 Rodekro, Denmark. An international forum for the exchange of experience and information among contributors and readers in about 50 nations. Essays about outstanding authors and illustrators from many countries.

Booklist. Barbara Elleman, children's books editor. American Library Association, published biweekly. Reviews of children's and adult's books and nonprint materials. Periodic bibliographies on a specific subject, reference tools, and commentary on issues are invaluable.

Bulletin of the Center for Children's Books. Betsy Hearne, editor; Zena Sutherland, associate editor. The University of Chicago Press, published monthly except August. Critical reviews of books rated as * (books of special distinction), R (recommended), Ad (additional), M (marginal), NR (not recommended), SpC (special collection), SpR (special reader). Curricular use and developmental values are assigned when appropriate.

CBC Features. Children's Book Council, published semiannually. A newsletter about current issues and events, free and inexpensive materials, materials for Children's Book Week, topical bibliographies, and essays by publishers and authors or illustrators.

Children's Literature Association Quarterly. Children's Literature Association. Roderick McGillis, editor for 1988, University of Calgary. Book reviews and articles on British and American children's literature, research, teaching children's literature, theater, and conference proceedings. Special sections on current topics of interest, poetry, censorship, awards and announcements.

Children's Literature in Education. Anita Moss, editor. Agathon Press, published quarterly. Essays on children's books, including critical reviews, research reviews, biographical studies, creators' views of their craft, and discussions of poetry and prose.

The Horn Book Magazine. Anita Silvey, editor. Horn Book, published bimonthly. Enlightened commentary by the editor, articles by creators of children's books, publishers, critics, teachers, and librarians. Starred reviews for outstanding books, comprehensive reviews of recommended books. Newbery and Caldecott acceptance speeches, biographical sketches of winners, *Boston Globe*-Horn Book Award winners, and other notable awards. Announcements of children's literature conferences and events.

Journal of Youth Services in Libraries (formerly *Top of the News*) Association of Library Services to Children and Young Adult Services Division. Joni Bodart-Talbot, editor. American Library Association, published quarterly. Articles of interest to teachers and librarians on current issues, specialized bibliographies, acceptance speeches by the Newbery and Caldecott Award winners, conference proceedings, and organizational news.

Language Arts. National Council of Teachers of English, published September through May. Janet Hickman's bookwatching column reviews current recommended books for children. Profiles on authors and illustrators, articles on using books in the classroom, response to literature, and writing as an outgrowth of reading literature.

The Lion and the Unicorn. Department of English, Brooklyn College. Articles on literary criticism, current issues, and themes in children's literature.

The New Advocate. Joel Taxel, editor; Christopher Gordon, publisher. Needham Heights, Mass. A lively journal that addresses current issues and topics of interest in the children's book world.

The New York Times Book Review. Weekly column of reviews, written by other authors, plus a Spring and Fall special section devoted to children's books. Annual list of ten best illustrated books of the year.

Phaedrus: An International Journal of Children's Literature Research. James Fraser, editor. Fairleigh Dickinson University, published semiannually. Essays on cross-cultural aspects of children's literature, research reviews, biographical studies of authors and illustrators, and international reports. For the serious student of children's literature.

Publisher's Weekly. Bowker, published weekly with a Spring and Fall special edition on children's books. Both positive and negative reviews of books and articles of interest to publishers, teachers, librarians, and authors.

The Reading Teacher. International Reading Association, published nine times a year. Monthly column of reviews of children's books. Articles on the use of books in the classroom, special bibliographies, cross-cultural studies, and research using children's books in reading programs.

School Library Journal. Lillian Gerhardt, editor. Bowker, eleven issues per year. Reviews of children's books, written by practicing school and public librarians, often include comparisons with other books on the same topic. Articles on current issues, conferences, library services, and special features. An annual "Best Books of the Year" column.

School Library Media Quarterly. American Association of School Librarians. American Library Association, published quarterly. Articles on censorship, using books in the classroom, research, library services, and current issues.

Science and Children. National Science Teachers Association, published eight times per year. Monthly column of reviews of informational books on science topics, plus an annual list of recommended books chosen by NSTA/Children's Book Council Liaison Committee.

The Web: Wonderfully Exciting Books. Charlotte Huck and Janet Hickman, editors. Ohio State University, published quarterly. Reviews of current books plus a "web of possibilities" for activities and related readings on a theme, topic, author, or illustrator.

Wilson Library Bulletin. Wilson, published monthly September to June. A monthly column of book reviews, articles on authors and illustrators, current issues, and news of interest to professionals. The October issue is devoted to children's books.

Children's Magazines and Newspapers

Boy's Life
Age range: 8–18. For boys, especially those involved in the Scouting world. *Boy's Life*, 1325 Walnut Hill Lane, Irving, TX 75038–3096

Chickadee
Age range: 4–9. Teaches children about the environment around them through interesting articles and outstanding illustrations. *Chickadee*, The Young Naturalist Foundation, 59 Front Street E, Toronto, Ontario, Canada M5E 1B3

Classical Calliope
Age range: 10–17. Contains "the classics" in literature. *Classical Calliope*, 20 Grove Street, Peterborough, NH 03458

Cobblestone
Age range: 8–14. The history magazine for young people. *Cobblestone*, 20 Grove Street, Peterborough, NH 03458

Cricket
Age range: 6–12. Contains quality literature and illustration for children. *Cricket*, Box 2670, Boulder, CO 80321

Current Events
Age range: 11–16. For students in social studies classes in the middle, junior, and early senior high school (grades 5–10). *Current Events*, 245 Long Hill Road, Middletown, CT 06457

Current Science
Age range: 11–16. For students in science classes in the middle, junior, and early senior high school (grades 5–10). *Current Science*, 245 Long Hill Road, Middletown, CT 06457

Dynamath
Age range: 5–12. Offers features that deal with basic math. *Dynamath* Scholastic Inc., 730 Broadway, New York, NY 10003

The Electric Company
Age range: 6–10. Contains general interest reading. *The Electric Company*, 200 Watt Street, P. O. Box 2923, Boulder, CO 80322

Faces
Age range: 8–14. Written and published in cooperation with the American Museum of Natural History of New York City about people from all over the world. *Faces*, 20 Grove Street, Peterborough, NH 03458

Highlights for Children
Age range: 2–12. Has "Fun with a Purpose" recreational yet educational features; the only all-purpose magazine for children of this age range.

Highlights for Children, P.O. Box 269, Columbus, OH 43272–0002

Junior Scholastic

Age range: 6–12. Contains features that pertain to social studies. *Junior Scholastic,* Scholastic Inc., 730 Broadway, New York, NY 10003

The McGuffey Writer

Age range: 5–14. Encourages children to write by providing an outlet for their work. *The McGuffey Writer,* 400 A McGuffey Hall, Miami University, Oxford, OH 45056

The Mini Page

Age range: 5–12. Offers general interest reading. Universal Press Syndicate, 4400 Johnson Drive, Kansas City, KS 66205

National Geographic World

Age range: 8–13. Outstanding illustrations and content in this nature and science magazine. *National Geographic World,* Department 01085, 17th and M Streets, NW, Box 2330, Washington, D.C. 20036

Odyssey

Age range: 8–14. For children with an interest in astronomy and space science; contains quality photography and illustration. *Odyssey,* P.O. Box 92788, Milwaukee, WI 53202

Owl

Age range: 8–14. Teaches children about the environment around them through quality articles and outstanding photography. *Owl,* The Young Naturalist Foundation, 59 Front Street E, Toronto, Ontario, Canada M5E 1B3

Penny Power

Age range: 8–14. Youthful version of *Consumer Re-* ports. *Penny Power* Magazine, P.O. Box 2878, Boulder, CO 80322

Pennywhistle Press

Age range: 5–13. Contains general interest features. *Pennywhistle Press,* Box 500–P, Washington, D.C. 20044

Ranger Rick

Age range: 6–12. Well-illustrated and reliable nature magazine. *Ranger Rick,* The National Wildlife Federation, 1412 16th Street, NW, Washington, D.C. 20036–2266

Science World

Age range: 7–10. Offers diverse features in the field of science. *Science World,* 730 Broadway, New York, NY 10003

Sesame Street

Age range: 2–6. Preschool prereading publication. *Sesame Street,* P.O. Box 2896, Boulder, CO 80322

Stone Soup

Age range: 6–13. Literary magazine written by children. *Stone Soup,* P.O. Box 83, Santa Cruz, CA 95063

3-2-1 Contact

Age range: 8–14. Offers interesting articles and activities in the fields of science and technology. *3-2-1 Contact,* Box 2933, Boulder, CO 80322

Turtle

Age range: 2–5. Health magazine for preschool children. *Turtle,* P.O. Box 10681, Des Moines, IA 50381

Your Big Backyard

Age range: 8–12. Outstanding photography and illustration in this nature magazine. *Your Big Backyard,* The National Wildlife Federation, 1412 16th Street, NW, Washington, D.C. 20036

Publishers of Children's Books

Abelard-Schuman
  257 Park Avenue
  New York, NY 10010

Abingdon Press
  201 Eighth Avenue, South
  Nashville, TN 37202

Addison-Wesley Publishing Co.,
Inc.
  Jacob Way
  Reading, MA 01867

Aladdin Books (an imprint of the
Macmillan Children's Book Group)
  866 Third Avenue
  New York, NY 10022

American Council on Education
  One Dupont Circle, NW
  Washington, D.C. 20036

American Library Association
  Publication Department
  50 East Huron Street
  Chicago, IL 60611

Ariel (a division of Farrar, Straus &
Giroux, Inc.)
  19 Union Square
  New York, NY 10003

Astor Honor
  48 East 43d St.
  New York, NY 10017

Atheneum Publishers (an affiliate
of the Macmillan Children's Book
Group)
  866 Third Avenue
  New York, NY 10022

The Atlantic Monthly Press
  8 Arlington St.
  Boston, MA 02116

Avon Books
  105 Madison Avenue
  New York, NY 10016

Bantam Books
  666 Fifth Avenue
  New York, NY 10103

Bobbs-Merrill
  4300 West 62d St.
  Indianapolis, IN 46206

R. R. Bowker Company
  245 West 17th Street
  New York, NY 10011

Bowmar
  Box 3623
  Glendale, CA 91201

Bradbury Press (an affiliate of Macmillan, Inc.)
  866 Third Avenue
  New York, NY 10022

Carolrhoda Books
  241 First Avenue North
  Minneapolis, MN 55401

Children's Book Council, Inc.
  67 Irving Place
  New York, NY 10003

Children's Press
  1224 West Van Buren St.
  Chicago, IL 60607

Clarion Books (a division of
Houghton Mifflin)
  52 Vanderbilt Avenue
  New York, NY 10017

William Collins Publishers, Inc.
  200 Madison Avenue
  New York, NY 10016

Coward, McCann & Geoghegan, Inc.
200 Madison Avenue
New York, NY 10016

Creative Education
123 South Broad St.
Mankato, MN 56001

Crowell Junior Books (Harper Junior Books Group)
10 East 53rd Street
New York, NY 10022

Crown Publishers, Inc.
225 Park Avenue South
New York, NY 10003

Delacorte Press
1 Dag Hammarskjold Plaza
245 East 47th Street
New York, NY 10017

Dell Publishing Co., Inc.
1 Dag Hammarskjold Plaza
245 East 47th St.
New York, NY 10017

Dial Books for Young Readers
2 Park Avenue
New York, NY 10016

Dodd, Mead & Co., Inc.
71 Fifth Avenue
New York, NY 10003

Doubleday & Co., Inc.
245 Park Avenue
New York, NY 10167

Dover Publications, Inc.
180 Varick St.
New York, NY 10014

E. P. Dutton
2 Park Avenue
New York, NY 10016

Elsevier/Nelson Books
2 Park Avenue
New York, NY 10016

Enslow Publishers
Bloy Street & Ramsey Avenue
Box 777
Hillside, NJ 07205

M. Evans & Co., Inc.
216 East 49th Street
New York, NY 10017

Farrar, Straus & Giroux, Inc.
19 Union Square West
New York, NY 10003

Follett Publishing Co.
1010 West Washington Boulevard
Chicago, IL 60607

Four Winds Press
866 Third Avenue
New York, NY 10022

Gale Research Company
Book Tower
Detroit, MI 48226

Garland Publishing, Inc.
136 Madison Avenue
New York, NY 10016

Garrard Publishing
1607 North Market St.
Champaign, IL 61820

Golden Books
850 Third Avenue
New York, NY 10022

Golden Gate Junior Books
1247 1/2 North Vista St.
Los Angeles, CA 90046

Golden Press (Western Publishing)
Mound Ave.
Racine, WI 53404

Greenwillow Books (a division of William Morrow & Co.)
105 Madison Avenue
New York, NY 10016

Grosset & Dunlap, Inc.
51 Madison Avenue
New York, NY 10010

Gulliver Books (an imprint of Harcourt Brace Jovanovich, Inc.)
1250 Sixth Avenue
San Diego, CA 92101

Harcourt Brace Jovanovich, Inc.
1250 Sixth Avenue
San Diego, CA 92101

Harper & Row, Publishers, Inc.
10 East 53rd Street
New York, NY 10022

Harper Trophy Paperbacks (Harper Junior Books Group)
10 East 53rd Street
New York, NY 10022

Harvey House, Publishers
20 Waterside Plaza
New York, NY 10010

Hastings House Publishers, Inc.
10 East 40th Street
New York, NY 10016

Holiday House
18 East 53rd Street
New York, NY 10022

Henry Holt and Company, Inc.
115 West 18th Street
New York, NY 10011

The Horn Book, Inc.
Park Square Building
31 St. James Avenue
Boston, MA 02116

Houghton Mifflin Co.
2 Park Street
Boston, MA 02108

Houghton Mifflin
52 Vanderbilt Avenue
New York, NY 10017

International Reading Association
800 Barksdale Road
Newark, DE 19714

The Jewish Publication Society
60 East 42nd Street, Suite 1339
New York, NY 10165

Joy Street Books (an imprint of Little, Brown & Co.)
34 Beacon Street
Boston, MA 02108

Alfred A. Knopf, Inc.
201 East 50th Street
New York, NY 10022

Larousse & Co., Inc.
572 Fifth Avenue
New York, NY 10036

Lerner Publications Company
241 First Avenue North
Minneapolis, MN 55401

J. B. Lippincott Junior Books (Harper Junior Books Group)
10 East 53rd Street
New York, NY 10022

Little, Brown & Co.
34 Beacon Street
Boston, MA 02106

Lodestar Books (an imprint of E. P. Dutton)
2 Park Avenue
New York, NY 10016

Lothrop, Lee & Shepard Books
105 Madison Avenue
New York, NY 10016

Margaret K. McElderry Books (a division of Macmillan Publishers)
886 Third Avenue
New York, NY 10022

McGraw-Hill Book Co.
1221 Avenue of the Americas
New York, NY 10020

David McKay
750 Third Avenue
New York, NY 10017

Macmillan Publishing Co., Inc.
866 Third Avenue
New York, NY 10022

Julian Messner (Simon & Schuster Juvenile Publishing Division)
1230 Avenue of the Americas
New York, NY 10020

Methuen, Inc.
733 Third Avenue
New York, NY 10017

William Morrow & Co., Inc.
105 Madison Avenue
New York, NY 10016

National Council of Teachers of English
1111 Kenyon Road
Urbana, IL 61801

National Education Association
1201 16th Street, NW
Washington, D.C. 20036

The New American Library, Inc.
1301 Avenue of the Americas
New York, NY 10019

Orchard Books (a division of Franklin Watts, Inc.)
387 Park Avenue South
New York, NY 10016

Oxford University Press
200 Madison Avenue
New York, NY 10016

Pantheon Books
201 East 50th St.
New York, NY 10022

Parents Magazine Press (a division of Gruner & Jahr USA, Publishers)
685 Third Avenue
New York, NY 10017

Pelican Publishing Company, Inc.
1101 Monroe Street
P.O. Box 189
Gretna, LA 70053

Philomel Books (a division of the Putnam & Grosset Group)
51 Madison Avenue
New York, NY 10010

Picture Book Studio
60 North Main Street
Natick, MA 01760

Platt & Munk
1055 Bronx River Avenue
Bronx, NY 10472

Plays, Inc.
8 Arlington St.
Boston, MA 02116

Pleasant Company
7 North Pinckney Street
Madison, WI 53703

Pocket Books
1230 Avenue of the Americas
New York, NY 10020

Clarkson N. Potter, Inc.
225 Park Avenue South
New York, NY 10003

Prentice-Hall Books for Young Readers (Simon & Schuster Juvenile Publishing Division)
Englewood Cliffs, NJ 07632

Puffin Books
40 West 23rd Street
New York, NY 10010

G. P. Putnam's Sons
51 Madison Avenue
New York, NY 10010

Harlin Quist Books
192 East 75 St.
New York, NY 10021

Rand McNally & Co.
P.O. Box 7600
Chicago, IL 60680

Random House
201 East 50th Street
New York, NY 10022

Schocken Books, Inc.
200 Madison Avenue
New York, NY 10016

Scholastic Book Services
730 Broadway
New York, NY 10003

Scott, Foresman and Co.
1900 East Lake Avenue
Glenview, IL 60025

Charles Scribner's Sons (an imprint of the Macmillan Children's Book Group)
866 Third Avenue
New York, NY 10022

Sierra Club Books
53 Bush St.
San Francisco, CA 94108

Stemmer House Publishers, Inc.
2627 Caves Road
Owings Mills, MD 21117

Ticknor & Fields (an imprint of Houghton Mifflin company)
52 Vanderbilt Avenue
New York, NY 10017

Tundra Books of Northern New York
51 Clinton St.
P.O. Box 1030
Plattsburgh, NY 12901

Unicorn Books (an imprint of E. P. Dutton)
306 Dartmouth St.
Boston, MA 02116

Viking Kestrel
40 West 23rd Street
New York, NY 10010

Walker & Company
720 Fifth Avenue
New York, NY 10019

Wanderer Books
Simon & Schuster Building
1230 Avenue of the Americas
New York, NY 10020

Frederick Warne & Co., Inc.
40 West 23rd Street
New York, NY 10010

Franklin Watts, Inc.
  387 Park Avenue South
  New York, NY 10016
Western Publishing Co.
  850 Third Avenue
  New York, NY 10022

The Westminster Press
  925 Chestnut St.
  Philadelphia, PA 19107
Windmill Books
  Simon & Schuster Bldg.
  1230 Avenue of the Americas
  New York, NY 10020

Yale University Press
  302 Temple Street
  New Haven, CT 06520

Holiday Books

GENERAL

Alexander, Sue. *Small Plays for Special Days.* Illustrated by Tom Huffman. New York: Seabury, 1977.

Burnett, Bernice. *Holidays.* New York: Watts, 1983.

Cole, Ann, et al. *A Pumpkin in a Pear Tree: Creative Ideas for Twelve Months of Holiday Fun.* Illustrated by Debby Young. Boston: Little, Brown, 1976.

Fisher, Aileen, ed. *Holiday Programs for Boys and Girls.* Boston: Plays, 1986.

Hautzig, Esther. *Holiday Treats.* Illustrated by Yaroslava. New York: Macmillan, 1983.

Larrick, Nancy, ed. *More Poetry for Holidays.* Illustrated by Harold Berson. New York: Garrard, 1973.

———. *Poetry for Holidays.* Illustrated by Kelly Oechsli. New York: Garrard, 1966.

Livingston, Myra Cohn, ed. *Celebrations.* Illustrated by Leonard Everett Fisher. New York: Holiday House, 1985.

———. *O Frabjous Day! Poetry for Holidays and Special Occasions.* New York: Atheneum, McElderry, 1977.

Quackenbush, Robert, ed. *The Holiday Song Book.* New York: Lothrop, Lee & Shepard, 1977.

Tudor, Tasha. *A Time to Keep: The Tasha Tudor Book of Holidays.* Illustrated by Tasha Tudor. New York: Macmillan, 1977.

HALLOWEEN

Adams, Adrienne. *A Halloween Happening.* New York: Macmillan, 1981.

———. *A Woggle of Witches.* New York: Macmillan, 1971.

Anderson, Lonzo. *The Halloween Party.* Illustrated by Adrienne Adams. New York: Scribner's, 1974.

Bright, Robert. *Georgie's Halloween.* Illustrated by Robert Bright. New York: Doubleday, 1971.

Brown, Marc. *Arthur's Halloween.* Boston: Atlantic, 1983.

———. *Witches Four.* New York: Parents, 1980.

Bunting, Eve. *Scary, Scary Halloween.* Illustrated by Jan Brett. New York: Ticknor & Fields, 1986.

Charles, Donald. *Shaggy Dog's Halloween.* Chicago: Children's Press, 1984.

Coombs, Patricia. *Dorrie and the Halloween Plot.* New York: Lothrop, Lee & Shepard, 1976.

Corwin, Judith. *Halloween Fun.* New York: Messner, 1983.

Dobrin, Arnold. *Make a Witch, Make a Goblin: A Book of Halloween Crafts.* New York: Four Winds, 1977.

Gibbons, Gail. *Halloween.* New York: Holiday House, 1984.

Godden, Rumer. *Mr. McFaddin's Halloween.* New York: Viking, 1975.

Guthrie, Donna. *The Witch Who Lives down the Hall.*

Illustrated by Amy Schwartz. San Diego: Harcourt Brace Jovanovich, 1985.

Herda, D. J. *Halloween*. New York: Watts, 1983.

Hoban, Lillian. *Arthur's Halloween Costume*. Illustrated by Lillian Hoban. New York: Harper & Row, 1984.

Katz, Ruth. *Pumpkin Personalities*. Illustrated by Sharon Tondreau. New York: Walker, 1979.

Leedy, Loreen. *Dragon Halloween Party: A Story and Activity Book*. New York: Holiday House, 1986.

Miller, Edna. *Mousekin's Golden House*. Illustrated by Edna Miller. Englewood Cliffs, N.J.: Prentice-Hall, 1964.

Prelutsky, Jack. *It's Halloween*. Illustrated by Marylin Hafner. New York: Greenwillow, 1977.

———. *Nightmares: Poems to Trouble Your Sleep*. Illustrated by Arnold Lobel. New York: Greenwillow, 1976.

Riley, James Whitcomb. *The Gobble-Uns'll Git You Ef You Don't Watch Out!* Illustrated by Joel Schick. Philadelphia: Lippincott, 1975.

Rose, David. *It Hardly Seems Like Halloween*. New York: Lothrop, Lee & Shepard, 1983.

Stevenson, James. *That Terrible Halloween Night*. New York: Greenwillow, 1980.

Titherington, Jeanne. *Pumpkin Pumpkin*. New York: Greenwillow, 1986.

THANKSGIVING

Alcott, Louisa May. *An Old Fashioned Thanksgiving*. Philadelphia: Lippincott, 1974.

Baldwin, Margaret. *Thanksgiving*. New York: Watts, 1983.

Brown, Marc. *Arthur's Thanksgiving*. Boston: Little, Brown, 1984.

Child, Lydia Marie. *Over the River and Through the Wood*. Illustrated by Brinton Turkle. New York: Coward, 1974.

Corwin, Judith. *Thanksgiving Fun*. New York: Messner, 1984.

Gibbons, Gail. *Thanksgiving Day*. New York: Holiday House, 1985.

Hopkins, Lee Bennett, ed. *Merrily Comes Our Harvest in: Poems for Thanksgiving*. Illustrated by Ben Schecter. New York: Harcourt Brace Jovanovich, 1978.

Janice. *Little Bear's Thanksgiving*. Illustrated by Mariana. New York: Lothrop, Lee & Shepard, 1967.

Kroll, Steven. *One Tough Turkey*. Illustrated by John Wallner. New York: Holiday House, 1982.

Livingston, Myra Cohn, comp. *Thanksgiving Poems*. Illustrated by Stephen Gammell. New York: Holiday House, 1985.

Markham, Marion. *Thanksgiving Day Parade Mystery*. Illustrated by Dianne Cassidy. Boston: Houghton Mifflin, 1986.

Prelutsky, Jack. *It's Thanksgiving*. Illustrated by Marylin Hafner. New York: Greenwillow, 1982.

CHANUKAH

Adler, David. *A Picture Book of Hanukkah*. New York: Holiday House, 1985.

Chaikin, Miriam. *Light the Candle: The Story and Meaning of Hanukkah*. Boston: Houghton Mifflin, 1981.

Greenfeld, Howard. *Chanukah*. New York: Holt, 1976.

Hirsh, Marilyn. *I Love Hanukkah*. New York: Holiday House, 1984.

CHRISTMAS

Adams, Adrienne. *The Christmas Party*. New York: Macmillan, 1978.

Anderson, Joan. *Christmas on the Prairie*. Photography by George Ancona. New York: Ticknor & Fields, 1985.

Bemelmans, Ludwig. *Madeline's Christmas*. New York: Viking, 1985.

Brett, Jan. *Twelve Days of Christmas*. New York: Dodd, Mead, 1986.

Briggs, Raymond. *Father Christmas*. New York: Penguin, 1977.

Broger, Achim, adapt. *The Santa Clauses*. Illustrated by Ute Drause. New York: Dial, 1986.

Brown, Marc. *Arthur's Christmas*. Boston: Little, Brown, 1985.

Carrick, Carol. *Paul's Christmas Birthday*. Illustrated by Donald Carrick. New York: Greenwillow, 1978.

Cazet, Denys. *Christmas Moon*. New York: Bradbury, 1984.

———. *December Twenty-Fourth*. New York: Bradbury, 1986.

Chapman, Jean. *Sugar-Plum Christmas Book*. Illustrated by Deborah Niland. Chicago: Children's Press, 1982.

Coskey, Evelyn. *Christmas Crafts for Everyone.* Illustrated by Roy Wallace. Photography by Sid Dorris. Nashville: Abingdon, 1976.

Cuyler, Margery. *The All-Around Christmas Book.* Illustrated by Corbett Jones. New York: Holt, Rinehart & Winston, 1982.

DeBrunhoff, Jean. *Babar and Father Christmas.* New York: Random House, 1949.

dePaola, Tomie. *Family Christmas Tree Book.* New York: Holiday House, 1984.

———. *Merry Christmas, Strega Nona.* San Diego: Harcourt Brace Jovanovich, 1986.

Dubanevich, Arlene. *Pigs at Christmas.* New York: Bradbury, 1986.

Duvoisin, Roger. *Petunia's Christmas.* New York: Knopf, 1963.

Ets, Marie Hall. *Nine Days to Christmas.* New York: Viking, 1959.

Gantschev, Ivan. *The Christmas Train.* Boston: Little, Brown, n.d.

Giblin, James. *The Truth About Santa Claus.* New York: Crowell, 1985.

Gibbons, Gail. *Christmas Time.* New York: Holiday House, 1985.

Godden, Rumer. *The Story of Holly and Ivy.* Illustrated by Barbara Cooney. New York: Viking, 1985.

Harrison, Michael, ed. *The Oxford Book of Christmas Poems.* Illustrated by Christopher Stuart-Clark. New York: Oxford University Press, 1984.

Hayes, Sarah. *Happy Christmas Gemma.* Illustrated by Jan Ormerod. New York: Lothrop, Lee & Shepard, 1986.

Haywood, Carolyn. *Santa Claus Forever.* Illustrated by Victor Ambrus. New York: Morrow, 1983.

Hoban, Lillian. *It's Really Christmas.* New York: Greenwillow, 1982.

Holabird, Katherine. *Angelina's Christmas.* Illustrated by Helen Craig. New York: Crown, 1985.

Hollyn, Lynn. *Lynn Hollyn's Christmas Toyland.* Illustrated by Lori Anazlone. New York: Knopf, 1985.

Hughes, Shirley. *Lucy and Tom's Christmas.* New York: Viking, 1986.

Hunt, Roderick. *The Oxford Christmas Book For Children.* New York: Oxford University Press, 1983.

Janice. *Little Bear's Christmas.* Illustrated by Mariana. New York: Lothrop, Lee & Shepard, 1964.

Keats, Ezra Jack. *The Little Drummer Boy.* Words and music by Katherine Davis, Henry Onorati, and Harry Simeone. New York: Macmillan, 1972.

Keller, Holly. *A Bear for Christmas.* New York: Greenwillow, 1986.

Kroll, Steven. *Santa's Crash-Bang Christmas.* Illustrated by Tomie dePaola. New York: Holiday House, 1977.

Lindgren, Astrid, and Ilon Wikland. *Christmas in Noisy Village.* Translated by Florence Lamborn. New York: Penguin, 1981.

Livingston, Myra Cohn, ed. *Christmas Poems.* Illustrated by Trina Schart Hyman. New York: Holiday House, 1984.

Lobel, Adrianne. *A Small Sheep in a Pear Tree.* New York: Harper & Row, 1977.

Merriam, Eve. *The Christmas Box.* Illustrated by David Small. New York: Morrow, 1985.

Menotti, Gian Carlo. *Amahl and the Night Visitors.* Adapted by Frances Frost, illustrated by Michele Lemieux. New York: Morrow, 1986.

Moeri, Louise. *Star Mother's Youngest Child.* Illustrated by Trina Schart Hyman. Boston: Houghton Mifflin, 1975.

Moore, Clement. *The Night Before Christmas.* Illustrated by Grandma Moses. New York: Random House, 1962.

———. *The Night Before Christmas.* Illustrated by Tomie dePaola. New York: Holiday House, 1980.

Noble, Trinka. *Apple Tree Christmas.* New York: Dial, 1984.

Northrup, Marguerite, ed. *The Christmas Story: From the Gospels of Matthew and Luke.* New York: Metropolitan Museum, 1966.

Parish, Peggy. *Merry Christmas, Amelia Bedelia.* Illustrated by Lynn Sweat. New York: Greenwillow, 1986.

Pearson, Tracey Campbell. *We Wish You a Merry Christmas: A Traditional Christmas Carol.* New York: Dial, 1986.

Pettit, Florence Harvey. *Christmas All Around the House: Traditional Decorations You Can Make.* Illustrated by Wendy Watson. New York: Crowell, 1976.

Potter, Beatrix. *The Tailor of Gloucester.* 1904. Reprint. New York: Dover, 1973.

Robinson, Barbara. *The Best Christmas Pageant Ever.* Illustrated by Judith G. Brown. New York: Harper & Row, 1972.

Rock, Gail. *The House Without a Christmas Tree.* New York: Dell, 1985.

Scarry, Richard. *Richard Scarry's Best Christmas Book Ever.* New York: Random House, 1981.

Seuss, Dr. *How the Grinch Stole Christmas*. New York: Random House, 1957.

Spier, Peter. *Peter Spier's Christmas*. New York: Doubleday, 1983.

Stevenson, James. *Night After Christmas*. New York: Greenwillow, 1981.

Tudor, Tasha. *Take Joy! The Tasha Tudor Christmas Book*. New York: Putnam's, 1980.

Van Allsburg, Chris. *Polar Express*. Boston: Houghton Mifflin, 1985.

Van Leeuwen, Jean. *The Great Christmas Caper*. Illustrated by Steven Kellogg. New York: Dial, 1975.

Vincent, Gabrielle. *Merry Christmas, Ernest and Celestine*. New York: Greenwillow, 1984.

Wells, Rosemary. *Max's Christmas*. New York: Dial, 1986.

Weiss, Ellen. *Things to Make and Do for Christmas*. New York: Watts, 1980.

Wilson, Robina B. *Merry Christmas! Children at Christmastime Around the World*. Illustrated by Satomi Ichikawa. New York: Putnam's, 1983.

VALENTINE'S DAY

Adams, Adrienne. *The Great Valentine's Day Balloon Race*. New York: Macmillan, 1987.

Brown, Fern. *Valentine's Day*. New York: Watts, 1983.

Brown, Marc. *Arthur's Valentine*. New York: Avon, 1982.

Bunting, Eve. *The Valentine Bears*. Illustrated by Jan Brett. New York: Clarion, 1983.

Carlson, Nancy. *Mysterious Valentine*. Minneapolis: Carolrhoda, 1985.

Cohen, Miriam. *"Bee My Valentine!"* Illustrated by Lillian Hoban. New York: Greenwillow, 1978.

Corwin, Judith. *Valentine Fun*. New York: Messner, 1982.

dePaola, Tomie. *Things to Make and Do for Valentine's Day*. New York: Watts, 1976.

Glovach, Linda. *Little Witch's Valentine Book*. Englewood Cliffs, N.J.: Prentice-Hall, 1984.

Greenwald, Sheila. *Valentine Rosy*. Boston: Little, Brown, 1984.

Hopkins, Lee Bennett, ed. *Good Morning to You, Valentine*. Illustrated by Tomie dePaola. New York: Harcourt Brace Jovanovich, 1976.

Kraus, Robert. *How Spider Saved Valentine's Day*. New York: Scholastic, 1986.

Livingston, Myra Cohn. *Valentine Poems*. Illustrated by Patience Brewster. New York: Holiday House, 1987.

Model, Frank. *One Zillion Valentines*. New York: Greenwillow, 1981.

Sopraner, Robyn. *Valentine's Day—Things to Make and Do*. Illustrated by Renzo Barto. Mahwah, N.J.: Troll, 1981.

EASTER

Adams, Adrienne. *The Easter Egg Artists*. New York: Macmillan, 1981.

Berger, Gilda. *Easter and Other Spring Holidays*. New York: Watts, 1983.

Friedrich, Priscilla, and Otto Friedrich. *The Easter Bunny That Overslept*. Illustrated by Adrienne Adams. New York: Lothrop, Lee & Shepard, 1983.

Heyward, DuBose. *The Country Bunny and the Golden Shoes*. Boston: Houghton Mifflin, 1939.

Kroll, Steven. *Big Bunny and the Easter Eggs*. Illustrated by Dick Gackenbach. New York: Scholastic, 1983.

Milhous, Katherine. *The Egg Tree*. Illustrated by Katherine Milhous. New York: Macmillan, 1981.

Stevenson, James. *The Great Big Especially Beautiful Easter Egg*. New York: Greenwillow, 1983.

Birthdays of Selected Authors and Illustrators

JANUARY

2	Isaac Asimov, Crosby Bonsall, Jean Little
3	Carolyn Haywood, J. R. R. Tolkien
4	Jakob Grimm
6	Carl Sandburg, Vera Cleaver
7	Kay Chorao
9	Clyde Robert Bulla
10	Remy Charlip
11	Robert O'Brien
12	Charles Perrault, Jack London
13	Michael Bond
14	Hugh Lofting
18	A. A. Milne, Raymond Briggs
19	Edgar Allen Poe
22	Blair Lent, Brian Wildsmith
25	James Flora
26	Mary Mapes Dodge
27	Lewis Carroll, Jean Merrill
28	Ann Jonas
29	Bill Peet
30	Lloyd Alexander

FEBRUARY

1	Langston Hughes
2	Rebecca Caudill
4	Russell Hoban
5	Patricia Lauber
7	Laura Ingalls Wilder
8	Jules Verne
9	Hilda Van Stockum
10	Elaine Konigsburg, Charles Lamb
11	Jane Yolen
12	Judy Blume
15	Norman Bridwell, Doris Orgel
16	Nancy Ekholm Burkert, Mary O'Neill
19	Louis Slobodkin
24	Wilhelm Grimm
25	Frank Bonham, Cynthia Voigt
27	Henry Wadsworth Longfellow, Uri Shulevitz
28	Sir John Tenniel

MARCH

2	Dr. Seuss, Leo Dillon
4	Meindert DeJong
5	Errol Le Cain
8	Kenneth Grahame
11	Wanda Gág, Ezra Jack Keats
12	Virginia Hamilton, Leo Lionni
13	Ellen Raskin, Dorothy Aldis, Diane Dillon
14	Marguerite de Angeli

16   Sid Fleischman
17   Kate Greenaway
20   Ellen Conford, Mitsumasa Anno, Lois Lowry
22   Randolph Caldecott
23   Eleanor Cameron
24   Mary Stolz, Bill Cleaver
26   Robert Frost
27   Dick King-Smith

APRIL

2   Hans Christian Andersen
3   Washington Irving
8   Trina Schart Hyman
9   Joseph Krumgold, Leonard Wibberley
10   David Adler
12   Beverly Cleary, Hardie Gramatky
13   Marguerite Henry, Genevieve Foster, Lee Bennett Hopkins
19   Jean Lee Latham
22   William Jay Smith
23   William Shakespeare
24   Evaline Ness
25   Walter De la Mare
26   Patricia Reilly Giff
27   Ludwig Bemelmans, John Burningham
29   Jill Paton Walsh
30   Dorothy Hinshaw Patent

MAY

7   Nonny Hogrogian
8   Milton Meltzer
9   Eleanor Estes, Sir James Barrie, Willian Pène du Bois, Keith Robertson
10   John Rowe Townsend, Margaret Wise Brown
11   Zilpha Keatley Snyder
12   Edward Lear
14   George Selden
15   Frank Baum
17   Eloise Greenfield
18   Lillian Hoban, Irene Hunt
21   Virginia Haviland
22   Arnold Lobel
23   Scott O'Dell, Susan Cooper
25   Martha Alexander
30   Millicent Selsam
31   Jay Williams, Elizabeth Coatsworth, Walt Whitman

JUNE

1   James Daugherty
2   Norton Juster, Paul Galdone, Helen Oxenbury
3   Anita Lobel
5   Franklyn M. Branley
6   Peter Spier, Verna Aardema
7   Gwendolyn Brooks, John Goodall
10   Maurice Sendak
12   James Houston
14   Penelope Farmer, Laurence Yep
18   Pat Hutchins, Chris Van Allsburg
24   John Ciardi, Leonard Everett Fisher
25   Eric Carle
26   Charlotte Zolotow, Lynd Ward, Robert Burch, Wallace Tripp, Walter Farley
27   Lucille Clifton
30   Mollie Hunter

JULY

2   Jean Craighead George
4   Nathaniel Hawthorne
6   Beatrix Potter
11   E. B. White, Helen Cresswell
12   Johanna Spyri, Herbert S. Zim
13   Marcia Brown
14   Isaac Bashevis Singer, Peggy Parish
15   Walter Edmonds
16   Arnold Adoff, Richard Egielski
17   Karla Kuskin
19   Eve Merriam, John Newbery
23   Robert Quackenbush
27   Scott Corbett, Hilaire Belloc
28   Natalie Babbitt, Beatrix Potter

AUGUST

1   Gail Gibbons
6   Matt Christopher, Barbara Cooney
7   Betsy Byars
8   Jan Pienkowski
9   José Aruego, Seymour Simon
10   Margot Tomes
11   Don Freeman, Joanna Cole
12   Mary Ann Hoberman
15   Walter Crane, Brinton Turkle
17   Myra Cohn Livingston, Ariane Dewey
19   Ogden Nash

21 Arthur Yorinks
26 Patricia Beatty
28 Phyllis Krasilovsky, Roger Duvoisin, Tasha Tudor
30 Virginia Lee Burton, Donald Crews

SEPTEMBER

2 Eugene Field
3 Aliki
4 Syd Hoff, Joan Aiken
7 C. B. Colby
8 Jack Prelutsky
9 Aileen Fisher
11 Alfred Slote
13 Roald Dahl, Else Minarik
14 William Armstrong
15 Robert McCloskey, Tomie dePaola
16 H. A. Rey
19 Arthur Rackham, Rachel Field, James Haskins
20 Donald Hall
23 Jan Ormerod
24 Harry Behn, Leslie Brooke, Jane Curry, Felice Holman
27 Bernard Waber, Paul Goble
28 Kate Douglas Wiggin
30 Alvin Tresselt

OCTOBER

3 Natalie Savage Carlson, Molly Cone
4 Julia Cunningham, Robert Lawson, Donald Sobol
5 Louise Fitzhugh
6 Steven Kellogg
7 James Whitcomb Riley, Alice Dalgliesh, Susan Jeffers
10 James Marshall
11 Russell Freedman
13 Katherine Paterson
14 Lois Lenski
19 Ed Emberley

21 Ursula Le Guin
23 Marjorie Flack
24 Bruno Munari
27 Constance Greene

NOVEMBER

1 Symeon Shimin
7 Armstrong Sperry
12 Marjorie Weinman Sharmat
13 Robert Louis Stevenson
14 Astrid Lindgren, William Steig
15 David McCord, Manus Pinkwater
16 Jean Fritz
20 William Cole
21 Elizabeth George Speare, Leo Politi
24 C. Collodi, Sylvia Engdahl, Frances Hodgson Burnett, Yoshiko Uchida
26 Doris Gates, Laurence Pringle
28 Tomi Ungerer
29 Louisa May Alcott, Madeleine L'Engle, C. S. Lewis
30 Mark Twain, Margot Zemach

DECEMBER

2 David Macaulay
5 Christina Rossetti, Harve Zemach
6 Elizabeth Yates
8 Padraic Colum, Edwin Tunis
9 Joel Chandler Harris, Joan Blos
10 Emily Dickinson, Rumer Godden, Ernest Shepard
12 Barbara Emberley
13 Leonard Weisgard
16 Marie Hall Ets, Arthur C. Clarke
18 Marilyn Sachs
19 Eve Bunting
22 William O. Steele
24 Feodor Rojankovsky, Margaret J. Anderson
28 Carol Ryrie Brink
30 Rudyard Kipling, Mercer Mayer

COPYRIGHTS AND ACKNOWLEDGMENTS

Chapter 1

Page 4 N. M. Bodecker, ''Hello Book'' from a bookmark for Children's Book Week (Children's Book Council, 1978). Used by permission of author. **27–28** From *A Wizard of Earthsea* by Ursula K. Le Guin. Copyright © 1968 by Elisabeth Covel Le Guin and Caroline Le Guin. Reprinted by permission of Houghton Mifflin Company. **32** ''The Little Turtle'' from *Collected Poems of Vachel Lindsay*. Copyright © 1920 by Macmillan Publishing Co., Inc., renewed 1948 by Elizabeth C. Lindsay. Used by permission. **32** ''Hold Fast Your Dreams'' by Louise Driscoll. Copyright © 1916 by The New York Times Company. Reprinted by permission.

Chapter 2

Page 44 ''Books Fall Open'' from *One at a Time* by David McCord. Copyright © 1961, 1962, 1965, 1966, 1970, 1974 by David McCord. Reprinted by permission of Little, Brown and Company. **55–56** Letter reprinted by kind permission of Mary Sirmons. **58** Chart reprinted by kind permission of William P. Casey. **60** ''Snow'' by Dorothy Aldis reprinted by permission of G. P. Putnam's Sons from *Everything and Anything* by Dorothy Aldis. Copyright © 1925–27, renewed 1953–55 by Dorothy Aldis. **60** Lines from ''Whistles'' by Dorothy Aldis, reprinted by permission of G. P. Putnam's Sons, from *Here, There and Everywhere* by Dorothy Aldis. Copyright © 1927, 1928, renewed © 1955, 1956 by Dorothy Aldis. **61** ''Hallowe'en'' from *The Little Hill*, poems and pictures by Harry Behn. Copyright © 1949 by Harry Behn, renewed 1977 by Alice L. Behn. Reprinted by permission of Marian Reiner. **61** ''My Friend Leona'' by Mary O'Neill from *People I'd Like to Keep*. Doubleday, 1964. **61** Excerpt from ''Jimmy Jet and His TV Set'' from *Where the Sidewalk Ends* by Shel Silverstein. Copyright © 1974 by Evil Eye Music, Inc. Reprinted by permission of Harper & Row Publishers, Inc. **74** From *The Pobble Who Has No Toes* by Edward Lear. Viking Penguin, 1978. **83**

From *The Ghost Eye Tree* by Bill Martin Jr and John Archambault. Holt, Rinehart & Winston, 1985.

Chapter 3

Page 96 ''Books'' from *One at a Time* by David McCord. Copyright © 1961, 1962, 1965, 1966, 1970, 1974 by David McCord. By permission of Little, Brown and Company. **101** From *Madeline* by Ludwig Bemelmans. Copyright © 1939 by Ludwig Bemelmans, renewed © 1967 by Madeleine Bemelmans and Barabara Bemelmans Marciano. Reprinted by permission of Viking Penguin, Inc. **101** Used by kind permission of Leanore Canepa.

Chapter 4

Page 150 ''Watch Out'' from *Near the Window Tree* by Karla Kuskin. Copyright © 1975 by Karla Kuskin. Reprinted by permission of Harper & Row Publishers, Inc. **155** Copyright © 1970 by Felice Holman. **158** ''The End'' from *Now We Are Six* by A. A. Milne. Copyright © 1927 by E. P. Dutton, renewed 1955 by A. A. Milne. Reprinted by permission of the publisher, E. P. Dutton, a division of NAL Penguin, Inc. **162** ''Us Two'' from *Now We Are Six* by A. A. Milne. Copyright © 1927 by E. P. Dutton, renewed 1955 by A. A. Milne. Reprinted by permission of the publisher, E. P. Dutton, a division of NAL Penguin, Inc. **179** ''Little'' by Dorothy Aldis. Reprinted by permission of G. P. Putnam's Sons. From *Anything and Everything* by Dorothy Aldis, copyright © 1925–27, renewed 1953–55 by Dorothy Aldis. **181** From ''Where the Sidewalk Ends'' by Shel Silverstein. Copyright © 1974 by Evil Eye Music, Inc. Reprinted by permission of Harper & Row, Publishers, Inc. **191** ''Listen Rabbit'' from *Listen Rabbit* by Aileen Fisher (Thomas Y. Crowell). Text Copyright © 1964 by Aileen Fisher. Reprinted by permission of Harper & Row, Publishers, Inc. **191** First stanza of ''Early Spring'' from *Rabbits, Rabbits*, poems by Aileen Fisher. Text copyright © 1983 by

E. P. Dutton, a division of NAL Penguin, Inc. **361** Reprinted by permission of Dodd, Mead & Company, Inc., from *The Complete Nonsense Book* by Edward Lear. **362** "The Night Will Never Stay" from *Eleanor Farjeon's Poems for Children* (J. B. Lippincott). Originally published in *Collected Poems* by Eleanor Farjeon, copyright © 1951 by Eleanor Farjeon. Reprinted by permission of Harper & Row, Publishers, Inc. **363** "Who Has Seen the Wind?" by Christina Rosetti in the *Scott, Foresman Anthology of Children's Literature*, edited by Zena Sutherland and Myra Cohn Livingston. Scott, Foresman, 1984. **364** "Haiku" Nos. 5 and 10 from *One at a Time* by David McCord. Copyright © 1961, 1962, 1965, 1970, 1974 by David McCord. By permission of Little, Brown and Company. **368** "Treehouse" by Ted Kooser, from *Pocket Poems* collected by Paul Janeczko. Bradbury Press, 1985. **368** "Snow" by Nan Fry, from *Pocket Poems*, collected by Paul Janeczko. Bradbury Press, 1985. **368** "Galoshes" by Rhoda W. Bacmeister in *Arbuthnot Anthology of Children's Literature*, 4th ed., edited by Zena Sutherland et al. Lothrop, Lee & Shepard, 1976. **369** From *If All the Seas Were One Sea* by Janina Domanska. Macmillan, 1987. **369** "The Fourth" from *Where the Sidewalk Ends* by Shel Silverstein. Copyright © 1974 by Evil Eye Music. Reprinted by permission of Harper & Row, Publishers, Inc. **369** From *Garbage Delight* by Dennis Lee. Copyright © 1977. Reprinted by permission of Macmillan of Canada, A Division of Canada Publishing Corporation. **369** From *One at a Time* by David McCord. Copyright © 1961, 1962, 1965, 1966, 1970, 1974 by David McCord. By permission of Little, Brown and Company. **370** Reprinted with permission of Macmillan Publishing Company. From *Circus* by Jack Prelutsky. Copyright © 1974 by Jack Prelutsky. **371** "Where Would You Be?" from *Dogs and Dragons, Trees and Dreams* by Karla Kuskin. Originally published in *The Rose on My Cake* by Karla Kuskin. Copyright © 1964 by Karla Kuskin. Reprinted by permission of Harper & Row, Publishers, Inc. **371** From *One at a Time* by David McCord. Copyright © 1961, 1962, 1965, 1966, 1970, 1974 by David McCord. By permission of Little, Brown and Company. **371** "From a Railway Carriage" and "Where Go the Boats?" in *A Child's Garden of Verses* by Robert Louis Stevenson. Scribner, 1905. **374** "My Knee Is Only Sprained" from *Sports Pages* by Arnold Adoff (J. B. Lippincott). Text copyright © 1986 by Arnold Adoff. Reprinted by permission of Harper & Row, Publishers, Inc. **375** From *A Sky Full of Poems* by Eve Merriam. Copyright © 1964, 1970, 1973 by Eve Merriam. All rights reserved. Reprinted by permission of Marian Reiner for the author. **375** "Dandelion" from *Poems by a Little Girl* by Hilda Conkling. Copyright © 1920 by J. B. Lippincott Co., © 1949 by Hilda Conkling. Reprinted by permission of the author. **375** From *The Dream Keeper and Other Poems* by Langston Hughes. Copyright © 1932 by Alfred A. Knopf, Inc., and renewed © 1960 by Langston Hughes. Reprinted by permission of Alfred A. Knopf, Inc. **375** Copyright © 1923, 1969 by Holt, Rinehart and Winston. Copyright © 1951 by Robert Frost. Reprinted from *The Poetry of Robert Frost*, edited by Edward Connery Lathem. By permission of Henry Holt and Company, Inc. **375** From *Moon-Whales and Other Poems* by Ted Hughes. Copyright © 1963, 1976 by Ted Hughes. Reprinted by permission of Viking Penguin, Inc. **376–77** "Reflections on a Gift of Watermelon Pickle Received from a Friend Called Felicity" by John Tobias. Copyright © 1961 by the University of New Mexico Press, assigned to John Tobias, 305 East 86th Street, New York, NY 10028. **378** Excerpted from "How to Eat a Poem" in *Jamboree: Rhymes for All Times* by Eve Merriam. Copyright © 1962, 1964, 1966, 1973, 1984 by Eve Marriam. All rights reserved. Reprinted by permission of Marian Reiner for the author.

Chapter 8

Page 389 Lillian Moore, "Reflections" from *Something New Begins*. Copyright © 1982 by Lillian Moore. Reprinted with the permission of Atheneum Publishers, an imprint of Macmillan Publishing Company. **410–11** Teaching idea used by kind permission of Diane Person.

Chapter 9

Page 458 "Ancient History" by Arthur Guiterman in *The Arbuthnot Anthology of Children's Literature*, 4th ed., edited by Zena Sutherland et al. Lothrop, Lee and Shepard, 1976.

Chapter 10

Page 525 "Buffalo Dusk" from *Smoke and Steel* by Carl Sandburg. Copyright © 1920 by Harcourt Brace Jovanovich, Inc., and renewed 1948 by Carl Sandburg. Reprinted by permission of the publisher.

Chapter 11

Page 574 "Saying Yes" by Diana Chang. Reprinted by permission of the author. **579** From *More Cricket Songs*, Japanese haiku translated by Harry Behn. Copyright © 1971 by Harry Behn. All rights reserved. Reprinted by permission of Marian Reiner. **580** Haiku from *Don't Tell the Scarecrow*, edited by Issa et al. Four Winds, Scholastic, 1969. **580** Haiku from *In a Spring Garden*, collected by Richard Lewis (Dial Press, 1965). "Grasshopper, Do not trample" by Issa from *Haiku* (Vol. 4) and "The moon in the water" by Ryota from *Haiku* (Vol. 3). The Hokuseido Press, trans. R. H. Blyth. **580** Sijo from *Sunset in a Spider Web: Sijo Poetry of Ancient Korea*, collected by Virginia Olsen Baron. Holt, Rinehart & Winston, 1974. **586** Activity used by kind permission of Domica Mazzochi. **588** From *Bringing the Rain to Kapiti Plain* by Verna Aardema. Text copyright © 1981 by Verna Aardema. Reprinted by permission of the publisher, Dial Books for Young Readers. **589** Excerpted from *Beat the Story Drum, Pum, Pum* by Ashley Bryan. Copyright © 1980 Ashley Bryan. Reprinted with the permission of the Atheneum Publishers, an imprint of Macmillan Publishing Company. **591** From *Honey, I Love and Other Poems* by Eloise Greenfield. Viking, 1972. **591** "Black

Is Brown Is Tan" (first 5 lines) from *Black Is Brown Is Tan* by Arnold Adoff. Text copyright © 1973 by Arnold Adoff. Reprinted by permission of Harper & Row, Publishers, Inc. **600** From *My Song Is a Piece of Jade* by Toni de Gerez. English translation copyright © 1984 by Organizacion Editorial Novaro, S. A. By permission of Little, Brown and Company. **602** From *The Hispanic Americans* by Milton Meltzer. Crowell, 1982. **606** Copyright © 1986 by Valerie Worth Bahlke. **606** Poem by Carol Adler. **610** Teaching idea reprinted form Hadassah Jewish Education Study Guide titled "Jewish Children's Books: How to Choose Them, How to Use Them" by Marcia Posner, Ph.D. **616** From *The Trees Stand Shining: Poetry of the North American Indians,* collected by Hettie Jones. Dial, 1971. **616** Excerpt from *Many Winters* by Nancy Wood. Copyright © 1972 by The Institute of American Indian Arts. Reprinted by permission of Doubleday, a division of Bantam, Doubleday, Dell Publishing Group, Inc. **617** Activity developed by Corie Adjmi. **618** "The Desert" by Daniel A. Poler. Reprinted by kind permission of the author. **625–26** Teaching idea developed by Lucy Rubin.

ILLUSTRATION CREDITS

Chapter 1

Page 6, top: © Elizabeth Crews; bottom: © Hays/Monkmeyer Press Photo Service. **7,** top: © Mimi Forsyth/Monkmeyer Press Photo Service; bottom: © Elizabeth Crews. **8** Text and art excerpts from *I'll Fix Anthony* written by Judith Viorst; illustrated by Arnold Lobel. Text copyright © 1969 by Judith Viorst. Pictures copyright © 1969 by Arnold Lobel. Reprinted by permission of Harper & Row, Publishers, Inc. **12** Illustration from *Little Bear* by Else Homelund Minarik, pictures by Maurice Sendak. Pictures copyright © 1957 by Maurice Sendak. Reprinted by permission of Harper & Row, Publishers, Inc. **21** © Elizabeth Crews. **22** Illustration from *The Doorbell Rang* by Pat Hutchins. Copyright © 1986 by Pat Hutchins. By permission of Greenwillow Books (A Division of William Morrow and Company, Inc.). **26** From *A Wizard of Earthsea* by Ursula K. Le Guin. Illustrated by Ruth Robbins. Parnassus Press, 1968. **29** Illustration from *Make Way for Ducklings* by Robert McCloskey. Copyright © 1941, renewed © 1969 by Robert McCloskey. All rights reserved. Reprinted by permission of Viking Penguin Inc. **30** Barbara Cooney. **31** Cover illustration by Garth Williams from *Charlotte's Web* by E. B. White, pictures by Garth Williams. Copyright © 1952 by E. B. White. Illustrations copyright renewed 1980 by Garth Williams. Reprinted by permission of Harper & Row, Publishers, Inc. **33** Illustration and excerpt from *Whiskers and Rhymes*, p. 48, by Arnold Lobel. Copyright © 1985 by Arnold Lobel. By permission of Greenwillow Books (A Division of William Morrow and Company, Inc.). **34** Reproduced with the permission of Charles Scribner's Sons, an imprint of Macmillan Publishing Company from *The Cour-*

age of Sarah Noble by Alice Dalgliesh, illustrated by Leonard Weisgard. Copyright © 1954 by Alice Dalgliesh and Leonard Weisgard, copyright renewed. **35** Illustration from *Commodore Perry in the Land of the Shogun,* p. 60, by Rhoda Blumberg. Text copyright © 1985 by Rhoda Blumberg. By permission of Lothrop, Lee & Shepard Books (A Division of William Morrow and Company, Inc.). **36** Illustration from *So Far from the Bamboo Grove* by Yoko Kawashima Watkins. Copyright © 1986 by Yoko Kawashima Watkins. By permission of Lothrop, Lee & Shepard Books (A Division of William Morrow and Company, Inc.). **37** American Library Association.

Chapter 2

Page 47 Illustration from *Becca Backward, Becca Forward* by Bruce McMillan. Copyright © 1986 by Bruce McMillan. By permission of Lothrop, Lee & Shepard Books (A Division of William Morrow and Company, Inc.). **48** Illustration by Donna Diamond from *Bridge to Terabithia* by Katherine Paterson, illustrations by Donna Diamond (Thomas Y. Crowell) Copyright © 1977 by Katherine Paterson. Reprinted by permission of Harper & Row, Publishers, Inc. **52** © Ed Lettau/Photo Researchers. **54,** top: HBJ photo, Larry Hoagland, Professional Photographic Services; bottom: From *In Coal Country* by Judith Hendershot, illustrations copyright © 1987 by Thomas B. Allen. Reprinted by permission of Alfred A. Knopf, Inc. **55** Courtesy Hilda L. Lauber, Baytown, Texas. **57** © Elizabeth Crews. **60** © Elizabeth Crews. **64,** top: © S. H. Smith; bottom: From *What's in Fox's Sack?* by Paul Galdone. Copyright © 1982 by Paul Galdone. Reprinted by permission of Clarion Books/ Ticknor & Fields, a Houghton Mifflin Company. **65,** left: Illustration by Nancy Ekholm Burkert from *Snow White and the Seven Dwarfs.* Copyright © 1972 by Nancy Ekholm Burkert. Reproduced by permission of Farrar, Straus & Giroux, Inc.; right, from *Snow White* translated by Paul Heims, illustrations by Trina Schart Hyman. Text copyright © 1974 by Paul Heims, illustrations copyright © 1974 by Trina Schart Hyman. By permission of Little, Brown and Company in association with the Atlantic Monthly Press. **66** Courtesy Weston Woods Studios. **67** From *Winnie the Pooh* by A. A. Milne, illustrated by Ernest H. Shepard. Copyright © 1926 by E. P. Dutton, renewed 1954 by A. A. Milne. Reproduced by permission of the publisher, E. P. Dutton, a division of NAL Penguin Inc. **71** Illustration from *Blueberries for Sal* by Robert McCloskey. Copyright 1948, renewed © 1976 by Robert McCloskey. All rights reserved. Reprinted by permission of Viking Penguin Inc. **72** © Elizabeth Crews/Stock, Boston. **78** Ginger Chih. **80** "January" text and illustration from *Chicken Soup with Rice* by Maurice Sendak. Copyright © 1962 by Maurice Sendak. Reprinted by permission of Harper & Row, Publishers, Inc. **82** © Elizabeth Hamlin/Stock, Boston. **85,** left: Courtesy Laurie Secord, Worthington Hills Elementary School, Worthington, Ohio; right : From *Pezzetino* by Leo Lionni. Copyright © 1975 by Leo Lionni. Reprinted by permission of Pantheon Books, a Division of Random House,

Inc. **86–87:** Courtesy Laurie Secord, Worthington Hills Elementary School, Worthington, Ohio.

Chapter 3

Page 101 Illustration from *Madeline* by Ludwig Bemelmans. Illustration copyright renewed © 1967 by Madeleine Bemelmans and Barbara Bemelmans Marciano. All rights reserved. Reprinted by permission of Viking Penguin Inc. **102** Reprinted with permission of Elizabeth Sulzby and the International Reading Association. **108** Illustration from *Spot Goes to the Farm* by Eric Hill, © 1987 by Eric Hill. Reprinted by permission of G. P. Putnam's Sons. **110** Illustration from *On Market Street* by Arnold Lobel. Text copyright © 1981 by Arnold Lobel. Illustrations copyright © 1981 by Anita Lobel. By permission of Greenwillow Books (A Division of William Morrow and Company, Inc.). **111** Reprinted with permission of Bradbury Press, an affiliate of Macmillan, Inc., from *Alphabatics* by Suse MacDonald. Copyright © 1986 by Suse MacDonald. **112,** top: From *The Z Was Zapped* by Chris Van Allsburg. Copyright © 1987 by Chris Van Allsburg. Reprinted by permission of Houghton Mifflin Company; bottom: From *Jambo Means Hello: Swahili Alphabet Book* by Muriel Feelings, pictures by Tom Feelings. Pictures © 1974 by Tom Feelings. Reprinted by permission of the publisher, Dial Books for Young Readers. **113** Illustration by Eric Carle reprinted by permission of Philomel Books from *The Very Hungry Caterpillar* by Eric Carle, copyright © 1969 by Eric Carle. **114,** left: Illustration from *Ten, Nine, Eight*, p. 5, by Molly Bang. Copyright © 1983 by Molly Garrett Bang. By permission of Greenwillow Books (A Division of William Morrow and Company, Inc.). **114** From *Animal Numbers* by Bert Kitchen. Copyright © 1987 by Bert Kitchen. Reproduced by permission of the publisher, Dial Books for Young Readers. **116** Courtesy Nancy Tafuri. Photo by Tom Tafuri. **118** Illustration from *Truck* by Donald Crews. Copyright © 1980 by Donald Crews. By permission of Greenwillow Books (A Division of William Morrow and Company, Inc.). **120** Eric Carle. **121** Illustrations from pages 26–27 in *King Bidgood's in the Bathtub* by Audrey Wood, illustrations copyright © 1985 by Don Wood. Reprinted by permission of Harcourt Brace Jovanovich, Inc. **122** From *Frog, Where Are You?* by Mercer Mayer. Copyright © 1969 by Mercer Mayer. Reproduced by permission of the publisher, Dial Books for Young Readers. **123** HBJ Photo by Diane Pella. **124** Photo by Carole Cutner. **126** Illustration from *Picnic* by Emily Arnold McCully. Copyright © 1984 by Emily Arnold McCully. Reprinted by permission of Harper & Row, Publishers, Inc. **127** Reproduced with permission of Macmillan Publishing Company from *The Milk Makers* by Gail Gibbons. Copyright © by Gail Gibbons. **130** Courtesy Harcourt Brace Jovanovich, Inc. **131** Illustration from *Frog and Toad Are Friends*, written and illustrated by Arnold Lobel. Copyright © 1970 by Arnold Lobel. Reprinted by permission of Harper & Row, Publishers, Inc. **132** Photo by Susan Hirschman. **134** Ian Anderson. Reproduced by permission of Harper & Row, Publishers, Inc. **135** Illustration from *Ramona and her Father* by Beverly Cleary. Illustration by Alan Tiegreen.

Text copyright © 1975, 1977 by Beverly Clearly. By permission of Morrow Junior Books (A Division of William Morrow and Company, Inc.).

Chapter 4

Page 152 From *The Tale of Peter Rabbit* by Beatrix Potter. London: Frederick Warne. **156** Illustration by José Aruego from *Leo the Late Bloomer* by Robert Kraus, pictures by José Aruego. Pictures © 1971 by José Aruego. Reprinted by permission of Harper & Row, Publishers, Inc. **159** Reprinted with permission of Macmillan Publishing Company from *Max* by Rachel Isadora. Copyright © 1976 by Rachel Isadora. **161** From *Ira Sleeps Over* by Bernard Waber. Copyright © 1972 by Bernard Waber. Reprinted by permission of Houghton Mifflin Company. **162** Illustration by Clement Hurd from *Goodnight Moon* by Margaret Wise Brown, pictures by Clement Hurd copyright © 1974 by Harper & Row Publishers, Inc., renewed © 1965 by Roberta Brown Rauch and Clement Hurd. Reprinted by permission of Harper & Row, Publishers, Inc. **165** From *Jumanji* by Chris Van Allsburg. Copyright © 1981 by Chris Van Allsburg. Reprinted by permission of Houghton Mifflin Company. **166** Houghton Mifflin Company. **167** Copyright © 1969 by William Steig. Reprinted by permission of Simon & Schuster, Inc. **168** © Nancy Crampton. **170** © by Candid Lang. Reproduced by permission of Harper & Row, Publishers, Inc. **171** Illustration from *Where the Wild Things Are*, written and illustrated by Maurice Sendak. Copyright © 1963 by Maurice Sendak. Reprinted by permission of Harper & Row, Publishers, Inc. **173,** left: Illustration by Barbara Cooney Porter from *Ox-Cart Man* by Donald Hall. Illustrations copyright © 1979 by Barbara Cooney Porter. All rights reserved. Reprinted by permission of Viking Penguin Inc.; right: Illustration from *An Evening at Alfie's* by Shirley Hughes. Copyright © 1984 by Shirley Hughes. By permission of Lothrop, Lee & Shepard Books (A Division of William Morrow and Company, Inc.). **175** From *Amifika* by Lucille Clifton, illustrated by Thomas DiGrazia. Illustrations copyright © 1977 by Thomas DiGrazia. Reproduced by permission of the publisher, E. P. Dutton, a division of NAL Penguin Inc. **178** Reproduced with the permission of Charles Scribner's Sons, an imprint of Macmillan Publishing Company, from *A Baby for Max* by Kathryn Lasky, Photographs by Christopher Knight. Copyright © 1984 by Christopher Knight. **183** From *Blackberries in the Dark* by Mavis Jukes. Illustrations copyright © 1985 by Thomas B. Allen. Reprinted by permission of Alfred A. Knopf, Inc. **186** Illustration by Maurice Sendak from *Let's Be Enemies* by Janice May Udry, pictures by Maurice Sendak. Pictures copyright © 1961 by Maurice Sendak. Reprinted by permission of Harper & Row, Publishers, Inc. **187** Reprinted with permission of Macmillan Publishing Company from *Willaby* by Rachel Isadora. Copyright © 1977 by Rachel Isadora. **197** Graham Oakley, illustration from *The Church Mice at Bay*. Copyright © 1978 Graham Oakley. Reprinted with the permission of Atheneum Publishers, an imprint of Macmillan Publishing Company. **202** Courtesy E. P. Dutton.

Chapter 5

Page 220 Illustration from *Tomie dePaola's Mother Goose,* © 1985 by Tomie dePaola. Reprinted by permission of G. P. Putnam's Sons. **226** From *Sing a Song of Sixpence.* Pictures by Tracey Campbell Pearson. Pictures copyright © 1985 by Tracey Campbell Pearson. Reprinted by permission of the publisher, Dial Books for Young Readers. **228** *Fairy Tales Told Again,* illustrated by Gustave Doré. London, Paris, and New York: Cassell, Petter and Galpin, 1872. **229** Culver Pictures. **233** ©Elizabeth Crews/Stock, Boston. **234** From the book *Strega Nona* by Tomie dePaola © 1975. Used by permission of the publisher, Prentice-Hall, Inc., Englewood Cliffs, New Jersey. **235** Photo: Jon Gilbert Fox. **237** Illustration from the title page in *Jump! The Adventures of Brer Rabbit* by Joel Chandler Harris, illustrations by Barry Moser, copyright © 1986 by Pennyroyal Press, Inc. Reprinted by permission of Harcourt Brace Jovanovich, Inc. **240** Bernie Goedhardt. **243,** left: Illustration by Arthur Rackham from *Grimm's Fairy Tales.* All rights reserved. Reprinted by permission of Viking Penguin Inc.; right: Reproduced with the permission of Charles Scribner's Sons, an imprint of Macmillan Publishing Company, from *Tom Tit Tot* by Evaline Ness. Illustrations copyright © 1965 by Evaline Ness. **246,** left: The Metropolitan Museum of Art, Rogers Fund, 1920 (20.81.1); right: From the book *The Lion and the Rat* by Brian Wildsmith. Copyright © 1963. Used with permission of the publisher, Franklin Watts. **252** Copyright © 1984 by Leonard Everett Fisher. Reprinted from *The Olympains* by permission of Holiday House. **262** Illustration from *Pecos Bill* by Steven Kellogg. Copyright © 1986 by Steven Kellogg. By permission of Morrow Junior Books (A Division of William Morrow and Company, Inc.).

Chapter 6

Page 280 Illustration by Garth Williams from *Charlotte's Web* by E. B. White. Copyright © 1952 by E. B. White. Pictures by Garth Williams. Illustrations copyright renewed 1980 by Garth Williams. Reprinted by permission of Harper & Row, Publishers, Inc. **283** Illustration by J. R. R. Tolkien from *The Hobbit* by J. R. R. Tolkien. Copyright © 1966 by J. R. R. Tolkien. Reprinted by permission of Houghton Mifflin Company. **286** Illustration from page 97 in *The Borrowers* by Mary Norton, illustrated by Beth Krush and Joe Krush, copyright © 1952, 1953 by Mary Norton, renewed by Mary Norton and Beth Krush and Joe Krush. Reprinted by permission of Harcourt Brace Jovanovich, Inc. **288** Illustration by Bernardo Bryson reprinted by permission of Coward-McCann, Inc. from *The Return of the Twelves* by Pauline Clark, illustrations copyright © 1963 by Coward-McCann, Inc. **289** A & C Black (Publishers) Ltd. **290** The New York Public Library. **291** Courtesy E. P. Dutton. **292** Reproduced with the permission of Charles Scribner's Sons, an imprint of Macmillan Publishing Company from *The Wind in the Willows* by Kenneth Grahame, illustrated by Ernest H. Shepard. Copyright © 1933 Charles Scribner's Sons; coyright renewed © 1961 Ernest H. Shepard. **300** © C. S. Lewis Pte. Ltd. 1950. Illustrated by Pauline Baynes.

Published by William Collins Sons and Co. Ltd. **304** Illustration by Alan E. Cober from *The Dark is Rising* by Susan Cooper. Illustration copyright © 1973 Alan E. Cober. Reprinted with the permission of Margaret McElderry Books, an imprint of Macmillan Publishing Company. **307** From *The High King* by Lloyd Alexander, map by Evaline Ness. Map copyright © 1968 by Holt, Rinehart and Winston, Inc. Reprinted by permission of Henry Holt and Company, Inc. **313** © Thomas Victor 1983. **315** Cover from *Beauty: A Retelling of the Story of Beauty and the Beast* by Robin McKinley. Reprinted by permission of Harper & Row, Publishers, Inc. **316** Reprinted with permission of Macmillan Publishing Company from Jules Verne, *20,000 Leagues Under the Sea,* illustrated by Charles Molina. Copyright © 1962 by Macmillan Publishing Company. **320** HBJ Photo, Larry Hoagland, Professional Photographic Services. Courtesy Colin Graham Young. **322** Kurt Muller. **328** Reprinted with permission of Atheneum, an imprint of Macmillan Publishing Company from *Z for Zachariah* by Robert C. O'Brien. Copyright © 1975 by Sally Conly.

Chapter 7

Page 340 Illustration: From *Peacock Pie* by Walter De la Mare. Illustrations copyright © 1961 by Barbara Cooney. Reprinted by permission of Alfred A. Knopf, Inc.; Text: The Literary Trustees of Walter De la Mare and The Society of Authors as their representative. **345** Courtesy Colin Graham Young. **347** "Ride a Purple Pelican" pp. 62–63 from *Ride a Purple Pelican* by Jack Prelutsky. Text copyright © 1986 by Jack Prelutsky. Illustrations copyright © 1986 by Garth Williams. By permission of Greenwillow Books (A Division of William Morrow and Company, Inc.). **350** Courtesy Thomas V. Crowell. **351** Courtesy Little, Brown & Company. **352** Piper Productions. Reproduced by permission of Harper & Row, Publishers, Inc. **353** Photograph by Marilyn Sanders. **354,** left: Photo by Bachrach; right: Reprinted by permission of Houghton Mifflin Company. **355,** left: Joan Glazer; right: Courtesy Harper & Row, Publishers, Inc. **363,** left: "A Seeing Poem" from *Seeing Things* by Robert Froman, lettering by Ray Barber (Thomas V. Crowell). Copyright © 1974 by Robert Froman. Reprinted by permission of Harper & Row, Publishers, Inc. **363** Myra Cohn Livingston, "Winter Tree" from *O Sliver of Liver and Other Poems.* Copyright © 1979 by Myra Cohn Livingston. Reprinted with the permission of Margaret K. McElderry Books, an imprint of Macmillan Publishing Company. **365** Reproduced with the permission of Charles Scribner's Sons, an imprint of Macmillan Publishing Company from *Fly with the Wind, Flow with the Water* by Ann Atwood. Copyright © 1979 Ann Atwood. **370** Illustration: From *The Random House Book of Poetry for Children,* edited by Jack C. Prelutsky, illustrated by Arnold Lobel. Copyright © 1983 by Random House, Inc. Reprinted by permission of the publisher; Text from *Tirra Lirra: Rhymes Old and New* by Laura E. Richards. Copyright © 1932 by Laura E. Richards. Copyright © renewed 1960 by Hamilton Richards. By permission of Little, Brown and Company. **373** Susie Fitzhugh.

Chapter 8

Page 391 From *Little Women* by Louisa May Alcott. Published by Little, Brown and Company. **395** James Shefcik. **399** Illustration from *Harriet the Spy* written and illustrated by Louise Fitzhugh. Copyright © 1964 by Louise Fitzhugh. Reprinted by permission of Harper & Row, Publishers, Inc. **401** Charles William Bush. **400** From the book *Blubber* by Judy Blume, Laurel Leaf Edition, 1978. Used by permission of Dell Publishing, A Division of Bantam, Doubleday, Dell Publishing Group, Inc. **403** Jacket illustration by Darryl Zudeck from *Crystal* by Walter Dean Myers. Copyright © 1987 by Viking Penguin Inc. All rights reserved. Reprinted by permission of Viking Penguin Inc. **404** Photo by Sandra Hansen. **406** Reprinted by permission of Houghton Mifflin Company. Photo by Amanda Smith. **409** Courtesy Dell Books. **419** From *Let the Balloon Go* by Ivan Southall. Illustrated by Ian Ribbons. 1968. Reprinted by permission of Methuen Children's Books Ltd., London. **420** © Dean Abramson/Stock, Boston. **422** Illustration by Robert Greiner from *Follow My Leader* by James B. Garfield. Copyright © 1957 by James B. Garfield and Robert Greiner. Copyright renewed © 1985 by Mrs. Jack Lazarus. All rights reserved. Reprinted by permission of Viking Penguin Inc. **423** *Guelph Daily Mercury.* Reproduced by permission of Harper & Row, Publishers, Inc. **426** From *The Westing Game* by Ellen Raskin. Copyright © 1978 by Ellen Raskin. Reproduced by permission of the publisher, E. P. Dutton, a division of NAL Penquin Inc. **430** Illustration by John Schoenherr from *Julie of the Wolves* by Jean Craighead George, pictures by John Schoenherr. Illustrations copyright © 1972 by John Schoenherr. Reprinted by permission of Harper & Row, Publishers, Inc. **431** Ellan Young Photography. Reproduced by permission of Harper & Row, Publishers, Inc. **436** © by Jill Paton Walsh. Reproduced by permission of Harper & Row, Publishers, Inc. **438** Illustration by Donna Diamond From *Beat the Turtle Drum* by Constance Greene. Illustrations copyright © 1976 by Viking Penguin Inc. All rights reserved. Reprinted by permission of Viking Penguin Inc. **441** Illustration by Ann Grifalconi from *The Midnight Fox* by Betsy Byars. Illustration copyright © 1968 by Viking Penquin, Inc. All rights reserved. Reprinted by permission of Viking Penguin, Inc. **444** Cover from *Me Too* by Vera and Bill Cleaver, cover art © 1985 by Ellen Thompson. Reprinted by permission of Harper & Row, Publishers, Inc. **445** Illustration by Ted CoConis from *Summer of the Swans* by Betsy Byars. Illustrations copyright © 1970 by The Viking Press, Inc. All rights reserved. Reprinted by permission of Viking Penguin Inc. **448** From *Fran Ellen's House* by Marilyn Sachs, jacket illustration by Vincent Nasta. Copyright © 1987 by Marilyn Sachs. Reproduced by permission of the publisher, E. P. Dutton, a division of NAL Penguin, Inc.

Chapter 9

Page 460 Illustration by Garth Williams from *Little House in the Big Woods* by Laura Ingalls Wilder, pictures copyright © 1953 by Garth Williams, renewed 1981 by Garth Williams.

Reprinted by permission of Harper & Row, Publishers, Inc. **466** Keary Nichols/MPBN. Reproduced by permission of Harper & Row, Publishers, Inc. **471** From *Castle* by David Macaulay. Copyright © 1977 by David Macaulay. Reprinted by permission of Houghton Mifflin Company. **476** From *Christopher Columbus* by Piero Ventura, based on the text by Gian Paolo Ceserani. Copyright © 1975 by Random House, Inc. Reprinted by permission of the publisher. **478** Reprinted with the permission of Atheneum Publishers, an imprint of Macmillan Publishing Company from *The Pilgrims of Plimouth* by Marcia Sewall. Copyright © 1986 Marcia Sewall. **482** Illustration from *My Brother Sam is Dead* by Karl W. Stuecklen. Written by James Lincoln Collier and Christopher Collier. Illustration copyright © 1974 by Scholastic, Inc. Reproduced by permission of Four Winds Press, a division of Scholastic, Inc. **483** Frontispiece illustration by Ellen Thompson from *The Fighting Ground* by Avi. Frontispiece copyright © 1984 by Ellen Thompson (J. B. Lippincott). Reprinted by permission of Harper & Row, Publishers, Inc. **486** Illustration by Trina Schart Hyman reprinted by permission of Coward, McCann & Geoghegan from *Why Don't You Get a Horse, Sam Adams?* by Jean Fritz, illustrations copyright © 1974 by Trina Schart Hyman. **487** © 1987 Janet Woodcock. **489** Illustration from *The Incredible Journey of Lewis and Clark* by Rhoda Blumberg. Text copyright © 1987 by Rhoda Blumberg. By permission of Lothrop, Lee & Shepard Books (A Division of William Morrow and Company, Inc.). **491** From *Sing Down the Moon* by Scott O'Dell. Copyright © 1970 by Scott O'Dell. Reprinted by permission of Houghton Mifflin Company. **496** National Portrait Gallery, Frederick Meserve Collection. **500** Jacket from *Sarah, Plain and Tall* by Patricia MacLachlan, illustration by Marcia Sewall. Jacket art © 1985 by Marcia Sewall. Reprinted by permission of Harper & Row, Publishers, Inc. **502** Illustrations copyright © 1986 by Deborah Kogan Ray. Reprinted from *My Prairie Year* by Brett Harvey by permission of Holiday House. **505** Cover from *After the Dancing Days* by Margaret I. Rostkowski. Cover art copyright © 1988 by Linda Benson. Reprinted by permission of Harper & Row, Publishers, Inc. **507** Courtesy Dial Books for Young Readers. **513** Catherine Noren.

Chapter 10

Page 528 Photograph from *Eat the Fruit, Plant the Seed*, p. 458, by Millicent E. Selsam. Text copyright © 1980 by Millicent E. Selsam. Illustrations copyright © 1980 by Jerome Wexler. By permission of Morrow Junior Books (A Division of William Morrow and Company, Inc.). **533** Copyright © 1985 by Olivier Dunrea. Reprinted from *Skara Brae* by permission of Holiday House. **534** Courtesy Macmillan Publishing Company. **540** Copyright © 1987 by Gail Gibbons. Reprinted from *Dinosaurs* by permission of Holiday House. **542**, left: Photograph from *A Children's Zoo* by Tana Hoban. Copyright © 1985 by Tana Hoban. By permission of Greenwillow Books (A Division of William Morrow and Company, Inc.); right: Ron Cohn/The Gorilla Foundation. **544** Courtesy Laurence Pringle. **548** Illustration by

Keizaburo Tejima reprinted by permission of Philomel books from *Owl Lake,* illustrations copyright © 1982 by Keizaburo Tejima.   **549** Illustration by Bob Marshall from *One Day in the Prairie* by Jean Craighead George. (Thomas Y. Crowell). Illustration copyright © 1986 by Bob Marshall. Reprinted by permission of Harper & Row, Publishers, Inc.   **551** Illustration by Irene Brady from *Peeping in the Shell* by Faith McNulty, illustrated by Irene Brady. Illustrations copyright © 1986 by Irene Brady. Reprinted by permission of Harper & Row, Publishers, Inc.   **552** Photograph and caption from *The Crocodile and the Crane* by Judy Cutchins and Ginny Johnston. Copyright © 1986 by Judy Cutchins and Ginny Johnston. By permission of Morrow Junior Books (A Division of William Morrow and Company, Inc.).   **558** NASA.   **563** Illustration from *Uranus* by Seymour Simon. Text copyright © 1987 by Seymour Simon. Illustrations copyright © 1987 by William Morrow & Co., Inc. By permission of Morrow Junior Books (A Division of William Morrow and Company, Inc.).   **583** Illustration from *Whales, Nomads of the Sea,* p. 89, by Helen Roney Sattler. Text copyright © 1987 by Helen Roney Sattler. Illustrations copyright © 1987 by Jean Day Zallinger. By permission of Lothrop, Lee & Shepard Books (A Division of William Morrow and Company, Inc.).   **584** © Mike Mazzaschi/Stock, Boston.

Chapter 11

Page 577 © Elizabeth Crews.   **582** Photo by Deborah Storms.   **585** Illustration from *The Land I Lost* by Huynh Quang Nhuong with pictures by Vo-Dinh Mai. Illustrations copyright © 1982 by Vo-Dinh Mai. Reprinted by permission of Harper & Row, Publishers, Inc.   **587** Web Developed by Domica Mazzachi.   **590** From *The People Could Fly: American Black Folktales* by Virginia Hamilton. Illustration copyright © by Leo and Diane Dillon. Reprinted by permission of Alfred A. Knopf, Inc.   **594** Web developed by Muriel J. Clarkston.   **598** Illustrations copyright © 1980 by Tomie dePaola. Reprinted from *The Lady of Guadalupe* by permission of Holiday House.   **604** Jerry Bauer.   **606** Illustration by Maurice Sendak from *Zlateh the Goat* by Isaac Bashevis Singer, pictures by Maurice Sendak. Pictures copyright © 1966 by Maurice Sendak. Reprinted by permission of Harper & Row, Publishers, Inc.   **614** Reproduced with the permission of Atheneum Publishers, an imprint of Macmillan Publishing Company from *The Enchanted Caribou* by Elizabeth Cleaver. Copyright © 1985 Elizabeth Cleaver.   **616** © Gale Zucker/Stock, Boston.   **617** Web developed by Corie Adjmi.   **619** National Archives, Smithsonian Institution.   **621** Photograph from *The Children We Remember* by Chana Byers Abells. Text copyright © 1983–1986 by Chana Byers Abells. By permission of Greenwillow Books (A Division of William Morrow and Company, Inc.).   **625** Web developed by Lucy Rubin.

Chapter 12

Pages 643, 645, 655, 658, 673 From *Yankee Doodle's Literary Sampler of Prose, Poetry and Pictures.* Selected from the Rare Book Collections of the Library of Congress and introduced by Virginia Haviland and Margaret N. Coughlan. Thomas Y. Crowell, 1974.   **644** Facsimile of a colonial horn book, reproduced by hand for The Horn Book, Inc., Boston, Mass.   **645** Historical Pictures Service, Chicago.   **646, 650, 658** The Rare Book Division, The New York Public Library, Astor, Lenox and Tilden Foundations.   **647** Culver Pictures.   **661, 670** The Bettmann Archive.   **662** Illustration by Rudyard Kipling.

Color Plates

Plate A-1 Reprinted with permission of Aladdin Books, an imprint of Macmillan Publishing Company from *Say Goodnight* by Helen Oxenbury. Copyright © 1987 Helen Oxenbury.   **A-2** Illustration from *Corduroy on the Go* by Don Freeman. Copyright © 1985 by Viking Penguin Inc. All rights reserved. Reprinted by permission of Viking Penguin Inc.   **A-3** Picture Book Studio, Saxonville, MA, 1986.   **A-4** Illustration by Tomie de Paola reprinted by permission of G.P. Putnam's Sons from *Giorgio's Village.* Illustrations Copyright © 1982 by Tomie de Paola.   **A-5** *Fat Mouse* by Harry Stevens (Penguin Books Ltd., 1987), copyright © Harry Stevens, 1987. Reproduced by permission of Penguin Books, Ltd.   **A-6** From *The Jolly Postman* by Janet and Allan Ahlberg. Copyright © 1986 by Allan and Janet Ahlberg. By permission of Little, Brown and Company.   **A-7** From *My Pillow Book* by Angela Ackerman. Copyright © 1988 by Angela Ackerman. Reprinted by permission of Random House, Inc.   **A-8** Illustration from *Building a House* by Byron Barton. Copyright © 1981 by Byron Barton. By permission of Greenwillow Books (A Division of William Morrow and Company, Inc.).   **A-9** Illustration from *Red, Blue, Yellow Shoe* by Tana Hoban. Copyright © 1986 by Tana Hoban. By permission of Greenwillow Books (A Division of William Morrow and Company, Inc.).

Plate B-1 Illustration from *Song to Demeter* by Cynthia and William Birrer. Copyright © 1987 by Cynthia E. and William Birrer. By permission of Lothrop, Lee and Shepard Books (A Division of William Morrow and Company, Inc.).   **B-2** From *The Polar Express* by Chris Van Allsburg. Copyright © 1985 by Chris Van Allsburg. Reprinted by permission of Houghton Mifflin Company.   **B-3** Illustration from *Where the Forest Meets the Sea* by Jeannie Baker. Copyright © by Jeannie Baker. By permission of Greenwillow Books (A Division of William Morrow and Company, Inc.).   **B-4** Illustration from *Dots, Spots, Speckles and Stripes.* Copyright © 1987 by Tana Hoban. By permission of Greenwillow Books (A Division of William Morrow and Company, Inc.).   **B-5** Illustration from *Jungle Walk* by Nancy Tafuri. Copyright © 1988 by Nancy Tafuri. By permission of Greenwillow Books (A Division of William Morrow and Company, Inc.).   **B-6** Illustration from *Frog and Toad Pop-Up Book* by Arnold Lobel. Copyright © 1986 by Arnold Lobel. Reprinted by permission of Harper & Row, Publishers.   **B-7** Illustration from *A Week of Lullabies* compiled and edited by Helen Plotz. Illustrated by Marisabina

AUTHOR AND TITLE INDEX

Numbers in *italics* indicate the pages on which illustrations appear.

SUBJECT INDEX

Activities: American Indians, 612, *617*; animal extinctions, 554; animals, 545; author interview, 425; babysitter's handbook, 164; Bible stories, 265; book character diary, 327; books for reading aloud, 61–63; brother or sister for sale bulletin board, 181; comparing stories about aging, 435; creatures from mythology, 253; Cupid and Psyche, 256; diorama, 287; dispel the myths, 485; early settlers, 477; evaluating media reports, 560; facts in fiction, 475; family tree, 184; favorite author or illustrator, 199; haiku cards, 365; Hansel and Gretel, 233; hero tales, 258; history through literature, 494; integrating literature and arts, 492; language of A. A. Milne, 293; literary analysis, 482; make a book, 115; matching maxims and fables, 247; "meet the character" radio script, 416; Middle Ages, 470; Mother Goose, 223; Mother Hubbard, 227; multicultural literature, 586, *587*; narrative poems, 358; nature in poetry, 192; new baby books, 179; Noah's ark, 266; Norse myths, 474; nuclear power, 329; observe and describe people, 398; parallel poems, 372; Persephone, 258; personification, 374; pioneer life, 499; poetry pageant, 377; race of the future, 326; snowmen, 190; songfest, 263; study the past through tombstones, 498; tall tales, 261; tape-recorded storytelling, 127; teddy bear week, 163; *The Westing Game* game, 427; time lines and maps,

465; tundra dwellers, 432; witch hunts, 480; word puzzles, 133; word search, 119; words from mythology, 259; World War II, 511
Adolescents, realistic fiction about, 402–406, 418
Adoption, 177–78
Advanced grades: poetry for, 357; read-aloud books for, 63; study units for, 558–64; suggested books for, 17
Adventure stories. *See* Quest stories
Aesthetic reading, 7
Age-appropriate books, 12
Aging, realistic fiction about, 433–35
Aliterates, 6–7
Alliteration, 368
Alphabet, as a framework for a story, 76
Alphabet books, 110–13
America: books originating from, 654–55; colonial times, 477–81; discovery of, 474–75; World War II in, 515
American Indians, 611–19; biographies of, 491–92; fiction of, *617*, 618; folklore of, 611–15; historical fiction of, 489–91; nonfiction of, 618–19; poetry of, 615–18
American Revolution. *See* Revolutionary War
American Sunday school movement, 654
Animal behavior, research into, 556–58
Animal books, 191–193
Animal fantasy, 290–98
Animals: farm animals, 543–46; wildlife, 546–47; zoo animals, 541–43; Web, *547*
Animal stories, realistic, 440–43

Anthropomorphism, 529
Art: in Mother Goose books, 225; in picture books, 196–205. *See also* Book illustration
Art activities, as a response to literature, 84–86
Arthurian legend, 304–305, 310–12
Asian-Americans, 577–87; biography of, 585–87; fiction of, 580–84; folklore of, 578–79; nonfiction of, 584–85; picture books of, 580–81; poetry of, 579–80
Assonance, 368
Astronomy, 561–62
Audiovisual presentations of literature, 65–69; advantages of, 68
Audubon Society, 550
Author interview, 428

Babies, books for, 107–108
Babysitter's handbook, 164
"Bad boy" literature, 659–60
Ballads, 366–67; literary, 366; reciting contemporary, 367
Ballet books, 195
Battledores, *645*
Bedtime fears, 162
Bedtime poems, 164
Beginning stories, 109–10
Beginning-to-read books, 129–33
Bible, 641; as literature, 264–66
Big books, 123
Biographies, 34, 459–61, 618–19; about American Indians, 491–92; about Asian-Americans, 585–87; about black Americans, 595–96; about the Civil War, 495–97; about colonial times, 478; about explorers, 476–77; about Hispanic Amer-

Touchstones in the History of Children's Literature

ILLUSTRATORS AND REPRESENTATIVE BOOKS

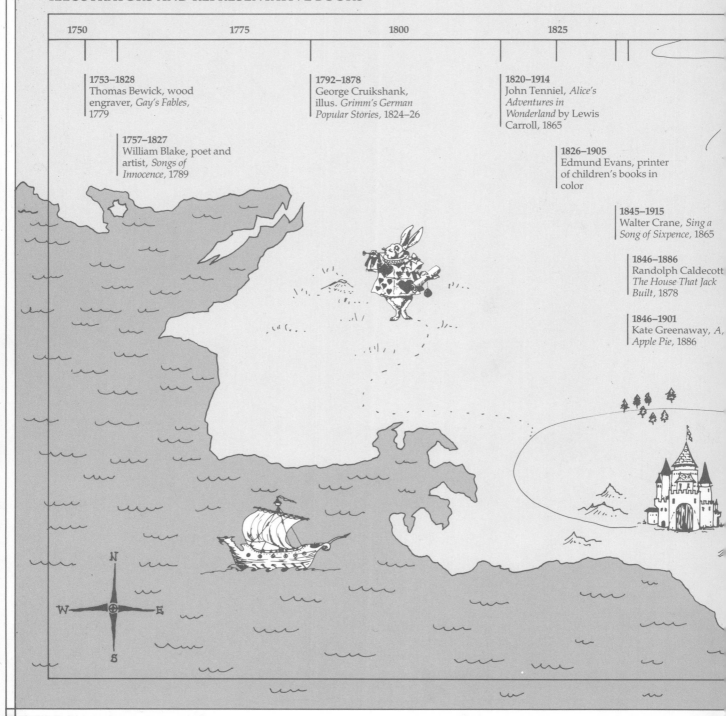

| 1750 | 1775 | 1800 | 1825 |

1753–1828
Thomas Bewick, wood engraver, *Gay's Fables*, 1779

1757–1827
William Blake, poet and artist, *Songs of Innocence*, 1789

1792–1878
George Cruikshank, illus. *Grimm's German Popular Stories*, 1824–26

1820–1914
John Tenniel, *Alice's Adventures in Wonderland* by Lewis Carroll, 1865

1826–1905
Edmund Evans, printer of children's books in color

1845–1915
Walter Crane, *Sing a Song of Sixpence*, 1865

1846–1886
Randolph Caldecott, *The House That Jack Built*, 1878

1846–1901
Kate Greenaway, *A, Apple Pie*, 1886

N W E S